D1626107

THE NORTH AMERICAN BUFFALO

THE NORTH AMERICAN BUFFALO

The
North American
BUFFALO

A Critical Study
of the Species in
its Wild State

FRANK GILBERT ROE

DAVID & CHARLES : NEWTON ABBOT

ISBN 0 7153 5679 8

© University of Toronto Press 1970, 1972

First Published in Great Britain 1972
by David & Charles (Publishers) Limited

Printed in Great Britain by
Redwood Press Limited
Trowbridge, Wiltshire

PREFACE

THE present work was put together during the leisure intervals of an exacting avocation, over a period of some fifteen years. Whatever may be the critical verdict on its final character, it was certainly not planned in any iconoclastic spirit. Actually, its origin was almost accidental. My excursus into buffalo history was meant to be an appendix to a study of the historical evolution of early English roads, for which I had already collected considerable material. This appendix was intended to illustrate my contention that the earliest English roads were probably *not* originally wild animal tracks; nor were the earliest human (Indian) trails of this continent buffalo tracks.* In the search for positive evidence on the latter phase of the question, I discovered something of the vast mass of historical evidence available concerning the buffalo. Its diverse and contradictory character, coming from witnesses of broadly equal inherent credibility, led me onward by degrees into classification and arrangement; and to a general critical appraisal of the witnesses themselves and of their testimony and opinions.

I have to acknowledge a deep indebtedness to several friends. First of all stands the late D. E. Cameron, for very many years Librarian of the University of Alberta, for introduction to much recondite source-material, for the critical advice and ripe judgment of a scholar, and above all for the unflagging kindness which spared no effort on behalf of one so entirely beyond academic circles as myself. Without his encouragement the book would probably never have been written. Without the aid of the late Hon. A. C. Rutherford, Chancellor of the University (and first Premier of the Province of Alberta) it probably never *could* have been written. Though I was a stranger to Dr. Rutherford before approaching him for assistance, I was at once given *carte blanche* in his magnificent library of early Canadiana and Americana, which included many very valuable original editions. From this rich collection I was even allowed to take away anything I chose to select.

I must also acknowledge the great kindness of Professors William Rowan, F. M. Salter, and M. H. Long, of the respective faculties of

*See F. G. Roe, "The 'Wild Animal Path' Origin of Ancient Roads," *Antiquity* (England), III, 1929, 299-311; "The Crooked Field," *ibid.*, X, 1936, 325-40; "The Winding Road," *ibid.*, XIII, 1939, 191-206.

Zoology, English, and History in the same University; the first for obtaining for me several valuable monographs from their authors and for the loan of important material from his own collections; and all three for critical advice and tireless effort on my behalf in bringing this work before the notice of public bodies in Canada and elsewhere. My grateful thanks are also due to my friend E. L. Hill, Esq., the first City Librarian of Edmonton, 1909-36 (and now of Victoria, B.C.), for similar services most ungrudgingly rendered; and in all the foregoing instances to the secretarial and library staffs of the City and University Libraries, together with Miss McKee, then in charge of the Provincial Legislative Library, all of Edmonton.

My cordial acknowledgements are likewise due to Professor G. W. Brown, now Editor of the University of Toronto Press and for many years editor of the *Canadian Historical Review* (in which certain chapters were printed as separate papers), to the late Dean W. Burton Hurd and to Dr. C. Cecil Lingard, who as Chairman and Secretary of the Publications Committee of the Canadian Social Science Research Council, brought the work to the notice of the Council. To the Council I am indebted for a generous grant-in-aid toward publication, as I am also to the University of Toronto Press Publication Fund for assistance toward the same end. I must further thank the editorial bodies of the *Canadian Historical Review* and of the Royal Society of Canada (Section II), for permission to reprint chapters VIII, XIII, XIV, and Appendices D, K; which originally appeared as separate papers in the *Review* and in the *Transactions of the Royal Society of Canada*, respectively.

Finally, my most sincere and grateful thanks must be tendered to the Editorial Department of the University of Toronto Press, particularly to Miss Eleanor Harman, Associate Editor and Production Manager, and Mrs. Ann Rabjohns, formerly of the same branch, and also to the printing-room staff, for the unstinted care and skill which have been bestowed upon the technical production of the book. Other incidental acknowledgements appear in the course of the work.

It is to be understood that the responsibility for all opinions expressed, and for the manner of their expression, is exclusively mine.

Cadboro Bay, Victoria, B.C. FRANK GILBERT ROE

PREFACE TO THE SECOND EDITION

DESPITE the utmost effort on the part of all concerned, a work of this comprehensive character can scarcely be expected to appear without any deficiencies being found. While nothing has revealed itself of any nature requiring revision of the broad final conclusions, it has been possible to add informative matter not previously known to the author or not even in print in 1951, notably with respect to the advance of the buffalo into the far Southwest. This possibility was recognized by the author and also noticed by several reviewers as the least satisfactory portion of the first edition. It is hoped that this deficiency has now been adequately supplied. A map has also been included, embracing the total area of the former buffalo range, together with the regions of early discoveries of the herds (giving dates), and also of the latest recorded encounters and the various eras and areas of extinction. This will enable readers to form a more intelligent idea of the highlights of buffalo history.

There remains only the pleasant duty of thanking the following for their very kind assistance and co-operation: Mr. Bruce Peel, Librarian of the University of Alberta; Mr. A. D. Ridge, Provincial Archivist of Alberta, for his ready co-operation in the loan of important photographic material from the Ernest Brown Collection, and to my old friend Miss Gladys Reeves (a niece of the late Mr. Brown) for formal permission to use the same; to Dr. Willard Ireland, Provincial Archivist of British Columbia, his Assistant Miss Inez Mitchell and her staff; to Dr. Hugh Dempsey, Director of the Glenbow Foundation of Calgary (Alberta), and his staff; and finally to the University of Toronto Press – including Miss Eleanor Harman, Miss M. Jean Houston, and Miss Jean Wilson. As with the first edition, the responsibility for statements made in this edition is exclusively my own.

FRANK GILBERT ROE

Cadboro Bay, Victoria, B.C.

CONTENTS

THE NORTH AMERICAN BUFFALO

NOTE

THE use of single inverted commas (' ') throughout this work denotes either paraphrases of quotations, or such local, proverbial, or technical (&c. &c.) expressions, not originally the author's own, as may require some distinctive indication other than italics. Double inverted commas (" ") indicate the exact language of the document quoted, word for word without any change whatever, apart from omissions of needless matter, shown by a hiatus (. . .). All italics occurring in quotations are those of the document quoted, unless specifically stated to be my own.

CHAPTER I

INTRODUCTION

THE bison of the North American continent (*Bison americanus, or some kindred designation*),[1] to which, following weighty precedent, I shall hereafter refer by its familiar name of buffalo,[2] is one of those important creatures like the horse, the dog,

[1]The doctors disagree. I find the following variations, and there may be others.

PRAIRIE BUFFALO

Bison Americanus: Allen, *American Bisons;* Hornaday, "Extermination of the American Bison"; Hewitt, *Conservation of the Wild Life of Canada,* 115; Kitto, "Survival of American Bison in Canada" (*Geographical Journal,* LXIII, 1924, 431-7); *Encyclopaedia Britannica,* 14th ed., *s.v.* Bison.

Bison Bison: Osborn, *Age of Mammals,* 481; Scharff, *Distribution and Origin of Life in America,* 65.

Bison Bison Americanus: Garretson, *American Bison.*

Bison Bison Bison: Rowan, "Canada's Buffalo" (*Country Life,* LXVI, 1929, 358-60). Dr. Rowan is professor of zoology in the University of Alberta.

Bison Bison (Linnaeus): Lucas, "Fossil Bisons of North America" (*Proceedings of the United States National Museum,* XXI, no. 1172, 755-71); Seton, *Life-Histories of Northern Animals,* I, 247; *Game Animals,* III, 641; Stone and Cram, *American Animals,* 66-70.

Bos Americanus: Dodge, *Plains of the Great West,* 129; Chittenden, *American Fur Trade,* II, 809; Coues, correspondence to Allen (*American Bisons,* 124).

Bos (Bison) Bison: Encyclopaedia Britannica, 11th ed., *s.v.* Bison.

For further early classifications, see Skinner and Kaisen, *Fossil Bison of Alaska,* 161.

WOOD BUFFALO

BISON BISON ATHABASCAE RHOADS: Seton, *Life-Histories of Northern Animals,* I, 250, Raup, *Range Conditions in Wood Buffalo Park,* 10, 18, 50.

BOS AMERICANUS ATHABASCAE (? after Raup): *The Times* (London), Nov. 18, 1937.

BOS (BISON) BISON ATHABASCAE: Garretson, *American Bison,* 7. See also Skinner and Kaisen, *Fossil Bison of Alaska,* 165.

[2]"In the United States, this animal has generally borne the name of *buffalo,* though discriminating writers persist that the name is erroneous, and that it should be called the American bison. The latter is undoubtedly its correct English cognomen, but probably among the people generally the name *buffalo* will never be supplanted. The term *American buffalo* is doubtless defensible for those who prefer it, and even *buffalo* is no more a misnomer than scores of the names of our common mammals and birds. . . . The name buffalo is of course strictly applicable only to the genus *Bubalus,* embracing the true African and Indian buffaloes . . ." (Allen, *American Bisons,* 51).

"Although *Bison Americanus* is a true bison, according to scientific classification, and not a buffalo, the fact that more than sixty millions of people in this

3

and the deer, which have exercised a great and far-reaching influence upon portions of the human race. In some respects, it occupied an almost unique position in this category. For although the range of some of the others is possibly greater, the horse and the dog had first to be domesticated, and the term 'deer' comprehends some hundred and fifty, perhaps more, species of the *Cervidae* in many lands. Moreover, the buffalo were virtually of one species—as some classifications insist they actually are in the most rigid scientific sense—and could be utilized in their native wild condition.

The presence of this animal has deeply affected the civilization of the North American continent—perhaps more vitally than has ever been the case with any other single species in its indigenous environment in any portion of the globe. The horse would probably occupy first place in such a category; but in the present state of our knowledge, we can scarcely be certain just where its indigenous home was; and as an historic force it has been most decidedly an importation everywhere. The camel and the African elephant have assuredly coloured and influenced the civilizations or human relationships of their respective habitats: the former, by its adaptability to the life of the autochthonous peoples inhabiting its range—or perhaps *vice versa;* the latter, by possibly being—for its ivory—the exciting cause of what Livingstone termed the 'open sore' of the Dark Continent, slavery. But the elephant, despite its large numbers and wide geographical range, does not appear ever to have flourished in such vast hosts, nor to have been so available as to constitute the almost sole source of subsistence to whole nations of aboriginal peoples. Except for food, these peoples apparently made little use of it. And neither the camel nor the elephant, save perhaps to a small extent the latter, can be considered to have materially influenced the civilization of the white race impinging upon its habitat. The Eskimo and the musk-ox might possibly be cited as a parallel instance *in esse.* But the same rejoinders would apply to them. Furthermore, the numbers of the Eskimo have in all historic times

---

country unite in calling him a 'buffalo,' and know him by no other name, renders it quite unnecessary for me to apologize for following, in part, a harmless custom which has now become so universal that all the naturalists in the world could not change it if they would . . ." (Hornaday, "Extermination of the American Bison," 371). After this brave declaration—which required some courage in a zoologist— it is amusing to find the old scientific Adam so strong in Dr. Hornaday that *bison* is still perhaps more frequently used by him.

I also prefer the name 'buffalo,' because there actually was a variety which in its local habitat the mountaineers called a 'bison'—the only use of the term which I have found, apart from scientists. It seemed well to preserve the distinction (see chap. III, notes 41, *seq.* Also Appendix II.).

been few; and, even more significant, the musk-ox has been classified by zoologists of high standing as simply an Arctic buffalo.[3]

The historic American buffalo (*Bison americanus*) occupies a fundamentally different position. It is the only known creature which has ever thronged in such prodigious hosts a geographical range which climatic and ecological characteristics or potentialities made a natural home for a really large white population. Here the buffalo has no parallel. The immense numbers, and the comprehensive and, for aboriginal requirements, literally inexhaustible resources which it furnished, contributed greatly to make the most independent (and consequently most intractable) of the aboriginal population what they were; and these in turn developed or accentuated characteristics in the white invaders which may long continue to be visible.

Our scientific knowledge of the buffalo has been obscured by circumstances almost peculiar to this species. The great game quadrupeds of the world have in most instances first been encountered—apart from natives of their habitats—by the big game hunter. Such persons are generally men of cultivated leisure, and frequently possess some scientific training. The acute observation which is essential in order to hunt successfully a new and unfamiliar animal—powerful, wary, and very frequently dangerous—almost instinctively extends itself beyond the purely utilitarian phases. An observer of this type is commonly aware of the scientific wisdom of avoiding hasty judgments. The late Theodore Roosevelt's fascinating work of African travel may be instanced as an appropriate illustration. Here the actual personal impressions of the moment are balanced against other considerations, such as comparative knowledge from a wide variety of sources, and a wise scientific caution.[4]

With the American buffalo, the case was entirely different. The scientific inquirer, instead of being among the first in the field, was among the last. The westward spread of settlement, and the utilization of the buffalo for subsistence and for gain, introduced the species to a large public, which could seldom by any stretch of imagination be termed scientific. Most of this public was nearly illiterate; for the mere

[3] See Appendix N.

[4] Roosevelt, *African Game Trails*. For variability in the habits of African buffalo, rhinoceros, giraffes, 'bongo' ('as big as bullocks'), etc., see 208, 219, 241, 362, 389, 400, 420. For general corroboration of Roosevelt, cf. Maxwell, *Stalking Big Game with a Camera*, 15-16, 65, 83, 93, 135-9, 141, 213, 226, 227; *Encyclopaedia Britannica*, 14th ed., *s.v.* Lion, etc. I since find that the frontiersmen's tales in Roosevelt's earlier work, *Winning of the West*, need to be taken with caution, as the author points out; see particularly I, 259. Cf. also below, chap. VI, notes 123-6.

ability to read after a fashion or to write one's name is but little removed, in the dearth of facilities or practice, from absolute illiteracy.
This 'frontiersman' type of mind is marked by two outstanding characteristics. The first—common to most persons who lack a certain breadth
of reading—is the failure to realize the importance of *comparative*
knowledge. The second is an utter disdain for anyone who might
chance to recognize the value of such criteria, and might seek to apply
them as a check upon the prairie eye-witness's first-hand assertions or
adopted conclusions. Unless such a man has himself observed a pronounced variability of conduct, such as we shall see is well attested in
the buffalo,[5] anything which he has *seen* the buffalo do, or leave un-
done, becomes something which they 'always' do or 'never' do.

It may be added that the border ruffians, outlaws, and bad men,
and other romantic phenomena of the West, have long been the subject-matter of a rather lurid type of fiction, which could relate any
extravagance with a fine disdain for the limitations of evidence or of
probability. The buffalo, having been contemporary denizens of the
same habitat, were often treated in the same manner. We find that any
yarn which anybody chooses to tell is placed on the same footing with
the most rigidly authenticated testimony of reputable eye-witnesses.
It is vain to turn from the white plainsman to the aborigine in the hope
of anything better; for this trait of sweeping generalization is, if anything, even more pronounced in the Indian.[6]

Unfortunately, in most instances the scholarly inquirers appear to
have been quite content to accept as final the confident dogmatisms of
the plainsmen. By a curious irony, in the one outstanding instance
where they did not, later scientific classification has vindicated the
contention of the unlearned.[7] That even scientific visitors to the buffalo
country should seek information from residents, or record their un-
solicited utterances, was natural; and it would be difficult to suggest
a better starting-point. But in many instances, even in the course of
one summer's observation, such visitors, in their day-to-day accounts,
remark upon occurrences which are hopelessly irreconcilable with the
uniformitarian pronouncements in their set 'descriptions' of the

[5]"The American bison presents a considerable range of what may be termed
individual variations . . ." (Allen, *American Bisons*, 48). Theodore Roosevelt,
whose knowledge of buffalo was apparently gathered outdoors, says something
similar (*Hunting Trips of a Ranchman*, 196).

[6]A very competent student seems to describe the Indian in general very aptly
as an acute and reliable observer, but a poor generalizer. Grinnell, *The Fighting
Cheyennes*, 270.

[7]See chap. III, "North American Variants of the Buffalo."

buffalo; and they seldom make any comment whatever on the discrepancy.[8]

In another respect, the buffalo have not been particularly fortunate in their historians. It is generally taken more or less for granted, reasoning from common experience, that a later, more modern historian in any field will be, on the whole, more full and more reliable. More recent research into facts, and a consequently better basis for sound critical conclusions, entitle students to expect this. In this particular field the student will be disappointed. Apart from those scholars such as Dr. (Sir John) Richardson, who have given us somewhat localized studies of some particular region—in his case surprisingly little diminished in value by the lapse of time[9]—there have been three serious historical generalizers on buffalo. These are Professor Joel A. Allen,[10] Dr. W. T. Hornaday,[11] and the late Ernest Thompson Seton.[12] Of these, Allen, the earliest, is also incomparably the best. He realized the prime importance of citing as many of the early travel-references as possible, and preferably in the witness's own words. Unfortunately, however, the date of his publication (1876) precluded any account of the final slaughter in the northern United States and Canada (1877-83). The next in chronological order is Hornaday, who wrote in 1889. Hornaday is a zoologist of the first order, but a very inferior historian. He is one of the most deplorable examples of that uncritical type of scientific inquirer to which I have alluded. Allen is his principal literary authority; but he does not hesitate to discard him at any moment when Allen's conclusions differ from those which Hornaday himself has adopted, from whom or for what reason the reader is seldom told. Hornaday has subjected his readers and himself to serious injustice by his refusal to utilize one of the best descriptions of the buffalo ever written—that of George Catlin.[13] The 'time-spirit' of nineteenth-century America-at-large was against Catlin;[14] and when

[8]"Contributing to the obvious unreliability in many cases are the basic facts that a large proportion of the published information is based not upon the writers' own observations, but upon the reports of natives, chiefly Indians, and that any estimate of the number of animals is bound to have been then, as it still is, purely conjectural . . ." (Raup, *Range Conditions in Wood Buffalo Park*, 8).

[9]Richardson, *Fauna Boreali-Americana*, I.

[10]Allen, *American Bisons*.

[11]Hornaday, "Extermination of the American Bison."

[12]Seton, *Life-Histories of Northern Animals*, I, 247-301; *Game Animals*, III, 640-712.

[13]Catlin, *Letters on the North American Indians*, I, 247-64.

[14]Despite the fact that they were based upon a longer and infinitely more intimate experience than those of almost any other writer of that day, George Catlin's opinions on anything Indian were damned by one fatal disqualification—

he sympathized with the Indians! To those propagandists and 'educators' of public opinion who coveted the Indian lands (see Thwaites (ed.), *Early Western Travels,* XIV, 21; and cf. below, Appendix FF.), it was of the first importance to decry Catlin as half liar, half fool. This embraced everything he said, and naturally included buffalo. While the wide and varied data necessary for adequate comparative study were not then so richly compiled as now, nevertheless, a sufficient amount was available, taken together with his own observations, to start Catlin— as it did—on the right track. The very diversities and contradictions of the buffalo cosmogony—which will be abundantly demonstrated to readers of the present essay—rendered it easy to find plainsmen who disagreed with Catlin; and, on the very usual supposition that only one can be right, Catlin was *Athanasius contra mundum.* The field was in the possession of those local and narrow generalizers from their own sole experience, of the 'always' and 'never' school, to which allusion has been made; and, however much they might disagree amongst themselves, their combined force against Catlin—the true cause of which, in my opinion, was often unsuspected—misled good men, whose own rejection of Catlin's opinions influenced others. Thus only can I explain the criticisms directed against Catlin, in a manner to which scarcely any other man has been subjected.

Had a more philosophic attitude prevailed, it might have been recognized that certain statements are inherently more credible than others, irrespective of who makes them. If a traveller returns from a savage land, through which he passed without injury, although unarmed and alone, and reports the natives to be bloodthirsty and treacherous, we may discount his characterization very considerably, since, if that had been the case, he probably would never have survived to tell such a tale. Even so good and acute a man as Parkman recorded his disquietudes at the dangers of his sojourn among the western Sioux, but seems, from his own account, never to have been in any danger. (*Oregon Trail,* 319, *et passim*).

If a well-armed expedition returns and states that but for a constant watchfulness, 'never leaving their rifles,' etc., they would have been murdered by the treacherous and bloodthirsty savages, we simply do not know whether this be true or not, since they never put it to the test. This is distinct from any question of provocation; and we know that some of the Indian-haters were men who would scarcely have been secure from a richly deserved retaliation, had the red men encountered them in the White House itself.

If the Livingstones, McDougalls, Lacombes, or Catlins tell us they have journeyed alone and unarmed through some such region, as Dr. Whitman did in 1835, and that the 'savages' are peaceable and friendly to those who treat them properly, their safe return is itself equivalent to proof of the truth of what they say.

General Chittenden is very severe with Catlin: "He was distrusted by those who knew him in the West, and was more than once taken to task by his contemporaries . . ." (but apparently only *re* Indians; *American Fur Trade,* II, 637-8, 642, 647). Chittenden buttresses his argument by an appeal to the great name of Parkman; but compare Parkman's own note (*Half-Century of Conflict,* II, 20-1). Colonel Dodge also criticizes Catlin, because of disagreement in their respective characterizations of Indians; as if men never varied! (*Our Wild Indians,* 54, 63, 64, 305.)

Among Western contemporaries, Catlin was endorsed (on his own appeal) by Maximilian, Prince of Wied, and James Kipp (Thwaites (ed.), *Early Western Travels,* ed. note, XXIII, 324; see also *ibid.,* ed. note, 189); likewise Brazeau, Hudson's Bay Company trader, to Southesk, 1859 (Southesk, *Travels,* 151, 159). Cf. also Palliser, a competent judge, who had been in the Western States, 1848 (*Journals,* 38, 40, 90, 93, 199). See also (pro Catlin) Blair (*Indian Tribes,* II, 311); Catlin 'accurate and trustworthy'; thus, a master-critic, Fiske (*Discovery of*

Hornaday was writing, the white heats of the Custer 'massacre' were still aglow. Apart from Hornaday's description of the northern extermination, of which he may be considered the authoritative historian (citing largely from contemporary sources and eye-witnesses' accounts), his essay contains little which has not been more judiciously told by Allen, from whom most of it is taken, sometimes without inverted commas. Including the important additional matter from 1876 onward, it is a much slighter production than Allen's. In respect of detail alone, apart from any questions of treatment, to speak of a monograph of 182 pages on the largest, most numerous, and most economically and socially important historic mammal of this continent, as 'exhaustive,'[15] 'thorough,'[16] and 'elaborate,'[17] can be considered only as an index of the critics' very superficial acquaintance with the subject or of their low standards of sufficiency.

The last of the three, the contribution of Ernest Thompson Seton, must be pronounced, in the light of his much wider opportunities, to be the most deficient of all. During the interval between the essay of Hornaday (1889) and Seton's earlier work (1910), a considerable number of invaluable sources for buffalo history were published. Foremost among these were the highly important publications under the skilled editorship of Dr. Elliott Coues,[18] and the magnificent series of Dr. Reuben Gold Thwaites,[19] incomparable store-houses of buffalo lore from early eye-witnesses. Among all these, practically—I believe actually—the only work cited by Seton which was not mentioned by Hornaday twenty years earlier is Dr. Coues's *Henry-Thompson Journals*. This particular work was enthusiastically hailed by Seton as meeting the precise need for "a series of observations made during a number of years at one point where the Buffalo abounded . . .," as the only sure method of deciding the question of migration.[20] He adds in this connection: "Twenty years ago we should have said, 'Too late for that,' but now the discovery of Alexander Henry's precious old 'Journal in Red River Valley' has shed some light on the Buffalo and most other bygone creatures in that now famous land of grain. . . ."[21]

America, I, 40); see also Gass, *Journal of Lewis and Clark Expedition*, introd., xxxix; and by implication, Seton (*Life-Histories of Northern Animals*, I, 262, 280, 285, 288, 290, 292). There were some contemporaries "of whom to be dispraised were no small praise. . . ."

[15]"An exhaustive treatise . . ." (Stone and Cram, *American Animals*, 68).
[16]"Hornaday's thorough work . . ." (Webb, *Great Plains*, 43).
[17]"An elaborate memoir . . ." (Garretson, *American Bison*, 1938, 193).
[18]Coues (ed.), *Lewis and Clark Journals*; Coues (ed.), *Expeditions of Pike*; Coues (ed.), *Henry-Thompson Journals*; Coues (ed.), *Journal of Jacob Fowler*.
[19]Thwaites (ed.), *Jesuit Relations*; Thwaites (ed.), *Early Western Travels*;

These utterances are by no means borne out by the very meagre and altogether unsatisfactory use which he made of the document in question, as we shall have occasion to note. Perhaps even less defensible is the implication of pontifical authority for this one source above all others. The section on buffalo in Seton's later encyclopaedic work, *Game Animals* (1929), is virtually a reprint of the earlier one, with some additions relating principally to the Northern wood buffalo. The critical remarks on the migration controversy remain unmodified. Seton, while a genius of the very first rank as a field observer with pen and pencil, is frequently an uncritical and careless historian of the buffalo.

The present essay is an attempt to remedy the defects of earlier works. While I do not deny that it is largely iconoclastic in form, it certainly was not commenced in any iconoclastic spirit. As the shortcomings of previous efforts in this field began to reveal themselves, both in respect of the lack (in the two later generalizers I have mentioned) of a true critical approach, and of anything like an adequate use of the available historical material, and as the project began to take shape in my mind, I laid down for my own guidance three fundamental principles. These were: (1) the insertion wherever practicable of any witness's testimony in his own words; (2) the inclusion of as many contributions as possible on any given topic, particularly where they tended to combat some existing but dubiously supported belief; (3) the rigid and accurate documentation of all statements or evidence of any character. I have earnestly striven throughout to observe these conditions, as I believe that in no other way can a reliable historical account of the buffalo be written.

One cannot lay claim to such a title as 'exhaustive.' I am only too acutely conscious of important, although inevitable, omissions from my list of sources consulted. What will probably be the most exact and important buffalo sources of all will not be available to students until the classification of the archives of the Hudson's Bay Company, in progress at Hudson's Bay House, London, is completed. But there comes a point where research, if it is to yield any fruit whatever, must give place to co-ordination. I can only say that I have spared no effort to make the present essay as complete as possible; and I do not think any *class* of evidence has been left unnoticed. I do not believe the actual testimony of any single eye-witness has been rejected, except-

---

also Hennepin's *New Discovery* (Thwaites (ed.), reprint of English trans. of 1698).

[20]Seton, *Life-Histories of Northern Animals*, I, 261-7.

[21]*Ibid.*, 265.

ing, possibly, where he has contradicted himself. But it has frequently proved necessary to distinguish carefully between the testimony and the opinions of a witness—a vital distinction which is all too often ignored. I have more than once rejected the uniform applicability of testimony to all situations; and for good reason, as will be seen. While supplementary evidence on points of detail will doubtless continue to appear, it is difficult to conceive that there will emerge any fundamental and authoritative evidence which would override the general conclusions presented.

Chapter II

EARLY BUFFALO IN NORTH AMERICA

THE present essay is not closely concerned with the question of buffalo origins in North America. The problems arising from this belong more properly to the fields of the biologist, the geologist, and the archaeologist. Certain tentative conclusions seem to arise, however, even from historical evidence; and these I shall briefly note. Merely because of its vastly greater numbers and immensely larger historic habitat, the Plains type was almost instinctively regarded as the parent, and the numerically smaller variants as the offshoots. Until little more than half a century ago, this view held the field practically unchallenged. Almost hand in hand went the belief that the buffalo species were indigenous to their historic Plains habitat. This has found frequent expression in early writers.[1] The influence of this attitude, which has almost become a tradition, has been so general that one appears to endorse it, even in the act of formal dissent, by the use of such phrases as the title of the following chapter. Considered as a deliberate expression of opinion, however, one or two items of evidence from history or observation may be noted. Professor William Rowan remarks: "There is no doubt that the wood bison have been isolated for many centuries. They are generally considered to be an offshoot from the plains race, but on what evidence I am unaware. . . ."[2]

The evidence apparently consists in the tacit adoption of opinions expressed long ago by various writers, some of whom did not even pretend to be offering any scientific conclusion,[3] and in the ignoring

[1]"At all times": Berlandier MS. on mammals of Mexico (1830), now lost, but cited by Allen, *American Bisons*, 129; Hornaday, "Extermination of the American Bison," 382. ". . . from time immemorial": Nuttall, *Early Western Travels*, XIII, 145, 211. ". . . for many ages": Irving, *Astoria*, 165. ". . . a thousand generations": Farnham, *Early Western Travels*, XXVIII, 94. ". . . thousands of years" (in Kentucky), "hundreds of years", "centuries ago": Hulbert, *Historic Highways*, I, 117, 124, 138. ". . . thousands of years": Hubbard, *Neolithic Dew-Ponds and Cattle-Ways*, 52. ". . . for uncounted ages": Stone and Cram, *American Animals*, 67. ". . . many hundreds of years": Maclean, *McDougall of Alberta*, 264.

[2]Rowan, "Canada's Buffalo," 358-60.

[3]As, for example, David Thompson, *circa* 1812: ". . . the Bisons that take to the Woods, become much larger than those of the plains . . ." *Narrative*, ed. Tyrrell, 558. On the growth of the opinion, see Soper, "History of the Northern Bison" (*Ecological Monographs*, XI, Oct., 1941, 347-412). I am indebted to the author's kindness for a copy of this most valuable and comprehensive study (see p. 354), on the above).

of divergent critical suggestions. A few expressions of the orthodox opinion are of interest: "From the observations made on the subject we may conclude that the buffalo inhabited the temperate zone of the New World, and that they inhabited it at all times. In the north they never advanced beyond the 48th or 58th degree [*sic*] of latitude. . . ." (Dr. Berlandier, *circa* 1830).[4] ". . . the great plains country of the West was the natural home of the species. . . ."[5] "The countless herds . . . were a product of the plains country, and but for the limitless expanse of grazing country, their existence in such enormous multitudes would have been impossible."[6] "Type-locality, Mexico. . . ."[7] "The true home of the buffalo was on the Great Plains . . . It is not maintained that buffaloes were confined to the Plains, but it is essential to understand that their occupation of the forest and mountains was merely incidental, an overflow from their natural habitat. Hornaday's study seems to imply that the herds were invading the East when the white man came. . . ."[8] Following upon this, the same writer curiously remarks: "The buffalo had few qualities, save size and gregariousness, that fitted it to the Plains. . . ."[9] Others, such as N. S. Shaler (1891),[10] or Dr. Clark Wissler (1922),[11] may perhaps have held similar opinions; but their pronouncements concerning 'origins' and environment may only have reference to the *development* of the Plains type as we know it, which is a different thing.

An early notice of the European species, from which modern scientific opinion derives the American types, comes to us from Maximilian of Wied, an observer who apparently knew both. He writes as follows (1843):

The American buffalo or bison has been supposed to be, if not identical, very nearly akin, to the bison (*wisent* or *zuhr*) which still exists in Russia; but from all that I know of the latter, the two animals appear to me to form two entirely different species. The American buffalo is characterized by its hair and colour. Its head is very large and is carried low, its neck short, the withers very high, the fore part of the body colossal and broad, the back part, in proportion, small and weak, the tail rather short, very smooth, with short hairs, and a tuft at the end. During the summer months, the head, neck, shoulders, fore part of the body, and thighs, till behind the shoulder

[4]Berlandier MS., in Allen, *American Bisons,* 129; Hornaday, "Extermination of the American Bison," 382.
[5]*Ibid.,* 377.
[6]Chittenden, *American Fur Trade,* II, 758.
[7]Seton, *Game Animals,* III, 641, 643.
[8]Webb, *Great Plains,* 43-4.
[9]*Ibid.,* 44.
[10]Shaler, *Nature and Man in America,* 183.
[11]Wissler, *American Indian,* 14, 374.

blade, are covered with longer hair, which there ceases, and is bounded by a strictly defined line from the hinder part of the body, the hair of which is short and smooth, looking, altogether, like a shorn poodle. The forehead and upper part of the head have smooth hair from twelve to eighteen inches long, and that on the forelegs is equally long, hanging down to the middle of the shins. In the winter the hair of the hinder part of the body is rather longer with a thicker wool under it.

The prints, representing the wisent or zuhr of the Poles, which is still to be found in the forest of Bialowieza, represent that animal as very different from the American buffalo. The figure given by Bojanus (Tab. XXI) represents the head of a bull six years old, without any long hair, and so does Tab. XX, where the hair of the forehead of the American buffalo is twelve inches long, and the beard hangs down to a great length. In these and other prints there is no long hair on the forelegs; while the tail, in Bojanus's prints, has much longer hair than that of the American animal. None of them have the long hair on the fore part of the body, nor the strictly defined limit of the longer hair. . . .[12]

Apart from the question of European origin, the northern variety was classified by Samuel N. Rhoads of Philadelphia in 1897 as a subspecies, to which the name of *Bison bison Athabascae Rhoads* or some kindred designation has been given,[13] and this has met with a very general acceptance in scientific circles. Bearing this in mind, it is somewhat startling to note the following from a publication in 1923 of the then Department of the Interior, Ottawa, which was the official trustee of the Northern Wood buffalo:

The now almost extinct European buffalo was a forest species, while the so-called American buffalo, which today is found only in our parks and zoological collections, is descended from a race that lived on the plains and differed from the true bison of Europe in having more abundant hair, relatively weaker hindquarters and shorter and more curved horns. The last remnants of true bison in Europe have supposedly been exterminated by the Bolshevists.[14] Canada, however, in the northern wood buffalo possesses

[12]Maximilian, *Early Western Travels*, XXIII, 173. There are excellent photogravures of the two species, European and American, in Garretson, *American Bison;* and compare his general summary, 1-5.

[13]See on this, Raup, *Range Conditions in Wood Buffalo Park,* 18; Soper, "History of the Northern Bison," 355-7, etc.; Skinner and Kaisen, *Fossil Bison of Alaska,* 150, 151, 165, etc. Cf. below, notes 52, 54.

[14]I have since found the following: "A Soviet experiment in crossing American bison with European buffalo is reported a success at the Askania-Nova state preserves in the Ukraine.

"Breeders there seeking by this method to build up forest buffalo herds which were exterminated in the First Great War, said they had raised 71 bulls and 63 cows" (*Edmonton Journal,* Dec. 18, 1940).

If they were 'exterminated,' as commonly accepted, from what European buffalo are the crosses derived?

I find the following note in Gibbon: "Without losing myself in a labyrinth of species and names—the aurochs, urus, bisons, bubalus, bonasus, buffalo, etc.

not only finer specimens than those which ranged in the Caucasus but also larger, darker, and handsomer animals than those which were formerly found in such numbers on the plains far to the south.

Owing to this difference in appearance our wood buffalo has been classified as a sub-species of the American bison and is referred to as *Bos (Bison) Bison Athabascae,* but whatever differences there are between it and the buffalo of the plains are largely owing to environment. . . .[15]

A somewhat later publication by another official of the same Department takes the case even more completely for granted:

From our joint observation,[16] verified by the evidence of many reliable residents of the districts, including the paid rangers, white and native trappers and hunters, missionaries, public officials, and others, we are satisfied as to the correctness of the following information:

True American bison to the number of at least 1500 and in all probably 2000 are roaming in a free state in this district. . . . In colour they are darker than the former plains bison, but this is probably merely due to the northern and more sheltered range . . . its northern exile has improved it physically. . . . It is reasonably certain that bulls of 2500 lbs. weight are quite common in these herds. This clearly indicates that the bison in his new environment is not diminishing but rather increasing in size. His vitality appears to be unimpaired and his shyness and alertness to danger increased manyfold. In short, he has learned to take better care of himself. . . .[17]

One cannot suppose the foregoing writers, representing the former Department of the Interior, to have been ignorant at least of the existence of the Eurasiatic-origin theory concerning the bison species; their arrival on the North American continent in the Pleistocene period is treated as an accepted truth at least as early as 1910, if not long before.[18] It still remains questionable what authority the absolutely

---

(Buffon, *Histoire Naturelle,* supplement, III, VI, also XI), it is certain, that in the sixth century, a large wild species of horned cattle was hunted in the great forests of the Vosges in Lorraine, and the Ardennes" (*Gregory of Tours,* tome II, lib. x, cap. x, p. 369). Theodebert, King of the Franks, was overthrown and slain by a wild bull while hunting in the Belgic or German forests (*circa* A.D. 538). Gibbon, *Decline and Fall,* vol. III, chap. XLI, p. 534.

[15]Graham, *Canada's Wild Buffalo,* 8. His conclusion is incorrect. See below, chap. III, note 93, on osteological variations by which skeletons can be differentiated.

[16]The plural has reference to F. V. Seibert, also of the (then) Department of the Interior, Ottawa, who discusses the subject in "Some Notes on Canada's So-Called Wood Buffalo" (*Canadian Field-Naturalist,* XXXIX, 1925, 204-6), which I have not seen; on whom cf. Soper, "History of the Northern Bison," 353. Seibert contributes an appendix to Graham (*Canada's Wild Buffalo,* 13-14), in which he merely says: ". . . the only remnants, in a wild state, of the millions which roamed. . . ." This is non-controversial.

[17]Kitto, "Survival of American Bison in Canada," 436, 437; cf. Soper, "History of the Northern Bison," 353.

[18]Osborn, *Age of Mammals,* 438. Classifications of Northern fossil bison go

unanimous agreement of residents, howsoever 'reliable,' could confer
in what is finally a problem in palaeobiology. The addition of the
testimony of even one competent zoologist would have strengthened
their case much more. Only three years later (1926) the same Department published a pamphlet, apparently for the purpose of attracting
tourists, from which scientific theories of origins could quite legitimately have been omitted altogether. It is there stated: "The species
is believed to have arrived in this continent in mid-Pleistocene times
or during the warm inter-Glacial period. It probably crossed from
Asia by the northern land route and gradually spread southwards
until it covered more than one-third of North America. . . ."[19]

The definition of Mexico (by Linnaeus) as the 'type-locality'[20] is
interesting, since a contemporary investigator would virtually exclude
the buffalo from Mexico at any period of their history. 'Type-locality'
does not signify (as a layman might pardonably imagine) some specially favoured or characteristic region of their choice, such as the
Plains, but the region in which the type was first identified for scientific
knowledge. The earliest authentic data are furnished by the scribes
of Coronado's expedition; Cabeza de Vaca, another early explorer, is
very vague on this subject. But while their probable encounters with
buffalo took place in what was Mexico in Linnaeus's day (eighteenth
century), it is no longer such, nor did it bear the name in the age of
those early Spanish explorers. This tends to fix the species in our minds
as characteristically sub-tropical, and to obscure one of the most predominant features of the Plains buffalo—their ability to endure intense
cold; much more readily, in fact, than excessive heat. Detailed evidence of the former capacity, particularly, will be presented in a later
chapter,[21] but two or three factors affecting their reaction towards
heat may be noted here.

The buffalo pelage points very strongly towards a species developed in a cold winter climate. It may be doubted if any animal ever
possessed a more effective cold-defying covering; and the buffalo was
no polar bear, kept warm by oily, fatty foods. Two facts may be em-

back before Richardson's time (1829, *et seq.*). See below in this chapter, notes
50-2.

[19]Canada, Department of the Interior, *Bringing Back the Buffalo*. Another
'official' publication, but of a very different class, is fully up-to-date: Jenness,
Indians of Canada, 238.

[20]Seton, *Game Animals*, III, 641, 643. Another Southern Plains authority
would practically bar them from Mexico altogether: Hallenbeck, *Journey of
Cabeza de Vaca*, 140-6, etc. Cf. Skinner and Kaisen, *Fossil Bison of Alaska*, 149,
154-5. See discussion *in extenso* below, chap. IX, note 24. For fossil bison in
Mexico, see note 43 below.

[21]See chap. VIII, "Buffalo and Snow."

phasized in this connection. (1) Down to the very last of the southern herds, the characteristic 'buffalo-robe' was obtainable, the quality being apparently subject to the same criteria of seasonal (that is, winter) conditions, age, sex, etc., that prevailed in the colder north. (2) The Wainwright Buffalo Park animals shipped to the north are reported to have weathered without undue suffering or loss, and they are ancestrally of the Central Plains section of the habitat. If such protective features have supposedly been acquired as a result of the same individuals trekking for generations between sub-arctic and subtropical zones, the historical evidence furnishes no support to that supposition. Their reaction towards heat, quite natural in a southern plains-dweller clad in so heavy a coat, seems logical enough; moving northward from Mexico in summer, and even deserting the incomparable pastures of central Texas—'because of the heat,' since no other reasonably probable explanation offers itself—is well attested. Hornaday observes: "Undoubtedly this northern migration was to escape the heat of their southern winter range rather than to find better pasture; for as a grazing country for cattle all the year round, Texas is hardly surpassed, except where it is overstocked. It was with the buffaloes a matter of choice rather than necessity which sent them on their annual pilgrimage northward. . . ."[22]

With reference to over-stocking, a later scholar comments very pertinently on the absurdity of any migratory creatures leaving in spring, the opening season of greater abundance, a region which had been able to support their food requirements during the winter.[23] An 'instinctive' movement has no application here; since it should be at least as instinctive for a northern-born species to travel northward whence ancestrally it came, as for a southerner to strike northward on an initial exploration into an unknown territory. The same relationship towards extreme heat—perfectly logical in a northern forest-bred species, but difficult to explain in an indigenous product of the hot Southwestern Plains region—is noticeable in their readiness to seek shelter from the sun in summer. This has been recorded by various observers in the most northerly portions and generally best-shaded localities, respectively, of their United States habitat,[24] and in widely sundered areas.

[22]Hornaday, "Extermination of the American Bison," 424. On Texas pasturelands, see also ibid., 382; Allen, American Bisons, 129; Dodge, Our Wild Indians, 285; Bancroft, North Mexican States and Texas, II, 551-63; Webb (descriptions by Texans), Great Plains, 161, 209-27.

[23]Rowan, Riddle of Migration, 48, etc. In extenso below, chap. IV, note 66.

[24]Hennepin, New Discovery, I, 148; Ashe, 1806 (in Allen, American Bisons, 109); Henry, Turtle Mountain, North Dakota, 1806 (in Coues (ed.), Henry-

It will be noticed in due course that the historical references to Wood and Mountain buffalo range from Colorado or southern Wyoming on the west to lower Red River (west of Fort Garry) on the east, in a roughly semi-circular or 'arched' form;[25] and do not occur at all, despite forest or mountainous environment, in the woodlands of the east or southeast,[26] or in the mountain regions of the far southwest.[27] If the historic species are actually indigenous to the plains west of the Mississippi, it is difficult to understand why they did not entirely over-run, long before the seventeenth century, a territory so generally favourable as that on the eastern side of the extreme lower Mississippi, and why in so doing a woodland variety was not evolved, as it supposedly was in the northland. These objections cannot be met by anything which might be urged concerning former climatic conditions, or the different habitat of any possible ancestral fossil species; since no remains of the historic B. americanus have been found as yet within a considerable distance of the established southern range of the fossil specimens.[28]

The careful studies of American scientists particularly have added immensely to our knowledge of prehistoric bison species on the North American continent. This I can only outline, under the guidance of palaeontologists of high standing. The classification of the fossil species, subject of course to later possible modifications, is broadly as follows. Seven 'valid species' of fossil bison have been recognized, ranging from Alaska to Florida.[29] These are the following: Bison bison

---

Thompson Journals, I, 409); cf. also *ibid.,* 64, 99, 119; Taylor, "Painted Woods," Missouri River, 1865 (*Frontier Life,* 125).

[25]See chap. III, "North American Variants of the Buffalo."

[26]I utterly decline to accept Colonel Shoemaker's classification of a 'Black Pennsylvania buffalo' (*B. pennsylvanicus*), in the total absence of historical information. *In extenso,* chap. III, notes 9-49, 161, 182, etc.

[27]I find a place-name, Buffalo Meadows, on Buffalo Creek, Washo County, western Nevada, *circa* 40° 45' N., 119° 50' W. Unless this is the site of some fossil discovery (as below, note 42), it is a most interesting circumstance, which invites further investigation. The distribution map in Skinner and Kaisen (*Fossil Bison of Alaska,* 158) gives the farthest south specimen of what they classify as one race of Bison—the 'Wood or Mountain bison'—as being from central Colorado. This is Hornaday's classification, which I discuss in detail in the following chapter (*ibid.,* 150, 157, 165-8).

[28]Compare A. S. Romer, 1932: "The living species (*B. bison*) is known to have ranged much more widely in the past than in historic times. . . ." (Jenness (ed.), *American Aborigines,* essays, 53). He cites no authority. Unless this indicates discoveries later than F. W. Hodge in *Encyclopaedia Britannica,* 14th ed., *s.v.* Bison, the statement awaits confirmation.

[29]Lucas, "Fossil Bisons of North America"; Osborn, *Age of Mammals,* 482; Scharff, *Distribution and Origin of Life in America,* 66-7; Hodge, A. L. Kroeber, *Encyclopaedia Britannica,* 14th ed., *s.v.* Bison, North American Indians, etc. See

(the recent or historic species, found in Kentucky and in Kansas);[30] *B. alleni* (found in Idaho and Kansas);[31] *B. antiquus* (found "not farther east" than Kentucky, and in California);[32] *B. crassicornis* (found in Alaska only);[33] *B. ferox* (found in Nebraska);[34] *B. latifrons* (found in Arizona, Florida, Georgia, Kansas, Kentucky, Mississippi, Nebraska, Ohio, South Carolina, and Texas);[35] *B. occidentalis* (found in Alaska and Kansas).[36] In addition to these, fossil bison remains of unidentifiable or disputable species have been found in the Don Valley near Toronto;[37] and also in Toronto itself.[38] Others are recorded in the Klondike region,[39] and in several localities in the United States. These last, which are even yet being increased by new discoveries, are very numerous and cover an extensive territory from east to west, includ-

also Supplementary Note at the end of this chapter. Skinner and Kaisen give some 22 classifications, which, however, overlap in certain instances. (*Fossil Bison of Alaska*, 163-205).

[30]Lucas, "Fossil Bisons of North America," 757. For Kentucky, below, chap. III, note 6.

[31]*Ibid.*, 756, 765-6, plates LXXVII-LXXX; Osborn, *Age of Mammals*, 464, 481, 483, 490. Lucas, "Fossil Bisons of North America," includes *Bos crampianus* Cope (in Kansas) under *B. alleni* Marsh.

[32]Lucas, "Fossil Bisons of North America," 756, 759-60, plates LXVII-LXX; Osborn, *Age of Mammals*, 466, 473, 478, 481-3. *B. californicus* Rhoads is classed by Lucas as *B. antiquus* Leidy.

[33]Lucas, "Fossil Bisons of North America," 756, 760-5, plates LXXIII-LXXV; Osborn, *Age of Mammals*, 481, 483, 490. *B. crassicornis* Richardson, the 'heavy-horned fossil bison,' in Richardson, *Polar Regions*, 296; classified by Leidy as *B. latifrons*, and by Allen (*American Bisons*, 21-6) as *B. antiquus;* by Rhoads, as *B. alaskensis* (this, with *B. crassicornis* and *B. occidentalis*, being the three Alaskan fossil species of Scharff, *Distribution and Origin of Life in America*, 66). Restored by Lucas, as Richardson, Leidy 1854 ("Fossil Bisons of North America," 760).

[34]Lucas, "Fossil Bisons of North America," 766-7, plate LXXXII; Osborn, *Age of Mammals*, 481, 483.

[35]Lucas, "Fossil Bisons of North America," 767-70, plates LXXXII-LXXXIII; Osborn, *Age of Mammals*, 440, 454, 466, 471, 478, 481-3; see also McGee and Thomas, *History of North America*, XIX, 22; *Encyclopaedia Britannica*, 14th ed. *s.v.* Bison. See also a most valuable monograph: Vanderhoof, "A Skull of Bison Latifrons" (*University of California Publications in Geological Sciences*, 1942, 1-23). This describes a truly colossal specimen, with horns of six-foot spread, found in Shasta County, North California, December, 1933. The illustration (pp. 14, 21, 23) is reproduced in Hamilton, Jr., *American Mammals*, 20.

[36]Lucas, "Fossil Bisons of North America," 756, 758, plates LXV, LXVI, LXXXIII; Osborn, *Age of Mammals*, map, 481, 483.

[37]*Ibid.*, 449, 451.

[38]A fossil bison skull, 'estimated to be at least 10,000 years old,' was unearthed during sewer excavations in the city of Toronto. *Edmonton Journal*, June 11, 1932.

[39]Seton notes the discovery there, *circa* 1905, of fossil remains of bison and other animals, "in the low, level, Creek Gravels, possibly Pleistocene. . . ." Seton, *Game Animals*, III, 604.

ing California,[40] Cape Cod, Massachusetts,[41] Nevada,[42] New and Old Mexico,[43] Pennsylvania,[44] Texas,[45] Oregon, and Washington.[46] Some have since been classified in what is apparently intended to be specific rank, but on rather unsatisfactory grounds.[47]

The mere unearthing of fossil bison specimens in these widely sundered localities might of itself offer little or no evidence as to which of these regions (if any) was the place of origin. But the general conclusions of modern palaeontologists indicate that some at least of the identifiable fossil species came ancestrally from Asia and Europe, and reached North America by way of Alaska, over the land-bridge which formerly joined the two continents.[48] Further, various accepted points

[40]Osborn, Age of Mammals, 477.

[41]In 1920, a discovery "of a fragment of the maxilla with two milk teeth of a Bison at Orleans, on Cape Cod, Mass." Seton, Game Animals, III, 646. See remarks below, chap. IX, note 78.

[42]Osborn, Age of Mammals, 468; cf. above, note 27.

[43]Seton refers to a discovery, circa 1906, of buffalo bones, horns, etc., on the upper Tularosa River, New Mexico: "This extends the range of them nearly to the western border of New Mexico. . . ." Seton (citing Marcus W. Lyon, Jr., Proceedings of the United States National Museum, 1906, 648), Game Animals, III, 646. Fossils have been found in Arizona, however, which have been classified by Blake, 1898, as Bos arizonica and by Lucas, 1899, as B. latifrons (Lucas, "Fossil Bisons of North America," 756, 767-8); as above, note 35.

In 1925 another (Pleistocene) skeleton, found near Folsom, New Mexico, almost identical with the Texas one, below: Hodge, Encyclopaedia Britannica, 14th ed., s.v. Indians. See also on this, Eiseley, "Did the Folsom Bison Survive in Canada?" (Scientific Monthly, LVI, May, 1943, 468-72). On fossil remains in Old Mexico, see Skinner and Kaisen, Fossil Bison of Alaska, 155, 157, 171, 177, 179, 181, 206, 210. For fossil bison remains in the Okanagan Valley, British Columbia, see below, Appendix L.

[44]Osborn, Age of Mammals, 471.

[45]"In 1923-1924, the nearly complete and articulated skeleton of a Pleistocene bison was found on Lone Way Creek, near Colorado, Mitchell County, Texas. . . ." with flint-chipped instruments beneath. Hodge, Encyclopaedia Britannica, 14th ed., s.v. North American Indians, Archaeology.

[46]Skinner and Kaisen, 168, 180; Osborn, Age of Mammals, 474.

[47]The New Mexico and Colorado (Texas) fossils are since classified as B. taylori and B. figginsi respectively. Romer, in Jenness (ed.), American Aborigines, 79-80. Such designations seem objectionable. If there are no variations from accepted fossil species definable in descriptive terms, as latifrons, crassicornis, they must surely align with some one of those, similarly with Bos arizonica (note 43 above). Alleni, taylori, figginsi, are mere appendages. For discussions bearing on this question, which has apparently produced many anomalies in classification, see Skinner and Kaisen, Fossil Bison of Alaska, 161, 179, 181-2, 189-90, 206, etc. Vanderhoof ("A Skull of Bison Latifrons," 4-6) notes also (1942) B. angularis, B. chaneyi, B. crampianus, B. regius, B. rotundus. See also Eiseley, "Post-Glacial Climate Amelioration and the Extinction of Bison Taylori" (Science, XCV, June 26, 1942, 646).

[48]See Osborn, "Eurasiatic Mammals," in Age of Mammals, 438-44, 481, 483; Scharff, Distribution and Origin of Life in America, 66-7; Hodge, Encyclopaedia

of resemblance led many of the older generation of zoologists to certain conclusions. These have in many respects been modified, of course, but may briefly be described as follows:

The earlier identification of the American buffalo with the "*urus* or *zorax* of Caesar" by Thomas Salmon in 1749[49] may doubtless be dismissed as a random shot, perhaps prompted by the somewhat affected classicism of his day, since exact zoological classification was only in its infancy, and Salmon was nothing more than a most voluminous geographical and politico-historical gazetteer. Cuvier, however, classified *Bison latifrons* as *Aurochs* in 1808, 1812, the earliest definition of that species noted by Lucas.[50] Buckland (*circa* 1830) classified *B. crassicornis* as *Bos urus*. The same species, *B. crassicornis*, was classed by Leidy, 1854, 1869, as *Bison priscus;* by Richardson, 1854, as possibly such; and by Lydekker, 1885, 1898, as *B. bonasus* or *priscus,* and as *Bos priscus,* respectively; uniting them on the grounds that the horns of the fossil *priscus* were frequently indistinguishable from the (then) 'living *bonasus*' or *aurochs*.[51] While somewhat hesitant in accepting this *in toto,* Lucas notes some resemblances in a cranium of *B. europaeus* (in Brussels) to *B. crassicornis,* and also a considerable resemblance between the Siberian *B. latifrons* of Fischer (1830) and the American *B. antiquus* Leidy.[52] It is of interest to observe also that in the table of 'Measurements of Metacarpals' of five species given by Lucas,[53] the European *B. bonasus* approximates more closely to the historic American *B. bison* than does the latter to *B. crassicornis, latifrons,* or *occidentalis,* in several respects.

Some further most interesting particulars are furnished by a present-day zoologist, whose vigorous essay, while anonymous, reveals a masterly grasp of the subject:

In Europe, too, there are, or were until the war years, two surviving herds of bison, the one in the Caucasus, the other in the forest of Bielowitza in Lithuania. These animals were at one time considered to be identical. Investigations however showed them to be separable, and they were accorded, like ours today, subspecific rank. But the more detailed work of

---

Britannica, 14th ed., *s.v.* Indians; Jenness, *Indians of Canada,* 233-48, etc.; Skinner and Kaisen, *Fossil Bison of Alaska,* 131.

[49]Salmon, *A New Geographical and Historical Grammar* (of the World), 537; the passage *in extenso* below, chap. X, note 108.

[50]Lucas, "Fossil Bisons of North America," 767.

[51]*Ibid.,* 759-65.

[52]*Ibid.,* 764, 769.

[53]*Ibid.,* 765; cf. Osborn, *Age of Mammals,* 408, 470, 503, 555. See also on this, Skinner and Kaisen, *Fossil Bison of Alaska,* 131, 161, 215.

Hilzheimer finally showed them to be full species. Further, Hilzheimer demonstrated that the Caucasian animal showed a closer affinity to the American plains bison than to the European form. As a matter of fact the long horns and rounded frontal region of the skull of the wood bison are more reminiscent of the other European species, the Lithuanian bison, than they are of our own plains animal. . . .[54]

It is curious to note that about 1860 Hind, after passing judgment on the question of separate varieties,[55] wrote as follows: "The skins of the so-called wood buffalo, which I saw at Selkirk Settlement, bore a very close resemblance to the skin of the Lithuanian bison, judging from the specimens of that species which I have since had an opportunity of seeing in the British Museum. . . ."[56]

H. F. Osborn's brief and non-technical description of B. occidentalis is of interest because of its human associations:

There lived also in Alaska, probably in late Pleistocene times, and ranged down into Kansas, the species B. occidentalis. This animal most closely resembled the living bison, with which it was probably contemporaneous for a time. A complete specimen of a bull of this species was discovered with seven or eight other skeletons near Russell Springs, Logan County, Kansas, in association with a flint arrowhead. The skeleton as mounted in the Kansas Museum . . . is considerably larger than that of the largest recent bison in length and height and in the length of the hind limbs. The horn cores are similar in shape and proportions. . . .[57]

Osborn observes elsewhere concerning the arrowhead discovery: "the evidence that man was contemporaneous with the extinct species of bison is of the greatest importance. . . ."[58] A later study[59] apparently holds that this may be overrated: "That the Folsom bison[60] belonged to an extinct species is, of itself, no reason for placing its human hunters into a past geological age. In its foothill range this animal might have been exterminated by the very same people whose descendants, with the help of horses, guns, and white men, terminated the plains bison. And with the animal gone, their culture would have had to end

[54]A Canadian Zoologist, "The Passing of the Wood Bison" (Canadian Forum, V, 1925, 301-5). The 'Roman profile' of the Wood buffalo is also stressed by Rowan, "Canada's Buffalo." These particulars hardly agree with Maxwell Graham's dictum, "whatever differences there are . . . are largely owing to environment . . ." (above, note 15). Cf. Skinner and Kaisen, Fossil Bison of Alaska, 131, 161, 215.
[55]On this, see chap. III, notes 59, 83.
[56]Hind, Narrative, II, 104. Not to be confused with his Report, 1858. See Bibliography.
[57]Osborn, Age of Mammals, 483. Allen notes a 'Fossil Creek,' west of Hays City, Kansas, 1871; 38° N., 99° 30′ W. (American Bisons, 62).
[58]Osborn, Age of Mammals, 463, 464, 497.
[59]Kroeber, Cultural and Natural Areas in Native North America, 88.
[60]Above, note 43.

by altering or betaking itself elsewhere, thus perhaps appearing also to be more ancient than it really was. . . ."

Although *B. occidentalis* (like every other particularized fossil species) was 'considerably larger' than the historic American buffalo, it was itself surpassed in size by the 'early and gigantic form, *B. latifrons,*' and also by the "giant northwestern bison found in Alaska, which may have existed also in eastern Siberia, *B. crassicornis.*"[61] In connection with Osborn's description of the horn-cores of *B. occidentalis* as being similar to those of the historic Prairie species (although to a layman the resemblance seems much more pronounced in one type of *B. antiquus* given by Lucas),[62] it may be noted that the horns of several species, *B. alleni, B. occidentalis,* and the widely-diffused *B. latifrons,* in appearance at least bear a very close general resemblance to the descriptions of the Wood buffalo given to (or by) Thompson, Hind, and Hector;[63] while *B. crassicornis,* the other far northern fossil species, derived its very name from its huge horns of some form.[64] We shall see that the living race of the northland Wood buffalo was described by Hearne[65] and possibly by Kelsey[66] as having short black horns like the Plains animal. Conversely, two very early accounts describe what apparently must have been the Prairie type as 'long-horned beasts';[67] and again, as having horns 'nearly two feet in length.'[68] While such accounts, taken as a whole, may perhaps be explained by the excited amazement of the beholder, like the 'three or four at a birth,'[69] one can scarcely suppose that, with herds of some size in view before them, the early French explorers transferred to the entire species exceptional features characteristic only of 'buffalo oxen' or other 'sports' so rare that most travellers appear never to have seen or even heard of them.[70] If they could be accepted as they stand (in any material numbers), they might indicate either a wider territorial spread of the Wood species—say southward from the Lake Winnipeg country—or a 'throw-back' tending to illustrate an ancestral form.

In conclusion, the situation may be broadly summarized as follows.

[61]Osborn, *Age of Mammals,* 482, 483.

[62]Lucas, "Fossil Bisons of North America," 762, 763, plates LXVI, LXX.

[63]*Ibid.,* plates LXIX-LXXXII. For the witnesses mentioned, see below, chap. III, notes 59, 98, 100.

[64]Richardson's 'heavy-horned fossil bison': *Polar Regions,* 296.

[65]*In extenso* below, chap. III, notes 96-7.

[66]See note on Kelsey, conclusion of chap. XII.

[67]Radisson and Groseilliers, 1661: see below, chap. XII, notes 44-57.

[68]Dablon and Allouez, 1671: Thwaites (ed.), *Jesuit Relations,* LV, 197; Fox River, Wisconsin; so Thwaites, ed. note, *ibid.,* V, 14.

[69]*Ibid.,* LV, 195-7: *in extenso* below, chap. IX, note 86.

[70]See chap. III, notes 175-86.

The indigenous origin in the southern Plains region is rejected by authoritative opinion, and we are confronted with the choice between two alternatives: (1) a descent from an Eurasiatic form, probably of the Lithuanian type, through the woodland species to the Plains animal, as was suggested by Seton well over half a century ago, and adopted by Samuel N. Rhoads in 1897;[71] or (2) a direct descent from a similar Eurasiatic ancestry to the Prairie form, followed by a later development of the woodland type. Apart from the logical improbabilities inherent in the supposition of an evolution to the Prairie species, followed by a secondary change *reproducing very closely the original* (Lithuanian) *parent form*—which places a great strain upon an ordinary faith—it seems doubtful if the available time would be sufficient for such a double process.[72]

SUPPLEMENTARY NOTE: All former productions on American fossil bison or vestiges of such have been superseded by the magnificent monograph of Messrs. Skinner and Kaisen, *The Fossil Bison of Alaska,* 1947 (see Bibliography), which came into my hands too late for detailed use in the text. This important work contains what must be an exhaustive presentation of maps, plates, and tables of measurement. The title scarcely indicates the completely comprehensive range of their survey, which embraces the entire North American continent. It is with no diminution of respect for a masterpiece of scientific analysis that I find myself unable to accept their findings in one or two detailed instances in relation to the present and following chapters; in which historical evidence in my view fails to support their conclusions. On this particularly, see Supplementary Note at the end of chap. III.

[71]"Rhoads believed that in systematic position within its genus the Wood bison probably stands between the plains animal and the most recent fossil species. He quotes a note made by Seton in 1886, in which the latter proposed a varietal designation for the Wood buffalo and suggested that it was of an ancient stock from which the plains bison had developed. . . ." Raup, *Range Conditions in Wood Buffalo Park,* 18. Rhoads, "Notes on Living and Extinct Species of North American Bovidae" (*Proceedings of the Academy of Natural Science,* Philadelphia, 1897, March, 483-502); Seton, "The Wood Buffalo" (*Proceedings of the Canadian Institute,* XXI, 1886, 114-17); neither of which I have seen. A very good summary of Seton and Rhoads in Soper, "History of the Northern Bison," 355-7.

It is regrettable that Seton, with what appears in the light of present knowledge to be the true solution in his grasp, should have relinquished it, in deference, it would seem, to the dogmatic and certainly not more informed pronouncements of Dr. Hornaday, by whom Seton's important contribution is not mentioned. It was my privilege to meet Seton in Edmonton, at the home of his host, Professor Wm. Rowan, September 28, 1939. The distinguished guest informed me, in conversation on this matter, that, being 'challenged' to produce a type-specimen showing structure, pelage, etc., he was unable to do so, and thus, so to speak, lost his case by default. But Hornaday was himself no better equipped. He admitted never having seen these variant forms (see below, chap. III, note 50); and he cavalierly ignored or distorted the evidence of those who had.

[72]The severely scientific palaeologist might hesitate to endorse the suggestion, but the lay mind might infer also a far greater likelihood of dispersion from an originating focal point over a broad lateral area, represented by the Florida-California base line, than the reverse movement, commencing at the extremities of such a vast 'triangle,' and converging upon its geographical apex.

CHAPTER III

NORTH AMERICAN VARIANTS[*] OF THE BUFFALO AND THEIR GEOGRAPHICAL DISTRIBUTION

WHEN any animal species has occupied for a long time[1] such a huge and widely diversified territory as the American buffalo, we may with reasonable probability anticipate the development of modifications, amounting virtually to distinct varieties; and we cannot feel surprised that a belief in such varieties was strongly entertained among the plainsmen (both red and white) in more than one locality along those frontiers where forest and prairie, or plain and mountain, abutted. As full a presentation as our evidence permits of the geographical distribution of such supposed varieties should not only furnish important data concerning the direction of the buffalo's earliest advance into its historical habitat, but also on the possible region of its (American) origin.

Before proceeding with the general inquiry concerning varieties, it may be noted that, although the physical characteristics of the areas east of the Mississippi differed from the Plains territory as fundamentally as did the Plains from the mountain regions or from the northern woodlands beyond the North Saskatchewan, I have found only one indication in Eastern United States territory of any belief in local variations in the buffalo species. This, moreover, is of an unsatisfactory character, since the early observers, upon whose accounts it is based, do not appear to have known both the supposed varieties; while others, who almost certainly must have known of them had they existed, are silent upon the subject.[2]

These considerations indicate that the appearance of the historic species cannot authentically be dated far enough back in the eastern regions for any possible variations to have had time to develop. This suggestion is supported by the historical fact that the animal was not found in 1540 in certain regions where it was a familiar sight in the seventeenth and eighteenth centuries. The further absence of any local traditions in Florida, Georgia, or Alabama *ante* 1540, offers reasonable proof that its advance southeastward after that era was its first appearance there, and not simply a return after an absence at a time that included the very years when De Soto passed through the region.[3]

[*]On 'variants,' see Supplementary Note, below, p. 68.

[1]See above, chap. II, note 1, for learned opinion on this.
[2]Below, notes 9-40.   [3]See below, chap. IX, notes 18-21.

Archaeological evidence also substantiates this, as the following extract shows, coming from an investigator of the first rank:

In the pre-European state of the country, probably down to some time after the year 1000, the American bison or buffalo appears to have been absent from all the region east of the Mississippi. It is doubtful if the creature existed for any distance east of the Rocky Mountains. There had been an earlier and less plentiful species of bison in the country; but he appears to have disappeared many thousands of years ago, perhaps before the coming of man to this continent.[4] Our well-known species probably was developed in some region far to the west of the Mississippi, whence it gradually spread to the eastward. The Mound-Builders apparently did not know the creature. We determine this point by the fact that we do not find bison bones about the old kitchen fires, and we fail to find any picture of the beast in the abundant delineations of animals made by these ancient people. They figured all the other important forms of land animals, including birds, snakes, and also many of those from the far-off waters of the Atlantic and the Gulf of Mexico; but they have given us no representation of this, which would have been to them the king of beasts. We therefore justly conclude that it was unknown to them. . . .[5]

The relatively recent advent of the buffalo into the Mississippi valley is well indicated by the facts disclosed in a section of the remarkable deposits which have been accumulated around the salt springs at Big Bone Lick, in Boone County, Kentucky. At this locality a number of springs whose waters are saline and therefore tempting to the larger herbivora emerge on the earth in the level bottom of a small valley. In the olden days these waters were evidently poured forth into a swampy field of some acres in extent. A section through the deposit shows us the following order of events in the later geologic days of this district. During and perhaps before the coming of the last glacial sheet upon the northern parts of this continent, these springs were greatly resorted to by the elephants which inhabited this district. When in 1868 the present writer made extensive excavations around these springs, he found at a depth of ten feet below the surface and thence downward for an unknown depth many remains of these gigantic pachyderms, the skeletons being broken to pieces by the pressure of the feet of the successive generations of these animals. Above that level, in the section which probably represents the time when the margin of the great glacier lay only a few miles to the north of the site, lay the remains of a musk-ox allied to the living form found in the Arctic regions and to the caribou or American reindeer. These remains were mingled with those of the elephant and mastodon. At about the same level occur the bones of a bison belonging to the same genus as our so-called American buffalo, but specifically quite distinct from that form. After all the above-named creatures had passed away, near the very top of the section, in positions which seem to indicate an exceedingly recent arrival in the district, we find the bones of our ordinary bison. The conditions in which their skeletons are found are such as to show that they could not well have been for more than

[4]Seton mentions an 'extinct Alleghanian bison': *Life-Histories of Northern Animals*, I, 250; cf. *ibid.*, I, 17-18.
[5]Shaler, *Nature and Man in America*, 183-4.

a few centuries in this part of the continent at the time when it was first
visited by Europeans. . . .[6]

The relatively recent date of the mounds, rather than the vastly
more remote eras formerly suggested, is now generally accepted.[7]
Such archaeological information, taken with the geological evidence
from investigations such as those of Shaler and others, is sufficiently
conclusive for the purpose of approximately 'dating' the historic buffalo
in that region.[8] Even were this evidence of late arrival rejected, there
would still be insufficient positive evidence of the development of any
new variety in the territory in question.

Before leaving the area, we may conveniently discuss the Pennsylvania 'Wood bison,' which its discoverer or champion, Henry W. Shoemaker, classifies as a separate variety or sub-species under the name
of *Bison americanus Pennsylvanicus*. Shoemaker's classification of the
Pennsylvania bison is based upon traditional particulars furnished by
the great-grandchildren of early settlers, principally in Clinton County,
Pennsylvania. There can be nothing but commendation for the effort
to secure such material before it is lost; but the use made of it in this

[6]*Ibid.*, 185, 186. The situation is about 20 miles southwest from Cincinnati,
Ohio. For some early descriptions, see Croghan (*Early Western Travels*, I, 135);
Captain Harry Gordon's Journal, in Mereness (ed.), *Colonial Travels*, 466;
Kenton, *Simon Kenton*, 63. *Cresswell's Journal*, 83-7; Cuming, *Early Western
Travels*, IV, 175. See also Allen, *American Bisons*, 112; Hornaday, "Extermination
of the American Bison," 387; Hulbert, *Historic Highways*, I, 116, 124; *B. antiquus*
Leidy and *B. latifrons* (Harlan) have been found in Big Bone Lick (Lucas,
"Fossil Bisons of North America," 756, 759, 767). See chap. II.

[7]Flagg, 1836, instanced the 'venerable oaks' on Monk Mound, St. Louis, as a
proof of immense antiquity (*Early Western Travels*, XXVI, 180-91). This means
little. A sound oak of 500 years would be immense, if there be such a thing. John
Nisbet, a practical forestry expert and also a historical student of the subject gives
less than 200 years for maturity (*Our Forests*, 88-132, 266), and another learned
historian, less than that (Albion, *Forests and Sea Power*, 95-100).

The important work of H. C. Shetrone, *The Mound Builders*, supersedes all
others and sums up our knowledge to date. He brings mound-building down to
circa 1650, and considers the wars of the League of the Iroquois (*post circa*
1570) to be the real cause of its abandonment (pp. 471-89). He seems needlessly
contemptuous of the hypothesis that the coming of the buffalo, by yielding an
easier subsistence than agriculture, arrested the upward trend toward a higher
civilization. Unless one can prove (1) that historically a thing *did* not occur, or
(2) that logically or physically it *could* not occur, then it *may* have occurred.
Meanwhile, his 'decay of mound-building' is virtually contemporaneous with the
buffalo advent east of the (southern) Mississippi. Even frequent exceptions prove
little contra, since such changes do not operate instantaneously, as if by legal
proclamation. Also, Shetrone himself notes as a 'puzzle' (p. 487) the complete
absence of mounds from Alabama to Mexico. Is it mere coincidence only that this
very region was in part the immemorial home of the buffalo?

[8]So accepted by Hulbert, *Historic Highways*, I, 101, to his own undoing, as it
seems to me.

case is uncritical and in my view unsatisfactory. Imputations of deliberate falsehood do not enter into this class of testimony; consequently the emphasis on the personal integrity of informants is no answer to critical objections.[9] And in any case, the objections are less against the informants than against the author's use of their material.

Shoemaker states that the Pennsylvania animal belonged to the type known as Wood bison, the hump was 'conspicuous by its absence,' and the 'heavy front and meagre hind-quarters of the western bison were not present.'[10] These features are decidedly present in the accepted Wood bison of northern Canada.[11] The colour is stated by Shoemaker to have been "very dark, many of the old bulls being coal-black, with grizzly white hairs around the nose and eyes. . . ."[12] Unfortunately, the only actual specimen recorded was a huge bull which the local settlers termed 'Old Logan,' the leader of *the last herd* in Pennsylvania. It had not been previously observed (in so far as we are informed), and left no successor.[13]

These recitals are not sufficient to decide colour for purposes of strict scientific classification. 'Black' is a favourite colloquial synonym for 'dark' or 'very dark.' Black bread, black poplar (*P. balsamifera*), Black Sea, Black Forest, Black River, Black Wood, etc.—none of these is *black*.[14] Father Binneteau, in the Illinois country, 1699, wrote that "the ox of these regions is of a blackish-brown. . . ."[15] Thompson Seton, describing a specimen skin of a northern Wood bison which ranged in colour from light brown to darker brown, becoming almost black on head, legs, and belly, says—". . . looking at head and legs you would say at once they were black. . . ."[16] Almost any range rider would agree that animals of any but the very lightest colours look black at a distance. In the absence of contemporary scientific examination, even the precise term 'coal-black,' after a century's filtering through the minds

[9]Shoemaker, *A Pennsylvania Bison Hunt*, 9, 28, 39, 43, 51; cf. below, note 166.
[10]*Ibid.*, 17.
[11]See photo in Graham, *Canada's Wild Buffalo*, 7-8; also Seton, *Game Animals*, III, 706. Professor Wm. Rowan, in conversation, further assures me there is no doubt about this.
[12]Shoemaker, *A Pennsylvania Bison Hunt*, 16-17. Seton, from this, classifies the entire 'race' as the 'Black Pennsylvanian Buffalo' (*Game Animals*, III, 643-6, 657, 658, 703). This is more than Shoemaker himself claims. Cf. also 'little or no hump' (*ibid.*, 643), and see below, note 114.
[13]Shoemaker, *A Pennsylvania Bison Hunt*, 30-3. If the 'grizzly white' hairs were actually noted in 'old Logan,' they might have been due merely to age.
[14]I have often heard folk of the same rural type describe whole meal bread (for example) as 'black as that stove!' It was not *white*.
[15]Thwaites (ed.), *Jesuit Relations*, LXV, 73, 105.
[16]Seton, *Game Animals*, III, 706. *In extenso* below, note 114.

of individuals who never saw these animals, is too indeterminate for any sound conclusions.

Their identification as a distinct variety in that particular corner of the buffalo habitat involves one of two hypotheses. Whether they are regarded as the parent stock from which the Plains buffalo later developed, or as a local variant evolved more or less in the Alleghany region (Shoemaker apparently favours the latter, since he speaks of the 'true bison of the plains'[17]), they must either (1) have penetrated to the region ages ago by way of the country south of the Great Lakes and up the Ohio Valley; or (2) have crossed from the Ontario side of the lakes by way of the Niagara peninsula or farther eastward along the St. Lawrence basin. We have seen the paucity of archaeological and geological evidence for the first supposition. Thus far, neither archaeological, geological, historical, nor traditional evidence has been discovered for the second one. Shoemaker himself recognizes Buffalo, N.Y. as the northern limit of their range.[18] From study of and intercourse with such scientific investigators as J. A. Allen and Samuel N. Rhoads, he should have realized the necessity for a co-ordination of all classes of available evidence—above all, both historical and geological chronology.

If a Pennsylvania variety could develop, there is, of course, no inherent reason why a 'bison of Louisiana' should not also do so, as Shoemaker believes was the case. But historical evidence indicates that in that general area the buffalo had not even reached the lower Mississippi in 1540 on their *original* eastward penetration of the Gulf States regions.[19]

After careful study of Shoemaker's remarks on the 'vast numbers' and 'vast herds' of the Pennsylvania buffalo,[20] I remain skeptical concerning their vastness. This phrase will receive more specific treatment later on,[21] but certain points arise at this place. An old man, one of the first settlers near (the later) Clarion, Pennsylvania, whose cabin was rubbed down by buffalo in a few hours (*circa* 1770),[22] is quoted from Thomas Ashe (1806) as being visited by buffalo "in such numbers that he supposed there could not have been less than two thousand there at a time. . . ."[23] On the following page (of Shoemaker), the same old

[17]Shoemaker, *A Pennsylvania Bison Hunt*, 9.

[18]*Ibid.*, 21. For this in detail, see below, chap. X, notes 167-85; and compare Seton's remarks, while also endorsing Shoemaker.

[19]See below, chap. IX, note 21.

[20]Shoemaker, *A Pennsylvania Bison Hunt*, 10, 26, 36.

[21]See below, chap. XIII.

[22]See below, chap. X, note 146.

[23]Shoemaker, *A Pennsylvania Bison Hunt*, 23.

man, apparently at the same time—'when he first settled there'—estimated that there could not have been less than *ten* thousand in the neighbourhood.[24] How much of this is Ashe, and how much is Ashe's old settler dealing with a period some thirty-five years earlier, is difficult to decide. Contemporary and later critics have recorded their opinions concerning Ashe,[25] and it may be noted here that Shoemaker quotes Ashe from J. A. Allen in respect of both numbers and trails, certainly implying the latter's endorsement, yet he fails to mention Allen's demolition of the trails 'observed to have been made by buffalo' around Onondaga Lake.[26]

The supposed numbers of this alleged sub-species rest upon no critical basis whatever. The 12,000 of 'the great northern herd' in 1773 are Shoemaker's figures, not his informants', for their impression which he adduces is regarding *families*, not numbers *in toto*. The families, which consisted of a bull and twenty or thirty cows, young animals, and calves, dropped off from the large herds in the spring and rejoined them in the autumn. There would certainly need to be a 'vast number of families' to account for 'tens of thousands' and 'vanished millions' in Pennsylvania.[27]

Ashe "met with a man who had killed two thousand buffaloes [in Pennsylvania] with his own hand, and others no doubt have done the

---

[24]*Ibid.*, 24.

[25]Ashe, *Travels in America* (1808). I have not seen this.

John Bradbury, the English naturalist who accompanied the Astorians westward, 1811, is very severe on Ashe's unreliability (*Early Western Travels*, V, 293). Cf. also Thwaites, ed. note, *ibid.*, V, 12.

[26]Allen has preserved a specimen of Ashe. *In re* Onondaga Lake, 1806, Ashe writes: ". . . the best roads to the lake were the 'buffalo tracks,' so called *from having been observed to be made* by the buffaloes in their annual visitations to the lake from their pasture-ground; and though this is a distance of above two hundred miles, the best surveyors could not have chosen a more direct course, or better or firmer ground . . ." (italics mine).

Unhappily for Ashe, however, Allen adds in a footnote: "The region about Onondaga Lake was thoroughly explored as early as 1670, and settlements made and a fort erected before 1705. Prior to 1738, lines of communication had been established between both the Susquehanna and Alleghany Rivers, but not a buffalo is mentioned as having been met with anywhere in the Onondaga region. Hence, Mr. Ashe was undoubtedly misinformed, in respect to the trail to Onondaga Lake having been made by buffaloes . . ." (Allen, *American Bisons*, 108, 109). Compare with Shoemaker, *A Pennsylvania Bison Hunt*, 13.

An uncritical 'popular' modern writer quotes (obviously) from Ashe on this; Allen is not mentioned: Moseley, *Our Wild Animals*, 182. Likewise, Ashe is 'the noted traveller and writer' to M. S. Garretson, who also ignores Allen's criticism, though he elsewhere utilizes Allen (*American Bisons*, 83-7). After twenty years' research, I find that most of those roads which 'everybody knows were old buffalo trails' vanish similarly into thin air.

[27]For all this see Shoemaker, *A Pennsylvania Bison Hunt*, 10-38.

same thing. . . ."[28] The Kentucky buffalo—which Shoemaker designates 'the true bison of the Plains'—have little relevance to *B. Pennsylvanicus.* Shoemaker, however, cites John Filson (1784) in support of his contentions on numbers.[29] We shall see that in 1775, when there were many more buffalo (so contemporary observers asserted), 'incredible numbers' at the Blue Licks signified 'a herd of 200 seen. . . .' There 'they were met in flocks of 150 to 200 in 1789.'[30] There also, about the same era, Simon Kenton once counted 1,500. Filson 'once heard a hunter assert that he had seen 1,000 there at once.' This was the preeminent place of resort, and these were unquestionably the maxima of the respective witnesses—their phraseology indicates that. In Pennsylvania, the 'countless numbers' and 'vanished millions' were hunted very prudently for subsistence only by the Indians, and not appreciably diminished—certainly not wasted; so says Shoemaker.[31] Yet by 1773, after only a year or two of settlement, these prodigious hosts of tens of thousands, "more prevalent in Pennsylvania than all the vast herds of various wild animals which were found by the first pioneers in South and South Central Africa"[32]—were 'cut in two' by the march of settlement. I have been unable to discover any evidence of this in any contemporary source available to me, unless the reader chooses to except Ashe's old settler.[33]

I allude elsewhere to a similar silence concerning variation in type,

[28]*Ibid.,* 26. Colonel John Kelly, who slew 'the last one' (January 19, 1801) was a mighty and famous hunter. "His specialty was buffaloes, and his friends stated that he killed over a hundred of these animals . . ." (*ibid.,* 39). It is very unlikely that either he or his friends would understate his exploits, and highly improbable that twenty times as many was a common record! Garretson, in his account of Kelly's achievement, omits the foregoing particular (*American Bison,* 84-9), and elsewhere (*ibid.,* 66-9) prints the dogmas of Shoemaker as of apparently equal value with the contemporary evidence of John McDonnell and Alexander Henry, Jr. (1797-1801).

[29]Shoemaker, *A Pennsylvania Bison Hunt,* 9, 26.

[30]For these witnesses and others *in extenso,* below, chap. X, *passim.*

[31]Shoemaker, *A Pennsylvania Bison Hunt,* 13, 22, 38.

[32]*Ibid.,* 24, citing no authority. This cannot be contemporary, even as a guess! 'South Central Africa' was unknown—certainly to Pennsylvanians—in 1773. Cf. the following, written 1889: "Even in South Central Africa, which has always been exceedingly prolific in grand herds of game, it is probable that all its quadrupeds taken together would never have more than equalled the total number of the buffalo in this country forty years ago [that is, *circa* 1850] . . ." (Hornaday, "Extermination of the American Bison," 389). It seems idle to consider Shoemaker's preposterous assertion as other than a plagiarism from Hornaday, whose phraseology he has elsewhere copied. It apparently made no difference to Shoemaker's critical standing, in the estimation of two of Hornaday's admirers, Seton and Garretson.

[33]Shoemaker, *A Pennsylvania Bison Hunt,* 13-14.

pronounced as it must have been.[34] Any buffalo encountered west of
the Alleghanies by such men as Dr. Walker, Boone, Henderson, or
Nicholas Cresswell (1750-75) must have been *B. Pennsylvanicus;* for
Shoemaker extends their migrations from the Great Lakes to Georgia
and Tennessee.[35] There was at least one man upon whose notice these
very specific differences must surely have forced themselves. Jacques
Legardeur de St. Pierre, on that westward journey of 1751 which
penetrated to the valley of the Saskatchewan,[36] could scarcely have
escaped seeing the hosts of the Plains buffalo at some point. In December, 1753, he was 'the one-eyed commander' at Fort Le Bœuf on the
Ohio—apparently the same mentioned by Shoemaker on the Rivière
des Bœufs—where Washington interviewed him.[37] It seems incredible
that such a man would not have made some comment on a striking
variation in the buffalo of the Pennsylvania region had any such variation existed. Such a reference would have left at least a casual allusion
in the French historical material which would have been detected by
Parkman, Allen, Theodore Roosevelt, or A. B. Hulbert, all of whom
ransacked the historical source-literature of this era and region for
their own respective purposes.

The scientific generalizers are also silent on the subject. Both Allen
and Hornaday were of the anti-variation school; and their failure "to
give anything like a description of the Pennsylvania bison"[38] perhaps
need not unduly surprise us. But we cannot suppose any aversions on
this score in Samuel N. Rhoads, who first raised the northern Wood
bison to the status of a sub-species.[39] His unwillingness to differentiate
the Pennsylvania bison—despite personal contact with its discoverer's
enthusiasms—[40] can only indicate dissatisfaction with the evidence for
variation.

In the Rocky Mountain territory and also in the far northland, the
case for variation is entirely different. Here we have evidence of variation from contemporary observers who had already traversed many
hundred miles of buffalo territory, and may in general be considered
to have been quite competent to form reasonably sound judgments
concerning their experiences. The same applies even more emphatically

[34]See below, chap. IX, note 139 *seq.*
[35]Shoemaker, *A Pennsylvania Bison Hunt,* 9, 13, 36.
[36]See below, chap. X, note 162.
[37]Shoemaker, *A Pennsylvania Bison Hunt,* 24; Hulbert, *Historic Highways,*
III, 104-17.
[38]Shoemaker, *A Pennsylvania Bison Hunt,* 8.
[39]So Raup, *Range Conditions in Wood Buffalo Park,* 18, 49.
[40]Shoemaker, *A Pennsylvania Bison Hunt,* 42.

to the judgment of those persons, white or red, who were almost life-long residents in the western or northern areas of the habitat. These considerations make the anti-variation attitude of our principal (earlier) scientific authorities on the buffalo the more surprising, and indeed very difficult to comprehend.

It would almost seem that for some reason now beyond discovery, they determined before-hand that, while local (that is, environmental) variation might be acknowledged as a hypothetical possibility, no such changes of any material significance had as yet actually occurred. In the most rigid sense, there was but one, unvaried species. In the light of this assumption, both literary and local accounts of the *smaller* 'mountain bison' and the *larger* 'wood buffalo,' instead of opening their minds to the possibility of *two* such variations from the Plains type being actually existent, were seized upon as exaggerated, contra-dictory, and mutually-destructive descriptions of what could only be the one Plains animal.[41] Whether it occurred to them or not, they neglected to follow up the vital factor that the two differing descrip-tions came from two widely sundered geographical regions. It is true that in each of these areas there were some among the more reliable literary authorities who dissented from the majority verdict in each of the respective territories.

Bodies of testimony comprising some twenty-five or thirty wit-nesses from the two territories, none of whom, however, appears to have known *both* types, are each in their own area unanimously agreed that the Mountain bison were much smaller and the northern Wood buffalo much larger than the ordinary Plains breed. There are a few exceptions to this generally held view which may be noted here. Sir Richard Burton, who apparently never encountered a Wood buffalo, speaks of the larger 'Buffalo of the Woods, which haunts the Rocky Mountains,' but later seems to identify them with 'Mountain buffalo' in the Wind River Range.[42] But Burton's work is not cited (by name) by any of the scientific authorities on the subject whom I have seen; and Allen, who somewhat grudgingly admitted the pos-sibility of an occasional variation in the 'Parks' and foothill country, so different from the common Plains territory—and also makes them larger while denying any really reliable grounds for accepting their existence at all—seems to have derived his ideas entirely from hunters' hearsay and one skin, sent to the Smithsonian Institution in 1875.[43]

[41]So, Allen, *American Bisons*, 39-41; Hornaday, "Extermination of the Amer-ican Bison," 407-9.
[42]Burton, *City of the Saints*, 50, 165. See below, note 47.
[43]Allen, *American Bisons*, 39-41.

Conversely, one man only among those northland witnesses who had actually seen the animals, D. W. Harmon, and one other who had not, J. W. ('Saskatchewan') Taylor, sometime United States consul at Fort Garry, describe the 'Wood buffalo' as being smaller.[44]

The earliest scientific writer to draw attention to the existence of any variant type was Sir John Richardson, who writes as follows:

The whole of this district [the 'limestone tract'] is well wooded; it yields the fur-bearing animals most abundantly; and a variety of the bison, termed from this circumstance the wood bison, comes within its western border in the more northern quarter. This animal has even extended its range to a particular corner, named Slave Point, on the north side of Great Slave Lake. . . .

The bison which frequent the woody parts of the country form smaller herds than those which roam over the plains, but are said to be individually of greater size. . . .[45]

The next, Professor Henry Youle Hind, was more detailed and more definitive:

The existence of two kinds of buffalo is firmly believed by many hunters at Red River; they are stated to be the prairie buffalo and the buffalo of the woods. Many old hunters with whom I have conversed on this subject aver that the so-called wood buffalo is a distinct species, and although they are not able to offer scientific proofs, yet the difference in size, colour, hair, and horns, are enumerated as the evidence upon which they base their statement. Men from their youth familiar with these animals on the great plains, and [with] the varieties which are frequently met with in large herds, still cling to this opinion. The plain[s] buffalo are not always of the dark and rich bright brown which forms their characteristic colour. They are sometimes seen from white to almost black. A gray buffalo is not at all uncommon. Buffalo emasculated by wolves, *the half-breeds say*,[46] are often found on the prairies, where they grow to an immense size; the skin of the buffalo ox is recognised by the shortness of the wool and by its large dimensions. The skin of the so-called wood buffalo is much larger than that of the common animal, the hair is very short, mane or hair about the neck short and soft, and altogether destitute of curl, which is the common feature in the hair or wool of the prairie animal.

The wood buffalo is stated to be very scarce, and only found north of the Saskatchewan and on the flanks of the Rocky Mountains. It never ventures into the open plains; the prairie buffalo, on the contrary, generally

[44]*Harmon's Journal*, 366 (along the Clearwater River; see chap. XII, note 105 *seq.*); Taylor, corresponding to Allen, 1873 (*American Bisons*, 172). The anonymous contributor to the *Encyclopaedia Britannica*, 14th ed., speaks of "a smaller woodland variety . . ." (*s.v.* Bison).

[45]Richardson, *Fauna Boreali-Americana*, I, xxvii, 282.

[46]The four words in italics (mine) are omitted by Hornaday (pp. 407-8), whose transcripts frequently omit words and alter syntax, punctuation, and capitalization under the aegis of inverted commas. Compare below, Appendix O.

avoids the woods in summer, and keeps to the open country, but in winter
they are frequently found in the woods of the Little Souris, Saskatchewan,
the Touchwood Hills, and the aspen groves on the Qu'Appelle. There is
no doubt that formerly the prairie buffalo ranged through open woods
almost as much as he now does through the prairies. . . .[47]

Since no observer, whether writer or plainsman, seems to have had
a knowledge of both the regions mentioned by Hind, such as would
enable him to compare the two variants, it is difficult to conceive on
what grounds a scientist such as he identified the two as one and the
same.

Too late for Hind or Allen, but in abundant time for Hornaday,
Colonel Richard Irving Dodge is our earliest really definitive authority
on the 'Mountain bison.' His description must be given in his own
words:

In various portions of the Rocky Mountains, especially in the region of
the parks,[48] is found an animal which old mountaineers call the 'bison.'
This animal bears about the same relation to a buffalo as a sturdy mountain
pony does to an American horse. His body is lighter, whilst his legs are
shorter, but much thicker and stronger, than the plains animal, thus enabling him to perform feats of climbing and tumbling almost incredible in such
a huge and unwieldy beast.

These animals are by no means plentiful, and are moreover excessively
shy, inhabiting the deepest, darkest defiles, or the craggy, almost precipitous,
sides of mountains, inaccessible to any but the most practiced mountaineers.

From the tops of the mountains which rim the parks the rains of ages
have cut deep gorges, which plunge with brusque abruptness, but nevertheless with great regularity, hundreds and even thousands of feet to the valley
below. Down the bottom of each such gorge is a clear cold stream of purest
water, fertilizing a narrow belt of a few feet of alluvial, and giving birth
and growth to a dense jungle of spruce, quaking asp, and other mountain
trees. One side of the gorge is generally a thick forest of pine, while the
other side is a meadow-like park, covered with splendid grass. Such gorges
are the favourite haunt of the mountain buffalo. Early in the morning he
enjoys a bountiful breakfast of the rich nutritious grasses, quenches his
thirst with the finest water, and, retiring just within the line of jungle,
where, himself unseen, he can scan the open, he crouches himself in the
long grass and reposes in comfort and security until appetite calls him to
his dinner late in the evening. Unlike his plains relative, there is no stupid
staring at an intruder. At the first symptom of danger, they disappear like
magic in the thicket, and never stop until far removed from even the
apprehension of pursuit. I have many times come upon their fresh tracks,

[47]Hind, *Report, 1858*, 105. The dates make it possible that Burton (above,
note 42) may have derived his identification of the two varieties as one from Hind,
almost the only one of our wood-buffalo authorities then in print.

[48]For the Parks, see Bancroft, *History of Nevada*, 322-37, 495, 629.

upon the beds from which they had first sprung in alarm, but I have never even seen one. . . .

Old mountaineers and trappers have given me wonderful accounts of the number of these animals in all the mountain regions 'many years ago,' and I have been informed by them that their present rarity is due to the great snow-storm of 1844-45, of which I have already spoken as destroying the plains buffalo in the Laramie country. . . .[49]

The foregoing accounts of Hind and Dodge are the only ones quoted by Hornaday with the apparent status of authorities; one can only say that his use of them has been peculiar. He rejects Hind's views on the larger size of the Wood buffalo, but endorses his opinion on the identity of the woodland and Mountain varieties; and he rejects Dodge's differentiation, but is prepared to accept on hypothetical grounds the *smaller* size of a Mountain variety, should such have had time to develop. This paradox can only be quoted in his own words:

The belief in the existence of a distinct mountain variety is quite common among hunters and frontiersmen all along the eastern slope of the Rocky Mountains as far north as Peace River. . . . Having myself never seen a specimen of the so-called 'mountain buffalo' or 'wood buffalo,' which some writers accord the rank of a distinct variety, I can only quote the descriptions of others. While most Rocky Mountain hunters consider the bison of the mountains quite distinct from that of the plains, it must be remarked that no two authorities quite agree in regard to the distinguishing characters of the varieties they recognise. . . .

In the absence of facts based upon personal observation, I may be permitted to advance an opinion in regard to the wood buffalo. There is some reason for the belief that certain changes of form may have taken place in the buffaloes that have taken up a permanent residence in rugged and precipitous mountain regions. Indeed, it is hardly possible to understand how such a radical change in the habits of an animal could fail, through successive generations, to effect certain changes in the animal itself. It seems to me that the changes which would take place in a band of plains buffaloes transferred to a permanent mountain habitat can be forecast with a marked degree of certainty. The changes that take place under such conditions in cattle, swine, and goats are well known, and similar causes would certainly produce similar results in the buffalo.

The scantier feed of the mountains and the great waste of vital energy called for in procuring it, would hardly produce a larger buffalo than the plains-fed animal, who acquires an abundance of daily food of the best quality with but little effort.

[49]Dodge, *Plains of the Great West*, 144 *seq.* It is quoted by Hornaday, 409. Dodge's characterization is corroborated by an old plainsman still earlier, who first saw these 'bison' (*sic*) in 1847. They were encountered in North and South Parks, and were 'not so vicious as buffalo'; which is much the same as the unanimous 'shyness.' Drannan, *Thirty-one Years on the Plains*, 55, 81, 123-6. For Dodge's Laramie snowstorm, see below *in extenso*, chap. VIII, note 9.

We should expect to see the mountain buffalo smaller in body than the plains animal, with better leg development and particularly with stronger hind quarters. The pelvis of the plains buffalo is surprisingly small and weak for so large an animal.

Beyond question, constant mountain climbing is bound to develop a maximum of useful muscle and bone and a minimum of useless fat. If the loss of mane sustained by African lions who live in bushy localities may be taken as an index, we should expect the bison of the mountains, especially the 'wood buffalo,' to lose a good deal of his shaggy frontlet and mane on the bushes and trees which surrounded him. Therefore we would naturally expect to find the hair on those parts shorter and in far less perfect condition than on the bison of the treeless prairies. By reason of the more shaded condition of his home, and the decided mitigation of the sun's fierceness, we should also expect to see his entire pelage of a darker tone. That he would acquire a degree of agility and strength unknown in his relative of the plain is reasonably certain. In the course of many centuries the change in his form might become well defined, constant, and conspicuous; but at present there is apparently not the slightest ground for considering that the 'mountain buffalo' or 'wood buffalo' is entitled to rank even as a variety of *Bison americanus*.[50]

Elsewhere, Hornaday writes somewhat similarly:

Had the buffalo remained a few centuries in undisturbed possession of his range, and with liberty to roam at will over the North American continent, it is almost certain that several distinctly recognizable varieties would have been produced. The buffalo of the hot regions in the extreme south would have become a short-haired animal like the gaur of India and the African buffalo. The individuals inhabiting the extreme north, in the vicinity of Great Slave Lake, for example, would have developed still longer hair, and taken on more of the intense hairiness of the musk-ox. In the 'wood' or 'mountain' buffalo, we already have a distinct foreshadowing of the changes which would have taken place in the individuals which made their permanent residence upon rugged mountains. . . .[51]

It might be urged that the 'liberty to roam' implies the habit of using it, and that according to Hornaday's own migration theory, there would probably be no buffalo of the south or of the north, but one herd, ranging over its entire western habitat. However, the crux of the question for the moment is—if a few centuries forward could occasion such profound changes, why could not some considerable number of centuries backward (aggregating, in Hornaday's own opinion, or in that of others endorsed by him, vastly more than a few),[52] have already produced similar changes?

One factor emphasized by Hornaday in his outline of the probable causes of possible change is "the scantier feed of the mountains and

---

[50]Hornaday, "Extermination of the American Bison," 407, 408-9.
[51]*Ibid.*, 377.   [52]See above, chap. II, note 1.

the great waste of vital energy called for in procuring it. . . ."[53] Yet his own premier authority for the region, Colonel Dodge, waxes enthusiastic concerning the unparalleled quality of feed and water in the very localities where the Mountain buffalo was actually to be found, and the luxurious ease with which it obtained its fill! An earlier explorer writes of this, almost in Dodge's precise area (Upper South Platte country, March 10, 1825): ". . . my horses retained their strength and spirits in a remarkable degree, which, with other circumstances confirms me in the opinion that the vegetation of the mountains is much more nourishing than that of the plains. . . ."[54]

The disagreement among the witnesses to which Hornaday recurs is not difficult to demonstrate on the gratuitous assumption that these testimonies have reference to the same animal; although one might have thought *a priori* that such discrepancies concerning a species occupying a vast and widely-diversified climatic and topographical environment, strengthened rather than weakened the probabilities for variation. Be this as it may, a similar disagreement is found among those whom Hornaday cites in support of his contention; in fact, a considerable majority are directly contrary to his views.

The present discussion may appear to some to be 'flogging a dead horse,' but that view would be incorrect. The latest generalizer on the American buffalo—in contradistinction to the monographical specialist—endorses Hornaday's dogmatic pronouncements and cites him with the finality of fifty years ago;[55] This makes his validity a living question. Hence, it is pertinent to quote those passages adduced by him as (presumably) supporting his argument. These I present in chronological order.

The passage of Richardson has been noted above. The next is also Canadian testimony, that of Hind, which I have quoted *in extenso*. Allen (whose work was constantly at Hornaday's elbow), in the very act of emphasizing the "different, exaggerated, and contradictory accounts of its distinctive features, [so] that it is almost impossible to believe in its existence, except in the imagination of the hunter and

[53]Above, note 50.
[54]General W. H. Ashley, in Dale (ed.), *Ashley-Smith Explorations*, 130; cf. *ibid.*, 137; cf. Henry (1810) below, note 76.
[55]The earliest criticism of Hornaday that I have found dates 1933: "Part of his account of the wood buffalo is somewhat confused because he treated it as being identical with the so-called mountain buffalo . . ." (Raup, *Range Conditions in Wood Buffalo Park*, 46). Seton's tone is identical in 1910 and 1929; and cf. above, chap. I, notes 15-17. Garretson (*American Bison*) writes in 1938 as though Hornaday's dicta were unquestionable; and this under the aegis of the American Bison Society. See also Supplementary Note at the end of the present chapter.

adventurer," states, nevertheless, that "the same characters of larger size, darker, shorter, and softer pelage are usually attributed to it. . . ."[56] That passage alone should have made Hornaday more cautious in identifying it so persistently with Dodge's *smaller* animal.

From Professor John Macoun he took the following: "In the winter of 1870 the last buffalo were killed north of Peace River; but in 1875 about 1000 head were still in existence between the Athabasca and Peace Rivers, north of Little [that is, 'Lesser'] Slave Lake. These are called wood buffalo by the hunters, but differ only in size from those of the plains. . . ."[57] 'Differing only in size' is ambiguous, but other Canadian witnesses specify more clearly. Hornaday says again (this time quoting from Miller Christy):

"The Hon. Dr. Schulz [Schultz[58]], in the recent debate on the Mackenzie River basin, in the Canadian Senate, quoted Senator Hardisty of Edmonton, of the Hudson's Bay Company, to the effect that the wood buffalo still existed in the region in question. "It was," he said, "difficult to estimate how many, but probably five or six hundred still remain in scattered bands. There had been no appreciable difference in their numbers, he thought, during the last fifteen years, as they could not be hunted on horseback on account of the wooded character of the country, and were, therefore, very little molested. They are larger than the buffalo of the great plains, weighing at least 150 pounds more. They are also coarser haired and straighter horned.

"Dr. Schulz [*sic*] further stated that he had received the following testimony from Mr. Donald Ross of Edmonton: The wood buffalo still exists in the localities named. About 1870 one was killed as far west on Peace River as Fort Dunvegan. They are quite different from the prairie buffalo, being nearly double the size, as they will dress fully 700 pounds.[59]

"The doctor also quoted Mr. Frank Oliver, of Edmonton, to the effect that the wood buffalo still exists in small numbers between the Lower Peace and Great Slave Rivers, extending westward from the latter to the Salt River in latitude 60 degrees, and also between the Peace and Athabasca Rivers. He states that 'they are larger than the prairie buffalo and the fur is darker, but practically they are the same animal. . . .' "[60]

[56]Allen, *American Bisons*, 39-40.

[57]Macoun, *Manitoba*, 342; Hornaday, "Extermination of the American Bison," 524. At 'Chimeroo's Prairie,' Peace River; so Butler, *Wild North Land*, 228.

[58]The source is fully indicated in Raup's bibliography (p. 50) in the Canadian Parliamentary papers. I have not seen these.

[59]Hornaday remarks (p. 524): "It will be apparent to most observers, I think, that Mr. Ross's statement in regard to the wood buffalo is a random shot. . . ." 'Twice as big' may be; but the 'dressing 700 lbs.' seems fairly definite. In any case, it may keep company with other random shots in Hornaday's essay; and an exaggeration scarcely justifies an assumption of a *smaller* variety.

[60]Christy, "The Last of the Buffaloes" (*The Field*, London, November 10, 1888, 698); in Hornaday, "Extermination of the American Bison," 524. Raup

In addition to the above, all partly defining the animal, he also quotes from a letter to himself from Harrison Young, Esq., an old Hudson's Bay Company officer. The allusion to Wood buffalo is as follows: "In our own district of Athabasca, along the Salt River, there are still a few wood buffalo killed every year, but they are fast diminishing in numbers and are also becoming very shy. . . ."[61]

Finally, Hornaday gives a mutilated quotation from a scientific field observer in the United States, otherwise unknown to me. For reasons which will be apparent, I use the term 'mutilated' advisedly, in preference to such phrases as abridged, condensed, or abbreviated. The quotation reads as follows:

"Upon examining the specimen, I found it to be an old bull, apparently smaller and very much blacker than the ones I had seen killed on the plains only a day or so before. Then I examined the first one I had shot, as well as others which were killed by the packer from the same bunch, and I came to the conclusion that they were typical representatives of the variety known as the 'mountain buffalo,' a form much more active in movement, of slighter limbs, blacker, and far more dangerous to attack. My opinion in the premises remains unaltered today. In all this, I may be mistaken, but it was also the opinion held by the old buffalo-hunter who accompanied me, and who at once remarked when he saw them that they were 'mountain buffalo,' and not the plains variety. . . .[62] These specimens were not actually measured by me in either case, and their being considered smaller only rested upon my judging them by my eye. But they were of a softer pelage, lighter in limb, and when discovered they were in the timber on the side of the Big Horn Mountains [in the autumn of 1877]. . . ."[63]

In the face of his own utterances concerning the general belief in varieties, and the detailed testimony of his own witnesses to its wide prevalence (among classes of men whose lives very frequently depended upon their powers of accurate observation), Hornaday lamented elsewhere that in the heyday of the buffalo hosts the hunters

---

(*Range Conditions in Wood Buffalo Park*, bibl., 50) states that 'most of Oliver's notes are from one Murdock McLeod. . . .'

[61]Hornaday, "Extermination of the American Bison," 524. Mrs. Harrison Young, who died 1945, aged ninety-two, was a sister of our invaluable buffalo authority, the Rev. Dr. John McDougall (Alberta, 1862-1917).

[62]The hiatus is an omission by Hornaday. But what 'opinion'? He should have printed this or indicated its tenor. It seems clear from the context that this observer is for the 'distinct variety' in the dispute. I think this deserves the term 'mutilation.'

[63]Shufeldt, "The American Buffalo" (*Forest and Stream*, June 14, 1888); Hornaday, "Extermination of the American Bison," 411. Compare Bancroft: "The Montana [sic] buffalo is said to have been smaller, less humped, and with finer hair than the southern animal. In 1865 a band of them were seen on the Hellgate River [that is, near Deer Lodge, Montana, circa 46° 5′ N., 112° 50′ W.] for the first time in many years . . ." (*History of Washington, Idaho and Montana*, 595). This must surely mean *Mountain* buffalo. Montana is well within the Prairie buffalo range. Similarly, Garretson, *American Bison*, 5.

were so entirely engrossed in slaughtering the animal that they had neither time nor inclination to study it.[64] While doubtless true enough of the extermination period, as a general proposition it is unjust and almost absurd. Those men, red or white, may not have studied it with a naturalist's enthusiasms or comparative knowledge, but in order to survive they had perforce to study their game animals most accurately. Knowledge acquired thus is, in many instances, as reliable as that of 'science' commonly so called. In fact, if Hornaday's own dicta furnish any criterion, it may at times be more so. I have no doubt that such a man as Henry Chatillon, Parkman's guide in 1846, was no isolated specimen: "He knew all their peculiarities; he had studied them as a scholar studies his books. Nothing excited his indignation so much as any wanton destruction committed among the cows, and in his view shooting a calf was a cardinal sin. . . ."[65]

We may compare others: McDougall's friend 'Muddy Bull' the Stoney hunter, 1864, ". . . a splendid hunter; he had made a study of the instincts of the animals within his range . . .";[66] a later student writes similarly, concerning 'Eagle foot,' a Chippewyan, and Philip Merasty, a half-breed, "Philip, without knowing it, was, like many an Indian, an unread wilderness naturalist. . . ."[67]

Such descriptions would apply to many men of the wilds whose knowledge was never enshrined in print. There can be no just comparison between the true plainsman, red or white, and the skin-hunting barbarian, the real savage, of the American seventies, from whom Hornaday's knowledge of so-called 'buffalo-hunters' seems clearly to have been derived, since he mentions no other type; of them it would be difficult to say anything good or very much too bad.[68]

Hind, Allen, and Hornaday himself all show that there were untutored but essentially scientific students of the buffalo to be found everywhere. Their long familiarity with everything about the animal susceptible of observation led them to certain conclusions, which they asserted with a strenuousness that might appear unscientific to the philosopher of the schools. Nevertheless, such conclusions were logically sound, in so much as they were wide and generally accepted

---

[64]Hornaday, "Extermination of the American Buffalo," 394.

[65]Parkman, Oregon Trail, 425.

[66]McDougall, Saddle, Sled, and Snowshoe, 119.

[67]Buchanan, Wild Life in Canada (northern Saskatche van area), 140. Compare also Butler's classic description of a moose-hunter's tactics (Wild North Land, 206-10).

[68]If my language be thought too severe, the reader may compare that of Hornaday himself. Below, chap. XV, notes 4-6.

inductions from a large mass of undisputed fact, in so far as the out-door observers were concerned. I am myself no more competent than were they to pronounce to what degree external, structural, or habitual modifications must progress in a species before they conform to the technical definition of a separate 'variety,' if indeed any accepted definition exists.[69] It is difficult to evade the conclusion that the real crux was that the conclusions in question clashed with opinions adopted beforehand by these scientists. The prairie students did not deserve the contempt with which their observations—the only real evidence at that time—were, not so much answered, as ignored.

The literature of the subject at large (including much, some of it very early, that was in print when Hornaday wrote, and which there-fore so definitive an authority should have seen) furnishes no more support to the anti-variation school than did that which Hornaday utilized. Commencing with Samuel Hearne[70] (1770-72), we find the following description:

> The buffalo in these parts, I think . . . are in general much larger than the English black cattle; particularly the bulls, which though they may not in reality be taller than the largest size of the English oxen, yet to me always appeared to be much larger. In fact they are so heavy, that when six or eight Indians are in company at the skinning of a large bull, they never attempt to turn it over while entire, but when the upper side is skinned, they cut off the leg and shoulder, rip up the belly, take out all the intestines, cut off the head, and make it as light as possible, before they turn it to skin the underside. The skin is in some places of an incredible thickness, particularly about the neck, where it often exceeds an inch. The horns are short, black, and almost straight, but very thick at the roots or base. . . .
> The buffalos chiefly delight in wide open plains, which in those parts produce very long coarse grass, or rather a kind of small flags or rushes, upon which they feed, but when pursued they always take to the woods. . . .
> Of all the large beasts in those parts, the buffalo is easiest to kill. . . ,[71]

[69]Although differences in size, colour, pelage, horns, and osteology are main-tained to be of no significance in the case of buffalo, analagous variations suffice to differentiate 'some forty varieties' of the American gopher (Scharff, *Distribution and Origin of Life in America*, 60). Compare also the '15 or 20 varieties' of the American rattlesnake: Ditmars (one of Dr. Hornaday's own staff at this time), *Reptile Book*, 425-65, 470; also *Encyclopaedia Britannica*, 11th and 14th eds., *s.v.* Rattlesnakes. While Hind was writing, Darwin was writing also on "the endless disputes whether or not some fifty species of British brambles are good species . . ." (*Origin of Species*, 456); cf. *ibid.*, 35-51, 113, 388, 397.

[70]In my note on Henry Kelsey, 1691, concluding chap. XII, I show that he may have alluded to Wood buffalo, but one cannot call it evidence.

[71]Hearne, *Journey*, ed. Tyrrell, 255-7. These are "the northern race of the bison, the so-called Wood Bison" (ed. note, p. 255). Hearne adds elsewhere (p. 258): "The weight, however, is by no means equal to what has been commonly reported" . . . "buffaloes at Hudson's House are much smaller" (p. 256). The

David Thompson, apparently on or near Ile à la Crosse Lake, records the following: "On the fourth of June [1812], we put ashore to hunt and killed two Bison Bulls. I have already mentioned that all the Bisons that take to the Woods, become much larger than those of the plains, these were so, their horns from tip to tip measured two feet, and on the curve 28 inches, and when fat [they] must weigh at least two thousand pounds. . . ."[72]

There are several allusions to Wood buffalo in the *Journal* of Alexander Henry the younger: "[Sept. 1, 1810] Deschamps came in with two cows; a few are seen about Fish Lake, but they are the wood buffalo, more shy and wild than those of the plains. When they have once been fired at, a second shot can seldom be got. . . ."[73] This notice is perhaps even more valuable than that of Thompson, cited above, but discussion may more conveniently be deferred until the conclusion of our historical references.

These creatures were also quite common on the Upper Saskatchewan and its adjacent territory above Edmonton. Henry noted a herd of 'strong wood buffalo' near Rocky Mountain House (close by the junction of the Clearwater River, about 50° 25′ N., 114° 50′ W.) in October, 1810; and they were 'numerous but as wild as moose' on the

---

reader must reconcile as best he can the 'ease of killing' with their shyness, as in Hearne himself and everyone else.

On weight, see below in this chapter, notes 119, 131-55.

[72]Thompson, *Narrative*, ed. Tyrrell, 558; cf. *ibid.*, 438. Tyrrell appends a zoological note by E. A. Preble: "A northern race of the bison has been separated as a sub-species under the name of *Bison bison Athabascae* Rhoads [Samuel N. Rhoads, 1897; so Raup, *Range Conditions in Wood Buffalo Park*, 49], the type being taken from the country immediately south of Great Slave Lake. . . . Before northern specimens had been examined by mammalogists, the animal had been extirpated over most of its former habitat, so that the exact limits of range of the northern race will never be known. In view of Thompson's intimate acquaintance with the bison of the plains, his statement that the two killed here were of the woodland form is of distinct scientific value. The locality was on Beaver River, in lat. 58° 18′ N., long. 109° W." (*ibid.*, 558).

The position given is some 40 or 50 miles south of Lake Athabaska, where their presence is undisputed, if anywhere. Preble was up there in 1907 (see Inspector Jarvis, Royal North West Mounted Police *Report*, 1907, App. N, 122-9); and may refer to some local 'Beaver River.' The only ones I can find are: (1) in the Kasha ('Cassiar') country, British Columbia, 60° N., 125° W. (see Jenness, *Indians of Canada*, 396; *Handbook of Canadian Indians*, 236), which is out of the question; (2) flowing into Great Slave Lake from the southwest, near the Mackenzie River outflow; (3) flowing into Ile à la Crosse Lake, about 55° 40′ N., 108° 40′ W., on which see Coues's note, *Henry-Thompson Journals*, II, 573.

[73]Coues (ed.), *Henry-Thompson Journals*, II, 622. "Fish Lake" is probably Whitefish or Goodfish Lake, closely adjacent, some 80 miles northeast from Edmonton, about 54° 25′ N., 112° W. See the same note *ibid.*, 573, and cf. Geographical Board of Canada, *Place-Names of Alberta*, 58, 134, and map.

upper stretches of the river that winter, and also below the Mountain House.[74] In the latter region, near the head of Wolf Creek,[75] in May, 1811, he observes ". . . strong wood buffalo must have been numerous here all winter, judging from the piles of dung I saw. . . ." His description of them during that winter is of interest: "Buffalo seem to be numerous; we saw the tracks of several herds which had crossed on the ice. These are of the strong wood kind, and as wild as moose; they never resort to the plains but delight in mountain valleys, where they feed on the short grass which seems to be of an excellent quality, as horses soon get fat on it . . . the back fat was nearly two inches thick, and the flesh more interlarded than I have ever observed that of the meadow buffalo to be. . . ."[76]

Richardson's remarks on the buffalo of the 'limestone tract' have been noted, and need not be reproduced.[77] Daniel W. Harmon was writing his work about the same time; he gives the following account: "Those that remain in the country between the Sisiscatchwin [sic] and Peace Rivers are called the wood buffaloes, because they inhabit a woody country; and they are considerably smaller than those which inhabit the plains. They are, also, more wild and difficult to approach. . . ."[78]

Washington Irving had evidently heard of the wary 'Mountain buffalo': "It is said, however, that the buffalo on the Pacific side of the Rocky Mountains are fleeter and more active than those on the Atlantic side; those upon the plains of the Columbia can scarcely be overtaken by a horse that would outstrip the same animal in the neighbourhood of the Platte, the usual hunting-ground of the Blackfeet. . . ."[79]

Dr. Hector, on one of the many 'Pipestone Creeks,' which he gives as 51° 38′ 5″ N. (and which is approximately 117° W. on the head-

[74]Coues (ed.), *Henry-Thompson Journals*, II, 639-41, 660, 682.

[75]This is the nearest definite notice known to me of Wood buffalo ranging near Edmonton to the westward. This is not the modern Wolf Creek, which joins the Macleod River at the Twin Bridges on the Canadian National main line east of Edson, Alberta. It is the present Blindman River, tributary of Red Deer River (see Coues (ed.), *Henry-Thompson Journals*, II, 637; *Place-Names of Alberta*, 21, 136, and map; 'Wolf's Trail,' Battle River to Blindman mouth, *Rundle's Journal*, May 15, 1847, etc.; *Palliser Journals*, 119, 176, etc.). The head is about 52° 45′ N., 114° 30′ W., near Hoadley, Alberta, southwest of Edmonton 50 miles or so.

[76]Coues (ed.), *Henry-Thompson Journals*, II, 739; cf. also 682-97. Re the mountain grass, cf. Ashley, above, note 54; also Dodge, above, note 49.

[77]See above, note 45.

[78]*Harmon's Journal*, 366; possibly along the Clearwater route (tributary of the Athabaska, Fort McMurray; *not* the river of note 74 above) where Thomas Simpson noted some in December, 1837 (*Narrative of Discoveries*, 60-1).

[79]Irving, *Captain Bonneville*, 343.

waters of the Bow River, east of Howes Pass, and north of the Canadian Pacific summit at Stephen),[80] was told by his guide in 1859 that: ". . . two years ago he killed a buffalo cow at this place, and that he saw at the time a band of seven—two bulls, four cows, and a calf. They were of the thickwood variety, which are larger and blacker, and with more spreading horns, than those of the prairies. They run swiftly through the woods, and are quite as wary and difficult to hunt as the moose deer. . . ."[81]

Buffalo Jones describes the 'Mountain buffalo' as being 'much smaller and darker, now extinct.' It is uncertain whether the latter statement is that of his editor, Colonel Henry Inman, or is taken from some earlier document; and he does not appear to have seen them.[82]

Our next account is from Sir William Butler's flowing pen: "The giant form of the wood buffalo no longer darkens the steep lofty shores [of Peace River]. . . . It is still a matter of dispute whether the wood buffalo is the same species as his namesake of the southern plains; but it is generally believed by the Indians that he is of a kindred race. He is nevertheless larger, darker, and wilder; and although the northern land, in which he is still found, abounds in open prairies and small plains, he nevertheless seeks in preference the thickest woods. Whether he be of the plain race or not, one thing is certain—his habits vary much from his southern cousin. . . ."[83]

It is, of course, difficult to correlate Indian thought to our terms—themselves somewhat vague—of 'kindred' and 'species,' but the existence of different words for the two in Indian languages signifies anything but identity.[84] In any case, I am very sceptical of general assertions concerning 'Indian' conceptions. Acute tribal individualisms forbid that.

Following is a most interesting reference to the buffalo's presence in what thus becomes the extreme southeastern corner of the Canadian Wood-buffalo habitat, and almost of the Canadian range in general. Its apparent presence here finds inferential support from the circumstance that it appears to have been from Red River hunters that Hind derived his knowledge of the animal, although of course they might

[80]See *Place-Names of Alberta*, 103, and map.
[81]Hector, in *Palliser Journals*, 148.
[82]*Buffalo Jones' Forty Years of Adventure*, 259.
[83]Butler, *Wild North Land*, 210. Cf. Alexander Henry, 1810: ". . . ranges of hills, covered with pine, aspens, and other woods, intersected by small spots of meadow, where the [Wood] buffalo appeared to rest . . ." (Coues (ed.), *Henry-Thompson Journals*, II, 684, 687).
[84]See below in this chapter, note 118.

have obtained it from old Hudson's Bay men of farther northern experience: "Formerly a variety called the wood buffalo was very numerous in the forests surrounding Lakes Winnipeg and Manitoba, the last survivor having been killed only two years ago [that is, in 1870] on Sturgeon Creek, ten miles west of Fort Garry. The wood buffalo is smaller than its congener of the plains, with finer and darker wool, and a superior quality of flesh. It more resembles the 'bison' of naturalists. . . ."[85]

This record, with its specific differences and precise dating, derives additional significance from the fact that at this time (and for some years previously) the Red River Hunt had had to travel increasingly long distances westward to find the ordinary Prairie buffalo, as is shown below. It may lend some weight to the possible interpretation of Alexander Mackenzie's utterance of 1789 as indicating buffalo at some recent era on the eastern side of Lake Winnipeg.[86]

Hornaday himself cites a letter from E. W. Nelson, Alaska, to Allen, dated July 11, 1877, in which, without specifying the Wood buffalo by that name, the writer observes concerning the buffalo along Hay River, Great Slave Lake, in 1871: "It is asserted that these buffalo are larger than those of the plains."[87]

Warburton Pike wrote as follows, 1889:

Scattered over this huge extent of territory are still a few bands of buffalo. Sometimes they are heard of at Forts Smith and Vermilion, sometimes at Fort St. John, close up to the big mountains on Peace River, and occasionally at Fort Nelson, on the south branch of the Liard. It is impossible to say anything about their numbers, as the country they inhabit is so large, and the Indians, who are few in number, usually keep to the same hunting ground. These animals go by the name of wood-buffalo, and most people are of the opinion that they are a distinct race from the old prairie buffalo so numerous in bygone days; but I am inclined to think that the very slight difference in appearance is easily accounted for by climatic influences, variety of food, and the better shelter of the woods. . . .[88]

Considering that Pike himself was the first to render a skin and

[85]J. W. ('Saskatchewan') Taylor, United States consul, Winnipeg, 1873, correspondence to J. A. Allen (*American Bisons*, 172). Printed also by Garretson (citing no source), *American Bison*, 7.

[86]For the Red River Hunt, see chap. XIV. For Mackenzie, chap. XII, note 54.

[87]Hornaday, "Extermination of the American Bison," 385. Raup's bibliography (*Range Conditions in Wood Buffalo Park*, 43) cites the letter as being printed by J. A. Allen in *American Naturalist*, XI, 1877, 624, which I have not seen.

[88]Pike, *Barren Ground*, 156; cf. 251.

[89]Raup's very full bibliography (*Range Conditions in Wood Buffalo Park*, 43-52) cites 101 sources; and even he omits David Thompson, Alexander Henry, Jr., and Dr. Hector.

skull of one of the species available for purposes of scientific examination, he would seem to have been strangely under the influence of the predominant, scientific conclusions of the time, as against local opinions based upon some degree of knowledge. He may be considered as the last of the earlier body of witnesses, at least of those whom I have been able to consult.[89] With the exceptions of the younger Alexander Henry and Warburton Pike himself, all of the foregoing either were cited or might have been cited by Hornaday (1887-89).

In connection with the geographical distribution of the buffalo, attention has been drawn above[90] to a definite notice of the Wood buffalo at Fish Lake, some eighty miles or so northeast of Edmonton. This is really a more valuable note than that of E. A. Preble concerning the range-limits of the animal. H. M. Raup observes that "Prof. William Rowan of the University of Alberta, who has studied the problem extensively . . . is perhaps right in doubting the authenticity of records for wood bison south of McMurray . . ." (that is, about 56° 40' N., 111° 30' W.). This is in reference to a statement of H. J. Moberly, then the Hudson's Bay Company's chief factor at Fort McMurray, that in 1887 a band still lived between McMurray and Lac la Biche (54° 50' N., 112° W.).[91] It may be noted that the late Professor James M. Macoun, a son of Professor John Macoun, informed Thompson Seton that in July, 1888, he saw the meat of eight buffalo bulls that were killed between Lac la Biche and Methy Portage,[92] (on the Saskatchewan-Churchill-Clearwater route to the Athabaska). These would surely be Wood buffalo. Lac la Biche is less than thirty-five miles north of the two 'Fish Lakes' indicated as the probable scene of Henry's reference of 1810, and about 130 miles south from Methy Portage. The region is (or was) of the precise topographical character favoured by the Wood buffalo.

I am informed by Dr. Rowan that there appears to be a sort of 'Debatable Land' extending from McMurray northward toward the Peace River, in which, so far as he can learn—and where, I understand, he has had local friends interested in the search—no buffalo bones have ever been found, and north of which the bones are exclusively those of Wood buffalo.[93] This, of course, would not necessarily apply to the eastern side of the Athabaska, as there is no Peace River entering there to constitute any barrier on that side. Butler speaks of the Buffalo

[90]See above, note 73.
[91]Raup, *Range Conditions in Wood Buffalo Park*, 11-12, 44.
[92]Seton, *Life-Histories of Northern Animals*, I, 297.
[93]*Ex. inf.* frequent conversations with Dr. Rowan, a close personal friend.

Hills, one day south of Peace River, being considered as their northern limit in 1873.[94] Dr. Hector, in 1858, placed their northern limit 'at least three degrees' south of Peace River.[95] He is in part corroborated by place-name evidence. Buffalo River and Bison Lake are situated some twenty-five and fifty miles respectively south of Buffalo Head Hills.[96] The term 'Peace River,' however, is unfortunately very vague, unless longitudes or definite localities are given. The course of the river is roughly eastward from the Rocky Mountains to about 56° N., 118° W., near the modern town of Peace River, northerly to 58° N., 117° W., thence about E.N.E. to its mouth. In its relation to Butler's localized limit of 1873, Hector's would possibly signify 'three degrees south' from the lower stretch of the river, between Fort Vermilion and Fort Providence. This, together with a total absence of (recorded) buffalo place-names across the entire territory from McMurray to the 116th meridian of longitude, tends strongly to corroborate Rowan's conclusions, *for the western side* of the Athabaska River. In his remarks, which would seem to apply Dr. Rowan's findings to both sides indifferently, H. M. Raup has perhaps overlooked Alexander Henry's reference, which he does not mention.[97] Actually, there seems good reason to suspect that the 'northern' limit of the two authorities cited (for 1858, 1873) was really a *southern* limit of the Northern species. The barren territory indicated by Rowan may very probably be estimated to begin (westward of a line roughly from Edmonton to Athabaska Landing) not very far north of the Sturgeon River, twelve or fifteen miles north of Edmonton.[98] Seton's informant, Elzear Mignault, a resident on Peace River, 1865-75, stated that only one Prairie buffalo— an old mangy bull, most probably an 'outlaw'—was ever seen in Peace River Valley (?) being slain there in 1866.[99] The assured identification of Prairie as against Wood buffalo is consonant with the fact that there is nowhere any hint of uncertainty among any of the early witnesses as to the type with which they were dealing. Had there been common and promiscuous crossing between the two types there should surely

[94]Butler, *Wild North Land*, 167, 168, 172. 'Buffalo Head Hills,' 57° 40′ N., 116° W.; some 60 miles south of Fort Vermilion, with Mustus Lake between the two (*mustus*, Cree = buffalo), and nearly 200 miles W.N.W. from McMurray: see *Place-Names of Alberta*, 26, and map.

[95]Hector, in *Palliser Journals*, 126.

[96]*Place-Names of Alberta*, 26, and map.

[97]Raup, *Range Conditions in Wood Buffalo Park* (1772-1897), 8-12.

[98]This question is examined in detail, in discussing the Canadian habitat at large. Below, chap. XII, note 222 *seq.*

[99]Seton, *Game Animals*, III, 661; cf. *Harmon's Journal, circa* 1819 (above, note 78).

have been some indeterminate 'transitional' hybrids, which the hunters would hesitate to classify. Yet none could have been better judges.

Another argument for the absolute identity of the two species has recently been brought forward. It is worth quoting here, if only as a specimen of the class of evidence which apparently satisfies the defenders of the anti-variation school. Garretson cites the following (1938):

> In 1888, the Hon. William Christie, ex-member of the Northwest Council and inspecting factor of the Hudson's Bay Company, stated before a Government Committee that he considered the wood buffalo was identical with the plains buffalo. Long ago the latter species was found as far north as Peace River in great numbers, and the plains Indians, the Sarcees and others, were then in the Peace River country. There is a place called Battle River in the Peace River valley, where these plains Indians had a tremendous battle, and it is called Battle River from that circumstance. The plains buffalo were in that country then in thousands, just the same as they were in the plains. As they got hunted by the Indians, they moved out, and the Indians moved out of the Peace River country also after this great battle and went into the plains. The battle in question was fought perhaps one hundred years previously. A number of the plains buffalo got into the woods and bred and remained there and are still living in the woods there. . . .[100]

It is difficult to decide whether the foregoing is a confused paraphrase of Christie's testimony, or a series of declarations from a dogmatist of no special competence, parading as a Northern authority before a body incompetent to criticize his evidence. It can only be examined point by point:

(a) '100 years previously' (that is, circa 1788): in 1771 Hearne found there what zoologists have identified from his description as Wood buffalo (above, note 71).

(b) Compare the historical testimony of Mignault and the osteological evidence of Rowan, together with the presence much farther south of a well-recognized 'Wood buffalo' as early as 1810 (above, note 73).

(c) The Plains Indians, the Sarcees and others, moving out from the Peace River country 'after circa 1788.' They are mentioned, on their way to their present locality near Calgary, Alberta, by Cocking, 1772; Alexander Mackenzie, 1789; Duncan McGillivray, 1794; and others; and their foremost authoritative student, Dr. Diamond Jenness, commences their drift southward about 1700. In 1794, McGillivray places the Sarcees in the Beaver Hills area, east of Edmonton.[101] About 1840,

[100]Garretson, American Bison, 7-8.
[101]Jenness, Sarcee Indians of Alberta, 1-7.

the 'Sarcee Hills' were some sixty miles southwest from Edmonton, near Battle Lake, the source of the Battle River.[102]

(d) There is only one Battle River discoverable in Plains Indian territory at any period, the well-known one (in (c) above) entering the North Saskatchewan at Battleford. The 'Battle River' which joins the Peace at 57° 20′ N., 117° W., is in the precise territory where the bones are exclusively those of Wood buffalo. There are the Peace *Hills*, south of Edmonton along the (first) Battle River, near Wetaskiwin (that is, in Cree = 'peace').[103] These were well known by that name in Christie's day at Edmonton.

(e) The Plains buffalo 'taking to the woods': this was common enough in winter, but they came forth again. David Thompson gave a somewhat similar explanation of the origin of Wood buffalo (above, note 72). This explanation was perhaps due to local contemporary gossip or folk-lore, and as such, was possibly the source of Christie's opinion. Such a belief is excusable in Thompson's time, in the absence of advanced comparative knowledge; it should not be offered as evidence by a modern 'authority' without critical comment.

(f) The existence of separate terms (doubtless of long standing) for the two types, in Indian languages (below, note 118).

The later evidence concerning habits seems at first sight to vary somewhat; but it resolves itself largely into the choice of language. Such characteristics as the greater shyness or wariness, or the darker colour of the Wood buffalo do not find a single dissentient at any period. Seton (following Mignault) describes them thus: "Its general habits differ a good deal from those of its prairie relative, rather resembling those of the Moose; although it is much less wary and difficult of approach than that animal. It is rarely found in herds, except in the fall. The greatest number my informant ever saw together was three. They were going down to the river as he rounded a point in a barge. As soon as he came in view, they scrambled up a bank and disappeared in the woods. . . ."[104]

Seton (or Mignault) considered them less wary than the moose (whose wariness itself varied),[105] yet this instant disappearance when something was sighted or smelled is related apparently as their normal conduct, although one could approach them within fifty yards, accord-

[102]*Rundle's Journal*, February 27, 1843.
[103]*Place-Names of Alberta*, 99, 133.
[104]Seton, *Game Animals*, III, 708. His original comments on them date in substance from 1886; so Raup, *Range Conditions in Wood Buffalo Park*, 10, 18, 50.
[105]See Thompson, *Narrative*, ed. Tyrrell, 197; cf. Seton, *Life-Histories of Northern Animals*, I, 144-86.

ing to others, if only seen and not smelled.[106] F. H. Kitto, who treats the wood buffalo as an immigrant from the Plains, says, "his shyness in his new environment has increased manyfold. . . ."[107]

Seton himself on his first encounter (June, 1907) described them as 'more shy than moose.' It was locally asserted about Fort Smith at that time that 'they were *not* being hunted.' Why, therefore, the shyness, asks Seton.[108] It seems possible that he under-rated the congenital shyness reported of both Wood and 'Mountain' buffalo (a woodsdweller) by practically everyone. Dr. Gordon Hewitt observes that, according to the Royal North West Mounted Police and other official reports, the Wood buffalo were not so shy in 1907, 1913, and 1916 as indicated by Seton.[109]

The different reports on their shyness appear to be largely caused by style and terminology. Seton and Inspector Jarvis agreed in 1907. I have not seen the later Police reports, but other observers, as noted above, confirm the general shyness. Jarvis, Graham, Rowan, and others note a poor eyesight, which enabled observers to creep up against the wind quite closely, but all agree on the immediate flight when the intruder was detected. Dr. Rowan, who carefully observed them in their haunts in September, 1925, says: ". . . for wariness they surpassed even the moose that we encountered in the park. . . . The beasts have new been protected for many years, and their disposition is without doubt inherent. And upon this as much stress may legitimately be laid as upon structural peculiarities in considering the validity of their separation from the plains animal. . . ."[110] Certainly the historical evidence from Hearne, the earliest observer, onward, supports Rowan beyond reasonable question. Even M. S. Garretson notes their wariness, as contrasted with the stupidity of their Plains relative, but nevertheless endorses the conclusions of 'the best authorities' (unspecified) that there is no difference.[111]

[106]See on this Seton, *Game Animals*, III, 658-62, 710; Inspector Jarvis, Royal North West Mounted Police *Report*, 1907, App. N, 122-9; Graham, *Canada's Wild Buffalo*, 9; Rowan, "Canada's Buffalo."

[107]Kitto, "Survival of the American Bison in Canada." This may be compared with note 113 below. That note describes a precisely opposite process in Plains buffalo which are *known* to be immigrants in the Northland. So far from any increased shyness, they infected the natives with their own indifference.

[108]Seton, *Arctic Prairies*, 318-20. For the 'not being hunted,' see Inspector Jarvis, Royal North West Mounted Police *Report*, 1907.

[109]Hewitt, *Conservation of the Wild Life of Canada*, 121-33.

[110]Rowan, "Canada's Buffalo." Dr. Rowan was doubtless contrasting them with the tameness of other animals after only twenty years or less of protection in Jasper Park, Alberta.

[111]Garretson, *American Bison*, 5, 8, 44.

Mention should be made at this point of the magnificent monograph of J. Dewey Soper on the Northern Bison.[112] This careful and detailed study of the Wood Buffalo Park animals in their own haunts brings together a large mass of scattered material from various published sources and is by far the most complete among recent productions. Unfortunately, as the author himself observes, the mingling of the two species in the Park since the transference of Plains animals from Wainwright, has gradually reduced the ratio of pure Wood buffalo to a not always recognizable and dwindling fraction, which is now probably not more than some 10 per cent. In these circumstances, it is futile to cite this important monograph in support of any contention regarding Wood buffalo.[113]

In the opening decades of the twentieth century (following upon Rhoads, 1897) scientific opinion on the classification of the buffalo underwent a reversal; a belief in the existence of various species became widely prevalent. It is doubtful whether the entire history of zoology presents a parallel instance of so complete a reversal in accepted scientific classification—particularly when this reversal constituted an adoption of opinions unanimously maintained from the first by the unlettered students of the wilderness. Thompson Seton was one of the first to adopt the latter classification. He gives an interesting scientific description of the animal, which reveals such visible differences from the Plains type as might attract a hunter's attention:

General Characters. Size larger, colours darker, horns slenderer, much longer and more incurved, and hair more dense and silky than in *B. bison.*

Description of type specimen from data furnished by Professors J. Macoun and H. A. Ward. "Pelage everywhere dense and silky; short and fine over much of hinder part of body, becoming very dense and curly and long anteriorly, especially on shoulders and neck, and also quite long on the frontal aspect. Colour along crest of hump and vertical line to rump 'light brown,' shading in all directions to darker brown, and becoming almost black on the whole head, legs and belly. 'Looking at head and legs you would say at once that they were black.' Ears, muzzle, hoofs and horns and distal half of tail black.

[112]Soper, "History of the Northern Bison," 347-412.

[113]I may instance a case in point. A later observer in the Park than Soper (though in print earlier) mentions an instance of a 'wood' buffalo charging *towards* the intruders, not away from them; which is implied as being common: Goodwin, "Buffalo Hunt, 1935" (*Natural History*, September, 1935, 156-63). This is also quoted by Soper (p. 397). This seems entirely foreign to the testimony concerning the true Wood buffalo of the ante-Wainwright era; but is recorded of the Plains animals in their 'aboriginal' environment, as is also the 'stolid indifference' which is now frequently noticeable among buffalo suddenly surprised in the Park (Soper, "History of the Northern Bison," 396-401). On these features in Plains buffalo, see below, chap. VI, at large.

"Horns [in mounted skin] very long and strongly recurved. . . ."[114]

We cannot feel surprised that Seton, confronted at first hand with an animal of this description, and himself so competent a naturalist, should be one of the first to adopt the later classification, in a work of popular appeal. In 1910, he wrote thus: "Covering, as it does, so many diverse faunal areas, we might naturally expect the Buffalo to split up into several corresponding races; and it is generally recognized that, in a measure, it did so. The far north produced the huge wood Buffalo (*B.B. athabascae* Rhoads); the Rockies, the small dark Mountain Buffalo; the Plains, the paler medium-sized Plains Buffalo. It is probable, too, that the extinct Alleghanian Buffalo had distinctive characteristics, but there is no available evidence to prove this. . . ."[115] In his later magnificent production, the Alleghanian buffalo and the Mountain buffalo do not appear, only the Plains and Wood buffalo and thirdly *B. pennsylvanicus* Shoemaker.[116]

Seton's original description, based on Mignault, is of outstanding interest. It is the first account given by an old resident to a questioning scientist during the earlier years before questions of scarcity or impending extinction, with their resultant possibilities of change in the aboriginal habits and mentality of the Wood buffalo, had arisen.[117] I quote his own much later extract from it:

Mignault maintains with the Indians that it is distinct, urging also in support of his opinion that the only Prairie Buffalo ever seen in the [Peace River] valley was killed in 1866. It was a solitary mangy bull, a complete outcast, which would probably not have been the case had the Wood Buffalo been his immediate kindred. All my informants agree that the Wood Buffalo differs from its prairie relative in being much larger and considerably darker in colour. Mignault adds that its legs are proportionately shorter, its horns less robust and more curved inwards, its hair, shorter, finer, entirely without curl, and all over of a very dark brown, almost a black in winter, but in the summer assuming a hue not unlike that of the prairie animal.

The two forms are not distinguished on the books of the Hudson's Bay Company.

When in 1875 Mignault left the Peace River, the Wood Buffalo were plentiful in the country between Dunvegan and Great Slave Lake, and the Liard and Athabaska Rivers. In 1884 he heard from a comrade that they were then still common.

[114]Seton, *Game Animals*, III, 706; cf. above, note 16.
[115]Seton, *Life Histories of Northern Animals*, I, 250; cf. *ibid.*, 17-18.
[116]Seton, *Game Animals*, III, 643.
[117]Seton, "The Wood Buffalo," (114-17), in Raup, *Range Conditions in Wood Buffalo Park*, 10, 18, 50. Seton antedated Rhoads by eleven years (*ibid.*, 18) in

The Indians, he said, call it *Ah-thuk-ard-Moos-toosh,* and consider it quite distinct from the Prairie Buffalo, which they call *Mas-kootay Moos-toosh.* . . .[118]

The occasional individual or group variations from any one form or habit which might possibly be assumed as a rigid standard of morphology, are interesting, and may be of value in considering origins or evolutionary development. The reader will not fail to notice the resemblance to the Plains animal in this respect. I quote Seton's description of the 'Radford' bull:

On May 29, 1914, I visited the Calgary Museum, and examined the Radford bull. It is about 6 feet at the withers, has no mane, no beard, no 'chaps.' But the hair all over the body is long and curly. It has immense horns, long and curved, is of enormous bulk, evidently larger than any Plains Buffalo, and much like an Aurochs. It weighed 2,460 pounds, or 2,402 pounds after bleeding. . . .

The longest horns of this buffalo [type] recorded in Rowland Ward's Book [Ward, *Records of Big Game,* p. 428] are in the American National Collection, and measure as follows: Length, 18¾ ins.; girth, 15 ins.; tip to tip, 27½ ins. (owner's measurements). . . .[119]

The observed variations in several particulars may be conveniently summarized for purposes of comparison. The type-specimen of Professors James M. Macoun and H. A. Ward displays much 'light-brown' along the spine, with which Mignault agrees, while the 'darker' character attracted most of the later observers[120] (to whom the present

---

suggesting a varietal designation for the Wood buffalo. One must regret that he deferred to uninformed dogmatism (as above, chap. II, note 63).

[118]Seton, *Game Animals,* III, 708. Language sometimes throws curious sidelights on many problems. The Indians would presumably be Chippewyans; but *Mas-kootay Moostoosh* is Cree, in a dialectal form. Lacombe gives *maskutewimustus* = bœuf des prairies, buffle; *pikwatchimustus* = bœuf sauvage (*Dictionnaire de la langue des Cris,* 247, 442; cf. *ibid.,* 44, 227, 461, etc.). The circumstance that these Northern Indians had apparently no native word for the Prairie type is strong presumptive evidence that it did not inhabit their country, precisely as Mignault asserted.

Father Morice uses this identical argument concerning the indigenous absence of buffalo from the Takulli ('Carrier') country in British Columbia; they also called it by a Cree word (below, chap. XII, note 153). The Stoneys (Assiniboine) likewise have the two type-names: *sena-tatanga* = prairie buffalo: *cha-tatanga* = wood-buffalo (*ex. inf.* my friend, the Reverend P. G. Sutton, formerly missionary, Paul's Reserve, Wabamun Lake, Alberta). Although his informants had never seen either, they were competent to answer his question without hesitation. Compare Butler (above, note 83).

[119]This animal was shot by Harry V. Radford, 1909 (Seton, *Game Animals,* III, 707, 710). George G. Goodwin notes a specimen shot in 1934, measuring 6½ feet high at the shoulders and another which escaped, 'must have been close to 7 feet . . .' ("Buffalo Hunt, 1935," 156-63).

[120]Graham, *Canada's Wild Buffalo;* Seibert, *Natural Resources* (both Canadian Department of the Interior). Kitto, "Survival of American Bison in Canada,"

summary is confined, with the exception of Mignault, who is really 'late' in print, his early appearance in 1886 being virtually forgotten). Macoun and Ward's specimen has the hair 'curly and long anteriorly'; the Radford bull is 'curly all over the body.' Rowan has 'the texture of the wool softer'; Seton, 'more dense and silky';[121] Raup, 'the coat more shaggy than the Plains buffalo';[122] and Mignault (obviously attempting a summary of many years' experience), 'the hair shorter, finer, and entirely without curl.'[123]

The testimony concerning herds (not estimates of total aggregates) prior to the advent of the Wainwright immigrants, is similarly variable. Corporal Mellor of the Royal North West Mounted Police records 'a large band' in September, 1909 (if we only knew what 'large' signifies).[124] In 1907 Inspector Jarvis (of the same force) and Thompson Seton never saw herds of more than thirteen and nineteen animals of all ages, respectively.[125] Maxwell Graham in 1922 encountered three herds of sixteen animals each, and one of nine.[126] More recently, a partial air census in the Wood Buffalo Park notices that, of more than 1,500 animals counted by the airmen, one herd had 100 animals, and in general they ranged from fifteen to twenty in a herd. In this case, it seems probable that what the airmen termed 'Wood buffalo' would include both types and their heterogeneous offspring; and no mention is made of any attempt to distinguish between aborigines and immigrants, even if such were possible.[127] As against all this, Mignault, during ten years' residence, never saw more than three together, and considered they 'rarely went in herds, except in the fall,' this, moreover, being in a period of greater general abundance.[128] Then again, Maxwell Graham's description of one or two seen, and 'pig-like grunting noises heard where nothing could be seen owing to thick underbrush,'[129] indicates that the observer might really be in the vicinity of

436. Rowan, "Canada's Buffalo"; Raup, *Range Conditions in Wood Buffalo Park*, 18, etc. Compare also some opinions cited by Soper, "History of the Northern Bison," 355-7.

[121]Rowan, "Canada's Buffalo"; Seton, *Game Animals*, III, 706.

[122]Raup, *Range Conditions in Wood Buffalo Park*, 18.

[123]Seton, *Game Animals*, III, 708.

[124]Raup, *Range Conditions in Wood Buffalo Park*, 15 (citing the Royal North West Mounted Police *Report* for 1919, which I have not seen). For the examination of 'large,' 'immense,' etc., see below, chap. XIII.

[125]Jarvis, Royal North West Mounted Police *Report*, 1907, 123, 124.

[126]Graham, *Canada's Wild Buffalo*, 8-9.

[127]*Edmonton Journal*, April 1, 1931. See above on this, note 113.

[128]Seton, *Game Animals*, III, 708; cf. Raup, *Range Conditions in Wood Buffalo Park*, 10-12.

[129]Graham, *Canada's Wild Buffalo*, 8.

a much larger herd than any numbers of (pure) Wood buffalo recorded. If Mackenzie's 'vast herds' along the Peace River in 1793 were Wood buffalo—as is very generally thought[130]—they can have had no inherent aversion to large numbers herding together, when they were plentiful enough to do so.

A great deal has been said about larger woodland and smaller mountain varieties; but only one or two direct references to size or weight have been noted. For the benefit of those who have probably never seen buffalo *en masse,* and may also be unaccustomed to judging the weight of cattle on the hoof, the matter may be rendered more intelligible if some estimates of approximate weights of buffalo from various parts of the continent are given. I subjoin such data as I have been able to collect.

Richardson: "The Bison, when full grown, is said to attain at times a weight of two thousand pounds, but twelve or fourteen cwt. [that is, English 'hundredweight' = 112 pounds] is generally considered a full size in the fur countries. Its length, exclusive of the tail, is about eight feet and a half, its height at the fore quarters upwards of six feet, and the length of its tail is twenty inches. . . ."[131]

Audubon: "A large Bison bull will generally weigh nearly two thousand pounds, and a fat cow about twelve hundred pounds. We weighed one of the bulls killed by our party, and found it to reach 1,727 pounds, although it had already lost a good deal of blood. This was an old bull, and was not fat. It had probably weighed more at some previous period. . . ."[132]

A bull killed by Hornaday himself (December 6, 1886) while procuring specimens for the Smithsonian Institution, was estimated by expert judges to be nearer 1,700 than 1,600 pounds. This animal was "in full vigor, superbly muscled and well fed, but he carried not a single pound of fat. . . ."[133] Hornaday also mentions a magnificent animal, 'Cleveland,' the bull of the Atchison, Topeka, and Santa Fé Railway Company's herd at Bismarck Grove, Kansas (*circa* 1887), which was believed to weigh fully 3,000 pounds. This herd is described

[130]Rowan, "Canada's Buffalo." Evidently so considered by Colin Fraser, Hudson's Bay Company, to Milton and Cheadle, 1863 (*North-West Passage,* 200). Canadian Zoologist ("The Passing of the Wood Bison") thinks 300 'were the largest number probably seen by a white man at one time.' Frank Russell (University of Iowa, 1894) says that forty were killed in the winter of 1892-93: Garretson, *American Bison,* 8.

[131]Richardson, *Fauna Boreali-Americana,* I, 283.

[132]Audubon and Bachman, *American Quadrupeds,* II, 44.

[133]Hornaday, "Extermination of the American Bison," 403.

as being 'in fine condition,'[134] which probably implies that its leader weighed more than he would have done in his natural freedom. F. H. Kitto says of the Plains buffalo that formerly "a 1600-lb. bull was considered a big fellow, and that, with thousands to choose from, a 2100-lb. specimen was the largest that American museum expeditions were able to secure. . . ."[135]

The opinions of our more empirical observers vary considerably, here as elsewhere. Nicholas Cresswell, a practical farmer and stockbreeder, remarks concerning 'a large bull' near the Blue Licks in Kentucky (May 17, 1775): ". . . from his breast to the top of his shoulder measuring 3 feet, from his nose to his tail 9 feet 6 inches . . . I am certain he would have weighed a thousand. . . . Some will weigh 14 to 15 hundred [that is, English 'hundredweight' = 112 lbs.]."[136] Fortescue Cuming, in the same region, 1809, was informed by his host, Captain Waller (re 'twenty years before') that "the males sometimes exceeded 1000 pounds in weight, but the females were seldom heavier than 500. . . ."[137] F. A. Michaux, Kentucky, 1802, gives them as weighing from 1,200 to 1,400 pounds at four years of age, but does not specify sex.[138] Edward Umfreville, writing concerning the Saskatchewan country, circa 1785, says that—"From the nose to the root of the tail, a full-grown male is about ten feet long. . . . The weight of a full-grown male is about one thousand pounds, English. . . ."[139] D. W. Harmon, who at this time (1801) is dealing with the prairie region at large, states that "the male buffalo, when fat, will weigh from 1000 to 1500 pounds, and the female from 800 to 1000. . . ."[140]

The younger Henry favoured a wider range between the sexes, and furnishes some valuable details:

It is common to see a bull exceed 1500 pounds, but a cow is seldom over 700 to 800 pounds, gross. . . .

A fat cow, killed in the autumn, weighs from 600 to 700 pounds. A lean cow seldom exceeds 300 pounds. I have weighed 150 cows, killed from September 1st to February 1st, and found they averaged 400 pounds each. Bulls in the same space of time average 550 pounds. Two-year-old heifers, in autumn, average 110 pounds. These weights are exclusive of the offals. But the total eatable meat of one full-grown bull, as received in the storehouse, weighed 800 pounds. This bull was in full flesh, but had neither inside tallow nor back fat, which gives me reason to suppose that a full-

[134]*Ibid.*, 461-2.
[135]Kitto, "Survival of American Bison in Canada," 437.
[136]*Cresswell's Journal*, 75, 85.
[137]Cuming, *Early Western Travels*, IV, 178.
[138]Michaux, *ibid.*, III, 234.
[139]Umfreville, *Present State of Hudson's Bay*, 158, 159.
[140]*Harmon's Journal*, 42.

grown bull, killed fat, about July 1st,[141] would weigh about 1800 pounds, offals included.

Buffalo are cut up into the following twenty pieces by the hunter: 1 grosse bosse (hump); 1 petite bosse; 2 depouilles; 2 shoulders; 2 lourdes epaulettes (shoulder pieces); 2 fillets; 2 thighs; 2 sides; 1 belly; 1 heart; 1 rump; 1 brisket; 1 backbone; 1 neck. The tongue generally belongs to the hunter. . . .[142]

Some of the given dimensions and weights hardly seem in keeping; but probably even a 'rolling fat' Prairie buffalo roaming at large might fall short of the compact mass of flesh on a stall-fed animal with the same size of frame. It appears possible at least that the more northerly Prairie buffalo in some regions may actually have been somewhat smaller in general than those to the south. Catlin observes that "the buffalo bull often grows to the enormous weight of 2000 pounds. . . ."[143] The Earl of Southesk, commenting on this statement (presumably as being contrary to his own experiences), remarks that "It is possible that the buffalo on the south of the Missouri, where Catlin hunted, may average a greater size than those roaming farther north in the Saskatchewan districts. . . ."[144]

Jonathan Carver—if one only knew whether to accept him—described those on the plains about Lake Pepin (Minnesota) in 1766, as 'the largest buffaloes of any in America.'[145] There is a curious circumstance which may perhaps strengthen this possibility of sectional

[141]That is, just before the rutting season; on which see below, chap. V. Norbert Welsh (1845-1933) says they killed cows then for pemmican: *Last Buffalo-Hunter*, 110. Perhaps a later practice.

[142]Coues (ed.), *Henry-Thompson Journals*, I, 171, 446. Cf. the descriptions by Harmon (*Journal*, 287) and by Clark Wissler (in Kidd, "Blackfoot Ethnography," unpublished MS., 99-100, 110). The usages evidently varied among tribes. Welsh gives a graphic description of the actual method of skinning and cutting up on the prairie, to keep the meat clean: *Last Buffalo-Hunter*, 106.

[143]Catlin, *Letters on the North American Indians*, I, 247.

[144]Southesk, *Travels*, 91: Seton is also for the lesser weights: *Life-Histories of Northern Animals*, I, 250.

[145]Allen, *American Bisons*, 103. Carver 'honest but credulous': so, Coues (ed.), *Expeditions of Pike*, I, 60, 198-201. His authority 'doubtful': Thwaites, ed. note, *Early Western Travels*, XXVIII, 155. Cf. Winsor, *Narrative and Critical History*, IV, 262; Hulbert, *Historic Highways*, I, 24. Cited without comment by Bryce, *Remarkable History*, 193; also Burpee (ed.), *Journals of La Vérendrye*, 108. Made up of 'scissorings from Charlevoix and La Hontan': so, Hart, "Imagination in History" (*American Historical Review*, XV, Jan., 1910, 230); compare La Hontan's own reputation!

Carver's authenticity is now maintained to have been vindicated by later research, including his journals recently found in the British Museum: Gates (ed.), *Five Fur Traders of the Northwest*, 38. La Hontan also found a very learned and capable defender, the late Dr. Louise Phelps Kellogg (*ibid.*, 33).

Meanwhile, we may note that Carver has nothing to say about those other

varieties other than Wood or Mountain buffalo. Long's party in 1820 killed ". . . a bull of most gigantic stature. . . . We have often regretted that we had not taken the dimensions of this animal, as it appeared to surpass in size any we had before killed, and greatly to exceed the ordinary stature of the bison. . . ."[146] This was in the upper Arkansas River country. There is a record from neighbouring territory in Kansas of a bull that weighed 3,000 pounds gross, and of cows going occasionally from 1,300 to 1,500 pounds.[147] R. G. Thwaites observes *re* the Washita River, some sixty or seventy miles southward of the Arkansas, that Washita "signifies possibly country of large buffaloes."[148]

On the other hand, the estimates of Harmon (*circa* 1800), dealing with the same general territory as Southesk, and coming also from one practically certain to be cognizant of any Western opinions on such possible variations, do not indicate any such pronounced difference; and Paul Kane, in December, 1847, shot what he specifies as a Prairie buffalo, not far from Edmonton, the head of which alone weighed 202 pounds.[149] In all instances of estimated weights, it will be wise to allow a margin for temperamentalisms in the observer. In addition, J. A. Allen remarks that "the American bison presents a considerable range of what may be termed individual variations,"[150] of which any or all of these cases might be examples. If such a regional variability were ever established in the Prairie buffalo, it would certainly drive another nail into the coffin of the Saskatchewan-and-Texas itinerary.

The unquestionably larger size of the Wood buffalo, as noted by so many observers, is strikingly illustrated by a modern traveller: "Hearne did not exaggerate the size of these great beasts. In 1910 I saw at Edmonton the unmounted skin of a bull that had been shot by an explorer. . . . The beast had weighed almost a ton and a half. The hide, even when dry, was almost an inch thick, and would have been a heavy load, even for a powerful man. . . ."[151] As we have seen, the

---

'largest buffalo in America,' the *B. pennsylvanicus* of Shoemaker, through whose habitat a British officer travelling almost anywhere westward, *circa* 1766, must perforce have passed.

[146]Long (that is, Edwin James), *Early Western Travels*, XVI, 168.

[147]Soper, "History of the Northern Bison," 376; citing a work of Garretson's, 1927, which I have had no opportunity to see.

[148]Thwaites, ed. note, *Early Western Travels*, XVI, 138.

[149]Kane, *Wanderings of an Artist* (Radisson Society ed.), 260.

[150]Allen, *American Bisons*, 48. The (presumably typical) specimen of a prairie bull exhibited mounted at Wainwright Station for many years did not suggest really immense size. I have seen larger living ones.

[151]Haworth, *Trailmakers of the Northwest*, 43. Garretson cites Frank Russell (1894) similarly, who says the Indians had to cut them in half for conveyance on their sleds. Garretson also states that it was an 'Indian' custom to split buffalo

weight of the Radford bull, about the same time, is given by Seton as 2,460 pounds.[152] Maxwell Graham states that "many of the animals are over a ton, and some weight at least two thousand five hundred pounds."[153] F. H. Kitto, writing in 1924, is even more specific. "A bull killed in 1910 near Fort Smith weighed 2432 pounds. Another, cut off and hamstrung by wolves just as the rangers arrived on the scene, weighed 2500 pounds. It is reasonably certain that bulls of 2500 pounds weight are quite common in these herds. . . ."[154]

The very competent student who writes anonymously as 'A Canadian Zoologist' believes, from a study of the data down to 1925, that 2,500 pounds may be accepted as the average weight for Wood buffalo bulls, with possibly much larger extreme instances.[155] Seton states that he has seen cows "which stood as high and looked as heavy as ordinary bulls. . . ."[156] Since the only buffalo he appears to have seen running wild were in the Northern Wood-buffalo region, the reference is probably to that type. To sum up the Wood-buffalo evidence as a whole, it seems clear that the 'random shot' was not that of Donald Ross, who knew the species, but that of his critic, who did not. The larger size of woodland varieties of wandering species would appear to be somewhat of a general principle, if observers are correct.[157]

It must not be forgotten that the identification of occasional individual animals of abnormal size is further complicated by the phenomenon of the so-called 'buffalo ox.' This creature is described by Hind, and again by Allen, as follows: "Buffalo emasculated by wolves, *the half-breeds say* [that is, of Red River], are often found on the prairies, where they grow to an immense size; the skin of the buffalo

hides down back and belly (*American Bison*, 8, 33). I have not found this elsewhere; and certainly neither Hearne's Indians (above, note 71) nor the Red River half-breeds practised it, if Alexander Ross can be accepted.

[152]Above, note 119.
[153]Graham, *Canada's Wild Buffalo*, 11.
[154]Kitto, "Survival of American Bison in Canada," 437.
[155]Canadian Zoologist, "The Passing of the Wood Bison," 301-5.
[156]Seton, *Life-Histories of Northern Animals*, I, 249; cf. his *Game Animals*, III, 642. A number of early weights also in Soper, "History of the Northern Bison," 357, 376.
[157]Warburton Pike considered the woodland caribou to be fully a third heavier then the Barren Ground animals: Pike, *Barren Ground*, 47. Cf. E. A. Preble, note in Thompson's *Narrative*, ed. Tyrrell, 98. Osborn, *Age of Mammals*, 422, etc.
After all this foregoing evidence, Dr. R. M. Anderson of the Canadian National Museum is reported as describing them at an international conservation gathering at Baltimore as being 'smaller than the ones which lived on the American plains . . .' (*Edmonton Journal*, February 14, 1938). Compared with Soper's remarks ("History of the Northern Bison," 357, 376, etc.) citing Anderson, this must surely be a misprint.

ox is recognized by the shortness of the wool, and by its large dimensions. . . ."[158] Allen writes: "Castrated buffaloes are said to be met with where the buffaloes are abundant, being castrated when quite young by hunters. They are reported to attain an immense size, being so much larger than the others as to be conspicuous from their large size. . . ."[159] Southesk describes them as "a variety of somewhat rare occurrence . . . standing half as high again as a male of the ordinary description. . . ."[160] I have found one reference only which appears to be that of an actual eye-witness, namely, John McDougall, somewhere between Fort Benton and the divide between the Missouri and South Saskatchewan River basins, early winter, 1873: "During this afternoon . . . I saw several buffalo oxen, huge brutes, towering above the others, and, as usual, in fine condition. . . ."[161]

Pending the production of some really reliable evidence, I am deeply suspicious of the suggested explanations concerning these monstrosities. What 'several' may have meant to McDougall, in the midst of 'dense masses,' as he then was, we do not know; nor why he alone should treat them as being so familiar a spectacle as to require no enlightenment to his readers. The general rarity of such a noticeable phenomenon may legitimately be inferred from the fact that the entire buffalo literature that I have read furnished only one eye-witness reference. I suspect that 'ox' is probably nothing more than a convenient colloquialism, since it is not found among those earlier writers who 'called a spade a spade.'[162] If these were really normal male animals which had suffered castration by wolves, why the rarity?—which may, I think, be agreed upon. Wolves were certainly not rare, as we shall later see.[163] No single wolf could overpower an active young or

[158]Hind, Report, 1858, 105. The italics are mine; these words are omitted in Hornaday's quotation of the passage ("Extermination of the American Bison," 407-8). See below, Appendix O.

[159]Allen, American Bisons, 41.

[160]Southesk, Travels, 105.

[161]McDougall, Western Trails, 79.

[162]It has often struck me as a form of prudery, among experienced American and eastern Canadian stock-breeders (who as a class may use 'technical' terms which might seem coarse in common speech, much like a student in Middle English), to find men conversing on breeding topics among themselves out in the fields where eavesdropping was impossible, and deliberately refusing (as inquiry elicited) to use the word bull, preferring 'your animal,' or in some instances the absurd phrase 'gentleman cow.' Whatever its origin, this form of fastidiousness was certainly not inherited from English usage. For these reasons, I decline to accept 'ox' as necessarily signifying, to those who might use it, a castrated normal male animal (gelding, emasculate, eviratus). At the same time, if the term were accepted as a convenient phrase, the attempt by others to explain the name along normal lines (that is, by castration) would soon follow quite logically.

[163]See chap. VII, "Agencies Destructive to Buffalo Other than Man."

partly grown bull calf without first resorting to the common method of wolf-attack, hamstringing, which the victim certainly would not survive. A band, under any conceivable parallel conditions, would assuredly tear it to pieces. Unless the animal were young at the time, the characteristic masculine appearance or size would not thus change. In respect of size, even in beef cattle castrated when very young, there is very seldom any pronounced increase in mere *size* of the bullock over his sire. These facts can be verified by any stock-breeder.

Further, how could a young calf small enough to meet these latter objections, small enough also to be completely overpowered and actually so mastered (even if the bulls or mothers of the herd drove off the wolves in the interval between the operation and the time required to devour the calf, if there would be any interval)[164] survive the three or four days of lassitude and weakness which usually follow castration, even in the very young, certainly with domestic species of the genus *Bos*. The smell of blood would preclude hiding from a wolf. We shall see that the buffalo mothers were not specially remarkable for their devotion to calves which could not follow them;[165] and a general sympathy for injured members of a herd is not a common animal characteristic. It is pertinent to note that in a fairly wide survey of the travel literature of buffalo, I have not found one single instance of any man either witnessing the operation, or meeting anyone else who either claimed to have seen it or even to have known any third party so claiming. Hind's account is the sole one, with the single exception of Shoemaker, relating to its occurrence in Pennsylvania.[166]

I am equally sceptical concerning castration by hunters, Indian or white. Audubon writes thus: "Young buffalo bulls are sometimes cas-

[164]See Frémont's account, 1842, of a calf pursued by wolves, and 'half devoured before it was dead . . .' (*Narrative*, 21).

[165]See below, chap. VII, notes 123-47.

[166]The inclusion of this idle tale (as though nothing ever related of buffalo must be omitted from *B. pennsylvanicus*) only serves to increase the deep suspicion already aroused by much of Shoemaker's other detail, on traditional authority. Such questions cannot be settled by appeals to somebody's moral probity, nor having been 'talked over again and again' (Shoemaker, *A Pennsylvania Bison Hunt*, 16). So also has the 'hoop-snake,' by similar good folk!

The Pennsylvania buffalo was 'a tremendous animal' (*ibid.*, 16); although the weights he gives, 'bulls often weighing a ton and mature cows half that much' (p. 17), do not support his wide differentiations from the Plains type. Possibly the contrasted Kentucky buffalo were smaller than the latter; but of this we have neither explicit nor implied evidence, certainly not from anyone who had seen both. But the 'buffalo oxen' (of *B. pennsylvanicus*), of 'still greater size than the biggest bulls' (p. 18), must have been incredibly huge. Perhaps it was one of these, 'a monster horrible, mis-shapen, vast,' that David Ingram described in 1569 (below, chap. IX). I fear that Colonel Shoemaker has unconsciously suggested too much of the answers to his own questionings. I since find Roosevelt repeatedly

trated by the Indians, as we were told, for the purpose of rendering them larger and fatter, and we were informed, that when full grown they have been shot, and found to be far superior to others in the herd, in size as well as in flavour. . . ."[167] This would entail a wait of two or three years for an animal they might never see again; and here also the calf would be exposed to the same danger from wolves immediately following the operation. This, moreover, would be to invest the Indian and the half-breed with those precise qualities of foresight and patient provision for the future which so many self-righteous censors among our buffalo authorities most emphatically deny them; including particularly the very class of plainsmen from whom our scientists derived their information. Here again, I have been unable to discover a single witness—to an alleged *human* practice—at first, second, or third hand. The only allusion that bears the least resemblance is as follows, from Nicholas Cresswell, in Kentucky, 1775 (May 24): "Caught two calves alive, whose ears we marked and turned them out again. . . ." (May 26): "Shot an old Buffalo Bull that had its ears marked. . . ."[168] There is a world of difference between that and castration, in the crucial factors governing survival. I fear that in these instances, some plainsman was 'pulling the leg' of the visitor from the East.[169] The one real authority cited here, Dr. John McDougall, makes no mention of these supposed origins. In my view, these creatures are more suggestive of a 'sport' of some character, probably hermaphroditic.[170]

Even the occasional 'Beaver robes' have been said to be a variety

emphasizing the need for critical caution in using the reminiscent material of this very age and region (*Winning of the West, passim*).

[167]Audubon and Bachman, *American Quadrupeds*, II, 46. I am surprised at a scholar and critic such as Maximilian of Wied blindly accepting this foolish yarn (*Early Western Travels*, XXIII, 175).

[168]*Cresswell's Journal*, 78, 79.

[169]Dodge notes the propensity in plainsmen, most particularly towards the questioning stranger, and the consequent need for caution in accepting some of their stories. Dodge, *Plains of the Great West*, 145.

[170]I leave my suggestion as first written in 1929. I have since found the following, showing the presence and recognition of such, for which the Cree had a name; *ayekkwe, wok* (plural), nom racine = male coupé eviratus; *v.g. ayekkewakim*, cheval ou chien coupé; *ayekkwe mustus*, taureau coupé (*mustus* = buffalo). "Aussi, on appelle ainsi celui qui n'est ni male ni femelle, ou plutôt, *qui utrumque sexum habent*, Hermaphrodite." Lacombe, *Dictionnaire de la langue des Cris*, 326.

The only instance I have found among the *ungulata* at large is of a hermaphroditic big-horn, shot by a well-known big-game authority, W. A. Baillie-Grohman (Seton, *Game Animals*, III, 529). Others, not seen by men of education, may be lost under some local term of the 'buffalo ox' order. J. H. Taylor, in the Gros Ventre country, Missouri River, 1869, mentions what is apparently a lake so named, "the lonely valley of the stagnant Hermaphrodite . . ." (*Frontier Life*, 81); probably after one seen there. I know of no other such place-name.

of the bison.[171] They are apparently the same as the 'silk robe' of McDougall[172] and others. Their origin has been variously explained. Sir Richard Burton writes (1855) of: "the glossy black accident called the 'silk robe,' supposed by Western men to be a cross between the parent and the offspring. . . ."[173] Other Westerners ascribed them to orphan 'mavericks,' which had been licked all over when young by members of their band.[174] M. S. Garretson, discussing this in one of the soundest items of criticism in his entire work, believes it to be a prairie folk-tale, biologically impossible.[175] While entirely agreeing with Garretson in this conclusion, I consider the true crux to be the inherent fallacy of explaining such extremely exceptional phenomena as the direct results of every-day commonplace causes.[176]

Garretson notes yet another supposed variety: "Old hunters have stated that there were two distinct breeds of buffalo in the Plains country, and distinguished them as the 'mealy noses' and the 'black noses,' the noses of the former being yellow or smutty brown and those of the latter very black. . . ."[177] I have found no other allusion to any such distinction.

The mere circumstance that the general verdict of many of the earlier writers and scientists on this subject has been reversed by later zoological classification is in itself of no importance. Accepted theses are being subjected to revision or dismissal every day, owing to the impact of later knowledge.[178] But Hornaday, as we have seen, after

[171]Audubon and Bachman, *American Quadrupeds*, II, 54.
[172]McDougall, *Western Trails*, 238.
[173]Burton, *City of the Saints*, 51.
[174]Denny MS., 39.
[175]Garretson, *American Bison*, 31-3.
[176]They were even rarer than white buffalo (*ibid.*, 31); John McDougall mentions no other specimen during twenty years. With the 'clan' system at least, Burton's 'origin' must have been a common occurrence (see below, chap. V, note 68), and Denny's even commoner.
[177]Garretson, *American Bison*, 24.
[178]The various categories may be summarized as follows: 'Not even a variety': Hornaday ("Extermination of the American Bison," 409). 'Identical, but for slight difference in appearance': Garretson, 'according to the best authorities' in *American Bison*, 5, 7. 'The two alleged species "not distinct"': Edmond Seymour, president, American Bison Society, 1932 (Raup, *Range Conditions in Wood Buffalo Park*, 52). 'Only one species': Shepstone, *Wild Beasts To-day*, 127. 'Very slight difference': Pike, *Barren Ground*, 156. 'A kindred race' (so Indians, 1873): Butler, *Wild North Land*, 210. 'Same species, "questionable"': (Butler himself in *Wild North Land*, 10). 'A variety': Henry, 1811, in Coues (ed.), *Henry-Thompson Journals*, II, 682. Thompson, 1812: *Narrative*, 558. Dr. Hector, 1858: *Palliser Journals*, 148. Hind, 1858: *Report*, 105. Allen, *American Bisons*, 48. Taylor, 1873: *ibid.*, 173. Seton, 1886 (see Raup, *Range Conditions in Wood Buffalo Park*, 18, 50); Stone and Cram, *American Animals*, 69; and *Encyclopaedia Britannica*, 14th

postulating, purely as a future possibility, the development of a smaller variety in a hitherto unvaried species, can quite casually cite in another connection in the same monograph a long-existent larger species. His essay abounds with contradictions, which cannot possibly be reconciled with his determined and rigid systematization of buffalo characteristics, and which are forgotten or ignored when no longer required to prove some immediate point.[179] It is idle to overlook the fact that, in a careful study of his paper, this persistent propensity detracts considerably from its value. Yet neither in himself nor in his followers can we perceive any awareness of the discrepancies between his various contentions. These details would be of historical interest only, were it not, as noted above, that modern students (including perhaps the foremost popular naturalist of the English-speaking world)[180] continue to utilize and proclaim Dr. Hornaday as the exhaustive and unimpaired authority, sometimes despite their own quite manifestly superior knowledge.

SUPPLEMENTARY NOTE: The exhaustive monograph of Skinner and Kaisen, *The Fossil Bison of Alaska* (1947) reached me (through the

---

ed., *s.v.* Bison. So also, by evident implication, Dr. R. W. Shufeldt, 1877 (Hornaday, "Extermination of the American Bison," 411). 'Distinct race': E. Mignault, *et al.* 1866 in Seton, *Game Animals*, III, 708. 'Several races': Seton, 1910 in *Life-Histories of Northern Animals*, I, 250. 'Two races': Tyrrell (ed. note), Hearne, *Journey*, 255; Hewitt, *Conservation of the Wild Life of Canada*, 123. 'Sub-species': S. N. Rhoads, 1897 (Raup, *Range Conditions in Wood Buffalo Park*, 18); E. A. Preble, 1916 (in Thompson, *Narrative*, ed. Tyrrell, 558); Canadian Zoologist, "The Passing of the Wood Bison," 301-5; Rowan, "Canada's Buffalo"; Seton, *Game Animals*, III, 643, 706; Raup, *Range Conditions in Wood Buffalo Park*, 18; Soper, "History of the Northern Bison," 375 (perhaps full species). 'Sub-species, doubtful': Graham, *Canada's Wild Buffalo*, 8. 'Perhaps full species': Canadian Zoologist, "The Passing of the Wood Bison"; Soper, "History of the Northern Bison," 375. 'Said to be an inferior species' (by whom? F. G. R.): Kitto, "Survival of American Bison in Canada." *Winnipeg Evening Tribune*, Aug. 21, 1937: the last an uninformed dogmatism of no authority whatever.

According to M. S. Garretson, 1938, 'the best authorities' are for identity, the distinctions of 'wood' or 'mountain' being "no more than a climatic or geographical variation." The best authorities are not named (*American Bison*, 5).

The latest authorities, Skinner and Kaisen (1947) classify 'two races': *B. (Bison) bison bison =* the prairie animal, and *B. (Bison) bison athabascae =* the northern Wood buffalo. (*Fossil Bison of Alaska*, 157, 159, 161, 242).

[179]The species are uniformly regular (Hornaday, "Extermination of the American Bison," 420, 423, 425, 442); utterly capricious (*ibid.*, 377, 382, 420, 422, 493, 508, 511); characterictically intelligent (*ibid.*, 417, 418, 426, 431, 480); or temperamentally stupid (*ibid.*, 389, 392, 399, 416, 429, 431, 480); purely as the argument of the moment may require, but 'always' thus.

[180]E. T. Seton. His section on the buffalo (*Game Animals*, III, 640-712) consists principally of the matter in his *Life-Histories of Northern Animals*, I, 247-301, reprinted *verbatim*. The same criticism applies also to Garretson, *American Bison*, frequently cited in these pages.

kindness of the authors) too late for incorporation into the foregoing chapter.

In discussing the living race, or races, the authors classify *Bison (Bison) bison athabascae*, Rhoads, 1897, as 'living woodland or mountain bison' (p. 164), and indicate a similar identity in their distribution map (p. 158). They also state that "this race was known as woodland or mountain bison previous to its being named by Rhoads. Considerable data referring to the large bison in the vicinity of Great Slave Lake and in the Yukon Territory have been published in the accounts of northern exploration . . ." (p. 165). They go on to add: "In the more southern portions of North America, particularly the Rocky Mountains, early writings of explorations often refer to the immense size of mountain bison and their solitary habits. The woodland or northern bison may have acquired their mountain habitat by extending their range southward down the Rocky Mountains until they reached the mountains of Colorado, Wyoming, Utah, and Oregon. The mountain or northern bison has been variously described" (p. 165).

I believe that readers of the foregoing chapter will agree that the above statement reveals a serious misconception in respect of the 'immense size of mountain bison' mentioned in early travel-writings. As I have pointed out (above, note 41), it is only by arbitrarily identifying the two variants beforehand as one, that one can state that the 'mountain or northern' bison have been 'variously described.' With respect to those narrators (and their informants) who first used the term *Mountain bison* for the animal of the regions indicated in the southerly Rocky Mountain foothill territory—and who were the first to bring the creature to the notice of scientific criticism—such a statement is in direct opposition to historical facts, of which the authors may not have been aware.

I cannot claim to have read everything of early date concerning that territory; but I have yet to find any reference from any resident or experienced plainsman, mountaineer, sportsman, or scientist, of or in the region, to 'immense' Mountain bison. With the exception of one passing visitor, Sir Richard Burton, the Oriental traveller, writing five years afterwards (see above, notes 42, 47), every writer mentioning size whom I have seen, makes them smaller. Even Hornaday's own hypothetical Mountain variety would also become smaller (above, note 50). Skinner and Kaisen add elsewhere: "The literature, both scientific and historic, is so extensive that little can be added concerning this [the living] race that is not already known. Both Allen and Hornaday, in their time, have presented excellent historical accounts concerning *Bison* distribution and habits . . ." (*ibid.*, 162). Following from this estimate, their historic distribution (with map) is based on the records of Allen and Hornaday (p. 157).

In making Hornaday in particular a primary authority, these authors have regrettably overlooked the fact that he denied the unimpeachably larger size of the northern Wood buffalo (which they accept) quite as strenuously as the equally well-attested smaller size of the Mountain bison, which they reject on his authority. In fact, the latter was the better attested of the two, since the witnesses included men of higher educational and critical standards than the first-hand northern witnesses of Hornaday's time. (See above, notes 49, 63, 82, 115.)

The title of the foregoing chapter was originally "North American *Varieties* of the Buffalo." The term *variant* seemed to be preferable for this reason: *variety* is a recognized technical term in zoological classification. As we have noted, its applicability in given cases relating to many species of flora and fauna has occasioned much controversy from which the buffalo have not been exempt (see note 178 above). Consequently its use in these pages seemed to the author to present the appearance of taking sides in disputes wherein a layman in biology is not competent to pronounce any opinion whatever on his own authority. The expression *variant* is not here intended by the author to signify any technical zoological classification whatever.

CHAPTER IV

THE CLIMATES AND TOPOGRAPHY OF THE BUFFALO HABITAT

IN a study such as the present, the varying physical conditions of the vast area occupied by the historic buffalo are of immense importance. In later chapters, while presenting evidence for the presence of buffalo in regions other than their familiar plains habitat during the three and one-half centuries from the time of their earliest known discovery, my object goes beyond a historical survey. While the account is almost necessarily historical in form, my main purpose is to show by sound evidence that the species had actually, during the period of contact with residents, explorers, scientists, and chroniclers (and of course during much longer prehistoric eras in the habitat as a whole), occupied the vast range of territory lying between the extreme limits which I shall indicate below. Many occurrences or characteristics will be found to be obviously or ultimately traceable largely to climatic influences, including the most notable of all supposed buffalo characteristics, the migratory habit. This circumstance would almost certainly necessitate a frequent recurrence to climatic data in illustration of some particular topic under consideration. It seemed well, therefore, to avoid much undesirable repetition by presenting this in homogeneous form in a chapter of its own to which brief reference could be made.

The wide-flung boundaries of the buffalo habitat include an immense variation in climates, since the entire territory lies on one side of the equator, and some 25° of latitude distant therefrom at its nearest point. These climates range from almost tropical to sub-arctic. In spite of the wide climatic variation, we are confronted with a species which is, broadly speaking, the same throughout this huge territory. With one possible exception of any significance (which I have discussed in an earlier chapter,[1] and which it will be seen in no way invalidates the present argument), any racial or temperamental peculiarities which might by chance differentiate one buffalo from another are quite as likely to occur in more or less homogeneous bands[2] that have all their

---

[1]See above, chap. III, "North American Variants of the Buffalo and Their Geographical Distribution."

[2]Seton considers the small herds into which the huge masses were often divided

lives apparently occupied the same general 'climatic belt' of territory, as in bands far distant one from another. In the case of widely separated herds, such peculiarities could with some show of reason be seized upon as indications (and perhaps as results) of discrepant climatic or topographical environmental influences. To bring the argument within the narrower specific confines of the present essay, all the climatic variation incident to so wide a territorial range did little or nothing to make the buffalo materially different in any one portion from what they were in another. Wherever we find the animal, he still is what he apparently always was—a cloven-hoofed, gregarious ruminant.

It should, nevertheless, be quite evident that a creature of these essentially uniform characteristics and fundamentally unchanging habits, will leave behind him a physical and a mental impression that will still differ widely according to the varying types of country in which he dwells. For purposes of illustration, we may take for the moment the familiar, and to many people orthodox, conception of one 'sole' trail, which is followed in undeviating single file by every member of a band of perhaps several hundred head.[3] It becomes immediately apparent that the resultant track will be by no means identical in every region of the buffalo habitat. The hard, sun-baked, rainless plateaus of Old or New Mexico, southwestern Kansas, Oklahoma, Utah, or similar regions;[4] the (then) undrained, spongy 'savannahs' of

to be 'clans' of related animals: *Life-Histories of Northern Animals*, I, 274-7, 287, 291. Cf. Garretson, (contra) *American Bison*, 59.

[3]See on this particularly, Hornaday, "Extermination of the American Bison," 416-18, etc. The supposition cannot sustain critical historical examination, and field-investigation with the camera is even more utterly fatal. The kindred fantasy of the buffalo-Indian-highway-railroad route proves equally baseless. The great apostle of this cult is Hulbert, *Historic Highways of America* (16 vols.). The first two volumes, in which he expounds this thesis, are a mass of incoherent contradictions. See below, note 71. Later, his work is of high value, embodying much research.

[4]On the 'Great American Desert' of the southwest, see the early explorations of Cabeza de Vaca, *circa* 1530; Coronado *et al.*, 1540; Pike, 1806; Nuttall, 1819; Long, 1819-20; Gregg, 1831-40; Farnham, 1839; Catlin, 1832-40; Parkman, 1846; Marcy, 1852; etc. The 'snake-dance' of the Hopi shown by anthropological research to be a prayer for rain (*Journey of Coronado*, ed note, 180; cf. *ibid.*, 93, 211, 241-4; see also Fynn, *American Indian*, 211-29, and *Handbook of American Indians*). See also two later scholars, Dr. E. L. Hewett, *Ancient Life in the American Southwest*, 23, 32, 127, 138-43; Webb, *Great Plains;* some valuable information in Hallenbeck, *Journey of Cabeza de Vaca*.

On the 'semi-arid' plains territory of Western Canada, see the very full *Palliser Journals*, 1857-60, Hind's admirable *Report* of 1858, Butler's report to the lieutenant-governor, 1871 (in his *Great Lone Land*, appendix), Professor John Macoun's *Manitoba* (to be compared with his very contradictory *Autobiography*);

the southeast;[5] the rich inviting plains of eastern Texas;[6] the deeper and softer soils of the (original) 'prairies' in the long-grass areas of Illinois, Iowa, Missouri, or southern Wisconsin,[7] and their more northerly counterparts, topographically—the parklands of the Portage Plains in Manitoba, or of the 'Garden of Alberta' between Fort Pitt and Edmonton;[8] the wide and fertile levels of the Dakotas and Nebraska;

an excellent survey in C. M. MacInnes, *In the Shadow of the Rockies* (history of Southern Alberta). A comprehensive description of the Western scene as a whole in the opening chapters of Morton's encyclopaedic *History of the Canadian West*. A very thorough survey of such territory in Dowling, "The Southern Plains of Alberta" (Canadian Geological Survey, Memoir 93, Ottawa, 1917). His work contains a list of publications of the Survey. See also the *Annual Reports* of the Canadian Conservation Committee, 1917, 60-74; 1918, 179-82; 1919, 248; etc. The Soil Bulletins of the Universities of Alberta and Saskatchewan (southern areas) are invaluable.

[5]The word originally denoted marshy ground. The tribe known as 'Swampy Crees' or 'Swampies' called themselves '*Muskegon*' (whence the familiar 'muskeg' = swamp), and were termed *Savannas* and *Savanois* by Chauvignerie, 1736, and Charlevoix, 1744; because, says the latter (*Histoire du Canada*, III, 181), "the country they inhabit is low, swampy, thinly wooded, and because in Canada these wet lands that are good for nothing are called Savanes. . . ." (Blair, *Indian Tribes*, I, 106). Father Marest, near Hudson's Bay, 1706: "a country wholly marshy and abounding in Savannas. . . ." (*Jesuit Relations*, LXVI, 111). See also Mooney, "Muskegon," in *Handbook of Canadian Indians*, 276.

[6]Cabeza de Vaca, *circa* 1530: "All over the land are vast and handsome pastures, with good grass for cattle, and it strikes me the soil would be very fertile . . ." (*Journey*, 97; also *Purchas his Pilgrimes*, XVII, 480). Similarly, Father Douay, and Joutel, 1686, in *Journeys of La Salle*, I, 237, 239; II, 78-83, 173; Parkman, *La Salle*, 395. As a modern pasture region, Hornaday, "Extermination of the American Bison," 424; Bancroft, *Northern Mexican States and Texas*, II, 559-63; Webb, *Great Plains*, 161, 209-27; Hallenbeck, *Journey of Cabeza de Vaca*.

[7]Joliet, 1673: "At first when we were told of these treeless lands, I imagined that it was a country ravaged by fire, where the soil was so poor that it produced nothing. But we have certainly observed the contrary; and no better soil can be found, either for corn, for vines, or for any other fruit whatsoever. . . ." (*Jesuit Relations*, LVIII, 105). Similarly, Marquette, 1673; also Hennepin, and the scribes of La Salle's party; Gravier, Marest, Vivier, etc., 1700-1750 (Hennepin, *New Discovery; Jesuit Relations*, LVIII, LXV, LXVI, LXIX).

Croghan, 1765: "Some mention those spacious and beautiful meadows as barren savannahs. I apprehend it has been the artifice of the French to keep us ignorant of the country. . . ." (*Early Western Travels*, I, 140, 145). Their rank, lush growth aroused fears of agues. See Evans, Flint, Hulme, Flower, Faux, Flagg, 1818-36 (*ibid.*, VIII, IX, X, XI, XXVI, XXVII). Flower and Woods, contra: *ibid.*, X, 142, 259. This was the earliest era of settlement.

Monroe to Jefferson, 1786: "A great part of the territory is miserably poor, especially that near Lakes Michigan and Erie, and that upon the Mississippi and the Illinois consists of extensive plains which have not had, from appearances, and will not have, a single bush on them for ages. . . ." (Turner, *Frontier in American History*, 151). For a modern appraisal, Jones and Bryan, *North America*, 165.

[8]Jones and Bryan classify the 'short grass area' (roughly the entire buffalo plains habitat west of the Missouri River in the United States and including South Saskatchewan and South Alberta) as 'semi-arid,' changing from black to brown

the stony and sterile ridges of the 'Missouri Coteau,' on both sides of the international boundary;[9] the soft clay lands of the northern woodlands beyond the North Saskatchewan River; or the heavily timbered, almost sunless mountain defiles of the northern Rockies—to expect all these widely sundered regions to exhibit the same effects from the presence of herds whose actual numbers varied greatly, would be unreasonable.[10] This fact is of fundamental importance, and must at all times be borne in mind in attempting to form any judgment concerning what at first sight appear to be hopelessly discrepant assertions concerning the buffalo *track*, from writers apparently intelligent and presumably speaking in good faith.

Although there is no lack of generalizing assertion concerning the supposed propensity in buffalo for moving, commonly 'north and south,' from one climatic belt (if I may use the term) to another at certain changes of the season, I have found one reference only which can reasonably be considered to support that view. I must not be misunderstood here. I do not mean mere movements to north or south;

soils (*ibid.*, 173, 215, 224, 374, 495, 498-502); Texas to Coahuila as 'arid' (*ibid.*, 29-32).

For Western Canada and the respective types, there is a vast mass of information. See on this, a long resident, John McDougall *re* 1868: "From the North Branch of the Saskatchewan, extending a hundred miles north (that is, from Carlton) and then west along its whole length, is to be found one of the richest portions of Canada. . . ." (written *ante* 1898: *Pathfinding*, 273).

Re scientists, see Palliser (*et al.*), Hind, Sandford Fleming, 1874, Macoun, etc. Travellers: Paul Kane, 1846-48; Southesk, 1859; Milton and Cheadle, 1863; Butler, 1871, 1873; G. M. Grant, 1872. See also Oliver, "The Beginnings of Agriculture in Saskatchewan" (*Transactions of the Royal Society of Canada*, Sec. II, 1935, 1-32); and for a general critical review, Roe, "Early Opinions on the 'Fertile Belt' of Western Canada" (*Canadian Historical Review*, XXVII, 1946, 131 *seq.*).

[9]Parkman, Platte Valley, 1846: "The vast plain waved with tall rank grass, that swept our horses' bellies . . ." (*Oregon Trail*, 82).

For the Missouri Coteau Region and its type of 'bald-headed prairie,' see Catlin, *Letters on the North American Indians*, II, 165-71, 201-6; Parkman, *Oregon Trail*, 40-2, 77-80, 157, 208, 359, 460; *Life of De Smet*, IV, 1585; Macoun, *Manitoba*, 26, 30, 76, 203, 287, 289; *Autobiography*, 142-6, 164-78; Turner, *Frontier in American History*, 130, 147, 239-320; an old resident, Isaac Cowie, *Company of Adventurers* (Hudson's Bay Company), 253 *seq.*; Roe, "Early Opinions on the 'Fertile Belt' of Western Canada"; including authorities cited in notes 4, 7, above.

[10]Since first drafting the above, I find this from a plainsman: "Extending over nineteen degrees of latitude, and varying in altitude from almost sea-level to eight thousand feet above, the Plains present an almost infinite variation of climate; and besides the variations due to latitude and altitude, there are others resulting from the absence of those natural protectors of the earth's surface, trees, and from the aridity of the high Plains. . . ." (Dodge, *Our Wild Indians*, 502). I have had no opportunity to see Ward's excellent *Climates of America:* cf. also in this, Brooks, *Climate Through the Ages; Encyclopaedia Britannica, s.v.* Climates and Climatology, North America; Jones and Bryan, *North America* (1928); etc.

of such, evidence exists, and will be presented in due course. I refer specifically to regions where a somewhat pronounced line of climatic demarcation may apparently be observed, and in which—presumably because of that circumstance—something deserving the name of 'migration' has been noted. The paucity of such cases is not surprising. The lines defining the bounds of higher or lower (mean) temperatures, or greater or lesser rainfall, or in the West, for example, the more prevalent or only occasional influence of 'Chinook' winds,[11] cannot be drawn with the precision that marks one fenced field from another. For this reason, unless the observer actually could and did follow the moving herd in the autumn from the colder northern belt to the warmer southern one, and could ascertain beyond doubt that the same individuals continued their pilgrimage until the more genial climate was reached, and that they did not attempt to retrace their steps northward until the return of spring, when they again selected the region abandoned by them in the previous fall, I cannot see with what degree of assurance their southward movement could be ascribed purely to climatic reasons.

The single instance I have mentioned is related by Father Hennepin: "In Autumn . . . having grazed all the Summer long in those vast Meadows, where the Herbs are as high as they, they are then very fat . . . for the Convenience of those Creatures, there are Forests at certain distances, where they retire to rest, and shelter themselves against the violence of the sun. They change their Country according to the Seasons of the Year; for upon the approach of the Winter, they leave the North to go to the Southern Parts. . . ."[12]

It may be noted that the worthy Récollet has been stigmatized by a not particularly uncharitable critic—one who certainly cannot be accused of any failure to appreciate the early Catholic missionaries—as "the most impudent of liars," for some of his vaingloryings in this very work[13] (that is, the second London issue of 1698), which did not appear in his first edition of 1683, when La Salle, whose reputation they

[11]"The Chinooks are warm, dry, west winds which occur both in summer and winter. The summer Chinooks frequently result in excessive evaporation and soil drifting, particularly in the southeast [that is, of Alberta] and it is this fact that has made that part of the prairie less well adapted for crop production than the west and north. . . ." MacInnes, *In the Shadow of the Rockies*, 7. A more technical description in Dowling, "Southern Plains of Alberta," 3-20. For soil-drifting, Canadian Conservation Committee, *Annual Report*, 1917, 62, etc.

[12]Hennepin, *New Discovery*, ed. Thwaites, I, 148.

[13]Parkman, *La Salle*, 136; cf. Gravier, *Jesuit Relations*, LXV, 173. It perhaps may be necessary in Father Gravier's case to make some allowance for the enmity, *circa* 1690, between the Récollets and the Jesuit order.

traduce, was still alive.[14] Yet Parkman also points out that "where his vanity or his spite was not involved, he often told the truth,"[15] and adds that his descriptions are generally accurate.[16] Unfortunately, when once a writer or traveller has been convicted of almost everything that can undermine a reputation, from exaggeration to sheer lying, it is not easy to determine in a given case whether we are listening to Dr. Jekyll or to Mr. Hyde. Fortunately, in the present instance, we have more than intuitions to assist us. Father Hennepin tells us elsewhere: "In Winter . . . it is then their [the Indians'] Custom to leave their Villages, and with their whole Families to go a hunting wild Bulls, Beavers, etc. . . ."[17] Similar testimony is given by several of the Jesuit missionaries; and as there was little love lost between Jesuits and Récollets, their evidence in this particular is unexceptionable.[18] In reference to the custom, Hennepin describes a certain place, editorially identified as Peoria Lake, Illinois, as follows: "The Savages call that Place *Pimiteoui*; that is in their tongue, *A Place where there is abundance of fat beasts.*"[19]

La Salle's early biographer, Father Christian Le Clercq, mentions the same place and gives the same interpretation.[20] His missionary colleague, Father Zenobius Membre, states: "It is remarkable, because the Illinois River, which for several months in winter is frozen down to it, never is from this place to the mouth. . . ."[21] Father Membre adds elsewhere (*re* 'Northern Illinois'): "the winter cold . . . is piercing in these parts, though of short duration . . ."[22]; and again (near modern Chicago): "Though the winter in these parts is only two months long,

[14]"The records of literary piracy may be searched in vain for an act of depredation more recklessly impudent. . . ." (Parkman, *La Salle*, 247); cf. *ibid.*, *passim*. It is only fair to add that Hennepin found a brilliant defender in John Gilmary Shea, whose work I have not seen; but his arguments did not convince such critics as Bancroft (*Northwest Coast*, I, 588), Fiske (*Discovery of America*, II, 540), Coues (ed., *Expeditions of Pike*, I, 64, 91), or Hennepin's own editor, R. G. Thwaites (*New Discovery*, ed. pref.). See also Winsor (ed.), *Narrative and Critical History*, IV, 247-56.
[15]Parkman, *La Salle*, 137.
[16]*Ibid.*, 247, 267.
[17]Hennepin, *New Discovery*, I, 153.
[18]Dablon and Allouez, 1669-71: *Jesuit Relations*, LIV, 189; LV, 195-7; Binneteau, 1699: *ibid.*, LXV, 73-5; Gravier, 1700: *ibid.*, LXV, 135; Marest, *circa* 1710: *ibid.*, LXVI, 253; Poisson, 1726: *ibid.*, LXVII, 285.
[19]*New Discovery*, I, 154. On Pimiteoui, Pimitoui, see also James Mooney, *Handbook of American Indians*, II, 254.
[20]Le Clercq, *Journeys of La Salle*, I, 100.
[21]Membre, *ibid.*, I, 133. I am informed by former local residents that Peoria Lake itself often freezes.
[22]*Ibid.*, I, 113.

it is, notwithstanding, very severe. . . ."[23] Father Marest says the same
of the Illinois country about 1712: "Although this country is farther
south than Provence, the winter here is longer; the cold weather, however, is somewhat mitigated. . . ."[24] John Woods, 1820, allots 'about
two months' winter' to Illinois;[25] and Captain Bonnecamp, *circa* 1750,
says the same even of Detroit.[26]

When we consider that Peoria (approximately 40° 35′ N., 89° 40′
W., although it was erroneously estimated by La Salle to be 33° 45′
N.[27]) is only some eighty miles or so south from Chicago, we are confronted with what would seem to be a highly pronounced and somewhat closely defined demarcation of climatic phenomena.[28] This demarcation is even more remarkable than that in the Province of
Alberta, where this was written. Here, the Bow River at Calgary not
infrequently remains entirely open throughout the winter; whereas I
have never known the Red Deer River in the 'Canyon' region about
eighty miles distant to do so in the course of more than fifty years. But
the much more pronounced influence of the Chinook winds in southern
Alberta has to be taken into account; I have found no indication of
any similar local phenomenon in Illinois. Situated as Peoria is, within
less than one hundred miles from the extreme northern (known) limit
of the buffalo habitat in that part (that is, the southern boundary of
the state of Michigan and the Great Lakes), if there was ever any
migratory movement attributable to climatic influences, it is precisely
within the zone of such sudden and striking change that we might
expect to discover it. I shall later present historical evidence to show
that even this reasonable expectation by no means finds uniform fulfilment in respect of directions.

In order that the basis for the commonly accepted belief on this
question, and likewise for my own attitude concerning the same, may
be made clear, I shall quote at some length the observations of perhaps the most scientifically minded writer who has ever discussed the
problem. Allen writes:

[23]*Ibid.*, 132.
[24]Marest, *Jesuit Relations*, LXVI, 223; cf. also Vivier, 1750: *ibid.*, LXIX, 217.
[25]*Early Western Travels*, X, 335.
[26]Bonnecamp, *Jesuit Relations*, LXIX, 193.
[27]So, Le Clercq in *Journeys of La Salle*, I, 100. There is some confusion here.
In Marquette's voyage, 1673, he mentions a place where Joliet and he took counsel
concerning pushing further south or not, as being 33° 40′ N., 'in a buffalo country
where the inhabitants never saw snow. . . .' (*Jesuit Relations*, LIX, 157). It may
have been some recognizable landmark or spot, which La Salle thought he had
reached.
[28]See Shaler, *Nature and Man in America*, 241.

The buffalo is quite nomadic in its habits, the same individuals roaming, in the course of the year, over vast areas of country. The habit of the buffaloes, too, of keeping together in immense herds renders a slow but constant movement necessary in order to find food, that of a single locality soon becoming exhausted. . . .

They are also accustomed to make frequent shorter journeys to obtain water. The streams throughout the range of the buffalo run mainly in an east and west direction, and the buffaloes, in passing constantly from the broad grassy divides to the streams, soon form well-worn trails, which, running at right angles to the general course of the streams, have a nearly north and south trend. These paths have been regarded as indicating a very general north and south annual migration of these animals. It is, indeed, a widespread belief among the hunters and plainsmen that the buffaloes formerly performed regularly very extended migrations, going south in autumn and north in spring. I have even been assured by former agents of the American Fur Company, that before the great overland emigration to California . . . divided the buffaloes into two bands, the buffaloes that were found in summer on the plains of the Saskatchewan and the Red River of the North spent the winter in Texas, and *vice versa*. The early Jesuit explorers reported a similar annual migration among the buffaloes east of the Mississippi River, and scores of travellers have since repeated the same statement in respect to those of the Plains. That there are local migrations of an annual character seems in fact to be well substantiated, especially at the southward, where the buffaloes are reported to have formerly, in great measure, abandoned the plains of Texas in summer for those further north, revisiting them in winter. Before their range was intersected by railroads, or by the great transcontinental emigrant route by way of the South Pass,[29] the movements of the herds were, doubtless, much more regular than at present. North of the United States, as late as 1858, according to Hind, they still performed very extended migrations, as this author reports the Red River bands as leaving the plains of the Red River in spring, moving first westward to the Grand Coteau de Missouri, then northward and eastward to the Little Souris River, and thence southward again to the Red River plains.

As already stated, a slight movement northward in summer and southward in winter is well attested as formerly occurring in Texas; the hunters report the same thing as having taken place on the plains of Kansas; further north the buffaloes still visit the valley of the Yellowstone in summer from their winter quarters to the southward; along the forty-ninth parallel they also pass north in summer and south in winter; there is abundant evidence also of a similar north and south migration on the Saskatchewan plains. Yet it is very improbable that the buffaloes of the Saskatchewan ever wintered on the plains of Texas; and absolutely certain that for twenty-five years they have not passed as far south even as the valley of the Platte.[30] Doubtless the same individuals never moved more than a few hundred miles in a north

[29]That is, the Oregon-California Trail.

[30]That is, since not later than 1851; Allen's work was published in 1876; his visit to the Plains, gathering local information, was in 1871. This question will be examined chronologically later (see below, chap. XIX). Hornaday, however, ascribed the 'division into two herds' (if they were ever one!) to the Union Pacific Railway, 1865 ("Extermination of the American Bison," 492).

and south direction, the annual migration being doubtless merely a moderate swaying northward and southward of the whole mass with the changes of the seasons. We certainly know that buffaloes have been accustomed to remain in winter as far north as their habitat extends. North of the Saskatchewan they are described as merely leaving the more exposed portions of the plains during the deepest snows and severest periods of cold to take shelter in the open woods. We have, for instance, numerous attestations of their former abundance in winter at Carlton House, in latitude 53°, as well as at other of the Hudson's Bay Company's posts. . . .[31]

A careful study of the foregoing reveals how flimsy is much of the evidence upon which various forms of the migration argument are based. The Saskatchewan-Texas journey, despite the authority of old plainsmen, was beyond Allen's digestive powers—as well it might be—although a later observer at the northern end endorses it *in toto*.[32] From Texas (even at its northern boundary along the Red River) to the Saskatchewan comprises over twenty parallels of latitude, from 33° to 53° N., that is, about 1,400 miles in a directly northward line. Adding to that something between twelve and fifteen degrees of longitude westward from central Texas (about 97° W.), and also the inevitable irregular detourings of such a journey, one begins to grasp something of the mere mileage to be covered! We presume their 'day's work' would be uniform—it would assuredly need to be; yet if 1871 was a normal year, Colonel Dodge found the buffalo 'early in May' only at the Arkansas River, west of the Great Bend and somewhere near Fort Larned, with less than one-sixth of the Great Trek accomplished. A generation before (1839) they were six or seven weeks later than that at the Arkansas crossing.[33] If we allow for one rest-day each week—which such intelligent creatures would probably take on the Sabbath—they would have to cover some ten or twelve miles every day for six months. The herds, to which reference has been made, which 'wintered on the Saskatchewan,' would be the footsore unfortunates who had just arrived from Texas; and those observed going south in summer, a similar caravan homeward bound. There was a logic of sorts in the dictum that "the buffaloes that were found in summer on the plains of the Saskatchewan and the Red River of the North spent the winter in Texas, and *vice versa*. . . ."[34] They could not possibly have accomplished the round trip in one summer; and one can almost imagine

[31]Allen, *American Bisons*, 59-61.

[32]Denny MS., introd., 14. On this and Denny's other MS. since printed (*The Law Marches West*, ed. W. B. Cameron, 1938), see Bibliography, note 2.

[33]Dodge, *Plains of the Great West*, 120 *seq.*; see also on this his *Our Wild Indians*, 283. In 1839, they were only two or three days north of the Arkansas crossing, as late as June 21-4 (Farnham, *Early Western Travels*, XXVIII, 94-6).

[34]Allen, *American Bisons*, 59-61 (above, note 31).

their thrill when it was their turn, every alternate year, to 'winter in the South'!

That 'scores of travellers have repeated' this or that concerning the Plains buffalo is quite true; all too commonly their generalizations are taken wholesale from some informant who was destitute of critical judgment, and they make no attempt to discover to what his sweeping implications lead. In many years, the late arrival in the northern winter-quarters would be a suicidal experiment. In the case of the 'pilgrim cattle' that were driven northward from Texas into Montana and southern Alberta in the eighties, it is well known that the owners took a chance on getting them in soon enough in the fall to give them a few weeks of warm weather in which to recover a little, and on the hopes of an open winter. The disastrous 'Cochrane winter' of 1882-83 derived its name from the almost complete extermination of the pilgrim cattle on the Cochrane Ranch on the upper Bow River above Calgary, through the failure of such expectations. The stock, numbering some 5,000 head, reached the ranch in September, 1882, in poor condition, as was usual after such trips. Before the end of that month, winter set in with unparalleled fury; and snow covered the ground unbrokenly until April. Practically the entire stock of the Cochrane Ranch, along with thousands of head belonging to others, was swept into the coulees and smothered in the drifts which filled them to the level.[35]

I have alluded to the need for definitely ascertaining, by actual observation, that the long journeys supposedly made by the buffalo on these 'migrations' were really performed beyond doubt by the self-same individuals. I have met with no evidence of any scientific attempt to demonstrate this; in fact, I have found no observed evidence of any nature (except one solitary instance) beyond the assumptions that because buffalo herds were seen to move northward or southward, it was for climatic reasons; and that they kept on moving for huge distances, until some warmer or cooler climate was reached. To those accepting the conventional traditions on this question, evidence was presumably superfluous. Since every trail, Indian or otherwise, which extends across the Plains, 'was once a buffalo track,' the buffalo *must* have travelled those immense distances, and each assumption proved the other.

In one case only have I discovered what at first appeared to be

[35]Always known among the old-timers as 'the Cochrane winter.' See MacInnes, *In the Shadow of the Rockies*, 208; Denny (a contemporary), *The Law Marches West*, 157, 186.

evidence tending to support the supposition that the same individuals covered these immense mileages; but further examination renders this worse than doubtful. In an unpublished memoir of early reminiscence by Sir Cecil Denny,[36] mention is made of a certain 'white buffalo,' which by hearsay report was said to have been traced northwards in the company of a herd for hundreds of miles; and which, when finally killed through plunging in panic over a cut-bank on the Bow River near Blackfoot Crossing (1876), proved to be a Texas long-horn which had taken up with the buffalo.[37] The entire value of this incident as evidence of individuals continuously travelling long distances, hinges upon two vital considerations. The first is: was it or was it not the same white animal throughout these hundreds of miles?

Cases of actual white buffalo—the term embraces also those of a dirty cream or clay colour,[38] as I believe is likewise the case with the 'white' elephant of Siam—are certainly historically rare enough to make them noticeable; yet not so utterly rare (despite Hornaday's *dicta*)[39] as to make it *certain* that it must have been the same animal in all these loosely reported instances. For identification purposes, 'white buffalo' may include domestic animals joining a band—Denny's instance being an actual case in point—or possibly the hybrid offspring of such. If one white animal could join a herd in Wyoming or Montana, another might do so in Alberta. The phenomenon was not uncommon;[40] it was not even confined to horned stock.[41] The second consideration is this: if the white Texas long-horn in this particular instance could be accepted beyond doubt as being the same animal throughout, that

[36]See above, note 32. Denny resided in Alberta, 1874-1928.

[37]Denny MS., 40.

[38]Hornaday, "Extermination of the American Bison," 414. Alexander Henry says: "There are also some of a dirty gray, but these are very rare . . ."; implying from his context an almost greater rarity than of really white ones (Coues (ed.), *Henry-Thompson Journals*, I, 159).

[39]See Appendix D, "Albinism in Buffalo."

[40]See Appendix C, "Buffalo Domestication."

[41]Evidence varies. In 1541, three horses, saddled and bridled, were lost and never seen again; so, Castañeda, and Coronado himself (*Journey*, 66, 195). 'Not uncommon with horses and mules. . . .' (Gregg, *Early Western Travels*, XIX, 213). 'Mr. Kipp's horse . . . saddled and bridled, joined a band of buffalo, and was never recovered. . . .' (Maximilian, *ibid.*, XXIV, 45). Henry mentions a lost horse being found 'in company with a large herd of buffaloes,' Plumb River, 1800 (Coues (ed.), *Henry-Thompson Journals*, I, 117); also at Rocky Mountain House, 1810, ". . . a small herd of cows was found among our horses near the fort. . . ." (*ibid.*, II, 666). Conversely, however, Paul Kane, Fort Pitt, January, 1848: "They [the buffalo] killed with their horns twenty or thirty horses in their attempt to drive them off from the patches of grass which the horses had pawed the snow from with their hoofs for the purpose of getting at the grass; and severely gored many others, which eventually recovered. . . ." (*Wanderings of an Artist*, orig. ed., 396).

circumstance would furnish no proof whatever that the herd in whose company he was first—or later--seen was the identical herd in whose company he was finally slain. If a long-horn, or a scion of any breed, could leave home and take up with one herd of buffalo, why not with another?[42] If there be anything in the 'clan'-theory among buffalo, it could not apply to an alien species; and since, after all, it is the habits of buffalo and not of long-horns that are under discussion, the identity of the *herd* must be decided first. Probabilities are valueless here; we require certainties, or the case is not proved.

I am extremely sceptical concerning the migration on this grand scale for climatic reasons, certainly as regards the general territory north of the Platte. It is really astonishing how some scientists write of huge continental areas as if they were mere bodies of water. Speaking broadly, sea longitudes within the same latitudes reveal only minor changes in temperature sometimes for vast distances. On land, conditions are entirely different. The interacting influences of varying altitudes, of mountain chains, high plateaus and low plains, of great forest belts, of some territories interspersed with large bodies of water, and of others consisting of immense and continuously unbroken land areas—all these profoundly affect climate; in fact, they are themselves the principal causes for the existence of *climates* in the pluralized sense. To speak, in reference to the vast North American continent as a whole, of 'moving north' or 'migrating south' as an almost automatic procedure in order to avoid a hot summer or a cold winter, is, in many cases, reduced to absurdity by more potent considerations than simple latitude.

For example, the Platte River lies about 850 miles south from Edmonton, Alberta, where the present study was written. In my earlier days in the province, half a century ago, I lived among many American settlers from the old treeless Nebraska of the eighties; our adjoining neighbours on the same section were actually from the town of North Platte, situated at the forks of the north and south branches. Their tales of blizzards and long-continued 'cold snaps,' together with their own eloquent comments on the contrast with the milder Central Alberta winters, speedily convinced me that nobody but an imbecile would migrate south to the Platte in search of an easier winter climate.[43] To migrate for the winter from Calgary or southern Alberta generally into many parts of Montana would be a poor exchange; and I doubt whether even a buffalo inhabitant of Prince Albert, on the

[42]Frémont mentions a red ox which broke away and returned home, after a long journey down the Platte Valley, 1842 (*Narrative*, 17).

Saskatchewan River, which is commonly considered to be one of the coldest places in a land of bitterly cold winters, would better himself appreciably by wintering in the Dakotas,[44] while the sheltered Northern woods were still available.[45] I shall have occasion to note, before concluding the present chapter, that writers in the United States, among whom this type of generalization has been rather prevalent, are perhaps themselves not wholly to blame for their misapprehension in cases where personal contact has not been practicable, or in some of those earlier instances where personal contact with a Western Canada 'only fit for Indians and fur traders' was apparently beneath attention.[46] In some cases, they have been misled by Canadians themselves.[47] Be the reason whatever it may, the fact remains; and it has occasioned some curious dogmatisms concerning the all-embracing character of north-and-south migrations—curious to western Canadians at least. Their only effect is to seriously weaken the arguments of which they form a part and to reveal the profound ignorance of the climates of the Canadian historical buffalo habitat on the part of those who have advanced them.

Frequently, these supposed seasonal migrations, even as put forward by the champions of the belief, do not, it appears to me, cover sufficient latitudinal distances to meet the demands of their own argument. In that particular portion of the Western Plains territory where

[43]See General Ashley's account of wintry weather over the Platte, December, 1824 to January, 1825 (Dale (ed.), *Ashley-Smith Explorations*, 118-26). Winter rigours at the Pawnee villages, 1819-20 (Edwin James, *Early Western Travels*, XV, 216). Fort Phil Kearney, Montana, December, 1866 to January, 1867 (Hebard and Brininstool, *Bozeman Trail*, II, 16, 39, 104-7). Cold weather apparently in Arkansas, December, 1540 (De Soto, in *Purchas his Pilgrimes*, XVIII, 16). On the Arkansas River, not only December but October 28, 1806, see both Pike and Wilkinson (Coues (ed.), *Expeditions of Pike*, II, 433, 547-56); also 1822 (*ibid.*, ed. note, 437). Likewise on the same, 1871-2 (Dodge, *Plains of the Great West*, 121). On the Cimarron, 1865, and the Republican, 1867 (*ibid.*, 39-42). Compare further Long (James), *Early Western Travels*, XV, 311.

[44]For Dakota (if there were any doubts!), see David Thompson's account of his trip, November 29 to December 30, 1797, Assiniboine House (near Brandon, Manitoba) to the Mandan villages, 238 miles in 32 days—usually 12 days (*Narrative*, ed. Tyrrell, 210-24, 244). See also in this region, 1833-4, Maximilian, *Early Western Travels*, XXIV, 53-5; *Lewis and Clark Journals*; Gass, *Journal of Lewis and Clark Expedition*; Masson, *Les Bourgeois de la Compagnie du Nord-Ouest*; *Palliser Journals*; Cowie, *Company of Adventurers*, 240, 253 seq.

[45]For historical evidence concerning this, see below, chaps. XII, XX.

[46]One is surprised, however, to find Shaler (in 1891!) saying of the Saskatchewan River valley: ". . . the length and severity of the winters make it too cold to profit by the rearing of horned cattle and sheep. . . ." *Nature and Man in America*, 220, 253-5. Cf. an earlier United States climatologist, below, note 90.

[47]See below, notes 79, 89, 90.

the two 'climatic zones' might roughly be said to meet, the alleged "fixed habit of the great buffalo herds to move from two hundred to four hundred miles southward at the approach of winter. . . ."[48]—the mean of which would take them from the Platte into Oklahoma, Texas, or New Mexico—might really introduce them to a radically different winter climatic environment.[49] But in no instance does there appear to be a sufficient improvement in wandering from central Oklahoma into central Texas; from Santa Fé or the Canadian River to the Rio Grande; from the Llano Estacado into Old Mexico. Or again, in the North, from the Battle or Red Deer River country into northern Montana; from Montana into central Wyoming; from the South Saskatchewan to the Missouri; from the Missouri to the Platte; all of which regions are situated roughly some three hundred miles, the one from the other. For a herd to leave the great forests and scrub-belts of northern Alberta or Saskatchewan to wander about the international boundary, would have been imbecile. I shall later cite historical testimony of the first order proving that, habitually at least, the buffalo did no such thing. Furthermore, Hornaday's subdivision of the western buffalo habitat into lateral sections, in which the extreme northern pasture ground of one detachment becomes the extreme southern winter range-limit of the next northernmost division, seems to me to involve inescapably the patent absurdity that the 'richer pastures' and 'better grass' which lured each buffalo column southward at the approach of winter must have been found in each several case on the 'parched brown plains' that its next neighbours to the south had scornfully deserted.[50]

In human affairs we might 'plead that 'one man's meat is another man's poison,' but Hornaday was himself the most strenuous and immovable opponent of any suggestion of individualistic tendencies or

[48]Hornaday, "Extermination of the American Bison," 420-6, passim; also Buffalo Jones' Forty Years, 95.

[49]Edwin James (Long's Expedition, 1819-20): "This barren and ungenial district appeared, at this time, to be filled with greater numbers of animals than its meagre productions are sufficient to support. It was, however, manifest that the bisons, then thronging in such numbers, were moving toward the south. . . . What should ever prompt them to return to the inhospitable deserts of the Platte, it is not perhaps, easy to conjecture. . . ." Early Western Travels, XV, 248). But compare Parkman on the Platte, 1846 (above, note 9); also Darwin on large numbers in 'desert' regions (chap. XVIII, note 24).

[50]The very comprehensive terms, 'prairie' and the 'Plains,' have been applied quite commonly to any and every type of country from the Mississippi to the Rockies. I have collected over 300 adjectival forms. Westward from the Missouri are the regions of the famous 'buffalo grass,' though few agree as to what it really is or was. Castañeda, 1541, says of it: ". . . the grass grows tall near these lakes; away from them it is very short, a span or less. . . ."; so short that it "straightened up again as soon as it was trodden down. . . ." (Journey of Coronado, 67, 110, 139,

of separate varieties in buffalo, such as might conceivably explain temperamental predilections of this nature, as between northern and southern herds.[51] In addition to this, previous to 1869 or thereabout,

140). A. B. Hulbert thus describes it (from contemporary observers, Oregon-California Trail, 1849): "Buffalo grass, 'killed' by the frosts of winter, is resuscitated in the spring by becoming green from the root up without casing its stubble or emitting new shoots. It rarely ever exceeds two inches in height and never four, and is green only about one month in the year—but is very nutritious at any time. It is cured 'on the hoof.' . . ." (*Forty-Niners*, 135; a 'composite' chronicle of very skilfully woven contemporary material).

Gregg, 1840, classifies it as of two kinds, both species of *grama*, and considers it the same as the 'mesquite grass' in Texas (*Early Western Travels*, XX, 248). Sir Richard Burton gives Buffalo grass as *Sisleria dactyloides*, gramma grass = *Chondrosium foenum*, mesquite grass = *Stipa spata*, bunch grass = *Festuca*, and 'buffalo clover' = *Trifolium reflexum* (*City of the Saints*, 7, 51, 138-40). Hornaday classifies Buffalo grass as *bouteloua* [sic] *oligostachyia* ("Extermination of the American Bison," 426-9).

According to General Chittenden, *boutelona* [sic] *oligostachyia* is gramma grass, buffalo grass being *buchloe dachtyloides*; and he also specifies 'bunch grass' as *poa tenuifolia*. "The gramma grass was often called 'buffalo grass'. . . ." (*American Fur Trade*, II, 816). Garretson also identifies buffalo grass as *Buchloë dactyloides*, "often mistaken for curly mesquite (*Hilaria belangeri*)." He specifies three kinds of grama grass: black g. = *Muhlenbergia porteri*; blue g. = *Bouteloua gracilis*; hairy g. = *Bouteloua parryi*; the last two 'usually found in company with buffalo grass' (*American Bison*, 43). McClintock, without specifying any species as 'buffalo grass,' says that the favourite feed of the buffalo was a luxuriant meadow grass, the *Soyotoiyis* (*Siksika* Blackfoot = *Carex nebraskensis praevia*: *Old North Trail*, 286). 'Buffalo grass,' bunch grass, and *gramma* are mentioned without further classification by Gregg, 1840 (*Early Western Travels*, XIX, 205; XX, 240), Bancroft (*History of Utah*, 728; *History of Arizona*, 597), Dodge (*Plains of the Great West*, 33), Dowling ("Southern Plains of Alberta," 7), MacInnes (*In the Shadow of the Rockies*, 195). The last says: "In the summer time the country was one vast pasture and the buffalo grass, blue-joint, timothy, oat, and other natural grasses that carpeted it . . . possessed the peculiar property of curing as they stood in the suns and winds of autumn. . . . He also observes "that one ploughing destroyed their quality of curing in the autumn. Even if the land were allowed to go back to its natural state, though the grasses which grew upon it made good summer pasture, they would never again cure in the old way as they stood. . . ." (*ibid.*, 195).

The cliché fifty years ago was that 'the country shoulda been left the same side up that God A'mighty made it!'

Dr. Robert Newton, then president of the University of Alberta, states (correspondence July 17, 1942) that MacInnes is mistaken here, there being "no true buffalo grass" in Canada. Dr. Newton does not himself identify the 'true' buffalo grass, and fails to recognize the apparent absence of any uniformly-accepted classification of such. This circumstance reduces definition to mere opinion.

There is an up-thrust of the short-grass territory to the North Saskatchewan near Vermilion, Alberta, where Umfreville may have seen it *circa* 1785 (*Present State of Hudson's Bay*, 153). 'Buffalo grass' is reported to be 'over-running' the Oklahoma-Kansas territory again: *Edmonton Journal*, August 19, 1933.

After all this, it is laughable (to a Westerner) to find 'dank buffalo grass' from an unreliable 'popular' writer (Shepstone, *Wild Beasts of To-day*, 132).

[51]See above, chap. III ("North American Variants of the Buffalo and Their Geographical Distribution").

there was neither northern nor southern herd in his buffalo catena. There was only one.

Thompson Seton's comment is interesting: "I conclude with Hornaday that the Buffalo did migrate from 300 to 400 miles northward in spring, and as far southward again in autumn, but that the regularity of this movement was often much obscured by temporary changes of direction to meet changes of weather, to visit well-known pastures, to seek good crossings of rivers or mountains, or to avoid hostile camps or places of evil memories. Furthermore, there were scattered individuals to be found in all parts of the range at all seasons. . . ."[52] Which may be not unjustly paraphrased thus: the buffalo followed a regular migration northward and southward, except when they did not.

While I remain extremely sceptical concerning these assumed migrations north of the Platte, possibly north of the Arkansas, on the grand scale that might be termed strategy, there seems to have been no lack of movement, of the minor order designated by the military phrase 'tactic.' Concerning the probable causes of this, like so many phases of our study, it is easy to ask questions, and difficult to furnish answers. While other factors may, of course, enter into the case, I suspect that these are much more probably the true migrations, or better, 'wanderings,' based in most instances not upon *climate* strictly speaking,[53] but upon local, temporary, or seasonal variations in weather conditions. While the broad main lines of climatic classification are

[52]Seton, *Life-Histories of Northern Animals*, I, 266; *Game Animals*, III, 654.

[53]At the time this chapter was drafted, I was unaware that any 'technical' definition of 'migration' existed, or 'was even considered necessary. I therefore coined a rough one for myself, 'periodical removal from one recognized haunt to another' (below, chap. XIX, note 31).

I have since noted the following: "But the ability to travel is not synonymous with migration, which is a particular type of travel with distinctive features. We can formulate a definition that clearly delimits the term. None better than Gadow's exists and this we propose to adopt. Migration 'is the wandering of living creatures into another, usually distant locality in order to breed there; this implies a return and the double phenomenon is annual. All other changes of the abode are either sporadic, epidemic, or fluctuating within lesser limits . . .'" (Rowan, *The Riddle of Migration*, 46, quoting Hans F. Gadow, "Migration in Zoology," *Encyclopaedia Britannica*, 11th ed., XVIII, 433-7).

This clearly excludes wanderings for pasture from the category of migrations, even if this were not expressly stated by another high authority to be the case. "Roaming movements in search of food are not migrations. . . ." (J. Arthur Thomson, *Encyclopaedia Britannica*, 14th ed., XV, 473). It may be noted that a number of authoritative writers assign this latter as the cause of the buffalo wanderings. See Hewitt (following Hornaday), *Conservation of Wild Life in Canada*, 115: "Migrations . . . purely for the sake of food . . ."; Borrodaile, *The Animal and Its Environment*, 352; Roamings of the American bison ". . . in search of pasture . . .

doubtless definable with very considerable certainty and precision, there appears to be—even among some scientists—a failure to recognize that in so vast a country as North America, the weather in a given season may be radically different in areas situated much less than a hundred miles, even less than fifty miles apart, and in the same latitudes within a very few miles.[54] An examination of local weather and crop reports in Western Canada in almost any season will substantiate this; localities in the same general climatic, latitudinal, and topographical zones will report astonishing variations in weather and consequent crop conditions. These diversities will sometimes persist throughout an entire summer season, this condition being what is described above as 'seasonal'; sometimes the normal time-scheme is reversed, with a dry growing season and a wet harvest-time. Anyone who has devoted any attention whatever to this question is aware that throughout Western Canada—a term embracing a territory roughly 900 miles long and 500 wide—there is no season in which crops are not somewhere well above the average, ranging from 'very good' to 'bumper,' as well as being, somewhere, far below the average; and also that such local variations may be noted both in the 'Dry Belt' of this southern and southwestern Canada plains areas, and in the commonly better-watered 'black soil' scrublands. For example, the almost daily thunderstorms[55] that gladden a farmer's heart in an ideal June or July

obviously a mere matter of commissariat. . . ." (Gadow, "Migration in Zoology"; cf. Thomson, *Encyclopaedia Britannica*, 14th ed., XV, 473).

It would of course be most unjust to attempt to pin anyone down to a definition apparently not promulgated in his day. But while neither Hornaday nor Seton (nor even Allen) propounded any formal definition of their own, it can be shown that their historical postulates lack support from their own evidence. The fact that the buffalo movements did not conform to the (later) 'technical' requirements of *migration* removes a most important anterior cause for that regularity upon which they and their followers insist.

[54]For climatic variations in comparatively short distances, in the southwestern United States, see Marcy, *Exploration of Red River*, 14, 90; and for variations in different seasons (in an almost sub-tropical land), *ibid.*, 42.

[55]Western travel-literature frequently mentions these. Parkman: ". . . all the morning the sun beats upon him with a sultry, penetrating heat, and . . . with provoking regularity, at about four o'clock in the afternoon, a thunderstorm rises and drenches him to the skin. . . ." (*Oregon Trail*, 41-2; cf. 35, 55-7, 60, 79, 243, 250, 341-2, 369, 427-9, 453).

Daily thunderstorms, 1839: Farnham, *Early Western Travels*, XXVIII, 73, 103; 1842, Frémont, *Narrative*, 114.

Palliser (*et al.*), west of Red River, July, 1857: "the usual afternoon thunderstorm. . . ." (*Palliser Journals*, 39; cf. 44, 46, 143). Hector, Bow and Belly Rivers, Alberta, July-August, "almost daily": *ibid.*, 269. June-July, 1900, scarcely a cloudy morning or a dry afternoon in the Red Deer Canyon district. So in Edmonton, July, 1930, August, 1931; cf. 'two showers only' for the summer of 1929, as I was informed, being absent that year; 1937, 1941 very similar.

come in the Edmonton district almost wholly from the westward.[56] In the season of 1926, a district within twenty miles west of Edmonton, whose visibly manifest prosperity endorses its enviable reputation, experienced what was virtually a crop failure from drought, while the city itself enjoyed abundance of rain; in 1937 the 'June rains' were a failure in the same district and in the city alike. I was informed many years ago by a thoroughly reliable authority, the late Honourable Frank Oliver, resident in Edmonton, 1876-1933, that during the calamitous 'Cochrane winter' of 1882-83, to which reference has been made, the unusual depth of snow extended only for some fifty miles or so north of Calgary, beyond which point the winter was neither abnormally long nor severe. In other words, it ceased just about at the very point where normally the more severe Alberta winter zone begins. We have made no special study of this question. In point of fact, these variations are so notorious, and the means of substantiating them are so familiarly accessible, being no farther away any summer than the nearest newspaper or any informed old-timer's personal reminiscences,[57] that unless one were attempting to compile a detailed meteorological history of the West, special study is hardly necessary.

It is needless and would be profitless to suggest that such local climatic or weather variations were in any form or age the original causes of the wandering propensity in the buffalo species; but I suspect them to be a very powerful and important cause of their wanderings in known historical times. Largely by reason of the very proximity and plenty of the buffalo, the principal native races in most constant association with the animal were not agriculturists. For this reason, they would probably take but little *connected* notice of summer

---

Hind, 1858: '17 thunderstorms in 23 days'; *Report*, 8; cf. 12, 13, 41 (three), 42, 46, 47, 52, 60, 63, 65, 125. See also Ross, *Red River Settlement*, 258, 268; Cowie (1868), *Company of Adventurers*, 344-6; Macoun, *Manitoba*, 646; and compare also Brooks, *Climate Through the Ages*, 186; *Encyclopaedia Britannica*, 11th, 14th eds., *s.v.* Climate and Climatology.

[56]See Lewis and Clark on this feature, Missouri River, 1806: *Journals*, III, 359-65.

[57]We were still using bob-sleighs, last week of April, 1907. April 4, 5, in 1920, I froze my face badly in Edmonton, and the spring thaw only began, April 23, 1920. On March 1, 1926, and February 23, 1931, gophers were noticed (by myself) at Bardo, and Kelsey, Alberta, respectively. Reported in *Edmonton Journal*, March 2, 1926; *Edmonton Bulletin*, February 25, 1931. December 15, 1930, thawing heavily at Mirror, Alberta, 12.30 P.M.; no thaw whatever at Bashaw, 10 miles north, on that day.

Marquis of Lorne (Winnipeg, 1881): "The Red Deer Valley is especially remarkable as traversing a country where, according to the testimony of Indian chiefs travelling with us, snow never lies for more than three months. . . ." (Tuttle, *Our North Land*, 546). This may be true in parts.

In the Red Deer Canyon district (east of Red Deer, Alberta), it lay for five

weather phenomena;[58] which might account for the non-development of any coherent traditions in their folk-lore to explain the buffalo's comings and goings. The process in their case may have been one of partial degradation from a higher stage of civilization. An American scientist of high standing writes as follows:

It appears from certain fragments of evidence, that some of our American Indians, a few centuries before the coming of the whites to the shores of this continent, were in a rather higher state of advance than that in which they were found by the first Europeans. . . . The Ohio and the Upper Mississippi valleys abound in the tumuli and fortifications which apparently indicate that the people had been more numerous than they were when our race first knew them; that they depended more upon agriculture and less upon the chase than their successors who met the white man when he first came to this country. . . .

The cause of this decadence is interesting. The explanation seems to be as follows: In the state of savagery men depend altogether upon the products of the chase, or upon the untilled resources of the vegetation about them. As the population increases, the game becomes less abundant, and the folk are gradually driven to tillage. They become sedentary; they exercise the forethought which agriculture requires, and so advance to the next higher stage in development, where they depend in the main upon the resources which the soil affords. Each further increase in the population diminishes the relative value of the hunter's art, and tends to separate the people from the vagarious and brutalizing habits of their ancestors, who lived by the chase. . . .[59]

and a quarter months in 1896-7, five in 1897-8, five and a half in 1906-7, six and a half in 1919-20, four in 1924-5, five in 1935-6, five and a half in 1942-3, with scarcely a single thaw.

Compare MacInnes's perfectly true general description of south Alberta winter weather (*In the Shadow of the Rockies*, 3-4, 195) with his accounts of winters in 1882-3, 1886-7 (*ibid.*, 210, 217). In our own district mentioned above, the ground was never frozen from April, 1896 until November, 1898. Numbers of people never used a sleigh from March, 1904 until November, 1906. Macoun describes his journey through the southern plains area from Moose Jaw, Saskatchewan, to Macleod, Alberta, May 18 to July, 1895, when practically no rain whatever fell (Macoun, *Autobiography*, 267-71). In central Alberta, 1895 was an excessively wet season. Most of the land was newly broken and growth extremely rank; few crops ripened sufficiently to thresh. It was said at the time that one machine threshed everything from three miles north of the Red Deer River, some twelve miles, and for ten miles eastward (then the limit!).

The following descriptions of the same route reveal similar fluctuations: St. Paul to Fort Garry, 1862, "a succession of prairies dotted with copses. . . ." (Milton and Cheadle, *North-West Passage*, 13); 1868, "luxuriant prairie grass. . . ." (Young, *Canoe and Dog-Train*, 10); 1870, "the vast sandy wastes of the Dakota Prairie. . . ." (Butler, *Great Lone Land*, 94); 1872, "vast expanse of prairie. . . ." (Butler, *Wild North Land*, 44).

[58]Indian predictions of mild or severe winters are very frequently falsified in fact; and cf. below, note 69. See on all this, *Encyclopaedia Britannica, s.v.* Climate and Climatology.

[59]Shaler, *Nature and Man in America*, 181-3.

When in his westward [sic; but surely 'eastward'?] movement the buffalo came to the semi-civilized inhabitants of the Mississippi system of valleys, he brought a great plenty of animal food to the people, who had long been in a measure destitute of such resources, for they had no other domesticated animals save the dog. Not yet firmly fixed in the agricultural art, these tribes appear, after the coming of the buffalo, to have lapsed into the pure savagery which hunting entails. . . . With the rehabilitation of the hunter's habit, and with the nomadic conditions which this habit necessarily brings about, came more frequent contest between tribes, and the gradual decadence of the slight civilization which the people had acquired. . . .[60]

Whether one accepts Shaler's highly probable view of the process or not, the fact remains that Indian folk-lore and the ascertained scientific knowledge of buffalo find practically no points of common convergence.[61] Certain Indian beliefs may be extravagant; to whom little is given, of him shall little be required. Even so, they are not more extravagant than some which men of scientific attainments have not been ashamed to advance without adducing evidence in support. I have at least found none to justify the fantastic supposition that buffalo may leave or hasten across some exhausted or temporarily drought-stricken area, 'knowing' that in such-and-such a locality ahead of them, good pasturage is to be had.[62] We have only to apply this idea to the aforementioned summer's journey from Texas to the Saskatchewan to demonstrate the absurdity of both. Unless they had some method of intelligible intercommunication, a sort of buffalo 'bush-telegraph,' which would enable those 'scattered individuals to be found in all parts of the range at all seasons'[63] to inform the north-bound herd (and soon enough to give them an opportunity to turn aside from that regular migration-route of theirs, perhaps somewhere about the Missouri) that the plains north of the forty-ninth parallel were scorched with drought, it passes understanding how a herd which left that territory behind it in June or July, 1830, could 'know' what lay ahead of it in August or September, 1831! Fairy tales of this character may keep company with the mythical nonsense about the shark that follows a ship for week after week *because* there is a sick person aboard. The historical evidence concerning buffalo intelligence

[60]*Ibid.*, 184.
[61]See below, chap. XXI, "The Influence of the Buffalo Environment upon Indian Mentality."
[62]". . . having learned that a journey south will bring him to. . . ." (Hornaday, "Extermination of the American Bison," 418). Edwin James, 1820, was more cautious: "Experience may have taught them. . . ." (*Early Western Travels*, XV, 248). Irving, 1836: ". . . guided on its boundless migrations by some traditionary knowledge. . . ." (*Captain Bonneville*, 300).
[63]Seton, *Life-Histories of Northern Animals*, I, 267; *Game Animals*, III, 654.

by no means indicates any such advanced stage of development.[64] On this general question of knowledge as an impelling factor in migratory movements, I may quote Professor Rowan's analysis of such assumptions concerning bird migration, since essentially it will apply to buffalo also. He writes:

As far as the southward flight of many northern species is concerned it may, perhaps, be classed as a feeding movement since continuance in the north means inevitable starvation, but it is only half the story. What of the return passage? Food is neither obviously, nor certainly, in spite of the assertions of many writers, a compelling factor. If birds find ample sustenance on their winter range, they should find even more there in the summer, the season of universal abundance.[65] The assumption that the bird can foresee a possible forthcoming shortage of food as a result of impending spring increase, and therefore moves elsewhere, is wholly gratuitous and unwarranted. Not even man can certainly state that such would be the case. . . .[66]

Professor Rowan adds elsewhere:

Many migration writers assume that birds are 'driven' south by fall indications of coming winter. Such as assumption credits birds with a knowledge of affairs that they cannot possibly possess. It infers, for instance, that they can discriminate between one type of food shortage and another—the irremediable shortage of fall and the temporary shortage occasioned by such phenomena as summer snow-storms, protracted droughts, fires, &c., some or all of which must at one time or another have brought them to temporarily straitened circumstances on their breeding grounds but without eliciting a migratory response. It infers further that they know when winter is coming, an inference equally unwarranted. If they are birds of the year they have never experienced a winter. If they are migratory, their parents for countless generations before them, have left the north before winter has materialized. How can they possibly arrive at the knowledge of the very existence of such a thing as a northern winter? If they do not know that it is coming, they can surely not flee from it. It assumes still further that they can intelligently distinguish north from south. Why should they proceed south? Why not east or west or north again? Whatever the solution, the performance is not peculiar to birds. . . . [citing sea-species].[67]

[64]See below, chap. VI, "Some Buffalo Characteristics."

[65]Hornaday has justly emphasized the absurdity of buffalo leaving Texas, an unexcelled pasture region, *in spring*, for reasons of pasturage ("Extermination of the American Bison," 424; cf. above, *in extenso*, chap. II, note 19). He ascribes it, with much more probability, to the desire to escape the heat. Cf. below, chap. IX, note 24.

[66]Rowan, *Riddle of Migration*, 48.

[67]*Ibid.*, 78-9. I must acknowledge a great satisfaction on seeing this passage, some years after my general conclusions as given above had been tentatively written out in draft. My friend Dr. Rowan's close logical insistence upon minute but vital details is essentially the critical method applied in the present essay, in a manner which might be thought captious, and for which I am glad to find such authoritative support.

In their general application to buffalo, such supposed powers can scarcely be described by the frequently idle term 'instinct,' since it seems inconceivable that the faculty we designate as instinct can develop from a very occasional experience of exceptional phenomena. It may be noted further, that those writers who speak of the buffalo 'knowing,' for example, that a prolonged drought since spring, or a devastating fire the week before, has destroyed their food in a region far ahead of them, are often the self-same persons who insist on an invariably uniform course of buffalo-procedure throughout all their days; which I, at least, find impossible to explain, except upon the supposition of a total incapacity in buffalo for knowing anything other than by instinct.

The regular annual itinerary of the 'great western herds,' furnished to Hind[68] in 1858 by the Red River half-breed hunters, followed a route which was almost entirely in the more arid regions. Its *regularity* involves certain implications which are clearly untenable. An *annual* route, followed for reasons of pasturage, commits us inescapably, it seems to me, to the view that the buffalo knew what pasture prospects lay ahead of them. Pasturage on a large scale obviously depends upon the weather of the season—and above all, in this, one of the most precarious of the 'dry belts' of the continent. Since weather in this very territory flanking the Rockies is a thing which not even modern meteorological science can yet predict with invariable accuracy in spite of all its appliances and long-distance communication,[69] the supposition that buffalo could do this is too fantastic to sustain scrutiny for a moment, quite irrespective of any general opinions concerning buffalo intelligence. Here again, however, the itinerary itself is entirely destitute of historical support.[70] It seems more sensible to suppose that the buffalo hastened across such uninviting tracts because there was no inducement to linger, and in that way sooner or later reached the end of the sterile lands. Wanderings of this character may take place

[68]Given below *in extenso*, in its historical setting, chap. XIV, "The Red River Hunt," notes 50-2.

[69]See remarks above, and cf. note 57, on seasonal and other weather variations. I kept a diary, with weather notes (observation only, without instruments), for many years *ante* 1909. My conclusions were, and are from continued later observation, that 'weather signs'—'red at night, the shepherd's delight,' etc.—are worthless in Alberta, practically as much so as 'ground-hogs,' 'muskrat houses,' and similar folk-phenomena, largely imported from other countries. The not-infrequently unfulfilled official forecasts of the Meteorological Bureau are a standing source of amusement to observant citizens of Edmonton, where this was written. The Honourable Frank Oliver (Edmonton, 1876-1933) was fond of saying that 'the man who foretells Alberta weather is either a newcomer or a fool.'

[70]See below, chaps. XIV, XX; "Red River Hunt," "Irregular Migrations."

and in historical fact actually have taken place in very considerable degree; perhaps, if our knowledge were more extensive, we could trace such movements east and west as much as north and south.[71]

In so far as the wanderings of the buffalo in their Canadian habitat are concerned—although I have little doubt that similar principles governed in large areas of the western states, and the leading Canadian authority on the species endorses the theory of 'one herd only' until 1867-69—[72] the failure of a zoologist of high standing like Hornaday to grasp adequately the climatic and topographical significance of certain Western Canadian data is not wholly his own fault. His monograph, "Extermination of the American Bison" (which, despite its many defects, is yet of much value), is devoted primarily to the history of the buffalo in the United States, the Canadian allusions being little more than are required by geographical continuity and for corroboration. It is even in part a political production; for the author, as a member of a national scientific body, adduces political evidence, and comments thereupon in a manner in which, without grave discourtesy, even a scientist could scarcely have done concerning a foreign government.[73] Hornaday's plan[74] did not, therefore, render it incumbent upon him to make even an approximately exhaustive examination of Canadian historical material. I am unaware how many Canadian works he may have consulted, bearing upon this subject; he cites only those of

[71]See chap. XIX, "The Regular Migration." It is not irrelevant to point out further, with reference to buffalo trails down to the great buffalo rivers, which of course are to be found on either bank, and are quite gratuitously seized upon as evidence, not merely of paths to the water, which they are, but of unbroken, through *crossing* routes, that certain geographical factors are overlooked. In addition to the Mississippi, which flows southward, several noted buffalo streams flow for long distances southeastward, as the Missouri, and the Bow and Red Deer in Alberta, or northeastward, as the two Saskatchewans and the Battle River. In many places, a definitely authenticated crossing of such rivers could quite as logically be an east and west movement, as a north and south one. A. B. Hulbert, after laying down two fundamental propositions, the north and south movement, and the buffalo path *across* and not *along* the river-valley—quite applicable to his own chosen scene, the Ohio Valley, or the Platte, Republican, Arkansas, etc.— involves himself in hopeless contradiction again and again in attempting to maintain (at the Mississippi crossings, for example) his other cherished thesis of the *buffalo origin of westbound* trail-highway-railroad routes. This can only be done by making a mass of exceptions—themselves mutually irreconcilable—which deprive his uniformities of any significance. (See his *Historic Highways*, I, 24, 112, 128-40; II, 89-90; III, 211; V, 15-34; VI, 93, 206; VIII, 34; XI, 26; XII, 22; XIII, 134, etc.

[72]Seton, *Life-Histories of Northern Animals*, I, 293.

[73]Hornaday, "Extermination of the American Bison," 486, 513-21.

[74]Hornaday's title is "The Extermination of the American Bison, with a *Sketch of Its Life History*." Messrs. Stone and Cram, and Professor W. P. Webb (above, chap. I, notes 13-14) claim more for Hornaday's essay than he does himself.

Franklin,[75] Alexander Ross,[76] Professor Henry Youle Hind,[77] Principal Grant,[78] Professor John Macoun,[79] Professor Kenaston,[80] and Mr. Miller Christy's important paper.[81] From none of these has he quoted anything not directly bearing upon buffalo, although they all contain incidental references, a mere glance at which should make anyone cautious of hasty generalization concerning an unknown land. In Professor Hind's *Report* are many highly valuable observations and forecasts from a keen and trained scientific mind, which might nevertheless in the search for buffalo evidence be passed over by an inquirer to whom the future potentialities of Western Canada (or the history of opinion in 1858 concerning them) was not the central thesis. Possibly for the same reasons, neither the premier document of all on that subject—the inestimable reports of Captain Palliser and his colleagues—[82] nor the fascinating and graphic recitals of such travellers as Father De Smet,[83] Paul Kane,[84] the Earl of Southesk,[85] Milton and Cheadle,[86] or Sir William Butler,[87] are even mentioned. The rather minute and—for the study of the buffalo at least—historically invaluable reminiscences of Dr. John McDougall had not then (in 1889) begun to appear.[88]

One of the books mentioned above as quoted by Hornaday, was in the eighties extremely popular. While the interest of the other authors I have named in the same period was in a manner sectional and confined—they were travellers, scientific or other, relating what they had seen, with comment thereupon—Macoun's work had a comprehensiveness to which they made no pretence. He was explorer, plainsman, land guide, meteorologist, botanist, agriculturist, chemist, and geol-

---

Something similar in *Buffalo Jones' Forty Years*, 6; and in Seton, *Life-Histories of Northern Animals*, I, 262, 266.

[75]Franklin, (First) *Journey to the Polar Sea*, (orig. ed., 1825). I give reasons below for my conviction that Richardson's *Fauna Boreali-Americana* was quoted at second-hand. See below, Appendix O.

[76]Ross, *Red River Settlement*, 1856.

[77]Hind, *Report, 1858*. Hornaday cites Hind, *Narrative*. This is the *Narrative of the Dawson and Hind Expedition*, 2 vols., 1860, a more popular literary account.

[78]Grant, *Ocean to Ocean* (orig. ed., 1873).

[79]Macoun, *Manitoba*, 1882.

[80]Kenaston, in Hornaday, "Extermination of the American Bison," 504-5 (below, chap. XVII, note 89).

[81]Christy, "The Last of the Buffaloes," 1888, 697.

[82]*Palliser Journals*, 1863.

[83]DeSmet, *Oregon Missions*, etc., 1847.

[84]Kane, *Wanderings of an Artist* (orig. ed., 1859).

[85]Southesk, *Travels* (orig. ed., 1875).

[86]Milton and Cheadle, *North-West Passage* (orig. ed., 1865).

[87]Butler, *Great Lone Land*, 1872; *The Wild North Land*, 1873.

[88]See bibliography for titles and dates of these.

ogist, and in addition, of certain episodes (either personally or by contributory hands) a fairly full political historian, or propagandist. If Macoun's accuracy—or his scientific caution where accuracy, strictly speaking, was inherently unattainable—had been equal to his industry, his work would still be a notable and historically valuable production.[89]

The later date of Hornaday's essay on the buffalo, and its dogmatic certainties, convincing to the uncritical, have enabled it to supersede Allen's more carefully considered, more scientifically cautious, more widely comprehensive, more fully documented, and (down to 1876) in every way superior production on the subject, and to take rank as the authoritative pronouncement. Hornaday's utterly inadequate knowledge of the geographical, topographical, and climatic conditions of Western Canada—[90] about which he might have learned much even from his own master, Allen—together with his definitive *dicta* on buffalo habits in that unknown land—have practically miscoloured the world's thinking on the North American buffalo, apart from a very few quite recent specialists.[91]

[89]For a detailed criticism of Macoun, see Roe, "Early Opinions on the 'Fertile Belt' of Western Canada" (*Canadian Historical Review*, XXVII, 1946, 131-49).

[90]Hornaday might have avoided much of this. Blodgett, the eminent American climatologist of the mid-nineteenth century, says: "The buffalo winter on the upper Athabaska at least as safely as in the latitude of St. Paul, Minnesota. . . . The higher latitudes certainly differ widely from the plains which stretch southward from the Platte to the Llano Estacado of Texas, and none of the references made to them by residents or travellers indicate desert characteristics. Buffalo are far more abundant in the northern plains, and they remain throughout the winter at their extreme border, taking shelter in the belts of woodland along the Upper Athabaska and Peace Rivers. . . . Not only in the earliest explorations of these plains, but now, they are the great resort for buffalo herds, which . . . remain on them and at these woodland borders throughout the year. The simple fact of the presence of these herds of wild cattle on plains at so high a latitude is ample proof of the climatological and productive capacity of the country. . . ." Cited by Macoun, *Manitoba*, 153; also the author is mentioned by Hind, *Report, 1858*, 124. These two are among Hornaday's authorities. The passage above is also quoted by Tuttle, *Our Northland*, 392-419.

[91]The earliest criticism of Hornaday that I have seen is not until 1933: "Part of his account of the woods buffalo is somewhat confused because he treated it as being identical with the so-called mountain buffalo. . . ." Raup, *Range Conditions in Wood Buffalo Park*, 46.

CHAPTER V

THE 'BUFFALO YEAR'

IT is difficult, in any comprehensive study, to avoid overlapping, since the same evidence may bear upon more than one question requiring detailed discussion. Certain of the data to be presented in this chapter may be open to that objection. But it seems desirable to give 'the daily round, the common task' of the buffalo as a homogeneous whole, for more convenient and orderly reference.

The buffalo cows gave birth apparently from about mid-April until practically the end of June, after a gestation period of nine and one-half months.[1] This protracted calving season seems a somewhat lengthy span for a wild species roaming in freedom in an environment presenting broadly uniform, seasonal climatic changes, and these of an extreme kind in a very large portion of their habitat. It is, however, substantially confirmed by incidental evidence.

Eye-witness reports about calves are somewhat scanty, particularly for the later portions of the period. Here again, as frequently happens, features of immense historical and scientific interest today were utterly commonplace to those who could best have enlightened us. Alexander Henry the younger mentions 'calves very numerous' on Red River (near the international boundary), April 19, 1802.[2] Alexander Mackenzie, on the upper Peace River, May, 1793, speaks of 'vast herds, with their calves frisking about them.'[3] These are the only direct allusions to the calving *season* that I have been able to discover; for Henry's notice of 'a calf of this year,' February 28, 1801,[4] proves clearly by its very nature—if we had no other data for our guidance—that it

[1]"Some time in April usually, though possibly as early as January and as late as August, the full-grown cow has finished her 9½ months' gestation. . . ." Seton, *Life Histories of Northern Animals*, I, 277-9. My 'earliest' calf is February 28, 1801; another case of two calves, March 23, 1801. Coues (ed.), *Henry Thompson Journals*, I, 171, 173.

[2]Coues (ed.), *Henry-Thompson Journals*, I, 195. On April 15, 1810, however, (North Saskatchewan River) 'not a calf to be seen' (*ibid.*, II, 593). Alexander Ross is quite definite, as usual: "The cows generally calve at one period, and that period later by a month than our tame cattle. The calving season is May, when the heat of the sun is sufficiently strong for the preservation of their young in the open air. . . ." (Ross, *Fur Hunters*, II, 126). Henry Inman is equally dogmatic (Kansas): 'rutting only during a single month . . . calves all born at a certain time. . . .' (*Old Santa Fé Trail*, 218).

[3]Mackenzie, *Voyages, 1789 and 1793*, 148.

[4]Coues (ed.), *Henry-Thompson Journals*, I, 171.

was a quite exceptional event. There are one or two other instances which might have furnished some useful information on the (approximate) uniformity, or otherwise, of the calving season in the same territory, had our chroniclers been somewhat more explicit.

In almost the same locality, just north of or on the Arkansas River, in the general vicinity of the Great Bend, we have two accounts of meeting with 'the great herd' of northward-bound buffalo in spring, on that 'annual migration' so dear to many hearts. As we shall see, this chances to be the precise region where a regular movement northward and southward is not utterly destitute of historical foundation. In 1839 (June 21-4), Thomas J. Farnham records buffalo along the Santa Fé Trail, just north of the Arkansas River.[5] Colonel Dodge's famous encounter with the immense host computed as probably four millions or more (which will be discussed in detail later on)[6] occurred near the Great Bend, 'early in May,' 1871.[7] Neither witness mentions anything about calves. This, of course, does not preclude their presence, but if they were—as they seemingly should have been—normally plentiful, the omission is rather strange in Farnham's case at least, for he was no seasoned plainsman, this being his first trip.

The general evidence for the southern buffalo habitat seems to indicate that the northward movement did not extend beyond what was known as 'the Republican country,' a favoured haunt.[8] If the term 'migration' was meant in earlier times to bear the modern meaning, a definite movement to another customary region in order to bring forth their young there, we find ourselves confronted with a curious situation. Farnham's host would be late in arriving at the Republican country for such a purpose, even if Dodge's could hope to reach the goal within the general limits of time. If the calves in either case were born before leaving their winter home or after reaching their summer one, the movement could be truly classed as a 'migration.' In other instances (cited for different purposes by firm believers in the migrations), cows remained throughout a winter in their summer haunt, and brought forth their calves there.[9]

The evidence for the general phenomena of reproduction not only indicates an extended period of time, as Seton and Alexander Ross have remarked; but the main or central period, when sexual activities

[5]Farnham, *Early Western Travels*, XXVIII, 94-6.
[6]See below, chap. XIII.
[7]Dodge, *Plains of the Great West*, 121; also his *Our Wild Indians* (with trivial variations), 283-5. Cf. March, 1871 (*Plains of the Great West*, 90).
[8]Dodge, *Plains of the Great West*, 131; cf. below, chap. XIX.
[9]Berlandier MS. (*re* Texas, in Allen, *American Bisons*, 129; Hornaday, "Ex-

would be at their height, apparently varied in different sections of the great habitat. The rutting or 'running' season, as Catlin calls it,[10] with its unmistakable accompaniment of fighting and bellowings,[11] is given by Thompson Seton as being in August and September, in which latter month the animals 'lose interest.'[12]

This agrees with Catlin,[13] whom Seton also cites. But Frémont noted these phenomena on the Upper Platte, July 7, 1842,[14] as of course might be expected if the cows gave birth in April after nine and one-half months' gestation. This, in the same generally southern territory, would be in good time for Dodge's northbound herd, 'early in May.' Yet again, Lewis and Clark noted such phenomena, on July 11-13, 1806;[15] practically the same season as Frémont, and this was in the Upper Missouri country, the general region of Catlin's northern sojourn. Lewis and Clark describe the bellowings as characteristic 'at this season,' which may perhaps be interpreted somewhat broadly, since this was their first July on the Plains.[16] Father Lacombe gives September as the season, and states that the month derived its designation in Cree from that circumstance.[17] This finds support from Alexander Henry, at the extreme eastern edge of the Canadian prairie

termination of the American Bison," 382); Powder River, Montana, Hornaday, *ibid.*, 511.

[10]Missouri River, 1835: "It was in the midst of the 'running season,' and we heard the 'roaring' (as it is called) of the herd when we were several miles from them. . . ." (Catlin, *Letters on the North American Indians*, II, 13-14). So also Henry, July 15, 1810: "plenty of buffalo . . . now rutting and perpetually in motion. . . ." (North Saskatchewan River; in Coues (ed.), *Henry-Thompson Journals*, II, 614).

[11]See Hornaday's account of their habits at this season ("Extermination of the American Bison," 415-16). Compare *Lewis and Clark Journals*, III, 172, 232, 266, 352 ('heard five miles away'); and Henry, also 1806: Coues (ed.), *Henry-Thompson Journals*, I, 308, 407. 'Bellowings' about Nashville, Tennessee, 1770: Allen, *American Bisons*, 114.

[12]Seton, *Life-Histories of Northern Animals*, I, 291.

[13]Catlin, *Letters on the North American Indians*, I, 249.

[14]Frémont, *Narrative*, 26.

[15]*Lewis and Clark Journals*, III, 172-4.

[16]*Ibid.*, III, 232, 266, 352.

[17]"SEPTEMBRE = *notjihituwipisim* (lune où les animaux sont en rut). *Onotchihituwipisim* = mois où les animaux sont en rut. . . ." (Lacombe, *Dictionnaire de la langue des Cris*, 249, 565). *Les animaux* are clearly the buffalo, 'the animals' of the Plains Cree country. Horses (whose gestation is eleven months) were probably too recent in that territory to mass in herds as *the* animals (see Roe, "From Dogs to Horses among the Western Indian Tribes" (*Transactions of the Royal Society of Canada*, 1939, Sec. II, 209-75), or for the fact to crystallize in linguistic form as a seasonal designation. *Les animaux* was used for buffalo, Fort Qu'Appelle, 1868: so Cowie, *Company of Adventurers*, 294. The Cree term seems also from its structure to contain the great Algonkian 'buffalo-root' *pisik*, *peecheek*, the *pisikious* of Dablon, Allouez, Marquette, 1670 (*Jesuit Relations*, LV, 195, 197; LIX, 111; etc.), which in wide territorial use outmatched the Cree

habitat, although he suggests it was the close of the rutting season, September 9, 1800, for he states that they were 'still bellowing all night.'[18] Yet in a more central section of the Plain Cree country, the 'rutting-month' was August.[19] Bearing in mind, however, that such 'months' would be computed from variable lunar phenomena, such as new or full moons, and certainly not from our rigid nomenclature, this is virtually equivalent to agreement. One would have liked some more precise elucidation, all the same, of the 'bellowing all night' in January (Red River, 1802).[20]

If there were any value in the annual itinerary of the 'great western herd' given to Professor Hind by the Red River half-breed hunters in 1858,[21] or in the 'undeviating routes from time immemorial,' those herds seen and breeding on the upper Missouri in July (1806) should not have been 'going south' at all, as the explorers say they were.[22] They should have been Alberta and Saskatchewan buffalo coming northward into the Blackfoot and Western Cree territory, to remain there for the winter months, not breeding until September. This is our characteristic experience with the many uniformitarian buffalo postulates. Singly, they could be true; collectively, they shatter one another. Two of the later writers on buffalo state: "The mating season was in the fall, when the Bison occupied their Southern feeding grounds, the pairs remained in company until the spring, when the cows went off by themselves to the most sheltered spots they could find, and gave birth to their calves. . . ."[23]

If this were authentic, the movement would virtually be equivalent—'technically'—to migration; actually, the evidence furnishes little

---

itself (Lacombe, *Dictionnaire de la Langue des Cris*, 43, 472). See Appendix A, "Buffalo Synonymy."

McClintock speaks of a Blackfoot 'Buffalo Song': "When summer comes, He will come down from the mountains. . . . The Buffalo likes to live in the Mountains during the Autumn; He comes down from the Mountains to the Plains. . . ." (meaning? 'to join the cows'). McClintock, *Old North Trail*, 81. On 'buffalo-calling' ceremonies among several tribes, see Lowie, "Ceremonialism in North America" (*American Anthropologist*, New Series, XVI, 1914, 602-31); also Appendix E below, "Buffalo Ritualism in Indian Life."

[18]Coues (ed.), *Henry-Thompson Journals*, I, 93.

[19]*Uskauhu-picim* = 'rutting month'; so, Skinner, "The Culture of the Plains Cree" (*American Anthropologist*, XVI, 1914, 87). Maximilian gives the Cree *anont-chicheto* as the rutting month for buffalo (July: which is apparently an incomplete form of Lacombe's *onotchihituwipisim*, note 17 above; Skinner's being materially variant). The Osage, much farther south, is *tschetoga kìrucha* = July-August (Maximilian, *Early Western Travels*, XXIV, 232, 300).

[20]Coues (ed.), *Henry-Thompson Journals*, I, 193.

[21]Below, *in extenso*, chap. XIV, notes 51-2.

[22]*Lewis and Clark Journals*, III, 174-98.

[23]Stone and Cram, *American Animals*, 69.

or no support to the southern (migrational) occupation at breeding-time,[24] nor to the 'pairs.'[25] Nor is the selection of the sheltered spots based upon any evidence I have been able to discover in the reports of those most likely to be informed. The analogy from domestic cattle is in favour of such selection in the case of young heifers with their first calf, with whom it is a well-recognized characteristic. An old cow, on the contrary, is the most 'shameless' creature about a farm-yard. And the evidence which will be presented in a later chapter (from another angle), will show what must almost certainly have been the case with the herds seen by Farnham and Dodge—that calving must have taken place anywhere and everywhere, whatever the regular season may have been.[26] It is somewhat curious to note that the mating season of the farthest northward variety of all, the Northern Wood buffalo, is given as being in July and August.[27]

The calves, when young, were of a bright tawny colour, bearing, in the absence of any pronounced 'hump,' a closer resemblance to domestic cattle than· do the adults.[28] The mothers do not appear to have suckled them for any very lengthy period, probably not more than three or four months; for the milk of the buffalo cow, although sometimes described as rich[29]—'far richer than that of the Jersey,' asserts one frequently positive writer[30]—is also admitted to have been scanty.[31] This, of course, is consonant with all experience of wild animals. The cow that continues to give heavy yields of milk almost the year round is an artificial product, a machine made for that purpose.

Since it will be necessary to examine in detail in a later chapter the evidence for maternal affection in the buffalo, in relation both to

[24]See below, chap. XIX, "The Regular Migration."
[25]See remarks on David Ingram (1569): chap. IX, note 64; also chap. VI, note 126. Audubon believed them to be monogamous (American Quadrupeds, II, 37). Hornaday, whom Stone and Cram take as their professed guide, did not ("Extermination of the American Bison," 416). Soper, 1932, notes instances in (mongrelized) wood buffalo in the Wood Buffalo Park, which might suggest the monogamous interpretation (Soper, "History of the Northern Bison," 390).
[26]See below, chap. XX, "Irregular Migrations."
[27]Hewitt, Conservation of the Wild Life of Canada, 131. Mackenzie's notice of 'calves in May' (1793) seems to suggest this (Voyages, 1789 and 1793, 148). Above, note 3. Soper finds from 'May 10 to early June' as the general time of birth: "History of the Northern Bison," 378.
[28]See on this, Hornaday, "Extermination of the American Bison," 412-20; for wood buffalo, Soper, "History of the Northern Bison," 377.
[29]Long, 1820 (Early Western Travels, XIV, 305); E. Hough, 1887, in Buffalo Jones' Forty Years, 244.
[30]Ibid., 49, 141, 244.
[31]Gregg, Early Western Travels, XX, 264.

physical and to animal perils, I shall here only remark that it does not point to any very highly developed form of the maternal instincts.[32]

Like most of the hairy-coated or fur-bearing species inhabiting principally the temperate zones, with their radical changes of season twice a year, the buffalo shed their coats towards spring-time. I have found no evidence whatever as to whether the winter condition, and consequently their value as pelts, varied with the severity of the winter, although there is abundance of testimony to prove that winter was the only season suitable for procuring 'robes.' It is, of course, well known that among the ordinary fur-bearing animals, the colder winter produces the better fur. The only references I find to the buffalo's powers of endurance throughout severe winters tend to indicate a rather surprising reaction in a denizen of such long standing. Audubon writes: "During severe winters the buffaloes become very poor, and when the snow has covered the ground for several months to the depth of two or three feet, they are wretched objects to behold. They frequently in this emaciated state lose their hair and become covered with scabs, and the magpies alight on their backs and pick the sores. The poor animals in these dreadful seasons die in great numbers. . . ."[33]

While there are other references to buffalo emerging from a hard winter in a somewhat emaciated condition,[34] this is the only detailed account I have found of their breaking out in sores. Unless these were the results of some catastrophe such as being caught in a fire, or frozen severely in a semi-hairless state, one might almost suspect this miserable predicament to have been the result of some epidemic disease, but here again, hardly one single authenticated instance of any trace of disease among wild buffalo has ever been recorded.[35]

Unlike many of our domestic animals such as cattle and horses whose new spring coat 'forces' the old winter hair out, so that the shedding of the one and the appearance of the other may be classed as one operation, it would appear that in the case of the buffalo, there

[32]See below, chaps. VI, VII.

[33]Audubon and Bachman, *American Quadrupeds*, II, 46. Henry (January, 1801) mentions 'scabby old bulls,' without giving further details; possibly the same thing: Coues (ed.), *Henry-Thompson Journals*, I, 169, 194.

[34]On bulls losing their pelage in cold hard winters, see Hornaday, "Extermination of the American Bison," 418-20; also Umfreville, *Present State of Hudson's Bay*, 159. This may explain in part why the bulls were not so hardy as the cows. Mackenzie, *Voyages, 1789 and 1793*, lxix; Coues (ed.), *Henry-Thompson Journals*, I, 169-71. Henry notes elsewhere (North Saskatchewan River, April 20, 1810): "Upwards of 60 dead buffalo seen. At this season many are so weak that if they lie down they cannot rise . . ." (*ibid.*, II, 594).

[35]See on this Appendix J, "Buffalo and Disease."

was a distinct interval of a few weeks, during which time they were literally naked. Unfortunately for them, this was the precise time when mosquitoes and all the various species of winged pests indigenous to the North American continent were at their worst. There can in my opinion be little doubt that it was the combination of the natural irritation incident to the growth of the new coat—at which time our domestic horses and cows particularly love to be brushed and curried—with the maddening onslaughts of the insect hosts,[36] that gave rise to the passion for wallowing, which was a marked characteristic of the summer season.

Flies, as the cause of wallowing, have been disputed. Seton asserts that wallowing was "much more popular with the bulls than with the cows—a fact which seems to prove that flies alone were not the cause of it. . . ."[37] On the other hand, the extremely hairless condition of the bulls, of which Seton does not seem to have been aware (since he makes no mention of it), might easily account for their greater activity. It is, of course, well known that the rutting season produces strange manifestations among the males of many species, but it is equally certain that in any normal season in the lands of early summer rains (approximately anywhere north of the Platte) the worst insect pests of all, the mosquitoes, are practically over before the breeding season comes on. It has also been stated that where large herds were found, mosquitoes were not bad.[38] Unless the observed instances chanced to

[36]See Hornaday, "Extermination of the American Bison," 412-20; *Buffalo Jones' Forty Years*, 259-60. Matthew Cocking, 1772, noted it as a habit in the breeding season, which is usually later than 'fly-time.' But he was not among them until September, and 1772 might even have been an exceptionally wet autumn.

[37]Seton, *Life-Histories of Northern Animals*, I, 286.

[38]McDougall, *Pathfinding*, 258; cf. Franklin, (First) *Journey to the Polar Sea*, 189; both, however, in the same general North Saskatchewan territory, and the latter a stranger within the gate. Cf. Audubon for the Missouri River country (*American Quadrupeds*, II, 89); also Hornaday, "Extermination of the American Bison," 412-20, *passim*.

It seems probable also, judging from the season in which such things have been observed, that the flies may have been the real reason for occasional sportiveness in buffalo. 'At times brisk and frolicsome'; so Audubon, *American Quadrupeds*, II, 48. 'The only instance known' to Seton was of a number sporting in a Texas river, 1886; jumping in, 'follow my leader' fashion, and scrambling out again in processional order, to repeat the performance (Seton, *Life-Histories of Northern Animals*, I, 287). Farnham notes them 'swimming and gambolling' in the Arkansas River, June, 1839 (*Early Western Travels*, XXVIII, 105). Hind mentions something similar with deer and elk, Souris River, Manitoba, June, 1858 (Hind, *Report*, 42). Possibly so with wood buffalo (flies); so, Soper, "History of the Northern Bison," 401.

be in dry seasons, which are unfavourable to mosquitoes, this must surely mean that the herds had licked up the stagnant surface water where those insects breed; or, possibly, that the mosquitoes devoted themselves so whole-heartedly to the unfortunate quadrupeds that the human victims got off almost scot-free.

Whether by reason of insect plagues or of some cause less readily detected, wallowing was one of the most prominent summer character-istics of buffalo and also one upon which a great confusion of ideas prevails. Almost any slight depression of the ground has been pointed out to somebody or other (often by old Westerners) as an 'old buffalo wallow.' These depressions are sometimes of such straitened dimen-sions that if animals ever got into them, they would have had to stay. Many of them are high up on almost precipitous hill-sides, where no buffalo could plough up the surface with one horn and shoulder with-out overbalancing and rolling to the bottom.[39] Just as often, a real buffalo-wallow has offered its irresistible delights, plainly visible after fifty or sixty years, but utterly unsuspected by one's eager misin-formant.

Buffalo-wallows were frequently a natural formation, as Colonel Dodge pointed out long ago,[40] and so far from being of an individual 'one-buffalo' size, some are of enormous dimensions, and are permanent physical features,[41] changing only from wet to dry under very pro-nounced variations in weather conditions. I suspect that in many cases the description—principally in fiction—of the buffalo bull 'preparing' or 'making' a wallow as if it must always be done anew, was really the first paroxysm of enthusiasm, like the swimmer's first joyous header, after reaching the tempting spot. And the enjoyment when the wallow was 'made,' almost buried at times in the luxurious mud, was the dreamy lassitude which one experiences in a hot bath after the more violent initial exercises have been performed.

Some of the large hay marshes, 'hay sloughs,' or—where there is a body of water in the centre—'hay lakes,'[42] which are well known in the

---

[39]Such places are commonly 'burn-outs,' where a small willow-clump has been. Owing to the semi-peaty character of the leaf-mould about the roots, roots and soil are consumed together in the second burning; leaving a saucer-like de-pression which in time grows another thin sod upon its surface. For these, on a large scale, see Canadian Conservation Committee, "The Burnouts of Southern Saskatchewan" (*Tenth Annual Report*, 1918, 179-82).

[40]Dodge, *Plains of the Great West*, 28.

[41]See below, note 44.

[42]Hay Lake, village near Edmonton, Alberta; another in the Northwest Territories, Canada.

western regions, are old buffalo-wallows of this 'permanent' character. Sometimes they are miles in length, of very considerable width, and, of course, of concave surface. The outer circumference, in the old, better-watered days, was heavily clothed with a rich grass, much valued as hay, from one to three feet (commonly) in height, standing on a close, resilient, dark-brown, peaty sod which would hold up any load of hay two horses could haul. Farther in, the grass could be mown, but owing to the wetter surface, no horse-rake could pick it up. Beyond this, constituting the centre if there was no 'lake' of open water, the tall grass seen at a distance presented no difference to the ordinary observer, although to an experienced eye it did not stand so closely together as on the outer areas. But the soft surface had been so cut up and torn away by the buffalo horns and hoofs, that the imaginary level was really an expanse of rounded hummocks upon which the grasses grew. These were often termed 'nigger heads,' and were so round and slippery that it was extremely difficult to walk across them in daylight, and virtually impossible in the darkness. Between these were quagmires of oozy filth of problematical depth, reminding one of Bunyan's Slough of Despond.[43]

Near Minburn, Alberta, about one hundred miles southeast from Edmonton, is a tract locally known as the 'Buffalo Wallow.' Twenty-five or thirty years ago it was very much in accordance with my description above, but owing to a prolonged cycle of much drier seasons the softer central portion is now as hard as any other. Between and upon the hummocks I have described, the grass grows thickly, and it is manifestly much favoured by the cattle, for it is never allowed to reach any great length and hence is perennially young and tender. With no long grass to obscure the formation, its unquestionable cause is clearly revealed, and, so far as cultivation is concerned, it will remain revealed for all time. For the suns and the later tramplings of the cattle have baked the mud into the solidity of brick; it can neither be ploughed nor mown because of the 'hard-pan' character of the soil and its utter irregularity of surface, and the tract stands a silent but eloquent memorial to the buffalo who made it.[44]

At other places where water-levels were more immediately variable, according to the time of the year or the fluctuating rainfalls of

[43]As an Albertan of two weeks' experience, 1894, I turned aside mistakenly from my course one night when afoot, and tackled such a place at its centre, escaping only with some difficulty, after much floundering through the muskeg. The buffalo were then only some ten years extinct in that locality, near the Red Deer Canyon. Neither cattle nor horses would ever cross this place, not then recognized by us as a buffalo wallow, despite speculations concerning its origin.
[44]It was formerly strewn with buffalo skeletons.

different summers,[45] a 'wallow' in wet periods formed a 'dust-pan' in dry ones. And in addition to these larger resorts, there were many smaller, such as may yet be seen in almost any part of the old buffalo country by those who know what to look for. And I suspect that far greater numbers than those still discernible have been obliterated along the 'buffalo rivers' of the West, through the filling of their inequalities with silty deposits during the occasional inundations. The consequent growth of the rank lush vegetation characteristic of such river 'bottom-lands' would soon create another sod, indistinguishable from that around it. Along the Battle River in Central Alberta, a famous buffalo resort of yore, there are countless *ings* and *hamms*[46]— now wild hay-meadows—whose surfaces are firm and almost as smooth as ploughed fields. It seems impossible that anything but the action of water could have effected this, and floods, or partial floods, are not by any means uncommon. Yet the buffalo hosts must have cut and churned such flats into semi-quagmires times without number through the ages.

Allen's description of the wallows is of interest (1871):

An excavation is made having a diameter of fifteen or twenty feet, and two feet in depth. These wallows thus become characteristic marks of a buffalo country, outlasting even the ordinary trails, while their effect is much more marked, rank vegetation growing about their borders and serving to indicate their positions when quite distant.

The buffaloes, however, do not always choose moist places in which to roll, and are quite content with wallowing in the dust when mud-and-water wallows are not conveniently to hand, wherever, in short, large herds have grazed, hollows formed by their indulgence in this propensity are of very frequent occurrence. These circular depressions, which are also usually called 'wallows,' are of smaller size than the water wallows, being from eight to ten or twelve feet or more in diameter, and a few inches to upwards of a foot in depth. These also are not effaced by natural agencies for many years, and hence remain a lasting evidence of the former existence of populous herds of buffaloes at the localities where these old 'wallows' are found. . . ."[47]

[45]The writer learned to swim in 1901, in a 'lake slough' eight feet deep in the centre, out of which we ourselves hauled the hay, in full loads, in 1897-8.

[46]A *hamm* (not to be confused with *ham* = home, *Scotticè* 'hame') is a tract enclosed in the bend of a stream; it signifies an 'enclosed possession or fold,' akin to 'hamm' = the bend of the knee, and common ham, and allied to the verb to 'hem in.' *Ings* are river-flats, or bottom-lands, as Deep-ing Fen, Lincolnshire, or Stock-ing-ford, Warwickshire (nothing to do with hosiery; *stock* as in stockade, Stockholm, a pillar, perhaps once an idol, as the Miltonic 'stocks and stones'). See Mawer, *Chief Elements in English Place-Names* (English Place Name Society, 1924, 32, 41-2). No connection with the '—ingham' and '—ington' names; these are patronymic home-names.

[47]Allen, *American Bisons*, 64-6; cf. Parkman, *Oregon Trail*, 77.

Thomas Nuttall (lower Arkansas River country, 1819), remarks: "We discovered them in a state of repose, and could perceive the places where they had been gratifying themselves by wallowing or rolling in the dust. . . ."[48] Dr. Gregg, on the upper Canadian River, 1831, notes ". . . the innumerable ponds which bespeckled the plain, and which kept us at least well supplied with water. Many of these ponds seem to have grown out of 'buffalo wallows'—a term used on the Prairies to designate a sink made by the buffalo's pawing the earth for the purpose of obtaining a smooth dusty surface to roll upon. . . ."[49] The foregoing quotation would tend to corroborate the view that both types of wallowings took place broadly in the same general localities, in mud if the ground were muddy, and in dust if it were not. Buffalo Jones, however, goes so far as to say: "Buffalo seldom roll in the mud, contrary to the general supposition, but excavate their wallows by pawing up the earth. The dust then blows away, and their shaggy coats are filled with dirt, which is shaken off at pleasure. . . ."[50]

Buffalo Jones is much more dogmatic than infallible concerning buffalo, which he only knew as a wild species in the drier Southwest, and never saw before 1871,[51] when—as he himself observes[52]—their habits had changed by reason of excessive hunting.[53] If words mean anything, one may ask how such a term as 'wallow' which is known to hosts of people who probably never heard of a 'buffalo wallow,' came to be applied to a mere pawing up the earth. Horses do this, and roll also, but I never remember hearing of a 'horse-wallow,' or of one 'wallowing.' Other writers, not of wholly negligible authority, make no allusion to 'dust-pans.'[54] But the general consensus of opinion seems to point quite clearly to low places, wet or dry. In concluding this phase of our subject, it is interesting to note that a much more significant and permanent effect than the leaving of ancient wallows has been ascribed by several students to the buffalo's habit—traceable to the same intolerable irritation which expressed itself in the wallow-

---

[48]Nuttall, *Early Western Travels*, XIII, 210.

[49]Gregg, *ibid.*, XX, 132; as water-reservoirs, so also Dodge, *Plains of the Great West*, 28.

[50]*Buffalo Jones' Forty Years*, 259. Garretson, who is equally certain, prints a photograph of what is evidently a dustpan on the high plains of western Kansas, which is made to apply to the entire habitat (*American Bison*, 34-6).

[51]*Buffalo Jones' Forty Years*, 37.

[52]*Ibid.*, 202, 224.

[53]See Hornaday on this, "Extermination of the American Bison," 422-31. *In extenso* below, chap. VI.

[54]Catlin (who gives a drawing of a bull in a wallow, dripping with mud), *Letters on the North American Indians*, I, 249-51; II, 77, 84; Dodge, *Plains of the Great West*, 28, 119-47; Hornaday, "Extermination of the American Bison,"

ings—of rubbing against trees. This resulted in much destruction of timber and, therefore, in the extension of the open prairie lands through their agency.[55]

Perhaps nothing in the entire buffalo economy has given rise to more discrepant testimony than their drinking habits. In this matter a critical investigator finds himself at variance with the great authority of Francis Parkman, perhaps the earliest 'classic' to popularize a knowledge of buffalo.[56] In his earliest work, which so graphically records his sojournings among the prairie tribes in 1846, Parkman writes: "From every gorge and ravine, opening from the hills, descended deep well-worn paths, where the buffalo issued twice a day to drink at the Platte. . . ."[57] Elsewhere he remarks again: ". . . twice a day, at sunrise and at noon, the buffalo came issuing from the hills, slowly advancing in their grave processions, to drink at the river. . . ."[58]

This, as first-hand testimony from a keen observer, might seem decisive enough for any purpose; but even here, evidence which cannot be ignored appears to indicate that what Parkman witnessed may have been a purely occasional and irregular event, or at best only one of many such manifestations, which he accepted as an invariable feature in the daily round, and afterwards transferred to other times and places.[59]

418-20; Denny MS., 40-3; Seton, *Arctic Prairies*, 52. Practically all immensely outweigh Jones.

Apropos of Seton (*Arctic Prairies*), Northern Wood buffalo wallows are mostly 'dust-pans' in sand: Graham, *Canada's Wild Buffalo*, with "Appendix" by Seibert (Pamphlet); Raup, *Range Conditions in Wood Buffalo Park*, 30-2; Rowan "Canada's Buffalo," 358-60; Soper, "History of the Northern Bison," 385-6.

[55]See below, Appendix K, "Buffalo and Prairie Lands."

[56]It should be recognized that the Parkman of the *Oregon Trail* does not carry quite the authority of the later historian. He was a lad of twenty-three, whose work was composed virtually at the time and has never since (thank heaven!) been altered. As a record of personal experiences, it is as valuable—sometimes contra Parkman—as it is delightful. As an authoritative generalization concerning a land he had never seen before, and an alien race against whom he harboured the common prejudices of his day and country (almost inevitably; see on the 'education' of Eastern United States opinion on the Indian, Bancroft, *North Mexican States and Texas*, II, 104 (1826); *History of Oregon*, II, 404; Thwaites, ed. note, *Early Western Travels*, XIV, 21; also below, Appendix FF), it is less convincing. One may respectfully suggest that four or five months' acquaintance is hardly sufficient. Compare on this, Bancroft, *History of Oregon*, I, 554; Fiske, prefatory essay to Parkman's *Complete Works*; Thwaites, ed. note, *Early Western Travels*, I, 105; Wrong, "Francis Parkman," *Canadian Historical Review*, IV, 289-303 (Parkman Centenary, 1923), a masterly short study.

[57]Parkman, *Oregon Trail*, 77.

[58]*Ibid.*, 418.

[59]'Following' Hennepin, he describes the buffalo as "trampling by in ponderous columns, or filing in long lines, morning, noon, and night, to drink at the river. . . ." Again ('following' Joutel) ". . . where the buffalo, descending daily

According to Hornaday and others, the species would seem to have possessed a camel-like capacity for enduring long periods without water. Hornaday writes:

In such broken country as Montana, Wyoming, and Southwestern Dakota, the herds, on reaching the best grazing grounds on the divides, would graze there day after day until increasing thirst compelled them to seek for water. Then, actuated by a common impulse, the search for a water-hole was begun in a business-like way. The leader of a herd, or 'bunch,' which post was usually filled by an old cow,[60] would start off down the nearest 'draw,' or stream-heading,[61] and all the rest would fall into line and follow her. From the moment this start was made, there was no more feeding, save as a mouthful of grass could be snatched now and then without turning aside. In single file, in a line sometimes half a mile long and con-

---

from their pastures in long files to drink at the river, made a broad and easy path for the travellers. . . ." (Parkman, *La Salle*, 197, 422). Cf. also *ibid.*, 228.

Neither Hennepin nor Joutel mentions any 'daily descent.' Joutel's full narrative is 'far more copious' (*ibid.*, ix, 400) than the Abstract of 1713, which I have had to use (see *Journeys of La Salle*: bibliographical note by the editor, Professor I. J. Cox, II, 248). But the daily descent is also absent from Dr. R. G. Thwaites's unabridged reprint of Hennepin's English translation of 1698 (2 vols., 1903).

Parkman did this deliberately and confessedly at times. See his description of La Vérendrye's journey to the Mandans, 1738. The Indians 'did thus and thus'; and in a footnote: 'at least they did so when he dwelt among their kindred' a century later! Potentially true, no doubt; but scarcely evidence of fact for La Vérendrye's trip (*Half-Century of Conflict*, II, 31).

[60]'Always an old cow': Seton, *Life-Histories of Northern Animals*, I, 274; *Game Animals*, III, 694. Fortescue Cuming's host, Captain Waller (Kentucky, *circa* 1789): ". . . he made it a rule to select the leader, who was always an old and fat female. When she was killed . . . the rest of the herd would not desert her, until he had shot as many as he thought proper. If one of the common herd was the first victim of his rifle, the rest would immediately fly. . . ." *Early Western Travels*, IV, 178.

De Smet, 1841: "The Indians say that the buffaloes live together as the bees, under the direction of a queen, and that when the queen is wounded, all the others surround and deplore her. . . ." *Ibid.*, XXVII, 266.

Alexander Henry the elder, 1776: "The Indians remark that in all herds of animals there are chiefs, or leaders, by whom the motions of the rest are determined. . . ." *Travels, 1760-1776*, 295.

Cows without bulls were common at certain seasons—who save a cow should lead them? See *Journey of Coronado*, 142, 193, 230; Burpee (ed.), "Cocking's Journal," 104, 105, 115; Coues (ed.), *Henry-Thompson Journals*, I, 98, 102, 108, 131, 134, 136, 155, 253; Coues (ed.), *Expeditions of Pike*, II, 438, 516; Simon Fraser, *First Journal* (in Doughty, *Report of Canadian Archives*, 1929, 109); Bradbury, 1811, *Early Western Travels*, V, 147; Brackenridge, 1811, *ibid.*, VI, 147; Pattie, 1824, *ibid.*, XVIII, 50; Gregg, 1831, *ibid.*, XX, 263; Parkman, *Oregon Trail*, 259, 266; Milton and Cheadle, *North-West Passage*, 58; Allen, *American Bisons*, 157, 189.

[61]A good sketch of this, Seton, *Life-Histories of Northern Animals*, I, 295; *Game Animals*, III, 684.

taining between one and two hundred buffaloes,[62] the procession slowly marched down the coulee, close alongside the gully as soon as the water course began to cut a pathway for itself. . . . After such a long journey to water, a herd would usually remain by it for some hours, lying down, resting, and drinking at intervals until completely satisfied.

Having drunk its fill, the herd would never march directly back to the choice feeding grounds it had just left, but instead would leisurely stroll off at a right angle from the course it came, and then wander off across the hills in an almost aimless[63] search for fresh fields [sic] and pastures new. When buffalo remained long in a certain locality, it was a common thing for them to visit the same watering-place a number of times, at intervals of greater or less duration, according to circumstances. . . ."[64]

It may be remarked here that Hornaday's essay presents no indication that he ever saw the buffalo in the days of their plenty. He describes the general region of his own (almost unsuccessful) search for living specimens in 1886.[65] For information concerning their habits, he appears to have depended upon the uncritical kind of informant I have discussed in my introductory chapter. To be precise, how do we know that it was *the same herd* which revisited some drinking-place again and again at these varying intervals?—or who even watched, and supposed it to be? We have seen the utterly unsatisfactory character of one such supposed identification by a man who *a priori*—as an educated man—was much more likely to be critically minded.[66]

Buffalo Jones, himself the most successful breeder of his day—perhaps of any day[67]—of buffalo and domestic cattle, in discussing the ideal type required for the western ranges, said: "What we want (among other qualities) is a race of cattle so clannish[68] as never to separate and go astray . . . the animal that can water every third day

---

[62]Simon Kenton is said to have counted 1500 at once in single file (Blue Licks, Kentucky, 1775). Kenton, *Simon Kenton*, 63.

[63]"No wild animal roams at random." Seton (*re* moose), *Life-Histories of Northern Animals*, I, 153.

[64]Hornaday, "Extermination of the American Bison," 416-18.

[65]*Ibid.*, 529-48.

[66]See on this, Denny's 'white buffalo' (chap. IV, note 37).

[67]See Appendix C, "Buffalo Domestication."

[68]Buffalo Jones states very emphatically that the small herds (of which the huge aggregates were composed) were 'clans' of related animals led by their sire; which knew one another by scent and sound, and "when separated . . . they never rest until they are together again. . . ." (*Buffalo Jones' Forty Years*, 50, 234). Seton supports this (*Life-Histories of Northern Animals*, I, 274-7, 287, 291); Dodge rejects the idea after nearly thirty years among the buffalo (*post* 1849), and much more careful observation of the formation and dispersal of large herds (*Plains of the Great West*, 123). Both men may be partly right, for nothing seems to be absolutely uniform concerning buffalo. Soper (1932) and apparently informed Northern opinion at large are for 'clans.' Soper, "History of the Northern Bison," 391.

and keep fat, ranging from twenty to thirty miles from water. . . ."[69] It is clear from this that Jones was looking to the buffalo-partner to produce something different from the morning-noon-and-night water-drinker; he wanted a hybrid with which successfully to stock the semi-arid lands.

Thompson Seton's description of buffalo drinking differs considerably, despite some general resemblances: "All the early morning they graze. Toward ten o'clock they lie down and chew their cud; about noon the old cow will arise and march toward the water with the band behind her. She does not go far among the many deep-worn Buffalo trails before finding one which is headed her way. She follows it, the others come stringing along single file behind her. The only exception to the single rank is made by the young calves, which run and frisk along beside their mothers. It may be miles to the watering-place, but the herd marches steadily and with purpose. . . ."[70]

If the habits described in the foregoing paragraph, as in that of Parkman, are considered uniform practice (whether of a three-times-daily, 'sunrise-and-noon,' or a 'once-a-day drinker,' especially if they had to travel miles to the water),[71] one wonders how they ever found

[69] In Hornaday, "Extermination of the American Bison," 457. In this connection, I have since found an interesting allusion, which I quote: "In 1875 occurred one of the most severe droughts that ever visited the Concho country in Texas. All the streams dried up except the main ones. Buffalo came to the South Concho from miles and miles to water and covered the ranges to such an extent that there was little room left for cattle. Hundreds died on the range that year and hundreds of others died in the stream or after they had staggered from the water. . . ." (Garretson, American Bison, 72).

Since Garretson inserts this in his chapter on 'natural enemies,' the 'hundreds' presumably have reference to buffalo. While of course we dare not assume that the species was literally and absolutely impervious to thirst under any conditions—and evidently these were exceptionally severe—the date of 1875 tends to arouse suspicion. Droughts must surely have occurred before, within the era of European contact with the species, and nothing appears to have been said in this case regarding the effects upon the range cattle, who should supposedly have suffered sooner and worse. In 1875 the remaining buffalo were being pursued more relentlessly than ever in the Southwest, and thirst had for some years been used as a weapon against them, by establishing cordons of hunters to bar the herds from drinking-places. (See below on this, chap. XV.) Hornaday mentions the hide-hunters' propagandist efforts to divert attention from their own terrible slaughterings (chap. XV, note 89, etc.). One would like to feel more certain that this was not an instance of making a drought the explanation for a mortality of which it was not the true cause. Cf. however chap. XIII, note 111, also the note at the end of chap. XX. It will there be seen that a resident of the Concho country at this very time makes no mention of such a catastrophe.

[70] Seton, Life-Histories of Northern Animals, I, 282; see his drawing, ibid., 295; also in his Game Animals, III, 684; an admirable delineation of such places (that is, the 'draws,' coulees, gullies, etc.).

[71] 'Once-a-day drinker' is Seton's expression (Life-Histories of Northern Animals, I, 282). Col. Henrý Inman says the same ". . . once a day and that late

the necessary time to graze or ruminate. It really seems as if at times they would be likely to 'meet themselves coming back.' We have another account, earlier than any and from no arm-chair stylist, but a man on the ground, doubtless describing in plain English what he knew. The younger Alexander Henry, in his account of the Bois Percé, a famous crossing-place on the Red River near the (later) international boundary, says: "The ground along the river is worn down by the buffalo, especially at every bend of the river westward, where the plains run down to the water, and where the herds come night and day to drink . . ." (1800).[72]

It is difficult to be sure to just what extent we are justified in accepting any analogy between buffalo and 'wild,' or range cattle (of domesticated breeds) in the former buffalo habitat. Colonel Dodge, a careful observer who dwelt on the plains for over thirty years from 1849 onward, states that "the habits of the buffalo are almost identical with those of domestic cattle."[73] In this he is largely corroborated by Buffalo Jones,[74] who is often one of his severest critics. Yet Dodge has devoted

in the afternoon. . . ." (*Old Santa Fé Trail*, 217). Inman, curiously enough, was the editor, perhaps compiler, of *Buffalo Jones' Forty Years*, frequently quoted by me, and a staunch upholder of Jones's dicta. And Jones is for every third day, apparently. See below, note 75.

[72]Coues (ed.), *Henry-Thompson Journals*, I, 88. It is evidently near to and perhaps identical with John McDonnell's 'Buffalo Ford' (Account of Red River, 1793-97, in Masson, *Les Bourgeois de la Compagnie du Nord-Ouest*, I, 269).

[73]Dodge, *Plains of the Great West*, 123.

[74]Jones states that domesticated buffalo drive like range cattle (*Buffalo Jones' Forty Years*, 246). Robert Wickliffe, a famous early cross-breeder of Lexington, Kentucky (1843), in correspondence with Audubon mentions in some of the hybrids a considerable trend toward domestic traits, and in others no material modification from buffalo usages. (Audubon and Bachman, *American Quadrupeds*, II, 51-4).

I was told by the Wainwright yard engine crew, who loaded the animals shipped north from the Buffalo Park in 1928, that 'they acted no different from a bunch of ordinary range cattle.' Somewhat similar testimony appears in Allen, *American Bisons*, 69; but at Wainwright in the latter years, visitors were forbidden to enter the Park afoot, which was formerly customary, even for children. This is, of course, identical with the danger from range cattle. Garretson cites several cases showing the danger of trusting 'domesticated' buffalo (*American Bison*, 47-51).

Cf. buffalo in a prairie fire, Bow River, Alberta, 1876: ". . . a large number were driven in the blind rush away from the fire right over the cut bank west of our camp, and plunged in a bellowing mass down some hundreds of feet on to the rocky shores of the river. . . ." (Denny MS., 40). Range cattle in Mexico: "A man once told me he had known a herd so wild that they ran right over the edge of a bluff, never even seeing it in their alarm; the result being that fifty-seven mangled carcasses were found at the bottom of the ravine. . . ." (Tweedie, *Mexico As I Saw It*, 43). 'Mountain buffalo' behaved similarly but were unharmed (Dodge, *Plains of the Great West*, 144-7).

several pages to the many and profound differences between the Texas wild cattle and the buffalo.[75] Concerning range—not 'wild'— cattle, the following may be noted:

> Cattle have curious ways of their own; for instance an ordinary herd will *string in* to water about nine or ten o'clock every morning. One of the old cows will start off generally to the same pool, and the others invariably follow in single file. They walk right into the water and drink, then go and lie down on the bank to chew the cud. They stay near water until about four o'clock in the afternoon in the summer, during which time they will drink, perhaps, three or four times. During the cool of the evening they begin to wander away, going in single file along the paths they have made. Many animals have their own particular feeding-ground, and travel, perhaps, three or four miles back to it, not stopping to eat anything by the way. They feed until it is quite dark, often indeed when it is dark,[76] and then lie down and go to sleep. By daylight they are busily eating again, and when satisfied trail off to the water.
>
> In summer cattle go every day to water, but in the cooler weather they do not drink for two or three days at a time, especially if they get lots of prickly pear. . . ."[77]

The above description furnishes partial support to both opinions, but obviously it can scarcely be adduced for cattle or buffalo throughout the enormous extent of the entire buffalo habitat. Moreover, these cattle were within daily reach of *the same* watering-place on their Mexican ranch, where Mrs. Tweedie observed them. Concerning others, she adds elsewhere: "The real wild cattle, which still exist in certain parts of Mexico, are weedy and small, with enormous horns, they live on the prickly pear and grass, never seek water like the ranch cattle, and never drink at all except when it rains and they find a puddle. . . ."[78]

There need be no doubt that every one of the foregoing statements describes practices in which buffalo have been seen at some time or other to indulge. But we are not told (in most cases) who our authorities' informants may have been, nor what degree of experience or

[75]Dodge, *Plains of the Great West*, 148-54. He states that cattle feeding on the high plains pasturage of short 'buffalo grass' back from the Arkansas River "return to the river for water only on alternate days. . . ." (*ibid.*, 33). See above, *re* this precise territory, note 71.

Compare also: "Cattle do not run at the sound of a gun; buffalo always do— that is a habit acquired since they have been hunted so much. . . ." (Hough, 1887, in *Buffalo Jones' Forty Years*, 146; cf. *ibid.*, 224, also Hornaday, "Extermination of the American Bison," 427-34). Buffalo, differing from domestic cattle, rise front feet first: Soper, "History of the Northern Bison," 401.

[76]Cf. similar variations in other lands, *re* nocturnal feeding, etc. Roosevelt, *African Game Trails*, 208, 219, 241, 362, 389, 400, 420, etc.; Maxwell, *Stalking Big Game with a Camera*, 15, 65, 83, 93, 135, 141, 213, 226.

[77]Tweedie, *Mexico As I Saw It*, 44-5.

[78]*Ibid.*, 46.

of discrimination they possessed. These may be assumed to have been broadly equal. But neither of our two principal secondary authorities here quoted, Hornaday and Seton, ever saw a herd of buffalo in the days of their glory, and the utterly irreconcilable character of the 'uniform practices' (expressed or implied) compels a careful critic to conclude that little uniformity existed. Perhaps the final reference, to the wild cattle of Mexico, comes nearest to the truth. The buffalo did as best they could; if there was water available, they drank, if not, they got along without it until a supply presented itself. The presence of 'trails to the water' proves little; without doubt, in the hot dry Southwest they must often have found little or none in the watering-places when they reached them, precisely as did men.

I am the more confirmed in this general conclusion by the well-authenticated buffalo habit of drinking anything and everything that was liquid, which I imagine would scarcely have been the case with an animal that was always within reach, thrice, twice, or even once daily, of rivers, creeks, or the larger and purer lakes. Nor is this a matter of a mere perverted taste, for they would drink just as eagerly of the very purest spring water from a mountain stream.[79] One is compelled to conclude that neither the quantity nor the quality of water was of serious importance to the buffalo. If no positive evidence to this effect remains, we must infer it from the mere circumstance that the buffalo, or vestiges of their presence, have been found on the great arid plains where water was almost invariably scarce, and frequently was not to be obtained at all.

In some instances, what a traveller on the plains would term 'bad'— that is, alkali—water would gratify the buffalo's craving for salt, as with range or domestic cattle today. Pedro de Castañeda, in 1541, noted a 'salt lake' which was clearly a buffalo resort, since he mentions an enormous pile of 'cowbones' (buffalo) there.[80] In a far distant territory, Henri Joutel writes: "The Indians showed us a spring of salt water, and made us go ashore to view it. We observed the ground about it was much beaten by bullocks' feet, and it is likely they love that salt water . . ." (1687).[81]

[79]See Dodge, *Plains of the Great West*, 144 *et seq.* (*in extenso* above, chap. III, note 49).

[80]Castañeda in *Journey of Coronado*, 140; for the passage *in extenso*, see chap. XIII, note 111. By contrast, Rev. John Mackenzie, the missionary colleague of Moffat and Livingstone in South Africa, describes how poor tortured oxen, maddened with thirst, nevertheless refused the foul brackish water in some of the holes in the Kalahari Desert (*Day-Dawn in Dark Places*, London, 1882).

[81]*Journeys of La Salle*, II, 207. For the Kentucky 'Blue Licks,' see the references cited above, chap. III, note 6; and for Georgia also, *circa* 1773, see Bartram, *Travels*, 55, 263.

In other cases, it was mere filth, and the buffalo apparently preferred it.[82] Long, 1820, notes them drinking at foul stagnant pools in the Canadian River,[83] and we know from other evidence that rivers in the Southwest were often very low in the summer-time, as was the Cimarron River in 1831.[84] Frémont, in 1843, mentions encamping "at a little pond of very bad water, from which we drove away a herd of buffalo that were standing in and about it."[85] Parkman (1846) speaks of ponds 'so badly mired by buffalo that their horses were afraid to approach.'[86] Sir Cecil Denny (1874) found the lakes in the Cypress Hills unspeakably polluted by buffalo;[87] and Seton describes this as a characteristic: "The sanitation of the buffalo is very low, its excretions being left anywhere. Such is the rule among creatures that have nothing of the nature of a nest or home-point. . . ."[88] The same propensity has bestowed a number of place-names at various points in the buffalo habitat.[89] While the buffalo were primarily a gregarious species, so much so that it has been said that they were 'never solitary except by accident,'[90] yet there seems to have been commonly a curious separa-

A salt lake, a marsh, apparently lower Red River, near 'the fork' (that is, Winnipeg), 1737; Burpee (ed.), Journals of La Vérendrye, 250, 251; cf. 'Stinking River' = La Salle River, near Winnipeg, perhaps the same. Several such, west of Red River, 'famous places for buffalo,' 1800: Coues (ed.), Henry-Thompson Journals, I, 138; Thompson, Narrative, 252 (the same spots).

[82]Lewis and Clark Journals, III, 180.

[83]Long, Early Western Travels, XVI, 132.

[84]The tragedy of Jedediah Smith, 1831; Gregg, ibid., XIX, 236; Chittenden, American Fur Trade, II, 552; Dale (ed.), Ashley-Smith Explorations, 296, etc.

[85]Frémont, Narrative, 99; cf. Cowie, Company of Adventurers, 207.

[86]Parkman, Oregon Trail, 230; cf. Hughes, Father Lacombe, 169; Hornaday, "Extermination of the American Bison," 417, 418.

[87]Denny MS., 193; see also Cowie on this, in the same general territory, 1868-70; Company of Adventurers, 207, 323, 374.

[88]Seton, Life-Histories of Northern Animals, I, 287.

[89]Yellowhead Lake, the summit in the pass of that name, was known 1859, 1872, as 'Cow Dung Lake': Palliser Journals, 129; Grant, Ocean to Ocean, 278. 'Buffalo Dung Lake,' 1863: Milton and Cheadle, North-West Passage, 245.

Chip Lake, 80 miles west of Edmonton, Alberta ('chips' = bois de vache) was 'Buffalo Dung Lake' in 1810 (Coues (ed.), Henry-Thompson Journals, II, 585, 652). 'Bull Dung Lake' alias 'Buffalo Chip Lake,' 1859 (Palliser Journals, 130, 182); and 'Dirt Lake,' 1859 or 1875 (map in Southesk, Travels, 1859, published 1875). I am ignorant whether the 'Dirt Hills' (a local name for the Missouri Coteau, north of Lat. 49° N., see Macoun, Autobiography, 164-9), had reference to this or not. It was no very special buffalo resort.

Grinnell states that the Pawnee name for the Republican river (a famous buffalo haunt) signifies 'dung' or 'filthy' from this cause: Grinnell, Fighting Cheyennes, 90, 299.

[90]So, Fletcher, s.v. Buffalo, Handbook of American Indians, I, 169. Buffalo 'seldom seen alone'; De Smet, Early Western Travels, XXVII, 265; Life of De Smet, IV, 1397.

tion of the sexes, except at breeding-time. The various accounts we have concerning this are not exempt from the usual contradictions; but it is possible that some of these may be such only in appearance, from the chronicler having omitted to specify the precise season of the year to which he refers. Other general statements, however, are hopelessly irreconcilable.

In the course of our inquiries in a later chapter into certain of the prominent buffalo 'characteristics' and their significance in buffalo

---

Lone animals were not so utterly uncommon, it would seem ('always bulls,' so Seton, *Life-Histories of Northern Animals*, I, 289, but see below). A bull, Illinois River, December, 1679: Hennepin, *New Discovery*, I, 146; Kentucky, 1750: Hulbert, *Historic Highways*, I, 114; Peace River, August, 1793: Mackenzie, *Voyages*, 375; two bulls only in 16 days, Wood Mountain to Qu'Appelle River, February, 1800: Coues (ed.), *Henry-Thompson Journals*, I, 4; 'a lone bull here and there' north of Missouri River, July, 1806: *ibid.*, I, 405; lone bull near Kootenay Pass, 1809: Thompson, *Narrative*, 408; two cows, Pembina River (Alberta), October, 1810: *ibid.*, 441; two young bulls, Upper Athabaska River, January, 1811: *ibid.*, 444; two cows, Upper Columbia River country, October, 1811: *ibid.*, 538; lone bull, lower Missouri River, May, 1811: Brackenridge, *Early Western Travels*, VI, 90; lone bull, Missouri headwaters, 1813: Ross, *ibid.*, VII, 226; lone bull, Athabaska River, below the Pembina, another below Lac la Biche, another below Fort Vermilion, North Saskatchewan River, all in June, 1814: Franchère, *ibid.*, VI, 365, 368, 372; lone bull, above Roche Miette, Upper Athabaska River (near modern Jasper, Alberta), June, 1817: Cox, *Columbia River*, II, 177; lone bull (twice), Platte River, 1819: Long, *Early Western Travels*, XV, 186, 256; 'two only' in 100 miles, Platte River, June, 1820: *ibid.*, XV, 225, 227; one bull, 'too ill-savoured to eat,' near Pike's Peak; 'one' (likewise, but eaten *nolens volens*) July, August, 1820: *ibid.*, XVI, 30, 103; lone bull, Cimarron River country, June, 1831: Gregg, *ibid.*, XIX, 179; solitary bull, Missouri River (twice), June, July, 1833: Maximilian, *ibid.*, XXII, 341; XXIII, 48; lone bulls, Bear River and near Fort Hall, July-August, 1833: Townsend, *ibid.*, XXI, 201, 210, 236; lone bulls, North Saskatchewan River above Battleford, October 7, 1840, June 14, 1841: *Rundle's Journal, sub diebus;* lone bull, near Chimney Rock, Platte River, June, 1845: Hancock, *Narrative*, 18; lone bull, Arkansas River country, 1846: Parkman, *Oregon Trail*, 415; lone bull (twice), Moose Mountain, 1857; one or two alone near Moose Jaw Creek, July, 1857; lone cow near High River, Alberta, August, 1858: *Palliser Journals*, 48, 49, 53, 91; lone bulls, on Qu'Appelle River, Saskatchewan River, and west of Touchwood Hills, July, November, 1859: Southesk, *Travels*, 69, 80, 81, 306; lone bull near Carlton, January, 1863: Milton and Cheadle, *North-West Passage*, 124; one bull only, Omaha to Cheyenne, Wyoming, 1867: Hornaday, "Extermination of the American Bison," 492; solitary bulls, 1865-8: McDougall, *Pathfinding*, 29, 44, 50, 65, 189; bulls killed, 'not eatable' (twice): *ibid.*, 194; 'prime meat,' *ibid.*, 213, 255 (as also Gregg, *Early Western Travels*, XX, 264); 'often coming across single ancients,' Northwest of Calgary, April, 1873: McDougall, *Western Trails*, 16; lone bull at Fort Bridger, Utah, 1875; 'said to be the first for thirty years': Allen, *American Bisons*, 125. 'Pairs of old bulls' not uncommon, besides singles: Soper, "History of the Northern Bison," 393.

Some very late Canadian instances in Seton, *Life-Histories of Northern Animals*, I, 256-8. These, however, belong to the era of final extermination as a

history, we shall see that the defence of the calves from various (principally animal) foes, is credited by some witnesses to the bulls, by others to the cows, while others again make bulls the protectors of both cows and calves.[91] Nor does even this exhaust the possibilities of contradiction. For others deny that the cows afforded their offspring any protection really worthy of the name. Yet we have very precise accounts from witnesses as trustworthy as any we possess, including the first essentially scientific observers of the species in their Plains habitat, of large herds of bulls without cows, just as we have seen masses of cows without bulls[92]—for the one of course implies the other, in great measure. These herds of bulls, moreover, have been seen both before the normal breeding season,[93] and after it should normally have closed.[94] Others cover the entire summer, or more than one.[95] In other words, these absences include the very periods when the calves were in the greatest need of protection: the early summer, when the young calves were at their very weakest, and late autumn and early winter when increasing cold and hunger made their assailants bolder, and the young animals were scarcely big enough to defy them. I suspect that, here again, sufficient allowance has not been made for those individual variations at which Allen hinted.[96]

The same factor may be responsible for the discrepant testimony concerning their mating habits. Thompson Seton, discussing the respective probabilities inherent in the suggestions of monogamous, promiscuous, or polygamous relations among them, apparently favours the last—or 'seraglio'—explanation; for although he does not say so specifically, he supports Buffalo Jones on the 'clan' supposition,[97]

---

wild species, when they were solitary for the best of reasons. See for these, below, chap. XVII, note 92 et seq.

[91]See below, chaps. VI, VII.

[92]See note 60 above.

[93]So, Castañeda, in Journey of Coronado, 73, 140; Purchas his Pilgrimes, XVIII, 64-5; Brackenridge, 1811, Early Western Travels, VI, 147; Pattie, 1824, ibid., XVIII, 50; Gregg, 1831-40, ibid., XX, 263; '4000 bulls at once': Paul Kane, 1846, Wanderings of an Artist, 58; McDougall, Western Trails, 48, 85, etc.

[94]Burpee (ed.), "Cocking's Journal," 104. Coues (ed.), Expeditions of Pike, 1806, II, 516. Milton and Cheadle, North-West Passage, 58. McDougall, Pathfinding, 224. Cf. also a fragment of a diary of old Fort Ellice (Hudson's Bay Company) 1860-63, in Hawkes, Saskatchewan and Her People, I, 181-8.

[95]Alexander Henry, 1800-5: Coues (ed.), Henry-Thompson Journals, I, 98, 102, 108, 131, 134, 155, 253. Parkman, Oregon Trail, 91, 235, 406, 415, 419.

[96]Allen, American Bisons, 48; so also (mongrelized) wood buffalo (Soper, "History of the Northern Bison," 398).

[97]Seton, Life-Histories of Northern Animals, I, 274, 287, 291; cf. on mating in moose, ibid., 173-6.

which scarcely seems intelligible on any other principle. Audubon believed the buffalo to be monogamous,[98] as do two modern writers, Stone and Cram,[99] although their professed mentor, Hornaday, apparently did not.[100] Under such circumstances, it certainly seems rather captious to conclude from the description of the buffalo (which he makes monogamous) and similar details, that David Ingram, the Elizabethan seaman of John Hawkins's 'marooned' crew in 1568, is to be discredited.[101] H. M. Brackenridge who went part way up the Missouri with the Astorians in 1811, writes that "the males at this season of the year always go in pairs, a singular fact in the natural history of the animal. . . ."[102] I have been unable to discover anything respecting the Plains buffalo that could be interpreted as confirmation for this statement, nor for the account of the winter 'pairing' given by Stone and Cram. We do not on that account reject the actual observations made by the monogamistic champions, however.

One would suppose the buffalo cows would bear occasional twin calves in somewhat the same ratio as our domestic breeds, although this is not by any means certain.[103] I have not found any allusion whatever to this, either of fact or opinion; they would not, however, be very easy to observe in the calving season. There is a description by Fathers Dablon and Allouez, *circa* 1670, of the *pisikious*, in which they are said to bear 'three or four calves at a time.'[104] It is unnecessary to discredit the integrity of our witnesses in partly rejecting their accounts of a new and strange creature. If the analogy with domestic cattle is of any value in this particular, they may have surprised three or four young calves lying down together while their mothers grazed. By some strange mental telepathy, domestic calves—presumably when replete and contented—can be induced to do this, and to remain quiet in the long grass for considerable periods of time. I have often dis-

---

[98]Audubon and Bachman, *American Quadrupeds*, II, 37-8.

[99]Stone and Cram, *American Animals*, 69 (above, note 23).

[100]Hornaday, "Extermination of the American Bison," 416.

[101]For Ingram in more detail, below, chap. IX, notes 53-65.

[102]Brackenridge, *Early Western Travels*, VI, 90. See above, note 90.

[103]The only allusion I have found to twins is of an indeterminate character. If a Sarcee woman bore twins it was commonly explained that she had 'eaten the flesh of a buffalo cow which had borne twin calves. . . .' Jenness, *Sarcee Indians of Alberta*, 27. See below, Appendix HH.

The domestic analogy cannot be pushed too far. For a species whose entire existence has probably been spent on lands infested with insect pests, compare the miserable tail of the buffalo (twenty inches 'maximum length,' Richardson, *Fauna Boreali-Americana*, I, 283) with the magnificent and effective instrument of domestic cattle.

[104]Thwaites (ed.), *Jesuit Relations*, LV, 195-7.

turbed them thus, before I was aware of their vicinity. Or they may even have been 'mavericks' which had lost their mothers, and were possibly clustered about some cow whose own calf was lost. If this was at all a common experience—and one fairly early observer thinks the occasional 'beaver' or 'silk' robes were made by orphans being licked by sympathetic elders of the band[105]—it might even explain the total silence concerning genuine twins. But we must always remember that so many of these curious details were utterly commonplace to the men best able to inform us.

In spite of much assertion pro and con, it appears to be broadly true that in summer-time the buffalo were not much harassed by the Indians. In later chapters,[106] I shall examine the question of aggregates of Indian consumption and of 'wastefulness,' by them and their half-breed kindred, by the comparative arithmetical method, which, in relation to a topic in which pseudo-statistics are flung about so recklessly, is in my view the only effective one. There was one form of summer slaughter which prevailed among the Indians from aboriginal times; but I have found no evidence beyond unsubstantial assertion—in some cases from manifestly tainted sources—that this was carried to a wasteful extent. I have alluded in the present chapter to the virtually hairless condition of the buffalo during the early summer. At this season the Indians replenished their stocks of 'summer skins,' to be used for the making of their tipis, or any other articles for which a hairless hide was required.[107] The grand object in summer appears to have been to retain 'their own buffaloes' on their own tribal territories as far as possible, an ideal which did not preclude the luring of their enemies' herds on to the ground likewise, if it could be done. The tribal organizations of 'soldiers' whose authority often exceeded that of any chiefs, have been found in many 'buffalo Indian' tribes.[108] The guarding of the herds from indiscriminate attack in calving-time was one of their primary functions; and it seems idle to suppose that such organizations would have continued to exist unless their powers had been recognized and vindicated during the ages by popular opinion.

[105]Denny MS., 39. Garretson discusses this supposed origin very judiciously, citing biological opinion, and showing the logical requirements of the argument, which he rejects; in my view, quite soundly (*American Bison*, 31-3). It is probably folk-lore, red or white.

[106]See chaps. XIV, XVIII, XXI.

[107]"Those skins which are obtained during this season are known by the name of *summer skins*, and are used for the construction of their skin lodges, and for personal cloathing [sic] for summer wear. . . ." Edwin James, in Long, 1820, *Early Western Travels*, XIV, 301.

[108]See below, chap. XIV, note 34.

It is possible to find instances in later days of the disregard of the call for prudence in respect of buffalo; but one cannot wonder that in 1868 tribal sanctions were less powerful than of yore; and concerning buffalo in particular, the young Indians could hardly be expected to refrain, simply in order to leave the more for outside intruders.[109] The anti-Indian spirit of the nineteenth century requires that no statement concerning Indian slaughter of the buffalo be accepted without a most careful scrutiny.[110] Assertions from fur-traders, in particular,[111] compel the reflection that in spite of what must have been aboriginal, age-old forms of 'extravagance,' which it is said destroyed immense hosts annually that never in any form came into a fur-trader's hands; yet questions of the possible extinction of the species never arose until after the white stranger made his appearance.

The late summer and autumn must be considered the Golden Age of the buffalo year. The season was at its best, with moderately warm nights and the glorious days of the Plains autumn, 'Indian summer'; the grass under average conditions was plentiful and good; the insect pests were no more; and the well-grown buffalo pelage (which was normally considered fit for robes by November) was now amply sufficient for any purposes of protection. It was customary at this season for the Indians to replenish their stocks of hides with the hair 'robes,'

[109]Isaac Cowie (Gull Lake, Saskatchewan, on the (later) main line of the Canadian Pacific Railway, June, 1868) mentions wasteful slaughter by Cree 'young men,' despite the warnings and entreaties of the elders: Cowie, *Company of Adventurers*, 297.

[110]Hornaday says they killed 'in season and out of season' ("Extermination of the American Bison," 506); 'in summer for the hairless hides' (499); cf. *ibid.*, 524, etc. Frémont talks of their 'thoughtless and abominable extravagance' (*Narrative*, 140); and similar expressions galore could be collected (see below, chap. XXI, "The Influence of the Buffalo Environment upon Indian Mentality").

Yet Hornaday himself admits: "Right well was this gift of the gods used by the Indians" (p. 437). "It was not until 1881 that hunting buffalo in summer became a wholesale business" (p. 507; although the statement is in itself incorrect). He also cites—without comment—a Western newspaper of 1881, which says, in part: "To the credit of the Indians, it can be said that they killed no more than they could save the meat from. . . ." (Hornaday, "Extermination of the American Bison," 503). All this is discussed in detail later.

[111]J. B. Sanford (American Fur Company) to Frémont: "It is during the summer months, and in the early part of autumn, that the greatest number of buffalo are killed, and yet at this time a skin is never taken for the purposes of trade. . . ." Frémont, *Narrative*, 142. *Re* the Hudson's Bay Company, compare Innis, *Fur Trade in Canada*, 336. *The Report of the Select Committee on the Hudson's Bay Company, 1857*, cited by Professor Innis in *Fur Trade in Canada* (p. 336), seems clearly to convey the insinuation that the American Fur Company *did* purchase summer skins, while the Hudson's Bay Company would not. Such rival recriminations are best taken with a grain of salt.

which were needed for such purposes as bedding and certain winter garments worn with the 'wool' inside. They also at this time, or as soon as the cows were in suitable condition, laid in a stock of buffalo meat for food. Hornaday says "they were too lazy and shiftless to cure much buffalo meat,"[112] but we shall dispute this later. Some writers treat the procuring of meat and hides as two separate forms of extravagance; but since cows only were used for each purpose, except in cases of dire necessity (as at Fort Ellice, November, 1863)[113] there can be no doubt that in countless cases the two purposes would be served by the same animals.

It has been charged by a reckless and ill-informed present-day writer, that the Indians slew thousands of cows for the unborn calves, which they considered a dainty.[114] That these were so regarded by the Indians is quite true, as we shall later see; and not by Indians alone. Apart, however, from the preference for the cows as food (in which their taste was endorsed by white epicures),[115] which together with the season of the year when their needs were greatest, necessarily involved the slaughter of many with young, I have found no other allusion to such an alleged practice, among a mass of sweeping and bitter accusations. Against this charge—as possessing any bearing upon the extermination of the species through any aboriginal methods or customs—may be set the considered judgment of a much more competent student, that up to *circa* 1750 the buffalo were increasing to the point of actual overcrowding.[116]

In most accounts of the buffalo a great deal is said about their 'annual migration' southward at the approach of winter. Some of the apparently inescapable implications of this theory have already been examined. This concept is so central and vital to the whole life and history of the species that it cannot be dealt with in the closing pages of any chapter. The actual historical evidence for such supposed practices will be reviewed in detail later.[117] The same applies to their adjustment to environmental winter conditions at large. These, like everything else about the buffalo, will be found to exhibit remarkable local, seasonal, and temperamental variations.[118]

[112]Hornaday, "Extermination of the American Bison," 499.
   [113]"Hunters returned to-day with the meat of twelve bulls; no cows seen. . . ." Diary of Fort Ellice (fragment): Hawkes, *Saskatchewan and Her People*, I, 187. Cf. above, note 90.
   [114]Kelly, *The Rangemen*, 106.
   [115]See below, chap. XIV, note 37.
   [116]Seton, *Life-Histories of Northern Animals*, I, 259-61, 292; also his *Game Animals*, III, 654-7. Examined in detail below, chap. XVIII.
   [117]Below, chaps. XIX-XXI.
   [118]See chap. VIII, "Buffalo and Snow."

CHAPTER VI

SOME BUFFALO 'CHARACTERISTICS'

IN the foregoing chapters, I have referred more than once to the contradictory nature of much of the evidence concerning the habits of buffalo, and to the difficulty—and also the unwisdom—of attempting to decide too definitely on their supposed characteristics. I shall have occasion to treat this theme again before concluding. Bearing in mind that upon the assumed uniformitarianism in the species is based a very considerable portion of the popular and traditional concepts which it is the purpose of this volume to examine, it seems desirable before proceeding further to present as a semi-homogeneous body of evidence some historical testimony concerning habits and mentality, in support of my general conclusions.

Much of the evidence to be presented in this and the two following chapters has little bearing on what might be thought to be the buffalo history *per se.* At the same time it has the very strongest bearing on the question of the universal applicability of much of the evidence for buffalo mentality at large. I shall begin with their much-extolled intelligence.

A good deal has been said, frequently in a highly rhetorical style, concerning this particular trait as exhibited in the 'selection' of buffalo-trail routes. While the present study is not directly concerned with the buffalo *trail,* which constitutes an important subject in itself—particularly in the light of Hulbert's sweeping postulates on the buffalo-trail origin of the American road-routes at large[1]—at the same time much of the argument in support of the case for intelligence in the species is in relation to these trails. It therefore becomes necessary to cite certain of these allusions, as without them much of the contrary evidence would be in part almost unintelligible to the reader. Lewis and Clark, Upper Missouri River, 1806, write:[2] "As these animals have a wonderful sagacity in the choice of routes, the coincidence of a buffalo with an Indian road[3] was the strongest assurance that it was the best. . . ."

[1] I have summarized a few of the logical, historical and topographical objections in my paper, "The 'Wild Animal Path' Origin of Ancient Roads" (*Antiquity,* III, Sept., 1929, 299-311). I hope to publish a full critical work on the same subject; it is already virtually completed.

[2] *Lewis and Clark Journals,* III, 208.

[3] 'Road': *i.e.* trail. *Trail* not used by Lewis and Clark; always *road* or *track.*

John Bradbury, the English naturalist who journeyed with the westbound Astorians for a distance, notes along the Niobrara River, 1811: "Along the bluffs . . . we observed excellent roads made by the buffaloes. These roads I had frequent opportunities of examining, and am of opinion that no engineer could have laid them out more judiciously. . . ."[4]

Washington Irving furnishes a very typical specimen of the generalizations about the buffalo which may appear in 'fine writing':

Buffalo—that ever-journeying animal, which moves in countless droves from point to point of the vast wilderness, traversing plains, pouring through the intricate defiles of mountains, swimming rivers, ever on the move, guided on its boundless migrations by some -traditionary knowledge.

These great migrating herds of buffalo have their hereditary paths and highways, worn deep through the country and making for the surest passes of the mountains, and the most practicable fords of the rivers. When once a column is in full career, it goes straight forward, regardless of all obstacles; those in front being impelled by the moving mass behind. At such times

---

'Road' commonly in the eighteenth century, as in Hulbert, *Historic Highways, passim*. The common early phrase, apart from *path*, is *trace* (from early French maps: so McGuire, *Handbook of American Indians*, II, 799-801). *Trace*, translated *track* or *trail*, in Thwaites (ed.), *Jesuit Relations*, XXIV, 286, 287; XXIX, 20, 23; 'The great buffalo trace, '(Kentucky Licks) 1772-3: Allen, *American Bisons*, 112; The same, as 'the old trace,' 1780: Fleming's *Journal* in Mereness (ed.), *Colonial Travels*, 673; 'Kenton's Trace,' Kentucky, *circa* 1790: Kenton, *Simon Kenton*, 263; 'The Osage Trace,' 1806: Coues (ed.), *Expeditions of Pike*, II, 396; 'The Natchitoches Trace,' to Texas, *circa* 1820: Coman, *Economic Beginnings of the Far West*, II, 95; 'Santa Fé Trace,' *circa* 1835: Gregg, *Early Western Travels*, XX, 229; 1852: Marcy, *Exploration of the Red River*, 87 (Marcy has 'Santa Fé Road': *ibid.*, 40; and 'trail,' *passim*). The Oregon Trail at Independence, Missouri, as 'The Independence Trace': Hancock, *Narrative*, ed. pref., x.

Nuttall, and Long (or Edwin James), both 1819, use *trace* without comment (*Early Western Travels*, XIII, 212, 213, etc.; *ibid.*, XVI, 95). Both again have 'trace, or path' (*ibid.*, XIII, 223; XVI, 247); Irving, 1832, has 'trace' (*Tour of the Prairies*, 443, 444, 447); later, 'trail,' given at first in inverted commas (Irving, *Astoria*, 213, 316); then, 'trail, or path' (*ibid.*, 261); 'road, or trail' (*ibid.*, 263, 361); and 'trail,' as now, without comment (*ibid.*, 221). In *Captain Bonneville*, 1836, he evidently assumes the reader's knowledge of *trail* (95, 301, et passim). Dr. Gregg, who nearly always uses *trail*, has *trace* as late as 1843 (*Early Western Travels*, XX, 229). Parkman (*Oregon Trail*) never uses *trace* in that sense; but Marcy does, 1852 (*Exploration of the Red River*, 21, 81, 87, 89).

The verb, 'to trail,' is far older. John Chilton, Panuco, Mexico, 1572: ". . . many wayes [*paths*] traled by the wilde beasts . . ."; Hakluyt, *Voyages* (Everyman ed.), VI, 274. "The Outlaw's Song of Traillebaston" *circa* 1300, in *Political Songs*, ed. Wright (Camden Society), 231-6. These ruffians 'trailed their bâtons' (clubs) behind them, as the Elizabethan or Cromwellian soldier 'trailed a pike.'

[4]Bradbury, *Early Western Travels*, V, 99. I have searched in vain for anything similar—from an engineer.

they will break through a camp, trampling down everything in their course. . . .[5]

Dr. John McDougall describes an experience in the central Battle River territory, Alberta; summer, 1865:

. . . we were very soon jogging down the winding saddle-path which was but the adoption and endorsation by man of the buffalo path of the preceding ages.

In the course of years I have travelled thousands of miles along buffalo paths, and often I have wondered at and admired the instinctive knowledge of engineering skill manifested in the selection of ground and route made by these wandering herds of wild cattle. If one was in doubt as to a crossing let him follow the path of a buffalo. Gladly have I often taken to these in the winter time, when the snow was deep. Taking off my snowshoes, I have run behind my dog-train on the packed trail made by the sharp hoofs of the migrating buffalo. . . .[6]

Elsewhere, speaking of a journey undertaken in December, 1873, from the upper Bow River Valley towards the Red Deer River and Edmonton by the foothill route, he says: "This time we travelled by a new route through the hills. Old buffalo trails were our bridle paths, and through spots and scenes wonderfully picturesque and intensely suggestive these instinctive engineers of nature led us on. . . ."[7]

The two foregoing quotations might seem to be decisive, but actually, as will be shown later, much of the evidence which leads one to doubt their general implications comes from John McDougall's own long experience.[8]

Allen writes thus: "Ordinarily, however, the buffalo shows commendable sagacity in respect to his choice of routes, usually choosing

[5]Irving, *Captain Bonneville,* 300-1; similarly, *Tour of the Prairies,* 430, 443, 466; *Astoria,* 233, 250, 358, etc. Irving is a 'classic,' whatever that may be; but scarcely a historian. See criticisms, Franchère, *Early Western Travels,* VI, 173, 402-10. Thwaites, ed. note, *ibid.,* V, 14. Coues (ed.), *Henry-Thompson Journals,* II, 842, 886. Bancroft (very severe), *Northwest Coast,* 138, 145, 168, 172, 207, 247, 568-75, 586. See also Harry Thurston Peck, *W. H. Prescott* (English Men of Letters Series, 1905), 134, 174-5.

[6]McDougall, *Pathfinding,* 104-5.

[7]McDougall, *Western Trails,* 108.

[8]Cf. his account of hunting for a ford, Red Deer Canyon, October, 1873. A bunch of buffalo bulls actually preceded him down the hillside, where according to the foregoing, the easiest and best of fords should have awaited him, with its three essentials, 'approach, ford, and departure.' He makes no mention of high water, which is uncommon in October in the Red Deer River. Yet he was all day finding a practicable ford! (McDougall, *Pathfinding,* 85-7). See Alexander Henry, who was in similar difficulties, Plumb River, Southern Manitoba, Mouse (Souris) River, North Dakota; July, 1806, a wet season: Coues (ed.), *Henry-Thompson Journals,* I, 285, 313, etc.

the easiest grades and the most direct courses, so that a buffalo trail can be depended upon as affording the most feasible road possible through the region it traverses. . . ."[9] Hornaday elaborates on this general statement, and describes the breaking-out of a buffalo-path down one of the 'coulées' or gullies which form the usual approach to the far western river-valleys: "When the gully curved to right or left the leader would cross its bed and keep straight on until the narrow ditch completed its wayward course and came back to the middle of the coulée. The trail of a herd in search of water is usually as good a piece of engineering as could be executed by the best railway surveyor, and is governed by precisely the same principles. It always follows the level of the valley, swerves around the high points, and crosses the stream repeatedly in order to avoid climbing up from the level. . . ."[10]

A. B. Hulbert also supports the champions for 'intelligence.' He quotes the passage cited above from Allen, and continues:

This was because their weight demanded the most stable courses and they were thus very sure of avoiding low grounds, preferring even difficult climbs to passage ways through soft ground. . . .[11]

The buffalo, because of his sagacious selection of the most sure and most direct courses, has influenced the routes of trade and travel of the white race. . . .[12]

. . . the buffalo found the points of least resistance with an accuracy as infallible as the sagacity of any savage. . . .[13]

The reader may compare Hulbert's buffalo with those of Hornaday. The latter, so far from 'preferring difficult climbs,' cross their streams repeatedly by fords which, if not soft and miry to begin with, would very soon be made so by bands of large heavy animals,[14] and apparently quite regardless of their need for 'stable courses.' And each writer is equally certain.

We have had occasion already to note that in one instance of this 'intelligent selection,' cited by Thomas Ashe, 1806, as "having been

[9]Allen, *American Bisons*, 63.

[10]Hornaday, "Extermination of the American Bison," 417.

[11]Hulbert, *Historic Highways*, I, 132-3.

Some of the portion from Allen (above, note 9) is given in inverted commas, without mentioning his source.

[12]Hulbert, *Historic Highways*, I, 137.

[13]*Ibid.*, II, 15.

[14]On miry buffalo-fords, and the difficulty of crossing such places at times, see Henry, 1800-6: Coues (ed.), *Henry-Thompson Journals*, I, 93-4, 134, 320, 376. See also Parkman, *Oregon Trail*, 230; Hughes, *Father Lacombe*, 169; Hornaday, "Extermination of the American Bison," 417, 418. According to Colonel Dodge, the buffalo's instinct 'deserted him in crossing rivers, plunging in anywhere. . . .' Dodge, *Plains of the Great West*, 123.

observed to be made" by the buffalo, the major fact of buffalo selection itself has been shown by a far superior critic to be without historical foundation.[15] Moreover, in large portions of this continent, both in the extreme southeast and southwest, the buffalo was far later than the Indian, and in other regions the species never reached there at all.[16]

Somewhat strangely, Hulbert remarks elsewhere: "For an animal credited with but little instinct, the buffalo found the paths of least resistance with remarkable sagacity. . . ."[17] We are not told who the buffalo's detractors are. With one exception only, he cites none but supporters of the high intelligence. The exception is George Washington (1784), and his case is interesting. Hulbert writes thus: "Thousands of traces were widened by early explorers and settlers who branched off from main traveled ways, or pushed ahead on an old buffalo trail; the path . . . which Washington followed was an old buffalo trail, but had received the name of an early pioneer, and was known as 'McCulloch's Path'. . . ."[18] He says again, with reference to the opening in 1827 of the first division of the Baltimore and Ohio Railway to Piedmont, that it ran "not far from the 'blind' trace Washington rode through far back in 1784, in search of a portage road from eastern to western waters. . . ."[19]

Since Hulbert repeats *ad infinitum* that Indians, white pioneers, early highways, and railroads, all 'followed the buffalo,' and since Washington knew he was on a buffalo path, this can only mean that after all his thirty years' experience of the wilds, he was not aware— or not so well aware as Hulbert—that he was *ipso facto* already on 'the most feasible' local route to the summit. Hence, presumably, the 'searching.'

Washington's *Journal* (cited by Hulbert himself) puts the case differently, however (Sandy Creek, West Virginia, 1784): "At the Crossing of this Creek, McCullock's path, which owes its origen to Buffaloes, being no other than their tracks from one lick to another & *consequently crooked and not well chosen*, strikes off from the New Road. . . ."[20]

Unconsciously supporting this expression of contemporary opinion on buffalo trail-intelligence as against later eulogy, a plainsman (in print prior to Hulbert) asserts that all buffalo trails are crooked:

[15]See above, chap. III, notes 25-6.
[16]See chaps. IX, X; also note on "Buffalo in California" (end of chap. XI).
[17]Hulbert, *Historic Highways*, I, 128.
[18]*Ibid.*, XI, 26.
[19]*Ibid.*, XIII, 134; cf. *ibid.*, X, 153; XII, 22.
[20]*Ibid.*, XII, 122 (the italics are mine): cf. *ibid.*, I, 22, 138-9, etc.

They never pursue a straight course in traveling. Their eyes are so placed in the head that it is impossible for them to see directly in front; and especially is this true on account of the heavy locks on their forehead. Neither can they look backward, on account of their immense shaggy shoulders, hence they are compelled to keep one side or the other turned in the general direction in which they are going. Not being good travelers sideways, they look ahead with one eye and to the rear with the other, deflecting to the right and then to the left for a distance of two or three hundred yards. . . .

The curious deviating from a straight course, as has been explained, is the cause of the crookedness of the buffalo trails to be seen on the prairies of the remote west. Colonel Jones positively affirms that a trail cannot be found anywhere that is longer than four hundred yards without a change of direction, yet the general course of the herd would be comparatively straight for a distance of thirty or forty miles. . . .[21]

This is apparently the habit described by Richardson: "When the bison runs, it leans very much first to one side for a time, and then to the other, and so on alternately. . . ."[22]

Other dissentients on 'intelligence' may also be found, and their testimony is interesting. Allen[23] designates the buffalo the stupidest animal of the plains, "manifesting in some respects an intense stupidity."[24] This opinion is the more credible, since he elsewhere observes that "the stupidity of the buffalo, as well as its sagacity, has been by some writers greatly overstated. . . ."[25] Allen considers—probably with much justice—the effect of numbers to be responsible for those cases in which whole herds stampeded over precipices or into bogs; leaders who might have seen the peril could not avoid it, and those behind who might have avoided it could not see it. "Their crowding forward into quicksands is presumably the blind action of more or less excited herds—a rashness a single animal or a few together would avoid. . . ."[26] We may compare Catlin on this: "The buffalo are very blind animals, and owing, probably, in a great measure, to the profuse locks that hang over their eyes, they run chiefly by the nose, and follow in the tracks of each other, seemingly heedless of what is about them; and of

[21]*Buffalo Jones' Forty Years*, ed. Inman, 260, 262. The Oregon-California Trail, which must (of course) have been a buffalo trail to begin with, is described by Hulbert's contemporary chroniclers as "never exactly straight for fifty feet at a stretch. . . ." (Hulbert, *Forty-Niners*, 52-3). Strangely enough, considering his literary antecedents, there is not one single allusion to buffalo-origins throughout the book, from chroniclers or editor.

[22]Richardson, *Fauna Boreali-Americana*, I, 282.

[23]Allen, *American Bisons*, 66.

[24]*Ibid.*, 67; cf. Sir Richard Burton (1855)—'Dull, surly, and stupid, also timid and wary' (*City of the Saints*, 52).

[25]Allen, *American Bisons*, 70.

[26]*Ibid.*, 70.

course, easily disposed to rush in a mass, and the whole tribe or gang to pass in the tracks of those that have first led the way. . . ."[27]

Arguing hypothetically, Allen's suggestion seems entirely reasonable and probable. It is typical of the erratic character of buffalo evidence in general that it by no means furnishes universal support in this respect. Colonel Dodge is quite clear: "The buffalo is the most stupid of any of the animal creation of which I have knowledge . . ." (he cites examples).[28] In view of his already recorded utterances on its intelligence, I quote Hornaday on this somewhat fully: "In his search for grass the buffalo displayed but little intelligence or power of original thought. Instead of closely following the divides between water-courses, where the soil was best and grass most abundant, he would not hesitate to wander away from good feeding-grounds into barren 'bad-lands,' covered with sage-brush, where the grass was very thin and poor. . . ."[29]

He says again:

The buffalo of the past was an animal of a rather low order of intelligence, and his dullness of intellect was one of the important factors in his phenomenally swift extermination. He was provokingly slow in comprehending the existence and nature of the dangers that threatened his life, and, like the stupid brute that he was, would very often stand quietly and see two or three score, or even a hundred of his relatives and companions shot down before his eyes, with no other feeling than one of stupid wonder and curiosity. Neither the noise nor smoke of the still-hunter's rifle, the falling, struggling, nor the final death of his companions conveyed to his mind the idea of a danger to be fled from, and so the herd stood still and allowed the still-hunter to slaughter its members at will.

Like the Indian and many white men also, the buffalo seemed to feel that their number was so great that it could never be sensibly diminished. The presence of such a great multitude gave to each of its individuals a feeling of security and mutual support that is very generally found in animals who congregate in large herds. . . .[30]

The buffalo owes his extermination very largely to his own unparalleled stupidity; for nothing else could by any possibility have enabled the still-hunters to accomplish what they did in such an incredibly short time. . . .[31]

The buffalo of the past possessed but little curiosity; his stolid indifference to everything he did not understand cost him his existence. . . .[32]

[27]Catlin, *Letters on the North American Indians*, II, 57.

[28]Dodge, *Our Wild Indians*, 291; very similarly, his *Plains of the Great West*, 119.

[29]Hornaday, "Extermination of the American Bison," 416; cf. 418—"Having learned that a journey southward will bring him to better pastures. . . ." etc. See above on these postulates, chap. IV, notes 62-7.

[30]Hornaday, "Extermination of the American Bison," 429-30.

[31]*Ibid.*, 465.

[32]*Ibid.*, 432.

It must be admitted that the buffalo of the past was very often a most stupid reasoner. He would deliberately walk into a quicksand, where hundreds of his companions were already engulfed and in their death-struggle. He would quit feeding, run half a mile, and rush headlong into a moving train of cars that happened to come between him and the main herd on the other side of the track. He allowed himself to be impounded and slaughtered by a howling mob in a rudely-constructed pen, which a concerted effort on the part of three or four old bulls would have utterly demolished at any point. A herd of a thousand buffaloes would allow an armed hunter to gallop into their midst, very often within arm's-length, when any of the bulls nearest him might easily have bowled him over and had him trampled to death in a moment. The hunter who would ride in that manner into a herd of the Cape buffaloes of Africa (*Bubalus caffer*) would be unhorsed and killed before he had gone half a furlong. . . .[33]

Dodge gives some particulars of their incapacity to adjust themselves to the phenomenon of the railway. In 1871-72, he states:

The Atchison, Topeka, and Santa Fé Railroad was then in process of construction and nowhere could the peculiarity of the buffalo . . . be better studied than from its trains. If a herd was on the north side of the track, it would stand stupidly gazing, and without a symptom of alarm, although the locomotive passed within a hundred yards. If on the south side of the track, even though at a distance of one or two miles from it, the passage of a train set the whole herd in the wildest commotion. At full speed, and utterly regardless of the consequences, it would make for the track on its line of retreat. If the train happened not to be in its path, it crossed the track and stopped satisfied. If the train was in its way, each individual buffalo went at it with the desperation of despair, plunging against or between locomotives and cars, just as its blind madness chanced to direct it. Numbers were killed, but numbers still pressed on, to stop and stare as soon as the obstacle had passed. After having trains thrown off the track twice in one week, conductors learned to have a very decided respect for the idiosyncrasies of the buffalo, and when there was a possibility of skirting a herd "on the rampage" for the north side of the track, the train was slowed up, and sometimes stopped entirely.[34]

Apropos of this passage, Dodge, in a letter to Hornaday (who had quoted it or intended to do so[35]), adds as follows: "There are at least a hundred reputable railroad men now employed on the Atchison, Topeka, and Santa Fé Railroad, who were witnesses of, and sometimes sufferers from, the wild rushes of the buffalo, as described. . . . I was at the time stationed at Fort Dodge, and I was personally cognizant of several of these 'accidents'. . . ."[36]

At a railway mechanical convention in Chicago in 1925, the present

[33]*Ibid.*, 431-2.
[34]Dodge, *Plains of the Great West*, 121.
[35]Hornaday, "Extermination of the American Bison," 392 (letter of September 21. 1887). The passage appears also in Allen, *American Bisons*, 66-7.
[36]Hornaday, "Extermination of the American Bison," 480.

writer had the pleasure of meeting veteran locomotive engineers who had worked on certain prairie divisions in the early days. While they told me nothing of a nature specifically corroborative of Dodge, their own reminiscences of trains stopped—sometimes for hours—and the danger of moving until the buffalo were 'in clear,' prepared one for anything connected with such an erratic brute; and, entirely apart from Dodge's own reputable standing,[37] there is nothing in his statement which is inherently incredible, whether we can explain it or not. The anxiety to be all together on one side of the track (more after the manner described by Hornaday, above) is an almost uniform phenomenon among domestic stock which have strayed on to the line, as all enginemen in the prairie territories are well aware.

In presenting supplementary (or discrepant) evidence concerning the foregoing testimonies or opinions, I do not, in any single instance, question the veracity of the narrative; but only, where it so occurs, the tenability of any theory of close uniformity in buffalo habits and traits. The conception that the buffalo were stupid in any way or degree is itself primarily an exception to a far more widely accepted belief in their high intelligence. Yet, even here, we find exception upon exception. Hornaday's broad generalizations on their apathy while their companions were being slain, and upon the easy complaisance with which they allowed themselves to be penned and slaughtered *en masse,* are in the main quite true. Yet this simple stupidity was not always exhibited. Hornaday himself observes: "It is some satisfaction to know that when the first [?] 'run' was made, the herd of two hundred buffaloes was no sooner driven into the pound than a wary old bull espied a weak spot in the fence, charged it at full speed, and burst through to freedom and the prairie, followed by the entire herd. . . ."[38]

The younger Henry mentions a similar occurrence among the Piegans, in 1811;[39] and apparently it was not uncommon, since John McDougall notes an apprehensiveness, in 'dedicating,' or first utilizing, a new buffalo-pound; for if this occurred at such a time, "the driver would be humiliated, the new pound made unlucky, and the whole camp sadly disappointed. . . ."[40]

Matthew Cocking, 1772-73, remarks that 'we' (that is, his Assiniboine and Cree associates, evidently) "are not so expert at pounding

---

[37]See on this, a critical scholar of the first order; Fiske, *Discovery of America,* I, 50.

[38]Hornaday, "Extermination of the American Bison," 480.

[39]Coues (ed.), *Henry-Thompson Journals,* II, 725.

[40]McDougall, *Saddle, Sled and Snowshoe,* 279; cf. Hind, *Report, 1858,* 55-6.

as the Architinue [Blackfoot] Natives. . . ."[41] In the following spring likewise (March 28-April 3, 1773), he laments the ill success of the 'Natives': "They bring droves to the pound, but only few enter into it. . . ."[42]

Along a similar line of reasoning, Thomas Ashe (1806), as we have seen, describes buffalo in Pennsylvania as shunning forever a spot where a great slaughter took place;[43] and J. A. Allen records something similar of the Laramie Plains country, 1845,[44] on the authority of Dodge.[45] Yet again, Thomas Simpson, perhaps a better early authority than any of those mentioned,[46] says concerning 'pounds': "In the vicinity [of Carlton House] were three camps of Assiniboines. . . . Each camp had its buffalo pound, into which they drove forty or fifty animals daily and I afterward learned that, in other places, these pounds were actually formed of piled-up carcasses! As might be supposed, the stores of Carlton were groaning with meat, and the very dogs were fed on beefsteaks. . . ."[47] At that season (January, 1840), a daily drive anywhere in central Saskatchewan would entail the piled-up carcasses—frozen solid!

Similarly with reference to great masses being pushed into quicksands which single animals would supposedly avoid: "In the summer of 1867, over 2000 buffaloes out of a herd of about 4000, lost their lives in the quicksands of the Platte River, while attempting to cross . . ." (near Plum Creek).[48]

Single animals were entrapped, however. The very first buffalo mentioned by Hennepin, 1679, the only one seen for '130 leagues,'

[41]Burpee (ed.), "Cocking's Journal," 108-10.
[42]Ibid., 116.
[43]Allen, American Bisons, 109-10. See chap. X, note 146.
[44]Ibid., 164-5.
[45]Dodge, Plains of the Great West, 129-30, 145.
[46]Bancroft is unjust to the two Simpsons, whom he lumps with their unscrupulous relative, Sir George (Northwest Coast, II, 523). Cf. Life of Thomas Simpson, by his brother Alexander, 331-96; McLean, Twenty-Five Years' Service, II, 311 seq.
[47]Simpson, Narrative of Discoveries, 402. Paul Kane, 1846, heard of one built of buffalo bones: Wanderings of an Artist (Radisson Society ed.), 81.
[48]Allen, American Bisons, 62; Dodge, Plains of the Great West, 122; Hornaday, "Extermination of the American Bison," 421; Seton, Life-Histories of Northern Animals, I, 271. I find a well known 'Plum Creek,' about 35 miles west of Fort Kearney; which is near Grand Island, Nebraska. W. F. Cody ('Buffalo Bill') was a stage-driver between the two points (Walsh and Salsbury, The Making of Buffalo Bill, 44, 94). This would be valuable chronological evidence for their presence so far east, supplementing Butler (chap. XIII, note 143); but Dodge (Plains of the Great West, 122), unfortunately says 'South Platte.' Garretson makes it 'Fort Kearney, on the South Platte' (American Bison, 45), which is mere nonsense. For buffalo near there, 1870, see chap. XV, note 40.

was an old bull mired near the Illinois River. Having killed him, Hennepin says: "We . . . had much ado to get him out of the Mud. . . ."[49] Parkman remarks of quicksands or other danger-spots crusted over with clay: "Places like this are numerous in the Rocky Mountains. The buffalo, in his blind and heedless walk, often plunges into them unawares. . . ."[50] He notes a very striking instance of one thus engulfed.[51] Audubon, shortly before, mentions something similar: "On one occasion, we saw an unfortunate cow that had fallen, or rather sank into a quicksand only seven or eight feet wide; she was quite dead, and we walked on her still fresh carcass safely across the ravine which had buried her in its treacherous and shifting sands. . . ."[52] Hancock, about the same time (1845), describes one of these danger-spots, near the summit of the South Pass: ". . . we found an ox mired in apparently solid ground, and in extricating him, observed a peculiarity of the earth, which seemed to be floating on the surface of the water, for in walking on it, one would be impressed with this belief, from its waving, rocking motion. . . ."[53] Thompson Seton sums up as follows: "The obstinate adherence to one course that characterized the Buffalo led many to their deaths in the treacherous bogs. . . . I doubt not that every great bog and quicksand in the Central Northwest will prove on drainage to be a Buffalo bone-yard, containing countless bones that date from the earliest days. . . ."[54]

Concerning uniformity of conduct, Seton's 'obstinate adherence' wins high praise from Buffalo Jones. "There was a constancy of action indicating a degree of intelligence only to be found in the most brainy of the brute creation. . . ."[55] He further states that they "seldom mire in swamps. . . ."[56] Such buffalo as his probably would not; for he elsewhere affirms—what I have found in no other source—that they ". . . would also linger a day or two before venturing to pass a creek, river, or cañon where there appeared any danger ahead. . . ."[57]

I have spoken of exception upon exception. I have collected several allusions concerning danger, both when the enemy was in front and again when he was behind them. Lewis and Clark, then westbound, near Great Falls, Montana (1805), observed: "They go in large herds

[49]Hennepin, New Discovery, I, 146.
[50]Parkman, Oregon Trail, 315.
[51]Ibid., 415.
[52]Audubon and Bachman, American Quadrupeds, II, 39.
[53]Hancock, Narrative, 21.
[54]Seton, Life-Histories of Northern Animals, I, 271.
[55]Buffalo Jones' Forty Years, 230.
[56]Ibid., 260.
[57]Ibid., 95.

to water about the falls, and as all the passages to the river near that place are narrow and steep [that is, 'coulees'], the foremost are pressed into the water by the impatience of those behind. . . ."[58] Hornaday comments similarly:

During the days of the buffalo it was a common thing for voyagers on the Missouri River to see buffaloes hopelessly mired in the quicksands or mud along the shore, either dead or dying. . . . Such accidents as these, it may be repeated, were due to the great number of animals and the momentum of the moving mass. The forced marches of the great herds were like the flight of a routed army, in which helpless individuals were thrust into mortal peril by the irresistible force of the mass coming behind, which rushes blindly on after its leaders. In this way, it was possible to decoy a herd toward a precipice, and cause it to plunge over en masse, the leaders being thrust over by their followers, and all the rest following of their own free will. . . .[59]

Such places were often utilized by the Indians instead of the artificial pounds made by enclosing an area with a fence.[60] McDougall also relates instances in which buffalo have jumped over precipices when pursued without any intention of pounding. In the winter of 1874-75, a herd of sixty or seventy which he was running jumped over the 'cut-bank' into the Bow River, and, breaking through the ice, were drowned.[61] Denny describes a stampede caused by a prairie fire, also along the Bow River, near Blackfoot Crossing, in 1876: "A large number were driven in the blind rush away from the fire right over the cut-bank west of our camp, and plunged in a bellowing mass down some hundreds of feet on to the rocky shores of the river. . . ."[62]

In spring, 1869, however, McDougall was running buffalo at a place very much like Dried Meat Lake, on the Battle River (Central Alberta;[63] apparently in that vicinity, whether it be that place or not),

[58]Lewis and Clark Journals, I, 352; cf. Patrick Gass, Journal of the Lewis and Clark Expedition, 102-7.

[59]Hornaday, "Extermination of the American Bison," 420-1. Father Lacombe, travelling by steamer down the Missouri, 1869, speaks of "watching herds of buffalo come crashing through the trees on the river bank, and precipitate themselves into the current. . . ." (Hughes, Father Lacombe, 172).

[60]'Jumping-pounds'; whence Jumping Pond, west of Calgary (Place Names of Alberta, 69). The Kootenai had one at 'Kootenay Parc,' Upper North Saskatchewan River, 1811; and the Piegans made one on Red Deer River, for Henry's post. Coues (ed.), Henry-Thompson Journals, II, 670, 691, 723, 725. 'Two Medicine River,' Montana, from a double piskun (that is, probably at a 'fork' or confluence); see view and description, McClintock, Old North Trail, 438, 520.

[61]McDougall, Western Trails, 236.

[62]Denny MS., 40. It was this occurrence which enabled Denny to identify the supposed 'white buffalo,' mentioned above (chap. IV, note 37).

[63]Dried Meat Lake is a widening of the Battle River, southeast from Camrose,

and they acted quite differently. "Along the foot of the hill, there was a long narrow lake with precipitous banks. At this the advance buffalo balked and turned, and soon we were met by the returning herd, dashing at full speed upon our line. . . ."[64] This is the only instance of this precise character that I have found;[65] but McDougall's testimony is unexceptionable, and what happened once might happen again.

When the enemy was in front, circumstances were different. Perhaps nothing about our subject has been more strongly stressed, or more generally accepted, than the difficulty (or hopelessness[66]) of turning aside an oncoming buffalo herd. As usual, however, in respect of opinion among plainsmen, of actual occurrences, and of the probable governing causes of such—inquiry tells another story. My earliest testimony recording their unchangeable persistence is from Richardson (1829) who is less reliable when dependent upon others' information than when observing at first hand. He remarks: "They are less wary when they are assembled together in numbers, and will then often blindly follow their leaders, regardless of, or trampling down the hunters posted in their way. . . ."[67] Irving (working from Bonneville's papers) writes thus:

When once a column is in full career, it goes straight forward regardless of all obstacles; those in front being impelled by the moving mass behind. At such times they will break through a camp, trampling down everything in their course.

It was the lot of the voyagers, one night, to encamp at one of those landing places, and exactly on the trail. They had not been long asleep, when they were awakened by a great bellowing and trampling, and the rush, and splash, and snorting of animals in the river. They had just time to ascertain that a buffalo army was entering the river on the opposite side,

Alberta. It might be thought to derive its name from the resemblance to a long thin strip of dried meat; but it is said to be from the hillside having once been covered with meat, drying (*Place Names of Alberta*, 44). Cf. Palliser's 'Dried Meat Camps' (*Palliser Journals*, 87, 90).

[64]McDougall, *Red River Rebellion*, 75. Cf. Buffalo Jones—". . . the leaders if shot at would never turn back any considerable distance, evidently persistently opposed to retracing their steps toward the place from whence they had started. . . ." (*Buffalo Jones' Forty Years*, 95). Henry notes cases essentially similar to McDougall's, of driven or 'led' buffalo *refusing* at the edge of a Piegan 'jumping-pound' (Coues (ed.), *Henry-Thompson Journals*, II, 725).

[65]I find a 'turning about face' of a somewhat different nature, recorded by General Sam Steele (*Forty Years in Canada*, 146). See chap. XVII, note 73.

[66]For example, Buffalo Jones—'Impossible to turn wild buffalo.' (*Buffalo Jones' Forty Years*, 247.) Yet he and others did it! (*ibid.*, 201, 231-4). M. S. Garretson cites instances of this being done for days together, in spite of his assertion that 'nothing in front stopped them' (*American Bisons*, 54-5, 146-8). See also below, chap. XX, note 89.

[67]Richardson, *Fauna Boreali-Americana*, I, 281.

and making toward the landing place. With all haste they moved their boat and shifted their camp, by which time the head of the column had reached the shore, and came pressing up the bank. . . .[68]

H. Y. Hind is even more emphatic: "It is almost needless to remark again that fires interfere with this systematic migration, but there are no other impedimenta which will divert the buffalo from their course. The Half-Breeds state that no slaughter by large parties of hunters or Indians can turn large herds from the general direction they have taken when on the march; want of food is alone able to make them deviate from the course they have taken. . . ."[69] Seton is more cautious: "An onset of hunters may swerve them for a time, but it does not change their main trend. . . ."[70] Seeing that the 'main trend' itself will be found to be highly problematical, both in the territory covered by these Canadian observers and elsewhere, such views do not advance our knowledge very materially.

These opinions find corroboration from certain early plains travellers in the central buffalo territory. Along the Platte, in May, 1832, J. B. or Nathaniel Wyeth writes: ". . . buffalo in frightful droves. Such large armies of them have no fear of man. They will travel over him and make nothing of him. . . ."[71] Farnham, along the Santa Fé Trail, June, 1839, says much the same: ". . . they spent the remainder of the night firing upon the buffalo, to keep them from running over them. Their situation was dangerous in the extreme, for when buffalo become enraged, or frightened in any considerable number, and commence running, the whole herd start simultaneously, and pursue nearly a right-line course regardless of obstacles. . . ."[72]

As against this view, an educated and philosophical observer with a much wider personal experience of the southern buffalo plains, states deliberately: "Even the largest droves (the opinions of some travellers to the contrary notwithstanding), though in the wildest career, are easily turned from their course by a single man who may intercept them. . . ."[73]

Dr. Gregg, who gives instances of this practice, is the only writer I have found who advances this as a thesis, so to say; but instances in

[68]Irving, *Captain Bonneville*, 300-1. Nicholas Cresswell (Kentucky, 1775) describes them similarly camping at a 'Crossing Place'; and the buffaloes jumped into their dug-out canoe and split it: *Cresswell's Journal*, 98; cf. *ibid.*, 84. Lewis and Clark mention an apprehensiveness of a similar occurrence: *Journals*, III, 236.

[69]Hind, *Report, 1858*, 106.

[70]Seton, *Life-Histories of Northern Animals*, I, 274.

[71]Wyeth, *Early Western Travels*, XXI, 51, 101.

[72]Farnham, *ibid.*, XXVIII, 94-6.

[73]Gregg, *ibid.*, XX, 270.

which buffalo were turned by a few men, or diverted by the mere presence of man, from an apparent line of route, are far from uncommon. Many writers have mentioned the keen scent of the buffalo,[74] which indeed is a common characteristic of wild species everywhere. Edwin James, the secretary and historian of Long's Plains expedition of 1819-20, affirms that the odour of the white man was apparently more terrifying to buffalo than that of the Indian, driving them mad, so that they swam rivers in their frantic desire to escape.[75] Butler says the same; but not, it would seem, from first-hand experience.[76] The younger Henry makes no such distinction. He remarks (1800):

We saw a great herd of cows going at full speed southward, but on coming to our track, which goes to the salt lake, they began to smell the ground, and, as suddenly as if they had been fired at, turned toward the mountain [that is, westward]. It is surprising how sagacious these animals are. When in the least alarmed they will smell the track of even a single person in the grass, and run away in a contrary direction. I have seen large herds, walking very slowly to pasture, and feeding as they went, come to a place where some persons had passed on foot, when they would instantly stop, smell the ground, draw back a few paces, bellow, and tear up the earth with their horns. Sometimes, the whole herd would range along the route, keeping up a terrible noise, until one of them was hardy enough to jump over, when they would all follow and run some distance. . . .[77]

Diron D'Artaguiette writes (Mississippi River, February 13, 1723): "We perceived on the other side of the river a herd of wild cattle [that is, buffalo] which were coming there to drink, a thing which induced us to cross over and to go ashore so as to kill some of them; but these animals, having scented us, we could not approach them. . . ."[78] Curiously enough in the Eastern territory also (1789), Fortescue Cuming was told by his Kentucky host, Captain Waller: ". . . the harmless and unsuspecting animals used to stand gazing with apparent curiosity at their destroyer until he was sometimes within twenty yards of them. . . ."[79] Cuming says nothing here of scent, nor of its terrors. Neither does Henry, on the North Saskatchewan, September, 1808: ". . . a plain, covered with buffalo, coming down to cross; but on observing us, they altered their course and slowly pro-

[74]Hornaday, "Extermination of the American Bison," 418. Hind, *Report, 1858*, 107; Irving, *Captain Bonneville*, 334; Gregg, *Early Western Travels*, XX, 268; De Smet, *ibid.*, XXVII, 266; etc.

[75]Long, *ibid.*, XV, 256; cf. Maxwell on African elephants: *Hunting Big Game with a Camera*, 35, 46, 83.

[76]Butler, *Great Lone Land*, 272.

[77]Coues (ed.), *Henry-Thompson Journals*, I, 136.

[78]Mereness (ed.), *Colonial Travels*, 53.

[79]Cuming, *Early Western Travels*, IV, 178.

ceeded in a body up river . . ." (crossing about a mile further up).[80]

An incidental allusion from Edwin James describes a great herd near the Big Bend of the Arkansas River (August, 1820) 'rushing madly away' as the scent of the white man reached them;[81] but it is not clear that this might not have occurred had the party consisted solely of Indians. Similarly, Buffalo Jones (re the 'peculiarly obnoxious' odour of the whites) states that "often a herd has been stampeded by the scent from a single hunter even four miles away;" and that herds have been known to scent water when miles distant.[82] Seeing that according to his own testimony they would stampede "on the slightest provocation, frequently without any assignable cause . . .,"[83] it is entirely pertinent to ask how, and by whom, the explanations assigned by him were *known* to be the correct ones.

Edwin James, again, remarks in another place: "Notwithstanding the immense numbers of bison, deer, antelopes, and other animals, the country is less strewed with bones than almost any we have seen; affording an evidence that it is not a favourite hunting-ground of any tribe of Indians. The animals also appear wholly unaccustomed to the sight of men. The bisons and wolves move off slowly to the right and left, leaving a lane for the party to pass, but those on the windward often linger for a long time, almost within reach of our rifles, regarding us with little appearance of alarm. . . ."[84]

There is little suggestion here either of 'panic' or of the danger or impossibility of getting past them. In the classic example of Dodge, on the Arkansas River in May, 1871 (to which I only allude here, as it must be quoted *in extenso* later in relation to numbers), there was abundance of panic, but the buffalo ran *towards* him,[85] as they did in the case of McDougall, noted above.[86] Then again, Joel Palmer on the Platte, June 15, 1845, writes thus: "At daylight a herd of buffalo approached near the camp; they were crossing the river, but as soon as they caught the scent, they retreated to the other side. . . ."[87] Pattie describes two such occurrences (1824), in one of which the herd ran

[80]Coues (ed.), *Henry-Thompson Journals*, II, 495.

[81]Long, *Early Western Travels*, XVI, 228.

[82]*Buffalo Jones' Forty Years*, 57, 246, 247.

[83]*Ibid.*, 230.

[84]Long, *Early Western Travels*, XVI, 140, 153; Dodge, an almost identical experience, through 'countless throngs,' 1872 (*Plains of the Great West*, 61).

[85]*Ibid.*, 120-1; also his *Our Wild Indians*, 283-6; see below *in extenso*, chap. XIII, notes 143-4.

[86]Above, note 64.

[87]Palmer, *Early Western Travels*, XXX, 53.

towards the party,[88] and in the other away from them.[89] I think it will be acknowledged that dogmatism on the 'uniform habits of buffalo' in this particular respect would be unwise.

So also when the buffalo, being frightened for whatever reason, rushed toward the intruders, or when without having been frightened or diverted from their route by any interference they were continuing in their original direction—even then they were turned aside: sometimes with, sometimes without, any apparent difficulty, as numerous witnesses testify. Matthew Cocking notes (September 2, 1772): "A large band of Female Buffalo from the Westward crossed the [Saskatchewan?] river near our tents, but were drove back by the Natives, who killed several. . . ."[90]

The elder Henry, somewhere not far distant (south of Carlton, February, 1776), writes as follows: "In the morning, we were alarmed by the approach of a herd of oxen [that is, buffalo], who came from the open ground, to shelter themselves in the wood. Their numbers were so great, that we dreaded lest they should fairly trample down the camp. . . . The Indians killed several, when close upon the tents; but, neither the fire of the Indians, nor the noise of the dogs, could *soon*[91] drive them away. Whatever were the terrors which filled the wood, they had no other escape from the terrors of the storm. . . ."[92] His nephew, the younger Henry, mentions 'twelve cows' crossing the North Saskatchewan in August, 1810; "but the noise of the dogs and children turned them. . . ."[93]

'Twelve,' or the mere indefinite mention of a 'number,' might very reasonably be held as hardly justifying any conclusions concerning really large masses. The following testimonies are consequently of additional value. Rundle the missionary records as under, Carlton to Edmonton, August 26, 1845, and following days: "On our way we passed or saw herds of buffalo more or less for five days. The immense quantity we saw would scarce be credited by an inhabitant of old England. They were in numbers—numberless.[94] The largest herd I

---

[88]Pattie, *ibid.*, XVIII, 56.
[89]*Ibid.*, 65.
[90]Burpee (ed.), "Cocking's Journal," 105.
[91]The italics are mine.
[92]Henry, *Travels, 1760-1776*, 280.
[93]Coues (ed.), *Henry-Thompson Journals*, II, 618; 'six bulls swimming across,' September 5, 1808 (*ibid.*, II, 490). Cf. Grinnell, *Fighting Cheyennes*, 209.
[94]A most interesting side-light on Rundle. In his day *the* poet of English Nonconformity was Milton, whom Rundle often quotes. Shakespeare, as a playwright, was anathema. Tennyson and Browning were scarcely known. This is

ever saw passed near our encampment. They had probably been startled near the river; my guide fired twice during the night to frighten them off from us. . . ."[95] Hancock relates a similar experience along the Platte, a few weeks earlier (June, 1845):

. . . while making preparations for crossing an immense herd of buffalo came in view; in fact the whole country as far as we could see presented a mass of buffaloes in a stampede, coming towards us; having heard of the danger of encountering these roving herds on their stampede, we immediately went to work as best we could, by driving the wagons around in a circle, to make a fortification for ourselves and animals, against the approach of these formidable travelers of the Plains. Several of our company more daring than the others took a position on an eminence and keeping an incessant firing of guns and pistols, succeeded in a diversion of their route to within two hundred yards of us, so that we shot quite a number of them. It was estimated that this army of buffaloes was at least two hours in passing our encampment. . . .[96]

G. B. Grinnell notices the following occurrence, at the Big Bend of the Arkansas, May 1857: "At the big bend . . . the [United States Army] command, with its beef-herd and mule-trains, was threatened by a stampeding herd of buffalo which swept down on them. The situation was critical. . . . The wagon-train was corralled, the beef-herd driven into the enclosure, and the troops opened fire on the approaching herd, splitting it, so that the two branches passed them on either side. It took this herd of buffalo about half an hour to pass the troops. . . ."[97]

Contrasted with these methods are those adopted by other plainsmen, white or red, indicating a divergence of opinion about the most advisable course in such contingencies. Duncan McGillivray, the Nor' West trader, was in almost the same locality[98] as Rundle, but half a century earlier (September 26, 1794): "Buffalo are exceedingly numerous—from the summit of a hill which afforded an extensive prospect, we observed the face of the Country entirely covered by them, in

---

clearly a Miltonic recollection:
> "He look'd, and saw what numbers numberless
> The city gates outpour'd. . . ."
> (*Paradise Regained*, III, 310-11)

[95]*Rundle's Journal, sub die.* Rundle was then no greenhorn; he had been five years on the Saskatchewan.

[96]Hancock, *Narrative*, 9-10.

[97]Grinnell, *Fighting Cheyennes*, 115-16; cf. also *Buffalo Jones' Forty Years*, 201.

[98]McGillivray's Fort George is about where Middle Creek enters the North Saskatchewan River, near the Canadian National Station of the latter name; about 30 miles east of St. Paul des Métis, Alberta. Buckingham House (Hudson's Bay Company) was near by. See Coues's note, *Henry-Thompson Journals*, II, 560.

short they are numerous as the locusts of Egypt, and to give us passage they were forced to range themselves on both sides and we were no sooner past than they closed their ranks as before. . . ."[99]

I have encountered two most interesting passages of particular relevance, since they indicate a general similarity in behaviour in those later days when buffalo are believed (as we shall see below) to have become more excitable through incessant persecution. Isaac Cowie describes an encounter in July, 1869:

> We followed the trail [from Fort Ellice, Sask.] leading to Touchwood Hills . . . and then headed northwesterly towards the north end of Last Mountain Lake [105° 15' W., 51° N.], round which we went and then fell in with buffalo innumerable. They blackened the whole country, the compact moving masses covering it so that not a glimpse of green grass could be seen. Our route took us into the midst of the herd, which opened in front and closed behind the train of carts like water round a ship, but always leaving an open space about the width of the range of an Indian gun in front, rear, and flanks. The earth trembled, day and night, as they moved in billow-like battalions over the undulations of the plain. Every drop of water on our way was foul and yellow with their wallowings and excretions. So we travelled among the multitude for several days (save when we shot a fat cow for food, or a bull made a charge and perhaps upset a cart before he was shot down) neither molesting nor molested . . . we reached the scattered fringe of the mass through which we had journeyed, marvelling at its myriads and their passive indifference to us. . . .[100]

General Sam Steele relates that in the early days of the Mounted Police in southern Alberta, they were on their way from West Butte to Macleod, when:

> . . . they were disturbed one night by mysterious rumblings, which were explained when morning came by vast masses of bison, which stretched as far as the eye could see. They crowded down in the coulées by hundreds, and on the advice of Jerry Potts,[101] the men were ordered not to fire a shot lest the sound of the gun might stampede the vast herd. If that had happened, the entire camp might have been trampled to death, or at the very least, many of the horses and oxen would have been swept away in the wild rush.[102] In order to ensure a sufficient supply of water for horses and men, the troops were ordered to drive the thirsty bison back from the springs as quietly as possible. That day the routine was changed, and the advance

---

[99]*McGillivray's Journal*, 28.

[100]Cowie, *Company of Adventurers*, 373-4.

[101]The famous half-breed Mounted Police guide, 1874-95. See Steele, *Forty Years in Canada;* MacInnes, *In the Shadow of the Rockies* (History of South Alberta); Denny, *The Law Marches West;* etc., etc.

[102]"On one occasion a train belonging to Healy and Hamilton [*circa* 1878] lost most of its strength in . . . a single night, owing to the fact that the oxen wandered away with a passing herd of buffalo. . . ." (MacInnes, *In the Shadow of the Rockies*, 178).

and rear guards were ordered to march along on either side of the main body, while the wagon train and guns were closed up to within one yard distance from each other. All day long the buffalo kept very close to the line of march, and from time to time a young bull would charge along close to the troopers, tossing his head and snorting defiance at these strange intruders. . . .[103]

Should the foregoing instances be considered insufficiently conclusive testimony concerning the successful handling of huge masses, I may again allude to the crowning example of Colonel Dodge. It is true that in this case he and his sole companion (his army servant) deemed it advisable to use their firearms to divert the immense host, but they had no body of troops to assist them; and the apparently continuous herd through which they were able to force their passage is computed to have contained not less—possibly many more—than four million buffalo.[104] The reader has doubtless noticed that in this latter category of testimony where the travellers quietly pushed their way through, they make no mention of the buffalo being abnormally agitated by the unwonted scent of the white man. In dividing a herd, however, they *must* have been smelt by animals on the leeward side. I do not dispute the initial statement; I dispute its universal truth.[105]

By reason of this very circumstance, the foregoing testimonies establish neither the intelligence nor the stupidity of the species. Hornaday emphasizes the noticeable change, wrought by their harrowing experiences, upon the last generation of the wild buffalo:

But with the approach of extermination, and the utter breaking up of all the herds, a complete change has been wrought in the character of the bison. At last, but alas! entirely too late, the crack of the rifle and its accompanying puff of smoke conveyed to the slow mind of the bison a sense of deadly danger to himself. At last he recognized man, whether on foot or on horseback, or peering at him from a coulée, as his mortal enemy. At last he learned to run. In 1886 we found the scattered remnant of the great northern herd the wildest and most difficult animals to kill that we had ever hunted in any country.[106] It had been only through the keenest exercise of all their powers of self-preservation that these buffaloes had survived until that late day, and we found them almost as swift as antelopes and far more wary. The instant a buffalo caught sight of a man, even though a mile

[103]Steele, *Forty Years in Canada*, 76-7.
[104]For all this *in extenso*, see below, chap. XIII, notes 143-4.
[105]". . . they seldom swerved from their well-trodden 'buffalo paths' for any obstacles. . . ." (Stone and Cram, *American Animals*, 69).
[106]I should wish to avoid injustice to Dr. Hornaday, and I am unaware in what lands he may have travelled; but I have found in his essay no allusion to personal experience of wild buffalo except in 1886. This discounts his generalizing observations heavily in my opinion.

distant, he was off at the top of his speed, and generally ran for some wild region several miles away. . . .

The last buffaloes were mentally as capable of taking care of themselves as any animals I ever hunted. The power of original reasoning which they manifested in scattering all over a given tract of rough country, like hostile Indians when hotly pressed by soldiers, in the Indian-like manner in which they hid from sight in deep hollows, and, as we finally proved, *in grazing only in ravines and hollows,* proved conclusively that, *but for the use of firearms,* those very buffaloes would have been actually safe from harm by man, and that they would have increased indefinitely. As they were then, the Indians' arrows and spears could never have been brought to bear upon them, save in rare instances, for they had thoroughly learned to dread man and fly from him for their lives. Could those buffaloes have been protected from rifles and revolvers the resultant race would have displayed far more active mental powers, keener vision and finer physique than the extinguished race possessed. . . .[107]

With the buffalo, fear of man is now the ruling passion, says Colonel Dodge: "He is as timid about his flank and rear as a raw recruit. When travelling nothing in front stops him, but an unusual object in the rear will send him to the right about (toward the main body of the herd) at the top of his speed. . . ."

It was very seldom that the buffalo evinced any courage save that of despair, which even cowards possess. Unconscious of his strength, his only thought was flight, and it was only when brought to bay that he was ready to fight. Now and then, however, in the chase, the buffalo turned upon his pursuer and overthrew horse and rider. Sometimes the tables were completely turned and the hunter found his only safety in flight. During the buffalo slaughter the butchers sometimes had narrow escapes from buffaloes supposed to be dead or mortally wounded, and a story comes from the great northern range south of Glendive [Montana] of a hunter who was killed by an old bull whose tongue he had actually cut out in the belief that he was dead. . . .[108]

The change, as Hornaday describes it, would seem entirely probable and logical—that is, forgetting for the moment his insistence elsewhere on the buffalo's normally high intelligence. But he himself cites evidence (together with other earlier observers) to show the workings of such change forty years earlier, long before the buffalo was exposed to the persecutions of the final extermination. He writes:

The pioneers who "crossed the plains" in those days [that is, of 1849] killed buffaloes for food whenever they could, and the constant harrying these animals experienced along the line of travel, soon led them to retire from the proximity of such continual danger. It was undoubtedly due to

[107]Hornaday, "Extermination of the American Bison," 430-1. His observations *re* firearms are a tacit admission that the Indians would (or could) never have exterminated them by any aboriginal methods of destruction. Unconscious confessions like this continually emerge.

[108]*Ibid.,* 432. In relation to danger from buffalo, see below, note 123.

this cause that the number seen by parties who crossed the plains in 1849 and subsequently was surprisingly small.[109] But, fortunately for the buffaloes, the pioneers who would gladly have halted and turned aside now and then for the excitement of the chase, were compelled to hurry on and accomplish the long journey while good weather lasted. It was owing to this fact, and the scarcity of good horses, that the buffaloes found it necessary to retire only a few miles from the wagon route to get beyond the reach of those who would gladly have hunted them. . . .[110]

In a few years the tide of overland travel became so great that the buffaloes learned to keep away from the dangers of the trail, and many a pioneer has crossed the plains without ever seeing a live buffalo. . . .[111]

Parkman also, whose observations covered a wide territory from the Black Hills to the Santa Fé Trail, remarked in 1846: "The frequent stupidity and infatuation of the buffalo seems the more remarkable from the contrast it offers to their wildness and wariness at other times. . . ."[112] It is difficult to decide which of these aspects Parkman regarded as the norm, but almost the latest generalizing writers I have seen concerning buffalo conclude thus: "While during the last few years of their existence buffaloes became wary and realized to some extent the danger of close contact with men, they were normally stupid to a degree. . . ."[113] This verdict, which appears to fit the broad facts about as well as any concise definition can, is the more notable, coming from two students who confessedly accept Hornaday as their guide.

In former times, when the buffalo's world was wide, when retreating from an attack he always ran against the wind, to avoid running upon a new danger, which showed that he depended more upon his sense of smell than upon his eyesight. During the last years of his existence, however, this habit almost totally disappeared, and the harried survivors learned to run for the regions which afforded the greatest safety. But even to-day [that is, 1887-89] if a Texas hunter should go into the Staked Plains and descry in the distance a body of animals running against the wind, he would without a moment's hesitation pronounce them buffaloes, and the chances are that he would be right. . . . I once discovered with the field glass a small band of buffaloes lying down at mid-day on the slope of a high ridge, and having ridden hard for several hours we seized the opportunity to . . . give our horses an hour's rest before making the attack. While we were so doing, the herd got up, shifted its position to the opposite side of the ridge, and again laid down, every buffalo with his nose pointing to windward. . . .[114]

[109]This will be examined later.
[110]Hornaday, "Extermination of the American Bison," 491; likewise (1855) Burton, *City of the Saints*, 48.
[111]Hornaday, "Extermination of the American Bison," 492.
[112]Parkman, *Oregon Trail*, 425.
[113]Stone and Cram, *American Animals*, 69.
[114]Hornaday, "Extermination of the American Bison," 418, 422-3.

The habit of running against the wind is asserted also by Gregg (1840),[115] by E. Hough (1887),[116] and ('when pursued') by Buffalo Jones.[117] Yet there is one vital consideration which must be remembered before assuming this to be a buffalo peculiarity adopted for reasons of safety. Big-game hunters invariably insist upon the primary necessity of the approach with the wind blowing from the game and into the hunter's face.[118] The natural direction for any wild creature to take when alarmed is directly away from the cause of the alarm; in other words, if the danger is *scented,* to windward. Again, in a land infested with insects, as was the buffalo range, when facing the almost invariable daily breeze of the plains the plague is rendered much less intolerable; and, as I have pointed out already, if the habits of semi-wild or of domesticated cattle furnish any criteria, this is unquestionably the uniform practice.[119] I have noted the fact that Hornaday's only personal allusions to buffalo experiences refer to the two Smithsonian Expeditions of 1886. Despite his remarks about the 'almost total disappearance' of the habit, this very herd displayed it, and he tells us it would be quite confidently expected by his Texas hunters. Thus the evidence he adduces does not support his own assertion, and what he offers as the *known* cause for their shifting movements seems little more than *post hoc ergo propter hoc.*

In another place he presents evidence of altered behaviour in certain given circumstances;[120] but it is no more irregular than much which has been shown concerning the species in the heyday of their unchanged 'normal' mentality. I do not dispute the evidence of fact,

[115]Gregg, *Early Western Travels,* XX, 268.
[116]E. Hough, in *Buffalo Jones' Forty Years,* 130.
[117]*Ibid.,* 186, 260.
[118]According to Colonel Dodge, 'most hunted animals face the wind when going to water' (*Plains of the Great West,* 353).
[119]'Habits of buffalo almost identical with domestic cattle.' *Ibid.,* 123; cf. *Buffalo Jones' Forty Years,* 246-65. Above, chap. V, note 73 *seq.*
[120]"Our buffalo-hunter declared that in chasing buffaloes we could count with certainty on their always running against the wind, for this had always been their habit. Although this was once their habit, we soon found that those who now represent the survival of the fittest have learned better wisdom, and now run (1) away from their pursuers, and (2) toward the best hiding-place. Now they pay no attention whatever to the direction of the wind, and if a pursuer follows straight behind, a buffalo may change his course three or four times in a ten-mile chase. An old bull once led one of our hunters around three-quarters of a circle which had a diameter of five or six miles. . . ." (Hornaday, "Extermination of the American Bison," 431). Even this could be done entirely against the wind on one of our variable 'box-the-compass' prairie days; and their hunter, who made his living by buffalo, seems to have been unaware of this pronounced change in the animals' habits.

but it cannot be reconciled with any conception of uniformity in behaviour. They were 'intelligent,' yet the locomotive taught them nothing of danger, virtually to the last. They were—most assuredly!— stupid, yet the same witness who discredits the possibility that any dawning perception of danger from man entered their minds until the final era, tells us again that they learned wisdom from a much feebler persecution long before. Others ignore this, thereby disputing it by implication,[121] while yet another considers both phases of mentality to be entirely characteristic.[122] And every one of these positions can be supported by testimony from early first-hand witnesses.

In view of evidence to be cited later concerning Indian depredations, it is of interest to note the tacit admission that it was not until the white 'buffalo butcher' appeared that the animal learned the fear of man. And, considering that with one striking exception, practically everyone else insists on the difficulty and danger of trying to turn aside an oncoming herd (this including those who actually succeeded in doing so), it is remarkable that in all the material I have consulted on the species, I have not encountered one single instance of anyone being killed or even injured by buffalo from this cause.[123] Perhaps

[121]Stone and Cram, *American Animals*, 69.

[122]Parkman, *Oregon Trail*, 425.

[123]In addition to 'many killed by tame buffalo' (on which see Garretson, *American Bison*, 47-51; also chap. V, note 74), Thompson Seton writes: "The Buffalo is a dangerous animal, the only really dangerous one in America. If we had exact figures to show, I believe we should find more human beings killed by Buffalo than by any other of our wild creatures . . ." (Seton, *Game Animals*, III, 672). Father Marquette, *circa* 1673 (who had only just encountered them, and whose account needs correction in other respects) thought them dangerous when attacked (Thwaites (ed.), *Jesuit Relations*, LIX, 111-13; *in extenso* below, chap. IX, note 88). Henry, 1810, says that 'lives are sometimes lost' when the leading buffalo in a pound 'refuses' the jump, and breaks through the crowd of Indians on either side; but specifies no actual instance (Coues (ed.), *Henry-Thompson Journals*, II, 725). Lewis and Clark, citing either Mandan or common opinion, 1804, say 'a wounded buffalo rarely attacks a hunter' (*Journals*, I, 198). According to two of Kidd's Blackfoot informants, "surrounding was not considered especially dangerous. . . ." (Kidd, "Blackfoot Ethnography," 93; cf. *ibid.*, 193). Norbert Welsh (1845-1933) says: "Never in all my buffalo chasing did I get hurt by buffalo, nor do I know of any other hunters who were ever attacked by buffalo. In the race, the buffalo were too frightened to stop for fight. Sometimes a wounded buffalo would make a dash at me, but I would let fly and knock him down. A man had to be quick with his gun. . . ." (*Last Buffalo-Hunter*, 109).

Contra, Duncan McGillivray was tossed by a wounded buffalo, September 20, 1794 (*Journal*, 25); as also Finan McDonald, June 2, 1827 (Ermatinger, "York Factory Express Journal," *Transactions of the Royal Society of Canada*, 1912, Sec. II, 87-8). Hind mentions a man tossed by a buffalo bull, 1858 (*Report*, 102). The hero in James Willard Schultz's book, *Apauk, Caller of Buffalo*, 1916— which the author insists is not fiction—meets his death from a herd he has just 'brought in' to the pound. Among several 'narrow escapes,' I have found one single

the most circumstantial description of buffalo ferocity is from Alexander Ross, whom I quote:

. . . there is perhaps not an animal that roams in this, or in the wilds of any other country, more fierce and formidable than a buffalo bull during the rutting season; neither the Polar bear, nor the Bengal tiger, surpass that animal in ferocity. When not mortally wounded, buffalo turn upon man or horse; but when mortally wounded, they stand fiercely eyeing their assailant until life ebbs away.

As we were travelling one day among a herd, we shot at a bull and wounded him severely—so much so, that he could neither run after us, nor from us; propping himself on his legs, therefore, he stood looking at us until we had fired ten balls through his body, now and then giving a shake of the head. Although he was apparently unable to stir, yet we kept at a respectful distance from him, for such is the agility of body and quickness of eye, and so hideous are the looks of buffalo, that we dared not for some time approach him: at last, one more bold than the rest went up and pushed the beast over; he was dead! If not brought to the ground by the first or second shot, let the hunter be on his guard! The old bulls,· when badly wounded and unable to pursue their assailant, prop themselves, as we have seen, and often stand in that position till dead; but the head of a wounded bull, while in that position, is invariably turned to his pursuer; so if the hunter is in doubt, let him change his position, to see if the bull changes his position also. The surest mark of his being mortally wounded and unable to stir, is when he cannot turn his head round to his pursuers; in that case you may safely walk up and throw him down. . . .[124]

I suspect that here (as frequently) Ross has recorded an incident and made it a law. In this very case, the bull died without the hunters in his company applying the test, or apparently even knowing of it. What most of the transient visitors regarded as their only salvation against ferocity on the stampede—firearms—Jerry Potts, a man of lifelong experience, considered to merely increase the danger. I suspect that in this matter the scientists quoted here have accepted too literally that use of 'always' and 'never' which is really little more than a colloquialism, particularly among illiterate men not given to wide inductions.[125] With reference to intelligence, even in regard to the mating

---

instance of death in my 'buffalo' reading. See Masson, *Les Bourgeois de la Compagnie du Nord-Ouest*, II, 397 (*c.* 1790).

[124]Ross, *Fur Hunters*, II, 125.

[125]Compare a most competent observer, the late Charles Sheldon, Alaska, 1906: Sheep 'do not always feed against the wind': found by him feeding with the wind (Sheldon, *The Wilderness of Denali*, 72-7). "It has been asserted that an animal never drops dead in its tracks from a heart shot"; yet he noted one which did (*ibid.*, 251). See also on *horned* cow caribou (one herd of fourteen): *ibid.*, 218, 219, 221, 259. Cf. also Roosevelt and Marius Maxwell on uniformity (cited above, chap. I, note 2). According to Hornaday ("Extermination of the American Bison," 431) buffalo only fed against the wind.

habits of the buffalo, we find the same, apparently, inevitable conflict of opinion. Audubon believed the buffalo to be monogamous.[126] Seton, commenting on the various divergent views, *re* monogamous, promiscuous, or polygamous-'seraglio' habits, apparently favours the last, although he does not say so specifically, for he considers the small herds to be 'clans' of relatives, which hardly seems explicable on any other principle.[127] Hornaday, without expressing any positive opinion, rejects the 'harem' or seraglio supposition as being merely fancy, for this would be "ascribing to the bison a degree of intelligence which he never possessed. . . ."[128]

The same propensity to generalize upon insufficient data is found in the matter of speed. The majority of our early witnesses describe the buffalo as swift, although they may mean swift as compared with known European creatures. This includes Coronado's scribes of 1541: ". . . when they had found a great multitude of these oxen, and would compasse them about and force them into inclosure or toiles, their enterprize prevailed but a little; they are so wild and so swift. . . ."[129] Their swiftness is emphasized also by Henry Hawks, 1572,[130] and by Hennepin, 1680: "They are so swift that no Savage can overtake them. . . ."[131] The 'ranger' with Oglethorpe in Georgia, 1739, says they could 'outrun and tire' a horse.[132] Hearne is somewhat contradictory concerning the northern Wood buffalo, thirty years later. He states that they could "plunge through deep snow faster than the swiftest Indian can run in snow-shoes. . . ." Yet, "of all the large beasts in those parts, the buffalo is easiest to kill. . . ."[133]

D. W. Harmon[134] and the younger Henry [135] agree on their wildness, which virtually implies, if it does not specify, swiftness, in an

---

[126]Audubon and Bachman, *American Quadrupeds*, II, 37-8. Brackenridge, May, 1811, has the *bulls* 'always going in pairs at this season' (*Early Western Travels*, VI, 90). Stone and Cram are also for the monogamous relation (*American Animals*, 69); cf. their professed authority, Hornaday, note 128. This is thought to be one reason for doubting David Ingram's journey and description, 1569 (Allen, *American Bisons*, 80; see below, chap. IX, note 64).

[127]Seton, *Life-Histories of Northern Animals*, I, 274-7, 287-8, 291; cf. various opinions on mating in moose: *ibid.*, I, 173-6.

[128]Hornaday, "Extermination of the American Bison," 416.

[129]*Purchas his Pilgrimes*, XVIII, 78.

[130]Relation in Hakluyt, *Voyages*, VI, 283 (*in extenso*, below, chap. IX, note 28).

[131]Hennepin, *New Discovery*, I, 150.

[132]Mereness (ed.), *Colonial Travels*, 219 (*in extenso* below, chap. X, note 89).

[133]Hearne, *Journey*, ed. Tyrrell, 257.

[134]*Harmon's Journal*, 366 (see chap. III, note 78).

[135]Coues (ed.), *Henry-Thompson Journals*, II, 622, 682 (see chap. III, notes 73-6).

animal roaming in freedom. This is corroborated later by Hector[136] and Butler.[137] Irving ascribes greater swiftness to the mountain buffalo than to the prairie species, presumably on Bonneville's authority.[138] Richardson says of buffalo in general: "It is dangerous for the hunter to shew himself after having wounded one, for it will pursue him, and although its gait may appear heavy and awkward, it will have no great difficulty in overtaking the fleetest runner. . . ."[139] General (then Captain) R. B. Marcy goes further: ". . . the buffalo has immense powers of endurance, and will run for many miles without any apparent effort or diminution in speed. The first buffalo I ever saw I followed about ten miles and when I left him he seemed to run faster than when the chase commenced. . . ."[140]

Marcy alludes elsewhere to his inability to overtake the buffalo cows which had an early start.[141] This widely supported opinion finds implied confirmation in the well-known superiority of the horses used by the Indians for buffalo running over the general stock, which struck one early observer so forcibly that he considered they must be stallions.[142] The reader must judge to what extent the foregoing testimonies of fact or of opinion justify generalizations such as the following, which cannot be estimated in the light of any collateral evidence adduced by its author, since he furnishes none whatever.

It was for the great game animals to mark out what became known as the first thoroughfares of America. The plunging buffalo, keen of instinct, and nothing if not a utilitarian, broke great roads across the continent on the summits of the watersheds, beside which the first Indian trails were but traces through the forests. Heavy, fleet of foot, capable of covering scores of miles a day, the buffalo tore his roads from one feeding-ground to another, and from north to south on the high grounds; hence his roads were swept clear of débris in summer and of snow in winter. . . .[143]

He says again:

The endurance and speed of the buffalo far exceeded that possessed by domesticated cattle. With a good start a swift horse could only with difficulty overtake a herd of buffaloes. Their gait was an awkward lumbering gallop, and the speed which they attained was much greater than it appeared to be. . . .[144]

[136]*Palliser Journals*, 148 (see chap. III, note 83).
[137]Butler, *Wild North Land*, 210, 211 (see chap. III, note 83).
[138]Irving, *Captain Bonneville*, 343 (see chap. III, note 79).
[139]Richardson, *Fauna Boreali-Americana*, I, 281.
[140]Marcy, *Prairie Traveller*, 236.
[141]Marcy, *Exploration of the Red River*, 24; cf. Audubon and Bachman, *American Quadrupeds*, II, 39, 41.
[142]*McGillivray's Journal*, lxix, 29.
[143]Hulbert, *Historic Highways*, I, 19.
[144]*Ibid.*, I, 107.

We may concede the necessity for a swift horse in pursuit of such an animal as Hulbert's buffalo, but where is the evidence for all this? Hulbert cites none, and I have found no vestige of support for such huge distances, Marcy's 'ten miles' being the extreme (estimated) distance based on any actual test. Here also, as too frequently throughout his work, Hulbert appropriates local and topographical evidence from anywhere to support a thesis supposedly dealing with the regions adjacent to the Ohio Valley, where the 'great buffalo roads' of his argument are or were to be found. If he is dealing then, with the territory between the Atlantic and the Mississippi, he himself, not to mention others, states that this vast area was formerly densely wooded.[145] My own long experience of heavily forested country makes it difficult to credit the high winds which swept its highlands clean, and I utterly disbelieve in the 'scores of miles per day' in such a region, if anywhere. If these phenomena relate to the plains buffalo range, what was the nature of the débris which its winds swept clear? Concerning the apparent and real speeds of the buffalo, an observer of much wider practical experience, whose field notes are in my opinion his most valuable contributions, says the precise contrary of wild animals in general; that hunters' estimates of speed are almost always too high.[146]

Hulbert mentions no authority of weight on the buffalo. When he wrote, Hornaday summed up the buffalo knowledge of the day. I shall therefore quote him, both as a criterion of Hulbert's acceptability and for his own intrinsic value: "It was a fixed habit with the great buffalo herds to roam southward from 200 to 400 miles at the approach of winter. Sometimes this movement was accomplished quietly and without any excitement, but at other times it was done with a rush, in which considerable distances would be gone over at the double quick. The advance of a herd was often very much like that of a big army, in a straggling line from four to ten animals abreast. Sometimes the herd moved forward in a dense mass, and in consequence often came to grief. . . .[147] But it is not to be understood that the movement of a great herd, because it was made on a run, necessarily partook of the nature of a stampede, in which a herd sweeps forward as a body. . . ."[148] He gives a description, furnished by a hunter, of an 'immense herd' moving southward (Beaver Creek, south of Glendive, Montana, about December 1, 1882): "The herd came on at a jog trot,

[145]*Ibid.*, I, 20; II, 80-1; III, 74-9; V, 15-34, 93; VII, 156; XI, 39-43, 125; etc. For others, see below, Appendix K, notes 17-37.
[146]Seton, *Life-Histories of Northern Animals*, I, 231, 233.
[147]Hornaday, "Extermination of the American Bison," 420.
[148]*Ibid.*, 421.

and moved quite rapidly. 'In the morning the whole country was black with buffalo.' It was estimated that ten thousand head were in sight. One immense detachment went down on to a 'flat' and laid down. There it remained quietly, enjoying a long rest, for about ten days. It gradually broke up into small bands, which strolled off in various directions looking for food, and which the hunters quietly attacked. . . ."[149]

Hornaday quotes a further description, given to him by a plainsman, James McNaney, the guide and hunter to the two Smithsonian Expeditions of 1886:

[Montana, winter of 1881-82] . . . one morning about daybreak a great herd which was travelling south began to pass their camp. A long line of moving forms was seen advancing rapidly from the northwest, coming in the direction of the hunters' camp. It disappeared in the creek valley for a few moments, and presently the leaders suddenly came in sight again at the top of a 'rise' a few hundred yards away, and came down the intervening slope at full speed, within fifty yards of the two tents. After them came a living stream of followers, all going at a gallop, described by the observer as a 'long lope,'[150] from four to ten buffaloes abreast. Sometimes there would be a break in the column of a few minutes' duration, then more buffaloes would appear at the brow of the hill, and the column went rushing by as before. The calves ran with their mothers, and the young stock got over the ground with less exertion than the older animals. For about four hours . . . did this column of buffaloes gallop past the camp over a course no wider than a village street. Three miles away toward the south the long dark line of bobbing humps and hind-quarters wound to the right between two hills and disappeared. . . .[151]

Somewhat curiously, he adds elsewhere:

It is probable, and in fact reasonably certain, that such forced-march migrations as the above were due to snow-covered pasture and a scarcity of food on the more northern ranges. Having learned that a journey south will bring him to regions of less snow and more grass, it is but natural that so lusty a traveler should migrate. The herds or bands which started south in the fall months traveled more leisurely, with frequent halts to graze on rich pastures. . . . Unless closely pursued, the buffalo never chose to make a journey of several miles through hilly country, on a continuous run. Even when fleeing from the attack of a hunter, I have often had occasion to notice that, if the hunter was a mile behind, the buffalo would always walk when going uphill; but as soon as the crest was gained he would begin to run, and go down the slope either at a gallop or a swift trot. . . .[152]

[149]*Ibid.*, 421; on 'trotting,' cf. Inman's remarks, chap. XV, note 62; see also chap. XVII, note 97.
[150]The Westerner's 'lope' is the English 'canter.'
[151]Hornaday, "Extermination of the American Bison," 422.
[152]*Ibid.*, 422. See note above (149) on 'trotting' which Hornaday endorses.

It is much to be regretted that Hornaday's personal observations—
as likewise those of his foregoing informants—were made in the final
days of the free wild species. Despite his remarks concerning buffalo
traits which he had 'often' noticed, a very cursory and partial examination of those passages reveals quite clearly (as in the reproduction
verbatim of the 'four to ten' animals abreast) the narrow and insufficient basis upon which his confident generalizations are founded. For
he himself insists, as we have seen, upon the profound changes
wrought in the buffalo mentality by the agonies of the closing years.
In the last quotation, he comments on the leisurely manner in which
the regular fall migration was normally conducted; the buffalo, 'unless
closely pursued, never choosing' to run far at once in a hilly country. A
page or two earlier, we are to understand that their movement 'for
considerable distances at the double quick' was an equally normal
optional variation, and McNaney is obviously cited as proof. Yet again,
what guarantee have we that this particular rapid journey was not an
abnormal galloping movement caused by close pursuit? For we shall
see later, on Hornaday's own authority, that the Montana range was
'crowded with hunters' at that precise time.[153] In spite of these considerations, which lie upon the surface and should be manifest to any
critic, these contradictory arguments are advanced as a supposedly
consistent contribution to our knowledge of uniform buffalo characteristics, and are similarly accepted—as a 'full examination'—by those
who should know better.[154] On Hornaday's own premises, however,
it is clear that they furnish very little support to Hulbert's pronouncements on speed habits in buffalo; and *a fortiori* the characteristics of
the earlier 'normal' times would furnish even less.

Even on the question of purely incidental references such, for example, as running uphill, generalization is vain. Some of our witnesses
seem to give complete support to Hornaday. Irving (reporting as an
eye-witness) says: "The immense weight of head and shoulders causes
the buffalo to labour up hill; but it accelerates his descent."[155] Others,
of superior authority, leave this less certain. Thompson, 1808, says of the
'bison cows': "These animals often frequent the gorges of the Mountains for the fresh grass, water, and freedom from flies; but are careful
not to be shut in by impassable rocks, and on being hunted uniformly

W. F. Drannan says the buffalo were slower and 'harder to frighten' in the fall,
being fat (*Thirty-One Years on the Plains*, 332).

[153]See below, chap. XVI, "The Destruction of the Northern Herd in the
United States."

[154]See Seton, *Life-Histories of Northern Animals*, I, 261-2.

[155]Irving, *Tour of the Prairies*, 493.

make for the open country; yet when found in a narrow place I have seen the Bisons take to the rocky hills and go up steep places where they could barely stand, the Bison is a headstrong animal. . . ."[156] Brackenridge (Missouri River, 1811) observed: "In some places the hills rose to the height of mountains. It contributed much to our amusement to observe the herds of buffaloe, ascending and descending by a winding path. . . ."[157]

Similarly, Maximilian (Bad Lands of the Missouri, September 18, 1833): The buffalo "turned into a lateral ravine, where we saw these heavy animals ascend the high steep mountains. It often appeared inconceivable how these colossal masses could make their way up the steep naked walls. . . ."[158] Frémont's testimony is almost identical (canyon of the North Platte, near 'Red Buttes,' about 106° 38′ W., July, 1842): "Immediately on entering we discovered a band of buffalo. The hunters failed to kill any of them . . . and in the meantime the herd clambered up the face of the ridge. It is sometimes wonderful to see these apparently clumsy animals make their way up and down the most rugged and broken precipices. . . ."[159]

McDougall gives a graphic description (Red Deer River, below Tail Creek, Alberta, 1867):

. . . finding a bunch of bulls right down on the river bottom near the water's edge, we made a big circuit and started the herd. They took up a deep ravine, and soon began to climb the almost perpendicular banks to the uplands above. These banks were not small affairs, but were hundreds of feet in height. In our eagerness we followed close on their heels, and some of them would stop and look around at us as if the next move would be in a charge down the steep upon us. . . . I am sure it must have taken from ten to fifteen minutes to follow those big monsters . . . up that hill. . . . I had already singled out mine, and was keeping dangerously near him, but it would not do to fire at any on such a hill; we must let them reach the top. . . . We reached the summit and the bulls jumped into a hard race at once, as if the climb had been nothing. . . .[160]

Dr. Elliott Coues thus described them (to Allen): "The buffaloes are more expert and venturesome climbers than their unwieldy forms would indicate. Upon the summits of the Sweet Grass Hills [Montana], inaccessible on horseback, and where a man can only go about by scrambling, their dung and bones are found, with those of the moun-

[156]Thompson, *Narrative*, ed. Tyrrell, 396-7.
[157]Brackenridge, *Early Western Travels*, VI, 148.
[158]Maximilian, *ibid.*, XXIII, 175.
[159]Frémont, *Narrative*, 59.
[160]McDougall, *Pathfinding*, 224; cf. De Smet (Missouri River, 1866), *Life of De Smet*, III, 850.

tain sheep. The hillsides here and the equally steep banks in places along the heads of the Milk River and its tributaries, too declivious in their natural state to afford footing to a horse or a mule, are cut by innumerable hoofs into a series of narrow terraces, each a buffalo trail. . . ."[161]

Two reliable observers specifically note a considerable speed on such occasions. Parkman, 1846, writes: ". . . over the sides of the hills long files of the frightened animals were rapidly ascending. . . ."[162] Catlin, observing buffalo who had just crossed the Missouri and were apparently not in any way frightened, mentions them "galloping up and over the bluffs. . . ."[163]

It is remarkable, however, that even the general concept of the buffalo as a swift creature in any situation finds contradiction from several witnesses, including some early ones. Sir Samuel Argall, apparently the first of English speech to observe the animals—if these were actually buffalo—in or near the Atlantic seaboard states, stated in 1613: ". . . they are easie to be killed, in regard they are heavy, slow, and not so wild as other beasts of the Wildernesse. . . ."[164] Father De Quens (south of Lake Ontario, September, 1654) records that "from those ownerless herds . . . our travellers killed eighteen cows [*vaches sauvages*] within less than an hour. . . .[165] Father Marquette, 1673, says of them: "As their legs are thick and rather Short, they do not run very fast, As a rule, except when angry. . . ."[166] Hennepin, 1680, after telling us[167] they 'are so swift that no savage can overtake them,' observes elsewhere: "Sometimes they [the Indians] would send the swiftest among them . . . who would drive whole Droves of wild Bulls before them and force them to swim the River. . . ."[168] Father Douay, 1687, described the chase as being "abundant and easy, especially for wild cattle . . .";[169] but whether he meant for horsemen or afoot is not clear.

Henry Kelsey, however, gives the earliest account known to me in English of a 'surround' made beyond doubt by footmen (August

[161]Correspondence to J. A. Allen; quoted in *American Bisons*, 159. The same phenomena are common along the Battle River, in Alberta.

[162]Parkman, *Oregon Trail*, 268.

[163]Catlin, *Letters on the North American Indians*, II, 13.

[164]*Purchas his Pilgrimes*, XIX, 91-2 (*in extenso*, chap. IX, note 39—if those are buffalo).

[165]*Jesuit Relations*, XLII, 37; cf. *ibid.*, LIX, 103, 107.

[166]*Ibid.*, LIX, 111-13 (*in extenso*, chap. IX, note 88).

[167]Hennepin, *New Discovery*, I, 150 (above in this chapter, note 131).

[168]*Ibid.*, I, 242.

[169]Douay, in *Journeys of La Salle*, I, 264.

23, 1691): "This Instant [that is, 'to-day'] ye Indians going a hunting Kill'd great store of Buffillo. Now ye manner of their hunting these Beast on ye Barren ground is when they see a great parcel of them together they surround them with men wch done they gather themselves into a smaller Compass Keeping ye Beast still in ye middle & so shooting ym till they break out at some place or other & so gett away from ym. . . ."[170] Michaux (1802) and Fortescue Cuming's informant, Captain Waller (1809), also appear to have thought them slow.[171] This, moreover, was in the same general territory (as were also, broadly, the others cited above, apart from Kelsey) of Hulbert's long-distance racers.

Seton says of the 'primitive Indian': "In winter, where the snow was deep, he could pursue the animals [that is, the buffalo] on snowshoes, and slay them easily enough. . . ."[172] This was the very thing Hearne (whose Indians were surely primitive enough) says he could not do;[173] but local circumstances might alter cases, and very probably both men are, broadly speaking, right.

The foregoing testimonies can scarcely be ignored; and yet they by no means justify the rejection of the equally circumstantial accounts of the swiftness of buffalo. The selective breeding of a superior strain of buffalo-running ponies by the prairie Indian tribes precludes any such attitude, in my view; even if the present chapter were not one long protest against any theory of 'sole explanations' of the various buffalo phenomena. On the other hand, we can hardly take literally some of the statements regarding the speed of the buffalo.[174] If their speed were so great, I cannot see how the Indians by buffalo-running on horseback could ever have accomplished much more than to secure the older and less agile animals for food. It is beyond dispute—it is in fact the head and front of their offending with more than one rigorous censor—that they did no such thing; but were satisfied with nothing less than the best except in cases of most urgent need.[175] It seems probable that Dodge furnishes the best clue to these apparent contradictions:

When travelling unmolested the buffalo is extremely careful in his choice of grades by which to pass from one creek to another; so much so indeed,

[170]*Kelsey Papers*, ed. Doughty and Martin, 13.
[171]Michaux, *Early Western Travels*, III, 234; Cuming, *ibid.*, IV, 178 (*in extenso*, chap. X, notes 45-6).
[172]Seton, *Life-Histories of Northern Animals*, I, 271.
[173]Hearne, *Journey*, 257 (above, note 133).
[174]'Few horses which can keep up with a buffalo' (E. Hough (1887!), in *Buffalo Jones' Forty Years*, 131).
[175]See below, chap. XIV, notes 32-40.

that, though a well defined buffalo-trail may not be a good wagon-road, one may rest well assured that it is the best route to be had. He seems to have a natural antipathy to the exertion of going up or down steep places. In crossing streams his instinct deserts him. He plunges in anywhere, without fear or care, and shows less sense in extricating himself from the difficulties incident to such action than any other animal, wild or tame.

His indisposition to travel over bad ground is by no means to be taken as inability to do so. When frightened he will, with perfect impunity, climb banks or plunge down precipices where it would be impossible, or certain death, for a horse to follow . . . such is his strength and power of resistance that he is rarely seriously injured by tumbles which would disable, if not kill, any other animal. . . .

A buffalo can run only about two-thirds as fast as a good horse, but what he lacks in speed he makes up in bottom or endurance, in tenacity of purpose, and in a most extraordinary vitality. . . .

If a herd is not overtaken in 500 or 600 yards, the chase had better be abandoned, if any regard is to be had for the horse. . . .

Among steep ravines or very broken ground the buffalo can travel better than the best horse. . . .[176]

After our general review of opinion, the latest generalization of all reads curiously: "The buffalo had few qualities, save massive size and gregariousness, that fitted it to the Plains. It is described *by all observers*, from Catlin on, as a stupid animal, the easiest victim to the hunter. The buffalo was slow of gait, clumsy in movement, and had relatively poor eyesight and little fear of sound. Though it had a fairly keen sense of smell, this sense was useless to it when it was approached from down the wind. . . ."[177]

It is even possible, in view of what has been urged by Hornaday and others concerning mental changes arising from the radical differences in later environmental conditions, that the super-swiftness of the animal may itself have been a modification of comparatively recent date. It may have had its origin—or pronounced development—in the utilization of the horse for buffalo-hunting by the Plains Indians. And what about hunters afoot? Despite the well-attested fleetness, of both forest and plains tribes,[178] it is difficult to conceive how footmen

[176]Dodge, *Plains of the Great West*, 122-3, 126, 127, 129; cf. *ibid.*, 424-6. Dodge's 'antipathy to steep places' may be compared with notes 153-161, above. Nothing about buffalo seems exempt from contradiction.

[177]Webb, *Great Plains*, 44, 53. The italics are mine.

[178]'Florida,' 1541: "They are so well used to runne, that without resting themselves, or standing still at all, they runne from Morning until the Evening, following a Deere, and in this manner they kill many, following them untill they tire them, and sometimes take them alive. . . ." (*Purchas his Pilgrimes*, XVII, 476). Captain John Smith, Virginia, 1607, on encompassing the game with fire: *ibid.*, XVIII, 444. Lescarbot, *History of New France* (Champlain Society ed.), III, 144. Mississippi River tribes, Hennepin, *New Discovery*, I, 147, 242; also Father

could ever have been able to encompass an animal swift enough to outstrip almost any horse. Yet we know that many tribes subsisted largely, and some almost entirely, on the buffalo before the coming of the horse among them. This fact almost forces us to some such explanation as that suggested by Dodge's account.

It is not pretended that the general opinions tentatively advanced in this chapter either exhaust the subject or offer a necessarily final explanation. But we have presented evidence based upon testimony of approximately equal authorities which, after duly allowing for possible explanatory circumstances not recorded or insufficiently emphasized, leaves a residuum of discrepancies. This variation must certainly be recognized and is, I believe, hopelessly irreconcilable with any process of facile and uniform generalization.[179]

Marest, 1710: ". . . men generally of tall stature, very lithe, and good runners, being accustomed from their tenderest youth to hunt wild beasts in the forests. . . ." (*Jesuit Relations*, LXVI, 229).

Castañeda on Indians of 'Quivira' refers to *overtaking* a soldier who 'fled from the camp on a mare' (*Journey of Coronado*, 114, 144). On Mandans and Assiniboines, 1738, *Journals of La Vérendrye*, ed. Burpee, 108. Sioux, 1801, 'extraordinarily swift': Coues (ed.), *Henry-Thompson Journals*, I, 162. On Cheyennes, Grinnell, *Fighting Cheyennes*, 1-7. Southwestern tribes (including women), Fynn, *The American Indian*, 142.

[179]A similar conclusion, *re* wood buffalo, long after the foregoing was written, in Soper, "History of the Northern Bison," 398.

CHAPTER VII

AGENCIES DESTRUCTIVE TO BUFFALO, OTHER THAN MAN. I

A GREAT deal has been said by various writers and publicists (partly expressing and, perhaps, partly creating a legend or tradition) to suggest that man, and particularly the red man, brought the buffalo to the verge of extinction by wastefulness and greed, long before the final butchery. This last, in fact, is considered by many, with reference to the period from 1849 onward, to have merely hastened an inevitable event. It may be well, therefore, to remind the reader that there were other and potent agencies inimical to the species, and to present some evidence of their workings.

The latest scientific writer on the subject whom I have been able to consult, remarks:

The primitive Indian was far from being the greatest enemy of the buffalo. Armed with bow and arrow or lance, and without the aid of a horse, he could scarcely count solely on the Buffalo for his livelihood. In winter, when snow was deep, he could pursue the animals on snow-shoes, and slay them easily enough. But there was rarely sufficient snow for this; all the circumstances precluded the possibility of great destruction of Buffalo life by this means. Moreover, the opportunities for such slaughter were confined to the north. On rare occasions, the tribes could unite and form a Buffalo pound. But there was usually a sufficiency of small game to make this great effort not worth while; and I doubt not that, before the coming of the horse and the rifle, the Red man did little harm to the great Bison herd. . . .[1] The chief enemies of the Buffalo herds, taking in[2] inverse order of importance, were blizzards, Wolves, prairie fires, bogs, the Indian, and rivers. Epidemic disease seems to have been unknown among them. . . .[3]

Seton says elsewhere, "By far the worst destroyer of the Buffalo in ancient days was treacherous ice in the spring. . . ."[4] The relative importance of other animals, fire, and water, as destroyers of the

---

[1]Seton, *Life-Histories of Northern Animals*, I, 271; also his *Game Animals*, III, 682. While I agree with Seton, it is not particularly for the reasons he gives. We shall find plentiful evidence for the buffalo usages of historic times long antedating the coming of the horse. Below, chap. XXI.

[2]So printed; but evidently 'taken in,' or 'taking them in. . . .'

[3]Seton, *Life-Histories of Northern Animals*, I, 267; but see below, Appendix J, "Buffalo and Disease."

[4]Seton, *Life-Histories of Northern Animals*, I, 271.

buffalo herds is of no significance in our present discussion. Taking them in order, we encounter, as usual, highly contradictory testimony.

1. ANIMAL FOES

Seton (as we have seen, ranks wolves among the lesser causes in the buffalo Bills of Mortality.[5] In another place in the same earlier work he considers "the number killed by wolves was not great. . . ."[6] By way of contradiction, in his later encyclopaedic production, he quotes without comment a passage from one of his premier authorities, Colonel Dodge, in which the grey wolves are described as being ". . . [excepting man] the most dangerous enemy of the Buffalo. . . ."[7] This is certainly (in reference to wolves) the very general consensus of opinion among the earlier travellers and students; and, apart from any question of inconsistency with himself, it is difficult to conceive upon what grounds Seton based any contrary opinion. Long (or Edwin James) writes, 1820: "In whatever direction they move, their parasites and dependents fail not to follow. Large herds are invariably attended by gangs of meagre, famine-pinched wolves, and flights of obscene and ravenous birds. . . ."[8]

Similar evidence is furnished by several others;[9] while more than one writer specifically alludes to the depredations of wolves among the calving cows and the young calves, as indeed one might expect if the species had any four-legged enemies at all.[10] Dr. Gregg ascribes the generally poor quality of the veal to the "scanty supply of milk which their dams afford, and to their running so much from hunters and wolves. . . ."[11]

[5]*Ibid.*, 267, above, note 3. This opinion may have been inspired or strengthened by his northern investigations. Soper states that wolves are no very serious menace among the wood buffalo. But as he points out, there is an abundance of easier prey ("History of the Northern Bison," 379, 402-3).

[6]Seton, *Life-Histories of Northern Animals*, I, 270.

[7]Seton, *Game Animals*, III, 696.

[8]Long, *Early Western Travels*, XV, 248; also 257; and *ibid.*, XVI, 140.

[9]Bradbury, *ibid.*, V, 118, 123, 147, 174; Brackenridge, *ibid.*, VI, 135; Gregg, *ibid.*, XX, 92; Catlin, *Letters on the North American Indians*, I, 253, 257; Hornaday, "Extermination of the American Bison," 422-6, 433; MacInnes, *In the Shadow of the Rockies*, 66-8, 220-1.

[10]See Charles Mackenzie, 1804, in Masson, *Les Bourgeois de la Compagnie du Nord-Ouest*, I, 331; Maximilian, 1833, *Early Western Travels*, XXIII, 249; De Smet, 1840 *seq.*, *ibid.*, XXVII, 267. According to Father De Smet, the Indians asserted that wolves slew one third of the buffalo calves annually (*Life of De Smet*, I, 205; II, 603); and compare an instance recorded above, chap. III, note 164. See also Audubon and Bachman, *American Quadrupeds*, II, 50; Marcy, *Exploration of the Red River*, 28, 104; *Buffalo Jones' Forty Years* ('the calves' worst enemy'), 248.

[11]Gregg, *Early Western Travels*, XX, 264. The richness of the milk is extolled by Long (*ibid.*, XIV, 305); also Buffalo Jones, 'infinitely richer than that of the

One can scarcely doubt that the wolves were abundant enough to be a nuisance to hunters and travellers.[12] Duncan McGillivray, on the south side of the Saskatchewan, near the present city of Prince Albert, remarks concerning them (1794): "He [that is, their hunter] carried the tongues of seven Buffaloes which he had killed, but we did not reap the benefit of his good fortune, the Wolves having devoured them in the night. . . ."[13] Wyeth, on the Platte River, 1833, likewise states: "Our company, after killing ten or twelve of them, never enjoyed the benefit of more than two of them, the rest being carried off by wolves before morning. . . ."[14] Alexander Ross also, in describing the Red River Hunt, tells us that after dark, "What then remains is lost and falls to the wolves";[15] or, according to another contemporary witness, to their almost equally savage half-bred descendants, the dogs.[16]

Richardson seems apparently to have thought such accounts over-rated; and his endorsement of what must surely have been merely general assertions by his Northland acquaintances illustrates afresh the constant need for caution in these matters. He says: "The buffalo hunters would be unable to preserve the game they kill from the wolves, if the latter were not as fearful as they are rapacious. The simple precaution of tying a handerchief to a branch, or of blowing up a bladder, and hanging it so as to wave in the wind, is sufficient to keep herds of wolves at a distance. At times, however, they are impelled by hunger to be more venturous. . . ."[17]

It is of course possible that Zebulon M. Pike, following the route of the (later) Santa Fé Trail, may have had to deal with a different and more courageous breed. He writes (October 15, 1806): "Killed two buffalo and left part of our clothing with them in order to scare away the wolves. . . ." But on the following day he notes: ". . . crossed to our two buffaloes; found a great many wolves at them, notwithstanding the precautions taken to keep them off. . . ."[18]

Jersey'; so likewise E. Hough, 1887 (in *Buffalo Jones' Forty Years*, 49, 141, 244). That of the 'cattalo' was even richer; but the nearer to the full-blooded buffalo the scantier (*ibid.*, 244); which latter supports Gregg.

[12]'Gangs,' Long, *Early Western Travels*, XV, 248; 'great gangs,' Hancock, *Narrative*, 10; 'troops,' Simpson, *Narrative of Discoveries*, 405, 407; 'dozens,' *Buffalo Jones' Forty Years*, 77.

[13]*Journal of Duncan McGillivray*, ed. Morton, 1929, 21-2.

[14]Wyeth, *Early Western Travels*, XXI, 51.

[15]Ross, *Red River Settlement*, 258.

[16]Kane, *Wanderings of an Artist* (Radisson Society ed.), 53; cf. *ibid.*, 61, 62, 82, 272.

[17]Richardson, *Fauna Boreali-Americana*, I, 63-4.

[18]Coues (ed.), *Expeditions of Pike*, II, 426. Yet in the same southern territory, we find Buffalo Jones leaving such things by his captured calves, and apparently with success, *Buffalo Jones' Forty Years*, 77, 186, 248).

In the latest era of the buffalo as a wild species, it is quite evident that wolves must have been numerous, for they furnished a living (on the northern range at least) to a tolerably large class of hunters, the 'wolfers.' Their numbers would imply that the calling paid well enough to be attractive. Their favourite method—itself clear evidence that *all* buffaloes could not outstrip a horse—was "to run a buffalo down, cut it open, throw in a dose of strychnine or arsenic, which the blood of the dying animal would carry to all parts of the body. Thus the wolves who devoured the carcass were killed, and it was believed that this was the only way in which they could be poisoned. . . ."[19] These 'wolfers' as a class were strongly opposed to the practice of the traders of furnishing the Indians with breech-loaders or repeating-rifles, thereby tending to exterminate the buffalo more rapidly; not, however, from any humane anxiety concerning the economic future of the red man, but because they feared buffalo and 'wolfing' would vanish simultaneously, as they did. The wolves increased at the expense of the range herds, until the ranchers took them in hand systematically.[20] All these things being considered, it is regrettable that Seton did not give more detailed reasons for coming to what can scarcely be re-garded as other than an untenable conclusion.

Audubon ranks the grizzly bear (*Ursus horribilis* Ord) as more dangerous to buffalo than the wolf, and next to the worst enemy, man.[21] This opinion finds considerable support from others, in par-ticular from a most authoritative source, Ernest Thompson Seton.[22] Here again, however, Seton offers practically no testimony of fact, and his testimony of opinion is somewhat contradictory.[23] Coming, as it

[19]MacInnes, *In the Shadow of the Rockies*, 66. In this they were certainly wrong. In the old days I can recall that numbers were poisoned (although the operation required great care) by strychnine poured into melted fat, which was then allowed to freeze and—unlike lean—could be bolted whole without chewing; commonly melting in the stomach before the taste could be detected. Compare Milton and Cheadle on an even more cunning animal, the wolverine (*North-West Passage*, 102-5, 109, 114-17). Yet even this was 'occasionally' poisoned or trapped (*ibid.*, 103). Sheldon, 1906, records one trapped, one poisoned (*Wilderness of Denali*, 289, 313).

[20]MacInnes, *In the Shadow of the Rockies*, 66-7, 220-1, 237; Steele, *Forty Years in Canada*, 121.

[21]Audubon and Bachman, *American Quadrupeds*, II, 50.

[22]Seton, *Game Animals*, II, 18, 24, on grizzly bears following the herds and preying on the buffalo.

[23]"The Cattle-killing Grizzly is the lineal descendant and natural heir of the Buffalo-killer. But he has an easier job, for a range steer is a light matter compared with an old Buffalo bull. Nevertheless the Grizzly could and did kill the latter . . . the only two that dared to face the Grizzly in open battle: the Buffalo bull and the Mountain Lion. . . . Deer and Buffalo in the form of carrion he always did eat, but the creatures themselves he did not kill because he could not catch

appears to do, principally from old plainsmen, it is remarkable that there is no confirmation in records of eye-witnesses, if they were so wide-spread—and hence so common—as our two great naturalists clearly imply. I have found only two direct references to bears preying on buffalo; one of which does not actually specify the grizzly,[24] while the other, although stating it to be a grizzly, tends to imply but does not specify, attack upon a living animal.[25] Of an attack under any conditions, by a grizzly bear, upon a living adult buffalo of either sex, I have found only a single recorded instance.[26] The black bear is stated to have been afraid of the buffalo.[27] And there we must leave it.

2. FIRE

While the actual amount of evidence that I have been able to collect concerning buffalo and prairie fires is not large, the fact that such evidence exists at all points to the probability that there were many similar catastrophes of which no records have survived. Hind writes as follows:

Blind buffalo are frequently found accompanying herds, and sometimes they are met with alone. Their eyes have been destroyed by prairie fires, but their quickened sense of hearing and smell, and their increased alertness, enable them to guard against danger and make it more difficult to approach them in quiet weather than those possessing sight. The hunters think that blind buffalo frequently give the alarm when they are stealthily approaching a herd in undulating country. When galloping over stony ground blind buffalo frequently fall, but when quietly feeding they avoid the stones and boulders with wonderful skill. . . .[28]

The firing of the prairies was common throughout the entire prairie buffalo range,[29] with the exception of the extreme northern (Wood) buffalo habitat—into which, apparently, Hind never penetrated. The reader, therefore, will probably share my own astonishment at learn-

them. . . ." (Seton, *Game Animals*, II, 27, 28, 71, 77.) Garretson prints a drawing (originally of 1871) of a combat between a buffalo and (apparently) a grizzly, in which the latter seems to be getting the worst of it (*American Bison*, 35). Theodore Roosevelt perhaps records Western traditional opinion *circa* 1885: suggesting the grizzly as only an occasional foe (Roosevelt, *Hunting Trips of a Ranchman*, 188).

[24]John McDonald of Garth, North Saskatchewan River, 1793. Cited below *in extenso* in another connection; see note 92.

[25]A grizzly bear devouring a calf; almost in the same locality, near Carlton, September 7, 1808 (Coues (ed.), *Henry-Thompson Journals*, II, 496).

[26]Professor John Macoun mentions one (Hand Hills, Alberta, 1877) 'caught in the act' of killing a buffalo cow (*Manitoba*, 337).

[27]Seton, *Game Animals*, II, 185.

[28]Hind, *Report, 1858*, 107. See below, Appendix I, p. 828.

[29]See below, Appendix K, "Buffalo and the formation of Prairie Lands."

ing that in all the not inconsiderable buffalo-reminiscence, travel-literature, or scientific generalization I have consulted, I have not found—with but one single exception, to be noted—an allusion to buffalo blinded in this way. Nor have I found any reference to the characteristics associated with them by Hind, nor to any hunters' tales concerning them; nor even to one solitary instance of any living animal, either alone or in company with a herd, being discovered, or so much as supposed, to be blind. Yet the phenomena attendant upon prairie or bush fires must have been familiar to every old plainsman, red or white. I cannot pretend to have attained exhaustiveness in my researches, but it is none the less curious that so little has survived concerning this subject. The one year in which blind buffalo are actually noted is 1804, and by two witnesses. Charles Mackenzie, on a journey from Fort Assiniboine (near Brandon, Manitoba) to the Missouri (October 11-24, 1804), writes: "In the course of a few days, we observed whole herds of buffaloes with their hair singed; some were blind, and half-roasted carcasses strewed our way. . . ."[30]

The younger Henry is more circumstantial (November 25, 1804): ". . . plains burned in every direction and blind buffalo seen every moment wandering about. The poor beasts have all the hair singed off, even the skin in many places is shriveled up and terribly burned, and their eyes are swollen and closed fast. It was really pitiful to see them staggering about, sometimes running afoul of a large stone, at other times tumbling down hill and falling into creeks not yet frozen over. In one spot we found a whole herd lying dead. . . . [we have] seen an incredible number of dead and dying, blind, lame, singed and roasted buffalo."[31] Rundle (Little Red Deer country, central Alberta, May 19, 1847) remarks: "It was about this time we saw the burnt buffalo. They had perished in the flames the preceding fall of the year, when that part of the country was on fire. They must have rushed through the flames, till overcome with the heat, they sank in the last gasp of agony. These poor animals probably under the Divine Providence, were the means of saving the lives of some Indians who were driven from the woods by starvation. . . ."[32] Denny records a stampede

[30]In Masson, *Les Bourgeois de la Compagnie du Nord-Ouest*, I, 328. 'Plains all burnt,' Souris River to the Missouri (Larocque, *ibid.*, I, 301); cf. *Harmon's Journal* (1804), 90.

[31]Coues (ed.), *Henry-Thompson Journals*, I, 253.

[32]*Rundle's Journal*, *sub die*. Denny (MS., 43) says that blind buffalo acted as sentinels, having exceptionally keen scent, but gives no instances. This is, obviously, from Hind. Denny cites no material not in the Alberta Legislative Library, Edmonton, and unfortunately omits much that is.

during a prairie fire, along the Bow River, 1876: ". . . a large number were driven in the blind rush away from the fire right over the cut bank west of our camp and plunged in a bellowing mass down some hundreds of feet on to the rocky shores of the river. . . ."[33]

There is nothing surprising in an easily affrighted animal being panic-stricken in such situations, and our knowledge of the terrible havoc wrought by prairie fires among range cattle[34] enables us readily to conceive its horrors to a species so much more heavily clothed with hair about the head and body; and particularly at so late a time as November, when Henry saw them, and when the winter coat was full-grown.[35] But I am sceptical about the 'blind guides.' Denny's statement presented as a *fact*, is only 'what the hunters think' in Hind; and it is doubtful whether the average buffalo needed any powers of super-scent to assist it in detecting the approach of enemies.

3. WATER

Finally, we shall deal with the last and most important item in Thompson Seton's classification—water. It will be found that the testimony of experienced eye-witnesses concerning this will not only seriously discount once again the supposed intelligence of the buffalo, but will be seen to be hopelessly irreconcilable with some of the essential and fundamental concepts of the 'buffalo trail' theory itself. I have referred above to the powers of the buffalo as a swimmer, as indicating that the ford (that is, the 'shallow') was not essential as a crossing-place. Catlin has left us a most graphic description illustrative of this, which I quote:

In one instance, near the mouth of the White River, we met the most immense herd crossing the Missouri River, and from an imprudence got our boat into imminent danger amongst them, from which we were highly delighted to make our escape. It was in the midst of the 'running season,' and we had heard the 'roaring' (as it is called) of the herd when we were several miles from them. When we came in sight, we were actually terrified at the immense numbers that were streaming down the green hills on one side of the river, and galloping up over the bluffs on the other. The river

[33]Denny MS., 40.

[34]See MacInnes, *In the Shadow of the Rockies*, 111, 220. He mentions 1901 as a bad year in Southern Alberta (p. 220). We had practically no fires in the Red Deer Canyon country from 1898 (our worst year) until 1905; for reasons given in detail in my paper, "The Extermination of the Buffalo in Western Canada" (*Canadian Historical Review*, XV, 1934, 1-23). See also below, Appendix J, "Buffalo and Disease."

[35]See Hornaday, "Extermination of the American Bison," 412-14; also above, chap. V, "The Buffalo Year."

was filled and in parts blackened with their heads and horns, as they were swimming about, following up their objects, and making desperate battle whilst they were swimming. I deemed it imprudent for our canoe to be dodging amongst them, and we ran it ashore for a few hours, where we laid, waiting for the opportunity of seeing the river clear, but we waited in vain. Their numbers, however, got somewhat diminished at last, and we pushed off, and successfully made our way amongst them. From the immense numbers that had passed the river at that place, they had torn the prairie bank of fifteen feet in height, so as to form a sort of road or landing-place, where they all in succession clambered up. Many in their turmoil had been wafted below this landing, and unable to regain it against the swiftness of the current, had fastened themselves along in crowds, hugging close to the high bank under which they were standing. As we were drifting by these, and supposing ourselves out of danger, I drew up my rifle and shot one of them in the head, which tumbled into the water, and brought with him a hundred others, which plunged in, and in a moment were swimming about our canoe, and placing it in great danger.[36] No attack was made upon us, and in the confusion the poor beasts knew not, perhaps, the enemy that was amongst them; but we were liable to be sunk by them as they were furiously hooking and climbing onto each other. I rose in my canoe, and by my gestures and hallooing kept them from coming in contact with us until we were out of their reach. . . .[37]

Lewis and Clark record a somewhat similar occurrence, also on the Missouri, August, 1806: "A herd happened to be on their way across the river. Such was the multitude of these animals, that although the river, including an island over which they passed, was a mile in length [sic], the herd stretched as thick as they could swim completely from one side to the other and the party was obliged to stop for an hour. . . ."[38] Some forty-five miles farther downstream, "two other herds, as numerous as the first," crossed the river;[39] and on another occasion, "the boats escaped with difficulty between two herds of buffalo which were crossing. . . ."[40] H. M. Brackenridge, travelling with the Astorians west-bound for a distance, also mentions buffalo swimming the Missouri in the summer of 1811;[41] which he elsewhere specifies as a wet season, with high water.[42] Prince Maximilian notes the

[36]Note above, the anxiety of Jerry Potts concerning gunfire (chap. VI, note 102).

[37]Catlin, *Letters on the North American Indians*, II, 13-14. Garretson records a similar experience of a Missouri River steamboat captain; the distance through the herd (which necessitated frequently stopping the boat) being over four miles. *American Bison*, 61-2.

[38]*Lewis and Clark Journals*, III, 237.

[39]*Ibid.*

[40]*Ibid.*, 238.

[41]Brackenridge, *Early Western Travels*, VI, 109.

[42]*Ibid.*, 132.

same condition in July, 1833,[43] and 'buffalo and antelope' again in the spring of 1834, near Fort Mandan.[44] These movements across so turbulent a stream were not invariably mass-impulses, for Bradbury (with the Astorians, 1811) observed three cows and a calf swimming across.[45]

Similar movements are recorded along several of the greater rivers of the continent. Charlevoix, in October, 1721, mentions "a great Number of Buffaloes, crossing the [Illinois] River in a great Hurry. . . ."[46] as also does Diron d'Artaguiette, two years later.[47] The latter explorer had seen them swim the mighty Mississippi itself, three months previously,[48] as also, apparently, had Hennepin, over a generation earlier (1680).[49] Captain Bonneville saw them crossing the Yellowstone in August, 1833.[50] The younger Henry, at his post on the upper Red River, notes (April 20, 1802), "Buffalo in abundance on the East side of the Red river and crossing opposite the fort. . . ."[51]

Concerning the two great western rivers of the Canadian habitat, our information is fairly full. Palliser found buffalo plentiful 'on both sides' of the South Saskatchewan, near the 'Elbow' (52° N., 107° W.) in September, 1857.[52] Hind saw them crossing near there in July, 1858;[53] and Southesk in July, 1859.[54] Denny, at some point below Calgary, in the autumn of 1874, saw "some thousands of buffalo swimming across the Bow River [that is, the South Saskatchewan], which at this point was a considerable stream and very swift. . . ."[55]

On the North Saskatchewan, they were observed by Mitchell Oman, in 1780 or 1781; perhaps below the Forks, where the feat would be a veritable trial of strength, unless the stream was exceptionally low.[56] Cocking also remarks them 'swimming the [Saskatchewan?] river,' September 2, 1772.[57] Alexander Henry, junior, noticed them swimming (northward) across that river in September, 1808,[58] and

[43]Maximilian, ibid., XXIII, 37.   [44]Ibid., XXIV, 86.
[45]Bradbury, ibid., V, 92.
[46]Allen, American Bisons, 106.
[47]Journal, June 30, 1723 (in Mereness (ed.), Colonial Travels, 83).
[48]March 19, 1723 (ibid., 62).
[49]Hennepin, New Discovery, I, 146, 242.
[50]Irving, Captain Bonneville, 301.
[51]Coues (ed.), Henry-Thompson Journals, I, 95.
[52]Palliser Journals, 55.
[53]Hind, Report, 1858, 52, 57, 63.
[54]Southesk, Travels, 78.
[55]Denny MS., 198.
[56]Cited by Thompson, Narrative, ed. Tyrrell, 322.
[57]"Cocking's Journal," ed. Burpee, 105.
[58]Coues (ed.), Henry-Thompson Journals, II, 490, 494-6, 504.

again in August, 1810.[59] In June, 1810, below Edmonton, David
Thompson relates: "As we descended many herds of the Bison were
crossing as the whim took them. They swim well, though slowly. . . ."[60]
Franklin's party, in 1820, noted their swimming powers.[61] Rundle
observed them crossing the Saskatchewan in October, 1840, but does
not indicate their direction.[62] Paul Kane saw them swimming the river
southward, May 26, 1848;[63] and Milton and Cheadle mention them
crossing northward near Carlton, in September, 1862.[64] As with the
Missouri, these were not invariably mass-movements; the instances
recorded by Henry in 1808 and 1810 mention 'six bulls' and 'twelve
cows' respectively.[65]

It must be considered remarkable that despite the conventional
view of these movements as 'regular migrations' in which the buffalo
forded the rivers on their routes at the same—and therefore presumably well-known—places, 'nothing being allowed to stop them,' many
of those who actually witnessed these passages regarded the sight as
an outstanding experience. This includes some who subscribed to the
aforementioned belief. Irving writes as follows (Yellowstone River,
1833): "It was a singular spectacle by the uncertain moonlight to behold this countless throng making their way across the river blowing
and bellowing, and splashing. Sometimes they pass in such dense and
continuous columns as to form a temporary dam across the river, the
waters of which rise and rush over their backs or between their squadrons. The roaring and rushing sound of one of these vast herds crossing a river, may sometimes, in a still night, be heard for miles. . . ."[66]

One perhaps need not be surprised at Irving (or his informants),[67]
Denny,[68] or John McDonald of Garth,[69] all of whom (when they wit-

[59]*Ibid.*, 618.
[60]Thompson, *Narrative*, 433.
[61]Franklin, (First) *Journey to the Polar Sea*, 197.
[62]*Rundle's Journal* (one week below Edmonton), October 11, 1840.
[63]Kane, *Wanderings of an Artist* (Radisson Society ed.), 292, 293; cf. *ibid.*,
82.
[64]Milton and Cheadle, *North-West Passage*, 59.
[65]Coues (ed.), *Henry-Thompson Journals*, II, 490, 618.
[66]Irving, *Captain Bonneville*, 301.
[67]Irving wrote from the papers of Bonneville and the Astorians, supplemented
by personal observation during his prairie tour of 1832.
[68]Denny MS., 198.
[69]*In extenso* below, note 92. He had then been only a year or so in the West.
See Bryce, *Remarkable History*, 161; MacInnes, *In the Shadow of the Rockies*, 40;
Wallace, "Biographical Dictionary of the Nor-Westers" in *Documents Relating to
the North West Company*, 464. In 1805, after fourteen years, McDonald's tone
is much less excited. On the South Saskatchewan River, from the 'Elbow' towards
Chesterfield House, he writes: "Almost run over by the buffaloes at our camp-

nessed such sights) were new to the buffalo country, writing in such a strain. But John McDougall, despite his lengthy experience, characterizes as 'a unique sight' the spectacle of some thousands crossing the North Saskatchewan some 200 miles below Edmonton, in July, 1863.[70] Yet according to the orthodox shibboleths on this topic, however 'unique' it might be to a newcomer in 1863, it should have been so no longer when McDougall wrote his book in 1896; for during nearly twenty years after 1863 he had, of course, only to proceed to the 'regular crossing-place' to witness the same performance twice a year or so!

It is equally strange that if buffalo had been following their regular routes from time immemorial, an observer so late as *circa* 1832 should be privileged to witness them (as Catlin relates above[71]) in the act of 'tearing down' a new road, or—perhaps even more remarkable—of getting off the track and finding themselves without any exit from the river-bed. The physical (that is, topographical) explanation of these facts is quite simple, and its truth will readily be recognized by Western readers or observant visitors. But it plays havoc with the legendary jargon concerning buffalo trails and fords.

In many—perhaps most—instances, our Western streams meander in crooked reaches from one side to the other of valleys sometimes very much more than a mile in breadth and usually deep; of which the actual streams may not occupy more than a quarter, or a tenth, or—as with the Battle River, for example—perhaps even less than a twentieth of the lateral area. Along the convex outer side of these curving reaches, the current in flood time sweeps with great force, scooping out the mud until the bank at such places is perpendicular or even somewhat concave. The direction of the curve frequently changes so suddenly in the smaller streams and creeks that within a few yards one may find a steep perpendicular bank and again an easy slope down to the river's brink, constituting in everything but depth—which depends upon recent weather conditions or rain, or heat in the case of mountain streams—a natural ford. But a natural approach and a natural easy exit facing each other on the opposite sides of such a stream are

ment. This is their rutting season also, and coming down like an avalanche, those behind pushed the others down the banks. We were obliged to keep on large fires and fire guns to keep them off. They came sometimes a few yards from our tents and canoes. . . ." (In Masson, *Les Bourgeois de la Compagnie du Nord-Ouest*, II, 30.) Compare Charles Mackenzie almost on the same day, 1805, northward-bound from the Missouri to the Souris River (*ibid.*, I, 251).

[70]McDougall, *Saddle, Sled and Snowshoe*, 63. Swimming not specified; this dependent upon the season.

[71]Above, note 37.

almost a physical impossibility. It is more common to find that both sides are in need of some 'cutting down' with a spade, as very high waters will even wash away portions of the narrow 'beaches' on the shallower side. At such places, I have witnessed young cattle jumping into deep water rather than take the ford, much as Dodge remarks concerning buffalo.[72] Since a flood season, of varying degrees of volume, occurs during some portion of practically every summer, the perpendicular or hollow banks will fall sooner or later of their own weight to the natural angle of repose, and will, of course, do so more readily if heavy animals walk too near the edge, as they very easily might among the lush and marshy grass common in such spots. These hide the exact margin very often; I have gone to swim in such creeks and have more than once found myself sliding over the brink into deep water before I was aware of my precise position. So far as heavier creatures are concerned, Henri Joutel says: "One of our horses, going along the edge of an upright bank, fell into the water . . ."; and caused them some ado to get it out again (1687).[73]

The frequent or general occurrence of these conditions throughout the prairie buffalo habitat is clearly shown by a number of allusions. Nuttall (1819) thus describes the 'bends' of the Arkansas River: "As in the Mississippi, the current sets with the greatest force against the centre of the curves; the banks of which are nearly perpendicular and subject to a perpetual state of dislocation."[74] Edwin James, of Long's expedition, 1820, notes the 'falling-in banks' of the Kansas River.[75] Dr. Gregg extends the process beyond water-courses. He speaks of the 'narrow breaks or ravines with overhanging banks'; and says "the tenacious turf of the buffalo grass retains the marginal surface and causes this. . . ."[76] Bradbury, who travelled along the Missouri River country with the Astorians, twenty years before Gregg, remarks: "In the valleys, the land floods, during the rainy season, have worn channels so deep and with the sides so precipitous, that a traveller is often under the necessity of proceeding a mile or two along one of these ravines before he can cross it. . . ."[77]

I am convinced that this is no exaggeration. Catlin records a personal experience along one of the creek beds. It was a deep creek;

[72]*In extenso* above, chap. VI, note 176.
[73]Joutel, in *Journeys of La Salle*, II, 116.
[74]Nuttall, *Early Western Travels*, XIII, 100.
[75]Long, *ibid.*, XIV, 185, 219.
[76]Gregg, *ibid.*, XX, 240, 241.
[77]Bradbury, *ibid.*, V, 71. Cf. Richardson's general remarks on this, in Franklin, (First) *Journey to the Polar Sea*, Appendix I, 499.

and, after walking 'many miles' looking for a ford, he swam his horse over, but found the bank too steep for the poor animal to clamber out. He was almost in despair when the lucky discovery of one of the 'roads, torn down by the buffalo' (after the manner of a city subway where the street level has had to be depressed in order to secure clearance overhead) solved his difficulty.[78] According to Parkman, such places were a favourite lair for the hunter in the old days: "The farther bank was about four or five feet high, and quite perpendicular, being cut away by the water in spring. . . . The hunter crouches under the bank . . . he sees a motion among the long weeds and grass just at the spot where the path is channelled through the bank. . . . Half sliding, half plunging, down comes the buffalo upon the river-bed below. . . ."[79] The reader may compare the younger Henry (on the 'Scratching River,' southern Manitoba, August, 1800): "We amused ourselves by lying in wait close under the bank, for the buffaloes which came to drink. When the poor brutes came to within about ten yards of us, on a sudden we would fire a volley of twenty-five guns at them, killing and wounding many, of which we took only the tongues. . . ."[80]

As might be expected, such places are not confined to one continent. An African traveller notes at least one "perpendicular bank, caused by the erosion in a hairpin bend. . . ."[81] One reads a good deal in travel-literature about the changeableness of fords, river-currents, and the like, but few non-geological observers have attempted to exhibit the processes. Yet in such places, erosion must surely be a prominent factor. Dr. Gregg notes the necessity for marking the ford of the Arkansas (on the Santa Fé Trail) with stakes to avoid the quicksands,[82] evidently suggesting that the river-bed was changeable. On the same river ten years previously, Long's secretary and historian, Edwin James, relates how, by turning slightly aside from an impassable spot, where one of their party was nearly drowned in the saddle, they got across without much difficulty.[83] J. K. Townsend in 1833 forded the Green (Colorado) River easily; at fifty yards' distance it was unfordable.[84] Near the Big Bend of the Missouri, in the same year (1833)

---

[78]Catlin, *Letters on the North American Indians,* II, 94. Henry records very similar experiences on the Park, Salt, and Turtle rivers (Coues (ed.), *Henry-Thompson Journals,* I, 134, 137, 138, 285, 313).

[79]Parkman, *Oregon Trail,* 419, 420.

[80]Coues (ed.), *Henry-Thompson Journals,* I, 67.

[81]Maxwell, *Stalking Big Game with a Camera,* 165.

[82]Gregg, *Early Western Travels,* XIX, 214.

[83]Long, *ibid.,* XVI, 249.

[84]Townsend, *ibid.,* XXI, 189.

Maximilian observed an island which had been formed after Lewis and Clark passed the spot in 1804-6.[85]

The bearing of historical and physical data of this character upon the supposed principles of the buffalo migration-route is obvious. Momentarily assuming, for the sake of the argument, that buffalo throughout their territory habitually followed the same routes to the same crossing-places, it is not difficult to visualize the possible results. Their trails must frequently have led them to places where last year's (or last spring's) 'wonderfully sagacious' easy ford with its 'road' had been washed away and, in order to attain the easy exit perhaps still visible on the farther shore they had to hurl themselves into a deep and raging torrent whose swiftness (as in Catlin's actual recital) took them far down the stream where they were confronted by a precipitous bank. They might easily enough by sheer weight 'tear a road' *down* to the water anywhere, but Catlin very plainly indicates an inability, in very many at least, to 'tear' such a road *up* the bank after crossing. It is the very keynote of the traditional buffalo-trail thesis that these roads—even if they had escaped the eroding influence of the flood times—were not to be found everywhere along the river-banks; they were only discoverable at certain selected spots—the best, of course, in the 'wonderful natural engineer' tradition. I have shown furthermore that the places where last year's road still remained on the hither side, inviting them—needlessly, of course, for they 'never swerved' in any case—by its easy access to the water's edge, are by reason of physical causes precisely the places most likely to lead to a high perpendicular bank on the farther shore. This is demonstrable by observation at the present day. I see no way to escape the conclusion that high water or flood in our Western rivers reduces the orthodox buffalo-trail dogmas to absurdity. It is an historical fact that large numbers of animals were drowned, as we shall shortly see; and, unless this was caused by some such occasional condition as high water, it is hard to understand how any got safely across. This means that the 'buffalo ford' was useless to many of its makers at the precise moment when they needed it most. At low water, of course, most of the rivers in the western Plains buffalo habitat could be crossed almost anywhere.

Although there seems to be no reasonable doubt that buffalo—possibly in considerable numbers—were drowned in summer time as a result of their own impetuosity under conditions such as those

[85]Maximilian, *ibid.*, XXII, 312; cf. on the Upper Mississippi, Coues (ed.), *Expeditions of Pike*, I, 56-60, 310.

described by Lewis and Clark and by Father Lacombe;[86] yet the great mass-destruction by water (or at least by rivers) would appear from the records of various observers to have occurred principally in the spring; and it may no doubt be ascribed to what Thompson Seton ranks as the worst enemy, 'treacherous ice.'[87] It is true that Paul Kane, the artist, on the North Saskatchewan between Edmonton and Carlton remarked (May 25, 1848): "We saw great numbers of dead buffaloes along the shore of the river, which from the long continuance of the snow covering the herbage, had become so exhausted, that they were drowned in attempting to swim across the river, in their accustomed migration to the south every spring, and now lay in thousands along the banks. . . ."[88]

Kane was of course a stranger; and we have no means of knowing whether the cause he assigns was based upon local information, or was pure assumption on his part or on the part of his companions from Edmonton. His remarks on 'long continuance of snow' point to a hard winter in 1847-48, and hence very possibly to a later break-up of the river ice than usual—these buffalo having perhaps perished in the icy waters in the more 'normal' spring-tide fashion. Buffalo certainly appear to have been plentiful along the Saskatchewan that winter,[89] which generally (but, as we shall see, not invariably) meant a hard winter; on the other hand, snow, if the animals had shelter, does not appear to have necessarily entailed starvation.

Certainly the great season for drowned buffalo was at the spring thaw; and, in many instances, these had probably met their doom some months previously by breaking through the ice. John McDonnell, descending the Qu'Appelle River, remarks in his Journal (May 18, 1795): "Observing a good many carcasses of buffaloes in the river and along its banks, I was taken up the whole day with counting them and, to my surprise, found I had numbered when we put up at night, 7360, drowned and mired along the river and in it. It is true, in one or two places, I went on shore and walked from one carcass to the other, where they lay from three to five files deep. . . ."[90]

Such recorded numbers find abundant corroboration. John Mc-

[86]Above, chap. VI, notes 58, 59.

[87]Above, note 4.

[88]Kane, *Wanderings of an Artist* (Radisson Society ed.), 292. Cf. Henry (1809): "Upwards of sixty dead buffalo seen; at this season [April] many are so weak that if they lie down they cannot rise . . ." (Coues (ed.), *Henry-Thompson Journals*, II, 594).

[89]Richardson, *Arctic Expedition, 1847-1850*, 38, 42.

[90]McDonnell, in Masson, *Les Bourgeois de la Compagnie du Nord-Ouest*, I, 294; cf. above, note 24.

Donald of Garth remarks concerning the Saskatchewan (above Carlton in 1793): "It was a grand Sight to me to see such a Grand River, the innumerable herds of Buffaloes and Deers & many grizle Bears on its Banks feeding & crossing in such numbers that we often got our canoes amongst them and shot hundreds without need.[91] There lay sometimes upward of a thousand dead on some low points drowned while crossing in Spring on the ice & washed ashore. Amongst them were to be seen often the Bears feeding upon the carcasses. . . ."[92]

The younger Henry also remarks (Red River, April, 1801) that 'drowned buffalo continue to drift by in whole herds throughout the month, and toward the end for two days and nights their dead bodies formed one continuous line in the current.' Thousands grounded along the bank; and the stench was so offensively strong that sometimes he could not eat because of it. The Indians told him that every spring it was 'about the same.'[93] It may doubtless be considered an indication of the variation in seasons, and probably also in the numbers wintering along the Red River, that Henry observes (March 25, 1803): "Very few drowned buffalo this spring."[94]

If so many buffalo were drowned in comparatively small rivers such as the Qu'Appelle or the Red, one cannot wonder that the spectacle drew notice on the mighty Missouri. Charles Mackenzie, at the Mandan villages, November, 1804 to April, 1805, notes: "Buffaloes and other animals are in immense numbers destroyed every winter by the Mississouri [sic] Indians. In stormy weather, whole droves run from the mountains and plains to seek shelter in the woods which form the margin of the Mississouri; many of them, attempting to cross when the ice is weak, sink and are drowned, and, in the spring, both sides of the river are in several places covered with rotten carcases and skeletons of buffaloes, elks, &c. . . ."[95]

These catastrophes were not always due to 'natural causes.' Mac-

[91]A not uncommon amusement; see Catlin, *Letters on the North American Indians*, II, 13-14; Irving, *Astoria*, 179; *Captain Bonneville*, 301; also Alexander Henry, above, note 80.

[92]"Memoir," of John McDonald of Garth, which I have not seen; quoted by A. S. Morton (ed.), *Journal of Duncan McGillivray*, introd., xlvii. The words above between 'innumerable' and 'need' (in a different spelling and capitalization, and followed by a hiatus or lacuna) are given (from McDonald) in Masson, *Les Bourgeois de la Compagnie du Nord-Ouest*, II, 18. See also *re* the Saskatchewan River (1846), Kane, *Wanderings of an Artist*, 75.

[93]Coues (ed.), *Henry-Thompson Journals*, I, 174-7. Coues (ed. note, I, 174) cites McDonnell (above, note 90), as corroborating Henry.

[94]*Ibid.*, 210. Compare below, note 98.

[95]Mackenzie, in Masson, *Les Bourgeois de la Compagnie du Nord-Ouest*, I, 337.

kenzie again, in a later expedition to the Mandans, November, 1805 to February, 1806, tells us:

The winter being far advanced and considerable drifts of snow on the ground, thousands of buffaloes resorted to the vicinity of the villages.[96] We had great pleasure in seeing the Indians go into the fields, surround and kill whole droves of them; the best parts only of the meat were taken home, the rest remaining to rot in the field. At times the Indians would congregate in great numbers and continue to drive large herds to the banks of the Missis-souri and, by gradual approaches, confine them into a narrow space where the ice was weakest, until, by their weight and pressure, large square[s] of ice, some of fifty yards, would give way and vast numbers of animals were plunged into the river and carried by the current under the solid ice to a 'mare' a little below, where they again emerged, floated and were received by crowds of women and children, provided with proper hooks and instruments to haul them on the ice, which, in a short time, became strewed with dead carcasses. Here they were left for some time to take flavor, then carried home and considered a great delicacy. . . .[97]

Mackenzie further informs us:

These dead animals, which often float down the current for hundreds of miles, are preferred by the Natives to any other kind of food. . . . So fond are the Mandans of putrid meat that they bury animals whole in the winter for consumption in the spring.
The water of the Mississourie [sic] this spring [1805] was uncommonly low, and in consequence drowned animals were not so abundant as usual at the breaking up of navigation.[98] However there were still plenty, and I had opportunity of observing the courage and dexterity of the young Mandanes among the floating ice, hauling ashore some scores of these nauseous carcasses, while the women, as active as they, were securing all the drift-wood within their reach for fire.
The Mandanes are excellent swimmers; I was no less surprised to see in the drift ice the men occasionally leap from one block to another, often falling between, plunging under, darting up elsewhere and securing themselves upon very slippery flakes; yet no serious accident happened. The women performed their part equally well; you would see them slip out of their leather smoks, despising danger, plunge into the troubled deep to secure their object. Nor did they seem to feel the smallest inconvenience from the presence of crowds who lined the beach. The men and women of this place do not seem to think it necessary to sew fig leaves together to make themselves aprons, and they are not ashamed to appear naked in public. . . .[99]

Mackenzie's recital finds confirmation in every particular. Brad-

[96]Compare this with McDonnell (1799): "There is so little snow at the Missouri that the natives run down the buffalos on horseback the entire winter . . ." (ibid., 272). This in Dakota!
[97]Mackenzie, ibid., 366.
[98]Cf. Henry, in the spring of 1803; above, note 94.
[99]Mackenzie, in Masson, Les Bourgeois de la Compagnie du Nord-Ouest, I,

bury, with the Astorians along the Missouri, noted many drowned buffalo near Leavenworth, April 16, 1811;[100] and on May 27 he remarked that 'the putrefying carcasses were very offensive.'[101] Maximilian also observed 'dead cows' floating down the Missouri in June, 1833,[102] and he states elsewhere: 'Whole herds were often drowned in the Missouri, and in some rivers, 1800 or more dead bodies have been found in one place. . . .' Later: "Complete dams are formed of the bodies of these animals in some of the morasses of the rivers; from this we may form some idea of the decrease of the buffaloes. . . ."[103] Maximilian corroborates the Mandan liking for putrid flesh,[104] as also does Henry (1806).[105] This has been noted as characteristic[106] of several Indian tribes.

The Missouri must have had an evil (and wide) reputation at an early date; for Flagg, who seems to have gone no farther west than St. Louis, mentions in 1836 that "Dead bodies are sometimes found floating upon the Missouri far down its course. . . ."[107]

The readiness of buffalo to take to the ice has been noted by many observers, and furnishes once again a curious commentary upon 'intelligence.' It has been recorded by Lewis and Clark,[108] and also by

337. Maximilian noted their skill in the water (*Early Western Travels*, XXIII, 346). Their immodesty is emphasized by Henry (Coues (ed.), *Henry-Thompson Journals*, I, 325); Thompson (*Narrative*, 234); and Gass (*Journal of the Lewis and Clark Expedition*, 72). Contra, Catlin (*circa* 1835) found them guarded, 'arrow on string,' while bathing (*Letters on the North American Indians*, I, 96, 121, 195-7).

[100]Bradbury, *Early Western Travels*, V, 68, 99; cf. Irving, *Astoria*, 141, 179.

[101]Bradbury, *Early Western Travels*, V, 68, 99.

[102]Maximilian, *ibid.*, XXII, 341.

[103]*Ibid.*, 382. I have since found the following from N. M. W. J. McKenzie (Hudson's Bay Company, Fort Ellice, 1876-1916): "I saw where buffalo in the fall had tried to cross the [South] Saskatchewan River, and had broken through the ice. Carcasses of dead buffalo completely bridged the river, the remainder of the herd passing over them. Buffalo always followed the leader like sheep . . ." (*The Beaver*, Hudson's Bay Company, December, 1920, 13-15). Sir George Simpson wrote (July, 1841): "In the year 1829 . . . I saw as many as ten thousand of their putrid carcases lying mired in a single ford of the Saskatchewan, and contaminating the air for many miles around . . ." (*Journey around the World*, I, 92). In March, 1866, Welsh mentions a herd of 1000 breaking through the ice of the South Saskatchewan River, and being frozen in (*The Last Buffalo Hunter*, 85). Perhaps McKenzie's herd.

[104]*Early Western Travels*, XXII, 346.

[105]Coues (ed.), *Henry-Thompson Journals*, I, 341.

[106]W. F. Wentzel and Geo. Keith (Northern tribes, 1807): in Masson, *Les Bourgeois de la Compagnie du Nord-Ouest*, I, 85; II, 69; Audubon and Bachman, *American Quadrupeds*, II, 41; McDougall, *Saddle, Sled and Snowshoe*, 132; *Western Trails*, 236.

[107]Flagg, *Early Western Travels*, XXVI, 280.

[108]*Lewis and Clark Journals*, I, 199.

Father De Smet,[109] along the Missouri; and by the younger Henry, on the Upper Saskatchewan between Rocky Mountain House and Kootenay Plain, in February, 1811.[110] The only description of the buffalo method of crossing ice—that I have seen—is from McDougall (January, 1875):

It was at this time that I saw the wonderful instinct of the buffalo in crossing an ice-bound river. The ice was very smooth and glassy, and many score jumped the high bank at the mouth of Ghost River and made to cross the Bow. I sat on my horse and thought they would balk at the smooth ice; but, to my great astonishment, the wise animals bunched to the centre, and in a packed, dense mass, went skating and sliding across the smooth ice to the other bank without a tumble. They braced each other across the hundred yards or more of glassy ice, and went on the run up the other bank as if this was a common experience in their history, and again I said to myself, "How wonderful is instinct. . . ."[111]

Taking the above as it stands, without comparative data of any kind, one might unhesitatingly endorse McDougall's verdict; but on the very same hunting-trip he describes a herd of 'sixty or seventy' (also on the Upper Bow) jumping the bank in the manner indicated, and sliding out on the smooth ice and into a deep hole in the stream, in which all were drowned.[112] Furthermore, it is impossible to doubt that this very process of 'bunching' must in many instances have been the cause of buffalo being drowned when the ice broke under them on frozen lakes. This is well attested, as, for example: "One winter a herd of nearly 100 buffaloes attempted to cross a lake called 'Lac-qui-parle' in Minnesota, upon the ice, which gave way and drowned the entire herd. . . ."[113]

McDougall himself (April, 1864) notes: "We passed Fort Pitt, and . . . came to Jackfish Lake, where we found the camp of Salteaux that frequented this lake feasting on the carcases of a great herd of buffalo that had been drowned in the lake the previous winter. Too many had got together in some stampede across the ice and had broken through and were drowned; and now that the ice was off the lake, the carcases were drifting ashore. . . ."[114]

What McDougall extols as 'wonderful instinct,' Allen designates

---

[109]*Life of De Smet*, III, 852.
[110]Coues (ed.), *Henry-Thompson Journals*, II, 682, 690.
[111]McDougall, *Western Trails*, 237.
[112]*Ibid.*, 236.
[113]Allen, *American Bisons*, 62; also Hornaday, "Extermination of the American Bison," 420-1.
[114]McDougall, *Saddle, Sled and Snowshoe*, 132.

as 'reckless fearlessness.'[115] The instinct which supposedly taught them that safety lay in numbers did not always prevent them from venturing when few. At the same Jackfish Lake, in December, 1857, Dr. Hector relates: "The slipperiness of the ice . . . was turned to good account the other day by the Indians, as they drove a band of buffalo cows so that they had to go out on the ice of the lake, when of course they fell and stumbled, and could make no progress, while their pursuers, approaching on foot, with ease killed the whole, to the number of fourteen."[116] Rundle relates very similar occurrences in the Beaver Hills country eastward from Edmonton: "A herd of buffalo appeared on a small lake which was partially covered with snow, so that travelling over it was very difficult. The consequence was that one of the buffalo, a cow, fell on the ice and was soon despatched. . . ."[117]

These winter-time propensities of the buffalo are significant in relation to the buffalo-trail theory. To those who know how topographical details may be obliterated by a winter of heavy snow and incessant driving storms and blizzards, there will be no difficulty whatever in realizing that such winter crossings might be attempted over some of the deepest reaches, or most dangerous eddies, or most hopeless quicksands. The hard-packed ice of the winter-made trail—invariably, from its nature, the last to disappear in the spring—if treated by some unwary early traveller as a 'path to the ford,' might lead him straight to disaster.

Collateral evidence of the readiness of other animals than buffalo to face what would seem to be deep reaches of the rivers, in the water or over the ice, is furnished in a curious Letter or Report to Lord Selkirk from Miles Macdonell, Selkirk's first Governor at Red River. Writing from York Factory, May 31, 1812, Macdonell says: "From 27th April to 15th May I daresay that no less than 3000 deer crossed the [Nelson] river below the Seal Islands, from North to South side in different herds some containing at least 100. I am told they equally abound all the way up this river and have regular crossing-places. Down here they crossed anywhere indiscriminately, without regarding the length or steepness of the banks or the roughness of the ice...."[118]

We seem to be confronted here by some local unconfirmed tra-

---

[115]Allen, *American Bisons*, 62-3.

[116]Hector, in *Palliser Journals*, 69.

[117]*Rundle's Journal*, January 15, 1841; so also *ibid.*, March 14, 1843. An almost precisely similar occurrence with a lone bull (McDougall, *Saddle, Sled and Snowshoe*, 23).

[118]*Report of Canadian Archives*, ed. Brymner, 1886, ccxxi.

dition concerning 'regular routes.' And, as far as buffalo are concerned, we have nothing to set off against the probable consequences I have mentioned, except Hulbert's idle generalization that buffalo 'never travelled in winter.'[119]

In the previous chapter I cited a number of passages from various writers endorsing the supposed buffalo-track origin of road and rail-way routes, many of which are supposed to have passed through an intermediate stage as Indian trails.[120] Hornaday goes even further than the common generalizations on this; he specifies in some detail those features in the buffalo trail which render it—I do not think I am distorting his views here—practically a ready-made route for any rail-way surveyor who might desire to go in that particular direction. I quote his own words:

When the gully curved to right or left the leader[121] would cross its bed and keep straight on until the narrow ditch completed its wayward course and came back to the middle of the coulee. The trail of a herd in search of water is usually as good a piece of engineering as could be executed by the best railway surveyor, and is governed by precisely the same principles. It always follows the level of the valley, swerves around the high points, and crosses the stream repeatedly in order to avoid climbing up from the level. . . .[122]

It is needless at the present moment to inquire whether this description finds general support from the evidence; nor need we pause to labour the point that 'swerving around' with the valley to maintain a level, and 'keeping straight on' when the gully curved, are contradictions in terms; while for 'a trail in search of water' to cross any stream and keep on is peculiar, to say the least. Accepting it—temporarily—what follows? The reader who is prepared to accept this propensity for crossing streams, and the stated manner of doing so, as an indication of high intelligence, may be somewhat startled on learning its frequent results.

There remains one final manifestation in the relationship of buffalo to water, which frequently constituted a very serious danger. Furthermore, this danger, being very often needlessly encountered, presents the strongest conceivable indictment of the intelligence of the species. I refer to the consequences of these river-crossings to their calves. The

[119]Hulbert, *Historic Highways*, I, 130. See below, chap. VIII, notes 96-123.
[120]Above, chap. VI, notes 1-20.
[121]'Usually an old cow' (Hornaday, "Extermination of the American Bison," 417); 'always an old cow' (Seton, *Life-Histories of Northern Animals*, I, 274). See above, chap. V, note 60.
[122]Hornaday, "Extermination of the American Bison," 417.

evidence concerning the degree of affection exhibited by the buffalo cows for their young is very contradictory. Allen writes:

> In respect to the degree of maternal affection possessed by the buffalo cow there seems to be a wide range of opinion among observers. Some deny that the mother has any affection for her offspring, stating that when frightened the buffalo cow will abandon her calf without the slightest hesitation. On the other hand, others report her as being not only constantly vigilant in the care of her young, but bold in its defence. Colonel Dodge, indeed, states that the duty of protecting the calves devolves wholly upon the bulls. . . .
>
> Audubon states, on the contrary, that the cow does not at such times desert its young, but tries to defend it, which statement is confirmed by many plainsmen and hunters who are thoroughly conversant with the habits of the buffalo. . . .[123]

Allen seems to have claimed more for Audubon's testimony than its language will warrant. The latter says: "When a large herd of these wild animals are crossing a river, the calves or yearlings manage to get on the backs of the cows, and are thus conveyed safely over. . . ."[124] I have met with this statement nowhere else. But this was not all. The bank had still to be climbed; and in spite of 'roads' (which we have seen even some of the adults were unable to break down for themselves after drifting below such roads as were perhaps previously formed by herds coming *down* into the river), it would seem that calves frequently came to grief. I again quote Audubon:

> Buffalo calves are often drowned from being unable to ascend the steep banks of the rivers across which they have just swam, as the cows cannot help them, although they stand near the bank, and will not leave them to their fate unless something alarms them. On one occasion, Mr. Kipp, of the American Fur Company, caught eleven calves, their dams all the time standing near the top of the bank. Frequently, however, the cows leave the young to their fate, when most of them perish . . . we may add that we were informed, when on the Upper Missouri River, that when the banks of that river were practicable for cows, and their calves could not follow them, they went down again, after having gained the top, and would remain by them until forced away by the cravings of hunger. When thus forced by the necessity of saving themselves to quit their young, they seldom, if ever, returned to them. . . .[125]

The foregoing passage, which Hornaday quotes,[126] evidently led him—more logically than Allen's, I should suggest—to the conclusion (which he himself adopts) that Audubon did *not* support the case for

[123]Allen, *American Bisons*, 58.
[124]Audubon and Bachman, *American Quadrupeds*, II, 39.
[125]*Ibid.*, 38-9.
[126]Hornaday, "Extermination of the American Bison," 400.

strong maternal affection. Hornaday considered it rather a minus quantity, shown occasionally but not often.[127]

Thompson Seton, after reading most of the foregoing, or possibly all of it.[128] apparently still regards the matter as undecided—and with much justice. He speaks of the 'dull wit' of the buffalo cow,[129] and adds: "Some observers think her negligent of her duties. There is, indeed, great individual variation in this respect; but, ordinarily, she is the best protector the little one can have and is afraid of nothing when the calf is threatened. Yet many times she acts in a dumb, cowed way, especially when the assailant of the youngster is a man. . . ."[130] Elsewhere in the same work, however, he appears to rely upon the testimony of the younger Henry: "Alexander Henry mentions expressly that the mothers come back in search of their young after the hunt is over. . . ."[131]

I have previously had occasion to point out, with reference to Seton's triumphant appeals to Henry, that these questions are not settled by the 'express mention' of any one man.[132] According to both Catlin[133] and Dodge,[134] if anything alarmed the cows, they readily abandoned their calves in any precarious situation; and Bradbury noted instances (1811) of cows running away when shot at, and deserting their calves.[135] Even Buffalo Jones, who strenuously asserts the defence of the calf by its mother (giving instances) and of the calves of the herd by both cows and bulls, admits that "the old buffalo would get away and abandon the calves if hard pressed, which they would not do in ordinary circumstances. . . ."[136]

Bradbury and Catlin, at least, can scarcely be assigned to any later period of supposedly changed buffalo mentality.[137] Audubon's in-

---

[127]*Ibid.*, 433-4.
[128]Seton, *Life-Histories of Northern Animals*, I, 277-81.
[129]*Ibid.*, 279.
[130]*Ibid.* In his later work, Seton remarks about the musk ox: ". . . the young are never left alone. Analogy with the Plains Buffalo inclines one to accept the latter account. The growth of the young closely parallels that of the Plains Buffalo calf. The mother is devoted and fearless in her care . . ." (*Game Animals*, III, 627; cf. *ibid.*, III, 693-700).
[131]Seton, *Life-Histories of Northern Animals*, I, 281.
[132]See remarks above, chap. I, notes 17-18.
[133]Catlin, *Letters on the North American Indians*. I, 255.
[134]Dodge, *Plains of the Great West*, 124-5, 150.
[135]Bradbury, *Early Western Travels*, V, 84, 147.
[136]*Buffalo Jones' Forty Years*, 59-61, 135, 141, 205, 248.
[137]It must be recognized that this circumstance (discussed above, chap. VI, notes 107-15) discounts Buffalo Jones' generalizations on wild buffalo (which he never saw until the 'latter days')—as distinguished from his field experiences—

formants asserted also—in direct opposition to Henry—that the cows 'seldom returned.' The statements of several travellers concerning the ease with which buffalo calves could be captured and induced to abandon their mothers cast some suspicion upon the cows as protectors. In addition to his remarks cited above, Audubon says: "A singular trait in the Buffalo, when caught young, was related to us as follows: When a calf is taken, if the person who captures it places one of his fingers in its mouth, it will follow him afterwards, whether on foot or on horseback, for several miles. . . ."[138]

Catlin says the same.[139] Umfreville, half a century earlier, writes: "They might also be tamed to the plough; and that with the greatest facility, by taking them young in the Month of April or May, which a man who is swift of foot may do without the assistance of a horse. . . ."[140] Dr. Gregg also considered them 'tame,'[141] but both Pattie[142] and Townsend [143] regarded them as intractable. If the defence of the calves by the *bulls*[144] somewhat as range steers have been known to act in later times, were established beyond question, it might be thought to constitute some evidence concerning the habits of the cows; but since some witnesses describe what could be either a defence of the calves by both sexes, or of cows and calves by the bulls alone,[145] the evidence is scarcely conclusive.

If we assume (with the very latest generalizing authority, Garret-

---

very considerably. Yet neither he nor his 'compiler,' biographer, editor, Colonel Henry Inman, apparently has the least perception of the fact; although they note the 'psychological' change (*Buffalo Jones' Forty Years*, 202, 224). The same applies to Hornaday; see above, chap. VI, note 107.

[138]Audubon and Bachman, *American Quadrupeds*, II, 47. Apropos of this (or some similar trait), Garretson prints a drawing ('from life,' 1867) of a calf following a rider to camp; apparently without any finger-exercises (*American Bison*, 38-41).

[139]Catlin, *Letters on the North American Indians*, I, 255.

[140]Umfreville, *Present State of Hudson's Bay*, 159. The history of buffalo domestication contradicts this. See Appendix C.

[141]Gregg, *Early Western Travels*, XX, 268.

[142]Pattie, *ibid.*, XVIII, 64. Cf. below, Appendix C, notes 51-2.

[143]Townsend, *ibid.*, XXI, 206; similarly *Buffalo Jones' Forty Years*, 65. Sir Richard Burton says the buffalo calf was tamed by the Flatheads, but never (so far as he knew) utilized. Townsend, of all early writers, should have known of it (Burton, *City of the Saints*, 51).

[144]So, by Dodge (*Plains of the Great West*, 125); cited also by Allen (*American Bisons*, 58), who further quotes an account by an eye-witness (*ibid.*); also on this, Hornaday ("Extermination of the American Bison," 433-4).

[145]Garretson says that, when in danger, "the calves would be gathered together and surrounded by a double ring, the cows forming the inside and the bulls the outer circle . . ." (*American Bison*, 39). According to the following, the bulls protected both: Bradbury, a witness (*Early Western Travels*, V, 147); Parkman (*Oregon Trail*, 422); Darwin (citing no authority, *Descent of Man*, 104).

son)[146] that the maternal affection of the buffalo mother was strong, we have, on the evidence, to disparage its intelligence. Indeed, Hulbert himself, who credits the buffalo with extremely high intelligence, admits: "The extensive courses of the buffalo often necessitated the crossing of large streams. This often caused a loss to many of the old and young members of the herds, especially if the stream was swift or swollen. Often, after having successfully battled their way entirely across the stream, a bluff or a miry landing-place proved disastrous. . . ."[147]

The 'necessity' of these crossings depended apparently upon the extensive courses; we have seen and shall again see that this initial premise itself is by no means universally true; and Hornaday again, somewhat ludicrously, makes these frequent crossings a feature in the 'search for water.' I do not know whether in the higher orders of the animal kingdom there is another example of a species leading its young deliberately into situations where their lives were constantly in danger from physical phenomena or animal foes, and were very often lost, merely in obedience to what was frequently a whim; since little which they did not already possess was to be obtained by crossing the streams. This puzzle cannot be solved by any reference to the 'migratory instinct,' even if that historically ill-supported supposition were to be conceded. How came any (presumably) acquired characteristic

---

Ross says that the cows after calving "as if with one accord, withdraw themselves from the mountains and rocks [?], and resort in large families to the valleys, where there is open ground, with small clumps of wood affording shelter and preservation; as there they can see the approach of an enemy from afar. The cows herd together in the centre, and the bulls graze in the distance: all in sight of each other . . . during which time the herds feed round and round the place as if to defend the growing calves from the approach of an enemy or from wolves. The resident Indian tribes seldom hunt or disturb the buffalo at this season, or before the first of July. The Indians often assured me, that, during the calving season, the bulls keep guard; and have been frequently known to assemble together, in order to keep at a distance any wolves, bears, or other enemies, that might attempt to approach the cows . . ." (Fur Hunters, II, 126). I suspect that in many cases, Indians (even if correctly understood) 'assured' questioners what the questioner wished.

[146]Stone and Cram (who consider Hornaday 'exhaustive' and scarcely cite anyone else), say strangely that "the calves were jealously guarded and defended from all dangers by their mothers . . ." (American Animals, 69). This is hardly Hornaday's conclusion (above, note 127).

Garretson writes thus: "It is the writer's opinion that there is no animal in which the maternal instinct of protection is as wonderfully developed as the buffalo cow—Col. R. I. Dodge to the contrary notwithstanding" (American Bison, 39). Dodge was one of the most careful everyday observers from 1849 onward for thirty-five years, and a supreme authority of Garretson's own mentor, Dr. Hornaday.

[147]Hulbert, Historic Highways, I, 108; cf. Audubon and Bachman, American Quadrupeds, II, 39.

to override that most fundamental of all passions, the maternal instinct? And it seems paradoxical to seize upon the mere methods or details of an inherently suicidal process and hold them up for our admiration as proofs of intelligence.

Our inquiry into this phase of buffalo mentality may be summed up in the words of three competent students; the last extract is particularly impressive, since the author was a scholar deeply read in the literature of Western history, a plainsman of wide experience in the buffalo era, and a critic of sane and balanced judgment.

In winter, when the ice has become strong enough to bear the weight of many tons, buffaloes are often drowned in great numbers, for they are in the habit of crossing rivers on the ice, and should any alarm occur, rush in a dense crowd to one place; the ice gives way beneath the pressure of hundreds of these huge animals, they are precipitated into the water, and if it is deep enough to reach over their backs, soon perish. Should the water, however, be shallow, they scuffle through the . . . ice, in the greatest disorder, to the shore. . . . Small herds, crossing rivers on the ice in the spring, are set adrift, in consequence of a sudden breaking of the ice. . . .   They have been seen floating on such occasions in groups of three, four, and sometimes eight or ten together, although on separate cakes of ice. A few stragglers have been known to reach the shore in an almost exhausted state; but the majority perish from cold and want of food rather than trust themselves boldly to the turbulent waters. . . .[148]

For generations the dwellers on the Missouri River were familiar with the yearly flood that bore countless Buffalo hulks to be packed away in the Mississippi mud, that in some far geological day will be the rock, all stored and storied with unnumbered bones. Now we know that all the northern rivers made their death-traps every spring; and since their sum of length must have been not less than 20,000 miles, we can form an estimate of the prodigious slaughter that was caused by rotten ice. Clearly the destruction by Nature's own means was so great that the Buffalo can have done no more than barely hold its own in the fight; and when the rifle also came upon the scene, its doom was sealed. . . .[149]

It is probable that the total number of buffalo killed by man in those days was insignificant in comparison with the destruction wrought by the warring of nature's elements against the poor brutes. . . .[150]

[148]*Ibid.*, 38.
[149]Seton, *Life-Histories of Northern Animals*, I, 274.
[150]Coues, ed. note, *Henry-Thompson Journals*, I, 174.

CHAPTER VIII

AGENCIES DESTRUCTIVE TO BUFFALO, OTHER THAN
MAN. II

SNOW

THOSE writers who have regarded the final disappearance of
the wild buffalo from the western plains as dramatically sudden have suggested that some more immediate and catastrophic
explanation was required than the progressive extermination by man.
Snow has been suggested as such a potent destructive force, and as
being possibly the true cause of their final extinction as a free wild
species in their more northerly habitat at least; and the view has been
expressed that an examination of the available evidence might yield
interesting and valuable results.[1] It seems logical to discuss this question as a feature in our general investigation of hostile physical
agencies, in preference to deferring it until we approach the general
history of the buffalo extermination at large. My purpose in this chapter is therefore to present such evidence as I have been able to find
on this point.

The idea that snow caused wholesale destruction of buffalo is not
new. Yet it does not seem to have occurred to the persistent advocates
of this theory that a similarly 'sudden' extermination took place in the
southern habitat, where no snowfall of the depth or duration required
for such a catastrophe has been recorded. I shall cite a number of expressions of opinion, approximately in chronological order, to illustrate the growth of the belief. A common characteristic of what I may
term the 'buffalo tradition' in various regions of their vast historic
habitat is that of some extraordinary catastrophe, following which
buffalo 'were never seen again' in this or that locality. There can be
no sounder criterion of the value of such stories than historical evidence showing whether the buffalo did finally disappear at the times
and places in question.

---

[1]This was the view expressed by the late Professor A. S. Morton of the
University of Saskatchewan, in reference to my paper on "The Extermination of
the Buffalo in Western Canada" (*Canadian Historical Review*, XV, 1934, 1-23;
Morton, *ibid.*, 213-18). The present chapter is identical in substance with a further paper, "Buffalo and Snow" (*ibid.*, XVII, 1936, 125-46). Sir Richard Burton
makes snow fundamental: "The buffalo is partially migratory in its habits; it
appears to follow the snow, which preserves its food from destruction . . ." (*City
of the Saints*, 51). This, from a visitor, possesses no special authority.

The earliest historical disappearance which is coupled with snow occurred in Utah. The passing of the buffalo there is dated by Hornaday on his map in 1838.[2] He remarks: "It is well known that buffalo, though in very small numbers, once inhabited northeastern Utah, and that a few were killed by the Mormon settlers prior to 1840 in the vicinity of Great Salt Lake. . . ."[3] The same approximate date is given by Allen. He mentions a very severe winter in Utah, 1837, ". . . when, according to the reports of mountaineers and Indians, the snow fell to the depth of ten feet on a level. The few buffaloes that escaped starvation are said to have soon afterwards 'disappeared.' . . ."[4] What is perhaps a variant version of the same event is cited by Bancroft in a very picturesque 'Wild West' form:

Many strange stories the old trapper, James Bridger, used to tell; for instance in the winter of 1830 it began to snow in the valley of the Great Salt Lake, and the snow fell for seventy days until the whole country was white-coated to the thickness of seventy feet. Vast herds of buffalo were caught by this snow, caught and pinched to death, and the carcasses preserved; and finally when spring came, all Bridger had to do was tumble them into Salt Lake, and have pickled buffalo enough to feed him and the whole nation, down to the time of their extermination. And this is why there have been no buffaloes in that region since. . . .[5]

It may be noted that in this yarn Hornaday's 'very small numbers' are 'vast herds.' In May, 1825, Ashley and Jedidiah Smith found northeastern Utah 'well supplied with buffaloe,'[6] whatever that expression might signify to men well acquainted with the Plains herds. In reference to 'none being seen' after the great snow, it was said that a solitary buffalo bull which appeared near Fort Bridger (124 miles northeast of Salt Lake City) in 1875 was the first one seen for thirty years.[7] Fort Bridger (*circa* 1843) was then about thirty years old. A picturesque but inaccurate writer states that the 'frequency of buffalo' was one reason for Bridger's choice of the site.[8]

[2]Hornaday, "Extermination of the American Bison," 548.

[3]*Ibid.*, 383. One of Hornaday's characteristic inaccuracies. Who were the "Mormon settlers prior to 1840"? The first reached there in 1847 (Bancroft, *History of Utah*). A certain 'Danite,' one Bill Hickman, 'claimed' to have killed the last buffalo in Salt Lake Valley, 1838 (Allen, *American Bisons*, 119). He was 'the notorious Bill Hickman,' a scoundrel, afterwards a Danite (Bancroft, *History of Utah*, 564, 663; *History of Nevada*, 205); cf. Burton, *City of the Saints*, 191, 344, 448, on Hickman.

[4]Allen, *American Bisons*, 119, 120.

[5]Bancroft, *History of Nevada*, 3-4.

[6]Dale (ed.), *Ashley-Smith Explorations*, 155.

[7]Allen, *American Bisons*, 125; '124 miles' to Salt Lake City (Burton, *City of the Saints*, 178).

[8]Laut, *Overland Trail*, 121.

182   THE NORTH AMERICAN BUFFALO

Dodge gives a most interesting account of a great snowstorm:

According to hunters' traditions the Laramie Plains were visited in the winter of 1844-45 by a most extraordinary snowstorm. Contrary to all precedent, there was no wind, and the snow covered the surface evenly to a depth of nearly four feet. Immediately after the storm a bright sun softened the surface, which at night froze into a crust so firm that it was weeks before any heavy animal could make any headway over it. The Laramie Plains, being entirely surrounded by mountains, had always been a favourite wintering-place for the buffaloes. Thousands were caught in this storm and perished miserably from starvation. Since that time not a single buffalo has ever visited the Laramie Plains. When I first crossed these plains, in 1868, the whole country was dotted with skulls of buffaloes, all in the last stages of decomposition and all apparently of the same age [or period of exposure], giving some foundation for the tradition. Indeed, it was in answer to my request for an explanation of the numbers, appearance, and identity of age [i.e. condition] of these skulls, that the tradition was related to me by an old hunter, who, however, could not himself vouch for the facts. . . .[9]

I recollect a somewhat similar condition of things in southern Alberta in November, 1896. Stories were current of range cattle bleeding to death owing to gashes from the hard-frozen crust, but a second timely 'Chinook' (wind)[10] mitigated the severity. Captain Palliser notes observing blood on the snow in the month of March;[11] so likewise (in winter) does Allen.[12] And in the northern Wood buffalo habitat, a similar cause was assigned (*circa* 1866) as the reason for an alleged serious decrease in the wild herds in the Peace River country.[13] This explanation, however (in the last instance), while not incredible in itself, is so bound up with mere guesswork concerning the actual numbers of the buffalo in any era, and with the appearance of various legends (wolves, etc.) to account for 'shrinkages' more probably due to slaughter by hunters—even to the extent of poaching in the latter days[14]—that it becomes unwise to pronounce too certainly.

There seems to be a suspicious family likeness about the Utah and Laramie snowstorms. Yet one hesitates to reject the story given to Dodge entirely, especially when coming from such cautious informants

---

[9]Dodge, *Plains of the Great West*, 129-30. Cited also by Allen (*American Bisons*, 164-5) from *Chicago Inter-Ocean*, Aug. 5, 1875. Sir Richard Burton (presumably upon local information) ascribes their disappearance from 'Utah Valley' to the 'severe winter of 1845' (*City of the Saints*, 50).

[10]On the Chinooks, see above; chap. IV, note 11.

[11]*Palliser Journals*, 12-13.

[12]Allen, *American Bisons*, 61-2 (Kansas, 1871).

[13]Raup, *Range Conditions in Wood Buffalo Park*, 19, 20, 48. See below, note 36.

[14]*Ibid.*, 8, 9, 11, 13; cf. also above, chap. I, note 6; and below, note 36.

as himself and his old-timer. At the same time, the circumstance that
the weather conditions were considered 'contrary to all precedent'
renders it somewhat doubtful that such occurrences as he describes
were a very common cause of destruction. Even although the very
latest generalizing authority on buffalo calls this 'a well-authenticated
tradition,' the statement—endorsed by him[15]—that the buffalo were
never again found at the Laramie Plains after that time is without
foundation. In the very next summer, 1845, a very competent Indianologist states that the Ogallala (Sioux) were obliged to go *to* the
Laramie Plains to find buffalo for subsistence, and makes no mention
of them being disappointed in this.[16] While he cites no direct authority
for this, the presence of buffalo in that region in 1845 and later is
established by contemporary testimony. In 1845, Samuel Hancock
noted 'a profusion of game,' including buffalo, from the Forks of the
Platte to Fort Laramie;[17] and in the same year Joel Palmer records
them practically all the way along the North Platte to the ford near
Independence Rock,[18] which is given as being 443 miles from the
Forks, and 213 miles westward from Fort Laramie.[19] In 1846, Parkman
found them 'rare' in the neighbourhood of Fort Laramie; so much so
that a projected intertribal Indian war had to be abandoned for lack
of food for the warriors.[20] But Palmer, returning eastbound apparently
somewhat earlier in the same summer, noted them much as in the
previous year.[21]

For 1847, although 'vast herds' were seen on the 'Mormon trail'
(which ran along the northern side of the Lower Platte from the
Missouri to the crossing of the main Oregon-California Trail at Fort
Laramie, Wyoming[22]), I have no special information concerning Laramie. In 1849, 'Buffalo Land' began at the Forks of the Platte.[23] A
'Forty-Niner,' Allen Varner, writing to Hornaday nearly forty years
later, says they saw only "small bunches, never more than forty or fifty

[15]Garretson, *American Bison*, 69. His account almost entirely reproduces
Dodge's language (as above, note 9), without inverted commas. When Dodge's
own caution and that of his informant are contrasted with Garretson's credulity
or inattention, the latter's comment on Dodge (above, chap. VII, note 146) is
very ill-timed.
[16]Grinnell, *Fighting Cheyennes*, 94-5.
[17]Hancock, *Narrative*, 15-22.
[18]Palmer, *Early Western Travels*, XXX, 48-66.
[19]"Itinerary" in Hancock, *Narrative*, ed. pref., xiv.
[20]Parkman, *Oregon Trail*, 159, 201, 203, 229.
[21]Palmer, *Early Western Travels*, XXX, 247.
[22]Bancroft, *History of Utah*, 253, 254, 260; for the trail, see Hulbert, *Forty-
Niners*, 119.
[23]*Ibid.*, 84, 89, 90, 102.

together,"[24] from the Forks to Fort Laramie. But his knowledge (or memory) of the Oregon Trail is incorrect in other particulars,[25] and may be so in this. Captain Howard Stansbury, of the United States Army, returning eastward over the same route, also in the summer of 1849, saw '. . . no buffaloes east of the Forks of the Platte, but found them in abundance west of that point. . . .'[26] Hulbert's chroniclers followed the cut-off up the South Platte, which avoided the dreaded 'Ash Hollow,' and they saw a large herd at 'Lower California Crossing,' near Brûlé, Nebraska, and again at 'Mud Spring,' near Simla, Nebraska.[27] In the same year, the Mormons encountered them at various points on the way to the South Pass, but not farther west.[28] Such records dispose fairly well of 'none being seen' on the Laramie Plains after 1844-45.

There are two or three generalizations on destruction by snow in the later years. Ernest Thompson Seton quotes a correspondent, R. N. Bunn of Chicago, who speaks of 'hundreds of thousands' which crossed the Missouri going northward in the winter of 1870-71, and again of huge numbers in the following winter, 1871-72, which "never returned; nor is there any evidence of them having been slain by hunters. . . ." Bunn also speaks of enormous numbers of skeletons having been found (in Kingsbury County, South Dakota), "on none of which were broken limbs or signs of bullet fractures. . . ." Large clusters of bones were also found in hollows in this locality. Bunn remarks in conclusion: "I believe that at all times the Dakota blizzard has taken heavier toll of the buffalo than ever the Dakota Indian did. . . ."[29] Upon this Seton comments:

No one who has seen the Northern blizzard will question its terrible power. I have lived through several and agree with Bunn that a long suc-

[24]Correspondence to Hornaday, "Extermination of the American Bison," 491.
[25]He says (*ibid.*) the Oregon Trail 'had been travelled very little previous to that year.' Actually it had been used since 1840 by thousands: '5000' in 1847; '20,000' in 1848; etc. For estimated numbers, 1845-65, see Bancroft, *History of Oregon*, I, 323-8, 394, 395, 448, 508, 511, 552, 623, 751; II, 82, 174, 463, 493-5; *History of California*, IV, 267-72; V, 554-7; VI, 143-63; VII, 497; *Early Western Travels*, ed. notes, XXVI, 15-16; XXVII, 190; XXX, 11, 72, 250; Hancock, *Narrative*, 2, 4; Coman, *Economic Beginnings of the Far West*, II, 163; Hebard and Brininstool, *Bozeman Trail*, I, 54, 58, 90; Laut, *Overland Trail*, 54-9, 177; Hulbert, *Forty-Niners*, 112. The last (pp. 18, 84) shows how the incessant prairie winds obliterated wheel-tracks, etc., which perhaps partly explains Varner's misconception.
[26]Allen, *American Bisons*, 146; cf. Bancroft, *History of Utah*, 467.
[27]Hulbert, *Forty-Niners*, 84, 89, 90, 102.
[28]Bancroft, *History of Utah*, 421-2.
[29]Seton, *Life-Histories of Northern Animals*, I, 267-9.

cession of these snow-siroccos might in certain circumstances destroy every Bison on the range before spring. But blizzards *did not happen every winter,* and they were restricted to a certain limited treeless area lying far north and of heavy snow.[30] So that I doubt whether, upon the whole, the destruction by blizzards was comparable with that of other agencies which were of more regular occurrence and covered a large part, or all, of the Bison range....[31]

It is not clear whether the hundreds of thousands mentioned by Bunn crossed the Missouri at points in Dakota or not. If that be what is meant, his evidence conflicts materially with other data on the last days of the northern herds. The western boundary of the two Dakotas is 104° W. The eastern limit of the buffalo about that time along the international boundary was about 107° W. If one could accept a very detailed 'annual itinerary' furnished by the Red River halfbreeds to Henry Youle Hind in 1858, the regular route of the Canadian herds at that time was southward in summer from the Qu'Appelle via the Missouri Coteau to the Missouri, thence westward along the Missouri and Yellowstone Valleys, and northward along the slopes of the foothills into Canada for the winter, which was spent in the Carlton country and between the two Saskatchewans.[32] But despite Hind's acceptance of this, its times and directions (and even the presence of buffalo) were disproved on the very trip wherein he records it; and its utter worthlessness, as a regular procedure, is demonstrated by a vast mass of evidence.

So too, while we must appreciate the apparent care with which the skeletons were examined for evidences of wounds, etc., we could wish that the type of country in which they were found had been described with similar precision. The mention of bones being "also found in hollows" seems to justify the inference that the main masses were on

[30]The non-Western reader may not be aware that although the term is often loosely so used, a 'blizzard' is not properly a storm of *falling* snow. It is a snow wind-storm, only possible on open plains, and often occurring under a cloudless sky. The intense cold and the violence of the wind, which swirls around seemingly from all quarters, cause one to turn this way and that for breath, until all sense of direction is often lost. When experienced residents of the plains perceive a blizzard coming, they very commonly stretch a line between house and barn, since the storm will often last three days and nights; lacking such a line, many persons have been lost and frozen to death within 200 yards or less of their own doors. On the blizzard, see Webb, *Great Plains,* 25, citing some historical studies; and for personal experiences and trail expedients in a dangerous region, Cowie, *Company of Adventurers,* 207, 244-8, 353, 387, etc.: also Thompson, Henry, McDougall, etc., at large. Seton's implication here, that the region north of the Missouri River lies outside (south of) the true blizzard area, cannot be accepted. That territory is the very home of them.

[31]Seton, *Life-Histories of Northern Animals,* I, 269.

[32]Hind, *Report, 1858,* 106. Given *in extenso* below, chap. XIV, note 52.

level ground; but whether on river bottom-lands or high prairie, woodland, scrub-land (or formerly such), or 'bald-headed' plains, is left
unmentioned, as is likewise their probable age. Furthermore, the implied supposition on Bunn's part that the absence of bullet-fractures,
etc., practically constitutes proof that these animals could not have
been slain by hunters, is untenable. It is often loosely assumed that,
from the first moment of their introduction, firearms completely superseded the aboriginal weapons of the Indians for hunting. I shall later
present strong evidence for an expert and manifestly continuous use
of the bow—and by tribes of this very region, broadly speaking—right
down to 1872, if not later.[33]

Unfractured bones might also indicate buffalo destroyed by fire.
Fires, as we have seen, have been considered an active danger, although only two actually fatal historical cases have proved discoverable; and in both those instances it is made quite clear that the animals
were not *consumed* by the fires which blinded or slew them.[34] And
whether slain by hunters, burned, or smothered by snow, there is still
the problem of how bones, presumably exposed, survived without further damage from fire, or from the depredations of wolves. Further
criticism may conveniently be deferred until a somewhat similar case
has been brought to notice. Sir William (then Captain) Butler wrote
in 1873:

> The giant form of the wood buffalo no longer darkens the steep lofty
> shores [of Peace River]. When first Mackenzie beheld the long reaches of
> the river [1793], the 'gentle lawns' which alternated with 'abrupt precipices'
> were 'enlivened' by vast herds of buffaloes. Thirty-three years later [1826]
> Sir George Simpson also ascended the river with his matchless Iroquois
> crew. Yet no buffalo darkened the lofty shores.
>
> What destroyed them in that short interval? The answer is not difficult
> to seek—deep snow. . . . During one winter of exceptionally deep snow,
> eighty buffaloes were killed in a single day in the vicinity of Dunvegan. The
> Indians ran them into the snowdrifts, and then despatched them with
> knives. . . .[35]

This would appear to be the event mentioned by an eminent and
well-known American scientist, E. W. Nelson, in a letter to J. A. Allen,
dated July 11, 1877, giving information from two travellers who had
crossed the mountains in 1871:

> These gentlemen descended the Peace River, and on about the 118th
> degree of longitude made a portage to Hay River, directly north. On this

[33]See below, Appendix T, "Late Survival of Indian Archery."
[34]See above, chap. VII, notes 30-32.
[35]Butler, *Wild North Land*, 210; cf. also Hornaday, "Extermination of the
American Bison," 423.

portage they saw thousands of buffalo skulls, and old trails, in some instances two or three feet deep, leading E. and W. They wintered on Hay River near its entrance to Great Slave Lake, and here found the buffalo still common, occupying a restricted territory along the southern border of the lake. They made inquiry concerning the larger number of skulls seen by them on the portage, and learned that about fifty years before, snow fell to the estimated depth of fourteen feet, and so enveloped the animals that they perished by thousands. . . .[36]

Dr. G. M. Dawson also stated in 1879: "It is reported that a few buffaloes were seen last year [1878] near Pine River, but the animal has now become in the Peace River country practically extinct; an event which according to the Indians, happened at a date not very remote, owing to a winter of exceptional severity, during which the snow 'reached to the buffaloes' backs.' . . ."[37] Dr. Hector, of the Palliser expedition, wrote in 1858: "When we compare the description given by Sir Alexander Mackenzie of the prairie country along Peace River, with its vast herds of buffalo and elks, when he passed in 1793, with the present northern limit of the large herds of these animals, at least three degrees of latitude farther south, the change is very striking; and still more so if it is true, as the Indians say, that the disappearance of the large quantities of game has only taken place within the last twenty years. . . ."[38]

These various events may really have been one and the same, but it is not certain. In any case, we cannot, I believe, rely upon the evidence of Indians in defining fairly precise periods of time and the exact particulars of catastrophes.[39] A competent Western authority seems to describe the Indian in general very aptly when he terms him an acute and reliable observer, but a poor generalizer.[40] This is not to throw any stones at the Indian. It is a well-known philological truism that in our own ancestral Old English, it is almost impossible to generalize, which doubtless indicates a lack of the capacity in those

[36]Printed by Allen, "The Northern Range of the Bison" (*American Naturalist*, XI, 1877, 624, which I have not seen). It seems curious that the disaster to the animals mentioned to Ogilvie in 1890 as having occurred *circa* 1866 (Raup, *Range Conditions in Wood Buffalo Park*, 19, 20, 48) was not alluded to (in the same general region) in 1871. See my remarks above, notes 13-14. Compare the next note.

[37]Dawson, in Macoun, *Manitoba*, 125.

[38]*Palliser Journals*, 126.

[39]For an examination of a similar native tradition, see F. G. Roe, "The Extermination of the Buffalo in Western Canada," *Canadian Historical Review*, XV, 1934, 1-10; also below, Appendix J, "Buffalo and Disease." On Indian tradition, see also an excellent article, by Swanton and Dixon, "Primitive American History" (*American Anthropologist*, New Series. XVI, 1914, 376-412).

[40]Grinnell, *Fighting Cheyennes*, 270.

who spoke it. Futile generalizations are, however, common enough not only in the writings of ancient chroniclers but in the speech of our own day.[41] The present essay is one long criticism of futile generalizations, many of them by learned scholars.

The mere circumstance that Simpson saw no buffalo along the Peace in 1826 proves nothing in regard either to the snow or to any other possible agent of wholesale destruction. Butler himself rode for hundreds of miles in the winter of 1870 through what he called the 'winter home of the buffalo,' and saw 'not one.'[42] These inscrutable fluctuations in their comings and goings are the one commonplace of travellers' everyday experiences with the buffalo since their discovery.[43] It is possible too that on this very journey in 1826 there might have been thousands a short distance back from the river banks beyond Simpson's ken; he was travelling up a canyon some 500 to 800 feet in estimated depth.

It will be noticed that there is a material, if not irreconcilable confusion in the details of these relations, which renders implicit acceptance of them difficult. Dawson's date, 'not very remote,' would hardly reach back to 1826, although (in 1878) it might do so for the aforementioned instance of 1866 in the same general territory, as recorded by Raup. But while this last was ascribed to a heavy winter thaw and rain followed by hard frost, the particulars given to Dawson were merely of extraordinarily deep snow—if four to five feet be considered such in that region. The account given by Hector or his informants of the 'disappearance of the larger quantities'—from unspecified causes— is 'within the last twenty years' (that is, about 1838). Moreover, the portage mentioned in Nelson's letter to Allen between the Peace and Hay rivers must surely have been not farther south than where the

---

[41]See in the *Anglo-Saxon Chronicle, circa* 1090-1125, wet seasons 'of which no man ever saw the like . . .' when perhaps the same scribe had bemoaned one only the year before. Compare our modern shibboleth, 'I never saw anything like it,' for the commonest occurrences.

[42]Butler, *Great Lone Land* (including his "Report"), 230, 358; cf. 304.

[43]These local fluctuations have given rise to much false generalization on the 'disappearance' of the buffalo. Frémont had them 'extinct' in this very region of the Upper Platte in 1842 (*Narrative*, 142). In summer, 1867, Major J. W. Powell and Professor A. H. Thompson saw only one old bull along the Platte, up to Cheyenne, Wyoming. Hornaday cites this as evidence of extinction in that territory ("Extermination of the American Bison," 492); yet in September, 1867, Sir William (then Captain) Butler encountered a herd near Fort Kearney (Grand Island, Lower Platte, not Fort *Phil* Kearney of the Fetterman 'massacre,' 595 miles distant, in Wyoming) which took 'two hours' hard riding' to pass through (*Autobiography*, 90-7). It was 1867 also when the 2000 head (out of 4000, so Garretson, *American Bison*, 44) were mired in the South Platte, though not at Fort Kearney, as he says. See chap. VI, note 48; chap. XV, note 40.

northward-bound Peace takes its great sweep to the eastward, some miles above Fort Vermilion (about 58° N., 117° W.); by going 'directly north' they would strike Hay River about 59° N. Dunvegan, however, would still be some 200 miles or thereabouts (56° N., 118° W.) to the southward of Hay River; and a slaughter of 'eighty in one day' among 'vast herds' scarcely amounts to extermination, without a great multiplication of such days. We may note that despite the skulls and bones on the portage, they were 'still common' on lower Hay River as late as 1871.

The attempt to reconcile the various accounts with Hector's northern limits in 1858 is yet further complicated by the circumstance that it is doubtful whether the Peace River herds of 1793 and those of 1858, 'some three degrees farther south,' are of the same specific type. Mackenzie's and all those north of the Peace are generally held to have been Wood buffalo. As we have seen, the evidence for the presence of Wood buffalo south of the Peace for some distance westward of the lower Athabaska, seems dubious in the light of modern field investigation.[44] Here too, a certain generic resemblance in these recitals forces itself upon our attention. In almost every instance, the burden of the lament is a contrast with the 'brave days of old'; and these legendary catastrophes are described as occurring so long ago that further questioning is futile, as it was perhaps meant to be. The Indian was no fool; and was probably not ignorant of what was going on far to the south. It was quite as obviously contrary to his interest in the 'seventies as it was in the 'nineties (when this perfectly natural form of 'deception,' if you will, is known to have been practised) to encourage the inquisitive stranger to suppose that the game was anything else than highly precarious, and becoming more so every year. As they stand, I do not feel that any of these alleged occurrences can justify our acceptance of snow as a materially destructive agent in the northlands.

And even these questions of the historical authenticity of some specific explanation leave one fundamental problem unsolved. As we have seen, Seton was content to accept Bunn's estimate of the blizzard at its deadliest, *when it occurred,* but discounted it as a really material force in the destruction of the buffalo, on the ground that such things 'did not occur every year.' As with extinction by disease, are we justified in supposing that certain physical phenomena appeared only in the last days of the buffalo? If deep snowfalls, or wild storms, have prevailed—as seems more logical—throughout the existing geological

[44]See detailed evidence above, chap. III, note 100.

and climatic eras in the buffalo habitat, we must assume that they were deadly at all times. If so, it seems somewhat doubtful whether the species could have so increased as to make any hypothesis of 'overcrowding' even seem probable.[45] Thus there seems to be little ground for any view that snow brought about a general destruction anywhere.[46]

The contrary belief is well represented by Hornaday, whose remarks on the question I quote, as follows:

A buffalo can weather storms and outlive hunger and cold which would kill any domestic steer that ever lived. When nature placed him on the treeless and blizzard-swept plains, she left him well equipped to survive whatever natural conditions he would have to encounter. The most striking feature of his entire *tout ensemble* is his magnificent suit of hair and fur combined, the warmest covering possessed by any quadruped save the musk-ox. The head, neck, and fore quarters are clothed with hide and hair so thick as to be almost, if not entirely, impervious to cold. The hair on the body and hind quarters is long, fine, and of that peculiar woolly quality which constitutes the best possible protection against cold. Let him who doubts the warmth of a good buffalo robe try to weather a blizzard with something else, and then try the robe. The very form of the buffalo—short, thick legs, and head hung very near the ground—suggests most forcibly a special fitness to wrestle with mother earth for a living, snow or no snow. A buffalo will flounder for days through deep snow-drifts without a morsel of food, and survive where the best range steer would literally freeze on foot, bolt upright, as hundreds did in the winter of 1886-'87. While range cattle will turn tail to a blizzard and drift helplessly, the buffalo faces it every time, and remains master of the situation. . . .[47]

In his description of the Atchison, Topeka, and Santa Fé Railway Company's herd at Bismarck Grove, Kansas (*circa* 1889), he says again: ". . . they don't take kindly to shelter, and whether a blizzard is blowing, with the mercury 20 degrees below zero, or the sun pouring down with his scorching rays, with the thermometer 110 degrees above, they set their heads resolutely toward storm or sun, and take their medicine as if they liked it. . . ."[48] Somewhat curiously he writes elsewhere: "In winter the buffalo used to face the storms, instead of turning tail and 'drifting' before them helplessly, as domestic cattle

---

[45]See Seton on this, *Life-Histories of Northern Animals,* I, 259-61; *Game Animals,* III, 654-7; discussed in detail below, chap. XVIII.

[46]According to Dodge (*Plains of the Great West,* 144), the disappearance of the 'mountain bison' of the Colorado 'Parks' country was due to the same great storm which destroyed the buffalo on the Laramie Plains, 1844. Yet he himself, who reached the West only in 1849, hunted the 'bison.' See chap. III; also on the Wood buffalo, Soper, "History of the Northern Bison," 374, 380, 400, etc.

[47]Hornaday, "Extermination of the American Bison," 453.

[48]*Ibid.,* 461-2.

do. But at the same time, when beset by a blizzard, he would wisely seek shelter from it in some narrow and deep valley or system of ravines. There the herd would lie down and wait patiently for the storm to cease. After a heavy fall of snow, the place to find buffalo was in the flats and creek bottoms, where the tall rank bunch grasses showed their tops above the snow, and afforded the best and almost the only food obtainable. . . ."[49]

As a description of something which buffalo were *observed*—or even believed—to do on occasion, the foregoing is of great interest; as a definition of their conduct in all cases under such conditions, it is woefully inaccurate and misleading. The words *always* and *never* should have been deleted from Hornaday's scientific vocabulary. Under his plastic touch, an incident becomes a practice, and a practice becomes a law. We may question the precise 'wisdom' of a course which led such well-protected animals to seek shelter in the one type of country wherein they ran the greatest risk of being buried alive— the coulees. In the case of the 'mountain buffalo,' these localities were described by our principal authority, Colonel Dodge, who had hunted them in such territory, as their typical habitat; and the same hunter emphasized their intelligence and wariness, by contrast with their stupid Plains relative.[50] Nor is the implied distinction between 'wisely seeking shelter' and fleeing for refuge altogether clear. So also the supposed superiority in the wintering capacity of buffalo over domestic stock is not unchallenged by evidence. W. P. Webb records that on the same fatal Laramie Plains in the winter of 1864-65, the oxen of a snowed-up train were 'turned out to die,' but were found again in the spring in much better condition, which (says Webb) first revealed the stock-wintering possibilities of the region.[51] Bancroft, however, mentions oxen similarly turned loose in the Platte Valley in the winter of 1858-59 (with like astonishing results) by one A. J. Williams, a pioneer who first drove Mexican cattle to the Platte (1866).[52] The same superiority over domestic stock was also claimed for the hybrid cattalo by Buffalo Jones,[53] and the claim was endorsed by Thompson Seton.[54] Jones was a reckless and uncritical generalizer, however, and Seton the

[49]*Ibid.*, 423.

[50]Dodge, *Plains of the Great West*, 144; Hornaday, "Extermination of the American Bison," 408; *in extenso* above, chap. III, note 61.

[51]Webb, *Great Plains*, 225.

[52]Bancroft, *History of Nevada*, 543. Raine and Barnes speak of this as a common legend or occurrence in the West, but cite no other instance than Bancroft's (*Cattle, Cowboys, and Rangers*, 202).

[53]*Buffalo Jones' Forty Years*, 243-5.

[54]Seton, *Life-Histories of Northern Animals*, I, 299.

historian falls far short of Seton the field observer, as we shall have occasion to note.

A species which could winter at all on the northern plains habitat were assuredly no weaklings. Yet the propensity to seek shelter in cold and stormy weather must surely have been noticeable, since this was a very generally accepted belief, as an abundance of evidence attests. It is noted by Alexander Henry the elder, apparently south of Carlton or near Batoche, in February, 1776.[55] Alexander Mackenzie writes as follows, describing the North Saskatchewan country, 1789: ". . . the country in general on the West and North side of this great river, is broken by the lakes and rivers with small intervening plains, where the soil is good and the grass grows to some length. To these the male buffaloes resort for the winter, and if it be very severe, the females also are obliged to leave the plains. . . ."[56]

David Thompson, between (the present) Brandon, Manitoba, and Fort Garry (that is, 'the Forks'), February 26-March 3, 1798, records meeting only ". . . a chance small herd of Bisons, for these animals avoid deep snow."[57] The younger Henry, however, crossing much the same territory on a diagonal route from (Lake) Manitoba House to Pembina River, January 28-February 3, 1803, was "never out of sight of herds. . . ."[58] Patrick Gass, of Lewis and Clark's expedition (on the Missouri, December 9, 1804), remarks: "Very cold. Buffalo coming into the woods. . . ."[59] D. W. Harmon, the Nor' Wester (March 15, 1806), records "a heavy winter in the Athabaska country. . . . Buffaloes have been found in plenty within a few miles of the fort all winter . . ." (South Branch Fort, at or near Batoche, Saskatchewan).[60] The younger Alexander Henry, describing the country near Fort à la Corne, below the junction of the two Saskatchewans, says: "It cannot be called an open country, as spots of wood are frequent. Buffalo abound in winter when the cold obliges them to leave the plains for shelter among the hummocks, where they find plenty of good long grass. . . ."[61]

In other instances, the woodland country served them as a merely temporary refuge. Henry writes elsewhere (Red River, February 1, 1801): "A terrible snowstorm. Stormy weather causes the buffalo to

[55]Henry, Travels, 1760-1776, 280.
[56]Mackenzie, Voyages, 1789 and 1793, lxix.
[57]Thompson, Narrative, ed. Tyrrell, 246.
[58]Coues (ed.), Henry-Thompson Journals, I, 208.
[59]Gass, Journal of the Lewis and Clark Expedition, ed. Hosmer, 59.
[60]Harmon's Journal, 119; for the fort, Coues's note (Henry-Thompson Journals, II, 484).
[61]Ibid., 483.

approach the woods for shelter, and it no sooner abates than they return to the plains. . . ."[62] Alexander Ross of Fort Garry mentions a 'storm of several days' in December, 1825, which 'drove the buffalo beyond the hunters' reach,' and starvation ensued.[63] Maximilian of Wied (at the Mandan villages on the Missouri, 1833-34) observes: "The buffalo herds do not appear in the immediate neighbourhood of Fort Clarke,[64] except when the winter is very severe. . . . The hunters of the fort are often obliged to ride twenty miles before they find them. In the cold snow-storms, so prevalent during the winter, these animals take refuge in the forests on the banks, when great numbers of them are killed, and it is often almost impossible to drive them out of the wood. . . ."[65]

This may be contrasted with John McDonnell, at the same place, 1793-97, possibly describing some particular winter: "There is so little snow at the Missouri that the natives run down the buffalos on horseback the whole winter through. . . ."[66] Citing what was presumably a general local opinion, Sir George Simpson,[67] Palliser,[68] Dr. Hector,[69] Milton and Cheadle,[70] and Sir William Butler,[71] all noted that the buffalo in winter were wont to approach the edge of the woods.

All these Canadian authorities indicate a definite reason for the winter movements of the buffalo; not in specified directions, but into a specific type of country—regardless of direction *per se*, but wherever shelter might be attained. This may be contrasted with the vague general assertions about 'southern migrations for the winter,' which are frequently neither authenticated nor even intelligible. For they are sweepingly applied to the entire historic habitat of the species; yet in numerous instances climate and topography (in addition to unimpeachable historical evidence) are definitely opposed to the orthodox seasons or directions of these migrations of buffalo tradition.[72] John

[62]*Ibid.*, I, 160.

[63]Ross, *Red River Settlement*, 100.

[64]Now Bismarck, North Dakota. The Mandan villages are commemorated in Mandan, North Dakota, across the Missouri River.

[65]Maximilian, *Early Western Travels*, XXIII, 245; cf. *ibid.*, 345-6; XXIV, 53-5; see also below, note 84.

[66]McDonnell, in Masson, *Les Bourgeois de la Compagnie du Nord-Ouest*, I, 272.

[67]Simpson, *Journey Around the World*, I, 92.

[68]*Palliser Journals*, 92, 201, 202.

[69]*Ibid.*, 68, 75, 120-2.

[70]Milton and Cheadle, *North-West Passage*, 83, 146.

[71]Butler, *Wild North Land*, 167.

[72]See above, chap. IV, on climate, etc.; and for historical evidence in detail, chap. XX, below, "Irregular Migrations."

McDougall writes: "It is still very hard for the inexperienced to understand that the colder the weather and harder the winter, further into the north did the great herds feed; but all through the sixties and seventies this was my knowledge of them. . . ."[73]

Sixty years before McDougall, Sir George Simpson wrote:

They make yearly migrations from one part of the country to another, reversing, in this respect, the ordinary course of birds of passage. During the winter, they go north in order to obtain the shelter of the woods against the severity of the weather, while, on the approach of summer, they proceed to the open plains of the south with the view of eluding the attacks of the musquitoes. At this time of the year, they had deserted the country through which we had been travelling of late [near Carlton, North Saskatchewan River, July, 1841].[74]

Allen mentions a westward winter 'migration':

In northern Kansas the old trails show that their movements were formerly in the usual north and south direction, the trails all having that course. Since the construction of the Kansas Pacific Railway, however, their habits have completely changed, an east and west migration having recently prevailed to such an extent that a new set of trails, running at right angles to the earlier, have been deeply worn. Until recently the buffalo ranged eastward in summer . . . but retired westward in winter, few being found at this season east of Fort Hays. . . .[75] Two reasons may be assigned for this change of habit; first, their reluctance to cross the railroad, and secondly, the greater mildness of the winters to the westward of Ellis as compared with the region east of this point. During the winter of 1871-'72 I found that for a period of several weeks, in December and January, the country east of Ellis was covered with ice and encrusted snow sufficiently deep to bury the grass below the reach of either the buffaloes or the domestic cattle. In the vicinity of Ellis the amount of ice and snow began rapidly to diminish, while a little further westward the ground was almost wholly bare. I was informed, furthermore, that this was the usual distribution of snow in this region whenever any fell there. Although occasionally the snow does not accumulate in sufficient quantity to render grazing difficult over any of the country west of Fossil Creek, the buffaloes regularly abandon this region in winter for the country further west, where snow is of more exceptional occurrence. . . .[76]

In this account we are confronted with the same dilemma as in the *destruction* of buffalo by blizzards: why some climatic influences manifestly age-old should have induced the buffalo to change age-old ways only at the eleventh hour. The alleged reluctance to cross the tracks

[73]McDougall, *Red River Rebellion*, 26.
[74]Simpson, *Journey Around the World*, I, 92.
[75]Now Hays, north-northeast of Dodge City, Kansas.
[76]Allen, *American Bisons*, 61-2. See above, note 36, for 'old trails' leading east and west; evidently very old ones.

and the frequently ascribed influence of railways in general as a barrier to buffalo movements lack confirmation, and in that very region most specifically.[77] Allen apparently only saw the buffalo first in 1871,[78] and may have been dependent upon loose assertions from uncritical informants for the supposition that east-and-west trails were an innovation of recent times. As I have pointed out already, Hulbert's sweeping postulates on the buffalo-trail origin of westbound transcontinental highway and railroad routes demand such trails as Allen mentions;[79] and westward movements, in a region where the buffalo were virtually extinct before any railway came, will be noted in the present chapter.[80] It is interesting to notice that Hornaday, with whom the orthodox north-and-south migration is an absolute fetish, ignores this passage entirely, although Allen is his principal authority. Another logical consequence of the northward winter movements is even more amusing. Blizzards come as a rule—always in Manitoba, says Thompson Seton[81]— from the north. Consequently the buffalo must either turn tail before the storm, which Hornaday and his loyal henchman, Seton, say they did not;[82] or they must march or migrate northward in winter, which both Hornaday and Seton say they did not.[83]

Whether it be that they fled for refuge or 'wisely sought shelter' on such occasions, we have historical evidence of their selection of the coulees in more than one instance, much as Dr. Hornaday suggests. Charles Mackenzie, on the Missouri (February, 1805), writes: ". . . we lost our way and were obliged to seek shelter under the banks of a small creek, where the severity of the weather detained us three days. Here we found plenty of buffaloes, they did not mind our presence, and we killed four of them for the sake of their hides. . . ."[84] Dr. Elliott

---

[77]For detailed evidence, see below, chap. XV, note 63; chap. XVIII, note 95.
[78]Allen, *American Bisons*, 55.
[79]Cf. above, chap. IV, note 69.
[80]See below, notes 116, 117, 119.
[81]Seton, *Life-Histories of Northern Animals*, I, 266.
[82]Hornaday, "Extermination of the American Bison," 423, 453, 461; Seton, *Life-Histories of Northern Animals*, I, 266; but he says of the (late) Stony Mountain (Winnipeg) herd: "When a blizzard comes on they lie down close together with their backs to the wind, and allow the storm to drift over them . . ." (*ibid.*, I, 298). Later (1929) he remarks quite casually: "Even the Buffalo suffered in a blizzard, but the Musk-ox is equipped to meet any measure of cold and wind . . ." (*Game Animals*, III, 634).
[83]Hornaday, "Extermination of the American Bison," 382, 420-5; Seton, *Life-Histories of Northern Animals*, I, 262, 266. Seton also discussed Bunn's suggestion without noticing the heretical northward winter movement.
[84]Mackenzie, in Masson, *Les Bourgeois de la Compagnie du Nord-Ouest*, I, 333 (that is, to protect themselves against the biting cold).

Coues notes, concerning some such spot: "In exploring the Sweet Grass Hills [Montana], I followed up one gorge where for a mile or so skulls and skeletons lay almost touching each other in the *cul de sac*. Here was evident indication that a drove, in attempting to cross from the hog-back on one side to the other, had sunk in the snow which filled the ravine, and lost many of their number. . . ."[85] The late Sir Cecil Denny (a member of the original Northwest Mounted Police force of 1874) records a personal experience in the Milk River country in March, 1875. The police party had camped in a river-bottom during a blizzard; and a herd of buffalo came crowding in for shelter and almost overwhelmed them.[86] Catlin alludes to such incidents;[87] and Palliser, near High River, in southern Alberta, in 1858, refers to a large quantity of bones near a spring, which might be traceable to such a cause.[88] Down to the very last, however, it was commonly around springs where the final remains of exposed bone-vestiges were to be seen in any quantity (1894 *seq.*); and this included flat spring-muskegs, where excessive depths of snow could scarcely occur. Dr. Jenness refers to the discovery of bone-deposits in ravines on the Sarcee reservation, some few miles southwest of Calgary, Alberta, 1919-20;[89] but it is not entirely clear whether these were ever seen and identified by competent zoologists as buffalo bones or not. There is at least a possibility that they may have been relics of the famous 'Cochrane winter' of 1882-83, which destroyed so many range cattle.[90] A. S. Morton mentions similar masses found in ravines in the Kamsack and Fort Pelly country in eastern Saskatchewan, by the earliest settlers in the locality; which by the date of their discovery must assuredly have been those of buffalo, even without evidence of examination.[91] I have been unable, however, to obtain any further more precise information concerning them.

Precise information is almost invariably the one thing lacking in these recitals; and, without it, the assumption that snow was the direct cause of destruction is without adequate foundation. We have eyewitnesses to attest the workings of every other hostile physical agency: bogs and quicksands, fire, water, and rotten ice. Nobody seems ever to

[85]Correspondence with J. A. Allen, 1874 (*American Bisons*, 159).
[86]Denny, *The Law Marches West*, ed. Cameron, 69.
[87]Catlin, *Letters on North American Indians*, I, 253.
[88]*Palliser Journals*, 91.
[89]Jenness, *Indians of Canada*, 58; *Sarcee Indians of Alberta*, 14.
[90]See on this, above, chap. IV, note 35; also my own remarks, in *Canadian Historical Review*, XV, 218.
[91]Correspondence from the late Professor Morton, *ibid.*, 213-18; cf. above, note 1.

have seen buffalo overwhelmed or buried in snow.[92] There is nothing in Coues's rather meagre description which precludes the possibility that his *cul de sac* was really an old 'jumping-pound' site, of which there are plenty in the old buffalo territory.[93] In the other cases, where topographical detail is even more general and less informative, the possibilities are increased. Then, too, herds in temporary difficulties in deep snow might be 'corralled' and slain by hunters in situations from which they could have escaped without serious injury had they been left alone. In the instance cited by Butler, this is the precise method asserted to have been used.[94] If there were any historical value in Hornaday's dictum that these ravines were the sure places in which to find buffalo after a storm, such contingencies must have occasioned a terrific mortality among them; since none could possibly be better judges of this than the Indians themselves, whose mastery of every phase of buffalo-lore is extolled by early travellers everywhere throughout the habitat.[95] We shall have an early opportunity to judge.

The logical corollary of the belief that the buffalo always sought shelter from the cold and the storms was the belief that they refused to come in so long as the winter weather remained mild. D. W. Harmon notes at one of his Saskatchewan River posts—it is not entirely clear which—on January 9, 1802, that the buffalo, "in consequence of the late mild weather," had 'removed into the large prairie,' and on February 22, 1804, he makes an almost identical observation.[96] At Edmonton, in January, 1821, it was recorded that buffalo were scarce, owing to a mild winter;[97] and at the self-same time, George Simpson remarks on 'buffalo and moose being hard to get in a mild season, owing to their acuteness of smell and hearing.'[98] In what was described as the open winter of 1868-69 the buffalo are similarly recorded as being 'far out' (eastward) from McDougall's mission at Pigeon Lake, southwest from Edmonton.[99] Under such conditions, the approach of

[92]Pattie found some dead in the snow, perhaps in the South Pass, May, 1825 (*Early Western Travels*, XVIII, 140).

[93]Jumping Pond Creek, west of Calgary, should properly, of course, be 'Jumping pound.' The Blackfoot original, *ninapiskan*, contains the root-form *piskan* (*Place-Names of Alberta*, 69).

[94]Above, note 35.

[95]This is treated in detail below, chap. XXI, "The Influence of the Buffalo Environment upon Indian Mentality."

[96]*Harmon's Journal*, 58, 81; see also Gates (ed.), *Five Fur Traders of the North-West*, 134-55.

[97]Davidson, *North West Company*, Appendix O, 303.

[98]*Simpson's Athabaska Journal* (Champlain Society ed.), 236.

[99]McDougall, *Red River Rebellion*, 26.

cold weather was viewed with satisfaction. John McDougall tells us that in the winter of 1865 they were far out from Victoria (now Pakan) on the North Saskatchewan below Edmonton, where the McDougalls' mission home then was; and the 'old men' said: "Cold weather is near ... and the buffalo will come into this north country. . . ."[100]

Sometimes these expectations were realized; sometimes not. The following winter, 1866-67, the buffalo were 'far out south and east' from Pigeon Lake the entire winter season, in spite of its exceptional severity.[101] McDougall describes a mid-winter journey in search of them (January, 1867) from Victoria via Birch Lake (Innisfree, Alberta) to the Battle River near Wainwright; but they were 80 or 100 miles farther south, "and had not yet attempted to come north," despite the bitter weather, with the result that Victoria was very short of food.[102] In 1867-68 they were again far out from Pigeon Lake and Edmonton, causing much destitution among the Indians throughout the district.[103] In winter, 1872-73, McDougall again relates: "The buffalo kept out beyond them, and notwithstanding the stress and storm of the rigorous winter, refused to come into the northern pastures on the Battle and Saskatchewan Rivers. . . ."[104] This last statement is corroborated in part by Butler. At the Forks of the Saskatchewan, October 31, 1872, buffalo were said to be 200 miles, or 'fifteen days' distant.[105]

The same uncertain disposition was noted in other localities. I have quoted Mackenzie on the evident superior endurance of the cows.[106] So also Henry (February 1, 1801, describing a Manitoba blizzard): "A terrible snow-storm. . . . It is surprising how the cows resist the piercing N. wind, which at times blows with such violence and raises such drifts over the bleak plains, that it cannot be faced; still, these animals graze in the open field. . . ."[107] Henry records again (November 15, 1805): "A terrible snow-storm. . . . Buffalo passing northward in as great numbers as ever I saw them. . . ."[108] The incidental jottings

[100]McDougall, *Pathfinding*, 11-12, 117, 120, 150.
[101]*Ibid.*, 183-210.
[102]*Ibid.*, 196, 210.
[103]*Ibid.*, 243, 248; so also Hughes, *Father Lacombe*, 142.
[104]McDougall, *Western Trails*, 9. Cf. Milton and Cheadle, whose Indian hunter, 'several years before' their acquaintance with him (1862), nearly starved to death near Carlton, because that winter the buffalo, despite the cold, 'did not come up to the woods' (*North-West Passage*, 146).
[105]Butler, *Wild North Land*, 44, 57.
[106]Above, note 56.
[107]Coues (ed.), *Henry-Thompson Journals*, I, 169.
[108]*Ibid.*, I, 273. See remarks above, notes 81-3.

of both Thompson and Henry concerning varying feast-and-famine conditions in winter, 1797-1805, in the regions of Lake Manitoba, Brandon, and the Pembina and Red rivers, fully substantiate the irregular attitude of the species toward snow and blizzards.[109] Thirty years later, Maximilian wrote (at the Mandan villages on the Missouri): ". . . in winter, when they approach the Missouri and seek shelter in the woods, a great number are often killed in a short time. If it is very cold, and the buffalo keep at a distance in the prairie, they [the Mandans] hunt but little. . . ."[110] He had experience of this refusal to come in, during a blizzard in January, 1834: ". . . exposure to the weather was painful both to man and beast. It was hoped, however, that it would soon cause the herds of buffalo to come nearer to us, but this expectation was not realized. . . ."[111]

This same region furnishes some striking commentaries on the supposed certainty of 'knowing where to find buffalo' after a storm. Patrick Gass has recorded that in December, 1804, buffalo were thought to be near, but could not be found.[112] About Christmas, however, they drew nigh in force; and likewise the following winter.[113] During the aforementioned blizzard of January, 1834, the Mandan hunters were out for a week in search of buffalo, but without success. Following shortly upon this, herds were discovered only six miles distant.[114] Such experiences are a commonplace in buffalo history in all seasons and localities, and may be instructively compared with the idle rhetoric I have quoted on the subject.[115]

True to their utterly unpredictable disposition, on other occasions the buffalo did as was expected of them. McDougall writes (January, 1876, near Morley, Bow River, west of Calgary): ". . . the snow was deepening and the weather becoming colder. This encouraged us, as we thought it would bring the wild herds nearer to the foothills. . . . The cold was intense and the buffalo were steadily heading for the hills. . . . We could see the herds moving westward. . . ."[116] These winter experiences serve as a corrective to supposed southerly migra-

[109]Compare Coues (ed.), Henry-Thompson Journals, I, passim.
[110]Maximilian, Early Western Travels, XXIII, 345.
[111]Ibid., XXIV, 53-4.
[112]Gass, Journal of the Lewis and Clark Expeditions, 55, 62.
[113]Mackenzie in Masson, Les Bourgeois de la Compagnie du Nord-Ouest, I 331, 366.
[114]Maximilian, Early Western Travels, XXIV, 55; cf. ibid., XXIII, 274; XXIV, 45, 53, 57, 63, 89, 94.
[115]Given in detail below, chap. XX, "Irregular Migrations."
[116]McDougall MS., 34, 36, 37.

tions as a uniform practice.[117] But they were not a mere 'hibernating' in some one selected spot. A. B. Hulbert in his usual sweeping style informs us that "the buffalo . . . did not travel in the winter. . . ."[118] As is not uncommon, historical evidence tells a different tale. General W. H. Ashley, the fur trader, writes at the 'South Fork of the Platte,' December 28, 1824: "The snow was now so deep that had it not been for the numerous herds of buffalo moving down the river we could not possibly have proceeded. The paths of these animals were beat on either side of the river and afforded an easy passage to our horses. . . ."[119] John McDougall tells us also: "If one was in doubt as to a crossing let him follow the path of a buffalo. Gladly have I often taken to these in the wintertime, when the snow was deep. Taking off my snow-shoes, I have run behind my dog-train on the packed trail made by the sharp hoofs of the migrating buffalo. . . ."[120] Such movements in themselves, apart from any following of trails, are well attested in all regions of the historic habitat west of the Mississippi, south,[121] north,[122] and also in the deep-snow territories west of the Rocky Mountains.[123]

It will occasion no surprise to the reader by this time to find that even the winter habits of the buffalo while grazing are not uniformly authenticated. Catlin speaks of them 'pawing through the snow';[124] but the passage occurs in a sort of general introduction to his very

[117]Compare above, note 80.

[118]Hulbert, Historic Highways, I, 130; XI, 31-2.

[119]Dale (ed.), Ashley-Smith Explorations, 124. An eastward movement in winter, nearly fifty years before those 'new trails' circa 1870. See above, note 76; also 'old' ones, note 36.

[120]McDougall, Pathfinding, 103.

[121]Coues (ed.), Expeditions of Pike, II, 474, 485-90; Marcy, Prairie Traveller, 234; Dale (ed.), Ashley-Smith Explorations, 124; Allen, American Bisons (correspondence from Coues), 159.

[122]Hearne, Journey, ed. Tyrrell, 255-76; Henry, Travels, 1760-1776, 278-80; Thompson, Narrative, ed. Tyrrell, 305. Henry, Jr., thought from finding dung only under the snow, Kootenay Park, North Saskatchewan River, February 8, 1811, that they went up there only in summer, but found buffalo three days higher up, February 11 (Coues (ed.), Henry-Thompson Journals, II, 686-91, 697). Richardson, Fauna Boreali-Americana, I, 281; also in Franklin, (First) Journey to the Polar Sea, 55. Hector in Palliser Journals, 69. Blodgett (U.S.A.), in Hind, Report, 1858, 122-4. Macoun, Manitoba, 153. Tuttle, Our North Land, 415. Allen, American Bisons, 59-61, 159. Hughes, Father Lacombe, 266. McClintock, Old North Trail, 81-3. Denny MS., 252, 274, etc. Above all, detailed accounts in Coues (ed.), Henry-Thompson Journals, I, 130, 162, 166, 230, 273 (Red River, 1799-1805); and in McDougall at large.

[123]1825: Dale (ed.), Ashley-Smith Explorations, 141; 1833: Irving, Captain Bonneville, 332; 1841-42: De Smet, Early Western Travels, XXVII, 334, 348, 349.

[124]Catlin, Letters on the North American Indians, I, 248.

valuable description of the animal, and while quite possibly representing his actual opinion, it is not sufficiently reasoned to justify critical
insistence upon it. Denny uses the same expression, perhaps copied
from Catlin, but apparently in the same loose sense.[125] Denny's general
observations, moreover, as apart from his personal experiences, are of
small scientific value by reason of an insufficient comparative criticism. The only really direct observations in favour of 'pawing' are from
Richardson, in so far as I can discover, and I am not certain whether
he had ever seen buffalo at close range in winter before 1829. He
writes thus: "In winter they scrape away the snow with their feet to
reach the grass. . . ."[126] He says elsewhere: "The wild buffalo scrapes
away the snow with its feet to get at the herbage beneath, and the
horse, which was introduced by the Spanish invaders of Mexico, and
may be said to have become naturalized, does the same; but it is
worthy of remark that the ox, more lately brought from Europe, has
not yet acquired an art so necessary for procuring its food. . . ."[127] *Per
contra,* Palliser, who would seem to have been acquainted with
Richardson's opinion, writes: "I have killed many fat buffaloes in the
months of January and February, after which I have invariably found
them lean, and sometimes seen the ground sprinkled with blood from
the hardness of the surface, which the animal tries to shovel aside with
its nose. If even the buffalo, whose nose is formed by nature for this
purpose, finds a difficulty in obtaining his food, how much more difficult for [domestic animals]."[128]

That excellent observer, Dr. Hector, confirms this by personal
scrutiny, in the Red Deer River country, near the present Innisfail,
Alberta, December, 1858: ". . . we saw a large band of buffalo and
approached them by crawling in the snow, by which I got the best
view I ever had of the animals when quietly feeding. The snow was
about twelve inches deep on the open ground, and in feeding I saw
that they used their noses like pigs to plough it up, and did not scrape
like horses with their fore feet. . . ."[129]

Contemporary observers of the northwest Wood buffalo say the
same of them.[130] Thompson Seton writes concerning the hybrid animal: "The *Cattalo* . . . has the advantage of being exceedingly hardy,
fearless of blizzards, able to paw and root through the snow for grass

[125]Denny MS., introd., 12.
[126]Richardson, *Fauna Boreali-Americana,* I, 281.
[127]Extract from Journal, in Franklin, (First) *Journey to the Polar Sea,* 55.
[128]*Palliser Journals,* 12-13.
[129]*Ibid.,* 122.
[130]Graham, *Canada's Wild Buffalo,* 7; Soper, "History of the Northern Bison,"
400.

when ordinary cattle would starve. . . ."[131] He cites Buffalo Jones as his authority, but Jones says, "they root in snow."[132] Professor Mac-Innes, who had available much evidence from 'old-timers,' speaks of the range cattle 'muzzling through the snow.'[133] This agrees with my own experience, which is, however, not wide, since we were compelled to feed our northern cattle entirely throughout the winters. The only pawing I have ever noticed was by bulls in the rutting season or when excited, much as Dr. Gregg described the buffalo bulls 'pawing the earth' when making a wallow.[134] Probably to old plainsmen, the feeding habits of the buffalo were so utterly familiar as to excite no remark; and most of the travellers to whom buffalo were a novelty, saw them in summer. Anthony Henday speaks of seeing them on the Saskatchewan prairies (September 13, 1754), "grazing like English cattle . . .";[135] but the expression can only be considered a general one, and though I have more than once seen the same country white with snow on that date, he makes no mention of such a condition. One might very easily have observed the living species at Wainwright, prior to the closing of the Park; but I have never chanced to be there in heavy snowfall, nor to see one single buffalo whenever I was there.[136] And since I share the opinion expressed by eminent zoologists, that a wild race are really living unnaturally under such conditions,[137] I deliberately refrained from going there while pursuing my buffalo researches more seriously. The point is not in itself of great importance, but my experience strikingly illustrates the frequently contradictory nature of so much of the evidence on the uniformity of buffalo behaviour.[138]

[131]Seton, Life-Histories of Northern Animals, I, 299.

[132]Buffalo Jones' Forty Years, 50. Garretson also is for the Buffalo 'rooting' in the snow (American Bison, 46).

[133]MacInnes, In the Shadow of the Rockies, 195, 218.

[134]Gregg, Early Western Travels, XX, 132.

[135]"Henday's Journal," ed. Burpee, 332.

[136]As a curious commentary on 'disappearance' (above, note 43), in 1924 the Wainwright Park contained nearly 9000 buffalo (see below, chap. XVIII). During four months that summer I spent every Sunday in Wainwright and visited the Park on at least three-fifths of them. Despite countless fresh tracks about the entrance lodge, I never once saw an animal.

[137]Osborn, Age of Mammals, 502; Scharff, Distribution and Origin of Life in America, 66. The late Dr. Gordon Hewitt was of the contrary opinion. See his account of the Wainwright Park "buffalo living under these eminently natural conditions"—inside fences! Hewitt, Conservation of the Wild Life of Canada, 134-6. The sequel scarcely vindicates the plea. See below, Appendix J, "Buffalo and Disease."

[138]Hewitt considered that the readiness of the Park animals to eat hay marked an approach toward semi-domestication (Conservation of the Wild Life of Canada, 136). At Carlton, January, 1840, Thomas Simpson found Patrick Small, the trader,. hastily getting in his stacks before the buffalo consumed them utterly (Narrative

To what extent can the foregoing evidence be thought to support any hypothesis of wholesale destruction by snow? I recall a conversation many years ago with a particularly well-informed 'old-timer,' the late Hon. Frank Oliver (Edmonton, 1876-1933), concerning the 'Cochrane winter' of 1882-83, which he well remembered. Mr. Oliver was emphatically of the opinion that snow had played no part worth considering in the extinction of the wild buffalo; and I am constrained to agree. As I have remarked, we have no direct proof that the supposed catastrophes traceable to snow were really caused by that; and the testimony of eye-witnesses indicates that the buffalo had a generally well-founded indifference to, and disdain for, snow.

The supposition that the final disappearance of the buffalo was sudden has led to suggestions that some catastrophic or other non-human agency must have been responsible. It had, however, been known to most people, broadly speaking, that the herds were dwindling away. My own view may be summed up in this way. We know as we grow older that almost certainly we shall need glasses as eyesight begins to fail. Despite our recognition of this entirely normal human process, I strongly suspect that when the day actually arrives when they can no longer be dispensed with, most of us feel a sense of sudden shock. Or we might take a case where one's utmost frugality cannot avoid having to slightly encroach upon his principal each year, in order to meet living expenses. Everybody knows the inevitable result of such a contingency. Yet I doubt whether anyone could make the final discovery that the cupboard was actually bare without a similar shock. I consider that only in some such sense can the final disappearance of the buffalo be regarded as sudden.[139]

NOTE

It is regrettable in relation to such a question as the buffalo reaction to snow, that since the commingling and interbreeding of the northern Wood buffalo and the Plains immigrants from the Wainwright Park (which has produced a hybrid mentality as well as appearance; see Soper, "History of the Northern Bison," 375-6, 396-9), the data on so-called Wood buffalo are inevitably somewhat unreriable. Various habits and traits, supposedly aboriginal in the region, may really be of Plains derivation, recorded as such long ago by our earlier literary authorities. See Skinner and Kaisen, *Fossil Bison of Alaska*, 168.

---

of Discoveries, 402). Similarly, at Fort Ellice, *circa* 1867, in hard winters, the haystacks required watchmen to keep the buffalo away (Cowie, *Company of Adventurers*, 182).

[139]See also my remarks (*Canadian Historical Review*, XV, 213-18).

Chapter IX

THE EUROPEAN DISCOVERY OF THE BUFFALO

M ORE than one virtually independent discovery of the buffalo was made by Europeans. This is not surprising, when we consider its vast habitat, probably exceeded only by those of the two great cats of the Old World and the African elephant. The African lion has been found from end to end of that huge continent, and in Asia as far east as Mesopotamia, and a closely related (maneless) form has been found in Gujerat (northwest India). The Asiatic tiger ranges (or ranged) throughout India proper on the west, to southern China, Indo-China, Burma, Siam, and certain large islands of the Malay Archipelago on the east and southeast, and as far as Mongolia and Manchuria in the north.[1] The *Canidae* and the *Cervidae* can hardly be acknowledged as competitors, since both families embrace many very widely differing species.

The buffalo habitat extended from Georgia in the southeast to the north of Great Slave Lake in the northwest;[2] and from the extreme south of the province of Neuva Biscaya (states of Chihuahua and Durango, Mexico[3]) certainly to the eastern end of Lake Erie, and possibly much farther east. From its northern limit, about 63° N., to its southern (if Durango City could be taken as the datum) on the Tropic of Cancer, 24° N., there is an enormous stretch of over 2700 miles. The limit commonly given, however, is nearer 28° N.[4] For the general delimitation of the buffalo range, I cannot do better than quote two admirable summaries, which differ slightly:

The range of the American bison extended over about one-third of the entire continent of North America. Starting almost at tide-water on the Atlantic coast, it extended westward through a vast tract of dense forest, across the Alleghany Mountain system to the prairies along the Mississippi, and southward to the Delta of that great stream. Although the great plains

---

[1]*Encyclopaedia Britannica*, 14th ed., *s.v.* Lion, Tiger. In the Natural History Museum, South Kensington (London), August 23, 1929, I saw a fine mounted specimen of a tiger from Mongolia, a rich tawny colour.

[2]Richardson, *Fauna Boreali-Americana*, I, 279.

[3]Berlandier MS., now lost, cited by Allen, *American Bisons*, 129; Hornaday, "Extermination of the American Bison," 382. Given *in extenso* below, chap. XIX, note 10.

[4]Berlandier MS. (in Allen, *American Bisons*, 129; Hornaday, "Extermination of the American Bison," 382).

country of the West was the natural home of the species, where it flourished most abundantly, it also wandered south across Texas to the burning plains of northeastern Mexico, westward across the Rocky Mountains into New Mexico, Utah, and Idaho, and northward across a vast treeless waste to the bleak and inhospitable shores of the Great Slave Lake itself. It is more than probable that had the bison remained unmolested by man and uninfluenced by him, he would eventually have crossed the Sierra Nevada and the Coast Range, and taken up his abode in the fertile valleys of the Pacific Slope. . . .[5]

According to another authority, the buffalo range was:

. . . chiefly between the Rocky and Alleghany mountains. While traces of the buffalo have been found as far east as Cavetown, Maryland—and there is documentary evidence that the animal ranged almost, if not quite, to the Georgia coast—the lack of remains in the shell-heaps of the Atlantic shore seems to indicate its absence generally from that region, although it was not unknown to some of the tribes living on the rivers. . . . At that time (i.e. *circa* 1530) the herds ranged from below the Rio Grande in Mexico, N.W. through what is now E. New Mexico, Utah, Oregon, Washington, and British Columbia, thence crossing the mountains to Great Slave Lake, they roamed the valleys of Saskatchewan and Red rivers, keeping to the W. of l. Winnipeg and l. Superior and S. of l. Michigan and l. Erie, to the vicinity of Niagara; there turning southward to W. Pennsylvania and crossing the Alleghanies they spread over the W. portion of Maryland, Virginia, North Carolina, South Carolina, Georgia, and N. Mississippi and Louisiana. All the tribes within this range depended largely on the buffalo for food and clothing, and this dependence, with the influence of the habits of the animal, profoundly affected tribal customs and religious rites. This is more clearly seen in the tribes W. of the Mississippi, where the people were in constant contact with the buffalo during the summer and winter migrations of the great northern and southern herds. These great herds were composed of innumerable smaller ones of a few thousands each, for the buffalo was never solitary; except by accident. . . .[6]

An earlier student than either, writing about 1871, says that "undoubted evidence exists to show that at some period the buffalo reached in his vast migrations the shores of the Pacific and the Atlantic. . . ."[7] It is regrettable that something of this evidence was not forthcoming. The years intervening since Butler's day have produced little enough in support of the opinion. We shall note a similar instance below, in relation to a supposed European discoverer.

[5]*Ibid.*, 376; cf. Allen, *American Bisons*, 72-4.
[6]Alice C. Fletcher, *s.v.* Buffalo, *Handbook of American Indians*, I, 170. As a summary of their presence, this is admirable; as a description of the actual routes of dispersion (if that be what is meant), both her account and Hornaday's outstrip our actual knowledge.
[7]Butler, *Great Lone Land*, 315; cf. Seton, *Game Animals*, III, 646, 703.

It seems possible that the very first Europeans to gaze upon the animal—although not at large—were Cortez and his companions upon their arrival in the city of Mexico in 1519.[8] The buffalo was described by the Spanish historian, De Solis (writing in 1684,[9] 1691,[10] or 1724[11]) as being in the zoological collection of the Aztec monarch, Montezuma; the sight of which so astonished the *conquistadores*. De Solis refers to the animal in his work as the 'Mexican Bull':[12] ". . . a wonderful composition of divers Animals. It has crooked Shoulders with a Bunch on its Back like a Camel, its Flanks dry; its Tail large, and its Neck covered with Hair like a Lion. It is cloven-footed, its Head armed like that of a Bull, which it resembles in Fierceness, with no less Strength and Agility. . . ."[13]

Strangely enough, this passage appears to have escaped the notice of the lynx-eyed Prescott—if one may apply the figure to an almost blind man. Among the commerce of the Aztecs he mentions 'hides, raw and dressed,'[14] which could surely have been only buffalo in 1519.[15] This, together with a brief reference in concluding to the range of the buffalo in or near the Mexican dominions, is his only notice of

[8]Hornaday ("Extermination of the American Bison," 373) and Seton (*Game Animals*, III, 644) have 1521. I have followed the date given by Prescott (*Conquest of Mexico*, I, 337).

[9]Seton, *Life-Histories of Northern Animals*, I, 251.

[10]Seton, *Game Animals*, III, 644.

[11]Allen, *American Bisons*, 231; Hornaday, "Extermination of the American Bison," 373.

[12]*Taurus Mexicanus* appears earlier; in *Rerum Medicarum Novae Hispaniae Thesaurus Francisci Hernandez* (Roma, 1651), 587; so Richardson, *Fauna Boreali-Americana*, I, xxxix, 279. Audubon and Bachman, *American Quadrupeds*, II, 33. Bancroft mentions the work of Dr. Hernandez as being written for Philip II of Spain (1527-98), *Native Races*, II, 165, 476; III, 728.

[13]Allen, *American Bisons*, Appendix, 231; Hornaday, "Extermination of the American Bison," 373.

[14]Prescott, *Conquest of Mexico*, I, 375; cf. Bancroft, *Native Races*, II, 378.

[15]Later exports of hides from New Spain and the Islands are well known. Martine Basanier of Paris says (1582): ". . . the Spaniards at their first entrance into Hispaniola found neither sugar-cane nor ginger growing there, nor any kind of our cattel. But finding the place fit for pasture they sent kine & buls and sundry sort of other profitable beasts thither . . . the hides of which oxen with sugar and ginger, are now the chief merchandise of that Island . . ." (Hakluyt, *Voyages*, VI, 229); cf. *ibid.*, 249, 289; VII, 92, etc.

So also Cuba. The Gentleman of Elvas says (of the 'many wild cows there'): ". . . so numerous likewise are the paths made by cattle, that no one can travel without an Indian of the country for a guide, there being everywhere high and thick woods . . ." (*Narratives of De Soto*, I, 14, 17).

Acosta (1588) states that 64,350 hides were exported from New Spain in 1587, of the two kinds, 'tame and wild kine.' Thousands of the latter were slain for the hides only, leaving the flesh; "so that in some places the aire hath beene corrupted with the abundance of these stinking carkasses . . ." (*Purchas his Pil-*

the species in his great work;[16] and a later (and most voluminous) historian is likewise silent.[17]

Several of the more notable among the Spanish explorers just missed being among the earliest Europeans to view the animal in its native haunts. Hornaday remarks: "Neither De Soto, Ponce de Leon, Vasquez de Ayllon, nor Pamphilo [sic] de Narváez ever saw the buffalo, for the reason that all their explorations were made south of what was then the habitat of that animal. At the time De Soto made his great exploration from Florida northwestward to the Mississippi and into Arkansas (1539-1541) he did indeed pass through country in northern Mississippi and Louisiana that was afterward inhabited by the buffalo, but at that time not one was to be found there. . . ."[18]

This failure to push on to the actual locality of the animal when they were within 'five or six leagues' of its presence[19] may possibly have been caused by the disease from which De Soto not long after-wards died, and its probable effects upon the morale of the expedition, or even, perhaps, to the 'cold' of the buffalo country,[20] which was discouraging to the Spaniards. It seems strange to us, however, when we consider that before leaving Spain for this expedition into Florida, De Soto had conferred with Alvar Nuñez Cabeza de Vaca concerning the wonderful beasts which the latter had seen.[21]

grimes, XV, 127). Oviedo says the same of Hispaniola (1525): "of Beeves . . . which I knew first carried thither from Spain" (ibid., XV, 224). In 1590 New Spain exported 100,000 hides (Hakluyt, Voyages, VII, 136).

[16]Prescott, Conquest of Mexico, II, 400-1.

[17]Bancroft (who includes De Solis in his Bibliography) never mentions him in his account of 'Montezuma's menagerie' and of Aztec commerce (Native Races, II, 163-7, 378-97).

[18]Hornaday, "Extermination of the American Bison," 375. The dates of the four explorers are respectively 1539-42, 1512, 1520, and 1524, 1528. See J. G. Shea, in Winsor (ed.), Narrative and Critical History, II, 231-98; Fiske, Discovery of America, II, 483-500; Brittain, History of North America, I, 496, etc.; and for De Soto, Purchas his Pilgrimes, XVII, 521-50; XVIII, 1-51; Narratives of De Soto, I, 128, 133, 140. Cf. also Allen, American Bisons, 100, 133.

[19]Purchas his Pilgrimes, XVIII, 31, 33; Narratives of De Soto, I, 128, 133, 140 (Elvas).

[20]Ibid. Cf. above, chap. IV, note 43.

[21]Purchas his Pilgrimes, XVIII, 45; also the Gentleman of Elvas (in Narratives of De Soto, I, 140). De Soto, "Letter to the Magistrates of Santiago de Cuba" (ibid., II, 162), implies this, and also that he himself did not see them: ". . . a town containing [among other things] herds of tame deer that are tended. What this means unless it be the cattle of which we brought the knowledge with us [from Spain, I take it], I do not understand. . . ."

These things make me somewhat suspicious about Cortez having seen the animal long before. Surely this would be known in Spanish court circles. Cortez was there in 1528 (Prescott, Conquest of Mexico, II, 339). De Solis wrote much

This last notable personage was the first of all known Europeans to behold 'the cows' in their natural freedom—in the course of his eight years of wandering, sometimes alone, sometimes with his companions, Andres Dorantes, Alonso del Castillo Maldonado, and Estévanico, a Moor or 'negro'—successively as slave, guest, or leader among the many Indian tribes of the lower North American continent, from the Gulf of Mexico to the Pacific slope, 1528-36. I quote from his description of the animals:

> They found Oxen there and I saw them three times, and eate of them; and (as I thinke) they are of the bignesse of those of Spaine. They have little hornes like the Moresche cattle, and very long haire, and some of them are ash-colour, and others blacke, and in my judgment they have better haire and much thicker than those of our Countries. Of those which are not great, they make Garments to cover them, and of the greater they make shoes and targets [that is, shields] and these came from the North further through the Land unto the Coast of Florida, and extend themselves farre within the Land more than four hundred leagues. And in this way, through the Vallies by which they come, the people that dwell there come downe and eat of them, and send great store of hides into the Countrie. . . .[22]

It is not certain, however, just where Cabeza de Vaca encountered the animals. While the general opinion of the older school concerning the locality of his shipwreck remains but little altered,[23] the region of his meeting with the buffalo, and the southern limits of the buffalo range itself, have occasioned discussion. While the views of the latest critic on this question must command respect by reason of his wide local knowledge and field experience, that portion of his argument which is based partly upon buffalo history is not wholly satisfactory, since it lacks the wide research given to the geographical, topographical, and ecological factors affecting the route of Cabeza.[24]

---

later; and Cortez was a most unlikely man to yield to anyone a prior knowledge of anything in the land *he* had discovered. Furthermore, it seems doubtful, *a priori*, whether any creature furnishing a commercial 'raw material' as indicated by Prescott (above, note 14) would also be a zoological curiosity, *among the same people*.

[22]*Purchas his Pilgrimes*, XVII, 449-507. *Journey of Cabeza*, ed. Bandelier, 94. See also Hallenbeck, *Journey of Cabeza de Vaca*, 65-6, 140-6, 200, etc.

[23]Allen (*American Bisons*, 131) cites Davis, *Spanish Conquest of New Mexico*, 1867 (which I have not seen), who puts the shipwreck of Narváez in 1528, at some point on the Louisiana coast, west of the Mississippi. Hallenbeck shows that Galveston Island (Cabeza's 'Malhado Island') is practically the only one that meets the conditions (*Journey of Cabeza de Vaca*, 119-27, 247 *seq.*). General conclusions varied between Galveston and Matagorda Bays.

[24]'Somewhere in S.E. Texas'; so Allen, *American Bisons*, 131. "In all probability, within fifty miles of the present city of Houston, Texas . . ." (Hornaday, "Extermination of the American Bison," 381). See also John Gilmary Shea, in

Winsor (ed.), *Narrative and Critical History*, II, 287. Fiske, *Discovery of America*, I, 251; II, 501. Brittain, *History of North America*, I, 498, etc. Bancroft sums up the attitude of the earlier school; see his *North Mexican States and Texas*, I, 60-70; also his *History of Arizona*, 16-19.

More recent (Texan) scholars route Cabeza much farther south than formerly. See on this, Webb, *Great Plains*, 95-102 (who himself seems uncertain about this); also Bishop, *Odyssey of Cabeza de Vaca*, who cites much original Spanish and local southwestern material and presents the outstanding biography of Cabeza. Cleve Hallenbeck is purely exegetical and interpretative. While I am incompetent, and do not propose, to offer any opinion on Cabeza's route *per se*, Hallenbeck's conclusions on the buffalo habitat seem untenable. He puts their 'normal southern limit' (itself a projecting 'tongue') at Austin, Texas (map, 306), on the strength of 'tradition.' Cabeza, as given above (note 23), has them 'unto the Coast of Florida,' which term Hallenbeck himself extends to the Rio Grande (*Journey of Cabeza de Vaca*, 33). These, however, are explained as being "only stragglers from the main herd" (*ibid.*, 140-2). I find no warrant for this in Cabeza himself. Similarly, Cabeza's four hundred leagues are explained as being northward from where he met them, whether in Texas or in Oklahoma (*ibid.*, 66). But how could Cabeza know this? Whatever '400 leagues' may be, something between 800 and 1200 miles (see on this, Hallenbeck, *ibid.*, 111, who reckons the old Spanish league as roughly equal to three miles), is it not as likely to mean across country which was in some degree known to Cabeza himself? With Cabeza at the southern limit, such a distance northward would take him close to modern Canada, of which he could know nothing. A mere random assertion would surely be in more indefinite round numbers—500 or 1000; '400' reads like at least an attempt at an estimate.

So also the testimony of any one old buffalo-hunter, even more so his mere opinion, belief, assurance (as Captain Poe, *ibid.*, 144, 145), while always acceptable as contributory evidence, is impossible as a final generalization; most assuredly so in relation to an epoch of some 350 years earlier. If the buffalo movements in or out of Texas were for pasturage and not for climate (as held by Poe, *ibid.*, 145), why did they not occupy those 'vast and handsome pastures' which Cabeza found 'all over the land' (*ibid.*, 140; *Journey of Cabeza*, ed. Bandelier, 97); and why did they ever leave Texas in spring, when pasturage was getting better, as Hornaday and Professor Rowan have very pertinently noted (see above, chap. IV, note 65)?

The absence of buffalo from any locality in a given year proves nothing whatever. The silence of tradition and of travel journals makes Hallenbeck's strongest point; but he himself comments on Cabeza's failure to note things 'that he must have seen' (*Journey of Cabeza de Vaca*, 106, 268, etc.; cf. on the silence, 144, 145). In fact, this argument would prove too much. Hallenbeck (p. 143) identifies the river where Hernando de Alvarado 'saw his first buffalo,' 1540, as the 'Canadian' and not the 'Pecos'; as Espejo thought erroneously, 1583 (says Hallenbeck); and Winship (ed., in *Journey of Coronado*, ix, 64, 228). Winship prints Alvarado's "Report" (*ibid.*, 241 *seq.*). The only river mentioned therein 'flows through a very wide open plain,' and is identified by the editor as the Rio Grande. Seeing 'the cows' is not referred to. In this work of Winship's, which contains (p. vi) 'many revisions and corrections' from his original translation of 1896 in the *Fourteenth Report, U.S. Bureau of Ethnology* (which I have not seen), neither Castañeda nor Jaramillo mentions any Rio de las Vacas. Hallenbeck does not specify *why* this is the Canadian River. Others have done so, as being the 'ravine' where the Spaniards camped near the buffalo (i.e. from the name *cañada* = gorge; see Webb, *Great Plains*, 95-102, citing Texan scholars on this; who place Quivira there, and Coronado 'never off the *Llano Estacado* of Texas'). But

We may compare another description by one of Coronado's party (1541): "These Oxen are of the bignesse of our Bulls, but their hornes lesse, with a great bunch on their foreshoulders, and more haire on their fore-parts than behind, which is like wool; a mane like a horses on their back-bone, and long haire from the Knees downward, with store of long haire at the chinne and throat, a long flocke also at the

Castañeda said this of the *rivers* (plural) 'which flow at the bottom of ravines' (*Journey of Coronado*, 111). This implies most or all of them. Whether this be correct or not, Alvarado, as I remark above, mentions no such type of river; and arguing from the 'silence,' so emphasized by Hallenbeck above, the 'Canadian' would hence be disqualified. Conversely, who would care to endorse the legendary 'hoop-snake' (in the same region) on the ground of persistent tradition, which is its only discoverable foundation?

Finally, Hallenbeck says that the trails of the region "were first broken out by the herbivorous animals of the southwest," and afterwards used by the Indians (*Journey of Cabeza de Vaca*, 110). He cites no authority for this in relation to circa 1530. Cabeza himself said, ". . . all through that country there are no trails . . ." (*Journey of Cabeza*, ed. Bandelier, 102; cf. 119, 128, 174, etc.). On the plains, Castañeda's only mention is of 'paths down into the ravines, made by the cows' (*Journey of Coronado*, ed. Winship, 111). Elsewhere he says (*ibid.*, 139-40) that the passage of hundreds of animals and men left no trace, as the short wiry grass straightened up behind them, and bones and cow dung had to be piled up as landmarks to guide those following after. This is corroborated by his comrades (*ibid.*, 195, 209, 210, 215, 231, 238). On the return journey from Quivira, Jaramillo says their guides led them 'by a good road' (*ibid.*, 238). But *road* here clearly signifies *route*; for Castañeda very carefully describes how the Indians kept their direction in a pathless region by successive arrows shot ahead of them (*ibid.*, 75). Yet this was the direct route between Quivira and Cibola, perhaps the two most important places in that country, wherever they might be situated; and *there was no visible road!* I doubt if the antelope—apparently the other herbivorous gregarious denizen of the Cabeza prairie-route (Hallenbeck, *Journey of Cabeza de Vaca*, 67, 141, 151)—was any trail-breaker. After many years' historical and field investigation, I utterly reject the *animal*-Indian-highway supposition; but the late A. B. Hulbert, its hierarch, would certainly have claimed such territory for buffalo! See below, note 84.

The lost Berlandier MS. (see above, note 3) states that the Franciscans in 1602 encountered 'numerous herds' near Monterey, in Nueva Leon, Mexico; and Pike included buffalo among the animals of Coahuila (perhaps other North Mexican states also) in 1807 (Coues (ed.), *Expeditions of Pike*, II, 738, 777). André Thevet, in his work *Les Singularitez de la France Antarctique* (1558), giving one of the very earliest drawings of the buffalo) mentions their home as "Floride et la rivière de Palme" (Rio Grande). He is classed as a 'mendacious writer' (Winsor (ed.), *Narrative and Critical History*, I, 115; III, 184); but there seems nothing very far-fetched about this, at least, and H. E. Bolton notes a reference to buffalo south of the Rio Grande in 1691 (*Handbook of American Indians*, II, 106). Bancroft also cites a reference to buffalo domestication in Mexico (*in extenso*, Appendix C, note 8). Cf. note at conclusion of chap. XX. The specific mention of Coahuila and Nueva Leon obviates any discussion whether *Mexico* signifies some former Spanish territory which is now part of Texas or New Mexico. The latest classificationists (1947) include northern Mexico in the range of the historic Plains buffalo (Skinner and Kaisen, *Fossil Bison of Alaska*, 149).

end of the males tailes. The Horses fled from them, of which they slue some, being enraged. They are meat, drinke, shoes, houses, fire, vessels, and their Masters whole substance. . . ."25

What may very probably have been the earliest description ever printed in English is also of interest: "There is a great number of beasts or kine in the country of Cibola, which were never brought thither by the Spanyards, but breed naturally in the countrey. They are like unto our oxen, saving that they have upon their shoulders a bunch like a camell, which is higher then the rest of their body. They are marvellous wild and swift in running. They call them the beasts or kine of Cibola. . . ."26 Doubtless Cabeza de Vaca's varied experiences made him a renowned figure in his day. But Hornaday is mistaken in assuming (or adopting from others) the belief that the buffalo provided the origin for his title. This had actually been borne by his family for more than three centuries.27

25*Purchas his Pilgrimes*, XVIII, 64-5; "Anonymous Document" ("Traslado de las Nuevas") in *Journey of Coronado*, ed. Winship, 194; "Relacion del Suceso," *ibid.*, 206, 210.

26'A Relation . . . of Nova Hispania . . . by Henry Hawks, merchant, which lived five yeeres in the sayd countrey, and drew the same at the request of M. Richard Hakluyt, Esquire, of Eyton in the County of Hereford, in the yeare 1572' (Hakluyt, *Voyages*, VI, 283).

27". . . afterwards called Cabeza de Vaca—or in other words, 'Cattle Cabeza,' the prototype of our own distinguished Buffalo Bill . . ." (Hornaday, "Extermination of the American Bison," 373, citing no authority). Actually, this was an ancestral name, derived from an exploit in the earlier Moorish wars. Just before the great battle of Las Navas de Tolosa, July 11-12, 1212, Martin Alhaja, then simply a peasant, disclosed a secret path through the mountain passes to the Christian forces. He placed the skull of a cow (*cabeza de vaca*) at the entrance to the defile, to identify the spot for those following. This manoeuvre proved to be the decisive factor in what has been called 'the greatest victory since Charles Martel,' at Tours, 732, and 'the most crushing of all over the Moslem.' The peasant guide, the maternal ancestor of Alvar Nuñez, was ennobled for his patriotism by the title of Cabeza de Vaca. See on this, Dunham, *History of Spain and Portugal*, II, 45-8; Ulick R. Burke, *History of Spain*, I, 205, 235; Bandelier (ed.), *Journey of Cabeza*, introd., x; Bishop, *Odyssey of Cabeza de Vaca*; Hallenbeck, *Journey of Cabeza de Vaca*, 17-18.

Hornaday's statement is either a wild guess or an uncritical adoption of somebody else's. It would be of no significance, were it not that such careless errors inevitably cast suspicion upon other unsupported assertions from the same source. For the general reader, Agnes Laut is almost as misleading: ". . . he of the Cow's Head, who had been raised to the nobility by the Spanish king for guiding the royal army through a mountain pass by a cow's head . . ." (Laut, *Pilgrims of the Santa Fé*, 16-17). Her sneers at the 'maps and study-chair men' (*Overland Trail*, 19, 32, 98, etc.) were scarcely becoming.

According to some, Cabeza de Vaca was one of those noble incompetents whose rank secured him a position his mediocrity could never have attained; whose later troubles as Governor of Paraguay, 1541, were largely of his own making. According to others, he was a high-minded and enlightened administrator,

When we remember that the presence of the buffalo in the southeastern United States is noted in the two summaries which have been quoted at the beginning of our present chapter (and which will be substantiated by reliable historical evidence), it is rather curious that at the precise period when historical light first breaks upon the region they should not be found there. Although a broad application of the historical name of 'Florida' is a well known fact, it is worth emphasizing that historically, the question of buffalo in Florida applies to much more than the territory comprised within the modern State of that name. The evidence concerning this will be found to have a most important bearing upon our inquiries. Some of the earlier Spanish explorers, between Ponce de Leon and De Soto (1512-39) are believed by competent critics to have sailed northward along the Atlantic coast as far as Massachusetts Bay, yet all this was the coast of 'Florida.' According to Pedro Menendez de Avila, who was Governor of Florida, 1565: "The Province and Government of Florida . . . is all that which lyeth from the River of Palmes . . .[28] which is near the tropicke in 22. degrees, unto the point of Bacallaos,[29] which falleth in 48 degrees and

ages before his time; another Las Casas, less prejudiced—and less fortunate—than the good Bishop of Chiapas. There seems to be some truth in both views; perhaps he was a good rather than a wise man. See the contemporary chronicle in *Purchas his Pilgrimes*, XVII, 25-39; also Helps, *Spanish Conquests in America*, IV, 273; Winsor (ed.), *Narrative and Critical History*, VIII, 387; Bandelier (ed.), *Journey of Cabeza*, xi; Graham, *Conquest of the River Plate;* and, above all, Bishop, *Odyssey of Cabeza de Vaca.*

Coronado's unfitness is less doubtful. See *Journey of Coronado*, ed. Winship, 10, 44, 68, 74, 130-4; Thomas, *History of North America*, II, 44-6; Fortier and Ficklen, *ibid.*, IX, 464; Aiton, *American Historical Review*, XXX, 1924, 298-304.

Doubts have been expressed—needlessly, it would seem—concerning the authenticity of Cabeza's "Relacion" of his wanderings. See Helps, *Spanish Conquests in America*, IV, 292; Bandelier (ed.), *Journey of Cabeza*, xiii; Graham, *Conquest of the River Plate*, 88, etc.; and particularly Bishop, *Odyssey of Cabeza de Vaca*, and Hallenbeck, *Journey of Cabeza de Vaca*. Buffalo Jones is almost grotesquely sceptical, however. He not only doubts De Solis, whom he calls De Soto, and the 'Mexican Bull,' but Cabeza also (*Buffalo Jones' Forty Years*, 3-11). Doubtless De Solis 'never did see a buffalo'; apparently he was never in Mexico (Prescott, *Conquest of Mexico*, II, 287-92). But Cabeza's cows—'much like those of Spain'—are thought by Jones to be more like Texas cattle than the 'much larger' buffalo. Jones enthusiastically accepts the 'unmistakeably authentic' descriptions of Coronado's party; yet they (and Hawks likewise) say practically the same as Cabeza. Finally, were there any 'cattle' other than buffalo in Mexico or Texas *circa* 1519-30? Oviedo crossed to the Indies in 1513 (*ibid.*, 55-9). Compare his statement on this (above, note 15).

[28]The Rio Grande.

[29]Newfoundland. About the earliest reference I have found is from Sebastian Cabot, *circa* 1550 (Hakluyt, *Voyages*, V, 89, 90); cf. *ibid.*, VI, 14, 19. Bacallaos = 'cod-land' (Spanish *bacallaos*, Portuguese *bacalhao* = cod); see *Canadian Historical Review*, XXIII, 1942, 261.

a half, in the which are 1258. leagues of Coast, and from thence to 73. degrees of altitude to the North by the Coast, and within the land all that which hee discovereth. . . ."[30]

Thus the description of 'Florida'—'from Labrador to Mexico'— is scarcely exaggeration;[31] and 'from Chesapeake Bay to beyond the Mississippi'[32] is well within the mark. At the same time, the only portions of this Florida which were colonized by other than Spaniards were along the Atlantic coast from the (modern) Florida peninsula northwards; and 'Descriptions of Florida' from non-Spanish pens must be understood in that sense.

The historical evidence for the presence of buffalo in any very near proximity to the Atlantic coast north of Georgia or the Carolinas is in my opinion dubious. I have found but three references of any significance to this effect. The first is in a letter from the same Pedro Menendez to Philip II of Spain, *circa* 1566: "In 1565, and for some years previous, bison-skins were brought by the Indians down the Potomac and thence carried along shore in canoes to the French about the Gulf of St. Lawrence. During two years 6000 skins were thus obtained. . . ."[33] Secondly, Hornaday (who must almost certainly have known of, and possibly rejected, the above) writes: ". . . the earliest discovery of the bison in Eastern North America, or indeed anywhere north of Coronado's route, was made somewhere near Washington, District of Columbia, in 1612, by an English navigator, Samuel Argoll [*sic*, commonly 'Argall']."[34]

Argall himself relates: "I set my men to the felling of Timber, for the building of a Frigat, which I had left half-finished at Point Comfort . . . and returned myself with the ship into Pembrook River and so discovered to the head of it, which is about 65. leagues into the land and navigable for any ship. *And then marching into the Countrie,*[35] I found great store of Cattle as big as Kine, of which the Indians that were my guides killed a couple, which we found to be very good and wholesome meate, and are very easie to be killed, in regard they are

---

[30]Translation (by Purchas) of Antonio de Herrera, 1601 (*Purchas his Pilgrimes,* XIV, 460). See also Shea, "Ancient Florida," in Winsor (ed.), *Narrative and Critical History,* II, 231-98; Fiske, *Discovery of America,* II, 483-500; Brittain, *History of North America,* I, 496, etc.

[31]Parkman, *Pioneers of France,* 103; cf. Fiske, *Discovery of America,* II, 73-91, 483-531.

[32]Hamilton, *History of North America,* III, 5.

[33]Parkman, *Pioneers of France,* 234, who seems doubtful about it. It is also quoted without criticism ("it is learned that . . .") by Fletcher, "Trading Posts," *Handbook of American Indians,* II, 798.

[34]Hornaday, "Extermination of the American Bison," 375.

[35]Italics mine.

heavy, slow, and not so wild as other beasts of the Wildernesse. . . ."[36]
Allen thinks this Pembrook River may have been the James River and
not the Potomac. Buffalo are stated, however (upon no authority that
I have been able to identify), to have actually been seen along the
Potomac itself by Henry Fleet, an English trader, in 1624: "As for
deer, buffaloes, bears, turkeys, the woods do swarm with them. . . ."[37]

In attempting to estimate the value of these testimonies, we are
met at the outset by some stubborn objections. Among a very considerable number of early descriptions of Florida or relations in narrative form, not one includes the buffalo among the animals of the
country. Yet the buffalo, or its general appearance, was almost certainly known by repute to the earliest of these authors, the Gentleman
of Elvas, one of De Soto's party, and possibly to others.[38] Lest readers
should question my implied identification of Florida and Virginia, it
may be pointed out that in a *Discourse on Virginia* (1625), the latter
is explicitly stated to be conterminous with Florida.[39] And in what I
may term the later Virginia, of the period of the foregoing references
to buffalo, there are again a number of descriptions, in none of which,
with the single exception of Sir Samuel Argall—if that be one—is there
any allusion to the animal.[40]

So far as Menendez is concerned, it is incredible that if the French
had been engaged in a traffic of such volume as early as 'previous to

[36]*Purchas his Pilgrimes,* XIX, 91-2.

[37]Cited by Hornaday, "Extermination of the American Bison," 378. Henry
Fleet, 1624, 1632, is mentioned (and his *Journal* cited) in Winsor (ed.), *Narrative
and Critical History,* III, 526, 561; IV, 165; but there is no mention of buffalo.

[38]Not mentioned in his description of the beasts of Florida (*Narratives of De
Soto,* I, 222); see also *Purchas his Pilgrimes,* XVII, 521-50; XVIII, 1-51). Nor by
the French, 1562-65 (*ibid.,* XVIII, 183; Lescarbot, *History of New France,* III,
227); John Hawkins, 1564 (in Hakluyt, *Voyages,* VII, 42-51); Martine Basanier
of Paris, 1586 (*ibid.,* VI, 232-45).

Compare 'Virginia' (identical with 'Florida' *post* 1584): not mentioned by
Philip Amadas and Arthur Barlow, 1584 (Hakluyt, *Voyages,* VI, 123, 131); Ralph
Lane, 1585 (*ibid.,* 140); Thomas Heriot, 1584-87 (*ibid.,* 170, 181, 194); Bartholo-
mew Gosnold, 1602 (*Purchas his Pilgrimes,* XVIII, 302-13); John Brereton, "Flora
and Fauna," 1602 (*ibid.,* 314-20); Martin Pring, 1603 (*ibid.,* 322-9); Bartholomew
Gilbert, (*ibid.,* 329-35); George Percy, 1607 (*ibid.,* 403-19); Captain John Smith,
"Description" and "Occurrents," 1607 (*ibid.,* 419-540). "Of beasts the chief are
Deare, nothing differing from ours . . ." (Smith, *ibid.,* 433).

[39]*Ibid.,* XIX, 228; cf. Alexander Whitaker, 1613 (Virginia) "situate within
the degrees of 34 and 47 . . ." (*ibid.,* 112)ͼ.

[40]The author of the "Discourse" (1625): "I might add the Shag-Haired Oxen
seen by Sir Samuel Argall . . ." (*ibid.,* 250). No buffalo mentioned by Sir Thomas
Gates, 1610 (*ibid.,* 5-72); Sir Samuel Argall, 1612 (*ibid.,* 73-84, 207-17); Alexander Whitaker, 1613 (*ibid.,* 109-16); Ralph Hamor, 1614 (*ibid.,* 95-102); none
in the above "Discourse" (*ibid.,* 218-67); none, is the conclusion of Purchas himself (*ibid.,* XX, 134).

1565,' the painstaking and generally trustworthy Lescarbot should not have heard of it.[41] H. H. Bancroft (who rejects the truth of the statement) says that "Menendez doubtless told the story in good faith, being deceived by an adventurer who took advantage of his enthusiasm. . . ."[42] This may have been so, but the name of Menendez is not conspicuously associated with good faith; and a master-critic calls him a 'matchless liar.'[43] It seems not improbable that Menendez (with needless circumspection, I should suggest) may have thought that even with a bigot like Philip the Second, it might do no harm to insinuate that the heretics were not only enemies of God, but enemies also to the material interests of His Most Catholic Majesty, the King of the Spains. One argument or another secured him Philip's warm approval.[44]

Concerning Argall's case, Hornaday remarks: "It is to be regretted that the narrative of the explorer affords no precise clew to the locality of this interesting discovery; but since it is doubtful that the mariners journeyed very far on foot from the head of navigation on the Potomac, it seems highly probable that the first American Bison seen by Europeans, other than the Spaniards, was found within 15 miles, or even less, of the capitol of the United States, and possibly within the District of Columbia itself. . . ."[45]

Argall's own relation says: ". . . and then marching into the Countrie . . ." the words which I have italicized above; even the approximate distance or direction not being stated. I do not understand what right any commentator possesses to assume that this means, 'he went just far enough not to endanger another very picturesque hypothesis that might be put forward concerning this episode.' We have seen that the identity of the Potomac itself with Argall's 'Pembrook River' was doubted by a generally much more cautious critic, J. A. Allen.[46] I have only one suggestion to make, and it may tend to increase doubt rather than to solve it. The word 'buffalo' in the accepted spelling of its reputed author using it (for the case of Henry Fleet is backed by no ascertained authority) is not found, so far as I can discover, in English writings earlier than Henry Kelsey's *Journal* of 1689-

---

[41]No mention of buffalo in his account of Menendez and the massacre of the Huguenots (*History of New France*, I, 121-43). Shea says nothing of buffalo in 1565, though he cites the letters of Menendez (Winsor (ed.), *Narrative and Critical History*, II, 270, 272, 277).

[42]Bancroft, *Northwest Coast*, I, 51.

[43]Fiske, *Discovery of America*, II, 513.

[44]Parkman, *Pioneers of France*, 134, 151.

[45]Hornaday, "Extermination of the American Bison," 375.

[46]Allen, *American Bisons*, 86.

91,[47] but *bufle* and *buffe* are found in English over a century earlier, and are applied to species other than *Bison americanus*; in fact, to any animal that might be thought to yield good 'buffe' for buff leather, or for the famed 'buff coats' of the Cromwellian era.[48] I quote a contemporary description of a moose:

There is also a certain Beast that the Natives call a Mosse [*sic*], hee is as big-bodied as an Oxe, headed like a fallow Deere, with a broad Palme, which he mues[49] every yeare, as doth the Deere, and neck like a Red Deere, with a short Mane running downe along the Ranes of his back, his haire long like an Elke, but esteemed to be better than that for Sadlers use, he hath likewise a great bunch hanging downe under his throat, and is of the colour of our blacker sort of fallow Deere, his legs are long, and his feet are as big as the feet of our Oxen, his tail is longer than the single of a Deere, and runneth almost downe to his Huxens, his skinne maketh very good Buffe, and his flesh is excellent good food, which the Natives use to Jerkin and keepe all the yeere to serve their turne, and so proves very serviceable for their use. . . .[50]

I do not propose to assert that Argall's 'shag-haired ox' was a moose, which species is not known to have wandered so far south along the Atlantic seaboard.[51] I say simply that we do not know how far he marched inland while his men were engaged with their shipbuilding;[52] and any discrepancy between his 'heavy and slow, easily

---

[47]'Buffilo'; see *Kelsey Papers*, ed. Doughty and Martin. Garretson ascribes the first use of the standard 'buffalo' to Mark Catesby, *A Natural History of Carolina*, 1754 (*American Bison*, 10, 233). Dr. Walker apparently used it in 1750; and a work in my possession, by Thomas Salmon, 1749 (see Bibliography) has buffaloe (*see* chap. X, notes 108, 131).

[48]*Buffles*, in "A Relation of Newfoundland" (Hakluyt, *Voyages*, VI, 23), *circa* 1583; also Ralph Fitch, East Indies, 1583-91 (*ibid.*, III, 287, 289, 307). *Bufs* or *Buffes*: Antony Parckhurst, Newfoundland, 1578 (*ibid.*, V, 347); Newfoundland, 1583 (*ibid.*, VI, 64); Fitch, East Indies (*ibid.*); Russia (*ibid.*, II, 294); Anthony Knivet, Brazil, 1597 (*Purchas his Pilgrimes*, XVI, 213); Herrera, *in re* Guatemala, 1601 (*ibid.*, XIV, 487); "Manati hides make good buffe": Robert Harcourt, 1608 (*ibid.*, 380); "Ellans or Stagges whereof good buffe be made . . ."; New France, 1610 (*ibid.*, XVIII, 246, 264; see also Lescarbot, *History of New France*, II, 281. I suppose our modern shade, 'buff-colour,' is derived from the colour of buff leather; perhaps also the silversmith's process of 'buffing' on a revolving leather polisher or disc.

[49]*Mues* = sheds or moults (verb). 'Mews' were not originally stables, but where the falcons moulted. Cf. Milton: "England . . . mewing her mighty youth . . ." (*Areopagitica*, ed. W. H. D. Rouse, 56).

[50]"A Relation of New England," 1607-22 (*Purchas his Pilgrimes*, XIX, 269-84), citing p. 281.

[51]Farthest south (*circa* 1850) about 43° 30' N.: Audubon and Bachman, *American Quadrupeds*, II, 192; cf. Seton, *Life-Histories of Northern Animals*, I, 148.

[52]*Purchas his Pilgrimes*, XIX, 91-2. Garretson is also dubious about the suggested locality, near Washington, D.C. (*American Bison*, 16-17).

killed' beast, and moose or elk, is no greater than between conflicting accounts of unquestionable buffalo, as we have had occasion to note in more than one connection. Argall's testimony is no more specific than that of some others I have cited. Fleet's case virtually stands or falls with Argall's, and must be considered to leave the question unproven.

In any circumstances, it is very probable that Argall was not the first European other than a Spaniard to see the buffalo, and in all likelihood the first meeting took place far enough from the neighbourhood of the Potomac. Perhaps David Ingram, one of those unfortunate men who were marooned by John Hawkins on the Mexican coast near the Rio de Minas or the River of Panuco, in October, 1568, may have seen the buffalo.[53] Ingram was more fortunate than some of his comrades, whose relations of their miseries after the Inquisition made its appearance in Mexico in 1574 are printed by Hakluyt;[54] for after a land journey of nearly a year[55] he eventually reached Cape Breton or St. John's River.[56] Thence a friendly French vessel carried him to France, whereby he finally got safely home to England.

Although some part of his long journey must have taken him through what is generally regarded as a portion of the buffalo habitat from time immemorial—the plains of Texas—the animal is not very readily recognizable from his description. Allen is apparently doubtful about it himself, since he includes this among a number of extracts cited from early travel literature for the express purpose of showing that many of these, which have been adduced as historical records of the animal's presence along the Atlantic seaboard from *circa* 1535 onward, are very uncertain or positively inadmissible.[57] Ingram's account reads: ". . . great plenty of Buffes . . . wch are Beastes as bigge as twoe Oxen in length almost twenty foote, havinge longe eares like a bludde hownde wth long heares about there eares, ther hornes be Crooked like Rames hornes, ther eyes blacke, ther heares longe blacke, rough and hagged as a Goate, the Hydes of these Beastes are sold verye deare. These Beastes doe keepe Company a male and a female and doe always fighte wth others of the same kind. . . ."[58]

[53]Hakluyt, *Voyages,* VI, 296-354; *Purchas his Pilgrimes,* XVI, 109, 112; Fiske, *Discovery of America,* I, 249, 251; Allen, *American Bisons,* 80.

[54]Hakluyt, *Voyages,* VI, 296-354.

[55]In "A Discourse upon the North partes of America": ". . . David Ingram, who travelled in these countries xi. Moneths and more. . . ." (*ibid.,* 51, 59).

[56]'Cape Breton in Acadia' (*Purchas his Pilgrimes,* XVI, 109, 112); 'St. John's River' (Fiske, *Discovery of America,* I, 249-51).

[57]Allen, *American Bisons,* 74-91.

[58]Quoted by Allen, *ibid.,* 80; as also photostatic copy in my possession.

It is perhaps worth noting that on their original publication by Richard Hakluyt in the first edition of the great collection of *Voyages,* certain of these relations aroused so much criticism that they were omitted from the second edition,[59] and are not now very accessible.[60] The contemporary criticisms have not lacked an echo in our own day;[61] and Allen remarks that while Ingram almost must have seen the buffalo somewhere, there is nothing in his narrative identifying the locality with the Atlantic slope.[62]

At the same time, it may be pointed out that Ingram was subjected to a rather minute examination by Sir Francis Walsingham and Sir George Peckham in 1582. This, while not professedly 'scientific' in purpose, involved considerable geographical detail in considering Hawkins's conduct, and it is probable that the two councillors were not

[59]"As for David Ingrams perambulation to the North parts, Master Hakluyt in his first Edition published the same, but it seemeth some incredibilities of his reports caused him to leave him out in his next Impression, the reward of lying being not to be beleeved in truths. . . ." (*Purchas his Pilgrimes,* XVI, 109).

[60]I cite the source for the benefit of students (see Bibliography, *s.v.* Ingram).

[61]See Winsor (ed.), *Narrative and Critical History,* III, 64, 170, 186. Not much value in these recitals, think contributor and editor (p. 186). Fiske apparently accepted them (*Discovery of America,* I, 249-51). A modern biographer, naturally—though perhaps not excessively—partial to Hawkins, scouts the whole tale (without mentioning the 'buffes'), and thinks Ingram was perhaps 'picked up by a French corsair in Mexican waters' (Williamson, *John Hawkins,* 201, 236-8).

The 'buffes' are the stumbling-block to any easy solution. In "A Discourse upon the North partes of America," *circa* 1585, is the following: "There is also a kinde of beast much bigger than an Oxe, whose hide is more than eighteene foote long, of which sort a countreyman of ours, one Walker a sea man, who was upon that coast, did for a trueth report in the presence of divers honourable and worshipfull persons, that he and his company did finde in one cottage above two hundred and fortie hides, which they brought away and solde in France for fortie shillings an hide; and with this agreeth David Ingram, and describeth that beast at large, supposing it to be a certaine kinde of Buffe . . ." (Hakluyt, *Voyages,* VI, 63). Compare Antony Parckhurst, Newfoundland, 1578: ". . . other mighty beastes like to camels in greatness, and their feet cloven, I did see them farre off not able to discerne them perfectly, but their steps shewed their feete were cloven, and bigger than the feete of Camels, I suppose them to bee a kind of Buffes which I read to bee in the countreyes adjacent, and very many in the firme land . . ." (*ibid.,* V, 347). Similarly, "A Briefe Relation of Newfoundland," 1583: "Beasts of sundry kindes, red deare, buffles or a beast, as it seemeth by the tract & foote very large in maner of an oxe . . ." (*ibid.,* VI, 23). If Ingram was too far south to see the buffalo, then *ipso facto* his creatures could not have been moose. What other huge species was there?

[62]Allen, *American Bisons,* 80. By implication, Allen (*ibid.,* 85-6), Hornaday ("Extermination of the American Bison," 375), and the latter's faithful follower, Seton (*Life-Histories of Northern Animals,* I, 253) appear to discredit Ingram. They all term Argall 'the first European north of Coronado's route.'

wholly ignorant of the American geography of their time.[63] Secondly, after making due allowance for the natural excitement of a very probably unlearned and uncritical mind, the 'incredibilities' concerning the buffalo have been matched in our own time in respect of his very particulars of size and habits, by naturalists and others;[64] and a century after Ingram's day, were surpassed by men of scholastic learning in describing what were unquestionably buffalo.[65] These factors make it unwise to ridicule Ingram too readily.

Although under favourable conditions the animal was equal to swimming even such rivers as the Mississippi, I doubt if its known swimming powers would justify the assertion current *circa* 1586, that buffalo were to be seen on the shores of the island of Anticosti, in the Gulf of St. Lawrence;[66] even apart from the complete absence of any

[63]Ingram's "Relation" (photostatic copy in my possession), from Weston; see Bibliography, *s.v.* Ingram.

[64]They were believed by Audubon (1854) to be monogamous (*American Quadrupeds*, II, 37); so also Stone and Cram (*American Animals*, 69). Brackenridge, 1811, had the bulls 'wintering or summering in pairs' (*Early Western Travels*, VI, 90). Even their huge and incredible size (from an unlearned and strange observer, as above, note 58) is no more preposterous than the monstrous *B. americanus pennsylvanicus* of Colonel Shoemaker's uncritical postulates; which are recorded by Ernest Thompson Seton without any suggestion of scientific doubt (see chap. III, notes 9-49).

[65]Fathers Dablon and Allouez, 1671, credited the buffalo with four calves at a birth (*Jesuit Relations*, LV, 195-7). See below, note 86.

.   [66]Thevet MS., 1586 (cited by Parkman, *Pioneers of France*, 234). "Thevet says that he had himself seen them. Perhaps he confounds them with the moose" (*ibid.*). Cf. Bancroft: "Here upon the St. Lawrence at this time furs were plentiful and easily obtained; it is said that even the bison then inhabited these parts . . ." (*Northwest Coast*, I, 383).

Whether the same as David Ingram's beast or not, those animals whose hides were seen and sold by 'one Walker, a sea man,' (above, note 61) must surely have been moose. But the problem is further complicated by another fearful and wonderful brute. Thomas James to Lord Burghley, September 14, 1591, writes thus concerning some creature recorded by Jacques Cartier in 1534: ". . . as big as Oxen and to have teeth in their mouthes like Elephants teeth. True it is they are called in Latin *Boves Marini* or *Vaccæ Marinæ* and in the Russian tongue *Morsses* the hides whereof I have seen as big as any Oxe hide, and being dressed I have yet a piece of one thicker than any two Oxe or Buls hides in England. The Leather-dressers take them to be excellent good to make light targets against the arrowes of the Savages. . . . The teeth of the said *fishes* [italics mine] whereof I have seen a dry fat full at once, are a foote and sometimes more in length . . . the graine of the bone is somewhat more yellow than the Ivorie. . . . The skinne of them is like Buffes leather . . ." (Hakluyt, *Voyages*, VI, 91-3).

A similar (but shorter) description of them by Richard Fisher, 1593, and allusions to them as encountered in the St. Lawrence Gulf waters by James, Fisher, George Drake, 1593, and Charles Leigh, 1597 (*ibid.*, 93-113).

These can be nothing but walrus. They were 'to be taken in April, May, and June' (Drake, 1593, *ibid.*, 97). '*Walrus* or *Morse* (*odobaenus rosmarus* = the

220 THE NORTH AMERICAN BUFFALO

notice concerning them in the intervening territory between Anticosti and the ascertained habitat. There is, however, one localized reference to an animal which is considered by Allen—with strong probability—to be unquestionably the buffalo, which may justify the extension of their habitat, at its extreme northeast corner, along the southern side of Lake Ontario and in the Adirondack region some two or three hundred miles. I shall cite a passage from an old work which I have had no opportunity to see for myself, Thomas Morton's *New English Canaan*. This passage was, I believe, first brought forward in this connection by R. B. Marcy in 1853,[67] and has since been quoted somewhat more fully by Allen. For this reason, I use Allen's citation. He writes:

The occurrence of a stream in western New York [State] called Buffalo Creek which empties into the eastern end of Lake Erie is commonly viewed as traditional evidence of its [the buffalo's] occurrence at this point, but positive testimony to this effect has so far escaped me.[68]

This locality, if it actually came so far eastward, must have formed the eastward limit of its range along the lakes. I have found only highly questionable allusions to the occurrence of buffaloes along the southern shores of Lake Ontario. Keating, on the authority of Colhoun, however, has cited a passage from Morton's *New English Canaan* as proof of their former existence in the neighbourhood of this lake. Morton's statement is based on Indian reports, and the context gives sufficient evidence of the general vagueness of his knowledge of the region of which he was speaking. The passage, printed in 1637, is as follows: "They [the Indians] have also made descriptions of great heards of well growne beasts that live about the parts of this lake [Erocoise[69]], such as the Christian world (untill this discovery) hath not bin made acquainted with. These Beasts are of the bignesse of a Cowe, their flesh being very good foode, their hides good lether, their fleeces very usefull, being a kind of wolle as fine almost as the wolle of the Beaver, and the Salvages doe make garments thereof. It is tenne yeares since first the relation of these things came to the eares of the English. . . ."

The 'beast' [says Allen] to which allusion is here made is unquestionably the buffalo, but the locality of Lake 'Erocoise' is not so easily settled. Colhoun regards it, and probably correctly, as identical with Lake Ontario. . . .[70]

'Atlantic' walrus; Norse *hvalros* = 'whale-horse') 'Found in the sixteenth century as far S. as the southern coast of Nova Scotia,' i.e. about 43° 20' N. (*Encyclopaedia Britannica*, 11th ed., *s.v.* Walrus. The 14th ed. *re* the same is impossibly condensed and altogether unsatisfactory.)

[67]Marcy, *Exploration of the Red River*, 104 (i.e. 'first' *re* Lake Champlain).

[68]This scholarly caution may be contrasted with Hulbert's certitude concerning such buffalo origins in this region (*Historic Highways*, I, 139, etc.).

[69]In Marcy's citation, after *Erocoise* are found the words "now Lake Champlain," within what should be Morton's own words, in inverted commas as though the identification as Lake Champlain was Morton's. For Morton's book, see Winsor (ed.), *Narrative and Critical History*, III, 348; Fiske, *Beginnings of New England* (*Complete Works*, III), 90-2. Morton was the New England agent of the colonizing magnates, Sir Edwin Sandys and Sir Ferdinando Gorges.

[70]Allen, *American Bisons*, 107-8. He notes Marcy's identification as Lake

Morton describes these creatures as having been known to the English 'tenne yeares' before the writing of his book, i.e. not later than 1627. Now it is undoubtedly true that Lake Ontario was known as the 'Lake of the Iroquois,' but the earliest reference I have found to Ontario under that name is not until 1654.[71] Its earlier name (1615) was 'Lake of the Onondagas.'[72] Long before 1654, however, in fact from the very beginnings of the settlement of New France, the 'Lake of the Iroquois' was Lake Champlain,[73] and at least as late as 1653, the Richelieu River, which drains Lake Champlain into the St. Lawrence, was known as the 'River of the Iroquois';[74] so it is possible that Marcy's identification is correct. If one could discover evidence of the phrase as a common expression current among various Indian tribes— it was from Indian sources that Morton's information was ultimately derived—it would be almost sufficient to vindicate Marcy's opinion, which was apparently shared by others.[75] The early use of the names by Champlain and the Jesuits, before they could have acquired the necessary local knowledge to bestow such names themselves, and Father Le Moine's phrase, "*we* call it. . . ." (if my interpretation of this be a legitimate inference[76]) would seem to point to some such general use, and to the consequent soundness of the association of

---

Champlain, without comment. Hornaday quotes the passage ("Extermination of the American Bison," 385) but ignores Marcy. Garretson cites it without direct comment (*American Bison*, 18). 'Iroquois' is apparently 'Ontario' in Jones and Bryan, *North America*, 43.

[71]Father Simon Le Moine, 1654: ". . . a great Lake called Ontario; we call it the lake of the Iroquois, because they have their villages on its southern side . . ." (*Jesuit Relations*, XLI, 95, 125). Le Moine also, 1661 (*ibid.*, XLVII, 71). Father Hierosme Lalemant, 1664: "the great Lake of the Iroquois, called Ontario . . ." (*ibid.*, XLIX, 151). So also on a contemporary map (*ibid.*, 266).

[72]*Champlain's Travels* (Champlain Society ed.), III, 62, 79; IV, 248, 251, 283.

[73]*Champlain's Travels*, ed. Bourne, I, 194, 198, 205, 216; Father Pierre Biard, 1610 (*Jesuit Relations*, I, 251, 319). I have not found it in Lescarbot.

[74]Lescarbot uses this habitually (*History of New France*, I, 104; II, 7, 87, 129-33, 137, 141; III, 10, 15, 21); *Champlain's Travels* (Champlain Society ed.), I, 103, 158; IV, 74, 89; Father Le Jeune, 1637: "the river of the Hiroquois, so called ,because it comes from their country . . ." (*Jesuit Relations*, XII, 131-3; ed. note, XII, 272). Father Bressani, 1653: ". . . named after the Iroquois, because it comes from their lake. . . ." (*ibid.*, XXXVIII, 233).

One might pardonably imagine 'Erocoise' to have been the parent form of Erie; but the latter is from the Erie or 'cat' tribe of the Iroquois; from "the prodigious number of Wild cats in their country. . . .": LeMercier, 1653; De Quens, 1656 (*ibid.*, XLI, 81; XLII, 179; cf XXXIII, 63). See also Taylor, *Names*, 119.

[75]'None east of Lake Champlain' (Hind, *Narrative*, II, 106).

[76]Father Le Moine's meaning seems to be, not 'we,' the French as distinct from the natives; but 'we,' the residents of the region in common, French or Indian indifferently, as against strangers, or possibly the English.

Lake Champlain with the buffalo; but this, unfortunately, while highly probable, is not proof.

In concluding this attempt to review and appraise the evidence for the presence of the buffalo in certain less familiar or disputed portions of the Eastern territory, it may be broadly true, as Allen expressed it in 1876, that the opinions in favour of its former existence 'in certain portions of the Atlantic seaboard region' have been substantiated by later research.[77] I know of no evidence that it ever was true of virtually the entire Atlantic coast of the United States, as Spencer F. Baird maintained in 1857.[78] The evidence for almost any part of the coast will be seen to be practically negligible—certainly in so far as numbers are concerned; and certain authorities make the Alleghanies[79] or Appalachians[80] the eastern limit in any significant sense.

I present this slight summary to make it clear that any arguments based upon buffalo origins in the Hudson or the adjacent valley-routes, so far from possessing evidence in support, have not even 'authority'— whatever force that may be thought to command against a lack of testimony—in their favour.

What may be termed the northwestern discovery of the buffalo (in the United States territory) occurred on or near the watershed which divides the western drainage basin of the Great Lakes from that of the upper Mississippi.[81] Allen, writing in 1876, was not disposed to extend its habitat very far to the northward in Wisconsin. He says:

[77]Allen, *American Bisons*, 74-5.

[78]*Ibid*. Audubon and Bachman, *American Quadrupeds*, II, 55; Garretson, *American Bison*, 18; likewise doubtful. Seton notes the discovery in 1920, "of a fragment of the maxilla with 2 milk teeth of a Bison at Orleans, on Cape Cod, Mass." (*Game Animals*, III, 646). It is not stated whether this was the historic *Bison americanus* or of some fossil species. Pending further discoveries in the intervening territory westward towards the Susquehanna Valley, it cannot really be considered to prove much.

[79]Allen, *American Bisons*, 55, 73, 92; Hornaday, "Extermination of the American Bison," 376; Fletcher, *Handbook of American Indians*, I, 170; Wissler, *American Indian*, 14.

[80]Stone and Cram, *American Animals*, 67.

[81]Hornaday, who had a weakness for these didactic inaccuracies, says that Father Hennepin (December 1679) was 'the first white man to see the buffalo in its northern habitat' ("Extermination of the American Bison," 375). He was many years behind, and was not even the first to record it. Father Le Moine, south of Lake Ontario, September 1654, records "large herds of wild cattle" (*Jesuit Relations*, XLI, 129). On the same trip Father De Quens says: ". . . our travellers killed 18 cows (*vaches sauvages*) within less than an hour, on Prairies prepared by nature alone for those ownerless herds. . . ." (*ibid.*, XLII, 37; cf. Chaumonot, 1656, *ibid.*, 63). These may not have been buffalo, but the 'herds' and the easy slaughter render it not impossible; and although *vache sauvage* was applied to deer, I am not aware that it was confined to them (see Appendix B).

"The buffalos may never have existed in northeastern Wisconsin, though they probably ranged over the prairies of the western and southern portion of the State. They were not met with, however, even there by the first European explorers of that region. . . . Father Marquette does not appear to have met with them in crossing from Green Bay to the Wisconsin River in 1673, nor did he see them in his subsequent descent of that river. . . . La Hontan, in 1687, also found none on either the Fox or Wisconsin River; first meeting with them on the Mississippi, not far above the mouth of the Wisconsin. . . ."[82] Hornaday, who makes no special comment on these statements, but who generally follows Allen, remarks that "a line drawn from Winnipeg to Chicago, curving slightly to the eastward in the middle portion, will very nearly define the eastern boundary of the buffalo's range in Minnesota and Wisconsin. . . ."[83]

Such a line, curving as described, would bring the buffalo virtually to the shore of Lake Superior near Duluth, which lies about three-

---

Hulbert thinks Radisson and Groseilliers were on the Mississippi in 1659 (*Historic Highways*, VII, 182), and they themselves on their fourth journey in 1661 describe their coming to 'a lake which had a great store of cows; the wild men kill not except for necessary use' (Bryce, *Remarkable History*, 5-6, believes this to be the Lake of the Woods). If Hulbert be correct concerning the buffalo origin of the Fox-Wisconsin portage (*Historic Highways*, I, 140), Father Ménard—who, had he lived, would very probably have been the discoverer of the Mississippi—very likely saw the buffalo before 1661. His death (August, 1661) took place in the Wisconsin buffalo territory, according to high Wisconsin authority; on Black River (so Blair, *Indian Tribes*, I, 172), or along the headwaters of Chippewa River (as Coues (ed.), *Expeditions of Pike*, I, 296; Winsor (ed.), *Narrative and Critical History*, IV, 286). Boucher mentions buffalo in 1663 (Thwaites, ed. note, *Jesuit Relations*, IX, 310); in which year occurs also their first direct notice in that series (Hierosme Lalemant, *ibid.*, XLVII, 147, 149, 316). Claude Allouez alludes to and describes them in the Illinois country, 1666 (*ibid.*, LI, 42, 43, 51); and again, either he, Dablon, or Marquette, 1669-70 (*ibid.*, LIV, 189). They are also described by Fathers Dablon and Allouez, 1671, along the Fox River, thinks Thwaites (ed., *ibid.*, LV, 14, 195); and by Joliet and Father Marquette, 1670-73, apparently along the Wisconsin or Mississippi (*ibid.*, LVIII, 99, 107; LIX, 103-13; also good notes on these two men, L, 322; LXXI, 400; cf. also, Hennepin, *New Discovery*, ed. Thwaites, II, 643; and contra, Allen, *American Bisons*, 104).

Daniel Greysolon Du Lhut also antedates Hennepin. He was a familiar figure, boasting of his influence with the Indians (see Bryce, *Remarkable History*, 78), in regions which Hennepin first saw as a terrified captive of the eastern Sioux, from whose clutches Du Lhut contrived to rescue the worthy Récollet (see Hennepin, *New Discovery*, I, 228 *seq.*; Parkman, *La Salle*, 263-8).

Allen's work alone, which cites many of these names and dates (80-2) should have saved Hornaday from this needless error. For a general discussion of these problems, see also Winsor (ed.), *Narrative and Critical History*, IV, 169-71, 201-46.

[82]Allen, *American Bisons*, 104.
[83]Hornaday, "Extermination of the American Bison," 385.

fifths of the distance northwestward from Chicago to Winnipeg. It would probably also serve as a rough line of demarcation between the differing types of country, prairie or parkland, and heavier coniferous timber areas, which may be the basis of the foregoing delimitation, although that is not stated to be the case. This line would strike Lake Michigan somewhere about Milwaukee or slightly south; and practically the whole of Black River to its headwaters, as also the Fox-Wisconsin portage near Portage, Wisconsin, and a portion of the upper Fox River, would be within the territory thus defined. With entire respect for Hulbert's careful research along purely historical lines, I cannot feel that his inclusion of the Fox-Wisconsin portage[84] (which would tend to push the buffalo habitat farther toward the northeast) is above suspicion; in his sweeping prehistoric generalizations on buffalo, all is grist that comes to the mill. But Dr. Reuben Gold Thwaites is of another calibre; and in a question affecting the historical topography of Wisconsin, he had also the enormous advantage of a wide local knowledge. He considers it to be along the Fox River (in Winnebago County) that Fathers Dablon and Allouez encountered the herds in 1671, which they described as follows:

All the prairie country, extending to our knowledge more than 300 leagues in every direction,—to say nothing of its farther extent, of which we have no knowledge,—affords ample sustenance to the wild *cows,* not infrequently encountered in herds of 400 and 500 each. These, by their abundance, furnish adequate provision for whole Villages, which therefore are not obliged to scatter by families during their hunting season, as is the case with Savages elsewhere.[85]

In these rich pasture lands are also found buffaloes (*buffes*) called Pisikiou, which greatly resemble our bulls in size and strength. They surpass our cattle, however,—first, in being more prolific, the female bearing three or four young at a time; secondly, in having larger horns, which are indeed very similar to those of our cattle in form and colour, but are of double their size, being nearly two feet long when the animal is fairly mature; and thirdly, in having thick, heavy, dark-coloured hair which somewhat resembles the wool of sheep, but is much coarser and thicker. Therefore it is made into robes and fur garments which afford greater protection from the cold than any other furs of this country. Its flesh is excellent; and buffalo, when mixed with wild oats, makes the most excellent of native dishes. . . .[86]

Father Marquette's description, on his first voyage (*circa* 1670), is even more detailed:

[84]Hulbert, *Historic Highways,* I, 139.
[85]From the context, this portion may possibly refer to deer.
[86]*Jesuit Relations,* LV, 195-7; and for the locality, Thwaites's note (*ibid.,* 14). *Re* the 'four at a birth,' I have suggested above (chap. V, notes 104-5) what may be a probable explanation of their misunderstanding.

We call them [that is, the 'Pisikious'] Wild Cattle [*bœufs sauvages*] because they are very similar to our domestic cattle. They are not longer, but are nearly as large again, and more Corpulent. When our people killed one, three persons had much difficulty in moving it. The head is very large; the forehead is flat, and a foot and a half Wide between the Horns, which are exactly like those of our oxen, but black and much larger. Under the Neck they have a sort of large dewlap, which hangs down; and on The back is a rather high hump. The whole of the head, the Neck, and a portion of the Shoulders, are Covered with a thick Mane Like That of horses; it forms a crest a foot long, which makes them hideous, and, falling over their eyes, Prevents them from seeing what is before Them. The remainder of the Body is covered with a heavy coat of curly hair, almost Like that of our sheep, but much stronger and Thicker. It fails off in Summer, and The skin becomes as soft as Velvet. At that season, the savages use the Hides for making fine Robes, which they paint in various Colors. The flesh and the fat of the pisikious are Excellent, and constitute the best dish at feasts. Moreover, they are very fierce; and not a year passes without their killing some savages. When attacked, they catch a man on their Horns, if they can, toss Him in the air, and then throw him on the ground, after which they trample him under foot, and kill him. If a person fire at Them from a distance, with either a bow or a gun, he must, immediately after the Shot, throw himself down and hide in the grass. For if they perceive Him who has fired, they Run at him, and attack him. As their legs are thick and rather Short, they do not run very fast, As a rule, except when angry. They are scattered about the prairie in herds; I have seen one of 400. . . .[87]

The precise locality of these respective encounters is somewhat uncertain. Allen believes that Marquette (? 1670) saw nothing of them on the Wisconsin River; and that his first view was on the Mississippi, about lat. 41° 28′ N., which is practically at Davenport, Iowa (41° 29′ N.).[88] R. G. Thwaites, however, considers that Marquette's description applies to the Wisconsin River, which joins the Mississippi at Prairie du Chien, a hundred miles or so above Davenport. Marquette says: "The country through which it flows is very fine; the Groves dispos'd at certain Distances in the Meadows, make a noble Prospect. . . . We saw no other Game in those Meadows but abundance of Wild-Goats and Wild-Bulls. . . ."[89]

It was on the upper Fox River in Thwaites's opinion, and consequently to the northward even of the Fox-Wisconsin portage, that Dablon and Allouez, of whom Allen makes no mention, saw buffalo in 1671.[90] In any case, both recitals would seem, by the linguistic evi-

[87]*Jesuit Relations*, LIX, 111-13. In all these comparisons of size with European cattle, from *circa* 1520 onward, the reader may remember that the huge modern beef-breeds had not then been developed.

[88]Allen, *American Bisons*, 104.

[89]Marquette, in Hennepin, *New Discovery*, ed. Thwaites, II, 643.

[90]*Jesuit Relations*, LV, 14, 195-7.

dence of the *pisikious,* to belong to the same tribal territory, broadly speaking; and Hornaday's slightly curved line would include the whole of the Wisconsin River within its boundary. Even if it were proven beyond question that none were seen along the Wisconsin by Marquette in 1673, nor by La Hontan in 1687, this fact would be of very little value in determining their habitual delimitation; unless it could be shown that neither the animals themselves, nor any indications of their former presence, had ever been found there. For practically all the important generalizing authorities on buffalo are agreed upon a propensity on the part of the herds to desert, sometimes for lengthy periods, regions which at other times were familiar ground to them.[91] I shall later present evidence which goes even further, and reveals a totally incalculable mental quality; as a result of which experienced hunters were often at a loss where to find buffalo which were commonly—and in many instances, as the sequel showed, actually—in the region at that season.[92] For these various reasons, and because his local knowledge of Wisconsin was so wide and exact, I incline to Thwaites's opinion in this matter. Allen himself notes that two buffalo were killed by the Sioux in 'upper Wisconsin' as late as 1832;[93] but that term is too vague for any definite conclusion, nor do we know from what direction they may have come, or been driven. Their final extirpation in northwestern Wisconsin is given on Hornaday's map as 1832;[94] which is no doubt approximately correct.[95]

It seems doubtful whether Henry Kelsey's 'discovery' of the buffalo in Canada in 1689-91 can correctly be termed such. There is an utter lack of any element of surprise in his quite casual remarks, in contrast with the attitude of the Jesuit missionaries cited above. Those men were manifestly describing a creature strange to themselves—apparently even by hearsay—and doubtless believed it to be equally strange to their superiors for whom they wrote. But their unfamiliarity by no

[91]On La Hontan, 1687, see Allen, *American Bisons,* 104. La Hontan, 'the Munchausen of his day' (so, Bancroft, *Northwest Coast,* I, 588) had a poor reputation (cf. Winsor (ed.), *Narrative and Critical History,* IV, 257-62; Coues (ed.), *Expeditions of Pike,* I, 67); but some later critics oppose this (see chap. III, note 161). For the erratic absences, see below; chap. XIV, note 13.
[92]See chap. XX, "Irregular Migrations."
[93]Allen, *American Bisons,* 117.
[94]Hornaday, "Extermination of the American Bison," map, 548. The outline of the buffalo habitat at this point does not correspond with his description—"Winnipeg to Chicago" (*ibid.,* 385).
[95]Catlin describes the 'Menomonies' (Fox River and western shores of Green Bay, Wisconsin) as being ". . . out of the reach of the buffaloes," *circa* 1835 (*Letters on the North American Indians,* II, 147).

means implies a similar unfamiliarity in fur-trading circles, even if the precise range of the animals was not definitely known. Kelsey found in a certain (unidentified) spot some 'beasts' which he was apparently quite prepared to find somewhere. In any case, I reserve the matter for a later chapter on the buffalo in Canada.[96]

[96]See note on Henry Kelsey, at conclusion of chap. XII.

CHAPTER X

THE BUFFALO HABITAT AND ITS HISTORICAL
CHRONOLOGY*: EAST OF THE MISSISSIPPI RIVER

THE former occupation by the buffalo of the westerly Lake states is beyond question, in so far as Illinois, Indiana, and Ohio are concerned. There seems, however, to be some uncertainty with respect to southern Michigan. Allen remarks: "Hennepin [1679], Marest [1710], Gravier [1700], Charlevoix [1720], and other Jesuit missionaries[1] appear not to have met with it on the St. Joseph's River, nor anywhere in Southern Michigan, although they found it abundant on the Kaskaskia, and further southward. . . ."[2] Hornaday agrees that it is doubtful "whether the former range of the species extended north of the northern boundary of Indiana, but since southern Michigan was as well adapted to their support as Ohio or Indiana, their absence from that State must have been due more to accident than design. . . ."[3]

This lack of evidence to establish clearly occupancy of a territory so closely contiguous[4] and so similar physically to regions where the buffalo are known to have ranged during many years may, in my view, be reasonably regarded as supporting the hypothesis of their comparatively recent arrival on the eastern side of the Mississippi, and in relatively scanty numbers. This factor will be found to be of some importance to our inquiry later on.

*In presenting the evidence for the former presence of buffalo in this territory, I use the term "historical (i.e. authenticated) chronology" advisedly, in preference to "chronological history." The latter term could embrace all those random assertions which have been only too common on this topic, provided that some date or other is attached to them.

[1]Hennepin was a Récollet, and an opponent of the Jesuits.

[2]Allen, *American Bisons*, 104-5. The dates given are mine.

[3]Hornaday, "Extermination of the American Bison," 385.

[4]Schoolcraft, citing no authority, has them in southern Michigan (Allen, *American Bisons*, 105). Based perhaps upon this, Allen's map shows an upward curve in that state, to about 43° N., near Lansing. Hornaday ("Extermination of the American Bison," map, 548) marks the boundary direct between the southern end of Lake Michigan and Lake Erie. E. L. Moseley, an uncritical 'popular' writer, presumably upon Allen's authority, but citing none, has them 'in southern Michigan only' (*Our Wild Animals*, 184).

So far as Illinois is concerned, it would almost seem that, although Hennepin was neither the first to see nor the first to record the northern buffalo in the United States habitat, he may have been the first—he was certainly among the earliest—to publish the knowledge. This must have been peculiarly associated with the country of the Illinois tribes. For they were termed 'Illinois cattle' by Bacqueville de la Potherie (*circa* 1700),[5] and this name was still in familiar use half a century later.[6] References to the animal in Illinois, so far as I can find, are somewhat scanty, but they may serve to convey some idea of eighteenth-century conditions. Father Gravier (1700) alludes to buffalo among the Illinois tribes;[7] this being, in Allen's opinion, along the Kaskaskia River,[8] or between Vandalia and St. Louis, where it was found as late as 1773.[9] Father Marest (1712) bears similar testimony to its presence among the Illinois,[10] and Vaudreuil (1718) found it 'abundant' on the Rock River.[11] Father Râle (*circa* 1720) says of the Illinois Indians that there is "no year in which they do not kill . . . more than 2000 oxen. . . ."[12] "Hamburgh's Journal" (1763) notes an abundance from Chicago River southward,[13] and similarly Colonel George Croghan records 'plenty' along the Little Wabash, June, 1765.[14] Another British officer, Captain Harry Gordon, notes at the mouth of the Wabash River, July 31, 1766: "The herds of Buffaloe are hereabouts Extraordinary large and frequent to be seen. . . ."[15] Pittman, writing about 1770, records abundance of buffalo in Illinois.[16] On George Rogers Clark's famous march to Vincennes in 1779, his party found 'numbers of buffalo' on 'Cot Plains,' near 'the two Wabashes.'[17]

[5]Blair, *Indian Tribes*, I, 366.
[6]Bonnecamp, 1750, in *Jesuit Relations*, LXIX, 177; 'ilinois oxen' and 'cows' are used, manifestly for domestic cattle, 1733-56, "Detroit Mission Acounts," *ibid.*, LXIX, 268-9, 291.
[7]*Ibid.*, LXV, 135, 159.
[8]Allen, *American Bisons*, 104-5.
[9]*Ibid.*, 116.
[10]*Jesuit Relations*, LXVI, 225, 227, 253, 287.
[11]Allen, *American Bisons*, 106. Rock River is an eastern tributary of the Mississippi, which it enters near Davenport, Iowa. Rock Island is at the confluence.
[12]*Jesuit Relations*, LXVIII, 169. Not necessarily all in modern Illinois, as these tribes followed the buffalo (so Hennepin, 1679, *New Discovery*, I, 153; Binneteau, 1699, *Jesuit Relations*, LXV, 73-5; cf. *ibid.*, LIV, 189; Gravier, Marest, *ibid.*)
[13]Printed in Mereness(ed.), *Colonial Travels*, 362, 363
[14]"Croghan's Journals," in *Early Western Travels*, I, 140.
[15]Mereness (ed.), *Colonial Travels*, 468, 469.
[16]Allen, *American Bisons*, 106.
[17]Hulbert, *Historic Highways*, VIII, 50-3; see also Bruce, *Daniel Boone*, 190. *Cot* thought to be *quatre*, or 'Four-Mile Prairie,' Clay County, Illinois. The 'two' are Little Wabash and Big Muddy Creek, or Little Wabash and Fox River (so Hulbert, *Historic Highways*, VIII, 50-3).

The statement of Thomas Ashe (1806) that there was "not one buffalt to be found at this time east of the Mississippi,"[18] is somewhat too sweeping, as was not uncommon with Ashe; but Hulme's inclusion of them among the animals of Illinois as late as 1819 is almost equally dubious.[19] Brackenridge (1814) says that at that time they had retired 'to the northward of the Illinois and westward of the Mississippi.'[20] This is accepted by others, and apparently by Allen, and may be taken as substantially correct.[21]

I have found very few references to Indiana, but, speaking generally, the various chronological data given above may be considered equally applicable to this state. Buffalo are mentioned in this region (in Allen's opinion) by Vaudreuil (1718) and Charlevoix (1720),[22] and they are also noted by Croghan near Vincennes in June, 1765.[23] Conditions in the greater woodland regions away from the larger rivers must have been conducive to their survival; for they are stated to have been seen near Vincennes in 1808;[24] and in southern Indiana—where a place-name, French Lick, almost on a line between Vincennes and Louisville, Kentucky, perhaps commemorates a former resort—one was killed in 1830,[25] the very latest of all our references east of the Mississippi.

Allusions to buffalo in Ohio are more plentiful. The southern shore of Lake Erie constitutes, in part, the northern limit of the known buffalo habitat. Baron La Hontan explored the southern shore of Lake Erie in 1687. He writes: "I cannot express what quantities of Deer and Turkeys are to be found in these Woods, and in the vast Meads that lye upon the South side of the Lake. At the bottom of the Lake we find beeves upon the Banks of two pleasant Rivers that disembogue into it, without Cataracts or Rapid Currents. . . ."[26]

[18]Allen, *American Bisons*, 110.

[19]Hulme, *Early Western Travels*, X, 287.

[20]Allen, *American Bisons*, 117. 'The Illinois' signifies the territory, not the river. Alexander Henry, Jr., uses the same phrase, 1806 (Coues (ed.), *Henry-Thompson Journals*, I, 384).

[21]'Extinct *circa* 1800': George Graham of Cincinnati (presumably a recognized authority) to Allen, *American Bisons*, 229. A post on the Wabash River, *circa* 1700, is stated to have secured 15,000 hides 'in a short time.' (Willson, *Great Company*, 183.) I doubt this. The figure is out of all proportion to the general ratios of buffalo-hide returns at that era.

[22]Allen, *American Bisons*, 106, 107.

[23]Croghan, *Early Western Travels*, I, 143; Hulbert, *Historic Highways*, II, 56.

[24]Moseley, *Our Wild Animals*, 184.

[25]Garretson, *American Bison*, 92.

[26]Allen, *American Bisons*, 107.

Vaudreuil also stated that 'buffaloes abound on the south shore of Lake Erie, but not on the north. . . .'[27] Allen cites other testimony to their presence in this state in the early eighteenth century;[28] but the importance of the Ohio Valley as a main route of westbound travel, from about 1750 onward, seems to have driven the buffalo down the valley to its western boundaries some noticeable time before their actual extinction within the limits of the state itself (as defined in later years). Considering also the importance of the Ohio Valley in its relation to Hulbert's great thesis, as almost the sole westward migration thoroughfare of the buffalo hosts east of the Mississippi, the references concerning either occasions or numbers are scarcely what we might expect. Croghan, in 1765, along the Little Kanawha River, a tributary of the Ohio from the West Virginia highlands, and perhaps actually more—or even entirely—within the latter state, notes 'Buffaloes very plentiful.'[29]

In 1766, Captain Harry Gordon says that buffalo were first seen on the Ohio River, one hundred miles below Fort Pitt (Pittsburgh), "but they are not so Common, until we pass the Scioto" (Portsmouth, Ohio).[30] This is corroborated by a reference from a learned American scholar, which I quote: "[In 1795] buffalo [are] nearly disappeared from this region, where, less than thirty years before Croghan had found them in such vast numbers. Butricke (Historical Magazine, viii, p. 259) says that in 1768 they were scarce above the Scioto River. The last buffalo was killed in the Great Kanawha Valley, about twelve miles below Charleston, West Virginia, in 1815."[31]

Captain Gordon observes concerning Fort Massac, which he gives as 120 miles below the mouth of the Wabash, on the Ohio River, and

[27]British-American Magazine (ed. H. Y. Hind, Toronto, 1863 et seq.) I, 628. I am indebted for this rather rare—and I believe short-lived— publication (an early attempt at a Canadian quarterly review) to my friend the late D. E. Cameron, formerly librarian of the University of Alberta.

[28]Allen, American Bisons, 106, 107. Also an undated reference, possibly Vaudreuil also, but certainly of the French period: "Thirty leagues up the Miamis River, at a place called La Glaise [later Fort Defiance], Buffaloes are always found . . ." (British-American Magazine, I, 628). What is a 'league'? If it be three miles, this would be near the head of the Miami, perhaps west of Bellefontaine, Ohio.

[29]Early Western Travels, I, 130, 132; see also Allen, American Bisons, 229-31.
[30]In Mereness (ed.), Colonial Travels, 465.
[31]Thwaites, ed. note, Early Western Travels, III, 37; cf. Michaux, ibid., III, 97. With sincere respect to Thwaites's memory, I must demur to 'vast numbers.' Croghan says 'very plentiful' (Early Western Travels, I, 130, 132); 'in great plenty' (p. 140); 'in plenty' (p. 143); all purely relative expressions. This is discussed in detail below. See chap. XIII.

11 miles below the confluence of the Tennessee River, at or near Paducah, Kentucky: "Hunters from this Post may be sent amongst the Buffaloe, any Quantity of whose Beef they can procure in proper Season. . . ."[32] At this point, however, they might, of course, be in some contact with the larger trans-Mississippi herds, which no doubt swam backward and forward to some extent.[33] One is stated to have been killed by Washington somewhere in the Ohio Valley territory in 1770—[34] no very great proof of 'vast numbers' at that era; and buffalo were seen, apparently, on the Ohio River in June, 1775.[35] Gallatin describes them as being 'abundant' between the Great and Little Kanawha Rivers in 1784-85; for eight months he lived principally on their flesh.[36] An army journal of 1787 records 'a buffalo brought in' to Fort Harmar, March 27, and 'five buffalo' (as something of an event) on October 4, of that year.[37] One was killed near Gallipolis, Ohio (which is near the mouth of the Kanawha River) in 1795.[38] In October, 1795, also, buffalo were 'seen' by André Michaux, the naturalist, near Fort Massac.[39] His use of this term does not suggest anything like the reputed numbers of thirty years before. A testimony cited from an old settler at Marietta, Ohio (mouth of Muskingum River), speaks of 'old inhabitants'—not himself—having killed buffalo about there, circa 1806; and another letter mentions reports of buffalo on 'Buffalo Fork,' 20 miles east of Zanesville, Ohio, circa 1808.[40] What must surely have been the very last recorded instance in the upper Ohio basin was a buffalo cow and her calf, killed at the head of 'Tygart's River' in the Kanawha headwaters country, in 1825. The sire is not mentioned.[41] Such isolated occurrences scarcely invalidate the general conclusions of Graham[42] and Allen,[43] who date the disappearance of the buffalo in Ohio about 1800 and 1805 respectively. It is of course in the same broad sense that Garretson considers them 'practically extinct' east of

[32]Mereness (ed.), Colonial Travels, 470. For the fort, see Michaux, Early Western Travels, III, 73; also Coues's note, Expeditions of Pike, II, 657; Thwaites, ed. note, Early Western Travels, XXII, 203.

[33]On swimming the Mississippi, see above, chap. VII, notes 48-9.

[34]Allen, American Bisons, 229-31.

[35]Cresswell's Journal, 87-90.

[36]British-American Magazine, I, 629.

[37]Ibid.

[38]Moseley, Our Wild Animals, 183.

[39]Michaux, Early Western Travels, III, 73.

[40]British-American Magazine, I, 629.

[41]Garretson, American Bison, 92.

[42]Allen, American Bisons, 229-31.

[43]Ibid., 116-18.

the Mississippi River by 1820.[44] This is probably as near to absolute truth as we can hope to attain.

With reference to buffalo in Kentucky, F. A. Michaux writes (1802):

> . . . a short time after the settling of the Europeans several species . . . wholly disappeared, particularly the elks and bisons. The latter, notwithstanding, were more common there than in any other part of North America. The non-occupation of the country, the quantity of rushes and wild peas, which supplied them abundantly with food the whole year round; and the licks (places impregnated with salt . . .) are the causes that kept them there. Their number was at that time so considerable that they were met in flocks of 150 to 200. They were so far from being ferocious, that they did not fear the approach of the huntsmen, who sometimes shot them solely for the sake of having their tongue, which they looked upon as a delicious morsel. . . . At present, there are scarcely any from Ohio to the river Illinois. They have nearly deserted these parts, and strayed to the right [that is, west] bank of the Mississippi. . . .[45]

This is corroborated by Fortescue Cuming (1809), who recounts a conversation with his 'old-timer' Kentucky host, Captain Waller:

> He said that buffaloes, bears, and deer were so plenty in the country [that is, twenty years previously *circa* 1789] . . . that little or no bread was used, but that even the children were fed on game; the facility of gaining which prevented the progress of agriculture, until the poor innocent buffaloes were completely extirpated, and the other wild animals much thinned. And that the principal part of the cultivation of Kentucky had been within the last fifteen years. He said that the buffaloes had been so numerous, going in herds of several hundreds together, that about the salt licks and springs they frequented, they pressed down and destroyed the soil to a depth of three or four feet, as was conspicuous yet in the neighbourhood of the Blue Lick, where all the old trees have their roots bare of soil to that depth. . . . He said that the whole country was then an entire cane-brake, which sometimes grew to forty feet high, but that the domestic stock introduced by the settlers have eradicated the cane, except in some remote and unsettled parts of the state. . . .[46]

These general summaries are borne out by a number of specific allusions at different dates. Croghan says (June, 1765): "In our way we passed through a fine timbered clear wood; we came into a large

[44]Garretson, *American Bison*, 92.

[45]F. A. Michaux (son of André), *Early Western Travels*, III, 234. His remarks about buffalo being more common in Kentucky than anywhere else on the continent were written before Lewis and Clark, Pike, and others, had explored the West. Flocks 'of 150 to 200'!

[46]Cuming, *Early Western Travels*, IV, 175-8; also Allen, *American Bisons*, 103. Such places were also called 'Buffalo Stamps'; so S. P. Hildreth, resident of Marietta, Ohio, 1806 *seq.* (*British-American Magazine*, I, 629).

road which the buffaloes have beaten, spacious enough for two wag-
gons to go abreast, and leading straight into the Lick. . . ."[47] Captain
Gordon, at the same place, 'Big Bone Lick,' about 20 miles southwest
from Cincinnati, writes one year later: "We Encamped opposite the
great Lick, and next day I went with a Party of Indians and Batteau-
Men to view this much talked of Place. The beaten Roads from all
Quarters to it easily Conducted us, as they resemble those to an Inland
Village where Cattle go to and fro a large Common. . . . The extent
of the Muddy part of the Lick is ¾ of an Acre. This Mud being of a
Salt Quality is greedily lick'd by Buffaloe, Elk, and Deer, who come
from distant parts in great Numbers for this purpose. . . ."[48] Simon
Kenton's account is also of interest:

> . . . a 'buffalo road' touched at Lawrence Creek and ended at the great
> salt springs of Licking River, called later the Blue Licks from the color of
> the bubbling water. 'When I first saw it,' said Kenton in one of his deposi-
> tions, 'it was a deep pond of salt water and sand—the drier the time the
> deeper the pond; the buffaloes trod it all into a mire and prevented it run-
> ning into the river . . . . at different times the waters would overflow and
> leave a considerable quantity of sand in the places where the pond stood,
> when numerous small springs burst up all along . . . when the buffaloes by
> treading it would soon make it a pond again.' The flats on both sides of the
> river were crowded with buffaloes come to lick the salty earth. . . .
> He crossed the Licking, and on the other side fell in with another
> buffalo trail which led to the Upper Blue Licks where again was evidence
> of game the like of which he had never seen. . . .[49]

In the same year (1775) a young English visitor writes (of Grinin's
Lick): "This is the largest Lick I ever saw. I suppose here is 50 acres
of land trodden by Buffaloes, but there is not a blade of grass upon it.
Incredible numbers come here to the Salt springs . . . a herd of two
hundred odd. . . . Springs of this sort have large roads made to them,
as large as most public roads in a populous country. . . ."[50]

"Henderson's Diary" notes the presence of 'bofelos' and 'bufelos'
along the 'Caintuck River,' April 18–May 1, 1775;[51] and although the

[47]Croghan, Early Western Travels, I, 135; Hulbert, Historic Highways, I, 116.
[48]In Mereness (ed.), Colonial Travels, 466-7.
[49]Kenton, Simon Kenton, 63.
[50]Cresswell's Journal, 85, 86.
[51]Hulbert, Historic Highways, VI, 115. The following is too good to be
omitted. "Abrams mair ran into the River with her load & Swam over he folowd
her & got on her and made her Swim Back agin it is a very raney Eavening
we take up Camp near Richland Crek they kill a beef [? buffalo] Mr. Drake
Bakes Bread without washing his hands we keep sentry this night for fear of
the indians . . ." ("Henderson's Diary," April 11, 1775: in Hulbert, ibid., 113).
'Abram' was Abraham Hanks, grandfather of Abraham Lincoln (Archibald
Henderson, American Historical Review, XX, 91-2).

settlers—or the more thrifty among them—put the buffalo products to many uses, even spinning the 'wool,'[52] as had been attempted among the French colonists around New Orleans about 1700 (by Royal Proclamation at the instigation of the Governor, d'Iberville[53]), yet very possibly the buffalo were almost as much of a nuisance as an asset. Kenton mentions 'two acres of corn' destroyed by them in 1776;[54] probably not the only instance. This may partly account for very little cultivation while the buffalo remained. But their doom was hastened also by the fearful winter of 1779-80, "when from the middle of November to the last of February all Kentucky was shrouded in snow and ice . . . and even buffalo would come so close to the settlements that they could be shot from the cabin doors. . . . Kentucky's herds of game were never again so great—thousands of deer and buffalo perished. . . ."[55]

This is corroborated by Colonel William Fleming (March 20, 1780): ". . . the earth for so long a time covered with snow and the water entirely froze . . . even the Buffaloes died starved to death. . . ."[56] Before this terrible winter, fresh buffalo meat is noticed as 'a ready dish.'[57] Yet after it, Kenton speaks of 'plenty' at the forks of the Licking River in September and October, 1782.[58] John Filson in 1784 writes as follows: "I have heard a hunter assert that he saw above one thousand buffaloes at the Blue Licks at once; so numerous were they before the first settlers had wantonly sported away their lives. . . . The amazing herds of buffalo which resort hither, by their size and numbers, fill the traveller with amazement and terror, especially when he beholds the prodigious roads they have made from all quarters, as if leading to some populous city; the vast space of land around these springs desolated as if by a ravaging enemy, and hills reduced to plains; for the land near these springs is chiefly hilly. . . ."[59]

[52]"Fleming's Journal" (1779-80), in Mereness (ed.), Colonial Travels, 629. The Mormons—perhaps in part the grandchildren of these settlers—"collected the hair of the buffalo from the sage-brush as they travelled . . ." (1847-48). Bancroft, History of Utah, 276.
[53]Winsor (ed.), Narrative and Critical History, V, 21.
[54]Kenton, Simon Kenton, 77.
[55]Ibid., 148.
[56]Mereness (ed.), Colonial Travels, 636.
[57]Hulbert, Historic Highways, VI, 196.
[58]Kenton, Simon Kenton, 160.
[59]Allen, American Bisons, 112-13; Hornaday, "Extermination of the American Bison", 386-7. Filson: 'that inaccurate and turgid amanuensis . . ." (Archibald Henderson, American Historical Review, XX, 86). Turgid, certainly! Note 'roads' from all these witnesses—i.e. trails. See above, chap. VI, note 2; also Cresswell (note 50 above). 'Public roads' in England circa 1775 were mostly bad trails.

Daniel Boone is stated to have declared concerning the Red River region, in Kentucky, *circa* 1770: "The buffaloes were more frequent than I have ever seen cattle in the settlements, browsing on the leaves of the cane, or cropping the herbage of those extensive plains, fearless because ignorant of the violence of man. Sometimes we saw hundreds in a drove, and the numbers about the salt springs were amazing. . . ."[60]

After all these vicissitudes, as late as 1786—and even this is earlier than the abounding era of Cuming's host (1789)—we find 'Buffalo plenty' at Kenton's Station.[61] And in so far as the 'hundreds' are concerned, we learn that on one occasion when he was there, in 1775, Kenton "counted fifteen hundred buffalo pacing in a single file to the Licks. . . ."[62]

Despite all this, however, 'hundreds,' and those mentioned almost with bated breath, do not convey any very vivid impression of such really large numbers as are commonly associated with buffalo; and amidst the early rhetoric on the subject, one or two observers said so quite plainly. "Henderson's Diary" notes (May 9, 1775): "We found it very difficult at first to stop great waste in killing meat. Some would kill three, four, five, or half a dozen buffaloes and not take half a horse load from them all. For want of a little obligatory law, our game as soon as got here, if not before, was driven off very much. Fifteen or twenty miles was as short a distance as good hunters thought of getting meat, nay, sometimes they were obliged to go thirty miles, though by chance once or twice a week buffalo was killed within five or six miles. . . ."[63]

It is worth while noting also in the recent and authentic biography of Simon Kenton (a careful production based upon original and family documents), that Kenton on coming to the Blue Licks—an acknowledged central rendezvous—although he had lived in the regions of so-called 'immense herds'[64] all his life, found "evidence of game *the like of*

---

[60]Allen, *American Bisons*, 112; Hornaday, "Extermination of the American Bison," 388; Hulbert, *Historic Highways*, VI, 32; Bruce, *Daniel Boone*, 96-100. Boone also speaks of 'thousands,' Kentucky, 1753 (*ibid.*, 29-30). But 'hundreds' in 1770 does not suggest one familiar with thousands, and the 'settlements' would not represent the hosts of the Texas, Montana, or Alberta ranges.

[61]Kenton, *Simon Kenton*, 178. Writing from the Boone MSS., Theodore Roosevelt notes buffalo-meat at 3*d* per pound, *post* 1784. At this era 'beef was plentiful'; hence the price of buffalo beef might indicate lesser demand, quite as much as plentiful supply (*Winning of the West*, III, 110).

[62]Kenton, *Simon Kenton*, 63.

[63]Bruce, *Daniel Boone*, 125.

[64]The phrase is applied by Allen to Kentucky, West Virginia, and Tennessee. (*American Bisons*, 72-3.)

which he had never seen."[65] If words mean anything, 'vast numbers' must be interpreted purely in a relative sense. The final extinction of the species in Kentucky is dated by both Allen and Graham *circa* 1800.[66]

I have found but few direct references to the buffalo in the adjoining State of Tennessee, which was ranked by Gallatin as the southern limit in the central territory east of the Mississippi River.[67] Broadly speaking, the general environmental conditions would be similar to those of Kentucky. As I have remarked, Allen uses the same phraseology, 'immense herds,' for both states. An early traveller in the region writes: "The open space around and near the sulphur or salt springs, instead of being an 'old field,' as had been supposed by Mr. Mausker, at his visit here in 1769, was thus freed from trees and underbrush by the innumerable herds of buffalo and deer and elk that came to these waters. . . ."[68]

This is not altogether so certain as the writer appears to have thought. Shoemaker, whether by reason of this passage or independently, speaks of many such buffalo 'clearings,' and cites the place-name of Clearfield, Pennsylvania,[69] as proof. Unfortunately for this thesis, old Indian fields were not uncommon in the south-eastern states area;[70] and Clearfields, Buckinghamshire,[71] and Clearwood, Wiltshire,[72] are English place-names dating back to 1305 and 1348 respectively and probably much further. It would scarcely be necessary to notice this, were it not that some writers have thought that the great plains and prairies of the North American continent have been produced by the action of buffalo rubbing down and destroying the trees. This will be dealt with in due course.[73]

Where the city of Nashville now stands, there were in 1770 "according to Ramsey . . . immense numbers of buffalo and other wild game. The country was crowded with them. Their bellowings sounded from

[65]Kenton, *Simon Kenton*, 63. The italics are mine.

[66]Allen, *American Bisons*, 113-18, 229-31.

[67]Garretson, *American Bison*, 23.

[68]Allen writes as if the rectification were his own (*American Bisons*, 114), but it is given by Garretson (*American Bison*, 22-3, 54) as from John Donelson, "Journal of a Voyage from Fort Patrick Henry on the Holston River to the French Salt Springs on the Cumberland River," 1780.

[69]Shoemaker, *A Pennsylvania Bison Hunt*, 30-3, followed by Garretson (*American Bison*, 54).

[70]*Travels of William Bartram*, 173, 314-15, etc.

[71]*Place-Names of Buckinghamshire* (English Place-Name Society), 119.

[72]*Place-Names of Wiltshire* (English Place-Name Society), 156.

[73]See Appendix K, "Buffalo and the Formation of Prairie Lands."

the hills and forest. . . ."[74] It may be noted, however, that neither Ramsey nor Boone (who as early as 1764 found 'vast herds' grazing in the valleys of eastern Tennessee, between the spurs of the Cumberland Mountains[75]) has much or anything to say about 'buffalo clearings.' Buffalo were included by André Michaux among the 'animals of Tennessee' in 1796.[76] Allen dates their extirpation in the state about 1800-10.[77]

Along the Mississippi Valley itself, the buffalo spread farther south than they appear to have done in the southeastern area. Probably along the river their numbers may have been augmented from the regions westward toward Texas. In the two Delta states of Mississippi and Louisiana, they have been noted from about 1685 onward, and according to Hornaday[78] were found in 'large numbers,' circa 1697-1722.

The evidence for the large numbers in the first quarter of the eighteenth century seems rather doubtful. In almost all these relations, it is often extremely difficult to identify the precise locality which is indicated under such terms as 'southern' or 'lower' Mississippi Valley. When Marest tells us (circa 1712) of "abundant herds of wild oxen along the Illinois, Mississippi, and Ouabache [Wabash] rivers,"[79] it is very possible that the other rivers may indicate the portion of the Mississippi territory to which the missionary refers; but when Father Vivier says (1750) that the plains and forests of the 'lower Mississippi' contain wild cattle which are found in herds,[80] this might mean anywhere for some hundreds of miles. We have, however, a number of localized allusions to assist us, falling within the period which has been mentioned.

Father Gravier, 1700, referring to the 'Toanikas' (Tunica) of the southern Mississippi, says: "As among the Illinois, whole families go together to Hunt the wild ox, which is seldom seen in this country. . . . It is a long time since either wild oxen, Deer, or bears, have been seen in this country. . . ."[81]

[74]Allen, American Bisons, 114; Hornaday, "Extermination of the American Bison," 388.
[75]Allen, American Bisons, 114; Hornaday, "Extermination of the American Bison," 388; Bruce, Daniel Boone, 46-7.
[76]Michaux, Early Western Travels, III, 63.
[77]Allen, American Bisons, 116-18.
[78]Hornaday, "Extermination of the American Bison," 380, 381; cf. Allen, American Bisons, 226-9.
[79]Jesuit Relations, LXVI, 225, 227, 253, 287.
[80]Vivier, Jesuit Relations, LXIX, 209.
[81]Gravier, Jesuit Relations, LXV, 135, 159; so also Marest, 1712, ibid., LXVI, 253. For the Tunica, see Handbook of American Indians, II, 838.

These statements find strong inferential corroboration in another historical fact, at this precise time. The attempt of d'Iberville, to which I have alluded, to prosecute under royal command the 'buffalo wool' industry, expressly included the domestication of the species for that particular purpose.[82] When we note that this was done at the instigation of d'Iberville himself, 'the man on the spot,' it can scarcely be supposed (even apart from fairly explicit testimony to the contrary) that at this time the wild race was locally available in really large numbers which might reasonably be expected to continue. Hornaday states that buffalo were recorded among the Natchez Indians, or around Natchez, Mississippi, in the period 1697-1722,[83] but cites neither any specific time nor any authority for the assertion. The French officer, Diron D'Artaguiette, says of the Natchez Indians (1722), "They also kill buffaloes, but they have to go a very long distance to find them. . . ."[84] The same officer enumerates among the needs of the colonists at New Orleans at this time, ". . . salted meat; the country in some seasons not being sufficiently supplied with buffaloes to support the colony. . . ."[85]

Even this 'local supply' perhaps came from a distance. Father Poisson writes as follows ('Aux-Akensas,' that is, 'Arkansaw,' 1726): "The hunters . . . at the end of summer ascend the Mississippi for 200 or 300 leagues to the country where there are cattle. . . . They begin to find wild cattle at only 30 leagues from here; these animals roam in herds over the prairies or along the rivers; last year a Canadian brought down to new Orleans 480 tongues of cattle that he and his partner alone had killed during the winter. . . ."[86]

[82]Winsor (ed.), *Narrative and Critical History*, V, 21.

[83]Hornaday, "Extermination of the American Bison," 380, 381.

[84]"Journal of D'Artaguiette," in Mereness (ed.), *Colonial Travels*, 47.

[85]*Ibid.*, 22.

[86]Poisson, *Jesuit Relations*, LXVII, 285. This is the earliest mention I have found of buffalo tongues in trade.

The long journey made by D'Artaguiette up the Mississippi in 1723 furnished a few facts relative to this question. February 8 (apparently near the northern border of modern Louisiana): ". . . numerous tracks of buffalo, all fresh, which induced us to go hunting . . ." (Mereness (ed.), *Colonial Travels,* 52). None until February 13, when "we perceived on the other side of the river a herd of wild cattle [*bœufs sauvages* = buffalo] which were coming there to drink, a thing which induced us to cross over and to go ashore so as to kill some of them; but these animals, having scented us, we could not approach them . . . ." No more for some time; then, February 17: "no hope of killing buffaloes from here to the Arkansas." This was five days, reaching there February 22. Buffalo first seen, March 9; one killed, March 12. Seen again, March 13, March 15-16, one killed each day; so also March 20, 23. March 25, 27, one and two, respectively. April 1, 2, one each day. April 8, two killed. April 10, one killed. None until June 29; one killed. June 30, five killed. July 1, 2, 3, 6, 8, one each day. July 14: "no

In the Gulf States of Mississippi (the inland regions back from the river), Alabama, and Florida, there is no record of the historic buffalo having ever been known. It appears not to have penetrated south of the Tennessee River,[87] or (roughly) south of Latitude 35° N., which might very nearly be indicated by a line drawn from Memphis to Chattanooga. Allen, while remarking on the entire absence of historical or other evidence relating to (modern) Florida,[88] considers it nevertheless possible that the buffalo may once have dwelt there.[89] In view of a broad similarity in climatic and ecological conditions to the neighbouring states, this is probable. Concerning Alabama, Hornaday goes a little further. Notwithstanding the fact (emphasized by himself) that there is no known reference of any kind to buffalo there, nor even to the use of buffalo products by the Alabama Indians, he believes the animal once inhabited the northern half of the state.[90] He bases his opinion, I should suppose, on the same general similarity of environment.

This suggests that there was no reason inherent in the region why the buffalo should not have advanced to the shores of the Gulf of Mexico, as they actually did on the western side of the Mississippi, in Texas. The only probable explanations that suggest themselves are that the species had not occupied the Southeast for a sufficiently long time, or in numbers great enough to withstand the attack of Indian hunting tribes. It seems to be almost unquestionable that De Soto's great expedition through 'Florida' in 1539-42 must have passed broadly across central Alabama on its westward course from the Savannah River to the Yazoo.[91] It is incredible that during this time the expedition was

---

longer the hope of killing any buffalo . . ." (Mereness (ed.), *Colonial Travels*, 52-66, 83-6). Theoretically, they should have been abreast of the 'north-bound migration' and seeing 'vast hosts' every day at this time.

[87]Allen, *American Bisons*, 55, 73, 102; cf. Appendix, *ibid.*, 229-31.

[88]*Ibid.*, 97-101.

[89]*Ibid.*, 225-6.

[90]Hornaday, "Extermination of the American Bison," 380.

[91]In this, I have largely followed Fiske (*Discovery of America*, II, 509-10), whose wide and balanced judgment in these critical questions is still of high value. The identification of the precise route followed by De Soto has baffled many inquirers. Nuttall (1819) thought the exploration of the 'immemorial trails' (if there are any!) might facilitate this (*Early Western Travels*, XIII, 145); but the difficulty is as great as ever, or was in 1922 (*Narratives of De Soto*, ed. note, II, 54). Almost all those whose works I have been able to consult confine themselves to taking the party through Florida, Georgia, Alabama, Louisiana, Mississippi, Arkansas, and Texas, which is fairly safe (see Shea, in Winsor (ed.), *Narrative and Critical History*, II, 250-4; Fiske, *Discovery of America*, II, 509-10; Brittain, *History of North America*, I, 361; Webb, *Great Plains*, 111-14).

on the fringe of (or actually within) a territory containing the readily recognizable 'kine of Cibola' or *vacas jorobadas*—of which their leader had heard from Cabeza de Vaca himself—if the animals were actually ranging at that time within those general limits, without the Spaniards even hearing of them. Even a tradition of their former presence would surely, one thinks, have been recorded.[92] This was done when they encountered news of the 'cattle' in the thinly populated area to the north, where it was so cold that maize could scarcely be grown.[93] It is equally incredible that the historic buffalo could have penetrated thither, flourished, passed, and left no memorials, visible, fossilized, or traditional, in the relatively brief period that has elapsed since informed scientific opinion admits them to the central states and the outlying territories on the eastern side of the Mississippi.[94] The firmly rooted practice of agriculture among the tribes of these lower southern states argues in my opinion very strongly against the suggestion.[95]

Hornaday mentions a Choctaw tradition—which he does not himself endorse—that the buffalo disappeared from what is now the state of Mississippi early in the eighteenth century, owing to a great drought, which was particularly severe in the prairie region. No rain is said to have fallen for three years. The Nownbee and Tombigbee Rivers dried up, and the forests perished. The elk and buffalo, which until then had been numerous, fled beyond the Mississippi, and never returned.[96] Indian traditions going back beyond the memory of living

---

Fiske notes one possible localization (whether his own or not) which has since been generally accepted. He places their fight at Mauvila, 'a few miles above the junction of the Tombigbee and Alabama rivers, and thinks that probably 'Mauvila,' or 'Maubila,' gave the name *Mobile* to the river formed by the two' (Fiske, *Discovery of America*, II, 509; see also *Handbook of American Indians*, I, 916; Graham, *The Horses of the Conquest*, 75-6; Bishop, *Odyssey of Cabeza de Vaca*, 30-2).

Confusion of 'b' and 'v' is frequent among the Gascons (Lescarbot, *History of New France*, III, 125), and the Spanish. The usual *Cibola* is *Civola, Cevola* (in *Purchas, his Pilgrimes*, XVIII, 62, 63; *Journey of Coronado*, 173), Havana-Habana, Quivira-Quibira, Ovando-Obando, Balparaiso, Baldivia, Saabedra, etc., are common in Hakluyt and Purchas. Compare Martavan, Malavar, in Hakluyt (*Voyages*, III, 240, 311; IV, 248).

[92]*Purchas his Pilgrimes*, XVIII, 45-6; also the Gentleman of Elvas; *Narratives of De Soto*, I, 140. Cf. De Soto himself, *ibid.*, II, 162 (chap. IX, note 21).

[93]*Purchas his Pilgrimes*, XVIII, 16, 31-3; *Narratives of De Soto*, I, 128, 133, 140.

[94]See on this, Shaler, "On the Age of the Bison in the Ohio Valley," in Allen, *American Bisons*, Appendix II, 232-6; also Shaler, *Nature and Man in America*, 181-8.

[95]*Ibid.*, 182, 187. On 'old Indian fields,' 1773, above, note 70.

[96]Hornaday, "Extermination of the American Bison," 381.

commentators are often very dubious, as some of the folk tales and unverified seasonal weather predictions tend to show;[97] and here, again, we find the familiar story of a bygone Golden Age.[98] In the present case, certain conclusions are inescapable. The period 'until then' of buffalo plenty (that is, *circa* 1700) must have begun after De Soto passed, for this region lies right across his line of march, in which none were encountered. No mention is made of this profusion in the period 1542-1700 in any source I have been able to consult, nor is there any mention of buffalo bone-deposits of the historic species found in the state.[99] I do not know what is—or was—the prairie region in Mississippi, but if this tradition were to be credited, the magnificent slow-growing hardwoods of the southern states would be little more than two hundred years old *at this present time*. Before dismissing southern tradition, William Bartram, the naturalist, mentions as an apparently familiar traditional belief in his own day (1773), "nations of Indians who emigrated from the west, beyond the [Mississippi] river. . . ."[100] There is a multiplicity of 'westbound' tradition on this point, in addition to movements accepted by science.[101] This assertion may find some confirmation in Bartram's observations on the Hispano-Indian 'Siminole' and 'Chactaw' horses.[102] These waves of emigration might have followed the buffalo, as is claimed for so many others, or the pressure of tribes with horses might conceivably turn buffalo eastward. In any event, the existing data are insufficient for any very valuable conclusions to be drawn.

In the Atlantic coast states, evidence appears to indicate that the buffalo not only penetrated much farther south than they did inland, but also approached "very nearly, if not quite to the Georgia coast."[103] Allen notes evidence concerning their presence in southern Georgia.[104]

[97]See an examination of one, Appendix J, "Buffalo and Disease."
[98]See remarks above, chap. VIII, notes 44-6.
[99]The fossil *B. latifrons* has been found there. Above, chap. II, note 35.
[100]Bartram, *Travels*, 185.
[101]According to Hulbert, the westbound pioneers over the Alleghanies 'followed the Indian, who followed the buffalo.' Both were originally southeast-bound; and the Indian reached the Southeast *first*, since the buffalo never reached some portions at all. On the westward dispersion of the Siouan Family, see Thomas and Swanton, *Handbook of American Indians*, II, 577-9; cf. below, note 130.
[102]Bartram, *Travels*, 185-6. See also Roe, "From Dogs to Horses among the Western Indian Tribes" (*Transactions of the Royal Society of Canada*, 1939, Sec. II, 209-75).
[103]Fletcher, "Buffalo," in *Handbook of American Indians*, I, 169.
[104]Allen, *American Bisons*, 225.

He also remarks: "Up to the time of Moore's voyage to Georgia the interior was almost wholly unexplored, and it is almost certain that had not the 'large herds of buffalo upon the mainland' existed within a distance of twenty or thirty miles or less from the coast, the colonists would have had no knowledge of them; nor would the Indians have taken to the war-path against the whites at Darien, under pretext of hunting buffalo. . . ."[105]

I am unaware of the exact date of Moore's voyage, but it was probably in the thirties of that century, since there is mention in 1736 of large herds upon the mainland near St. Simon's Island, which is not far from Darien.[106] Oglethorpe in 1733 includes 'deer, elks, bears, wolves, and buffaloes' among the animals of Georgia (and South Carolina);[107] and Thomas Salmon, a voluminous gazetteer of his day, says of 'Carolina' (1749), which in his classification included both the Carolinas and Georgia: "Among their Native Animals, they have the *Urus* or *Zorax* [? Aurochs] described by Cæsar, which the *English* improperly call a Buffaloe. . . ."[108]

They appear to have been fairly plentiful there at one time, as 'plenty' is to be understood in the eastern territories. An early writer says. ('Great Ogechee River,' Georgia, 1739): "Killing buffaloes . . . of which there is a very great Plenty, and they are very good Eating. Though they are a very heavy Beast, they will out Run a Horse and Quite Tire him. . . ." Again, (Oconee River, 1739) "Buffaloes, of which there are abundance, We Seeing Several Herds of sixty or upwards in a herd. . . ."[109]

I have no precise information regarding their final disappearance in Georgia, though Allen's (implied) date, *circa* 1770, is probably none too soon.[110] For David Taitt (1772) makes no mention of the living animal, although he notes places named after buffalo;[111] and William Bartram (1773) says: ". . . the buffalo (*urus*), once so very numerous, is not at this day to be seen in this part of the country. . . ."[112] He

[105]*Ibid.*, 96; Hornaday, "Extermination of the American Bison," 379-80.
[106]*Ibid.*, 379-80. The two are about 32° N.–32° 10′ N.
[107]Allen, *American Bisons*, 96; Hornaday, "Extermination of the American Bison," 379-80. See also John Wesley's *Journal*, I, 62 (1737).
[108]Salmon, *A New Geographical and Historical Grammar*, 537.
[109]"Travels with Gen. Oglethorpe, 1739-1742" (in Mereness (ed.), *Colonial Travels*, 219-20). I cannot comprehend Garretson here: 'abundant in Georgia' (*American Bison*, 15); 'not unknown in Georgia' (*ibid.*, 19).
[110]Allen, *American Bisons*, 225.
[111]"Journal of David Taitt" (Mereness (ed.), *Colonial Travels*, 562).
[112]Bartram, *Travels*, 62. An editorial note to a recent reprint has them merely 'scarce' in the Southeast, where they formerly 'ranged in great numbers.'

further mentions seeing near Fort James on the Savannah River, "heaps of white gnawed bones of ancient buffalo, elk, and deer . . .";[113] and he also alludes to the 'Great Buffalo Lick,' on the "Great Ridge, which separates the waters of the Savanna and Alatamaha, about eighty miles distant from Augusta. . . ."[114]

The presence of buffalo in the upland districts of the two Carolinas in the first three quarters of the eighteenth century seems to be well established, even apart from *a priori* probabilities arising from contiguity to Georgia.[115] Hornaday cites a gentleman who (in 1857) asked an old resident of some seventy years how 'Buffalo Ford' on the Catawba River, near Statesville, North Carolina, got its name. "He told me that his grandfather told him, that when he was a boy the buffalo crossed there." The longitude is given as 81° W., and the date would be approximately 1740-50.[116] In South Carolina, buffalo were 'abundant' in the first half of the eighteenth century; and some of the settlers in the Abbeville district, which is on the upper waters of the Savannah River and not far from the Georgia line, are said to have found them there in 1756.[117] This is the 'upland country' along the flank of the southerly Alleghanies, and Allen alludes to it in somewhat conflicting terms. The buffalo, he says, were found "only to a limited extent east of the Alleghanies, chiefly in the upper districts of North and South Carolina. . . ."[118] Later, we read: ". . . its existence on the Atlantic slope of the continent being confined to the highlands of North and South Carolina. . . ."[119]

The latter statement is obviously incorrect, even upon its learned author's own showing; but I quote it as tending to illustrate the general

---

In the first settlement of Georgia they were 'as abundant as they were in Tennessee and Kentucky, 10,000 being seen in a herd' (where?). Georgia, apparently, was 'well supplied with buffalo tongues as late as up to 1774.' Adair, *History of the American Indians* (1775), ed. Williams (1930), 445-6.

[113]Bartram, *Travels*, 263.
[114]*Ibid.*, 55.
[115]Allen, *American Bisons*, 55, 72-4, 92-7.
[116]Hornaday, "Extermination of the American Bison," 379. This may or may not have been the case, despite Hulbert's certainties as to *why* such names were bestowed (*Historic Highways*, I, 139). Folk-etymology is a perilous thing. See below on 'Buffalo Cross Roads,' note 157. There was an idle tale current at Kenilworth (Warwickshire) that Chesford Bridge over the Avon was so named (i.e. Chesterford) 'because the Bishop of Chester's carriage was almost swept away in the ford' during a flood *circa* 1840 (itself an actual fact). It was *Chessfordbrugge*, etc., 1272-1427 (Jusserand, *Wayfaring Life*, 418; Duignan, *Warwickshire Place-Names*, 42; *Place-Names of Warwickshire* (English Place-Name Society), 191.
[117]Hornaday, "Extermination of the American Bison," 379.
[118]Allen, *American Bisons*, 55.
[119]*Ibid.*, 73.

obscurity of the question in relation to the Atlantic states. A later student furnishes the only suggested approximate date that I have found for the final disappearance of the buffalo: "Down to the outbreak of the Revolution herds of buffaloes grazed in the grassy prairie regions. And if the last of them disappeared beyond the mountains by 1775, their deep-worn trails leading to favored licks and ranges persisted for many years afterwards, as was the case with piles of bones of the slaughtered animals. . . ."[120]

Something has already been said about buffalo in Virginia. Hornaday states that they are said to have been more numerous in Virginia than in any other of the Atlantic states.[121] Michaux, as we have seen, said they were more numerous in Kentucky[122] than in any other part of North America. In each case, this may be regarded as somebody's opinion—or random assertion—and nothing more. It is regrettable that we have not some really precise and positive evidence of their supposed early discovery, to which allusion has been made. Hornaday mentions that a certain Colonel William Byrd and his party found buffalo 'in thick wooded country' along the Virginia and North Carolina boundary, at a point (given as 78° 40′ W.), only 155 miles from the Atlantic coast, in 1620.[123] The date must be an error or a misprint, for elsewhere he gives it as 1729-33,[124] and the last is supported by Allen,[125] and seemingly by other authorities.[126] The locality mentioned by Hornaday is at or near the junction of the Staunton and Roanoke Rivers. The presence of buffalo in this region, perhaps about 1730 or

[120]Bagot, "The South Carolina Up-Country at the End of the Eighteenth Century," *American Historical Review*, XXVIII, 682-98. It reads as if Bagot were for 'driving out' rather than extermination. Allen is strongly for the reverse, and the evidence seems to support him (*American Bisons*, 117). On trails in the Carolina and Virginia woodlands, *ibid.*, 86. There are certain editorial references to buffalo in the southeastern region as late as 1774, in Adair, *History of the American Indians*, ed. Williams, 445-6; but the editorial assumptions of a considerable plenty are neither supported by Adair himself, 1761-68 (*ibid.*) nor by Bartram, 1773 (see above, notes 110-14). Roosevelt, whose period begins only in 1774, uses much conventional phraseology about 'thundering herds,' etc., for which there seems inadequate support. His general attitude toward large numbers is very soundly critical; and he himself notes an instance—evidently considered phenomenal—of a party in that year having 'seen 300 buffalo,' (*Winning of the West*, I, 187).

[121]Hornaday, "Extermination of the American Bison," 379.

[122]Above, note 45.

[123]Hornaday, "Extermination of the American Bison," 378-9.

[124]*Ibid.*, 376.

[125]1733, in Allen, *American Bisons*, 85. On buffalo in the Shenandoah Valley *circa* 1730, *ibid.*, 225.

[126]Turner (*Frontier in American History*, 84, 98) mentions Captain William Byrd, 1679, and Colonel William Byrd, *circa* 1730. One of these must be the man. The William Byrds were a dynasty.

earlier, is indicated by a 'large Buffalo Lick,' which the emigrating Moravians noted in 1753, about ten miles from Roanoke.[127] I do not understand the emphasis placed by Hornaday on this encounter, when he had already proved (to his own satisfaction) that they were found much nearer the Atlantic coast a century or more earlier;[128] and he himself mentions further that as early as 1701 buffalo had been caught and domesticated by the Huguenot settlers on the James River, above Richmond, also apparently nearer to the coast.[129] This latter fact in itself scarcely points to their being very numerous. Indeed, despite what has been said about numbers in the Atlantic states, it has been pointed out that Lawson (1709) 'thought it worth while to record' that two buffalo were killed in one season on Cape Fear River, North Carolina;[130] and Dr. Walker notes on his four or five months' journey from Virginia to Kentucky and back, March to July, 1750, that besides "8 Elks, 20 Deer, 53 Bears, and many birds, they killed 13 Buffaloes. . . ."[131]

Concerning numbers, in the same region and the same year, Captain Bonnecamp, one of the French officers, is more caustic than complimentary. He says:

It was in the neighbourhood of the river that we began to see the Illinois cattle; but here and elsewhere they were in such small numbers that our men could hardly kill a score of them. It was, besides, necessary to seek them far in the woods. We had been assured, however, at our departure, that at each point we should find them by hundreds, and that the tongues alone of those which we should kill would suffice to support the troops. This is not the first time when I have experienced that hyperbole and exaggeration were figures familiar to the Canadians. . . .[132]

No doubt big 'fish stories' of this character were not uncommon. James Flint, writing in 1820, says of Kentucky: "The buffaloes, when Kentucky was first settled, were shot, by the settlers, merely for their tongues; the carcase and skin being thought worth nothing, were left to rot where the animal fell. . . ."[133] This implies a profusion, as well

---

[127]"Diary of the Moravians," in Mereness (ed.), *Colonial Travels*, 344.

[128]See above, chap. IX, note 45.

[129]See Appendix C, "Buffalo Domestication."

[130]Richardson, *Fauna Boreali-Americana*, I, 279; Audubon and Bachman, *American Quadrupeds*, II, 54-5. Lawson also describes the Tutelo, a Siouan tribe of Virginia and North Carolina, as having plenty of buffalo *circa* 1710, although they were also agriculturists. Mooney, "Tutelo," *Handbook of American Indians*, II, 855.

[131]"Walker's Journal," in Hulbert, *Historic Highways*, VI, 53.

[132]Bonnecamp, *Jesuit Relations*, LXIX, 177-9.

[133]Flint, *Early Western Travels*, XII, 19.

as the settlers' wastefulness. But we have seen above that, together with this somewhat legendary plenty, Captain Waller declared that the settlers subsisted almost exclusively on buffalo and other game; and Colonel Fleming, a contemporary observer, remarked in 1780 that practically every portion of the buffalo was utilized, even to the wool. This careful conservation of buffalo resources scarcely seems consistent with the abundance implied in the taking of tongues alone; and it was the tongues, seventy years previously, which were to be sufficient to maintain Bonnecamp's force.

I am ignorant upon what ground Allen applies the somewhat hackneyed phrase, 'immense herds,' to West Virginia.[134] He himself does not cite a single reference to large numbers, and I have found none elsewhere. It is worth noting also that Bonnecamp's highly competent editor, Dr. R. G. Thwaites, considers 'this river' in the passage quoted above concerning scarcity, to be in Virginia (which in this relationship practically necessitates *West* Virginia) or Ohio.[135] In 1750 the immense numbers should have been practically unimpaired, for that was virtually the beginning of the white invasion of the westward slope of the Alleghanies. Bonnecamp specifically ridicules the 'immense numbers,' of which he had *heard*; and Dr. Walker's party, whose route traversed both the traditional lands of plenty, shot thirteen buffalo in four or five months! Allen dates their extinction as occurring about 1772.[136] But we have noted references to buffalo in a region which is certainly on the borders, and may be within the very territory, of West Virginia as late as 1795, 1815, and even 1825.[137]

Although Maryland is considered to be the farthest point eastward reached by the buffalo in that approximate latitude,[138] references to the locality are few and vague. Father Andrew White is said to have

[134]Allen, *American Bisons*, 72-3, 110-11.

[135]Thwaites, ed. note, *Jesuit Relations*, LXIX, 298.

[136]Allen, *American Bisons*, 110-11. Flint (*Early Western Travels*, XII, 19) notes that buffalo robes cost $5.00 each in Wheeling, West Virginia, in 1820; but they were then being imported from the West. Miss Coman says that buffalo skins ('*temp.* J. J. Astor,' *circa* 1814?) were worth $1.00 to $1.50 on the plains; $5.00 to $10.00 'in the States.' Coman, *Economic Beginnings of the Far West*, I, 353, 394. In the Saskatchewan country then, an Indian would receive a *fathom* of tobacco (three-quarters of a pound) or two horn combs or 20 charges of powder and ball for a buffalo (Davidson, *North-West Company*, 223). An Oglala (Sioux) woman was worth six buffalo robes (Walker, "Oglala Kinship Terms," *American Anthropologist*, XVI, 1914, 96-109.

[137]Above, notes 31, 36, 38, 41.

[138]". . . as far east as Cavetown [east of Hagerstown] Maryland . . ." (Fletcher, 'Buffalo,' *Handbook of American Indians*, I, 169).

seen buffalo there in 1632,[139] and Ogilby in 1680.[140] I have been unable to discover anything whatever concerning disappearance. This may not unreasonably be placed at about the same period as in Virginia; perhaps, if anything, rather earlier, by reason of the nearness of the Atlantic littoral, with its likelier chances of landing parties from ships, and earlier colonization. Similarly, too, the geographical position of Maryland as a definitely unalterable limit of their range eastward, would prevent any 'reinforcement' of their numbers by migrating herds which could thus contribute to defer their extermination, since none could come from practically any direction save from the westward alone.

The 'buffalo boundary' in western Pennsylvania is thought to be indicated by a marsh which is called 'Buffalo Swamp' on Peter Kalm's map of 1771.[141] The boundary is said to be shown on this map (which I have not seen) as being situated between the Alleghany River and the west branch of the Susquehanna, near the heads of Licking Creek and Toby's Creek (apparently now Oil Creek and Clarion Creek respectively). In this locality we are told there were once 'buffaloes in thousands.'[142] Hornaday writes thus: "While there is not at hand any positive evidence that the buffalo ever inhabited the southeastern portion of Pennsylvania, its presence in the locality mentioned above, and in West Virginia generally, furnishes sufficient reason for extending the boundary so as to include the southwestern portion of the State, and connect with our starting-point, the District of Columbia. . . ."[143]

Whatever may be thought of this assumption, it seems to be clear that in northwestern Pennsylvania the buffalo were at one time to be found in fair numbers:

In the vicinity of the spot where the town of Clarion now stands, in northwestern Pennsylvania, Mr. Thomas Ashe relates that one of the first settlers built his log cabin near a salt spring which was visited by the buf-

---

[139]Allen, *American Bisons*, 78, 84. I have been unable to see Father White's *Relatio Itineris in Marylandiam* (Maryland Historical Society Fund Publication No. 7). I have read his topographical description from this, with no allusion to buffalo, in a later work to which I have lost the reference.

[140]Allen, *American Bisons*, 84. For Ogilby, *Handbook of American Indians*, II, 1208 (1671).

[141]Allen, *American Bisons*, 84.

[142]Hornaday, "Extermination of the American Bison," 386.

[143]*Ibid.* The reader's acceptance of this facile procedure must depend largely on his opinions regarding the District of Columbia itself (see above, chap. IX, note 45).

faloes in such numbers that he 'supposed there could not have been less than two thousand in the neighbourhood of the spring.' During the first years of his residence there, the buffaloes came in droves of about three hundred each. They sought for no manner of food, but only bathed and drank three or four times a day, and rolled in the earth, or reposed, with their flanks distended, in the adjacent shades;[144] and on the fifth and sixth days, separated into distinct droves, bathed, drank, and departed in single files, according to the exact order of their arrival. . . .

In the first and second years, this old man, with some companions, killed from 600 to 700 of these noble creatures, merely for the sake of their skins, which to them were worth only 2s. each; and after this 'work of death' they were obliged to leave the place till the following season, or till the wolves, bears, panthers, eagles, rooks, ravens, &c., had devoured the carcasses, and abandoned the place for other prey. In the two following years, the same persons killed great numbers out of the first droves that arrived, skinned them, and left their bodies exposed to the sun and air, but they soon had reason to repent of this, for the remaining droves, as they came up in succession, stopped, gazed on the mangled and putrid bodies, sorrowfully moaned or furiously lowed aloud, and returned instantly to the wilderness in an unusual run, without tasting their favourite spring, or licking the impregnated earth, which was also once their most agreeable occupation; nor did they, nor any of their race, ever revisit the neighbourhood. . . .[145]

Ashe's literary reputation—perhaps also his native capacity for sifting his informants' wheat from the chaff—being somewhat dubious,[146] the reader may take or leave the picturesque details about 'exact order,' etc. But since it is upon such recitals that the 'thousands' apparently depend, I believe a forensic cross-examiner would ask one or two questions. Who established the identity of those separate herds *at the time of their arrival,* and observed the unbroken continuity of each in the confusion of the slaughter of several hundreds, in preparation for an 'exact order' of departure which the old man and his friends—then strangers to buffalo habits—could not possibly have foreseen? And why did not the buffalo shun the spot after the first year's slaughter, which was essentially identical—being for hides only—with the third and fourth? Apart from these *cruces,* one would gladly have exchanged what Carlyle would have called the 'water' in Ashe's lucubrations for a hint of dates. We must suppose, however, that there were at least buffalo in the region, and possibly in some numbers. It would seem also that they were found even farther east than Hornaday sug-

[144]On buffalo seeking the shade, see below, Appendix K.
[145]Allen, *American Bisons,* 109-10. Hornaday, "Extermination of the American Bison," 387, 420, gives a part of this passage from Ashe. He states also that in the first and second years the buffalo rubbed the old man's cabin down in a few hours (p. 420).
[146]On Ashe, see above, chap. III, notes 25-6.

gests. Allen alludes to their presence (*circa* 1790-1800) near Lewis-burg,[147] not far from the main Susquehanna Valley; which might indicate that stream as the possible eastern boundary, broadly speaking, of their main habitat in this territory.

It seems to me doubtful whether the buffalo were ever really very numerous in Pennsylvania. Thompson Seton remarks:

It is hard to realize now that the woods of Pennsylvania contained thousands of buffalo as late as 1750. Their pathways through the woods were the most convenient ways for travel for mankind.

As late as 1773, when Philip Quigley settled on the West Branch [of the Susquehanna] Clinton County, Pa., the great Northern herd of Buffalo 'still numbered about 12,000 animals'. . . .[148]

I must frankly acknowledge that after a considerable study of comparative data on eastern buffalo history, I am deeply suspicious of these numbers at that era. I have also studied some of Shoemaker's researches at first-hand.[149] If anyone ever saw that (estimated) number at once, he would surely have mentioned it, and Seton would scarcely have failed to notice it. The 'two or three hundred' at once, and the prodigious maximum of 'not less than two thousand' of Ashe's informant, who dwelt in the same general region as Quigley and was broadly of the same generation historically (one of the first settlers), would have been utterly eclipsed. If Philip Quigley saw herds of two thousand, or droves of only two or three hundred each, what proof does this furnish that the Pennsylvania buffalo range contained six, or forty, such aggregations in 1773?

Another factor may be noted. While it has been convenient in the present historical survey to deal as nearly as is practicable with one state at once, the conception of the summer migration from Georgia or Tennessee to the Great Lakes and return[150] eliminates such artificial boundaries. So that the implied or specified scantiness recorded by Dr. Walker and Bonnecamp in 1750—before the huge masses had been cut in two by the westward march of settlement[151]—according to Shoe-

---

[147]Allen, *American Bisons*, 223. Lewisburg, Pennsylvania, lies approximately 41° 20′ N., practically on a line between Rochester, New York, and Baltimore, Maryland.

[148]Seton, *Game Animals*, III, 657. On Ashe's supposed 'buffalo highways' about Onondaga, compare above, chap. III, note 26.

[149]Shoemaker, *A Pennsylvania Bison Hunt; Extinct Pennsylvania Animals.* Compare also Rhoads, *Mammals of Pennsylvania and New Jersey*, and Seton, *Game Animals*, III, 646, 659, 703, 709.

[150]Shoemaker, *Pennsylvania Bison Hunt*, 22-38, etc.

[151]*Ibid.*, 10-22, 38, etc.

maker's own thesis must have affected Pennsylvania buffalo just as much (at some season or other) as if their journeyings had been in that state. Former students of our present subject, and others such as Justin Winsor's collaborators, and also Parkman, Roosevelt, Hulbert, and Thwaites, who ransacked the historical source-material of this region for their own particular needs, have presented no indications of such an abundance, which could hardly by any possibility have entirely escaped notice. Theodore Roosevelt, whose *Winning of the West* deals with the same age and region, and frequently with the same uncritical type of informant, warns his readers repeatedly against the danger of accepting the *details* of these recitals too readily, particularly in relation to numbers. I consider this account from Ashe to be a highly relevant illustration of this need for caution.

Then again, the numbers mentioned by Ashe's informant were at a favoured place of common resort, precisely as with the 'Blue Licks' of Kentucky. Licking Creek, mentioned above, and Ashe's 'salt spring' (if indeed they be not one and the same) are the only allusions to salt licks or creeks in Pennsylvania that I have been able to find. There are a number of other buffalo place-names, almost undoubtedly indicative of their former presence,[152] but not such as to justify any pronounced inferences concerning large numbers. The Moravians in 1753 record a Buffalo Creek (possibly named by themselves) somewhere near the Pennsylvania and West Virginia boundary.[153] Allen also mentions one in Pennsylvania—whether the same or another—the exact locality of which is not clear.[154] Allen and Shoemaker note a Buffalo Valley of the eighteenth century, in which was a place known as Buffalo Cross Roads.[155] This type of name has furnished the school of Hulbert with material for much disquisition on 'north and south buffalo highways, with here and there a great cross route. . . .'[156] But this very place derived its name from *one* buffalo![157]

Seton observes concerning the Pennsylvania buffalo: "This Buffalo appears to have been much like the Wood Buffalo, but larger, and darker—almost black. Although the first race seen by English-speaking

[152]See below, Appendix K, note 4.
[153]"Diary," in Mereness (ed.), *Colonial Travels*, 340, 342.
[154]Allen, *American Bisons*, 108, 110.
[155]*Ibid.*, 87; Shoemaker, in Seton, *Game Animals*, III, 657, 658.
[156]Hulbert, *Historic Highways*, I, 131, etc.
[157]Seton says (*Game Animals*, III, 658) the 'last buffalo in Pennsylvania' was killed at Buffalo Cross Roads *circa* 1800. But his authority, Shoemaker (*Pennsylvania Bison Hunt*, 40) says *it was afterward called so*, from this occurrence! So also Garretson, *American Bison*, 89 (giving the date, January 19, 1801).

folk, it was the last to be described. Col. Henry W. Shoemaker gave it the name *pennsylvanicus* in 1915. . . ."[158]

I am unaware whether or no this is the race referred to by Seton in his earlier work as the 'extinct Alleghanian buffalo.'[159] One or two considerations must be noticed, however. If this *B. pennsylvanicus* were really the first to be seen by English-speaking folk, it must certainly be identical with the species of Argall and others—if theirs were truly buffalo.[160] I have met with no indication of any character tending to suggest the presence of more than one *historic* species in the territory east of the Mississippi between the Great Lakes and the Gulf of Mexico. Now if *B. pennsylvanicus* were really larger than the Northern Wood buffalo (*B. bison athabascæ*, Rhoads), it must have been a truly gigantic brute.[161] It is extraordinary that among our earlier witnesses, such as Dr. Walker, Henderson, Boone, Kenton, Filson, etc., there seem to be no allusions to the vastly larger size of the Pennsylvania animal as compared with the buffalo elsewhere in the territory east of the Mississippi; or—if the herds in that region were all of this huge type—to the striking difference between those and the true Western or Plains buffalo of the Mississippi Valley and westward, which Boone, Kenton, and others lived to see. If they never saw the Pennsylvania buffalo themselves, surely among so many traditions relating to its numbers there should have been some concerning its enormous size. Neither of these men, nor our early Western travellers such as Legardeur de Saint-Pierre (who must have seen both kinds[162]), nor those in Thwaites's invaluable collection, nor the early settlers—many of them doubtless grandchildren of old Pennsylvanians[163]—offer the least hint that I have been able to discover. These questions await answers. One cannot wonder that such men as S. N. Rhoads, who was certainly no enemy to the theory of distinct varieties, apparently found the evidence unsatisfactory.[164] Concerning the extinction of the buffalo

[158]Seton, *Game Animals*, III, 657. On blackness, above, chap. III, notes 110-23.

[159]Seton, *Life-Histories of Northern Animals*, I, 250.

[160]Above, chap. IX, notes 45-52.

[161]See above, chap. III, "Variants of the Buffalo."

[162]This man, in 1751-52, travelled to 'within sight of the Rocky Mountains,' where he or his colleague, Niverville, founded the famous but elusive 'Fort La Jonquière.' He was later the 'one-eyed commander' at Fort Le Bœuf, with whom Washington treated in December, 1753 (Hulbert, *Historic Highways*, III, 104-17.)

[163]Cf. above on probably inherited knowledge, note 52.

[164]Shoemaker's own admission (*Pennsylvania Bison Hunt*, 8, 42). He offers the personal integrity of his informants as 'proof' of things their great-grandfathers possibly saw or did!

in Pennsylvania, the latest mention of a herd that I have seen is in the 'White Mountains of Union County,' 1799, where it was destroyed.[165] The 'last buffalo' was killed in various localities, 1801, 1808, 1810.[166]

With reference to the eastern territory abutting on the Great Lakes, the actual presence of the buffalo about the eastern end of Lake Erie, and its connection with the origin of the name of the great city so called, were apparently not considered certain by Allen: "The occurrence of a stream in Western New York, called Buffalo Creek, which empties into the eastern end of Lake Erie, is commonly viewed as traditional evidence of its [the buffalo's] presence at that point, but positive testimony to this fact has thus far escaped me. . . ."[167] In this connection, the following is of interest:

The oldest of the Seneca Indians residing on the Buffalo Creek reservation in 1820, near this city [? Buffalo, New York] stated positively to persons now living that when . . . [the Senecas] came here to reside (which was probably not until after Sullivan's expedition in 1799), the bones of the buffalo, with those of other animals, were found at the 'Salt Lick,' on the banks of the Buffalo Creek, within four miles of the City Hall. That it was a tradition among the Indians, of the truth of which they had no doubt, that the buffalo visited the Salt Lick in great numbers at no very distant period before that time. . . .[168]

It may be the same locality to which Charlevoix alludes: "He also speaks of their [? the buffaloes'] attempts to enter the mouth of the *Rivière aux Bœufs*, on Lake Ontario, a few leagues below the entrance to the River Niagara, in which they failed by reason of the shallowness of the water. . . ."[169]

The presence of the buffalo along Lake Ontario—perhaps farther east—has been noticed already.[170]

In his later work, Seton mentions the discovery of a buffalo skull beneath the streets of Syracuse, New York, in 1889. He does not specify whether it was of the historic (*B. americanus*) or of some fossil species, though his general tone tends to indicate the former.[171] Syracuse is situated just north of a tributary of the east branch of the Susquehanna. If the river valley at large could be ascertained as the general

[165]Seton, *Game Animals*, III, 658.
[166]*Ibid.*, 657-8.
[167]Allen, *American Bisons*, 107. This origin of Buffalo, New York, is considered as virtually conclusive by Hornaday, "Extermination of the American Bison," 385; Hulbert, *Historic Highways*, I, 103; and apparently by Seton, *Life-Histories of Northern Animals*, I, 258.
[168]*British-American Magazine*, I, 628-9 (1863).
[169]*Ibid.*, 628.
[170]See chap. IX, notes 67-76.
[171]Seton, *Game Animals*, III, 646.

buffalo boundary in that territory, there would be fair presumptive evidence that its two main sources constitute a possible route both to the district around Buffalo, New York, and along the east branch northeastward toward Lake Champlain.

Champlain himself gives a description of some region which, according to his latitudes, would certainly be in modern Canada, since he at the time was in Ontario, north of Lake Erie, and the country he describes was yet farther north: "To the north of this great river, extending some hundred leagues westward towards the Attigouatans [Hurons], there are very high mountains; the climate is more temperate than in any other of the said regions, being in latitude 41°. All these . . . regions abound in animals of the chase, such as stags, caribou, moose, does, buffalos [buffles], bears, wolves, beaver, foxes, weasels, martens, and several other species of animals. . . ."[172]

While *B. americanus* could no doubt be found about latitude 41°, that parallel runs through central Pennsylvania and northern Ohio; and where Champlain then was—not to mention farther north along the Laurentian range[173]—was about 44° N. So that Champlain's testimony is unavailing to prove any case for buffalo in Ontario, where the historic species has never been recorded.[174] Thompson Seton, discussing this, writes as follows: "We find that in the East the Buffalo followed the deciduous forests, and yet appeared to avoid the coniferous woods. A study of the conditions prepares me for a future find of Buffalo bones on the north side of Lake Erie. . . ."[175] Buffalo skulls of unidentified fossil species have been found near and within the city of Toronto (*ante* 1910, 1932);[176] hence Seton's forecast seems inherently not improbable of fulfilment.

There is no reason, however, to reject Champlain's account of the *Cheveux Relevés*, whom he met on the same journey in 1615, and who carried "a round buckler of tanned leather which comes from an animal like the buffalo. . . ."[177] These were the Ottawas, whose home

[172]*Champlain's Voyages* (Champlain Society ed.), III, 115-16; IV, 297.

[173]*I.e.* the 'very high mountains' mentioned (ed. note, *ibid.*, III, 116). The 'great river' is apparently the Ottawa.

[174]Charlevoix and Vaudreuil both mention 'vast herds,' or abundance, south of Lake Erie; the latter adds specifically, 'but not on the north' (*British-American Magazine*, I, 628). See Richardson, *Fauna Boreali-Americana*, I, 279; Allen, *American Bisons*, 73, 107; Hornaday, "Extermination of the American Bison," 385; Thwaites (ed. note), *Jesuit Relations*, IX, 310; Fletcher, "Buffalo," *Handbook of American Indians*, I, 169.

[175]Seton, *Life-Histories of Northern Animals*, I, 258; *Game Animals*, III, 650.

[176]See above on this, chap. II, notes 32 and 33.

[177]*Champlain's Voyages* (Champlain Society ed.), III, 105; IV, 287-8.

was "somewhere south or south-west of Georgian Bay"[178] (near where he met them), or in Bruce and Grey counties, Ontario,[179] which is much the same thing. The probability of these being truly buffalo-hide shields is much increased by the circumstance that the *Cheveux Relevés* obtained them by trade "from people in those northern parts," at a distance of some forty days' journey in either direction.[180] This region lay, in the opinion of Champlain's editors, past the Great Lakes, and probably on the buffalo plains of the upper Mississippi. That they did not procure the hides by a much shorter journey to the southern side of the Great Lakes might be explained either by the enmity of the Iroquois or by their economic necessity, if the latter needed the buffalo for themselves.[181] So long a trip to the westward at that relatively early date implies a shortage—for whatever reason—which seems to accord with our general conclusions. A scholarly critic rejects Champlain's account of the buffalo land of plenty, quoted above, on the ground that it was 'too far east' at this date, and considers that he was probably misled by seeing buffalo-skins obtained in trade.[182] This would, of course, be quite true in Canada, but if Morton's 'lake Erocoise' be actually Ontario and not Champlain in 1627, 'tenne yeares' before he wrote,[183] this puts the buffalo farther east only a dozen years later than when Champlain supposedly saw them. There seems therefore no valid reason for doubting that they penetrated as far east as Buffalo, New York, at the very least.[184] Concerning their final disappearance in the Great Lakes region, I have no positive information.[185]

[178]*Ibid.*, III, 43-5, 96; IV, 280.

[179]Parkman, *Pioneers of France*, 404, 405.

[180]*Champlain's Voyages* (Champlain Society ed.), III, 105; IV, 287.

[181]On buffalo-hunting among the Iroquoians, see Wissler, "Material Cultures of the North American Indian," *American Anthropologist*, XVI, 1914, 447-505.

[182]*Champlain's Voyages* (ed. Bourne, *American Explorers*, 1922), II, 66, 115.

[183]See above, chap. IX, notes 67-70.

[184]See Fletcher, "Buffalo," *Handbook of American Indians*, I, 169.

As an example of what has too often passed for evidence, cf. Taylor (*Names and Their Histories*, 77-8) on the origin of Buffalo, New York: ". . . founded in 1801, when the region was still frequented by the bison or North American buffalo. The city of Buffalo is at the eastern end of Lake Erie, where the vast herds of buffaloes would easily pass the chain of lakes in their annual migrations . . . ."

Taylor was no ignoramus nor shallow pretender, but a deeply learned scholar in his own province, and a man of wide historical and philological research, yet here the 'annual migration' answers for everything. Its own authenticity has yet to be established.

[185]Seton (*Game Animals*, III, 646) cites Miller (? Gerrit S. Miller, Jr.), *Mammals of New York*, which I have not seen; *post* 1801: so Taylor, in the preceding note.

In concluding our inquiry relative to the regions east of the Mississippi as a whole, one is compelled to say (what is not commonly the case) that in his observations on numbers Allen is much less scientific in tone than is his principal successor in this field. 'Immense herds' or synonymous phrases,[186] coming from one who had himself seen the Western myriads in the evening of their heyday,[187] would be interpreted, in the absence of specific qualification, as meaning what the same expression meant on the Great Plains. Hornaday's phraseology, "in some places it was so abundant as to cause remark,"[188] is much more cautious and likewise much more convincing, and one cannot but regret that so eminent a naturalist did not always adopt a similarly guarded attitude. He concludes that while the numbers of the buffalo seemed considerable to dwellers east of the Mississippi, they were 'mere stragglers from the innumerable mass' of the Plains areas.[189] The majority of generalizers on buffalo agree with him.[190]

[186]Allen, *American Bisons*, 72-3.

[187]Allen remarks that he himself had simply disbelieved the accounts of vast numbers, enormous hosts, etc., until he saw them on the plains in 1871 (*American Bisons*, 55). This acceptance scarcely justifies the automatic application of such terms to another region and era.

[188]Hornaday, "Extermination of the American Bison," 387.

[189]*Ibid.*, 388.

[190]Seton (*Life-Histories of Northern Animals*, I, 258): 'In all this wooded country, however, its numbers were small . . . ." So in 1910; in 1929 he evidently accepts the 'thousands' without hesitation (*Game Animals*, III, 657). I cannot follow him there. Stone and Cram, 1913, narrow his earlier estimate down even more: ". . . decidedly rare . . . everywhere east of the Appalachian Mountains . . ." (*American Animals*, 67). Wissler, 1922: "The bison of the prairies found its way as far east as the Alleghanies, but except in the open country was not an important item . . ." (*American Indian*, 14). From the foregoing, possibly the late Dr. Wissler did not concede its presence in the Atlantic states in any measure whatsoever. He never once mentions Hulbert. Webb, 1931: ". . . the important fact is that buffalo were rare in the Eastern woodland area, not numerous enough to exert any influence either on the native races or on the newcomers from Europe. It was not until the settlements approached the prairies, the tall grass lands, which stretched along the margin of the timber-line, that the buffalo appear in sufficiently large numbers to make an impression on human life . . . . It is not maintained that buffaloes were confined to the Plains, but it is essential to understand that their occupation of the forest and mountains was merely incidental, an overflow from their natural habitat. Hornaday's study seems to imply that the herds were invading the East when the white man came . . ." (*Great Plains*, 43-4). Garretson, 1938, is rather non-committal: "While the buffalo were found in considerable numbers east of the Alleghany Mountains as far as central Pennsylvania, the herds on the west side in Ohio, Kentucky, and the Illinois country were much larger; but the Great Plains country west of the Mississippi . . . was the center of vast herds of really countless numbers . . ." (*American Bison*, 58-9).

CHAPTER XI

THE BUFFALO HABITAT AND ITS HISTORICAL CHRO-NOLOGY: WEST OF THE ROCKY MOUNTAINS IN THE UNITED STATES

SINCE the title of the present chapter might conceivably give rise to misconceptions, it may be well to note at the outset that although it is quite common to speak of the 'Rockies' as if there were but one mountain chain to be crossed between the Plains and the Pacific coast, as a matter of fact there are in various areas two,[1] three,[2] or even four such chains.[3] The Rocky Mountains proper are only the first or easternmost of these. This loose phraseology is not, however, commonly used either by travellers, explorers, or scientists, nor even by those not ordinarily mindful of such distinctions, where they themselves happen to be present or former mountain dwellers. So that in this chapter, an allusion to the buffalo at some period 'west of the Rocky Mountains' should not necessarily be taken to signify 'along the Pacific Coast,' as might otherwise be assumed.

I have already noted Hornaday's forecast of the ultimate probability of the species journeying to the Pacific littoral, perhaps actually to tidewater, 'had they remained unmolested and uninfluenced by man.'[4] An eminent lady archaeologist, who wrote after Hornaday's monograph appeared, would almost convey the impression, in the absence of corrective data, that the buffalo did reach almost if not absolutely to Pacific tidewater, as long ago as Cabeza de Vaca's day, or shortly afterwards: "At that time [that is, *circa* 1530] the herds ranged from below the Rio Grande in Mexico, N.W. throughout what is now E. New Mexico, Utah, Oregon, Washington, and British Columbia. . . ."[5]

[1]The Grand Trunk Pacific (now Canadian National) route from Edmonton to Prince Rupert, B.C., through the Yellowhead Pass, crosses only two.
[2]Hornaday ("Extermination of the American Bison," 376-7) mentions three in the Southwestern U.S.: the Rockies, Sierra Nevada, and the Coast Range.
[3]The Canadian Pacific route crosses four: the Rockies, Selkirks, Cascades or Gold Range, and Coast Range.
[4]See above, chap. IX, note 5.
[5]Fletcher, *s.v.* Buffalo, *Handbook of American Indians*, I, 169.

I shall attempt in this chapter to set forth the actual evidence for the presence of the buffalo within the limits indicated by my title, taking as my datum the summit and western slope of the Rocky Mountain chain proper, although the reader must be warned that it may not always be possible to avoid slipping over to the eastern side at times, since it is frequently difficult to be quite sure of the actual location of some given episode. Many of the early travellers themselves were uncertain of their position, along or between rivers unmapped or unnamed, and sometimes wrongly identified by their own guides, and not infrequently their observations of latitude and longitude have been found to be inaccurate.[6]

R. B. Marcy, writing in 1852, is somewhat vague on the subject of the buffalo's westward range, particularly for a student with a considerable knowledge of some of the less familiar buffalo and travel literature. He considers it doubtful "whether the buffalo ever ranged beyond the Rocky Mountains, yet they have been found as far west as the western slope. . . ."[7] It seems improbable that a scientifically minded observer like Marcy, who had lived on the southwestern plains for many years, should be ignorant of the existence of two (or more) mountain ranges, or of the many published or common reports of the animal's presence in the western mountain territories. If we knew exactly what he intended by 'beyond,' or the 'western slope,' we might find that where he seems to contradict he really confirms these reports.

The available evidence indicates a westward extension of the buffalo habitat in a manner which resembles the animal's progress eastwards from the Mississippi toward the Atlantic. On this side, unfortunately, we have no record of any explorer either crossing the continent from the Pacific slope (at any point south of the forty-ninth parallel) or penetrating inland to any extent at a sufficiently early period to furnish adequate data concerning the numbers or local habitat of buffalo previous to the first decade of the nineteenth century. The only comparatively early Far Western explorers, such as La Vérendrye, *circa* 1738, penetrated no farther west than the central regions in the buffalo habitat; and La Vérendrye, the earliest northern plains visitor known to me, was two centuries later than Coronado or

[6]*In re* Long, 1819-20, see Thwaites, ed. note, *Early Western Travels*, XV, 250-1. Compare Champlain, 1615 (above, chap. X, note 172). Cases of Indian guides being lost are not infrequent in the literature, and too well authenticated for doubt. As pathfinders, they varied as we do, although, naturally, they were generally superior to white men.

[7]Marcy, *Exploration of the Red River*, 104.

De Soto.[8] Even before the advance of the white men into the Rocky Mountain territory, the westward advance of the buffalo must have been much impeded by the 'economic pressure' of the Indian tribes beyond the actual buffalo range. For many Indians journeyed through the passes to procure buffalo meat and hides, either by hostile forays or by trade. This is attested by the earliest observers and by many others, and was clearly a long-established practice.[9]

It was not very long after Lewis and Clark, that the furtrader made his appearance. Together with the earlier demands made upon them by Indian hunters for legitimate purposes of subsistence, the buffalo then became subject to an additional strain upon their numbers; and this was heightened by the constantly increasing use of the more deadly firearms of the whites. It is somewhat improbable, in my opinion, that at any time after the (buffalo) fur-trading era with the whites

[8]Bancroft mentions a tradition of Spaniards in Wyoming, *ante* 1650, which he thinks baseless, as then they had not, in his opinion, penetrated north of the Arkansas River (*History of Nevada*, 672). A broadly similar viewpoint in Webb, "The Spanish Approach to the Great Plains" (*Great Plains*, 83-139). There were Spaniards on the Platte, near the Forks, 1721; perhaps the same as those under Villazur, 1720 (see Burpee (ed.), *Journals of La Vérendrye*, 417; Wissler, *American Anthropologist*, XVI, 1914, 2).

[9]Flatheads, Salish, Sahaptin, Kootenais, Nez Percés, Snakes, Walla-Walla: see on this Gass, *Journal of the Lewis and Clark Expedition*, 1805, which says 'no buffalo in the Walla Walla country' (p. 150). *Lewis and Clark Journals*, III, 164. Thompson, *Narrative*, ed. Tyrrell, 417, 419, 424, 492, 529, 551. Coues (ed.), *Henry-Thompson Journals*, II, 707, 709-13, 819. Franchère, *Early Western Travels*, VI, 339, 341. Ross, *ibid.*, VII, 215. Townsend, *ibid.*, XXI, 232. Frémont (1843), *Narrative*, 140. Paul Kane (1847), *Wanderings of an Artist* (Radisson Society ed.), 199. Wissler thinks the 'Northern Shoshoneans' ('Snakes,' etc.) made more use of the buffalo than the Nez Percés (*American Anthropologist*, XVI, 1914, 447-505). Cf. below, note 98.

Clark's River, 1806, as *Cokalahiskit*—'river of the road to buffalo': so *Lewis and Clark Journals*, III, 164. This reversed by Patrick Gass: *Isquet-co-qual-la—* 'the road to the buffaloes'; Gass, *Journal of the Lewis and Clark Expedition*, 254. Bancroft mentions the 'southern Nez Percé trail to the buffalo grounds' along the north side of the south fork of the Clearwater. Also the 'Lolo trail' "to the buffalo country by the Lolo fork of the Clearwater" (in the Missoula-Lewiston region): *History of Washington, Idaho, and Montana*, 240, 506. For further details on dress, etc. (from buffalo), see also his *Native Races*, I, 258-67, 273, 461.

'Kootanie Plain,' Upper North Saskatchewan River, above Rocky Mountain House, as a trading-place: Thompson, *Narrative*, ed. Tyrrell, 431, 557. Coues (ed.), *Henry-Thompson Journals*, II, 707, 709-13, 819. *Palliser Journals*, 14-6, 112, 158, 159. Southesk, *Travels*, 255. Cf. McClintock, *Old North Trail*, 2, 9, 40, etc.

War-parties of Kootenais and Flatheads attacked Pigeon Lake and Edmonton as late as 1867 and 1868: McDougall, *Pathfinding*, 239, 261.

began, the number of hides available for market would be governed purely by the food requirements of the hunters, although Hornaday thinks otherwise in reference to this region: "The extirpation of the bison west of the Rocky Mountains was due to legitimate hunting for food and clothing rather than for marketable peltries. . . ."[10]

This would be to concede a capacity for moderation which Hornaday strenuously denies to Indians as a race. But perhaps the greater difficulties of transport and fewer numbers in the mountain territory might lessen the possibilities of exploitation.

The general evidence, considered as a whole, in my opinion leaves little room for doubt that owing to such causes as those indicated, the buffalo never advanced much farther westward after the coming of the white men, but remained where the invaders first found them; apart from trifling movements which will be noted in one or two localities. From the earliest days of what might be termed scientific inquiry concerning the species in this region, it appears to have been a very generally accepted belief that their appearance west of the Rockies was comparatively recent. Richardson says: "The bison are supposed to have found their way across the mountains only very recently, and they are still comparatively few in numbers, and confined to certain spots. . . ."[11] He says again:

Their migrations to the westward were formerly limited by the Rocky Mountain range, and they are still unknown in New Caledonia [that is, British Columbia] and on the shores of the Pacific to the north of Columbia River; but of late years they have found out a passage across the mountains near the source of the Saskatchewan, and their numbers to the westward are said to be annually increasing. In 1806, when Lewis and Clark crossed the mountains at the head of the Missouri, bison skins were an important article of traffic between the inhabitants on the east side and the natives to the westward.

Farther to the southward, in New Mexico and California,[12] the bison appears to be numerous on both sides of the Rocky Mountain chain. . . .[13]

It by no means follows, in speaking of an advance 'westward,' that the actual line of march was in all cases necessarily in that precise direction along some river valley or its dividing watershed. It may very easily have been a northerly movement (for example), which

[10]Hornaday, "Extermination of the American Bison," 486.

[11]Or, "in particular passes only" (Richardson, *Fauna Boreali-Americana*, introd., I, xxxi).

[12]On buffalo in California, see Note at the end of the present chapter.

[13]Richardson, *Fauna Boreali-Americana*, I, 280. Quoted also by Audubon and Bachman, *American Quadrupeds*, II, 54. For its misuse by Allen and Hornaday, see below, Appendix O.

brought them to some point west of where a previously recorded 'western limit' has been noted, and where possibly no direct communication (by buffalo) between the two localities has ever been observed. In fact, if Hulbert's emphatic insistence on 'north-and-south migration-routes' were to be accepted rigidly, we should be driven to adopt something like this as the only feasible explanation of movements in any direction except north and south. In such a rough and broken territory, it is quite conceivable—and indeed, actually happened—that travellers might record at some point that buffalo were no longer to be seen, or that vestiges of their former presence ceased to be noticeable, while at the same time they were found by others in considerable force in some adjacent valley, along which buffalo (or evidence of their recent occupation) could be traced for some distance beyond their supposed longitudinal limit in that region. For example, Lewis and Clark, in 1806, note (in northwestern Montana): ". . . signs and tracks of the buffalo; from which it seems that those animals do sometimes penetrate to a short distance within the mountains. . . ."[14]

It might very readily be supposed from their language that the explorers were endeavouring to correct an impression, prevalent *circa* 1805, that the buffalo were *not* to be found, say, west of the Plains area. They were travelling eastward on their return journey at this time (July, 1806), when the advent of the buffalo would—as it did—turn privation into plenty, and when these indications would be the *first* encountered. These factors make it fairly certain that they would not mistake the place at which they observed them, and that this was really (for them) the farthest westerly point.[15] Yet it seems to be unquestionable that shortly afterward—and probably at this very time—the animal had penetrated to points considerably westward of those specified by Lewis and Clark.[16] The eastward-bound Astorians, in October, 1812, note as follows, at a point south of the Lewis and Clark route, and apparently near the headwaters of the streams that rise near the South Pass, though still then on the westward side: "The riverbanks were deserted; a few old tracks showed where a herd of old

[14]*Journals*, III, 170; cf. Gass, *Journal of the Lewis and Clark Expedition*, 254-66.

[15]Lewis and Clark place the westward limit, 1805, not far from Great Falls, Montana (say about 112° W.): *Journals*, I, 374, 378, 397; II, 88, 108, 110, 116, 121, 132, 174; III, 164, 170, 224. Cf. Gass, *Journal of the Lewis and Clark Expedition*, 102-9. See Webb's comments on the vagueness of the Lewis and Clark data, *Great Plains*, 142-4.

[16]Bancroft has buffalo 'common in aboriginal times' in eastern Oregon and Boisé Valley (*History of Utah*, 15, 258). He cites no authority. 'Aboriginal times' in that region could mean down to 1805, or 1811.

bulls had some time before passed along; but not a horn nor hump was to be seen in this sterile landscape. . . ."[17]

Farther eastward, a few days later, in the same month of October, they noted again, 'No buffalo,' although large quantities of bones were scattered about at a deserted Indian camp, which was thought to have been abandoned about a month previously.[18] But on their journey westward in the year previous, they found the animals much farther west than this. On Spanish River, in September, 1811, they found herds, which were expected to be the last the Astorians would see; these were being hunted by the Snakes, who had come across the mountains to get winter meat.[19] Yet they found at 'Henry's Fort' on a tributary of the Columbia, that "tracks of buffalo were to be seen in all directions, but none of a fresh date . . ." (October, 1811).[20]

They noted farther on a tributary of the 'upper' (really central) Columbia, which is given as 'two hundred and eighty miles since leaving Fort Henry': "These prairies at certain seasons are ranged by migrating herds of the wide-wandering buffalo, the tracks of which, though not of recent date, were frequently to be seen . . ." (November, 1811).[21] Later in the same month, on the Snake River, they remarked that "there were signs of buffalo having been there, but a very long time before . . ." (November, 1811).[22]

Allen also observes concerning Lewis and Clark's 'western limit' of the buffalo, that there was "evidence of their former existence in immense herds on the Jefferson Fork . . ." (of the Missouri; one of its three main heads).[23] What this evidence was he does not specify, but taken together with the foregoing, the presence of the buffalo in the first decade of the nineteenth century at points much farther west than those of Lewis and Clark may be considered clearly established. After all, the latter could only follow a relatively narrow path across the region, and they had absolutely no comparative data by which to check their own observations.

[17]Irving, *Astoria*, 358. Few things are harder to identify than Irving's localities, but surely such broad statements must be true, though how they knew them to be 'tracks of old bulls' is incomprehensible.

[18]*Ibid.*, 360-1.

[19]*Ibid.*, 236-8.

[20]*Ibid.*, 247.

[21]*Ibid.*, 250; quoted (without comment) by Allen, *American Bisons*, 123. 'Henry's Fort' must refer to what was afterwards known as Andrew Henry's post, since it was not seemingly until 1817 that he came there. See Coues, ed. notes, *Henry-Thompson Journals*, II, 842, 882; also Long, *Early Western Travels*, XV, 245.

[22]Irving, *Astoria*, 262.

[23]Allen, *American Bisons*, 122-3.

In all probability, neither Stephen H. Long nor Edwin James, his secretary and historian, had much knowledge of the history of the Astorians—beyond possible hearsay—when Long's *Voyages and Travels* first appeared (1823). They write as follows (1820):

They [that is, buffalo] have not yet crossed the entire breadth of the mountains at the head of the Missouri, though they penetrate, in some parts, far within that range, to the most accessible fertile valleys, particularly the valley of Lewis's River. It was there that Mr. Henry and his party wintered, and subsisted chiefly upon the flesh of these animals, which they saw in considerable herds, but the Indians affirmed that it was unusual for the bisons to visit that neighbourhood. This would seem to fix the date of their arrival at the headwaters of the Columbia River between 1805, when Lewis and Clark visited them, and Mr. Henry's visit, about 1817. . . .[24]

Concerning their supposedly 'comparatively recent' arrival west of the Rockies, Frémont, writing a quarter of a century later, has this to say:

In travelling through the country west of the Rocky Mountains, observation readily led me to the impression that the buffalo had, for the first time, crossed that range to the waters of the Pacific[25] only a few years prior to the period we are now considering [that is, *circa* 1824], and in this opinion I am sustained by Mr. Fitzpatrick[26] and the older trappers in that country. In the region west of the Rocky Mountains, we never meet with any of the ancient vestiges which, throughout all the country lying upon their eastern waters, are found in the *great highways,* continuous for hundreds of miles, always several inches and sometimes several feet in depth, which the buffalo have made in crossing from one river to another, or in traversing the mountain ranges. . . .[27]

We have seen that this opinion was also that broadly held by Dr. Richardson.[28] It is furthermore that of H. H. Bancroft: ". . . indeed the buffalo once found its way westward as far as the plains of the upper Columbia, but its residence there was of short duration. . . ."[29] Frémont further observes: "In that region lying between the Green or

[24]Long (that is Edwin James), *Early Western Travels,* XV, 245.
[25]Meaning evidently 'those rivers draining into the Pacific,' which is the sense of Bancroft's title, *Native Races of the Pacific States.*
[26]Major Thomas Fitzpatrick, "the man who knew more about the mountains than any other man, except possibly Bridger . . ." (Hebard and Brininstool, *Bozeman Trail,* I, 38-9); cf. also Frémont himself, *Narrative,* 93, 110, 141; De Smet, *Early Western Travels,* XXVII, 248; Dale (ed.), *Ashley-Smith Explorations,* 89-93.
[27]Frémont, *Narrative,* 141.
[28]*Fauna Boreali-Americana,* I, xxxi, 280 (above, notes 11, 13).
[29]Bancroft, *Northwest Coast,* I, 411. Long, Irving, Allen and Bancroft, all speak of the 'upper Columbia,' or the 'headwaters of the Columbia' (which are south of Yellowhead Pass, about 53° N.) when they evidently mean its U.S. tributaries.

Colorado River and the headwaters of the Rio [Grande] del Norte, over the *Yampah, Kooyah, White,* and *Grand* rivers—all of which are the waters of the Colorado[30]—the buffalo never extended so far to the westward as they did on the waters of the Columbia; and only in one or two instances have they been known to descend as far west as the mouth of White River. . . ."[31]

This view is endorsed by Allen;[32] and it is perhaps not necessary to search for any recondite cause. Probably it may be explained by the contrast between the verdant valley-lands of the northerly regions and the sterile sandy wastes of the more southerly Rocky Mountains territory, in Utah, for example, concerning which Hornaday remarks: "There is no evidence that the bison ever inhabited the southwestern half of Utah; and considering the general sterility of the Territory as a whole prior to its development by irrigation, it is surprising that any buffalo in his senses should ever set foot on it at all. . . ."[33]

But, while the opinion is quite probably sound in itself, the reader should note one important distinction, which may easily be obscured. The Rocky Mountains lie, not north and south, but northwest and southeast. Edmonton, Alberta, for example, lies about 200 miles eastward from the entrance to the Rockies, yet it is some 430 miles farther west than Denver, Colorado, which is situated in the very heart of the mountains, and at a far higher altitude.[34]

Consequently 'farther west' and 'farther into the mountains' do not necessarily mean the same thing, and we may also recollect that many of these early explorers (including Frémont), ascertained their position by longitude, rather than by mileage from the Rocky Mountain summit, which would tend to increase the confusion. The place mentioned by Frémont as the western limit in the central territories, White River, at its confluence with Green (Colorado) River lies about 109° 30′ W. A line along this position in the latitude of Edmonton would be about 450 miles east of the Rocky Mountain summit. Continued south, it would enter the Pacific Ocean practically at the southernmost extremity of the Lower California peninsula. The mouth of White River itself is well to the west of the Rockies proper, and nearer to the Wahsatch Range. The ultimate source of most of the later

---

[30]The Yampah is 'Mary's' (or Bear) River. Dale (ed.), *Ashley-Smith Explorations*, 146.

[31]Frémont, *Narrative*, 141.

[32]Allen, *American Bisons*, 122.

[33]Hornaday, "Extermination of the American Bison," 383.

[34]Edmonton, 53° 36′ N., 113° 5′ W.; Denver, 39° 48′ N., 105° W. At 40° N., one degree of longitude = 53.6 miles.

generalizations on buffalo in the regions west of the Rockies seems to be the opinions of Frémont, writing in 1844, which I shall again quote:

. . . my information is derived principally from Mr. Fitzpatrick, supplemented by my own personal knowledge and acquaintance with the country. Our knowledge does not go farther back than the spring of 1824, at which time the buffalo were spread in immense numbers over the Green River and Bear River valleys, and through all the country lying between the Colorado, or Green River of the Gulf of California and Lewis's Fork of the Columbia, the meridian of Fort Hall[35] then forming the western limit of their range. The buffalo then remained for many years in that country, and frequently moved down the valley of the Columbia, on both sides of the river, as far as the *Fishing Falls*. Below this point they never descended in any number. About 1834 or 1835 they began to diminish very rapidly, and continued to decrease until about 1838 or 1840, when, with the country we have just described, they abandoned all the waters of the Pacific, north of Lewis's Fork of the Columbia. At that time the Flathead Indians were in the habit of finding their buffalo on the heads of Salmon River and other streams of the Columbia; but now they never meet with them farther west than the three forks of the Missouri or the plains of the Yellowstone River. . . .[36]

While any student of buffalo history must acknowledge an indebtedness to Frémont for even the attempt to furnish data concerning the appearance and disappearance of the species in a somewhat obscure portion of its habitat, we are still compelled to recognize that 1844 is much too early for any authoritative pronouncement on the subject, almost anywhere west of the Mississippi. Frémont's utterances belong really to the history of opinion. The travel-literature bearing upon buffalo, while fairly copious even then, had not undergone even a semblance of co-ordination. Allen's monograph of 1876, which in my opinion is still the best essay on their chronological history that I have seen, was also the first to attempt the study in anything like adequate detail. The Carsons, Fitzpatricks, Bridgers, *et al.*, master-plainsmen as they were, would for that very reason probably be the last men in the world to concede any necessity for checking *their* experience on what may be termed academic questions relating to buffalo chronology, with that of anyone else. It is much to be regretted that we have no continuous record of buffalo comings and goings in the Oregon

[35]Fort Hall, 43° 31′ N., 112° 29′ W. Given on Alexander Ross's map (*Fur Hunters*) as about 42° N., 113° W. Straight north of Great Salt Lake, 218 miles from Fort Bridger, at the junction of Lewis's River and Portneuf River, or a little north of that point, according to Bancroft, *Northwest Coast*, II, 585. According to Townsend, 1833, they were west of Fort Hall at that time. Below, notes 40, 64, 65.

[36]Frémont, *Narrative*, 140.

Territory.[37] As the case stands, reappearances, which have been noted at various periods considerably later than 1840 or 1844, may belong to either class of phenomena already mentioned:[38] to an actual re-appearance after an absence of some duration, or to that erratic wandering propensity which often made buffalo very difficult for experienced hunters to find in a district from which they were never at that particular time really absent. Furthermore, there are numerous references in the travel-literature which, without careful co-ordination with other historical evidence, could easily result in grave misconceptions. If the following, for example, were uniformly the case, it might serve to explain 'disappearances' from other localities ('Bayou Salade,' headwaters of South Platte River): "The buffalo have for ages resorted here about the last days of July, from the arid plains of the Arkansas and the Platte; and thither the Eutaws and Cheyennes from the mountains around Santa Fé, and the Shoshonies or Snakes and Arrapahoes from the west, and the Blackfeet, Crows, and Sioux from the north, have for ages met and hunted and fought. . . ."[39]

J. K. Townsend (1833) mentions 'the Buffalo Plains,' northwest from Fort Hall, 'where the Blackfeet hunt.'[40] Father De Smet, however, writing about 1846, gives the name of 'the Blackfeet Plains' to the region more usually associated with the Blackfoot, "from the Sascatshawin to the Yellowstone."[41] A traveller, meeting the Blackfoot in either of the two former localities in the thirties, or a modern critic after reading Townsend or Farnham, might very naturally suppose the 'Blackfeet Plains' of De Smet to have been entirely abandoned by the herds *circa* 1833-39, and the tribe forced to seek subsistence elsewhere.

Here, too, as I have previously remarked concerning the territory east of the Mississippi, it will be wise to regard references to numbers in the light of relative rather than absolute terms. At the same time it may be noted that the *actual* number of an 'immense herd' is probably much greater than the same phrase would connote in the eastern territory;[42] the occasional estimates of herds encountered tend to prove

[37]Lieutenant Wilkes's Report to the Secretary of the Navy (1842) defines 'Oregon' as extending west from the Rockies to the Pacific Ocean (*Early Western Travels*, XXIX, 94).

[38]See above, chap. IX, note 91; also below, chap. XIV, note 13.

[39]Farnham (1839), *Early Western Travels*, XXVIII, 209, 266.

[40]Townsend, *ibid.*, XXI, 232-6.

[41]De Smet, *ibid.*, XXIX, 365.

[42]Bancroft (writing *circa* 1875): "Buffalo are now never found west of the Rocky Mountains, and there are but few localities where game has ever been

that, in my opinion. This of course is entirely what might be expected, since they were much nearer to the main 'source of supply' east of the Rockies, with numerous fairly convenient lines of communication in the river valleys whose headwaters met along the Atlantic-Pacific watershed. And such allusions here are from men who, with few exceptions, had already seen the true Plains hosts.

I give below, in chronological order, such references to buffalo in the 'Oregon Territory' as I have been able to collect. For the reasons I have mentioned in connection with the Blackfoot, our very earliest instance emphasizes the danger of using historical notices too dogmatically. Alexander Henry the younger, mentions in his *Journal* on several occasions that the Flatheads and the Kootenays had 'gone to the south-east to hunt buffalo' (*circa* 1811).[43] We have no means of knowing whether this really indicates that there were none in their own country, or whether such excursions were in the nature of reprisals on the Blackfoot or other tribes for hunting in the Flathead Country.[44]

Alexander Ross (Salmon River, western Idaho, May to June, 1824) remarks as follows: "Buffalo were abundant, immense herds of these animals being seen in every direction in one of the valleys through which we passed, there could not have been less than ten thousand in one herd, out of which our hunters killed sixty. . . ."[45]

In the same season, Ross records buffalo also in 'Day's Valley,' Goddin River, in June;[46] and at the head of Salmon River, in October, 1824.[47] Frémont, as we have seen, makes 1824 the commencement of an era marked by a profusion of buffalo[48] from central Green River northward to the lower central Columbia. So far as Green River is concerned, along its lower stretches in northern Utah, or in its upper portions in Wyoming, there is nothing really noteworthy about recording buffalo. It was in the latter state that the very last wild herd known to be in existence in the United States was ranging in 1889.[49] Ashley and Smith's party along Mary's River (the Yampah or Bear River), a

abundant, at least since the country became known to white men . . . . Buffalo never pass to west of the Rocky Mountains . . ." (citing various authorities; surely meaning 'since some particular era'?): *Native Races*, I, 263, 264.

[43]Coues (ed.), *Henry-Thompson Journals*, II, 707, 710, 712-13, 819.

[44]On wars and treatment of Blackfoot prisoners by Flatheads, see Cox, *Columbia River*, I, 232-45; II, 160; Bancroft, *Native Races*, I, 268.

[45]Ross, *Fur Hunters*, II, 60.

[46]*Ibid.*, 69.

[47]*Ibid.*, 138.

[48]Frémont, *Narrative*, 140. We may remember that when he speaks of 'immense numbers,' he had seen the Plains hosts, and knew what numbers meant!

[49]Hornaday, "Extermination of the American Bison," 522.

tributary of the Green River in eastern Utah, noted "a number of buffaloe" on May 8, 1825;[50] and not long afterwards they found the mountainous country farther north "well supplied with buffaloes, elk, bear, antelope, and mountain sheep."[51] Along Green River again, in southern Wyoming, they noted on April 25, 1825: "Game continues abundant, particularly buffaloes. There is no appearance of these animals wintering on this river; but they are at this time travelling *from the West* in great numbers. . . ."[52]

In southwestern Wyoming also, in mountainous country, in the following June (1825) Smith noted "no scarcity of buffalo . . ."; "very plenty," as far as he penetrated, almost anywhere.[53] It is as a mountain animal, west of the Rockies, that the foregoing instances are of present interest to us. On the Bitter Root River (a tributary of Clark's Fork of the Columbia), there were 'a few buffaloes' in October, 1831;[54] and in December, 1831, they were 'scarce' on Salmon River,[55] where Ross had noted 'immense herds' in 1824.

Irving remarks that Captain Bonneville, in 1833 ". . . had confidently expected to find buffalo in abundance on the headwaters of the Portneuf; but on reaching that region not a track was to be seen. . . . At length, one of the scouts, who had made a wide sweep away to the headwaters of the Blackfoot River, discovered great herds quietly grazing in the adjacent meadows. . . ."[56]

J. K. Townsend on his journey westward in 1833, noted that buffalo were 'rarely seen' on Sandy River, a tributary of the Green (or Colorado) River, in June;[57] but on the Green River itself, in the same month, he found them 'abundant.'[58] On Bear River, in July, they were 'very scarce: one or two seen';[59] and a small herd was observed near Fort Hall, also in July.[60] They discovered 'immense numbers,' however, along Snake River and Ross Creek, one of its tributaries, about three days (some 60 or 70 miles) back from Fort Hall on their incom-

[50]Dale (ed.), *Ashley-Smith Explorations*, 146.
[51]*Ibid.*, 155.
[52]*Ibid.*, 141 (italics mine). See above, on 'north and south' travelling, note 13.
[53]*Ibid.*, 158.
[54]Bancroft, *Northwest Coast*, II, 517.
[55]*Ibid.*, II, 518.
[56]Irving, *Captain Bonneville*, 311. Irving says 'near Fort Hall,' but that post was at (or near) the mouth of the Portneuf, as we have seen (above, note 35).
[57]Townsend, *Early Western Travels*, XXI, 187.
[58]*Ibid.*, 194.
[59]*Ibid.*, 200, 201.
[60]*Ibid.*, 210, 213.

ing route[61]—a similar experience to that of Bonneville's scouts, cited above; which illustrates what I have emphasized as the need for critical caution before too readily accepting accounts of extermination or disappearance in reference to specified localities at improbably early dates. On the aforesaid 'Buffalo Plains . . . where the Blackfeet hunt,' Townsend's party were 'much disappointed' at seeing no buffalo save a solitary straggling bull, August, 1833.[62] It may have been here also where Bonneville's confident expectations went unrealized. In November, 1833, either on the headwaters of the Portneuf, or near Fort Hall— it is not clear which, as Irving makes these two distinct localities into one—buffalo were found in 'immense numbers.'[63] Hornaday states that in 1834 ". . . the presence of herds near the Mallade and Boisé and Salmon Rivers, ten days' journey—200 miles—west of Fort Hall, is recorded in J. K. Townsend's *Narrative of a Journey across the Rocky Mountains. . . .*"[64]

While this is not literally correct, since Townsend mentions only 'ones' and 'twos,' and says nothing of 'herds,'[65] yet it is of interest to note that according to Frémont (writing twenty years after the date he specifies), Fort Hall was their westward limit in 1824.[66] Yet Ross recorded 'immense herds' on Salmon River at that very season—May and June, 1824![67] Also in November, 1833, Bonneville (or Irving) says: "The people upon Snake River having chased off the buffalo before the snow had become deep, immense herds now came trooping over the mountains. . . ."[68] In 1835, Rev. Samuel Parker, the missionary, observed 'great herds' on the east fork of Salmon River;[69] and conversely westbound travellers in 1836 recorded that the buffalo failed after Bear River was passed.[70]

We have now reached the period, 'about 1838 or 1840,' when (according to Frémont) they 'entirely abandoned all the waters of the Pacific.'[71] Farnham, on his journey westward in 1839, found 'buffalo in plenty' in North Park (the source of the North Platte; and known as the 'Bull Pen,' presumably because the animals were common

[61]*Ibid.,* 212-19.
[62]*Ibid.,* 232-6.
[63]Irving, *Captain Bonneville,* 332.
[64]Hornaday, "Extermination of the American Bison," 383.
[65]Townsend, *Early Western Travels,* XXI, 230-74.
[66]Frémont, *Narrative,* 140 (above, notes 35, 36).
[67]Above, note 45.
[68]Irving, *Captain Bonneville,* 333.
[69]Allen, *American Bisons,* 124.
[70]Coman, *Economic Beginnings of the Far West,* II, 143.
[71]Above, note 36.

there), July 31, 1839.[72] 'Plenty of buffalo' were also recorded at Fort Hall, in August, 1839.[73] Father De Smet observed 'immense herds' in the Mussel-Shell Mountains, in western Montana, September 12, 1839;[74] and noted also that they were 'abundant' in the Bitter Root Mountains, in October and November, 1841.[75] From December 23, 1841, until February, 1842, 'none were to be seen along the Bitter Root River; then, over a mountain ridge, herds of them were found, and 155 killed in one day' (February 6, 1842).[76]

In Lieutenant Wilkes's Report to the Secretary of the Navy (1842) concerning the features and potentialities of Oregon—which then denoted the entire territory west of the Rockies to the Pacific Coast— he states that "in the eastern section, buffalo abound. . . ."[77] Frémont in 1843 noted that, after leaving the Sweetwater (which rises in or very near the South Pass), the buffalo 'entirely disappeared.'[78] Travellers in the previous year (1842) had also observed them on the Sweetwater.[79] But on his return journey eastward by another route in the early summer of 1844, Frémont first encountered them on St. Vrain's Fork of the Green River,[80] a locality which, if not exactly 'west' of South Pass,[81] is well over the summit on the western slopes, and consequently farther into the mountains.

Hancock's party in 1845 saw no buffalo after leaving the neighbourhood of Fort Laramie.[82] Joel Palmer, who either closely preceded or closely followed Hancock in the same summer,[83] remarks as follows (west of South Pass, July, 1845; 320 miles west of Fort Laramie[84]): "We are now out of the range of the buffalo. . . . There have been so many companies of emigrants in advance of us that they have frightened the buffalo from the road. . . ."[85] Travelling eastbound in the

[72]Farnham, *Early Western Travels*, XXVIII, 209, 266; apparently the 'Buffalo Bull Pen' of Bancroft, *Native Races*, I, 460.
[73]Farnham, *Early Western Travels*, XXVIII, 258, 303, 308.
[74]De Smet, *ibid.*, XXIX, 349.
[75]*Ibid.*, XXVII, 334.
[76]*Ibid.*, 348, 349.
[77]Wilkes, *ibid.*, XXIX, 94.
[78]Frémont, *Narrative*, 70, 80.
[79]Bancroft, *History of Oregon*, I, 260.
[80]Frémont, *Narrative*, 308, 309; Allen, *American Bisons*, 120-1.
[81]See remarks above, note 34.
[82]Hancock, *Narrative*, 22.
[83]*Ibid.*, introd., viii. Palmer was a Canadian, born 1810, 'near the foot of Lake Ontario,' who afterwards became a prominent public character in Oregon. See Bancroft, *History of Oregon*, I, 522, etc.; Thwaites, (ed.), introd., *Early Western Travels*, XXX.
[84]Hancock, *Narrative*, editorial "Itinerary," xiv-xv.
[85]Palmer, *Early Western Travels*, XXX, 72.

following year, Palmer found 'a few' at the South Pass, May 26, 1846,[86] and he observes: "The buffalo seldom range beyond the South Pass, and never west of Green River. . . ."[87]

Palmer's language implies quite clearly—either that buffalo *were* encountered (though he does not mention any such occurrence) or that in common opinion they *might be* met with in 1846 up to Green River. Buffalo having been 'frightened from the road' seems to have been the stock explanation if the emigrants failed to encounter them;[88] an explanation designed, perhaps, to cover up the falsified predictions of enthusiastic 'boosters' and propagandists. Yet they were encountered later than 1845 or 1846, at least up to the South Pass, in apparently large quantities.[89]

Bonneville marked the Cœur d'Alene country as being in 1833 "the extreme western limit of the buffalo range."[90] In practically the same longitude (approximately 117° W.) and not very far north, in the Pend d'Oreille region, Father De Smet remarked in 1845: "Buffalo and beaver *are becoming* every year more scarce. . . ."[91] In mountain country in western Montana or Idaho (seemingly in the Bitter Root Mountains vicinity) in 1846, the same careful observer records a valley 'clouded with buffalo.'[92]

Paul Kane, the artist, observed in 1847 (obviously citing an opinion of the time, since he had no previous personal experience of the coun-

[86]*Ibid.*, 247.

[87]*Ibid.*, 260.

[88]Cf. 1843, on the Oregon Trail: "Toward the last of June the buffalo country was reached, where it was expected to obtain abundance of game; but a hunting expedition from New Orleans having preceded them, the buffaloes were driven from the line of travel . . ." (Bancroft, *History of Oregon*, I, 396); see also *ibid.*, 128.

Those buffalo, which 'nothing could turn aside from their path!'

Cf. 1844: "When they reached the buffalo grounds, Captain Cornelius Gilliam (the leader) used to dash off after the game, to the disappointment of those left in charge of the train . . ." (Bancroft, *History of Oregon*, I, 450).

[89]According to the Mormon reports, in 1847 (practically up to the South Pass) ". . . there roamed such vast herds of buffaloes that it was often necessary to send parties in advance and clear the road before the teams could pass . . ." (Bancroft, *History of Utah*, 253, 254, 260).

[90]Irving, *Captain Bonneville*, 86.

[91]*Life of De Smet*, III, 995 (italics mine). So also, Captain Blakiston, told by the Stoneys, Southern Alberta, 1858: 'The animals are getting every year more scarce . . .' ("Report on the Exploration of the Kootanie and Boundary Passes of the Rocky Mountains in 1858," in *Occasional Papers of the Royal Artillery Institution*, 1860, 118-20, 237-54, 240). I am indebted for a knowledge of this almost unknown document to my friend the late D. E. Cameron, then Librarian of Alberta University.

[92]*Life of De Smet*, I, 362.

try): "Several years back . . . the Walla-Wallas[93] used to go in annual buffalo hunts, and herds of these immense animals frequented the west side of the mountains, though now rarely seen. . . ."[94]

Here again, 'rarely seen' scarcely implies a total and final disappearance, although I have found no record of them in this region at any subsequent date. At the time of the troubles arising from the Whitman massacre by the Cayuse Indians in 1847, we read that Ellis, a noted Cayuse chief, was 'absent in the buffalo country' in March, 1848;[95] but how far distant that was, I cannot say. The latest definite notices of the buffalo that I have found are in December, 1853, from Dr. Suckley and Lieutenant Mullan. Suckley writes: "For a number of years none had been seen west of the mountains; but, singular to relate, a buffalo bull was killed at the mouth of the Pend d'Oreille River, on the day I passed it. The Indians were in great joy at this, supposing that the buffalo were coming back to them. . . ."[96]

Mullan writes: "Just east of the mountains separating the sources of the Jefferson [Fork, that is, of the Missouri] and Salmon Rivers, buffalo 'in immense numbers . . .'; 'hundreds of thousands' slain by the Nez Percés 'and all Indians' east and west of the mountains; and small game innumerable. . . ."[97]

Bancroft speaks of the Mormons in Idaho 'among the buffalo-hunting Nez Percés,' in 1854,[98] but he also says in relation to the very same time (circa 1854): "The buffalo which once grazed on the Snake River plains had long been driven east of the Rocky Mountains. . . ."[99]

Allen (writing before the publication of the histories of Bancroft) cites and seemingly endorses an opinion that by 1855 the buffalo 'were not then beyond the Rocky Mountains.'[100] The only item of evidence known to me which might seem to contradict this is that in a treaty made at Fort Hall in 1868 it was specified that the Bannock Indians at Fort Hall reservation "were to be permitted to go to the buffalo grounds. . . ."[101] This would seem to indicate some customary huntingground; but since we are ignorant of its location, the circumstance

    [93]If Walla Walla (Washington) indicates the centre of their former domain, it is in 46° 8' N., 118° 50' W. For their tribal limits, see Bancroft, Native Races, I, 292-321; ('Columbians').
    [94]Wanderings of an Artist (Radisson Society ed.), 199.
    [95]Bancroft, History of Oregon, I, 719.
    [96]Allen, American Bisons, 124.
    [97]Ibid., 124-5.
    [98]Bancroft, History of Washington, Idaho, and Montana, 402, above, note 9.
    [99]Ibid., 400.
    [100]Allen, American Bisons, 125 (citing Dr. Newberry). Hornaday's map ("Extermination of the American Bison," 548) gives 1838-40.
    [101]Bancroft, History of Washington, Idaho, and Montana, 515.

proves nothing; and the general conclusion of Allen, who utilized every opportunity of consulting an immense mass of living tradition and experience, such as is not now available, and in addition made a wide study of the documentary evidence, may be accepted as being substantially accurate. Perhaps the very farthest known point westward was thought to have been attained by the solitary buffalo whose bones were discovered in 1873 by Professor O. C. Marsh, on Willow Creek, Malheur County, eastern Oregon, in the eastern foothills of the Blue Mountains. These range approximately north and south, from about 43° 30′ N. and from 118° W. to 120° W. The bones were found about 44° N., so the finder informed Professor Allen, and apparently (from the designation 'Malheur Cave') on the upper waters of the North Fork or Middle Fork of Malheur River.[102] Ernest Thompson Seton, however, writes as follows in 1929:

"In 1826, according to Vernon Bailey (in *Journal of Mammalogy*, November, 1923, 254), Peter Skene Ogden, in charge of a party of trappers, discovered Harney Lake, which he graphically describes in his journal entry of November 1st, and he says 'Buffalo have been here, and heads are to be seen.' This carries them fifty miles farther west than the Malheur Cave, and I believe gives the westernmost record for Buffalo in the United States. . . ."[103]

There is a reference in Bancroft's *History of Oregon*, which may possibly mean that such vestiges were found at a point farther west still, unless a much later place-name has been antedated in the account of certain of the Indian wars, which hardly appears to be the case. Bancroft's map shows a 'Cow Creek,' a tributary of one of the forks of the Umpqua River, rising about 42° 40′ N., 123° 15′ W.;[104] and also a 'Cowhead Lake' in southern Oregon.[105] If the latter, as seems probable, was named from the finding of a cow skull, a sufficiently early date might indicate buffalo remains. The analogous history of such names renders these conclusions at least possible; and I note a place-name, Skullspring, in Malheur County, in southeastern Oregon, near the southern flank of the Cedar Mountains, about 117° 45′ W., 43° 30′ N.[106] This does not affect the uniqueness of the Harney Lake remains,

[102]Allen, *American Bisons*, 119, 121; Hornaday, "Extermination of the American Bison," 384; Hulbert, *Historic Highways*, I, 103 (who says '1875').

[103]Seton, *Game Animals*, III, 646. Harney Lake, about 43° 15′ N., 119° 10′ W. See further on this discovery, Skinner and Kaisen, *Fossil Bison of Alaska*, 166, 168.

[104]Map, *History of Oregon*, II, 380.

[105]*Ibid.*, 504. I find a Cow Creek Lake, about 43° N., 117° 20′ W.

[106]According to the laws of nomenclature, if it be suggested that this was a later name, dating from the era of domestic cattle, what becomes of the

being about fifty miles eastward; but it perhaps tends to suggest that there may be such vestiges farther westward still, and in some material quantity.

It will not have escaped the reader's notice that even such fragmentary evidence as I have been able to collect is quite irreconcilable with the generalizations of Frémont and of Bancroft respectively; the one concerning the chronological history of the local range of the buffalo and their disappearance therefrom; and the other respecting their numbers in the territory west of the Rocky Mountains. Frémont, as I have pointed out, wrote too soon even to attempt the task successfully. Bancroft, however, was indefatigable in collecting information from every available source. His inaccuracy in this particular was caused in my opinion by the inherent impossibility of formulating any general truth concerning buffalo which should be uniformly applicable over a wide range of territory, or during an extended period of years. This will be demonstrated beyond reasonable doubt before the present essay is concluded.

I have hitherto dealt principally with the northern portion of the transmontane area. The recorded buffalo history of the southern section is unfortunately slight. The history of the buffalo in New Mexico can scarcely be said to belong to the territory 'west of the Rocky Mountains,' in the sense in which we commonly use that phrase. Antonio de Espejo encountered buffalo in that state in 1583,[107] as also did Vargas.[108] Even these were not the first after Coronado's party; for Martin Lopez de Ibarra records seeing buffalo in 1564-65,[109] and Barrundo and Escalanté[110] (or Escalona[111]) in 1581. Later explorers include Vicenté de Zaldívar in 1598,[112] Juan de Oñate in 1604,[113]

---

earlier one; given—as such names are—for purposes of identification by the first comers (*i.e.* first using that particular language, whatever it may be)? Moreover, the 'Cow Creeks,' like the Red Rivers, Clearwaters, Beaver Creeks, etc., are of the precise type of toponymous (that is, self-explanatory) *first* names, to eliminate the endless confusion of which Post Offices and railways bestow later ones.

[107]Espejo ". . . returned in July, 1583, by another way, downe a River, called De la Vaccas, or Kine [considered to be the Pecos River], an hundred and twenty leagues, still meeting with store of those cattell . . ." (*Purchas his Pilgrimes*, XVIII, 65-7); cf. also Bancroft, *History of Arizona*, 80-91, and *North Mexican States and Texas*, I, 127; Thomas, *History of North America*, II, 44-6. For doubts about this, see Hallenbeck, *Journey of Cabeza de Vaca*, 142.

[108]Bancroft, *History of Arizona*, 72.

[109]Bancroft, *North Mexican States and Texas*, I, 109.

[110]Bancroft, *History of Arizona*, 75, 77, 89.

[111]*Ibid.*, bibliography, xxix.

[112]*Ibid.*, 138.

[113]*Ibid.*, 346-8.

and Diego de Vargas in 1694.[114] Like New Mexico, old Mexico is not usually considered to be 'west of the Rockies'; however, it may be worth noting that Pike included buffalo among the animals of Coahuila or the northern Mexican States in 1807.[115]

While there appear to have been no inherent reasons for not extending the buffalo range from a generally similar and adjacent region into Arizona, the evidence for this having actually occurred is very frail and unsatisfactory. Allen remarks concerning this: ". . . notwithstanding the location of the famed kingdom of Cibola by the early explorers, there do not seem to be any well-authenticated accounts of the existence of these animals west of the Rio Grande. . . . Dr. Elliott Coues stated [1868]: '. . . there is abundant evidence that the buffalo (*Bos americanus*) formerly ranged over Arizona, though none exist there now'; but in correspondence (1875) could not undertake to substantiate the statement. . . ."[116]

Bancroft states that Vildosola's expedition in 1758 found the Apaches in Arizona obtaining buffalo skins from a people (supposed to be Moqui) seven days northward from the Gila River, 'where there were many cattle and cultivated lands.' The present Hopi-Moqui Reserve (1924) is situated some 180 miles north of the upper Gila River. In this precise territory, on the boundary between the Moqui and Navajo reservations, and on a line directly north from Winslow, Arizona, there is *Mesa la Vaca,* that is 'Cow Plain(s).' Reasoning *a priori,* it seems unlikely that the Spaniards would apply such a name from domestic cattle which they themselves had taken with them to such a locality. It seems equally improbable also that early parties— the more likely to bestow the name—would convey cattle with them. It may further be noted that the *vaca* place-names as a class are identified with the buffalo by practically all Southwestern scholars. *Circa* 1758, buffalo were perfectly familiar to the Spaniards. This circumstance appears to render confusion with cowhides impossible; and we have no historical evidence of which I am aware, to indicate that 'seven days northward from the Gila River' there were any domestic cattle in 1758, even if Vildosola's more southerly informants possessed

---

[114]*Ibid.,* 210.

[115]Coues, (ed.), *Expeditions of Pike,* II, 738, 777.

[116]Allen, *American Bisons,* 125-8. 'Cibola' is generally accepted as Zuni, New Mexico (35° N., 109° W.). On Zuni as 'the buffalo province,' at the time of Philip II of Spain, see Bancroft, *History of Arizona,* 42, 44, 85, 195, 229; *History of Utah,* 1-5; *Native Races,* IV, 673. It is so accepted by later scholars: Coues (ed.) *Expeditions of Pike,* II, 630; Hodge, *s.v.* Zuni, *Handbook of American Indians,* II, 1015-20; Webb, *Great Plains,* 102.

any at that date. The foregoing particulars may therefore possibly be considered to establish the historical presence of buffalo in Arizona.[117]

R. B. Marcy writes concerning the Comanches (*circa* 1850): "The knowledge they possess of their early history is very vague and limited, and does not extend farther back than a few generations. They say that their forefathers lived precisely as they do and followed the buffalo: that they came from a country toward the setting sun, where they expect to return after death. . . ."[118]

It must be left to anthropological scholars, more competent than myself, to pronounce whether such traditions would justify any extension of the buffalo habitat beyond their authenticated range. I should hesitate to venture upon the hazardous task of vindicating Indian traditions at large concerning buffalo, although I shall notice a number of them later on.[119] Some Indian traditions appear to have been established by scientific investigation,[120] while, in other cases, tradition has

[117]Bancroft, *North Mexican States and Texas*, I, 558. For *vaca*, etc., see Appendix I, "Buffalo Place-Names." There were fossil species in Arizona. On *B. arizonica*, see Skinner and Kaisen, *Fossil Bison of Alaska*, 150, 204, 207, 210.

[118]Marcy, *Exploration of the Red River*, 107; also Bancroft, *Native Races*, III, 528.

[119]See below, chap. XXI, "Influence of the Buffalo Environment." On Mandan and Sioux traditions and buffalo legends in which the buffalo were on the earth before the first man see Maximilian, *Early Western Travels*, XXIII, 252-395; Catlin, *Letters on the North American Indians*, I, 178-81; II, 168. Both tribes are Siouan, whose ancestral home is in the Carolinas (*Handbook of American Indians*, II, 577), where buffalo hardly penetrated at all until a very late day and in small numbers. Blackfoot traditions are considered unsatisfactory, often contradictory; so Kidd, "Blackfoot Ethnography," 10. On Indian oral tradition at large, see Swanton and Dixon, *American Anthropologist*, XVI, 1914, 376-412.

[120]See Fiske's remarks on the tradition of the negro Estévanico, the 'Black Mexican,' preserved after 350 years (since Coronado) in the Southwest: Fiske, *Discovery of America*, II, 507; also Bishop, *Odyssey of Cabeza de Vaca*, 161.

There seems also to be topographical tradition preserved in the name of the Blackfoot (Siksika), 'perhaps from moccasins blackened by the ashes of prairie fires'; so Mooney, *s.v.* Siksika, *Handbook of American Indians*, II, 568. I am surprised that Dr. Mooney did not perceive that this would be about the last reason for bestowing a *distinctive* appellation (which is the basis of all nomenclature) upon any one tribe of Indians, since prairie fires have been general from unknown times. According to McClintock, an adopted son of the tribe, their own tradition is "that ages ago their people lived far to the north of their present country, where the dark fertile soil so discoloured their moccasins that they were called *Siksikaua* or Black Moccasins" (McClintock, *Old North Trail*, 2). The contrast between the light clean sandy soils of the Blackfoot country in Alberta or Montana and the black sticky loam of the northern scrublands—where this was written—might impress anyone. See on this, Henry, 1808 (Coues (ed.), *Henry-Thompson Journals*, II, 545); also Jones and Bryan, *North America*, 165, 172, 215, 224, 374, 495-502.

failed to preserve any memory of what must have been really striking events.[121] In the present instance, unfortunately, coming 'from the west' could be quite legitimately said in the region of the upper or central Red River (of Texas) without by any means removing this distant ancestral home beyond the western confines of the historically established and acknowledged buffalo habitat.

In the State of Nevada, which was once included within 'California,'[122] nothing whatever has apparently been recorded about the historic buffalo at any time,[123] although fossil species have been found there.[124] Two present-day writers give their 'original range' as being 'to Nevada.'[125] It is difficult to decide just what this means. Possibly it is intended to include that state, or to signify western Utah; but there seems at present to be no extant evidence of buffalo in either,[126] except possibly in a small section northwest of Great Salt Lake. In Washoe county, Nevada, about 40° 15′ N., and just inside the western state line, I find a place-name, 'Buffalo Meadows,' on Buffalo Creek. This possibly commemorates the discovery of the fossil vestiges I have mentioned, of whose actual original whereabouts I am unaware. Otherwise, it might furnish a clue, if the date could be ascertained.

Concerning Utah, Hornaday remarks: "It is well known that buffaloes, though in very small numbers, once inhabited northeastern Utah, and that a few were killed by the Mormon settlers prior to 1840 in the vicinity of Great Salt Lake. . . ."[127] I am unaware who 'the Mormon settlers prior to 1840' may have been,[128] but Ashley and Smith's

Mooney and Thomas, s.v. Cree, Handbook of American Indians, I, 359-62, themselves support the driving of the Siksika southwest by the Crees and Assiniboine.

[121]Coronado's expedition of 1541 was found to be entirely forgotten at Cibola, from accounts given to Juan de Oñate, 1596. The visits of Cabrillo, 1542, and Drake, 1579, were not remembered in California, according to Fathers Crespi and Serra, 1769. So, Bancroft, Native Races, III, 27.

[122]Bancroft, History of Nevada, 66.

[123]Ibid., 247-8.

[124]Above, chap. II, notes 35, 36. See further Skinner and Kaisen, Fossil Bison of Alaska, 185, 186.

[125]Stone and Cram, American Animals, 66. I have since noted a reference by Sir Richard Burton (1860) which one could wish were more precise. He speaks of buffalo being in 'Utah Valley' "fourteen to fifteen years ago . . . and later still upon the Humboldt River . . ." (City of the Saints, 50). The Humboldt River apparently rises in Nevada, north of Elko; approximately 41° 10′ N., 116° W. Burton also mentions a certain Skull Valley, which may possibly be west of the Utah-Nevada line, the allusion not being very specific (ibid., 330, 454, 511).

[126]See Hornaday (above, note 33).

[127]Hornaday, "Extermination of the American Bison," 383.

[128]The earliest arrived in 1847 (Bancroft, History of Utah).

party found that very region 'well supplied with buffaloe' in May, 1825.[129] What is perhaps more curious, in view of evidence which has been noted for a relatively recent invasion of the transmontane area at large, and a less forward (westerly) advance in its more southern portions, is that the buffalo occupation of the Salt Lake Valley has been thought by an eminent American palaeontologist to date back to a very remote period, ". . . since their skulls occur wholly buried in the marshes about the lake, where the deposition appears to have been quite slow. . . ."[130] Allen sums up the scientific evidence for their final disappearance as follows:

> The buffalo seems, however, to have lingered longer on the headwaters of the Colorado than in either the Great Salt Lake Valley, or the valley of Bear River, or on the head-waters of the two main forks of the Columbia. Frémont found them on St. Vrain's Fork of Green River, and on the Vermilion in 1844, and Stansbury in 1849 found them on the northern tributaries of the Yampah [that is, Bear River] and the upper tributaries of Green River,[131] but the scarcity of water seemed to have forced the greater part of them southward. . . . They have, however, long since disappeared from the head-waters of Green River, and, indeed, from all the country drained by the tributaries of the Colorado. Although their bleached skulls are still found throughout the valleys, I was informed by old hunters whom I saw there in the autumn of 1871, that no buffaloes had been seen in this region for more than twenty years. . . .[132]

What may be termed the local or popular history of their final disappearance is less clear. There were no buffalo among the 1229 wild animals of various species slain by the Mormon 'hunting companies for the extermination of wild beasts' in the winter of 1848-49.[133] In a discussion of various routes in the vicinity of Salt Lake City, neither buffalo nor buffalo place-names appear,[134] nor are they mentioned by John W. Gunnison in 1852.[135] A well-known (later) 'Danite,' one Bill Hickman,[136] afterwards 'claimed' to have killed the last buffalo in Salt Lake Valley in 1838,[137] but I can find no evidence that he was there at

[129]Dale (ed.), *Ashley-Smith Explorations*, 155.
[130]Professor H. W. Henshaw, quoted by Allen, *American Bisons*, 119-20.
[131]About long. 110° W.; N.E. Utah and S.W. Wyoming. Green River lower down becomes the Colorado.
[132]Allen, *American Bisons*, 120-1.
[133]Bancroft, *History of Utah*, 287.
[134]*Ibid.*, 258.
[135]*Ibid.*, 323.
[136]'The notorious Bill Hickman': Bancroft, *History of Utah*, 564, 663; *History of Nevada*, 205.
[137]Allen, *American Bisons*, 119; whence presumably the date, 1838, on Hornaday's map ("Extermination of the American Bison," 548).

that early date. Putting aside his Münchausen-like details, one presumes there must have been some factual basis for the prodigious buffalo mortality described by Bridger.[138] If we accept his date, the animals had vanished in 1830, years before.

A solitary bull appeared in 1875 near Fort Bridger (Uinta county, Wyoming, in the extreme southwest corner of the state, about 41° 25′ N., 110° 20′ W.), where it was said to have been the first one seen for thirty years.[139] The 'last one' in the adjoining northeastern portion of Utah is declared to have been shot on Henry's Fork of the Green River (which it joins about 109° 35′ W. on the Utah-Wyoming state line; some thirty miles southeast of Fort Bridger) in 1844.[140] Since Fort Bridger itself dates from 1843 only, this report compares curiously with the unsupported assertion of a characteristically hasty writer, that the 'frequency of buffalo' was one reason for Bridger's selection of the situation.[141]

Hornaday sarcastically observes concerning the final extirpation (of 1883) in the United States, that the 'last buffalo' "has already been killed about a score of times."[142] The history of 'the last wolf' in England inclines one to agree with him.[143]

[138]*In extenso* above, chap. VIII, note 5.
[139]Allen, *American Bisons*, 125.
[140]*Ibid.*, Professor O. C. Marsh to Allen. Waldo R. Wedel, discussing bison remains in Promontory Cave, Promontory Point, Utah (which is 'full of them'), says that "bison occurred in some number in the area until about 1832" (*Smithsonian Miscellaneous Collections*, vol. 100, 472). See on fossil remains from Utah, Skinner and Kaisen, *Fossil Bison of Alaska*, 167.
[141]Laut, *The Overland Trail*, 121.
[142]Hornaday, "Extermination of the American Bison," 521, 525.
[143]An old tradition, repeated in several books, has the last wolf in England slain by John of Gaunt (1340-99) in Oulton Woods, Yorkshire, a few miles south of Leeds (Green, *The Making of England*, II, 7; Williams, *History of the Midland Railway*, 452, etc.). Another places the last wolf at Wormhill, Peak of Derbyshire (Harting, *Extinct British Animals*, 146). Longstaff (*Wiltshire Place-Names*, I, 82) has wolves in the 'English' forests as late as 1680, which is too late for England and too early for 'Britain,' for they were in Scotland as late as 1743 or 1756 (Harting, *Extinct British Animals*, 158-85). There are many fifteenth-century references. In the *York Records, circa* 1413, "Thei ete men that have ben hanged when thei fal from the galows . . ." (Wylie, *Henry V*, I, 206). "The Bohemian visitors to England in 1466 were amazed at the absence of wolves . . ." (*ibid.*, I, 358); but most mediaeval visitors saw only the 'civilized' England of the southeast shires, and saw it from the highways. The probable date for the extermination of the wolves is about 1500: ". . . no wolves in England . . ." (*Italian Relation of England, circa* 1500, ed. Sneyd, 10).
    See also Pearson, *Early and Middle Ages of England*, I, 206; *Notes and Queries*, Series 2, VIII, 296, 402; Cox, *Royal Forests of England*, 32; and above all, Harting, *Extinct British Animals*, 115-209, who collected practically all the evidence extant.

Note on Buffalo in Modern (Coastal) California

It is almost impossible to be sure just what any one person may have meant, at any precise period, by 'California'; it is almost as vague as 'Florida' or 'Louisiana.' (See on all this, Bancroft, *History of California*, I, 64-8, 138, 199, etc., V, 18; Winsor (ed.), *Narrative and Critical History*, VIII, 257; Taylor, *Names*, 81; *Encyclopaedia Britannica*, 14th ed., *s.v.* California, etc.) At one time 'California' included Nevada (Bancroft, *History of Nevada*, 66); and since the name was bestowed from the south or southwest, it might easily extend northeastward into the established buffalo habitat. It is doubtless in this wide and uncertain sense that Richardson used the term in 1829 (above, note 12).

It is also possible, however, that he may have intended California as we know it to-day, and had reference to the supposed mention of buffalo to Juan Rodriguez Cabrillo, the Portuguese voyager (in the Spanish service), in 1542. The Coast Indians spoke to him of many 'cows' in the 'interior,' wherever that may be. These a modern scholar considers to be 'buffalo' (Thomas, *History of North America*, II, 366-7). According to Bancroft's account of Cabrillo (*History of California*, I, 69-81), the word is "*cae*, which the voyagers understand to be cows . . ." (p. 72). No doubt, if they could be considered as 'cows' in 1542, buffalo (vac-*cae*) would be the only cows in that region; but I suspect that after Cabeza's 'cows,' any strange animals to the northward would be 'cows' for some years.

Francis Drake was off the California coast (which he named New Albion) on his famous voyage around the world, in June and July, 1579. According to one account, ". . . inland . . . infinite was the company of very large and fat Deere which there we sawe by thousands, as we supposed, in a heard . . ." (*World Encompassed*, which I have not seen, cited by Bancroft, *History of California*, I, 83). Another description states: "Our necessarie businesse being ended, our Generall [that is, Drake] with his companie traveiled up into the Countrey to their villages, where we found heardes of Deere by a thousand in a companie, being mostly large and fat of body . . ." (Hakluyt, *Voyages*, VI, 245; the same also, word for word, *ibid.*, VIII, 66).

While it is true that 'deer,' in Elizabethan times, could still be used in the Old English sense of 'wild animals,' as in Shakespeare, "mice

---

A full-grown grey wolf was killed on the Midland Railway (later L.M.S.) at Cumwhinton, near Carlisle, December 29, 1904 (*Railway Magazine*, XVI, 169).

and rats and such small deer . . ." (*Lear,* III, 4), yet others used it manifestly in our modern sense; for example Captain John Smith, Virginia, 1607, spoke of "Deare, nothing differing from ours" (*Purchas his Pilgrimes,* XVIII, 433). These animals may therefore quite legitimately be taken as deer (*cervidae*).

Cabrillo also saw, about 'San Mateo,' 33° 20′ N. (perhaps San Diego, though Bancroft thinks not) ". . . broad grassy plains, high and rolling land, and animals in droves of 100 or more, resembling Peruvian sheep with long wool, small horns, and broad round tails. . . ." (Bancroft, *History of California,* I, 70).

Bancroft, in his account of Father Juan Crespi's journey of 1772 (March 26, near Alameda, California), remarks: ". . . deer and bears are plentiful, and traces are seen of animals which the friar imagines to be buffaloes, but which the soldiers pronounce *burros* or 'jackass deer' such as they had seen in New Mexico . . ." (Bancroft, *History of California,* I, 185; cf. *ibid.,* 285). Anza (near Carquinez, April, 1776) saw 'vast herds of elk or jackass deer' (*ibid.,* 285, 288).

I am led to doubt the presence of buffalo in California within any historic period because they are not mentioned in any of the early descriptions of the animals of the country. While the earliest printed English accounts of the buffalo—the 'kine of Cibola'—are apparently later than 1579, they were very probably known by hearsay among many seafaring folk in England. In Spain, Cabeza's 'cows' were most likely known even earlier. Certainly they were known well enough by 1769, the period of the Spanish settlement of California. They are not mentioned by any of the following explorers or visitors: description of animals, etc., by Torquemada and Ascension, in Viscaino's voyage of 1595 (Bancroft, *History of California,* I, 96-105); Juan Crespi, 1769, 1772 (*ibid.,* 132-63, 183-97); Pedro Fages, governor of California, 1775 (*ibid.,* I, 486; II, 44); La Perouse, 1786 (*ibid.,* I, 428-38); Vancouver, 1792 (*ibid.,* 510-29, 702-4).

Bancroft, in his chapter on "Inland Explorations," mentions the following, none of whom allude to buffalo: Anza, 1774; Garces, 1775; Rivera, Gonzales, Arguello, Moraga, Velasquez, 1776, 1781, 1783; Arillaga, Martin, Maitorena, Sanchez, Zalvidea, Munez, 1804-6 (*History of California,* II, 43-57); and Langsdorff, 1806 (*ibid.,* 139).

This brings us to 1812. Ross Cox, the fur trader, writes as follows: "The Spaniards at San Francisco informed our traders that in the year 1812 they were obliged to kill upwards of 30,000 (wild) horses in California in order to preserve sufficient grass for the buffalo, the fat of which forms an article for exportation" (*Columbia River,* II, 96).

The immense numbers of wild horses are well authenticated: Bancroft, *Pastoral California* (*circa* 1820-40), 336, 346-7; Frémont, who saw them in the San Joaquin Valley, 1844 (*Narrative*, 270-2). So likewise are the slaughterings: Bancroft, *History of California*, II, 182-3 (1805-10); p. 418 (1810-20); pp. 668-9 (1820-30). Also the exports of tallow: *ibid.*, 420, 669; *Pastoral California*, 466-72. The 'buffalo' are not mentioned in the descriptions of Captain Shaler, 1808 (Bancroft, *History of California*, II, 23-4); Von Chamisso, with Otto Von Kotzebue, 1816 (*ibid.*, 281), or Von Kotzebue again, 1824-25 (*ibid.*, 523-5); José Romero, from Tucson, Sonora, to California and back, 1822-24 (*ibid.*, 507-9); Captain Morrell, 1825 (*ibid.*, 588); Captain F. W. Beechey, R.N., 1826-27 (*ibid.*, III, 120-5); Duhaut-Cilly and Botta, 1827 (*ibid.*, 128-30); David Douglas, botanist and scientist, 1830-32 (*ibid.*, 403-5); nor in hunters' recitals, 1830 *et seq.* (*ibid.*, 389-95). The traders of 1812 possibly confused the two common uses of *vacas*—'cows' or 'buffalo.'

I am confirmed in my doubts by the almost immediate introduction of domestic cattle into Alta California (1772, Bancroft, *History of California*, I, 194, 261), a thing scarcely necessary, perhaps not practicable, while buffalo roamed in any number. Cattle were raised at the missions in immense numbers (*ibid.*, 331, 388, 457-500, 556-77, 657, 682-3, 706-24; II, 107-23, 138-81, 346-68, 395, 418, 505, 554-623; III, 348-66, 619-57, 732, etc. A reference to 'too many cattle': *ibid.*, I, 611; horses and cattle, figures for 1800: *ibid.*, 621; and export of hides: III, 641, 732, etc.).

Among Spanish place-names in Father Juan Crespi's diary, 1769, and elsewhere (*History of California*, I, 142-6; II, 28; etc.), I find *Cañada de los Osos* (and bears seen there): *ibid.*, I, 144, 149, 200; but not a single *ojo*, *rio*, *llano*, or *cañada* (etc.) *del vacas* or *cibolo*.

There seems, in short, to be no real evidence of any character for the presence of the historic buffalo in (modern) California at any time. Some further notes in corroboration in Bancroft, *North Mexican States and Texas*, I, 130-201, 276-304, 407-91, *passim*; II, 705 *seq.*

CHAPTER XII

THE HISTORICAL HABITAT OF PLAINS AND WOOD
BUFFALO IN CANADA

ALTHOUGH the title of the present chapter embraces the whole area of Canada, it may be well to specify at the outset that only the more remote and less familiar regions of the historical buffalo range in the Dominion will be dealt with here. The historic presence of the species in the Canadian plains territory is unquestioned; and requires chronological rather than geographical examination.

Perhaps the best summary of the ultimate range of the buffalo in Canada is still that of Sir John Richardson, which I quote:

> Great Slave Lake in latitude 60° was at one time the northern boundary of their range; but of late years, according to the testimony of the natives, they have taken possession of the flat limestone district of Slave Point, on the north side of that lake, and have wandered to the vicinity of Great Marten Lake, in latitude 63° or 64°. As far as I have been able to ascertain, the limestone and sandstone formations, lying between the Rocky Mountain ridge and the lower eastern chain of primitive rocks, are the only districts in the fur countries that are frequented by the bison. In these comparatively level tracts there is much prairie land, on which they find good grass in the summer, and also many marshes overgrown with bulrushes and carices, which furnish them with winter food. Salt springs and lakes also abound on the confines of the limestone, and there are several well-known salt-licks where bison are sure to be found at all seasons of the year. They do not frequent any of the districts formed of primitive rocks, and the limits of their range to the eastward within the Hudson Bay Company's territories may be nearly correctly marked on the map by a line commencing in longitude 97° on the Red River, which flows into the south end of Lake Winnipeg, crossing the Saskatchewan to the westward of the Basquiau Hill,[1] and running from thence by the Athapescow [sic][2] to the east end of Great Slave Lake. Their migrations to the westward were formerly limited by the Rocky Mountain range, and they are still unknown in New Caledonia and on the shores of the Pacific to the north of the Columbia River; but of late

---

[1]"The Pasquia Hill or Pasquia Mountain is the low ridge upon which The Pas (northern Manitoba: where the Hudson's Bay Railway crosses the Saskatchewan)—always called today 'The Paw'—stands . . ." (Tuttle, *Our North Land*, 336). 'The Paw,' 1846: Kane, *Wanderings of an Artist*, 74.

[2]Probably, but not necessarily, Athabaska; see below, note 83.

years they have found out a passage across the mountains near the source of the Saskatchewan, and their numbers to the westward are said to be annually increasing. . . .[3]

In his own pronouncements on the same subject, Hornaday apparently accepts Richardson (the only early traveller whom he cites concerning the region) as his principal authority for the western side of the Canadian mountain territory; in this respect he followed Allen, both in his text and on his map. Yet there are some serious discrepancies between the two. Richardson says again: "The bison are supposed to have found their way across the mountains only very recently; and they are still comparatively few in numbers, and confined to certain spots . . . in particular passes only. . . ."[4]

This would seem to be natural in such a rough and broken country; and for those who subscribe to the doctrine of the buffalo paths 'following the lines of least resistance,' etc., such a belief is, in fact, almost obligatory. However, although Hornaday is himself one of the leaders in that particular *cultus*, he marks the boundaries of his buffalo habitat with a continuous line in that region. If he encountered any new light on the subject, subsequent to Richardson's day, he has not told us what it was.

It would appear to be quite correct—in so far as a non-geological critic, dependent almost entirely on historical evidence, may judge— that the ultimate bounds of the buffalo habitat on its northern sides were determined largely, perhaps principally, by various geological phenomena. However, it by no means follows that the buffalo necessarily attained to those ultimate geological frontiers on every side of their northern range. In the southern portions of their territory, abundant evidence shows that the historic *Bison americanus* never penetrated into certain regions, virtually identical in climate, pasturage, and topography, with adjacent districts actually occupied by them in fair numbers. If the delimitations indicated by Allen and Hornaday are based upon anything other than geological data, it is regrettable that they did not present their evidence. Although I cannot profess to have exhausted the sources of information, it is also remarkable that I have nowhere found a hint of any such evidence. As a conjectural or tentative suggestion for certain localities, their suggested buffalo

[3]Richardson, *Fauna Boreali-Americana*, I, 279-80; quoted by Allen, *American Bisons*, 166-8, in a mangled fashion; and so reproduced by Hornaday, "Extermination of the American Bison," 384. See below on this, Appendix O.

[4]Richardson, *Fauna Boreali-Americana*, introd. I, xxxi; see also his *Arctic Expedition, 1847-1850*, 100.

boundary might be accepted; as a definite historical record, it is un-reliable.

Hornaday's boundary crosses the forty-ninth parallel at a point about longitude 115° 40′ W., that is, a little eastward of Bedlington, British Columbia, and·south of Kootenay Lake. It then curves north-westward towards the Columbia Valley,[5] up which it proceeds to the source of that river, about 53° N. This is a region which is familiar to those who have travelled by the Canadian National route from Edmon-ton through the Yellowhead Pass, either to Vancouver or to Prince Rupert, for the line is just south of Mount Robson. The same railway route to Vancouver, after leaving the Upper Fraser Valley, follows for a time the Canoe River, which is the headwater of the Columbia. Assuming the buffalo to be travelling northward or southward, as his line would indicate (and as his strenuous insistence on those 'invari-able' directions would demand[6]) the crossing of the racing and turbulent Fraser at this point is a typical illustration of the problems of the 'continuous line.' It is much more likely that instead of crossing it somewhere between Tête Jaune Cache and Red Pass, the buffalo would keep up its banks and cross more easily (if they ever crossed at all) near the summit, around Yellowhead Lake, which at some time *circa* 1800 was clearly a buffalo haunt.[7]

From the headwaters of the Columbia the line follows the western side of the main Rocky Mountain range to latitude 55° N. At this pre-cise point, the summit level, longitude 120° W., and latitude 55° N., all coincide; at least upon a map. It also marks the boundary line of the provinces of Alberta and British Columbia, following the 120th meridian of longitude north to latitude 60° N., and the summit level southward to the international boundary.

From 55° N., where it crosses the Rockies, Hornaday's buffalo boundary proceeds almost north, with a slight curve to the eastward, to its northernmost extremity, on an upper arm of Great Slave Lake, about 63° 30′ N.

The only name I can find on modern maps at all resembling 'Great Marten Lake' is Lake la Martre, about 63° N. and 120° W., to the west of Slave Point.[8] This last has generally been accepted, since the

---

[5]It may have been Hornaday's intention to specify the main Columbia Valley as his boundary, but it would be unreasonable to expect such precise delimitation on a small map like his ("Extermination of the American Bison," 548).

[6]*Ibid.*, 382, 420-5, etc.   [7]See below, note 151.

[8]Perhaps *marthe* = 'marten'; as in Champlain, *Voyages*, ed. Biggar, III, 116.

first expedition of Franklin and Richardson, as the buffalo's farthest recorded point to the northward.[9]

From this point, Hornaday's line now turns about and runs almost directly in a south-southeast course, to a point on the headwaters of the Churchill River, on the eastern side of Buffalo Lake and La Crosse Lake, about 56° N., and 107° 30′ W. This line cuts straight across Great Slave Lake, east of the northwesterly arm of the lake on which Fort Rae is situated, to a point on the southern shore, perhaps some fifty miles east of Fort Resolution and near what is marked as the 'Rivière du Rocher' or Rocky River. It also cuts straight across Lake Athabaska almost at its widest part, in the direction I have mentioned. As I have observed, neither scientist offers the least hint whence this very precise information was derived. In Hornaday's case, particularly, the adoption of this continuous line involves him in a curious dilemma. Such great bodies of water could only have been crossed in this direct fashion on the ice in winter; but Dr. Hornaday is never tired of insisting that on the approach of winter the buffalo uniformly and invariably migrated to the south.[10] And this, despite the fact that Richardson

---

Marten Lake, 1793, in Masson, *Les Bourgeois de la Compagnie du Nord-Ouest*, I, 95; so also Innis, *Fur Trade in Canada*, 204. I do not know what other it can be.

[9]"The Buffaloes are abundant in all parts of North America, where cultivation has not interfered with their range; they are also extremely numerous on the plains of the Saskatchewan, and are also found, though less plentifully, in the woods, as far north as Great Slave Lake; a few frequent Slave Point, on the north side of the Lake, but this is the most northern situation in which they were observed by Captain Franklin's party . . ." (Joseph Sabine, in Franklin, (First) *Journey to the Polar Sea*, Appendix V, "Zoology," 668): So also, Allen, *American Bisons*, 166; Hornaday, "Extermination of the American Bison," 384; cf. Bancroft, (1875): "Immense herds of buffalo roam over the bleak grassy plains of the eastern Tinnéh, but seldom venture far to the west of the Rocky Mountains . . ." (*Native Races*, I, 39, 114).

Other limits may yet be passed. An Edmonton airman, W. Leigh Brintnell, reported buffalo 'roaming in thousands' in the Nahanni country, northern British Columbia (*Edmonton Journal*, October 2, 1934). They were presumably emigrants from Wood Buffalo Park, N.W.T. Again Soper notes a Wood bison skull found by Harry V. Radford, 1911, on the winter trail between Fort Rae (63° N., 115° W.) and Fort Providence (62° N., 118° W.), considered by its finder "doubtless the most northern point from which even a fragmentary specimen of *B. b. athabascae* has been collected" (Soper, "History of the Northern Bison," 359). But as Soper shows (*ibid.*, 358), and as will be seen below, this record was surpassed 120 years or more earlier.

[10]Hornaday, "Extermination of the American Bison," 382, 420-5. Cf. Stone and Cram: "In winter time the herds migrated regularly to the Southern portion of their range . . ." (*American Animals*, 69). Similarly, Seton, *Life-Histories of Northern Animals*, I, 261-7. Again: "Herds that would be along the North Saskatchewan in the summer of one season would be in the State of Texas in the following . . ." (Denny MS., 13). The two first follow Hornaday; the last repeats idle tradition; none cites any evidence whatever.

(who is Hornaday's principal—or sole—source as well as that of his own confessed mentor, J. A. Allen) takes them around the eastern end! Richardson beyond doubt wrote, if not from personal investigation in this particular phase, at least from careful inquiry, to the utmost of his opportunities. So far as the Canadian Northwest is concerned, Hornaday in 1889 could have had no first-hand information, as his frequent and deplorable errors prove; nor did he have many resources in the form of carefully ascertained testimony to guide him.

From the point last noted on the upper Churchill, the line bends, bearing more directly eastward, apparently along the course of that river, which here is merely a series of narrow lakes, or perhaps along the higher lands which roughly parallel the river valley. Somewhere near Lac la Ronge the line turns southeastward toward the Saskatchewan River, which it crosses a few miles to the west of Cumberland Lake. After crossing the Saskatchewan, it bends in a more east-south-east direction, and passes by the northern end of Lake Winnipegosis, to a point about half-way down Lake Winnipeg almost opposite the mouth of Beren's River, keeping all this time—upon what authority I know not—about equidistant between Lake Winnipeg and Lakes Winnipegosis and Manitoba. Thence it trends rather more to the southward and touches the extreme southern point of Lake Winnipeg at Selkirk. From here it proceeds almost directly, but with a slight easterly convexity or 'bulging,' southeastward to the Lake of the Woods, where it crosses the international boundary, whence it continues almost directly to the southern end of Lake Michigan.

It may be noted that Richardson's line, from The Pas on the Saskatchewan River (approximately 53° 40′ N., 103° 30′ W.) to the eastern end of Great Slave Lake, would not only pass almost directly by the eastern end of Lake Athabaska, but would also include a larger portion of Churchill River, and would embrace, rather than exclude, Cumberland Lake. I am unaware what may have been Richardson's authority for this; but I incline to believe that Cumberland Lake was included deliberately by Richardson, and did not merely chance to be within a straight line drawn between two far distant points. This would seem to be opposed to their own personal experience in 1819-20, and hence was possibly derived from local

---

Thomas Simpson states that at Carlton, January, 1840, three camps of Assiniboines had each their separate pound, into which they drove 40 to 50 animals daily (*Narrative of Discoveries*, 402, 404). This is cited by Allen (*American Bisons*, 206), who merely says '1840'. It is faithfully so copied by Hornaday, as proof of Indian wastefulness ("Extermination of the American Bison," 480), in blissful ignorance of the season, when, according to his own dictum, there were no buffalo within 300 or 400 miles of Carlton, southward!

information. Franklin's expedition found no buffalo near Cumberland House, which was one of their ports of call on their journey westward, and states that they were 'not found' in that locality at that date;[11] their first notice being of the 'plentiful buffalo steaks' at Carlton House, January 31, 1820.[12]

The actual historical references to buffalo at any point east of the Forks of the Saskatchewan are, almost without exception, very vague. Henry Kelsey, the very first English-speaking explorer to see the species in their northern habitat,[13] was assuredly—and perhaps purposely—obscure enough.[14] Although the next earliest, and the first whom it appears possible to localize, Anthony Henday (1754-55), was travelling to the South Saskatchewan country, he apparently left the river itself and struck overland at a more easterly point than was afterwards common on westbound journeys,[15] probably to avoid the French post at Fort à la Corne. If the route marked on Burpee's map, accompanying his edition of 'Hendry's' (that is, Henday's) "Journal"[16] be correct, Henday must have seen his first herd not far south of Melfort, Saskatchewan, August 15, 1754;[17] and in a territory where, in so far as physical and (presumably) geological characteristics are concerned, the buffalo habitat could certainly be pushed eastward for a considerable distance. On his return journey, Henday noted buffalo as common along the banks of the South or North Saskatchewan[18]

[11]Franklin (First) *Journey to the Polar Sea*, 89.
[12]*Ibid.*, 103.
[13]Even apart from David Ingram (? 1568-69) and possible New Englanders, he was hardly the first Englishman to see the species in the more northerly parts. There was apparently one in La Salle's second expedition, in 1686, who must have seen the buffalo. *Journeys of La Salle*, I, 52.
[14]See note on Henry Kelsey at the conclusion of this chapter.
[15]There was a post, 'La Montée,' the N.W. Company post adjacent to Carlton, of the H.B. Company, (see *Simpson's Athabaska Journal*, ed. Rich, Appendix A, 414). Coues thinks this (the 'mounting-place') was where travellers exchanged boats for horses: *Henry-Thompson Journals*, II, 490; see also Franklin (First) *Journey to the Polar Sea*, 117.
[16]*Transactions of the Royal Society of Canada*, 1907, Sec. II, 307-54. On the change in the name, see *Canadian Historical Review*, XVII, 1936, 145, 200.
[17]"Journal of Antony Henday," ed. Burpee, 329. Wherever he be, he is clearly far enough from the Touchwood Hills and Qu'Appelle headwaters, where Agnes Laut has him on August 15 (*Conquest of the Great Northwest*, I, 343). She also has 'red deer in myriads' on the 'Mosquito Plains, 100 miles south of the Pas'—which is almost in Lake Winnipegosis!—August 1 and 2 (*ibid.*, I, 343). Burpee's Henday says nothing of all this, however, and Henday's own 'Muscuty Plains' (probably *mascouten*, = swampy, 'muskeg'; not *mosquito* at all) are reached August 13, and continue until October 29, 1754 ("Henday's Journal," ed. Burpee, 328, 341). Her book, published 1908, 1918, is actually subsequent to Burpee's edition of Henday!
[18]Morton insists that the return was via the North Saskatchewan. See his note, *Canadian Historical Review*, XVII, 200, incorporated in his monumental

practically all the way to Fort à la Corne, which is perhaps some forty or fifty miles below the Forks of the Saskatchewan, and about the same from Melfort northwestward.[19] Matthew Cocking, journeying up the Saskatchewan in August, 1772, encountered no buffalo until August 23, twelve days above Fort à la Corne.[20] On his return trip, he noted them intermittently from April 3 until May 19, 1773, on which latter date he reached the Forks, after which no more were seen.[21]

Alexander Henry the elder (1775-76) makes no mention of buffalo along the Saskatchewan before his arrival at 'Fort des Prairies,' which from its situation would appear to be roughly in the general vicinity of the later Carlton (established 1795).[22] His is one of the first allusions to the traditional plenty of the region: "The quantity of provisions, which I found collected here, exceeded everything of which I had previously formed a notion. In one heap I saw fifty ton of beef, so fat that the men could scarcely find a sufficiency of lean. . . ."[23]

Edward Umfreville, writing of the period *circa* 1784-87, says the buffalo are not found "till you are considerably higher up the [Saskatchewan] river . . ." than Cedar Lake.[24] Since Cedar Lake was only some three days from Lake Winnipeg, this might mean almost anything; and his only other geographical reference to them is even more vague. He speaks of 'innumerable herds' in 'Hudson's Bay,'[25] which (even without the allusion previously cited) could only mean the Hudson Bay Territory at large.

I have noted the inclusion by Richardson of the Cumberland House region within the limits of the northern buffalo habitat. In a fragment of the Diary of William Tomison[26] are some entries relating to buffalo, October-December, 1801. The editorial extracts are absurdly

---

History of the Canadian West, 1939, 245-50. His strongest point is in reference to the canoe flotilla. This deserves consideration; but I am deeply suspicious of minute topographical identifications of regions probably burned over repeatedly in a period of nearly 200 years, and of the supposed description of the North Saskatchewan, the largest river in his Western itinerary, as 'a creek.'

[19]April 28 to May 23, 1755: "Henday's Journal," 350-1.

[20]"Journal of Matthew Cocking," 1772-73 (*Transactions of the Royal Society of Canada*, 1908, Sec. II, 89-121; ed. Burpee), citing 101-3.

[21]*Ibid.*, 116-18.

[22]'Fort des Prairies' was a kind of generic name (like 'railhead' or 'end of steel' in later times) applied to the frontier post, whatever that was. See on this, Coues (ed), *Henry-Thompson Journals*, II, 481; *Handbook of Canadian Indians*, 511. Apparently Edmonton, *circa* 1800: *Harmon's Journal*, 38, 41, 107, 122, 123; and as late as 1825: Ross, *Fur Hunters*, II, 209, 211.

[23]Henry, *Travels, 1760-1776*, 273. See also below, Appendix M.

[24]Umfreville, *Present State of Hudson's Bay*, 150.

[25]*Ibid.*, 37, 103.

[26]*The Beaver*, October, 1920, 31; December, 1920, 7-8.

headed "Life at York Factory." Neither buffalo nor Blackfoot, 'Stone' (Assiniboine) or 'Fall' (Gros Ventre, Atsina[27]) Indians have ever been recorded at Hudson Bay. It is well known that it was precisely because those tribes could not be induced to make the journey that the Great Company had to advance westward. Tomison was 'Inland Chief' for many years,[28] and in this capacity he 'remained continuously' at Cumberland House from August, 1801, until 1803.[29] Even this does not settle the problem of buffalo near Cumberland, for we find that during the period 1774-92 there were apparently none in that locality.[30] The mention of the 'French House,' apparently near by (possibly Fort à la Corne),[31] seems to render it probable that the entries for October to December, 1801, are from some post at or near, perhaps beyond, the Forks of the Saskatchewan. There is nothing whatever to indicate that the fragment, though belonging to Tomison's district, was actually written by himself, or even at his place of residence during the years indicated. The only other notice contiguous to Cumberland may fittingly be given here, although chronologically out of place. It is recorded by Paul Kane at the mouth of Cumberland River, two days above The Pas (and going upstream), August 28, 1846: "We passed a large quantity of the bones of buffaloes which had been drowned in the preceding winter in attempting to cross the ice. The wolves had picked them all clean. . . ."[32] Kane makes no mention of any comment whatever from the more experienced critics in whose company he was travelling. We have no means of knowing whether the buffalo were drowned at—or even near—the spot where their bones were observed. We do know that the whole carcasses often floated considerable distances down stream, and these may have done so before grounding on the river flats. And there we must leave this question; the allusion is too vague to furnish any definite conclusions.

Duncan McGillivray notes buffalo on the south side of the Saskatchewan, apparently near Prince Albert, September 11 to 16, 1794.[33]

[27]Not to be confused with the 'Gros Ventres' (Minatari, Hidatsa) of the Missouri. These are the 'Big Bellies' from whom the Belly River, Southern Alberta, derived its name. See *Handbook of American Indians*, I, 113; *Place-Names of Alberta*, 18; *McGillivray's Journal*, ed. Morton, 27; Henry, in Coues (ed.), *Henry-Thompson Journals*, II, 531, 718-20, 733-6, etc.; Maximilian, *Early Western Travels*, XXIII, 70-6; also cf. *ibid.*, VI, 371.

[28]*Hearne and Turnor Journals*, ed. Tyrrell, 581-91.

[29]*Ibid.*, 589.

[30]*Ibid.*, 37, 53, 117, 177. There are also allusions to 'Grass [*i.e.* Prairie] Indians, from the Buffalo Country . . .' (117, 177).

[31]*Ibid.*, 583; *The Beaver*, December, 1920, 7.

[32]Kane, *Wanderings of an Artist* (Radisson Society ed.), 75.

[33]*McGillivray's Journal*, 21-2.

Alexander Henry, Jr., in the same month in 1808, appears to have encountered none until reaching the vicinity of Carlton,[34] and coming up again in the summer of 1809 he notes that buffalo were 'not expected' until reaching that neighbourhood.[35] I have noticed that the Franklin party met them in the same locality in 1820.[36] The only references to buffalo made by Edward Ermatinger in 1827 refer to the country above Carlton. The animals were found, apparently, near Fort Pitt, May 30 to June 2, Carlton being reached on June 4.[37] Later that year, coming upstream, the party obtained buffalo meat from 'a man from Carlton,' three days below that point, and similarly the day before reaching Carlton on August 23. They saw their first buffalo on the 29th, two days below the Battle River confluence.[38]

The pioneer missionary, Rev. Robert Terrill Rundle, proceeding up the Saskatchewan on his initial journey to Edmonton, saw them (doubtless for the first time in his life) two days above Carlton, October 4, 1840; and subsequent first allusions in the same general locality are on June 14, 1841, and August 26, 1845.[39] Paul Kane, then eastbound (1848), remarks concerning the region between Carlton and Cumberland House, "we were now out of the buffalo country altogether. . . ."[40] Some locality between Cumberland House and the Forks had apparently always been their northeastern frontier in the Canadian West since 1754-74, and perhaps at all times; and from about 1800 onward Carlton may be considered such until their final extermination as a free wild species in the northern prairie territory.

At the same time, it must not be forgotten in any attempt to particularize localities, that almost every observer I have cited was a traveller, a bird of passage and not a resident. Most of these travelled in the summer, moreover, when the herds of the Saskatchewan territory commonly moved southward. The banks of the river are in most places forest-clad or precipitous, leading up to the high 'bench' or prairie levels. It is not impossible that some of the eighteenth-century witnesses may have journeyed through regions which were still buffalo resorts at certain seasons, without seeing any. Even at Carlton, where

[34]Coues (ed.), *Henry-Thompson Journals*, II, 490-8, 502-7. The buffalo about this time were 'generally expected' about La Montée, or at most the Elbow of the South Saskatchewan; and pemmican was supplied to serve until then (Innis, *Fur Trade in Canada*, 235).

[35]Coues (ed.), *Henry-Thompson Journals*, II, 539.

[36]Franklin, (First) *Journey to the Polar Sea*, 89, 103.

[37]Ermatinger, "York Factory Express Journal," 1827-28 (*Transactions of the Royal Society of Canada*, 1912, Sec. II, 67-132), citing 87-8.

[38]*Ibid.*, 100-1.

[39]*Rundle's Journal, sub diebus.*

[40]Kane, *Wanderings of an Artist* (Radisson Society ed.), 305.

every one of the more transient passers-by (prior to Thomas Simpson, January, 1837[41]) notes an abundance of buffalo, Rundle records a scarcity, and their supplies nearly exhausted; which points to a scarcity of some duration at this time, July 19, 1845.[42] The following year, during a journey from Carlton to Fort Pitt (August 25 to 29, 1846), through a stretch of country proverbial then and later for its unfailing plenty, there were 'no buffalo seen.'[43] It is at least twenty-five years too early at this era to suggest that these instances of scarcity indicated 'the beginning of the end.'

Tracing the eastern border of the Canadian habitat from the Saskatchewan to its ultimate point at the Lake of the Woods, where it crosses the international boundary, I have noted that Hornaday (following Allen) places the line midway between the two lakes—they are almost one—Winnipegosis and Manitoba, and Lake Winnipeg itself. One would like to learn the authority for this very precise demarcation, for it is not altogether certain, judging from various fragmentary items of evidence, that the species were not at one time to be found on the eastern side of Lake Winnipeg, along its lower extent. On their 'fourth journey' of 1661, Radisson and Groseilliers recorded in their journal: "This place hath a great store of Cows. . . . The wild men [sauvages] kill not except for necessary use. . . ."[44]

The identifications of both the locality and the species referred to in this quotation are difficult, and have given rise to controversy. The two sides have been picturesquely summarized as the 'French' and the 'English' arguments: the first of these contending for the explorers having reached Hudson Bay, and for the cows as probably signifying caribou;[45] while the second (apparently basing their case on the 'cows' being buffalo) are for some spot within the recognized buffalo habitat, on the ground that buffalo could not possibly have been found in the James Bay region or farther north. The latter school are well represented by Dr. George Bryce, who is for the cows as buffalo and the

---

[41]Simpson, Narrative of Discoveries, 48 ("Carlton starving").

[42]Rundle's Journal, sub die.

[43]Ibid., sub diebus. This last is corroborated by Kane, a fellow-pilgrim (Wanderings of an Artist (Radisson Society ed.), 76, 77). They were found some ten or fifteen miles west of Fort Pitt, September 7, 1846 (ibid., 84, 89).

[44]Bryce, Remarkable History, 6.

[45]The phraseology is apparently the coinage of Agnes Laut, Pathfinders of the West, 101-31. She is of the opinion indicated, and seemingly not without reason. There is no mention of buffalo (B. americanus) in Father Albanel's very circumstantial account of his journey to Hudson Bay in 1672 (Jesuit Relations, ed. Thwaites, LVI, 169-213, etc.). The latest scholar to discuss the problem is also in favour of Hudson Bay (Morton, History of the Canadian West, 44).

place as the Lake of the Woods.[46] Lawrence J. Burpee, in discussing this thorny problem, remarks:

This, too, has been seized upon as evidence against a journey to James Bay, on the ground that buffalo could not possibly have been seen around the shores of James Bay. Assuming that Radisson meant buffalo, and that is not altogether certain, there is no particular reason why he should not have found buffalo in the wooded country south or southwest of James Bay. Dr. A. P. Low, Director of the Canadian Geological Survey, who is thoroughly familiar with the region, says that wood buffalo may easily have ranged through that country at the time of Radisson's journey. In any case, Radisson constantly refers to the buffalo in earlier parts of his voyages as 'Buff,' and may have meant one of the deer family by 'cows'. . . .[47]

Burpee was certainly on firm ground in refusing to identify 'cows' or 'wild cows' (vaches sauvages) as necessarily buffalo. Those were the conventional French terms for different varieties of deer before they became acquainted with the buffalo.[48] He and Dr. A. P. Low are, in my view, probably right in their opinion, although I have found no direct historical evidence in support. There are, however, certain historical allusions which possibly support their conclusion. La Vérendrye in 1730 writes of Winnipeg River: "the left [that is, south] bank is inhabited by the Assiniboin and the Sioux; the country is rich in metals and buffalo are abundant. . . ."[49] I add Burpee's editorial note concerning this:

The primitive range of the buffalo, according to Hornaday, Allen, Seton, and other authorities was confined on the north to a line extending from the western extremity of Lake Superior, in a general north-westerly line, to the southern shore of Lake Winnipeg, and thence to Lake Athabaska. Alexander Henry, the elder, travelled from Grand Portage to Lake Winnipeg in 1775, but says nothing about buffalo; nor do any later travellers over the same route. In his Account of the Countries adjoining Hudson Bay (1744), however, Arthur Dobbs gives the narrative of Joseph La France, who travelled from Grand Portage to Lake Winnipeg in 1740,[50] and who reports buffalo along Rainy River, and even as far east as Grand Portage. La Vérendrye's statement may probably be taken in a broad sense as referring to the country of the Sioux and Assiniboin, south of the Winnipeg river, but

---

[46]Bryce, Remarkable History, 4-7. He notes that Miller Christy, an eminent English buffalo student, "and others," are opposed to his views.

[47]Burpee, Search for the Western Sea, 213-19.

[48]See below, Appendix B, "Buffalo and Wild Cows." The first direct reference to B. americanus in Jesuit Relations is 1663 (XLVII, 147, 149, 316).

[49]Journals of La Vérendrye, ed. Burpee, 59-60.

[50]Bryce (Remarkable History, 73) has "to Hudson's Bay"; perhaps signifying 'via Lake Winnipeg.' I have not seen Dobbs's book. It is worth noting that Major Robert Rogers (1767) speaks of Rivière du Bœuf and La Rivière Ouinipeck as being apparently contiguous: Innis, Fur Trade in Canada, Appendix E, 421.

not necessarily in its immediate neighbourhood. That would embrace a district unquestionably within the known range of the buffalo. . . .[51]

John Long, the fur trader, has one or two stray references to buffalo (1768-82) which might possibly indicate their presence in localities much farther east than has usually been supposed, and would render their appearance about Grand Portage quite credible. Long resided for a lengthy period in the region northeast of Lake 'Alempigon.' He describes buffalo-hunting methods, and also mentions bands of Indians 'arriving with their fall hunt.'[52] If this occurred near what is thought to be Lake Nepigon or Nipigon,[53] it would most certainly necessitate a recasting of our ideas concerning the Canadian buffalo range. In addition to this, Sir Alexander Mackenzie, in the *General History of the Fur Trade* prefixed to his *Voyages,* in his description of the country near Lake 'Winipic' (apparently *circa* 1789), mentions the presence of ". . . herds of the buffalo and elk, *especially on the Western side.*"[54]

It is perhaps neither just nor wise to apply too rigid a logic to passages not written for argumentative purposes, but the inference seems fair that such language from a practised writer may be interpreted in the usual grammatical sense, to indicate some at least on the eastern side of the lake; or perhaps a local belief in their presence, not wholly without foundation, whether actual specimens proved discoverable or not. An interesting item of information cited by Allen may lend some support to that suggestion: "Formerly a variety called the wood buffalo was very numerous in the forests surrounding Lakes Winnipeg and Manitoba, the last survivor having been killed only two years ago [that is, in 1871] on Sturgeon Creek, ten miles west of Fort Garry. The wood buffalo is smaller than its congener of the plains, with finer and darker wool, and a superior quality of flesh. It more resembles the 'bison' of naturalists. . . ."[55]

[51]*Journals of La Vérendrye,* ed. note, 60. Grand Portage is practically (a trifle south of the point) where the international boundary conjoins Lake Superior on the west. The boundary is Pigeon River, whose falls the portage avoids. See Coues (ed.), *Henry-Thompson Journals,* I, 6; Burpee (ed.), *Journals of La Vérendrye,* 7, 53; and the latter's excellent paper, "Grand Portage" (*Proceedings of the Minnesota State Historical Society,* 1931, 359-77).

[52]Long, *Early Western Travels,* II, 135, 148.

[53]*Alempigon* = Nepigon; so Thwaites (*ibid.,* II, 87; also *Jesuit Relations,* LI, 63); and Long himself (*Early Western Travels,* II, 121). Burpee (ed., *Journals of La Vérendrye,* 55) is for Lake Winnipeg (? the same root = *winipigon*). Thwaites (*Early Western Travels,* ed. notes, II, 14, 196) recognizes the difficulty of identifying Long's localities, but 'fall hunt' scarcely suggests the smaller fry among furry creatures.

[54]Mackenzie, *Voyages, 1789 and 1793,* lix, lxi (italics mine).

[55]*Ex inf.* J.W. ('Saskatchewan') Taylor, U.S. Consul, Winnipeg, 1873, to Allen, *American Bisons,* 172.

Whether or no the foregoing constitutes very likely evidence for the presence of buffalo east of Lake Winnipeg the reader may decide for himself; it certainly cannot be considered proof. A recent scientific writer, Dr. A. S. Romer, states that "the living species [B. bison, identical with B. americanus] is known to have ranged much more widely in the past than in historic times."[56] Dr. Romer cites neither documentary authority nor examples. Unless he is referring to discoveries subsequent to those summarized by F. W. Hodge (1930) and much later authorities on the subject, his assertion awaits confirmation, since our present knowledge points in an entirely opposing direction.[57] And there we must leave the matter.

The buffalo were certainly at some period on the eastern side of Red River at points south of Fort Garry, as the younger Henry records more than once,[58] and as, of course, they must have been, in order to extend to the Lake of the Woods. But when we speak of the 'known range' of the buffalo, it may be noticed that Father Aulneau, in his letter of 1736, which rather minutely describes the Lake of the Woods region, makes no mention of buffalo.[59] There is also a curious passage in David Thompson's Narrative which appears to refer to this locality, and the value of which will probably depend largely upon the reader's previous opinions concerning the acceptability of Indian traditions at large. Thompson found that the Mandans had apparently no traditions ". . . beyond the days of their great, great Grandfathers, who formerly possessed all the streams of the Red River and head of the Mississippe [sic], where the Wild Rice, and the Deer were plenty, but then the Bison and the Horse were not known to them."[60]

Allen states that the buffalo were exterminated east of Red River by 1850.[61] Elliott Coues is broadly in agreement, it would seem; for writing in 1875 he says ". . . so long since, that the traces of their former presence have become effaced. . . ."[62] Hind (who is cited by Allen himself) scarcely implies complete extinction at so early a date. He visited the West in 1857-58, and says: ". . . their skulls are also seen on

[56]American Aborigines, ed. Jenness, 53.

[57]Encyclopaedia Britannica (14th ed.), s.v. Bison, North American Indians. The magnificent monograph of Skinner and Kaisen, Fossi' Bison of Alaska, demonstrates the soundness of my contention even more widely. I am much indebted to the authors for the gift of this important production.

[58]Coues (ed.), Henry-Thompson Journals, I, 70, 89, 103, 168, 195, 230 (1800-03).

[59]Jesuit Relations, LXVIII, 287-305, 334.

[60]Thompson, Narrative, ed. Tyrrell, 230-1.

[61]Allen, American Bisons, 144, 156.

[62]Cited by Allen, ibid., 158.

the eastern side of the Red River of the North, in Minnesota, but the living animal is very rarely to be met with. . . ."[63]

Some further analogous evidence from the adjacent United States' territory may be of value. At this very time (1858), Assistant-Surgeon Asa Wall (U.S. Army) is cited by Allen as stating that buffalo were 'still common' about Fort Abercrombie, which was established in August of that year at a point somewhere near the modern Breckenridge, Minnesota.[64] Considering the general trend of settlement in the fifties, northward from the Mississippi River, it is on the whole probable that if an American army officer found them 'common'—or found them at all—on the Upper Red River, they would still be discoverable for some distance farther down. As between the east and west sides of the river, Hornaday (following Allen) marks them on his map as extinct in Dakota, 1840, ten years earlier than on the right (Minnesota) bank.[65] For the actual neighbourhood of the Lake of the Woods, he gives no date; nor have I found any mention of such elsewhere. This phase of the subject, however, belongs more properly to the Red River Hunt.[66] In concluding the survey of this particular corner of the buffalo habitat (that is, east of Red River), I am personally disposed to doubt whether it ever saw very much of the really immense numbers, judging from the approximate estimates mentioned by Pike in his northern expedition up the Mississippi in 1805.[67]

If the object of the foregoing discussion had been to formulate some connected and consistent theory on the buffalo advance or prevalence, pro or con, the available testimony could scarcely be said to be very helpful. One is encouraged to look forward by one item of evidence, and is thrust backward by the next. The same may be said of such data as I have been able to find concerning the history of the species along the shores of Lake Winnipeg and westward, and thence into the Northland.

It occasions no surprise to find buffalo plentiful along Lake Manitoba in 1803. Speaking apparently of Manitoba House,[68] January, 1803,

[63]*Ibid.*, 169-70.

[64]Situated 'above the mouth of Wild Rice River, some twelve leagues' below the Cheyenne River at Moorhead, Minnesota (Coues (ed.), *Henry-Thompson Journals*, I, 143-8). Butler, 1870, has it at the junction of Buffalo and Red Rivers, 180 miles from St. Cloud, 300 miles from Fort Garry (Winnipeg), just north of Breckenridge Prairie, or 'B. Flats' (Butler, *Great Lone Land*, 87-104).

[65]Hornaday, map ("Extermination of the American Bison," 548).

[66]See below, chap. XIV, "The Red River Hunt."

[67]Coues (ed.), *Expeditions of Pike*, I, 102, 110, 113, 318, 343-5, etc.

[68]Latitude 51°N.; east of Laurier, Manitoba; some 40 miles southeast of Lake Dauphin.

the younger Alexander Henry says: "Here we found Mr. McDonnell, Junior, starving with buffalo at his door. . . . Our course was about South for three days to Portage la Prairie, and thence about S.E. for four hard days to Panbian [Pembina] river, where we arrived Feb. 3. Through all this country we never marched a day without passing herds of buffalo; even along the shore of the lake they were very numerous. . . ."[69]

This condition of plenty did not apparently continue for long. D. W. Harmon observes that as early as *circa* 1819, the Saulteaux (who occupied this general territory, west of Lake Winnipeg) 'were becoming agriculturists';[70] a circumstance which in a tribe formerly hunters from time immemorial, could surely indicate only a most serious diminution of game. Yet again, we need not assume any rapid decrease on so large and general a scale as this might be thought to imply. The Swan River country to the west of Lake Winnipegosis, where Harmon noted 'buffalo numerous' in September, 1802,[71] appears to have been pretty well stocked in 1832.[72] As late as *circa* 1840, R. M. Ballantyne— then a resident at Norway House—specifies the 'Swan River District' as apparently being considered a chief source of (buffalo) supply for the Norway House and Hudson's Bay establishments.[73]

Hind observes (1858): "In the memory of many Red River hunters, the buffalo were accustomed to visit the prairies of the Assiniboine [river] as far north as Lake Manitobah, where in fact their skulls and bones are now to be seen. . . ."[74] Butler makes a similar remark in

[69]Coues (ed.), *Henry-Thompson Journals*, I, 208.

[70]*Harmon's Journal*, 288. Some data in Oliver, "The Beginnings of Agriculture in Saskatchewan" (*Transactions of the Royal Society of Canada*, 1935, Sec. II, 1-32).

[71]*Harmon's Journal*, 70.

[72]In 1832, Chief Trader William Todd, Fort Pelly, was instructed that the trade in 'provisions' (*i.e.* dried buffalo meat) was to be 'discouraged'; but to secure 'all the clean rendered tallow he could collect' (*The Canadian North-West*, ed. Oliver, I, 679).

[73]Ballantyne, *Hudson Bay*, 101, 149. This district (1830-43) comprised— with occasional alterations here and there—Forts Pelly, Dauphine, Shoal River, Manitoba. Fort Ellice was established in 1831, to keep the Assiniboine and Cree trade from the Missouri River posts (Oliver (ed.), *Canadian North-West*, I, 646-79; II, 695-856, *passim*). In 1856, Egg Lake, Qu'Appelle Lakes, and Touchwood Hills posts are included (Bryce, *Remarkable History*, Appendix C, 489-90).

But according to the Minutes of Council for the Northern Department, Hudson's Bay Company, 1830-43, printed by the late Professor Oliver, requisitions of buffalo provisions for Norway House (and presumably for points farther distant, this place being the Depot) were entirely from the Saskatchewan District at that time. (Oliver (ed.), *Canadian North-West*, I, 645, 660, 678; II, 694-870, *passim*). Cf. Innis, *Fur Trade in Canada*, 365.

[74]Hind, *Report, 1858*, 106.

1871: ". . . men [are] still living who remembered to have hunted the buffalo on the shores of Lake Manitoba. . . ."[75] 'Men still living' is hopelessly vague; and in 1871 could carry the period backwards practically to the younger Henry's days. Hind, in the year of his visit, notes the case of a man living at that time near Lake Manitoba, who was "tossed by a buffalo bull during the past summer . . ."[76] (that is, 1858); but he does not say where this occurred. In the following year at Fort Pelly, some considerable distance westward on the headwaters of the Assiniboine River, the Earl of Southesk writes (December, 1859): "Buffalo never come within several days' march. . . ."[77]

Sir William (then Captain) Butler also stated them to be 'no longer existing' in the Saulteaux country, west of Lake Winnipeg, in 1870;[78] yet in 1873, a Saulteaux chief merely said to Rev. Egerton Ryerson Young, in (and referring to) that precise region: "The buffalo and deer once so abundant are fast disappearing. . . ."[79] The last utterance may of course have been one of a type of which the historical 'buffalo' literature presents frequent examples; whenever (as in this case) the influx of the whites had caused uneasiness. Frequently in such contingencies, the Indians confidently believed (as in 1885),[80] that if the expulsion of the white man or some such momentous event could be brought to pass, 'the buffalo would return.' As it stands, I doubt if we have any right to read such a meaning into it, where none such has been suggested by a careful and competent observer of Indian habits of thought and language. On the other hand, if it be really the expression of a statesmanlike mind, consciously and deliberately put forward in relation to actually existing facts, then we must conclude that at this time the buffalo were not so completely exterminated in the Saulteaux country as Butler or his informants believed. It is in the face of uncer-

[75]Butler's Report for Governor Archibald (*Great Lone Land*, 358).

[76]Hind, *Report, 1858*, 102.

[77]Southesk, *Travels*, 306. Fort Pelly epitomizes the fluctuations of buffalo movement. Allen writes: "Coxe, 1812, found buffalo in small numbers on the headwaters of the Assiniboine and its tributaries . . ." (*American Bisons*, 168). If this be Ross Cox, it should be 1817, as in 1812 he was on the Pacific Coast. Thomas Simpson, from Carlton to one day from Pelly, January, 1840, found 'myriads' (*Narrative of Discoveries*, 406-7). This precise direction, southeast from Carlton, bore the name of 'Buffalo Robe Plain' in 1825; probably indicating a traditional plenty (Governor Simpson's Journal, 1824-25, in *Fur Trade and Empire*, ed. Merk, 155). In March, 1863, 'starving'; so Milton and Cheadle, *North-West Passage*, 160. I know nothing more concerning buffalo specifically, but cf. Cowie, 1867 *seq.* (*Company of Adventurers*, 356-69).

[78]Butler's Report (*Great Lone Land*, 372, 376).

[79]Young, *Canoe and Dog Train*, 239; for Young, see Morris, *Treaties with the Indians of Manitoba*, 147, 348.

[80]Hughes, *Father Lacombe*, 304.

tainties of this character that one feels anew the general need for continuous local chronological records.

We are confronted with the same discouraging lack of precise information in attempting to establish the bounds of the northern habitat on its eastern side from the lower Saskatchewan to its ultimate extremity beyond Great Slave Lake. Hornaday's line (following Allen) seems too far to the west, if we are to accept evidence such as would scarcely be disputed for ordinary processes of investigation. Samuel Hearne, on his way back towards Hudson Bay in the early months of 1772, presents positive testimony to the presence of buffalo[81] for fourteen days from 'Lake Clowey'[82] in a direction which he gives as east-southeast, but which his editor, J. B. Tyrrell, feels compelled by a careful study of Hearne's localities (based upon a wide personal knowledge of the region) to change to south-southeast, south, and—for a short distance along Slave River below Fort Resolution—almost to south-southwest.[83] Hearne describes the party as journeying from Lake Clowey, from February 14th to February 29th, through a country "abounding with moose and buffalo";[84] but none were seen after the latter date.[85]

[81]Whether Wood or Plains buffalo is here immaterial; doubtless the former.

[82]Lake Clowey is given by Hearne as 62° 50′ N., 113° 30′ W. The latitude is probably near enough; so, Tyrrell (Hearne, *Journey*, ed. note, 132); but the longitude would place it, not near Artillery Lake (say 63° N., 107° W.) as on Hearne's map (see *Journey*) but almost on a line between Fort Resolution on Great Slave Lake and the southwest point of Lake Mackay, and very near the latter. After the breaking of his quadrant, Hearne's observations became unreliable, as is well known. See Tyrrell's notes (*ibid.*, 29-32, 150, 161, 164, 222, 270, 283, etc.).

[83]The reconciliation of Hearne's positions, directions, and dates, would be, I should suppose, as difficult a task as a critical editor—in this case blessed (or cursed) with independent knowledge of his own—would ever have to face. It seems absurd to suggest that a naval officer was uncertain whether he was going east-southeast or not; but Tyrrell often has to show that a given direction could not have landed him in places which are unmistakably identified by their Indian names. Hearne speaks of buffalo as plentiful, south of Lake 'Athapuskow' (Great Slave Lake; so Tyrrell, *ibid.*, 226, 234, 253); and 'seeing them every day,' then on his way home, January 1772 (*ibid.*, 255, 263). Yet in February he was northeast—or north—and east-southeast; still going! (*ibid.*, 271, 276).

Hearne's 'Athapuscow' is Lake Athabaska (so *Handbook of Canadian Indians*, 48); but Tyrrell's identification seems more reliable. Richardson's 'Athapescow' (above, note 2) is really immaterial to the discussion, as his line from The Pas would pass by the eastern end of either lake. There is an Athapupuskow Lake, 55° N., 102° W., northeast from Cumberland Lake; and Coues identifies David Thompson's 'Athapupuskow or Mr. Small's river' as Cold River, a tributary to the Misinipi from Cold Lake (? northeast of Edmonton, 54° 40′ N., 110° W.): *Henry-Thompson Journals*, II, 577.

[84]Hearne, *Journey*, ed. Tyrrell, 271.

[85]*Ibid.*, 276.

We have no warrant for assuming that Hearne was then travelling at the period indicated exactly on the fringe of the buffalo habitat; nor can we be sure that, had he journeyed a day or two eastward (?) and then travelled on a line approximately parallel, he would not have seen buffalo or traces of them. But the fact remains that after February 29 the party saw no more during their remaining journey of exactly four months to Hudson Bay, where they arrived June 29. During this time they travelled (according to Tyrrell's map reproducing their route as nearly as may be[86]) approximately along the 61st parallel for a distance of about nine degrees of longitude from near Slave River to Wholdiah Lake (say 113° W. to 104° W.), equivalent at latitude 61° N. to over 300 miles,[87] before crossing Richardson's buffalo 'boundary line.' Throughout all this wide stretch of territory they make no mention of the animals, nor of any sign, vestige, indication, or even tradition of them.

The fact that no other writer does so (whom I have had the opportunity to consult) is not surprising. Even for travellers whose ultimate destination might be the Lake Athabaska region, or as far east as Fort Reliance on the eastern end of Great Slave Lake, the usual route was via Isle à la Crosse, Buffalo Lake,[88] and Methy Portage, and down the Clearwater River to the Athabaska at Fort McMurray. This circumstance will account quite sufficiently for the fact that in the entire territory north from the Saskatchewan to Lake Athabaska, the localities mentioned as constituting the conventional route from Carlton to the lower Athabaska country and beyond, are the farthest eastward portion of the Northland in which I have found any definite notice of buffalo. This very silence raises the question of the basis of validity for the 'point-to-point' delineation of our various generalizers. Even if their boundaries could be shown to conform positively or hypothetically to a topographical or geological frontier[89]—and it is highly improbable that such a frontier would be defined in any clean-cut, 'survey-line' fashion—we are not necessarily justified in assuming (in the virtually complete absence of other evidence) that the buffalo at some time or another actually reached those limits.

[86]Map, in his edition of Hearne, *Journey*.

[87]Given as 34.67 miles at 60° N. Nine degrees at 60° N. = 312.03 miles.

[88]One of the many Buffalo Lakes. Now Peter Pond Lake; see Tyrrell, ed. note, *Hearne and Turnor Journals*, 367; *Place-Names of Alberta*, map (56° N., 109° W.).

[89]The operation of such physical frontiers is not certain. In some of the Lake regions, Seton thinks the boundaries of deciduous and coniferous forest regions marked the buffalo limits (above, chap. X, note 175). To judge from

As I have suggested, there are other instances in the Southern States, and also in the Lake States, of a failure on the part of the buffalo to occupy regions which for no visible or conceivable reasons—except very possibly time—they should not have occupied. In fact, apart from any implications arising from the 'traditional' conceptions of the 'line of least resistance' route for buffalo journeyings—which I do not accept, pending the production of some really reliable evidence—, if we are to draw a line between two (or more) far distant points which buffalo are known to have visited, and include the entire territory within that frontier as their known habitat, we might as well ignore the restrictions of evidence and assume that because Europeans, for example, were at The Pas and also at Fort Reliance, they must have occupied all the territory lying directly between those respective places! The commonly delineated northeastern 'buffalo frontier' north of the Saskatchewan, certainly north of the Churchill, may be accepted as a greater or lesser probability, very much according to the individual point of view. In my opinion, it cannot be regarded as established on the basis of acknowledged evidence.[90]

I am confirmed in this conclusion by the evidently scanty numbers which are more commonly indicated in the testimonies of travellers through those northern regions where buffalo were seen at all. There are no accounts of 'immense numbers' or of 'vast hosts,' seen at one time, and no attempts to compute the herds, or the space of ground they occupied, such as are found here and there in the descriptions of more southerly observers, from the Saskatchewan to the Pecos. Such a term as 'abundance' is a relative expression; in this question of buffalo, its significance lies wholly in how wide a need, or what particular purpose, the 'abundance' in question was competent to satisfy. There is scarcely a single traveller through the southern plains territory, although frequently he has heard long before of the great herds that swarmed there, but stands aghast at the actual spectacle itself, when seen for the first time.[91] The northern explorer must surely have been

the views of Low (above, note 47) and from the physical character of much of the Northern Wood buffalo range, this is questionable, for Wood buffalo at least. See Soper, "History of the Northern Bison," *passim.*

[90]Tyrrell, in the bibliography to his edition of Hearne, cites some modern travellers and scientists whom I have had no opportunity to consult. It is probable that if they had found buffalo indications eastward towards Hudson Bay, he would have quoted them. I am informed by Dr. R. C. Wallace, Principal of Queen's University (Canada), who has geologized in a portion of the territory, that he had never heard of any such discoveries being made in that region, up to 1930.

[91]See the case of Professor Allen himself (above, chap. X, note 187).

made of more phlegmatic stuff, excepting on the supposition that what he saw was very different! 'Saw a buffalo,' or 'a few buffalo,' constitutes his very common form of reference. Sometimes travellers are 'informed' or 'assured' by the Indians of goodly numbers to be found somewhere else, very much as was Bonnecamp (1750), two thousand miles away.[92] And in those occasional instances where the phraseology of really large numbers is actually used, a comparison with other examples from the less richly stocked territories should again enjoin caution in forming our conclusions.

I give below, in general chronological order, such testimonies as I have been able to collect, concerning the presence of buffalo in the territory under discussion, along the Athabaska River Valley, north of Athabaska Landing,[93] and in the country at large on its right (eastern) bank. Some of the very earliest references concerning 'buffalo' may not have been to Bison at all.[94]

It is needless to recapitulate Hearne's references to buffalo; after the various considerations are balanced, their precise locality remains somewhat problematical. For reasons which I specify below, however, we may accept not only his allusions but those of practically every one else, concerning buffalo seen in this territory, probably anywhere north of 54° 39' N., as being Wood buffalo. Peter Fidler and Malcolm Ross, in June, 1791, on the Carlton-Athabaska route by way of Isle à la Crosse, note their presence, though evidently in scanty numbers on this journey at least. They write: ". . . the Jepewyans [Chippewyans] has proposed another track where they say there is a plenty of buffaloe and Moose and no European has ever gone that way before."[95] This was what was called 'the South way' from Isle à la Crosse to the Athabaska, via Garson River and Lake, rather than the Methy Portage, a cut-off following 'string instead of bow.'[96] The party noted buffalo vestiges, 'much of their dung laying about the banks,' and 'many fresh tracks' were seen in 'a fine country for cattle,' but no 'plenty'; only odd ones for two weeks until June 17.[97]

[92]*In extenso*, above, chap. X, note 132.
[93]Now Athabaska, Alberta, the apex of the great southward sweep of the river finally turning north; 90 miles north from Edmonton.
[94]See on these confusions, Appendix N.
[95]*Hearne and Turnor Journals*, ed. Tyrrell, 370, 371.
[96]Previous to 1911, Garson Lake (56° 20' N., 110° W.) was one of the countless 'Whitefish Lakes' of the Northwest (*Place-Names of Alberta*, 56).
[97]*Hearne and Turnor Journals* (as also Philip Turnor, July, 1791), 373, 379, 381, 383, 386, 414. Turnor's map marks the region: 'Some buffalo.'

I have already noted, in discussing the two varieties, an instance of Wood buffalo being found at a point some 130 miles south of Garson Lake, in 1810.[98] This is of particular interest, as being the earliest description known to me from a contemporary observer *who knew the two kinds* of buffalo.[99] This fact fixes the locality mentioned as the southernmost point recorded in the territory more immediately east of Edmonton. On general principles, I should have classed this region as the (winter) Plains buffalo range, only some twenty-five miles north of the Saskatchewan River, which they are frequently recorded to have crossed hereabouts. But while Plains buffalo sheltered in the woodlands (as in this region), it is unanimously agreed by all early observers that the Wood buffalo would not go out on the Plains.[100]

Along the main stream of the Athabaska (lower down towards Athabaska Lake and Fort Chipewyan), the region is described by Fidler, Ross, and Turnor, particularly on the western side, about 57° N., as 'a fine country for Buffalo and Moose.'[101] They do not, however, mention seeing any. Harmon says there were 'a few buffaloes found,' *circa* 1807-10;[102] and their general prevalence along the main fur traders' route between the Athabaska and the Saskatchewan water-systems is indicated at an earlier period in Mackenzie's *General History of the Fur Trade* (*circa* 1778-89): "All this country, to the South Branch of the Saskatchiwine, abounds in beaver, moose-deer, fallow-deer, elks, bears, buffaloes, &c. . . ."[103]

Like every other buffalo resort, however, regardless of its local or popular reputation, the region experienced its ups and downs. This precariousness is well described by Governor Simpson:

Throughout this country everything is in extremes—unparalleled cold and excessive heat; long droughts, balanced by drenching rain and destructive hail. But it is not in climate only that these contrarieties prevail; at some seasons both whites and natives are living in wasteful abundance, on venison, buffalo, fish and game of all kinds; while at other times they are reduced to the last degree of hunger, after passing several days without food.

[98]Above, chap. III, note 100.

[99]Hearne, at the time of his great Northland journey, evidently did not.

[100]See *Harmon's Journal*, 366; Coues (ed.), *Henry-Thompson Journals*, II. 682; Hind, *Report 1858*, 105; Hector, in *Palliser Journals*, 148; Butler, *Wild North Land*, 211; Macoun, *Manitoba*, 342; Seton, *Arctic Prairies*, 36-142.

[101]*Hearne and Turnor Journals*, 392.

[102]*Harmon's Journal*, 138; cf. James McKenzie, in Masson, *Les Bourgeois de la Compagnie du Nord-Ouest*, II, 397.

[103]Mackenzie, *Voyages 1789 and 1793*, lxxix-lxxxii. On the route is Lac du Bœuf = Buffalo Lake, near La Crosse Lake (*ibid.*, lxxx). In a sparse region, such names probably indicate 'a buffalo seen'; in a good one, a host!

In the year 1820, our provisions fell short at our establishment, and on two or three occasions I went for two or three whole days and nights without having a single morsel to swallow, but then again, I was one of a party of eleven men and one woman which discussed at one sitting meal no less than three ducks and twenty-two geese!

On the Saskatchewan the daily rations are eight pounds of meat a head, whereas in other districts our people have been sent on long journeys with nothing but a pint of meal and some parchment for their sustenance....[104]

The establishment of 1820, to which Simpson refers, was Fort Wedderburn, the Hudson's Bay Company rival post to the closely adjacent Fort Chipewyan of the Nor'Westers. It was at Fort Wedderburn that Simpson, secretly clothed with unsuspected powers, spent his year's 'novitiate,' from which he was shortly to emerge as the executive head of the two amalgamated companies in Canada. The incidental references in his *Journal* of that year regarding buffalo bear out his general review, as likewise do those of other early observers, as we shall later see.

Concerning the Athabaska Valley, south of Lake Athabaska to the Clearwater (or possibly to Athabaska Landing), Dr. Richardson wrote: ". . . a plain extends from near Athabaska Lake to the Clear Water River, tolerably well wooded and frequented by buffaloes. . . ."[105] A few specific notices remain, relating to the territory at large. About Berens House and Red River (a western tributary of the Athabaska), which places cannot have been very far apart,[106] Simpson's Report for 1820-21 states that "the country abounds with Buffalo and Deer"; and the Indians about there and Fort Wedderburn were "desired to devote themselves" to buffalo hunting during the summer of 1821, doubtless to avert the uncertainties and privations occasionally experienced during the previous winter.[107] Here again it is not easy to discover what 'abounding' meant to a newcomer. Various notices, prior even to Simpson, do not suggest really large numbers. A little farther up, just above or just below Athabaska Landing (that is, in a region less travelled by the fur traders than was the case below the Clearwater confluence) Gabriel Franchère, the Astorian, eastward-

[104]Simpson, *Journey Around the World*, I, 98-99.

[105]"Geognostical Observations," in Franklin (First) *Journey to the Polar Sea*, Appendix I, 514; also Richardson, *Arctic Expedition, 1847-1850*, 78, 82.

[106]Berens House given as sixty miles from Fort Chipewyan, 'near Fort McKay, (*Place-Names of Alberta*, 18). Red River is 57° 10′ N., also near Fort McKay. Not to be confused with Red River, flowing northward to its confluence with the Peace at Little Red River Post, 58° 30′ N., 114° 40′ W. Simpson, however, speaks of buffalo being 'about four days from Fort Wedderburn towards Berens house' (*Simpson's Athabaska Journal*, 288).

[107]*Ibid.*, 302, 306, 312, 337, 343, 362, 364.

bound in June, 1814, records a solitary buffalo;[108] and in the latter vicinity, Ross Cox, also eastbound, observed 'some buffalo' just three years later, June 10, 1817.[109] Both travellers repeated the experience somewhere near the Lac la Biche country in the same respective months, Franchère again encountering a lone animal[110] and Cox a small number.[111] In the same region, as far back as the winter of 1798-99, David Thompson met some about Lac la Biche, but only 'a few bulls.'[112]

The Clearwater country furnishes an illustration of the fluctuations of the buffalo at different eras, which here, as so frequently elsewhere, elicited one of the characteristic jeremiads on their disappearance. At the Forks of the 'Pembina' (another of the many Pembinas, now re-named the Christina[113]), a tributary of the Clearwater, twelve miles east of the later Fort McMurray, Simpson noted 'plenty of buffalo' in September, 1820, and again in May, 1821.[114] It may be pointed out that 'the South way' followed by Turnor's party in 1791 would almost certainly lie along the lower Christina, yet they saw only odd ones, despite various indications.[115] Travelling along the Clearwater in 1833, John McLean remarks that "in former times these hills were covered with herds of buffaloes, but not one is to be seen now. . . ."[116] On January 26, 1837, however, Thomas Simpson saw along the same river "a band of five wood buffaloes, sunning their fat sides"; and their tracks were 'numerous in every direction.'[117] And forty years after McLean, in 1873, Sir William Butler recounts how they made merry "over the countless wood-buffalo steaks" at the Fort (McMurray) on the Athabaska and Clearwater Rivers.[118] It was in this general territory that one of the last herds in Canada south of the (present) Northern Wood buffalo reserve was slaughtered (1888).[119]

[108]He merely says "below the Pembina river," Early Western Travels, VI, 365.

[109]Cox, Columbia River, II, 188, 189.

[110]Franchère, Early Western Travels, VI, 368.

[111]Cox, Columbia River, II, 190; a few more on the Beaver River, near Cold Lake (II, 193).

[112]Thompson, Narrative, ed. Tyrrell, 305.

[113]Since 1911, Place-Names of Alberta, 34. Not the Pembina of note 108, above.

[114]Simpson's Athabaska Journal, 69, 344.

[115]Above, notes 95-8.

[116]McLean, Twenty-Five Years' Service, orig. ed., II, 227; ibid., Champlain Society ed., 136.

[117]Simpson, Narrative of Discoveries, 60-1.

[118]Butler, Wild North Land, 122.

[119]See below, chap. XVII, "The Final Extermination in Western Canada."

The final section of the Canadian buffalo habitat to engage our attention is comprised in the Rocky Mountain territory from the international boundary to the extreme northern limit of their range, about latitude 63° 30′ N., and west of the Athabaska and Slave Rivers, and of a line drawn from Athabaska Landing to Macleod; with the proviso that, in the southern plains territory, this area would embrace some of its most typical prairie range, which (as stated at the outset) it is not the intention to discuss here.

Hornaday's continuous line indicating the buffalo boundary northward from the forty-ninth parallel to approximately latitude 55° N., where it crosses the summit apparently about the headwaters of the Wapiti River, a tributary of the (upper) Peace River, is in this region in my opinion peculiarly inapplicable. For, although he is supposedly following Allen in his map, yet he disregards—while professing to accept—Allen's principal authority, Richardson, who advances the entirely reasonable suggestion that the advent of the buffalo across the Canadian Rockies into British Columbia was "in particular passes only."[120] Hornaday likewise entirely ignores contemporary information furnished to Allen by a competent field observer, which I shall cite in due course, and which strongly tends to support Richardson's conclusions. Whether Hornaday fell a victim to the temptation to depict the extreme buffalo boundary in its northwestern corner as a typical specimen of a 'north-and-south' migration-route, and in pursuance of this idea was led to exclude contradictory evidence, as he does elsewhere; or whether his assertions were caused merely by haste and a resultant failure to consider and co-ordinate material unquestionably known to him, I cannot say. Such historical evidence as I have been able to collect, in addition to general conclusions suggested by topographical and physical conditions in the mountain territory, furnishes considerable support to Richardson's opinion, and virtually none to that of Hornaday, as expressed in his map of the buffalo habitat.[121] His map and his text are widely contradictory. He writes as follows:

At two or three points only did the buffaloes of the British Possessions cross the Rocky Mountain barrier toward British Columbia. One was the pass through which the Canadian Pacific Railway now runs, 200 miles north of the International Boundary. According to Richardson, the number of buffaloes which crossed the mountains at that point were sufficiently noticeable to constitute a feature of the fauna on the western side of the range.[122]

[120]In extenso above, note 4.
[121]Hornaday, "Extermination of the American Bison," 548.
[122]See below on this, Appendix O, "Buffalo in the Rocky Mountain Passes."

It is said that buffalo also crossed by way of the Kootenai Pass, which is only a few miles south of the boundary line, but the number which did so must have been very small. . . .[123]

It is regrettable that Hornaday did not adduce some authority for the statement on the use by buffalo of the Kootenay Pass. There seems to be some confusion of terminology among certain of the early explorers concerning this place. Captain Thomas Blakiston, who travelled through the region in semi-independent conjunction with the Palliser expedition in 1858, describes the Kootenay Pass thus: ". . . where another of the branches of the Belly River issues from the mountains. Here we struck a narrow but tolerably well beaten track, which the Indians informed us was the Kootanie trail. . . ."[124]

He gives the position at the eastern entrance as 114° 34′ W., and 49° 34′ N., extending to 115° 24′ W.[125] This situation, on a modern map, can only indicate the Crow's Nest Pass by the presence of the Canadian Pacific Railway (so named) along its course. Yet Blakiston himself mentions also the 'Crow's Nest Pass,' and a trail running through it, but without any suggestion of their identity with the Kootenay Pass and Trail, which nevertheless would appear to be the case.[126] What Blakiston calls the 'Flathead Pass' (49° N.) must surely be the same as Dr. G. M. Dawson's 'South Kootanie Pass.'[127] The pass of this name is given on an authoritative official map as being about 49° 5′ N., and there are two others, the Middle and North Kootenay passes, between this one and the Crow's Nest Pass.[128] Blakiston traversed these passes in the summer and autumn of 1858, yet he says nothing whatever regarding their use by buffalo at that or any other time, nor of ancient or recent buffalo vestiges, nor of any Indian tradition of the presence of buffalo formerly; although he mentions seeing a herd in the upper Belly River Valley, August 18, 1858,[129] and relates that the Stoneys (Assiniboine) told him buffalo 'were getting every year more scarce.'[130] He does observe, however, that "there is little or no game on the west side of the mountains"; and that the 'Flathead Pass' was used "by the Flathead Indians when crossing to the Sas-

[123]Hornaday, "Extermination of the American Bison," 384-5.
[124]Blakiston, *Report*, 243 (by courtesy of the late D. E. Cameron, formerly librarian, University of Alberta).
[125]*Ibid.*, 243, 246.
[126]*Ibid.*, 254. "The present Crowsnest mountain is in latitude 49° 42′, longitude 114° 35′ . . ." (*Place-Names of Alberta*, 39-40).
[127]Blakiston, *Report*, 254; Dawson to Allen (*American Bisons*, 174).
[128]Map in *Place-Names of Alberta*.
[129]Blakiston, *Report*, 241.
[130]*Ibid.*, 240.

katchewan Plains for the purpose of obtaining buffalo meat. . . ."[131]
The use of this and other passes across the Rockies by the 'Flatheads'
(commonly a generic term applied to any of the 'head-flattening'
tribes) and others, is well attested, and was doubtless an immemorial
usage before the first white men appeared in the territory.[132] This fact
tends to support Richardson's surmise that the buffalo advance across
the Rockies, in the northern and central regions at least, might in 1829
be dated "only very recently."[133]

The natural inferences to be drawn from the foregoing particulars
are directly confirmed by Dr. G. M. Dawson, the well-known Canadian explorer and scientist of the seventies, in correspondence with
Professor Allen himself: "We saw abundant traces of the passage of
great herds in spring on the upper branches of Milk River, and they
come in to the foot of the Rocky Mountains. I do not think they ever
cross the mountains in the vicinity of the Forty-Ninth Parallel, though
I have seen their bones as far up the South Kootanie Pass as the last
grassy meadow. . . ."[134]

There is, of course, nothing far-fetched in the supposition that these
middle passes *may* have been used by the buffalo to penetrate into
British Columbia in the district near Field, on the Canadian Pacific
Railway. John McDougall noted their presence, and their trails, well
up the Bow River Valley, the (later) main line route of that system,
in April and also at Christmas time, 1873;[135] and the earlier missionary, Rundle, recorded 'buffalo numerous' at a point thought to be near
Banff, Alberta, April 14, 1841, and in addition made various incidental
references to herds in the region flanking the Bow Valley on the northern side,[136] where a southward movement would bring them into this
region at points generally contiguous to the locality of McDougall's
allusions of 1873.

Furthermore, in the latest days of the Plains buffalo in western
Canada, a newspaper notice, cited by a careful historian, instances
them 'coming down from the mountains' in great numbers,[137] in what
must apparently have been the precise intermediate territory, from

[131]*Ibid.*, 251, 252, 254.

[132]For this *in extenso*, see above, chap. XI, note 9.

[133]Richardson, *Fauna Boreali-Americana*, introd. I, xxxi.

[134]Dawson, Correspondence to Allen (in *American Bisons*, 174).

[135]McDougall, *Western Trails*, 21-4, 108. In January, 1876, he writes (as
from near Calgary) on seeing the buffalo in an intense cold snap ". . . moving
steadily westward . . . into the hills . . ." (McDougall MS., 34-7).

[136]*Rundle's Journal*, April 14 to May 1, 1841.

[137]*Saskatchewan Herald* (Battleford, Saskatchewan), February 10, 1879;
quoted by Black, *History of Saskatchewan*, 184-5.

about 49° to 52° N. None of this material, however, was very readily accessible when Hornaday wrote; much of it was not yet printed. The unbroken silence of travellers, and the failure to discover any buffalo vestiges on the western side of the mountain range[138] (in so far as I can ascertain); the declared opinion of other careful observers that buffalo actually did not penetrate through passes farther south and contiguous to a region always much more heavily stocked (in Hornaday's own opinion[139]) than the similar Canadian territory to the northward; these factors must in my view outweigh an assertion which is at variance with the very authority upon which it is professedly based. These factors, I consider, establish my conclusion that the buffalo boundary line along the Columbia Valley south of latitude 52° N. is pure speculation, unwarranted in the present state of our knowledge. I have been (later) informed by Dr. G. Clifford Carl, of Victoria, B.C., Provincial Zoologist, that a fossilized skeleton (or a portion of one) was discovered near Kelowna in the Okanagan district of British Columbia, in 1919. It was identified as being that of a buffalo.[140] Accepting this identification as correct, we have no ground for any assumption from a solitary specimen that either historic or fossil species are thereby proved to have ever occupied the intervening territory between Kelowna and the present westward limits in the Rocky Mountain summit passes. This particular specimen could—much more probably—have come northward from the lower Columbia territory in Washington.

It is by no means certain that the actual buffalo territory in British Columbia even extended as far south as latitude 52° N., and it may really have to be placed, in so far as our present knowledge tends to indicate, near latitude 54° or 55° N. While I shall adduce evidence of the former presence of the animals along all the principal 'eastward-bound' river valleys, extending to points well within the mountains and evidently not far from the summit region, the southernmost point on the western side of the Canadian Rockies, of which I have found any record, is that noted by Mackenzie in 1793[141] on the upper Parsnip

[138]Surely nothing could surpass railway construction, laying bare wide areas foot by foot, for the exposure of superficial vestiges, at least. I was informed in 1941 that buffalo vestiges had been found at points along the route of the recently constructed Jasper–Banff highway; which extends their eastern mountain range perhaps as far south as the Canadian Pacific main line. It is possible that these may be Wood buffalo. See below, notes 160, 172-4.

[139]Hornaday, "Extermination of the American Bison," 441, 509. The historical evidence scarcely supports this view.

[140]See Appendix L.

[141]Mackenzie, *Voyages 1789 and 1793*, 365.

River, the farthest southern branch of whose headwaters rises in Summit Lake, about 54° N., 122° 30′ W. This place is a few miles northward from Fort (now Prince) George, and on the well-known Giscombe Portage route from the Peace to the Fraser River.[142] D. W. Harmon, in his general description of the Northland in his day, says: "Buffaloes are found in great numbers, in all of the plain or prairie countries, on both sides of the Rocky Mountains, as far north as about latitude 56° or 57°. . . ."[143]

Harmon's statement is that of a northern resident, who dwelt for a portion of his time in the very region mentioned above, at Fort McLeod and Stuart Lake;[144] and it will be noted that while he mentions the buffalo range to the northward, he says nothing of the south, where he had never lived. He had to skirt the western side of the Rockies for some distance southward from Peace River Pass and along the Parsnip River to reach those localities. From Giscombe Portage the way to the Pacific (whether via the Fraser or not) lay well to the westward of the main Rocky Mountain range, along which the region southeastward (that is, from Giscombe) to the Yellowhead (or 'Leather' Pass)[145] and thence onward to the Athabaska Pass, was at that time an unknown land to white men, and very probably to Indians also; whose own routes in such extremely rough and broken country usually lay along the river valleys. Even if one were to concede in its fullness the

---

[142]Giscombe, the fourth station east from Prince George, B.C., on the Canadian National route to Prince Rupert, perpetuates the name, and is no great distance from the old portage trail. See Morice, *Northern Interior of British Columbia*, 59, 328; Haworth, *Trailmakers of the Northwest*, 204.

[143]*Harmon's Journal*, 365.

[144]*Ibid.*, 150, *seq.*

[145]So called from leather products being sent that way for the 'New Caledonia' (British Columbia) fur posts. See McLean, *Twenty-Five Years' Service*, (orig. ed.), I, 274; Milton and Cheadle, *North-West Passage*, 183; Bancroft, *Northwest Coast*, II, 530, *Place-Names of Alberta*, 75, 137. Although in the early material the 'Leather Pass' always signifies the Yellowhead, it is difficult to see why that alone got the name, for although so used, 1835, 1836 (Oliver (ed.), *Canadian North-West*, II, 714, 720), yet leather was also sent from Jasper House to Okanagan by way of Columbia Portage, or 'Boat Encampment,' 1830, 1836, etc. (*ibid.*, I, 651; II, 729, 736).

This pass does not appear in the *Report of the Select Committee on the Hudson's Bay Company, 1857*. The veracious John Miles, an officer of the H.B. Company, asked if there were any other pass north of the boundary line save 'Boat Encampment,' answered: "The only one is through the Peace River to the north. I never heard of any other" (*ibid.*, 261). This man had travelled from Jasper to Norway House, via Edmonton, 1852. Cf. A. K. Isbister, *ibid.*, 355-6. It was 'well-known,' so Merk (ed.), *Fur Trade and Empire*, 350; and it was certainly known to the Hudson's Bay Company people at Edmonton 1863; (see Milton and Cheadle, *North-West Passage*, 192).

theory of the buffalo origin of trails in general,[146] the lack of incentive in the buffalo species, which I have elsewhere emphasized,[147] would in my opinion invalidate the application of this theory in areas beyond these northern summits of the higher Rocky Mountain passes. The human invader of these regions, red or white, had definite and obvious incentives—sustenance or gain. Unless we are to suppose a conscious knowledge by the buffalo of its 'mission' as a surveyor of the wilds for the future highway or railway route,[148] it could have had no motive conceivable by gods or men for turning its back on the plains and fertile scrublands, and instead, looking to where the grass grew poorer with every mile. Not only that, the buffalo must attempt to force its way past a certain point along these rocky defiles, sometimes narrowing into mere dingles, almost devoid of pasturage, where a tiny stream runs for much of the way between shelves of solid rock, and where avalanche or fire has blocked the route again and again with an impassable *renversé* of fallen timber![149] This would be a curious commentary on the much-belauded instinct of the buffalo, 'knowing where the best pastures were to be found,' etc.[150] Furthermore, the theory of the buffalo's mountain penetration leads principally in a direction which is utterly irreconcilable with the stringent requirements of the 'north-and-south migration' route as postulated by the self-same champions!

It is rather unfortunate, both for the buffalo highway theory *per se,* and for the invasion of British Columbia by any of the only three passes (from the prairies) as yet traversed by railways, that while in each case the buffalo have entered, and in one at least appear to have actually reached the summit,[151] in no instance of the three is there any record of them passing through to the western side. I have found no record of buffalo having actually been seen in the Yellowhead Pass. The nearest approach to such a record is set forth by Governor Simp-

[146]See above, chap. VI, notes 1-22, on buffalo 'intelligence.'

[147]Roe, "The 'Wild Animal Path' Origin of Ancient Roads" (*Antiquity,* III, September 1929, 299-311).

[148]Scarcely an exaggeration of the thesis of Hulbert (above, chap. VI).

[149]Compare 'Embarras River,' Alberta = 'impassable owing to driftwood' (*Place-Names of Alberta,* 48). *Embarras* and *renversé* = 'fallen in every direction,' are frequent as common nouns in the fur traders' journals. See Milton and Cheadle, on Thompson River, B.C., 1863 (*North-West Passage,* 276).

[150]See above, chap. VI, notes 1-22; also Dr. Rowan's trenchant examination of this supposition, chap. IV, notes 62-7.

[151]Yellowhead Lake, in the pass of that name (the summit), was formerly Cow Dung Lake, or Buffalo Dung Lake. See *Palliser Journals,* 129; Milton and Cheadle, *North-West Passage,* 192, 245; Grant, *Ocean to Ocean,* 278. For 'Cowdung River,' see next note.

son, October 14, 1824 (if this really refers to the Pass itself): "Our route is about due West through defiles in the Mountains; the track for Cranberry [present Moose] Lake takes a northerly direction [actually westerly] by Cow Dung [Miette] River which falls into the Main Stream at Henry's House [modern Jasper]. Our Road was rugged and bad frequently covered with fallen Timber the country having been over run by Fire; it appears well stocked with Animals as we found many tracks of Buffalo & Deer. . . ."[152]

We are not left wholly dependent upon negative inferences such as the silence of travellers. We are told by a savant of unrivalled authority, whose profound knowledge of the region is derived both from scientific investigation and from long familiarity with an immense mass of native lore and tradition, only accessible to such as he, that "The buffalo was never indigenous to the Carrier country, and the Stuart Lake Indians call it by a Cree word. . . . The Sekanais have a native name of their own for the buffalo, which circumstance confirms Mackenzie's account of its being originally found west of the Rockies. He also mentions having seen several inclosures to drive in and capture the larger game. . . ."[153]

Pending further enlightenment, therefore, the presence of buffalo at any historic period[154] on the western side of the Canadian Rockies

[152]Merk (ed.), Fur Trade and Empire, 32. The identifications in square brackets are mine.

[153]Morice, Northern Interior of British Columbia, 38. He cites John Stuart, 'none among the Carriers,' 1815 (ibid., 95). So also, there were 'none in New Caledonia,' circa 1815 (Stuart to Ross Cox, Columbia River, II, 47). The 'Carriers' (Takulli) occupy the Upper Fraser, Upper Skeena, Stuart Lake country; the 'Sekani,' the region of the Upper Peace and tributaries (Handbook of Canadian Indians, 413, 445).

After this, prices around Stuart Lake seem remarkably cheap, circa 1825: best buffalo robes, 5 shillings each; tongues, sixpence each ($1.20 and 12 cents respectively: Morice, Northern Interior of British Columbia, 130). Of course, we require other prices with which to compare these. See Red River prices, 1825-42, below, chap. XIV, note 29.

[154]Dr. Jenness remarks, however, that according to the Tahltan and 'Kaskas' (or Kashas), there were buffalo in their country—'plentiful' among the latter—in pre-European times; so, native tradition (Indians of Canada, 370, 396). The Tahltan dwelt on the Stikine River, whose northern branch rises near Dease Lake, south of Cassiar, about 59° N., 130°W. (Jenness, ibid., 13, 370; Handbook of Canadian Indians, 444); and the Kaskas or Kasha, on the upper Liard and Dease Rivers, north of the Sekani, and near Beaver River, about 60° N., 125° W. According to Father Morice, the former 'McDame Creek' got from the tribes mentioned above its famous (for gold) name of 'Cassiar' ('Kasha'; so Jenness, Indians of Canada, 396; Handbook of Canadian Indians, 236).

But were these truly buffalo? The mere use of an Indian 'loan-word' buffalo name is no proof of B. americanus or B. athabascae (see below on this, Appendix

remains unsubstantiated by evidence for any locality south of 55° N. latitude or thereabouts.

There are a number of historical references to buffalo in the Upper North Saskatchewan country above Edmonton, and also on the Upper Athabaska, and in certain of the intervening localities. In practically all these cases, as we get away from the more open prairie territory, we find less and less indication of the really large numbers. Even such a term as 'numerous' seems to convey merely a sense of a relative improvement on a general sparsity, tending to suggest that a migration over the mountain passes would be neither large in itself nor likely to arise here as a result of excessive demands upon insufficient pasturage resources. I give such references as I have found, approximately in chronological order.

David Thompson noted the presence of buffalo along the upper North Saskatchewan (two cows) in October, 1808, and again in August, 1809, roughly in the same locality, near the headwaters of the 'Saskatchewan' (Howse) Pass.[155] Lower down, 'two days above Edmonton'—a considerable distance when coming downstream—he observed a lone bull, June, 1810, and remarks with satisfaction: "We are now in the land of the Bison [and] we hope no more to be in want of Provisions. . . ."[156] He appears to classify this region roughly from Kootenay Plain (near the junction of Cline River, about 52° 10′ N., 116° 30′ W.) downward. His incidental allusions, however, are only to 'ones' and 'twos,' and this fact may be taken into account in our general speculation on numbers. For he mentions 'two Cow Bisons' once again, somewhere near Cline River between the Saskatchewan and Athabaska headwaters, late in 1810.[157] Alexander Henry the younger, some months later, found buffalo 'numerous,' well above Rocky Mountain House.[158] Both he and Thompson specify the animals

N). This region, however, is fairly close to that aforementioned (above, note 9), as having somewhat recently been occupied by an immigrant host of Wood buffalo, as observed by Brintnell (note 9); which at least indicates a region where buffalo presumably *could* have subsisted. Can it possibly be that we have here some vague tradition of their *aboriginal* appearance in the region, long ages ago? This deserves careful anthropological investigation. See on the possibility of an Indian aboriginal knowledge of the mammoth, *Canadian Historical Review*, XVI, 121; XVIII, 117 (1935, 1937).

[155]Thompson, *Narrative*, ed. Tyrrell, 396, 408; cf. Masson, *Les Bourgeois de la Compagnie du Nord-Ouest*, II, 53.

[156]Thompson, *Narrative*, ed. Tyrrell, 305, 432. On river-speeds upstream and down, see below, note 179.

[157]*Ibid.*, 441.

[158]Coues (ed.), *Henry-Thompson Journals*, II, 639-41, 653-61, 681-97, etc.

in this region as the 'strong wood buffalo,' or 'Bison of the Woods';[159] and in the territory above Rocky Mountain House (and well toward the summit) they were found as late as 1858 or later.[160]

From the time of Thompson and Henry there is a noticeable paucity of travel references relating to the Saskatchewan route. The reason would appear to be that the Hudson's Bay parties—and most visitors travelled under their aegis—had a choice of two routes by using the Athabaska River, the Yellowhead Pass to the upper Fraser, or the 'Columbia' (or 'Athabaska') Pass, by way of 'Boat Encampment,' to the headwaters of the Columbia River. This latter pass had also to be used, or was preferred, by those transmontane voyagers journeying up the upper Saskatchewan, who pursued a devious route from Kootenay Plain to Jasper House, which—by the map at least—must have followed rather closely the recently completed Banff-Jasper highway. This was known as 'Old Cline's Trail,' after Michael Cline, who was in charge of Jasper House intermittently from about 1824 to 1834,[161] and who is said to have broken out this trail on his autumnal provision-hunts. This circumstance again tends to cast doubt on any supposed plenty of buffalo, probably of other game also, in the Jasper House or Yellowhead Pass region in 1830 or thereabouts.[162] There is, of course, the possibility that the increasing traffic along the Athabaska since 1825, when Simpson, after examination of various possible alternatives, made this the 'main line' via Edmonton,[163] may have tended to frighten

[159]Henry, *ibid.*; Thompson, *Narrative*, ed. Tyrrell, 438.

[160]See below, notes 172-4; also note 138, above.

[161]Cline, Clyne, Kline, Klyne, Klein, etc. (*Place-Names of Alberta*, 35). Governor Simpson and Alexander Ross met him at Jasper, 1825 (Merk (ed.), *Fur-Trade and Empire*, 29, 148; Ross, *Fur Hunters*, II, 203); Ermatinger, 1827 ("York Factory Express Journal," 103-5); left there 1833; so Oliver (ed.), *Canadian North-West*, I, 645, 661; II, 693, 694. Cline River, tributary North Saskatchewan River, named after him. 'Cline's Trail,' 1859: Hector, *Palliser Journals*, 112.

[162]Colin Fraser (Jasper, 1839-56: Oliver (ed.), *Canadian North-West*, II, 778, etc.) told Milton and Cheadle that 'when he first went there,' deer and bighorns (buffalo not mentioned) were very plentiful (Milton and Cheadle, *North-West Passage*, 200).

[163]Southwest of Edmonton, the Pembina (tributary of the Athabaska River) and the Saskatchewan run roughly parallel, 7 to 12 miles apart, for some 30 miles. Near Entwistle, the Canadian National Railway crosses the former and the Sturgeon (tributary of the Saskatchewan River) within six miles. Thompson used one of these portages, apparently the former, in 1799; and Donald McKenzie in 1814 (Coues (ed.), *Henry Thompson Journals*, I, 279; II, 566, 761). In 1824, Governor Simpson had the trail from Edmonton to Fort Assiniboine (Athabaska River, 100 miles northwest) widened to make a pack-trail, the 'Fort Assiniboine Portage Trail'; and the two places were made depots for pack-ponies. There are some unflattering descriptions of the route. See Merk (ed.),

the wild creatures back from the main valley. Such factors may partly account for the scantiness of the buffalo references in the period, say, *ante* 1860, when something of the supposed aboriginal degree of plenty should still have prevailed.

One notable exception to the almost universal use of the Athabaska River route was Father De Smet, who reached Edmonton via Rocky Mountain House, after crossing the mountains probably by way of White Man Pass (50° 45′ N., 115° 29′ W., southwest of Calgary; so called after his passage).[164] His remarks, however (Fort Edmonton, 1845-46), might lead us to suppose that buffalo were extinct in virtually the entire western Alberta region at that early date, which of course was not the case for nearly forty years more. He writes: "What I here saw of beavers is applicable to almost all the Hudson territory [*sic*]. When the reindeer, buffalo, and moose abounded, the Crees were their peaceful possessors. These animals have now disappeared. . . ."[165]

This was quite evidently a local and temporary fluctuation, and as such, is corroborated by De Smet's Protestant friend Rundle, whose acquaintance he made at this time. Rundle observes in his *Journal*, at Rocky Mountain House: "Assinaboines starving here. . . . For two or three autumns the Assinaboines have been starving here. . . ."[166]

The foregoing comments by the two missionaries are of much more than mere passing interest, for they furnish unexceptionable contemporary testimony to local conditions in a region which is found, several years later, to have borne a reputation for unfailing abundance at this very time; until the onslaughts of a disastrous epidemic disease exterminated the game, after which the former plenty was never again known. I quote Dr. Hector's account of this (North Saskatchewan River, near the headwaters, September, 1858):

Fur Trade and Empire, 22-9, 38, 69, 150; Ross, *Fur Hunters*, II, 205; Ermatinger, "York Factory Express Journal," 84-6, 93; Kane, *Wanderings of an Artist* (orig. ed.), 363; *Rundle's Journal*, November 18 to 20, December 24 to 28, 1841. See Minutes of Council, Northern Department, H.B. Company, 1830-43, in Oliver (ed.), *Canadian North-West*, I, 646, 661; II, 694, 714, 729, 761.

I journeyed there in September, 1939. Certain unimproved sections of it were sufficiently villainous even then.

[164]De Smet, *Early Western Travels*, XXIX, 234-51; *Place-Names of Alberta*, 134.

[165]De Smet, *Early Western Travels*, XXIX, 250; *Life of De Smet*, II, 533. Yet he noted at Edmonton, New Year, 1846, the '500 buffalo' in the ice-house (see below, Appendix M) with no hint of any foreboding from his hosts that it 'might be the last time,' or the like.

[166]*Rundle's Journal*, October 18, 1845.

Near our camp we found some old buffalo dung, and the Indians told us that not many years ago there were many of these animals along the valley of the North Saskatchewan, within the mountains. Eleven years ago, they say, there were great fires all through the mountains, and in the woods along their eastern base; and after that a disease broke out among all the animals, so that they used to find wapiti [that is, elk], moose, and other deer, as well as buffalo, lying dead in numbers. Before that time there was abundance of game in all parts of the country, but since then there has been great scarcity of animals, and only the best hunters can make sure of killing. I have heard the same description of the sudden change that took place from half-breed hunters in different parts of the country; so there is little doubt that there is some foundation for the accounts given by the Indians. . . .[167]

It will be seen later, in a detailed examination both of contemporary testimony and of comparative data at large, that the theory of epidemic disease among buffalo is untenable; and that the suppositions of an extraordinary profusion of game before this alleged epidemic, and of a pronounced shortage after it within the period indicated by Dr. Hector (that is, 1847-58), have little or no basis in historical fact.[168]

Hector found the buffalo 'far out' at Rocky Mountain House on January, 1858.[169] A year later, in January and February, 1859, Palliser himself noted 'plenty' between Edmonton and that point.[170] I incline to think that the phraseology used by those reporting to Hector, 'far out,' indicates here—as commonly in this foothill territory—'on the plains' to the southeastward, and that this observation may be accepted as referring to the Plains variety. The same, by reason of the route between Edmonton and the 'Mountain fort,'[171] very probably applies to Palliser's reference also. As we have seen, however, with respect to David Thompson and Henry, another allusion at this time from Hector is almost certainly to the Wood buffalo. In August, 1859, Hector observed a fresh buffalo track along the Sifleur River,[172] which rises far above Rocky Mountain House, in about 51° 45′ N., 116° 10′ W., directly north of Lake Louise. Hector does not specify exactly where

[167]Hector in *Palliser Journals*, 111. Yet Hector himself mentions the case of a Stoney hunter at Rocky Mountain House, January, 1858, who in one recent season had killed fifty-seven moose—the most difficult quarry of all! (*ibid.*, 76, 102, 107-8).

[168]Roe, *Canadian Historical Review*, XV, 1-10 (1934); also below, Appendix J, "Buffalo and Disease."

[169]*Palliser Journals*, 74, 75, 79, 202.

[170]*Ibid.*, 117.

[171]This is pretty thoroughly covered in Rundle's journeys between the two points, 1840-48.

[172]Hector in *Palliser Journals*, 149.

on the Sifleur River; but on the same journey, and not very far distant, on one of the numerous 'Pipestone Creeks' of the West,[173] which he gives as being 51° 38′ 5″ N. (and which is approximately 117° W., on the headwaters of the Bow River, east of Howse Pass and north of the Canadian Pacific Railway summit at Stephen), he was told by his guide: ". . . two years ago he killed a buffalo cow at this place, and that he saw at the time a band of seven,—two bulls, four cows, and a calf. They were of the thickwood variety, which are larger and blacker, and with more spreading horns, than those of the prairies. They run swiftly through the woods, and are quite as wary and difficult to hunt as the moose deer. . . ."[174]

This notice is of immense interest, for it is the southernmost instance known to me in the Canadian forest-and-mountain territory in the West of what seems undoubtedly to be the Northern Wood buffalo, conforming in its description to the living animal in the Peace River Northlands. The next emergence to the southward of any variant form from the common Plains type is of the smaller creature[175] which was recognized among hunters from the Montana to the Colorado Rockies as the 'mountain bison' or 'mountain buffalo.' This latter animal is the sole instance I have found of the term *bison* being used on this continent by any but scientific writers.[176]

For reasons already discussed in relation to other remote corners of the Canadian habitat, I have said that I find little ground for associating the headwaters of these prairie streams (with one possible exception, shortly to be dealt with) with any really large numbers of buffalo. The very fragmentary notices of their history along the neighbouring valley of the upper Athabaska, from the summit downward, furnish nothing to contradict that conclusion. We have seen that an experienced early resident at Jasper House deemed it advisable to make a long journey across rough country, apparently in preference to relying upon local food resources. Although I cannot lay claim

[173]Like its French equivalent, 'Pierre au Calumet,' one of the commonest of place-names, signifying where stone for making Indian pipes was to be obtained.

[174]Hector in *Palliser Journals*, 148; cf. below, chap. XVII, note 108.

[175]Hellgate River, near Deer Lodge, Montana (about 46° 30′ N., 113° W.), 1865: Bancroft, *History of Washington, Idaho, and Montana*, 595. Big Horn Mountains, Wyoming, 1877: Dr. R. W. Shufeldt, in Hornaday, "Extermination of the American Bison," 411. It will be remembered that the two killed west of Fort Garry, 1871, are stated to have been 'smaller' than the Plains buffalo (above, note 55). See note at conclusion of chap. III.

[176]See my remarks above, chap. I, note 1. I include David Thompson among these.

to possessing a guide's knowledge of the region, I have seen sufficient of the upper Athabaska Valley at several points to form some idea of the probable wisdom of such a course. I doubt whether any cautious observer would associate such a locality with herds of any material numbers.

Here again our earliest references are from the observant and accurate David Thompson. Between January 1 and January 6, 1811, he notes 'two young bulls,' and where a herd had been feeding, 'four days' from the summit of the Athabaska Pass.[177] Nine months later, October 7, 1811, he mentions 'two Cow Bisons' at a point which almost seems to have been *west* of the summit.[178] If this be correct, it is the only such recorded encounter with the living animal, known to me, at any point in British Columbia south of the Pine River Pass (about 55° N.). A modern historian states that there were buffalo at 'Prairie de la Vache' (given as 'far beyond the Miette' = the present town of Jasper[179]) in 1814.[180] He cites no authority for this, but it is quite probable. For Ross Cox, who mentions that the place derived its name from buffalo having been killed or seen there, speaks of seeing a buffalo well above Roche Miette in June, 1817.[181] Hind included the Athabaska Valley as a portion of the common wintering-ground for the 'great western herds' from the Missouri northward in his day;[182] but it is not certain whether he embraced the upper Athabaska within (or very near) the mountain territory in this designation. In view of the fact that the 'annual itinerary' of his halfbreed informants is demonstrably inaccurate in itself,[183] the point is not of great importance. The younger Henry states that the country of the 'Snares' (Indians), which was apparently along Snaring River, the first tributary of the Athabaska from the west below Jasper;[184] was 'nearly destitute of animals' in

[177]Thompson, *Narrative,* ed. Tyrrell, 444, 445.

[178]*Ibid.,* 538.

[179]About half-way between the mouths of the Miette and Whirlpool Rivers (Ermatinger, "York Factory Express Journal," 81, 109). He was three days going upstream, and one going down. Cf. *Palliser Journals,* 128.

[180]Blue, *Alberta Past and Present,* I, 90.

[181]Cox, *Columbia River,* II, 175, 177, 181. Cox's 'Roche Miette' is not the well-known landmark of today, so familiar to travellers; but the present Roche de Smet.' So, Ermatinger, "York Factory Express Journal," ed. note, 108.

[182]The Athabaska Valley is mentioned in Hind, *Narrative of the Dawson and Hind Expedition,* II, 107-9. This is quoted by Allen, *American Bisons,* 170. Not in the (otherwise identical) passage in Hind, *Report, 1858,* 106.

[183]See below, *in extenso,* chap. XIV, "The Red River Hunt."

[184]*Place-Names of Alberta,* 117. Near Snaring station, Canadian National Railway.

April, 1810.[185] This, together with the noticeable paucity in the numbers actually seen, may be considered a pertinent commentary on 'Cline's trail' and local food resources.

In the intervening territory westward from Edmonton towards the Athabaska, which was once even more heavily wooded than it is now, I have only found one direct eye-witness reference to buffalo. Thompson observed 'two cow Bisons' along the upper Pembina Valley in October, 1810, in a locality probably not far from the two possible portage-routes across to the Saskatchewan waters.[186] There are, however, several place-names which indicate the former presence of buffalo, and the most important of these certainly implies numbers. The lake now known as Chip Lake (that is, 'buffalo chip' = *bois de vache*[187]), eighty miles or so westward from Edmonton and ten miles beyond the Pembina River mentioned above, was Buffalo Dung Lake in 1810,[188] Bull Dung Lake or Buffalo Chip Lake in 1859,[189] and Dirt Lake in 1859 or 1875.[190] There was a Buffalo River near it in 1859,[191] and either in the upper Pembina or upper North Saskatchewan country neighbouring, a Buffalo Rapid in 1811.[192]

To the scientific inquirer, one circumstance must be thought regrettable. Somewhere in their passage up or down the Athabaska or the Saskatchewan, our early voyagers crossed what all our information tends to show was a fairly definite border line between the Plains and Wood buffalo territory, beyond which the Wood buffalo at least never apparently ventured.[193] We have to bear in mind, of course, that in many cases an animal seen on the shore by a voyager on these great rivers would be too far from the centre of the stream for any but an experienced observer to detect such variations; and even to such a man, unless he chanced at the moment to be interested in questions of perceptible differences or geographical limits, a buffalo seen would be 'a buffalo' and nothing more. Two of our very earliest witnesses,

[185]Coues (ed.), *Henry-Thompson Journals*, II, 596.

[186]Thompson, *Narrative*, ed. Tyrrell, 441.

[187]*Place-Names of Alberta*, 33.

[188]Coues (ed.), *Henry-Thompson Journals*, II, 585, 652.

[189]*Palliser Journals*, 130, 182.

[190]Map in Southesk, *Travels* (1859, published 1875).

[191]*Palliser Journals*, 182; perhaps now Lobstick (*i.e.* 'lop-stick,' a lopped or topped tree) River, flowing from Chip Lake to the Pembina (*Place-Names of Alberta*, 78). Chip Lake often 'Lobstick Lake,' *circa* 1897, though seldom heard now.

[192]Coues (ed.), *Henry-Thompson Journals*, II, 683.

[193]See above, note 100.

Franchère (1814) and Ross Cox (1817), had never yet seen the Plains buffalo, having journeyed to Astoria by sea, so that specific definition could not be expected from them. I am informed that large masses of buffalo bones were (and perhaps still are) to be seen up the McLeod River, on Lambert Creek, near Weald, on the Coal Branch of the Canadian National system; and also lower down, some ten miles above the confluence with the Athabaska at Whitecourt, Alberta.[194] Of what species these may be I am ignorant, as they have not (to my knowledge) been examined by competent zoologists. The lines of geographical demarcation would nowhere be uniformly drawn, but with respect to this more southerly section of the Wood buffalo territory, if the Whitecourt locality (say 54° 10′ N., 115° 40′ W.) be considered too far east for Wood buffalo, we may recall that Henry in May, 1811, noted their presence about the head of Wolf Creek (modern Blindman River, Alberta), which lies forty miles or so farther eastward (about 114° 30′ W., 52° 45′ N.),[195] near Hoadley, Alberta. This is less than forty miles west of a direct line between Calgary and Edmonton, and would on general principles doubtless be classed unhesitatingly in the Prairie buffalo territory.

The concluding section of the Canadian habitat to be considered, north and west of the lower Athabaska and from the Peace River prairies up to their extreme northern limit, appears in some localities at least to have been occupied by considerable numbers. The author of the *General History of the Fur Trade* (*circa* 1789) would restrict the northern limit of the animals to a region 'still farther south' than latitude 60° N. in the Chipewyan country, but adds. "That animal is well known to frequent an higher latitude to the Westward of their country. . . ."[196] We have already seen good reason for maintaining that along the main route northward by the Slave and Mackenzie Rivers the buffalo were found well to the northward of latitude 60° N., even apart from the country 'to the westward.'

In the country about the present Fort Smith, which is on the 60th parallel, Philip Turnor in 1791 described the buffalo on his map as 'plenty'; although in his journal they are merely occasional.[197] They were killed by his party from 60° 35′ N., to 61° 11′ ('a good part for Buffalo'[198]), and he was 'informed' that they were to be found at least

[194]*Ex inf.* H. Powers, Esq., Edmonton (1937).
[195]See above, chap. III, notes 102-3.
[196]Mackenzie, *Voyages 1789 and 1793*, cxxi.
[197]*Hearne and Turnor Journals*, ed. Tyrrell, map; also, 410.
[198]*Ibid.*, 410, 412.

as far as 61° 22′ N.[199] They were found even farther north at an earlier date. Along Slave River, which flows northwestward from about 59° N. to 61° N., Mackenzie writes in 1789: "The Indians informed me that at a very small distance from either bank of the river, are very extensive plains, frequented by large herds of buffaloes. . . ."[200] In his famous voyage down the great river that bears his name, Mackenzie noted a tributary joining the larger stream from the northward and having its rise in the Horn Mountains, about latitude 63° N. His Indian guide informed him that "there are very extensive plains on both sides of it, which abound in buffaloes and moose deer. . . ."[201] On his return journey some months later, at a point near the confluence, about 61° 35′ N., he notes: "The fresh tracks and beds of buffalo were very perceptible. Near this place a river flowed in from the Horn Mountains, which are at no great distance. . . . The English chief [an Indian guide] arrived with the tongue of a cow, or female buffalo, while four men and the Indians were dispatched for the flesh. . . ."[202]

The Horn Mountains are also stated by Richardson to have been the northern limit of the buffalo in 1848.[203] This puts their range nearly 150 miles beyond what he—without doubt the zoological observer on the earlier occasions—defined as the boundary, Slave Point, in 1821.[204] Actually they were encountered by Turnor's party *in propriae personae* (which does not appear to have been the case with Richardson or Franklin in 1821 at the point they mention[205]) fully as far north, or farther, in 1791-92. Peter Fidler records that in autumn, 1791, "they was a little to the Westward of the [Great] Slave Lake in fine plains full of Buffalo."[206] He also mentions herds along 'Buffalo River,' 1791-92,[207] which is presumably the Buffalo River that enters Great Slave Lake about 61° N., 115° W. He later notes them 'very few,'

[199]*Ibid.*, 414.

[200]Mackenzie, *Voyages 1789 and 1793*, 8; possibly a summer absence (see Soper, "History of the Northern Bison," 361).

[201]Mackenzie, *Voyages 1789 and 1793*, 23.

[202]*Ibid.*, 103, 108. Discrepancies of this character between the *General History of the Fur Trade* and the *Voyages* (as above, note 196) make one wonder whether the former is really Mackenzie's own or by another hand; in either case perhaps written long before, and inserted without further revision.

[203]Richardson, *Arctic Expedition, 1847-1850*, 111.

[204]Franklin, (First) *Journey to the Polar Sea*, 668 (*in extenso* above, note 9).

[205]Cf. the (First) *Journey to the Polar Sea*, at this time. A single buffalo, south of Slave Lake, was hailed as 'a valuable prize' (p. 197).

[206]*Hearne and Turnor Journals,* ed. Tyrrell; Turnor, 447, 448, 452; also Fidler's "Journal," *ibid.*, 500.

[207]*Ibid.*, 502-8.

about 61° 4′ N.[208]; and in January, 1792, he describes the locality where he then was: "Several fine plains of Grass land & no woods a fine place for the Buffalo . . . ," but apparently only 'ones' and 'twos' were seen. [209] Since the men on the ground might not have been conversant in 1821 with the data of Mackenzie or Turnor, the limit then given to Franklin's party may represent the ultimate point where buffalo had actually been seen by the guides of the expedition or its hosts at the various northern fur posts.

On his second great journey of exploration, Mackenzie observed 'extensive herds' along the Peace River prairie belts, if these references really mean anything more than that buffalo were seen from the canoes along the brink of a river whose banks are estimated in various localities to be from 300 to 800 feet in height.[210] For it seems unlikely that the distinction he specifies below, doubtless true enough in itself, could have been ascertained from direct observation on a hurried trip up a river-gorge, and it probably represents general experience or opinion. On the upper Peace River, May, 1793, he noted ". . . vast herds of elks and buffaloes; the former choosing the steeps and uplands and the latter preferring the plains. At this time the buffalo were attended with their young ones, who were frisking about them . . ."[211]

On his return journey from the Pacific, along the lower stretches of Peace River, his party saw a single animal, August 20, 1793. This was followed, two days later, by 'abundance,' although he says, ". . . as we neared the Fort [Chipewyan] the cattle appeared proportionately to diminish. . . ."[212] D. W. Harmon's description of the Peace River prairies (circa 1807-10) agrees with that of Mackenzie: "Through the whole course, from this fall, nearly to the Rocky Mountains, at a little distance from the river, on each side, there are plains of considerable extent, which afford pasture for numerous herds of the buffalo . . . ."[213]

He also records a scantiness, apparently similar to that reported by Mackenzie in the vicinity of Fort Chipewyan,[214] which is not at all surprising in view of the inevitably greater local strain upon the

[208]Ibid., 526, 530, 535, 538.

[209]Ibid., 540-52. Similarly, Turnor's map, and 410 (above, note 197).

[210]Macoun and Charles Horetzky, C.E.; in Sandford Fleming, Explorations and Surveys for a Canadian Pacific Railway (up to January 1, 1874), 70-7, cf. ibid., 38, 46. See also Hugh M. Raup, Phytogeographic Studies in the Peace and Upper Liard River Regions, 8-10, 25, 34-42, etc.

[211]Mackenzie, Voyages 1789 and 1793, 148; cf. ibid., 118, 123, 155-8, 377.

[212]Ibid., 375, 377, 378.

[213]Harmon's Journal, 141; cf. ibid., 153, 156, 226, 285.

[214]Ibid., 138.

buffalo resources there. It is revealed also in Simpson's references to buffalo, written at the contiguous Fort Wedderburn, in the winter of 1820-21. In his report to the chiefs of the Company, covering that period, Simpson is somewhat indefinite. Buffalo 'are not now so close as formerly, rarely within six or eight days'; but 'generally plentiful within a few days' march.'[215] Yet in that winter, when the afore-mentioned scarcity occured, which led Simpson to recommend strongly that more attention be paid to garden produce after the manner of the rival North West Company, for the subsistence of the posts,[216] he records buffalo being slain 'six days' distant, December, 1820; 'three days,' January, 1821; 'about three days,' February, 1821; about four days,' and 'not far away,' in March, 1821.[217] Franklin observes that during the same winter they were 'at some distance' from Fort Chip-ewyan;[218] but mentions that 'numerous tracks' were seen near the place on Christmas Day, 1820. [219] This fact, which was doubtless unknown to Simpson, illustrates the hostile relations which existed between the two *châteaux malvoisin*, to which his *Journal* bears such frequent testimony. It seems probable that Richardson considered the current scarcity to be one of those erratic fluctuations of buffalo move-ment of which their history presents abundant evidence, if we may judge from his later pronouncements.[220] Simpson (probably also basing his decision upon more experienced local information) apparently thought the same. For he desired the Indians at Fort Wedderburn and Berens House to 'devote themselves wholly to buffalo hunting' during the summer of 1821.[221]

The general statements of Mackenzie and Harmon concerning the Peace River territory are borne out by in some detail by evidence (contemporary with the latter) concerning Dunvegan and its vicinity. Clearly the 'cows' mentioned by Simon Fraser, apparently above that point in 1806, can only have been buffalo,[222] and they would seem to have been fairly plentiful. For Fraser's "Dunvegan Journal" (April 18 to October 14, 1806) has '42 bags of pemmican made' (that is about 3800 pounds), May 2; 'some hundreds of pounds of meat'

[215]*Simpson's Athabaska Journal*, ed. Rich, 355, 360, 380.
[216]*Ibid.*, 27, 263, 280, 364, 373, 379, 380.
[217]*Ibid.*, 178, 212, 271, 288, 290.
[218]Franklin, (First) *Journey to the Polar Sea*, 154.
[219]*Ibid.*, 280.
[220]Richardson, *ibid.*, 514 (*in extenso* above, note 105).
[221]*Simpson's Athabaska Journal*, ed. Rich, 302, 306, 312.
[222]Fraser, "First Journal," April 14, 1806; in *Report of Canadian Archives*, 1929, 109-59.

brought there by squaws of the Flux (?) tribe, July 14; buffalo at Dunvegan, August 23; 'meat again brought in by Indians,' September 7, 1806.[223] Lower down, at Fort St. Mary's, near the junction of the Smoky River with the Peace (later Peace River Landing, now the town of Peace River[224]), Simpson stated (1820) that "the adjacent woods and plains abound with buffalo and deer."[225] Colville House (near the Loon River confluence, and apparently the later Fort Vermilion) had 'Buffalo very numerous in the neighbourhood.'[226] The Fort Liard country, southwestward from Fort Simpson and the Horn Mountains (about 61° N., 124° W.) was 'well stocked,' having 'a considerable number' of buffalo.[227] Buffalo were also noted along the Smoky River in 1826;[228] and in the roughly rectangular territory formed by the lower Smoky and Peace rivers, the lower Athabaska, and the fifty-fifth parallel, there are a number of 'buffalo' place-names, which suggest their prevalence here at an earlier period.[229]

Dr. Hector wrote concerning the buffalo range in 1858: "Until a few years ago, these prairies supported large bands of buffalo and elk . . . . When we compare the descriptions given by Sir Alexander Mackenzie of the prairie country along Peace River, with its vast herds of buffalo and elks, when he passed in 1793, with the present northern limit of the large herds of these animals, at least three degrees of latitude further south, the change is very striking; and still more so if it is true, as the Indians say, that the disappearance

[223]J. N. Wallace, The Wintering Partners on Peace River, 123-33.
[224]Place-Names of Alberta, 100.
[225]Simpson's Athabaska Journal, ed. Rich, 364.
[226]Ibid., 383, 384.
[227]Ibid., 387, 394.
[228]Franklin, Second Journey to the Polar Sea, 311.
[229]I find the Buffalo Hills ('one day' south of Peace River; so Butler, Wild North Land, 167, 168, 172) probably the same as the Buffalo Head Hills (so Place-Names of Alberta, 26, and map). There is also a Buffalo River flowing northwest from these, whether Back's 'Buffalo River' of 1820 or not (Franklin, (First) Journey to the Polar Sea, 284), I am unaware. This rises in or near Buffalo (elsewhere Bison) Lake (57° 10′ N., 116° W.). There is also a Buffalo Lake River flowing north into Great Slave Lake, about 114° 30′ W. Wood Buffalo River, flowing into Loon River, rises 56° 30′ N., 113° W. near the eastward sweep of the Athabaska toward Fort McMurray. There is also Mustus Lake (mustus = buffalo, in Cree) south of Peace River, 58° 6′ N., 116° 25′ W., and quite probably there are others. I have also found an allusion to a Buffalo Bay Lake, apparently in the Lesser Slave Lake area (Edmonton Journal, April 22, 1938). If this name actually owes its origin to the historic buffalo, it would indicate their former presence in a locality which has furnished no other evidence of any kind. Harmon mentions that the Beaver Indians were "formerly clothed with the skins of buffalo . . ." (Journal, 149); and Jenness has noted the ancient use of 'buffalo pounds' among them (Indians of Canada, 383), both implying fairly large numbers, I judge.

of the large quantities of game has only taken place within the last twenty years . . . ."[230]

This question of supposed limits in various eras is one of much obscurity. Even with an observer as cautious and reliable as Hector, the entirely natural tendency in one who was not here long enough to amass the necessary comparative data for himself—or as much of it as was then available—to believe the local accounts given by native residents 'who ought to know,' more than once misled him. Added to this was the fact that practically throughout the nineteenth century, apart perhaps from a very few specialists, the scientific belief reigned unchallenged that the buffalo were absolutely indigenous to the North American continent; that the plains animal, *Bison americanus*, was the parent form among the various historic types known or believed to exist;[231] and that any questions of 'advance' or of geographical limits must necessarily be discussed from the standpoint of an originating 'type-locality' in some southern-central area.[232] Under such conditions of belief, many conclusions were confidently or mournfully pronounced which today are little more than historical landmarks in the records of opinion concerning the buffalo. What may be termed the geographical history of this particular portion of the Canadian habitat is yet more confused by reason of it being the frontier line—the 'march'—along which Prairie and Wood buffalo territory met.

It is difficult to offer anything except a hypothetical suggestion concerning the precise boundaries, or the actual routes by which either species may have reached those limits from their 'starting point.' Hector's instance is a case in point. We do not positively know whether his stated limit of 1858 represented a northern advance of true Plains buffalo; or a southern penetration of the Northern Wood buffalo from their aboriginal range. This uncertainty is increased by the loose phraseology often employed, not only by men on the ground who commonly lacked scientific training and whose familiarity bred carelessness, but also by men of education, like Butler. When he says, for example, that in 1873 'buffalo' were scarce along the southern shores of Lake Athabaska,[233] while 'wood buffalo' were numerous on the northwestern and southwestern shores of the same

[230]Hector in *Palliser Journals*, 126.

[231]See on this, Allen, *American Bisons*, 129-30; Hornaday, "Extermination of the American Bison," 377, 382 (both citing Berlandier MS., 1830, now lost); Chittenden, *American Fur Trade*, II, 758.

[232]Seton gives this as Mexico, following Linnaeus, 1758 (*Game Animals*, III, 641, 643); see also Skinner and Kaisen, *Fossil Bison of Alaska*, 161.

[233]Butler, *Wild North Land*, 142.

lake,[234] it would be vain to attempt any conclusions from these statements without further information.

For our present purpose, although I repeat that we do not actually know, the probabilities are overwhelmingly in favour of Hector's 'three degrees' of supposed shrinkage, 1793-1858, constituting a southbound push rather than a northbound retreat. Not only have we the archaeological, osteological, and historical evidence cited already in relation both to varieties[235] and to snow as possibly a prime cause of extinction;[236] but the critic dissenting from those implications will have to face some strong historical objections in relation to the intermediate territory farther south. Hector's reduction of three degrees 'within the last twenty years' (that is, *circa* 1838) from the penetration-limit of a supposed northbound movement, logically necessitates a more or less unbroken occupation of the territory to the rear of the buffalo 'march,' southward to the true buffalo plains area. Almost within the very period, and certainly near enough to be in close touch with its traditions, Rundle was making his missionary journeys betwen Fort Edmonton and Lesser Slave Lake Post, and as far north as Utikuma (= Whitefish[237]) Lake, nearly 56° N., 115° 30′ W. (1840-48). Starvation, or its imminent approach, was an almost uniform experience toward the close of winter in those localities. Amid all their hopes or fears concerning the prospects of moose, deer, elk, etc., there is not the faintest allusion to buffalo—even in the past tense; neither from Rundle's host, George McDougall (who was clerk-in-charge at the post, 1831-46[238]), nor from anyone else. Nor is there any encounter with buffalo, nor implied expectation or even reminiscence of such, at any point on the journeys to or from Edmonton. The only reference I have noted to buffalo north of Edmonton about that time is from Paul Kane, who saw a small band on the Sturgeon River—a famous buffalo haunt of yore, lower down—about ten miles northwestward from Edmonton, in October, 1846.[239]

[234]*Ibid.*, 139.

[235]See above, chap. III, notes 91-103.

[236]See above, chap. VIII, at large.

[237]Poisson blanc = *attikamek:* Lacombe, *Dictionnaire de la Langue des Cris*, 225, 318. Commonly in the fur-trade, *tickameg* (as in *Hearne and Turnor Journals*, ed. Tyrrell, 37, 319-23, 359, 454, 480); *tittemeg* (*ibid.*, 128); or *tittameg* (*ibid.*, 178; Ross, *Fur Hunters*, II, 202, etc.). For the lake, *Place-Names of Alberta*, 128 and map.

[238]See W. S. Wallace (ed.), *Documents Relating to the North West Company*, "Biographical Dictionary," 467; also *Simpson's Athabaska Journal*, ed. Rich, 274, 390. See above, however, note 229.

[239]Kane, *Wanderings of an Artist* (Radisson Society ed.), 97.

Two considerations incline me to doubt whether, in historic times at least, the two buffalo frontiers north of the Saskatchewan ever abutted closely one upon another. If the official reports of the amicable relations existing between the 'cousins' in the Northern Wood Buffalo Park are actually correct—which there seemed at one time some reason to doubt[240]—then surely two species (or varieties) which could so quickly 'make a match of it' in an artificial liberty would long since have done so in their aboriginal freedom. The inevitable result would have been the production in these border regions of an intermediate cross-bred or hybrid type, combining in various details the general appearance of either parent. If it were genetically possible for the progeny of one pair to reproduce exclusively the appearance of the sire (or the dam) in all cases, even that could scarcely apply to buffalo, a gregarious species whose breeding habits were apparently— and by the 'law of battle' almost necessarily—promiscuous. Still less could mentality be made to conform to a definite order in such a manner, so that the 'pro-prairie' youngster might be relied upon to make for the prairies, while the 'pro-forest' creature remained in the deep woods. Even without postulating such an ultra-uniformity, the appearance of the prairie-like animal in the woods in winter might arouse little comment; but the spectacle of his almost-woodland cousin or brother in the open would certainly have called forth excited notice in a land where all agreed that the Wood buffalo shunned the open country.[241] This ere long would have had its almost inevitable repercussion in some written form. For it must be remembered that the very frontier regions where alone such phenomena would probably be found are the same ones which are most intimately described (and by residents) in our early historical source material. I cannot, of course, pretend to have exhausted this; but in much reading I have nowhere found the slightest hint that any one of those old plainsmen or traders felt the least vestige of doubt concerning the racial identity of the particular buffalo or buffaloes upon which he was gazing. It has been claimed by some that such a radical or specific fusion has occurred in the past in the territory adjacent to the (present) Wood Buffalo Park area, but as I have said, no his-

[240]It is known that when one consignment of Plains buffalo from Wainwright Park encountered one of the local (aboriginal) herds of Wood buffalo for the first time, they swam the Peace River in panic, and made off southward. An additional large area was added to the Buffalo Park to permit them to remain there undisturbed. This, I understand, is the local version (ex inf. Professor William Rowan to the writer). Cf. Seton's account, Game Animals, III, 661.

[241]See above, note 100.

torical reference appears to exist in regard to anything of the kind in the free aboriginal times of the two species, and there are other weighty reasons against it.[242]

The second consideration is this: Although the general winter trend of the herds in the Saskatchewan territory was northward, the existing visible evidence of trails in the Edmonton district offers no encouragement to any supposition of a great winter movement *en masse* (or summer one either) beyond the height of land separating the Saskatchewan drainage basin from that of the Athabaska, at the farthest. There has been an abundance of fine writing on 'buffalo routes' and lines of least resistance. A glance at any map will show that along north-and-south river-valley routes into the Athabaska country there is one spot *par excellence*. Athabaska (Landing) is about ninety miles north of Edmonton. It is the southern apex of a huge double triangular zigzag in the river's course, extending from well above the junction of the Pembina in the west, to the great northward sweep from Athabaska Landing to Fort McMurray and Lake Athabaska on the east. The natural routes from Lesser Slave Lake and the Smoky River country on the northwest, and from the Lower Athabaska territory to the north and northeast, converge directly—the first downstream, the second upstream—on Athabaska Landing. At that precise spot also, Tawatinaw River (or Creek[243]) debouches into the great stream from the south. The distance from the height of land at Legal, Alberta, to the Athabaska River is about sixty miles, following the windings of the creek, almost directly northward. The entire distance furnishes a remarkably easy grade for the railway which runs along the valley floor.[244] For buffalo there are shelter, water, and a manifest abundance of rich pasturage along the slopes and flats of the valley—the latter probably at all seasons—as well as on the plateau (or 'bench') above. Here surely, if anywhere, one of the larger multi-paralleled, 'main line,' north-and-south migration-trails into the Northland should be found.[245] Although the valley floor is not so closely cultivated as to preclude their presence being still

---

[242]See above, chap. III, note 100; also Appendix J, "Buffalo and Disease." The latest investigator, J. Dewey Soper, 1932-34, finds it "difficult to imagine how this conception originated, as there appears to be nothing to support it . . ." ("History of the Northern Bison," 358).

[243]'River' on maps; 'the creek' (more fittingly) to local residents.

[244]At Nestow, mile-post 55 from Edmonton, the railway head of the creek-valley proper = 2083 feet; Athabaska station-platform, mile-post 96.7 = 1690 feet; a fall of 393 feet in 41.7 miles = a fraction under 9½ feet per mile (396 feet): White (ed.), *Altitudes in Canada* (National Geographic Board), 279.

visible, I have discovered no indication of such trails. The occasional paths descending from the 'bench' above are merely single ones, and there are few enough of them. They present a readily noticeable contrast to the multitudes that 'gridiron' the hillsides along the Saskatchewan, Battle, or lower Sturgeon rivers, or even the central Pembina, west of Lac Ste Anne; and quite probably an equal contrast to those which Dr. G. M. Dawson found in 1879 'scoring and rutting' the Peace River prairies.[246] I can see no real indication that this was ever a 'buffalo-migration thoroughfare.'

It is fortunate that questions of extinction in the northern territory do not arise, since the buffalo as a free wild species have not been exterminated. For it would be found no easy task to reach conclusions purely from the literary evidence. A short specimen of this will suffice. Butler, wriitng in 1873, says 'the last buffalo north of Peace River' was killed at a place called 'Chimeroo's Prairie,' in 1870.[247] Yet in the same work he also writes: "The range of the Wood buffalo is much farther north than is generally believed. There are scattered herds even now on the banks of the Liard River as far as sixty-one degres of north latitude . . . ."[248] Even had they been extirpated later in this northern country evidence already cited shows that 1870 would be a much too early date.[249]

Note on Henry Kelsey

The publication of the *Kelsey Papers* (ed. A. G. Doughty and Chester Martin) has relegated much controversy to oblivion, as the editors observe (introd., xi). For the present essay, they have rendered needless a note I had prepared discussing the bearing of Kelsey's journey of 1691 upon the actual delimitation of the northeastern corner of the Canadian buffalo habitat. Kelsey's journey supposedly began at Hudson Bay, according to the earlier writers. Had this belief proved to be correct, the Canadian buffalo range must either have been pushed back farther toward the northeast than our other

[245]I am hesitant concerning unsupported Indian tradition, after some examination of such; but according to Mackenzie's informants in 1793, the buffalo made their appearance in the upper Peace River from the *east*: (Mackenzie, *Voyages 1789 and 1793*, 143; cf. *ibid.*, 365). In any case, the statement is too vague to convey any real information.

[246]Dawson, in Macoun, *Manitoba*, 125; cf. Macoun, *ibid.*, 342.

[247]Butler, *Wild North Land*, 228; Macoun, *Manitoba*, 342; Hornaday, "Extermination of the American Bison," 524.

[248]Butler, *Wild North Land*, 211.

[249]See above, chap. III, notes 62, 112-17, etc.; chap. VIII, notes 35-43.

information would seem to warrant, or Kelsey's mileages—and with them much of his topography—must have been abandoned.

The journey of 1691, however, starts from Deering's (or Dering's) Point. The actual situation of this place is perhaps not satisfactorily settled. The suggested sites range from Cedar Lake to The Pas, and the editors of the *Kelsey Papers* show that none of them entirely meets the required conditions (pp. xxxviii-xxxix). A later scholar identifies the place as "the sharp bend of the [Saskatchewan] river twelve miles below the Pas . . ." (Morton, *History of the Canadian West*, 111; see also Innis, *Fur Trade in Canada*, 125). In so far as my own case is concerned, however, taking as my datum any point within the limits mentioned, the mileages as given by Kelsey present no problem whatever, as they all fall easily enough within the bounds of what is well established on other authority as the Canadian buffalo habitat in historic times.

It is extremely mortifying not to be able positively to identify the locality where Kelsey saw the real buffalo, since he was most probably the first European observer in the Canadian North-West. Dr. J. B. Tyrrell apparently believes that this has successfully been done, and that Professor W. H. Holmes's interpretation of the Indians —the *Naywatamee poets*—as the Mandans, is established. He also considers that the country can be recognized beyond doubt as "somewhere near the banks of the Assiniboine or South Saskatchewan Rivers . . ." (Hearne, *Journey,* ed. Tyrrell, introd. 12). Seeing that this territory constitutes a huge irregular triangle, whose apex would be about Prince Albert, Saskatchewan, while its extreme base-line points would be at Winnipeg and at Banff, Alberta (some 900 miles apart) the statement involves little danger of contradiction. I cannot pretend to rival Professor Holmes or Dr. Tyrrell on the various probabilities derivable from distinctive Indian tribal details, which might tend to assist identification; Of the lack of this kind of data, as factors in their decision, a critic may quite justly complain. (Innis, *Fur Trade in Canada*, 125). But before the argument reaches that particular stage, are there any sufficient grounds for associating the Mandans with the territory indicated?

Less than fifty years after Kelsey (1738), La Vérendrye found the Mandans—to all appearance well-established—in the upper or central Missouri River territory; and this they still occupied when the various nineteenth-century travellers visited them, from Lewis and Clark onward. Apparently at all times they were a semi-sedentary and rather timid people, apprehensive of powerful enemies around them. And if their own traditions are credible, they came from a region between the Mississippi-Red River headwaters and the Great Lakes (Thompson, *Narrative*, ed. Tyrrell, 230). The 'Mandan Trail' in Southern Manitoba (see Bryce, *Remarkable History*, 324) has been brought forward to prove that they were travellers. The history and laws of nomenclature rebut this. This is the trail *to*—not *of* or *by*—the Mandans. One might as well classify the trails so called as having been made by the Santa Fés, the Oregons, the Jaspers, or the Fort Assiniboines. As to the possibility of recognizing a particular locality in a territory described as vaguely as this, with its woods and more woods and open land between, in a region whose general topographical characteristics are its continual repetition and monotonous sameness— and probably burnt over again and again in the two centuries from Kelsey to Tyrrell—I am utterly sceptical. (See editorial remarks, *Journal of Henry Kelsey*, ed. Bell, 27.)

The reference to the buffalo ". . . not like those to the northward, their horns growing like an English Ox, but black and short . . ." (*Kelsey Papers*, 13) may bear two possible interpretations. They might be actual Plains buffalo in the country south of the Saskatchewan River, 'not like' the (Wood) buffalo to the north, which Kelsey might possibly have seen, not so very far from Dering's Point. Or, they might themselves be Wood buffalo, not like those (supposed) buffalo to the north, that is, the musk-oxen he had already termed 'buffalo' in 1689 (*Kelsey Papers*, xix, 27-9; *Journal of Henry Kelsey*, ed. Bell, 36). It may be noted also that Kelsey's description in his "Rhymed Introduction," "a black, a Buffillo great . . ." (*Kelsey Papers*, 3), as well as his rather precise account of the horns, 'short and black,' etc., corresponds to a considerable extent with Hearne's account of the huge Wood buffalo (Hearne, *Journey*, 255). We do well, none the less, to remember, in relation to the 'huge,' 'prodigious,' 'enormous' buffalo of various observers, that in the days of Kelsey, Hearne, Cresswell, etc., the great modern domestic beef breeds had not been developed. Any attempt to fix the point at which Kelsey saw buffalo in 1691 must be based upon either Dr. Bell or the editors of the *Kelsey Papers*. The former attempts precise localization; the latter (in my view more judiciously) do not. Even if we concede Dr. Bell's identification in all particulars, the result, "somewhere in the Touchwood Hills" (*Journal of Henry Kelsey*, 30-5), is disappointingly vague and inconclusive.

There is one final point of interest. Is it absolutely certain that either August 10 (*Hudson's Bay Company's Annual Calendar*, 1928), or August 18, 1691 (Burpee, *Search for the Western Sea*, 109), is actually the date when Kelsey saw the true Plains buffalo for the first time? When we consider that he was, almost beyond reasonable doubt, the first of native English speech to see not only the buffalo, but also, probably, the grizzly bear (though Burpee doubts it being a grizzly: *ibid.*, 103), his description of the former, apart from its horns (August 20, 1691), is astonishingly casual, as compared with his endeavours to make the other—presumably—equally unknown monster intelligible to his readers or (probably critical) superiors at Hudson Bay. During practically the whole time, from abandoning his canoes and "setting forward into the woods" on July 19, 1691, probably along the Saskatchewan or Carrot River, he was within what has already been shown to be, down to later eras, a portion of the Canadian buffalo range.

On the journey overland, from July 19 onward, there are occasional allusions to 'beasts.' There are 'two' on July 20; 'five' on July 26; 'one' on July 29; and 'a great store of Beast' on August 10, the same term which he uses for the 'Buffilo' on August 19, and again also on August 23 (*Kelsey Papers*, 6-13). Dr. Bell, upon what authority I know not, writes: ". . . the many 'beasts' he records as being killed by the party being red deer (when he killed a moose he named it as such) . . ." (*Journal of Henry Kelsey*, 24). An example of this is 'Buck Muse,' July 24, yet he also termed this a 'Beast' (*Kelsey Papers*, 7, 8). Why a man who knew and used the foreign (that is, Indian) term for a non-English species of deer could not use the familiar English name of 'deer' for another species indistinguishable from those familiar in his native land,[250] is not apparent. One of these 'Beasts,' moreover, was adequate to 'suffice' a starving troop; a circumstance which alone makes 'red deer' a highly improbable interpretation. On another occasion, there was 'great store of Beast'; Kelsey camping 'where they lay thickest' (August 10: *ibid.*, 11). This points either to an unrecorded 'surround' of deer, such as that of 'Buffillo' on August 23, which he carefully describes (*ibid.*, 13); or to the possibility of these 'Beasts' themselves being buffalo, from July 20 onward.

Now it may be pointed out that in England *beast* was—and probably still is, for I heard it commonly so used in my boyhood days there—not merely a synonym for 'animal,' as it is in literary and

[250]Much more familiar than today. See Macaulay's *History of England*, chap. III, 'State of England in 1685.' For the general resemblance to English deer, cf. Captain John Smith, Virginia, 1607, ". . . deare, nothing differing from ours . . ." (*Purchas his Pilgrimes*, XVIII, 433).

everyday usage wherever English is spoken; but also, in farmer's or butcher's colloquial terminology the established 'professional' or technical phrase both for the living beef-animal 'on the hoof,' and also for the dressed carcass. It is applied to beef cattle only, and never to sheep or pigs. It is at least possible that this may have been the sense in which it was used by Kelsey;[251] and that it therefore indicates buffalo. If this were the case, his discovery might be dated accord ingly.

A later scholarly critic, now deceased, Rev. J. W. Whillans, writing with forty years' close acquaintance with the territory, believes Kelsey's first encounter with the buffalo occurred after crossing the South Saskatchewan, and somewhere in the long peninsula between the two branches, between Clark's Crossing on the Fort Garry and Edmonton Trail (*circa* 52° 30′ N.) and the Forks near Prince Albert. I am informed that Mr. Whillans' identification of the river topography from Kelsey's description is endorsed by competent local topographers of the University of Saskatchewan, whose headquarters at Saskatoon are in the near locality. I am indebted for these details to Mr. Whillans himself (1952).

[251]Henry Hawks, 1572, ". . . Beasts or Kine"; Thomas Morton, **1637**, ". . . Beasts of the bignesse of a Cowe . . ." (in Allen, *American Bisons*, 107; *in extenso* above, chap. IX, notes 26, 50, 69-70. Matthew Cocking, Saskatchewan or Battle River, January 22, 1773; "the beast pound . . ." ("Cocking's Journal," ed. Burpee, 113). Also applied to buffalo, Georgia, 1739 (above, chapter X, note 109).

The term is apparently confined to *large* animals, some of which were probably buffalo (as Ingram, 1569: above, chap. IX, note 58); while others probably or certainly were not (Antony Parckhurst, Newfoundland, 1578: above, chapter IX, note 61; also a moose, 'a beast as big-bodied as an Oxe'; New England, *circa* 1607-22, above, chap. IX, note 50).

CHAPTER XIII

THE NUMBERS OF THE BUFFALO:
GENERAL REFERENCES FROM THE EARLIEST TIMES

THE topic of the present chapter constitutes a very important phase of buffalo history. It cannot be treated, with even approximately satisfactory results, except at some length. For this reason I shall, in this chapter, confine myself to such general historical references to numbers as I have been able to collect; a later chapter will consist of such data (with comment thereupon) as have been compiled by various authorities concerning the possible total aggregate existent on this North American continent at different times. Some of the existent statistics, together with estimated figures based in most instances upon very careful and commonly conservative calculations, may serve to check—more frequently to corroborate—the purely conjectural computations which are all that we can obtain (or indeed expect) from most observers.

Ernest Thompson Seton complains: "The early explorers who describe the buffalo bands do not give us anything more explicit than superlative expressions, such as 'countless herds,' 'incredible numbers,' 'teeming myriads,' 'the world one robe,' etc. . . ."[1] This is scarcely just, as we shall see; nevertheless the student must be thankful for this misconception on Seton's part, since it led him to attempt a general estimate of his own, which is of high value. Nor can we really feel surprised that superlative expressions are about all that many of our witnesses yield; in most instances they were not trained or scientifically minded observers nor did they often possess any exact criteria upon which statistical data could be based. Mere assertions of precise numbers, without some criterion, could scarcely be thought to convey the exactitude desiderated by Seton. Still we are not left wholly without means of comparison. The almost excited and sometimes apparently incredible utterances of many of our travellers can be examined in the light of later official records: and also in the light of the matter-of-fact recitals or reminiscences of men who quite coolly relate or even boast of the numbers of buffalo they have

[1] Seton, *Life-Histories of Northern Animals*, I, 259.

slaughtered—numbers which a self-respecting traveller might have been expected to falsify for very shame, if self-respecting men could have done such deeds.[2] There are of course in the buffalo literature many somewhat vague and detached allusions to 'vast herds,' 'immense hosts,' etc., not containing otherwise informative matter, which it would be wearisome to reproduce as a mere catalogue. In this section I confine myself as far as practicable to actual historical recitals where some effort has been made to illustrate the size and significance of the host recorded.

If certain of the *felidae* have ranged over a wider habitat, perhaps no species of any family ever occupied the earth in vaster quantities than did the buffalo.[3] J. A. Allen observes:

> The American bison is, as is well known, pre-eminently a gregarious animal. At times herds have been met with of immense size, numbering thousands, and even millions, of individuals. The accounts given by thoroughly veracious travellers respecting their size sound almost like exaggerations. . . . I myself must confess to slight misgivings in respect to their thorough truthfulness until I had, in 1871, an opportunity of seeing the moving multitudes of these animals on the plains of Kansas, when I was convinced of the possibility of the seemingly most extravagant reports being true. Only when demoralized and broken up by constant persecution from hunters do the herds become scattered. . . .[4]

Sir William Butler, shortly before this, wrote: "The earth had never elsewhere such an accumulation of animal life as this northern continent must have exhibited five or six centuries ago, when, from the Great Slave Lake to the Gulf of Florida, millions upon millions of bisons roamed the wilderness. . . ."[5] Hornaday is even more emphatic:

> Of all the quadrupeds that have ever lived upon the earth, probably no other species has ever marshaled such innumerable hosts as those of the

[2]See below, chaps. XV, XVI, at large.

[3]Some northern travellers think the caribou may have exceeded them. See on this, Appendix F, "Caribou."

"The indications are that mastodons were extraordinarily abundant; it is estimated . . . that they may have been at one time as numerous as the bison." Remains of mastodons at Big Bone Lick, Kentucky, "one hundred times those of bison" (Osborn, *Age of Mammals*, 481). *Bison antiquus* = 2, *B. latrifons* = 1, per 100 (remains of) mastodon (*ibid.*, 478).

[4]Allen, *American Bisons*, 55. Seton: "during the migrations alone that the very large herds were seen . . ." (*Life Histories of Northern Animals*, I, 274). Stone and Cram: "[they] returned north in the spring in scattered herds, making their migration march less conspicuous . . ." (*American Animals*, 69). For an 'inconspicuous' northbound herd of 4,000,000, May, 1871; see below, note 144.

[5]Butler, *Wild North Land*, 211.

American bison. It would have been as easy to count or to estimate the leaves in a forest as to calculate the number of buffaloes living at any given time during the history of the species, previous to 1870. Even in South Central Africa, which has always been exceedingly prolific in great herds of game, it is probable that all its quadrupeds taken together on an equal area would never have more than equaled the total number of buffalo in this country forty years ago [that is, *circa* 1850]. . . . To an African hunter such a statement may seem incredible, but it appears to be fully warranted by the literature of both branches of the subject. . . .[6]

He adds elsewhere:

Twenty years hence, when not even a bone or a buffalo chip remains above ground throughout the West to mark the presence of the buffalo, it may be difficult for people to believe that these animals ever existed in such large numbers as to constitute not only a serious annoyance, but very often a dangerous menace to wagon travel across the plains, and also to stop railway trains, and even to throw them off the track. The like has probably never occurred before in any country, and most assuredly never will again, if the present rate of large game destruction all over the world can be taken as a foreshadowing of the. future. . . .[7]

In dealing first of all with the Mississippi River region and the territories to the eastward, we must not be misled by the fact that the early observers of the animal in those portions of its habitat use virtually the same phraseology to describe the numbers seen by them as is employed by travellers on the Great Plains. 'Large' and 'small' and their various synonymous forms are purely relative terms, as is frequently quite strikingly exemplified in this present field of our inquiry.[8] I am glad to note that I am not alone in thus emphasizing this relative significance, and in the general conclusions to be drawn therefrom. Hornaday remarks:

Judged by ordinary standards of comparison, the early pioneers of the last [that is, eighteenth] century thought buffalo were abundant in the localities mentioned. . . . But the herds which lived east of the Mississippi

[6]Hornaday, "Extermination of the American Bison," 387.
[7]*Ibid.*, 391-2.
[8]Compare Father Marquette, *circa* 1670: "They are scattered about the prairie in herds. I have seen one of 400" (*Jesuit Relations*, LIX, 111-13) cf. *ibid.* LVIII, 99; LIX, 103, 107. Contrast Seton: "It was during the migrations alone that the very large herds were seen. Bands of a few thousands were found at all seasons, but the millions came together only on some great general impulse . . ." (*Life-Histories of Northern Animals*, I, 274).
    Charles Dickens, 1842: "From St. Louis we cross to Chicago, traversing immense prairies . . ." (*Letters*, 62). Audubon, also *circa* 1842, having meanwhile seen the 'Great Prairie' of the Missouri: "the small and beautiful prairies of Indiana and Illinois . . ." (Audubon and Bachman, *American Quadrupeds*, II, 36). Edmund Flagg, 1836, calls them 'the lesser prairies' (*Early Western Travels*, XXVI, 340).

were comparatively only mere stragglers from the innumerable mass which covered the great western pasture region from the Mississippi to the Rocky Mountains, and from the Rio Grande to Great Slave Lake. Between the Rocky Mountains and the States lying along the Mississippi River on the west, from Minnesota to Louisiana, the whole country was one vast buffalo range, inhabited by millions of buffaloes. . . . They lived and moved as no other quadrupeds ever have, in great multitudes, like grand armies in review, covering scores of square miles at once. They were so numerous that they frequently stopped boats in the rivers, threatened to overwhelm travellers on the plains, and in later years derailed locomotives and cars, until railway engineers learned by experience the wisdom of stopping their trains whenever there were buffaloes crossing the track. . . .[9]

The general soundness of his interpretation (and my own) is established beyond question by those occasional testimonies where mention of some estimated number indicates clearly enough what constituted a vast herd east of the Mississippi. Father Hennepin, a man not excessively averse to exaggeration,[10] remarks: "There must have been innumerable quantity of Wild Bulls in that Country, since the earth is covered with their Horns. . . ."[11] Elsewhere he speaks of the 'meadows' (prairies) along the Mississippi—"covered with an infinite number of Wild Bulls. . . ."[12] Yet when he attempts to specify numbers, 'droves of about four or five hundred together,'[13] represent his conception of the herds. Father Marquette, who encountered them in 1670-73, uses almost identical phraseology about 'abundance'[14] and 'infinite numbers,'[15] and evidently feels that he has reached the limits of human credulity in asserting (as it were with bated breath) that he has 'seen four hundred together.'[16] Similarly, La Salle and his companions on their way down the Mississippi in 1680, speak of 'large numbers,'[17] 'abundance,'[18] and 'prodigious quantities.'[19] But on their

[9]Hornaday, "Extermination of the American Bison," 388. His conclusion is shared by Seton, 1910 (Life-Histories of Northern Animals, I, 258); although in 1929 he accepts 'thousands' without any hesitation. Cf. Stone and Cram, American Animals, 67. Wissler, American Indian, 14. Webb, Great Plains, 43-4.

[10]See above, chap. IV, notes 12-19.

[11]Hennepin, New Discovery, ed. Thwaites, I, 146. 'Wild Bull' (taureau sauvage) is his generic term for the species, and does not here indicate the sex.

[12]Ibid., 185; cf., 211, 212.

[13]Ibid., 151. J. Peter Turner, (Geographical Magazine, England, August, 1936) has Hennepin "doing his missionary work among countless thousands where later Chicago was to rise . . ." (Montreal Gazette, August 13, 1936).

[14]Marquette, in Hennepin, New Discovery, II, 641-3.

[15]Ibid., 644.

[16]Ibid., 646; Jesuit Relations, LIX, 111-13; cf. ibid., LVIII, 99; LIX, 103, 107.

[17]Tonty in Journeys of La Salle, I, 26; Father Christian Le Clercq, ibid., 216.

[18]Father Zenobius Membre, ibid., 134.

[19]La Salle, Father Anastasius Douay, ibid., 195, 224.

second journey, when they landed in the 'Bay of St. Louis'[20] (Matagorda Bay, near Galveston, Texas),[21] in the Gulf of Mexico and in the very heart of the southern buffalo country, their astonishment finds more definite expression. The 'infinite number of beeves,'[22] and 'multitude of beeves,'[23] were such that "the smallest herd seemed to contain two or three hundred";[24] and these shortly became 'herds of thousands.'[25]

The testimony of eighteenth-century travellers in the territory east of the Mississippi reveals quite plainly that 'vast numbers,' in the Western prairie sense, are a misnomer. Many of these allusions are very vague. A post "on the Wabash River" (which could mean almost anywhere in the State of Indiana) is stated, *circa* 1700, to have secured 15,000 buffalo hides 'in a short time';[26] an instance for which I can find no contemporary authority, and which is widely disproportionate to general buffalo hide figures at that period. Vaudreuil found buffalo 'abundant' along Rock River, 1718;[27] and Father Râle says of the Illinois Indians about the same time that there is "no year in which they do not kill . . . more than 2000 oxen . . ." (buffalo).[28] But these were not necessarily all in modern Illinois; since the tribes thereabouts followed the buffalo.[29] Hamburgh's "Journal" (southward from Chicago River, 1763)[30] and Pittman (Illinois, 1770)[31] note 'abundance' of buffalo. But for what purpose (as with Vaudreuil, 1718) were they 'abundant'? Colonel George Croghan (June, 1765) mentions "great plenty" along the Little Wabash,[32] and "plenty" near Vincennes, Indiana;[33] where George Rogers Clark, on the famous expedition of 1779, records 'numbers.'[34]

[20]Douay, Henri Joutel, *ibid.*, I, 237; II, 78.
[21]Parkman, *La Salle*, 374, 379; Hornaday, "Extermination of the American Bison," 381.
[22]Joutel, in *Journeys of La Salle*, II, 78, 79.
[23]Joutel, *ibid.*, 100.
[24]Douay, *ibid.*, I, 224.
[25]Douay, Joutel, *ibid.*, 264; II, 69.
[26]Willson, *Great Company*, 183.
[27]Allen, *American Bisons*, 106. For Rock River, see above, chap. X, note 11.
[28]*Jesuit Relations*, LXVIII, 169.
[29]See on this, Hennepin, 1680 (*New Discovery*, I, 153); Father Binneteau, 1699 (*Jesuit Relations*, LXV, 73-5); Gravier, 1700 (*ibid.*, 135, 159); Marest, 1712 (*ibid.*, LXVI, 225, 227, 253, 287); cf. also *ibid.*, LIV, 189.
[30]Mereness (ed.), *Colonial Travels*, 362, 363.
[31]Allen, *American Bisons*, 106.
[32]Croghan, *Journals*; in *Early Western Travels*, I, 140.
[33]*Ibid.*, 143; Hulbert, *Historic Highways*, II, 56.
[34]*Ibid.*, VIII, 50-3; Bruce, *Daniel Boone*, 190. In 1787, seeing 'five buffaloes' near Vincennes, was an event (*British-American Magazine*, Toronto, 1863, I, 629).

A British officer, Captain Harry Gordon, notes at the mouth of the Wabash River, July 31, 1766, that "The herds of Buffaloe are hereabouts Extraordinary large and frequent to be seen. . . ."[35] The same observer writes concerning Fort Massac (which is probably at or near Paducah, Kentucky[36]): "Hunters from this Post may be sent amongst the Buffaloe, any Quantity of whose Beef they can procure in proper Season. . . ."[37] Here again, it is quite pertinent to ask by what standard they appeared "Extraordinary large" to a newcomer in the region. And at Fort Massac, they were within the neighbourhood of the larger trans-Mississippi bands, which apparently swam back and forth indifferently.[38]

In the upper Ohio Basin, supposedly the greatest buffalo haunt and thoroughfare of the territory east of the Mississippi,[39] we again find various generalizations concerning 'vast herds'; there are also a few rather more precise accounts. But these latter do not furnish much evidence in support of the generalizing writers. Captain Bonnecamp, 1750, somewhere about the Virginia-Ohio boundary, according to Thwaites,[40] had heard of them. I quote his own words: "It was in the neighbourhood of this river that we began to see the Islinois cattle; but here and elsewhere, they were in such small numbers that our men could hardly kill a score of them. It was, besides, necessary to seek them far in the woods, We had been assured, however, at our departure, that at each point we should find them by the hundreds, and that tongues alone of those which we should kill would suffice to support the troops. This is not the first time when I have experienced that hyperbole and exaggeration were figures familiar to the Canadians. . . ."[41]

Dr. Walker, traversing much the same country in the same year on his journey from Albemarle County, Virginia, to Kentucky and back again (March to July, 1750), recorded that in addition to '8 Elks, 20 Deer, 53 Bears, & many Birds,' they killed '13 Buffaloes'![42] George Croghan, in what must broadly have been in the same region as Bonnecamp, on the Little Kanawha River, June, 1765, speaks of the buffalo

[35]Mereness (ed.), *Colonial Travels*, 468, 469.
[36]For Fort Massac, see above, chap. X, note 32.
[37]Gordon, in Mereness (ed.), *Colonial Travels*, 470.
[38]Seen by Hennepin, 1680 (*New Discovery*, I, 146, 242); also Diron D'Artaguiette, 1723 (*Journal*, in Mereness (ed.), *Colonial Travels*, 62; cf. *ibid.*, 83).
[39]Hulbert's great thesis in the 'prehistoric' portion of his *Historic Highways*.
[40]Thwaites, ed. note, *Jesuit Relations*, LXIX, 298.
[41]Bonnecamp, *ibid.*, 177.
[42]Quoted by Hulbert, *Historic Highways*, VI, 53.

as 'very plentiful.'[43] In the following year, Captain Gordon saw none until a hundred miles below Fort Pitt (Pittsburgh); and they were not common until after passing the Scioto River (Portsmouth, Ohio).[44]

Kentucky is mentioned as a land of absolutely prodigious hosts. I quote a typical generalization of this character, referring to the famous Blue Licks:

> For ages the buffalo had come to these licks to find salt. Instinct had taught them the necessity of periodical visits to these saline springs, where nature had provided this essential to animal life, and for hundreds of years, along these narrow paths, cut out of the woods by the ceaseless trampings of these mighty herds of buffalo, had come millions of these animals to find health and life in the waters which gushed from the Licking bottom. When they had satisfied nature's call for salt, these herds would climb the adjacent hills or lie down and rest through the day and sleep through the night. On these eminences thousands of them would stand and watch the incoming buffaloes as they emerged from the trace on the western side, and, plunging into the waters of the Licking, [would] swim across the stream and slake nature's demand for this necessary product, which here the Great Power for all animal life had laid up in unlimited quantity. . . .[45]

Judging from one or two indications, as it appears in his work, the passage is not certainly from Hulbert's own pen. Its insertion, however, without critical comment of any nature, implies his endorsement of its views. It is unfortunate that the author did not identify at least one witness of the 'thousands,' not to say 'millions'; in any case, some much more specific testimony is to be found. Daniel Boone is cited as referring to 'thousands' in Kentucky in 1753.[46] In 1770, he is quoted as follows, concerning the Red River region in that state: "The buffaloes were more frequent than I have ever seen cattle in the settlements, browsing on the leaves of the cane, or cropping the herbage of those extensive plains, fearless because ignorant of the violence of man. Sometimes we saw hundreds in a drove, and the numbers about the salt springs were amazing. . . ."[47] I shall venture to say that this is scarcely the language of one familiar with 'thousands': and 'more than he had seen in the settlements' does not necessarily signify the immense numbers of the Alberta or Texas ranching country.

[43]Croghan, *Early Western Travels*, I, 130, 132; also Allen, *American Bisons*, 229-31.
[44]Mereness (ed.), *Colonial Travels*, 465.
[45]Hulbert, *Historic Highways*, I, 124.
[46]Bruce, *Daniel Boone*, 29-30.
[47]Allen, *American Bisons*, 112; Hornaday, "Extermination of the American Bison," 388; Hulbert, *Historic Highways*, VI, 32; Bruce, *Daniel Boone*, 96-100.

Allen quotes an account of 'innumerable herds' along the Cumberland River, in Kentucky-Tennessee, prior to 1769; but does not specify his authority.[48] And where Nashville now stands, there were in 1770 ". . . according to Ramsey . . . immense numbers of buffalo and other wild game. The country was crowded with them. Their bellowings sounded from the hills and forests. . . ."[49] Daniel Boone also mentions 'vast herds of buffalo' grazing among the spurs of the Cumberland Mountains in East Tennessee, about 1764 and perhaps later.[50] F. A. Michaux, the naturalist, writes as follows (1802): ". . . a short time after the settling of the Europeans [circa 1750] several species . . . wholly disappeared, particularly the elks and bisons. The latter, notwithstanding, were more common there than in any other part of North America. . . . Their number was at that time so considerable that they were met in flocks of 150 to 200. . . ."[51] This is corroborated by Fortescue Cuming, who gives an account derived from his 'old-timer' Kentucky host, Captain Waller, in 1809:

He said that buffaloes, bears, and deer were so plenty in the country [twenty years before: circa 1789] that little or no bread was used, but that even the children were fed on game. . . . And that the principal part of the cultivation of Kentucky had been within the last fifteen years. He said that the buffaloes had been so numerous, going in herds of several hundreds together, that about the salt licks and springs they frequented, they pressed down and destroyed the soil to a depth three or four feet, as was conspicuous yet in the neighbourhood of the Blue Lick, where all the old trees have their roots bare of soil to that depth. . . . He said that the whole country was then an entire cane-brake, which sometimes grew to forty feet high, but that the domestic stock introduced by the settlers have eradicated the cane, except in some remote and unsettled parts of the state. . . .[52]

[48]Allen, American Bisons, 114.
[49]Ibid.; Hornaday, "Extermination of the American Bison," 388.
[50]Allen, American Bisons, 114; Hornaday, "Extermination of the American Bison," 388; Bruce, Daniel Boone, 46-7.
[51]F. A. Michaux (son of André), Early Western Travels, III, 234.
[52]Cuming, ibid., IV, 175-8; see also Allen, American Bisons, 113. It is curious, to say the least, that the settlers' stock should have 'eradicated' in some twenty years what the 'mighty herds' and the 'millions' (of the same genus bos, and almost certainly of similar food-habits) had been unable to extirpate in 'hundreds of years' and 'ages.' Boone (above, note 47) speaks of them "browsing on it": and no less a person than John Wesley noted in Georgia, 1737, that the "cane-swamps . . . are the best feeding for all kinds of cattle . . .": Wesley's Journal (Everyman ed.), I, 62. I find the following, however: "In the first settlement of Georgia, they were as abundant as they were in Tennessee and Kentucky . . ."; '10,000' seen in a herd; and establishments 'constantly supplied with buffalo tongues until as late as 1774': Adair, History of the American Indians (1775; new ed., 1930), ed. note, 445. These reminiscent statements go back to the third or fourth generation of commonly uncritical

One of our earlier witnesses, Captain Gordon, speaks of buffalo, elk, and deer coming to the Blue Lick in "great numbers" (1766).[53] Nicholas Cresswell, a young English visitor in Revolutionary times (1775-77), who crossed the Alleghanies into Kentucky, had heard of the immense herds about the Great Lick, and promised himself meat on arrival there; but in actual fact found none to kill (June, 1775).[54] Later on, he records "incredible numbers . . . a herd of two hundred odd. . . ."[55] Simon Kenton, at the same place in the same year, although he had lived in the lands of "immense herds" all his life, found 'evidence of game *the like of which he had never seen*'; and on one occasion counted fifteen hundred buffalo 'pacing in single file to the Licks. . . .'[56]

Evidently their numbers were not sufficient to stand the strain very long. Henderson's "Diary" notes (May 9, 1775): "We found it very difficult at first to stop great waste in killing meat. Some would kill three, four, five, or half a dozen buffaloes, and not take half a horse load from them all. For want of a little obligatory law, our game as soon as we got here, if not before, was driven off very much. Fifteen or twenty miles was as short a distance as good hunters thought of getting meat, nay, sometimes they were obliged to go thirty miles, though by chance once or twice a week buffalo was killed within five or six miles. . . ."[57] John Filson writes in 1784: "I have heard a hunter assert that he saw above one thousand buffaloes at the Blue Licks at once, so numerous were they before the first settlers had wantonly sported away their lives. . . . The amazing herds of buffalo which resort thither, by their size and numbers, fill the traveller with amazement and terror. . . ."[58]

The same conception of 'great numbers' is found in Georgia at an even earlier date. There were 'large herds' there in 1736.[59] In 1739, on the Great Ogechee and Oconee Rivers, respectively, there were

informants. This in my view discounts 'thousands,' which I personally disbelieve. The contemporary traveller Bartram found *none* in Georgia in 1773 (*Travels*, 55, 62, 263). Adair himself, writing probably 1761-68, speaks of buffalo as 'scarce' (*History of the American Indians*, xviii, xxiii, 445). Cf. below, note 60.

[53]*Journal* (in Mereness (ed.), *Colonial Travels*, 466).
[54]*Journal of Nicholas Cresswell, 1775-1777*, 85-90.   [55]*Ibid.*, 86.
[56]Kenton, *Simon Kenton*, 63. The italics are mine.
[57]Quoted by Bruce, *Daniel Boone*, 125.
[58]Allen, *American Bisons*, 112; Hornaday, "Extermination of the American Bison," 386. Filson: "that inaccurate and turgid amanuensis . . ." (so, Professor Archibald Henderson, *American Historical Review*, XX, 1914, 86).
[59]Allen, *American Bisons*, 96; Hornaday, "Extermination of the American Bison," 379.

'great plenty,' and 'abundance'; an eye-witness records "Seeing Several Herds of sixty and upwards in a Herd. . . ."[60] When such modest figures have to do duty for 'huge,' 'immense,' 'vast,' 'amazing,' or 'incredible' numbers, when a hunter sees a thousand at one time, or another (amid such plenty as he had never seen before) counts fifteen hundred, and both of these, moreover, being in the generally accepted region of greatest resort, it seems clear that these expressions can be interpreted only in a relative sense. Common sense assumes that if the witnesses had seen greater maxima they would have mentioned them. With the one single exception, even the numbers are only estimates, not likely to be understated. They do not furnish much support for 'thousands' or 'millions.'

It might be less necessary to emphasize this in such detail, were it not that more recently Shoemaker has made a patriotic but quite uncritical attempt to establish Pennsylvania as the home—up to about 1770—of 'tens of thousands,' and 'vanished millions.'[61] Shoemaker's principal literary authority is a certain Thomas Ashe, the author of *Travels in America.* Shoemaker quotes Ashe largely at second-hand from Allen, without noticing either Allen's remarks[62] or those of other critics, contemporary and later, on Ashe's utter unreliability.[63] In addition, Shoemaker cites traditional testimony from then living descendants of the early settlers, some of whom never saw the ancestors for whom they vouch; and considers his case 'proved' by the persistence of the tradition of vast numbers, and by the personal integrity of his informants.[64] Ashe mentions an old man who "supposed there could not have been less than 2000" at a certain spring.[65] Following this, the same old man, apparently at the same time— "when he first settled there"—estimated there could not have been less than *ten* thousand in the neighbourhood of the spring.[66] The same pioneer, in the first and second years, with some companions, killed 'from 600 to 700' buffalo.[67] Ashe met with another 'who killed 2000 buffaloes in Pennsylvania with his own hand, and others no

[60]"Travels with General Oglethorpe, 1739-1742" (in Mereness (ed.), *Colonial Travels,* 219). Cf. above, note 52.

[61]Shoemaker, *Pennsylvania Bison Hunt,* 1915.

[62]Allen, *American Bisons,* 108-9.

[63]For contemporary and other criticisms of Ashe *in extenso,* chap. III, notes 25-6.

[64]Shoemaker, *Pennsylvania Bison Hunt,* 9, 28, 39, 43, 51, etc.

[65]Allen, *American Bisons,* 109; also (in part) Hornaday, "Extermination of the American Bison," 387, 420; Shoemaker, *Pennsylvania Bison Hunt,* 23.

[66]*Ibid.,* 24.

[67]See authorities cited in note 65.

doubt have done the same thing."[68] About the same time, Shoemaker himself mentions a certain Colonel John Kelly, a mighty hunter; "his specialty was buffaloes, and his friends stated that he killed over a hundred of these animals."[69] He also states that the 'countless numbers'[70] and 'vanished millions'[71] were hunted very prudently, for subsistence only, by the Indians; and not appreciably diminished—certainly not wasted—in Pennsylvania.[72] Yet by 1773, after only a year or two of settlement,[73] these vast hosts of 'tens of thousands'[74] were 'cut in two' by the westward march of settlement.[75] They were, he says, "more prevalent in Pennsylvania than all the vast herds of various wild animals which were found by the first pioneers in South and Central Africa."[76] The northern section of this unimaginable host was estimated by a certain Philip Quigley in 1773 to contain twelve thousand animals.[77] With the possible exception of Ashe's old settler —if he be considered contemporary, dealing with some thirty or forty years earlier—I can find nothing of these vast hosts in any contemporary source I have been able to discover. The historical material of this era and region was ransacked by Parkman, Allen, Theodore Roosevelt, and Hulbert for their own respective purposes; there is not even the most casual allusion to millions. Shoemaker's pronouncements on the 'Black Pennsylvania buffalo' as a distinct species (*Bison americanus Pennsylvanicus*) do not properly belong to the present subject; but their utterly contradictory nature involves his entire argument on buffalo in suspicion. One cannot wonder that his classification found no support among zoologists at large.[78]

[68]Shoemaker, *Pennsylvania Bison Hunt*, 26. I have already noticed Roosevelt's repeated warnings to his readers against a too-credulous acceptance of this class of evidence in this precise region and era (*Winning of the West, passim*).

[69]*Ibid.*, 39. It is extremely improbable that either Colonel Kelly or his admirers would *under*state the total.

[70]Shoemaker, *Pennsylvania Bison Hunt*, 13.

[71]*Ibid.*, 10, 38.

[72]*Ibid.*, 22.

[73]*Ibid.*, 38.

[74]*Ibid.*, 22.

[75]*Ibid.*, 38.

[76]*Ibid.*, 24; citing no authority. It seems idle to consider this anything but a plagiarism from Hornaday (above, note 6). It cannot be contemporary, even as a guess. 'South Central Africa' was unknown in 1773; and Hornaday's figure is *the entire total* on the North American continent *circa* 1850.

[77]Shoemaker, *Pennsylvania Bison Hunt*, 18. It is astonishing to find this wild farrago of unsubstantiated guesswork accepted *in toto*, without discussion, by Seton (*Game Animals*, III, 657). But Seton the field observer and Seton the buffalo historian are widely different.

[78]Shoemaker, *Pennsylvania Bison Hunt*, 8, 42. Above, *in extenso*, chap. III, notes 47-9, 182.

It is interesting and significant to note that the same conception of 'large numbers' which I have emphasized was obviously present to the minds of many of the early travellers in the truly plentiful range westward of the Mississippi; men who had been reared in the regions of "abundance—herds of sixty or more";[79] or whose only knowledge, derived from hearsay, was evidently on a similarly limited plane. There is an unmistakable timidity and caution about their statements, uttered, as I have expressed it, with bated breath; the numbers they 'solemnly assert' or 'dare to affirm' they have seen, might almost be said to have been beneath the notice of the later witnesses—who were dealing with a species which had by their time become familiarly associated in the popular mind with really huge quantities. Lewis and Clark, ascending the Mississippi, 1804, observed ". . . buffalo in such multitudes that we cannot exaggerate in saying that at a single glance we saw three thousand of them before us. . . ."[80] Pike's language is identical (Cimarron River, November 4, 1806): "I do not think it an exaggeration to say there were 3000 in one view. . . ."[81] A fortnight later he remarks: "I found the hunters had killed without mercy, having slain 17 buffalo and wounded at least twenty more. . . ."[82]

Lieutenant Wilkinson, also of Pike's expedition, descending the Arkansas River, independently (November 8, 1806) states as follows: ". . . the herds of buffalo, elk, goat [that is, antelope] and deer, surpassed credibility. I do solemnly assert that, if I saw one, I saw more than 9000 buffaloes during the day's march. . . ."[83] A relation which does not even attempt the (entirely credible) round figure of 'ten thousand at once,' as seen by Lewis and Clark along the Missouri, 1804, 1806,[84] instinctively commands confidence. Lewis and Clark themselves found their standards increasing. On their return journey, near White River, August, 1806, they write: "Buffalo now so numerous that from an eminence we discovered more than we had ever seen before at one time; and if it be not impossible to calculate the moving multitude, which darkened the whole plains, we are convinced that twenty thousand would be no exaggerated number. . . ."[85]

[79]Above, note 60.
[80]*Lewis and Clark Journals*, I, 122.
[81]Coues (ed.), *Expeditions of Pike*, II, 438.
[82]*Ibid.*, 447.　　　　　　　　　　[83]*Ibid.*, 548
[84]*Lewis and Clark Journals*, 1805, 1806 (I, 370; III, 192); ". . . infinitely more than we had ever seen before at one view . . ." (I, 338); "at least a thousand" (I, 344); but compare even earlier, 1804: '52 herds at one view' (I, 165).
[85]*Ibid.*, III, 267.

Harmon (Edmonton District, 1801) tells us he saw "in different herds, at least a thousand buffaloes grazing. . . ."[86] On another occasion (in the same general territory): "In this excursion, we saw buffaloes in abundance, and when on a small rise of ground, I think I may with truth affirm that there were in view, grazing on the surrounding plains, at least five thousand of them . . . ."[87] Again (apparently near Fort Qu'Appelle, 1803) he says: "in the course of this pleasant ride, I saw thousands of buffaloes. . . ."[88] John Bradbury, the English naturalist, on the Missouri with the westbound Astorians (1811) was apparently struck by seeing a herd of '600 to 800'; perhaps, however, because they were mostly cows and calves.[89] Dr. Edwin James of Long's expedition of 1819-20, mentions as a phenomenon 'a herd of several hundreds' near Sioux River.[90] Later, he records "immense herds of bisons . . . at least ten thousand," at the Forks of the Platte, June, 1820.[91] Long's party also mentions the use of 'buffalo chips' (bois de vache) for fuel, as a novelty;[92] a circumstance which might possibly indicate—in addition to the treelessness of the plains—a profusion of that commodity unknown in the Central United States regions.

If internal evidence is of any value at any time, it here proves pretty conclusively that the foregoing passages were not written by men—nor were they addressed to a public—familiarized by either experience or authenticated reports with the idea of really large herds, ranging from scores or hundreds of thousands, up to millions. No doubt in the course of many centuries, the aggregate of these simultaneous thousands would approach millions, much as in Great Britain, for example, the railways carry over a thousand million passengers per annum, out of a population of some forty millions; but I doubt whether that is the meaning of the passage cited above from Hulbert.[93] Taken as it stands, the quotation is a very typical specimen (in my view) of the idle and baseless rhetoric with which this topic has been peculiarly afflicted; and which constitutes altogether too large a portion of Hulbert's 'prehistoric' speculations.[94] Shoemaker's dicta on numbers consist of little else.[95]

[86]*Harmon's Journal*, 41.   [87]*Ibid.*, 45.
[88]*Ibid.*, 103.   [89]*Early Western Travels*, V, 147.
[90]*Ibid.*, XIV, 278.   [91]*Ibid.*, XV, 239.
[92]*Ibid.*, 240. On 'buffalo chips,' see below, chap. XXI, note 24.
[93]Above, note 45.
[94]Hulbert's first two volumes are largely 'prehistory,' and swarm with contradictions; the others are historical and immensely valuable, embodying much resesarch.
[95]Compare above, chap. III, notes 47-9, 182, etc.

When we turn our attention to the typical buffalo habitat on the western side of the Mississippi, we cannot truly say that the language of our witnesses changes very materially; for it is difficult to expand a superlative. But judged in the light of several attempts at an accurate computation, we feel that in this great region superlatives actually have real meaning.

It does not appear that Alvar Nuñez Cabeza de Vaca was of the scientific temperament; and his position as a captive did not conduce towards leisurely and minute investigation. He merely furnishes general information without specific data; and would often be scarcely worth quoting, were he not the earliest European witness of all. He encountered the buffalo apparently in Texas, in 1528-30; perhaps near the mouth of the Pecos (which he calls 'Cow River'; and which is thought by some to be the same as Antonio Espejo's *Rio de las Vacas* of 1582-83).[96] Cabeza says of the buffalo: "These come from the North further through the Land unto the Coast of Florida, and extend themselves farre within the Land more than foure hundred leagues. . . ."[97]

Francisco Vasquez Coronado's expedition to 'Quivira'[98] in 1541 travelled under somewhat happier auspices. Its members were at least in some sense masters of their own fates; and evidently they felt that their sovereign and their fellow-countrymen, at least, would expect a description of what they had seen. Their various accounts must be considered the earliest essentially scientific descriptions that we possess of the buffalo and their plains environment.

The most detailed recital is furnished by Pedro de Castañeda who was not a member of the secondary expedition to Quivira.[99] It is true that, unlike some of the others, he wrote in the later years of his life; but he makes no attempt to hide this fact. He says, concerning some of the remarkable occurrences he mentions: "I dare to write of them because I am writing at a time when many men are still living who saw them, and who will vouch for my account. . . ."[100] This is the language of an honest man who does not fear criticism. The authenticity of the various descriptions of scenery, flora, fauna, Indian customs, etc., has been endorsed by competent modern critics; and a full share of this commendation has been accorded to

[96]On Cabeza de Vaca, see above, chap. IX, notes 21-7.
[97]*Purchas his Pilgrimes*, XVII, 478; *Journey of Cabeza*, ed. Bandelier, 94, 150-4.
[98]On the various identifications of 'Quivira,' see chap. IX, note 24.
[99]*Journey of Coronado*, ed. Winship, 1-148.
[100]Castañeda, *ibid.*, 139.

Castañeda.[101] He speaks of ". . . such great numbers of cows [that is, buffalo in general] that already it seemed incredible. . . . They came across so many animals that those who were on the advance guard killed a great number of bulls. As these fled they trampled one another in their haste until they came to a ravine. So many of the animals fell into this that they filled it up, and the rest went across on top of them. The men who were chasing them on horseback fell in among the animals without noticing where they were going. Three of the horses that fell in among the cows, all saddled and bridled, were lost sight of completely. . . ."[102] Castañeda says again: "In twenty leagues they had seen nothing but cows and the sky. . . ."[103] He estimated that during one fortnight they killed five hundred bulls; "the number of those that were there without any cows is something incredible. . . ."[104]

In his detailed description of the male animals, he writes as follows: "Another thing worth noticing is that the bulls travelled without cows in such large numbers that nobody could have counted them, and so far away from the cows that it was more than forty leagues from where we began to see the bulls to the place where we began to see the cows. . . ."[105]

Bulls without cows were not uncommon,[106] except in the breeding season; but while many travellers treat a great preponderance of bulls as the norm[107]—as one might, of course, expect from the vastly greater use of cows both for flesh and for hides[108]—Pike (1806) remarks as follows: ". . . it is worthy of remark that although the male buffaloes were in great abundance, yet in all our route from the Osage [villages] to the Pawnees we never saw one female. I

[101]See Winship (ibid., ed. preface, etc.); Bandelier (ed.), Journey of Cabeza, 89, 92, 100, 113, 154, 174, 175. On Castañeda in particular, see also Buffalo Jones' Forty Years, ed. Inman, 6-11; Fynn, American Indian, 100, 171; Aiton, "The Later Career of Coronado," American Historical Review, XXX, 1924, 298-304; "The Muster Roll of Coronado," ibid., XLIV, 1938, 556-70.

[102]Castañeda, in Journey of Coronado, 66.

[103]Ibid., 67.

[104]Ibid., 73.

[105]Ibid., 140-2; Purchas his Pilgrimes, XVIII, 64-5.

[106]See references on this, chap. V, notes 93-5; and for cows without bulls, the same chapter, note 60.

[107]Seton, Life-Histories of Northern Animals, I, 261. 'Ten to one': so, Dr. F. V. Hayden, Upper Missouri, 1861; 'a fair estimate,' thinks Allen, judging from Kansas, 1871 (American Bisons, 189). Surely this is not the natural ratio? This is presumably about equal. Some cows bear calves of one sex invariably, sometimes male, sometimes female. I have owned such. See remarks in Darwin, Descent of Man, chap. VIII, 251-68.

[108]See below on this, Appendix P.

acknowledge myself at a loss to determine whether this is to be attributed to the decided preference the savages give to the meat of the females, so that consequently they are almost exterminated in the hunting-grounds of the nations, or to some physical causes; for I afterwards discovered the females with young in such immense herds as gave me no reason to believe they yielded to the males in numbers. . . ."[109] To return to Castañeda: He remarks in another place:

Another thing was a heap of cowbones [that is, buffalo at large], a cross-bow shot long or a very little less,[110] almost twice a man's height in places, and some eighteen feet or more wide, which was found on the edge of a salt lake in the southern part, and this in a region where there are no people who could have made it. The only explanation of this which could be suggested was that the waves which the north wind must make in the lake had piled up the bones of the cattle which had died in the lake, when the old and weak ones which went into the water were unable to get out. The noticeable thing is the number of cattle that would be necessary to make such a pile of bones. . . .[111]

His accounts are corroborated by others of the expedition. The "Anonymous Document" relates: "Four days from this village [Cicuye[112]] they came to a country as level as the sea, and in these plains there was such a multitude of cows that they are number-less. . . ."[113] The "Relacion del Suceso" states, similarly:

[109]Coues (ed.), *Expeditions of Pike*, II, 516.

[110]Perhaps 400 to 500 yards. The range of the crossbow reckoned, I believe, about 50 per cent. farther than that of the English longbow. Froude cites the Statute, 33 Henry VIII, cap. 9 (1542); giving 220 yards as the required range for the heavy arrow: *History of England* (Everyman ed.), I, 42. At this time, old William Harrison bemoans the decadence of English archers (*Description of England*, ed. Furnivall, I, 279); but Shakespeare gives "fourteen or fourteen-and-a-half-score paces" = 280 or 290 yards (*2 Henry IV*, III, ii). But such comparisons are only guesses. We shall discuss some similar guesses below. See chap. XVIII.

[111]*Journey of Coronado*, ed. Winship, 140. Compare Darwin's account (derived in part from eye-witnesses) of great droughts in South America, along the Parana River, etc.; resulting in great mortality—and consequently similar bone-deposits—owing to drownings of animals exhausted by hunger and thirst: *Voyage of the 'Beagle,'* 125-7. Possibly Castañeda was not so very wide of the mark.

He was much nearer at least than a modern writer, who absurdly says of 'Pile o' Bones' (now Regina, Saskatchewan): "The real source of that name was of course the pile of buffalo bones stacked along the railway line to be loaded in freight cars for St. Paul . . ." (Gibbon, *Steel of Empire*, 236). Adjacent to Regina is 'Wascana Lake'; in Sioux, *Wascana* = 'pile of bones' (G. H. Armstrong, *Origin and Meaning of Place-Names in Canada*, 238). Thus is 'history' made in the year 1935!

[112]Pecos, New Mexico; so, *Journey of Coronado*, ed. preface, ix.

[113]*Ibid.*, 193.

It is fifteen leagues away from the [Rio Grande[114]] river to the east, toward the plains where the cows are. . . . [Hernando de] Alvarado . . . proceeded forward to these plains, and at the borders of these plains he found a little river which flows to the southwest,[115] and after four days' march he found the cows, which are the most monstrous thing in the way of animals, which has ever been seen or read about. He followed this river for one hundred leagues, finding more cows every day. . . . There is such a quantity of them that I do not know what to compare them with, except with the fish in the sea, because on this journey, as also on that which the whole army made when it was going to Quivira, there were so many that many times when we started to pass through the midst of them, and wanted to go through to the other side of them, we were not able to, because the country was covered with them. . . ."[116]

The "Relacion del Suceso" remarks that on the way northward to Quivira: ". . . they killed a world of bulls and cows, for there were days when they brought sixty and seventy head into camp, and it was necessary to go hunting every day. . . ."[117] Coronado himself, in his "Letter to the King" (Charles V) says: "I reached some plains, so vast that I did not find their limit anywhere that I went, although I travelled over them for more than three hundred leagues. And I found such quantity of cows in these . . . that it is impossible to number them, for while I was journeying through these plains, until I returned to where I first found them, there was not a day that I lost sight of them. . . ."[118] The "Narrative of Jaramillo" observes: ". . . we began to enter the plain where the cows are, although we did not find them for some four or five days, after which we began to come across bulls, of which there are great numbers, and after going on in the same direction and meeting the bulls for two or three days, we began to find ourselves in the midst of very great numbers of cows, yearlings and bulls, all in together. . . ."[119] The same narrator, speaking of the potential wealth of the newly discovered region, says: "Indeed, there is profit in the cattle ready to the hand, from the quantity of them, which is as great as one could imagine. . . ."[120] These explicit statements, coming from different members of the same expedition, with its inevitable mutual jealousies and criticisms, and occasional slight contradictions, agree so closely that one cannot doubt their authen-

[114]*Ibid.*, ed. note, 204.
[115]The Pecos River (*ibid.*, map).
[116]*Ibid.*, 205-6.
[117]*Ibid.*, 208.
[118]*Ibid.*, 213-21.
[119]*Ibid.*, 230.
[120]*Ibid.*, 237.

ticity. We may compare the "Relacion" of Antonio de Espejo: ". . . [they] returned in July, 1583, by another way, downe a River, called de la Vaccas, or of Kine, an hundred and twenty leagues, still meeting with store of those cattell. . . ."[121]

While it adds little concerning numbers specifically, the following is of interest, as being probably the very earliest description of the buffalo ever printed in English: "There is a great number of beasts or kine in the countrey of Cibola, which were never brought thither by the Spanyards, but breed naturally in the countrey. They are like unto our oxen, saving that they have long hair like a lion, and short hornes, and they have upon their shoulders a bunch like a camell, which is higher then [sic] the rest of their body. They are marvellous wild and swift in running. They call them the beasts or kine of Cibola. . . ."[122] The Franciscans are recorded to have encountered 'numerous herds' near Monterey, in Nueva Leon (Mexico) in 1602.[123] Here again, however, we do not know what constituted 'numerous' in their minds.

Dr. Josiah Gregg was inclined to be somewhat sceptical of the very great numbers, as being mere travellers' tales. In the Cimarron River country, June, 1831, he remarks:

Not even a buffalo was now to be seen to relieve the dull monotony of the scene; although at some seasons (and particularly in the fall) these prairies are literally strewed with herds of this animal. Then, "thousands and tens of thousands" might at times be seen from this eminence [that is, the "Round Mound"[124]]. But the buffalo is a migratory animal, and even in the midst of the Prairies where they are generally so very abundant, we sometimes travel for days without seeing a single one; though no signs of hunter or Indian can be discovered. To say the truth, however, I have never seen them anywhere upon the Prairies so abundant as some travellers have represented—in dense masses, darkening the whole country. I have only found them in scattered herds, of a few scores, hundreds, or sometimes thousands in each, and where in the greatest numbers, dispersed far and wide; but with large intervals between. Yet they are very sensibly and

[121]*Purchas his Pilgrimes*, XVIII, 65-7. Davis's version, *The Spanish Conquest of New Mexico*, 1867, which I have not seen, is quoted by Allen, *American Bisons*, 134; Hornaday, "Extermination of the American Bison," 383.

[122]"A Relation . . . of Nova Hispania . . . by Henry Hawks, merchant, which lived five yeeres in the sayd countrey, and drew the same at the request of M. Richard Hakluyt, Esquire, of Eyton in the County of Hereford, 1572 . . ." (Hakluyt, *Voyages*, VI, 283-4).

[123]Berlandier, MS. on the Mammals of Mexico, now lost, cited by Allen, *American Bisons*, 129; Hornaday, "Extermination of the American Bison," 382.

[124]A well-known landmark on the old Santa Fé Trail. See Gregg's Table of Mileages, *Early Western Travels*, XX, 93; and Chittenden's "Itinerary," *American Fur Trade*, II, 535-43.

rapidly decreasing. There is a current notion that the whites frighten them away; but I would ask, where do they go to? To be sure, to use a hunter's phrase, they 'frighten a few out of their skins'; yet for every one killed by the whites, more than a hundred, perhaps a thousand, fall by the hands of the savages. From these, however, there is truly 'nowhere to flee'; for they follow them wheresoever they go; while the poor brutes instinctively learn to avoid the fixed establishments, and, to some degree, the regular travelling routes of the whites. . . .[125]

He adds elsewhere:

Were they only killed for food, however, their natural increase would perhaps replenish the loss; yet the continual and wanton slaughter of them by travellers and hunters, and the still greater havoc made among them by the Indians, not only for meat, but often for the skins alone . . . are fast reducing their numbers, and must ultimately effect their total annihilation from [sic] the continent. It is believed that the annual 'export' of *buffalo rugs* from the Prairies and bordering "buffalo range" is about 100,000; and the number killed wantonly, or exclusively for meat, is no doubt still greater, as the skins are fit to dress scarcely half the year. The vast extent of the prairies upon which they now pasture is no argument against their total extinction, when we take into consideration the extent of country from which they have already disappeared; for, it is well known, that, within the recollection of our oldest pioneers, they were nearly as abundant east of the Mississippi as they now are upon the western prairie; and from history we learn that they once ranged to the Atlantic coast. Even within thirty years [that is, *circa* 1810], they were abundant over much of the present States of Missouri and Arkansas; yet they are now rarely seen within two hundred miles of the frontier. Indeed, upon the high plains they have very sensibly decreased within the last ten years. Nevertheless, the number of buffalo upon the Prairies is still immense. But as they incline to migrate *en masse* from place to place, it sometimes happens that, for several days' travel together, not a single one is to be met with; but in other places, many thousands are often seen at one time. . . .[126]

One would not wish to disparage the independent reflections of any observer (least of all, perhaps the most cultured and philosophic of all our early witnesses) merely on the grounds of a minority opinion. My own central thesis in everything relating to buffalo is the high importance and (inherently) equal value of precisely such discrepant evidence. It is nevertheless regrettable that Dr. Gregg should have

[125]Gregg, *Early Western Travels*, XIX, 243.
[126]*Ibid.*, XX, 264. Compare Maximilian, Prince of Wied, a contemporary: "There is another point on which I differ from Mr. [Hon. Albert] Gallatin, namely, his denial of the great decrease in the number of buffaloes in general. For when we consider how far these animals have been driven up the country, and that in these very parts [*i.e.* apparently near St. Louis] they are even less numerous than formerly, we have a fact which at once proves a very great decrease, of which nobody in the interior of the country can entertain a doubt . . ." (*Early Western Travels*, XXIV, 130).

reserved his criticism for the 'vast hosts of the prairies'; and bestowed none upon the 'almost equal abundance' east of the Mississippi. Disregarding for the moment the cumulative effect upon the present-day reader of the co-ordinated evidence which has been presented in the foregoing pages—since Dr. Gregg could probably have had no access to much of it—it is difficult nowadays, at least, to perceive any distinction in the respective evidence relative to the two viewpoints, to a man of 1830-40 or thereabouts. The two concepts were both, in a sense, traditions; both in need of authentic verification. The balance of inherent credibility, in fact, is in favour of the prairie 'tradition,' as I term it. For it was that of men in their prime, asserting (doubtless in some numbers) *what they claimed to have seen*; rather than recollections or hearsay recitals, at times perhaps tinged with senility, of the wonders of a vanished age.

If practically all evidence had perished save that of chronology, one bare fact alone should suffice. In spite of the increase, beyond all comparison, in the scale of destruction—1830 being the precise era dividing the 'desultory' from the 'systematic' extermination[127]—it took longer from 1830 onward to annihilate the western prairie herds than it did from the time of the supposed 'almost equal abundance' east of the Mississippi (according to Gregg, say *circa* 1780) up to 1830. Moreover, Dr. Gregg was not a permanent resident. He was a traveller through a portion of the southern buffalo habitat; first going westward along the Santa Fé Trail in 1831, and finally returning in 1839 or 1840. What he witnessed was almost certainly one of those imponderable absences to which he himself alludes in the very passages I have quoted; and which find corroboration in a far-distant region from an observer equally philosophic and more experienced: "There were millions of these cattle, and yet so big was the field that you might travel for days and weeks and not see one of them. But their tracks were everywhere . . . paths and dust-pans. . . ."[128]

My interpretation is (I believe) confirmed by a curious coincidence. The very earliest—so far as I am aware—of those "mathematical" attempts at an estimate (the great lack of which Thompson Seton bewailed) is furnished by Farnham, on the Santa Fé Trail, June 21 to June 24, 1839, at a point about three days prior to reaching the Arkansas River, westbound; that is to say, in the

[127]Hornaday's classification: 1730-1830; 1830- *circa* '83 ("Extermination of the American Bison," 484).

[128]McDougall, *Pathfinding*, 248.

same general region of which Gregg wrote; and about the very time when the latter was traversing it, eastward-bound. It is remarkable that they did not meet. Farnham writes thus: "The buffalo during the last three days had covered the country so completely, that it appeared oftentimes extremely dangerous even for the immense cavalcade of the Santa Fé traders to attempt to break its way through them. We travelled at the rate of 15 miles a day. The length of sight on either side of the trail, 15 miles; 15 x 3 = 45 x 30 = 1350 square miles of country so thickly covered with these noble animals, that when viewed from a height it scarcely afforded a sight of a square league of its surface. . . ."[129]

Pattie mentions such huge numbers, also on the Santa Fé Trail, July 1, 1825, that Dr. Willard, one of the party, believed there "could not have been less than 100,000 seen, before noon!"[130] We may compare J. K. Townsend (Platte River, May, 1833): "The whole plain, as far as the eye could discern, was covered by one enormous mass of buffalo. The vision, at the very least computation, would certainly extend ten miles, and in the whole of this great space, including about eight miles in width from the bluffs to the river bank, there was apparently no vista in the incalculable multitude. . . ."[131] The testimony of John Bradbury, the English naturalist with the Astorians (Missouri River, near modern Bismarck, North Dakota, May, 1811), is of much greater significance than its suggested numbers alone would indicate:

I observed the preceding days a sufficient number of buffaloes to induce me to credit the hunters in their reports of the vast numbers they had seen; but this day afforded ample confirmation . . . we saw before us a beautiful plain, as we judged, about four miles across, in the direction of our course, and of similar dimension from east to west. . . . The whole of the plain was perfectly level, and, like the rest of the country, without a single shrub. It was covered with the finest verdure, and in every part herds of buffalo were feeding. I counted seventeen herds, but the aggregate number of the animals it was difficult even to guess at: some thought upwards of 10,000. . . .[132]

The interesting factor in this case is that Bradbury had travelled across the Atlantic and Central States to the Missouri River; through a region where buffalo still existed, or had but very recently been exterminated. On Gregg's hypothesis, he would have been quite

[129]Farnham, *Early Western Travels*, XXVIII, 96.
[130]Pattie, *ibid.*, XVIII, 334.
[131]Townsend, *ibid.*, XXI, 161.
[132]Bradbury, *ibid.*, V, 148, 149.

familiar with the 'abundance' then or formerly true of the eastern habitat; and his suspensions of judgment would logically have been not concerning western numbers *per se,* but concerning their reported density on the prairies in comparison with their notorious (former or present) density east of the Mississippi. It seems impossible that such a criterion would not have been mentioned by an observant scientifically minded man; yet some ten thousand or so furnished 'ample confirmation' for anything he had heard!!

In the same general territory, the famous frontiersman, James Kipp, told Audubon, the naturalist, in 1842 that ". . . travelling from Travers Bay[133] to the Mandan nation in August [? 1841] . . . he passed through herds of buffalo for six days in succession. At another time he saw the great prairie near Fort Clark [that is, Bismarck, North Dakota], on the Missouri River almost blackened by these animals, which covered the plain to the hills that bounded the view in all directions, and probably extended farther. . . ."[134] About this time, Frémont records another vast host on the Platte, July 4, 1842:

As we were riding slowly along this afternoon, clouds of dust in the ravines, among the hills to our right, suddenly attracted our attention, and in a few minutes column after column of buffalo came galloping down, making directly to the river. By the time the leading herds had reached the water, the prairie was darkened with the dense masses. Immediately before us, when the bands first came down into the valley, stretched an unbroken line, the head of which was lost among the river hills on the opposite side, and still they poured down from the ridge on our right. From hill to hill the prairie bottom was certainly not less than two miles wide; and allowing the animals to be ten feet apart, and only ten in a line, there were already 11,000 in view. Some idea may thus be formed of their number, when they had occupied the whole plain. In a short time they surrounded us on every side; extending for several miles in the rear, and forward as far as the eye could reach; leaving around us, as we advanced, an open space of only two or three hundred yards. . . .[135]

Here also, as in Dr. Gregg's case, the peculiar significance of these huge masses lies in Frémont's comments concerning this particular period:

The extraordinary abundance of the buffalo on the east side of the Rocky Mountains, and their extraordinary diminution, will be made clearly evident from the following statement: At any time between the years 1824 and

[133]Traverse Lake (Minnesota) is the source of Red River; but this is more probably the Traverse Lake constituting the boundary line in northeast South Dakota.

[134]Audubon and Bachman, *American Quadrupeds,* II, 47.

[135]Frémont, *Narrative,* 21-2.

1836, a traveller might start from any given point south or north in the
Rocky Mountain range, journeying by the most direct route to the Missouri
River, and during the whole distance, his road would be always among
large bands of buffalo, which would never be out of his view until he arrived
almost within sight of the abodes of civilization. . . .[136]

In 1842, I found the Sioux Indians of the Upper Platte *démontes*, as
their French traders expressed it, with the failure of the buffalo; and in
the following year, large villages from the Upper Missouri came over to the
mountains at the heads of the Platte, in search of them. The rapidly progressive failure of their principal and almost their only means of subsistence
has created great alarm among them; and at this time there are only two
modes presented to them, by which they see a good prospect for escaping
starvation: one of these is to rob the settlements along the frontier of the
States; and the other is to form a league between the various tribes of the
Sioux nation, the Cheyennes and Arapahoes, and make war against the Crow
nation, in order to take from them their country, which is now the best
buffalo country in the west. This plan they now have in consideration. . . .[137]

The general opinion expressed in the first of the foregoing passages
is historically unsound, as a mass of evidence reveals; nor is Frémont's
competence to judge so widely at that early date, anywhere made
clear. The second one reads curiously, seeing that it was above the
Forks of the Platte that the immense host (of which 11,000 were but
a fraction) was seen by Frémont in that same year, 1842. The common
explanation for any failure to see buffalo along the Platte after 1840
was that they had been 'frightened from the trail by the emigrants.'
But indications point to this argument being used by propagandist
guides to explain away any lack of buffalo, which the disappointed
pilgrims had been led to expect in perpetual swarms.[138] In any case,
the number of travellers over the Oregon trail for 1842 is given as
only 125;[139] and Frémont himself did not consider that the use of
the 'excellent roads' from the mouth of the Platte to Fort Laramie
". . . would in any way interfere with the range of the buffalo, on
which the neighbouring Indians mainly depend for support. . . ."[140]

There is an interesting instance of large numbers at a rather late
date for the particular locality (1853):

Governor Stevens, in speaking of the abundance of the buffalo on the
Shayenne River,[141] near Lake Zisne [North Dakota] says: "About five miles

[136]*Ibid.*, 141. Frémont's besetting sin is hasty generalization.

[137]*Ibid.*, 142; cf. Grinnell, *Fighting Cheyennes*, 94.

[138]Cf. Palmer in *Early Western Travels*, XXX, 72; Bancroft, *History of
Oregon*, I, 128, 396.

[139]Hebard and Brininstool, *Bozeman Trail*, II, 163.

[140]Frémont, *Narrative*, 51-3.

[141]Shayenne, Sheyenne, Cheyenne; a western tributary of the Red River
which it enters below Fargo, North Dakota. Not to be confused with the Big
Cheyenne, of South Dakota.

from camp, we ascended to the top of a high hill, and for a great distance ahead every square mile seemed to have a herd of buffalo upon it. Their number was variously estimated by members of the party, some as high as half a million. I do not think it any exaggeration to set it down at 200,000. I had heard of the myriads of these animals inhabiting these plains, but I could not realize the truth of these accounts until to-day, when they surpass everything which I could have imagined from the accounts I had received. . . ."[142]

It is a rather curious fact that what appears to have been the largest herd ever recorded as being seen together in the buffalo country, was not seen until as late as 1871. This is the classic instance related by Colonel Richard Irving Dodge; and as this appears to be the stock example of numbers in the opinion of some authorities, and has also led to some interesting estimates of the possible aggregate, I shall quote his own acount of it:

In May, 1871, I drove in a light wagon from old Fort Zara to Fort Larned, on the Arkansas, thirty-four miles. At least twenty-five miles of this distance was through one immense herd, composed of countless smaller herds of buffalo then on their journey north. The road ran along the broad level "bottom," or valley, of the river.

The whole country appeared one great mass of buffalo, moving slowly to the northward; and it was only when actually among them that it could be ascertained that the apparently solid mass was an agglomeration of in-numerable small herds of from fifty to two hundred animals, separated from the surrounding herds by greater or less space, but still separated. The herds in the valley sullenly got out of my way, and, turning, stared stupidly at me, sometimes at only a few yards' distance. When I had reached a point where the hills were no longer more than a mile from the road, the buffalo on the hills, seeing an unusual object in their rear, turned, stared an instant, then started at full speed directly toward me, stampeding and bringing with them the numberless herds through which they passed, and pouring down upon me all the herds, no longer separated, but one immense compact mass of plunging animals, mad with fright, and as irresistible as an avalanche. The situation was by no means pleasant.

Reining up my horse (which was fortunately a quiet old beast that had been in at the death of many a buffalo, so that their wildest, maddest rush only caused him to cock his ears in wonder at their unnecessary excitement), I waited until the front of the mass was within fifty yards, when a few well-directed shots from my rifle split the herd, and sent it pouring off in two streams, to my right and left. When all had passed me they stopped, appar-ently perfectly satisfied, though thousands were yet within reach of my rifle and many within less than one hundred yards. Disdaining to fire again, I sent my servant to cut out the tongues of the fallen. This occurred so frequently within the next ten miles, that when I arrived at Fort Larned I had twenty-six tongues in my wagon, representing the greatest number of buffalo that my conscience can reproach me for having murdered on any

[142]Cited by Allen, *American Bisons*, 156.

single day.[143] I was not hunting, wanted no meat, and would not have voluntarily fired at these herds. I killed only in self-preservation, and fired almost every shot from the wagon. . . .[144]

Colonel Dodge, in correspondence with Hornaday (who presumably must have signified an intention of quoting this passage, as he does[145]), adds the following (September 21, 1887):

The great herd on the Arkansas, through which I passed, could not have averaged, at rest, over fifteen or twenty individuals to the acre, but was, from my own observation, not less than twenty-five miles wide, and from reports of hunters and others it was about five days passing a given point, or not less than fifty miles deep. From the top of Pawnee Rock[146] I could see from six to ten miles in almost every direction. The whole space was covered with buffalo, looking at a distance like one compact mass, the visual angle not permitting the ground to be seen. I have seen such sights a number of times, but never on so large a scale. . . .[147]

That was the last of the great herds [that is, "Southern herd"]. . . .[148]

Hornaday subjoins a most interesting comment, which I give in his own words:

With these figures before us, it is not difficult to make a calculation that will be somewhere near the truth of the number of buffaloes actually seen in one day by Colonel Dodge, on the Arkansas River during that memorable drive, and also of the number of head in the entire herd.

According to his recorded observations, the herd extended along the river for a distance of twenty-five miles, which was in reality the width of the vast procession that was moving north, and back from the road as far

[143]It is to be feared that this 'appeal to conscience' was written for the public. Colonel Dodge was in command at North Platte, Nebraska, where Sir W. F. Butler met him in September, 1867: "We told him of the week's hunting we had had on the Platte prairies. More than thirty buffalo bulls had been shot by us, and I could not but feel some qualms of conscience at the thought of the destruction of so much animal life; but Colonel Dodge held different views. 'Kill every buffalo you can,' he said; 'every buffalo dead is an Indian gone.' . . ." (See Butler, Autobiography, 97; cf. also his Great Lone Land, 63, 241, 318.)

[144]Dodge, Plains of the Great West, 120-1; also in his other work, Our Wild Indians, 283-5, with some immaterial variations. Something very similar, in March, 1871 (Plains of the Great West, 90).

[145]Hornaday, "Extermination of the American Bison," 389-90.

[146]Pawnee Rock and Larned are consecutive stations on the Santa Fé main line, east of Dodge City, Kansas.

[147]Dodge to Hornaday, "Extermination of the American Bison," 390.

[148]Ibid. This statement seems palpably incorrect. The slaughter grew progressively worse until 1874, on Dodge's own authority (Plains of the Great West, 138, 142). In December, 1872, says an old-timer, the Santa Fé system at Dodge City never turned a wheel for three days while a herd crossed their tracks (George W. Reighard, in Edmonton Journal, January 3, 1931). In 1873, sixteen hunters (out of 'thousands': Reighard, ibid.; '8000 or 10,000' hunters: Stuart N. Lake, in Saturday Evening Post, March 8, 1930) slew 28,000 buffalo! Scores claimed '100 per day.' See chap. XV, at large, on this.

as the eye could reach, on both sides. It is making a low estimate to consider the extent of the visible ground at one mile on either side. This gives a strip of country two miles wide by twenty-five long, or a total of fifty square miles covered with buffalo, averaging from fifteen to twenty to the acre.[149] Taking the lesser number, in order to be below the truth rather than above it, we find that the number actually seen on that day by Colonel Dodge was in the neighbourhood of 480,000, not counting the additional number taken in at the view from the top of Pawnee Rock, which, if added, would easily bring the total up to a round half-million!

If the advancing multitude had been at all points fifty miles in length (as it was known to have been in some places at least), by twenty-five miles in width, and still averaged fifteen head to the acre of ground, it would have contained the enormous number of 12,000,000 head. But, judging from the general principles governing such migrations, it is almost certain that the moving mass advanced in the shape of a wedge, which would make it necessary to deduct about two-thirds from the grand total, which would leave 4,000,000, as our estimate of the actual number of buffaloes in this great herd, which I believe is more likely to be below the truth than above it.[150]

Hornaday concludes by saying: "No wonder that the men of the West of those days, both white and red, thought it would be impossible to exterminate such a mighty multitude. . . . And yet, in four short years, the southern herd was almost totally annihilated. . . ."[151]

Lest any reader should feel incredulous concerning Colonel Dodge's relation at large, he himself cites corroborative evidence from a once well-known sportsman, William Blackmore of London (a personal friend of Dodge): "In the autumn of 1868, while crossing the plains on the Kansas Pacific Railroad, for a distance of upwards of 120 miles, between Ellsworth and Sheridan, we passed through an

[149]Hornaday adds: "On the plains of Dakota, Rev. Mr. Belcourt once counted 228 buffaloes . . . feeding on a single acre of ground. This of course was an unusual occurrence with buffaloes not stampeding but practically at rest. It is quite possible also that the extent of the ground may have been under-estimated . . ." (citing Schoolcraft, North American Indians, IV, 108: Hornaday, "Extermination of the American Bison," 391 note).

[150]Ibid., 390-1. Webb (Great Plains, 44) makes the extraordinary comment on this: "Hornaday estimates that herds [sic] might total 12,000,000, and that they certainly would reach 4,000,000 as a minimum estimate . . ." (italics mine). The estimate is of this herd alone, to which there is no parallel case in Hornaday. Garretson, however, writing in 1938, says "this was only one of the numerous herds in existence at that time . . ." (American Bison, 62). Scattered over the entire remaining habitat, this is no doubt quite true; but certainly not so, as implying other herds containing 4,000,000 each. Colonel Dodge, then on the ground, thought his the last (above, note 148). Garretson ignores Dodge, except in one instance (American Bison, 39), where he contemptuously contradicts him.

[151]Hornaday, "Extermination of the American Bison," 391.

almost unbroken herd of buffalo. The plains were blackened with them, and more than once the train had to stop to allow unusually large herds to pass. . . .[152] In 1872, whilst on a scout for about 100 miles south of Fort Dodge to the Indian Territory, we were never out of sight of buffalo. . . ."[153]

It may also be pointed out that while Hornaday's deduction of two-thirds from his grand total does justice to his evident desire for moderation (likewise indicated by his adoption of the minimum number per acre), such a proportion does not necessarily follow from the premises. It is obvious that the possible aggregate in his 'wedge' depends upon precisely whereabouts in the fifty-mile extent from front to rear Colonel Dodge happened to cross its path. Hornaday has assumed the twenty-five miles as the base line of his triangular wedge which is not necessarily the case. It is extremely probable that he is 'below the truth, rather than above it.'

Hornaday appears—if I interpret him correctly—to have entertained the misconception that the buffalo hosts were never very large in the western Canadian portion of the habitat, as compared with those in the United States. If he signifies by this their total aggregate, it is scarcely natural that they should be so, in some five or six parallels of latitude (that is, from latitude 40° to, say, 55° north; beyond the Saskatchewan River), as in a latitudinal range of twenty-four or thereabouts, from Durango northward. He says:

In the British possessions and Canada, the frontier business was largely monopolized by the Hudson's Bay Fur Company [sic], although the annual 'output' of robes and hides was but small in comparison with that gathered in the United States, where the herds were far more numerous. . . .[154]

At the time of the great division made by the Union Pacific Railway, the northern body of buffalo extended from the valley of the Platte River northward to the southern shore of Great Slave Lake, eastward almost to

[152]See remarks above, note 148. The Kansas Pacific, from its frequent experience of such occurrences, was known in 1873 as the 'Buffalo Route.' Seton, Game Animals, III, 423.

[153]Dodge, Plains of the Great West, introd. by Blackmore. xvi. Garretson notes a similar case, 1859, between the North and South Platte in extreme western Nebraska; 'over 200 miles through buffalo, millions would be inadequate to express it . . .' (American Bison, 61). Reighard (1867 et seq.): "On one of our trips in the spring from Fort Hays [Kansas] southward, we met the advancing herd at Pawnee . . . and from there clear on to Fort Supply, 175 miles, we travelled through a continuous mass of buffaloes grazing slowly northward . . ." (Edmonton Journal, January 3, 1931). Supply is in Oklahoma, near the boundary of Harper and Woodward counties, 36° 35' N., 99° 35' W. Garretson (p. 64) and others mention another, quite impossible host, which I discuss later in relation to the total aggregate (see chap. XVIII).

[154]Hornaday, "Extermination of the American Bison," 441.

Minnesota, and westward to an elevation of 8000 feet in the Rocky Mountains. The herds were more numerous along the central portion of this region, and from the Platte valley to Great Slave Lake the range was continuous. The buffalo population of the southern half of this great range was, according to all accounts, nearly three times as great as that of the northern half. At that time, or let us say, 1870, there were about 4,000,000 buffaloes south of the Platte River, and probably about 1,500,000 north of it.[155]

I am aware that the estimate in the number of buffaloes in the great northern herd is usually much higher than this,[156] but I can see no good grounds for making it so. To my mind the evidence is conclusive that, although the northern herd ranged over such an immense area, it was numerically less than half the size of the overwhelming multitude which actually crowded the southern range, and at times so completely consumed the herbage of the plains that detachments of the United States Army *found it difficult to find sufficient grass for their horses and mules. . . .*[157]

This statement, with its portentous italics, is supported by a quotation from an article in *Forest and Stream*: "Horace Jones, the interpreter here [that is, at Fort Sill[158]], says that on his first trip along the line of the 100th meridian, in 1859, they passed continuous herds for over sixty miles, which left so little grass behind them that Major Thomas was seriously troubled about his horses."[159]

As we have seen, the supposed 'crowding' of the southern range did not preclude the phenomenon, at a quite early date, of travellers seeing few buffalo or none whatever for days at a time; which in the parallel instances in the north would, according to the foregoing argument probably be cited as 'proof' of this relative scarcity.

Secondly, if the range be 'continuous' from the Platte to Great Slave Lake, in any sense in which it is not (topographically) con-

[155]There seems to be some confusion here. Hornaday begins by discussing the 'northern body' and 'northern range' (*i.e.* north from the Platte). The 'southern half of this great range' logically signifies the northern United States as against Canada; then suddenly the contrast is between north and south of the Platte. His figures are impossible. According to his own estimate, Dodge's herd alone contained 4,000,000 (perhaps far more) *after 1870*; and it would be absurd to suppose it literally included *every buffalo* from Texas to the Platte! Against the increase of calves for 1871, we must set the hunting seasons of 1870-71, which were devastating. His estimate (on p. 493) is 'twice as many' south of the Platte, but which of his present totals is to be adjusted to suit that ratio is not stated. Buffalo Jones has 14,000,000 in 1870 (*Buffalo Jones' Forty Years*, 255). This will be examined in our chap. XVIII on aggregates; but the statistics of slaughter, cited by himself, render Hornaday's estimates impossibly low.

[156]'By most authors . . .' (Seton, *Life-Histories of Northern Animals*, I, 296).

[157]Hornaday, "Extermination of the American Bison," 503-4.

[158]Now in Comanche County, Oklahoma; about 34° 30′ N., 98° 30′ W.

[159]Hornaday, "Extermination of the American Bison," 504, note. The citation is from *Forest and Stream*, II, 184; no date being given.

tinuous throughout its entire extent from south to north, this almost inevitably implies a migration between the points mentioned. Since Hornaday considers that the 'great herd' was only divided into two as late as about 1867 by the Union Pacific Railway,[160] this physical continuity logically entails something not easily distinguishable from the famous Texas-and-Saskatchewan itinerary, so dear to many hearts. And according to that concept, the southern buffalo near Fort Sill this year were the northern hosts on the Saskatchewan next year; and *vice versa*. They were only United States or Canadian buffalo by the chance of that year's march.

Thirdly, while there is nothing incredible in such vast hosts as were seen (or with reasonable probability computed), eating down the pasturage, the circumstance proves nothing about relative numbers in certain respective territories; for the occurrence is not isolated, as Hornaday appears to have thought. Joel Palmer noted it, June 7, 1845: "We find in our sixteen miles travel to-day that the grass is very poor in the Platte bottoms, having been devoured by the buffalo herds. . . ."[161]

Rather curiously, Canada actually furnishes more of this particular kind of testimony than does the United States buffalo territory. Captain Palliser in 1857 found the buffalo in such vast herds between the Elbow of the South Saskatchewan and Carlton (in September)[162] that he began to entertain fears for his horses; for the grass "was eaten to the earth, as if the place had been devastated by locusts"; and he observed this more than once.[163] John McDougall mentions a similar experience, somewhat farther westward, July, 1865[164]; and Sir Cecil Denny, on the original journey of the Mounted Police westward, notes about September 1, 1874, not very far east of the Cypress Hills: "The further we travelled the more plentiful became the buffalo. We came to places where, as far as the eye could reach, thousands and tens of thousands were in sight; the country being fairly black with them. They had eaten the grass very short, making the feed very scarce, and the lakes were polluted with them. . . ."[165] Alexander Henry the

---

[160]*Ibid.*, 492, 503.

[161]Palmer, *Early Western Travels*, XXX, 48. Cf. Parkman, on the Platte, 1846: ". . . tall rank grass, that swept our horses' bellies . . .," but no buffalo! (*Oregon Trail*, 81, 82.)

[162]*Palliser Journals*, 54, 57, 84. Compare this with their 'annual itinerary' given to Hind in 1858 (chap. XIV, notes 51-2). They should have been hundreds of miles farther west at this season.

[163]*Ibid.*

[164]McDougall, *Pathfinding*, 93.

[165]Denny, *The Law Marches West*, 27-31.

younger, commenting on the fact, states—as we might expect—that it
was not an uncommon experience at any time.[166]

The inference of large numbers in various localities in Canada,
is confirmed by direct mention from eye-witnesses. Paul Kane, the
artist, who wintered in Edmonton, 1847-48, observed: "Outside the
buffaloes range in thousands close to the fort . . . extremely numerous
this winter, and several had been shot within a few hundred
yards. . . ."[167] an enormous band . . . probably numbering nearly
10,000 [December, 1847]."[168] Along the North Saskatchewan, between
Edmonton and Fort Pitt, a distance of over 200 miles, Kane noted on
a journey in January, 1848:

> The animals had, we were told, never appeared in such vast numbers,
> nor shown themselves so near the Company's establishments; some have
> even been shot within the gates of the fort [Pitt]. . . . These remarks con-
> vey but a faint idea of the astonishing numbers of these animals; within the
> whole distance we had travelled on this journey we were never out of sight
> of large herds of them, and we had not found it necessary to go a step out
> of our direct course to find more than we required for our use. They were
> probably migrating northwards to escape from the human migrations which
> are so rapidly filling up the southern and western regions, which were
> formerly their pasture grounds. . . .[169]

McDougall, south of Carlton in the summer of 1862, speaks of
gazing from a ridge ". . . which enabled us to look down and across a
plain or open country, some ten by twenty miles in size, and which
seemed to be literally full of buffalo. . . ."[170] The same observer, travelling northward from the Battle River country, apparently near
Wetaskiwin, Alberta, toward his home at Victoria (now Pakan) on
the North Saskatchewan, in July, 1865, remarks once again:

> During the afternoon I had a revelation given me as to the number and
> nomadic character of the buffalo. I had by this time spent three years in the
> buffalo country, and I thought I knew something about them. . . . But that
> afternoon, as we steadily trotted northward across country, and ever and
> anon broke into a canter, I saw more buffalo than I had ever dreamed of
> before. The woods and plains were full of them. During the afternoon we
> came to a large round plain, perhaps ten miles across, and as I sat on my
> horse on the summit of a knoll overlooking this plain, it did not seem pos-
> sible to pack another buffalo into the space. The whole prairie was one

---

[166]Coues (ed.), *Henry-Thompson Journals*, I, 193.

[167]Kane, *Wanderings of an Artist* (Radisson, Society ed.), 256.

[168]*Ibid.*, 258.

[169]*Ibid.*, 277, 278. Note the presence of such great masses on the North
Saskatchewan (in winter!) in its relation to the supposedly 'regular southward
migration' at that season.

dense mass, and as . . . I rode around this large herd I could not but feel
that my ideas concerning buffalo and the capability of this country to sustain them were very much enlarged. I had in the three years seen hundreds
of thousands of buffalo, and had travelled thousands of miles over new
trails, but I had seen only a small number of the great herds, and but a very
small portion of the great North-West. Truly these were God's cattle upon
a thousand hills, and truly this greater Canada is an immense country. . . .[171]

An old Hudson's Bay man states that there were 'moving millions'
about Last Mountain Lake, northwest from Fort Qu'Appelle, in 1869.
One could wish the expression were more precise; but coming from
an experienced resident, it must at least signify extraordinarily large
numbers.[172] Another Hudson's Bay man, Andrew McDermott, of Selkirk, told United States Consul ('Saskatchewan') Taylor in 1873:
'Quite recently a party of hunters . . . in longitude 110°, latitude 51°,
was seven days in passing through a herd. . . .'[173] The position given
is between Medicine Hat, Alberta, and the Forks of the Red Deer and
South Saskatchewan Rivers.

In the summer of 1875, we have one of the most interesting estimates of all; this time south of the International Boundary. But even
without subscribing to the theory of the long-distance migration—for
which I find no adequate evidence in the north—it needs no labouring
that a purely political division meant nothing to them; in that vicinity
the American herd of today could easily be the Canadian herd of to-
morrow. John McDougall journeying from Fort Benton, Montana, to
his home at Morley, in the Upper Bow Valley, writes thus:

I very well remember our coming out upon the summit looking down
upon the Valley of Sun River. Approximately, it would be from twelve to
fifteen miles across to the limit of our range of vision on the sister summit,
and from fifteen to twenty miles up and down the valley, which I could
cover with my eye as I surveyed the plain before me.
Immediately opposite to our gentle descent was the annual round-up. . . .
As I found out later in the day from . . . the captain of the round-up, there
were over twenty-three thousand head of cattle in the bunch down there
at our feet. These were being held for the cut-out in a natural corral made
by the eccentric windings of the river. The spot on which these twenty-three
thousand cattle and horses and men were situated was, in the landscape
before me, about as a single fly would be on the ceiling of a large audience
room.

[170]McDougall, *Forest, Lake, and Prairie*, 202.
[171]McDougall, *Pathfinding*, 94-5.
[172]Cowie, *Company of Adventurers*, 373, 379.
[173]In Allen, *American Bisons*, 173.

Several times in my wanderings[174] I had found myself on the summits of hills much higher than those of Sun River, and commanding a wider expanse, and the whole country was like a tremendous round-up. The cattle of God had gathered upon these spots, and while what I had seen I knew would be but a small fraction of the whole herd, nevertheless, here were millions. Many times, from hills and range summits, I had seen more than half a million of buffalo at one time, judging of the number of cattle before me and of the shape of the country they were in. As I beheld them that glorious day in 1875, I was abundantly assured that my statement was a very modest estimate. . . .[175]

I have myself seen a photograph of five thousand buffalo in the Wainwright Buffalo Park, Alberta (not corralled), occupying an extraordinarily small space of ground; a spot which, as McDougall very justly says would be insignificant in the huge panorama which the eye could encompass across some wide valley. Such a reasoned estimate of distances or areas, coming from one well used to judging of these matters under the spur of necessity,[176] makes 'millions' of buffalo not inherently incredible.[177]

One is compelled to acknowledge, of course, that however carefully and cautiously the various foregoing estimates appear to have been framed, they are, none the less, in the final analysis, conjecture; and as such there may be critics whom they fail to convince. I shall therefore supplement them in a later chapter by data showing that there must have been some such enormous numbers for the species to have endured as long as it did; and this at least involves the possibility of huge portions of the total, agreeing broadly with the numbers estimated by our witnesses, being actually seen as they assert, at some time in some one place.

[174]This was McDougall's first trip south of the international boundary.

[175]McDougall, *Western Trails,* 266.

[176]Compare Father De Smet, whose credibility, like McDougall's, is above suspicion: "On many of my travels I have seen, so far as I could discern on these immense plains, thousands and thousands . . ." (*Life of De Smet,* III, 1027). In 1851 "thousands of buffalo, the whole space between the Missouri and the Yellowstone was covered as far as eye could reach" (*ibid.,* II, 657). On the Piegan method of computation, 'by the space of ground they stood on,' see Thompson, *Narrative,* ed. Tyrrell, 366.

[177]Parkman, *Oregon Trail,* 95, 101. Allen (1876): "Lieut. M. E. Hogan, 22nd United States Infantry, informed me in 1873 that the buffaloes had recently crossed the Marion and Teton Rivers, in north-western Montana, and were abundant throughout the region about Fort Shaw, and that there were 'millions of buffaloes' on Milk River (*American Bisons,* 157). General Stewart Van Vliet to Professor Spencer F. Baird of the Smithsonian Institution, March 10, 1887: "General Sheridan and I have seen millions of buffalo on the plains in former times [*i.e. post* 1867] . . ." (Hornaday, "Extermination of the American Bison," 403).

Meanwhile, it may be laid down with some confidence that the available evidence furnishes no support for any theory of invariably larger numbers in any one portion of the Western plains habitat than in another.

CHAPTER XIV

THE NUMBERS OF THE BUFFALO: THE RED RIVER HUNT

W E come now to the consideration of the extermination of the buffalo as a free wild species. Hornaday[1] classifies this process under two descriptions: The first he describes as 'desultory extirpation.' This was of a more or less legitimate kind, caused by the western march of settlement and its resultant demand upon the species for food and clothing. This he dates about 1730 to 1830. The second was 'systematic destruction,' on a vastly larger scale, for the sake of robes, hides, or tongues[2] (and in its latest manifestations—beyond any reasonable doubt—as a deliberate political and military policy),[3] which dates from 1830 onwards.

It may perhaps be open to question to which of these categories the Red River Hunt really belongs. It was at all times apparently regarded (despite its alleged wastefulness), at least by those engaged in it, as a means of procuring annually what they considered as their staple food supply; rather than as a mere robe-hunting expedition. Hornaday, however, has classified the Red River Hunt as the earliest phase of the systematic destruction:

The disappearance of the bison from the eastern United States was due to its consumption as food. It was very gradual, like the march of civilization, and, under the circumstances, absolutely inevitable. In a country so thickly peopled as this region speedily became, the mastodon could have survived extinction [sic] about as easily as the bison. Except when the latter became the victim of wholesale slaughter, there was little reason to bemoan his fate save upon grounds that may be regarded as purely sentimental. He served a most excellent purpose in the development of the country. . . .[4]

The period of the systematic slaughter of the bison naturally begins with the first organized efforts in that direction, in a business-like wholesale way. Although the species had been steadily driven westward for a hundred years by the advancing settlements, and had during all that time been hunted for the meat and robes it yielded, its extermination did not begin in earnest until 1820 or thereabouts. As before stated, various persons had

[1]Hornaday, "Extermination of the American Bison," 484.
[2]Ibid., 484-6.
[3]See on this, Appendix H, "Buffalo, Indian, and Legislation."
[4]Hornaday, "Extermination of the American Bison," 486.

previous to that time made buffalo killing a business in order to sell the skins,[5] but such instances were very exceptional. By that time the bison was totally extinct in all the region lying east of the Mississippi River except a portion of Wisconsin, where it survived until about 1830. In 1820, the first organized buffalo-hunting expedition on a grand scale was made from the Red River settlement, Manitoba, in which 540 carts proceeded to the range. Previous to that time the buffaloes were found near enough to the settlements around Fort Garry that every settler could hunt independently, but as the herds were driven farther and farther away, it required an organized effort and a long journey to reach them.[6]

Perhaps the pertinacity with which the Red River Hunt was maintained so long as any buffalo were to be found, to the serious neglect of agriculture in one of the garden spots of the earth, the Red River Valley and Portage Plains, justifies his classification. In any case, the abstract question is scarcely worth disputing. I include the Red River Hunt because of its natural intrinsic importance; because certain of its actual statistical data fall logically within the scope of the present essay; and because this information represents a valuable Canadian contribution to a subject whose statistics are otherwise taken almost entirely from the United States.

Hornaday's somewhat rapid and scanty summary of the causes and inception of the regular Hunt scarcely admits of very accurate chronology. I suspect furthermore, that in addition he has overlooked certain political events, which doubtless exerted some influence on the available buffalo resources.

Alexander Ross, the settlement's principal early historian, says concerning the Red River Valley near Fort Garry, that "all this part of the country was over-run by the wild buffalo, even as late as 1810."[7] This is borne out by a letter to Lord Selkirk, dated October 1, 1811. It is from no less a person than Miles Macdonell, who became Selkirk's first governor of Red River in the following year, 1812, when his first host of settlers arrived there; it evidently was written with that project in view. Macdonell says there "could be no apprehension of any want of Buffalo meat [in Red River] . . . from the vast abundance of the Country. . . ."[8] The following year, 1812, witnessed the arrival of Lord

[5]For traffic in skins, circa 1700 (?), Wabash River, Indiana, see chap. X, note 21.
[6]Hornaday, "Extermination of the American Bison," 487-8.
[7]Ross, Red River Settlement, 15; cf. 83.
[8]Report of Canadian Archives, 1886, cxciv. E. H. Oliver prints a letter, Selkirk to Macdonell (1811), to which the foregoing is probably the answer: "It is probable that at Y[ork] F[actory] you may meet people well acquainted with the Red River, from whom you can obtain intelligence what supplies of buffalo meat may be reckoned upon . . ." (Oliver (ed.), Canadian North-West, I, 170).

Selkirk's first contingent of settlers at Red River; and a modern authority remarks: "Strange to say, this was the first year when the Buffalo did not graze over the site of the modern Winnipeg. . . ."[9]

This influx, which was followed by more colonists in the years up to 1815,[10] represented not only more mouths to be fed; it consisted of a type of folk of little use at first in a buffalo hunt, and of no use at all to go forth 'independently' in search of such game. In the winter of 1812, although according to Hornaday's version, provision for the wants of each household was still possible in the independent fashion, Governor Macdonell deemed it advisable to move a number of the colonists to Pembina, on the present-day international boundary, some sixty miles southward, where buffalo were more easily to be obtained.[11] In the following winter (1813-14) the step was repeated.[12]

Comparing these historical facts with the glowing terms of dependable permanency in Macdonell's letter to Selkirk, which I have quoted, it is not difficult to perceive in the light of evidence already presented—of which more will follow—that Macdonell had been misled in his confident anticipations by the vague assurances of unfailing plenty, of whose frequent untrustworthiness the historical evidence presents abundant proof. There can be little doubt that an agricultural settlement planted right across the frontier line of the northeastern corner of the buffalo range in that latitude would ultimately bar the further movements of the herds in that region. But the actual history of the few years after 1812, in my opinion, indicates clearly that these earliest shortages around Fort Garry (while buffalo were still reasonably plentiful near Pembina) are not to be ascribed to any uniformly-progressive 'retreat' or shrinking of the buffalo frontier; but to those inscrutable fluctuations of buffalo movement which all students of the species have recognized.[13] For in 1817, buffalo were 'far off' from Fort

[9]Seton, Life-Histories of Northern Animals, I, 254.
[10]Their numbers given in Bryce, Remarkable History, 213.
[11]Ibid., 212; Willson, Great Company, 395.
[12]A Proclamation by Governor Macdonell, Fort Daer (i.e. Pembina, named after one of Selkirk's titles, Baron Daer), January 8, 1814, reads in part: ". . . in the yet uncultivated state of the country, the ordinary resources derived from the Buffalo and other wild animals hunted within the Territory are not deemed more than adequate for the requisite supply . . ." (Oliver (ed.) Canadian North-West, I, 185).
[13]See Audubon and Bachman, American Quadrupeds, II, 40; Marcy, Exploration of the Red River, 154; Dodge, Our Wild Indians, 379; Hornaday, "Extermination of the American Bison," 377; Allen, American Bisons, 61; Coues (ed.), Henry-Thompson Journals, I, 410, 416, 420, 421; Chamberlain, Handbook of Canadian Indians, 175. An old Hudson's Bay Company man says that the scarcity or plenty, nearness or remoteness of the buffalo "was the great topic

Garry,[14] yet in 1818 a large band was seen but a short distance west of that place.[15]

From about this time onward—as of course might be expected after the institution of the annual hunt about 1820—the retreat of the buffalo frontier from the permanent settlement at Fort Garry becomes clearly noticeable. Still, there is abundance of evidence to prove that out upon the great plains it was neither so rapid nor so uniform as Hornaday's language might suggest.

In 1819, according to Wilhelm Ferdinand Wentzel, "fire having overrun the plains in Red River, buffalos had become so scarce that none were to be found nearer than at the upper part of Pembina River, so that the poor colonists were reduced to great distress and want. . . ."[16] Ross, however, says "they could still kill some buffalo in the country adjacent to Fort Pembina."[17] In 1821, they were 'scarce' there.[18] An Indian said to Ross in 1825 (at the mouth of Red River): "The buffalo have deserted our lands. . . ."[19]

We find, however, that in addition to the much larger demand upon the buffalo for food which the influx of settlers entailed—pending the sufficiency of agricultural resources, which it is well known failed at first, from locusts and other causes[20]—other agencies operated in the same direction. Among several unsuccessful efforts put forth by the Hudson's Bay Company to assist the Red River colony[21] was the

of conversation among the fur-traders, and that the price of pemmican in the Qu'Appelle country, 1867, rose and fell with the plentifulness and scarcity of the herds . . ." (Cowie, *Company of Adventurers*, 221, 226).

Maximilian says the same of hunters' wages, which varied accordingly as buffalo were 'numerous' or 'distant': Fort McKenzie, Upper Missouri River (at or near the later Fort Benton), 1833 (*Early Western Travels*, XXIII, 93).

[14]Ross, *Red River Settlement*, 47.

[15]"According to tradition . . . within a day's ride . . ." (Seton, *Life-Histories of Northern Animals*, I, 254). 'Two miles west' (personal testimony of Andrew McDermott, formerly of the Hudson's Bay Company, Selkirk, Manitoba, to U.S. Consul J. W. 'Saskatchewan' Taylor, 1873), in Allen, *American Bisons*, 172.

[16]Letters of W. F. Wentzel, in Masson, *Les Bourgeois de la Compagnie du Nord-Ouest*, I, 129.

[17]Ross, *Red River Settlement*, 50.

[18]*Ibid.*, 58. It is stated (by later writers) that they were scarce again in 1822-23. MacKay, *The Honourable Company*, 179; Bryce, *Remarkable History*, 269.

[19]Ross, *Fur Hunters*, II, 251; cf. however, his own account of starvation owing to the great storm of December, 1825, which drove the buffalo beyond the hunters' reach (*Red River Settlement*, 100).

[20]Bryce, *Remarkable History*, 346; Mackay, *Honourable Company*, 258 (1818, 1819, 1820; also later, 1857, 1864).

[21]Bryce, *Remarkable History*, 351.

abortive 'Buffalo Wool Company,' which was inaugurated in 1821 and failed in 1822.[22] This created for a time an extraordinary demand which the settlers sought to supply by a buffalo slaughter upon a scale much larger than hitherto; and which could not fail to exert an abnormal influence upon the local extirpation of the species.

In fact, when we compare the stated date (1820) of the commencement of the regular annual hunt on a large scale with carts, with the institution of the Buffalo Wool Company in the following year, it seems highly probable that this projected local industry may have been the true underlying cause of the annual hunts.[23] It certainly does not appear to have arisen from a scarcity in any serious sense: It is true that in 1826, according to Alexander Ross, buffalo were not found until 150 or 200 miles 'beyond Pembina,'[24] in what direction we are not told; but this would seem to be only another instance of the common fluctuations of this or that year. For Dr. George Bryce, who utilized a large mass of contemporary historical material which I have had no opportunity to consult, says of the period *post* 1826:[25] "Pemmican from the plains was easy to get. . . ."[26]

[22]Ross, *Red River Settlement*, 69-72; Allen, *American Bisons*, 197-200; Bryce, *Remarkable History*, 350; MacKay, *Honourable Company*, 179; not mentioned by Hornaday. Dr. E. Melchior Eberts, of Montreal, informs me that Miss Juliette Gauthier, of Ottawa, has recently revived the production, which is being worked up into art-craft fabrics (1937).

[23]General Sam Steele (*Forty Years in Canada*, 58) attributes the Red River organization to fear of the Indians. This seems doubtful, since small parties also went out; and I have found no record of any clash, or apparently near imminence of such since the beginning of the Hunt, until about 1857 (see below on this, note 70). Indian raids in the region, of course, long antedated the Hunt. See Coues (ed.), *Henry-Thompson Journals*, I, 435; *The Journal of F. A. Larocque*, ed. Burpee. Cowie, contra, says the Sioux were afraid of the Métis, who had always defeated them (*Company of Adventurers*, 329-30).

There are some sinister implications concerning Indian hostility. Certain murders by the Sioux, 1822, were alleged to have been incited by 'free traders' (Minutes, 1822, in Oliver (ed.), *Canadian North-West*, I, 640). Governor Semple to Duncan Cameron (letter, March 31, 1816) alleged that the North-West Company's people "encouraged Indian tribes to make war upon British subjects attempting to colonize . . ." (*ibid.*, 203). Contra, Cowie states that evidence exists in the Dominion Archives (*Selkirk*, and *Bulger Papers*) that Selkirk himself opened negotiations with the Sioux in his conflict with the North-West Company, and in other dubious schemes (*Company of Adventurers*, 447). Innis mentions disaffected traders long before, fomenting trouble between 'Scioux and Chippawa,' 1775-80 (*Fur Trade in Canada*, 184).

[24]Ross, *Red River Settlement*, 99.

[25]See Bryce's bibliography (*Remarkable History*, 481-6). This precise time is dated by the Red River flood of 1826. On buffalo and floods, 1806, see Coues (ed.), *Henry Thompson Journals*, I, 420 (*in extenso* below, note 143).

[26]Bryce, *Remarkable History*, 353; McLean, *Twenty-Five Years' Service* (Champlain Society ed.), 373.

After some comparison of Agnes Laut's work with her authorities, I should not attach overmuch value to the statement, in her sweeping journalistic style, that about this time "all the Northwest brigades depended on the buffalo meat of Red River for their food. . . ."[27] For some thirty years previously, John McDonald of Garth tells us (what we should naturally expect) that this came also from the Saskatchewan territory. Concerning a trip down that river in 1793, he says: "We all got safe to Cumberland Depot, Deposited the Pemican, &c, safe for the Northern Departments where nothing of the kind can be much procured. This is the usual way of supply . . . a second supply also came from Red River. . . ."[28]

A contemporary record of prices at Red River in 1825 is also of interest; although without other comparative standards it is difficult to estimate the actual values: "Buffalo tongues, 9d. each; prime robes, 5s. each; common, 2s. 6d. each; 1000 dressed skins and 200 robes requisitioned from Red River [for that year]."[29] Whether the latter very moderate numbers indicate a difficulty in obtaining more is not clear; one would scarcely think so when these figures are compared with the statistics of slaughter (and of robe export) at much later dates. It may have been a feature in the Hudson's Bay Company's local policy (like the famous 'guaranteed market' for the settlers' surplus grain, of some eight bushels per annum per man) not to purchase too many skins from any one hunter.[30]

[27]Laut, *Conquest of the Great Northwest*, II, 146.

[28]Masson, *Les Bourgeois de la Compagnie du Nord-Ouest*, II, 18; also *McGillivray's Journal*, ed. Morton, introd., xlviii; Innis, *Fur Trade in Canada*, 237. Compare also above, chap. XII, notes 72-4.

[29]Innis, "Rupert's Land in 1825" (*Canadian Historical Review*, VII, 1926, 318). MacKay quotes the same prices for 1835 (*Honourable Company*, 357). The late Professor Oliver prints the following also: 1836 = 'prime robes,' 5s., 'common,' 2s. 6d.; 'dressed buffalo skins,' 2s. 6d.; 1841 = robes, 10s.; skins, 5s.; tongues, 9d.; 1842 = robes, 7s. 6d. (Oliver (ed.), *Canadian North-West*, II, 735, 835, 851). Cf. prices of the same, Stuart Lake, etc. British Columbia. *circa* 1825 (chap. XII, note 153). See further, prices obtained by Norbert Welsh (1845-1933) 1872, 1875, = $5.00, $10.00 (*The Last Buffalo Hunter*, ed. Weekes, 137, 154-6).

[30]Ross tells us that "when the expedition arrived, the Hudson's Bay Company, according to usual custom, issued a notice that it would take a certain specified quantity of provisions, not from each fellow that had been on the plains, but from each old and recognized hunter . . ." (*Red River Settlement*, 273). Rather a sinister qualification—themselves of course being the judges!

For the 'eight bushels per annum,' Bryce, *Remarkable History*. 353; from McLean, *Twenty-Five Years' Service* (orig. ed.), II, 308 (Champlain Society ed., 381). Governor Simpson in 1857 repudiated McLean's assertions, "We purchase all their surplus agricultural produce . . ." (*Report of the Select Committee on the Hudson's Bay Company, 1857,* 50). Simpson's testimony is a

The Red River Hunt has furnished our two United States authorities upon the buffalo, particularly, with a topic for lofty and needlessly severe reflections. As these commentators have exercised a much more direct influence upon the buffalo knowledge of the world at large than have those local chroniclers upon whom their statements are professedly based, it will be well to compare their general assertions with other historical facts unknown to, or ignored by them. I quote the two scientists first. Allen writes: "The Red River half-breed hunters have undoubtedly done more to exterminate the buffalo than any single cause, and have long since wholly extirpated them throughout not only this vast region, but also over the extensive prairies of the Assiniboine, the Qu'Appelle, and the lower Saskatchewan. . . ."[31]

This must be considered a caustic judgment, coming from one fully cognizant—and possibly in part an eye-witness—of the frightful southern slaughter of 1870-74. Hornaday is even more dramatically severe:

Probably never before in the history of the world, until civilized men came in contact with the buffalo, did whole armies of men march out in true military style, with officers, flag, chaplains, and rules of war, and make war on wild animals. No wonder the buffalo has been exterminated. So long as they existed north of the Missouri in any considerable number, the half-breeds and Indians of the Manitoba Red River settlement used to gather each year in a great army, and go with carts to the buffalo range. On these great hunts, which took place every year from about the 15th of June to the 1st of September, vast quantities of buffalo were killed and the supply was finally exhausted. As if Heaven had decreed the extirpation of the species, the half-breed hunters, like their white robe-hunting rivals further south, also killed *cows* in preference to bulls so long as a choice was possible,

---

catalogue of similar shufflings, which did not deceive the Committee (*ibid.*, 45-51, 56-71, 76-7, 83-5, 90-104, etc.). For a specimen purchase, 1824: 200 hundredweight of flour, 100 bushels barley, 1200 pounds hulled barley, 100 bushels peas, 1000 bushels 'Indian corn,' 20 kegs butter of 60 pounds per keg (Minutes, in Merk (ed.), *Fur Trade and Empire*, 225). In 1843, "in order to afford a market to a certain extent to the Agriculturists of Red River Settlement," 2000 bushels of wheat were purchased by the Hudson's Bay Company (Minutes, in Oliver (ed.), *Canadian North-West*, II, 857). The population total for that year (*ibid.*, I, 74) is 5143; on the usual ratio of adult males to population, about *two* bushels per man! Many criticize McLean, but his facts match his reflections as some of theirs frequently do not; cf. Cowie (pro McLean), *Company of Adventurers*, 461, 475. Actually, McLean anticipated by a century the rapidly-crystallizing modern verdict on Simpson. See *Simpson's Athasbaska Journal*; the *Colin Robertson Correspondence* (both Champlain Society); Merk (ed.), *Fur Trade and Empire*; also *Canadian Historical Review*, XX, 1939, 319; and two less severe critics, W. L. Morton, "Agriculture in the Red River Colony," *ibid.*, XXX, 1949, 305-21; J. S. Galbraith, "The Hudson's Bay Company under fire," *ibid.*, 322-35.

[31] Allen, *American Bisons*, 208.

the very course best calculated to exterminate any species in the shortest possible time.

The army of half-breeds and Indians which annually went forth from the Red River settlement to make war on the buffalo was often far larger than the army with which Cortez subdued a great empire.[32] As early as 1846, it had become so great that it was necessary to divide it into two divisions, one of which, the White Horse Plain division, was accustomed to go west by the Assiniboine River to the "rapids crossing-place," and from there in a south-westerly direction. The Red River division went south to Pembina, and did most of their hunting in Dakota. The two divisions sometimes met, but not intentionally. . . .[33]

The foregoing short summary contains so much of what is doubtless pure misapprehension, and so much which, while true in fact is misleading in inference, that one scarcely knows where to begin. I shall discuss the various phases of Hornaday's argument in the order given by himself, commencing with the 'rules of war.'

While in other relations we recognize the necessity for discipline among large masses of men, which alone can differentiate armies from mobs, Hornaday actually appears to regard it as an aggravation of the offence that this feature accompanied the hunt. It may truly enough never have been seen on quite so large a scale 'previous to civilized man'; but it seems to have been in use among a number of Indian buffalo-hunting tribes for a long time;[34] and it is more probably derived from that custom. In the case of the Indian tribes, this is stated to be for the purpose of protecting the buffalo and preserving them for the

---

[32]An idle comparison, and perhaps untrue, if we compare *combatants*. Given by Prescott as 166 before, and 1100 after the clash with Narváez (*Conquest of Mexico*, II, 26, 49). Fiske: 'Narváez with not less than 1200 soldiers; Cortez' total about 450, but only 300 with him; the remainder with Alvarado in Mexico' (*Discovery of America*, II, 282); '250 with Cortez,' contra Narváez (*Purchas his Pilgrimes*, XV, 515).

[33]Hornaday, "Extermination of the American Bison," 474-5.

[34]Hornaday himself notes that the Omahas had laws for the buffalo hunt (*ibid.*, 477). Compare also, 'soldiers' (*i.e.* social organizations; see *Handbook of American Indians*, II, 611, 614) and their authority; In 1776 (Alexander Henry the elder, *Travels, 1760-1776*, 288-92, 309); Piegans, *circa* 1800 (Thompson, *Narrative*, ed. Tyrrell, 358); Mandans, 1833 (Maximilian, *Early Western Travels*, XXIII, 293): Saulteau, *circa* 1877 (Morris, *Treaties with the Indians of Manitoba*, 82). Jenness, *Sarcee Indians of Alberta*, 41-6; Kidd, "Blackfoot Ethnography," 134, etc.

On prudence concerning buffalo, see also Ross, *Fur Hunters*, II, 125; Mandans, 1806, in Coues (ed.), *Henry-Thompson Journals*, I, 366; Cheyennes and Arapahoes, *circa* 1850, in Dodge, *Plains of the Great West*, 266, 277, 353; *Our Wild Indians*, 576; perhaps also Kiowas and Comanches, and his remarks in general (*ibid.*, 287, 576). See above, chap. V, notes 109-11.

Cowie mentions wasteful slaughter by Cree 'young men,' Gull Lake (main line of C.P.R., Saskatchewan), June, 1868; but this was 'despite the warnings and entreaties of the elders': *Company of Adventurers*, 297; cf. Sioux, *ibid.*, 188.

use of the tribe at large, instead of allowing one or two ungovernable individualists to stampede them at their pleasure. Can any unbiassed critic doubt that with the Red River Hunt, such rules as those forbidding any person to "fork off, lag behind, or go before, without permission" or to "run buffalo before the general order"[35] were for the purpose of restricting, not encouraging, an indiscriminate slaughter (a propensity which in any society seldom needs encouragement)? The very name by which the hunt captain's auxiliary police were designated—'soldiers'—was that used by the Indians (or some of them) long before. We must remember also that these men were engaged in providing for their own subsistence and that of their families during a long hard winter; and that waste under such conditions would be something more than the mere indifference of a nomad—who could follow the game almost indefinitely—towards a more remote future (for which Hornaday elsewhere castigates the Indians). These laws are, in any case, considered by most students in the sense which I have suggested; including at least one, Dr. Bryce, who was in living touch with veterans of the bygone Red River days.[36]

Precisely the same arguments apply to the preference for the cows. This, too, was an inheritance from Indian usage from the earliest historic times; and one which, whatever other disparities of taste between Indian and white man might prevail in foods, very speedily commended itself to the whites. Bull meat was scarcely ever eaten except by those *in extremis*, when most men so circumstanced are not particularly fastidious.[37]

It is easy for us, who have witnessed the final scenes of the tragedy, to rant about "criminal folly" and so forth, but Hornaday himself acknowledged—in some places, not uniformly—that the men of that era were quite justified in regarding the possible extinction of the buffalo as an idle chimera.[38] Whichever of his contemporary utterances

[35]For these, see Ross, *Red River Settlement*, 249; Hind, *Report, 1858*, 111; Bryce, *Remarkable History*, 368; Haworth, *Trailmakers of the Northwest*, 145-9.

Oliver shows that the Buffalo Hunt regulations were framed by the 'General Quarterly Court of Red River' (*Canadian North-West*, I, 80, 129). Gabriel Dumont, Riel's lieutenant, organized a 'Government' on the general lines of the Buffalo Hunt in the Duck Lake district, Saskatchewan, 1873 (*ibid.*, II, 1038); Stanley, *Canadian Historical Review*, XVII, 1936, 399-412; also his *Birth of Western Canada*, 179-82.

[36]Bryce, *Remarkable History*, 264, 364-72; Haworth, *Trailmakers of the Northwest*, 145-9.

[37]See Appendix P on this.

[38]"No wonder that the men of the West of those days, both white and red, thought it would be impossible to exterminate such a mighty multitude . . ." (Hornaday, "Extermination of the American Bison," 391).

"Like the Indian and many white men also, the buffalo seemed to feel that

on this question the reader may prefer to accept, an abundance of evidence exists proving that such was the actual belief of the Indians, and quite logically, doubtless of many, or most, of the half-breeds also.[39]

This being the case, I can conceive of no reason why they should not select the most palatable, or the most readily workable, of the buffalo products for their own use. We should undoubtedly have done the same; and to speak of it as "a course best calculated" to exterminate the species, or to produce any other effect, when it is quite evident that calculation of any long-sighted economic character was seldom or never an Indian trait,[40] is wholly without justification.

Concerning the numbers and general conduct of the Hunt, Alexander Ross says: ". . . the hunters make two trips to the plains annually; the proceeds of the first are sold off to supply their wants in clothing and other necessaries for the year, but the second furnishes their winter stock of food. . . ."[41]

Hornaday appears to have misconceived what I take to be Ross's meaning: that is, two expeditions at different seasons. He says: "The two great annual expeditions of the Red River half-breeds which always took place in the summer, went in two directions from Winnipeg and Pembina—one, the White Horse Plain division, going westward along the Qu'Appelle into the Saskatchewan country, and the other, the Red River division, southward into Dakota. . . ."[42]

In the quotation previously cited from his pen on this matter,[43] he certainly conveys the impression (which seems to be the true one) that the actual centre and starting point for the Hunt was Red River, whence it derived its name. John McLean (1849) tells us there were

---

their number was so great that it could never be sensibly diminished . . ." (ibid., 429).

"Although half a million buffaloes were killed by Indians, half-breeds, and whites, the natural increase was so very considerable, as to make it seem that the evil day of extermination was yet far distant . . ." (ibid., 466).

[39]My friend Dr. E. A. Corbett (then of the University of Alberta) was told by a man living circa 1933, grandson of an old Hudson's Bay Company man, that the buffalo were not 'exterminated,' either by disease (on which, see Appendix J, "Buffalo and Disease") or by man, the latter being preposterous. Man 'never could have exterminated them; they went back into the earth whence they had come'!

[40]In Hornaday's own opinion at least. See his paper ("Extermination of the American Bison," 391, 465, 480-3, 490-2, 499, 506, 512).

[41]Ross, Red River Settlement, 98-9; cf. Steele's remark, Forty Years in Canada, 94-6.

[42]Hornaday, "Extermination of the American Bison," 425.

[43]See above, note 33.

two trips generally, the latter in August.[44] When Milton and Cheadle were at Fort Garry, in 1862, the accepted phraseology was 'Spring and Fall Hunt'; and they mention Milton 'going out' with the Fall Hunt in 1860.[45] Paul Kane, the artist, who saw Fort Garry on his way westward in 1846, writes:

Their buffalo hunts are conducted by the whole tribe, and take place twice a year, about the middle of June and October, at which periods notice is sent around to all the families to meet at a certain day on the White Horse Plain, about twenty miles [westward] from Fort Garry. Here the tribe is divided into three bands, each taking a separate route for the purpose of falling in with the herds of buffaloes. These bands are each accompanied by about 500 carts, drawn either by an ox or a horse. . . .[46]

Southesk also noted this division at White Horse Plain, in June, 1859.[47] Hornaday jumbles chronology and locality indiscriminately, as though immediately after 1846 buffalo could not be found westward nearer than 'the Saskatchewan country' beyond the Qu'Appelle. This of course is nonsense; but at the same time, what might be called the local or geographical history of the Red River Hunt will be found to furnish some curious comment upon any theory of regularity in buffalo movement. I shall quote the description given by Hind, as it is the most elaborate I have seen concerning the Red River Hunt, and is also the chief basis for the generalizations of Allen[48] and Hornaday[49] respectively on this particular phase. Hind's description is as follows:

Red River hunters recognise two grand divisions of buffalo, those of the Grand Coteau and Red River, and those of the Saskatchewan. . . . The north-western buffalo ranges are as follows, and first with respect to the Red River Range: The animals winter on the Little Souris, and south-easterly towards and beyond Devil's Lake [that is, in Dakota] and thence on to Red River and the Shayenne.[50] Here, too, they are found in the spring. Their course then lies west toward the Grand Coteau de Missouri, until the month of June, when they come north, and revisit the Little Souris from the west, turning round the west flank of Turtle Mountain to Devil's lake, and by the main river (Red River) to the Shayenne again. In the memory

[44]McLean, *Twenty-Five Years' Service* (orig. ed.), II, 302; so also McDougall, *Saddle, Sled, and Snowshoe*, 141.

[45]Milton and Cheadle, *North-West Passage*, 43-4, 60; cf. Hind, *Report, 1858,* 7.

[46]Kane, *Wanderings of an Artist* (Radisson Society ed.), 51.

[47]Southesk, *Travels*, 41.

[48]Allen, *American Bisons*, 170.

[49]Hornaday, "Extermination of the American Bison," 474-5.

[50]A tributary of the Red River, which it joins at Moorhead, Minnesota, about 47° N., 97° W. Not to be confused with the Big Cheyenne, of South Dakota. I use the spelling of the document quoted in all cases. See below, notes 54, 91.

of many Red River hunters, the buffalo used to visit the prairies of the Assiniboine as far north as Lake Manitobah; where in fact their skulls and bones are now to be seen; their skulls are also seen on the east side of the Red River of the North, in Minnesota, but the living animal is very rarely to be met with. A few years ago they were accustomed to pass on the east side of Turtle Mountain through the Blue Hills of the Souris, but of late years their wanderings in this direction have ceased; experience teaching them that their enemies the Half-breeds have approached too near their haunts in that direction. . . .

The great western herds winter between the South and the North Branches of the Saskatchewan, and south of the Touchwood Hills; they cross the South Branch in June and July, visit the prairies on the south side of the Touchwood Hill range, and cross the Qu'Appelle valley anywhere between the Elbow of the South Branch and a few miles west of Fort Ellice on the Assiniboine. They then strike for the Grand Coteau de Missouri, and their eastern flank often approaches the Red River herds coming north from the Grand Coteau. They then proceed across the Missouri, up the Yellow Stone, and return to the Saskatchewan as winter approaches, by the flanks of the Rocky Mountains. We saw many small herds, belonging to the western bands, cross the Qu'Appelle Valley and proceed in single file toward the Grand Coteau in July last [that is, 1858].[51]

The eastern bands which we had expected to find on the Little Souris were on the main river (Red River is so termed by the Half-breeds hunting in this quarter). They had proceeded early thither, far to the south of their usual track, in consequence of the devastating fires which swept the plains from the Rocky Mountains to Red River in the autumn of 1857. We met bulls all moving south, when approaching Fort Ellice; they had come from their winter quarters near the Touchwood Hill range. As a general rule the Saskatchewan bands of buffalo go north during the autumn and south during the summer. The Little Souris and main river bands [Red River] go north-west in summer and south-east in autumn. . . .[52]

The foregoing is an admirable specimen of a type of general description which might be considered highly informative or even convincing, if we had no other source of information. It goes without saying that the men who were able to formulate for Hind's benefit

[51]In his daily jottings, Hind records them as 'going east' at the time (Report, 1858, 52, 57, 63). As an instance of a 'regular migration route,' Hind's two points "between the Elbow of the South Branch (of the Saskatchewan) and a few miles west of Fort Ellice," are five degrees of longitude apart, just about 230 miles (at circa 51° North).

[52]Ibid., 106. John Macdonell records 'incredible numbers' on the Qu'Appelle Plains, or east of there, October 7, 1793; where they ought not to have been at that season, according to the above (Journal, in Gates (ed.), Five Fur Traders of the North-West, 115). What was doubtless the general consensus of local opinion at Fort Qu'Appelle, 1868, knew nothing of these routes. Cowie says: "The annual northern migration of the buffalo herds from across the Missouri [had been diverted westward] . . ." (Company of Adventurers, 290, 302, 458). Unfortunately, this 'annual' event itself is only another tradition, lacking historical confirmation.

such a clear description of the annual buffalo itinerary in their own local territory should never have had the least difficulty in locating the herds at any time during their annual hunts. But alas! "facts are chiels that winna' ding an' daurna' be disputed"; and historical evidence tells a totally different tale.

It is rather unfortunate that in the midst of all this uniformity, Hind himself should have had to record his own party's failure to find buffalo on the Little Souris "as they had expected." It is true that he ascribed this to 'devastating fires' (of which I have found no mention in this wide-spread sense in the Palliser papers of 1857); and he remarks on the same page that nothing but fire would divert the buffalo from their route. Even granting this, fires were no exceptional occurrence; and would, in their acknowledged frequency, be sufficient to upset all buffalo calculations about three times out of four.

Hind, too, writing in the present tense, *circa* 1858, has them around Devil's Lake (North Dakota) in winter and springtime. Hornaday says, however: "In 1840, the site of the present city of Jamestown, Dakota, was the northeastern limit of the herds that summered in Dakota, and the country lying between that point and the Missouri was for years the favorite hunting-ground of the Red River division. . . ."[53] Jamestown is about eighty miles south of Devil's Lake!

I shall call a witness more authoritative than either of the above. Alexander Ross says:

Of late years, the chase has been far distant from Pembina; and the hunters do not so much as know in what direction they may find the buffalo, as these animals frequently shift their ground. It is a mere leap in the dark, whether at their outset the expedition takes the right or the wrong road; and their luck in the chase, of course, depends materially on the choice they make. The year of our narrative [that is, 1840] they travelled a south-west or middle course; being the one generally preferred, since it leads past most of the rivers near their sources, where they are most easily crossed. The only inconvenience attending this choice is the scarcity of wood, which in a dry season is but a secondary consideration.

Not to dwell on the ordinary routine of each day's journey, it was the ninth day from Pembina before we reached the Chienne river, distant only about 150 miles; and as yet we had not seen a single band of buffalo. On the third of July, our nineteenth day from the settlement, and at a distance of little more than 250 miles, we came in sight of our destined hunting ground; and on the day following . . . we had our first buffalo race. . . .[54]

He says elsewhere concerning the same journey: "After leaving the Missouri River . . . we turned to the west, where we had a few

[53] Hornaday, "Extermination of the American Bison," 425 (citing no authority).   [54] Ross, *Red River Settlement*, 255.

races with various success. We were afterwards led for some time backwards and forwards at the pleasure of the buffalo, often crossing and
recrossing our path until we had travelled to almost every point of the
compass. . . ."[55]

Although the very essence of Ross's recital is the utter unreliability
of buffalo movement, and although he makes it equally clear (in my
opinion at least) that the route he mentions was merely that of 'the
year of our narrative,' 1840, yet it would seem that Hornaday, in his
positive passion for systematization, makes the ephemeral experiences
of that year his authority—he cites no other—for another of his uniformitarian dicta. Yet both he and Hind (whose words he copies
verbatim) tell us that "the two divisions sometimes met but not intentionally. . . ."[56]

Either those children of the plains were hopelessly lost; or else this
means precisely what Ross tells us in so many words, that the locality
of the buffalo was entirely problematical, "taking a leap in the dark."
How far afield from Hornaday's uniform routes and territories the
hunters sometimes had to go is shown by the fact (cited by himself)
of the White Horse Plain division being in Dakota territory in 1849[57];
while in the following year, 1850, when Father Lacombe accompanied
them, the "Pembina Hunt"—which can signify only the southern, or
what Hornaday calls the Red River division—travelled westward, I
should suppose upon good report of plenty, and found buffalo about
Turtle Mountain, some 150 miles distant.[58]

Hind's elaborate generalization would excite less comment had it
been written before his own plains' experience, instead of after. As it
stands, one is amazed that a scientist could calmly write such a paragraph, with no suggestion of critical query other than the one single
remark about the fires. For his incidental daily jottings reveal unmistakably the truth of Ross's description, and the inaccuracy of his own.
One would like to know what those old plainsmen really told to some
of these visitors. One suspects something of that weakness in uncultivated pioneers for very definite but unauthenticated assertion; perhaps also a touch of the fondness for 'pulling the leg' of the tenderfoot-
inquirer, against which Theodore Roosevelt and Dodge warn their
readers.[59]

[55]Ibid., 265. Seton, citing the foregoing, erroneously dates it '1849' (Life-
Histories of Northern Animals, I, 254).
[56]Hind, Report, 1858, 106; Hornaday, "Extermination of the American Bison,"
475.   [57]Ibid.   [58]Hughes, Father Lacombe, 23-33.
[59]Roosevelt, Winning of the West, passim; Dodge, Plains of the Great West,
145.

At the very outset of his journey, Hind mentions "the failure of last year's autumn buffalo hunt" (that is, 1857);[60] no general cause, such as fires, being indicated. He was also told that "the buffalo this year are far south";[61] and (acting no doubt upon sound advice) he tells us: "At White Horse Plains, 22 miles from Fort Garry, we purchased an ox, to serve as a *dernier resort* [*sic*] in case we should not meet with buffalo. . . ."[62] They needed the ox. At Little Souris River (June, 1858), he found occasion to remark: "Here we expected to find buffalo, but not a sign of any living creature could be detected with the aid of a good glass. The prairie had been burnt last autumn, and the Buffalo had not arrived from the south or west to people this beautiful level waste. . . ."[63]

At the 'Souris Sand Hills' (July 1, 1858), he observed: "The *Bois de Vache* [that is, 'buffalo-chips'] . . . is distributed very abundantly in the prairie and through the Sand Hills and ranges near to the [Hudson's Bay Company's] post. In fact the buffalo were very numerous during the whole of the winter of 1856 and spring of 1857 on the banks of the Souris, but the great fires during the autumn of last year, have driven them south and north-west, and between the two branches of the Saskatchewan. . . ."[64]

On the following day he notes "an abundance of last year's *bois de vache*" and "the first fresh buffalo tracks were seen to-day. . . ."[65] On July 3, they made an excursion southward to the Souris Lakes (in Dakota), ". . . in the hope of finding buffalo to replenish our stores; but although fresh tracks were seen, and skulls and bones in large numbers, the remains of last year's 'run,' yet no living animal but a 'cabri' [antelope] was visible. . . ."[66]

According to his general description which I have quoted at length, the southern (Grand Coteau and Red River) herds wintered from the Little Souris to the Cheyenne, in a general southeasterly direction. The 'Saskatchewan' herds wintered in the Carlton country and between the two Branches. Fort Ellice in this itinerary is purely a 'summer resort,' as is likewise the Touchwood Hills region. But Palliser, writing

[60]Hind, *Report, 1858,* 7.
[61]*Ibid.,* 8.
[62]*Ibid.,* 39.
[63]*Ibid.,* 42.
[64]*Ibid.,* 43. In June, 1857, Palliser's party travelled 'hundreds of miles' through this very region without seeing any; later finding 'buffalo in great numbers' west of Moose Jaw Creek (*Palliser Journals,* 48, 54-5).
[65]Hind, *Report, 1858,* 44.
[66]*Ibid.,* 45.

about the same time, says: "During the winter, as the herds of buffalo seek the shelter of the partially wooded country, the Plains Indians tent near the North Saskatchewan and toward the Touchwood Hills and Fort Carlton. . . ."[67]

Hind himself remarks incidentally: "Ponds and lakes are numerous on the Grand Coteau side [that is, of the Qu'Appelle River—apparently] and it is probably on this account that the Buffalo cross the Qu'Appelle valley near the Moose-Jaws Fork and west of Buffalo Pound Hill Lake; in the winter they keep toward the Touchwood Hills for the sake of shelter. . . ."[68]

"Buffalo congregate in the beautiful prairie south of the fort [that is, Touchwood Hills] every winter, sometimes in vast numbers. . . ."[69] I have noted before that Hind writes in the present tense. Hornaday comments on Hind as follows:

In 1857 the Plains Crees, inhabiting the country around the headwaters of the Qu'Appelle [250 miles due west from Winnipeg] assembled in council, and determined that in consequence of promises often made and broken by the white men and half-breeds, and the rapid destruction by them of the buffalo they [the Crees] fed on, they would not permit either white men or half-breeds to hunt in their country or travel through it, except for the purpose of trading for their dried meat, pemmican, skins or robes. . . . In 1858 . . . Professor Hind's expedition saw only one buffalo in the whole course of their journey from Winnipeg, until they reached Sand Hill Lake, at the head of the Qu'Appelle, near the south branch of the Saskatchewan, where the first herd was encountered. Although the species was not totally extinct on the Qu'Appelle at that time, it was practically so. . . .[70]

[67]*Palliser Journals*, 202.
[68]Hind, *Report, 1858*, 53.
[69]*Ibid.*, 69. Cowie mentions that it was frequently necessary at Fort Ellice to station watchmen around the hay corral in winter when the snow was deep, to keep the buffalo from the stacks (*Company of Adventurers*, 182). But what about those buffalo, 'which nothing could turn from their course!'
[70]Hornaday, "Extermination of the American Bison," 489-90. For his first paragraph, printed within inverted commas, he cites no authority. It is in Hind, *Report, 1858*, 52. Charles Pratt, missionary at Fort Qu'Appelle, 1857, himself a pure Cree (Palliser) or Stoney (Hector), or half-breed (Hind, 48), but said to be actually a Cree-Assiniboine (so Cowie, who knew him well, *Company of Adventurers*, 235), reported the Crees as 'beginning to apprehend scarcity of buffalo' (*Palliser Journals*, 51). Cowie notes the tribes in the Cypress Hills locality. 1868, resenting the 'half-breed whites' (which must mean the Red River Hunt) coming to hunt in that region; they thought 'the entire British nation was living on their pemmican' (Cowie, *Company of Adventurers*, 301-5, 445, 483). Norbert Welsh says that about the same time the half-breeds were warned by the Indians not to hunt buffalo about Red Deer Lake (some 50 miles south of Prince Albert. Saskatchewan) unless they paid a 'duty' on every buffalo of which there were 'lots,' about 1866-68 (Welsh, *The Last Buffalo-Hunter*, ed. Weekes, 97-100). See also Black, *History of Saskatchewan*, 180.

The Earl of Southesk, at Fort Qu'Appelle, June, 1859, says: "Not a buffalo to be seen, though for the last two days we had been travelling, constantly finding the skulls and bones of former herds."[71] George M. Grant, however, in August, 1872, met a half-breed and his family, whose six carts were laden with the spoils from sixty buffaloes, on the Qu'Appelle River above Fort Ellice; and one hundred miles farther up (down?) the river, buffalo were encountered 'in swarms.'[72]

We have seen the Touchwood Hills country described by Hind[73] both as a summer 'port of call' and ('near there') as a wintering ground. Touchwood Hills post was 'starving' in February, 1863;[74] but buffalo were plentiful near there in August, 1864.[75] Grant, in August also, 1872, records quantities, "where the buffalo have not come on this route for many years. . . ."[76]

[71]Southesk, *Travels*, 58, 70. In the foregoing work of Welsh which appeared too late for inclusion in my text, there is abundant proof that buffalo were plentiful in the territory between Fort Qu'Appelle and well up towards Prince Albert in the later sixties. In fall and winter, 1865-66, they were 'plentiful' near the Round Plain (Dundurn, Saskatchewan); this man's own share being '50 cows.' In a winter hunt in a blizzard, '80 buffalo' were shot. Early in 1866, the plains were 'black with buffalo,' 700 being killed in two 'runs' by 25 men; and in March, 1866, 1000 fell through the ice into the South Saskatchewan River, and were frozen in. There was 'a big herd' about 100 miles southwest of Red Deer Lake (*i.e.* near modern Saskatoon); and later, 'large herds, 1000 and more in a herd' in the same region (Welsh, 1845-1933, *The Last Buffalo-Hunter*, 73-8, 82-5, 105-10), etc.

Near Qu'Appelle itself, there was 'abundance,' 1869; and 'moving millions' about Last Mountain Lake that summer. The following winter, 1869-70, there were 'scattered bands' from the Qu'Appelle River to the Elbow of the South Saskatchewan River (Cowie, *Company of Adventurers*, 373, 379, 388). In 1870, the hunt failed, and there were no buffalo about Fort Qu'Appelle that winter, 1870-71 (*ibid.*, 411-18); although at Round Plain, "where the buffalo used to winter and travel there more than at any other place on the plains," they had one hunt that winter, after which the buffalo 'went south into American territory' (Welsh, *The Last Buffalo-Hunter*, 118, 129); although Fort Qu'Appelle apparently saw nothing of them.

[72]Grant, *Ocean to Ocean* (Radisson Society ed.), 123. There were buffalo near Fort Qu'Appelle in 1872, but 'few' (Cowie, *Company of Adventurers*, 454). A recent historian notes the vagaries of the buffalo hunt, 1860-70 (MacKay, *Honourable Company*, 284). But they were still enjoying 'buffalo steaks' at Fort Qu'Appelle, in the winter of 1879-80 (Stanley, *Birth of Western Canada*, 220).

[73]I believe it will tax the ingenuity of any critic to reduce the foregoing discordant data into any systematic movement, Hind's or any other (see above, notes 52, 67-9).

[74]Milton and Cheadle, *North-West Passage*, 157.

[75]McDougall, *Saddle, Sled, and Snowshoe*, 163.

[76]Grant, *Ocean to Ocean*, 126, 137. Last Mountain Lake (1869: above, note 71) is about 30 miles or so west of the Touchwood Hills, on or south of the old Carlton trail from Fort Garry.

Similarly, with regard to Fort Ellice, situated at the junction of the Qu'Appelle and the Assiniboine (about 50° 30′ N., 102° W., near Lazare, Manitoba, on the main line of the Canadian National, formerly Grand Trunk Pacific, and just east of the Manitoba-Saskatchewan boundary): in July, 1858, Hind found them 'numerous' only some thirty miles west of the fort;[77] and Southesk also found buffalo near there in July, 1859.[78]

From a precious fragment of a Diary of the Fort (1860-63) found near there in a decayed condition and printed by a recent and pains-taking historian of Saskatchewan,[79] we find the following: "Men starv-ing at the Fort" (April 2, June 9, 1860); buffalo "a short distance beyond Moose Mountain"[80] (April 9, June 26, 1860);[81] "Sent off hunt-ers" (October 22, 1860); "Hunters returned with meat of thirty buffalo cows" (November 12, 1860);[82] "Hunters returned with meat of twelve bulls; no cows seen" (November, 1863).[83]

Acting presumably upon local advice at Fort Garry, Milton and Cheadle tell us that Lord Dunmore and a party from Montreal, going buffalo hunting on the plains in August, 1862, started for Fort Ellice as their base;[84] but unfortunately we have no information where they found their buffalo, and the two travellers mentioned seem to have encountered none that same year earlier than near Carlton.[85] In July, 1864, Fort Ellice was certainly 'badly off for food.'[86] It is in keeping with these fluctuations that about Turtle Mountain, where the Hunt found them in 1850,[87] and Palliser's party saw none in 1857,[88] Lord Southesk records them in 1859.[89] There can be little doubt that a care-

[77]Hind, Report, 1858, 46, 51, 106.
[78]Southesk, Travels, 51, 52.
[79]Hawkes, Saskatchewan and her People, I, 181-8.
[80]Fort Ellice to Moose Mountain, approximately 60 miles southwest.
[81]Hawkes, Saskatchewan and her People, I, 182, 183, 185.
[82]Ibid., 186.
[83]Ibid., 187. But see above, note 69, on buffalo and haystacks there. Cowie certainly writes as though it came within his own time. See note 166.
[84]Milton and Cheadle, North-West Passage, 45.
[85]Ibid., 50, 58. But compare Governor Simpson's experience over the same route, Fort Ellice to Carlton, July, 1841: "For three or four days the soil has been absolutely manured with the dung of the buffalo, so that myriads of these animals must have recently passed over the ground; and we hoped soon to meet with a herd of them . . ." (Journey Around the World, I, 74). They were not seen until two or three days after Carlton (ibid., 99). The earlier allusion refers to the famous 'Buffalo Robe Plain,' southeast of Carlton (another 'unfailing haunt'). See Merk (ed.), Fur Trade and Empire, 135.
[86]McDougall, Saddle, Sled, and Snowshoe, 157.
[87]Hughes, Father Lacombe, 23-33.
[88]Palliser Journals, 48.
[89]Southesk, Travels, 343, 344.

ful historian is right in thinking that as regards the Red River Hunt: "the place of rendezvous varied from year to year, according to the variations in the movements of the migrating buffalo. . . ."[90] His conclusion seems to me inevitable.

It may be urged by some critics that these erratic variations of movement were in themselves purely a result of the incessant attacks of the Red River hunters. Hornaday would certainly support such a suggestion:

Although the bison formerly ranged to Fort Garry, near Winnipeg, they had been steadily killed off and driven back, and in 1840 none were found by the expedition until it was 250 miles from Pembina, which is situated on the Red River at the International Boundary. At that time the extinction of the species from the Red River to the Cheyenne was practically complete.[91] The Red River settlers, aided, of course, by the Indians of that region, are responsible for the extermination of the bison throughout northeastern Dakota, as far as the Cheyenne River, northern Minnesota, and the whole of what is now the Province of Manitoba. More than that, as the game grew scarce and retired farther and farther, the half-breeds, who despised agriculture so long as there was a buffalo to kill, extended their hunting operations westward along the Qu'Appelle until they encroached upon the hunting-grounds of the Plain Crees, who lived in the Saskatchewan country.

Thus was an enormous inroad made into the northern half of the herd which had previously covered the entire pasture region from the Great Slave Lake to central Texas. This was the first visible impression of the systematic killing which began in 1820. Up to 1840 it is reasonably certain, as will be seen by figures given elsewhere, that by this business-like method of the half-breeds, at least 652,000 buffaloes were destroyed by them alone. Even as early as 1840 the Red River hunt was prosecuted through Dakota southwestwardly to the Missouri River and a short distance beyond it. Here it touched the wide strip of territory bordering that stream, which was even then being regularly drained of its animal resources by the Indian hunters, who made the river their base of operations, and whose robes were shipped on its steam boats.

It is certain that these annual Red River expeditions into Dakota were kept up as late as 1847,[92] and as long thereafter as buffaloes were to be

[90]Black, History of Saskatchewan, 63.

[91]Meaning, presumably, from the Red River Settlement to the Cheyenne. The Cheyenne is itself a tributary of Red River, entering it at Fargo, North Dakota, and Moorhead, Minnesota; and is the Shayenne of Hind, 1858 (Report, 106). There is the town of Sheyenne (North Dakota), south of Devil's Lake, and on the river. The tribe of that name (pronounced 'Shy-an' in the West, as Henry, 'Schians,' 1806; Coues (ed.), Henry-Thompson Journals, I, 354), formerly lived in this locality, reaching the Missouri, circa 1676; so Grinnell, Fighting Cheyennes, 1-4; Burpee (ed.), Journals of La Vérendrye, 407; Maximilian, Early Western Travels, XXII, 333. A later scholar prefers 'some time after 1700': Waldo R. Wedel, "Culture Sequences in the Central Great Plains" (Smithsonian Miscellaneous Collections, vol. 100, 1940), 327. See above, note 50.

[92]He himself instances 1849 ("Extermination of the American Bison," 475); above, note 57.

found in any number between the Cheyenne and the Missouri. At the same time the White Horse Plains division, which hunted westward from Fort Garry, did its work of destruction quite as rapidly and thoroughly as the rival expedition to the United States. . . .[93]

I shall have occasion before concluding this chapter to offer some criticisms concerning the inaccuracies of fact in the foregoing, and the almost inevitable resultant misapprehensions.

Other men seem to have held similar views; not about the Red River Hunt specifically, so much as to the tendency of hunting in general to drive the buffalo herds backward like a wall. Palliser remarks on this: "The great plains of the North Saskatchewan, which, within the last fifteen years, were every winter teeming with buffalo, have now only a few large bands, numbering, it is true, tens of thousands, but no longer to be found all over the country as in former times. The large bands, indeed, in which these animals are now met with, are a sure sign of their being overhunted, and the result is already being felt."[94]

Southesk held much the same opinion; except that he did not regard the large bands as a late manifestation, dating only from the time when the approach of extermination had become imminent; in which view he was historically correct. He observes (1859):

Large as were the herds I saw in July, they were nothing to what I have heard and read of, and there is reason to believe that I then beheld all the buffaloes belonging to the two Saskatchewan valleys and the intervening country pressed from various quarters into one great host. There were none near Edmonton, none near Pitt; none near Carlton; during the whole winter—the inhabitants meanwhile almost starving. And now I learn that the Blackfeet have been compelled to leave their usual settlements, and go far south in pursuit of their means of existence. . . .[95]

It is of course obvious that if the buffalo of the Western Canadian territory were literally "pressed into one great host," they could be in only one place at once; and quite apart from the fact that they would be constantly driven about by hunters,[96] it is very unlikely that the herd would always be in the same place. This being so, it might tend to establish the general hypothesis of Palliser and Southesk as the true explanation of their fluctuating appearances and disappearances in certain recorded localities of which I have given some instances, but

[93]*Ibid.*, 489.
[94]*Palliser Journals*, 202.
[95]Southesk, *Travels*, 255.
[96]The Stoneys (Assiniboine) about Rocky Mountain House intimated something like this to Hector, 1859: that one tribe had to wait until the members of another had satisfied themselves (*Palliser Journals*, 145).

for two factors of vital importance. The first of these is that the 'one great host' itself, at the very time of which Southesk writes, as well as later, does not appear to have had any historical basis in fact.[97]

The second is that so far as the general territory of the Red River Hunt is concerned, we possess abundant historical evidence to show that these fluctuations were a common experience, long before the institution of the annual hunts in 1820, and before the appearance even of a body of resident settlers, whose needs brought the Red River Hunt into being. The Journals of Alexander Henry the younger—the very work which Thompson Seton hailed with such enthusiasm, as meeting our precise need of a fairly continuous buffalo record in some one locality[98]—will be found to present some remarkable testimony along the lines I have indicated. Thompson Seton remarks concerning Henry's post on Park River,[99] some thirty-five miles south of the (later) international boundary: "The buffalo lived in that region the year round, though less numerous there than higher up the river. . . ."[100]

[97]Southesk himself records buffalo near Fort Ellice (*Travels*, 51, 52); none at Fort Qu'Appelle (58, 70); 'a great band' crossing the South Saskatchewan River, near the 'Elbow,' 51° N., 107° W. (p. 78); 'vast quantities' from the Elbow to near Carlton (p. 92 *seq.*); to say nothing of his mention of buffalo at Turtle Mountain (p. 343). Why were these not in one single great host?

Similarly, plenty between Edmonton and Rocky Mountain House, January and February, 1859; and near Fort Pitt, April, 1859 (Palliser, Hector, in *Palliser Journals*, 117, 132). Compare Palliser *et al.*, 1857: none westward from Fort Garry for 'hundreds of miles' (p. 48); "in great numbers,' west of Moose Jaw Creek (pp. 54-5); 'scarce' thence to the Elbow or west of there; 'buffalo plentiful, country covered with them,' some 20 miles past the Elbow to near Carlton (pp. 55-8, 247). Plenty ('immense herds' near Fort Pitt) from two days west of Carlton to two days east of Edmonton; 393 miles = 13 days (Hector, pp. 67-71). Between these, Carlton itself was short (pp. 20, 81, 202). 'Plenty' at Edmonton (pp. 72, 78, 80, 202); starvation at Rocky Mountain House (pp. 74, 75, 202).

Concerning scarcity at Carlton, 1858, Hind agrees with Southesk (*Report, 1858*, 52); but Palliser has plenty for that year (*Palliser Journals*, 202). As early as September 5, 1824, Simpson wrote: "In the event of a failure of the Buffalo Hunts at Carlton, which is not unusual . . ."(Merk. (ed.), *Fur Trade and Empire*, 17).

Regarding my allusion to later times than Southesk: In the spring of 1872 buffalo were in great plenty southeastward from Edmonton, 'hundreds being killed in one hunt' (McDougall, *Red River Rebellion*, 228). Grant found them 'in swarms,' upper Qu'Appelle River, August, 1872 (*Ocean to Ocean*, 123); 'plenty,' Touchwood Hills and westward (*ibid.*, 126, 137, 145); 'vast numbers,' south of Fort Pitt (*ibid.*, 173; cf. also Butler, *Wild North Land*, 47). Imagine this huge territory covered with 'one herd'!

[98]Seton, *Life-Histories of Northern Animals*, I, 261-7.

[99]"Park River, near which we are settled, derived its name from the fact that the Assiniboines once made a park or pound on this river for buffaloes . . ." (Coues (ed.), *Henry-Thompson Journals*, I, 93; cf. *ibid.*, 88-95).

[100]Seton, *Life-Histories of Northern Animals*, I, 266.

'That region' is somewhat indefinite; and we shall see that it by no means invariably followed that buffalo could be obtained at all times, as might be inferred. Henry himself says, concerning the country, which lies between 'the Sale' (that is, La Salle River[101]) and the Assiniboine: ". . . Moose and red deer are very numerous at all seasons, and in the winter buffaloes resort here for shelter from storms and cold. . . ."[102]

This might roughly be described as constituting the region between the Assiniboine and the international boundary for some considerable distance westward of the Red River. The locality itself by no means agrees with Hind's relation of the wintering-ground;[103] but that might of course change considerably in some sixty years. What is of more importance is that its incidental history does not agree with Henry's own generalization. He tells us (February, 1800): ". . . 'Hunger' was the general cry at our establishments along the Assiniboine . . .: only 'two bulls in sixteen days' being found between Wood Mountain and the Qu'Appelle."[104]

In August, 1800, there were "many herds there";[105] this again scarcely agreeing with Hind's itinerary. In September, 1800, Henry writes: "Notwithstanding buffalo and other animals are [meaning, I suppose, 'have been'—or 'usually are'] so numerous, we are again obliged to depend upon our hooks and lines. . . ."[106]

On September 8, 1800: ". . . the buffaloes were all in motion, crossing from the east to the west side of the [Red] river, and directing their course toward the Hair Hills as fast as they could walk [that is, westward]. . . ."[107]

---

[101]Some 12 or 15 miles southwest of Winnipeg; locally known as 'Stinking River'; cf. Henry, 1801 (Coues (ed.), Henry-Thompson Journals, I, 55).

[102]Ibid., I, 56; also along Reed River, a tributary of Red River, on the eastern side (ibid., 70).

[103]Above, notes 50-2.

[104]Coues (ed.), Henry-Thompson Journals, I, 4.

[105]Ibid., 57, 61, 64-5, 67-9.

[106]Ibid., 77.

[107]Ibid., 89. The 'Hair Hills' are the 'Pembina Mountains,' southern Manitoba (ibid., 81; mentioned as a good 'Bison resort' by Thompson, Narrative, 252). Cf. Hairy Hill, Alberta (Place-Names of Alberta, 61). These 'hair' names are thought to be from very scrubby tangled regions, where the buffalo left much of their 'wool' sticking to the shrubbery. The 'Hairy Bag,' a valley near McDougall's mission home at Victoria (Pakan, Alberta) was a famous buffalo haunt (McDougall, Saddle, Sled, and Snowshoe, 104). The Mormons, on the exodus to Utah, 1847, "collected the hair of the buffalo from the sage-brush as they travelled . . ." (Bancroft, History of Utah, 276).

On September 26, 1800, he writes: "No buffalo to be seen on the west side [of Red River]; they appear to have gone toward the Hair Hills. . . ."[108] He furthermore notes "immense herds moving southward slowly," September 18, 1800;[109] "moving southward in one body," October 5, 1800;[110] "great herd of cows going at full speed southward," November 7, 1800.[111] Intermittently, between September, 1800, and January, 1801, we find 'more buffalo than ever,'[112] which, coupled with these sporadic southward and westward movements, seems clearly to indicate a condition of anything but regularity.

In December, 1800, Portage La Prairie was 'starving':[113] this might be cited in support of Hind's 'wintering-grounds,' but can scarcely be made to agree with Henry. On New Year's Day, 1801, the latter again records that "the plains were covered with them" near his post on the Red River, moving in a body from north to south.[114] A week later, January 8, 1801, the buffalo were 'at a distance';[115] but on January 14, 1801, Henry notes 'incredible numbers . . . close up, and moving north-ward. . . .'[116] January 19, 1801, he remarks that buffalo were "as numer-ous on the east side of the Red River as on the west":[117] and in the following March he observes that they have "for some time been wandering about in every direction. . . ."[118]

The foregoing extracts summarize the buffalo movements (or a number of them) in one particular region during a year. As I have remarked above, we have not yet reached the era of 'systematic ex-termination,' according to Hornaday's own classification; and its par-ticular feature in that territory, the Red River Hunt, had not yet been inaugurated. In short, there are no grounds whatever for considering this as a particularly abnormal season. Since Henry's notes on buffalo indicate that the Lower Red River Valley and neighbourhood was a good buffalo country, the occasional erratic scarcities become the more

[108]Coues (ed.), *Henry-Thompson Journals*, I, 103. He also mentions 'Plumb River' (? Plum Coulee, southern Manitoba), near the 'Loge des Bœufs,' a noted buffalo resort (*ibid.*, 68).

[109]*Ibid.*, 99.
[110]*Ibid.*, 112.
[111]*Ibid.*, 136.
[112]*Ibid.*, 98-9, 112-20, 138, 161, 167, 169-70, 173.
[113]*Ibid.*, 161; again in 1806 (p. 421).
[114]*Ibid.*, 162.
[115]*Ibid.*, 166.
[116]*Ibid.*, 167. See remarks below, note 130.
[117]Coues (ed.), *Henry-Thompson Journals*, I, 168.
[118]*Ibid.*, 171.

noticeable. For convenience, I group a number of references to abundance, or otherwise, topically instead of chronologically.

ABUNDANCE: 'numerous herds' from 'the Forks' (that is, Winnipeg) to Pembina, August, 1801;[119] 'Grand Marais' (southwest from Winnipeg), September, 1801;[120] 'abundant' near the Fort (that is, Park River); December, 1801 to January, 1802;[121] similarly, September, 1802 to January, 1803;[122] and again, September 27, 1803;[123] previous to which he noted them 'in abundance' along the Pembina River, May 31, 1803.[124] In November, 1803, 'several herds' along Tongue River, 'in stormy weather';[125] and the same again, in April and May, 1804.[126] 'Plenty' near 'the Forks' (Winnipeg), September, 1804;[127] the same near the post, October, 1804,[128] and also on the upper 'Rivière Sale' (La Salle River), August 20, 1805.[129] November 15, 1805: "A terrible snowstorm. . . . Buffalo passing northward in as great numbers as ever I saw them . . .";[130] and in December, 1805, he was 'laying in thirty cows per day.'[131] 'In abundance' to the westward of Red River, May, 1806;[132] and in the following July (1806), 'some herds' travelling westward, on the west of Turtle Mountain.[133] This last is a most interesting notice, for they were westbound almost at the very place and time when, according to Hind (or his informants) they travelled eastward and south.[134] 'In abundance, the prairie covered with herds' (between the Missouri and Fort Assiniboine, near Brandon, Manitoba) August 1 to 4, 1806.[135] 'Buffalo abounded' in the winter of 1806-7,

[119]*Ibid.*, 185, 186.
[120]*Ibid.*, 191.
[121]*Ibid.*, 192-3.
[122]*Ibid.*, 205-8.
[123]*Ibid.*, 225.
[124]Not to be confused with the Alberta 'Pembina River.' Given as 'a corruption of *neepimenan*' (Cree = 'cranberry'): *Place-Names of Alberta*, 100. For the latter, see Coues (ed.), *Henry-Thompson Journals*, II, 661. Henry calls both rivers the 'Panbian'; and mentions elsewhere that "choke-cherries and panbians abound" (North Saskatchewan River, 1808: *ibid.*, 486). For another Alberta (former) 'Pembina River,' see above, chap. XII, note 113.
[125]Coues (ed.), *Henry-Thompson Journals*, I, 230.
[126]*Ibid.*, 241, 244.
[127]*Ibid.*, 250.
[128]*Ibid.*, 251.
[129]*Ibid.*, 265.
[130]*Ibid.*, 273. Note this reference. This quite incidental remark of Henry's involves Hornaday and Thompson Seton in the logical dilemma to which I have drawn attention *re* buffalo and snow (see above, chap. VIII, notes 81-3). Cf. above, note 116.
[131]Coues (ed.), *Henry-Thompson Journals*, I, 273.
[132]*Ibid.*, 275.
[133]*Ibid.*, 309, 310.   [134]Above, notes 50-2.

on the Red River[136] and were also 'abundant,' the following winter (January 1, 1808).[137]

SCARCITY: In November and December, 1803, there were 'few buffalo' on the Plumb River—the very region where their normal abundance was (we must suppose) commemorated in the *Loge des Bœufs*—and the XY post in that locality was 'starving.'[138] Charles Mackenzie found Henry's post on Red River in August, 1805, 'in a state of starvation.'[139] At the Gratias River, in July, 1806, on his journey of that summer to the Mandan villages on the Missouri, Henry noted that "cows there are none, and even bulls are scarce. . . ."[140] At Fort Assiniboine (near Brandon, Manitoba), also in July, 1806, there were 'no buffalo,' and the post was 'starving.'[141] On his return, at Fort Assiniboine again (August 9 to 10, 1806), he says: "There has been no trade whatever this summer. The Indians are starving all over the country, no buffalo being found within their limits. . . ."[142]

As he drew nearer home, the same conditions prevailed. He says of the plains along the Pembina, near Red River: "I have many times beheld these plains covered with buffalo at all seasons of the year; now not one solitary old bull enlivens the prospect. This summer's extraordinary rain, having overflowed the low country, has caused the buffalo to resort to the high lands southward. . . ."[143]

The reflection seems inevitable that if Henry knew *why* the buffalo had deserted the Assiniboine and Pembina plains, and whither they had gone, the Indians, native dwellers in that region, should have known also. When he reached Fort Assiniboine on August 9, 1806, and found them still starving, the prairie only five days' distance to the southward was—and had been—'covered with herds.'[144]

[135]Coues (ed.), *Henry-Thompson Journals*, I, 407-10.

[136]*Ibid.*, 422.

[137]*Ibid.*, 428.

[138]*Ibid.*, 231.

[139]Masson, *Les Bourgeois de la Compagnie du Nord-Ouest*, I, 353; but this scarcely agrees with Henry himself (Coues (ed.), *Henry-Thompson Journals*, I, 265); see above, note 129.

[140]Coues (ed.), *Henry-Thompson Journals*, I, 286.

[141]*Ibid.*, 302-3.

[142]*Ibid.*, 416; see also starvation at Portage La Prairie (p. 421).

[143]*Ibid.*, 420.

[144]*Ibid.*, 410 (August 4, 1806). Charles Mackenzie, over (probably) the same route, June to July, 1806, noted 'immense herds' along the Missouri tributaries (Masson, *Les Bourgeois de la Compagnie du Nord-Ouest*, I, 377). The Indians *may* have known, but feared to go. F. A. Larocque, crossing the Missouri Coteau, 1805, says they saw 'quantities of buffalo, but did not dare to fire at them because of the Sioux' (*Journal of Larocque*, ed. Burpee). But surely Henry would have known of and mentioned such a condition.

This very local variation is paralleled by another which he mentions three winters previously. Referring apparently to Manitoba House on Lake Manitoba (January, 1803), he says: "Here we found Mr. Mc-Donnell, Junior, starving with buffalo at his door. . . . Our course was about South for three days to Portage la Prairie, and thence about S.E. for four hard days to Panbian [Pembina] river, where we arrived Feb. 3. Through all this country we never marched a day without passing herds of buffalo; even along the shore of the lake they were very numerous. . . ."[145]

Stormy weather in that bitter region in wintertime might account for McDonnell's ignorance of the near vicinity of the buffalo; but this could scarcely apply in the month of August. As an interesting commentary on the general uncertainty in the same district (broadly speaking) we may note David Thompson's winter journey from Assiniboine House (that is, the 'Fort Assiniboine' of Henry) to the Mandan villages and back again. On his trip of thirty-two days, November 29 to December 30, 1797, he saw 'very few buffalo; no herd above twenty.'[146] Returning, January 10 to February 3, 1798, he saw 'very few' again;[147] and 'but a few' on the trip from (virtually) Brandon to Winnipeg, of ten days, February 26 to March 7, 1798,—right across Henry's later track, when Henry saw such numbers.[148] And an even earlier explorer, who antedated Henry by twenty years more than Henry antedated Hind, La Vérendrye on his return from the Mandan villages, in December, 1738, found the same region (where they had been told of its abundance all the year round[149]) at starvation point.[150]

At the same time that Henry was recording his experiences, and at no great distance from the southern limits of the Red River Hunt, Zebulon M. Pike, on his journey toward the sources of the Mississippi, found the first indication of buffalo near Little Rock River, October 13, 1805. Although he elsewhere describes the spot as the resort of 'immense herds of elk and buffalo,'[151] he saw 'one buffalo sign' only.[152]

By comparing the dates mentioned in the Red River and adjacent regions, with the resultant revelations of movements, small or great,

---

[145]Coues (ed.), *Henry-Thompson Journals*, I, 208.
[146]Thompson, *Narrative*, ed. Tyrrell, 210-24 (ones and twos; four bulls).
[147]*Ibid.*, 240.
[148]*Ibid.*, 246.
[149]*Journals of La Vérendrye* (ed. Burpee), 240, 251, 303, 310.
[150]*Ibid.*, 352-9; cf. Fort Maurepas starving, 1750 (Burpee, *Search for the Western Sea*, 272).
[151]Coues, (ed.), *Expeditions of Pike*, I, 316.
[152]*Ibid.*, 102.

in any direction at any period of the year, and apparently regardless of annual seasons or immediate weather conditions, I am at a loss to conceive upon what basis the generalizer can postulate any regularly recurring seasonal or annual movement in certain uniform directions, of any character whatsoever. The mere fact that such assertions happen to be made (almost invariably on the strength of a passing traveller's experience during one season) by critics who themselves had also seen the buffalo at some time is of very slight importance. It is the testimony of other men (of equal inherent credibility) to the contrary, gathered from experiences under precisely similar conditions, that robs any one utterance of any claim to pontifical authority.

How curiously local certain of these fluctuations were after the year 1820 is illustrated by two citations from independent sources. Dr. George Bryce relates that in June, 1823, ". . . from the Upper Red River it was stated that on account of prairie fires the buffalo were few, and that the wild Assiniboines had betaken themselves to the Saskatchewan to enjoy its plenty. . . ."[153]

In the very same year, and in the month following (July, 1823), Major Stephen H. Long reached Pembina, where the Red River crosses the forty-ninth parallel. I quote Bryce again: "On the day after Long's arrival he saw the return of the buffalo hunters from the chase. The procession consisted of one hundred and fifteen carts, each loaded with about eight hundred pounds of the pressed buffalo meat. There were three hundred persons, including the women. The number of horses was about two hundred. . . ."[154]

Even if these had not been obtained on the Upper Red River (which is of course possible), Long's expedition saw 'herds numbering thousands' about the sources of the Red and Minnesota Rivers, in spring and early summer, 1823.[155]

After that, the following (quoted by Hind from the history of the same expedition) reads somewhat strangely:

[Keating] Every year this animal's rovings are restricted. In 1822, the limit of its wanderings down the St. Peter was Great Swan Lake. . . . In 1823, the gentlemen of the Columbia Fur Company were obliged to travel five days in the northwest direction from Lake Travers [that is, the source of the Red River] before they fell in with the game, but then they succeeded in killing sixty animals. There can be no doubt but this constant subtraction

[153]Bryce, *Remarkable History*, 269. Above, note 22.
[154]*Ibid.*, 328. The first is quoted from official documents of the Hudson's Bay Company; the second from Keating's account of Long's expedition which I have unfortunately had no opportunity to see.
[155]Allen, *American Bisons*, 143.

from his roamings must affect his numbers; certainly more so than the practice of killing only the cows and leaving the bulls; a custom which has probably prevailed among the Indians for a long time, and which we cannot therefore consider as the source of the great modern diminution in their numbers. . . .[156]

The distance and direction specified would bring the gentlemen practically to the (Dakota) Cheyenne River; in the region of which even the similar jeremiad of Hornaday postpones buffalo extermination until about 1840, when it is ascribed to the Red River hunters 'and the Indians of that region.'[157] As a matter of fact, it seems probable that both generalizations are incorrect. The region mentioned by Long would be roughly along the Cheyenne River, east of Jamestown, North Dakota, approximately some three hundred miles from St. Paul. Allen cites evidence that buffalo were 'abundant' within fifty miles of St. Paul in 1836.[158] He also states (on the authority of Pope) that buffalo were killed in the immediate vicinity of the settlements at Pembina, in 1850;[159] and according to Assistant-Surgeon Asa Wall (U.S. Army), they were 'still common' about Fort Abercrombie, on the Red River, as late as 1858.[160]

Concerning Hornaday's description of the 'buffalo frontier' being at the Cheyenne—not to say 'beyond it to the Missouri'— in 1840, we may compare the following:

[1853] Governor Stevens, in speaking of the abundance of the buffalo on the Shayenne River, near Lake Zisne, . . . says: "About five miles from camp, we ascended to the top of a high hill, and for a great distance ahead every square mile seemed to have a herd of buffalo upon it.[161] Their number was variously estimated by the members of the party, some as high as half a million. I do not think it is any exaggeration to set it down at 200,000. I had heard of the myriads of these animals inhabiting these plains, but I could not realize the truth of these accounts until to-day, when they surpass everything which I could have imagined from the accounts which I had received. . . ."[162]

[156]Hind, *Report, 1858,* 106. There is another Lake Traverse, in the extreme northeast corner of South Dakota; but the date makes it clear that is not the one.

[157]Hornaday, "Extermination of the American Bison," 489; above, notes 91-3. That river rises in Sheridan County, but attains its northernmost point in Benson County, North Dakota, southwest of Devil's Lake.

[158]Allen, *American Bisons,* 142. Yet they are said to have been 'exterminated or driven off from Fort Snelling' (*i.e.* St. Paul) soon after it was built, 1819 (Coues (ed.), *Expeditions of Pike,* I, 58, ed. note).

[159]Allen, *American Bisons,* 143, 155.

[160]*Ibid.,* 156. For the situation of Fort Abercrombie, see chap. XII, note 64.

[161]Compare Lewis and Clark, Missouri River, 1804: 'Fifty-two herds at one view . . .' (*Journals,* I, 165).

[162]Cited by Allen, *American Bisons,* 156.

It seems incredible that Hornaday had this work almost hourly in his hand while writing his own essay!

In the more central territory usually associated with the Red River Hunt, some of Hornaday's 'buffalo frontiers' are equally misleading, considered in the definite sense which his language must be thought to intend. Despite the fact that the expedition of 1840 had to go some 250 miles (from Pembina) for its first buffalo, and the expressed opinion of Alexander Ross that in 1852 'the end of the buffalo was not far distant;'[163] we find the following, derived from a contemporary source: "Nevertheless, there were at that time many Buffalo still roaming the Big Plain where Carberry [Manitoba] now stands; Captain John Schott remembered finding plenty there in 1852. . . ."[164]

Similarly, although Hornaday has the buffalo 'practically extinct, if not actually so,' as far west as the Qu'Appelle River in 1857,[165] yet they were seen much farther east some years later. Seton says again: "The last Buffalo band seen in Manitoba by John Schott was in 1861, when an immense herd was discovered in Grand Valley. They completely covered the site of the present town of Brandon. . . ."[166]

Thompson Seton further remarks: "In 1867 a trader, J. L. Lagare, went on a journey from Winnipeg toward Wood Mountain. He told me in conversation that he saw the first Buffalo at Oak Lake;[167] and during the winter of 1867-1868 he and his partner lived on Buffalo killed on the Souris Plains, although they were then scarce, and only small bunches were to be seen. The great herd kept farther west, about Cypress Hills. . . ."[168]

[163]Ross, *Red River Settlement*, 267.
[164]Seton, *Life-Histories of Northern Animals*, I, 254; cf. his *Arctic Prairies*, 7. Carberry is 106 miles west of Winnipeg. Events of 1852 are rather more definite than some, as the great flood of that year might 'date' them. See Ross, *Red River Settlement*, 413-16; and the account of them having to cut a road for that year's Red River Hunt through the 'Bad Woods,' west of Portage La Prairie (Hind, *Report, 1858*, 41).
[165]Hornaday, "Extermination of the American Bison," 490 (above, note 70). Hind found about 140 miles west of Souris—say Moose Mountain—to be the western limit of acquaintance of his Red River half-breeds in any hunts up to 1858. "They were most of them familiar with the country south of the Great Prairie, the Grand Coteau de Missouri . . ." (*Report, 1858*, 46).
[166]Seton, *Life-Histories of Northern Animals*, I, 256. Brandon is 133 miles west of Winnipeg. According to Cowie, Brandon House (a little down the Assiniboine River, I believe) was considered 'too far from buffalo' in 1830; and Fort Ellice similarly, 1867 (*Company of Adventurers*, 187, 458, 483). Compare above, note 83.
[167]Oak Lake, 32 miles west of Brandon; 165 from Winnipeg. In 1867, Archbishop Taché said the Red River hunters were 'starving' (Stanley, *Birth of Western Canada*, 53, 415).
[168]Seton, *Life-Histories of Northern Animals*, I, 256. Sometime, apparently

The gradually increasing distances from Red River are, of course, sufficiently well authenticated. Ross says (1850): ". . . Buffalo, the only inducement to the plains, are falling off fast. They are now like a ball between two players. The Americans are driving them north, the British south. The west alone will furnish them a last and temporary retreat. . . ."[169]

McDougall, also, notes on one of his hunting trips that his companion, born in the Red River settlement, and then about twenty years of age, "had never seen buffalo" until 1864, on the plains between the Battle and Saskatchewan rivers;[170] and ten years later, a Hudson's Bay officer, 'born in the Red River Valley,' participated in a buffalo-run for the first time (1874).[171] McDougall, too, records meeting the Spring Hunt in early June, 1864, working northwestward along the Saskatchewan trail, east of Fort Ellice;[172] and they apparently followed the same route in 1872.[173] In 1873, according to the testimony of an old Hudson's Bay man, the nearest point westward from Fort Garry was the 'Woody Hill,' three hundred miles southwest by his computation, and meaning presumably Wood Mountain. For 'large bands' it was necessary to go five hundred miles; this latter region would be about Cypress Hills.[174] The same informant stated (also in 1873) that ". . . quite recently a party of hunters, in the district adjoining the

1866-67, Norbert Welsh has 'Buffalo Bill' (W. F. Cody) coming up into the Qu'Appelle or Long Lake country, buffalo-hunting (*The Last Buffalo-Hunter*, 85). At that time, Cody was a lad of 21, who had just reached Kansas. His famous beef contract, which brought him name and fame, was of 1867-68 (see Walsh and Salsbury, *The Making of Buffalo Bill*). He would have had to cross hundreds of miles of buffalo-thronged country to reach one which was becoming very short of buffalo at that time. Welsh's own total for the winter's trade (1865-66) was only 160 robes (*ibid.*, 87).

In January, 1868, Cowie found no buffalo from Fort Qu'Appelle until after crossing the Missouri Coteau (southwestward); thence a few, to Wood Mountain and Old Wives' Lake (*circa* 108° W.). At the two places named, the winter returns were 485 and 90 robes respectively (Cowie, *Company of Adventurers*, 249-61, 290). The Indians, however, were living in abundance (*ibid.*, 259). In June, 1868, Cowie saw no buffalo from Qu'Appelle to Gull Lake, Saskatchewan, (main line of C.P.R.) some 200 miles. At that place, they had 'a grand buffalo hunt' (*ibid.*, 290, 328-30).

[169]Ross, *Red River Settlement*, 267.

[170]McDougall, *Saddle, Sled, and Snowshoe*, 221.

[171]McDougall, *Western Trails*, 234.

[172]McDougall, *Saddle, Sled, and Snowshoe*, 140.

[173]Grant, *Ocean to Ocean*, 145.

[174]Andrew McDermott (formerly of the Hudson's Bay Company), Selkirk, to U.S. Consul J. W. ('Saskatchewan') Taylor, 1873 (in Allen, *American Bisons*, 172). On buffalo about Cypress Hills, 1871-72, see Cowie, *Company of Adventurers*, 433; cf. also Steele, *Forty Years in Canada*, 43, 75-7.

country of the Blackfoot Indians, in the longitude 110°, latitude 51°, was seven days in passing through a herd. . . ."[175]

Thompson Seton writes: "In 1874 Dr. E. Coues passed along the International Boundary without seeing any buffalo until he got to Frenchmen's River, Montana, about Long. 107° 20'. . . ."[176] In the same year the Red River Hunt had to go as far as Cypress Hills before finding buffalo; for the original force of the Northwest Mounted Police met them just east of that region on the homeward journey, at the end of August, 1874. The police encountered buffalo shortly afterward, and killed their first, September 1, 1874.[177]

Concerning this, Denny remarks: "The further we travelled west, the more plentiful became the buffalo. We came to places where, as far as the eye could reach, thousands and tens of thousands were in sight; the country being fairly black with them. They had eaten the grass very short, making the feed very scarce, and the lakes were polluted with them. These immense bands seemed to be travelling north, and there seemed to be no end to them. . . ."[178]

This finds general corroboration in a modern history of the southern Alberta territory:

The boundary survey parties in that year [that is, 1874] were held up for several hours on at least two occasions by the passing herd. Under date of September 23, 1874, Colonel French, on his way to Fort Benton, wrote in his diary that he passed an immense herd of buffalo which he and [Colonel] Macleod computed at between seventy and eighty thousand. About the same time the secretary of the United States Boundary Commission described another herd:

"The number of animals was beyond estimation. Looking at the herd from an elevation of about 1800 feet above the plains, I was unable to see the end in any direction. The half-breeds, Sioux, Assiniboines, Gros Ventres of the prairie, and the Blackfeet followed the outskirts of this herd, but for all their wastefulness they made little impression on it."

[175]Allen, *American Bisons*, 173. The position given lies between Medicine Hat, Alberta, and the Red Deer Forks (old Chesterfield House) on the South Saskatchewan River. North of that, towards Sounding Lake and Battleford, 1871-72, see Welsh (*Last Buffalo-Hunter*, 131-2) and near Little Devil's Lake (Manitou Lake, Watrous, Saskatchewan, by the context), 'plenty,' moving west, November, 1872 (*ibid.*, 138). Cowie speaks of 'plentifulness of buffalo being anticipated,' March, 1873; but does not say why (*Company of Adventurers*, 481).

[176]Seton, *Life-Histories of Northern Animals*, I, 256.

[177]Denny, *The Law Marches West*, ed. Cameron, 29-30.

[178]*Ibid.*; cf. Steele, *Forty Years in Canada*, 75-6. General Steele was a comrade of Denny in the original North West Mounted Police force of 1874. Buffalo were very erratic in this region. Cowie, winter 1871-72: "Next morning that plain, which had been vacant the whole day before, was filled with scattered herds of buffalo . . ." (*Company of Adventurers*, 433).

The same historian goes on to say that it was generally believed at the time by "the Fort Benton traders that owing to the destruction of the wolves,[179] the number of buffalo was actually increasing. . . ."[180]

I have been unable to discover any authentic reference to expeditions of the Red River Hunt later than the year in question (1874).

Before concluding the present chapter, the question of "wastefulness'—an almost universal allegation by writers on the Red River Hunt —must be examined. This has given rise to a good deal of what is not readily distinguishable from cant; to which our leading buffalo authority, Hornaday, has assuredly contributed his full share. While it is quite possible that wastefulness may be a common characteristic in any large body of men having Indian blood (although this must be proved, instead of being simply assumed) there are certain factors which must in common justice be noticed. One of these has been mentioned; that is, that there was no visible need for frugality in buffalo consumption, particularly in the earlier buffalo days when the Indian psychological attitude toward them was in process of development.

Secondly, the Indians had no opportunity to present a case for themselves, but have been judged by alien critics. It so chances that almost all the local and literary authorities on Red River belonged to a proverbially thrifty race, to whom waste, in the white man's connotation, was peculiarly abhorrent; and one can scarcely doubt that many passing travellers not themselves of Scottish blood became tinged with the Hudson's Bay man's attitude on this question. Thirdly, we have to reckon with the conscious and deliberate hatred for the Indian and all of his kin which was rampant in the United States virtually throughout the nineteenth century, which even corrupted many of her scientists—Hornaday himself is a deplorable case in point—and which a high-minded band of her students and education-

[179]*I.e.* by 'wolfers,' a fraternity who trapped or caught wolves by means of poisoned buffalo in a particularly skilful manner. Their methods are best described by MacInnes (*In the Shadow of the Rockies*, 66). The opinion quoted may be contrasted with Seton's dictum on the number of buffalo killed by wolves 'not being great' (*Life-Histories of Northern Animals*, I, 270), which is contrary to every contemporary authority I have seen, and they are not few. On wolves, see chap. VII, notes 5-20.

[180]MacInnes, *In the Shadow of the Rockies*, 143. See above, however, note 34. Note the attitude of the elders toward waste. Yet the persistence of the 'young men' cannot be wondered at. Why *should* they economize, *circa* 1868, merely for others to take the more!

ists are now endeavouring to dispel. Canada has not been so entirely free from this infection as some of us would like to believe.[181]

Before proceeding with our detailed examination, it may be noted with respect to the usual generalization (by every writer but one or two) defining 'the half-breeds' as perpetrators of this or that—always as vague and essentially meaningless as 'the Indians,' 'the Europeans,' or 'the Orientals'—that one of the exceptions, who chances to be perhaps the most competent judge, divides them into three classes, as follows:

". . . (1) those who have their farms and homes; (2) those who are entirely identified with the Indians, living with them and speaking their language; (3) those who do not farm, but live after the habits of the Indians, by the pursuit of the buffalo and the chase. . . ."[182]

Hornaday's definition is much more comprehensive and concise: ". . . the half-breeds, who despised agriculture as long as there was a buffalo to kill. . . ."[183]

Palliser remarked in June, 1857, on Pembina being "deserted for the annual hunt, just when the labour of the population in the fields would be most effective";[184] and others have made similar observations.[185] McDougall writes as follows, concerning the Red River settlement at large: "Here, as everywhere in the North-West, the influence of the great herds of buffalo on the plains, and big shoals of fish in the lakes and rivers, was detrimental to the permanent prosperity of

[181]"The American dictum that the only good Indian is a dead Indian has never prevailed on this side of the line . . ." (Hawkes, *Saskatchewan and her People*, I, 84). It may not have 'prevailed'; but one of the earliest Canadian newspapers I ever saw, six weeks after my arrival in the West, thought it a 'smart' thing to headline a notice of an Indian found dead on the prairie, 'A Good Indian Found' (*Manitoba Weekly Free Press*, Winnipeg, August 9, 1894). Compare Burpee on this: Kane, *Wanderings of an Artist* (Radisson Society ed.), introd., xiii-xiv; a Canadian settler's hatred of the 'red-skins,' Northern Ontario, 1868 (Butler, *Autobiography*, 104); white settlers' contempt for the Carrier Indians, B.C. (Jenness, *Indians of Canada*, 368); and Jenness's general remarks on "Interaction of Indians and Whites" (*ibid.*, 249-64).

[182]Morris, *Treaties with the Indians of Manitoba*, 294; something similar in McLean, *Twenty-Five Years' Service*, orig. ed., II, 303. See also Cowie's very full and instructive classification (as Morris): *Company of Adventurers*, 61-6; and Stanley, *Birth of Western Canada*, 5-10. Cf. below, note 225.

[183]Hornaday, "Extermination of the American Bison," 489.

[184]*Palliser Journals*, 41.

[185]McLean, *Twenty-Five Years' Service*, II, 297; Ross, *Red River Settlement*, 242, 252, 307; Richardson, *Arctic Expedition, 1847-1850*, 275; Kane, *Wanderings of an Artist*, 51; Hind, *Report, 1858*, 40, 75; Grant, *Ocean to Ocean*, 123; Bryce, *Remarkable History*, 366.

a people. You cannot really civilize a hunter or a fisherman, until you wean him from these modes of making a livelihood. . . ."[186]

The same entirely logical and predicable factor, the nomadic instinct, has been noted among the Indians of the east,[187] west,[188] north,[189] and south.[190] While it is naturally regrettable in the eyes of a missionary, one would think that to a scientist it should be purely a characteristic, certainly not demanding a tone of lofty moral reprobation.

In recording his encounter with the westbound Spring Hunt in 1864, McDougall reflects as follows: "These were the men who owned the rich portions of Manitoba, the Portage plains, and the banks of the Assiniboine and Red Rivers; but what cared they for rich homesteads so long as buffalo could be found within five or six hundred miles?"[191]

People who live in glass houses should not throw stones. In the self-same work, McDougall himself (having described their own tedious efforts to grind some meal in a small hand-mill) concludes thus: "So long as we can get buffalo within three hundred miles we would prefer buffalo steaks to barley-meal. . . ."[192] After this, from a scion of a meal-eating ancestry, who had then spent only two years among the buffalo, who shall blame the Indian or his kin!

Traveller after traveller has expatiated on the exciting joys of buffalo-running.[193] Professor Macoun goes so far as to say: "After

[186]McDougall, Forest, Lake, and Prairie, 76.

[187]The Jesuit fathers noted that the Indians' nomadic habits hindered missionary work. See Father Le Jeune, 1637-39 (Jesuit Relations, XII, 169; XIV, 127, 205, 215; XVI, 233, 249): ". . . the same thing in a Savage to wish to become sedentary and to believe in God" (XIV, 215). Cf. Father Morain, Acadia, 1677 (ibid., LX, 269).

[188]Spokan Indians, 1847 (Kane, Wanderings of an Artist, 215).

[189]Professor John Macoun (Peace River, 1872), in Fleming et al., Explorations and Surveys for a Canadian Pacific Railway, up to January 1, 1874, 94.

[190]Attempts of the Spanish Government (Texas, circa 1807) to convert buffalo-hunting tribes—in part—towards agriculture (Coues (ed.), Expeditions of Pike, II, 785).

[191]McDougall, Saddle, Sled, and Snowshoe, 141.

[192]Ibid., 250.

[193]See on this, Long (i.e. Edwin James), Early Western Travels, XV, 257; Gregg, ibid., XX, 112, 214; Catlin, Letters on the North American Indians, I, 24-6, 251-3; Frémont, Narrative, 17-21, 29; Parkman, Oregon Trail, 402-13; Life of De Smet, IV, 1376, 1397; Kane, Wanderings of an Artist, 56-60; Ross, Red River Settlement, 255-62; Southesk, Travels, 91-107; Milton and Cheadle, North-West Passage, 60-3; McDougall, Saddle, Sled, and Snowshoe, 221; also his Western Trails, 234; Cowie, Company of Adventurers, 329-30; Allen, American Bisons, 202, 210; Hornaday, "Extermination of the American Bison," 470-8; Garretson, American Bison, 99-104; etc.

According to Colonel Dodge, 'it soon palled' on an old resident (Plains of

witnessing one buffalo hunt, I cannot blame the half-breed and the Indian for leaving the farm and wildly making for the plains when it is reported that buffalo have crossed the border. . . ."[194]

Hornaday actually quotes this passage,[195] presumably as the most striking testimony he has found to the quite extraordinary fascination of buffalo hunting, which communicated itself from men[196] even to the horses;[197] yet without a single hint of endorsement of the shrewd insight and kindly tolerance of one who made no pretense of being a sportsman.

The only mitigation of Hornaday's severity that I have found is one statement, which I quote: "From all accounts, the Red River half-breeds, who hunted almost exclusively with fire-arms, never dreamed of the deadly still-hunt, but always killed their game by 'running' it. . . ."[198]

Precisely as dates are the soundest criteria by which to consider buffalo movements, so figures are the best standard by which to estimate wastefulness. We have, unfortunately, no continuous record; but actual or computed numbers at various times are given by several writers. Alexander Ross furnishes the following census of the carts assembled in camp for the 'first' (that is, spring) hunt at five different periods.[199]

---

the Great West, 127); but cf. Catlin's account (an eye-witness) of General Leavenworth meeting his death, near the False Washita River, 1834, through being unable to resist the temptation (Letters on the North American Indians, II, 49-51, 79).

[194]Macoun, Manitoba, 344.

[195]Hornaday, "Extermination of the American Bison," 476-7.

[196]See Dr. Gregg on 'buffalo running-fever' in novices; 'the sight of buffalo too much for most hunters; killing for the sake of killing, and for the excitement of it.' He himself pleads guilty to the latter (Early Western Travels, XX, 112, 214). Something similar in Dodge (Plains of the Great West, 126). Norbert Welsh says that Buffalo Bill shot 500 'just for fun' (Last Buffalo-Hunter, 85). No doubt somebody did it, even if it was not Cody (see above, note 168).

[197]On the wonderful training and intelligence of the Indian 'buffalo runners,' see Bradbury, Early Western Travels, V, 174; Catlin, Letters on the North American Indians, I, 251; Hind, Report, 1858, 107; Hornaday, "Extermination of the American Bison," 474; Kidd, "Blackfoot Ethnography," 93; Welsh, Last Buffalo-Hunter, 109. See Dodge on the two Mexicans who always drove their buffalo into camp (Plains of the Great West, 129, cf. 424). It was by some such tactics that Buffalo Bill was said to have out-classed his rivals and made his fame (Walsh and Salsbury, Making of Buffalo Bill, 106-19). My first saddle-horse was descended from the old buffalo-running stock, a most prairie-wise old veteran. The qualities of these horses led Duncan McGillivray (1794) to think them stallions, which is possible (Journal, ed. Morton, lxix, 69).

[198]Hornaday, "Extermination of the American Bison," 470.

[199]Ross, Red River Settlement, 246. The percentages are mine.

1820 ....540 carts
1825 ....680 carts (An approximate increase of 24 per cent)
1830 ....820 carts (an approximate increase of 22 per cent)
1835 ....970 carts (an approximate increase of 18 per cent)
1840 ....1210 carts (an approximate increase of 25 per cent)

After the division in about 1846 into the two respective contingents of approximately equal size (presumably), to which reference has been made above,[200] it is difficult to decide whether some of our informants refer to one only of these two (and which), or to the aggregate total. The latest figures given by Ross are for 1840; and they will be found to be substantiated by his precise itemized description. About 1845, according to John McLean, each hunter had "at least six carts, some twelve; perhaps 5000 carts," the number of hunters not being specified.[201] The strict average of nine would yield 555 hunters, not of course necessarily *families*, but approximating that result, if the Red River half-breeds followed Indian ratios at all closely. The hunters may be accepted; the carts are impossible. The average rate of increase during the five-year periods covered by Ross (1820-40) is roughly about 22 per cent. The figure suggested by McLean represents an increase in a practically similar five-year period of some 410 per cent which in the absence of confirmation I consider incredible.

In Sibley's paper on the buffalo (which I have unfortunately been unable to see)[202] is set forth an account by a well-known worthy among the earlier Western missionaries, Reverend Father George Belcourt, dated November 25, 1845, of an expedition which he accompanied in that year. The expedition was a comparatively small one, like others which were on the range that season. It started from Pembina, and 'very generously'—or prudently—took care not to spoil the prospects of the great Red River division, which was taking the field about the same time; but, although 'small,' it comprised 213 carts with 55 hunters and their families.[203] We have here a fraction less than four carts per hunter.

Allen speaks of "1200 carts going south in a body" to Devil's Lake, North Dakota, in 1847.[204] In this case we have a rather sudden descent to what is approximately Ross's total of 1840. In 1849 ". . . a Mr. Flett

[200]See above, notes 42-7.
[201]McLean, *Twenty-Five Years' Service*, II, 298; '1500' in 1846 (Kane, *Wanderings of an Artist*, 51; above, note 46). See remarks below, note 236.
[202]The paper is in Schoolcraft, *North American Indians*, IV, 92-110.
[203]Allen, *American Bisons*, 155; Hornaday, "Extermination of the American Bison," 475.   [204]Allen, *American Bisons*, 155.

took a census of the White Horse Plain division in Dakota territory, and found that it contained 603 carts, 700 half-breeds, 200 Indians, 600 horses, 200 oxen, 400 dogs, and 1 cat. . . ."[205]

These are evidently approximate figures; but if one could accept the time-honoured ratio of one man in five persons, this would yield about 180 men, or somewhere between three and four carts per hunter.

In the following year, 1850, the "Pembina Hunt"—which would apparently indicate what Hornaday calls the "Red River division," travelled westward and found buffalo at Turtle Mountain, some 150 miles distant. It was estimated by Father Lacombe, who accompanied it, at from 800 to 1000 carts, and over 1000 men, women, and children.[206]

In 1852, when owing to the notable floods of that year the trail along the Assiniboine was impassable, and they were obliged to cut a road through the 'Bad Woods' west of Portage la Prairie, the western division consisted of 400 carts.[207]

About 1862, Milton and Cheadle, speaking in round figures, state that "the number of hunters frequently exceeds 500, . . . the number of carts often reaches 1500 or 1600. . . ."[208]

When McDougall met them in late May or early June, 1864, he says, ". . . they must have had five hundred or more carts, besides many wagons. Then this number would be very much augmented from Fort Ellice and other points eastward. . . ."[209]

This last proviso leaves one wondering whether any proportion in other years dwelt elsewhere than along Red River, but even if this were so, it could not seriously affect averages.

The apparent ratio of carts per hunter varies between practically four, in Father Belcourt's account, and somewhere about three, in the general estimate of Milton and Cheadle. One might feel inclined to favour the higher figure, since it is contained in a specific enumeration, were it not that the most precise and detailed computation we possess actually shows an average of less than two carts per hunter. This is Ross's table of the hunt which left Fort Garry for Pembina on June 15, 1840, in which he states not merely the numbers, but also the suggested monetary value of the expedition. This is as follows:

[205]Hornaday, "Extermination of the American Bison"; probably from Hind's *Narrative*, II, 110. Not in his *Report, 1858*.
[206]Hughes, *Father Lacombe*, 23-33.
[207]Hind, *Report, 1858*, 41.
[208]Milton and Cheadle, *North-West Passage*, 44.
[209]McDougall, *Saddle, Sled, and Snowshoe*, 141.

1210 carts at £1 10s. 0d. each	£1815
620 hunters (2 months) at 1s. per day	1860
650 women (2 months) at 9d. per day	1460
360 boys and girls (2 months) at 4d. per day	360
403 buffalo runners (i.e. horses) at £15 each	6045
655 carthorses at £8 each	5240
586 draught oxen at £6 each	3516
Guns, gunpowder, knives, axes, harness, camp equipment, and utensils (approximate estimate)	3700

£23,996 or £24,000[210]

This expedition, according to Ross's estimate, brought back an average of 900 pounds per cart—1000 pounds being considered a 'full load'—the resultant total being 1,089,000 pounds of meat, or something over 200 pounds for each person,[211] Ross says of this hunt: "The main party arrived on the return journey at Pembina on August 17th. . . . In due time the settlement was reached, and the trip being a successful one, the returns on this occasion may be taken as a fair annual average. . . ."[212]

From data furnished almost entirely by one witness, Alexander Ross—of whose social attitude towards the half-breeds, or whose temperamental attitude toward waste by other folk, we know something—Hornaday attempts to form a general judgment on the wastefulness of the Red River hunters, I do not think such clear-cut and definite conclusions as his can safely be drawn from the evidence available; nor do I consider him justified in so wide and sweeping an application of his averages over many years, and in relation to an entire (and large) body of hunters who are historically known to have imposed upon themselves various restrictive regulations. He writes:

In Ross's Red River Settlement, pp. 242-273, and Schoolcraft's North American Indians, Part iv, pp. 101-110, are given detailed accounts of the conduct and results of two hunting expeditions by the half-breeds, with many valuable statistics. On this data we base our calculation.

Taking the result of one particular day's slaughter as an index to the methods of the hunters in utilizing the products of the chase, we find that. . . .[213]

[210]Ross, Red River Settlement, 244; also cited by Hornaday, "Extermination of the American Bison," 488; Bryce, Remarkable History, 366.

[211]Ross, Red River Settlement, 272-3; Bryce, Remarkable History, 372.

[212]Ross, Red River Settlement, 273.

[213]Here follows a somewhat involved combination of Hornaday and Ross intermingled. For the sake of clearness, I give the passage from Ross herewith: "As a proof of the most profligate waste of animals, we might mention that during the first and second races [i.e. 'runs'] it was calculated that not less than

Hornaday then continues:

A bundle of dried meat weighs 60 to 70 pounds, and a bag of pemmican 100 to 110 pounds. If economically worked up, a whole buffalo cow yields half a bag of pemmican (about 55 pounds) and three-fourths of a bundle of dried meat (say 45 pounds). The most economical calculate that from 8 to 10 cows are required to load a single Red River Cart. The proceeds of 1776 cows once furnished 228 bags of pemmican, 213 bales of dried meat, 166 sacks of tallow weighing 200 pounds each, 556 bladders of marrow weighing 12 pounds each, and the value of the whole was $8160. The total of the above statement is 132,657 pounds of buffalo product for 1776 cows, or within a fraction of 75 pounds to each cow. The bulls and young animals killed were not accounted for. . . .[214]

The expedition described by Mr. Ross [that is, of 1840] contained 1210 carts and 620 hunters, and returned with 1,089,000 pounds of meat, making 900 pounds for each cart and 200 pounds for each individual in the expedition,[215] of all ages and of both sexes. Allowing, as already ascertained, that of the above quantity of product every 75 pounds represents one cow saved and two and one-third buffaloes wasted, it means that 14,520 buffaloes were

---

2500 animals had been killed, and out of that number only 375 bags of pemmican and 240 bales of dried meat were made. Now, making all allowance for waste, 750 animals would have been ample for such a result. What then, we may ask, became of the remaining 1750? Surely the 1630 mouths, starving as they had been for the month before (not forgetting a due allowance for the dogs), never consumed that quantity of beef in four or five days! The food, in short, was wasted. . . . Scarcely one-third of the animals killed in number is turned to account . . ." (ibid., 264).

We may contrast other instances, alleged and actual. A well-known case is mentioned by Catlin at the mouth of the Teton River, Dakota, just before his arrival, circa 1832. 'An immense herd' was attacked by 500 Sioux and surrounded. They brought back 1400 buffalo tongues (Catlin, Letters on the North American Indians, I, 256); also another instance of a herd 'of several hundred head' slain in toto by the starving Minatarees or Gros Ventres (ibid., 199).

Dodge: "A white hunter, considered very reliable, told me that he had once seen nearly 300 buffalo killed in one [Indian] surround, that the whole affair occupied less than ten minutes after the signal was given, and that not a single buffalo escaped . . ." (Plains of the Great West, 355).

Buffalo Jones, describing a surround of a herd 'of at least 2000 buffalo' by the Pawnees (spring, 1872), concludes thus: "After the Indians had departed, I counted up their day's work. I supposed, of course, from their demonstrations and hurrahs, I would find at least a hundred dead buffaloes, but imagine my disgust when the total numbered only forty-one!" (Buffalo Jones' Forty Years, 97-102.)

[214]This is Father Belcourt's party; above, note 203. No 'young animals' are mentioned. The bulls are accounted for; "not even a tongue was taken" (Hornaday, "Extermination of the American Bison," 475). This is wastefulness, in a sense, but it proves nothing concerning utilization by hunters of those parts they did consider fit to eat. On Hudson's Bay Company's post standards, 1868, see Cowie (in extenso, below, Appendix M); and on the use of buffalo offals by half-breeds, 1809, see Coues (ed.), Henry-Thompson Journals, II, 572, etc.

[215]"In the settlement" (so Ross, Red River Settlement, 273; italics mine); '1630 souls' x 200 pounds = 326,000 pounds of meat only.

killed and utilized, and 33,250 buffaloes were killed and eaten fresh or wasted, and 47,770 buffaloes were killed by 620 hunters, or an average of 77 buffaloes to each hunter. The total number of buffaloes killed for each cart was 39.

Allowing what was actually the case, that every buffalo killed would, if properly cared for, have yielded meat, fat and robe worth at least $5, the total value of the buffaloes slaughtered by that expedition amounted to $238,850; and of which the various products actually utilized represented a cash value of $72,600 added to the wealth of the Red River half-breeds.

In 1820 there went 540 carts to the buffalo plains; in 1825, 680; in 1830, 820; in 1835, 970; in 1840, 1210.

From 1820 to 1825 the average for each year was 610; from 1825 to 1830, 750; from 1830 to 1835, 895; from 1835 to 1840, 1090.

Accepting the statement of eye-witnesses that for every buffalo killed two and one-third buffaloes are wasted or eaten on the spot, and that every loaded cart represents 39 dead buffaloes, which were worth when utilized $5 each, we have the following series of totals:

From 1820 to 1825 five expeditions of 610 carts each killed 118,950 buffaloes, worth $594,750.

From 1825 to 1830 five expeditions of 750 carts each killed 146,250 buffaloes, worth $731,250.

From 1830 to 1835 five expeditions of 895 carts each killed 174,525 buffaloes, worth $872,625.

From 1835 to 1840 five expeditions of 1090 carts killed 215,550 buffaloes, worth $1,062,750.

Total number of buffaloes killed in 20 years, 652,275; total value of buffaloes killed in 20 years, $3,261,375; total value of the product utilized and added to the wealth of the settlements, $978,412.[216]

To begin with 'eye-witnesses,' there is just one. And since he could have been an eye-witness, whether he actually was one or not, why could Ross not tell us plainly what *was* done in this concrete instance with the surplus of buffalo, instead of asking questions and furnishing hypothetical answers? He does tell us certain things, however, which perhaps he forgot on this particular occasion, and which Hornaday ignores. This hunt in question, which consisted of two 'races' or runs, of which the first resulted in '1375 tongues being brought into camp' the first evening,[217] was in the nature of things a protracted affair of several hours. After dark, says Ross: ". . . what then remains is lost, and falls to the wolves; hundreds of animals are sometimes abandoned,

[216]Hornaday, "Extermination of the American Bison," 436, 437. Such arithmetical legerdemain abundantly justifies the philosopher's classification of lies in four categories: "lies, damned lies, 'facts', and statistics"! Garretson is not satisfied even with this figure. Citing no authority, he makes it 40,000 annually for the same twenty years = 800,000! (*American Bison*, 93-4.)

[217]Ross, *Red River Settlement*, 257; see also Bryce, *Remarkable History*, 371.

for even a thunderstorm, in one hour, will render the meat useless. . . ."[218]

Abundant evidence proves the prevalence at this very season, of the 'almost daily thunderstorm' in several sections of the western buffalo habitat, including this one.[219] Ross speaks also of 'making a due allowance for the dogs.' But the evidence seems to indicate that these animals could provide for themselves, though whether they conformed to Ross's conception of a due allowance is not so certain. Paul Kane observes: "They are always accompanied by an immense number of dogs which follow them from the settlements for the purpose of feeding on the offal and remains of the slain buffaloes. These dogs are very like wolves, both in appearance and disposition, and are, no doubt, a cross breed between the wolf and the dog. A great many of them acknowledge no particular master, and are sometimes dangerous in times of scarcity. I have myself known them to attack horses and eat them. . . ."[220]

Ross himself tells us that there were 542 of these brutes on this very expedition;[221] and in a kill of some 2500 from one herd, whether in 'one day' or in 'two races,' it is perfectly certain that wolves and semi-wolves would account for a large amount of meat, even without any waste arising from thunder-storms. While it may be taken for granted that under such general conditions every *large* kill would involve a quite considerable destruction of meat, it is pure assumption to imply that their entire product from the hunt was derived from large herds, necessarily too great for the meat to be saved the same evening. All our buffalo history indicates the very common presence of small herds.[222] In fact, the initial premises of Ross upon which

[218]Ross, *Red River Settlement*, 258, 268. On buffalo-meat and thunderstorms, see also Henry, Jr.: Coues (ed.), *Henry-Thompson Journals*, I, 99-100; II, 618.

[219]Western travel literature is fairly copious on this. See a large number of references *in extenso* (above, chap. IV, note 55). Colonel Dodge states furthermore that buffalo meat would turn bad overnight if the intestines were not removed (*Plains of the Great West*, 116).

[220]Kane, *Wanderings of an Artist*, 53, 61, 62, 82, 272. Kane records that one night at Fort Edmonton, 1847, five or six dogs attacked Rundle, the missionary, and had got him down and would certainly have killed him, had not an Indian woman come to his assistance. The clamour called out Harriott, then in charge, who shot the dogs.

[221]Ross, *Red River Settlement*, 246. Flett's enumeration of the 1849 party gives an even higher average: 400 dogs to 603 carts! (Hornaday, "Extermination of the American Bison," 475.) Above, note 205.

[222]Buffalo "were frequently found in small herds . . ." (Ross, *Red River Settlement*, 263).

Hornaday bases his very precise calculations are nothing but a series of assumptions. The 'not less than 2500 killed' are somebody's guess, we know not whose; the computation that only 750 out of 2500, or three-tenths of the buffalo slain were saved in every hunt during twenty years is pure guesswork again, as is likewise the supposition that this was the ratio in each of the 'runs' during even this one season. But perhaps the most glaring of all is the facile implication that not merely the ratio, but the *aggregate* was invariably maintained during so long a period. In his conception of the probable ratio of averages, Hornaday compares fittingly with Alexander Ross himself. That authority selects a 'successful' year, with the carts carrying 90 per cent of their accepted maximum load, as one which "may be taken as a fair annual average."[223] This predicates a uniformity in buffalo harvests which neither his own evidence nor anyone else's supports.

Hornaday's calm transference of the averages of one expedition to the aggregates of another is entirely without warrant, so likewise is his implied extension of the results to 'the half-breeds' at large. The results from Father Belcourt's expedition, 132,657 pounds of buffalo product from 1776 cows, or an average of about 75 pounds per cow, are nearly three and one-half times the average resulting from the kill as described by Ross. If Ross's 2500 animals yielded only 375 bags of pemmican and 240 bales of dried meat, the total on Hornaday's own figures would be 40,250 pounds of pemmican and, say, 15,600 pounds of dried meat, a total of 55,850 pounds, or about 22½ pounds per animal.

If this wide discrepancy between the respective figures proves anything at all, it assuredly proves a considerable variation in the luck of different expeditions in finding buffalo, in their general conditions when found, and in the various circumstances affecting the competence, judgment, and good fortune of the hunters; and exposes the utter absurdity of Hornaday's purely arithmetical conclusions.[224] Dis-

---

[223]*Ibid.*, 273; above, note 211. Isaac Cowie gives the Indian 'average' in a buffalo run as two animals per man: the Métis, 'better armed and mounted' (*i.e.* in 1867), as five (*Company of Adventurers*, 217).

[224]Hornaday himself ("Extermination of the American Bison," 475) notes that the average per family in the Belcourt expedition was 'about 35 buffaloes,' which he satirically observes "was very moderate slaughter." As we have seen, he has given the total in 1840 as '77 per hunter.' Grant (*Ocean to Ocean*, 123) records meeting a half-breed family on the Qu'Appelle in 1872: man, wife, and seven children. Their six carts were laden with the meat and robes from sixty buffaloes. Hornaday quotes this instance (p. 476). We have here three varied averages, which might arise from a number of causes. These make no impression whatever on his rigid uniformitarianism.

regarding for the moment, therefore, his application of 75 pounds (from Belcourt's figures) to the hunt described by Ross, and substituting the resultant average of 22½ pounds which follows from Ross's ascertained or suggested numbers, it is curious to notice that this utterly incredible waste—which they may believe who can!—occurred under a captain of the hunt whom Ross himself extols for his 'good sound sense.'[225]

Another curious circumstance may be noted. Dr. George Bryce and others consider, as we have seen,[226] that the rules of the expedition were meant, among other objects, 'to preserve the buffalo from wanton destruction'; and certainly their nature ill accords with the concept of a mere body of callous and unrestrained killers. This essentially differentiates the enterprise—and hence in all probability the mental attitude of its leaders at least—from an Indian buffalo hunt by nomadic tribes who could follow the buffalo at any time, and who by no method of reckoning could have anything like a capital sum of £24,000 invested in their undertaking. I suspect this last factor had something to do with the restrictive regulations of the hunt.

Now the reader will have observed (as noted by Hornaday) that in 1845 there were numerous small expeditions on the Pembina buffalo range, of which Father Belcourt's company was only one, starting about the same time as the great Red River division. Why could not these parties join the main hunt? Are we to suppose that such careless and prodigal folk (who slew 33 buffalo per family) stayed apart from the larger expedition because its waste and prodigality disgusted them?

I have no warrant for any direct assertion, but I suggest that it is highly probable that these smaller parties consisted of men to whom the restrictions of the larger body were irksome and intolerable.[227] Yet however this may be, they not only brought back a higher average amount per animal than that implied by Ross for the hunt of 1840, but also a very considerable aggregate of buffalo products other than tongues and choice portions. I have already adduced abundant evidence to show the uncertainty of the buffalo, both within the twenty-year period covered by Ross and by Hornaday, and long before.

---

[225]Ross, *Red River Settlement*, 247-8. This man, whose name was Wilkin or Wilkie, was one of that superior type known at Red River as 'English half-breeds' (*i.e.* a type or class, regardless of actual European descent), who were of Governor Morris's class (1), see above, note 182; so Cowie, *Company of Adventurers*, 64-6. He was also 'captain' in 1850, when Father Lacombe accompanied the Hunt (Hughes, *Father Lacombe*, 25, 33).

[226]See above, notes 35-6.

[227]There were such men: see Ross, *Red River Settlement*, 271-2.

According to McLean, writing presumably about 1848, they "returned with empty carts, these two years past"; the Indians having fired the prairie.[228] In 1850 there were apparently only some 800 buffalo killed.[229]

In addition to these fluctuations, there was the inevitable backward shrinkage of the approximate 'buffalo frontier,' with its resultant increase in meat consumed between the close of actual hunting and the arrival home. There was furthermore the natural increase[230] in a population "which despised agriculture so long as there was a buffalo to kill." Yet we are asked to believe that these men, despite the annually increasing strains on the supply of buffalo, were able to impose restrictions of that character on the mere *killing* of buffalo in the very heyday of their plenty; but were not concerned or were not able to place any whatever on the individual percentage of waste per buffalo, when dead, down to the very last days of the Hunt. Without some real evidence I decline to accept this.

I suspect that such general assertions as those of Kane[231] and Allen[232] have as their basis, in the final analysis, Ross's arithmetic. In any case the legend of Red River wastefulness has become so embedded in popular belief that it is apparently considered to be an indispensable feature on any allusion whatever to the Hunt. An 'old-timer' in Western Canada (reckoning by modern standards), who met the expedition just once, in the very latest year of its activities of which I have found any satisfactory evidence, and who never saw any of its

---

[228]McLean, *Twenty-Five Years' Service*, II, 302. It is one of the insoluble problems of our inquiry, what difference that need make (unless through fear of the Indians, above, notes 23, 144) to men who, of course, must have known where the buffalo were, 'on their regular migration,' at any given time, according to the orthodox jargon.

Father Morice (without any mention of fires) says that 200 carts returned empty in the *annus mirabilis*, 1840, out of 1700. He cites no authority for so wide a disagreement with Ross's carefully tabulated (and contemporary) totals. He may have included some outside parties, like Belcourt's of 1845. Morice, *Catholic Church in Western Canada*, I, 155.

[229]The 'Pembina Hunt': Hughes, *Father Lacombe*, 23-33.

[230]In 1836, 5000; in 1845, about 7000; so McLean, *Twenty-Five Years' Service*, II, 296; but see the statistical table at the conclusion of this chapter. In 1839, prisoners were to be allowed 'one pound of pemican per day, or its equivalent' (possibly in itself an indication of uncertainty in supply); in 1862, the allowance was 'one pound of flour and half a pound of pemican,' no equivalent being mentioned (Oliver (ed.), *Canadian North-West*, I, 291, 501).

[231]'. . . 30, 000 killed annually by half-breeds alone' (Kane, *Wanderings of an Artist*, 161).

[232]'Quite probably' 20,000 annually killed in the country of the Chippewas and Sioux, South of latitude 49°, by Red River hunters (also *circa* 1847: Allen, *American Bisons*, 144, 155).

members kill a buffalo, must nevertheless have a fling at the 'wastefulness of the half-breeds.'[233]

Apart from such actually known causes of waste as have been mentioned, I do not deny the probability of a certain amount, perhaps a considerable amount, in the case of folk living under such conditions in the field. Considering the flimsy nature of the evidence when carefully examined, however, I entirely disbelieve in the figures put forward. They are utterly preposterous, and in my opinion serve only to discredit the accuracy and trustworthiness of those who advance them.

On Hornaday's argument of uniformly diminishing numbers in a given area, it is clear that the fewer buffalo there were to slay, the more these men must have slain; not in any sense relatively, but absolutely; and this undeviating increase in slaughter was maintained during twenty years! But why stop at 1840? I have found no evidence—nor does Hornaday cite any—marking that year as a grand climacteric, after which a decline set in. So far as specific mention is concerned, we are as fully warranted in assuming the maintenance of the increase of some 22 per cent for each five-year period in the number of carts after 1840 as before; and beyond any question, as entirely justified in assuming the continuance of the ratio of 77 buffalo per hunter and 39 buffalo per cart as Hornaday was in his original computation. The Red River hunters might as well be hung for a sheep as for a lamb. Tabulated in Hornaday's own form, this would result as follows:

From 1841 to 1845 five expeditions of 1343 carts each killed 261,885 buffalo.

From 1846 to 1850 five expeditions of 1648 carts each killed 321,360 buffalo.[234]

From 1851 to 1855 five expeditions of 1999 carts each killed 389,805 buffalo.

From 1856 to 1860 five expeditions of 2436 carts each killed 475,410 buffalo.

From 1861 to 1865 five expeditions of 2980 carts each killed 581,140 buffalo.

From 1866 to 1870 five expeditions of 3641 carts each killed 709,995 buffalo.

[233]Denny MS., 13, 191. Compare note 180, above, re the Secretary of the U.S. Boundary Commission (apparently our invaluable Elliott Coues, the editor of Pike and the younger Henry), on Indians: ". . . but for all their wastefulness. . . ." etc. Of this he gives no indication; it has become a formula! (1874).

[234]As we have seen above (note 201) McLean would have the number for 1845 alone equal to three times the total for this period. None of the other writers mentioning numbers say whether they gave the grand total for the year in question or not, though presumably they did so.

From 1871 to 1874 four expeditions of 4354 carts each killed 679,224 buffalo.

Grand total of buffalo 'killed in 34 years': 3,418,819.[235] It is perhaps worth noting that even this huge aggregate of hypothetical carts from 1871 to 1874 does not equal ninety per cent of John McLean's easy estimate of 'perhaps 5000 carts' for about 1845.[236]

The meticulously-minded may demur to the above, on the ground that extant evidence explicitly denies it. Precisely the same objection applies to Hornaday's computations covering 1820-40. Evidence in quite sufficient abundance was available when he wrote, and an 'exhaustive' authority should have seen it.

The same injustice marks the language in which Hornaday, in particular,[237] has clothed his arguments in certain cases. After all, the Red River folk slew the buffalo for subsistence; and if we were to concede *in toto* the argument in regard to waste, even so, the Settlement did subsist principally on buffalo—on the authority of its harshest critics—for over half a century after the inception of the annual Hunt on the grand scale. To speak of the 'business-like method' of the half-breeds, 'best calculated' to extirpate the species in a short time, is logically inaccurate; for Hornaday himself has noted that they refrained from the more deadly method of killing, at which such admirable marksmen would certainly have excelled,[238] and which was adopted later by other hunters who did not even pretend to kill buffalo for subsistence.[239]

[235]It is pertinent to note that while the actual or supposed achievements of the Red River half-breeds in buffalo slaughter have been characterized by Allen—usually so moderate and judicious—as "having undoubtedly done more to exterminate the buffalo than any single cause" (*American Bisons*, 208; above, note 31), other 'statistics' (save the mark!) cited by himself, tell another story. Even on Hornaday's extravagant basis of computation, the Red River hunters would have taken thirty-four years to slay 3,418,819 buffalo. Spencer F. Baird asserted that in the fifties, 'the Upper Missouri tribes alone' were slaughtering *annually* 3,500,000 buffalo! The Upper Missouri tribes of Indians were estimated about 1850 at 54,550 souls (Maclean, *Canadian Savage Folk*, 1896, 293). Professor Baird's assertion is recorded by Allen (*American Bisons*, 186-7) without a word of critical comment. For an arithmetical examination of this and other reckless anti-Indian extravagances, see below, chap. XVIII.

[236]See above, note 201.

[237]Allen, while equally unjust in this, is somewhat less unctuous.

[238]See on this, Ross, *Red River Settlement*, 257; cf. Hornaday himself, above, note 198.

[239]See Hornaday's detailed description of the systematic extermination of the southern and northern herds in the U.S., 1870-75 and 1880-83 ("Extermination of the American Bison," 464-528).

The moral justification for Hornaday's attitude may perhaps be estimated from two facts, which are in very sharp contrast. He empties the vials of his wrath upon the 55 hunters who slew 1776 cows to fill 213 carts, and upon the 620 hunters who—so he says—slew 77 buffaloes per man in some months. While he undoubtedly administers a general castigation to the buffalo-destroyers of his own land and time, he fraternized with those whom he met; and he reports as a mere item in his argument what is perhaps the worst single case of all, that of a party "of sixteen hunters [who] report [which apparently signifies 'boast'] having killed 28,000 buffaloes during the past summer. . . ." (1873).[240] But these were neither half-breeds nor Indians! We may in conclusion compare General Sam Steele (Buffalo Lake, Alberta, winter 1874-75):

Vast numbers of buffalo covered the country. . . . Many buffalo were killed. . . . White hunters were few in number, but when they went to hunt for the purpose of obtaining a supply of fresh meat, they committed the most wanton destruction, killing enough for a whole settlement, or a regiment of soldiers. They were, as a rule, poor horsemen, and did their hunting on foot. Concealed in a bluff of timber or behind a snow-drift, they would shoot down hundreds. . . .

The Métis and Indians gave the buffalo a chance for its life; they were splendid horsemen . . . and killed the game from the saddle. . . .[241]

[240]This statement, from the *New Mexican*, a newspaper published in Santa Fé, New Mexico, was read by the Clerk of the House, in Congress, March 1, 1874 (Hornaday, "Extermination of the American Bison," 516).

[241]Steele, *Forty Years in Canada*, 87.

RED RIVER SETTLEMENT
SUMMARY OF CENSUS STATISTICS, 1831-1846

Year	Men		Women		Sons		Daughters		Servants		Totals	Houses	Stables	Barns
	Married	Unmarried	Married	Unmarried	Above 16	Under 16	Above 16	Under 16	Male	Female				
1831	398	113	401	82	128	622	81	602	....	....	2427	375	265	134
1832	448	108	452	91	120	753	74	705	....	....	2751	445	385	188
1833	482	94	480	74	147	838	116	751	....	....	2982	456	391	170
1834	557	132	567	89	143	922	108	842	....	....	3360	567	469	211
1835	595	80	595	66	176	1085	123	959	....	....	3679	574	516	227
1838	630	53	630	52	165	1177	155	1021	43	46	3972	641	630	230
1840	654	44	654	39	192	1240	178	1072	....	....	4073	627	632	254
1843	780	44	780	47	403	1384	452	1253	....	....	5143	730	924	295
1846	691	86	691	79	348	1144	325	1095	....	....	4459	674	1045	337

(Taken from E. H. Oliver (ed.), *Canadian North-West*, I, 74).

RED RIVER SETTLEMENT

SUMMARY OF CENSUS STATISTICS, 1831-1846

| | LIVE STOCK | | | | | | | | IMPLEMENTS, etc. | | | | | |
Year	Horses	Mares	Oxen	Bulls	Cows	Calves	Pigs	Sheep	Ploughs	Harrows	Carts	Boats	Canoes	Acres Cultivated
1831	241	169	887	71	1194	801	2362	....	187	243	302	15	289	2152
1832	279	198	1141	81	1538	878	2483	....	212	284	372	17	332	2631
1833	268	224	1219	83	1673	817	2033	....	238	314	486	13	273	3237½
1834	334	296	1592	116	2084	1211	2053	....	275	353	608	12	349	3230½
1835	443	323	1398	79	1664	1727	1995	....	311	400	709	11	316	3405
1838	599	534	1592	115	1683	1950	1698	457	382	476	1199	17	373	3862½
1840	656	627	1697	121	1851	2037	2092	1897	398	461	1371	368	26*	3955
1843	821	749	2307	107	2207	1580	1976	3569	429	536	1677	28	410	5003
1846	1218	1098	2240	107	2422	1125	3738	4188	438	541	1436	373	15*	5199½

*So in Oliver (I, 74); but the totals of boats and canoes in these years are surely transposed.

CHAPTER XV

THE NUMBERS OF THE BUFFALO: THE DESTRUCTION
OF THE SOUTHERN HERD

WE have now to consider an epoch concerning which the applicability of the phrase 'systematic destruction' of the buffalo could not possibly be disputed. In this and the two following chapters, I shall present such evidence as I have been able to collect regarding their final extermination (as a free wild species) in the southern and northern areas respectively of their latest Western habitat, the Plains; taking them in the order here specified, which is the chronological order also. Since I have hinted, in my concluding remarks in the previous chapter, at a certain supineness in Hornaday's attitude toward many of the buffalo-slayers, I cannot in justice omit his magnificent protest concerning the period of systematic slaughter in general; which he dates largely, 1830-88[1]—intensively, for the Southern herd 1870-74,[2] and for the Northern herd 1876-83.[3] This must be given in his own words:

We come now to a history which I would gladly leave unwritten. Its record is a disgrace to the American people in general, and the Territorial, State, and General Government in particular. It will cause succeeding generations to regard us as being possessed of the leading characteristics of the savage and the beast of prey—cruelty and greed. We will be likened to the blood-thirsty tiger of the Indian jungle, who slaughters a dozen bullocks at once when he knows he can eat only one.

In one respect, at least, the white men who engaged in the systematic slaughter of the bison were savages just as much as the Piegan Indians, who would drive a whole herd over a precipice to secure a week's rations of meat for a single village. The men who killed buffaloes for their tongues and those who shot them from the railway trains were murderers. In no way does civilized man so quickly revert to his former state as when he is alone with the beasts of the field. Give him a gun and something which he may kill without getting himself into trouble, and, presto! he is instantly a savage again, finding exquisite delight in bloodshed, slaughter, and death, if not for gain, then solely for the joy and happiness of it. There is no kind of warfare against game animals too unfair, too disreputable, or too mean

[1]Hornaday, "Extermination of the American Bison," 486.
[2]Ibid., 493-502.
[3]Ibid., 502-13.

416

for white men to engage in if they can only do so with safety to their own precious carcasses. They will shoot buffalo and antelope from running railway trains, drive deer into the water with hounds and cut their throats in cold blood, kill does with fawns a week old, kill fawns by the score for their spotted skins, slaughter deer, moose, and caribou in the snow at a pitiful disadvantage, just as the wolves do; exterminate the wild ducks on the whole Atlantic seaboard with punt guns for the metropolitan markets; kill off the Rocky Mountain goats for hides worth only 50 cents apiece, destroy wagon loads of trout with dynamite, and so on to the end of the chapter.

Perhaps the most gigantic task ever undertaken on this continent in the line of game-slaughter was the extermination of the bison in the great pasture region by the hide-hunters. Probably the brilliant rapidity and success with which that lofty undertaking was accomplished was a matter of surprise even to those who participated in it. . . .[4]

Hornaday remarks elsewhere:

A continuation of the record we have lately made as wholesale game butchers will justify posterity in dating us back with the mound-builders and cave-dwellers,[5] when man's only known function was to slay and eat.

The primary cause of the buffalo's extermination, and the one which embraced all others, was the descent of civilization, with all its elements of destructiveness, upon the whole of the country inhabited by that animal. From the Great Slave Lake to the Rio Grande, the home of the buffalo was everywhere overrun by the man with a gun; and, as has ever been the case, the wild creatures were gradually swept away, the largest and most conspicuous forms being the first to go.

The secondary causes . . . may be catalogued as follows:

Man's reckless greed, his wanton destructiveness, and improvidence in not husbanding such resources as come to him from the hand of nature, ready made.

The total and utterly inexcusable absence of protective measures and agencies on the part of the National Government and of the Western States and Territories. . . .[6]

These are hard sayings, but they are only too abundantly justified by the relations of reputable eye-witnesses, and others conversant with facts which in many instances the participants themselves apparently did not consider as discreditable, and saw no reason to hide. We read of men so disgustingly greedy that they had not even patience to skin the numbers they slew by any ordinary method, but must needs

[4]*Ibid.*, 486-7.

[5]Indignation here outstrips knowledge, 'and panting time toils after him in vain.' The juxtaposition of cave-man and mound-builder illustrates the haziness concerning the mound-builders common fifty years ago. See chap. III, notes 5-7.

[6]Hornaday, "Extermination of the American Bison," 464. Compare Stone and Cram: "Its extermination was one of the most shameful examples of man's greed and a nation's lethargy that is furnished in the history of our country . . ." (*American Animals*, 67); so also Garretson, *American Bison*, 154.

attempt to remove the hide—the one thing they valued—by means of a team of horses and a rope or chain; usually (one is delighted to add) ruining the skin and despoiling themselves in the process.[7] We read of men so wickedly wasteful that 'thousands upon thousands' of buffalo were killed for their tongues alone, and not even skinned; so that it was 'no uncommon thing' for a man to bring in two barrels at once of salted buffalo tongues without another pound of meat or a single skin.[8] Even from the lesser sin of mere ignorance, it was considered by careful observers that every buffalo robe that went to market from the southern territory in the years 1871 and 1872 represented as many as three or four, and even as high as five dead buffalo![9] We read of men so infamously and shamelessly cruel in their avarice that they formed themselves into cordons to guard the rivers and watering-places where the famishing animals sought to drink. They mowed them down with guns by day and frightened them back by fires at night; and this procedure was repeated again and again as the poor thirst-maddened creatures attempted to break through, until they were finally destroyed.[10]

An English sportsman and plainsman already mentioned, William Blackmore, of London, travelled in the autumn of 1873 'for some thirty or forty miles along the north bank of the Arkansas River,' to the east of Fort Dodge. He declares: ". . . there was a continual line of putrescent carcasses, so that the air was rendered pestilential and offensive to the last degree. The hunters had formed a line of camps along the banks of the river, and had shot down the buffalo, night and morning, as they came to drink. In order to give an idea of the number of these carcasses, it is only necessary to mention that I counted 67 on one spot not covering four acres. . . ."[11]

This peculiar fiendishness was perpetrated along the Arkansas, the

[7]Dodge, *Plains of the Great West*, 137; Hornaday, "Extermination of the American Bison," 494.

[8]*Ibid.*, 496; cf. *Buffalo Jones' Forty Years*, 37 *seq.*

[9]Dodge, *Plains of the Great West*, 132; Hornaday, "Extermination of the American Bison," 494.

[10]Dodge, *Plains of the Great West*, 133; also his *Our Wild Indians*, 295; Allen, *American Bisons*, 179; Hornaday, "Extermination of the American Bison," 496; *Buffalo Jones' Forty Years*, 256-62.

[11]Dodge, *Plains of the Great West*, introd. (by Blackmore), xv. 'It was said along the Arkansas River, a man could jump from carcass to carcass without touching the ground' (John Peter Turner, *Geographical Magazine*, England, August, 1936; *précis* in *Montreal Gazette*, August 13, 1936). The same was said along the Santa Fé railroad right-of-way (Garretson, *American Bison*, 107, 114). See below, chap. XVII, note 85. It was a common figure of speech, familiar in the English forests for centuries: 'From Nottingham to Welbeck' through Sher-

Republican, the South Platte, and other streams;[12] doubtless wherever opportunity presented itself. One cannot wonder at Hornaday's remark that if the southern buffalo range could have been roofed over at that time, it would have made 'one vast charnel-house.'[13]

It may help to bring home to us the stupendous figures of the slaughter, to remark that the number given above on 'a spot not covering four acres,' which Blackmore manifestly regarded as almost incredible without very precise particularization, dwindles almost into insignificance when compared with other well-authenticated records. Colonel Dodge tells us: "I have myself counted 112 carcasses of buffalo inside of a semi-circle of 200 yards radius, all of which were killed by one man from the same spot, and in less than three-quarters of an hour. . . ."[14]

---

wood Forest, or (Cheshire) 'From Blacon Point to Hillree a squirrel might hop from tree to tree' (Cox, *Royal Forests of England*, 132, 204, 220).

In contradistinction to Blackmore, who wrote at the time, and whose Introduction was accepted by Dodge who was a very competent first-hand critic, Garretson prints an idle tale from Brigadier-General Dangerfield Parker, concerning the precise locality of Dodge's immense herd of 1871. In 1869, 'approaching a small stream, he saw what he took to be a small herd of buffalo in the act of fording it. When he drew nearer he saw that they were dead animals, all mired during an attempt to cross. They had simply dried up in the pure air of the plains, without decaying. The animals were still standing in an upright position and had thus given the impression of being alive . . .' (Garretson, *American Bison*, 45-6). Such an event must have been notorious, yet apparently no contemporary has mentioned it; and it never came to the ears of Hornaday nor those tireless inquirers (three of them Army men), Dodge, Allen, Coues, and Chittenden. It may keep company with Bridger's nonsense about 'auto-pickling' in Salt Lake, 1830 (chap. VIII, note 5). Compare Sir Richard Burton (1860): "I have been gravely told of a herd of bison which arrested the course of the Platte River, causing its waters, like those of the Red Sea, to stand up, wall-fashion, while the animals were crossing. Of this Western order is the well-known account of a ride on a buffalo's horns . . ." (*City of the Saints*, 83).

Daniel Ott, forty years afterward, to Colonel Shoemaker (*Pennsylvania Bison Hunt*, 50-60) asserted likewise, 'no smell from decaying buffalo' in Kansas, 1873; but as the same witness says that buffalo 'always ran with the wind, nothing could turn them,' *i.e.*, right into the hunter's arms; and that at Fort Dodge (a prairie town where space was abundant and high Kansas winds prevalent) there were 'piles of hides 100 feet high stacked in all parts of the town,' one remains unconvinced. The average country grain elevator is about 75 feet high (cf. Garretson, *American Bison*, 110).

Garretson furthermore quotes from Blackmore, and from Dodge also (without acknowledgement) *re* the Northern slaughter of 1880, to which the authors in 1877 could not refer, and to which their remarks would not apply (*ibid.*, 153, 110).

[12]Hornaday, "Extermination of the American Bison," 496.

[13]*Ibid.*

[14]Dodge, *Plains of the Great West*, 136; cited also by Hornaday, "Extermination of the American Bison," 470.

Another southern hunter, Harry Andrews, 'made big money' in the slaughter of the mere remnants of the Southern herd in 1874-76, at prices ranging from 65 cents each for cow robes to $1.15 for bull robes; and on one occasion fired 115 shots from the same stand, and killed 63 buffalo 'in about an hour.'[15] On the Northern range later, 'Vic' Smith, 'the most famous hunter in Montana,' "in the winter of 1881-1882, killed 107 animals in one 'stand' in about an hour, and without shifting his point of attack. . . ."[16] 'Doc Aughl' and John Edwards, in the same season and locality, killed respectively 85 and 75 at one 'stand';[17] and in Montana also, a nameless hunter was stated by James McNaney, Hornaday's guide in 1886, to have slain in one stand 91 buffalo.[18] After these examples, there is nothing incredible in the statement of General W. B. Hazen: "I knew a man who killed with his own hand 99 buffaloes in one day, without taking a pound of the meat. . . ."[19]

Like the 'last buffalo,' more than one claim has been made to the highest number of kills in one day. A certain Dr. Carver disputed the precedence of 'Buffalo Bill' Cody as a buffalo-slayer, claiming 166 for one day's run. But while this is believed by a critically minded historian to be wholly fictitious, it is by reason of personal disqualifications affecting the claimant, rather than any inherent incredibility in the figures. In any case he is utterly eclipsed by an early resident of Dodge City, 'noted for his truthfulness,' who stated that he had killed 250 buffalo in one day.[20]

Nor are these figures, asserted or actual, merely the harvest of one crowded hour of glorious life. They are buttressed by kindred claims of aggregates which, taken broadly at least, can scarcely be doubted. Hornaday writes: "There are many men now living who declare that during the great slaughter they each killed from 2500 to 3000 buffaloes every year. . . ."[21] The *fact* of these assertions can be substantiated

[15]*Ibid.*, 469, 502.
[16]*Ibid.*, 510. For descriptions of 'still-hunting' methods, see Dodge, *Plains of the Great West*, 134-7; Allen, *American Bisons*, 211-15; Hornaday, "Extermination of the American Bison," 465-70; and a very good one in Garretson, *American Bison*, 115-19.
[17]Hornaday, "Extermination of the American Bison," 510.
[18]*Ibid.*, 469.
[19]Letter from General Hazen, read in Congress, March 10, 1874 (Hornaday, "Extermination of the American Bison," 516).
[20]For Dr. Carver, Walsh and Salsbury, *The Making of Buffalo Bill*, 223; for the truthful resident, Garretson, *American Bison*, 114.
[21]Hornaday, "Extermination of the American Bison," 501.

without difficulty. Buffalo Jones himself says: "I had been a successful buffalo-hunter, had killed thousands simply for their hides. . . ."[22]

Allen wrote similarly: ". . . one hunter informed me that he had himself killed over 3000 buffaloes a year for several years, and I met other persons who claimed to have each killed an equal number. . . ."[23] He cites another instance, on the authority of an early Western journalist, of a hunter who killed 3000 in the winter of 1873-74; '85 one day, 64 another,' etc.[24]

In a reminiscent magazine article, depicting the vanished splendours of Dodge City in the seventies, a certain individual, 'the noted Billy Tilghman,' is credited with 'thirty-three hundred hides in one season';[25] and even this is surpassed by another hunter working from Dodge City, an evident expert, Tom Nixon, who "once . . . killed twenty-six hundred in twenty-four days. . . ."[26]

An approximately equal number is claimed by another old hunter, George W. Reighard, also of Dodge City, where he was living as late as 1931. He says: "In 1872, when I went down into the Texas Panhandle with a buffalo-hunting outfit. . . . I killed a little over 3000 buffaloes in one month, which was an average of about 100 a day. . . ."[27]

Such daily or monthly aggregates must inevitably have resulted in most appalling totals, in the case of parties at all numerous or keeping the field for any length of time. The statement was read in Congress (March 10, 1874) that ". . . one party of sixteen hunters report having killed twenty-eight thousand buffaloes in the past summer . . ." (that is, of 1873).[28] This represents an average of 1750 each, slain at a season of the year when meat was difficult to save and often quite worthless as food, and when hides brought only a third (or less) of their winter

[22]*Buffalo Jones' Forty Years*, 37; cf. *ibid.*, 83-102.
[23]Allen, *American Bisons*, 189.
[24]*Ibid.*, 179.
[25]*Saturday Evening Post*, Philadelphia, March 8, 1930, 146. According to Garretson (who gives him the title here mentioned) 'the best authenticated total for a season' (*American Bison*, 114). Authenticated by the claimant, probably.
[26]*Saturday Evening Post*, March 8, 1930, 146.
[27]*Edmonton Journal*, January 3, 1931. Mr. Reighard also says: "I have often heard of still hunters killing one hundred and more in one stand. . . . Pity? No, I did not feel it. It was business with me. I had my money invested in that outfit; if it did not butcher the buffaloes there were many other hunting outfits all around me that would, so I killed all I could. . . ."
[28]From the *New Mexican* (newspaper, of Santa Fé, New Mexico): Hornaday, "Extermination of the American Bison," 516.

price.[29] The aforementioned Dr. Carver, in preferring his claim to the proud position of champion killer, 'the lifetime record for buffalo killing . . .,' "says that his total was 30,000, that he killed 5700 in a single winter, and 166 in a single day's run. . . ."[30]

These figures are believed by the historian to be fictitious; but, so far as their inherent possibility is concerned, they are not incredible. The achievements that—popularly at least[31]—made the reputation of

[29]"The hide . . . shot in warm weather was unfit for a robe; the hair was too thin then . . . on the Texas prairies it brought from 50 to 60 cents for a cow hide, and up to $1.00 for a bull hide. Good robes came from buffaloes killed in cold weather, and brought from $2. to $3. . . ." (Reighard, *Edmonton Journal,* January 3, 1931.)

Cf. Hornaday: "It was not until 1881 . . . that hunting buffalo in summer as well as in winter became a wholesale business. What hunting can be more disgraceful than the slaughter of females and young in summer, when skins are almost worthless! . . ." ("Extermination of the American Bison," 507.)

Edwin James, 1820: "Those skins which are obtained during this season are known by the name of *summer skins,* and are used in the construction of their skin lodges, and for their personal cloathing for summer wear. . . ." (*Early Western Travels,* XIV, 301.)

[30]Walsh and Salsbury, *The Making of Buffalo Bill,* 223.

[31]Time, and modern critical standards, have not dealt kindly with Buffalo Bill. Hornaday, writing in the heyday of his fame, says: "I regret that circumstances have prevented my obtaining the exact figures of the great kill of buffaloes that Mr. Cody [whom on p. 373 he calls "our own distinguished Buffalo Bill"] once made in a single run, in which he broke all previous records in that line, and fairly earned his title. In 1867 he entered into a contract with the Kansas Pacific Railway, then in the course of construction through western Kansas, at a monthly salary of $500, to deliver all the buffalo meat that would be required by the army of laborers engaged in building the road. In 18 months he killed 4280 buffaloes . . ." (Hornaday, "Extermination of the American Bison," 478). Inman has 'nearly five thousand' (*The Old Santa Fé Trail,* 210). Buffalo Bill, to whom the work is dedicated, contributes a preface, lauding Inman's authenticity.

According to a recent Canadian historian, "the notorious Buffalo Bill, whose claim to immortality seems to have been a singularly negative one, is said to have killed 4280 buffaloes in eighteen months, and forty-eight in fifty minutes . . ." (MacInnes, *In the Shadow of the Rockies,* 143).

Between these extremes lies modern United States opinion, well summed up by Walsh, whose researches leave little about Cody that is very certain, except the showman. While he considers the 4280 buffalo acceptable, he points out (p. 203) that 'no contemporary record can be found'; and Hornaday's failure to obtain 'exact figures' was practically the experience of everyone who ever tried. The criticisms of William E. Connelley, sometime Secretary of the Kansas State Historical Society, are damaging, if not damning (see Walsh and Salsbury, *The Making of Buffalo Bill,* vi, 38, 46, 67, 73, 79, 202-4). He doubts if Cody ever killed an Indian in his life! Cody's methods in buffalo-running seem to have been very skilful, enabling him to kill his buffalo in compact order on a small space; and his own time for the 4280 was *seventeen* months (*ibid.,* 106-9).

Compare Dodge on the two Mexicans who always drove their buffalo into camp to shoot them (*Plains of the Great West,* 129). Grinnell, a very well-informed critic, simply calls him 'William Cody' (*Fighting Cheyennes,* 300). Garretson says he was neither the first nor (by many!) the only 'Buffalo Bill.'

'Buffalo Bill' (W. F. Cody), in a more legitimate slaughter, while naturally not greater (since Dr. Carver doubtless provided for that) are still great enough to remove Carver's claim from the region of the impossible; and even Buffalo Bill's average, if not his aggregate, was out-done by another worthy at this time.[32]

Hornaday himself, who made the personal acquaintance of many of the hunters of this era, says: "There are many men now living [that is, in 1889] who declare that during the great slaughter they each killed from twenty-five hundred to three thousand buffaloes every year. With thousands of hunters on the range, and such possibilities of slaughter before each, it is, after all, no wonder that an average of nearly a million and a quarter of buffaloes fell each year during that bloody period. . . ."[33]

We must also remember that the practices mentioned were not mere occasional aberrations from a higher general standard of conduct, but, without doubt, were simply characteristic examples of the every-day attitude of an overwhelming proportion of a large class of men.[34] The immense numbers destroyed in so short a time prove this conclusively, as the huge totals could never have been attained by fair sport or lawful consumption for subsistence. Having regard to these facts, I not only consider Hornaday's language to have been in no wise excessively severe; I cannot even conceive what choice of language could be so. I must also add that while his strictures are directed towards the United States, whence his supporting evidence is derived, I believe that had the flow of population turned towards Canada, the human history would have been little different. The United States has no monopoly in the so-called 'sportsman,' the type of man who can see nothing in the wild creature except a target.[35]

In a contest to decide the claim, Cody's winning total in eight hours for three 'runs' was 69, which were counted. Garretson apparently doubts the 'American legend' (*American Bison*, 138-45). He may have been only the *first* super-slayer.

[32]Captain Jack Brydges is said to have killed 1142 in six weeks (Hornaday, "Extermination of the American Bison," 465); and the Tilghmans, Nixons, Reighards, and all the host of 3000 per season hunters, must have far surpassed him. I doubt if any of these men allowed anybody's record to eclipse his own!

[33]*Ibid.*, 501. Compare General Sam Steele (Buffalo Lake, Alberta, winter 1874-75): "The most successful of the half-breed hunters during that winter was Abraham Salois, who killed 600; in one run 37 fell to his rifle, no doubt the best on record . . ." (*Forty Years in Canada*, 87). He is very probably nearer the truth.

[34]Reighard: "I often hear it said that it was a wilful waste to butcher the buffalo as we did. . . . I and the other thousands of buffalo hunters had no high-minded motives in slaughtering the buffalo. We were after his hide and the money it would bring . . ." (*Edmonton Journal*, January 3, 1931).

[35]General Steele writes as follows (Buffalo Lake, Alberta, 1875): "White hunters were few in number, but when they went to hunt for the purpose of

I doubt whether at any time one could accurately classify the entire aggregate of buffalo as one 'herd.' Even those who thus write have presented no evidence that the whole mass were ever present together in one body, since their numbers acquired any significance; and I have not the slightest doubt that in historical times at least such was never the case.[36] In the era of their final extermination it is known that there were at least two grand aggregates, known respectively as the 'Northern' and the 'Southern' herd. The opening of the Oregon Trail, along the general line of which the Union Pacific Railway, for some distance at least, was later built, either foreshadowed this division,[37] or, as Allen thinks, caused it.[38]

Hornaday says: "In a few years the tide of overland travel became so great that the buffaloes learned to keep away from the dangers of the trail, and many a pioneer has crossed the plains without ever seeing a live buffalo. . . ."[39]

A later and very competent student writes as follows:

"The year 1841 was a turning-point in the history of the plains tribes, for that season the first emigrant train passed up the Platte on its way to Oregon. Hitherto the fur men had been almost the only ones who crossed the northern plains, and they were few in number; but from this year on an annually-increasing swarm of emigrants poured up the Platte. The Indians, at first astonished, soon became alarmed, and with good reason. The emigrants cut down and wasted the scant supply of wood along the road; their herds of oxen, horses, and mules gnawed the bottoms bare of grass; the buffalo were shot down and left to rot on the ground, and worse still, the herds were frightened from the country. In 1835, the Ogallala were hunting at the Forks of the Platte. Ten years later, to get meat they were obliged to go to the Laramie plains and among the mountains in hostile Snake country. They went with no good will toward the emigrants who had driven away the buffalo. . . ."[40]

---

obtaining a supply of fresh meat, they committed the most wanton destruction, killing enough for a whole settlement, or a regiment of soldiers. They were, as a rule, poor horsemen, and did their hunting on foot. Concealed in a bluff of timber or behind a snow-drift, they would shoot down hundreds without the poor animals having a chance to see the direction from which the shots came . . ." (*Forty Years in Canada*, 87).

[36]If we accept the lower Platte as the rough geographical centre of the more important buffalo habitat, 'one herd' there inescapably involves a lengthy eastward and westward emigration for the purpose; a possibility emphatically denied by some, and rather grudgingly admitted by others, in the evil days of 'the beginning of the end,' but not before. Characteristically, the champions of the 'north-and-south' propensity are also for 'one herd'; as Hornaday, "Extermination of the American Bison," 492; cf. Allen (contra), *American Bisons*, 59-61.

[37]Hornaday, "Extermination of the American Bison," 492.

[38]Allen, *American Bisons*, 144.

[39]Hornaday, "Extermination of the American Bison," 492.

[40]Grinnell, *Fighting Cheyennes*, 94-5. Father De Smet, who was along the Oregon Trail in 1840 (*Early Western Travels*, XXVI, 15-16) accompanied this

It is curious to note that in the following year (1842) Frémont apparently did not consider that the use of the 'excellent roads' from the mouth of the Platte to Fort Laramie would ". . . in any way interfere with the range of the buffalo, on which the neighbouring Indians mainly depend for support. . . ."[41]

It is difficult to define the approximate buffalo frontier on the eastern side at the time when the systematic slaughter may be said to have commenced in earnest; so many of the statements are distressingly vague and general without local knowledge wherewith to check them. Chittenden states as follows: "It was a common saying in the era of the fur trade that the buffalo was retreating before the white man at the rate of ten miles a year, and this is perhaps not an exaggerated measure of his certain and continuous disappearance. . . ."[42]

The obvious question arises—what was the 'era of the fur trade,' and where was the buffalo frontier at that precise time? Allen and Hornaday date their extinction in eastern Kansas about 1840,[43] and

---

first train in 1841 (ibid., XXVII, 190). He notes 'an immense herd' on the Platte (where?) June, 1841 (ibid., XXVII, 265). The supposed absence from Laramie Plains after 1844, and its inaccuracy, have been discussed re snow (above, chap. VIII, notes 9-28). This instance of Grinnell's seems really to be one of the frequent fluctuations of the herds, for Father De Smet remarks in 1858: "The race is not yet extinct in these parts, though it is becoming more rare to find the buffalo on the highway across the plains, which its instinct must have taught it to avoid. We met our first herds near Fort Kearney" (Grand Island, Nebraska: Life of De Smet, II, 723). As late as 1867, Sir William Butler met a herd there, which took 'two hours' hard riding to pass through . . .' (Autobiography, 90-7). Even later, in July, 1870, a party of Burlington survey engineers saw 'tens of thousands of buffalo' southwest from Fort Kearney, with one day's march. Thomas M. Davis, "Building the Burlington through Nebraska" (Nebraska History, XXX, December, 1949, 317-47; citing p. 322). There may quite easily have been yet later instances, which have not been recorded.

[41]Frémont, Narrative, 51-3. Below the Forks, June, 1842, 'buffalo swarming in immense numbers,' (pp. 16-17). Along the South Platte, buffalo, July 4; 'scarcer,' July 5-6; 'abundance,' July 7-8; 'scarce,' July 8-13; herds again, July 13; 'scarcity,' July 14-16; (ibid., 21-37). Preuss, along the North Platte, Forks to Fort Laramie and to longitude 105° W. 'practically none' (ibid., 37-55). Buffalo again from 105° 50' 45" W. to three days west of Independence Rock (ibid., 55-63). 'Entirely disappeared' beyond the Sweetwater (ibid., 70). Frémont must have considered these fluctuations quite normal, or surely he would not have written as above, without mentioning them.

[42]Chittenden, American Fur Trade, II, 816; Coman, Economic Beginnings of the Far West, II, 34, 56. Garretson (American Bison, 92) says this 'has often been stated' re the Middle West, east of the Mississippi. I have found no such statement anywhere, concerning that territory.

[43]Hornaday, map ("Extermination of the American Bison," 548). Bob Davis ("Canada Cavalcade," Magazine Section, Winnipeg Free Press, September 11, 1937) speaks of '300,000 buffalo' at Brownsville, Nebraska, on the banks of the Missouri River (? Brownville, Nemaha County, southeast Nebraska) 'thundering by for three days and nights, fifty-four years ago,' i.e. 1883. There is not a fragment of evidence for their presence—and in such incredible numbers—so far down

Father De Smet, referring to the country about Fort Leavenworth (1851), remarks: ". . . nor is it much longer ago that these fields were the pasture of enormous herds of buffalo. . . ."[44]

It would seem that the 'ten miles a year' can be taken only in a loose sense, if indeed it be anything more than a generalization based upon localized observations which extended over a period of a year or two. For Dr. Gregg, dealing with the period *circa* 1830, writes thus: "A few old buffalo have sometimes been met with about Cottonwood;" and in the year of his journey they encountered their first (May 30, 1831) on the second day after leaving Cottonwood[45] (that is, near Durham, Kansas[46]).

Gregg adds: "The buffalo are usually found much further east early in the spring, than during the rest of the year, on account of the long grass, which shoots up earlier in the season than the short pasturage of the plains. . . ."[47]

It may be noted that Cottonwood Creek, the place in question, was 192 miles on the Santa Fé Trail from Independence, the starting-point near the modern Kansas City; from thence to the Little Arkansas was 42 miles, and to the main Arkansas River was a further 36 miles, a total distance of only 78 miles from Cottonwood to the main river.[48] According to the 'ten miles a year' theory, in the forty years which elapsed from Gregg to Colonel Dodge's immense herd (1831-71), the buffalo frontier would have ⌐ ɾed backward from near Durham (about 97° W.) to about the longitude of Pueblo, Colorado (104° 40′ W.).[49]

Colonel Dodge himself, writing of a period of profusion which came to an end in 1874, says concerning the 'great spring migration': "The line of march of this great spring migration was not always the same, though it was confined within certain limits. I am informed by old frontiersmen that it has not within twenty-five years crossed the

---

the Missouri at that late date; nor of such a host anywhere in the buffalo territory of the United States after the early spring of 1883. See on this class of testimony on buffalo, below, chap. XVII, note 112. Hornaday notes them extinct about here, *circa* 1840 (map, "Extermination of the American Bison," 548). Some dates below, chap. XX, note 108.

[44]*Life of De Smet*, II, 720.

[45]Gregg, *Early Western Travels*, XIX, 205; cf. Coues (ed.), *Expeditions of Pike*, II, 400, 521, ed. notes.

[46]Thwaites, ed. note, *Early Western Travels*, XIX, 205; also Coues's excellent notes, *Expeditions of Pike*, II, 400-5, 517-22.

[47]Gregg, *Early Western Travels*, XIX, 205.

[48]Itinerary of the Santa Fé Trail, in Chittenden, *American Fur Trade*, II, 535-43; also Gregg's Table of Mileages, *Early Western Travels*, XX, 93.

[49]A degree of longitude at latitude 38° is given as 54.89 miles.

Arkansas River east of Great Bend, nor west of Big Sand Creek. The most favoured routes crossed the Arkansas at the mouth of Walnut Creek, Pawnee Fork, Mulberry Creek, the Cimarron Crossing, and Big Sand Creek. . . ."[50]

The vast host is described by Dodge as being 'constantly depleted' as it moved northward, "numbers wandering off to the right and left . . .,"[51] as of course we might expect; and Hornaday states that "on the east, even as late as 1872, thousands of buffaloes ranged within ten miles of Wichita. . . ."[52] Wichita, Kansas, is situated in 97° 12′ W.; for all practical purposes as far east (or within a very few miles) as the buffalo were *circa* 1830. The ten miles may perhaps represent a rude measure of the annual advance of settlement westward across a wide front. Similarly, if their 'constant and continuous disappearance' signifies merely a progressive reduction of the buffalo aggregate without even a temporary pause or increase, it may pass without criticism; but if it means a sort of 'sweeping back,' whereby they never again reappeared in any region they had once 'left' in these latter days, it will be shown that this opinion is unwarranted by the evidence. Hornaday observes:

Until the building of the transcontinental railway[53] made it possible to market the 'buffalo product,' buffalo hunting as a business was almost wholly in the hands of the Indians. Even then, the slaughter so far exceeded the natural increase that the narrowing limits of the buffalo range was [*sic*] watched with anxiety, and the ultimate extinction of the species confidently predicted. Even without railroads the extermination of the race would have taken place eventually, but it would have been delayed perhaps twenty years. . . .[54]

So far as the earlier part of this statement is concerned, speaking in the broad sense, as compared with the later squadrons of white buffalo-hunters, it is quite true. Even in the earlier pre-railway days, however, there were in certain regions in the Southwest sufficient white hunters to make a serious local impression, and to irritate if not to injure the Indians depending upon the herds for subsistence. In 1863, S. G. Colley, Indian Agent for the Upper Arkansas, reported as follows: "There was not a buffalo within two hundred miles of the

[50]Dodge, *Our Wild Indians*, 285.
[51]*Ibid.*
[52]Hornaday, "Extermination of the American Bison," 492, 500; quoting the *Wichita World* (Kansas), February 9, 1889, as authority for the statement.
[53]The Union Pacific, commenced at Omaha, Nebraska, in 1865.
[54]Hornaday, "Extermination of the American Bison," 492. The Indian rate of slaughter, and the 'anxiety' will be examined later.

reservation, and but little game of any kind, and that starvation caused most of the depredations committed by the Indians. . . . Thousands and thousands of buffalo are killed by hunters during the summer and fall merely for their hides and tallow, to the displeasure and injury of the Indians. . . ."[55]

The following is also recorded by Grinnell: "The officer at Salina, at the mouth of Salina Fork, on the Smoky Hill [River], 1864, reports that one hundred men on Salina alone made a living by killing buffalo for hides and tallow, and recommends that an order be issued forbidding such slaughter of game, as it angers the Indians. . . ."[56]

Whatever may have been perpetrated before the railways opened up the buffalo range, it was insignificant in comparison with the perfect orgy of murder that broke loose afterward. "The building of the Union Pacific Railway began at Omaha in 1865; and during that year 40 miles were constructed. The year following saw the completion of 265 miles more, and in 1867, 245 miles more were added, which brought it to Cheyenne. In 1868, 350 miles were built, and in 1869 the entire line was open to traffic. . . ."[57]

The Kansas Pacific was being built further to the south about the same time; and the Atchison, Topeka, and Santa Fé, approximately but not always closely paralleling the Santa Fé Trail,[58] reached Fort Dodge, now Dodge City, in September, 1872.[59]

Colonel Dodge has very graphically described the workings of that passion for killing to which Hornaday had reference,[60] and which at any time (among the larger herds) has cost the buffalo dear; a passion which a recent writer—with what degree of scientific sanction I know not—has traced to an age-old instinctive longing for revenge, reaching back to the primitive eras when man endured unutterable things from the 'dragons of the prime.'[61]

The enemy still approaching, some bull will face him, lower his head, and start on a most furious charge. But alas for brute courage! When he

[55]Grinnell, *Fighting Cheyennes*, 124; cf. 129. 'Indian thievery,' *circa* 1864, often the negligence of cattle herders (so, Kit Carson, *ibid.*, 132).

[56]*Ibid.*, 125. Inman (*The Old Santa Fé Trail*, 154) cites an early plainsman as stating (1861) that the Indians 'ate everything, even to the intestines,' and that their grievance was not what the whites *ate* but what they wasted. At this time the Indians were 'not hostile.'

[57]Hornaday, "Extermination of the American Bison," 492.

[58]Chittenden, *American Fur Trade*, II, 530, 534; Coues (ed.), *Expeditions of Pike*, II, 517.

[59]"Straight-Shooting Dodge," *Saturday Evening Post*, March 8, 1930, 146.

[60]Hornaday, "Extermination of the American Bison," 486-7 (above, note 4).

[61]"Big Game in Africa," *Chicago Record-Herald*, November 7, 1931.

has gone twenty or thirty yards, Mr. Bull thinks better of it, stops, stares an instant, and then trots[62] back to the herd. Another and another will try the same game, with the same result; and if, in spite of these ferocious demonstrations, the hunter still approaches, the whole herd will incontinently take to its heels.

This bullying proclivity, combined with his natural indisposition to get out of the way, has been the cause of the death of thousands of buffalo at the hands of men to whom buffalo-killing was no novelty, who needed no meat, and who would not have gone fifty yards out of their way to kill, but in whom opportunity so roused that spirit of murder which is inherent in every sportsman's breast, that the temptation was too strong to be resisted. . . .[63]

Catlin describes the thing, when with the United States troops along the Canadian River, June to August, 1834: "From morning till night, the camp has been daily almost deserted; the men have dispersed in little squads in all directions, and are dealing death to these poor creatures to a most cruel and wanton extent, merely for the pleasure of destroying, generally without stopping to cut out the meat. During yesterday and this day, several hundreds have undoubtedly been killed, and not so much as the flesh of half-a-dozen used. . . ."[64]

The confessions of such men as Gregg[65] and Parkman[66] show that even high-minded men were not exempt from this. We may conceive of its effect upon a motley host, among whom very many were far from being high-minded, and who, in one form of 'sport' particularly, did not even bring away the hide or the tongue for which alone others took the field. I quote a recent discriminating writer:

Buffalo hunting was the rage. No longer needed for meat or hides, the bison were falling in countless thousands in the name of sport. A contemporary writer draws the disgraceful picture:—

[62]I am unaware whether *trot* is deliberate or a casual phrase. Colonel Henry Inman says: "When you read of buffaloes 'trotting off,' you may rest assured that the author of the statement knows nothing of the habits of the animal. They invariably walk or gallop . . ." (so in *Buffalo Jones' Forty Years*, 260). Garretson, Secretary of the American Bison Society, whose publishers claim for him an exceptionally wide range of buffalo knowledge, gives their 'three gaits' as trot, gallop, and pace (*American Bison*, 57). For other trottings, related by Westerners, see chaps. VI, note 149, and endorsed by Hornaday himself, note 152; XVII, note 97. I have seen domestic cattle trot considerable distances; and Inman himself is utterly unreliable, as we shall see. Soper notes the trot as one of the gaits of the Northern Wood Buffalo ("History of the Northern Bison," 401).

[63]Dodge, *Plains of the Great West*, 126; compare Denny's account of Colonel Macleod and the savage old bull, 1875 (*The Law Marches West*, 67-8).

[64]Catlin, *Letters on the North American Indians*, II, 76.

[65]Gregg, *Early Western Travels*, XIX, 112, 214 (*in extenso*, chap. XIV, note 196).

[66]Parkman, *Oregon Trail*, 91, 419 (*in extenso*, below, Appendix P).

"all over the plains lying in disgusting masses of putrefaction along valley or hill, are strewn immense carcasses of wantonly slain Buffalo.

"Probably the most cruel of all bison-shooting pastime, is that of firing from the cars. During certain periods in the spring and fall, when the large herds are crossing the Kansas Pacific Railroad, the trains run for a hundred miles or more among countless thousands of the shaggy monarchs of the plains. . . . The rate per mile [sic] of passenger trains is slow upon the plains, and hence it often happens that cars and buffalo will be side by side for a mile or two. . . . During these races, the car-windows are opened, and numerous breech-loaders fling hundreds of bullets among the densely-crowded and flying masses. Many of the poor animals fall, and more go off to die in the ravines.[67] The train speeds on, and the scene is repeated every few miles until Buffalo Land is passed. . . ."[68]

So far as the general history of the extermination is concerned, one cannot hope to improve upon the vivid descriptions of our frequently cited authorities, gathered largely from eye-witnesses and sometimes recorded at first-hand. Hornaday's account deserves reproduction in his own words:

The geographical center of the great southern herd during the few years of its separate existence previous to its destruction was very near the present site of Garden City, Kansas. On the east, even as late as 1872, thousands of buffaloes ranged within ten miles of Wichita, which was then the head-quarters of a great number of buffalo-hunters, who plied their occupation vigorously during the winter.[69] On the north the herd ranged within 25 miles of the Union Pacific,[70] until the swarm of hunters coming down from

[67]The usual practice of wounded buffalo; so, Hornaday, "Extermination of the American Bison," 426.

[68]Walsh and Salsbury, The Making of Buffalo Bill, 165 (cf. above, note 11).

[69]The Wichita World (Kansas), February 9, 1889: "In 1871 and 1872 the buffalo ranged within ten miles of Wichita, and could be counted by the thousands. The town, then in its infancy, was the headquarters for a vast number of buffalo-hunters, who plied their occupation vigorously during the winter. The buffalo were killed principally for their hides, and daily wagon trains arrived in town loaded with them. Meat was very cheap in these days; fine, tender buffalo steak selling from 1 to 2 cents per pound. . . . the business was quite profitable for a time, but a sudden drop in the price of hides brought them down as low as 25 and 50 cents each. . . . It was a very common thing in those days for people living in Wichita to start out in the morning and return by evening with a wagon load of buffalo meat . . ." (cited by Hornaday, "Extermination of the American Bison," 500). See above (chap. VII, note 77) a long passage from Allen, stating that the buffalo 'regularly abandoned' the region east of Fort Hays and Ellis (in Ellis County) some 125 miles west of Wichita.

For prices, cf. Dodge, 1872-73: One gallon of watered whisky for five Indian-dressed buffalo robes; 7 to 9 cups of sugar for one robe; a red Mackinac blanket for two or even three robes; 'one measure of Indian cloth, or five or six measures of calico, was the equivalent of one robe' (Plains of the Great West, 322, 362).

[70]Given as '50 miles,' in Hornaday, "Extermination of the American Bison," 492.

the north drove them farther and farther south. On the west, a few small bands ranged as far as Pike's Peak and the South Park, but the main body ranged east of the town of Pueblo, Colorado. In the southwest, buffaloes were abundant as far as the Pecos and the Staked Plains [*Llano Estacado*], while the southern limit of the herd was about on a line with the southern boundary of New Mexico. . . .

During the years from 1866 to 1871, inclusive, the Atchison, Topeka and Santa Fé Railway, and what is now known as the Kansas Pacific, or Kansas division of the Union Pacific Railway, were constructed from the Missouri River westward across Kansas, and through the heart of the southern buffalo range.[71] The southern herd was literally cut to pieces by railways, and every portion of its range rendered easily accessible. There had always been a market for buffalo robes at a fair price,[72] and as soon as the railways crossed the buffalo country the slaughter began. The rush to the range was only surpassed by the rush to the gold mines of California in earlier years. The railroad builders, teamsters, fortune-seekers, "professional" hunters, trappers, guides, and every one out of a job turned out to hunt buffalo for hides and meat. The merchants who had already settled in all the little towns along the three great railways saw an opportunity to make money out of the buffalo product, and forthwith began to organize and supply hunting-parties with arms, ammunition, and provisions, and send them to the range. An immense business of this kind was done by the merchants of Dodge City [Fort Dodge],[73] Wichita, and Leavenworth, and scores of smaller towns did a corresponding amount of business in the same line. During the years 1871 to 1874 but little else was done in that country except buffalo killing.[74] Central depots were established in the best buffalo country, from whence hunting parties operated in all directions. Buildings were erected for the curing of meat, and corrals were built in which to heap up the immense piles of buffalo skins that accumulated. . . .

At first the utmost wastefulness prevailed. Every one wanted to kill buffalo, and no one was willing to do the skinning and curing. Thousands upon thousands of buffalo were killed for their tongues alone, and never skinned. Thousands more were wounded by unskillful marksmen and wandered off to die and become a total loss. . . .

The slaughter which began in 1871 was prosecuted with great vigor and enterprise in 1872, and reached its height in 1873. By that time, the country fairly swarmed with hunters,[75] each party putting forth its utmost efforts to destroy more buffaloes than its rivals. By that time experience had taught the value of thorough organization, and the butchering was done in

[71]The Kansas Pacific was known in 1873 as 'the Buffalo Route' (Seton, *Game Animals*, III, 423).

[72]Dodge says rather strangely: "In 1872 some enemy of the buffalo race discovered that their hides were merchantable . . ." (*Plains of the Great West*, 131).

[73]See on this, *Saturday Evening Post*, March 8, 1930, 146.

[74]"There was hardly a man in Kansas who had not killed his buffalo . . ." (E. Hough, in *Buffalo Jones' Forty Years*, 114).

[75]"Thousands': Hornaday, "Extermination of the American Bison," 501; so also, Reighard, *Edmonton Journal*, January 3, 1931; '8000 or 10,000': *Saturday Evening Post*, March 8, 1930, 146.

a more business-like way. By a coincidence that proved fatal to the bison,
it was just at the beginning of the slaughter that breech-loading, long-range
rifles attained what was practically perfection. . . . Before the leaden hail
of thousands of these deadly breech-loaders the buffaloes went down at the
rate of several thousands daily during the hunting season.[76]

There can be no doubt of the excessive wastefulness of the earlier
years. Colonel Dodge (an eye-witness) declares: "Though hundreds
of thousands of skins were sent to market, they scarcely indicated the
extent of the slaughter. Through want of skill in shooting and want of
knowledge in preserving the hides of those slain, on the part of these
green hunters, one hide sent to market represented three, four, or even
five dead buffalo. . . ."[77] Colonel Dodge says again:

The skinners and curers knew so little of the proper mode of curing
hides that at least half were lost of those actually taken. In the summer and
fall of 1872 one hide sent to market represented at least *three* dead buffalo.
This condition of affairs rapidly improved but such was the furor for
slaughter, and the ignorance of all concerned, that every hide sent to market
in 1871 represented no less than five dead buffalo.[78]

By 1873 the condition of affairs had somewhat improved, through better
organization of the hunting-parties and knowledge gained by experience in
curing. For all that, however, buffaloes were still so exceedingly plentiful,
and shooting was so much easier than skinning, the latter was looked upon
as a necessary evil and still slighted to such an extent that every hide
actually sold and delivered represented two dead buffaloes. . . .[79]

In 1874 the slaughterers began to take alarm at the increasing scarcity
of buffalo, and the skinners, having a much smaller number of dead animals
to take care of than ever before, were able to devote more time to each
subject and do their work properly. . . . During 1874, and from that time
on, 100 skins delivered represented not more than 125 dead buffaloes . . .
but no parties have ever got their proportion lower than this. . . .[80]

I again quote Hornaday:

Of course the slaughter was greatest along the lines of the three great
railways—the Kansas Pacific, the Atchison, Topeka and Santa Fé, and the
Union Pacific, about in the order named. It reached its height in the season
of 1873. During that year the Atchison, Topeka and Santa Fé Railroad
carried out of the buffalo country 251,443 robes, 1,617,000 pounds of meat,
and 2,743,100 pounds of bones. The end of the southern herd was then
near at hand. Could the southern buffalo range have been roofed over at

[76]Hornaday, "Extermination of the American Bison," 492-4; also Reighard,
Edmonton Journal, January 3, 1931.
   [77]Dodge, *Plains of the Great West*, 132; also his *Our Wild Indians*, 295.
   [78]Dodge, *Plains of the Great West*, 141.
   [79]*Ibid.*, 142.   [80]*Ibid.*, 138, 142.

that time it would have made one vast charnel-house. Putrifying carcasses, many of them with the hide still on, lay thickly scattered over thousands of square miles of the level prairie, poisoning the air and water and offending the sight. The remaining herds had become mere scattered bands, harried and driven hither and thither by the hunters, who now swarmed almost as thickly as the buffaloes. . . .[81]

White hunters were not allowed to hunt in the Indian Territory,[82] and the southern boundary of the State of Kansas was picketed by them, and a herd no sooner crossed the line going north[83] than it was destroyed. Every water-hole was guarded by a camp of hunters, and whenever a thirsty herd approached, it was promptly met by rifle-bullets.[84]

The promulgation of a law and its enforcement are not necessarily the same thing, particularly when the custodians of the law are more in sympathy with its violators than with those whom it was intended to protect. The edict in question was evidently accorded scant respect. G. B. Grinnell writes concerning this very situation, as follows:

The Comanches were much irritated by the pushing southward of the hide-hunters from the neighbourhood of Fort Dodge, for it was well understood in 1873 and 1874 that no hunting should be done south of the Arkansas River. That was regarded as the Indian country, and the terms of the Medicine Lodge treaty [that is, of 1867] provided that white hunters should not cross that stream, which was patrolled at intervals by troops. So long as buffalo were plenty north of the Arkansas, the hunters respected this feeling, but after buffalo got scarce the dead-line, in their estimation, was moved down to the Cimarron, where buffalo were found abundant, and when the great beasts were killed off there, they followed them still farther south.

The Indians strongly objected to the farther movement south of the white hunters, realizing, of course, that the extermination of the buffalo meant starvation for themselves. . . .[85]

[81]Hornaday, "Extermination of the American Bison," 496. It was said that on the Santa Fé route one could have journeyed 100 miles along the right-of-way without stepping off the carcasses of slaughtered buffalo (Garretson, *American Bison,* 114).

[82]Now the State of Oklahoma.

[83]Note the 'going north.' The hunting season was between October-November, and February (Hornaday, "Extermination of the American Bison," 511, 512); Hornaday never tires of insisting that they invariably *went south* in winter. Inman speaks of a train on the Kansas Pacific Railroad being held up for eight hours by an immense herd stretching as far as eye could see 'as they rushed onward to the south' in the *spring* of 1869! (*The Old Santa Fé Trail,* 203-4.) Garretson, immediately after noting September to April as the period of Billy Tilghman's prodigious exploits, unaccountably specifies May to December as the still-hunting season (*American Bison,* 115).

[84]Hornaday, "Extermination of the American Bison," 496.

[85]Grinnell, *Fighting Cheyennes,* 310.

I quote Hornaday's graphic recital once again:

During this entire period the slaughter of buffaloes was universal. The man who desired buffalo meat for food almost invariably killed five times as many animals as he could utilize, and after cutting from each victim its very choicest parts—the *tongue alone*, possibly, or perhaps the hump and hind quarters, one or the other, or both—fully four-fifths of the really edible portion of the carcass would be left to the wolves. It was no uncommon thing for a man to bring in two barrels of salted buffalo tongues, without another pound of meat or a solitary robe. The tongues were purchased at 25 cents each, and sold in the markets farther east at 50 cents. . . .

Judging from all accounts, it is making a safe estimate to say that probably no fewer than fifty thousand buffaloes have been killed for their tongues alone, and the most of these are undoubtedly chargeable against white men, who ought to have known better.[86]

The buffalo slaughter attracted big-game hunters from the Eastern States and also from European countries. There were 'dude parties' on the plains, which included New York millionaires and titled Englishmen,[87] and at least one Russian Grand Duke.[88] For the good name of the true sportsman all the world over, of whatever race—as distinguished from the mere slayer—and of the British sportsman in particular, it is highly gratifying to an English-born Canadian to be able to add the following:

A great deal has been said about the slaughter of buffaloes by foreign sportsmen, particularly Englishmen; but I must say that from all that can be ascertained on this point, this element of destruction has been greatly exaggerated and overestimated. It is true that every English sportsman who visited this country in the days of the buffalo always resolved to have, and did have, "a buffalo hunt," and usually under the auspices of United States Army officers. Undoubtedly these parties did kill hundreds of buffaloes, but it is very doubtful whether the aggregate slain by foreign sportsmen would run up higher than ten thousand. Indeed, for myself, I am well convinced that there are many old ex-still-hunters yet living, each of whom is accountable for a greater number of victims than all buffaloes killed by foreign sportsmen would make added together. The professional

[86]Hornaday, "Extermination of the American Bison," 496. In 1872 two carloads of tongues were shipped from Dodge City; and 'a number of fortunes were made' in killing buffalo for their tongues only, at 25 cents each (so, Garretson, *American Bison*, 114). The buffalo-hunters of Dodge were estimated at *circa* 2600; that season 'over 75,000 buffalo' were killed in the Dodge area, *i.e.* an amount perhaps equal to $20,000—among 2600 hunters. Fortunes!

[87]Walsh and Salsbury, *The Making of Buffalo Bill*, 165-9, 177.

[88]*Ibid.*, 168-9. The guest of W. F. Cody, North Platte, Nebraska (1872) or Fort Hays, Kansas, according to Inman (*The Old Santa Fé Trail*, 209); a somewhat serious discrepancy, considering that each of these men endorses the other's accuracy. For some particulars of this event in relation to Indian archery, see below, Appendix T.

butchers were very much given to crying out against "them English lords," and holding up their hands in holy horror at buffaloes killed by them for their heads, instead of for hides to sell at a dollar apiece; but it is due the American public to say that all this outcry was received at its true value and deceived very few. By those in possession of the facts, it was recognized as a "blind," to divert public attention from the true culprits.[89]

Hornaday adds (what is beyond doubt[90]) that notwithstanding this, many calling themselves sportsmen indulged in excessive slaughter, but he continues:

As a general thing, however, the professional sportsmen who went out to have a buffalo hunt for the excitement of the chase and the trophies it yielded, nearly always found the bison so easy a victim and one whose capture brought so little glory to the hunter, that the chase was voted very disappointing, and soon abandoned in favour of nobler game.[91] In those days there was no more to boast of in killing a buffalo than in the assassination of a Texas steer.[92]

It was, then, the hide-hunters, white and red, but especially white, who wiped out the great southern herd in four short years. The prices received for hides varied considerably, according to circumstances, but for the green or undressed article it usually ranged from 50 cents for the skins of calves to $1.25 for those of adult animals in good condition. Such prices seem ridiculously small, but when it is remembered that, when buffaloes were plentiful it was no uncommon thing for a hunter to kill from forty to sixty head in a day, it will readily be seen that the *chances* of making very handsome profits were sufficient to tempt hunters to make extraordinary

[89]Hornaday, "Extermination of the American Bison," 497. Garretson has much to say about this (*American Bison*, 111, 130), without noticing Hornaday's qualifying remarks. Cf. Sir Richard Burton, *City of the Saints*, 51, 73.

[90]Sir George Gore (at Fort Berthold, Missouri River): "He became a general favourite, but such a slaughter did he and his men make among the buffalo herds during the winter of 1855-56 that the attention of the United States Government was drawn thereto, and steps were taken to prevent any further annihilation by the Gore party . . ." (Hebard and Brininstool, *Bozeman Trail*, II, 228). Garretson says only 2500 buffalo; and considers the Government (which never interfered elsewhere in buffalo slaughter) was more concerned about protecting them from the Indians than about conserving the buffalo (*American Bison*, 101). In 1855, however, the policy of starving the Indians into submission by destroying their food had not been adopted; the U.S. troops were still thought to be their equals in the field, and the buffalo would be needed to feed the subjugated tribes.

On sportsmen, cf. Dodge, 1872: "In the fall of that year three English gentlemen went out with me for a short hunt, and in their excitement bagged more buffalo than would have supplied a brigade" (*Plains of the Great West*, 132; *Our Wild Indians*, 294. Quoted also by Hornaday, "Extermination of the American Bison," 498).

[91]Compare below, chap. XVII, notes 88-9.

[92]Rather an unhappy parallel, according to Dodge: "The domestic cattle of Texas, mis-called tame, are fifty times more dangerous to footmen than the fiercest buffalo . . ." (*Plains of the Great West*, 119).

exertions.[93] Moreover, even when the buffaloes were nearly gone, the country was overrun with men who had nothing else to look to as a means of livelihood, and so, no matter whether the profits were great or small, so long as enough buffaloes remained to make it possible to get a living by their pursuit, they were hunted down with the most determined persistency and pertinacity. [94]

Various attempts have been made to compute the numbers of the southern slaughter. The subject is necessarily a very complex and difficult one, and the most careful estimates cannot escape a large element of conjecture. I have met with no inquiry into this problem more judicious and apparently reliable than that of Colonel Richard Irving Dodge. It combines personal observation during the period of the slaughter itself, together with a previous buffalo experience of twenty-five years. Dodge carried out at the time a considerable amount of first-hand investigation among actual participants; he also made use of as large and complete a mass of statistics from those most competent to furnish them, as he was able to secure.

In forming this conclusion I have the advance endorsement of Hornaday, who has made this branch of the subject peculiarly his own; and who himself enjoyed the material advantage of personal intercourse with many buffalo-hunters of that era.[95] For this reason, I include remarks by Hornaday on Dodge's figures, as being more on an equal plane of independent authority than that of mere criticism of another's findings.

Dodge states that on approaching the officials of the Kansas Pacific and Union Pacific Railways respectively, in his search for statistical data concerning the quantities of buffalo products handled by their roads, they either could not or would not—more probably the latter in his opinion, which upon his facts seems to be well founded—furnish any statistics of this traffic. The officers of the Atchison, Topeka, and Santa Fé Railway, however, immediately placed at Dodge's disposal their traffic returns under this head for the years 1872, 1873, and 1874; and it is upon their figures that his calculations are based, treating the traffic upon the two recalcitrant roads as being approximately equal in volume.[96] Hornaday, after careful investigation, is prepared to accept this process of reasoning as essentially satisfactory:

[93]Robert Armstrong, Gleichen, Alberta, 1931, states that he made 'some $4000' in two years' buffalo-killing at this time; killing once '126 in five hours' ("Reminiscences" (aged 82) Edmonton Journal, February 14, 1931). Another hide-hunter at this time said he shot down 120 animals in forty minutes (M. I. McCreight, Buffalo Bone Days, 10). I am very greatly indebted to Mr. McCreight, a former bone-buyer, now a banker, for a copy of his most interesting (and partly reminiscent) booklet.   [94]Hornaday, "Extermination of the American Bison," 498.   [95]Ibid., 498-502.   [96]Dodge, Plains of the Great West, 139-40.

Inasmuch as the Kansas Pacific road cuts through a portion of the buffalo country which was in every respect as thickly inhabited by those animals as the region traversed by the Atchison, Topeka and Santa Fé, it seemed absolutely certain that the former road hauled out as many hides as the latter, if not more, and its quota is so set down.[97] The Union Pacific line handled a much smaller number of buffalo hides than either of its southern rivals, but Colonel Dodge believes that this, "with the smaller roads which touch the buffalo region, taken together, carried about as much as either of the two principal buffalo roads."

Colonel Dodge considers it reasonably certain that the statistics furnished by the Atchison, Topeka and Santa Fé road represent only one-third of the entire buffalo product,[98] and there certainly appears to be good ground for this belief. It is therefore in order to base further calculations upon these figures.[99]

Following is Dodge's table, based upon the actual figures furnished, and their application to the other non-consenting roads, on the basis indicated above:

Year	Atchison, Topeka, and Santa Fé	Union Pacific, Kansas Pacific, and all other railroads	Total
	Hides-Number	Hides-Number	Hides-Number
1872	165,721	331,442	497,163
1873	251,443	502,886	754,329
1874	42,289	84,578	126,867
Total	459,453	918,906	1,378,359
	Meat-Pounds	Meat-Pounds	Meat-Pounds
1872	none	none	none
1873	1,617,600	3,235,200	4,852,800
1874	632,800	1,265,600	1,898,400
Total	2,250,400	4,500,800	6,751,200
	Bones-Pounds	Bones-Pounds	Bones-Pounds
1872	1,135,300	2,270,600	3,405,900
1873	2,743,100	5,486,200	8,229,300
1874	6,914,950	13,829,900	20,744,850
Total	10,793,350	21,586,700	32,380,050[100]

[97]It was called 'the Buffalo Route' in 1873: Seton, *Game Animals*, III, 423.

[98]*I.e.* carried by railways only.

[99]Hornaday, "Extermination of the American Bison," 499-500.

[100]Dodge, *Plains of the Great West*, 140; also cf. Allen, *American Bisons*, 190. These totals are also accepted by McCreight, *Buffalo Bone Days*, 10.

This table, with all its stupendous aggregates, by no means exhausts the subject. These are only certain products, finding their way to market in a form that can be at least partly checked, and by one particular channel only. It is beyond doubt (as we have seen) that a given number of hides shipped signifies a much greater number of buffalo slain, be the actual ratio what it may. We have seen that according to evidence gathered at the time, by Dodge, that competent judge believed that every single hide marketed in 1872 represented three dead buffalo; in 1873, two; and in 1874, 100 skins delivered represented 125 dead animals. On this basis, he compiled the following table:

Year	Hides shipped by Atchison, Topeka & Santa Fé Railway	Hides shipped by other roads in same period (estimated)	Total number of buffaloes utilized	Total number killed and wasted	Total number of buffaloes slaughtered by whites
1872	165,721	331,442	497,163	994,326	1,491,489
1873	251,443	502,886	754,329	754,329	1,508,658
1874	42,289	84,578	126,867	31,716	158,563
Total	459,453	918,906	1,378,359	1,780,371	3,158,710[101]

Even with respect to white hunters alone, our inquiry is not terminated. The foregoing table merely applies the ratios adopted by Dodge for these three years (the worst of which was an improvement of 40 per cent over the appalling 5 to 1 proportion for 1871[102]) to those hides which were actually marketed. We have not yet included the white settlers living on or near the southern buffalo range. So long as the supply lasted, these folk slew for food as they chose, often starting out of a morning, and bringing home a wagon-load by night.[103] It is needless to take such sayings literally, but the currency of the aphorism *circa* 1877, that "there was hardly a man in Kansas that had not killed his buffalo"[104] proves conclusively the wide prevalence of the pursuit, in one form or another. Hornaday makes the following suggestion:

[101]Dodge, *Plains of the Great West*, 142. See below, Appendix Q.
[102]Dodge, *Plains of the Great West*, 132, 141.
[103]Hornaday, "Extermination of the American Bison," 492, 500.
[104]Hough, in *Buffalo Jones' Forty Years*, 114.

Unquestionably a great many thousand buffaloes were killed annually by the settlers of Kansas, Nebraska, Texas, New Mexico, and Colorado. . . . The number so slain can only be guessed at, for there is absolutely no data on which to found an estimate. Judging merely from the number of people within reach of the range, it may safely be estimated that the total number of buffaloes slaughtered annually to satisfy the wants of this heterogeneous element could not have been less than fifty thousand, and probably was a much higher number. This, for the three years, would make one hundred and fifty thousand . . .[105]

The skins from such promiscuous hunting are not included in the foregoing tables. One of this class of hunters informed Hornaday personally that owing to their ignorance of curing skins, 'hardly any' were saved.[106]

Finally there are the Indians of the southern buffalo range to be considered. Hornaday observes:

During all this time the Indians of all tribes within striking distance of the herds killed an immense number of buffaloes every year. In the summer they killed for the hairless hides[107] to use for lodges and for leather, and in the autumn they slaughtered for robes and meat, but particularly robes, which was all they could offer to the white trader in exchange for his goods. They were too lazy and shiftless to cure much buffalo meat, and besides, it was not necessary, for the Government fed them. . . .[108]

Concerning the probable number of the southern buffalo killed by the southern Indians (which may include wanderers who hunted both—or any—ranges), Dodge attempts an estimate, as follows:

[105]Hornaday, "Extermination of the American Bison," 501. He includes in this 'the mountain Indians living west of the great range.' This makes his estimate perfectly safe.

[106]*Ibid.*, 486, 500.

[107]In early summer, the buffalo were almost naked, and their wallowing, rolling, scratching, rubbing, etc., was to seek relief from insect pests. See above, chap. V, note 36 *seq.*; and for 'summer skins,' note 29 of this chapter. Early telegraph lines were often rubbed down: Fort Benton, 1873 (in John McDougall, *Western Trails*, 76, 263; cf. Garretson, *American Bison*, 36). Some interesting particulars on this: "The West's First Telegraph," from Selkirk, Manitoba, to somewhere near Leduc, south of Edmonton, 1876 (W. Everard Edmonds, *Edmonton Journal*, August 30, 1930). A tale is told, which is really too good to be omitted in relation to buffalo rubbing habits. The first telegraph lines suffered much from poles being rubbed down. A high 'Eastern' official, who had never seen a buffalo, suggested driving spikes into the poles—'That'll keep 'em off!' This was done over a section, and a report requested concerning the results. 'Fine! They were willing to wait their turn before; now they fight like hell over who's to get to the poles first!'

[108]Hornaday, "Extermination of the American Bison," 499. This last assertion concerning laziness, which is contradicted by much historical evidence, will be examined later. See chap. XXI. Furthermore, I know of no evidence that 'the Government fed them,' *until after the buffalo were gone.*

It is much more difficult to estimate the number of dead buffalo represented by the Indian-tanned skins or robes sent to market. This number varies with the different tribes, and their greater or less contact with the whites.

Thus the Cheyennes, Arapahoes, and Kiowas of the southern plains, having less contact with whites, use skins for their lodges, clothing, bedding, par-flèches, saddles, lariats, for almost everything. The number of robes sent to market represent only what we may call the foreign exchange of these tribes, and is really not more than one-tenth of the skins taken. To be well within bounds I will assume that one robe sent to market by these Indians represents six dead buffaloes.

Those bands of Sioux who live at the agencies, and whose peltries are taken to market by the Union Pacific Railroad, live in lodges of cotton cloth furnished by the Indian Bureau. They use much civilized clothing, bedding, boxes, ropes, &c. For these luxuries they must pay in robes, and as the buffalo range is far from wide, and their yearly 'crop' small, more than half of it goes to market.

The wilder Indians of the Upper Missouri yet use many skins, though their contact with whites has given them a taste for civilized luxuries, for which robes must be paid. I have no personal knowledge of the proportion, but I am informed by persons who profess to know, that about one robe is sent to market for every five skins. . . .[109]

The tables drawn up respectively by our two investigators[110] in each instance contain items not included in the other. I have therefore compiled the following table, and have indicated such items as are not given by both men.

Sources	Sent to market	Number of dead buffaloes represented
Kiowas, Comanches, Cheyennes, Arapahoes, and other Indians whose robes were marketed over the Santa Fé system	19,000	114,000
Sioux at agencies, Union Pacific Railway	10,000	16,000
Indian tribes of Upper Missouri	55,000	275,000[111]
Total	84,000	405,000

[109]Dodge, *Plains of the Great West,* 142-4. Drannan dates the first shipment of robes from the Kiowa and Comanche only in 1851 (*Thirty-One Years on the Plains,* 120).

[110]Hornaday, "Extermination of the American Bison," 500; Dodge, *Plains of the Great West,* 143.

[111]Dodge only.

405,000 per year ·for 1872-1873-1874 =   1,215,000
Killed by hide-hunters in the three years: 3,158,710[112]
                                             ───────
                                             4,373,710[113]
Killed by white settlers, etc., in the three years: 150,000[114]
                                             ───────
                                      Total   4,523,710

Dodge remarks in conclusion:

Nor is this all. No account has been taken of the immense number of buffalo killed by hunters, who came into the range from the wide frontier and took their skins out by wagons; of the immense numbers killed every year by hunters from New Mexico, Colorado, Texas, and the Indian territory; of the number killed by the Utes, Bannocks, and other mountain tribes, who every year make their fall hunt on the plains. Nothing has been said of the numbers sent from the Indian territory by other roads than the Atchison, Topeka, and Santa Fé, to St. Louis, Memphis, and elsewhere; of the immense numbers of robes which go to California, Montana, Idaho, and the Great West, nor of the still greater numbers taken each year from the territories of the United States by the Hudson's Bay Company.

All these will add another million to the already incredible mortuary list of the nearly extinct buffalo. . . .[115]

Considered as figures for the three fatal years only, I think it will be very generally acknowledged that the careful and cautious manner in which both investigators have refrained from utilizing anything like their own maxima as the basis for their calculations goes far to commend their acceptability to later critics. Allen's belief that in the season of 1872-73 'not less than 200,000 were killed in Kansas for hides alone,'[116] is easily within the mark, as the actual statistics of hides *saved* clearly prove; and his suggestion of a slaughter of 2,500,000 annually for the years 1870-75[117] would, perhaps, prove to be not very

[112]3,158,710; Hornaday's grand total ("Extermination of the American Bison," 500).

[113]4,373,710; Dodge's grand total (*Plains of the Great West,* 143).

[114]Hornaday only; he allows 130,000 x 3 (years) = 390,000 by Indians ("Extermination of the American Bison," 501).

[115]Dodge, *Plains of the Great West,* 143-4. The reader will observe that some of these channels of consumption are probably covered already by certain of the items in the final table above; also that while supposedly dealing with the southern slaughter, Colonel Dodge has included phases which can scarcely be classed under that head—as the reference to the Hudson's Bay Company, which at this time was rather in the reverse position to that mentioned by Dodge (see below, chap. XVII). I have quoted his passage intact, however, as it brings before our notice certain factors which may have no logical place elsewhere; and which certainly must have played a part in the *general* buffalo extermination.

[116]Allen, *American Bisons,* 178.

[117]*Ibid.,* 191.

far astray, if our knowledge were more complete. The acceptance of the estimates quoted above, representing one business firm in one town only, would almost necessitate the adoption of a higher aggregate still.[118]

While it appears that the close of the hunting season of 1875-76 saw the last of the buffalo-hunting upon any large scale, incidental items of evidence seem to indicate that a larger number of buffalo were still in existence in the southwestern regions than some students have supposed. I shall cite Hornaday's concluding words on this final phase. They probably give a fairly accurate idea, which later details tend to emphasize rather than diminish. He writes:

By the close of the hunting season of 1875 the great southern herd had ceased to exist. As a body, it had been utterly annihilated. The main body of the survivors, numbering about ten thousand head, fled southwest, and dispersed through that great tract of wild, desolate, and inhospitable country stretching southward from the Cimarron country across the "Public Land Strip," the Pan-handle of Texas, and the Llano Estacado, or Staked Plain, to the Pecos River. A few small bands of stragglers maintained a precarious existence for a few years longer on the headwaters of the Republican River and in southwestern Nebraska near Ogalalla, where calves were caught alive as late as 1885. Wild buffaloes were seen in southwestern Kansas for the last time in 1886,[119] and the two or three score of individuals still living[120] in the Canadian River country of the Texas Pan-handle are the last wild survivors of the Great Southern herd.

The main body of the fugitives which survived the great slaughter of 1871-'74 continued to attract hunters who were very "hard up,"[121] who pursued them, often at the risk of their own lives, even into the terrible Llano Estacado. . . .

[118]See Appendix Q.

[119]Hough, 1887: "It will be the cool, calculating, picayunish, fiendish, skinhunter who will make the last 'stalk' . . ." (*Buffalo Jones' Forty Years*, 165, 166). As usual, there are several 'last buffaloes': 1879, at 'Point of Rocks,' apparently in Morton County in the extreme southwest corner of Kansas (Garretson, *American Bison*, 125). The honour is claimed by or for one Joe Briggs, 1883, in Ford County, in which is Dodge City (*Saturday Evening Post*, March 8, 1830); also 1886, as above.

[120]*I.e.* in 1888-89, Bancroft cites a resident as stating that there were 'great numbers' in the Panhandle in 1876 (*North Mexican States and Texas*, II, 559). For 1879, see Webb, *The Texas Rangers*, 413; also *Mississippi Valley Historical Review*, XXIII, 1936, 289; for 1886, 1889, some particulars in Seton, *Game Animals*, III, 664-7; Garretson, *American Bison*, 126, 217. Below, note 130.

[121]Compare, however, Hornaday's own statement about Harry Andrews, making 'big money' among the mere remnants of the Southern herd in 1874-76; killing on one occasion 63 at one stand 'in about an hour.' This from Andrews personally in 1886 ("Extermination of the American Bison," 469, 502). A buffalo-hunter's standard of 'big money' was probably not a low one; and it cannot be supposed that Andrews was the only one.

In 1880 buffalo hunting as a business ceased forever in the Southwest, and so far as can be ascertained, but one successful hunt for robes has been made in that region since that time. That occurred in the fall and winter of 1887, about 100 miles north of Tascosa, Texas, when two parties . . . attacked the only band of buffaloes left alive in the Southwest, and which at that time numbered about two hundred head. The two parties killed fifty-two buffaloes . . . [122]

He supplements the information elsewhere:

In Texas a miserable remnant of the great southern herd still remains in the "Pan-handle country," between the two forks of the Canadian River. In 1886 about two hundred head survived, which number by the summer of 1887 had been reduced to one hundred, or less. In the hunting season of 1887-'88 a ranchman named Lee Howard[123] fitted out and led a strong party into the haunts of the survivors, and killed fifty-two of them. In May, 1888, Mr. C. J. Jones again visited this region for the purpose of capturing buffaloes alive.[124] His party found, from first to last, thirty-seven buffaloes, of which they captured eighteen head, eleven adult cows and seven calves; the greatest feat ever accomplished in buffalo-hunting. It is highly probable that Mr. Jones and his men saw about all the buffaloes now living in the Pan-handle country, and it therefore seems quite certain that not over twenty-five individuals remain.[125] These are so few, so remote, and so difficult to reach, it is to be hoped no one will consider them worth going after, and that they will be left to take care of themselves. It is greatly to be regretted that the State of Texas does not feel disposed to make a special effort for their protection and preservation. . . .[126]

Such was the end of the great southern herd. In 1871 it contained certainly no fewer than three million buffaloes; and by the beginning of 1875[127] its existence as a herd had utterly ceased, and nothing but scattered, fugitive bands remained.[128]

[122]*Ibid.*, 501, 502. Garretson, *American Bison*, 126.

[123]Some particulars on this individual, first Buffalo Jones's competitor, and afterward (by a clever ruse) his colleague or assistant in the calf-catching enterprise (*Buffalo Jones' Forty Years*, 138, 183, 203).

[124]Five consecutive seasons, 1884-88; so, Hornaday, "Extermination of the American Bison," 456, 459; cited also in *Buffalo Jones' Forty Years*, 223. According to Inman, three only before Hornaday wrote, and one after: April, 1886 (*ibid.*, 50-82); May, 1887 (described by Hough, who accompanied it; *ibid.*, 111-66); 'Spring,' 1888 (*ibid.*, 181-93); May, 1889 (*ibid.*, 201-24). The first of such enterprises recorded (to my knowledge) was hereabouts. Vicenté Zaldívar, along the Pecos River, September to November, 1598: ". . . a grand buffalo hunt with brilliant but not very successful attempts to catch some of the *cibolos* alive . . ." (Bancroft, *History of Arizona*, 138). [125]Written in 1888-89.

[126]"Extermination of the American Bison," 523. See Buffalo Jones's efforts then and later (*Buffalo Jones' Forty Years*, 262-5).

[127]Hornaday (p. 501) has "close of the season of 1875." Does he mean by this term, 1875-76? See above, note 119.

[128]Hornaday, "Extermination of the American Bison," 502. Compare Dodge, "During 1872-73-74 at least 5,000,000 buffalo were slaughtered for their hides . . ," (*Our Wild Indians*, 295)

The inferential evidence derivable from the figures given by Andrews concerning his own experience, seems to find confirmation from other incidental testimony; and even more strongly from evidence mentioned by Hornaday himself. Two years later than Andrews' time, hide-hunters were still out on the range; for a competent historian of the Cheyenne mentions the fact of Little Wolf's northern Cheyennes, on their famous march in 1878 from their uncongenial southern reserve back to their northern home, taking buffalo from hide-hunters at the Arkansas River.[129] North of that region, they are also described as being 'plentiful,' in the late summer or fall of the same year (1878·).[130]

Hornaday states that in the same year, also, Professor Thompson saw a pile of baled buffalo-skins in a corral at Dodge City, the solid cubic contents of which he calculated to equal 120 cords.[131] I have not found the faintest vestige of an allusion to any practice of keeping these over in stock from one season to another; it is almost certain that a summer in that climate would have ruined them. These therefore may be considered as the harvest of the hunting season of 1877-78. Such statistics or estimates of the buffalo-bone gathering industry as I have been able to collect furnish no information whatever concerning the dates of any possible survival of comparatively large numbers; and as they have been made the basis of attempts to compute the total aggregate of the buffalo, I reserve them for a later chapter, dealing with that subject.

NOTE

I must candidly confess to a very considerable hesitancy in seeming to endorse certain quasi-historical material by inserting it in my text on the same apparent standing with unquestionably reputable sources. This applies in varying degrees to both the two reminiscent articles occasionally cited in this chapter. They are both—necessarily—derived from or written by men at an age when memory is frequently treacherous. That of George W. Reighard contains beyond question (in my judgment) a certain amount of actual first-hand

[129]Grinnell, *Fighting Cheyennes*, 393.

[130]*Ibid.* So also Garretson, who states that it was estimated that in 1877 there were over 1500 hunters on the Texas range, which extended 400 miles south from the northern State line; and that in the final season of 1877-78 over 100,000 hides were obtained (*American Bison*, 125-6). Frank Dobie cites reminiscence which gives 5000 hunters on the Texas Plains in 1876; in which year Colonel Charles Goodnight 'drove 10,000 buffalo' out of Palo Duro Canyon; and mentions Fort Griffin, Clear Fork of the Brazos River, as the headquarters of the buffalo-hunters, 1875-79 (*The Flavor of Texas*, 225-34).

[131]Hornaday, "Extermination of the American Bison," 493. See Appendix R.

reminiscence by an actor in some of the scenes of the drama; but it is idle to overlook the fact that it also contains—in a very skilfully condensed form, the work either of Reighard himself, or more probably of some experienced journalistic hand—a quite masterly resumé of that part of Hornaday's essay so often cited dealing with the extermination proper.

This resumé is written in precisely the same style of first-hand intimacy as the Reighard reminiscences pure and simple; it contains matter, both of fact and of reflection, which is Hornaday's own, instantly recognizable by any student who has read his paper; and it includes items of information and philosophical parallels such as I have found in no other generalizing writer on the buffalo, except perhaps in one or two instances where Hornaday is frankly acknowledged as the source. This practically limits the origin of the material to two alternatives: either Hornaday copied from Reighard; or Reighard— or some journalistic collaborator, *vulgarisateur,* or what you will— copied from Hornaday. Which is the more probable may be left to the reader's judgment. It may furthermore be noticed that this material extends to regions which Reighard makes no mention of ever having seen, and of which Hornaday alone is the acknowledged authoritative historian (that is, *post* 1876). Reighard—or the writer—also has Hornaday "out here on the plains in an early day" to study the buffalo. This would, I think, naturally signify 'in the southern [Fort Dodge] territory.' Hornaday himself makes no allusion to any personal contact with the animals in freedom other than his two Smithsonian expeditions of 1886 to the northern buffalo range, at a very late day.

The article in the *Saturday Evening Post* is less complex in character. Its statements, when compared with actual official figures, render it fairly clear in my opinion that it is a combination of truthful, perhaps failing memory, and of that incorrigible propensity among plainsmen to 'pull the leg' of the stranger, above all of the *questioning* stranger, to which Colonel Dodge alludes (*Plains of the Great West,* 145-6). As comparative, hypothetical illustration of standards, tendencies, habits of thought, it is not without value; as literal, historical fact (concerning buffalo), it cannot be accepted without qualifications, or support.

I have since encountered other reminiscent material of the same class, relating to both the United States and Canada. I have had occasion to refer to Daniel Ott (see note 11 of the foregoing chapter); also in Canada to Norbert Welsh (chap. XIV, note 168). Later we shall cite the case of H. M. Starkey (also in Canada, below, chap. XVII, notes 84-6). In the second instance particularly, the picture presented of an Indian trader's life in the old days is of immense interest and of distinct value as clothing the dry bones of historical evidence with life. But in relation to well-known public characters or events, where we possess abundant data for purposes of verification, careful editorial criticism is frequently needful.

Another glaring example presents itself. An old army scout, twenty years Buffalo Bill's senior on the Plains, speaks (as with bated breath at such a distinction) of meeting him in 1861; when Cody was a country lad of fifteen years, in his native Kentucky! (Drannan, *Thirty-One Years on the Plains*, 399-404).

Such lapses in specific individual relationships are entirely natural in aged memories very seldom reinforced by diaries;[132] but they rob precise details of identification, chronology, or numbers, of all authority. The last, above all, are a constant source of suspicion in the free-and-easy, uncritical plains atmosphere.

[132]While engaged on the present production, I noted a case of an old lady, then aged 98, who was 'a girl friend of the great John Wesley, and often accompanied him on his journeys . . .' (*Edmonton Journal*, March 9, 1934). She was born in 1836; John Wesley died in 1791! In February, 1948, I myself met an old gentleman, a publisher of international repute and a cultured man, then 80 (*i.e.* born 1867-68); who told me he had *borne a personal share* in the acceptance of R. D. Blackmore's *Lorna Doone* for publication, after repeated rejections. *Lorna Doone* was published 1869-70.

CHAPTER XVI

THE NUMBERS OF THE BUFFALO: THE DESTRUCTION OF
THE NORTHERN HERD IN THE UNITED STATES

THE story of the destruction of the Northern herd could
scarcely be told, and certainly could not be told with any
degree of fullness, without recourse to Hornaday's collection
of invaluable material. No other writer has approached him in this
particular phase of the extermination. Our two important authorities
for the south, Allen and Dodge, both wrote before the final northern
slaughter had commenced, and practically everyone since Hornaday
has confessedly copied him almost exclusively. So far as historical narrative is concerned, I am very largely under the same necessity. Hornaday summarizes the extent and habitat of the northern herd as follows:

At the time of the great division made by the Union Pacific Railway
the northern body of buffalo extended from the valley of the Platte River
northward to the southern shore of Great Slave Lake, eastward almost to
Minnesota, and westward to an elevation of 8000 feet in the Rocky
Mountains. The herds were most numerous along the central portion of
this region . . . and from the Platte valley to Great Slave Lake the range
was continuous. The buffalo population of the southern half of this great
range was, according to all accounts, nearly three times as great as that
of the northern half.[1] At that time, or let us say, 1870, there were about
four million buffaloes south of the Platte River, and probably about one
million and a half north of it. . . .[2]

Hornaday continues: "I am aware that the estimate of the number
of buffaloes in the great northern herd is usually much higher than this,
but I can see no good ground for making it so. To my mind the evidence is conclusive that, although the northern herd ranged over such
an immense area, it was numerically less than half the size of the overwhelming multitude which actually crowded the southern range . . ."[3]

[1]"twice as many": Hornaday, "Extermination of the American Bison," 493.

[2]*Ibid.*, 503. See remarks above (chap. XIII, notes 150, 155) on the entire
contradiction between this and other estimates for 1871.

Professor MacInnes, usually very accurate, has curiously erred here. He
writes: "About 1870 the vast herd of bison which still remained was divided
into two by the American hunters. The southern division roamed over the territory south of the Missouri, while the northern was to be found in the country
between that river and the Saskatchewan . . ." (*In the Shadow of the Rockies*,
143).

[3]Hornaday, "Extermination of the American Bison," 503, 504.

It is in this connection that he cites, as 'proof,' the eating down of the prairie pasturage to starvation point on the southern range in certain places; but I have shown above that this was equally characteristic of Canada.[4] Further, the stupendous estimates of buffalo numbers cited by himself or by other authorities known to and accepted by him, at later periods than 1870,[5] must mean either that there were in 1870 far more than a million and one half; or that the common talk about slaying at that time—before the commencement of the final northern slaughter—'far above the natural rate of increase,' etc., must be disregarded; and with it about nine-tenths of the unctuous pharisaism about Indian wastefulness. So far as 'continuous range' is concerned, the entire habitat is necessarily continuous; but if he means that buffalo herds consisting of the same individuals ranged between these distant points, we have seen that this rests upon no firmer basis than rhetorical assertion.[6]

Until the building of the Northern Pacific Railway, there were but two noteworthy outlets for the buffalo robes that were taken annually in the Northwestern Territories of the United States. The principal one was the Missouri River, and the Yellowstone River was the other. Down these streams the hides were transported by steamboats to the nearest railway shipping point. For fifty years prior to the building of the Northern Pacific Railway in 1880-'82, the number of robes marketed every year by way of these streams was estimated variously at from fifty to one hundred thousand. A great number of hides taken in the British Possessions fell into the hands of the Hudson's Bay Company and found a market in Canada. . . .[7]

[4]See above, chap. XIII, notes 157-66.
[5]See below in this chapter, notes 27-42.
[6]See above, chap. IV, notes 30-52, etc.
[7]Hornaday, "Extermination of the American Bison," 502-3. This is illustrative of the contradictoriness of the buffalo history, and also of the very general haziness in the United States concerning western Canada in the nineteenth century. To Colonel Dodge, afar off, Canada was apparently draining the very life-blood of the United States fur trade. He notes the 'immense numbers' sent here and there, to say nothing of "the still greater numbers taken each year from the territories of the United States by the Hudson's Bay Company . . ." (Dodge, *Plains of the Great West*, 143). Cf. Lieutenant G. K. Warren (United States Army Report, 1858). He speaks of "the Prairie Crees, the Blackfeet, and the Assiniboines, who yearly cross the 49th parallel to hunt the buffalo . . ." (*British-American Magazine*, Toronto, 1863, I, 336).

Their actual competitors on the ground spoke differently, it would seem. Frémont quotes John B. Sanford of the American Fur Company—'for the last eight or ten years' (say 1834-44), the total was about 90,000 robes per annum: American Fur Company, 70,000; Hudson's Bay Company, 10,000; other companies, probably 10,000. Sanford adds: "In the north-west, the Hudson's Bay Company purchase from the Indians but a very small number—their only market being Canada, to which the cost of transportation nearly equals the produce of the furs;

The Northern Pacific Railway reached Bismarck, [North] Dakota, on the Missouri River, in the year 1876; and from that date onward received for transportation eastward all the buffalo robes and hides that came down the two rivers, Missouri and Yellowstone. . . .[8]

The end which so many observers had for years been predicting really began (with the northern herd) in 1876, two years after the great annihilation which had taken place in the South, although it was not until four years later that the slaughter became universal over the entire range. . . .[9]

The building of the . . . Railway across Dakota and Montana hastened the end that was fast approaching; but it was only an incident in the annihilation of the northern herd. Without it the final result would have been just the same, but the end would probably not have been reached until about 1888. . . .

The first really alarming impression made on our northern herd was by the Sioux Indians, who very speedily exterminated that portion of it which had previously covered the country lying between the North Platte and a line drawn from the centre of Wyoming to the centre of Dakota. All along the Missouri River, from Bismarck to Fort Benton, and along the Yellowstone to the head of navigation, the slaughter went bravely on. All the Indian tribes of that vast region—Sioux, Cheyennes, Crows, Blackfeet, Bloods, Piegans, Assiniboines, Gros Ventres, and Shoshones—found their most profitable business and greatest pleasure (next to scalping white settlers) in hunting the buffalo. . . .

The Indians of our northwestern Territories marketed about seventy-five thousand buffalo robes every year so long as the northern herd was large enough to afford the supply. If we allow that for every skin sold to white traders four others were used in supplying their own wants, which must be considered a very moderate estimate, the total number of buffalos slaughtered annually by these tribes must have been about three hundred and seventy-five thousand.

The beginning of the final slaughter of our northern herd may be dated about 1880, by which time the annual robe crop of the Indians had diminished three-fourths, and when summer killing for hairless hides began on a large scale. The range of this herd was surrounded on three sides by tribes of Indians, armed with breech-loading rifles and abundantly supplied

---

and it is only within a very recent period that they have received buffalo robes in trade . . ." (Frémont, *Narrative*, 141-2).

Hornaday: "In the British Possessions and Canada, the frontier business was largely monopolized by the Hudson's Bay Fur [*sic*] Company, although the annual "output" of robes and hides was but small in comparison with that gathered in the United States, where the herds were far more numerous. Even in their most fruitful locality for robes—the country south of the Saskatchewan—this company had a very powerful competitor in the firm of I. G. Baker & Co., of Fort Benton, which secured the lion's share of the spoil and sent it down the Missouri River . . ." ("Extermination of the American Bison," 441). Similarly, McDougall, *Western Trails*, 212. 'I. G. Baker' (in Canada) bought out by the Hudson's Bay Company in 1892 (Blue, *Alberta Past and Present*, I, 81). See chap. XVII.

[8]Hornaday, "Extermination of the American Bison," 507.
[9]*Ibid.*, 505-6.

with fixed ammunition. Up to the year 1880, the Indians of the tribes previously mentioned killed probably three times as many buffaloes as did the white hunters, and had there not been a white hunter in the whole Northwest the buffalo would have been exterminated there just as surely, though not so quickly by perhaps ten years, as actually occurred. Along the north, from the Missouri River to the British line, and from the reservation in northwestern Dakota to the main divide of the Rocky Mountains, a distance of 550 miles as the crow flies, the country was one continuous Indian reservation, inhabited by eight tribes, who slaughtered buffalo in season and out of season, in winter for robes and in summer for hides and meat to dry. In the Southeast was the great body of Sioux, and on the Southwest the Crows and Northern Cheyennes, all engaged in the same relentless warfare. It would have required a body of armed men larger than the whole United States Army to have withstood this continuous hostile pressure without ultimate annihilation.[10]

The running commentary in the foregoing passages is so inextricably intertwined with factual material that it is impossible to separate the two. The passages comprise about as extraordinary a collection of half-truths as one could wish to encounter. It will be necessary in a later chapter to examine in detail the psychological attitude of the Indian towards buffalo, so I shall summarize my present criticisms very briefly so far as Indians are concerned.

I doubt whether any reader not possessed of some knowledge of the development of Indian trade would suspect from the passage quoted above that it was the advent of the white trader that first gave the buffalo a value to the Indians over and above what it possessed as a source of food, clothing, etc. by acquainting them with hitherto unknown needs which buffalo skins might supply. No doubt the introduction of modern firearms had some bearing on the rapidity of the slaughter, although it may not have been so fundamental a cause as some would have us believe.[11] It seems probable that the chief effect of firearms was to increase the proportion of buffalo slain by the Indian. But, whatever the bearing of firearms on the slaughter, it was the white man, once again, who introduced them among the tribes. Further, in view of the fact that Dr. Hornaday himself instances needs

[10]*Ibid.*, 505-7.

[11]MacInnes, who considers the use of repeating rifles a disaster to the red man, writes: "And with these weapons the hunting of the buffalo became a mere slaughter, and undoubtedly, one of the causes which help to explain the extraordinary disappearance of this animal from the plains in the course of a few years, was the widespread use of such weapons by the Indians . . ." (*In the Shadow of the Rockies*, 73). The white hunters would have used them if the Indians had not; the principal explanation is the official attitude. See Appendix H, "Buffalo, Indian, and Legislation."

which the Indians supplied in both winter and summer from buffalo, the words 'slaughtering in season and out of season' are scarcely applicable; on this topic—as on others—he does not even agree with himself.[12] Then again we are asked to believe that—even without the addition of thousands of white hunters who, with their almost incredible daily or monthly or seasonal records, had been largely responsible for the rapid annihilation of the Southern herd (and who came prepared, as we shall shortly see, to repeat the slaughter in the North)—we are asked to believe that, even without this devastating influx, the buffalo in the North would have been exterminated in another five years (that is, *circa* 1888). When one remembers that most students of earlier Indian populations[13] enlarge on the extinction of whole tribes after the arrival of the white races, one might ask why such large numbers of the aborigines as must previously have existed had not extinguished the buffalo species, wholly or partly, long before. It is obvious, however, that such a feat was impossible previous to the appearance of the white man with his demands and his methods. I am at a loss to decide whether Hornaday's language concerning the end "which so many observers had for years been predicting," arises from *malice prepense* against the Indians, or results merely from a vagueness of thought and diction; but it certainly conveys a subtle implication that the Indian was the evil-doer responsible for this consummation long looked for, come at last!

It is highly instructive to note a few such predictions by white observers, as recorded in works cited by Hornaday, and to compare them with other opinions, some of them in the very same sources but ignored by him. Allen observes:

A century ago the rapid extermination of the buffalo had begun to attract the attention of travellers, Romans,[14] as early as 1776, alluding to the wanton destruction of 'this excellent beast, *for the sake of perhaps his tongue only*.' As early as 1820 Major Long thought it highly desirable that some law should be enforced for the preservation of the bison from wanton destruction by the white hunters, who, he said, were accustomed to attack

[12]Hornaday, "Extermination of the American Bison," 506: on p. 499 'they slaughtered in season and out of season, in summer for meat to dry'; *ibid.*, 437, we read: "If any animal was ever designed by the hand of nature for the express purpose of supplying at one stroke, nearly all the wants of an entire race, surely the buffalo was intended for the Indian. And right well was this gift of the gods utilized by the children of nature to whom it came. . . ."

[13]See below, Appendix G, "Indian Populations Subsisting on Buffalo."

[14]Bernard Romans, *A Concise Natural History of East and West Florida*, volume I (volume II unpublished), New York, 1775. I regret to say I have not seen this work and know nothing further concerning the author.

large herds, and from *mere wantonness* slaughter as many as they were able and leave the carcasses to be devoured by the wolves and birds of prey. . . .[15]

Gregg, in 1835, also alludes to the wanton slaughter of these animals by travellers and hunters, and the still greater havoc made among them by the Indians, who often kill them merely for the skins and tongues. Their total annihilation he regarded as only a question of time, although he believed that if they were only killed for food, their natural increase would perhaps replenish the loss. Almost every intelligent traveller who has crossed the Plains or spent much time in the buffalo country has also called attention to this exterminating slaughter, and predicted their complete annihilation at no very distant date. Some writers believed twenty or thirty years ago that they would hardly survive to the present time unless protected by the government. . . .[16]

Frémont is, I presume, a case in point. He remarks (1843):

The extraordinary rapidity with which the buffalo is disappearing from our territories will not appear surprising when we remember the great scale on which their destruction is yearly carried on. With inconsiderable exceptions, the business of the American trading posts is carried on in their skins; every year the Indian villages make new lodges, for which the skin of the buffalo furnishes the material; and in that portion of the country where they are still found, the Indians derive their entire support from them, and slaughter them with a thoughtless and abominable extravagance. . . .[17]

Such historical extracts as these might seem to prove the case for 'prediction' beyond question; but other facts (with some of which the reader has already been acquainted) put a somewhat different complexion on the matter. As I have confessed (in note 14), I know nothing of Romans, but the date, 1776, very strongly suggests the territory east of the Mississippi, where it has been shown that 'vast numbers' will bear only a relative (and limited) interpretation,[18] and where the not very difficult process of extermination was in visible and substantial progress at that time. Concerning actual prairie travellers, it is a curious fact, to which the reader's attention has already been drawn, that only one of them appears to have encountered really large herds, that is, Long (or his secretary, Dr. Edwin James, who apparently wrote the account of their travels); and he directs his strictures at the *white* hunters. Gregg, as I have remarked in some detail above,[19]

[15]Allen, *American Bisons*, 183; for the remarks mentioned, see Long, *Early Western Travels*, XV, 256.

[16]Allen, *American Bisons*, 183-4; the passage is in Gregg, *Early Western Travels*, XX, 264.

[17]Frémont, *Narrative*, 140.

[18]Compare above, chap. XIII.

[19]Chap. XIII, notes 125-6.

because he did not encounter any very large masses, actually disbelieved in their existence; as Allen himself confesses to having almost done—despite his almost unrivalled acquaintance with the literature of 'numbers'—until he saw them on the plains for himself in 1871.[20] Frémont, also, is an outstanding example of that perfectly natural propensity in the traveller to reason generally from what he sees; he has usually no other criteria for comparison until later, and what else is he to do? It is for the critic to apply comparative tests to his isolated phenomena. Frémont, both in the passage just quoted and above,[21] speaks of the 'disappearance of the buffalo' as a final and irrevocable fact in regions where it is well known they did not finally disappear until long after. In the minds of such men, an observed scarcity in localities where perhaps only a year before some traveller of established veracity noted 'immense herds,' or an observed slaughter of large numbers from a much smaller aggregate than they had been led to expect—such experiences accelerate the rate of 'extermination' enormously.

Allen quoted other expressions of opinion, which it apparently suited Hornaday to ignore: It was thought by General Meigs and General Sheridan that around 1870-71 there were 'more buffalo than ever before,' possibly because the use of strychnine in the slaughter of wolves for their hides had considerably curtailed the ravages of these animals on the buffalo, and because the preoccupation of the Indians with war had kept them from hunting as freely as usual for some years past.[22] Other men of Western experience concur broadly in this opinion concerning buffalo numbers.[23] Denny, whose opinions based upon personal observation are much more valuable than his scientific generalizations on buffalo, states that "If hunted by the Indians alone they would never have disappeared. . . ."[24] Other competent authorities have also been cited[25] above, who considered the Indian as by no means the buffalo's worst enemy; and, to crown all, there is Hornaday himself:

Notwithstanding the merciless war that had been waged against the buffalo for over a century by both whites and Indians, and the steady

[20]Allen, *American Bisons*, 55.
[21]Chap. XIII, notes 136-7.
[22]Allen, *American Bisons*, 176.

[23]*In re* wolves, this was the explanation given by the Fort Benton traders, 1874: MacInnes, *In the Shadow of the Rockies*, 144; cf. General Sam Steele, 'peace, rather than war,' a menace to the buffalo; "when everyone was at peace with his neighbour and could go where he liked, the buffalo would soon disappear . . ." (*Forty Years in Canada*, 110).
[24]Denny MS., introd., 13.
[25]Above, chaps. VII, VIII; "Agencies Destructive to Buffalo."

decrease of its numbers, as well as its range, there were several million head on foot, not only up to the completion of the Union Pacific Railway, but as late as the year 1870. Up to that time the killing done by white men had been chiefly for the sake of meat, the demand for robes was moderate, and the Indians took annually less than one hundred thousand for trading. Although half a million buffaloes were killed by Indians, half-breeds, and whites, the natural increase was so very considerable as to make it seem that the evil day of extermination was yet far distant.[26]

Although Hornaday (apparently quite justly) considers 1880 as the beginning of the final 'intensive' slaughter of the Northern herd, yet the figures for some ·few years prior to that date are sufficiently impressive; and it was quite probably the success of the older established traders in the Missouri territory, together with the sudden termination of the buffalo-hunting business in the South and the evident conviction which possessed the hunters that no opposition to the wholesale slaughter need be anticipated from the Federal government, that brought it to pass in the North. There are various allusions to very considerable numbers in the northern country in the middle and later seventies. Allen states that:

Lieutenant M. E. Hogan, 22nd, United States Infantry, informed me in 1873 that the buffaloes had recently crossed the Marias and Teton Rivers, in Northwestern Montana, from the northward, and were abundant throughout the region about Fort Shaw, and there were 'millions of buffaloes' on Milk River. . . .[27]

Denny also noted 'many large herds' in the Milk River country, in March, 1875;[28] and near the international boundary on both sides in the years from 1874 to 1879 there are a number of incidental references to them.[29] While some of the figures given concerning robe export at this time may be reasonable,[30] others are simply fantastic. L. V. Kelly asserts that in spring, 1874, I. G. Baker and Company shipped "from Benton alone 250,000 prime buffalo hides. . . ."[31] Kelly's inaccuracy elsewhere renders these figures incredible in any exact or literal sense.[32]

[26]Hornaday, "Extermination of the American Bison," 466. See below, Appendix P.

[27]Allen, American Bisons, 157. Fort Shaw, in Cascade County, Montana, west of Great Falls. Cf. this with a total of only 1,500,000, north of the Platte, 1870 (above, note 2).

[28]Denny, The Law Marches West, 68-70, etc.

[29]Ibid., 126, 131, 135, 143, etc.; McDougall, Western Trails, 202, 267; Steele, Forty Years in Canada, 76-80, 110, 114, 146-8; MacRae, History of Alberta, I, 377; MacInnes, In the Shadow of the Rockies, 72, 144.

[30]See below, chap. XVII, notes 35-72.

[31]Kelly, The Rangemen, 111.

[32]Kelly has the McDougalls at Morley, 1871 (ibid.), but John McDougall himself says, 1873, "for the first time in our lives . . ." (Western Trails, 17). MacInnes has strangely adopted Kelly, although he also utilized McDougall at

The American Fur Company's figures from Fort Benton in 1857 are 3,600 bales or 36,000 robes.[33] Messrs. I. G. Baker themselves stated in a letter to Hornaday (October 6, 1887) with reference to Fort Benton also, "There were sent East for the year 1876 from this point about 75,000 buffalo robes. . . ."[34]

Considering that a traffic of this description seldom diminishes while the source of supply remains unexhausted, an increase of approximately double in some twenty years is not incredible. However, as there was no such authenticated—or even asserted—phenomenal increase in the traffic in buffalo hides by any one firm at the time, and as it seems quite certain that such intensive slaughter was not widely prevalent before 1880 or even 1881, one cannot accept such figures as Kelly's without strong confirmation.

An extract (quoted by Hornaday) gives a vivid impression of the buffalo-skin traffic as it appeared to contemporaries, at a time when it had hardly even yet attained its short-lived maximum:

"It is estimated by competent authorities that one hundred thousand buffalo hides will be shipped out of the Yellowstone country this season [that is, 1881]. Two firms alone are negotiating for the transportation of twenty-five thousand hides each. . . . Most of our citizens saw the big load of buffalo hides that the *C. K. Peck* brought down last season, a load that hid everything below the roof of the hurricane deck. There were ten thousand hides in that load, and they were all brought out of the Yellowstone on one trip and transferred to the *C. K. Peck*. How such a load could ever have been piled on the little *Terry* not even the men on the boat appeared to know. It hid every part of the boat, barring only the pilot-house and smoke-stacks. But such a load will not be attempted again. For such boats as ply the Yellowstone there are at least fifteen full loads of buffalo hides and other pelts. Reckoning one thousand hides to three car loads, and adding to this fifty cars for the other pelts, it will take at least three hundred and fifty box-cars to carry this stupendous bulk of peltry East to market. These figures are not guesses but estimates made by men

---

first hand (*In the Shadow of the Rockies*, 193, 194), and even goes farther, and has George McDougall at Morley in 1864! (*ibid.*, 266, 274). MacInnes also cites Kelly (*The Rangemen*, 111: MacInnes, *In the Shadow of the Rockies*, 193) as making the McDougalls the first to drive in both range and domestic stock to Morley in 1871 (1873); but Kelly himself stresses the danger of buffalo to domestic cattle, and has 1875 or 1877 for domestic or range cattle (*The Rangemen*, 110-13; as likewise Denny, *The Law Marches West*, 79, 88, 89, 100, 128; McDougall MS., 25).

For an even more serious item of unsubstantiated assertion by Kelly, see Appendix BB, "Indian Wastefulness with Buffalo."

[33]Allen, *American Bisons*, 188.

[34]Hornaday, "Extermination of the American Bison," 506. According to Bancroft, 60,000 robes were exported from Fort Benton in 1878 (*History of Washington, Idaho, and Montana*, 753).

whose business it is to know about the amount of hides and furs awaiting shipment.

"Nothing like it has ever been known in the history of the fur trade. Last season the output of buffalo hides was above the average, and last year only about thirty thousand hides came out of the Yellowstone country, or less than a third of what is there now awaiting shipment. The past severe winter caused the buffalo to bunch themselves in a few valleys where there was pasturage, and there the slaughter went on all winter. There was no sport about it, simply shooting down the famine-tamed animals as cattle might be shot down in a barn-yard. To the credit of the Indians it can be said that they killed no more than they could save the meat from.[35] The greater part of the slaughter was done by white hunters, or butchers rather, who followed the business of killing and skinning buffalo by the month, leaving the carcasses to rot."[36]

Hornaday goes on to state:

The year 1881 witnessed the same kind of a stampede for the northern buffalo range that occurred just ten years previously in the south. . . . At that time the hunters and hide-buyers estimated that there were five hundred thousand buffaloes within a radius of 150 miles of Miles City [that is, Montana, on the Yellowstone, at the mouth of Tongue River, 46° 35′ N., 106° 15′ W.], and that there were still in the entire northern herd not far from one million head. The subsequent slaughter proved that these estimates were probably not far from the truth. In that year [1881] Fort Custer was so nearly overwhelmed by a passing herd that a detachment of soldiers was ordered out to turn the herd away from the post. In 1882 an immense herd appeared on the high level plateau on the north side of the Yellowstone which overlooks Miles City and Fort Keogh in the valley below. A squad of soldiers from the Fifth Infantry was sent up on the bluff, and in less than an hour had killed enough buffaloes to load six four-mule teams with meat. . . .

In 1882 there were, so it is estimated by men who were in the country, no fewer than five thousand white hunters and skinners on the northern range. Lieut. J. M. T. Partello declares that "a cordon of camps, from the Upper Missouri, where it bends to the west, stretched toward the setting sun as far as the dividing line of Idaho, completely blocking in the great ranges of the Milk River, the Musselshell, Yellowstone, and the Marias, and rendering it impossible for scarcely a single bison to escape through the chain of sentinel camps to the Canadian northwest. Hunters of Nebraska, Wyoming, and Colorado drove the poor hunted animals north, directly into the muzzles of thousands of repeaters ready to receive them. . . . as late as 1883, a herd of about seventy-five thousand crossed the Yellowstone River a few miles south of here [Fort Keogh], scores of Indians, pot-hunters,

[35]This must be considered unequivocal testimony, coming as it ultimately did from Western sources, where the Indian was hated. The significance of this will recur later, requiring consideration in detail (see chap. XXI).

[36]*Sioux City Journal*, Iowa, May (no date), 1881; in Hornaday, "Extermination of the American Bison," 503. For meat being left to rot, see below, note 52.

and white butchers on their heels, bound for the Canadian dominions, where they hoped to find a haven of safety. Alas! not five thousand of that mighty mass ever lived to reach the British border line."[37]

Hornaday remarks that it was difficult to decide—at least to the satisfaction of old hunters—which were the best hunting-grounds of the northern range.[38] This fact seems curious in the light of the tradition of the 'regular migration-route.' He goes on to say:

Lieutenant Partello states that when he hunted in the great triangle bounded by the three rivers, Missouri, Musselshell, and Yellowstone, it contained to the best of his knowledge and belief, two hundred and fifty thousand buffaloes. Unquestionably that region yielded an immense number of buffalo robes, and since the slaughter *thousands of tons* of bones have been gathered up there. Another favorite locality was the country lying between the Powder River and the Little Missouri, particularly the valleys of Beaver and O'Fallon Creeks. Thither went scores of "outfits" and hundreds of hunters and skinners from the Northern Pacific Railway towns from Miles City to Glendive. The hunters from the towns between Glendive and Bismarck mostly went south to Cedar Creek and the Grand and Moreau Rivers. But this territory was also the hunting ground of the Sioux Indians from the great reservations farther south.

Thousands upon thousands of buffaloes were killed on the Milk and Marias Rivers, in the Judith Basin, and in northern Wyoming.[39]

Hornaday further states:

As was the case in the south, it was the ability of a single hunter to destroy an entire bunch of buffalo in a single day that completely annihilated the remaining thousands of the northern herd before the people of the United States even learned what was going on. . . .[40] Where buffaloes were at all plentiful, every man who called himself a hunter was expected to kill between one and two thousand during the hunting season—from November to February[41]—and when the buffaloes were to be found it was a comparatively easy thing to do.

[37]Hornaday, "Extermination of the American Bison," 509. On repeating rifles, see remarks above, note 11.

[38]Hornaday, "Extermination of the American Bison," 511.

[39]*Ibid.*, 509-10.

[40]This seems doubtful, on Hornaday's own evidence (*ibid.*, 513-21). I cannot believe these hunters would have been so frank in their declarations as 'Vic. Smith' —and to a scientist! (see below, note 48)—unless they had felt a contemptuous assurance that a majority of public opinion was on their side. Only a few scientists and humanitarians cared.

[41]On the 'buffalo year,' see above, chap. V. For a specimen of the loose idle rhetoric noted in chap. XV, compare the above. Five thousand hunters (note 37) and 1500 per man ('1000 to 2000 per man') equals 7,500,000 buffalo per season. Yet it required *three* seasons to extirpate a supposed total of 1,500,000 (above, note 2) with their increase!

During the year 1882 the thousands of bisons that still remained alive on the range indicated above . . . were distributed over that entire area very generally. . . . a correspondent . . . wrote as follows: "It is truly wonderful how many buffalo are still left. Thousands of Indians and hundreds of white men depend on them for a living. At present nearly all the buffalo in Montana are between Milk River and Bear Paw Mountains. There are only a few small bands between the Missouri and the Yellowstone."[42] There were plenty of buffalo on the Upper Marias River in October, 1882. In November and December there were thousands between the Missouri and the Yellowstone Rivers. South of the Northern Pacific Railway the range during the hunting season of 1882-'83 was thus defined by a hunter . . . : "Then [October, 1882] the western limit was defined in a general way by Powder River and extending eastward well toward the Missouri and south to within 60 or 70 miles of the Black Hills. It embraces the valleys of all tributaries to Powder River from the east, all of the valleys of Beaver Creek, O'Fallon Creek, and the Little Missouri and Moreau Rivers, and both forks of the Cannon Ball for almost half their length. This immense territory, lying almost equally in Montana and Dakota, had been occupied during the winters by many thousands of buffalo from time immemorial, and many of the cows remained throughout the summer and brought forth their young undisturbed."[43]

Hornaday states that the party of which the foregoing writer was a member went from Miles City in October, 1882, due east to the 'bad lands' between Powder River and O'Fallon Creek, and were out all winter. They found comparatively few buffalo, and secured only 286 robes. The entire range in which they hunted was 'fairly infested with Indians and half-breeds, all hunting buffalo.'[44] He adds:

The hunting season which began in October, 1882, and ended in February, 1883, finished the annihilation of the great northern herd, and left but a few small bands of stragglers, numbering only a very few thousand individuals all told. A noted event of the season was the retreat northward across the Yellowstone of the immense herd mentioned by Lieutenant Partello as containing seventy-five thousand head; others estimated the number at fifty thousand; and the event is often spoken of by frontiersmen who were in that region at the time. Many think that the whole great body went north into British territory, and that there is still a goodly remnant of it in some remote region between the Peace River and the Saskatchewan, *or somewhere there*,[45] which will yet return to the United States. Nothing could be more illusory than this belief. In the first place, the herd never

[42]*Forest and Stream*, February, 1882, in Hornaday, "Extermination of the American Bison," 511.
[43]"Confessions of a Buffalo Butcher," *Forest and Stream*, XXIV, 489 (in Hornaday, "Extermination of the American Bison," 511).
[44]*Ibid.*
[45]Italics mine. A delightfully vague expression; a very fair index of the quite common U.S. ignorance of Western Canada fifty years ago.

reached the British line, and if it had, it would have been promptly annihilated by the hungry Blackfeet and Cree Indians, who were declared to
be in a half-starved condition through the disappearance of the buffalo, as
early as 1879. [46]

The great herd that "went north" was utterly extinguished by the white
hunters along the Missouri River and the Indians living north of it. The
only vestige of it that remained was a band of about two hundred individuals
that took refuge in the labyrinth of ravines and creek bottoms that lie west
of the Musselshell between Flat Willow and Box Elder Creeks, and another
band of about seventy-five which settled in the bad lands between the head
of the Big Dry and Big Porcupine Creeks, where a few survivors were
found by the writer in 1886. . . .[47]

In the southeast the fate of that portion of the herd is well known. The
herd which at the beginning of the hunting season of 1883 was known to
contain about ten thousand head, and ranged in western Dakota, about half
way between the Black Hills and Bismarck, between the Moreau and
Grand Rivers, was speedily reduced to about one thousand head. Vic.
Smith, who was "in at the death," says there were eleven hundred, others
say twelve hundred. Just at this juncture (October, 1883), Sitting Bull and
his whole band of nearly one thousand braves arrived from the Standing
Rock Agency, and in two days' time slaughtered the entire herd. Vic. Smith
and a host of white hunters took part in the killing of this last ten thousand,
and he declares that "when we got through the hunt there was not a hoof
left. That wound up the buffalo in the Far West, only a stray bull being seen
here and there afterwards."[48]

Hornaday concludes by saying what admits of no doubt, since he
had exceptional opportunities of judging:

Curiously enough, not even the buffalo-hunters themselves were at the
time aware of the fact that the end of the hunting season of 1882-'83 was
also the end of the buffalo, at least as an inhabitant of the plains and a
source of revenue. In the autumn of 1883 they nearly all outfitted as usual,
often at an expense of many hundreds of dollars, and blithely sought "the
range" that had up to that time been so prolific in robes. The end was in
nearly every case the same—total failure and bankruptcy. It was indeed
hard to believe that not only the millions, but also the thousands, had
actually gone, and forever. . . .[49]

[46]On all this, see the chapter following.

[47]Hornaday, "Extermination of the American Bison," 511-12. 'The writer' is
Hornaday himself, the head of the two Smithsonian expeditions of May and
September, 1886 (ibid., 402, 529-48; see also a good brief account in Garretson,
American Bison, 190-5). The region lies north of Billings, Montana, in Musselshell
and Fergus Counties. The Musselshell River joins the Missouri about the north-
east corner of Fergus County.

[48]Hornaday, "Extermination of the American Bison," 512. It is such 'declarations'—or better, boastings—to which I referred above, note 40.

[49]Hornaday, "Extermination of the American Bison," 512; also, George W.
Reighard, Edmonton Journal, January 3, 1931. I suspect, however, the latter
derived this from Hornaday, although it appears as 'reminiscence.' See note at
conclusion of chap. XV.

For a long time the majority of the ex-hunters cherished the fond delusion that the great herd had only "gone north" into the British Possessions, and would eventually return in great force. Scores of rumors of the finding of herds floated about, all of which were eagerly believed at first. But after a year or two had gone by without the appearance of a single buffalo, and likewise without any reliable information of the existence of a herd of any size, even in British territory, the butchers of the buffalo . . . sought other means of livelihood. Some took to gathering up buffalo bones and selling them by the ton, and others became cowboys.[50]

The somewhat meagre statistics that are available for the later years from about 1876 onward—principally gathered through the industry of Hornaday—tend to show that at least he has probably not over-rated the figures. He quotes a letter addressed to himself from J. M. Hannaford, the then traffic manager of the Northern Pacific Railway, dated September 3, 1887. I give this in part below:

"I regret that our accounts are not so kept as to enable me to furnish you accurate data; but I have been able to obtain the following general information, which may prove of some value to you:

"From the years 1876 and [to?] 1880 our line did not extend beyond Bismarck, which was the extreme easterly shipping point for buffalo robes and hides, they being brought down the Missouri River . . . for shipment from that point. In the years 1876, 1877, 1878, and 1879 there were handled at that point yearly from three to four thousand bales of robes, about one-half the bales containing ten robes, and the other half twelve robes each. During these years practically no hides were shipped. In 1880, the shipment of hides, dry and untanned, commenced, and in 1881 and 1882 our line was extended west, and the shipping points increased, reaching as far west as Terry and Sully Springs in Montana. During these years, 1880, 1881, and 1882, which practically finished the shipments of hides and robes, it is impossible for me to give you any just idea of the number shipped. The only figures obtainable are those of 1881, when over seventy-five thousand dry and untanned buffalo hides came down the river for shipment from Bismarck. Some robes were also shipped from this point that year, and a considerable number of robes and hides were shipped from several other shipping points.[51]

"The number of pounds of buffalo meat shipped over our line has never cut any figure, the bulk of the meat having been left on the prairie, as not being of sufficient value to pay the cost of transportation.[52]

[50]Hornaday, "Extermination of the American Bison," 513.

[51]Meaning presumably on the Northern Pacific. There must surely have been others which went farther down than Bismarck by boat, and were placed on other railways. See the quotation from the *Sioux City Journal* (above, note 36). Sioux City is far below Bismarck.

[52]This may be considered 'official.' Mentioned also by the *Sioux City Journal*, and by Joseph Ullman, fur buyer of New York, as common knowledge (Hornaday, "Extermination of the American Bison," 440). Yet Hornaday himself rather

"The names of the extreme eastern and western stations from which shipments were made are as follows: In 1880 Bismarck was the only shipping point. In 1881, Glendive, Bismarck, and Beaver Creek. In 1882, Terry and Sully Springs, Montana, were the chief shipping points, and in the order named, so far as numbers and amount of shipments are concerned. Bismarck on the east and Forsyth on the west were the two extremities. . . .

"Since 1882 there have, of course, been occasional shipments both of hides and robes, but in such small quantities and so seldom that they cut practically no figure, the bulk of them coming probably from North Missouri [River] points down the river to Bismarck."[53]

Messrs. I. G. Baker furnished the following to Hornaday, in reference solely to the trade from Fort Benton, Montana: "There were sent East for the year 1876 from this point about seventy-five thousand buffalo robes. In 1880 it had fallen to about twenty thousand; in 1883 not more than five thousand; and in 1884 none whatever. . . ."[54]

Following is a memorandum of buffalo robes and hides bought by Messrs. J. and A. Boskowitz, New York and Chicago, from 1876 to 1884:

Year	Buffalo robes		Buffalo hides	
	Number	Cost	Number	Cost
1876	31,838	$ 39,620	none	....
1877	9,353	35,660	none	....
1878	41,268	150,500	none	....
1879	28,613	110,420	none	....
1880	34,901	176,200	4,570	13,140
1881	23,355	151,800	26,601	89,030
1882	2,124	15,600	15,464	44,140
1883	5,690	29,770	21,869	67,190
1884	none	....	529	1,720
Total	177,142	$709,570	69,033	$215,220[55]

A memorandum furnished to Hornaday from the firm of Joseph Ullman, fur buyers of New York, Chicago, and St. Paul, gives the following information:

---

strangely says: "it is some gratification to know that the shocking and criminal wastefulness which was so marked a feature of the southern butchery was almost unknown in the north . . ." (*ibid.*, 510). It is possible that Hornaday was referring to the skins. [53]*Ibid.*, 507-8.

[54]Correspondence to Hornaday, October 6, 1887 (*ibid.*, 506).

[55]*Ibid.*, 439.

"In 1881 we handled about 14,000 hides . . . and 12,000 robes . . .

"In 1882 we purchased between 35,000 and 40,000 hides . . . and about 10,000 robes . . .

"In 1883 we purchased from 6,000 to 7,000 hides and about 1,500 to 2,000 robes . . .

"In 1884 we purchased less than 2,500 hides, and in my opinion these were such as were carried over from the previous season in the Northwest, and were not fresh-slaughtered skins. The collection of robes this season was also comparatively small, and nominally robes carried over from 1883.

"In 1885 the collection of hides amounted to little or nothing. . . ."[56]

Mr. J. N. Davis, a large fur-buyer of Minneapolis, in response to a request for statistics which he regretted his inability to furnish, estimated the shipments on the Northern Pacific Railway between Miles City and Mandan at about 50,000 in 1881, some 200,000 in 1882, and 40,000 in 1883. He concluded by saying: "In 1884 I shipped from Dickinson, Dakota Territory, the only carload of robes that went east that year, and it was the last shipment ever made."[57]

In addition to the foregoing, Hornaday names five other leading firms in the business, and mentions 'many others whose names he was then unable to recall.' Considering the Eastern fur buyers apart from traders like the I. G. Baker people, I have met with nothing to indicate that those firms who were able or willing to furnish some figures greatly exceeded the others in the magnitude of their operations. The wide variations in the aggregates of Messrs. Boskowitz and Ullman respectively during the years 1881-84 tend to establish that; and in fact the reverse is more likely: the greater the dealings in the harvest of slaughter, the less likelihood of courting publicity, at least from a scientific inquirer. This probability may be remembered later, when we attempt to form some conception of the total aggregates.

The statement quoted above,[58] from the notorious 'Vic.' Smith, that the slaughter of the herd in October, 1883, 'wound up the buffalo in the Far West,' while it is broadly true, is, of course, not literally so. Hornaday has devoted a section to a discussion of the "Completeness of the Extermination" up to May 1, 1889, covering the United States and Canada. With reference to Canada—which will be discussed shortly—this is supplemented considerably from other sources. I quote Hornaday below:

[56]*Ibid.*, 440-1.

[57]Correspondence to Hornaday, September 27, 1887 (*ibid.*, 513). I have found the statement from Davis nowhere except in Hornaday. Garretson (citing no authority) makes it *two* carloads (*American Bison*, 152).

[58]See note 48, above.

Although the existence of a few widely-scattered individuals enables us to say that the bison is not yet absolutely extinct in a wild state, there is no reason to hope that a single wild and unprotected individual will remain alive ten years hence. The nearer the species approaches to complete extermination, the more eagerly are the wretched fugitives pursued to the death whenever found. Western hunters are striving for the honor (?) of killing the last buffalo, which, it is to be noted, has already been slain about a score of times by that number of hunters.

The buffaloes still alive in a wild state are so very few, and have been so carefully "marked down" by hunters, it is possible to make a very close estimate of the total number remaining. . . .

In the United States the death of a buffalo is now such an event that it is immediately chronicled by the Associated Press and telegraphed all over the country. By reason of this, and from information already in hand, we are able to arrive at a very fair understanding of the present condition of the species in a wild state.

In December, 1886, the Smithsonian expedition left about fifteen buffaloes alive in the bad lands of the Missouri-Yellowstone divide, at the head of Big Porcupine Creek. In 1887, three of these were killed by cowboys, and in 1888 two more, the last death recorded being that of an old bull killed near Billings. There are probably eight or ten stragglers still remaining in that region, hiding in the wildest and most broken tracts of the bad lands, as far as possible from the cattle ranches, and where even cowboys seldom go save on a round-up. From the fact that no other buffaloes, at least so far as can be learned, have been killed in Montana during the last two years, I am convinced that the bunch referred to are the last representatives of the species remaining in Montana.

In the spring of 1886, Mr. B. C. Winston, while on a hunting trip around 75 miles west of Grand Rapids, Dakota, saw seven buffaloes—five adult animals and two calves; of which he killed one, a large bull, and caught a calf alive. On September 11, 1888, a solitary bull was killed 3 miles from the town of Oakes, in Dickey County. There are still three individuals in the unsettled country lying between that point and the Missouri, which are undoubtedly the only wild representatives of the race east of the Missouri.[59]

Even this comprehensive sketch does not entirely exhaust the history of the 'last buffaloes.' Perhaps because this was the final territory-at-large of the mass-slaughterings, and greater publicity was given to late encounters with the animals; and probably, also, because of the wild and broken nature of the country where the latest of the better-known remnants were found, small herds or occasional individuals, in addition to those mentioned by Hornaday, were recorded contemporaneously. One herd is also mentioned at a much later date.

[59]Hornaday, "Extermination of the American Bison," 521-2. Dickey County lies on the southern border of North Dakota, between 98° and 99° west longitude.

An old plainsman who was in the Dakota territory at the time speaks of 'the last wild herd ever seen' as being on the Rivière du Lac in September, 1882. This river flows southeastward along the eastern flank of the Missouri Coteau, joining the Mouse (Souris) River near Minot, North Dakota. The same writer states that along the lower stretches of the Coteau du Missouri, near the well-known 'Dog Den,' they had been extinct since 1874.[60] About the same time, a small herd still remained on the headwaters of Dismal River (boundary of Grant and Hooker counties), Nebraska, where it was destroyed by the Sioux in the fall or winter of 1882.[61]

In 1887, apparently in late autumn or early winter, a buffalo was killed on the Big Porcupine, in Montana. This stream joins the Yellowstone near Forsyth, westward from Miles City. This event is verified by the attempt of the American Museum of Natural History of New York to secure the skin for mounting. Its own expedition of that year, after a wide exploration of the region of Hornaday's successful hunt of 1886, had failed to find a single living specimen.[62] Farther south, however, in the same year (1887), there were still buffalo, as we learn from Hornaday; who quotes from a letter addressed to himself by Dr. William Stephenson (U.S. Army), from Pilot Butte, some thirty miles north of Rock Springs, Wyoming, April 28, 1887, as follows: "There are undoubtedly buffalo within fifty or sixty miles of here, two having been killed out of a band of four seen near there. I hear from cattlemen of their being seen every year north and northeast of here."[63]

The directions and distances suggested come very near to the famous South Pass,[64] between which and the vicinity of Fort Bridger buffalo were 'extinct' over forty years previously.[65] Hornaday adds, concerning the foregoing herd or herds:

This band was seen once in 1888. In February, 1889, Hon. Joseph M. Carey, member of Congress from Wyoming, received a letter informing

[60]Taylor, *Frontier Life*, 41, 262.
[61]Garretson, *American Bison*, 154.
[62]*Ibid.*, 193-5.
[63]Hornaday, "Extermination of the American Bison," 522.
[64]This famous highway of the Oregon-California Trail lies very near the junction of Fremont, Sublette, and Sweetwater counties, Wyoming. It there crosses the continental divide; and has inspired many rhapsodies on the 'buffalo-Indian-trail-highway-railroad succession.' The Union Pacific found a better route via the South Platte, Lodge Pole Creek, and Sherman Pass. South Pass is the one important pass which no railroad surveyor has utilized; so I was informed in 1942, by Dr. R. C. Overton, Professor of Commerce, Northwestern University, Evanston, Illinois, who knows the territory well. *Sic transit gloria!*
[65]See above, chap. XI, notes 139-40.

him that this band of buffaloes, consisting of twenty-six head, had been seen grazing in the Red Desert of Wyoming, and that the Indians were preparing to attack it. At Judge Carey's request the Indian Bureau issued orders which it was hoped would prevent the slaughter. So, until further developments, we have the pleasure of recording the presence of twenty-six wild buffaloes in southern Wyoming.[66]

There are no buffaloes whatever in the vicinity of the Yellowstone Park, either in Wyoming, Montana, or Idaho, save what wander out of that reservation, and when any do, they are speedily killed.[67]

In the farther north United States buffalo territory, there is a reference about the same time to what was evidently a quite considerable herd in North Dakota. A recent historian quotes the following item from *The Nor'-West Farmer and Miller* (Winnipeg) for 1888:

Bismarck, Sept. 13, 1888. John Whiteside, a hunter who came in from the north to-day says that while on a hunting expedition sixty miles north he saw herds of over sixty buffaloes and killed one. The animals were stampeded for water, and he had a narrow escape from being caught in their path in a ravine leading to the river. The buffalo did not stop for the river, but swam to the opposite shore, and when he last saw them they were going in a northwesterly direction. This is the first herd of any numbers seen in the valley for some years. . . .[68]

I have found no Bismarck in any portion of the northern range save the one in North Dakota. The probability that this is the Bismarck referred to is increased by the fact of buffalo being recorded in another portion of that State in the very same month, as we have seen.[69] Any incredulity one might feel concerning a reference to so late a period in that territory applies more or less to any testimony from an unknown witness after, say, 1883 or thereabout; and there we must leave the matter.

There is a most interesting final notice in respect of late survivors in Colorado. Hornaday writes:

[66]Hornaday, "Extermination of the American Bison," 522; so also on his map (*ibid.*, 548). I am glad to record the name of any intercessor on their behalf. Compare also Jones's efforts (*Buffalo Jones' Forty Years*, 262.)

[67]Hornaday, "Extermination of the American Bison," 522. Of the Park, he says: "Their heads alone are worth from $25 to $50 each to taxidermists, and for this reason every buffalo is a prize worth the hunter's winning. Had it not been for stringent laws, and a rigid enforcement of them by Captain Harris [the Superintendent], the last of the Park buffaloes would have been shot years ago, by Vic. Smith, the Rea Brothers, and other hunters, of whom there is always an able contingent around the Park" (*ibid.*, 521-2). See also—including an amusing example of 'rigid enforcement'—Garretson, *American Bison*, 196-202.

[68]Hawkes, *Saskatchewan and her People*, I, 57.

[69]Above, note 59.

There is a rumor that there are ten or twelve mountain buffaloes still on foot in Colorado, in a region called Lost Park, and while it lacks confirmation, we gladly accept it as a fact. In 1888 Mr. C. B. Cory, of Boston, saw in Denver, Colorado, eight fresh buffalo skins, which it was said had come from the region named above. In 1885 there was a herd of about forty "mountain buffalo" near South Park, and although some of the number may still survive, the indications are that the number of wild buffalo in Colorado does not exceed twenty individuals.[70]

M. S. Garretson states that a small herd, at one time containing twenty or thirty animals, actually did survive in Lost Park to as late a date as February, 1897, when the final remnant, two bulls, one cow, and one calf, were slain by vandal hunters as the climax of many such efforts which had gradually diminished their numbers, despite local attempts to protect them.[71] To the reader of the present essay, Hornaday's allusion to these being 'mountain buffalo' possesses an added significance, since he had already strenuously denied the existence of such a race.[72] Garretson, who does concede such a creature, states that they were extinct in the late sixties.[73]

When it is remembered that these last hunts could have no possible significance in relation to the 'economic independence of the Indian while the buffalo remained';[74] and also that the last hapless remnants had fled into regions where for long enough they could not constitute any menace to the crops or property of settlers, I consider that the pertinacity of the final miserable persecution, no less than the main slaughter, entirely justifies Dr. Hornaday's language concerning the butchery and the butchers.

[70]Hornaday, "Extermination of the American Bison," 522-3.
[71]Garretson, American Bison, 155.
[72]See above, chap. III, "North American Variants of the Buffalo."
[73]Garretson, American Bison, 5. Since he declares, however, on the same page, that there is but 'one species known to science'—mountain, wood, and plains bison, being all one—it is difficult to see how it can have become extinct.
[74]See below, Appendix H, "Buffalo, Indian, and Legislation."

CHAPTER XVII

THE NUMBERS OF THE BUFFALO: THE FINAL
EXTERMINATION IN WESTERN CANADA

WHEN the final extinction of the buffalo as a wild species roaming in freedom came to pass in the northwestern United States in 1883, the disappointed hide hunters, who had 'outfitted' as usual in the fall of that year, could not bring themselves to believe it. The popular explanation was that the disappearance was a mere passing phase; the great herd had 'gone north into Canada,' and would shortly return in force.[1] Contrary to this opinion, however, the virtual extermination in Canada actually preceded the final slaughter in the United States.

It may be said that, up to about 1870, there never was any progressive 'extermination' for robes alone in Canada, as there was in the United States. Whether among Indians or whites (practically all of the latter being, almost to the end, Hudson's Bay Company employees only), the utilization of buffalo embraced almost all the principal uses to which the animal had ever been put by those Indians who depended upon it almost exclusively, the first and predominant use of course being meat. The reasons for this difference between the two countries are in my opinion as follows. Since settlement of the plains territories was confined at first to the United States, 'extermination' first became a pressing question there; either as a necessary prelude to or a consequent result of occupation, or as a semi-political *desideratum* for other reasons. Secondly, the Hudson's Bay Company's deliberate and persistent opposition to settlement in western Canada, even to the latest moment, retarded the opening up of 'bulk transportation' routes. The virtually prohibitive cost of transporting buffalo in larger quantities than local uses necessitated discouraged the commercial interests from promoting or fostering a policy of extermination. Especially was this the case since long-distance transportation facilities were already taxed to the utmost in conveying less bulky and more valuable fur products. The easiest and most natural outlet by land from the upper Saskatchewan country was over the watershed of the Missouri basin,

[1]Hornaday, "Extermination of the American Bison," 511-13.

southward to Fort Benton, Montana. But it was not until about 1870[2] that the determined hostility of the northern (that is, Canadian) Blackfoot and their confederated tribes was overcome, and passage through their country made feasible.[3] When this was effected, the (buffalo) fur trade made its appearance in Canada; and, as historical students of this era are well aware, it was the accompanying introduction of 'bad men' and other demoralizing border elements so characteristic of the development of other sections of the Great West, which resulted in the inauguration of the North West Mounted Police in 1874.[4]

It has been noticed that Lord Southesk, as early as 1859, believed the buffalo to have decreased so greatly that they were reduced to one herd—of considerable numbers, of course.[5] Although this view is demonstrably unsound for Southesk's day,[6] and was never literally true

[2]Miss Diller gives 1866 as the first year in which American traders came across the line from Fort Benton ("Early Economic Development of Alberta," chap. III, 12; chap. IV, 3). I note that Father Lacombe went east that way in 1869, presumably indicating by then an established route (Hughes, *Father Lacombe*, 172).

[3]Although the record of the Hudson's Bay Company's relationships with the Indians has been generally good (as I have endeavoured impartially to show: Roe, "The Hudson's Bay Company and the Indians," *The Beaver*, Sept., 1936), such rhapsodies on the Company's 'mission' as those of Lord Strathcona (Willson, *The Great Company*, introd. xi-xiii) are idle and preposterous. This applies particularly to the southern country, after 1840. The only men who dared to go through there alone were Rundle and De Smet. Compare Sir George Simpson's tremors in 1841 (*Journey Around the World*, I, 58-9, 110). Lefroy in 1844 would 'not have been afraid to go through the Blackfoot country with Rowand for his escort'; and Butler wished to go back that way in 1871, but the Company officials at Edmonton would not risk it. They foretold disaster to the McDougalls' new southern missionary enterprise at Morley, on the upper Bow River, in 1873; and later re-established themselves, near the old Bow Fort, under the McDougalls' protection (McDougall, *Western Trails*, 15, 21, 200). Yet a modern 'historian' actually says of travel in the Blackfoot country (1857): "Under the protection of the Hudson's Bay Company, it could be done with perfect safety . . ."! (MacKay, *The Honourable Company*, 260). A likelier reason is given by Southesk, who says the Blackfoot "are very fond of Englishmen, and call them *na-pi-quan*, which means 'white man' as a term of honour . . ." (*Travels*, 151). The men who really paved the way for the Police in Alberta were Rundle, Woolsey, Scollen, Lacombe, and the McDougalls. See my review of Horan, *On the Side of the Law*, 1944; in *Canadian Historical Review*, XXVIII, March, 1947. (Below, note 103.)

[4]On the Cypress Hills massacre of Assiniboines by Americans, 1872, see McDougall, *Western Trails*, 253; Steele, *Forty Years in Canada*, 55; Hawkes, *Saskatchewan and her People*, I, 145; Denny, *The Law Marches West*, 65, 78. On ruffians of Fort Benton and Southern Alberta, see McDougall, *Western Trails*, 75, 128-30, 257-60; Steele, *Forty Years in Canada*, 53-8; MacRae, *History of Alberta*, I, 263; Denny, *The Law Marches West*, 76, 139, 150; MacInnes, *In the Shadow of the Rockies*, 66, etc.

[5]Southesk, *Travels*, 254-5.

[6]See above, chap. XIV, note 97.

until the very last days of all, something more nearly approximating that condition (in a territorial sense at least), may be said to have come to pass by about 1874. In the preceding half-century, the annual expeditions of the Red River Hunt had gradually pushed back the buffalo frontier to the Cypress Hills region, nearly 600 miles westward, where the original force of the Mounted Police, then on their way west, first encountered them in 1874.[7] The inauguration of the traffic between southern Alberta and Fort Benton produced a similar result in the southwestern area of the Canadian prairie buffalo range. There was thus a 'frontal attack' on the buffalo territory from the eastward, along a line extending from the 49th Parallel to the Saskatchewan River near Carlton or Battleford, and a turning movement along their flank practically to the entire depth of their 'formation' from the Cypress Hills westward to the foot of the Rockies. In such circumstances their disappearance seemed—as it was—inevitable, and no catastrophe is required to explain it.[8] At the same time, the testimony of competent observers, who must have known what had happened in the United States, is so cautious and conservative as to justify the assumption that a very great number of buffalo still remained in the Canadian Plains region in the earlier seventies.[9]

Denny states that there were 'no buffalo except wood buffalo' north of the North Saskatchewan River in 1874.[10] While quite possibly correct, this was hearsay only, for at that time Denny had only just reached southern Alberta with the original body of the Mounted Police, and there are some indications that buffalo were—or were believed to be by men deeply interested in their presence—still 'tolerably numerous' about Carlton as late as 1876.[11] John McDougall says that

[7]A very few were seen about Old Wives' Lakes, some distance east, on August 8; the first were killed in the Cypress Hills region on September 1: Denny, *The Law Marches West*, 27-31; Steele, *Forty Years in Canada*, 75-6.

[8]George McDougall, in McDougall, *Forest, Lake and Prairie*, 195; also McDougall MS., 10; Crowfoot (Blackfoot chief) to Denny, 1875: *The Law Marches West*, 99; Governor Laird, in Morris, *Treaties with the Indians of Manitoba*, 92, 93, 169, 170, 177, 183, 185, 188, 233, 262, 268, 284.

[9]Expected to be "nearly extinct after ten years" (Governor Laird, 1877: *ibid,.* 262); "within the next twenty-five years" (Allen, 1876, *American Bisons*, 55, 71).

[10]Denny MS., 38 (not in the printed version).

[11]For information concerning half-breeds selling their land in Red River (1876) and moving to the Duck Lake-Batoche-Carlton country to engage in the buffalo-hunting and pemmican trading. Unfortunately I have been unable, despite inquiry, to learn to what extent the reports of buffalo were verified (see Morton, *Canadian Historical Review*, XV, 1934, 213-18; also G. F. G. Stanley, "The Half-Breed 'Rising' of 1875," *ibid.*, XVII, 1936, 399-412).

There were some buffalo in that region in August 1877, but Governor Laird noted regretfully that the herds were small (Morris, *Treaties with the Indians of Manitoba*, 189, 192, 229).

the Indians between Edmonton and Victoria (now Pakan) some eighty miles down the Saskatchewan, were still 'living chiefly on buffalo' in 1875,[12] and General Sam Steele noted that the herds were 'not far' from Victoria in the autumn of 1874, and that Edmonton enjoyed 'plenty of fresh buffalo meat' in the winter of 1874-75.[13] During the same winter also, between Buffalo Lake and the Hand Hills in central Alberta, 'vast numbers of buffalo covered the country.'[14] So that although the buffalo (in the judgment of a hunter of both northern and southern experience on the Canadian buffalo range) were 'disappearing fast' as early as 1872,[15] there were still absolutely, if not relatively (in comparison with former times), a great many left in the general northern-central territory. Denny notes, however, that on a journey from Calgary to Fort Saskatchewan (below Edmonton) in the Christmas week of 1875, no buffalo were seen north of the Red Deer River, or about half-way,[16] although that winter there were plenty to the south.[17] At Edmonton, however, in January, 1876, Denny found quantities of dried buffalo meat taken in trade the previous summer, and a warehouse at the Fort 'stacked to the roof' with pemmican.[18] His observations confirm the accounts of McDougall and General Steele.

The testimony concerning southern Alberta is similar. John McDougall records 'great herds' and 'dense masses' near Fort Kipp (west of Lethbridge); 'buffalo numerous' near Morley (upper Bow River) and eastward, 'far out' from High River, in the summer of 1874.[19] That autumn, in September and October, Denny likewise records 'thousands' near Whoop-Up (southwest of Lethbridge[20]); and he speaks of them in large bands along Milk River in March, 1875,[21] and again along the Bow River near—apparently east of—Calgary in the

[12]McDougall MS., 20.
[13]Steele, *Forty Years in Canada*, 72, 84-5, 87.
[14]*Ibid.*
[15]Welsh, *The Last Buffalo Hunter*, 136. We may recollect that it was in the more southerly portion of this area that the enormous herd of 1873 took a party 'seven days to travel through it' (above, chap. XIV, note 175).
[16]Denny, *The Law Marches West*, 91.
[17]See below, notes 19 *seq.*
[18]Denny, *The Law Marches West*, 91-2.
[19]McDougall, *Western Trails*, 69, 79, 194, 233.
[20]For Fort Kipp and Whoop-Up, see *Place-Names of Alberta*, 72, 135; also authorities cited above, note 4. On buffalo there in 1874, see Denny, *The Law Marches West*, 36-9, 41, 44, 59-60; Steele, *Forty Years in Canada*, 76; MacInnes, *In the Shadow of the Rockies*, 143-5.
[21]Denny, *The Law Marches West*, 69; *in extenso* (*re* snow), above, chap. VIII, note 86.

following autumn.[22] At the same time (autumn, 1875), McDougall notes 'plenty' just south of High River.[23] He also mentions 'plenty' near Calgary in January, 1876;[24] and another contemporary source states that "that winter the buffalo roamed over the neighbouring plains in countless thousands."[25] It was also in the autumn of that year that Denny mentions buffalo about Blackfoot Crossing, east of Calgary, where the herd containing the supposed white buffalo met their deaths.[26] In the following spring and summer (1877) there were 'plenty,' east of Blackfoot Crossing.[27] Up to this time, the McDougalls lived chiefly on buffalo-meat at Morley,[28] as likewise did the Police (on first-hand authority) up to 1878.[29]

In western Saskatchewan, which constitutes the more easterly portion of this final (southern) Canadian buffalo range, their general history is very similar, although more meagrely localized, since our principal contemporary witness was less of the literary type. Norbert Welsh (1845-1933) recalls that there were buffalo near Fort Walsh (south of the Cypress Hills, practically on the Alberta-Saskatchewan boundary), and apparently in fair quantity, for he alone got one hundred.[30] They were 'travelling westward' near Cypress Hills in December, 1875, when there was a big hunt, and also another in February, 1876.[31] In the spring of 1876, however, his winter's trafficking only yielded fifty robes.[32] In the autumn of 1877, somewhere northeast of Wood Mountain (49° N., 105-107° 30' W.), he saw a herd of seven, of which he shot three, the others being 'too lean.'[33] Next year, 1878, 'there were no buffalo' at Cypress Hills; and at Milk River, there were none "between there and across the Missouri River, whither all the hunters, Indians, half-breeds, and traders, had chased them. . . ."[34] While we shall find that this is not literally correct for the Cypress Hills-Fort Walsh territory as a whole, yet it exhibits a sufficiently lifelike picture of the advance of the final extermination, as it presented

---

[22]Denny, *The Law Marches West*, 83.
[23]McDougall MS., 29.
[24]*Ibid.*, 36-8, 42, 48.
[25]Hughes, *Father Lacombe*, 266.
[26]Denny MS., 40 (discussed above, chap. IV, note 37).
[27]Denny, *The Law Marches West*, 105, 106.
[28]McDougall MS., 33.
[29]Denny MS., 316.
[30]Welsh, *The Last Buffalo Hunter*, ed. Weekes, 150.
[31]*Ibid.*, 158, 166.
[32]*Ibid.*, 169-70.
[33]*Ibid.*, 172.
[34]*Ibid.*, 172, 174, 200-6.

itself to an observer whose base was near Qu'Appelle, to the north-eastward. Those herds which appeared after his dates came from other directions.

During these years the fur traders were exporting large numbers of robes from southern Alberta, and in some cases the situation of the various posts at which these were traded is about the only guide we have to the localities (or tributary localities) where the last buffalo were found in any material numbers. Even in the earlier years of our present inquiry the figures are placed very high. Allen expresses the opinion on the basis of data furnished by J. W. ('Saskatchewan') Taylor, United States consul at Winnipeg (1873), that "it is evident that the destruction of buffalo in the Saskatchewan region in 1872 must have amounted to considerably more than a million, and these mainly cows. . . ."[35] Allen also states (apparently on testimony from the same informant): "The Saskatchewan district sent 17,930 buffalo robes through Minnesota to market during the year ending September 30, 1872; while an equal number was either consumed in the country or despatched to Europe by vessels from York Factory, on Hudson's Bay. . . ."[36]

While the numbers of furs sent southward seem not unreasonable (although one would have liked a more definite basis for his figures[37]) the 'equal number' otherwise disposed of has a rather happy-go-lucky air about it, as if it were let fall by one who did not much care where he allocated these buffalo robes, provided that he could show a sufficiently respectable grand total. Anyone able to indicate with such precision one channel of export should have had a more exact knowledge of the others. Obviously, with these extraordinary numbers, we seem to be all at once in a different world from that of the last decade of the Red River Hunt. I consider that an authenticated disposal of even some 36,000 hides through the United States (doubling the stated amount through Minnesota to allow for the traffic from Fort Benton,

---

[35]Allen, *American Bisons*, 191.

[36]*Ibid.*, 173, 191.

[37]Innis mentions 3500 robes sold at St. Paul (Minnesota) in some years in the fifties by the Red River settlers (*Fur Trade in Canada*, 336). Welsh gives an account of a trip with 300 carts laden with furs, in 1864 (*Last Buffalo Hunter*, 57-65). While the Red River cart carried 900-1000 lb., I have nowhere been able to ascertain its load in numbers of buffalo hides, and other furs were also carried, besides provisions and camp equipment.

The exportation of buffalo robes via Hudson Bay was suggested by Nicholas Garry *circa* 1822 (Innis, *Fur Trade in Canada*, 292). The above is the earliest (suggested) shipment known to me, in any quantity. Cowie mentions robes being sent to Montreal via the U.S., 1870 *seq.* (*Company of Adventurers*, 359).

which was in 1872 much nearer the Canadian field of supply) does not justify an estimate of the destruction as aggregating 'considerably more than a million' buffalo in one year. This estimate appears all the more disproportionate when we take into account the very meagre population of the Saskatchewan territory (even with the Red River hunters included) in 1872. In the terrific southern slaughter taking place in the United States in the very same year, 'thousands of hunters' much better armed than the Indians and half-breeds of Saskatchewan,[38] and certainly not less insatiable in their lust for killing, did not on the highest computation[39] much more than double the suggested Canadian total. This may be classed with the loose rhodomontade of the smoke-room, offered as evidence in the Court of History and accepted without examination.

Exception has been taken to my rejection of this prodigious total, principally on the ground that (in my critic's judgment) I have overlooked the enormous numbers of buffalo killed for food. Particularly, it was pointed out, in relation to the prime article of pemmican that the proportion of fat to the 'beat meat' (amongst which the melted fat is poured) was far greater than was the proportion of fat to lean in the average buffalo cow. Consequently, in order to make a given quantity of pemmican, a large additional number of cows had to be slain for the sake of their fat alone.[40]

This argument overlooks certain very pertinent considerations: (1) It was within the period when *robes*, rather than pemmican, had become the prime consideration, that this alleged holocaust occurred. (2) There is no reason why the additional cows killed *for fat alone* could not furnish a hide just as well as those cows whose entire product of fat and lean was needed. It was in the fall and winter that the buffalo were slain for both robes and food; the season of the 'summer skin,' which was unsuitable for a robe, was considered a season equally unsuitable for meat, almost without exception.[41] (3) In the worst days of the butchery of the 'southern herd' below the Platte, it was computed that not more than one hide in five reached the market.[42] The

---

[38]For estimates of their numbers, see above, chap. XV. notes 33, 69-94, etc.
[39]That of Allen: '2,500,000 per year,' 1870-75 (*American Bisons*, 191).
[40]On the importance of fat for making pemmican, see above, chap. XII, note 72. Such entries recur constantly in the Minutes (1830-43).
[41]For the season of making pemmican, see Simon Fraser, 1806 (above, chap. XII, note 223); also Henry, 1809, in Coues (ed.), *Henry-Thompson Journals*, II, 593. I have found one reference only to the contrary: shooting 'two-year-olds in June and July for pemmican' (Welsh, *Last Buffalo Hunter*, 110). This is *circa* 1867.
[42]See above, chap. XV, notes 77-80.

Saskatchewan hunters included a high proportion of experts reared among buffalo who never resorted to the wasteful methods of the worst of the southern slaughter, such as tearing off the hides with a team and chain. Yet their average of marketed hides (36,000 ? out of 'more than a million') is only about one in twenty-eight! Such a discrepancy is utterly incredible. (4) My critic[43] did not mention what is perhaps the crux of my contention; the impossible variation in the respective ratios of hunters (together with their equipment) to slaughter between the one territory and the other. I can see no reason for revising my original conclusion. At the same time, of course, whether such a huge figure as one million be literally admissible or not, the bare mention makes it virtually certain that a very large number were destroyed.

The opinion was expressed by Governor Alexander Morris, that in 1873 the American traders exported from the Canadian West buffalo robes to the value of fifty thousand dollars.[44] If these were obtained at the prices variously stated as prevailing in 1876 at Fort Macleod and elsewhere, this would represent about 18,000 to 22,000 robes.[45] Professor MacInnes, however, remarks elsewhere concerning this: "There are no reliable figures for the number of buffalo robes exported from Canada by the whisky-traders. After the police came, however, an attempt was made to collect duty on these exports, and though this was attended with a certain measure of success, it is almost certain that between 1874 and 1879 many thousands of robes were exported of which the Police knew nothing, not to mention the bison that were killed by the Indians for their own use. . . ."[46]

Denny (whether upon any sounder authority than popular estimates of the day, I do not know) affirms that in 1875 Messrs. I. G. Baker and Company shipped out '40,000 buffalo-robes and wolf-skins,' the proceeds of their winter's trade, from Macleod and Calgary.[47] Fifteen thousand were later specified (by the same author) as coming

[43]The late Professor R. O. Merriman (of Queen's University) whose courteous criticism and rejoinder by myself are in *Canadian Historical Review*, XV, 1934, 213-18.

[44]MacInnes, *In the Shadow of the Rockies*, 72.

[45]"Enormous numbers of buffalo robes were taken, the Indians receiving not more than two dollars in trade, while the robes realized five times that amount in Chicago . . ." (Steele, *Forty Years in Canada*, 110). A contemporary says: 'Two to three dollars'; but even in 1884!—'only three dollars for a prime robe' (Denny, *The Law Marches West*, 60, 182); 'Scores of thousands' slain during a number of years (McDougall, *Western Trails*, 128).

[46]MacInnes, *In the Shadow of the Rockies*, 145. The smuggling may partly explain the fact that the North-West Territories' customs receipts, from March, 1877, to July, 1878, totalled $526.00! (Black, *History of Saskatchewan*, 196.)

[47]Denny MS., 272.

from Macleod in that year's returns.[48] Without mentioning any exact figures, Steele states that 'enormous numbers' of buffalo-robes were taken at Macleod, and 'a good trade' was done at Fort Calgary, in 1876,[49] since the buffalo were plentiful near both points. Denny also records that during the same year (that is, 1875-76) 'an indefinite quantity' was taken in the north by the Hudson's Bay Company,[50] as the immense quantity of pemmican seen by him at Fort Edmonton in January, 1876, would naturally tend to suggest.[51] One of the earlier historians of Alberta states that there were 'about 30,000' robes sent from Macleod and Fort Walsh conjointly in 1878, and 'less than 14,000' in 1879.[52] A later scholar quotes what are evidently the same estimates in more detailed form.[53]

Year	Fort Macleod	Fort Walsh
1877	30,000	....
1878	13,000	18,375
1879	5,767	8,617

Although they have not survived in more precise form, some figures may possibly be added for Fort Walsh in 1877.[54]

Despite the serious inroads which slaughter on such a scale made upon the Indians' principal source of food, and although the authorities in the West were ill equipped to feed the Indians when that supply should fail, nothing was done for years towards conserving the buffalo resources. The date of the first attempt at conservation (1877) makes it difficult to resist the conclusion that nothing would have been done merely as a check to the hide hunters. In that year, however, an important political event increased the numbers of the buffalo-using Indians in Canada very considerably. In 1877, after having defeated the rash and foolhardy Custer and his force on the Little Bighorn in June of the previous year, Sitting Bull and a large number of his Sioux followers crossed the border into Canada. To what extent the law

[48]Denny, *The Law Marches West*, 60, 86. Messrs. I. G. Baker estimated their entire total from Fort Benton in 1876 as 'about 75,000' (correspondence to Hornaday, in "Extermination of the American Bison," 506).

[49]Steele, *Forty Years in Canada*, 110.

[50]Denny, *The Law Marches West*, 86.

[51]Above, note 18.

[52]MacRae, *History of Alberta*, I, 377.

[53]MacInnes, *In the Shadow of the Rockies*, 145; Diller, "Early Economic Development of Alberta," chap. IV.

[54]'Plenty meat there,' spring, 1877 (Denny, *The Law Marches West*, 126).

which was enacted that year reflected the wishes or influence of the hide hunters, it is impossible to say. It was, perhaps, not unnatural that while the Indians ardently desired protection for the buffalo against white hunters, protection against themselves was very distasteful.[55] The ordinance of 1877 forbade:

. . . the use of buffalo pounds, the wanton destruction of buffalo at any season, the killing of animals under two years of age, or the slaughter of female buffalo during a stated close season—briefer for Indians than for others. This law was framed in the best interests of the Indians and halfbreeds, but their very destitution made the protection of the waning herds a hardship, and it was found necessary to repeal the measure in the following year. . . .[56]

The condition of the buffalo herds in 1877 seems to have varied from one locality to another. Professor John Macoun speaks of the hills, 'covered by countless thousands';[57] a general expression probably, but surely indicating considerable numbers. A later Report (of 1881 and 1882) by Commissioner Irvine, observes: "In 1877 it must be remembered that large numbers of buffalo were to be found in the country . . .";[58] and Denny mentions 'plenty of buffalo' near Fort Walsh in October of that year.[59] Denny was evidently at Fort Walsh when the famous conference between Sitting Bull and the representatives from the United States was held there; and was an eye-witness to the contempt with which the famous chief treated General Terry and his colleagues in the presence of Colonel Irvine (or Macleod—whichever was the commanding officer at the post on this occasion).[60] What 'plenty' precisely signified it is difficult to say, but Lieutenant-Governor Laird's report of his journey from Battleford to Blackfoot Crossing (on the Bow River, about 60 miles east of Calgary) reads in part:

For the first day we followed a trail leading southward, but afterward our course was directed across the trackless plains until we approached

[55]Morris, Treaties with the Indians of Manitoba, 191, 193, 227, 228, 236, 237, 241, 258, 259, 267, 271, 272.
    [56]Black, History of Saskatchewan, 196; cf. ibid., 247; see also Oliver (ed.), Canadian North-West, II, 1046, 1054; MacInnes, In the Shadow of the Rockies, 145; Stanley, Birth of Western Canada, 222.
    [57]Macoun, Manitoba, 342.
    [58]Quoted by Denny, The Law Marches West, 168.
    [59]Ibid., 120-7.
    [60]'Irvine' in Black, History of Saskatchewan 186; see also Blue, Alberta Past and Present, I, 77; Steele, Forty Years in Canada, 123-30; Denny MS., 299 (the last—and perhaps Steele also—an eyewitness); 'Col. Macleod' in Denny, The Law Marches West, 126. On Sitting Bull, cf. Red Cloud and U.S. Army officers, 1866 (Hebard and Brininstool, The Bozeman Trail, I, 267).

nearer our destination. On the third day out we first sighted buffalo, and every day subsequently that we travelled, except the last, we saw herds of the animals. Most of the herds, however, were small, and we remarked with regret that very few calves of this season were to be seen. We observed portions of many buffalo carcasses on our route, from not a few of which the peltries had not been removed. From this circumstance, as well as from the fact that many of the skins are made into parchments and coverings for lodges, I concluded that the export of buffalo robes from the territories does not indicate even one-half the number of those valuable animals slaughtered annually in our country. . . .[61]

The failure of the afore-mentioned conference to induce the self-expatriated Sioux to return to their former haunts led to the adoption of a policy by the government at Washington or its military chiefs in the West, which is somewhat caustically described by a recent Western historian:

In 1878 the United States Government decided to starve Sitting Bull and his followers into surrender. A cordon of half-breeds, Indians, and American soldiers was therefore formed, and ordered to drive the buffalo back whenever the herds started to come north, and it was there, shut in by this cordon from their favourite grazing grounds on the Bow River, that the last great slaughter of the bison took place.[62] Had such a policy been adopted by the Canadian Government, it can be well imagined how furious their neighbours would have been. It seems rather unjust, to put it mildly, that because the Americans had failed to handle their own Indians success-fully, Canadian Indians were therefore to be afflicted with famine, and the task of the Canadian Mounted Police rendered almost impossible; for the Canadian Indians, as well as the Sioux, looked to the buffalo for their food. . . .[63]

While this was only too true of the buffalo as a whole, there must have been a certain number remaining in the country, perhaps in isolated bands, for Steele states that 'many Indians were hunting buf-falo' near Fort Walsh in May, 1878.[64] Possibly there was more 'hunting' than finding, for Denny says about the same time that the buffalo were 'gone' from the Macleod country and but 'few' were about Fort Walsh.[65] Yet, as we have seen, the following winter's returns totalled 14,384 robes from those very points.[66] The supply was not sufficient,

[61]Morris, *Treaties with the Indians of Manitoba*, 252; cf. 'one-half' with one in 28!

[62]This, of course, is incorrect. The 'final' slaughter in the U.S. had barely begun in 1878, as we have seen in the preceding chapter.

[63]MacInnes, *In the Shadow of the Rockies*, 146. On 'military' reasons for extermination in the U.S., see Appendix H, "Buffalo, Indian, and Legislation."

[64]Steele, *Forty Years in Canada*, 131.

[65]Denny, *The Law Marches West*, 133.

[66]See above, note 53.

however, to serve the hungry Indians for very long. Their predicament is described in an excerpt from the Press of the time:

The principal event that has brought about the existing state of things is undoubtedly the presence on the hunting-grounds formerly occupied by our own people, of the large bands of United States Indians who recently entered upon them. Their numbers are variously estimated at from 6000 to 10,000 souls, and the buffalo killed amount to hundreds daily. This wholesale slaughter and the exclusion of our Indians from their hunting-grounds, are undoubtedly the cause of much distress that prevailed last summer, and gave rise to rumours of coming trouble. Providentially, great bands of fat buffalo came down from the mountains in the autumn, and furnished a good supply of food for the winter, thus removing all cause of apprehension for the present. . . .[67]

Denny writes: "It became apparent in 1879 that the day of the buffalo was over, although for a few years afterwards small bands of stragglers drifted north into Canada. . . ." He adds that in that year the great herds had moved south, never to return, and that many Canadian Indians followed the buffalo to Montana. He says that "the main herd of buffalo now remaining were surrounded by most of the southern Indians, together with those of Canada, in a section of country south from Milk River to the Little Rockies and the Bear Paw Mountains, and across the Missouri River to the Judith Basin; and the state of the tribes of plain Indians of Canada in their own country was bordering on starvation. . . ." In July, 1879, "there were no buffalo in the country."[68] Here again, while this was not quite literally correct, it was substantially so. Professor Macoun, who was in the West at the time, confirms the broad outlines of the picture. "Where the hills were covered with countless thousands in 1877, the Blackfeet were dying of starvation in 1879. . . ."[69] Elsewhere he gives a graphic description of the starvation conditions in the Hand Hills country (south of Buffalo Lake, central Alberta) in September, 1879, and of the Indians' almost miraculous relief by the sudden appearance of a herd.[70] This may have been the herd mentioned by Colonel Macleod in his Report for 1879: "Once during the summer a very large herd crossed the line, east of the Cypress Hills, and smaller bands have come into the country, in some instances making their way north to the South Saskatchewan. . . . During the spring and early summer the condition of our Indians was

[67]*Saskatchewan Herald* (Battleford, Saskatchewan), February 10, 1879; in Black, *History of Saskatchewan*, 184.
[68]Denny, *The Law Marches West*, 135.
[69]Macoun, *Manitoba*, 342.
[70]Macoun, *Autobiography*, 149-50.

desperate in the extreme. Buffalo, their only source of supply, had moved south, and their horses were too weak to follow. . . ."[71]

Elsewhere, Denny himself writes: "In the fall and winter of 1879 the Indians belonging to Canada began to return from the American side where they had gone to follow the buffalo, who had now left the North West Territories for ever. True, a few scattered animals were found on rare occasion in the country between Wood Mountain and Battleford as late as 1884, but the buffalo as a means of subsistence for the Indian was gone. . . ."[72]

General Sam Steele states that in November, 1879, the buffalo were on their way northward, returning into Canada, when the Canadian Indians, in their uncontrollable hunger and impatience, got in front of the herd and hunted it, turning it back into Montana, whence it never again returned.[73] I should not be disposed to question this on any general grounds of the 'impossibility of turning buffalo from their course.' Investigation resolves that supposition into thin air, as we have seen.[74] Perhaps another buffalo authority may be quoted by way of comment. Buffalo Jones says:

. . . the buffalo always migrate two or three hundred miles north in the spring, returning late in the fall to their winter feeding grounds. Aware of this fact, I had learned by years of experience that when they were thus on their annual move it was easier to kill those animals at the head of the herd than those at the rear, as the latter always stampeded and rushed by if I opened fire upon them, while the leaders if shot at would never turn back any considerable distance, evidently persistently opposed to retracing their steps toward the place from whence they had started. . . .[75]

In so far as credibility is concerned (despite their double contradiction, in time-direction and in conduct) I am prepared to take both statements as they stand. For it is quite conceivable that one or two hunters might fail to turn a herd which a large band might turn with little difficulty. and in that respect the behaviour of Steele's herd merely furnishes an additional commentary on those mythical throngs which nothing could divert. As a historical movement, however, it lacks confirmation, and seems to conflict with the general consensus of testimony at this time. It is possible that Steele may have applied the

[71]Denny, *The Law Marches West*, 135.   [72]*Ibid.*, 143.
[73]Steele, *Forty Years in Canada*, 146-8. 'Practically extinct,' 1879 (Blue, *Alberta Past and Present*, I, 178). Dr. John Maclean (Edmonton, 1926) 'saw a herd of perhaps 100,000,' apparently autumn, 1879 (*Edmonton Journal*, November 17, 1926). But *where*? Seemingly somewhere in Montana, northward from the Missouri River. This could still be a usual sight in that vicinity then.
[74]See above, chap. VI, notes 66-82, etc.
[75]*Buffalo Jones' Forty Years*, 95.

tactics of the 'Cordon' described above to a different year and to other Indians.[76]

Denny sums up the situation in this region at this particular time: "For a year or two, the Indians continued to leave their reserves in large numbers in search of the vanished buffalo. It was hard to make them believe that they were gone for ever, and for years they believed that they would re-appear. They had a legend that the buffalo came originally from a hole in the ground in the centre of a lake in the north, and that on the advent of the white man they had re-entered it and would ultimately re-emerge. . . ."[77]

In 1880, in the Wood Mountain country, the buffalo were gone, and in 1881 in the south, the Indians were still looking for them where none existed. "It was late in the summer of 1881 that the Assiniboines and Crees left Fort Walsh, and went south in the hopes of still finding buffalo along the Missouri River,"[78] whence they returned in a starving condition. Another resident in the country at that time says: "During the winter of 1881, when the buffalo on the Missouri were returning to the Chinook region of Southern Alberta, the Crow and other [sic] Sioux Indian tribes set the prairie on fire, and the herds were driven southwards towards the Missouri and Yellowstone rivers, where they were corralled by the Indians and white people and exterminated. . . ."[79]

There were apparently buffalo yet remaining in noticeable quantity. A modern historian of Saskatchewan writes thus:

Senator John G. Turriff states that in 1881 there were herds of buffalo on the open plain between Moose Mountain and the American Boundary. In May, 1882, as he was coming from Manitoba into the Territories, he met the last buffalo hunt. They had been west of Moose Mountain and were returning. There were several hundred Red River carts, and they had stores of buffalo robes and pemmican. The Senator ought to know, as he bought supplies of these commodities. This would be the last organized buffalo hunt. . . .[80]

[76]Denny should surely have known of this occurrence. He was feeding the starving Indians at the time (*The Law Marches West*, 143 seq.; MacInnes, *In the Shadow of the Rockies*, 88, 147, 155, 162; Hughes, *Father Lacombe*, 243).

[77]Denny, *The Law Marches West*, 147, 152, 202. In 1885, 'if the white men could be driven out, the buffalo would return' (Hughes, *Father Lacombe*, 304).

[78]Denny, *The Law Marches West*, 127, 262, etc.

[79]Maclean, *Canadian Savage Folk*, 108. Fires are mentioned in 1878 (Diller, "Early Economic Development of Alberta," V, 5); also in 1879, 'Chief One Spot,' Blood Indian, (cited *Edmonton Journal*, January 27, 1932) is reported as saying, 'Buffalo go south like always do for winter feed.' In the passage quoted in the present note from Maclean, they were going north.

[80]Hawkes, *Saskatchewan and her People*, I, 57. The author's comments seem to indicate some skepticism, which I share concerning 'herds' of any size, and even more deeply, of the 'Hunt.' His phraseology certainly implies the Red

The same student cites the well-known missionary, Father Hugonard, as stating that the last buffalo he saw were one or two along Moose Jaw Creek in 1881, but that he believed there were stragglers as late as 1884.[81] An even more recent historian says that about 400 head were killed south of Wood Mountain (about 49° N., 107° W.) 'in the middle of 1882.'[82] This *could* have occurred in the locality mentioned, up to the close of hunting (February) in the winter of 1882-83. But it conflicts very materially with a mass of more credible contemporary testimony, which mentions the cordon formed along the northern border of the remaining buffalo range at that time. Both for public and private reasons, such a line, we may well believe, would certainly be maintained so closely that a herd 400 strong would have little chance of escape.[83] I suspect there has been some exaggeration of the numbers or a confusion in the date. There is a further fundamental objection with which I shall deal shortly.

In a letter which appeared in the press more recently than any of the foregoing (1938), the question of the possible extirpation of the Canadian buffalo by disease was again raised. The discussion of disease *per se* will receive attention before the conclusion of the present essay.[84] What here concern us are (1) the apparent date of the evidence adduced by the correspondent in support of his contention; and (2) the numbers of buffalo which were encountered at that era. According to the correspondent, when he was a lad of about twenty (in a year which is not specified, but which from the context, grammatical and otherwise, can only be 1883), he accompanied his father, a surveyor, on a trip between the Cypress Hills and Battleford, following a fairly direct route along which (judged by 'old-timer' standards) travellers were fairly numerous. They found masses of dead buffalo covering several acres so closely "that one could jump from one carcass to another." They also saw living buffalo: "four different herds and several small bunches from six to ten in number." When such round numbers are specified for 'small bunches' as distinct from 'herds,' surely the latter term must indicate some respectable and material size, say 50 to 100 in a herd.[85]

River Hunt, of which 1874 is my latest notice. They had only been west of Moose Mountain, and were *returning* in May! Compare the chronological and geographical evidence in chap. XIV, and the present chapter, at large.

[81]Hawkes, *Saskatchewan and her People*, I, 366.

[82]MacInnes, *In the Shadow of the Rockies*, 145.

[83]See above, chap. XVI, note 37.

[84]See below, Appendix J, "Buffalo and Disease."

[85]H. M. Starkey (of Seattle), *Regina Daily Star*, July 28, 1938; reply by the present writer, *ibid.*, August 26, 1938. I am much indebted to Mrs. Margaret Complin of Regina for bringing this to my attention. See below, note 98.

There is one damning and unanswerable objection to the acceptance of almost all of this vague and immensely post-dated reminiscence. It is perhaps particularly applicable where the memorable phenomena were encountered by men of education, like the correspondent's father. At that era the disappearance of the buffalo, and whether it was transitory, exaggerated, local, or final, were prime topics of the hour; yet this type of witness had nothing to say of these matters when they were of current importance. As we have seen, men were in general much more disposed to antedate than to postpone 'the finish of the buffalo,' because they based their opinions upon accounts of narrow local conditions. Yet these last first-hand observers of the buffalo neither perceived any significance themselves in their experiences, nor happened to mention them to anyone who would; their observations aroused no contemporary press publicity, like that produced by other testimonies which thus have gone upon permanent record. A 'conspiracy of silence' could scarcely effect more. The evidence presented to support their theories fifty-five years later is nothing more than the familiar argument of 'periodic recurrence': the mere repetition of certain assertions supposedly proves their truth.[86] One wonders if the famous legend of the 'hoop snake' has yet ceased to 'recur.' Geography, chronology, and details appear to be hopelessly jumbled.

Hornaday sums up the evidence on the extermination of the buffalo in Western Canada in the following passage. I prefer to quote his own words:

In the British Possessions, where the country was immense and game of all kinds except buffalo very scarce indeed; where, in the language of Professor Kenaston, the explorer, "there was a great deal of country around every wild animal," the buffalo constituted the main dependence of the Indians, who would not cultivate the soil at all, and of the half-breeds, who would not so long as they could find buffalo. Under such circumstances the

---

[86]In this instance, the recurrence of the explanation of "some disease, the same thing that killed them all over the west . . . ." (H. M. Starkey, *Regina Daily Star*, July 28, 1938). My request for evidence of this (in rebuttal of data furnished by myself) elicited no response. See note on "Reminiscence"; conclusion of chap. XV.

With reference to the same (?) year, 1883, Dr. Edmond Melchior Eberts of Montreal, in a most interesting letter informs me that when he visited the Hudson's Bay Company's warehouse in Winnipeg with his father at that time, there were said to be 250,000 buffalo robes stored there. Dr. Eberts does not himself vouch for these figures. As a stock, held for higher prices pending the (actually contemporaneous) termination of the slaughter, such a total is credible, but not as any one year's returns at that era. On the spectacular rise in prices, about 1884, see Garretson, *American Bison*, 157.

buffaloes of the British Possessions were hunted much more vigorously and persistently than those of the United States, where there was such an abundant supply of deer, elk, antelope, and other game for the Indians to feed upon, and a paternal government to support them with annuities besides.[87] Quite contrary to the prevailing idea of the people of the United States, viz., that there were great herds of buffaloes in existence in the Saskatchewan country long after ours had all been destroyed, the herds of British America had been almost totally exterminated by the time the final slaughter of our northern herd was inaugurated by the opening of the Northern Pacific Railway in 1880. The Canadian Pacific Railway played no part whatever in the extermination of the bison in the British Possessions, for it had already taken place. The half-breeds of Manitoba, the Plains Crees of Qu'Appelle, and the Blackfeet of the South Saskatchewan country swept bare a great belt of country stretching east and west between the Rocky Mountains and Manitoba. . . . The buffalo had disappeared from that entire region before 1879 and left the Blackfeet Indians on the verge of starvation. A few thousand buffaloes still remained in the country around the head-waters of the Battle River, between the North and South Saskatchewan, but they were surrounded and attacked from all sides, and their numbers diminished very rapidly until all were killed.

The latest information I have been able to obtain in regard to the disappearance of this northern band has been kindly furnished by Prof. C. A. Kenaston, who in 1881, and also in 1883, made a thorough exploration of the country between Winnipeg and Fort Edmonton for the Canadian Pacific Railway Company. His four routes between the two points named covered a vast scope of country, several hundred miles in width. In 1881, at Moose Jaw, 75 miles southeast of The Elbow of the South Saskatchewan, he saw a party of Cree Indians, who had just arrived from the northwest with several carts laden with fresh buffalo meat. At Fort Saskatchewan, on the North Saskatchewan River, just above[88] Edmonton, he saw a party of English sportsmen who had recently been hunting on the Battle and Red Deer Rivers, between Edmonton and Fort Kalgary [sic], where they had found buffaloes, and killed as many as they cared to slaughter. In one afternoon they killed fourteen, and could have killed more had they been more blood-thirsty. In 1883 Professor Kenaston found the fresh trail of a band of twenty-five or thirty buffaloes at the Elbow of the South Saskatchewan. Excepting in the above instances he saw no further traces of buffalo, nor did he hear of the existence of any in all the country he explored. In 1881 he saw many Cree Indians at Fort Qu'Appelle in a starving condition, and there was no pemmican or buffalo meat at the fort. In 1883, however, a little pemmican found its way to Winnipeg, where it sold at 15 cents per pound; an exceedingly high price. It had been made that year, evidently in the month of April, as he purchased it in May for his journey.[89]

[87]See on this, Appendix S.

[88]So in Hornaday; it is twenty miles below Edmonton.

[89]Hornaday, "Extermination of the American Bison," 504-5. I have been unable to obtain any further information concerning Professor Kenaston. Rev. Father Doucet, O.M.I., states that "the last large herd was killed by a band of Cree Indians near Red Deer in 1880" (Edmonton Journal, March 16, 1935).

484   THE NORTH AMERICAN BUFFALO

Hornaday has sketched the appalling consequences of the extermination among some of the Canadian Indians:

During the winter of 1886-'87, destitution and actual starvation prevailed to an alarming extent among certain tribes of Indians in the Northwest Territory who once lived bountifully on the buffalo. A terrible tale of suffering in the Athabaska and Peace River country has recently (1888) come to the minister of the interior of the Canadian government, in the form of a petition signed by the bishop of that diocese, six clergymen and missionaries, and several justices of the peace. It sets forth that "owing to the destruction of game, the Indians, both last winter and last summer, have been in a state of starvation. They are now in a complete state of destitution, and are utterly unable to provide themselves with clothing, shelter, ammunition, or food for the coming winter." The petition declares that on account of starvation, and consequent cannibalism, a party of twenty-nine Cree Indians was reduced to three in the winter of 1886.[90] Of the Fort Chippewyan Indians, between twenty and thirty starved to death last winter, and the death of many more was hastened by want of food and by famine diseases. Many other Indians—Crees, Beavers, and Chippewyans—at almost all points where there are missions or trading posts, would certainly have starved to death but for the help given them by the traders and missionaries at those places. It is now declared by the signers of the memorial that scores of families, having lost their heads by starvation, are now perfectly helpless, and during the coming winter must either starve to death or eat one another unless help comes. Heart-rending stories of suffering and cannibalism continue to come in from what was once the buffalo plains.

If ever thoughtless people were punished for their reckless improvidence, the Indians and half-breeds of the Northwest Territory are now paying the penalty for the wasteful slaughter of the buffalo a few short years ago. The buffalo is his own avenger, to an extent his remorseless slayers little dreamed he ever could be.[91]

'Large' is, of course, a relative term, and there might have been more than one 'last herd.' The locality suggests that this might possibly have been the band mentioned by Professor Kenaston.

[90]Hornaday subjoins a footnote ("Extermination of the American Bison," 527): "It was the Cree Indians who used to practice impounding buffaloes, slaughtering a penful of two hundred head at a time with the most fiendish glee, and leaving all but the very choicest of the meat to putrefy." Not the Crees alone, as we shall see.

He writes elsewhere: "And now, as we read of the appalling slaughter, one can scarcely repress the feeling of grim satisfaction that arises when we also read that many of the ex-slaughterers are almost starving for the millions of pounds of fat and juicy buffalo meat they wasted a few years ago. . . . People who are so utterly senseless as to wantonly destroy their own source of food, as the Indians have done, certainly deserve to starve . . ." (ibid., 480-1, 482). One need envy no man the satisfaction that arises in his bosom, however momentarily, at such a retribution as that!

[91]Ibid., 526-7. Cf. the following (Blackfoot): "In 1883-'84 some 600 of those in Montana died of sheer starvation in consequence of the sudden extinction of the buffalo . . ." (Mooney, "Siksika," in Handbook of American Indians, II,

It is difficult to transcribe such a passage calmly, half a century afterward. After reading the above and nothing else, who would suppose that a white skin hunter had even been heard of on the American continent!

Considering the ruthlessness of the commercial slaughter (that is, for hides) and the desperate plight of the unfortunate people in consequence, occasional individuals or small herds of the species survived to astonishingly late dates in various parts of Western Canada. Concerning Manitoba, Seton writes: "In 1882, when I first went to live in Western Manitoba, the prairie everywhere was dotted with old Buffalo skulls. Many had horns on them, but none had hair. Their condition and local tradition agree in fixing from 1860 to 1865 as the epoch when the last Buffalo were killed on the Big Plain . . ." (that is, near Carberry, Manitoba, 106 miles west of Winnipeg).[92]

He adds elsewhere, however, "In 1875 a few stragglers were said to be on the Big Plain. . . ."[93] The records of distance travelled from Fort Garry in 1862, 1864, and other years before encountering (or apparently expecting to encounter) any,[94] may lead us to believe that the buffalo of 1865 as well as those of 1875 were mere stragglers. Seton gives further interesting instances:

In 1879, about November 7, Dr. F. W. Shaw of Carberry, tells me that as he was going to Rapid City from the Big Plain, he saw the tracks of three buffalo at a place about four miles north of Grand Valley [that is, Brandon, Manitoba]. They had been travelling northward, and a few hours before had been seen . . . crossing the Assiniboine [River]. . . .[95]

In 1882, C. C. Helliwell, of Brandon, saw eight in the Souris region. . . .[96]

In the fall of 1883, according ot A. S. Barton, of Boissevain [about 100 miles southwest of Winnipeg] an old Buffalo Bull crossed the Souris Plain from the southeast, going northwesterly toward Plum Creek. It was pursued . . . on the Antlers of the Souris, but was never overtaken. About this time an old bull, probably the same, was seen near the site of the present town of Souris. My informant, H. W. O. Boger, says he saw it in daylight as it crossed his farm. It was trotting . . .[97] and went off north-west. . . . This was the last seen in the region. It was recorded in all the newspapers. . . .[98]

570-1). "In 1885, the Métis (half-breeds) of Wood Mountain and Willow Bunch were in a half-starving condition, owing to the recent collapse of the trade in buffalo skins . . ." (Black, *History of Saskatchewan*, 389).

[92]Seton, *Life-Histories of Northern Animals*, I, 256.   [93]*Ibid.*, I, 256.

[94]See above, chap. XIV, notes 83-5, 167-72, etc.

[95]Seton, *Life-Histories of Northern Animals*, I, 256.   [96]*Ibid.*

[97]Re 'trotting,' see Inman (chap. XV, note 62); and cf. chap. VI, note 149.

[98]Seton, *Life-Histories of Northern Animals*, I, 256-8; *Game Animals*, III, 649. *In re* newspapers, cf. my remarks above (notes 85-6), on H. M. Starkey, 1883 (?).

Farther west, in what we have seen was more properly the region of the last of the Canadian wild plains buffalo, there are several notices which appear to be well authenticated and reliable. In June or July, 1884, Dr. J. B. Tyrrell, the eminent Canadian geologist and explorer, while 'hunting for dinosaur fossils' in the region south of the Hand Hills along the lower Red Deer River valley—where they have since been unearthed in such numbers—encountered a band of about twenty buffalo.[99] Another Canadian scientist writes:

In October, 1884, a Canadian Pacific tri-weekly train from Calgary to Winnipeg was boarded at way-stations by passengers laden with rifles, saddles, and other equipment till it was crowded to capacity. Inquiry elicited the information that *seven* buffalo had been reported in the Cypress Hills. This was undoubtedly the last remnant of the vast herd which had once roved the prairies of Western Canada, and, inspired by a desire to slaughter at least fifty and probably one hundred, hunters immediately started for the town of Maple Creek, as being the nearest station on the Canadian Pacific—then the only railway in what is now the province of Saskatchewan.

It is gratifying to note that, so far as known, these sportsmen were unsuccessful, and this small herd survived for several years. It is believed that it increased to twenty or twenty-five, but eventually it was exterminated by Indians. . . .[100]

A gentleman whose Western recollections reach back to the buffalo era, states that six animals—locally considered as 'the last herd'—were killed in Wood Mountain, south of Indian Head, Saskatchewan, in 1886.[101] The early files of Alberta's first newspaper, contain the following notice (August, 1887): "The *Medicine Hat Times* reports the finding of a fresh trail of fifty buffalo near that town. . . ."[102] This notice must also belong to 1887: "An Indian just in [? to Winnipeg] from Manitou or Devil's Lake, about 100 miles west of Battleford, reports having seen four buffalo and tracked fourteen others in that neighbourhood. . . ."[103]

[99]Loundon, *A Canadian Geologist*, 53.

[100]J. W. (? James White, Ottawa), footnote in Hewitt, *Conservation of the Wild Life of Canada*, 121.

[101]*Ex inf.* Dr. Edmond Melchior Eberts, Montreal, to the author. I am very much indebted to Dr. Eberts for his courtesy in furnishing a total stranger with this information.

[102]"Fifty Years Ago," *Edmonton Bulletin*, August 6, 1937. From the files of the *Edmonton Bulletin*, established 1880, by the late Hon. Frank Oliver (Edmonton, 1876-1933).

[103]*Nor'-West Farmer and Miller*, January, 1888, quoted by Hawkes, *Saskatchewan and her People*, I, 57. Manito Lake is one of the commonest Western place-names. This is the Manito Lake, situated about four miles east of the Alberta-Saskatchewan provincial boundary. It is visible from the train at Artland,

A recent writer in a British periodical states that in July, 1888, "three gaunt bulls were killed in the valley of the Red Deer River, east of the Edmonton-Calgary trail. . . ."[104] Seton writes as follows: "James M. Macoun tells me that in 1888 (early July) he saw the meat of eight Buffalo Bulls that were killed between Methy Portage and Lac la Biche. They were the last seen there. . . ."[105] In a contemporary history of southern Alberta, I find the following: "The Game Report for 1888 states that of all the countless herds of bison that had formerly roamed the Territories, only six animals were known to be in existence, two old bulls in the Wood Mountain district; three cows and a bull between the Red Deer and Battle Rivers. . . ."[106]

Seton further notes an occurrence, which may refer to the latter band in the preceding instance: "In 1889, according to the Rev. J. A. McLoughlin [should be McLachlan], missionary at Victoria, north of the Saskatchewan,[107] and W. Hine, a band of eleven was found in the Hand Hills, five hundred miles west of Manitoba. Five were killed by Indian acquaintances of McLoughlin's. He saw part of the spoils, including a head, which sold at Winnipeg for $120.00. The other six were not accounted for. . . ."[108]

Some years ago the Alberta Press recorded the death of Samuel McKay, aged 80, 'ex-fur trader,' of Wild Horse, who was "believed to

Saskatchewan, on the main line of the Canadian National (ex-Grand Trunk Pacific). This is Henry's 'Lac du Diable,' of 1809. 'South of Battle River and southeast of Fort Vermilion' (its exact situation): Coues (ed.), *Henry-Thompson Journals*, II, 553, 606. Farther south toward Swift Current (Saskatchewan), J. D. Nicholson, then of the Police, records a small herd of five, also in 1887 (Horan, *On the Side of the Law*, 22).

[104]John Peter Turner, *Geographical Magazine* (England), August, 1936; *précis* in *Montreal Gazette, August* 13, 1936. For this and several other clippings, I am much indebted to my friends, Mr. and Mrs. D. Walter Thomson, of Ottawa. This is the exact locality where my parents settled six years later, July, 1894. There were no residents within twenty miles of us who dated back to 1888. Big game was still plentiful along the Red Deer River; but I never heard any allusion to buffalo as recently as 1888.

[105]Seton, *Life-Histories of Northern Animals*, I, 297; *Game Animals*, III, 669.

[106]MacInnes, *In the Shadow of the Rockies*, 145.

[107]Victoria is now Pakan, Alberta, some 80 miles or so northeast from Edmonton; the McDougalls' original mission home, founded by them in 1863. See *Place-Names of Alberta*, 98.

[108]Seton, *Life-Histories of Northern Animals*, I, 297; *Game Animals*, III, 669. I have since received the following from my friend, Henry Stelfox, Esq., of Rocky Mountain House, who is in close touch with Indian sources: "Many years ago an Indian told me that nine years after the last wild buffalo was killed on the prairies south and S.E. of here, they discovered about 300 buffalo in the Clearwater Valley about 70 miles southwest of here . . ." (correspondence to the author, July 22, 1942). It seems almost certain that in this territory they would be wood buffalo (see above, chap. XII, notes 171-95); also note 89.

have killed the last buffalo in Alberta."[109] Such claims are inherently incapable of proof, and may be relegated to the familiar 'last buffalo' category of which we have seen something.[110]

One cannot but regret profoundly that McDougall's invaluable reminiscences remained uncompleted at their venerated author's death in 1917. The latest instalment, upon which he was then at work, brings his life-story down only to 1876.[111] It is very probable that his detailed recitals of the years of the buffalo extermination in Western Canada would have added considerably to our reliable historical evidence for that epoch.[112]

[109]*Edmonton Journal,* April 15, 1932.

[110]See above, chap. XI, notes 137-43; chap. XV, note 119; chap. XVI, note 59.

[111]Cited in these pages as McDougall MS. (in Alberta Provincial Legislative Library, Edmonton, Alberta).

[112]There has been a considerable amount of loose, irresponsible rhetoric on this subject, linked with the buffalo at large, in 'popular' journalism: "The Story of the Buffalo" (*Montreal Gazette,* August 13, 1936); "The Story of the Bison" (editorial, in *The Times* (London), November 18, 1937); "I Re-Discover Canada" (Harwood Steele, *Winnipeg Evening Tribune,* August 21, 1937); "Ivanhoe," *in re* Donald Culross Peattie (a review, citing the *Winnipeg Tribune;* in *Edmonton Journal,* April 21, 1938). A later one yet has buffalo about James Bay, Ontario! G. C. Porter, "Revive Buffalo Hunts" in *Vancouver Province,* May 26, 1944).

In these productions as a class, chronology, geography, and caution are flung away, even by Canadians writing on Canada. There is an incredible slovenliness: 'overland trains' between Manitou and Morden (southern Manitoba) in 18-3 (1803 in *Canada Cavalcade*); in 1883 an unfinished branch line! 'Douglas, 120 miles *north* of Winnipeg on the C.P.R. main line' (*ibid.*). The people of Manitoba in the 1870's 'knew them so well that half the population lived on buffalo' (Steele; see above, chap. XIV, notes 170-1). These matters are not, of course, strictly relevant to the history of the buffalo, but they cast suspicion on other really relevant particulars from these sources. The least impossible is the editorial in *The Times;* the most utterly extravagant is *Canada Cavalcade.*

I have noted some of their assertions above, in the particular relationships in which they apply. As history, their dogmatisms make them worthless; they have some value as a reflection of a state of mind, which in respect of buffalo thinks in superlatives and to which nothing is impossible. Compare my note at the conclusion of chap. XV, on loose, undocumented reminiscence; the foregoing, at second-hand or worse, is inferior even to that.

Chapter XVIII

THE NUMBERS OF THE BUFFALO: SOME SUGGESTIONS
TOWARDS THE TOTAL AGGREGATE

I T is not my intention in the present chapter to attempt to present any definite conclusion of my own concerning an approximate total number of buffalo at any period. In the nature of the case, such conclusions could only be highly conjectural, the more so since the data upon which they must be based are also exceedingly conjectural and in some instances—in my opinion—more than a little improbable. So far as I have been able to discover, two attempts to estimate total numbers have been made. They are of very unequal value: only the second, by Ernest Thompson Seton, is scientific in method. Along with these two broader surveys I shall present to the reader a number of miscellaneous records of buffalo slaughter for specific years, which have been gleaned incidentally from various sources. Here again, while they may have come down to us as fairly specific accounts—as, for instance, a statement from some witness of personally good reputation that the American Fur Company handled so many thousand buffalo robes in a certain year—we have no means of knowing upon just what authority this information reached our witness, whether from the books of the company, or as the irresponsible estimate of some unknown attaché, or in some other form.

Despite the difficulties involved, however, some picture must be presented of buffalo numbers. A work of the present character would scarcely be complete without the inclusion of such data as would at least enable the reader to make some approximate estimate for himself of the once vast numbers of the buffalo on this continent.

The earliest of the two computations mentioned is by Buffalo Jones (1899): Buffalo "roaming over the Great Plains, and the number slaughtered outside the National Park, during the years specified."[1]

It may be doubted whether a more worthless table of statistics was ever compiled for public information. Buffalo Jones does not specify 'bulls only'; but it is manifest that according to him not a single calf could have been born during the last nineteen years! We might be

---

[1]*Buffalo Jones' Forty Years*, 255.

enumerating nine-pins: so many knocked over, so many left standing;
and this from the very man who killed almost the last wild herd slain
in the United States, on a trip whose express object was to secure

Year	Number of Buffalo	Number Killed in the past year	Number Killed for Hides
January 1, 1865	15,000,000	1,000,000	40,000
” 1, 1870	14,000,000	1,600,000	800,000
” 1, 1871	12,400,000	4,500,000	3,500,000
” 1, 1872	7,500,000	4,000,000	3,200,000
” 1, 1873	2,500,000 [sic]	1,000,000	700,000
” 1, 1874	1,500,000	500,000	350,000
” 1, 1875	1,000,000	300,000	240,000
” 1, 1876	700,000	100,000	75,000
” 1, 1877	600,000	75,000	60,000
” 1, 1878	525,000	70,000	50,000
” 1, 1879	455,000	60,000	52,000
” 1, 1880	395,000	70,000	60,000
” 1, 1881	325,000	80,000	70,000
” 1, 1882	245,000	85,000	77,000
” 1, 1883	160,000	90,000	80,000
” 1, 1884	70,000	50,000	46,000
” 1, 1885	20,000	15,000	13,000
” 1, 1886	5,000	4,000	3,500
” 1, 1887	1,000	500	450
” 1, 1888	500	350	300
” 1, 1889	150	150	130[2]

calves, which was successfully accomplished.[3] Buffalo Jones (or his
compiler, Colonel Inman) quotes with great approval the essay of
Hornaday.[4] That one paper alone contains abundantly sufficient detailed information to have saved them from offering such a production.
For the years 1871-72, the totals of slaughter 'for hides' are raised to
figures which far surpass the outside estimates of any other serious
investigator, and in 1873—when according to Dodge's carefully compiled records there was a considerable increase in the marketed percentage of hides per aggregate of buffalo slain—we have a sudden
decrease of about 75 per cent in the aggregate slaughtered, and

[2]*Ibid.* This is printed by Seton, but without the third column (hides): *Game
Animals*, III, 667.
[3]*Buffalo Jones' Forty Years*, 201-24.
[4]*Ibid.*, 223-4.

also a decrease of 12½ per cent in the ratio of marketed hides. This may have been necessary to Jones, in order to make the existence of this sterile species, whose birth-rate was nil, last out until 1889; but I have found no hint of such a spectacular reduction at that date in any contemporary (or other) source I have been able to consult. Then again in the north, their figures are demonstrably impossible. In 1874, while the Southern butchery was yet at its height, Messrs. I. G. Baker and Company are said to have shipped 250,000 hides from Fort Benton alone.[5] Jones's grand total killed for hides in 1876 exactly equals the number of hides which the same firm themselves told Hornaday they had shipped from Benton alone in that year.[6] In 1878, 60,000 robes are stated to have been exported from Benton;[7] another firm alone purchased over 41,000 hides out of a supposed total of only 50,000![8] In 1881 this buyer bought nearly 50,000 robes and hides of a supposed total of 70,000; in the same year another firm purchased 26,000; and there were many firms in the business for whom we have no figures. Thus again Jones's total is completely eclipsed.[9] Further, whereas Jones's total for 1881 and 1882 combined is only 147,000, a fairly competent judge believed that the Northern Pacific Railway handled in 1882 alone some 200,000 hides between Miles City, Montana, and Mandan, North Dakota, where that system encounters the Missouri River;[10] the Northern Pacific's own figures for 1881 exceed Jones's total for that year by over 5000.[11] Mr. J. N. Davis shipped 'the only carload of robes that went East' in 1884,[12] at which time the Northern, as well as the Southern herd, had been exterminated. Yet from some unknown reserve, of which no other student has ever heard, Jones produces a slaughter of 50,000 for that year—46,000 'for hides'! The only conceivable effect of such statistics is to completely discredit their author as a scientific generalizer, and their endorsement by Inman lends them no additional weight.[13] The full measure of their ineptitude becomes apparent when it is realized that almost every one of my

[5]Kelly, The Rangemen, 111. As I have remarked above, Kelly is inaccurate; but I question him for more weighty reasons than his disagreement with Jones (see chap. XVI, note 34).

[6]Hornaday, "Extermination of the American Bison," 506 (above, chap. XVI, note 34).

[7]Bancroft, History of Washington, Idaho, and Montana, 753.

[8]Hornaday, "Extermination of the American Bison," 439 (above, chap. XVI, note 55).

[9]Ibid., 440-1 (above, chap. XVI, note 56).

[10]Ibid., 513 (above, chap. XVI, note 57).

[11]Ibid., 507-8 (above, chap. XVI, notes 51-3).

[12]Ibid., 513 (above, chap. XVI, note 57).

[13]On Inman, see notes 99-100, 109 seq.

own foregoing comparisons is drawn from Hornaday's paper, with which these men were familiar.

As I have remarked, Thompson Seton's treatment of the problem is entirely different. As an outstanding example of careful reasoning from conjectural data, it deserves to be quoted in full. Considering the inherent impossibility of obtaining more exact criteria, it will probably never be superseded. He writes as follows:

The total area inhabited by the Buffalo was about 3,000,000 square miles. Of this area open plains constituted about one-half. According to figures supplied to me by A. F. Potter, of the Forest Service, the ranges of North and South Dakota, Montana, Wyoming, Nebraska, Kansas, Colorado, Texas, and Oklahoma (a total of about 750,000 square miles, or half of the plains) carried at the time of the last census (1900) about 24,000,000 head of cattle and horses and about 6,000,000 head of sheep. This means that, when fully stocked, these plains might sustain a number of Buffalo at least equal to the number of cattle and horses. But the Buffalo had to divide their heritage with numerous herds of Mustang, Antelope, and Wapiti. On the other hand, a Buffalo could find a living where a range animal would starve. Moreover, many of the richest bottom lands are now fenced in, and we have taken no account of the 6,000,000 sheep. On the whole, it seems that we are safe in placing the number of Buffalo formerly living on the entire Plains area as about 40,000,000.

The range of the species on the prairies was a third as large as that on the Plains, but it was vastly more fertile; indeed, the stockmen reckon one acre of prairie as equal in fertility to four acres of the Plains. Doubtless, therefore, the prairies sustained nearly as many head as the Plains; we may safely set their population at 30,000,000.

The forest region of the Buffalo supported a relatively sparse population. For its 1,000,000 square miles we cannot allow more than 5,000,000 buffalo.

Summing up these totals, we arrive at the conclusion that the primitive number of Buffalo was about 75,000,000. Let us consider the question from another standpoint. There were 1,500,000 square miles of the Plains; it takes 30 acres of such range to support an ordinary range beast, which needs as much as, or more than, a Buffalo. There were as many of the latter as the food could sustain; therefore the Plains had 30,000,000, but take off one-third to allow for the herds of other creatures, and we have 20,000,000 as the number of the Plains Buffalo. On the prairies and in the woods 10 acres a head is the usual range allowance; but doubling this to allow for Deer, &c.,[14] it would give us a population of 45,000,000, or a total of 65,000,000 Buffalo.

Again: Col. C. J. Jones estimated the Buffalo in 1870 at 14,000,000. They were then occupying less than one-third of their range and were not nearly so crowded as in ancient times; their original total, therefore, must have been at least 50,000,000.

[14]G. B. Grinnell thinks the antelope exceeded the buffalo in 'normal times,' say circa 1800 (Seton, Game Animals, III, 423-6).

Yet again: All the evidence available goes to show that the Buffalo herds travelled from 100 to 400 miles in search of food; and that these herds broke speedily to find sustenance, and therefore that the herds never went more than 300 or 400 miles from their home region. Hornaday estimates at 4,000,000 a herd which Col. Dodge saw travelling on the Arkansas in May, 1871. If this herd had been gathered from the extreme distance from which they are known to congregate, it would represent an area of 200,000 square miles. There would be room enough to repeat this about 15 times on their range, and thus yield a population of about 60,000,000 as the sum of the Buffalo in primitive days, when their whole range was stocked as fully as the food-supply would permit. From these facts it will appear very safe to put the primitive Buffalo population at from 50,000,000 to 60,000,000.

In 1800 there were practically no Buffalo east of the Mississippi. Their range had shrunken by one-eighth; their numbers doubtless shrunk in even greater degree; 40,000,000 head would be a fair estimate at that time.

The total of buffalo in captivity in 1889 was 256; since then they have added as nearly as possible 10 per cent. *per annum* in spite of many disadvantages, such as isolated animals, over-feeding, over-production of males, &c. If, therefore, we set the rate of increase in the wild herds at 5 per cent., as long as they are within the limit set by food-supply, we shall probably be near the facts. In early days the Buffalo held their own well against the Indians with their primitive weapons. But, in the full splendour of the Buffalo days, say about 1830, the Indians, aided now by horses and armed with rifles, killed, as will be seen later, at the rate of over 2,000,000 each year. Allen estimates the destruction by Indians at 2,000,000 annually in the earlier '40's. Baird puts it at 3,500,000 in the '50's on the Missouri alone. Other means of destruction added at least half as many more to the number, so that 3,000,000 a year may have been reached as a total of loss in the '30's. To stand such a drain with their slow rate of increase, the herds would have had to be at least ten times as numerous as they were. But they could not stand it and they were plainly diminishing. Therefore, they must have fallen below 40,000,000 even as early as the beginning of the nineteenth century. Nevertheless, they could not have been much less than that, or they would have vanished far faster than they did. . . .[15]

Without attempting a 'constructive' total of my own, there are nevertheless certain criticisms arising from this most valuable discussion, which lead me to think that Seton has by no means overestimated the probable aggregates he suggests for different periods. Assuming the numbers he sets forth to very nearly represent certain maxima, which were imposed by limitations of food supply, from which condition his 'crowding of the range' would naturally follow, I do not consider the historical evidence of the earlier buffalo times that we possess would justify the assumption of 'crowding.' It has been noticed already that certain portions of the southern United States,

[15]Seton, *Life-Histories of Northern Animals*, I, 259, 292; *Game Animals*, III, 654-7.

broadly similar in climate and topography to contiguous regions where buffalo were found in the earliest historic times, were not visited by the species before 1540. If we explain this circumstance in terms of overcrowding, we are confronted with a dilemma, by no means easy to solve. To assume that between 1540 and, say, 1750 overcrowding for the first time reached an acute stage would, in effect, be to postulate an incredibly recent date for their appearance—as the historic buffalo—in their historic habitat. To push the era of their origin far enough back to meet other historical requirements would be to render probable a much earlier arrival at a state of overcrowding, if overcrowding were ever to be a factor. By the time the white man came, it would have been impossible to visit any portion of the buffalo habitat without finding it so thickly crammed with animals that the grass would have been eaten off entirely or trodden into the ground. Both the orthodox 'migration' theory and the explanation in terms of 'capricious shiftings' are faced with the same problems. Where could the buffalo migrate (or shift) to? If the condition of overcrowding existed, it seems probable (in so far as our evidence enables us to judge) that it must have developed progressively until the time that the 'normal' causes of diminution—that is, physical phenomena and Indian slaughter for subsistence—were re-enforced by non-indigenous agents. It might logically be expected that from about 1750, as a result of the demands upon the buffalo for subsistence by white settlers (or garrisons), and above all, of the commercial demands of the fur trade, overcrowding would be progressively, although at first only slightly checked. That means that in the eighty or one hundred years previous to that date overcrowding must have been at its very worst, and could scarcely have failed to force itself upon the notice of even the least observant of travellers. Since these 'artificial' demands upon the buffalo increased only very gradually at first, it also means that it should have taken a considerable time for the relatively slight additional strain upon the buffalo resources to produce local scarcities which would be noticed any great distance away. These hypotheses seem to follow logically from the theory of overcrowding; but not one of them finds support from the known historical evidence.

It has been shown that this intermediate period, 1670-1750, furnishes evidence precisely similar to that which, in later times, supposedly constituted 'proof' of scarcity or final disappearance. As we have seen, the superlative phraseology of 'vast numbers,' etc., used by Marquette or Hennepin resolved itself in specific instances into 'having seen herds of four hundred,' or similar less imposing and modest numbers.[16] La Salle's followers, working their way northeastward from Texas toward the central Mississippi River territory in 1687, were in a good buffalo country practically all the way. Henri Joutel says: "The hunting of bullocks had failed us, and we had seen none from the place where our leader had been murdered. . . ."[17]

We have also seen that along the Lower Mississippi, where, about the year 1700, they were apparently so plentiful that D'Iberville, the French Governor, endeavoured to inaugurate a 'buffalo wool' industry, their numbers were also sufficiently precarious or insufficiently large that he proposed to supplement the buffalo resources by domestic propagation of the species.[18] Diron D'Artaguiette noted this precariousness in 1722 in the vicinity of New Orleans; and Father Poisson in 1726 found that the hunters had to ascend the Mississippi for '200 or 300 leagues' to obtain buffalo for that settlement.[19] It is true that all the instances I have specified belong to the 'long grass' region where overcrowding would not so easily occur; but surely the herds should have flocked more thickly into these favoured localities (particularly on the much-lauded theory of intelligence in this very respect). The earlier history of the short-grass plains territories presents no noticeable difference. La Vérendrye, on his return journey in 1739 from the Mandan villages to Red River, nearly starved;[20] and in the Southwest in 1806—which for this purpose (since there was as yet no fur trade there[21]) is broadly parallel to the period ante 1750 in the region east of the Mississippi—Pike and his colleagues speak of numbers which 'exceeded imagination'; and 'solemnly assert' that they have seen 3000 'in one view,' or 9000 in a day's march.[22] I am dubious concerning the herd seen by Dodge, inasmuch as the calculation is based upon the 'extreme distance from which they are known to congregate'; and nobody knows what this may be. Further, I have pointed out above not only that Hornaday has deliberately taken the minimum basis for his computation, but also that there remains an insoluble question to be considered: where, in its span from front to rear, did Dodge cross this wedge-shaped formation which was twenty-five miles wide at his own particular crossing-point? That very herd may have contained far

[16]See above, chap. XIII, notes 11-19.
[17]Joutel, *Journeys of La Salle*, II, 132.
[18]Winsor (ed.), *Narrative and Critical History*, V, 21 (above, chap. X, note 82).
[19]See above, chap. X, notes 84-6.
[20]Above, chap. XIV, notes 149-50.
[21]Chittenden, *American Fur Trade*, II, 483-553.
[22]Coues (ed.), *Expeditions of Pike*, II, 438, 440, 548 (above, chap. XIII, notes 81-3).

more than 4,000,000 buffalo. In fact, if we are to accept the theory of 'one sole herd' migrating *en masse* to the South for the winter (a theory which, in connection with the Southern herd, is perhaps more applicable about 1870 than at any other time) of which this would be the host returning in spring, it *must* have contained far more. Otherwise, the terrific slaughtering that, it is almost universally agreed, was carried on during the next four years would not have been possible; and 'fifteen times' its total (mentioned by Seton, above) would result in a very considerable advancement in the entire aggregate.[23] At the same time, I freely acknowledge the difficulty I have in reconciling my own critical suggestions with Seton's calculations, which are based upon an apparently fixed relationship—the capacity of a given area of pasturage to maintain a certain number of *herbivora*. It is not the only difficulty of the kind to be encountered in an inquiry such as this.

Seton's argument and general broad conclusions from his own premise seem logically unexceptionable. However, the premise itself is possibly unsound. In relation to the question of buffalo pasturage and food-supply, two major difficulties not necessarily connected with the problem of buffalo aggregates have always arisen; to neither of these could I discover a satisfactory solution.

The first difficulty arises out of the following circumstances: in the buffalo's characteristic and most crowded habitat, the plains, the 'buffalo grass' was extremely short and consequently scanty (as expressed in crop-growth per acre); whereas, in the scrubland regions which were their common winter haunts (for instance, north-central Alberta in its former state), while the grass was far longer it stood much thinner upon the ground, because the masses of poplar and willow forest and scrub growth crowded it out and hence the soil was excessively shaded. These conditions were sufficient to offset the greater natural fertility of the semi-woodland regions. In gazing over an expanse of this kind, in localities known to have been former winter haunts, one could not but speculate on the relative sparsity and insignificance of the open patches of grass or carices; and in winter time, when once eaten over, they were exhausted for that season. It baffled imagination to conceive of such a territory furnishing a food-supply sufficient for really material numbers during any extended period of a long northern winter; certainly it would be impossible on any scheme of computation analogous to that used to determine the resources required for the wintering of domestic cattle in such a climate.

[23]See our examination below in this chapter, notes 80-100.

Over a century ago, however, Darwin challenged the view which would seem to underlie Seton's calculation; and with the usual Darwinian wealth of factual illustration. He wrote:

That large animals require a luxuriant vegetation has been a general assumption which has passed from one work to another; but I do not hesitate to say that it is completely false, and that it has vitiated the reasoning of geologists on some points of great interest in the ancient history of the world. . . . There can be no doubt, however, that our ideas respecting the amount of food necessary for the support of large quadrupeds are much exaggerated; it should have been remembered that the camel, an animal of no mean bulk, has always been considered as the emblem of the desert. . . .[24]

The allusion to the camel shows that these conclusions are relevant not only to vanished geological epochs, but to historic eras. Darwin's historical and ecological evidence was largely derived from the South Africa of his own time—a region considered to be unequalled in the size and number of its herbivorous quadrupeds, and at the same time virtually a desert.[25] It would be impertinent for a writer like myself even to endorse an opinion of Darwin's on such topics; his facts are scarcely open to question. It may be that the semi-'regular' life of domesticated cattle has induced changes not inherent in the wild species.

Secondly, it is possible that the unquestionably superior initial fertility of the prairie lands—foolishly believed to be 'inexhaustible' and shamefully misused in pursuance of that delusion[26]—is partly to be traced to the heavy and constant manuring and the trampling of the same content into the soil. This automatic process of 'scientific farming,' which most certainly went far toward returning to the soil what it had taken from it, may have distilled a richer nutritive capacity into the pasturage than can be conferred solely by climatic agencies.[27] These

[24]Darwin, *Voyage of the 'Beagle,'* 80, 82. But what is a 'desert'?
[25]*Ibid.*, 80-4; cf. on 'overcrowding,' *ibid.*, 166-7.
[26]A scientist of the first rank, whose findings have suffered surprisingly little from the passage of time, stated (1891) that—in contradistinction to certain 'poor soils' in the Eastern States—"the prairie ground steadily diminishes in its productiveness under cultivation. . . .": Shaler, *Nature and Man in America*, 226, 254. On this subject, compare (amongst others) Bulletins 14, 16, of the College of Agriculture, University of Alberta; *Soil Surveys: Medicine Hat Sheet*, December, 1926, 40; *Sounding Creek Sheet*, December, 1927, 32; particularly.
[27]Darwin cites a writer in *Silliman's Journal* on pasturing by cattle changing coarse grass on the North American prairies into 'common pasture land': *Voyage of the 'Beagle,'* 112-13. Dr. Rowan, Professor of Zoology, Alberta University, questions (in conversation) the relevance of South African evidence to the North American buffalo habitat; partly by reason of the great increase in food

considerations might perhaps postulate a somewhat higher aggregate of buffalo than that suggested by Seton, for the era *circa* 1830; and indeed a greater total is demanded by certain assumptions of slaughter which he endorses or does not dispute. But where all else is hypothesis, such an addition could possess no higher claim.

The statistical material for determining the aggregates at different periods in the nineteenth century is exasperatingly meagre. It consists principally in assertions of figures. Upon what authority these are based other than observation or hearsay it is impossible to discover. The numerical variations are so wide that one suspects that many of them originated largely in their authors' personal attitudes towards the Indian. Those that I give have been collected from various sources.

The American Fur Company, we are told, "established trading posts along the Missouri River, one at the mouth of the Teton River, and another at the mouth of the Yellowstone. In 1826 a post was established at the eastern base of the Rocky Mountains, at the head of the Arkansas River, and in 1832 another was located in a corresponding situation at the head of the South Fork of the Platte, close to where Denver now stands. . . ."[28]

The early returns in robes could not have been large, as judged by later standards. About 1790-1800, the annual receipts at St. Louis were 'about 40,000 pounds of beaver, 8000 otter, 5000 bear, 150,000 deer, and a few hundred buffalo robes.'[29] Edwin James (*circa* 1822) states, with bated breath as it were, that a well-known early trader, Manuel Lisa, 'once sent to St. Louis 15,000 buffalo skins in a single year.'[30] About 1820, according to a modern historian, the number of buffalo slaughtered was about 200,000 per annum; of which only 5000 were slain by whites.[31] The returns at New York from 1830 to 1840, were stated to be 90,000 buffalo robes per annum.[32] Sanford, of the American

consumption noted by himself among his captive birds of wild species in a colder winter climate. Compare Soper, on both Wood Buffalo Park animals in winter and on the question of natural manuring ("History of the Northern Bison," 388).

[28]Hornaday, "Extermination of the American Bison," 488; cf. also Chittenden, *American Fur Trade*, I. The four are Fort Pierre, Fort Union, Bent's Fort, and St. Vrain's Fort, in the order given. See Chittenden, *ibid.*, II, 543; Bancroft, *History of Nevada, Colorado, and Wyoming*, 352; Grinnell, *Fighting Cheyennes*, 60.

[29]Bancroft, *History of the Northwest Coast*, I, 507. Note the meagre proportion of buffalo-skins in Henry's fur returns, 1800-6 (Coues (ed.), *Henry-Thompson Journals*, I, 184, 198, 201, 221, 245, 259, 281, 284, 420, 440-4). Cf. another early enumeration: 787,865 skins of 21 species; 2 buffalo skins! (Davidson, *The North-West Company*, Appendix J, 282).

[30]*Early Western Travels*, XIV, 313.

[31]Coman, *Economic Beginnings of the Far West*, II, 34.

[32]Bancroft, *History of the Northwest Coast*, I, 521. Cf. note 38 below.

Fur Company, told Frémont that their returns for 1834-44 were some 70,000 per annum; the Hudson's Bay 'and other companies' accounted for about 20,000 more. As he stated that "out of the great number of buffalo annually killed throughout the extensive regions inhabited by the Comanches and other kindred tribes, no robes whatever are furnished for trade," it may be assumed that these came principally from points on the Missouri River.[33] The figures suggested by Maximilian as the American Fur Company's annual average *circa* 1835 (possibly from those points) are from 40,000 to 50,000; 42,000 were sent out 'in a recent year'—cowskins at a price of $4.00 each.[34] He also notes a shipment of 7000 buffalo skins from Fort Pierre, on June 2, 1833.[35] In 1839, 'a very favourable year,' the American Fur Company received 45,000.[36] A careful student of the subject states that this company's shipments of robes to St. Louis were 67,000 in 1840; whereas in 1848 it shipped 110,000 robes and skins, 'mostly buffalo,' and 25,000 tongues.[37] George Catlin, writing about 1840, speaks of '150,000 or 200,000 robes annually.'[38] This appears to be an exaggeration, in comparison with other robe statistics of the same general era; but is scarcely so, if compared with some of the estimates of the total buffalo slaughter about this time. Allen mentions 100,000 as the shipment to St. Louis in 1850;[39] and in 1857 there were sent from Fort Benton 3600 bales or 36,000 robes; from Fort Union, 2700 to 3000 bales—about 30,000 robes; and from Forts Berthold and Clarke, 500 bales each— 10,000 robes; totalling some 75,000, 'then about the annual average.'[40] Another diligent inquirer gives the 'annual yield,' 1840-50, as 90,000 robes; 1850-60, 100,000.[41] In 1861, Dr. F. V. Hayden, who visited the Upper Missouri country several times between 1850 and 1860, wrote:

As near as I could ascertain, about 250,000 individuals are destroyed every year, about 100,000 being killed for robes. At the present time, the number of males to the females seems to be in the ratio of ten to one, and this fact is readily accounted for from the fact that the males are seldom killed when the cows can be obtained. Skins of females only are used 'for robes and are [sic] preferred for food. Besides the robes which are traded to the whites by the Indians, each man, woman, and child requires from

[33]Frémont, *Narrative*, 141-2.
[34]Maximilian, *Early Western Travels*, XXII, 380, 382.
[35]*Ibid.*, 327.
[36]*Life of De Smet*, I, 179.
[37]Chittenden, *American Fur Trade*, II, 817.
[38]Catlin, *Letters on the North American Indians*, I, 263.
[39]Allen, *American Bisons*, 186.
[40]*Ibid.*, 188.
[41]Coman, *Economic Beginnings of the Far West*, I, 366.

one to three robes a year for clothing.[42] A large quantity are employed in the manufacture of lodges, and an immense number of animals, which it would be difficult to estimate, are annually destroyed by wolves and by accidents. . . .[43]

Hornaday, whose figures can signify only robes marketed by Indians, sums up thus: 'For 1830-80, robes estimated variously at from 50,000 to 100,000 annually';[44] or, 'up to 1870 less than 100,000 annually.'[45]

The percentage of robes made or marketed out of the total number slain by Indians in a season has been variously estimated. Sanford (cited above) informed Frémont as follows:

During only four months of the year, from November to March, the skins are good for dressing; those obtained in the remaining eight months being valueless to the traders; and the hides of bulls are never taken off, or dressed as robes, at any season. Probably not more than one third of the skins are taken from the animals killed, even when they are in good season, the labour of preparing and dressing the robes being very great, and it is seldom that a lodge trades more than twenty skins in a year. It is during the summer months and in the early part of autumn, that the greatest number of buffalo are killed, and yet at this time a skin is never taken for the purposes of trade. . . .[46]

Dodge, as we have seen,[47] placed the ratio of slain buffalo much higher—up to six times—among those tribes in less intimate intercourse with the whites, and hence putting products from buffalo to wider domestic use. This would be the case with the Northern tribes in the earlier days. Allen,[48] Dr. Hayden,[49] and Hornaday,[50] however, adopt the general ratio of one robe for three animals suggested by Sanford,

[42]This seems a fair estimate; more for bedding than for clothing, strictly. Apart from buffalo robes (worn as such) buffalo skin was too heavy and unsatisfactory, and deerskin was preferred (see Coues (ed.), *Henry-Thompson Journals*, II, 525; Jenness, *Sarcee Indians of Alberta*, 19; Kidd, "Blackfoot Ethnography," 79 (who cites also Krieger, *American Indian Costumes*, 626).

[43]*Transactions of the American Philosophical Society*, vol. XII, (New Series), 151 (in Chittenden, *American Fur Trade*, II, 817; cf. Allen, *American Bisons*, 189).

[44]Hornaday, "Extermination of the American Bison," 502-3.

[45]*Ibid.*, 466. Cf. his remarks *in extenso* (*ibid.*, 505; above, chap. XVI, note 10).

[46]Frémont, *Narrative*, 142. On the readiness of rival fur companies to hurl this charge at one another while repudiating it themselves, see above, chap. V, note 111.

[47]Dodge, *Plains of the Great West*, 142-4 (above, chap. XV, note 109).

[48]Allen, *American Bisons*, 188.

[49]Above, note 43.

[50]Hornaday, "Extermination of the American Bison," 500. But compare 'one in five' *ibid.*, 505; (above, chap. XVI, note 10).

and we may accept that as a rough basis. The general rhodomontades on Indian wastefulness which so frequently accompany those estimates,[51] may be checked in part by two items of historical evidence. Hugh Glenn and Jacob Fowler's party on the Arkansas River in 1821 found 20,000 Indians—Arapahoes, Snakes, Comanches, and Kiowas—in 400 'tepees,' consuming one hundred buffalo per day.[52] Maximilian, on the Upper Missouri in 1833, noted with disapproval the wastefulness of the American Fur Company's men, slaughtering for tongues alone;[53] as likewise did Edwin James (or Long, or both) a dozen years previously,[54] when Katherine Coman ascribes 2½ per cent of the annual slaughter—a total of 5000—to white men![55]

Certainly, if slaughter by Indians even approached the figures suggested by some scholars, Indian wastefulness in the worst sense would be virtually indisputable. Seton, as we have seen, accepts the total of 'over 2,000,000 each year' from about 1830 onward.[56] Allen similarly endorses the computation of Frémont of 1,800,000 per year by Indians alone, which is based upon the American Fur Company's statistics;[57] and sets the slaughter at about 1,500,000 annually in the Upper Missouri country, as late as 1873.[58] General Sibley, in 1854, placed the figures at from 250,000 to 500,000 per annum—"evidently quite too low an estimate," says Allen in citing it,[59] although the higher figure considerably exceeds what the ratio adopted by Allen would require as the total slain, on the basis of the number of robes accepted by himself for that period. At the same time, he offers no criticism whatever (nor does Seton[60]) of the utterly incredible figures advanced by Spencer F.

[51]'Thoughtless and abominable extravagance': Frémont, Narrative, 140. '. . . perhaps the Indian himself who commits the mischief wantonly . . .': Dr. Leidy, 1852 (in Allen, American Bisons, 184). See also Gregg, Early Western Travels, XX, 264; in extenso, chap. XIII, note 125); Hornaday, "Extermination of the American Bison," 526-7 (in extenso, chap. XVII, notes 90-1).

[52]Coman, Economic Beginnings of the Far West, II, 77. I regret not having seen The Journal of Jacob Fowler, (ed. Coues, 1898). One hundred per day is one for each 200 persons: scarcely 'waste!' All the numbers are doubtless guesses; but the cultus of deliberate statistical anti-Indian propaganda was then scarcely born.

[53]Maximilian, Early Western Travels, XXII, 382.

[54]Long, ibid., XV, 257.

[55]Coman, Economic Beginnings of the Far West, II, 34 (see above, note 31).

[56]Seton, Life-Histories of Northern Animals, I, 261.

[57]Allen, American Bisons, 185. Seton has this (Life-Histories of Northern Animals, I, 261) as '2,000,000 annually in the earlier '40's' (see above, note 15).

[58]Allen, American Bisons, 188. Hornaday allows only 1,500,000 North of the Platte in 1870 ("Extermination of the American Bison," 503).

[59]Allen, American Bisons, 187, note.

[60]See above, note 15.

Baird, who held that 3,500,000 were slain by the Upper Missouri tribes alone, *circa* 1852.[61] This, as an annual performance by a body of hunters representing (on the not uncommon Indian family basis of two children per wife and after making some allowance for polygamy) almost certainly not more than 25 per cent of a probable total of from fifty to sixty thousands,[62] let them believe who can! It would be of immense interest to know how two men, both presumably dependent upon the same methods of investigation—these constituting, in the absence of an exact census, a combination of personal observation (if any) and of the accounts or criticisms of others—could differ concerning a broadly uniform annual estimate by nearly 90 per cent. From every point of view, Sibley is the more credible witness; he was a plainsman and an accepted authority on other phases of buffalo history. Baird's preposterous total would require—on the basis of an Indian population estimated at 54,550, and assuming a ratio of one hunter to every four individuals—that each hunter slay annually an average of 256⅝ buffalo. Or, if we were to adopt Henry's ratio for the Blackfoot of one man in five individuals, each adult male would have to slay more than 320⅝ per annum.[63]

If we accept the mean of Seton's different calculations, or broadly 60,000,000, as the aggregate of the primitive buffalo, his proportions of the numbers exterminated before and after 1800 seem scarcely logical. He holds that their range was 'shrunken by one-eighth.' Accordingly, he reduces their total numbers, *circa* 1800, by one-third, even though evidence as reliable as any of our buffalo evidence has shown that really great masses of buffalo have never been seen in historical times in the particular region which this eighth includes.

[61]Allen, *American Bisons*, 186-7. Professor Baird does not appear as a conspicuous exponent of scientific caution. He maintained (1857), despite the existing lack of evidence, that the historic buffalo penetrated eastward to practically the entire Atlantic seaboard of the U.S. So far as I am aware, nothing discovered since tends to establish this. (See above, chap. IX, note 78.)

[62]The Indians of the Upper Missouri and tributaries were estimated in 1850 at 54,550 (Maclean, *Canadian Savage Folk*, 293). The adult male ratio of the Blackfoot, according to Henry, 1809, was 1420 warriors to 7100 souls (*ibid.*, 294; Coues (ed.), *Henry-Thompson Journals*, II, 530). See on this, Appendix G.

[63]13,637 (hunters) x 256⅝ = 3,500,164; 10,910 (hunters) x 320⅝ = 3,499,928. Angus Buchanan estimates the northern Saskatchewan average caribou kill at 40 per male hunter per winter, as against Seton's 20; and ridicules the idea of wastefulness (*Wild Life in Canada*, 131-8).

For a definite enumeration of Indians, cf. Pike, August 30, 1806: "I last evening took the census of the Grand [Osage] village, and found it to be: men, 502; boys, 341; women and girls, 852; total, 1695; lodges, 214" (Coues (ed.), *Expeditions of Pike*, II, 582, 589).

Considering his estimates in terms of chronology, we arrive at even more startling results. Seton's figures for the century of what Hornaday terms 'desultory extirpation' of an essentially legitimate character, which he dates from 1730 to 1830,[64] require that in its first (and hence its lightest) seven decades, the meagre white population west of the Alleghanies and the Great Lakes, together with the Indian tribes which were not yet armed with rifles, reduced the total aggregate by one-third.[65] On the other hand, they would lead us to believe that the residue was able to survive an infinitely more terrific onslaught, whose shameful features have been made clear to the reader, for nearly eight and one-half decades longer! I consider this to be impossible.[66]

A great deal has been said also about the Indian and the rifle as a prime agent in the faster extermination of the herds. It is apparent that the Indian is the villain of the piece to many of the American publicists of the nineteenth century. Since they have already found the Indian guilty, the rifle is too telling an item of evidence for them to neglect. The moment it made its appearance in the mechanical world every Indian had, of course, at least one, with unlimited ammunition; and where the red-skinned Saul had slain his thousands, the copper-coloured David slew his ten thousands! Few scholars in those halcyon days asked for proof concerning anything attributed to Indians. If they did, 'the vast numbers' slain by the Indians 'proved' this charge to any reasonable man's satisfaction. The general evidence on Indian archery by no means indicates such a rapid abandonment of the bow.[67]

In the absence of definite statistics, which the nature of the case renders impossible, the best test of estimated totals is to note in what measure the figures advanced for annual slaughter correspond to them. The following table presents the actual increase in numbers at the Wainwright Buffalo Park during a period of twenty years. I have been unable to obtain any figures on the numbers of male and female calves

[64]Hornaday, "Extermination of the American Bison," 484-6.

[65]These authorities contradict themselves. Cf. Allen: "The Indians prior to the discovery of the continent by Europeans, appear not to have seriously affected the number of buffaloes, their natural increase equalling the number destroyed by the Indians and the wolves . . ." (*American Bisons*, 182); and Seton himself: ". . . before the coming of the horse and the rifle, the Red man did little harm to the great Bison herds. . . ." He dates the influence of these agencies from *circa* 1800, after which 'the epoch of extirpating slaughter' began (*Life-Histories of Northern Animals*, I, 274). For the horse, see Roe, "From Dogs to Horses among the Western Indian Tribes" (*Transactions of the Royal Society of Canada*, 1939, Sec. II, 209-75).

[66]I have ignored natural agencies. They operated in a like manner before and after 1800.

[67]See on this, Appendix T, "Late Survival of Indian Archery."

born each year, or of the exact proportion of adult males and females. Therefore, the percentages given (which, within one-half of one per cent, are my own) indicate the ratio of increase in the total numbers only.

Year	Numbers	Increase	Ratio of increase	Slaughtered for sale	Shipped north (To the Wood Buffalo Park at Fort Smith)
1909	716	50	7 per cent	....	....
1910	766	110	14 "	....	....
1911	876	172	20 "	....	....
1912	1048	208	20 "	....	....
1913	1256	236	19 "	....	....
1914	1492	202	13½ "	....	....
1915	1694	442	26 "	....	....
1916	2136	356	16½ "	....	....
1917	2492	537	21½ "	....	....
1918	3029	665	22 "	....	....
1919	3694	1148	30½ "	....	....
1920	4842	543	11 "	....	....
1921	5385	1075	20 "	....	....
1922	6460	997	15½ "	264	....
1923	7193	1825	25 "	1847	....
1924	7169	1800	25 "	....	....
1925	8969	2337	26 "	....	1634
1926[68]	9672	1600	16½ "	2000	2011
1927	6027	1200	20 "	1000	1940
1928[69]	4241	not given	....	....	1088
1929	....	....	....	....	....
1930[70]	5016	....	....	....	....

Average of annual increase, 1909-27 = 18 per cent

On the basis of the figures for 1927 (46 animals out of an aggregate of from 4000 to 6000—see note 69), the rate of 'natural decrease' may be taken as roughly one per cent. Many, perhaps most years there were gifts of buffalo to public bodies in various parts of the world, always including one or more cows. The actual rate of increase is, therefore, probably slightly higher than the figure I have given and would agree with the estimate of the wardens patrolling the Wood

[68]Report of the Department of the Interior, Parks Branch (Dominion of Canada), for the year ending March 31, 1927, 92-3.

[69]Add to the decrease of 2940 above, a 'natural decrease' of 46: thus, 6027 − 2986 + 1200 = 4241 (Report of Department of Interior, March 31, 1928, 93).

[70]Report of Department of Interior, March 31, 1930, 101.

Buffalo Park at Fort Smith, North-West Territories, who place the annual increase at from 20 to 25 per cent.[71] Altogether, Seton's estimate of 10 per cent seems inadequate as a starting-point, without reducing it to 5 per cent. Moreover, it would appear that he omitted certain known factors from his calculation, which would of themselves point to a greater natural increase than he allows.[72]

After allowing for the annual losses by wolves, which we have seen reckoned as high as one-third,[73] and for the occasional influences of hard winters[74] or other agencies from which animals running wild would probably suffer more severely, I would suggest that an average increase of 18 per cent would not be too high for buffalo in a primitive state. Following Seton's example, I base my calculations on the numbers of cows only, halving the indicated increase over a number of years, and then doubling the ratio, since female calves alone furnish any future increase. In order to be well within the mark, and to take no unfair advantage of Seton's arguments, I have assumed the following:

1. The existence of 40,000,000 buffalo, one half of them cows, as late as 1830.

2. That, in the absence of exact corroborative data, the annual increase consisted of male and female calves in equal numbers.[75]

[71]*Ibid.*, 151.

[72]On poachers around the Yellowstone Park, cf. above, chap. XVI, note 67. again, '250 out of 300' in the Park, slain by poachers, 1895-96 (*Buffalo Jones' Forty Years*, 264). This was known to Seton, but not mentioned by him (above, note 15). In his later work, however, Seton puts the increase at 20 per cent (*Game Animals*, III, 656, 671).

[73]So estimated by the Indians to De Smet (*Life of De Smet*, I, 205; II, 603).

[74]The evidence is uncertain. It may be noted that the terrible seven-months winter of 1919-20 was followed by the lowest increase recorded at Wainwright, 11 per cent. The 7 per cent of 1909 is perhaps hardly relevant, as the cows were unduly excited by the rounding-up and railway travelling; but 1908-9 was also a hard winter in the West. But the next lowest percentage (13½ per cent) follows the fairly mild winter of 1913-14 at Wainwright; while the one following in percentage order (15½ per cent) succeeded the similarly moderate winter of 1921-22. There are two of 16½ per cent, one for the extremely cold and stormy winter of 1915-16, and the other for the abnormally mild and short winter of 1925-26, only surpassed in some forty years by 1930-31 and 1941-42. (See references in detail; above, chap. IV, note 56). Finally, the highest of all (30½ per cent) occurred after a not particularly severe winter (1918-19); while the two next highest percentages (26 per cent) follow, respectively, the moderate winter of 1914-15, and the very cold winter of 1924-25, when there was no thaw from early November to the end of February. All these winters referred to were in the Wainwright locality, in which I was working during those years.

[75]Seton (above, note 15) associates 'over-feeding' in captivity with over-production of males. I am ignorant of current scientific opinion on this obscure question; but in 1910, when Seton was writing, it was rather the other way. See Henry Fairfield Osborn, *The Age of Mammals* (1910), 408, 414, 503, etc.

3. That 90 per cent of the female adult aggregate of each year produced calves.[76]

4. That one-eighth (12½ per cent) of the 'two millions slaughtered each year by the Indians' were bulls.

5. That the annual increase may be estimated, for reasons already given, at 18 per cent of the total female aggregate (less the 10 per cent 'unproductive') for each year.

I think the reader will acknowledge that the foregoing ratios are considerably higher than those laid down by Seton. Moreover, apart from the allowance made for natural or animal inroads upon the annual *increase,* there is no provision made for adult animals slain each year by snow, rivers, lakes, bogs, or fires, or by white hunters. These agencies, so we have been assured by a mass of testimony equal in value to any, accounted for a huge yearly total.[77] In the case of the hunters, there can be no doubt that their annual 'bag' increased considerably from 1830 onward. Yet, despite the advantages thus conceded to his figures, Seton's asserted 'Indian slaughter alone' would have totally exterminated the females by the year 1853 and have left only a mass of twenty or thirty million bulls.[78] Since we know that no such effect was produced, the only conclusion open to us in my opinion is that the average anti-Indian generalization concerning buffalo slaughter—be the author of it who he may—may be dismissed as rubbish![79]

There is one other item of so-called historical evidence to be examined. If it could be considered authentic, it would involve a recasting of all other ideas concerning the buffalo aggregate in their latter days, and possibly throughout their entire history. This testimony is unique because it admits of no relationship to anything hitherto presented on buffalo numbers; and, since it has apparently been accepted by some critics who ought to have known better, it requires careful

[76]It is almost certain that the buffalo heifer, running wild, would bear at two years old. This would leave two unproductive years, out of much less (probably) than twenty.

[77]Seton (above, note 15) considers this to be 'at least half as many more' to be added to the Indian slaughter total; this makes 3,000,000 annually.

[78]See table of figures at the end of this chapter.

[79]Seton cites J. A. Allen as estimating that in 1845, "probably 2,000,000 a year is much less than half the number killed at this time by the Indians alone . . ." (*Game Animals,* III, 656). See my Appendix G, on Indian Populations. Add to the above, white hunters and natural agencies, say another 2,000,000 odd, making a total of 6,000,000 *plus,* per annum. The statistically minded reader may find amusement calculating how long *before* 1853 the race must inevitably have disappeared!

examination. M. S. Garretson, whose account is apparently not the first, but is probably the most circumstantial,[80] prints the following:

Mr. Robert M. Wright, a well-known citizen of Dodge City, Kansas, who had lived for fifty years in the heart of the buffalo country and who in 1866 was appointed post trader at Fort Dodge, told the writer [that is, Garretson] that one night General Sheridan and Major Henry Inman, having just made the trip from Fort Supply, were occupying his office at Fort Dodge. They called him in to discuss how many buffalo there were between Fort Dodge and Fort Supply.

The buffalo were moving north and it was known that the great herd extended more than one hundred miles in width and was of unknown length.

Taking a strip fifty miles east and fifty west over the trail by which they had come, they first estimated ten billion animals. General Sheridan said, "That won't do!" They figured it again and made it one billion. Finally they reached the conclusion that there must be considerably over one hundred million, but said they were afraid to give out these figures lest they might be accused of something worse than prevaricating. Nevertheless they believed the last number to be a conservative one.[81]

Before entering upon direct arithmetical criticism, we may note certain chronological considerations. This occurred after 1867, apparently between then and 1870.[82] Dodge's account of his vast herd of 1871 in the Arkansas Valley not far distant, was published in 1877 as the climax of nearly thirty years' observation. It is incredible that no knowledge of this book ever penetrated to the place named by (or from) its author; or if it had done so, that it should have aroused no comment concerning an immeasurably greater host, which would certainly be a standing buffalo prodigy while any old-timer remained. Even if Dodge were so uncandid as to ignore anything of the kind (if only for contemptuous rejection) in his next book of 1883-86, where the 1877 recital is reprinted almost verbatim, there were others. Allen's diligent inquiries never discovered this. It should have been familiar in Army circles; yet it never filtered through to such men as Spencer F. Baird or Hornaday, who were in touch with General Sheridan or his friends,[83] yet still continued to regard Dodge's relatively insignificant host as the unsurpassed instance in all buffalo history.

[80]McCreight (*Buffalo Bone Days*, 4) says this was cited by E. A. Brininstool in *Fighting Red Cloud's Warriors*. I do not know the date of that publication; but in an apparently chronological list of Brininstool's writings, it comes long before *The Bozeman Trail* (Hebard and Brininstool, 1922). Moreover, Garretson's account is supposedly coming from a principal in the computation.

[81]Garretson, *American Bison*, 63-4.

[82]*Ibid.*, 63.

[83]See Hornaday, "Extermination of the American Bison," 403. (Above, chap. XIII, note 177.)

The distance from Fort Dodge to Fort Supply is almost exactly 76 miles in a direct line; we may call it 80 in round numbers. It is described as 'a good day's riding apart.'[84] The herd was 'known' (how?) to be over 100 miles wide, and must have been even larger than the mass they saw on their journey, being of 'unknown length.' But we have here a 'known' area of 8000 square miles. Dodge's herd was computed to have occupied a rough triangle (or 'wedge') 50 miles deep by 25 miles at its base. This constituted 625 square miles, or 400,000 acres, with an average of ten buffalo to the acre (calculated on the basis of the 4,000,000 judged by Hornaday to be the total number of the herd). Such a number would not, of course, preclude driving through them; and as we have seen, Dodge records them closing in on him at a gallop. In the case of Sheridan's herd, we are confronted with the same difficulty that we encountered in Dodge's description. At what point was Sheridan's vast host 'known' to be 100 miles wide? The adoption by Hornaday of the wedge formation as typical of a herd was doubtless based upon fairly sound reasoning;[85] the wedge is certainly more probable than a rectangular form, if domesticated breeds furnish any analogy. But taking the area of Sheridan's herd as Garretson gives it, we have nearly thirteen times the area suggested for Dodge's four millions ($625 \times 13 = 8125$); the excess of 'considerably over' one hundred million will take care of the excess area of 125 square miles. On this area of thirteen times the land, however, we have twenty-five times the buffalo aggregate. This proportion would not be impossible so far as mere standing space is concerned, whatever effect it might have on pasturage. But another point should be considered. Their only *calculation* produced a result of ten billion animals.[86] We have no hint that they detected or even suspected any error in this estimate; it was regretfully rejected, together with its reduction to one billion, simply because they were afraid people would not believe it. Quite evidently, if they could have felt that their original estimate would have been accepted, they would have retained it; and we are therefore justified in ascertaining what these authorities would have liked us to believe. Eight thousand square miles contain 5,120,000 acres. To accommodate ten billion would mean an average of a fraction more than 1953.12 animals per acre. If the figure were reduced to one billion (1,000,000,000) it would still necessitate 195.31 per acre. We have seen

[84]On the dust-cover on Garretson's *American Bison*.
[85]See Hornaday's remarks (chap. XIII, note 150).
[86]The American billion is one thousand millions (Funk and Wagnall's *Standard Dictionary*).

that Father Belcourt is said to have once counted 228 buffalo on an acre. Hornaday—not without reason, apparently—considered that he must either have seen standing animals in repose or must have under-estimated the computed area.[87] But imagination reels at the thought of any such totals (not to say eight and one half times as many— 1953.12) on a continuous tract of 5,120,000 acres! Such figures are truly astronomical. But what would be thought of an astronomer who for any conceivable reason save detected error, reduced the sun's distance from the earth to *one per cent* of his original and still unrepudiated estimate.[88]

Judging from the fact that he makes no critical comment of any character, even the first of the colossal totals is not beyond Garretson's heroic faith. Several observers have spoken of such large masses that 'when viewed at an angle' the ground could not be seen.[89] This is without doubt the condition described to Garretson by an old plains-man, relating to 1851: "*It looked as if* not another buffalo could have found room to squeeze in, and a man might have walked across the valley on their huddled backs as on a floor. . . ."[90] Presumably on the strength of this, the author has made a drawing of 'Buffalo on the march; from eye-witness accounts,'[91] and has inserted it in his book. According to his picture, a dance-floor could certainly be laid on the platform of closely-packed backs. This representation is 'supported' by letters from old-timers on the buffalo plains, who extol the 'life-like accuracy' of the drawings and cite their own experience in corrobora-tion.[92] Unfortunately, however, their testimony by no means agrees with Garretson's portrayal of these phenomena. Colonel Goodnight states that the herd was 'probably' twenty-five miles through and fifty

[87]Hornaday, "Extermination of the American Buffalo," 391. (Above, chap. XIII, note 149.)

[88]McCreight's account of this, taken from Brininstool (*Buffalo Bone Days,* 4) omits the ten billion; and gives *one* billion as 'the first calculation.' Probably the earlier version represents the chrysalis growth of the tale, and the second the butterfly.

[89]See above, chap. XIII, notes 129, 144, 147.

[90]Garretson, *American Bison,* 60 (italics mine).

[91]*Ibid.,* 45; cf. *ibid.,* 97. This drawing calls for brief comment. It is marked "*Drawing by M. S. Garretson*" (*ibid.,* 45). Garretson's work was reviewed by myself, in the *Canadian Historical Review,* XIX, 1938, 323-5. In March, 1939, in the private museum of Ernest Brown, Esq. of Edmonton, Alberta, an old-timer photographer and historian (whose collection has since been made the nucleus of a Provincial Museum of Alberta), I saw the same drawing poster-size, but without any artist's name or signature. I recognized it immediately. Mr. Brown informed me that the poster had been in his possession since about 1912.

[92]Colonel Charles Goodnight, Judge O. H. Nelson (in Garretson, *American Bison,* Appendix, 235-8).

miles long (which itself has a familiar ring) *and as thick as they could graze.*[93] In Garretson's sketch, grazing would be out of the question. Moreover, according to Goodnight, the buffalo left a lane from a quarter to half a mile in width, and the command 'generally went straight through,' although the buffalo would 'close up' if they became excited.[94] If Garretson's representation is according to fact, the command could not have gone straight through or gone at all. There could have been neither 'lane' or closing up; and to split such a host by rifle-fire, in the event of a stampede (as Goodnight speaks of doing) would have been a physical impossibility, since there was no vacant space to split them into! Another 'eye-witness,' in endorsing Garretson's 'life-like accuracy,' refers to trains which were delayed from one-half to two hours while buffalo crossed the track.[95] If a train had ever got in front of such a herd as Garretson's 'floor of buffaloes' backs' it would not only have been derailed (which did sometimes occur[96]), but the light wooden coaches of those days would have been crushed and ground into the very earth, together with their passengers, by the weight of the moving mass: the buffalo in the front of the herd could not have stopped, if they would, while their fellows thrust them onward from behind.

One is almost ashamed to dignify this 'Munchausen' nonsense about 'billions' by giving it serious arithmetical analysis. The entire history of the buffalo on the Southern range would have to be rewritten in a revolutionary fashion to take into account the slaughter and marketing of these impossible myriads, had they existed. It is extraordinary that Garretson should record this absurdity without comment and yet discuss elsewhere a fairly good rough field-test of buffalo numbers—which was suggested by General Sheridan, and which was related to Garretson by a participant in the experience. The test was made in what is today Oklahoma, between the Cimarron and Canadian Rivers. Sheridan's command had been marching from daybreak until 4:00 p.m.; and because most of the march had been through 'immense herds,' the question arose of how many buffalo had been seen. Sheridan asked the eleven staff officers, of whom 'Buffalo Bill' Cody was one, to record their estimates separately. The average of the eleven was 243,000,[97] which is not quite the same as 'billions.' In another place,

[93]*Ibid.*, 236 (italics mine).
[94]Goodnight, *ibid.*, 237.
[95]Nelson, *ibid.*, 237.
[96]Hornaday, "Extermination of the American Bison," 391-2, 388-9. (Above, chap. XIII, notes 7, 9).
[97]Garretson, *American Bison*, 63, 235.

Garretson puts the numbers 'which formerly inhabited the North American continent' at sixty millions.[98] To appraise Inman's position in estimating the one hundred, one thousand, or ten thousand millions of some year following 1867, it is sufficient to say that this is the same Colonel Henry Inman whose table quoted above [99] gives the buffalo *total*, January 1, 1865, as 15,000,000! In the field of buffalo history, distrust of Inman is the beginning of wisdom.[100]

Attempts have been made to estimate the total buffalo aggregate on the basis of the quantities of bones collected in various regions of their wide range. It is difficult to find reliable data for our purpose, or to reduce what we have to a satisfactory common denominator. One account describes in terms of pounds; others in terms of cars, or wagon-loads, or numbers of skeletons, or animals, or the estimated dimensions of some piled-up stack of bones. Many of these estimates are expressed, moreover, in the round numbers and loose phraseology of uncritical minds. Such recitals have too often been accepted literally and made the basis of rather close calculation by incautious critics who should have known better. Our efforts to reduce broad estimates and general dimensions to cords, pounds, car-loads, or numbers of animals will only approximate the truth, and more cannot be hoped for.

An old-timer gives us this picturesque description of the buffalo-bone trade:

. . . a market had developed in the east for the millions of buffalo skeletons that lay out on the plains. They were made into phosphate fertilizer and into carbon used in the refining of sugar, and sold for $7. to $10. a ton at the railroads. At first a man with a team could make big wages gathering and hauling the bones. I saw them so thick on the prairies west of Hays City that a wagon could be filled with all that two horses could haul from less than an acre of ground.[101]

I saw a pile of buffalo bones alongside the railroad track that was ten feet high, fifteen or twenty feet wide, and a quarter of a mile long. Col. Henry Inman made an investigation of the buffalo bone business, gathered statistics of shipments of bones on the railroads, and announced that 31,000,000 buffalo skeletons were shipped out of Kansas alone.

[98]*Ibid.*, 58.

[99]See above in this chapter, note 2. Garretson remarks (*American Bison*, 62) that estimates by Army officers 'would be somewhat more accurate than those of the casual traveller.' See next note.

[100]General H. M. Chittenden might well say that Inman was 'much better at telling a story than at relating facts' (*American Fur Trade*, II, 509, 538, 550).

[101]The photograph in Garretson (*American Bison*, 160) shows that in certain places at least, this would be no exaggeration.

I doubt if you could find on all the prairies of Kansas to-day one buffalo bone or any vestige of a buffalo. . . .[102]

The last statement is quite credible, for as long ago as 1889 Hornaday wrote: "This trade continued . . . until the plains have been gleaned so far back from the railway lines that it is no longer profitable to seek them. For that matter, however, it is said that south of the Union Pacific nothing worth the seeking now remains. . . ."[103]

Reighard's suggested dimensions do not seem incredible; but this 'fifteen or twenty' is one of those colloquialisms which make accurate computation very difficult, particularly when they add, as this does, 33 per cent as a mere afterthought.

Garretson writes in a similar vein about the Fort Worth and Denver route in the Panhandle of Texas in 1887: "At every way station, side-track or switch for one hundred and fifty miles, monster piles of bones were stacked up like cordwood. Many of these stacks were eight or ten feet high and more than half a mile long. . . ."[104] Elsewhere, he is even more specific, upon what authority we are not informed: "Twenty miles from Grenada, Colorado, on the Santa Fé Railroad right-of-way, was a rick of buffalo bones twelve feet high, twelve feet wide and a half a mile long—and this was but one of many."[105] It may be observed, however, that, at the time of which Garretson wrote, side-tracks of half a mile in length or longer (like those required by the enormous locomotive power of modern days) had not yet made their appearance;[106] and it is not probable that the bone-freighters would extend their piles beyond the length of a siding and thus make double handling necessary, when they could quite conveniently increase them in width, to such dimensions as Reighard indicates. So we may consider that 'half a mile' signifies merely a long pile. Let us consider quantities of buffalo bones in terms of cords. A square 12 feet by 12 feet contains 9 cords in each 8 feet of length; one half mile, 2640 feet, (not to say 'more than') would yield a total of 2970 cords. It is stated, on the authority of a firm of buffalo-bone shippers in North Dakota in the years 1884-91 (though we are not told by what process they ascertained this so definitely) that a carload comprised the bones from 850 animals.[107] This computation makes no allowance for

[102]Reighard, *Edmonton Journal*, January 3, 1931.
[103]Hornaday, "Extermination of the American Bison," 445.
[104]Garretson, *American Bison*, 163.
[105]*Ibid.*, 161.
[106]Perhaps I may add that I speak as a locomotive engineer of thirty-five years' railroad experience.
[107]McCreight, *Buffalo Bone Days*, 39.

different-sized skeletons, nor for conditions which might cause break-
ages and, therefore, closer packing. Differences in age or length of
exposure would result in varying degrees of brittleness, and brittle
bones stacked in the lower portion of a heavy pile would be apt to
break, and thereby pack still more closely. However, despite its
defects, as this is the only definite criterion of space which I have
encountered, we must be thankful for it. The standard box-car of that
era was a 40,000 pound or twenty-ton car, commonly 33 feet in length,
8 feet wide, and 7 high. This contains 1848 cubic feet, nearly 14½ cords.
Since it would not be possible to load such a commodity literally 'to
the roof,' we may allow about 14 cords per car; on the basis of 850
skeletons per carload, we arrive at a rough average of sixty buffalo
skeletons per cord. The pile above equals 212 cars and 180,200 buffalo.

In calculating quantities of buffalo bones in terms of weight, we
may start with the statement that it required about 100 skeletons to
make a ton of bones.[108] These proportions would naturally vary with
length of exposure, etc.; and in the latter days a greater number of
skeletons would no doubt be necessary to make up a ton. The latter
fact may make some of the statements which are expressed in terms
of carloads more credible. There is a record that someone (not named)
shipped 3000 carloads from Dodge City or near by apparently in two
years; the total weight, on Garretson's basis of calculation, would be
approximately 25,500 tons,[109] instead of the nominal 60,000, in 'twenty-
ton' cars.

It has been noted above that, according to their own figures (furnished to Colonel Dodge at his request), the Santa Fé system shipped
out 10,793,350 pounds of buffalo bones in the three years from 1872
to 1874. Dodge's assumption of an equal amount of bone-traffic on all
other railroads in the Southwest at that time—following upon their
inability or unwillingness to assist his inquiries—has also been noted.[110]
His hypothetical totals have been accepted by critics other than myself.[111] Since there were in those days no motor transport and no rival
facilities in the Southwest comparable to the Missouri River steam-

[108]Garretson, *American Bison*, 164; probably based on Inman, *The Old Santa
Fé Trail*, 203.

[109]Garretson, *American Bison*, 162.

[110]Above, chap. XV, note 100. Garretson (*American Bison*, 163) has
'1,350,000 lbs.'—in three years—probably a misprint. It is to be hoped so; since
the one individual recorded in note 109, who commenced bone-gathering 'about
the time the Santa Fé reached Dodge City' (December, 1872), shipped out
about 51,000,000 pounds of bones (25,500 tons) in *two* years!

[111]Hornaday, "Extermination of the American Bison," 499-500; McCreight,
Buffalo Bone Days, 10.

boats, it is safe to assume that the railways handled the entire long-distance shipments of buffalo products. We shall use this assumption as a starting-point for a discussion of the 31,000,000 buffalo skeletons which, according to Colonel Inman, were exported 'from Kansas alone,' in the years from 1868 to 1881.[112]

Thirty-one million skeletons represent 310,000 tons of bones, at the proportion of 100 to a ton; and 310,000 tons over a period of thirteen years give us an annual average of 23,846 tons, or 47,692,000 pounds, of bones per annum during that time. Inman appears to have taken a price of $8.00 per ton—the mean between the high and low extremes of $10.00 and $6.00 respectively which are given for that time—as the basis for his cash total of $2,500,000[113] (that is, $2,480,000) for the thirteen-year period. Now it will have been noted that in 1874 there is a really spectacular increase in bone shipments of over 250 per cent above the figures for 1873. This indicates clearly that by 1874 the bone industry was getting 'well into its stride.' It is quite probable that after 1874, when butchering on the colossal scale had put an end to intensive hunting proper, large numbers of former buffalo hunters plunged into the bone-gathering business, much as Hornaday has described; and for a year or two there might easily be a considerable advance in bone shipments over the figures for 1874. However, this inflation in amounts gathered in the industry would rapidly reduce the quantity of bones per man per day which it would be possible to bring from the increasingly distant deposits on the plains to a given place in a given time. Railways were few in the Southwest, and the bone industry is a story of long-distance hauls to the tracks. There were no doubt peak years to mark the height of the buffalo-bone industry, but Inman's averages for thirteen years would have to take into account two or three leaner years in the infancy of the traffic and also the years of its decline. Moreover, we have no accurate data from which to determine what proportion of the bones gathered from 1868 to 1881 represent animals *slain* during that period. The data we do possess appear to indicate that, prior to the final days of super-massacre, large masses of bones were exceptional phenomena *on the open plain*.[114] It appears that the only (relatively) large masses remaining from normal slaugh-

[112]Inman, *The Old Santa Fé Trail*, 203.

[113]Garretson, *American Bison*, 163; McCreight, *Buffalo Bone Days*, 8.

[114]Garretson says that 'in the early Sixties, portions of the plains were fairly white with bones' (*American Bison*, 160); but again, it seems illogical to suppose that Dodge, an old plainsman, would have noticed the bones on the Laramie Plains, 1868 (chap. VIII, note 9) had such sights been common: But cf. McCreight, *Buffalo Bone Days*, 22-4.

ter were about ancient pound-sites. It is nowhere made clear how long bones which were exposed to the weather, to the chances of lesser or greater destruction by prairie fires, and to the gnawing of wolves could withstand utter disintegration or even a partial decay which would render it impracticable or profitless to handle them.[115] So long as the great hosts remained, large quantities of bones must surely have been broken, crushed, and stamped into the earth.[116]

If, then, it is correct to assume that the greater portion of the 31,000,000 buffalo were actually slain from 1868 onward, we can distribute the bone-gathering over the thirteen years on an average basis of 2805 carloads, 23,846 tons, or 47,692,000 pounds per annum. However, it is not probable that the actual annual figures would approximate these averages for some years after bone-collecting superseded slaughter; and to make such averages an arithmetical possibility, there must have been four or five seasons for which the aggregates were not less than twice the general average. During those years, the totals must have been around 100,000,000 pounds, or 5882 carloads with a capacity of about 8½ tons each. The reader must again be reminded that all this was 'in Kansas alone.'

Let us compare these figures with Dodge's carefully considered estimate of buffalo-bone shipments for 1874. It is hardly credible that a rate nearly 500 per cent higher than his was maintained for four or five seasons. No contemporary nor any other reminiscent source that I have been able to discover mentions the visible traffic movements that would be required to attain such figures; and, if these have any foundation whatever, the silence of such men as Allen, Dodge, Horna-

[115]See preceding note. The bones there cannot be considered as any evidence of twenty-three years' survival, 1845-68; since the legend of 'no buffalo after 1845' has been shown to be without historical foundation. The bones seen by Dodge might have been much more recent (see chap. VIII, notes 15-28). Dr. Jenness notes a deposit of bones in a narrow gulch on the Sarcee reserve near Calgary—an old pound-site—whence they collected and sold several tons in 1918-20. These must have lain there nearly forty years (Jenness, *Sarcee Indians of Alberta*, 14; also his *Indians of Canada*, 58). These may have been protected by a deposit of some kind; otherwise, why had the Sarcees not discovered them long before?

My own parents settled in 1894 in the 'Red Deer Canyon' district, where the buffalo were little more than ten years extinct. Although I have often found fairly complete isolated skeletons, I have never, even around springs or such likely spots, seen more than five or six together (and even this number but seldom). Yet I never heard of any bone-gathering in our region, where the Calgary and Edmonton Railway (Canadian Pacific) was only three years old.

[116]This also may have some bearing on the enrichment of the soil (as above, notes 24-7). A chemical analysis of Kansas virgin prairie soils might yield some interesting information.

day, Coues, Chittenden, and Grinnell, cannot be easily explained away. I consider that Inman's estimate is another example of the loose talk of the smoke-room or the mess-table crystallized in print as serious history. A critic who does not appear to have allowed sufficiently for this tendency to interpret hearsay as fact writes:

It is fair to assume that bone collecting in the Kansas section continued for at least four years beyond 1881 even though on a less pretentious scale, therefore to arrive at a fair total for the Kansas field, we may add to the figures of Major Inman *at least* another million dollars, in doing which, we have a total sum of $3,500,000. . . .[117]

That is to say, although this period of acknowledged decline (when a given bulk of bones, owing to dessication by longer exposure would weigh less than ever) is less than one-third as long as the period of heavy traffic, he would increase the financial returns by two-fifths; and this also is from Kansas alone! That such an increase ever occurred is so highly improbable as to be virtually impossible.

As we have seen, we have good reason to believe that this prodigious bone-harvest represents for the most part buffalo killed in 1868 and later. But the averages of slaughter cannot be spread by any arithmetical process over any period of thirteen years; for, in Kansas at least, the great holocausts were over by 1874-75.[118] This necessitates that the 31,000,000 were slain in some seven years; and in conformity with the general historical character of the increasing slaughter after 1868, they might be allocated thus: 1868—1,500,000; 1869—2,500,000; 1870—5,000,000; 1871—6,000,000; 1872—7,000,000; 1873—6,000,000; 1874—3,000,000. No such gargantuan figures are so much as suggested, even by the loose-talking, uncritical old-timers of more recent years, as we have seen.[119] One such writer states (sixty years afterward) that Colonel Inman "gathered statistics of shipments of bones on the railroads"; as does Inman himself.[120] But two others, both of whom accept Inman's financial total,[121] say nothing about his statistical inquiries, a circumstance which does not increase one's confidence; and we have seen that at this very time, two of the three railways through the buffalo country refused such information to Dodge,[122] who gives us a

[117]McCreight, *Buffalo Bone Days*, 8. The italics are mine.
[118]Above, chap. XV, at large.
[119]See above, chap. XV, and read note 101.
[120]Reighard, *Edmonton Journal*, January 3, 1931 (*in extenso* above, note 102); Inman, *The Old Santa Fé Trail*, 203.
[121]Garretson, *American Bison*, 163 (who does not mention the 31,000,000). McCreight, *Buffalo Bone Days*, 8, 10, strangely accepts both Dodge's total for 1872-74 (chap. XV, note 100) and Inman's 31,000,000.
[122]See above, chap. XV, notes 96-100.

contemporary record, published in 1877. To sum up, in Inman's case it is difficult to separate the testimony from the witness; and the same witness, as I have noted already, compiled or endorsed a table of buffalo numbers for the entire habitat which showed a total of 15,000,000, as of January 1, 1865![123]

On the northern buffalo range, the bone-gathering industry appears to have followed a course essentially similar to that on the southern range. As before, much of our evidence consists of loose generalization which is not easily converted into concrete forms. Hornaday writes:

> The building of the Northern Pacific Railway made possible the shipment of immense quantities of dry bones. Even as late as 1886 overland travellers saw at many of the stations between Jamestown, Dakota, and Billings, Montana, immense heaps of bones lying alongside the track, awaiting shipment. In 1885 a single firm shipped over 200 tons of bones from Miles City.
>
> The valley of the Missouri River was gleaned by teamsters who gathered bones from as far back as one hundred miles and hauled them to the river for shipment in the steamers. One operator had eight wagons in the business. . . .[124]

Elsewhere, concerning 'the great triangle bounded by the three rivers, Missouri, Musselshell, and Yellowstone,' Hornaday remarks: ". . . since the slaughter *thousands of tons* have been gathered up there. . . ."[125]

'Thousands of tons' from 'millions of buffalo' (if the territory were gleaned with anything like completeness) involves no great strain upon our credence. It may perhaps be inferred that when Hornaday wrote, the Northern bone-traffic was yet in its infancy. For Garretson men-

[123]See above, notes 2, 99, 100. It can only be Inman's total which is responsible for the following. In a review of *Apache Agent, the Story of John P. Clum* (Woodworth Clum, Boston, 1936), J. P. Clum is credited with saying (p. 108): "Kansas must have supported at least thirty millions of buffalo at the time I was driving through . . ." (which appears to be not before 1874). This was very justly characterized by the reviewer as 'extravagant assertion' (*Mississippi Valley Historical Review*, XXVIII, 1936, 268). It could be defined in even shorter terms.

[124]Hornaday, "Extermination of the American Bison," 446. The earlier travel-literature of the Canadian Pacific Railway used to mention the 'picturesque sight' of stacks of buffalo bones to be seen at stations in the (then) North-West Territories. There were still some when I came West with my parents in July, 1894. For a photograph of a pile at Saskatoon (August, 1890) estimated to represent over 25,000 buffalo, see Hewitt, *Conservation of the Wild Life of Canada*, 114. This is on the basis of 850 skeletons per car, is only 30 car-loads, or some 250 tons.

[125]Hornaday, "Extermination of the American Bison," 510; cf. McCreight, *Buffalo Bone Days*, 38.

TABLE OF BUFFALO DECREASE

Year	Number of Males	Females			Increase (18 per cent—equal)		Killed	
		Total	Unproductive (10 per cent)	Productive (90 per cent)	Males	Females	Males	Females
1830	20,000,000	20,000,000	2,000,000	18,000,000	1,620,000	1,620,000	250,000	1,750,000
1831	21,370,000	17,870,000	1,787,000	16,083,000	1,447,470	1,447,470	250,000	1,750,000
1832	22,567,470	17,567,470	1,756,747	15,810,723	1,422,965	1,422,965	250,000	1,750,000
1833	23,740,435	17,240,435	1,724,043	15,516,392	1,396,475	1,396,475	250,000	1,750,000
1834	25,136,910	16,886,910	1,688,691	15,198,219	1,367,840	1,367,840	250,000	1,750,000
1835	26,254,750	16,504,750	1,650,475	14,854,275	1,336,885	1,336,885	250,000	1,750,000
1836	27,591,635	16,091,635	1,609,163	14,482,472	1,303,422	1,303,422	250,000	1,750,000
1837	28,645,057	15,645,057	1,564,505	14,080,552	1,267,250	1,267,250	250,000	1,750,000
1838	29,662,507	15,162,307	1,516,230	13,646,077	1,228,147	1,228,147	250,000	1,750,000
1839	30,640,654	14,640,454	1,464,045	13,176,409	1,185,897	1,185,897	250,000	1,750,000
1840	31,576,551	14,076,551	1,407,655	12,668,716	1,140,184	1,140,284	250,000	1,750,000
1841	32,466,735	13,466,735	1,346,673	12,120,062	1,090,806	1,090,806	250,000	1,750,000
1842	33,307,541	12,807,541	1,280,754	11,526,787	1,037,411	1,037,411	250,000	1,750,000
1843	34,094,952	12,094,952	1,209,495	10,885,457	979,691	979,691	250,000	1,750,000
1844	35,074,643	11,224,643	1,122,464	10,102,179	909,196	909,196	250,000	1,750,000
1845	35,733,839	10,383,839	1,038,384	9,345,455	841,091	841,091	250,000	1,750,000
1846	36,574,930	9,474,930	947,493	8,547,437	769,269	769,269	250,000	1,750,000
1847	37,094,199	8,494,199	849,420	7,644,779	688,030	688,030	250,000	1,750,000

TABLE OF BUFFALO DECREASE (Cont'd)

Year	Number of Males	Females			Increase (18 per cent equal)		Killed	
		Total	Unproductive (10 per cent)	Productive (90 per cent)	Males	Females	Males	Females
1848	37,532,229	7,432,229	743,225	6,688,999	602,010	602,010	250,000	1,750,000
1849	37,884,239	6,284,239	628,424	5,655,815	509,023	509,023	250,000	1,750,000
1850	38,125,216	5,043,262	504,326	4,538,936	408,504	408,504	250,000	1,750,000
1851	38,277,720	3,701,766	370,176	3,331,589	299,843	299,843	250,000	1,750,000
1852	38,327,563	2,251,609	225,161	2,026,448	182,380	182,380	250,000	1,750,000
1853	38,259,943	683,989	68,399	615,590	55,403	55,403	250,000	739,392
1854	38,065,346	......	......	......	......	......	250,000	

NOTE: 1853 = 683,989 females + 55,403 heifer calves; the entire female 'total' then in existence. The totals of the bulls shown are purely mechanical, no attempt having been made to allow for any 'natural decrease' of the males (that is, from old age), or for the physical accidents of flood and field.

Another point should not be forgotten. For a hypo-thetical calculation such as the foregoing, one has to start from a necessarily artificial datum. It is perfectly certain that the Indian preference for cows was of great antiquity; and the white hunters followed this, both for flesh and for robes. Hence it follows inevitably, that whatever the buffalo grand total might have been in 1830, the proportion of females would be much less than fifty per cent.

tions a man in the South who had "three big ox-teams and hauled about twelve to fifteen tons each trip."[126] At that rate, 200 tons would not take long. M. I. McCreight (himself an ex-bone buyer) mentions a pile at the western end of Devil's Lake, North Dakota, which was found to contain 250 carloads (2125 tons); another at Mouse (or Souris) River, yielding over 300 carloads (2550 tons); and a third at Fort Totten, on the southern shore of Devil's Lake, of 150 carloads (1275 tons).[127] Garretson mentions a pile at Minot, which was estimated at more than 5000 tons;[128] but, since Minot is on the Mouse River (where it is crossed by the Great Northern Railway), this may be an exaggerated estimate of the pile referred to by McCreight, whose figures represent, apparently, actual carload shipments. All these aggregates added together are eclipsed by the *annual* figures of one firm for seven years (1884-91); which averaged 1000 cars per annum with a resultant total of 5,950,000 buffalo skeletons.[129] And there were many firms in the business.[130]

Such figures as the foregoing point unquestionably to almost inconceivable numbers in the heyday of the living herds; we can only regret, however, that no attempt at precise computation, even after the utmost critical caution has been exercised, can be regarded as definitive.

[126]Garretson, *American Bison*, 161. McCreight (*Buffalo Bone Days*, 25) speaks of Red River carts carrying, 'according to the cart,' from 500 to 1000 or 1200 lbs.' This range is too wide to mean much. The 'load' of a Red River cart (in heavier wares, moreover) was 1000 pounds. They were much of a size.

[127]*Ibid.*, 19.

[128]Garretson, *American Bison*, 164.

[129]McCreight, *Buffalo Bone Days*, 39. The aggregate numbers are their own or McCreight's; since it was this firm which gave the car-load capacity as 850 skeletons.

[130]*Ibid.*, 38-9. While it is of course true (as McCreight, *ibid.*, Garretson, *American Bison*, 160, etc.) that bones were taken in trade for supplies furnished to new settlers in the buffalo territory, to describe them as 'legal tender,' as was done in local newspapers (Garretson, *ibid.*, 164) and by old-timers (*Saturday Evening Post*, March 8, 1930) is another example of the loose colloquial phraseology in which so much of our evidence is stated; and which it is extremely rash to accept too literally.

CHAPTER XIX

THE 'REGULAR MIGRATION'

I F mere repetition could raise any concept from the plane of pure assertion to that of established truth, surely it should have done so by this time for the 'regular,' 'annual,' 'general,' 'seasonal,' 'periodic,'[1] 'systematic,'[2] 'constant,'[3] 'orderly,'[4] or 'boundless'[5] migration of the buffalo, which is the origin of the theory of the regular trail, and the fundamental basis of the assumptions of road-origins from animal paths. This reiteration is perhaps not altogether illogical, in those who have already accepted the general implications of the buffalo-track argument. Their deductive process of reasoning requires a fact to fit their theory; and that fact is conveniently discovered in the 'regular migration of the buffalo.' If anyone desires proof of this, he is referred to any and every road which is not definitely known to have been surveyed by professional engineers within recent historical times; and such early roads are presented as 'evidence' of the regular migration. In this manner, the question has ceased to be an opinion, and has become a creed. Dissent from this, instead of being accepted on its merits as a reasonably cautious and considered divergence from the scientific viewpoint of other inquirers in the same field, becomes heresy. As with most other heresies, the answer to reason is authority. It is considered abundantly sufficient to reiterate the proposition at issue. It may no doubt be thought somewhat presumptuous even to postpone acceptance of such a widely entertained belief. There is one method only of ascertaining whether this conception is a sound one or not, and that is by an examination of the available evidence. I shall proceed with such an examination in the present chapter, citing to begin with one or two more or less detailed descriptions of the movement. A manuscript on the mammals of Mexico, which is now lost, but has been quoted by Allen,[6] and apparently copied from him by Hornaday,[7] states as follows:

[1]Thomas Nuttall, *Early Western Travels* XIII, 145; Edwin James, in Long, *ibid.*, XV, 256.

[2]Hind, *Report, 1858*, 106.   [3]Richardson, *The Polar Regions*, 275.

[4]Seton, *Life-Histories of Northern Animals*, I, 153. Used of buffalo not specifically, but by implication: "the moose have no orderly migration. . . ."

[5]Irving, *Captain Bonneville*, 300.   [6]Allen, *American Bisons*, 129-30.

[7]Hornaday, "Extermination of the American Bison," 382-3.

In 1602 the Franciscan monks who discovered Nueva Leon encountered in the neighbourhood of Monterey numerous herds of these quadrupeds. Also in Nueva Biscaya (States of Chihuahua and Durango) and sometimes to the extreme south of that country.[8] In the eighteenth century they concentrated more toward the north, at the beginning of the nineteenth receding more into the interior. . . . Every year in the spring, in April or May, they advance toward the north, to return again to the southern regions in September or October. The exact limits of these annual migrations are unknown; it is, however, probable that in the north [?] they never go beyond the banks of the Rio Bravo; or at least in the States of Coahuila and Texas. Toward the north, not being checked by the currents of the Missouri, they progress even as far as Michigan, and they are found in summer in the Territories and interior States of the United States of North America. The route which these animals follow in their migrations occupies a width of several miles, and becomes so marked that, besides the verdure destroyed, one would believe that the fields had been covered with manure.

These migrations are not general, for certain bands do not seem to follow the general mass of their kin, but remain stationary throughout the whole year on the prairies covered with a rich vegetation on the banks of the Rio de Guadeloupe and the Rio Colorado of Texas,[9] not far from the shores of the Gulf. . . .

From the observations made on this subject, we may conclude that the buffalo inhabited the temperate zone of the New World, and that they inhabited it at all times. In the north they never advanced beyond the 48th. or 58th. degree of latitude; and in the south, although they may have reached as low as 25°, they scarcely passed beyond the 27th. or 28th. degree (north latitude) at least in the inhabited and known parts of the country. . . .[10]

I have been unable to ascertain the precise date of Dr. Berlandier's work, but it was evidently written some time between 1828 and 1847, since he mentions the former date and also refers in an identical form to 'the States of Coahuila and Texas,' and the 'States of Chihuahua and Durango'—obviously as if they were two sister provinces under Spanish rule. This renders his suggestion concerning the indigenous origin of the buffalo out of date. In reference to Mexico at large, one must accept the broad statements of a scientific student concerning a land which he manifestly knew, and of which his present critic is ignorant.

[8]Presumably 'the extreme south' of Durango.

[9]The Rio Colorado of Texas debouches into Matagorda Bay, south of Galveston; the 'Espiritu Santo' of Cabeza de Vaca (Hallenbeck, *Journey of Cabeza de Vaca*, 127, 135), and generally accepted as the scene of La Salle's landing in 1686-87.

[10]Berlandier MS. (in Allen, *American Bisons*, 129-30; Hornaday, "Extermination of the American Bison," 382-3). Re the movements being 'not general,' J. D. Soper says of the movement of the wood buffalo westward in spring: "At no time does the westward trek appear to be generally in concert . . ." ("History of the Northern Bison," 384).

I am compelled to remark, however, that his observations on the northern regions of the buffalo range are either too vague or definitely wrong. They indicate an ignorance of the history of the buffalo in the northern territories which would be pardonable in the 'man in the street'; but is less excusable in a scientist writing presumably for public enlightenment; and particularly since he must apparently have written after the appearance of Richardson's *Fauna Boreali-Americana* in 1829.[11]

Berlandier has assumed without knowledge that because buffalo started northward from Mexico they kept on going northward indefinitely. This assumption is clothed in the same definite language that he employs in his references to Mexico, with which he was well acquainted. While he is in one place too definite, he is in another too vague. If 'Michigan' refers to the lake, Berlandier's statement that 'they progress as far as Michigan' may pass, since there could have been buffalo there at some time; but we have seen that the actual evidence for their presence in that State is very slight.[12] Whatever Berlandier may have meant, his language clearly implies that the same animals ranged all the way from Texas to Michigan, returning to Texas at the approach of winter. To speak of a 'route' of several miles' width seems curious, to say the least; and 'verdure destroyed' is palpably a mere misnomer for 'trampled down,' or 'eaten off.' If the vegetation were actually destroyed on an annual migration, a new route would be necessary each year; and it would become an interesting question whether the entire pasturage of the plains, or the species which depended upon it for subsistence, would perish first. Lastly, Berlandier's assertion that the northern limit of the buffalo was '48° or 58° N.,' is in the first place inaccurate; he should have verified his facts before speaking with authority. Moreover, while in computations of astronomical distance or geological time one is accustomed to margins of a few millions or scores of millions, a 700-mile margin in a total of only some 2,500 seems a mere slovenliness that robs his statement of any scientific value whatever. This inaccuracy in matters on which we possess the requisite data for independent judgment inevitably raises doubts whether some of his statements concerning Mexico and the phenomena of the southern migration may not be tinged with the same tendency towards hasty induction or sweeping generalization from insufficient facts. However, since two learned inquirers accept Ber-

[11]Four vols., 1829-37. The first volume, including the buffalo, appeared in 1829.

[12]On this, see above, chap. X, notes 1-4.

landier, I feel that I am justified in doing the same for his statement that the annual migrations 'were not general.' This assertion will find corroboration in the course of our investigations.

It will be of interest to quote the two inquirers mentioned and to note their respective attitudes toward the question. Allen writes:

> The buffalo is quite nomadic in its habits, the same individual roaming, in the course of the year, over vast areas of country. The habit of the buffaloes, too, of keeping together in immense herds renders a slow but constant movement necessary in order to find food, that of a single locality soon becoming exhausted. . . .[13]

We shall see that, according to other authorities, the buffalo did not keep together for very long; furthermore, 'roaming over vast areas of country' is not necessarily the same as travelling long distances northward and southward. Allen then gives a highly rationalized explanation of the north-and-south tendency; an explanation unknown to, or ignored by, some other publicists on buffalo.

> The streams throughout the range of the buffalo run mainly in an east-and-west direction, and the buffaloes, in passing constantly from the broad grassy divides to the streams, soon form well-worn trails, which, running at right angles to the general course of the streams, have a nearly north-and-south trend. These paths have been regarded as indicating a very general north and south migration of these animals. It is, indeed, a very wide-spread belief among the hunters and plainsmen that the buffaloes formerly performed very extended migrations, going south in autumn and north in spring . . . that . . . the buffaloes that were found in summer on the plains of Saskatchewan and the Red River of the North spent the winter in Texas and *vice versa*. That there are local migrations of an annual character seems in fact to be well established, especially at the southward, where the buffaloes are reported to have formerly, in great measure, abandoned the plains of Texas in summer for those further north, revisiting them in winter . . . the hunters report the same thing as having taken place on the plains of Kansas. . . . Yet it is very improbable that the buffaloes of the Saskatchewan plains ever wintered on the plains of Texas. . . . Doubtless the same individuals never moved more than a few hundred miles in a north and south direction, the annual migration being doubtless merely a moderate swaying northward and southward of the whole mass with the changes of the season. . . .[14]

[13]Allen, *American Bison*, 59.
[14]*Ibid.*, 59-61. Similarly 'improbable' from Saskatchewan to Peace River, thinks Macoun (*Manitoba*, 342); and with justice, as we have seen (above, chap. XII, notes 231, 243). The Denny MS. (p. 13) has them 'forever on the move' from Saskatchewan to Texas, like Allen's plainsmen. Seton (*Life-Histories of Northern Animals*, I, 262, 266) follows Allen's opinion, but credits it to Hornaday.

In my opinion, Allen in the foregoing puts his finger on the real cause of the north-and-south main trend of the trails. His reasoned explanation is in striking contrast with Hulbert's illogical insistence upon two mutually-destructive propositions—the north-and-south direction and the ridge-trail, paralleling the stream, rather than crossing it.[15] Hornaday, however, ignores Allen's topographical elucidation and is apparently all for 'instinct.' Hornaday says:

Unlike most other terrestrial quadrupeds of America, so long as he could roam at will the buffalo had settled migratory habits. While the elk and black-tail deer change their altitude twice a year, in conformity with the approach and disappearance of winter, the buffalo makes a radical change of latitude. This was most noticeable in the great western pasture region, where the herds were most numerous and their movements most easily observed.

At the approach of winter the whole great system of herds which ranged from the Peace River to the Indian Territory moved south a few hundred miles, and wintered under more favorable circumstances than each band would have experienced at its farthest north. Thus it happened that nearly the whole of the great range south of the Saskatchewan was occupied by buffaloes even in winter.

The movement north began with the return of mild weather in the early spring. Undoubtedly this northward migration was to escape the heat of their southern winter range rather than to find better pasture; for as a grazing country for cattle all the year round, Texas is hardly surpassed, except where it is overstocked. It was with the buffaloes a matter of choice rather than necessity which sent them on their annual pilgrimage northward. . . .[16]

Dodge, to whom we are already indebted for much valuable information concerning the history of the buffalo in the south, furnishes the following description of the migration on its northward march:

Fifty years ago [that is, *circa* 1836] the buffalo ranged from the Plains of Texas to far north beyond the British line; from the Missouri and upper Mississippi to the eastern slope of the Rocky Mountains. Every portion of this immense area, called the Plains, was either the permanent home of this animal, or might be expected to have each year one or more visits from migratory thousands. . . . These migrations were exceedingly erratic, depending somewhat on climate, but principally on the supply of grass.

From 1869 to 1873 I was stationed at various posts on the Arkansas River. Early in spring, as soon as the dry and apparently desert prairie had begun to change its coat of dingy brown to one of palest green, the horizon would begin to be dotted with buffalo, single, or in groups of two or three, forerunners of the coming herd. Thicker and thicker and in larger groups

[15]See remarks above, chap. IV, note 71.

[16]Hornaday, "Extermination of the American Bison," 423, 424. On Texas as a pasture region, see also Bancroft, *North Mexican States and Texas,* II, 559 *seq.*; Webb, *Great Plains,* 161, 209-27, etc. (citing much material).

they come, until by the time the grass is well up the whole vast landscape appears a mass of buffalo, some individuals feeding, others standing, others lying down, but the herd moving slowly, moving constantly, to the north-ward. . . .

Some years, as in 1871, the buffalo appeared to move northward in one immense column, oftentimes from twenty to fifty miles in width, and of unknown depth from front to rear. Other years the northward journey was made in several parallel columns, moving at the same rate, and with their numerous flankers covering a width of a hundred or more miles.

The line of march of this great spring migration was not always the same, though it was confined within certain limits. I am informed by old frontiers-men that it has not within twenty-five years crossed the Arkansas River east of Great Bend nor west of Big Sand Creek. The most favored routes crossed the Arkansas at the mouth of Walnut Creek, Pawnee Fork, Mulberry Creek, the Cimarron Crossing, and Big Sand Creek.

As the great herd proceeds northward it is constantly depleted, numbers wandering off to the right and left until finally it is scattered in small herds far and wide over the vast feeding-grounds where they pass the summer. . . .

When the food in one locality fails they go to another, and toward fall, when the grass of the high prairie becomes parched by the heat and drought, they gradually work their way back toward the south, concentrating on the rich pastures of Texas and the Indian Territory, whence, the same instinct acting on all, they are ready to start together on the northward march as soon as spring starts the grass. . . .[17]

Hornaday has also quoted the above *in extenso*[18] and comments upon it as follows:

So long as the bison held undisputed possession of the great plains, his migratory habits were as above—regular, general, and on a scale that was truly grand. The herds that wintered in Texas, the Indian Territory, and New Mexico probably spent their summers in Nebraska, southwestern Dakota, and Wyoming. The winter herds of northern Colorado, Wyoming, Nebraska, and southern Dakota went to northern Dakota and Montana, while the great Montana herds spent the summer on the Grand Coteau des Prairies lying between the Saskatchewan and the Missouri. . . .

The herds which wintered on the Montana ranges always went north in the early spring, usually in March, so that during the time the hunters were hauling in the hides taken on the winter hunt the ranges were entirely deserted. It is equally certain, however, that a few small bands remained in certain portions of Montana throughout the summer. But the main body crossed the international boundary, and spent the summer on the plains of the Saskatchewan, where they were hunted by the half-breeds from the Red River settlements and the Indians of the plains. It is my belief that in this movement nearly all the buffaloes in Montana and Dakota participated, and that the herds which spent the summer in Dakota, where they were annually hunted by the Red River half-breeds, came up from Kansas, Colorado, and Nebraska.[19]

[17]Dodge, *Our Wild Indians*, 282-6.
[18]Hornaday, "Extermination of the American Bison," 424.

The foregoing passage, which in the absence of comparative data might pass—as it has passed—for a valuable summary of buffalo movement over the plains territory, diminishes enormously in value under critical analysis. Hornaday's besetting sin is an unscientific propensity to elaborate a too broad and comprehensive thesis from insufficient material. Under his plastic touch, an incident becomes a practice, and a practice becomes a law, operating with rigid uniformity over immense and widely varying tracts of a huge continent. The above extract consists of the unhistorical, the anachronistic, and the illogical in roughly equal parts.

As I have previously had occasion to point out, I have found nothing whatever in Hornaday's paper, expressed or implied, indicating that he had any first-hand acquaintance with buffalo in their native haunts in the West prior to the two Smithsonian expeditions of 1886. The very purpose of those expeditions was to secure specimens of the buffalo for the nation before they were literally exterminated and so few[20] were discovered after much searching that Hornaday's opinions upon great masses were necessarily as dependent upon the testimony of other observers as are my own. Hornaday himself assures us more than once[21] that the harrowing experiences of the buffalo in the last few years wrought a considerable change in their mentality, as well they might! His own experience and most of the testimonies of fact or opinion that he cites belong to this later day, when the great mental change he postulates in the buffalo was already an accomplished fact, if it occurred at all. On his own argument, it could have had little or no bearing on the age-long characteristic mentality of the species.

Except for one observer, whom he cites only to chastise with contemptuous severity for his unbelief, Hornaday is much readier to extol the authority of earlier students than to record their opinions, if these chance to clash with his own. He calls the migrations 'general'; Berlandier, whom he cites (from Allen) without a single adverse criticism, says they were 'not general.' In his comment on Dodge, Hornaday calls them 'regular,' and indicates that changes in climate rather than questions of pasturage were the motivating cause. Dodge himself terms them 'exceedingly erratic,' arising largely from the need for better pasture. Hind is Hornaday's principal authority for the supposed annual itinerary of the buffalo on the western plains of Canada. Hind's description has been given in full above;[22] despite that, Hornaday's

[19]*Ibid.*, 425.
[20]*Ibid.*, 529-48.
[21]*Ibid.*, 422, 429-34. [22]Chap. XIV, note 52.

'summer' buffalo in Dakota hail principally from south of the Platte! Allen, his own chosen mentor, is ignored entirely again and again.

Hornaday's chronology is equally elastic. He is dealing either with the period before the great extermination, or during that era; judging from the commencement of the passage I have quoted, I should suppose the former. Yet, if he is writing of the earlier period, of what value is the testimony concerning the deserted condition of the Montana ranges 'when the hunters were hauling in the hides taken in the winter hunt'?—as if the killing and the securing of the hides were ever, until the final days of frenzy, two separate operations, months apart.[23] If he is dealing with the later era, the herds which were 'slain annually by the Red River half-breeds' in Dakota have no logical place in this passage; for he insists elsewhere that the buffalo in that territory had been extinguished or driven forth by the same folk in the 'forties.'[24]

I have shown above, in my remarks on the climatic bearings of Hornaday's migration argument, the inherent absurdity which it involves—the northern host finding their better winter pasture or a more tolerable climate in the same Wyoming or southern Dakota which the southern tribe had been glad to abandon because of its lack of these *desiderata*.[25] The quotation we are now considering will at least show the reader that my interpretation is not strained, but follows literally from Hornaday's words, whatever he may have meant. The plain truth is that the argument for the direction, the regularity, or the supposed causes of the migration would remain in a highly indeterminate and contradictory condition if it were dependent solely upon Hornaday's assembly of factual evidence to establish it.

A southbound return would seem to be inextricably bound up with an annual northward migration; and yet, absurd as it may appear, many of those authorities whose testimony is at other times often considered to be unexceptionable denied that a return journey was made. Referring to the opinions he has advanced in the quotation given above, Dodge observes:

It is but fair to say that this view is in direct conflict with the ideas of most 'old Plainsmen,' and of the Indians, who positively aver that the buffalo never returned south, and that each year's herd was composed of animals which had never made the journey before, and would never make it again. All admit the northern migration, that being too pronounced for any doubt or dispute, but refuse to admit the southern or return migration. Thousands

[23]See on this, Hornaday, "Extermination of the American Bison," 510.
[24]See chap. XIV, notes 91-3, 157, etc.
[25]See above, chap. IV, notes 43-50.

of young calves were caught or killed every spring, proving that they were produced during this migration, and accompanied the herd northward, but because the buffalo did not return south in one vast body, as they went north, it was stoutly maintained that they did not go south at all. The white frontier advocates of the 'no return' theory were easily confounded in argument, as they could give no reasonable hypothesis on which to account for the origin of the vast herd which yearly made its march northward. The Indian, however, was equal to the occasion. . . .[26]

One must acknowledge that it seems almost as idle to defend the theory of the southern return as to attack it. Irving, in virtually the same territory, in October, 1832, remarks:

We were now coming upon the tracks of buffaloes and wild horses. Those of the former tended invariably to the south, as we could perceive by the direction of the trampled grass. It was evident we were on the great highway of these migratory herds, but that they had chiefly passed to the southward. . . .[27]

Curiously enough, although Dodge appears to have found the northern migration 'too pronounced for any doubt,' Allen records the following:

General Meigs writes that a conductor of the Kansas Pacific Railway informed him in the winter of 1872-'73, that "while he had been several times delayed by the crossing of immense herds going south, he had never seen any buffalo returning. . . ."[28]

A more recent reminiscent old-timer remarks:

[From 'the highest point of land within the limits of Dodge City,' Kansas] I've seen a million buffalo in this valley, in a single herd. . . .
Fifty-seven years ago it was; early in December of '72. The Santa Fé records will show that for three days and nights all traffic west of Dodge was suspended while that one herd of buffalo was crossing the tracks. . . .[29]

One must suppose that this herd was travelling southward (a little overdue) at that time. It is interesting to note, *apropos* of contradictory evidence on this topic, that if it was, both the plainsmen's argument for 'no return,' and Dodge's explanation about not returning south 'in one vast body,' are shattered simultaneously; and if it was

---

[26]Dodge, *Our Wild Indians*, 286. The Indians believed in the supernatural origin of the buffalo. See on this, chap. XXI, notes 237-54.

[27]Irving, *Tour of the Prairies*, 466; corroborative testimony, Cimarron River, November, 1806, Coues (ed.), *Expeditions of Pike*, II, 436; Texas, *circa* 1853, Allen, *American Bisons*, 139; near Bent's Fort, November, 1858, Drannan, *Thirty-One Years on the Plains*, 332, 343. See also (1869), chap. XV, note 83.

[28]General Meigs, MS. notes on the buffalo (in Allen, *American Bisons*, 152); cf. George W. Reighard, *Edmonton Journal*, January 3, 1931.

[29]*Saturday Evening Post*, March 8, 1930.

not going south, the validity of the thesis of a uniform northbound spring migration is hopelessly destroyed. Truly a pretty dilemma![30] I do not think it is captious to suggest also, that, when it is used with reference to the characteristics of an animal species, the term 'general' signifies both etymologically and in common acceptation, a much nearer approach to 'universal' than would be permissible in reference to a body of human beings, of much higher individualized intelligence than the animal creation. 'General but not universal' could be said quite logically of human traits; but Hornaday, particularly, has by his sweeping systematizations placed himself in direct opposition to any such individualizing of the buffalo and has relinquished his right to enter a plea of individual variability in defence of any of his contentions.

Apart from mere details of time or season, direction or number, however, even the sacrosanct concept of the 'regular migration,' *per se,* has not been immune from sacrilegious assault; and by critics some of whom cannot lightly be disregarded. Allen is eclipsed by the iconoclastic Catlin. It may be of interest to observe, as illustrating the growth of my own opinions on the subject of migration, that I did not encounter Catlin's great work until after I had entered somewhat fully upon the reading essential to the present inquiry; but I had long before, in the course of a considerable amount of browsing in Western travel literature for its own intrinsic interest, formed certain tentative opinions. It then appeared to me that, if the term 'migration' was to bear the sense very usually applied, for example, to migratory birds— that of periodical removal from one recognized haunt to another[31]— the expression must frequently be a misnomer as applied to buffalo. I was therefore immensely interested to find that Catlin, a particularly competent observer in my opinion,[32] did not concede the fitness of the

[30]The whole question bristles wth these inconsistencies. Berlandier apparently takes all the 'starters' through to Michigan. Dodge distributes them along the road and returns them piecemeal; while Seton has it that only during the 'migrations' were the 'millions' ever seen (*Life-Histories of Northern Animals,* I, 274). Cf. Stone and Cram: "In winter time the herds migrated regularly to the southern portion of their range. After reaching their winter pastures in the South, they separated more or less and returned north in the Spring in scattered herds, making their migration much less conspicuous. The mating season was in the fall when the bisons occupied their Southern feeding grounds, the pairs remained in company until the spring, when the cows went off by themselves . . . and gave birth to their calves . . ." (*American Animals,* 69). They cite no authority; I doubt if they have any. Cf. chap. V at large.

[31]I leave this as it was originally framed. For an accepted scientific definition of 'migration,' see above, chap. IV, note 53.

[32]See on Catlin, chap. I, note 14.

expression. In the course of what is perhaps the very finest description of the animals in their native haunts ever written,[33] he characterizes them as follows:

These animals are, truly speaking, gregarious, but not migratory—they graze in immense and almost incredible numbers at times; and roam about and over vast tracts of country, from East to West, and from West to East, as often as from North to South; which it has often been supposedly they naturally and habitually did to accommodate themselves to the temperature of the climate in the different latitudes. The limits within which they are found in America are from the 30th to the 55th degrees of North Latitude; and their extent from East to West, which is from the border of our extreme Western frontier limits, to the Western verge of the Rocky Mountains, is defined by quite different causes, than those which the degrees of temperature have prescribed to them on the North and the South. Within these 25 degrees of latitude, the buffaloes seem to flourish, and get their living without the necessity of evading the rigour of the climate, for which Nature seems most wisely to have prepared them by the greater or less profusion of fur, with which she has clothed them.

It is very evident that, as high North as Lake Winnipeg, seven or eight hundred miles North of this, the buffalo subsists itself through the severest winters; getting its food chiefly by browsing amongst the timber, and by pawing through the snow,[34] for a bite at the grass, which in those regions is frozen up very suddenly at the beginning of the winter, with all its juices in it, and consequently furnishes very nutritious and efficient food; and often, if not generally, supporting the animals in better flesh during these difficult seasons of their lives, than they are found to be in, in the 30th degree of latitude, upon the borders of Mexico, where the severity of winter is not known, but during a long and tedious autumn, the herbage, under the influence of a burning sun, is gradually dried away to a mere husk, and its nutriment gone, leaving these poor creatures, even in the dead of winter, to bask in the warmth of a genial sun, without the benefit of a green or juicy thing to bite at. . . .[35]

These heresies move Hornaday to wrath. He declares: "Had Mr. Catlin resided continuously in any one locality . . . he would have found that the buffalo had decided migratory habits. The abundance of proof on this point renders it unnecessary to enter fully into the details of the subject."[36]

The only conclusive answer to ignorance or error such as that of which Catlin is here accused, is evidence. If the 'abundance of proof' is so great, it should not have been difficult to cite some of it; the

[33]Catlin, *Letters on the North American Indians*, I, 247-64.

[34]This is Catlin's contribution to the 'pawing' versus 'rooting' controversy, to which reference is made above, chap. VIII, notes 124-38.

Catlin, *Letters on the North American Indians*, I, 248; cf. *ibid.*, I, 261, 262.

[36]Hornaday, "Extermination of the American Bison," 423, note.

needlessness of 'entering fully' is scarcely a sufficient reason for not entering at all. I am of the opinion that there is a super-abundance of proof to show that Hornaday is wrong, and Catlin right. How many observers does the former cite who dwelt longer in any one locality in the West than did Catlin? With one notable exception, Hornaday's quotations are from passing travellers or visitors for a season or two—not necessarily scientists; observers who do not even wholly agree among themselves concerning buffalo, as we have seen again and again. The exception, of course, is Dodge, whose observations, valuable as they are, suffer in certain respects from insufficient comparative knowledge;[37] a result of that precise continuous residence for long periods in one locality, which alone, according to Hornaday, could have bestowed the crown of wisdom upon Catlin. We have seen in Dodge's case that despite his possession of the supreme qualification, Hornaday rejects his opinions concerning the 'regular migration.' Moreover, the latter's most-quoted authorities belong to a period from twenty to forty years later than Catlin; when on Hornaday's own argument, the introduction of superior firearms, the influx of settlement, the rush to Oregon and California over the two famous western trails, the advance of railways across the territory, and the resultant abnormal demand upon the species for 'sport,' subsistence, or profit—had already produced a noticeable change in the buffalo temperament, as compared with its virtually aboriginal character in Catlin's day on the Plains. If it were to be urged that Hornaday's authorities drew from the lifetime experiences of an earlier generation than themselves, may not Catlin have done the same? By virtue of a sympathy which Hornaday manifestly never felt—he scarcely ever mentions Indians without contempt—Catlin acquired an intimacy with the red men which laid open to him the stores of their traditional knowledge, and I really know of no reason why George Catlin should not have been equally entitled with anyone else to comment upon the facts he had collected, unless it be an intellectual incompetence for the task. In that particular respect, Catlin's remarks on the Canadian winter habitat of the buffalo, when compared with Hornaday's own, made a half century later in the light of wider and more available historical knowledge, indicate a capacity at least equal to that of his critic.

So far as other plainsmen are concerned, I have already had occasion to point out that virtually the only use which Hornaday and

[37]Some of Colonel Dodge's most intimate criticisms of 'Indian' psychology are drawn almost exclusively from the Cheyennes and Arapahoes, a confined view which led him into serious errors.

some other fellow-scientists have apparently been willing to make of those unlettered students who had spent lifetimes among the buffalo has been to accept from their facts based upon experience such as might support the pre-conceived theory of the critic; the conclusions of these observers have been contemptuously rejected or ignored if they failed to serve this purpose. It does not become any scientific student to reject the conclusions of eight years' careful observation on the mere ground that eight years is not long enough, especially if he is not prepared to replace them with the fruits of a much longer period of study.

The following passage in reference to other than north-and-south migrations is of interest, particularly since it was seen (and ignored) by Hornaday:

In northern Kansas the old trails show that their movements were formerly in the usual north and south direction, the trails all having that course. Since the construction of the Kansas Pacific Railway, however, their habits have completely changed, an east and west migration having recently prevailed to such an extent that a new set of trails, running at right angles to the earlier, have been deeply worn. Until recently the buffalo ranged eastward in summer to Fort Harker, but retired westward in winter, few being found at this season east of Fort Hays. In summer and early autumn, hunting-parties as late as 1872[38] made their headquarters at Hays City, later in the season at Ellis and Park's Fort, while in mid-winter they had to move their camps as far west as Coyote, Grinnell, and Wallace, or to a distance of one hundred to one hundred and fifty miles west of their fall camps, in consequence of the westward winter migration of the buffaloes. Two reasons may be assigned for this change of habit; first, their reluctance to cross the railroad,[39] and secondly, the greater mildness of the winters to the westward of Ellis as compared with the region east of this point. During the winter of 1871-72 I found that for a period of several weeks, in December and January, the country east of Ellis was covered with ice and encrusted snow sufficiently deep to bury the grass below the reach of either the buffaloes or the domestic cattle. In the vicinity of Ellis the amount of ice and snow began rapidly to diminish, while a little further westward the ground was almost wholly bare. I was informed furthermore, that this was the usual distribution of the snow in this region whenever any fell there. Although occasionally the snow does not accumulate in sufficient quantity to render grazing difficult over any of the country west of Fossil Creek, the buffaloes regularly abandon this region in winter for the country further west, where snow is of more exceptional occurrence.[40]

[38]Now Hays City, Ellis County, Kansas; N.N.E. from Dodge City, 38° N., 99° 30' W.

[39]This 'reluctance' lacks confirmation, Reighard, at that precise time a resident of Fort Hays, decidedly contra (*Edmonton Journal*, January 3, 1931). Cf. above in this chapter, notes 28-9; also chap. VI, notes 33-4; chap. XV, note 68.

[40]Allen, *American Bisons*, 61-2.

Dodge, then stationed in the vicinity, at or near Fort Dodge, mentions this severe winter but gives different consequences: "The winter of 1871-2 was unusually severe on the Arkansas. The ponds and smaller streams to the north were all frozen solid, and the buffalo were forced to the river for water. Their retreat was to the northward."[41]

Other evidence appears to indicate that if these trails were so pronounced as early as 1871, when Allen visited Kansas, they must have existed prior to a railway built about 1870. He says himself in another place:

After two or three years the results of this wholesale slaughter began to be apparent in the thinning of the herds and in their erratic movements and changed habits, especially in respect to their migrations. . . . In consequence of this east and westward migration, they had already worn deep trails running in this direction, and at right angles to the older set made when their migrations were *mainly*[42] from the north southward in autumn and from the south northward in spring. From the great persecution they had suffered from the hunters . . . their movements were already less regular than formerly. . . .[43]

The old-timer cited previously states that in 1867 and for some years afterward he was an army teamster between Fort Hays and Fort Supply, Oklahoma, about two hundred miles to the south. He adds: "On one of our trips in the spring, from Fort Hays southward, we met the advancing herd at Pawnee, fifty miles south of Fort Hays, and from there clear on to Fort Supply, 175 miles, we travelled through a continuous mass of buffaloes, grazing slowly northward."[44]

These particulars show that the 'cross-trails' must have been older than was thought by Allen's informants, and that the suggested change of route was by no means as uniform and complete as he (or they) would seem to have supposed.

Explanations based on 'persecution' can hardly be made to apply to Catlin's day, or to Canada. Even that hardy champion of the north-and-south trail, Hulbert, says (of his Central States territory): "And here, as in the Far West, the routes of the buffalo are north and south, with here and there a great cross trail. . . ."[45]

To crown all, Hornaday himself, it seems to me, yields the whole case by default in such passages as the following:

The capricious shiftings of certain sections of the great herds whereby large areas which for many years had been utterly unvisited by buffaloes

[41]Dodge, *Plains of the Great West*, 121.
[42]Italics mine.   [43]Allen, *American Bisons*, 152.
[44]Reighard, *Edmonton Journal*, January 3, 1931.
[45]Hulbert, *Historic Highways*, I, 131.

suddenly became overrun with them, could be followed up indefinitely, but to little purpose. . . .[46]

In 1880 the northern buffalo range embraced the following streams: The Missouri and all its tributaries, from Fort Shaw, Montana, to Fort Bennett, Dakota, and the Yellowstone and all its tributaries. Of this region, Miles City, Montana, was the geographical center. The grass was good over the whole of it, and the various divisions of the great herd were continually shifting from one locality to another, often making journeys several hundred miles at a time. . . .[47]

I differ emphatically concerning the 'little purpose,' for it is often only by an investigation of these unconsidered trifles that truth can be ascertained; it will seldom result from dogmatically or carelessly thrusting them aside. Also, once the presence of capricious impulse is conceded, 'regularity' falls to the ground *ipso facto*; and who can undertake to define the precise limits of such caprice in action? It would no longer be caprice. The periods during which the buffalo were alternately present and absent to which Hornaday alludes above, were quite as likely to appear at much shorter intervals, in Catlin's day as in his, and without any semblance of regularity in any respect. The phenomena upon which Hornaday principally bases his argument for regularity—the weather in the northern buffalo territory—are themselves notably and characteristically irregular. I have quoted above, in relation to buffalo and snow[48] (and need not repeat here at length), a number of accounts of herds in Montana moving south in winter which Hornaday explains as follows: "It is probable, and in fact reasonably certain, that such forced-march migrations . . . were due to snow-covered pastures and a scarcity of food on the more northern ranges. Having learned that a journey south will bring him to regions of less snow and more grass, it is but natural that so lusty a traveler should migrate. . . ."[49]

These particular movements may have been caused by snow; but apart from the futility of attempting to base conclusions applicable to buffalo during all time upon any conduct observed subsequent to that era of changed mentality of which we have heard so much, it is utterly unwarrantable to found any theory of 'regular' or 'annual' practice upon Montana or Western Canada weather conditions as I have shown above.[50] Anyone having an average knowledge of our north-

[46]Hornaday, "Extermination of the American Bison," 377.

[47]*Ibid.*, 508; cf. Dodge on this 'regular irregularity,' which apparently indicates the same thing (*Plains of the Great West*, 129).

[48]See above, chap. VI, note 152.

[49]Hornaday, "Extermination of the American Bison," 422.

[50]See chap. IV, notes 50-5.

western winters over a lengthy period of years will, I believe, agree that the very fact that weather is advanced as the exciting cause of such a movement, at once and without any need for further corroborative data, destroys the claim for migration to be considered a uniform process. For no such authority would be imbecile enough to maintain that there is anything like uniformity in our meteorological history. During fifty years in central Alberta, only once have I seen two abnormally severe winters follow consecutively (1896-97 and 1897-98); and likewise once only, two abnormally mild ones (1904-5 and 1905-6).[51]

Ernest Thompson Seton is the only one of our generalizing authorities upon buffalo who wrote upon the subject subsequent to Hornaday. For that reason he should be quoted at some length. I consider his contribution to the 'regular migration' inquiry[52] to be the most unsatisfactory portion of his entire section on the buffalo. He writes:

All observers agree that the Buffalo in great herds visited parts of the country where at other times they had been unknown, and they remained for a time until impelled by [to] another change of residence. The questions arise: Were these regular movements up and down certain routes? Was the change made under stress of weather, or famine, or both? In other words, was the Buffalo truly migratory?

To this question Catlin gives an emphatic 'No'. . . .[53]

Seton then gives part of the quotation from Catlin cited above and continues as below:

There is, furthermore, abundant proof that the herds were found summer and winter over most of the animal's natural range. That is all the proof I can find for the non-migratory theory.

On the other hand, all records, even those of Catlin, refer to the coming and going of the Buffalo, not perfectly regular, but quite seasonal, while most records speak especially of summer and winter ranges as regions where herds were to be found at set times. . . .

Colonel Dodge tells of a herd estimated at over 4,000,000 that he saw on the Arkansas in May 1871, *moving northward.* At Beaver Creek, 100 miles south of Glendive, Jas. McNaney says that the Buffalo began to arrive *from the north* in the middle of October, 1882; that about the first of December an immense herd came; that by Christmas all [?] had *gone southward,* but, that a few days later another great herd came *from the north,* and *followed* the rest. . . .[54]

    [51]See on this *in extenso,* chap. IV, note 55.
    [52]Seton, *Life-Histories of Northern Animals,* I, 266; also reprinted word for word in *Game Animals,* 1929, III, 650-4.
    [53]Seton, *Life-Histories of Northern Animals,* I, 261.
    [54]*Ibid.,* I, 262.

Hornaday, after a very full investigation of the subject writes: "It was a fixed habit with the great Buffalo herds to move southward from 200 to 400 miles at the approach of winter. . . ."[55]

Yet Seton immediately afterward adds the following, without even mentioning its utter irreconcilability with Hornaday's thesis: "It is remarkable that the Saskatchewan herd should have wintered in its coldest region. Probably the explanation is that this happened to comprise the best feeding grounds. . . ."[56] It was 'the best' in the sense of being the most sheltered, as Catlin had learned from some source seventy years earlier, but according to Hornaday (who had also read Seton's authority, Hind), they did *not* winter in their coldest region and there could be no 'best feeding grounds' in the farther north.

Seton's examination of the evidence for Red River migration is even more inexplicable. He writes:

The half-breeds and old hunters along the Red River have often told me of the northward coming of the Buffalo in spring, and of their southward migration in the fall. . . .[57]

There is only one sure way to determine the question of migration . . . a series of observations made during a number of years at one point where the Buffalo abounded. Twenty years ago we should have said, 'Too late for that', but now the discovery of Alexander Henry's precious old 'Journal in Red River Valley' has shed some light on the Buffalo and most other by-gone creatures of that now famous land of grain. . . .[58]

I have already protested against the attempt to invest the testimony of any one witness with final authority which should surpass all others; and in particular against giving to Henry any supposedly superior title to the pontifical position.[59] Unquestionably however, if Henry is to be the premier witness, the whole of his available testimony must be considered; and not merely that which may serve to support some pet prepossession. Seton goes on to say:

"Alexander Henry's record, given below, shows that, in 1800, the stream of migration, both northward and southward, moved parallel with and close to the Red River. The change to the route near Turtle Mountain began in 1812, when the first settlers came to Lord Selkirk's land grant, and it was directly caused by the increase of hunters in the neighbourhood. . . ."[60]

[55]*Ibid. All* had gone south, to be followed by *others!*
[56]*Ibid.*, I, 265.
[57]*Ibid.*, I, 262.
[58]*Ibid.*, I, 265 (*i.e. The Henry-Thompson Journals*, ed. Coues, 3 vols., 1897).
[59]See chap. I, notes 20-1.
[60]Seton, *Life-Histories of Northern Animals*, I, 265.

Seton cites a number of instances of buffalo movements noted near Henry's post on Red River, 1800-5, which I have given above, much more fully.[61] He includes eight notices, of which six indicate buffalo in that region in the dead of winter.[62] Three others (which I quote) reveal a northward movement in winter: "Jan. 14, 1801:–'Country covered with buffalo moving northward. . . .' Jan. 15, 1801:–'The plains were still covered with Buffalo moving slowly northward. . . .' Nov. 15, 1805:–'Terrible snow storm. Buffalo passing northward in as great numbers as I ever saw them. . . .' "[63]

Concerning the final entry (November 1805) Seton strangely observes: "This is the only record in Henry's *Journal* that contradicts the idea of a regular migration, but the writer expressly says that it was during a blizzard. In Manitoba blizzards come always from a northerly point. The Buffalo always faced the storm, hence, perhaps this irregular movement. . . ."[64] Yet on the very same page of his own work he has recorded the entries of January 15, 1801; with no mention from Henry or himself of any blizzard to account for 'this irregular movement'!

Even these do not exhaust the notices (by Henry) of movements equally 'irregular,' of which Seton says nothing. "Sept. 8, 1800:–'The buffalo were all in motion, crossing from east to west side of the [Red] river, and directing their course toward the Hair Hills [that is, Pembina Mountain, westward] as fast as they could walk. . . .' Sept. 26, 1800:–'No buffalo to be seen on the west side [of Red•River]; they appear to have gone toward the Hair Hills. . . .' Mar. 1801:–'Buffalo have for some time been wandering in every direction. . . .' July 1806:–'Herds, going from east to west. . . .' [noted west of Turtle Mountain]."[65]

We have here eastward and westward movements, just as Catlin described them, mingled indiscriminately with those to north or south; and a record, exactly as authentic as any other in the whole mass of buffalo evidence, of such movements in the Turtle Mountain region long before 1812. Seton concludes his discussion of migration thus:

[61]See chap. XIV, notes 98-143.

[62]Seton, *Life-Histories of Northern Animals*, I, 266 (citing Coues (ed.), *Henry-Thompson Journals*, I, 83, 136, 162, 166, 208, 273).

[63]Seton, *Life-Histories of Northern Animals*, I, 266 (*Henry-Thompson Journals*, I, 166, 273).

[64]Seton, *Life-Histories of Northern Animals*, I, 266; cf. *ibid.*, 298. See above (chap. VIII, notes 81-3), for the logical dilemma in which this involves Seton and Hornaday.

[65]Coues (ed.), *Henry-Thompson Journals*, I, 89, 103, 171, 309, 310.

I conclude with Hornaday that the Buffalo did migrate from 300 to 400 miles northward in spring, and as far southward again in autumn, but that the regularity of this movement was often much obscured by temporary changes of direction to meet changes of weather, to visit well-known pastures, to seek good crossings of rivers or mountains, or to avoid hostile camps or places of evil memories. Furthermore, there were scattered individuals to be found in all parts of the range at all seasons.

Theoretically, the Buffalo must have been migratory. Although it covered a vast region it continued of one species, whereas, it would probably have split up into several distinct species had it not been continually mixed as a result of migration. . . .[66]

Comparing this example of 'agreement with Hornaday' with that authority's own strenuous arguments for a regular and general migration, the latter well might cry, 'Save me from my friends!' I do not think I am distorting the sense of Seton's words (whatever his meaning may be) in suggesting that they may be paraphrased thus: the buffalo followed a regular migration, except that they did not always travel the same approximate routes at the same approximate times, season by season; their migration was general, except that some accompanied it, and others remained behind; and that (as Hulbert also states)[67] they invariably maintained a uniform northward and southward direction, except when they did not. To arrive at such a result by the suppression of evidence—one can call it nothing else, considering the ostentatious parade of the work containing it, as a decisive factor in the problem—leaves one wondering whether the critic's object was the elucidation of the facts or the vindication, at all costs, of Hornaday's opinions.

Concerning the final statement, it may be remarked in passing that opinion, as we have seen, is by no means unanimous on the buffalo having continued of one species.[68] What is of more significance here—

---

[66]Seton, *Life-Histories of Northern Animals*, I, 266. Concerning 'scattered individuals,' Hornaday says of the northwestern range: "This immense territory, lying almost equally in Montana and Dakota, had been occupied during the winters by many thousands of buffaloes from time immemorial, and many of the cows remained during the summer and brought forth their young undisturbed" ("Extermination of the American Bison," 511).

It is interesting to note the progressive dilution or distortion of opinion. Seton follows (?) Hornaday, who follows (?) Dodge. I quote Dodge: "That animal, though regular in his migrations, (going north in spring, and south in fall, or winter), was exceedingly erratic, his visits to any particular section of country depending on his own food supply, the condition of the grass. One year, the country of a tribe of Indians might be overrun by herds whose numbers were simply incalculable; the next year, the same territory might be visited by scarcely a single animal . . ." (Dodge, *Our Wild Indians*, 379-80).

[67]See above, note 45.   [68]See chap. III.

since it may perhaps throw some light on the actual origin and meaning of the migration controversy—is the almost universal application
of the term 'migration' to movements of any description. For it is
obvious at a glance that for purposes of general inter-breeding and
the avoidance of any sectional development of varieties through local-
ised isolation, the *regular* migration (whereby it is difficult to see how
certain herds could ever hold any intercourse with some other distant
ones, any more than a train crew, 'regularly migrating' between Calgary and Edmonton, or Vancouver and Seattle, could see anything of
men in Montreal or Chicago) becomes needless; Catlin's 'aimless
wanderings' being equally good, or rather, far better, for unless the
'continued mixing' were wide and promiscuous, sectional varieties, on
Seton's argument, would certainly result. Conversely, having demonstrated the truth of 'migration' *per se* by applying the term to any class
of movement in any direction, the uniformity of the 'north and south'
migration is proved by the precisely opposite process. If the trail, or
the apparent objective of the herd, is observed to lie in those directions,
this indicates a 'migration'; otherwise, it is merely an 'irregular movement.' Under this convenient system, the invariable uniformity of the
north-and-south migration becomes so self-evident as to render superfluous the portentous italics with which Seton impresses those directions upon his readers.[69] I consider that this grandiloquent phrase has
given rise to much misunderstanding and confusion; a much better
term would have been 'wanderings.'

It must at the same time be clearly recognized that what I have
contested in the foregoing pages is not the probable actuality of the
more or less regular migration *in certain regions*; but its applicability
to the whole of the buffalo range. This I continue to deny; and shall
proceed in the following chapter to disprove in detail. I have already
cited a considerable mass of evidence from residents or informed
travellers, tending to establish the authenticity of an approximately
regular migration in the southwestern buffalo territory, northward in
spring, and southward toward winter. This evidence comprises belief
in, or direct assertion of, a common tradition to that effect among long
or aboriginal residents; records of huge masses of buffalo actually
observed by reasonably credible eye-witnesses in circumstances which
seem to admit of no other explanation; and the existence of trails, if
we may rely upon the descriptions of observers who are accepted
practically unanimously for any other purpose, of a character not
mentioned by the more northern authorities, and such as my own

[69]See above, note 54.

investigations have not so far revealed in my own portion of the buffalo habitat. To reject such a volume of evidence concerning a region
I have myself never seen would be to convict me of that precise offence
of sweeping generalization which I have more than once condemned
in others. Accepting, therefore, the general implications of this body
of testimony, not necessarily in each minute detail, the real question
remaining is: How far northward did this migration extend, and what
was its purpose?

I have mentioned above the general evidence which seems (to a
non-biological inquirer, compelled to depend upon external and historical evidence) to indicate that the peculiarities of pelage and habit
in the buffalo point to a hyperborean animal gone southward rather
than to an original product of a sub-tropical or hot climate.[70]

Hornaday has very pertinently emphasized the anomaly of buffalo
leaving—and starting from—one of the very finest pasture regions of
the world for reasons of pasture;[71] and suggests that the motive for the
spring migration was to escape from the heat. Having regard to the
considerations mentioned at the commencement of this paragraph, and
which seem—broadly—to be supported by scientific conclusions not
reached when Hornaday wrote, I can see no more probable explanation. Given such a hypothesis, the migration (as a general movement)
must logically pause somewhere, where the excessive summer temperature would be mitigated, yet not far enough from the wintering region
to be beyond the compass of a round trip each season; for the tremendous journey each year from Mexico or Texas to the central Missouri or to Michigan—not to say the Saskatchewan—is climatically and
inherently improbable, and is destitute of historical support. Such a
region, broadly meeting these requirements, seems to be found in what
was called 'the Republican country,' which Dodge thus describes in
relation to the Southern herd:

> . . . their most prized feeding-ground was the section of country between
> the South Platte and the Arkansas Rivers, watered by the Republican,
> Smoky, Walnut, Pawnee and other parallel or tributary streams, and gen-
> erally known as the Republican country. Hundreds of thousands went south
> from here each winter, but hundreds of thousands remained. It was the
> chosen home of the buffalo. . . .[72]

Pattie, in the latter half of August, 1824, noted them "in such
prodigious numbers, as literally to have eaten down the grass of the
prairies. . . ."[73] Pike's expedition records them along the Osage and

---

[70]See above, chap. II, notes 18-20.   [71]See above, note 16.
[72]Dodge, *Plains of the Great West*, 131; see also Grinnell, *Fighting Cheyennes*,
90, 125, 127, 156, 259, 264, 299, 307.
[73]Pattie, *Early Western Travels*, XVIII, 49-65.

Republican Rivers at a time (September 12 to November 1, 1806)[74] when the southward journey should be commencing, and shortly after which other herds were seen travelling south.[75]

Such explicit testimony as that of Dodge, a general supporter of the regular migration theory, and who was when he wrote a resident of nearly thirty years' standing in that very region, cannot be ignored or easily explained away; and whatever the source of his information, the form of the foregoing statement makes it his own assertion. It may also be very instructively compared with Seton's generalization (considering that the latter 'follows' Dodge) on the 'scattered individuals' which remained on the range. Other testimony of a varied character certainly seems to point to central and western Kansas as being in a peculiar sense the characteristic region of the great herds, where buffalo were to be found in more or less abundance at practically all times.[76] If words have any meaning, it would seem to follow inevitably that a regular or general migration to the far northern regions must have restricted the presence of the buffalo in any locality along their route to twice a year, going and returning, these seasons depending, of course, upon just where the particular district happened to be situated along the 'buffalo highway.' If herds were found in Kansas (for instance) at any other, or at almost all times, the migration could not be regular; if any material number were so found at all, it could not be general; and if, in consequence, those terms require to be qualified, explained, interpreted afresh for each instance under consideration, they are better left unused.

Assuming for the moment the accuracy of the two hypotheses, that the buffalo are an earlier hyperborean species gone south, and that the regular migration northward arose from the heat, I freely acknowledge my utter inability even to offer a suggestion regarding the original pilgrimage to the south, or the persistent annual return to a region so soon afterward to again become uncongenial to them. It perhaps only adds one more to those numerous instances in which the *origin* of some recognized and powerful impulse is the despair of the inquirer.

[74]Coues (ed.), *Expeditions of Pike*, II, 401-35.
[75]*Ibid.*, II, 436.
[76]See some dates and particulars in Grinnell, *Fighting Cheyennes* (cf. references above, note 72). It was very probably in this region that the immense herds were seen by Coronado's party, April to August, 1541. See above on this, chap. IX, note 24. Compare also the statements on buffalo-bone traffic (chap. XVIII, note 100 *seq.*). Whether accurate or not, such assertions seem to point to a wide conviction that for numbers Kansas could not be surpassed.

Chapter XX

IRREGULAR MIGRATIONS

1. South of the Platte

FOR the purposes of the present chapter, the term 'irregular,' as applied to buffalo movements, bears two specific and distinct meanings, which it is well to make clear to the reader before proceeding further. Accepting the implied restriction of the phrase 'regular' to migration movements northward in spring and southward in autumn, 'irregular' signifies (1) movements possibly quite as regular in themselves, but not necessarily or usually in those directions at those seasons; and (2) movements in any direction at any time or season which are essentially irregular and erratic in the usual acceptation of those terms. These will be dealt with first in the southern territory in the United States and then in the northern States and finally in Canada; treating the valleys of the Platte and of the South Fork as the dividing line between the two first-named areas.

The wide extent of the historic buffalo habitat from east to west renders it inevitable that there must have been at some period an original movement of some character—whether we term it a migration or not—in one or other of those directions, to populate the two extremities of the range; unless, in order to preserve inviolate our allegiance to the north-and-southward concept, we prefer to suppose they evolved (or were created) contemporaneously at all points along their northern or southern boundary and moved forward as one buffalo to possess the land. As I have more than once had occasion to note, this 'original' migration movement was still incomplete in certain of the southeastern States as late as A.D. 1540; and this one, which was at least as much eastward as southward, is, curiously, the only such actual original migration of which we can be said to possess any chronological historic knowledge, amid all the mass of assumption and argument from the doughty champions of the invariable north-and-south! It seems to follow logically that a species which migrated —or wandered—eastward or westward once might do so again, and it will be seen that this was actually the case. Although the evidence seems incontestable (as I have observed in the previous chapter) for a movement in the southern territory much more regular in seasons and directions than any movement of that description north of the Platte, yet even the south is not exempt from these irregular manifestations. As I myself view the problem, I see no reason why it should be.

Although the recorded presence of buffalo in the southwestern mountain territory, either in the prairie foothills or on the eastern slope of the Rockies, is of course no guarantee in itself that they reached those localities by means of a westward-bound journey, yet a little careful analysis shows that such a direction is virtually inevitable. Although the great 'buffalo rivers'—if I may employ the term— such as the Platte and the Arkansas, do not literally flow directly east, their general direction is eastward, precisely as one speaks of eastbound or westbound trains between Winnipeg and Edmonton, although the latter place lies some 240 miles farther north.[1] According to the argument of the most rigid traditionalists, the buffalo 'invariably followed the line of least resistance'; and while their excessive emphasis on this will be shown to have been unwarranted, it is sufficiently true that the buffalo would not—and did not—disdain to use the westward river routes. Pike, in the mountainous country about Pike's Peak, in the headwaters of the Arkansas and South Platte Rivers, speaks of a route which he followed between certain of their tributary feeders (December 27, 1806): "Marched over an extremely rough road. . . . From there being no roads of buffalo, or signs of horses, I am convinced that neither those animals, nor the aborigines of the country, ever take this route, to go from the source of the river out of the mountains. . . ."[2]

Yet he records another of the numerous 'Buffalo Creeks' of the continent in that very region;[3] and the party found buffalo by Cheyenne Mountain, east of Pike's Peak, November 26, 1806;[4] as well as buffalo farther in the mountains, among the snow, January 18 to 25, 1807,[5] where their climbing powers excited his astonishment.[6] They encountered buffalo in varying small quantities all the way westward to the mountain localities mentioned, after first meeting with them near the Cottonwood Fork of the Neosho River on September 12, nearly two months out from St. Louis (July 15, 1806).[7] Pike's

---

[1]Winnipeg, 50° N.; Edmonton, 53° 36' N.
[2]Coues (ed.), *Expeditions of Pike*, II, 474.
[3]*Ibid.*, 468.   [4]*Ibid.*, 457.
[5]*Ibid.*, 485-90.   [6]*Ibid.*, 517; cf. also, 426-7.
[7]*Ibid.*, 401-73. The Neosho rises near Marion, Kansas, about 38° N., 97° 30' W., and flows generally S.S.E. into the Arkansas River at Muskogee, Oklahoma. This is probably the 'Cottonwood Creek,' 192 miles from Independence on the Santa Fé Trail (Chittenden, *American Fur Trade*, II, 537). Cf. above, chap. XV, note 48.

colleague, Lieutenant Wilkinson, records passing through herds for four or five days (November 8 to 12, 1806) during a detached expedition along the Arkansas, farther down, but as he does not specify the direction in which the buffalo may have been travelling at the time, the notice is not strictly relevant to our present inquiry.[8]

There are other records which are. Thomas Say, the naturalist, in his account of Captain Bell's journey down the Arkansas, in August, 1820 (detached from Long's expedition),[9] writes (August 9, 1820) "During these last few days past, the bisons have occurred in vast and almost continuous herds, and in such infinite numbers as seemed to indicate the great bend of the Arkansas as their chief and general rendezvous. . . ."[10] He further notes: (August 13, 1820) "Bison yet numerous. . . ."[11] (August 15, 1820) "Only five seen. . . ."[12] (August 16, 1820) "We have now passed the boundary of the summer bison range . . ." (at 37° N., 97° 30′ W.; Arkansas River).[13]

The last assumption was by no means verified by their experience. The point indicated is some miles south of Wichita, Kansas (37° 42′ N., 97° 12′ W.). The party had for some time been travelling eastward,[14] and directly across the supposed 'regular migration' route in its best-attested region, near the Great Bend; at the very time when the Arkansas River country should have been deserted and all the buffalo up near the Platte, at least. Yet after another fortnight's journey down the river, during which they were 'starving,' the party again encountered buffalo at the junction of the Verdigris and the Arkansas Rivers (35° 40′ N., 95° 20′ W. practically at Muskogee, Oklahoma; near where the Neosho River also debouches).[15]

To what extent Say's remarks may be warranted, clearly implying as they do an eastward summer and westward winter journey into the mountain territory, *circa* 1820, is difficult to decide, particularly in relation to the summer movement. Gregg writes: "The buffalo are usually found much further east early in the spring than during the rest of the year, on account of the long grass, which shoots up earlier in the season than the short pasturage of the plains. . . . A few old buffaloes have sometimes been met with about Cottonwood. . . ."[16]

---

[8]Coues (ed.), *Expeditions of Pike*, II, 548, 549.

[9]In Long, *Early Western Travels*, XVI, 192-291.

[10]*Ibid.*, 228.   [11]*Ibid.*, 238.

[12]*Ibid.*, 241.   [13]*Ibid.*, 242.

[14]Dodge City lies exactly west from Wichita (37° 46′ N.) across the Great Bend of the Arkansas River.

[15]*Early Western Travels*, XVI, 265, 267. For the Neosho River, see above, note 7.

[16]Gregg, *Early Western Travels*, XIX, 205.

In 1831 (May 30) buffalo were seen two days past Cottonwood. Gregg remarks on a later page, being then eastbound, in early May, 1839: ". . . we saw no buffalo after crossing the Arkansas river. It is true that owing to their disrelish for the long dry grass of the eastern prairies, the buffalo are rarely found so far east in autumn as during the spring; yet I never saw them so scarce in this region before. In fact, at all seasons, they are usually very abundant as far east as our point of leaving the Arkansas river. . . ."[17]

It may be considered improbable that they could reach a point within two days of Cottonwood (or some 170 miles) by May 30, of that year.[18] The frequent presence of great numbers on the Arkansas River at times considerably later than early May (when Gregg found none in 1839, and where Dodge saw his immense herd in 1871) is attested by Dr. Willard on the Santa Fé Trail, June 1, 1825. He says there "could not have been less than 100,000 before noon. . . ."[19] This at the usual rate of about fifteen miles per day,[20] and reckoning from May 1, would still be on the northern side of the Arkansas, as the Cimarron cut-off was not commonly used previous to 1834.[21] This conjectural distance (as well as the similar presence of buffalo) finds confirmation from Gregg (Santa Fé Trail, near the Ford of the Arkansas, that is, 'the Cimarron Crossing,' June 10, 1831). He remarks: "Although the buffalo had been scarce for a few days they soon became exceedingly abundant. . . ."[22]

Farnham likewise, in 1839 (June 21 to 23), remarks concerning the same locality (one day before reaching the Arkansas, westbound): (June 22) "The whole circle of vision was one black mass of those animals. . . ." (June 23) ". . . more numerous than ever. . . ." (June 24) "The buffalo during the last three days had covered the country so completely, that it appeared oftentimes extremely dangerous even for the immense cavalcade of the Santa Fé traders to attempt to break its way through them. . . ."[23]

[17]*Ibid.*, XX, 92; 122 miles from the Ford (Gregg, Table of Mileages, *ibid.*, 93; Chittenden, *American Fur Trade*, II, 537).
    [18]Gregg, *Early Western Travels*, XX, 93; Chittenden, *American Fur Trade*, II, 537.
        [19]*Early Western Travels*, XVIII, 334.
        [20]Gregg, *ibid.*, XX, 93; Chittenden, *American Fur Trade*, II, 525.
        [21]Gregg, *Early Western Travels*, XX, 91-3; Chittenden, *American Fur Trade*, II, 531, 541, 775.
        [22]Gregg, *Early Western Travels*, XIX, 213.
        [23]Farnham, *ibid.*, XXVIII, 94-6; similarly, about the same vicinity, June 1847: Drannan, *Thirty-One Years on the Plains*, 36.

Conversely, on the southern side of the Arkansas, and near the Cimarron River, where Jedidiah S. Smith met his tragic death at this time, and in the region of the innumerable 'criss-crossing' of buffalo trails,[24] Gregg observes again (end of June, 1831): "Not a buffalo to be seen . . . at some seasons (and particularly in the fall) the prairies are literally strewed with herds of these animals. . . ."[25]

The fall, or early winter, would of course be the appropriate time for the returning southbound hosts; yet Dodge himself, although he maintained the theory of a southward return in small unnoticeable bands,[26] remarked as a noteworthy event that they were 'rather scarce' along the Arkansas, just below the mouth of Sand Creek, in the Fall of 1870.[27] This might possibly be ascribed at that late date, to the 'beginning of the end'; yet Irving, in much the same locality, in the fall also (of 1832) observes that "the deep and frequent traces of buffalo showed it to be one of their favourite grazing grounds; yet none were to be seen. . . ."[28]

A dozen years before Irving, Long's party record the following, south of the Arkansas, apparently August, 1820: "Few traces of bison, either old or recent, were to be seen [only some antelopes and mustangs, all wild and shy]. . . . From these facts we inferred that we were on the frontiers of some permanent settlement . . ." (either of Spanish or Indians, which apparently they were not).[29]

Farnham, in the same region—broadly—mentions as a typical feature of the evening camp-life, 'argumentative plainsmen' . . . "delivering sage opinions about the destination of certain bands of buffalo . . .";[30] a thing plainly problematical! Farnham also (1839) describes a summer westward migration to the famous Bayou Salade, on the Upper South Platte: "The buffalo have for ages resorted here about the last days of July from the arid plains of the Arkansas and the Platte; and thither the Eutaws and Cheyennes from the mountains around Santa Fé, and the Shoshonies or Snakes and Arrapahoes from

---

[24]See Dale (ed.), *Ashley-Smith Explorations*, 295; Farnham, *Early Western Travels*, XXVIII, 94; Gregg, *ibid.*, XIX, 236; etc. Smith's party nearly died of thirst, *en route* to the Cimarron River; in a land 'criss-crossed with buffalo trails'; which according to the Hulbert school, 'invariably led to water'!

[25]Gregg, *ibid.*, XIX, 243.

[26]Above, chap. XIX, notes 17, 26.

[27]Dodge, *Plains of the Great West*, 375.

[28]Irving, *Tour of the Prairies*, 447. *Trace* here signifies trail. See above, chap. VI, note 2.

[29]Long, *Early Western Travels*, XVI, 83, 96.

[30]Farnham, *ibid.*, XXVIII, 172.

the west, and the Blackfoot, Crows, and Sioux from the north, have for ages met, and hunted, and fought. . . ."[31]

Even this, however, like practically everything else about the buffalo, was apparently open to exception. Farnham himself noted that they were becoming fewer along the Upper Arkansas in July 1839,[32] when they should presumably have been hastening thither; and Edwin James, of Long's party, records 'some bisons'—which can only indicate fewness—also on the Upper Arkansas, in the same month of 1820.[33] James again, in the neighbourhood of Pike's Peak, describes ". . . a large and much frequented road [that is, 'trail'[34]] passes the springs, and enters the mountains, running to the north of the high peak. It is travelled principally by the bisons, sometimes also by the Indians, who penetrate here to the Columbia. . . ."[35]

Yet in spite of these indications of buffalo, the actual evidence reveals clearly enough that finding them was purely a chance affair. Long's party, after seeing none for several days, found buffalo near Castle Rock, Colorado.[36] Following this, there were none for many days between the headwaters of the South Platte and the Arkansas, except one solitary bull, "too ill-savoured to eat." Later they discovered another of like evil savour, which in their starving condition they ate, nevertheless.[37] Long and his party were strangers in the mountains, losing themselves on occasion; and their troubles in finding buffalo might be hastily ascribed to this cause. Frémont, however, in the same region, between the headwaters of the same two rivers about the middle of July, 1843, speaks of them "hoping to fall in with buffalo . . ."; yet they found ". . . no indication of buffalo having recently been in the neighbourhood. . . ."[38]

Frémont's guide on this occasion was the famous Thomas Fitzpatrick, ". . . whom many years of hardship and exposure in the western territories had rendered familiar with a portion [including this precise portion] of the country it was designed to explore. . . ."[39]

---

[31]Ibid., 209, 266; also Chittenden, American Fur Trade, II, 750.

[32]Farnham, Early Western Travels, XXVIII, 97-106.

[33]Long, ibid., XV, 313. In July, 1694, Diego de Vargas found buffalo in the 'Yuta country' northward from Taos, about the Colorado and New Mexico State line; but the numbers are not indicated (Bancroft, History of Arizona, 210).

[34]See above, on road and trail, chap. VI, note 2.

[35]Long, Early Western Travels, XVI, 24, 72.

[36]Ibid., XV, 307. 'Near Pueblo' (sic); but Castle Rock is placed a few miles directly south of Denver, both being on longitude 105° W.

[37]Ibid., XVI, 30, 103.   [38]Frémont, Narrative, 102-4.

[39]Frémont to his chief, Colonel J. J. Abert, ibid., 93, 110, 140. Thomas Fitzpatrick was probably the discoverer of the famous South Pass (1822). See Dale (ed.), Ashley-Smith Explorations, 89, 102, 153, 319.

This absence of buffalo is not attributable to poor pasturage, for this is the very region of the 'Parks' already mentioned, and the explorers noted that 'buffalo grass' (*sesleria dactyloides*)[40] was the most abundant of a rich variety of grasses.[41]

These facts, on the supposition of any really seasonal movements, would seem to point towards this mountain territory as a winter, rather than as a summer resort. Edwin James observes concerning the very region where they were in such dire extremities: ". . . All the mountains which we ascended were more or less strewed with the dung of these animals about the lower parts; a conclusive evidence that this portion of the range had been traversed by the bisons. . . ."[42]

General (then Captain) R. B. Marcy, a competent observer, says: "Although generally regarded as migratory in their habits, yet the buffalo often winter in the snows of a high northern latitude. Early in the spring of 1858 I found them in the Rocky Mountains, at the head of the Arkansas and South Platte Rivers and there was every indication that this was a permanent abiding place for them. . . ."[43]

Pike's editor, Dr. Elliott Coues, himself both an experienced plainsman and a profound student of Western historical literature, endorses this; and adds the following description: "Between Salida and Brown Cañon the country is open and park-like among the mountains—just the sort of place where buffalo would herd in the winter. . . . The mountain fastnesses about the headwaters of the Arkansaw long continued to be wintering-grounds for the buffalo. . . ."[44]

Yet Frémont again, on the eastbound journey after his fearful trip through the Sierra Nevada, found buffalo (his 'first sight') on St. Vrain's Fork in June, 1844;[45] and he notes 'abundance in the Parks,' shortly afterward in the same month.[46] This might suggest buffalo there either in summer or winter; but Edwin James says after all

[40]This is Frémont's classification; but for a number of such, see above, chap. IV, note 50.

[41]Frémont, *Narrative*, 104.

[42]Long, *Early Western Travels*, XV, 245.

[43]Marcy, *The Prairie Traveller*, 234.

[44]Coues, ed. note, *Expeditions of Pike*, II, 472. Salida (38° N., 106° 30' W.) is on the Upper Arkansas River, southwest of Pike's Peak, between Pueblo and Leadville, Colorado. They were noted near (modern) Pueblo, Colorado, 'in abundance,' November, 1847 (Drannan, *Thirty-One Years on the Plains*, 54). They varied, as elsewhere. On buffalo about Bent's Fort, 1852, 1858, 1859 ('best season for years'), *ibid.*, 154, 332, 354.

[45]Frémont, *Narrative*, 308-9.

[46]*Ibid.*, 309-13. St. Vrain's Fort was situated a little north of Denver, and east of Long's Peak; almost exactly 40° 15' N., 105° W. The 'Fork' was a small tributary feeder, flowing into the South Platte. See Chittenden, *American Fur Trade*, II, 543.

this: "This band of Kaskaias [or 'Bad Hearts'] occupy the country about the sources of the Platte, Arkansa, and Rio del Norte, and extend their hunting excursions to Red River, and the sources of the Brases" (Brazos).[47]

Such testimonies as the foregoing can scarcely be said to advance the case for uniformity of movement in any direction or at any season to a really material extent.

Some interesting evidence also reveals the presence of considerable numbers along the Canadian River in those summer months when, according to the orthodox theory of a general migration, that locality should have been virtually deserted during the absence of the buffalo in their northern haunts. Long's expedition, descending the Canadian in August, 1820, record a few on the upper river, 'becoming more numerous' about 36° N.; 100° W. (which is there the modern state boundary between Texas and Oklahoma; a high prairie region west of the famous 'Cross Timbers'[48]) being followed by 'astonishing numbers' and 'immense herds' for several days; these growing smaller along the lower river.[49] Gregg, at the end of March, 1839, found them (after a scarcity) where the Canadian and the 'North Fork' begin to approach closer to each other, about 99°-100° W.[50] Marcy also found buffalo on the northern side of the Canadian in June, 1852.[51] Gregg sums up for us in this region by saying that buffalo were 'abundant on the Canadian, sometimes. . . .'[52]

Even the peculiarly favoured territory between the Arkansas and the Platte—'the Republican country'—was not exempt from similar fluctuations, and here too (as we shall find to be the case throughout the entire western buffalo habitat), the observed scarcities are not to be explained by 'disappearance,' excessive hunting, or 'the beginning of the end.' For it will be seen that scarcities follow plenty at periods too early for such explanations to apply; and are again followed, sometimes at considerably later eras, by the former condition of abundance. On the Republican River itself, where Pattie found 'immense numbers' in August, 1824,[53] and Frémont also in June,

[47]Long, *Early Western Travels*, XVI, 117.
[48]On these, see below, note 422.
[49]Long, *Early Western Travels*, XVI, 130-48, 164.
[50]Gregg, *ibid.*, XX, 118. In that locality, this would apparently be the Washita (*i.e.* North Fork of Red River), unless there was a 'North Fork' of the Washita itself, not discoverable on ordinary maps. See below, note 426.
[51]Marcy, *Exploration of Red River*, 43.
[52]Gregg, *Early Western Travels*, XX, 213. So found by Catlin, 1834 (*Letters on the North American Indians*, II, 76).
[53]Pattie, *Early Western Travels*, XVIII, 49-65.

1843,[54] (as he likewise did on the main Kansas River in July, 1844[55]), Edwin James in January, 1820—despite the supposed plenty throughout the year—records ". . . the Otoes on the Republican fork of the Konza [that is, the Kansas] river going after bison on the Pawnee Loup river; said to be plenty there."[56]

Shortly afterward, Long's party saw a herd of several hundreds on the Sioux River. When they broke up their winter camp in the spring,[57] they were advised by the Indians to try the Pawnee Loup river themselves, as 'there were no bisons on the Platte.' The explorers were suspicious of this information—having themselves possibly heard of that familiar legend of invariable plenty, but later found the warning intimation to be quite true.[58] They actually saw none, other than two solitary bulls about a hundred miles apart,[59] until they reached the Forks of the Platte, where they encountered 'immense herds, at least 10,000,'[60] followed by more large herds along the South Platte (June, 1820).[61]

James records two curious occurrences which reveal very clearly the utterly erratic nature of buffalo movements; the more remarkable in that this particular region has been so frequently extolled as one of ultra-uniformity. He writes (South Platte River, June, 1820):

This barren and ungenial district appeared at this time to be filled with greater numbers of animals than its meagre productions are sufficient to support. It was, however, manifest that the bisons, then thronging in such numbers, were moving toward the south. Experience may have taught them to repair at certain seasons to the more luxuriant plains of Arkansa and Red Rivers. What should ever prompt them to return to the inhospitable deserts of the Platte, it is not, perhaps, easy to conjecture. . . .[62]

These were presumably a detachment of those sagacious hosts who 'always knew where were the best pastures'; but this certainly could not have been the 'regular' southward autumn migration; for we have seen that even in late June they were often only at the Arkansas, coming northward. Again, in describing the 'Grand Pawnee village' (a permanent one on the Platte[63]), James relates the following

[54]Frémont, Narrative, 98-9.
[55]Ibid., 318.
[56]Long (James), Early Western Travels, XIV, 276.
[57]Ibid., 278.
[58]Ibid., XV, 207.
[59]Ibid., 225, 227.
[60]Ibid., 239.
[61]Ibid., 242-58.
[62]Ibid., 248.
[63]See on the Pawnees and their villages, Coues (ed.), Henry-Thompson Journals, I, 334, 338, 348; also his Explorations of Pike, II, 533. Long, Early

curious occurrence: ". . . immediately about the towns we saw many heads and skeletons of such as had been killed there the preceding spring. They had come in while the Pawnees were absent on their winter's hunt, and at their return, we were informed, they found the bisons immediately about their villages. . . ."[64]

The above must be acknowledged to constitute a striking commentary on the familiar shibboleths about experienced hunters 'always knowing where the buffalo could be found.' Although we shall meet with later examples, this is perhaps the most astonishing.

The foregoing mass of evidence exhibits clearly an utterly incalculable irregularity in buffalo movements in the very region which (even in my own opinion) presents a not inconsiderable volume of testimony to something approaching a regular or general migration; certainly more so than any other large territory known to me. It will be found as we work our way northward that this irregularity by no means diminishes.

In view of the fact that Texas in particular has been regarded by many writers as a sort of southern terminal, in which they scarcely 'resided,' merely flocking thither in winter and hurrying thence in spring, I include a note at the end of the chapter (too detailed for practicable abbreviation, and too long for quotation in the body of the chapter) containing a valuable synopsis, taken from Allen, on buffalo variations in that State after 1840.

2. The Platte Region

The evidence concerning migrations for the main valley of the Platte and the territory immediately adjacent on the northern side— along which from about 1840 the Oregon Trail ran—is of the same general character as that for the South. The earliest notice I have found is of the eastbound Astorians, who noted 'abundance of buffalo, which seemed absolutely to cover the country,' on the main stream below the Forks, during the period from December, 1812, to March, 1813.[65] Later, at the Pawnee villages on the Lower Platte, the hunters had 'gone south after buffalo.'[66] To winter on the Platte when they should have been

---

Western Travels, XV, 203, 209, 216, 233; Gregg, *ibid.*, XX, 91, 140, 351; Irving, *Astoria*, 381; also his *Captain Bonneville*, 80; Frémont, *Narrative*, 318; Parkman, *Oregon Trail*, 74, 78; Dale (ed.), *Ashley-Smith Explorations*, 119-22; and an admirable modern summary by W. R. Wedel, *Smithsonian Miscellaneous Collections*, vol. 100, 1940, 339-41.

[64]Long, *Early Western Travels*, XV, 256.
[65]Irving, *Astoria*, 379-80.
[66]*Ibid.*, 381.

in Texas (or Saskatchewan) is bad, but worse remains behind! James thus remarks on their absence in summer (June, 1820):

In the afternoon a single bison was seen at the distance of several miles, being the second since we had left the Pawnee villages, which were now about one hundred miles distant, and we were beginning to fear that the representations of the Indians, in relation to the difficulty of procuring game to subsist so large a party as ours, would prove true. We found, however, that every part of the country, which we had recently passed, had, at no distant period, been occupied by innumerable herds of bisons. Their tracks and dung were still to be seen in vast numbers; and the surface of the ground was strewn with skulls and skeletons, which were yet undecayed. . . .[67]

General Ashley, the well-known early fur trader, found buffalo at the Forks of the Platte, December 23, 1824: "The weather was fine, the valleys were literally covered with buffaloe. . . ."[68] Five days later, going up the South Platte, he says: "The snow was now so deep that had it not been for the numerous herds of buffaloe moving down the river, we could not possibly have proceeded. The paths of these animals were beat on either side of the river, and afforded an easy passage to our horses. . . ."[69]

Pattie, eastbound in early May the following spring (1825), records 'immense droves' on the Upper North Platte.[70] In the same month in 1832, Nathaniel or John B. Wyeth found buffalo 'in frightful droves' along the main river.[71] Captain Bonneville, a month later (June, 1832) found none; but Irving remarks concerning this: "There were certainly evidences, however, that the country was not always equally destitute of game. At one place they observed a field decorated with buffalo skulls, arranged in circles, curves, and other mathematical figures, as if for some mystic rite or ceremony. They were almost innumerable. . . ."[72] Along the North Platte, very shortly afterward (again recounting Bonneville's experience): "As far as his eye could reach the country seemed absolutely blackened by innumerable herds. No language . . . could convey an adequate idea of the vast living mass thus presented to his eye."[73]

[67]Long, Early Western Travels, XV, 227.
[68]Dale (ed.), Ashley-Smith Explorations, 123.
[69]Ibid., 124. Cf. the following (Green River, southern Wyoming, April 25, 1825): "Game continues abundant, particularly buffaloe. There is no appearance of these animals wintering on this river; but they are at this time travelling from the West in great numbers . . ." (ibid., 141).
[70]Pattie, Early Western Travels, XVIII, 141.
[71]Wyeth, ibid., XXI, 51.
[72]Irving, Captain Bonneville, 39.
[73]Ibid., 40.

Again in May, in the year following (1833) Townsend saw plenty of buffalo along the Platte.[74] Farnham records herds along the 'Upper Platte' (meaning apparently upper North Platte), July 21, 1839,[75] and in North Park, the source of the North Platte (nicknamed the 'Bull Pen' because of its traditional abundance) he found 'plenty,' July 31, 1839.[76] Father De Smet mentions seeing 'an immense herd on the Platte' (if we only knew where!) in June, 1841.[77] In June, 1842, Frémont's party found buffalo east of the Forks of the Platte. He says: "A few miles brought us into the midst of the buffalo, swarming in immense numbers over the plains, where they had left scarcely a blade of grass standing. Mr. Preuss, who was sketching at a little distance in the rear, had at first noted them as large groves of timber. . . ."[78]

I have already noticed the fluctuations of the buffalo between the Forks and the Sweetwater.[79]

The foregoing particulars might make out a very plausible case for the buffalo having retreated or disappeared practically up to the Forks by this time. In 1845, however, Samuel Hancock's party encountered an immense herd at the crossing of the Platte, which is given on the contemporary map as being at Grand Island, 115 miles east of the Forks.[80] In their case, the local appearances of buffalo almost exactly reversed those recorded by Frémont in 1842; Preuss finding practically none from the Forks to Fort Laramie,[81] while Hancock indicates 'abundance' in that section of his journey.[82] Hancock saw no buffalo after leaving the neighbourhood of Fort Laramie;[83] nor did Preuss from there up to 105° W.,[84] at which point he again met with them intermittently all the way to the Sweetwater, the head of which is the famous South Pass.[85] Joel Palmer, who apparently preceded Hancock by only a short time (being one of the 'wagon-masters' in the

[74]Townsend, *Early Western Travels*, XXI, 157-62.

[75]Farnham, *ibid.*, XXVIII, 205.

[76]*Ibid.*, 209, 266.

[77]De Smet, *ibid.*, XXVII, 265.

[78]Frémont, *Narrative*, 16-17; see also Allen, *American Bisons*, 148.

[79]Above, chap. XV, notes 39-40.

[80]Hancock, *Narrative*, 9-10. Map (1846) and mileages in the "Itinerary" (*ibid.*, xiv). Actually, the North Platte Crossing was at Platte Bridge, that is, modern Casper, Wyoming.

[81]Preuss, in Frémont, *Narrative*, 37-41.

[82]Hancock, *Narrative*, 15.   [83]*Ibid.*, 22.

[84]Preuss, in Frémont, *Narrative*, 54. Since Fort Laramie is about 104° 30' W., this is only 25 or 30 miles. *Fort* Laramie not to be confused with modern Laramie, Wyoming, 105° 50' W.

[85]Given in Hancock, *Narrative* ("Itinerary," xiv) as 109° 10' W., and about 42° 30' N.; 107 miles west from Independence Rock.

first division of the immigration of 1845, while Hancock occupied a similar position in the second division[86]), noted buffalo practically all the way from some point west of Fort Laramie to Independence Rock— a distance of 213 miles; at which latter place they "literally covered" the plains—and thence to South Pass.[87] Returning in the following year (1846) about two months earlier, from South Pass to Independence Rock, and most of the way to the Forks of the Platte, he found quantities; and at the latter place he again mentions the plains "literally covered with buffalo," so that "tens of thousands were to be seen at one view. . . ."[88]

Palmer, journeying down the lower Platte in June, 1846, must have almost met Francis Parkman travelling up it. We have seen that Hancock, only the year before, records an immense herd at the Crossing. Parkman, also following the Oregon Trail at this time, writes in disgust: "Four days on the Platte, and yet no buffalo! Last year's signs of them were provokingly abundant. . . ."[89]

Hornaday's correspondent, Allen Varner, describes his experiences in 1849:

"We left Independence on May 6, 1849, and struck the Platte River at Grand Island. The trail had been traveled but very little previous to that year. We saw no buffaloes whatever until we reached the forks of the Platte, on May 20, or thereabouts. There we saw seventeen head. From that time on we saw small bunches now and then; never more than forty or fifty together. We saw no great herds anywhere, and I should say we did not see over five hundred head all told. The most western point at which we saw buffaloes was about due north of Laramie Peak, and it must have been about the 20th of June. We killed several head for meat during our trip and found them all rather thin in flesh. Plainsmen who claimed to know, said that all the buffaloes we saw had wintered in that locality, and had not had time to get fat. The annual migration from the south had not yet begun, or rather had not yet brought any of the southern buffaloes that far north."[90]

[86]See Hancock, *Narrative*, ed. preface, viii.

[87]Palmer, *Early Western Travels*, XXX, 48-72.

[88]*Ibid.*, 247. Pattie, May 1825, found some dead in the snow; (perhaps in the South Pass; so, Thwaites, ed. note, *ibid.*, XVIII, 140).

[89]Parkman, *Oregon Trail*, 81. Next year, 1847, on the 'Mormon Trail' (north side of the Platte, from the Missouri to Grand Island) ". . . roamed such vast herds of buffaloes that it was often necessary to send parties in advance and clear the road before the teams could pass . . ." (Bancroft, *History of Utah*, 254). "The Mormons lived on buffalo meat and other game . . ." (*ibid.*, 260, note). Observe 'clearing the road,' the thing so often pronounced 'impossible.' Cf. chap. VI, note 66 *seq.*

[90]Hornaday, "Extermination of the American Bison," 491. Laramie Peak is about 42° 20′ N., 105° 30′ W. The spot is practically Douglas, Converse county, Wyoming.

Hornaday's own explanation of this scarcity, as we have seen,[91] is that the traffic along the Oregon Trail frightened the wary animals back from the highway. This was undoubtedly a contemporary opinion, for in 1845 Palmer writes as follows (not doubting the ability of an entire stranger to interpret the why and wherefore) concerning this (west of South Pass, July, 1845): "We are now out of the range of the buffalo. . . . There have been so many companies of emigrants in advance of us that they have frightened the buffalo from the road. . . ."[92]

Comparing this with Varner's statement, four years later, about the paucity of travel previous to 1849, one realizes the utterly empirical guess-work character of these general assertions.[93] Father De Smet, a much better informed and more reliable authority, says only (1858): ". . . it is becoming more rare to find the buffalo on the highway [that is, the Oregon Trail] across the plains, which its instinct must have taught it to avoid. . . ."[94]

Contrasted with Varner's experiences, Captain Howard Stansbury in the very same summer (1849), although he too 'saw no buffaloes' east of the Forks of the Platte, yet he 'found them in abundance west of that point, and only some four or five miles from the road'; which finds corroboration elsewhere.[95] There were other scarcities which do not admit of this explanation, and which point once again to that utterly erratic and unpredictable wandering propensity of which we have seen many previous examples. Parkman, in his summer sojourn among the Western Sioux in 1846, furnishes some interesting evidence of this. He relates particulars concerning a projected intertribal war; and he remarks that the enterprise was conditioned upon the plenty of buffalo, ". . . and buffalo this season were rare in this neighbourhood [that is, near Fort Laramie]. . . .[96] The scarcity of buffalo in the vicinity of La Bonté's camp had prevented them [the Indian allies] from assembling there. . . . We climbed the highest butte we could find, and could not see a buffalo nor an Indian; nothing but prairie for

[91]See above, chap. VI, note 109.
[92]Palmer, *Early Western Travels*, XXX, 72, 260; cf. chap. XI, note 88.
[93]For some estimated figures, above, chap. VIII, note 25.
[94]*Life of De Smet*, II, 723. See below, note 102.
[95]For Stansbury, see Allen, *American Bisons*, 144-6. In 1849 'Buffalo Land' began at the Forks of the Platte (where Long first found them, 1820, as above, note 60); and a large herd was seen at Lower California Crossing (South Platte, near Brulé, Nebraska), May 29, 1849. Again at Mud Spring (Simla, Nebraska), June 3-4; Hulbert, *Forty-Niners*, 84, 89, 90, 102. This agrees with Varner's account; above, note 90. In October, 1849, the Mormons found none in South Pass (Bancroft, *History of Utah*, 421).
[96]Parkman, *Oregon Trail*, 159.

twenty miles around us. . . ."[97] On another occasion, shortly afterward, Parkman remarks: "Not a buffalo nor an Indian was visible for many miles . . . yet the ground immediately around us was thickly strewn with the skulls and bones of buffalo. . . ."[98]

There are other references to buffalo on the Platte, however, and much later than Parkman, showing that 'Buffalo Land' began farther east than the Forks, considered to be their eastward limit in 1849. On the Mormon 'hand-cart emigration' of 1856, in August or September, at Wood River on the main Platte, east of the Forks, the country was 'alive with buffaloes,' which stampeded their yoke-cattle.[99] A considerable herd was encountered in 1857 at Plum Creek, a point about thirty-five miles west of Kearney.[100] Marcy, writing in the following year (1858), says of this precise locality ('one stage west of Fort Kearney'): ". . . here the buffalo generally begin to be seen. . . ."[101] Father De Smet, in the same year, makes a virtually identical observation: "The race is not yet extinct in these parts, though it is becoming more rare to find the buffalo on the highway across the plains [that is, the Oregon Trail] which its instinct must have taught it to avoid. We met our first herds near Fort Kearney. . . ."[102]

As late as 1867, Dodge relates an instance of some 2000, out of a herd of about 4000, losing their lives that summer in the quicksands of the Platte, while attempting to cross.[103] The exact situation of this Plum Creek is somewhat uncertain,[104] but Sir W. F. Butler encountered a herd in September of that year (1867) which took 'two hours'

[97]*Ibid.*, 201, 203.
[98]*Ibid.*, 229.
[99]Bancroft, *History of Utah*, 425.
[100]Walsh and Salsbury, *The Making of Buffalo Bill*, 52. They mention that W. F. Cody was once a stage-driver between the two points (pp. 44, 94) which identifies this Plum Creek.
[101]Marcy, *Prairie Traveller*, 234.
[102]*Life of De Smet*, II, 723. Fort Kearney not to be confused with Fort *Phil* Kearney on the Little Piney, a tributary of the Powder River, Montana (44° 40′ N., 106° 40′ W.), the scene of the so-called 'Fetterman Massacre' of December 21, 1866. They were 595 miles apart; and the latter was not built in 1858 (see Hebard and Brininstool, *Bozeman Trail*, II, 119). Sir Richard Burton in 1855 noted the 'first sign of buffalo' at Plum Creek, and 'buffalo abounding' some 25 miles farther west. About 50 miles west, Cottonwood Station, was the 'western limit at this season'; and the final mention of 'buffalo chips' for fuel is near 'Lower Crossing' on the South Platte (*City of the Saints*, 50, 506-7).
[103]Dodge, *Plains of the Great West*, 122.
[104]Plum Creek, 'on the Platte'; so Allen, *American Bisons*, 62, and Hornaday, "Extermination of the American Bison," 420. South Platte in Dodge, *Plains of the Great West*, 122, and 'Upper South Platte' in Chittenden, *American Fur Trade*, II, 579. Garretson has the impossible combination, 'Fort Kearney on the South Platte' (*American Bison*, 45).

hard riding' to pass through. As this was only five or six miles from Kearney,[105] and as Allen and Hornaday give about 1870 as the date of their extinction north of the Lower Platte,[106] the Plum Creek in question may have been the one mentioned above for the year 1867.

3. THE MISSOURI RIVER, AND ITS TRIBUTARY TERRITORIES

As one might naturally expect, seeing that the Missouri River was the natural avenue into the heart of the buffalo country, and the route along which the earliest explorers, traders, and travellers proceeded westward, the evidence concerning early buffalo movements is unusually plentiful; and—most fortunately—particularly so for those very early times when 'disappearance' or 'extinction' as an explanation of absence or scarcity is out of the question. The earliest historical notices we possess of buffalo on the Missouri (in working upward from its mouth) are from the Lewis and Clark expedition of 1804-6. In their case, being the first explorers, localities are often difficult to identify,[107] but this is here of relatively slight importance, as the presence of buffalo on the Missouri, apart from questions of irregularity, scarcely needs verification. Patrick Gass gives some dates and details, at times more illuminating than the official *Journals*. His earliest allusions are to 'several gangs of herds,' and 'a great many during the day,' on September 9 to 10, 17, 1804,[108] then following on October 19, 1804; and so far

[105]Butler, *Autbiography*, 90-7. A railway survey party (July, 1870) noted 'tens of thousands' of buffalo some few miles southwest of Fort Kearney: T. M. Davis, "Building the Burlington through Nebraska," *Nebraska History*, XXX, 1949, 317-47.

[106]Hornaday's map (following Allen), "Extermination of the American Bison," 548.

[107]References to large numbers are scattered throughout the first volume of the *Lewis and Clark Journals*, covering their first winter on the Missouri. I have since found Professor W. P. Webb commenting somewhat severely on the vagueness of their localities (*Great Plains*, 142).

[108]Gass, *Journal of Lewis and Clark Expedition*, ed. Hosmer, 30-3. Thwaites says their first encounter with buffalo was near Leavenworth (*Early Western Travels*, ed. note, VI, 68). I regret having had no opportunity to see either Coues's annotated edition of the Biddle *Lewis and Clark Journals* or Thwaites's critical edition of the originals.

Since our present inquiry takes us entirely away from the Leavenworth region, which we shall not again touch, I may here summarize the dates of their final disappearance about there.

H. M. Brackenridge (1811) notes a 'Buffalo Island,' somewhere below the Platte confluence (*Early Western Travels*, VI, 68); thought to be the same as *Isle au Vache*, now Cow Island, near Leavenworth, mentioned by Edwin James, 1819 (*ibid.*, XIV, 175). No buffalo were seen prior to that point, May, 1811. Brackenridge also mentions an Isle aux Bœufs, apparently rather lower down the Missouri (*ibid.*, VI, 38).

as one may judge from the lapse of time this latter occurrence[109] must have been somewhere near (perhaps above) the mouth of the Niobrara River, or Fort Randall.[110] This is of interest, as the party apparently saw few or none even about the mouth of the Platte, evidently a region of such traditional plenty at all seasons that Long's party, fifteen years later, could not believe it possible that there were 'none on the Platte,' as we have seen.[111]

Bradbury, the English naturalist travelling with the westbound Astorians, first saw buffalo near the Platte, May 2, 1811.[112] What direction this herd may have been following at that season it is difficult to guess; for Brackenridge, who was only a few days behind the Astorians, found buffalo bones strewed about at Wilson P. Hunt's camping-ground on May 16, 'six days old;' but saw no buffalo then nor for another week, getting his first view of them on May 23, and the first being killed next day, May 24, 1811.[113] Some years later this locality was, or was thought to be, the buffalo frontier, at least in journeying up the Missouri River, for James remarks (May, 1820): "Remains of bisons, as bones, horns, hoofs, and the like, are often seen on these plains; and in one instance, in a low swamp surrounded by forests, we discovered the recent track of a bull; but all the herds of these animals have deserted the country on this side [that is, south of] Council Bluffs. . . ."[114]

Farther up, Bradbury speaks of 'numberless herds on both sides' of the Missouri;[115] and this is corroborated by Brackenridge, who says

Westward from that locality, James tells us that in the winter of 1818-19, "a large herd of bisons was seen near the Grand Pass . . ." (*ibid.*, XIV, 166). Grand Pass was the divide between Salt Fork and the Missouri bottom, followed by the Osage Trace [? from St. Louis] leading to the Santa Fé Trail (Thwaites, ed. note, *ibid.*, XIV, 164). The Osage River joins the Missouri near Jefferson City; and the place would perhaps be somewhere south of Sedalia, Missouri.

Father De Smet says of Fort Leavenworth, 1851, ". . . nor is it much longer ago that these fields were the pasture of enormous herds of buffalo . . ." (*Life of De Smet*, II, 720). 'Not long ago' is a vague and purely relative expression. Parkman, on his way from Leavenworth to the Platte, 1846, speaks of "journeying for a fortnight and not seeing so much as the hoofprint of a deer . . . only the whitened skulls of the buffalo, once swarming in this now deserted region . . ." (*Oregon Trail*, 41). Yet Audubon says that buffalo were killed within forty miles of Leavenworth (direction not specified) in 1843 (Audubon and Bachman, *American Quadrupeds*, II, 50).

[109]Gass, *Journals of Lewis and Clark Expedition*, 51.
[110]On Louison Creek, South Dakota—Nebraska boundary.
[111]Above, notes 58, 59.
[112]Bradbury, *Early Western Travels*, V, 76.
[113]Brackenridge, *ibid.*, VI, 80-90.
[114]Long, *ibid.*, XV, 186.   [115]Bradbury, *ibid.*, V, 184, 185.

they were 'never out of sight,' June, 1811.[116] These relations certainly do not suggest that this region was dependent for its buffalo population upon the arrival of herds which did not leave Texas until springtime.

We come now to the region of the famous Mandan villages in the neighbourhood of the later posts, Fort Mandan and Fort Clarke; the present sites of Mandan and Bismarck, North Dakota, on the western and eastern banks respectively of the Missouri. The evidence concerning these is of unsurpassed value, for they are the earliest permanently settled habitations of Indian peoples known to me in any portion of the western buffalo range continuously occupied by the species, since our historic knowledge of them begins. The evidence, while far from being as continuous as one could wish, is nevertheless sufficiently full to constitute a very satisfactory test of the supposed predicable uniformity in buffalo movement; and—what is even more fortunate—even the very latest is early enough to render suggestions of final disappearance manifestly inapplicable in the light of the various data already placed before the reader.[117] I shall first quote the general descriptions of two philosophic observers concerning this locality and its people, and follow these with chronological evidence. Maximilian writes as follows:

The buffalo herds do not appear in the immediate vicinity of Fort Clarke, except when the winter is very severe, because they are too much disturbed by the numerous Indians of the neighbourhood. The hunters of the fort are often obliged to ride twenty miles before they find them. In the cold snowstorms, so prevalent during the winter, these animals take refuge in the forests on the banks, when great numbers of them are killed, and it is often almost impossible to drive them out of the wood. . . .[118]

In the summer time, if the herds of buffaloes are disposed to great distances on the prairie, the chase . . . requires more time and exertion; but in the winter, when they approach the Missouri and seek shelter in the woods, a great number are often killed in a short time. If it is very cold, and the buffalo keep at a distance in the prairie (which happened in the winter of 1833-34), they hunt but little, and would rather suffer hunger, or live only on maize and beans, than use any exertion. . . .[119]

He further states, concerning the Mandans:

The Indians residing in permanent villages have the advantage of the roving hunting tribes, in that they not only hunt, but derive their chief subsistence from their plantations, which afford them a degree of security

[116]Brackenridge, ibid., VI, 110, 111, 133, 134, 137.

[117]The last known car of hides ever shipped came from Dickinson, North Dakota (only 90 miles west of Mandan) in 1884. Above, chap. XVI, note 57.

[118]Maximilian, Early Western Travels, XXIII, 245.

[119]Ibid., 345; but compare below, note 136.

against distress. It is true, these Indians sometimes suffer hunger when the buffalo herds keep at a great distance, and their crops fail; but the distress can never be so great among the Missouri Indians, as in the tribes that live further northwards. . . .[120]

Catlin, who was in the vicinity about the same time, says: "Buffaloes, it is known, are a sort of roaming creatures, congregating occasionally in huge masses, and strolling about the country from east to west or from north to south, or just where their whims or strange fancies may lead them; and the Mandans are sometimes by this manner most unceremoniously left without anything to eat. . . ."[121]

These recitals suggest an uncertainty which the incidental evidence entirely substantiates. The circumstance of their earliest recorded visitor, La Vérendrye, starving on his return journey to Red River in the winter of 1738-39,[122] while it undoubtedly indicates uncertainty *per se*, may or may not directly concern Fort Mandan; yet even here, one may ask why he had not encountered the buffalo before leaving, during their "great annual migration to the south"[123] and thereby been enabled to make preparation beforehand, or why he had not met them— perhaps a little belated—on the way.

Patrick Gass records 'buffalo very numerous near Fort Mandan,' and by reason of 'very cold' weather, 'coming into the woods,' December 7 to 9, 1804. On December 17 to 18, they were 'thought to be near, but could not be found.'[124] About Christmas, 1804, says the Nor-West Company's trader Charles Mackenzie, who was at the Mandan villages that same winter, "the buffalo drew near, and we lived on the fat of the land."[125] In the following winter, Mackenzie was again there. He says: "The winter being far advanced and considerable drifts of snow on the ground, thousands of buffaloes resorted to the vicinity of the villages. . . ."[126]

Concerning this period, Lawrence J. Burpee writes: ". . . countless herds of buffalo came periodically to their [the Mandans'] very doors. . . ." (1804) "The Mandan villages were revelling in plenty, buffalo having passed an unusually long time around the Missouri, on their great annual migration to the south. . . ."[127]

[120]*Ibid.*, 274.
[121]Catlin, *Letters on the North American Indians*, I, 127.
[122]Above, chap. XIV, note 150.
[123]As postulated below, note 127.
[124]Gass, *Journal of Lewis and Clark Expedition*, 59, 62.
[125]Mackenzie, in Masson, *Les Bourgeois de la Compagnie du Nord-Ouest*, I, 331.
[126]*Ibid.*, 366.
[127]Burpee, *Search For the Western Sea*, 357, 363.

It is painful to find a careful and critical scholar, who spared no pains to place the most accurate information before his readers, compelled as it were, by the mechanical repetition of unsupported assertion, or the shortcomings of so-called 'investigations' by reputed authorities, to accept such unhistorical chaff, for which not a figment of actual evidence (covering that locality) exists to my knowledge, in place of the solid grain of truth.

On his journey up the Missouri in 1833, Maximilian, then just below the mouth of Jacques (or James) River, May 10, 1833, remarks as follows: "At the spot where we now are, it is said that large herds of buffalo are seen in the winter; but we had not yet met with one of these animals. . . ."[128]

On May 14, he writes: ". . . where, in the preceding year, the whole prairie was seen from the steamer to be covered with herds of buffaloes, but there were now no living creatures except [a few birds]. . . ."[129]

The first buffalo was seen, eight days above James River, on May 18;[130] and there were 'numerous herds' on June 3, two days before reaching Fort Pierre,[131] although Maximilian had been told some days previously (May 21) that the herds 'were said to have left the Missouri.'[132] Preposterous as these local explanations seem now, unaccompanied as they were by anything in the nature of comparative study of the species at large, we have to remember that amid the parrot-like reiteration, even then, of the 'regular migration,' some such suggestion almost forced itself upon the inquirer. The frequent fluctuations are revealed by some of Maximilian's casual jottings on the subject, at Forts Clarke and Pierre:

At Fort Clarke: buffalo were 'near,' November 26, 1833;[133] and 'distant,' December, 1833;[134] and in the first week of January, 1834, he writes as follows, concerning a blizzard then raging: ". . . exposure to the weather was painful to man and beast. It was hoped, however, that it would soon cause the herds of buffalo to come nearer to us; but this expectation was not realized. . . ."[135]

[128]Maximilian, *Early Western Travels*, XXII, 281. The James (or there the Dakota) River enters the Missouri at Yankton, South Dakota (42° 57′ N., 97° 20′ W.).

[129]*Ibid.*, 294.

[130]*Ibid.*, 298.

[131]*Ibid.*, 328.

[132]*Ibid.*, 300.

[133]*Ibid.*, XXIV, 27, 32, 36.

[134]*Ibid.*, 53-5, 57.

[135]*Ibid.*, 55.

Maximilian gives an account of the Mandans being out for a week in below-zero weather hunting for buffalo at this time; but without success.[136] Following upon this, they were found only six miles distant, January 23, 1834;[137] 'plenty' on February 10, 1834;[138] 'scarcity' in March, 1834.[139] Yet again, buffalo were seen in some number crossing the Missouri, three days below Fort Clarke, in April, 1834.[140]

It may be noted, apropos of the 'annual migration to the south,' that not a single one of the references I have collected on buffalo *crossing* the Missouri indicates the direction;[141] and a glance at the river's course on the map will show that in very many localities—the above being one—the crossing of the Missouri could quite as logically indicate a migration east-and-westward as north-and-south. By way of contrast with this occasional sufficiency, at Fort Pierre, seven days below Fort Clarke, and at the 'Sioux Agency, below the Big Bend,' two days beyond Fort Pierre, 'no buffalo were seen during the whole winter.'[142] At the latter place, April 27, 1834, ". . . hunters arrived with twenty horses, who had been absent about three weeks on a buffalo chase, but returned with only one horse-load of meat. . . ."[143]

Catlin remarks also, concerning this period: "The Minatarees [*Gros Ventres,* or *Hidatsa*], as well as the Mandans, had suffered for some months past for want of meat, and had indulged in the most alarming fears that the herds of buffalo were emigrating so far off that there was great danger of their actual starvation, when it was suddenly announced through the village one morning at an early hour that a herd of buffaloes was in sight. . . ."[144]

Maximilian, in describing the deserted villages of the Arickarees on the Missouri, says that it was ". . . a dry unproductive season, when the crops entirely failed; as well as the absence of the herds of buffaloes, which hastened their removal. . . ."[145]

Even Allen and Hornaday (who are not disposed—the latter particularly—to postpone that event) do not place the disappearance of

---

[136]*Ibid.* This scarcely agrees with his characterization above (note 119).
[137]*Ibid.,* 62.
[138]*Ibid.,* 66.
[139]*Ibid.,* 76-7.　　　　[140]*Ibid.,* 86.
[141]Above, chap. VII, notes 36-45.
[142]Maximilian, *Early Western Travels,* XXIV, 89, 94.
[143]*Ibid.,* 91.
[144]Catlin, *Letters on the North American Indians,* I, 199. Cf. Henry, *re* the Mandans, 1806: "They went away yesterday, and found buffalo in great abundance, near at hand . . ." (Coues (ed.), *Henry-Thompson Journals,* I, 336); see also Maximilian, *Early Western Travels,* XXIII, 368.
[145]*Ibid.,* XXII, 335 (*circa* 1832).

the buffalo on the northeastern bank of the Missouri near Fort Pierre or Fort Clarke earlier than 1870.[146]

Along the Missouri between Fort Clarke (or Fort Mandan) and Fort McKenzie (also called Fort 'Piekann,' from being in or near to the Piegan country); which was situated somewhere near Great Falls, Montana, Gass noted 'many buffalo' on both sides, April 17 to 21, 1805;[147] apparently near the mouth of the Yellowstone, where Fort Union was built later. On May 11 he records 'several great gangs'[148] in a locality which, in so far as the lapse of time is any guide, would possibly be near the mouth of Milk River. In the general vicinity of Great Falls, on either side, he notes considerable quantities, June 20, 26, July 3 to 5;[149] after which, the buffalo appear to have 'gone out into the plains,' July 7 to 10, 1805.[150] There would of course be nothing worthy of note in buffalo along the Missouri at that early date, except for purely comparative purposes, such as my own.

Where Gass saw large numbers, Maximilian some two months later in the season, found fewer. 'Some buffalo were seen' near Wild Onion Creek;[151] also between Fort Clarke and Fort Union, at the mouth of the Yellowstone, in June, 1833.[152] Along the Upper Missouri thence to Fort McKenzie, a distance of 850 miles by the river (although by land 'it had been done in ten days'[153]), during July and August, there are casual allusions to buffalo seen;[154] but nothing like the hosts recorded by Lewis and Clark on their return journey in 1806. Although these latter explorers speak of herds 'travelling uniformly in the same direction' (down the Missouri) 'with great method and regularity;[155] their incidental references reveal very little of those qualities: (July 11, 1806) ". . . buffalo in such numbers, that on a moderate computation there could not have been fewer than ten thousand within a circuit of two miles. At this season they are bellowing in every direction, so

[146]Hornaday's map, "Extermination of the American Bison," 548.
[147]Gass, *Journal of Lewis and Clark Expedition*, 76-7.
[148]*Ibid.*, 83.
[149]*Ibid.*, 102, 104, 107; cf. *Lewis and Clark Journals*, I, 352.
[150]Gass, *Journal of Lewis and Clark Expedition*, 107, 109.
[151]Maximilian, *Early Western Travels*, XXII, 366.
[152]*Ibid.*, 371, 380, 382, 387.
[153]*Ibid.*, 377. Katherine Coman must surely be mistaken in identifying this place with 'Fort Benton, at the mouth of the Big Horn' (*Economic Beginnings of the Far West*, I, 344, 349). It may be Fort Benton; but the Big Horn flows into the Yellowstone, not the Missouri.
[154]Maximilian, *Early Western Travels*, XXIII, 37-63, 81; cf. Gass, *Journal of Lewis and Clark Expedition*, 280-2.
[155]*Lewis and Clark Journals*, I, 376.

as to form an almost continuous roar. . . ."[156] (July 13) "The buffalo are leaving us fast, on their way to the southeast."[157] (July 14) "The buffalo have now nearly disappeared. . . ."[158]

Following this, for several days there was a great shortage of game, and food became very scarce; then on July 27, 'immense herds' were seen for twenty miles.[159] On August 3, there were 'very few buffalo,' and on August 4 'several herds' were seen.[160] Lest the reader might erroneously suppose that the aforementioned disappearance 'on their way to the southeast' furnishes evidence in support of a regular southward autumn migration, I shall cite other instances of the presence of the animals in force in this very region at seasons too late for them to be the southbound herds not yet departed, and apparently too early to be those Saskatchewan wanderers arriving for the mild Missouri winter. Maximilian makes several general allusions to buffalo along the Upper Missouri on his return trip from Fort McKenzie to Fort Union, September 10 to 29, 1833;[161] these notices include 'vast numbers' at the mouth of Judith River, and 'great herds' in the Bad Lands, September 17 to 18, 1833.[162] He also refers to herds around Fort Union during the month from September 29 to October 30;[163] during which season of the year Father De Smet also records 'large herds' on both sides of the Missouri at Fort Union on October 13, 1839,[164] and 'continuous vast herds' there in September, 1841.[165] Yet curiously enough, there were none near there in January, 1834: "The hunters had been absent nearly a month, in which time they killed only two bulls, two cows, and a calf. . . ."[166]

In November, 1833, Maximilian saw no buffalo between Fort Union and Fort Clarke.[167] We are not left to rely merely upon the inherent

[156]Ibid., III, 172; cf. III, 232, 266. For the bellowings in rutting-time, see chap. V, notes 10-20.

[157]Ibid., 174.

[158]Ibid., also Gass, Journal of Lewis and Clark Expedition, 259 (Bear Islands, Missouri River).

[159]Lewis and Clark Journals, III, 194; mouth of Marias River (so Gass, 266).

[160]Lewis and Clark Journals, III, 198; Gass, Journal of Lewis and Clark Expedition, 270.

[161]Maximilian, Early Western Travels, XXIII, 167-87.

[162]Ibid., 173-5.   [163]Ibid., 194-6.

[164]De Smet, ibid., XXIX, 367, 400-5.   [165]Ibid., XXVII, 183.

[166]Maximilian, ibid., XXIV, 63. Fort Union was a centre where the American Fur Company's annual average was 40,000 to 50,000 skins, circa 1835. The fort itself consumed from 600 to 800 buffaloes per annum (Maximilian, ibid., XXII, 380). On this last, see also Appendix M.

[167]Maximilian, ibid., XXIII, 213.

absurdity of supposing their final disappearance at this early date. His route led him by Fort Berthold (about 47° 40′ N., 102° W.) below the confluence of the Little Missouri; where Sir George Gore and his merry men played such havoc among the buffalo in the winter of 1855-56.[168] Furthermore, General W. F. Raynolds said of the country above Fort Pierre in 1859: "The whole country, for 140 miles was a dry desolate tract, a few antelopes forming the only living things met with; but buffaloes . . . have evidently been here, and may return at more favourable seasons of the year. . . ." He added further: "As late as 1866 they occupied much of the country between Fort Union and Fort Pierre. . . ."[169]

Father De Smet records the buffalo as 'disappeared' from the Missouri River, from Yankton Agency to 'above Fort Randall' on Louison Creek, in 1867;[170] but the previous citation would seem to indicate that the disappearance was recent. Similar fluctuations and irregularities reveal themselves between the lines in many recorded testimonies concerning the later years in the Upper Missouri region. De Smet wrote about 1846 or 1847: "The buffalo field is becoming narrower from year to year, and each succeeding hunt finds the Indians in closer contact It is highly probably that the Blackfoot plains, from the Sascatshawin [sic] to the Yellow Stone, will be the last resort of the wild animals twelve years hence. Will these be sufficient to feed and clothe the hundred thousand inhabitants of these western wilds?"[171]

De Smet was probably as competent an authority as any one man then living; but we have seen good reason to believe that without the frantic slaughter of the two respective exterminations, the buffalo herds could have withstood the 'normal' impact of Indians and fur traders of *circa* 1840 for a long time.

De Smet himself wrote in a similar strain in 1849.[172] Dr. Hayden, either on his own authority or quoting General Raynolds—it is not clear which—wrote in 1861: "They occur in large bands in the valley of the Yellowstone River and in the Blackfoot country, but their numbers are decreasing at a rapid rate. . . ."[173]

In 1864 an officer of the U.S. Army, whose name is not given, wrote that there were 'no buffalo, except along the Yellowstone; there numer-

[168]Hebard and Briminstool, *Bozeman Trail*, II, 228 (see chap. XV, note 90).
[169]Allen, *American Bisons*, 161.
[170]*Life of De Smet*, III, 872.
[171]De Smet, *Early Western Travels*, XXIX, 365; see also *Life of De Smet*, III, 948.
[172]*Ibid.*, 1187-9.
[173]Allen, *American Bisons*, 161.

ous.'[174] Father De Smet once again described them as 'fast disappearing' in 1868.[175] Such specific localized mention as that of the officer in 1864—particularly—might easily be seized upon in the absence of comparative data as historical evidence that, apart from the one region mentioned, the species was extinct. Yet Father De Smet himself speaks of 'countless herds' in the sixties, precisely as he had done in the forties.[176] The very same phraseology which he employs in the effort to describe the 'innumerable,' 'numberless,' 'vast,' 'immense,' and 'enormous' herds of 'thousands' on the Upper Missouri,[177] or the Yellowstone,[178] or in the Black Hills,[179] in the forties or fifties, or in the Blackfoot country in 1846,[180] is pressed into service again to depict the hosts in the Bad Lands,[181] or along the Upper Missouri,[182] in the late sixties; where in the earlier sixties the army officer mentioned above found 'none.' While such a man as Father De Smet could in 1868 (and doubtless did, as a result of thirty years' experience on the Plains) take a broad philosophic view, and conclude that the buffalo were undoubtedly fast disappearing, the visible evidence of the moment could scarcely have furnished uniform support to that conclusion. Two modern historians observe: "That there were at this time seemingly an unlimited number of buffalo for the hunt is witnessed by the fact that in the summer of 1868 General Sherman and his command rode for three days through one continuous band of buffalo. . . ."[183] Some essentially identical testimony comes from General Sheridan. In his Report to the Secretary of War, 1878, he wrote: "Having traversed the plains

[174]*Life of De Smet*, IV, 1585.
[175]*Ibid.*, 1221.
[176]*Ibid.*, II, 601; III, 828, 1032; *Early Western Travels*, XXIX, 349.
[177]*Life of De Smet*, I, 231 (1840); II, 657 (1851); III, 1188 (1849).
[178]*Ibid.*, I, 243 (1840); II, 657 (1851); III, 1188 (1849). An instance on the Yellowstone, 1854: 'not out of sight of large herds for 400 miles' (in Allen, *American Bisons*, 161). General W. F. Raynolds, 1859: "This [Yellowstone] valley has long been the home of countless herds. . . . I estimated that about 15 miles in length of the wide valley was in view. The entire tract of 40 or 50 square miles was covered with buffalo. . . ." Similarly, 1861 (*ibid.*, 161). On its tributaries, the Powder River country, 1865 ('the very cream of the buffalo range'), and the Big Horn, near Fort C. F. Smith, 1866, see Hebard and Brininstool, *Bozeman Trail*, I, 251-7; II, 146, 177; Grinnell, *Fighting Cheyennes*, 209-10. See also above, chap. XVI, notes 35-47.
[179]*Life of De Smet*, I, 210 (1840); cf. in the Black Hills, 1868, 50 tons of buffalo meat in one day for army use (Allen, *American Bisons*, 164).
[180]*Life of De Smet*, II, 588.
[181]*Ibid.*, III, 850, 851, (1866).
[182]*Ibid.*, 828, 850 (1866); 1027, 1188 (1849). Some particulars on herds along the Missouri basin, 1853-75: Allen, *American Bisons*, 156-166.
[183]Hebard and Brininstool, *Bozeman Trail*, II, 260.

ten or fifteen times since that date, I can bear personal testimony that where in 1868, millions of buffalo could be found, not a single one is now seen. . . ."[184]

If—as appears to be the case, judging from the selected fields of the authors respectively quoted—these unidentified references apply to the northern territory, they show that while the buffalo were unquestionably on the wane, there was nevertheless a vast aggregate still remaining; and observed scarcities in the central or upper Missouri River territory clearly find their true explanation in that incalculable irregularity to which I have frequently referred. This erratic propensity has been recorded incidentally by many travellers; many of whom date—like much of our other evidence—too early for 'disappearance' or 'extinction' to be in the least degree applicable, while others are recorded, as it were by an unintentional slip of the pen, by those who in their considered utterances labour to establish, or at least reveal themselves as firm believers in, the regular migration. In their day-to-day jottings, however, these instances of absence or plenty reveal themselves plainly for what they were: occurrences of 'this year'; and as such entirely unconnected with the fortunes of the previous or the prospects of the following season. I quote a number of such in chronological order: 'Scarce this summer . . .' (Red River to the Missouri, 1806: Alexander Henry the younger).[185] "This year the buffalo were scarce" (Red River, 1821).[186] "When buffalo are very numerous, as was the case this year . . ." (Red River, west and south, 1840).[187] "Scarce this season . . ." (the Platte River, 1846).[188] "Extremely numerous this winter . . . " (Edmonton, 1847-48).[189] "This year these animals are within a few days of the fort, and it is accordingly well off; but many years there is a great scarcity, and even starvation here . . ." (Edmonton, 1857).[190] "The buffalo this year are far south . . ." (west of Fort Garry, 1858).[191] "The past winter had been so hard . . ." (Edmonton, 1861-62).[192] "This year the buffalo had come up closer

---

[184]Quoted by P. E. Byrne, *Red Men's Last Stand*, 10. We have seen that some plainsmen (including Sheridan) believed that owing to certain causes, buffalo *circa* 1870 were 'more numerous than ever' (above, chap. XVI, notes 22-6).

[185]Coues (ed.), *Henry-Thompson Journals*, I, 306, 416.
[186]Ross, *Red River Settlement*, 57.
[187]*Ibid.*, 262.
[188]Parkman, *Oregon Trail*, 159.
[189]Kane, *Wanderings of an Artist* (Radisson Society ed.), 256.
[190]Hector, *Palliser Journals*, 72.
[191]Hind, *Report, 1858*, 8; cf. *ibid.*, 39, 42,
[192]Hughes, *Father Lacombe*, 89-90.

than usual . . ." (Carlton district, September, 1862).[193] "That winter buffalo did not come up to the woods . . ." (Carlton district, year unspecified, 'several years' before 1862).[194] ". . . very numerous this year . . ." (Upper Missouri River, 1866).[195] "Not numerous this year . . ." (Alberta, January, 1868).[196] "That winter the buffalo . . . in countless thousands . . ." (Calgary district, Bow River, January, 1876).[197]

The following are from Indian sources, for whose authenticity I cannot answer, but they have been accepted by students of long Indian experience: 'Buffalo very plenty' (1816-17); 'Sioux make medicine to bring the buffalo' (1843-44); 'Great abundance of buffalo meat' (1845-46); 'Buffalo very plenty' (1861-62).[198] I quote also from Blackfoot 'Winter Counts': 'The winter when it was necessary to eat dogs to keep from starving'; 'The winter when buffalo were scarce' (no dates).[199]

I think most critics will agree that special mention of such a character points to something exceptional (in the chronicler's estimation at least) in the buffalo economy; a circumstance which in this province of the supposedly ultra-uniform, is of more moment than the precise nature of the exception itself. Such general inferences, unmistakable as I consider them to be, are not the sole evidence, even for such critics as may be disposed to deny my interpretation of the testimony adduced, concerning the Missouri River territory at large. Maximilian has recorded the fact that the rates of pay for hunters at Fort McKenzie (1834) were different 'when buffalo are numerous' from those 'when they are distant.'[200] That such irregularities should have, as it were, crystallized into customary law points unmistakably, I consider, to a condition in which neither event was regarded as abnormal. Surely with a regular migration those variant payments would have expressed themselves in terms of regularly recurring seasons. Finally, if such

---

[193]Milton and Cheadle, *North-West Passage*, 58.

[194]*Ibid.*, 146.

[195]*Life of De Smet*, III, 850.   [196]Hughes, *Father Lacombe*, 142.

[197]*Ibid.*, 266. Cf. on all this, above, note 144.

[198]'A Sioux Calendar, 1799-1870' (in Dodge, *Our Wild Indians*, 401-4). I know nothing of this. Some measure of accuracy is suggested by its quite close agreement with such events as the appearance of Texas cattle on the Northern buffalo range.

[199]From an adopted member of the tribe, Walter McClintock (*Old North Trail*, 422).

[200]Maximilian, *Early Western Travels*, XXIII, 93. Similar conditions governed the prices of pemmican, Fort Qu'Appelle, 1867: Cowie, *Company of Adventurers*, 221, 226.

evidence is still deemed to be merely inferential and hence inconclusive, the precariousness of the buffalo at early dates is stated explicitly by Wyeth (1832),[201] De Smet (1846),[202] and McDougall (circa 1862).[203] The two latter, in particular, are experienced observers not lightly to be ignored or explained away. As the present inquiry embraces only the main prairie buffalo range, this concludes the subject, so far as the United States territory is concerned.[204]

4. THE SASKATCHEWAN TERRITORY

For the purposes of the present (final) section dealing with 'irregular migrations,' the Saskatchewan Territory comprises the region lying west of a line running roughly from the Cypress Hills country to the Elbow of the South Saskatchewan, and following that river thence to the Forks near the later city of Prince Albert; and lying entirely east of the Rocky Mountains and for some indeterminate distance (from forty to perhaps a hundred miles, which can only be indicated by occasional mention of localities) north of the North Saskatchewan River. The territory west of the Rockies is not included in our present discussion, which deals only with the prairies and plains, the natural scene of the immense hosts and of their supposed migratory tendencies. In dealing with the territory indicated, in order to present the evidence concerning the Red River Hunt in connected and homogeneous form, I included in my discussion of it a considerable amount of evidence referring primarily to the territory covered by the Hunt, of a character identical in essence with that given in the present chapter. It is therefore needless to repeat this here; but its corroborative weight should not be overlooked by the reader in estimating the general force of the argument for the wide-spread manifestations of buffalo irregularity.

We have seen that Hornaday laid it down as something of a principle that eight years (particularly when spent in wandering about the buffalo country) constituted an insufficient period to confer any authority upon Catlin.[205] So be it. We in Western Canada are happily fortunate in possessing the unadorned reminiscences of more than one long resident; one, in particular, who spent five-and-fifty years on the plains and foothills and lived among the buffalo from day to

---

[201]"Very uncertain; sometimes plenty enough . . ." (Wyeth, *Early Western Travels*, XXI, 101); cf. Gregg, 1831-39: "Abundant on the Canadian [river]—sometimes . . ." (*ibid.*, XX, 213).

[202]De Smet on their precariousness: *ibid.*, XXIX, 413.

[203]"Very precarious . . ." (McDougall, *Forest, Lake, and Prairie*, 150).

[204]See chap. XI, for similar evidence west of the Rocky Mountains.

[205]Above, chap. XIX, notes 35-40.

day during the last two decades of their free existence, and who has left us invaluable gleanings from that experience. Although he was not a scientific observer in the common acceptation of the term, he was at least a careful and competent eye-witness of what he relates, and a man whose high character gives an unimpeachable authority to his assertion; the more so that on this topic he had no thesis to maintain, and, curiously enough, seems to have given to the migration theory a loose general assent of which his own day-to-day narratives furnish the very strongest refutation. I refer to the late Reverend Dr. John McDougall.[206]

As we have seen, Hornaday has extended his migration argument to Western Canada with a precision equally definite with that applied to any portion of the general buffalo range. Hornaday could know nothing of McDougall's books, which were not written until after his own essay; although, as a matter of fact, they affirm little in principle concerning buffalo that could not have have been found long before. It is somewhat more disquieting that another professed man of science, Ernest Thompson Seton, should idly support Hornaday's *dicta* (on the strength of the so-called 'full investigation') concerning a land which Seton himself knew far better, and in which it is quite probable that he met McDougall himself, of whose writings he could or should in any case have known. We shall see, on the strength of detailed evidence, that in Western Canada, while there was a well-recognized migratory movement, it was in no sense regular; the uniform south-bound winter movement which Hornaday and his followers affirm, *did not take place*; and the east-and-westerly wanderings, which they deny, *did take place*. I shall not be so foolish as to dispute that movements in the directions maintained by Hornaday and his supporters did occur; but I consider that such movements were merely a manifestation of those utterly unpredictable impulses which led any band of buffalo, at any season or at any place, to move in any direction, and under any conditions, in any manner, and for any reason; which is the same as no reason at all.

I shall deal first with the northward migration in winter. McDougall says, in reference to the 'open winter' of 1868-69: ". . . the herds kept far out on the plains, or as much so as the weather permitted them to

---

[206]On the McDougalls, father and son (the latter, John, 1842-1917, Alberta, 1862 *seq.*) see Morris, *Treaties with the Indians of Manitoba*, 256, 362; MacRae, *History of Alberta*, I, 4, etc.; Steele, *Forty Years in Canada*, 110, 213; Blue, *Alberta Past and Present*, I, 181, 227-33; Hawkes, *Saskatchewan and her People*, I, 83; MacInnes, *In the Shadow of the Rockies*, 28, 63, 266; Maclean, *McDougall of Alberta*, etc.

do. It is still very hard for the inexperienced to understand that the colder the weather and harder the winter, farther and farther into the north did the great herds feed; but all through the sixties and seventies this was my knowledge of them. . . ."[207] He adds in another place: "Most of the Indians, the regular nomads . . . remained out in the border country . . . watching also for the buffalo to come farther north as was their habit at this season; for, contrary to outside ideas, the trend of the great herds was northward and westward during autumn and winter, and southward and eastward during spring and summer."[208]

Probably what the 'inexperienced' failed to realize—among other things—was that because of the geographical juxtaposition of the bare plains and the sheltered scrublands of the Saskatchewan territory it was northward and westward, towards the scrub belt, that the buffalo must perforce turn if they sought *shelter*. This is a factor of much deeper significance than mere distance from the Equator, which appears in some minds to be the sole datum. Their naïve insistence upon this fundamental applicability of north and south reminds one of those guileless innocents we sometimes meet even yet, who are convinced that the North Pole is very cold and the South Pole very hot.

I am not disposed even to attempt to bestow upon McDougall that final and supreme authority which I have denied to Alexander Henry, and which I should dispute against any one sole claimant. In Mc-Dougall's case, however, he is not the only one, nor even the first, to advance what I may term the 'thesis' of the northward winter movement; in fact, in date of publication, he is almost the last. Traveller after traveller has specified some particular area or other (upon well-informed local authority) as 'the winter home of the buffalo.' The second earliest English-speaking visitor to the Canadian 'Far West,' Matthew Cocking, near the Forks of the Saskatchewan, August 15, 1772, wrote: "The Indians tell me that in Winter buffalo are plenty here, which is confirmed by the quantity of Dung on the ground. . . ."[209]

The younger Henry says virtually the same for the Red Berry Hills, northwest of Carlton on the northern side of the Saskatchewan.[210] Butler applies the term to the 'Fertile Belt'—Carlton being roughly

[207]McDougall, *Red River Rebellion*, 26.

[208]*Ibid.*, 86. So also, (Sir) George Simpson, *Journey Around the World*, I, 92.

[209]"Cocking's Journal" ed. Burpee, 102.

[210]Coues (ed.), *Henry-Thompson Journals*, II, 548; cf. below, note 223.

the centre.[211] Sandford Fleming, 1874, says of the country along the eastern base of the Rockies: "Here is found the favourite wintering ground of great herds of buffalo . . ."[212]

Professor John Macoun describes the Tramping Lake and Eagle Hills region, lying south of Battleford, as the 'winter home of the buffalo;[213] and elsewhere not only uses precisely the same term for the 'exposed hills' in the Bow River country;[214] but again says that the Hand Hills district in Central Alberta was formerly noted for "the enormous herds of buffalo wintering in its neighbourhood."[215]

Others who do not specify any particular locality make mention of their general prevalence in the northern Saskatchewan territory during the winter. Palliser writes as follows (Aug. 15, 1858): "This is now nearly the time, too, when these [Blackfoot] Indians commence to arrive from the plains in the southeast, for the buffalo in winter approach the edge of the woods, and so also do the Indians, seeking fuel and thickwood animals, in case of the buffalo failing them during the winter. . . ."[216] He states also that the 'Thickwood Crees' " . . .occasionally in autumn make short excursions to the plains for buffalo, when the herds come close to the edge of the woods. . . ."[217]

This is corroborated by Dr. Hector. He states that the 'Thickwood Indians' north of Carlton ". . . sometimes make short excursions to the plains for buffalo when the herds come north of the Saskatchewan River. . . ."[218] Hind, as we have seen,[219] describes the buffalo (in a work which Hornaday had, or might have, read, since he quotes Hind) as wintering "between the south and north branches of the Saskatchewan, south of the Touchwood Hills, and beyond the North Saskatchewan in the valley of the Athabaska; they cross the South Branch [that is, going south] in June or July. . . ."[220] Milton and

[211]Butler, *Great Lone Land*, 230.

[212]*Explorations and Surveys for a Canadian Pacific Railway, up to January 1, 1874*, 39.

[213]Macoun, *Manitoba*, 104.

[214]*Ibid.*, 254.

[215]*Ibid.*, 255. A Plains Indian to Sergeant-Major Spicer, N.W.M. Police (*circa* 1885): "Our nation were camped on the [lower] Red Deer for the winter, for, as you know, the buffalo would go there for the winter, as the grass was good, and we used to follow them . . ." (Hawkes, *Saskatchewan and her People*, I, 113). The Hand Hills are described by Palliser as a sort of isolated patch of exceptionally luxurious vegetation in a semi-arid region (*Palliser Journals*, 11, 37).

[216]*Ibid.*, 92; and cf. *ibid.*, 202; also Hector, *ibid.*, 65, 68, 75, 120.

[217]Palliser, *ibid.*, 201.

[218]Hector, *ibid.*, 65.

[219]Above, chap. XIV, notes 51-2.

[220]Hind, *Report, 1858*, 106.

Cheadle use language almost identical with that of Palliser, and his colleague, Hector. Describing the Wood Crees in their own neighbourhood, some eighty miles northwest of Carlton (winter, 1862-63), they say: "They are most expert trappers and hunters of moose, and occasionally seek buffalo when they enter the skirts of the woods in severe winters. . . ."[221]

This is another of those examples where the 'changed mentality' of the latter days cannot apply; for precisely the same movements are recorded from fifty to seventy years earlier. Mackenzie, in describing the country on the northern side of the Saskatchewan, *circa* 1789, says: ". . . the country in general, on the West and North side of the great river, is broken by the lakes and rivers with small intervening plains, where the soil is good and the grass grows to some length. To these the male buffaloes resort for the winter, and if it be very severe, the females also are obliged to leave the plains. . . ."[222] The younger Henry remarks also of Fort à la Corne (1808): "It cannot be called an open country, as spots of wood are frequent. Buffalo abound in winter, when the cold obliges them to leave the plains for shelter among the hummocks, where they find plenty of good long grass. . . ."[223]

The foregoing citations are, after all, essentially of the character of generalizations; and as such, be the standard or experience of their authors what it may, could command only a very qualified assent from the present critic, were they not abundantly supported by incidental day-to-day relations of actual experiences. So far as the swimming of the Saskatchewan is concerned, this has already been dealt with in detail, in its relation to other phases of buffalo mentality, and need not here be repeated.[224] Other features of the northward winter movement, and of the presence of the buffalo in the country during that season, must be noticed in order to establish an historical basis for the declarations cited above.

Rejecting (as I do) the uniform southward autumnal migration, I am under no obligation to furnish any (approximate) date for its supposed commencement from the North Saskatchewan territory. Taking one year with another, however, I suggest about September 15, as a mean period when any buffalo of average wisdom would surely deem it advisable to go south and enjoy the balmy airs of

[221]Milton and Cheadle, *North-West Passage*, 83; cf. *ibid.*, 59, 146.
[222]Alexander Mackenzie, "General History of the Fur Trade," in *Voyages 1789 and 1793*, lxix.
[223]Coues (ed.), *Henry-Thompson Journals*, II, 483; cf. above, note 210.
[224]Above, chap. VII, notes 52-70.

Dakota or eastern Montana until spring. The uncompromising contender for the winter in Texas will of course need to get his bovine caravan under way much earlier. So also, while it is palpably impossible to fix any precise date for the northbound herds of the traditionalists to reach the Saskatchewan for their summer sojourn, I believe those best qualified to judge will agree that June 1 is not unduly late for that purpose. I shall therefore treat all references to buffalo between September 15 and June 1 as indications of their presence in the northern prairie territory in the winter season; making due note, at the same time, of any recorded movements, with their indicated directions, that I have been able to find.

The first English-speaking traveller of whom we have any knowledge in the (western) Saskatchewan territory was Anthony Henday (1754-55), whose general route has been discussed already.[225] At the very commencement of our historical buffalo evidence for the buffalo's most characteristic Canadian habitat, it is curious to note at such an early date the appearance of those fluctuations which are the essential topic of our present chapter. For after seeing his first herd, apparently somewhere south of Melfort, Saskatchewan (about 53° N., 105° W.), on August 15, 1754, Henday saw no more—excepting two only on August 26—until September 10.[226] From September 13 to October 13, we find the following remarks: "Many herds . . ." (September 13); ". . . so numerous obliged to make them sheer out of our way" (September 15); "very numerous . . ." (September 16); "in great droves. . . . great plenty . . . numbers of buffalo" (October 3-13).[227]

These would apparently be in the region south and east of Carlton, or south of the Forks, and working thence up the general direction of the South Saskatchewan toward the Blackfoot country, where Henday wintered among that tribe. During that winter he records buffalo intermittently between October 16 and November 8, December 19 to 30, 1754; January 12 to 31, February, and on April 13, 1755.[228] On his return journey in the spring, he notes buffalo perhaps along the Red Deer River from about Tail Creek,[229] and along the two Saskatchewans, practically all the way to Fort à la Corne, April 28 to May 23, 1755.[230]

[225]See above, chap. XII, notes 17-18.
[226]"Henday's Journal," ed. Burpee, 329-32.
[228]*Ibid.*, 340-9.   [227]*Ibid.*, 332-7.
[229]Tail Creek is the outlet of Buffalo Lake (on earlier maps as 'B. Hide Lake,' *i.e.* the 'tail of the hide') into the Red Deer River. But cf. chap. XII, note 18.
[230]"Henday's Journal," 350.

Matthew Cocking travelled over the same territory (broadly speaking, though perhaps not quite so far to the southwest) between almost the same dates in the years 1772-73. His party saw their first buffalo on August 23, twelve days up the river from Fort à la Corne, from which date until about October 26, the entries vary: "Herds . . ." (August 25); ". . . plenty of buffalo in sight on all sides . . . in small and large herds intermittently" (August 25 to September 2); "a large drove of Female Buffalo" (September 2); "None seen . . ." (September 2 to 17); "several killed" (September 17); "None" (September 17 to 27); "In great droves" (September 27 to October 21).[231]

Then follows an account of the 'Archithinue' (Blackfoot) Indians 'pounding buffalo' in a permanent pound—itself a fairly reasonable indication of buffalo more or less usually in this region at this season of the year—between the South Saskatchewan and Battle Rivers, October 21 to 26. In November to December, 1772, there were 'hardly any'; and in January, 1773, there were 'none,' and the 'Archithinue Natives' were starving.[232] On January 22, he writes as follows: "A young man joined us from the Beast pound to the Eastward of us, where we intended to go. He says the Buffalo are so scarce that the Indians are distressed for want of food; & therefore had unpitched intending to build a pound further on to the Eastward, where Buffalo are said to be numerous. . . ."[233] During the month of February, 1773, he records that buffalo were found 'intermittently' in the country lying roughly between Scott, Saskatchewan, and Lloydminster, on the Alberta-Saskatchewan boundary line. On February 25, he notes: "Two Natives joined us from the Westward . . . they say that Female Buffalo are plenty with them & that they abound in provisions . . . " (that is, somewhere near the Fort Pitt 'land of plenty,' judging from Burpee's map).[234]

There were 'droves' between March 28 and April 3; and on Cocking's homeward journey down the Saskatchewan, buffalo were seen intermittently all the way to the Forks, April 3 to May 19, 1773.[235]

Three years later, in February, 1776, Alexander Henry the elder mentions large herds—'too numerous to be counted'—south of 'Fort des Prairies.'[236]

[231]"Cocking's Journal," ed. Burpee, 103-9.
[232]Ibid., 110-13.
[233]Ibid., 113.   [234]Ibid., 114.
[235]Ibid., 116-18.
[236]Henry, Travels, 1760-1776, 278-80, 293-6, 309. 'Fort des Prairies' then probably near the Forks.

David Thompson relates that in October, 1787, he found none all the way from Manchester House, on the North Saskatchewan,[237] to the Bow River: "For three and twenty days we marched over fine grounds looking for the Indians without seeing any other animal than a chance Bull Bison, from the killing of a few we procured our provisions. . . ."[238]

Duncan McGillivray, on his journey up the Saskatchewan in September, 1794, found buffalo on the south side, near the present city of Prince Albert, and some little way above the Forks (September 11 to 16). He observes, however: "Tho' we kill abundance of animals to maintain the people, yet the Buffaloes are not so numerous as usual in these parts, we are therefore of opinion that some Tribe of Indians hover about us and frighten away the animals to some other place less frequented by man. . . ."[239] Later, however (September 26), he relates that "Buffalo are exceedingly numerous,—from the summit of a hill which afforded an extensive prospect, we observed the face of the Country entirely covered by them, in short they are numerous as locusts of Egypt, and to give us passage they were forced to range themselves on both sides and we were no sooner Past than they closed their ranks as before. . . ."[240] On October 10, he notes 'animals very scarce' at his post, Fort George, but ten days later is "happy to learn that the Buffaloes are very numerous at a short distance. . . ." On October 30 he relates: ". . . a *Strong Wood* Assiniboine Cheif [*sic*] arrived: he reports that vast herds of Buffaloes are at the Paint [that is, Vermilion[241]] River, where he intends to make a *Pound* in the course of the winter. . . ."[242]

The supply was apparently plentiful all winter: (November 16) "Mr. Hughes and myself are just arrived from the Hunters Tent but with 20 Buffaloes. The Hunters have been very successful for some time past and there is a fine quantity of fresh meat in the Hangard, notwithstanding the great consumption of about 80 men with near as many Women & children. . . ." (January 27, 1795)

[237]Twelve miles north of Birling, Canadian National Railways, Saskatoon-Vermilion-Edmonton. (So, Tyrrell, in Thompson, *Narrative*, introd., xxix).

[238]*Ibid.*, 325.

[239]*McGillivray's Journal*, ed. A. S. Morton, 21-4.

[240]*Ibid.*, 28; similarly, McDougall, *Western Trails*, 79.

[241]The Vermilion River joins the North Saskatchewan about 53° 30′ N., 110° 20′ W., a little below the mouth of Middle Creek, where apparently Fort George was situated as per Morton's map. There is a present 'Paint-Earth Creek,' a tributary of the Battle River; confluence about 52° 30′ N., 112° 30′ W. See *Place-Names of Alberta*, 98, 129.

[242]*McGillivray's Journal*, 33-8.

"We have finished a Glacière [that is, ice-house] containing 500 Thighs and Shoulders for the consumption of April and the beginning of May. . . ." (February 19, 1795) ". . . by examining the Meat account it appears 413 animals must have been carried this Winter to the Fort, but a sufficient quantity of Meat, Still remains to maintain us 'till the middle of May. . . ."[243]

John McDonald of Garth notes at his post on the Bow River (1797) that "Buffaloe were scarce this season [that is, winter, when the annual store was laid in if possible] near the Post and more so in spring"; but in 1798 he remarks "the fine valley of the [South] Saskatchewan [that is, the Bow] abounding with buffaloes. . . ."

There were 'plenty' about Chesterfield House, in summer or autumn, 1805.[244]

There are some interesting notices in Harmon's *Journal,* if only one could always identify his localities more exactly. There is some uncertainty as to whether some of the following refer to the Swan River region,[245] or to 'Alexandria,' ". . . among the Prairies, one hundred miles west of Carlton;"[246] but in any case they clearly indicate the frequent but uncertain presence of buffalo in the north in winter.

He notes a southward summer movement: "Buffaloes have now returned several days' march from this into the spacious prairies" (June 1, 1801).[247] "The buffaloes, in consequence of the late mild weather, have gone to a considerable distance, into the large prairie" (January 9, 1802).[248] "Buffaloes numerous in the large prairies, two days' march from this . . ." (Alexandria, September 28, 1802).[249] In another instance, we find 'starvation,' ". . . as the buffaloes at that time,

---

[243]*Ibid.,* 41-54. See below, on buffalo consumption at the fur posts, Appendix M. Kane gives us an interesting account of the making of the 'ice-pit' (*Glacière*) at Edmonton, 1847-48: "This is made by digging a square hole, capable of containing 700 or 800 buffalo carcases. As soon as the ice in the river is of sufficient thickness, it is cut into square blocks of uniform size with saws; with these blocks the floor of the pit is regularly paved, and the blocks cemented together by pouring water between them and allowing it to freeze solid. In like manner, the walls are solidly built up to the surface of the ground. The head and feet of the buffalo, when killed, are cut off, and the carcase, without being skinned, is divided into quarters, and piled in layers in the pit as brought in, until it is filled up, when the whole is covered with a thick coating of straw, which is again protected from the sun and rain by a shed. In this manner the meat keeps perfectly good through the whole summer, and eats much better than fresh-killed meat, being more tender and better flavoured . . ." (Kane, *Wanderings of an Artist* (orig. ed.), 367).

[244]Masson, *Les Bourgeois de la Compagnie du Nord-Ouest,* II, 20-2, 30, 33.
[245]*Harmon's Journal,* 57.
[246]*Ibid.,* 31, 46, 61.
[247]*Ibid.,* 51.
[248]*Ibid.,* 58-9.   [249]*Ibid.,* 70.

in consequence of the mild weather, were at a great distance, out in the large plains . . ." (February 22, 1804).[250] Again, 'almost starving for a month'; then suddenly "a plenty of buffalo within a day's march" (January, 1805).[251] At the 'South Branch Fort,' south of Prince Albert, he writes: "I am informed that buffaloes are in plenty within half-a-day's march from this" (September 21, 1805).[252] After 'a heavy winter in the Athabaska country,' "Buffaloes have been found in plenty within a few miles of the fort, during the whole winter" (March 15, 1806).[253]

Alexander Henry the younger, on his journey up the North Saskatchewan on September, 1808, found buffalo 'abundant' between Carlton and Fort Vermilion.[254] At Fort Vermilion, a year later (October, 1809), they were 'coming northward,' and there were 'plenty' south from the fort then, and also in April, 1810;[255] as was likewise the case about Egg Lake in February, 1810.[256] The following July (1810) they were 'plentiful' along the river territory practically all the way from Fort Vermilion (near the modern Vermilion, Alberta) to Edmonton, [257] but 'north of Battle River'—meaning, I should judge, in the general region south of the two Saskatchewan River points just named—there were 'none,' and the Indians were starving, in August, 1810.[258] On the 'Wolf' (that is, Blindman[259]) River, he found them 'numerous,' November 23, 1810.[260]

Gabriel Franchère, on his homeward journey from Astoria, mentions buffalo along the North Saskatchewan, below Fort Vermilion, in June, 1814.[261] Franklin's party noted 'some herds' west of Carlton, February 13, 1820.[262]

[250]*Ibid.*, 81.

[251]*Ibid.*, 102-3.

[252]*Ibid.*, 116. South Branch Fort was at or near the modern Batoche, Saskatchewan. So, Coues (ed. note, *Henry-Thompson Journals*, II, 484).

[253]*Harmon's Journal*, 119.

[254]Coues (ed.), *Henry-Thompson Journals*, II, 490-8, 502-7.

[255]*Ibid.*, II, 552, 558, 594.

[256]*Ibid.*, II, 586. Egg Lake, near Victoria (now Pakan) some 90 miles N.E. from Edmonton; see McDougall, *Saddle, Sled, and Snowshoe*, 178. 'Egg Lake' in *Place-Names of Alberta* (p. 47), is given as Tp. 67, Rg. 15, W. of 4th. Meridian. This would be near Lac la Biche, and beyond the known range of the prairie buffalo. See above, chap. XII, note 196, *seq.*

[257]Coues (ed.), *Henry-Thompson Journals*, II, 614.

[258]*Ibid.*, 620.

[259]A tributary of the Red Deer River, which it enters a mile or two south of Blackfalds, Alberta, east of the Calgary and Edmonton highway bridge.

[260]Coues (ed.), *Henry-Thompson Journals*, II, 665.

[261]Franchère, *Early Western Travels*, VI, 373.

[262]Franklin, (First) *Journey to the Polar Sea*, 121.

Thomas Simpson, between 'Moose Woods'[263] and Carlton, Christmas Day, 1836, observes that "the country is completely intersected by buffalo roads . . ." (that is, trails).[264] This, in the depth of a Saskatchewan winter, must either indicate a mild winter with little snow, or recently made tracks. According to his own dictum, the former resulted in plenty of supplies being brought to the trading posts; although Harmon in February, 1805, gives that precise weather condition as the reason for the post starving, in what was broadly the same climatic belt.[265] On the latter supposition, it reads strangely that at Carlton, on New Year's Day, 1837, "Provisions were unusually scarce this year, the great fires in autumn having driven the buffalo to a distance. . . ."[266]

On Simpson's return from the Arctic coast three years later, things were different. (Carlton, January 13, 1840) "The buffaloes were so numerous about this place that I found Mr. Small removing his haystacks to the fort, to save them from being entirely devoured. . . ."[267] He states further that for six days southeastward from Carlton towards Fort Pelly (January 15 to 21, 1840) ". . . we travelled amongst the buffaloes which covered the open country in myriads. . . ."[268]

Our next testimony comes from a resident; disqualified (alas!) by the fatal eight years' proviso. Rundle, the well-known pioneer missionary, noted buffalo 'numerous' and 'still numerous' westward from a point two days farther up the North Saskatchewan, October, 1840.[269] On October 11, he mentions buffalo 'crossing the river,' the direction not being indicated.[270] In December, 1840, and January, 1841, 'vast quantities' of meat were being brought into Fort Edmonton from

[263]'Moose Woods' (*Bois d'orignal*) given as 52° 4' N., on the South Saskatchewan River; practically at the present city of Saskatoon.

[264]Thomas Simpson, *Narrative of Discoveries*, 45. On 'roads,' cf. chap. VI, note 2.

[265]". . . the comparatively mild [???] climate of the Saskatchewan, where the mounted plain hordes often glut the establishments with the spoils of myriads of buffaloes. . . ." (Simpson, *Narrative of Discoveries*, 78). For Harmon, above, note 250.

[266]Simpson, *Narrative of Discoveries*, 48.

[267]*Ibid.*, 402.

[268]*Ibid.*, 406-7. This locality, S.E. from Carlton, had a famous reputation as the 'Buffalo Robe Plain': presumably from the abundance of buffalo robes (a *winter* crop) to be obtained there. Above, chap. XII, note 77.

[269]*Rundle's Journal*, October 4-11, 1840.

[270]*Ibid.* A pretty dilemma; if they were only going south (for 300 miles) at this late date, this contravenes regularity of movement, if north, regularity of direction; unless they were, in the latter event, those weary pilgrims just arriving from Texas!

the 'Hunters' Tent' near Beaver Lake.[271] In the following spring buffalo were 'numerous,' apparently somewhere below Banff, Alberta;[272] and 'plentiful' between the Bow River and Edmonton.[273] In midsummer, Rundle again records them in the Carlton-Battleford-Fort Pitt territory.[274] That winter (1841-42), 'starvation was imminent' in the Edmonton district, at White Fish Lake, and he remarked in April that it "prevails to a shocking extent among the Indians. . . ."[275]

In the autumn of 1842, Rundle notes that he saw "immense herds of buffalo," one day south or southeast of Edmonton;[276] and there were buffalo seen (on a frozen lake) in the Beaver Hills, during the following winter.[277] The next entry concerning buffalo notes a scarcity at Carlton two summers later: "Meat nearly out at the Fort. Expect to be scarce until buffalo are brought. . . ."[278]

Rundle left Carlton on his return to Edmonton, August 26, 1845. "On our way we passed or saw herds of buffalo more or less for five days. The immense quantity we saw would scarce be credited by an inhabitant of Old England. They were in numbers—numberless. . . ."[279] At Rocky Mountain House, that autumn, he records: "Assinaboines starving here. . . . For two or three autumns the Assinaboines have been starving here. . . ."[280]

This scarcity could not have prevailed at Edmonton. At the Rocky Mountain House, Rundle met Father De Smet; who later came on to Edmonton, where he spent the winter, in most cordial and delightful friendship with the Protestant missionary.[281] Rundle makes no mention of supplies at this time; but De Smet records '500 buffalo in the ice-

---

[271]*Ibid.*, December 19, 1840; January 15-16, 1841. Henry describes the routine (November, 1809): "I sent . . . Crevier and Perrin to haul the meat in, put it on a stage, and take care of it until it should be brought home. This is called making the *quart de loge*; each man is obliged to put 20 animals on the stage, and haul nearly the same number into the fort. Each man must also raise buffalo hides enough to make 20 pemmican bags (*taureaux*) for which purpose their women generally go with them to make their *quart de loge*, as they then get the tallow and other offals, which are of great service in their ménage . . ." (Coues (ed.), *Henry-Thompson Journals*, II, 572).

[272]*Rundle's Journal*, April 14, 1841.
[273]*Ibid.*, April 26-30, 1841.
[274]*Ibid.*, June 14-18, 1841.
[275]*Ibid.*, December 13, 1841; March 18, April 13, 1842.
[276]*Ibid.*, September 2, 1842.
[277]*Ibid.*, March 14, 1843.
[278]*Ibid.*, July 19, 1845.
[279]*Ibid.*, *sub die.*
[280]*Ibid.*, October 18, 1845.
[281]*Ibid.*, October 4, 1845 to March 18, 1846.

house at Edmonton,' Christmas, 1845, ". . . the ordinary amount of the winter-provisions . . .", and 30,000 white-fish, averaging four pounds each.[282]

For the late summer and fall of 1846, Rundle's relations are corroborated by those of Paul Kane, the artist. Rundle records 'no buffalo seen' between Carlton and Fort Pitt, August 25-29.[283] Kane, about September 7, remarks: "The buffaloes are here abundant, as is evident from the immense accumulation of their bones, which strew the plains in every direction. . . .[284]

The living animals were scarce there, however, just at that time; but Kane noted some west of Carlton, along the river.[285] Rundle, between Fort Pitt and Edmonton, "saw a great many buffalo by the way";[286] and Kane records 'immense numbers,' ten or fifteen miles west of Fort Pitt, shortly afterward.[287] In October, 1846, Kane found buffalo on the Sturgeon River, a few miles northwestward from Edmonton.[288] In the winter of the following year, Kane was at Edmonton again, on his return journey from the Pacific coast. He remarks that during that winter (1847-48) as a general spectacle: "Outside the buffaloes range in thousands close to the fort . . . extremely numerous this winter, and several had been shot within a few hundred yards."[289] In December, 1847, he mentions "an enormous band . . . probably numbering nearly ten thousand. . . ."[290] Of their numbers along the North Saskatchewan, during a journey of seven days from Edmonton to Fort Pitt, he writes as follows (January, 1848): ". . . within the whole distance we had travelled on this journey we were never out of sight of large herds of them, and we had not found it necessary to go a step out of our direct course to find more than we required for our use. They were probably migrating northwards to escape from the human migrations which are so rapidly filling up the southern and western regions, which were formerly their pasture grounds. . . ."[291] Notwithstanding this explanation, on his final journey homeward, he records on May 26, 1848: "We

[282]De Smet, *Early Western Travels*, XXIX, 234-51; cf. Hector, 1857: two buffaloes or 526 pounds per day served out at Edmonton (Hector, *Palliser Journals*, 72, 78).

[283]*Rundle's Journal, sub die.*

[284]Kane, *Wanderings of an Artist* (Radisson Society ed.), 77.

[285]*Ibid.*, 76, 84.

[286]*Rundle's Journal*, September 24-29, 1846.

[287]Kane, *Wanderings of an Artist*, 89.

[288]*Ibid.*, 97.

[289]*Ibid.*, 256.

[290]*Ibid.*, 258.

[291]*Ibid.*, 277.

saw several large herds of buffaloes swimming across the [Saskatche-wan] river, all going south. . . ."[292]

Precisely as we have seen with their kindred in the south, the north-ern herds were not even content with the heresy of reversing the ortho-dox direction of the winter migration and vice versa in summer; they actually dared, in addition, to indulge in 'irregular movements' east-and-westerly. The very first recorded observer in the Upper North Saskatchewan territory, Henday, remarks in his *Journal*, September 5, 1754: "The buffalo has taken the route upward"[293] [that is, up the Saskatchewan]. To this Burpee subjoins an editorial note: "This was always a favourite route of the buffalo, whose deep-worn trails and hollows may still be seen along the banks of the North Saskatche-wan. . . ."[294]

Hector records that they were 'far out on the plains,' owing to the open winter, in January, 1858; which in his then situation, along the Upper Saskatchewan, southwest of Edmonton, meant eastward.[295] The same careful observer notes them 'close to the woods' in the Little Red Deer Country (west of the present towns of Olds or Didsbury, Alberta) in December, 1858.[296] McDougall notes them as being 'far out' (eastward again) from the Pigeon Lake country 'in spite of a hard winter' in December, 1866, and at New Year, 1867;[297] as also in the winter of 1867-68.[298] McDougall later tells us that the Indians in 1875 objected to Fort Calgary at the Bow and Elbow Forks "being placed right in the path of the buffaloes. . . ."[299] This points to a tra-dition of movements up and down those rivers, which evidence from the same authority seems to substantiate: (Near Morley, Upper Bow River, January, 1876) ". . . the snow was deepening, and the weather becoming colder. This encouraged us, as we thought it would bring the wild herds nearer to the foothills. . . . The cold was intense, and the buffalo were steadily heading for the hills. . . . We could see the herds moving westward. . . ."[300]

[292]*Ibid.*, 293.

[293]"Henday's Journal," ed. Burpee, 331.

[294]*Ibid.* The trails are generally north and south into the river-valleys as described above (chap. XIX, note 14; chap. IV, note 71); but in many places this river is flowing northeast, and the trails could be either north and south or east and west.

[295]Hector, *Palliser Journals*, 75.

[296]*Ibid.*, 120-2.

[297]McDougall, *Pathfinding*, 183; cf. his *Western Trails*, 9, 120.

[298]McDougall, *Pathfinding*, 243.

[299]McDougall MS. (uncompleted), 9.

[300]*Ibid.*, 34, 36, 37.

One of the very last large herds ever recorded on the Canadian prairie range was described at the time as 'coming down from the mountains in the autumn' (of 1878), as we have seen.[301] Objection might with some show of reason be urged against these very late examples, as not being truly typical. John McDougall, however, speaks of them 'following old buffalo trails' along the Upper Bow Valley in 1873;[302] and a United States Indianologist (himself an adopted son of the 'Siksikaua') cites a Blackfoot 'buffalo song' of the Montana Foothills region: ". . . the buffalo come down from the mountains in summer . . .,"[303] which it is more than probable dates back many generations. McDougall also mentions a practice in impounding buffalo which clearly shows that in the opinion of the Indians they were just as likely to go west as north (and hence, presumably, the reverse of either direction): "If the migration of the buffalo was west, then the mouth of the pound was west also. If this was north, then the mouth of the pound was placed to the north, as it seemed to be the instinct of the buffalo when startled to run back in the direction whence he had recently come. . . ."[304]

This is specifically stated by McDougall to be a practice of long standing—as indeed we might expect. In passing, it may be contrasted with the dictum of Buffalo Jones, that to turn about was precisely the very thing they would not do.[305]

The foregoing mass of evidence clearly establishes a sound historical basis for the generalizations of McDougall and others, concerning the winter northward movement particularly.[306] Finally, an abundance of testimony (perhaps stronger here than anywhere, since we have the invaluable observations of McDougall's long experience to supplement those of passing travellers) will show that however closely experienced observers may agree concerning movements and their directions among the western Canadian prairie herds whenever anything like a general movement occurred, this event was itself in the highest degree erratic and problematical.

I am aware that contrary opinions have been expressed by men of scientific standing. Hind wrote: "The ranges of the buffalo in the northwestern prairies are still maintained with great exactness, and old

[301]*Saskatchewan Herald*, Battleford, February 10, 1879 (in Black, *History of Saskatchewan*, 184). Cited *in extenso* above, chap. XVII, note 67.

[302]McDougall, *Western Trails*, 21, 108.

[303]McClintock, *Old North Trail*, 83.

[304]McDougall, *Saddle, Sled, and Snowshoe*, 272.

[305]*Buffalo Jones' Forty Years*, 95; *in extenso* above, chap. XVII, note 75.

[306]See instances, from McDougall himself: *Saddle, Sled, and Snowshoe*, 123, 238, 244, 249, 255, 270, 272; *Red River Rebellion*, 95, 203, 214, 222, etc.

hunters, if the prairies have not been burnt, can generally tell the direction in which herds will be found at certain seasons of the year. If the prairies have been extensively burnt in the autumn, the search for the main herds during the following spring must depend on the course the fires have taken."[307]

Allen also wrote as follows: "The local movements of the buffaloes are said to have been formerly very regular, and the hunters conversant with their habits knew very well at what points they were most likely to find them at the different seasons of the year. Of late, however, the buffaloes have become much more erratic, owing to the constant persecutions to which they have been for so long a time subjected. . . ."[308]

We have seen above, in the land of the Red River Hunt, Hind's own failure to accomplish the supposedly easy task of locating the buffalo, despite the advice and guidance of old hunters;[309] and Ross's specific declaration that certainty was the one thing unattainable, it was 'taking a leap in the dark.'[310] We have also seen Gregg, Wyeth, and Catlin saying in the thirties the precise opposite to Hind and Allen;[311] concerning which time there is no evidence, so far as I am aware, of any great 'persecution' and its resultant mental changes wrought in the buffalo.

So far as Canada is concerned, I doubt whether anything that could be termed persecution was ever true, until the very last days, which were after Allen wrote (in 1876); if indeed it could be called true then. It most certainly had no bearing in Canada over a century ago. There is a reference to prairie fires, from Henry (January 24, 1811): "The plains being burned, buffalo are to be found only at a great distance beyond Bow river, which has been the cause of their not coming in as usual . . ." (that is, northward).[312]

Twenty-five years before Henry, David Thompson noted the following somewhat remarkable experience, without any fires to explain the case (1787, south from Manchester House, North Saskatchewan River[313]):

For three and twenty days we marched over fine grounds, looking for the Indians without seeing any other animal than a chance Bull Bison, from the killing of a few we procured our provisions.

[307]Hind, *Report, 1858*, 106.
[308]Allen, *American Bisons*, 61.
[309]Above, chap. XIV, notes 51-2, 60-6.
[310]Above, chap. XIV, notes 54-5.
[311]Above, notes 17, 185-203.
[312]Coues (ed.), *Henry-Thompson Journals*, II, 671.
[313]Above, note 237.

We found a Camp on the south side of the Bow River from its tender grass the favourite haunts of the Bisons, yet this camp had only provisions by daily hunting, and our frequent removals led us over a large tract of country, on which we rarely found the bisons to be numerous, and various camps with whom we had intelligence were in the same state with the Camp we lived with. . . . The Bisons are vagrant, wandering from place to place over the great Plains, but the Moose and other Deer are supposed to keep within a range of ground, which they do not willingly leave, but all were much lessened in number. A few years after I passed over nearly the same grounds, and found the Bisons far more numerous . . . (October, 1787).[314]

As Thompson himself notes, these absences were taken by those in the country at the time to be permanent; for he writes concerning the smallpox outbreak of 1781:[315] "I have already mentioned that before that dreadful disease appeared among the Indians they were numerous, and the Bison, Moose, Red, and other Deer more so in proportion . . . it was noted by the Traders and Natives, that at the death of the latter, and their being thus reduced to a small number, the numerous herds of Bison and Deer also disappeared both in the Woods and in the Plains. . . ."[316]

Father De Smet remarks similarly (Edmonton, 1846): "What I here saw of beavers is applicable to almost all the Hudson territory [sic]. When the reindeer, buffalo, and moose abounded, the Crees were their peaceful possessors. These animals have now disappeared. . . ."[317]

It is curious that De Smet did not see at the time that the well-filled ice-house at Edmonton should have given pause to such conclusions,[318] unless he actually supposed—of which there is no hint—that that winter's supplies were literally the last of the buffalo. A modern historian, no professed specialist on buffalo, by reason of a keen imaginative insight too often conspicuously lacking in our buffalo authorities, hits the nail squarely on the head. Referring to Thompson's aforementioned experience in 1787, MacInnes says: "Some idea of the precarious nature of the life of the Indians may be gathered

[314]Narrative, ed. Tyrrell, 325. Thought by the editor (p. 325) to be somewhere between High River and The Gap, on the upper Bow River.

[315]On this, see below, Appendix G, "Indian Populations."

[316]Thompson, Narrative, 323, 325, 337. The Indian explanation was that 'they were taken away by the Great Spirit, as they were not needed owing to so many Indians dying of small-pox' (ibid., 325). Chittenden states that by reason of the small-pox epidemic of 1837, buffalo were unusually abundant then on the Upper Missouri (American Fur Trade, II, 626).

[317]De Smet, Early Western Travels, XXIX, 250; Life of De Smet, II, 533.

[318]Above, note 282.

from the fact that even at this early date, the buffalo were scarce. This was undoubtedly only a temporary condition, but it is none the less significant. . . ."[319]

The reader will have noted above, that the very evidence which proves the frequent practice of a northward winter movement, proves also (despite its incompleteness) how varied and unreliable that movement was. Contrasted with idle generalities about hunters 'always knowing where buffalo were to be found,' etc., McDougall's books, for example, are a storehouse of testimony to the precise contrary. To quote all the instances he mentions during twenty years, of the uncertainties of skilled hunters in finding buffalo where by all experienced reasoning they felt entitled to expect them, would almost entail copying whole pages of his works.

In his earliest book, dealing with *circa* 1860, he describes the buffalo as being then "very precarious,"[320] "the buffalo might fail us."[321] He says of the local Plain Crees: "You might strike the camp soon, or you might be weeks looking for them, and when you found the Indians, they might be in a worse condition as to provisions than you were. This all depended on the buffalo in their migrations—sometimes here, and again hundreds of miles away. . . ."[322] Of the same people, he remarks elsewhere: "They were constantly moving with the buffalo, so that the place that knew them to-day might possibly never know them again for ever. . . ."[323] He says likewise of the Cree chieftain, Masképetoon:[324] "Winter or summer, his people had "no abiding-place". . . ."[325]

In a later book, McDougall describes the average condition in winter time: ". . . buffalo from fifty to two hundred miles away from your camp,—the rigor of the winter and the condition of grass and wood forbidding the camp moving any nearer to them. . . ."[326]

The younger Henry said precisely the same of the Piegans, over half a century earlier: "The buffalo regulates their movements over

[319]MacInnes, *In the Shadow of the Rockies,* 57; cf. Henry, 1811: 'Slave tribes' (*i.e.* Blackfoot Confederacy) starving. See above, note 312.

[320]*Forest, Lake, and Prairie,* 150.

[321]*Ibid.,* 235.

[322]*Ibid.,* 233.

[323]McDougall, *Saddle, Sled, and Snowshoe,* 32.

[324]A famous character. Maximilian met him at Fort Union, June, 1833: *Early Western Travels,* XXIII, 13. See on him, *Rundle's Journal, passim;* also below, chap. XXI, note 295.

[325]McDougall, *Saddle, Sled, and Snowshoe,* 196.

[326]McDougall, *Pathfinding* (*circa* 1865), 16.

THE NORTH AMERICAN BUFFALO

this vast extent of prairie throughout the year, as they must keep near these animals to obtain food. . . ."[327] Palliser noted the same fact, shortly before McDougall's arrival: "As a rule the bison hunters do not suffer from want of food, but they were kept constantly following the migrations of the buffalo. . . ."[328]

It appears to have been the custom with the McDougalls to organize a hunt in October or thereabouts, seeking the herds on the great plains and parklands southward from their home at Victoria (now Pakan) on the North Saskatchewan.[329] This was apparently lest a mild winter should ensue, and the herds remain 'far out' without striking for the shelter of the northern woodlands at all.[330] In some of these cases, the hunters apparently passed no great distance from the buffalo, in ignorance of their proximity,[331] and the Indians also, despite vigilant scouting, would sometimes be gone from Victoria for a month, and then report finding herds only two or three days distant from the Mission.[332] These testimonies are corroborated by other travellers, in addition to numerous incidental references in various books from McDougall himself.[333] The members of the Palliser expedition more than once record such experiences. Palliser himself writes (Turtle Mountain, June or July, 1857): "We have been disappointed by the entire absence of buffalo from the plains in this neighbourhood, where they are so frequently found. . . ."[334]

[327]Coues (ed.), *Henry-Thompson Journals*, II, 723. Catlin, also, speaks of the Indians "following the immense herds of buffaloes, as they range over these vast plains, from east to west, and north to south . . ." (*Letters on the North American Indians*, I, 43).

[328]*Palliser Journals*, 199, 201, 205.

[329]McDougall, *Saddle, Sled, and Snowshoe*, 80, 104, 117, 218, 220, etc.

[330]See extracts from *Harmon's Journal* (above, notes 245-53). McDougall gives instances where they stayed out, despite intense cold (above, chap. VIII, notes 99-104, etc.).

[331]McDougall, *Saddle, Sled, and Snowshoe*, 27-9. See above (chap. XI, notes 56-70) for similar experiences in the northwestern United States territory, 1830-45.

[332]McDougall, *Saddle, Sled, and Snowshoe*, 20, 29, 117. Cf. also the case of the Pawnees on the Platte (1819), where the buffalo came right up into the villages while the Indians were seeking them elsewhere (above, note 64).

McDougall says specifically: "There were millions of these cattle, and yet so big was the field that you might travel for days and weeks and not see one of them. But their tracks were everywhere . . . paths and dust-pans . . ." (*i.e.* 'dry wallows'), *Pathfinding*, 248.

[333]McDougall, *Saddle, Sled, and Snowshoe*, 21, 53, 111; *Red River Rebellion*, 132; *Western Trails*, 9. They were going northward in June-July, 1865 (*Pathfinding*, 74, 92); but—lest the Philistines should rejoice—he also records them going westward, February, 1865 (*ibid.*, 24).

[334]*Palliser Journals*, 44; cf. Henry, 1808 (Coues (ed.), *Henry-Thompson Journals*, I, 436).

He records similar 'disappointments' in the Moose Mountain region, August, 1857 (in which his half-breeds participated[335]), and in the Buffalo Lake—Hand Hills country, two summers later (1859).[336] Dr. Hector relates a like experience among the Stoneys in 1859;[337] and Sullivan, the secretary of the expedition,[338] describes two such occurrences, one in the Eagle Hills, southeast of Battleford, in June, 1858,[339] and the other north of the Bow River in July, 1858.[340] This last was of a very similar character to those noted above, where after a long search buffalo were found near the starting-point.[341] Milton and Cheadle also relate a number of similar revelations of buffalo unreliability.[342] There is nothing extraordinary in all this, to those who know anything of the very localized and varied topography of the so-called 'level prairies'; but it plays havoc with the theory of the regular migration, 'following the same route,' 'always knowing where they were to be found,' and so on, according to the familiar and well-known shibboleths. What this really meant in terms of distance—frequently enough at least to create a state of mind—is revealed by an incidental utterance from McDougall, apropos of their tedious endeavours to grind some meal in a small hand-mill: "So long as we can get buffalo within three hundred miles we would prefer buffalo-steaks to barley-meal."[343]

Precisely the same utter irregularity is revealed by such comparisons as I have been able to make between certain traditionally famous localities and their actual experiences. Butler, as we have seen, described the 'Fertile Belt'—the centre, roughly, being about Carlton—as 'the winter home of the buffalo.'[344] Yet in the self-same book, he states that he traversed this very region in the fall or early winter of 1870, the very season when the northward movement for shelter from severe weather might supposedly be in progress across or near his route; and in the whole of that journey of some twelve hundred miles, saw 'not one.'[345] Similarly, Macoun states that the Hand Hills district

[335]*Palliser Journals*, 48.
[336]*Ibid.*, 136.
[337]*Ibid.*, 145.
[338]Sullivan, like Hector, led detached expeditions (*ibid.*, 83-90, 160-2).
[339]Sullivan, in *Palliser Journals*, 83-4.
[340]Sullivan, *ibid.*, 89-90.
[341]See above, note 332.
[342]*North-West Passage*, 59, 77, 83, 124, 127, 142-6.
[343]McDougall, *Saddle, Sled, and Snowshoe*, 230. Cf. Butler, October-November, 1872, setting out on a hunt, 200 miles or more, or 'fifteen days,' westward from the Forks of the Saskatchewan (*Wild North Land*, 44, 57).
[344]Butler, *Great Lone Land*, 230.
[345]Butler's "Report to the Governor" (*ibid.*, 358).

in Central Alberta was formerly noted for "the enormous herds of buffalo wintering in its neighbourhood."[346] In this very locality, however, in February, 1871, John McDougall found the Indians in apprehension of starvation.[347] Macoun further states that between the Hand Hills and the Red Deer River, and also around Tail Creek (the outlet southward from Buffalo Lake into that stream) "buffalo in the palmy days of the past were never wanting";[348] yet it was in the latter region precisely that Palliser (who may also have heard something of the kind) experienced one of the aforementioned 'disappointments' at finding none in the summer of 1859.[349] It is rather a coincidence that Macoun himself found the Indians (Blackfoot, etc.) starving in the former district, between the Hand Hills and the Red Deer, in 1879;[350] but neither this fact, nor the almost miraculous appearance of a herd, at this time, could fairly be considered relevant at so late a period, the very eve of their extinction.

Palliser notes that in 1857 buffalo were plentiful between Edmonton and Fort Pitt, while Carlton and Rocky Mountain House were starving. In 1858, these local conditions were exactly reversed.[351] Fort Pitt itself was regarded as a peculiarly favoured locality, in Milton and Cheadle's day, though it may not always have been so considered.[352] The two travellers in question remark as follows: "This establishment furnishes the largest quantity of pemmican and dry meat for the posts more distant from the plains. The buffalo are seldom far distant from Fort Pitt, and often whilst there is a famine at Carlton and Edmonton, the people of the 'Little Fort,' as it is called, are feasting on fresh meat every day. . . ."[353]

[346]Macoun, *Manitoba*, 258.

[347]McDougall, *Red River Rebellion*, 160, 184.

[348]Macoun, *Manitoba*, 259, 260.

[349]*Palliser Journals*, 136. He mentions finding a great scarcity in the upper Bow Valley (*ibid.*, 92); the very region of McDougall's old paths (*Western Trails*, 21, 108), and where the McDougall family were 'still living chiefly on buffalo' as late as 1875 (McDougall MS., 20, 33). The *Palliser Journals* note many of these localized variations of feast and famine (Palliser, 20, 43, 44, 56, 63, 92, 116, 117, 134 *seq.*; Hector, 65, 69, 70, 72, 75, 78, 80, 81, 145, 149; Sullivan, 89-90).

[350]Macoun, *Autobiography*, 149-50.

[351]*Palliser Journals*, 202.

[352]Paul Kane, Fort Pitt, Jan. 1848: "The animals had, we were told, never appeared in such vast numbers, nor shown themselves so near the Company's establishments; some had even been shot within the gates of the fort . . ." (*Wanderings of an Artist*, Radisson Society ed., 277). Also on the Battle River, southwest of Edmonton, April, 1848: "We found buffaloes in places where the Indians said they had never been seen before . . ." (*ibid.*, 286).

[353]Milton and Cheadle, *North-West Passage*, 169-70.

Dr. Hector says, similarly, that buffalo "are never far distant, *even in the summer . . .*";[354] and McDougall (*circa* 1860) speaks of "the great herds coming closer and oftener to this point than to any other . . ." (of the Hudson's Bay Company's posts on the Saskatchewan).[355] Rundle noted buffalo about there in June, 1841, in August, 1845, and in September, 1846;[356] at which latter time Kane also records them.[357] Hector observed 'immense herds' near there in December, 1857; and he refers to buffalo there again in April, 1859.[358] Yet in 1858, this favoured spot was 'starving';[359] 'nearly starving' in July, 1859; they were 'far off' in November, 1859 (although there were some along the river toward Carlton at that time[360]), and there were "none near Pitt during the whole winter" of 1858-59 or 1859-60.[361] When Milton and Cheadle were at Fort Pitt in April, 1863, there were apparently none, despite their own expressed opinion on its plenty; nor are any mentioned along the entire route from Carlton to Edmonton.[362] Yet in the winter of 1863-64 a great herd was drowned in Jackfish Lake near there, showing some numbers in that neighbourhood.[363] There were 'vast numbers,' south, in 1872.[364]

It would have been of immense interest and value, had it been practicable to secure an uninterrupted journal of one (or more) of the Saskatchewan fur-trading posts from about 1790 or 1800 onward; and to note its 'buffalo history.' I give below such notices of this character as I have been able to collect, concerning a few of the more important centres.

CARLTON: 'abundance,' January, 1776; 'large herds,' south of Carlton, February, 1776;[365] 'numerous,' Prince Albert to beyond Carl-

[354]Hector, *Palliser Journals*, 70 (italics mine). These words clearly reveal the normal trend of movement. See below, note 408.

[355]McDougall, *Forest, Lake, and Prairie*, 142.

[356]*Rundle's Journal*, June 18, 1841; August 29-31, 1845; September 24-5, 1846.

[357]Kane, *Wanderings of an Artist*, 89; cf. above, notes 287-92, 352.

[358]Hector, *Palliser Journals*, 69, 132.

[359]So, Hector, and Palliser; *ibid.*, 71, 202.

[360]Southesk, *Travels*, 100, 285, 295-8.

[361]*Ibid.*, 254. It is not clear which. Southesk's book did not appear until 1875, and he may have utilized information obtained subsequent to his visit; but mention of 'none in the *winter*' shows clearly enough that in winter they were normally present.

[362]Milton and Cheadle, *North-West Passage*, 165-78 (April 6-May 14).

[363]McDougall, *Saddle, Sled, and Snowshoe*, 132.

[364]Grant, *Ocean to Ocean*, 173.

[365]Henry, *Travels, 1760-1776*, 273, 278-80, 309.

ton, September, 1794;[366] 'abundant,' Carlton and beyond, September, 1808;[367] 'plentiful,' Carlton and west, January and February, 1820;[368] 'unusually scarce,' January 1, 1837;[369] 'numerous . . . in myriads,' January 15, 1840;[370] 'numerous,' two days above Carlton, October, 1840; 'buffalo seen,' June, 1841; 'scarce,' July, 1845; 'immense quantities,' west of Carlton, August, 1845; 'no buffalo seen,' west of Carlton, August, 1845;[371] 'scarce,' September, 1846; 'buffalo seen,' west of Carlton, September, 1846; 'large herds,' apparently not far west of Carlton, May, 1848;[372] 'immense herds,' south of Carlton, September, 1857;[373] 'five days out,' October, 1857;[374] 'plenty,' two days west of Carlton until two days east of Edmonton (393 miles = 13 days), December, 1857;[375] 'distant,' nearest south of the Eagle Hills, winter, 1857-58;[376] 'starving,' 1857; 'plentiful,' 1858;[377] 'buffalo very scarce,' between North and South Branches (that is, Saskatoon to Carlton), summer, 1858;[378] 'none near Carlton,' apparently winter, 1858-59; 'plenty,' about two days south of Carlton, summer, 1859;[379] 'within a hundred miles of Carlton, or less than two days out,' summer, 1862;[380] (south of Carlton) "a ridge which enabled us to look down and across a plain or open country, some ten or twenty miles in size, and which seemed to be literally full of buffalo . . .," autumn, 1862;[381] 'often far distant,' 1862;[382] 'close up,' September, 1862; 'far out . . . starvation,' February, 1863;[383] 'far out,' November, 1870;[384] 'plenty,' November, 1872.[385]

[366]McGillivray's Journal, ed. A. S. Morton, 21-8.

[367]Coues (ed.), Henry-Thompson Journals, II, 490, 502.

[368]Franklin, (First) Journey to the Polar Sea, 103, 121.

[369]Thomas Simpson, Narrative of Discoveries, 48.

[370]Ibid., 402.

[371]Rundle's Journal, October 4-5, 1840; June 14, 1841; July 19, August 26-30, 1845; August 25-9, 1846.

[372]Kane, Wanderings of an Artist, 76, 77, 84, 293.

[373]Palliser, in Palliser Journals, 55-8; M. Bourgeau, ibid., 247.

[374]Hector, ibid., 65.

[375]Ibid., 67-72.

[376]Palliser, ibid., 63.

[377]Ibid., 20, 202; Hector, ibid., 81.

[378]Hind, Report, 1858, 52.

[379]Southesk, Travels, 91-127, 254.

[380]McDougall, Forest, Lake, and Prairie, 136.

[381]Ibid., 202.

[382]Previous to 1862—"vast herds covered the ground in every direction from Red River to Carlton . . ." (Milton and Cheadle, North-West Passage, 58). In 1863—"the days gone by when one could subsist with gun and net on the North Saskatchewan . . ." (ibid., 50, 68, 157).

[383]Ibid., 58-9, 141-57.

[384]Butler, Great Lone Land, 229, 358.

[385]Butler, Wild North Land, 47, 57.

VICTORIA:[386] 'many herds,' south of Whitefish Lake (that is, north of the Saskatchewan River), January, 1863: 'far south,' December, 1863; 'two days southeast,' January, 1864; 'vast herds,' second day south from Victoria, spring, 1865;[387] 'far out,' south from Victoria, winter, 1865-66; 'far out,' spring, 1866; 'far out,' south and east despite bitter cold, winter, 1866-67;[388] 'close up,' winter, 1869-70;[389] 'far out,' Christmas, 1870;[390] 'plenty,' November, 1872;[391] 'far out,' winter, 1872-73;[392] 'not far away,' winter, 1874-75;[393] 'none north of the Saskatchewan River, after 1874.[394]

EDMONTON (and district, including Pigeon Lake and Upper Saskatchewan territory): 'plentiful,' Horse Hills district adjacent to Edmonton, July, 1810; 'none north of Battle River: Indians starving,' August, 1810; 'buffalo seen,' Upper North Saskatchewan, October, 1810 and February, 1811;[395] 'buffalo scarce owing to a mild winter,' Fort Augustus (Edmonton), January 26, 1821;[396] 'abundance, meat in vast quantities,' Edmonton (from the hunters' camp near Beaver Lake), December, 1840;[397] 'buffalo' in Beaver Hills, eastward from Edmonton, January, 1841;[398] 'plentiful,' southward from Edmonton, spring, 1841; 'starvation imminent,' winter, 1841-42; 'starvation,' Whitefish Lake, spring, 1842; 'immense herds,' one day south or southeast, autumn, 1842; 'buffalo encountered,' Beaver Hills, March, 1843; 'Assiniboines starving; and have been starving for two or three autumns here,' Rocky Mountain House, October, 1845;[399] 'buffalo disappeared,' Edmonton district at large, October, 1845;[400] 'great many,' Fort Pitt to Edmonton,

---

[386]Rev. George McDougall's first mission, Saskatchewan River, 90 miles below Edmonton; founded 1863, and their headquarters for many years.

[387]McDougall, *Saddle, Sled, and Snowshoe*, 27, 106, 117, 271.

[388]McDougall, *Pathfinding*, 117-20, 150, 192, 196, 210.

[389]McDougall, *Red River Rebellion*, 95.

[390]Butler, *Great Lone Land*, 304. [391]Butler, *Wild North Land*, 47.

[392]McDougall, *Western Trails*, 9.

[393]Steele, *Forty Years in Canada*, 72; McDougall MS., 20, 33.

[394]Denny MS., 38; hearsay only, I suspect.

[395]Coues (ed.), *Henry-Thompson Journals*, II, 614, 615, 620, 653, 656, 661, 681-97.

[396]G. C. Davidson, *The North West Company*, Appendix O, 303.

[397]*Rundle's Journal*, December 19, 1840.

[398]*Ibid.*, January 15-16, 1841. McDougall states that when he came to Edmonton in 1862, it was known to the Indians as Beaver Hills House (*Forest, Lake, and Prairie*, 218; see also Coues (ed.), *Henry-Thompson Journals*, II, 611.

[399]*Rundle's Journal*, April 26-30, December 13, 1841; March 18, April 13, September 2, 1842; March 14, 1843; October 18, 1845.

[400]De Smet, *Early Western Travels*, XXIX, 250; *Life of De Smet*, II, 533. Cf., however, his own description of the plentiful supplies: above, notes 282, 317, 318.

autumn, 1846;[401] 'buffalo,' Sturgeon River, twelve miles northward, October, 1846; 'an enormous band, probably numbering 10,000,' Fort Edmonton, December, 1847; 'extremely numerous,' winter, 1847-48; 'plenty,' Edmonton to Fort Pitt, January, 1848;[402] 'plenty,' within two days eastward, January, 1857; 'plenty,' 1857;[403] 'far out,' Rocky Mountain House, January, 1858;[404] 'scarcity'—or 'none,' Edmonton, winter, 1858-59;[405] 'plenty,' toward Rocky Mountain House, January-February, 1859;[406] 'nearly starving,' Edmonton, July, 1859;[407] 'starving,' Edmonton, June-July, 1859;[408] 'starvation,' winter, 1861-62;[409] 'far out,' winter, 1862-63;[410] 'great herds,' near Beaver Lake, September, 1863;[411] October-November, 1864, January, 1865;[412] 'far out,' eastward from Pigeon Lake, December, 1866 to January, 1867; 'far out,' from Pigeon Lake, winter, 1867-68;[413] 'not numerous,' January, 1868;[414] 'far out,' from Pigeon Lake, winter, 1868-69 (an open winter); 'quite numerous,' on the 'big plains' southeast from Edmonton, spring, 1871; 'hundreds killed in one hunt,' southeast from Edmonton, spring, 1872;[415] 'far out,' winter, 1872-73;[416] 'plenty of fresh buffalo meat,' Edmonton, winter, 1874-75.[417]

The mass of evidence presented in this and the foregoing chapters at large is in my opinion fatal to any supposition of a regular or general migration among the species as a whole. The one resultant factor that emerges from our inquiry is the direct antithesis of any conception of regularity; an imponderable, incalculable, wholly erratic and unreliable caprice. I suspect that this irregularity, manifested for longer

[401]*Rundle's Journal*, September 24-9, 1846.

[402]Kane, *Wanderings of an Artist*, 97, 256, 258, 277.

[403]Hector and Palliser, in *Palliser Journals*, 69-72, 202. Hector remarks (p. 72): "This year these animals are within a few days of the fort, . . . but many years there is a great scarcity and even starvation here. . . ."

[404]Hector, *ibid.*, 75.

[405]'Scarcity': Palliser, *ibid.*, 15, 202; 'none': Southesk, *Travels*, 254.

[406]*Palliser Journals*, 117.

[407]Southesk, *Travels*, 100.

[408]*Palliser Journals*, 138. Hector observes *re* women and children left at home when the spring brigades departed: "and if the buffalo are distant they will certainly suffer a summer of great privation" (*ibid.*, 133), as they did. Cf. above, note 354.

[409]Hughes, *Father Lacombe*, 89-90.

[410]McDougall, *Forest, Lake, and Prairie*, 260.

[411]McDougall, *Saddle, Sled, and Snowshoe*, 78.

[412]*Ibid.*, 220-6, 255-7.

[413]McDougall, *Pathfinding*, 183-6, 243.

[414]Hughes, *Father Lacombe*, 142 seq.

[415]McDougall, *Red River Rebellion*, 26, 189, 203, 228.

[416]McDougall, *Western Trails*, 9.

[417]S. B. Steele, *Forty Years in Canada*, 84-5.

or shorter periods of duration, is the true explanation—as in the case of Father De Smet in the Edmonton district in 1845-46[418]—of many or most of the early references to the 'disappearance of the buffalo,' which are so frequently encountered in the contemporary literature of Western travel. Statements or complaints of this nature, made to passing travellers by the Indians, who were not given as a whole to long views or exactly-recorded philosophical data,[419] and accepted in good faith— which a scarcity at the moment, appearing to corroborate the assertions of their informants, might readily justify—are countered so often by equally reliable testimony to the presence of the species in great numbers at periods much later than the supposed 'final disappearance,' that the inquirer is driven to some such explanation as that which I have suggested.

My own deliberate conclusion, based upon the carefully collated evidence of aborigines, old-timers, travellers, sportsmen, and scientific observers, is that the buffalo were highly erratic;[420] and that no statement presupposing uniformity of action in their wanderings—if in anything—can be relied upon beyond the actual, observed matters of fact it may contain. In the following chapter I shall defend this opinion by presenting a mass of closely allied evidence—essentially a continuation of the present chapter—exhibiting the workings and influence of this erratic spirit upon the aboriginal human occupants of the buffalo range.[421]

Note

Buffalo Variations in Texas after 1840

The following note, which is taken from Allen, *American Bisons* (pp. 137-141), is of great historical value; in as much as it largely consists of references to 'disappearances' at early dates, in the very regions wherein the last wild buffalo hunt recorded in the United States actually occurred, as late as 1889.

---

[418]Above, notes 282, 317, 318, 400.

[419]Compare a competent Indianologist: "The old-time Indian was a far better observer than most white men. He saw more clearly what was happening, and usually reported facts more accurately. On the other hand, he was weak in reasoning from what he saw . . ." (Grinnell, *Fighting Cheyennes*, 270).

[420]Even in such a noted resort as the 'Great Licks' in Kentucky, this uncertainty existed. Nicholas Cresswell twice speaks of 'intending to kill some buffalo meat there'; and on his arrival finding none to kill!: *Cresswell's Journal*, 86, 90 (June 14, 24, 1775).

[421]See some evidence concerning another supposedly 'regularly migratory' species; below, Appendix F, "Caribou."

Beginning with the year 1841 . . . Kendall, in travelling north from Austin, Texas, first met with buffaloes seventy-five miles north of Austin, on Little River, a southern tributary of the Brazos, where he found them in immense herds. . . . Kendall also found them numerous on the Brazos, and states that they occasionally took shelter in the Cross Timbers,[422] and that he last met with them in going westward, on the upper part of the Big Washita, one of the sources of the Red River (near 100° W.).

Kennedy, writing in the same year [that is, 1841], says: 'The bison is still to be met with, in the mountainous districts between the Guadaloupe and the Rio Grande.' According to Gregg, however, they had already disappeared *east of the Cross Timbers* as early as 1840.[423]

In 1849, in an expedition from Fort Smith, Arkansas, to Santa Fé, Lieut. J. H. Simpson first saw buffaloes near the 97th. meridian, a few miles south of the Canadian, but adds that he saw not more than two buffaloes on the whole journey . . .[424] he says: "In regard to the buffalo, there can be no question that they have been in the habit of infesting the route in places during certain seasons of the year. Indeed, Gregg mentions them as swarming on the plains, on his return from Santa Fé, in the spring of 1840."[425]

[Ferdinand] Roemer, in 1849, says that the buffalo was then found only in the hilly parts of the State, far from the coast, and that herds of a thousand together were still seen between the Brazos and Austin. It would seem, however, that at this time there were very few buffaloes south of the Red River, as during the years 1849, 1850, and 1851 a series of military recon-

[422]The Cross Timbers are described by my earliest source, Washington Irving (October, 1832), as "a grand belt of open forest. . . . which ranges nearly north and south from the Arkansas to Red River . . ." (*Tour of the Prairies*, 402).

Dr. Gregg writes as follows (1838-39): "As the forest of Cross Timbers was now beginning to be seen in the distance, and fearing we might be troubled to find a passway through this brushy region, south of the Canadian, we forded this river . . ." (*Early Western Travels*, XX, 217).

"The Cross Timbers vary in width from five to thirty miles, and entirely cut off the communication betwixt the interior prairies and those of the great plains. . . . The underwood is so matted in many places with grapevines, greenbriars, &c, as to form almost impenetrable 'roughs,' which serve as hiding-places for wild beasts, as well as wild Indians; and would, in savage warfare, prove almost as formidable as the hummocks of Florida . . ." (Gregg, *ibid.*, 254-6). Compare a description by Chittenden (*American Fur Trade*, II, 803). Marcy (contra Gregg) says that he had crossed them at five different points, and without difficulty; 'open enough [as Irving, above] to take a wagon through without felling trees' (*Exploration of Red River*, 80, 84). A place might be open enough for peaceful passage, yet easily made 'impenetrable' when stoutly defended.

[423]See Gregg, *Early Western Travels*, XX, 118, 213, 217-56 (the italics are Allen's).

[424]This must have been east of the Cross Timbers. According to Allen, "The central portion of the wooded belt known as the 'Cross Timbers' lies along this meridian" (97° W.: *American Bisons*, note 138). Thwaites, however, has it beginning near the 99th meridian, and '400 miles long, extending from the Arkansas to the Brazos . . .' (ed. note, *Early Western Travels*, XVI, 142).

[425]I cannot identify this. Gregg's only 'swarms' (*sic*) are above Ash Creek, north of the Arkansas River, outward bound, June, 1831 (*ibid.*, XIX, 213).

naissances were made in Texas, forming a network of lines covering a large part of the State, during the running of which no buffaloes seem to have been met with. Lieut. Michler surveyed a line from Fort Washita southward along the 97th. meridian from 34° 30′ N. to about 31° N., and thence southwestward, in a nearly direct line to the Pecos River, striking it in longitude 103° and latitude 31° 20′. A line was continued from this point eastward again to the 100th. meridian, and thence southeastward to Corpus Christi Bay, in longitude 96° and latitude 28° 40′. Another line was carried down the Pecos to longitude 101° 40′, and thence to the headwaters of the Nueces, and down this river also to Corpus Christi Bay. The narratives of these expeditions make no mention of buffaloes, as they doubtless would if buffaloes had been met with. In 1850 Marcy met with a few stragglers south of the Canadian, near the divide between the Canadian and the Washita Forks of the Red River,[426] and saw their tracks and other indications of their presence there. He reports that the Kiowas and Comanches went north in summer to hunt the buffalo on the plains of the Arkansas, only a few buffaloes crossing at this time to the south of the Canadian.[427]

In 1852, according to the "Topographical Sketches of the Military Posts in Texas," buffaloes had entirely disappeared from the region about Fort Worth (on the west fork of the Trinity, just west of the 97th. meridian); they are not mentioned among the animals found at this date about Fort Belknap (on the Brazos, longitude about 98° 30′), neither were they found about Fort Terret (on the 100th. meridian). Very few are said to have been seen as far south as Fort Phantom Hill, since 1837. At Camp Johnston, on the Concho River (near the present Fort Concho), only one is reported as having been seen [that is, presumably, 1852] and the region is said to have been then not within their favourite range; but they are at the same time enumerated among the animals met with at Fort McKavett, situated some fifty miles to the southward of Fort Concho.

Lieut. Whipple, in his report of the survey of the 35th. parallel, made in 1853, found buffalo bones bleaching near a brackish spring, just west of the Cross Timbers, and nearly on the 99th. meridian. A few days later they saw the first living buffalo, and met with a few stragglers on succeeding days, on the sources of the Washita Branch of the Red River. He speaks of seeing buffalo signs as far west as Camp 44, a little east of the 102nd meridian. The main herds, however, were north of the Canadian, from which these were merely stragglers.[428] Professor Jules Marcou (Whipple's geolo-

[426]Just about where Gregg first encountered them, after a long interval of scarcity; working eastward, April, 1839 (*ibid.*, XX, 118). Above, note 50.

[427]There may have been more later on. See above (chap. XIII, note 159) the account by Horace Jones, Fort Sill, 1859 (about 100 miles south of the Canadian) of 'grass eaten down' along the 100th meridian: *Forest and Stream*, II, 184 (no date; cited by Hornaday, "Extermination of the American Bison," 504).

[428]North of the Canadian, June, 1852: Marcy, *Exploration of Red River*, 43. Buffalo above Cache Creek, Red River (of Texas) 1852: *ibid.*, 187; cf. also 104.

gist) informs me that the first bones of the buffalo were met with as far east as the Cross Timbers, or near the 98th meridian; but the region appeared not to have been visited by these animals for ten or twelve years. The first living buffalo was seen between Camps 33 and 34, about 99° 40', just south of the Canadian. The next day many carcasses were observed, and two days later five old bulls were seen. An old bull was killed between Camps 36 and 37, near the meridian of 100° 25', but no living buffalo were seen west of the 101st meridian, and no fresh signs were seen west of the 102nd. All the recent indications of buffalo were thus met with between the meridians of 98° 30' and 102°. The journey being made in September, the herds had not returned from the north, the individuals met with being only stragglers which had wandered somewhat to the southward of the usual southern limit of the summer range.[429]

Captain (now Major-General) Pope in 1854 surveyed the 32nd. parallel from El Paso and Doña Oña, on the Rio Grande, to Preston, on the Red River, passing northerly, and crossing the Pecos, and the head-waters of the Colorado, Trinity, and Brazos Rivers. Mr. J. H. Byrne, in his diary of the expedition, reports meeting *bois de vache* "for the first time" at Camp No. 10, near the Ojo del Cuerbo, or Salt Lakes, west of the Guadaloupe Mountains, and in the valley of the Rio Grande. This is the only allusion to buffalo or buffalo 'sign' contained in the narrative, although the kinds and quantity of game met with each day appear to be duly chronicled. We are further led to infer the entire absence at this time of buffaloes in Texas by some remarks made by Captain Pope, in his General Report, respecting the Comanche Indians whose country was the head-waters of the Canadian and Red Rivers, in the extreme northern part of Texas. He says: "During the summer months nearly the whole tribe migrates to the north, to hunt buffalo and wild horses on the plains of the upper Arkansas."[430]

Captain H. M. Lazelle, 8th U.S. Infantry, informs me that in 1859 there were no buffaloes in New Mexico, nor in Texas west of the 99th meridian; but that there were vast numbers in northern Texas between the meridians of 90° and 96°; but that they did not extend so far south as Pope's old trail of 1854.[431]

[429]A 'summer range' along the Canadian! Either Marcou or Allen evidently did not believe in the northward migration being general. Catlin, June-August, 1834, found them forty miles east of the junction of the False Washita and Red Rivers; also on the Canadian (*Letters on the North American Indians*, II, 46, 76); cf. above, notes 48-52.

[430]Cf. Marcy, 1852: The Northern and Middle Commanches were known among other Indians as 'buffalo-eaters,' ". . . and are generally to be found at their heels, migrating with them from place to place upon these vast and inhospitable plains of the West, the greater portions of which are incapable of cultivation, and seem destined in the future, as in the past, to be the abode of the wandering savage, possessing as they do, so few attractions to civilized man . . ." (*Exploration of Red River*, 94).

[431]Allen adds in a footnote (*American Bisons*, 140): "Pope's trail crosses the 90th meridian in about latitude 33° 30', and strikes the Pecos in longitude 103° 30' at Emigrant Crossing. . . ."

There is some confusion or carelessness here. East of longitude 100° W., the northern boundary of Texas is the Red River, about 34° N. (see map).

Hence it appears that for quite a number of years the buffaloes nearly abandoned Texas, or visited only its northwestern portions, and were of somewhat uncertain occurrence in summer at least, as far north as the Canadian. Of late, however, they have again become common over a considerable portion of the northwestern part of the State, occasionally extending southward along the 100th. meridian almost to the Rio Grande. Major-General M. C. Meigs, Quartermaster-General of the United States Army, says in some valuable MS. notes on the buffalo, that in the winter of 1869-'70 he saw their carcasses near Fort Concho, Texas, "showing that the buffalo had been abundant in that neighbourhood the previous year." The prairies having been extensively burned that winter about Concho, the buffaloes had not appeared within twenty miles of that post [? twenty miles northward or westward] that season. He also states that in the winter of 1871-'72 they extended their migrations westward to the Staked Plains.

Respecting their present southern limit in Texas, . . . Mr. J. Stevens, in answer to my inquiries on this point . . . states . . . for the last two or three years at Fort Concho, that buffaloes have of late been quite numerous there in winter, and that they were especially so last winter (? 1875-76 or 1874-75). He says that "after severe storms, they come in from the north in large numbers," at which times he has seen larger herds there than anywhere else, not excepting Kansas and the Indian Territory. East of Fort Concho he says they do not go south of the latitude of that post, but that to the westward they go twenty to fifty miles further to the southward, *but only occasionally*.[432] Mr. Stevens adds that none are found very far to the westward of Fort Concho, and that none have been found for a long time in any part of New Mexico, and that probably none ever will be found there again. From the best information I have been able to obtain, their present western limit seems to be the eastern border of the Staked Plains [Llano Estacado; about 102° 30′ W.].

There are certain discrepancies in the foregoing remarks, despite their high general value, which cannot be overlooked; and which prevent any one of these accounts from having the right to override other testimony. These considerations tend to indicate that here also, many of the 'disappearances' simply mean that the witness in question saw none on that particular journey; Gregg, 'east of the Cross Timbers,' being a case in point. In other instances, trained scientific observers

---

90° W. lies on a line between Memphis, Tennessee, and New Orleans; and the mean of '90° and 96°' (*i.e.* 93° W.) would be midway through the State of Louisiana. Hornaday has them extinct in Mississippi, 1720; southern Arkansas, 1820; southern and eastern Texas, 1837, 1850 (map, "Extermination of the American Bison," 548). The foregoing vagueness tends to cast doubt on accompanying statements and dates. Bancroft mentions 'diminution,' *circa* 1854; apparently in the Fort Belknap region, where in 1852 there were 'none.' *History of the North Mexican States and Texas*, II, 406. His only other reference to the species is to buffalo-hunting in Navarre County (northeast of Waco), in 1838 (*ibid.*, II, 311).

[432]Italics mine.

include data concerning buffalo vestiges recent or remote; and these testimonies furnish circumstantial evidence covering an approximate period of years. Allen (apparently on the authority of General Meigs' MS. notes) has them 'of late' *occasionally* 'extending southward along the 100th. Meridian almost to the Rio Grande'; this being supported by references to Fort Concho, 1869-70. Yet Mr. Stevens, the local authority quoted concerning Fort Concho, says that 'eastward they do not go south of that latitude.' Fort Concho is about 102° W.; some 110 miles west of the 100th meridian. Mr. Stevens also adds that none were (*circa* 1875) to be found in any part of New Mexico, nor had been for a long time. Allen endorses this by the western limit being given as the eastern border of the Llano Estacado. Yet he himself shortly afterwards prints a statement from a scientist of high standing, showing their presence considerably westward of the Staked Plain at this time.[433] There are, moreover, considerable gaps left untouched; 1841-49, and again, 1854-69. They may have 'appeared and disappeared,' once or more, regularly or irregularly, during these *lacunae*. Even the testimony as we have it, makes mention more than once of certain movements 'occasionally'; and everything considered, it appears to constitute little more than further corroborative evidence for the irregularity I have demonstrated throughout their habitat generally.

[433]"In 1873 they ranged westward to within one hundred miles of Santa Fé." Professor H. W. Henshaw: correspondence to Allen (*American Bisons*, 154). One could 'prove' their disappearance from New Mexico much earlier. Dr. Gregg, 1839, *re* the Yutas or Eutaws (*i.e.* Utes): "The habits of this tribe are altogether itinerant. A band of about 1000 spend their winters in the mountain valleys northward of Taos, and the summer season generally in the prairie plains to the east, hunting buffalo . . ." (*Early Western Travels*, XX, 83). Northward of Taos in the 'Yuta' country is the precise region where buffalo were found in July, 1694 (above, note 33).

Again: "Dr. (A.) Wislizenus reports that on Colonel Doniphan's march across the plains [1846] all signs of the buffalo, including even the *bois de vache*, disappeared near the meridian 101°, between the Arkansas and the Cimarron . . ." (Allen, *American Bisons*, 148). Gregg, 1839, 'saw none west of Spring Valley,' some 80 miles west of Chouteau's Fort (? Chouteau Island), about the same region (*Early Western Travels*, XX, 111, 115). Compare these observations with those of 1873!

CHAPTER XXI

THE INFLUENCE OF THE BUFFALO ENVIRONMENT
UPON INDIAN MENTALITY

1.

THE supreme plastic agencies in the formation and development
of what we may call the ingrained characteristics of type are,
of course, heredity and environment. Without attempting to
formulate a minutely detailed and closely defined classification of their
respective spheres of operation, capable of sustaining a keen philosophic scrutiny at all points, it may be permissible to suggest, along
broader and more general lines, that heredity is possibly the master-
force in the moulding of individual temperament; while environment
is the controlling influence in the evolution of tribal character. Whether
this loose and tentative demarcation of their activities be considered
acceptable or not, the general fact of the very great influence of environment upon human mentality is not denied.

This being the case, the assertion will scarcely even be questioned,
that the buffalo, since the earliest era of their impact upon the peoples
dwelling within their wide territorial range, must have exerted an
enormous influence upon Indian character.[1] When we reflect what
profound changes the advent of the horse wrought among the Plains
tribes in the three and one-half centuries from Coronado to the death
of Sitting Bull (1540-1890), in much less than half of which period
many tribes passed from sheer terror at the mere sight of the animal
into the select class of the two or three foremost equestrian peoples
of the world;[2] when we consider that in the uncounted ages before
they became acquainted with the horse, these tribes evidently contrived to get along quite well without it, as their eastern, western and
northern forest kindred have always done; when we compare this
facile assimilation of new conditions by the Indians in their wild state,

[1]Two eminent American archaeologists are inclined to rank the deer even
higher in this respect. McGee and Thomas, "Prehistoric America" (History of
North America XIX, 20-1).
[2]See on this, F. G. Roe, "From Dogs to Horses among the Western Indian
Tribes," Transactions of the Royal Society of Canada, 1939, Sec. II, 209-75.

with their manifest helplessness against the rigorous climatic and other environmental forces of the major portion of the western buffalo habitat when deprived of the resources which the buffalo furnished; we are enabled to form some conception of the far-reaching and complex character of the influence of the buffalo upon the Indian race extending from the physical to the mental domain.[3]

I know of no other instance throughout the entire world wherein from one single source so many commodities of primary importance were derived. Here, at least, the buffalo surely eclipsed the deer. Among the really fundamental needs of mankind, there was practically none which the former did not furnish. It supplied food for immediate and later use, clothing, bedding, shelter, fuel, tools, weapons (in part), household utilities, means for personal or ritualistic adornment, and even the outer 'ecclesiastical' symbols of worship.[4]

It is, of course, well recognized that Indian food-stuffs were not obtained literally from meat alone. A learned contributor to the great work already often cited, says:

Animal food was obtained from the game of the environment, and the settlement and movements of some tribes depended largely on the location or range of animals such as the buffalo, capable of furnishing an adequate food supply. No pure hunter's stage can be found, if it ever existed, for while the capture of animals devolved on the man, and the preparation of food on the woman, the latter added to the diet substances derived from the vegetable kingdom. Similarly, no purely agricultural stage with an exclusively vegetable diet existed. . . . .[5]

In the exact scientific sense, this is, of course, true, but for all practical purposes, the vegetable food of the Indians in winter in the central portions of the prairie buffalo range was almost nil;[6] and even in

---

[3]"The bison of the western plains made the Indian of that immense area emphatically a hunter. It did more. It brought out and developed certain physical and mental characteristics, naturally growing out of that region and the mode of life upon it . . ." (A. J. Fynn, *The American Indian as a Product of Environment*, 244).

"In the Plains area lived one animal that came nearer to dominating the life and shaping the institutions of a human race than any other in all the land, if not in the world—the buffalo . . ." (W. P. Webb, *Great Plains*, 33). Cf. also Wissler, *American Indian*, 370-4.

[4]On the last item, see Appendix D, E.

[5]Walter Hough, "Food," *Handbook of American Indians*, I, 466-9.

[6]Meat 'the sole diet of the Plains tribes nine months in the year'; so, Dodge, *Wild Indians*, 271. Even among those of the Atlantic territory, where cultivation was easy and productive, and much more common, meat was of high importance (see Hough, *Handbook of American Indians*, I, 466-9; also Fiske, *Discovery of America*, I, 27-9, 182). In New France, Lescarbot noted that in mild winters, which spoiled the moose-hunting, starvation ensued. *History of New France*, III, 28. Cf. Cyrus Thomas, "Maize," *Handbook of American Indians*, I, 790.

summer it can scarcely be doubted that the great preponderance of their food was meat.[7] There were exceptions to this general condition, even among tribes living in the very heart of what Indianologists have classified as the plains area, or bison area,[8] which a foremost authority describes as follows: "The chief traits of this culture are the dependence upon the buffalo or bison, and the very limited use of roots and berries; absence of fishing; lack of agriculture; the tipi as a movable dwelling; transportation by land only, with the dog and the travois (in historic times with the horse). . . ."[9]

Whether as a tribal custom brought with them from some former habitat, or for some other reason,[10] a number of tribes practised agriculture to a very considerable extent; among them being the Mandans,[11] Minatari[12] (Hidatsa, better known popularly as the 'Gros Ventres'), and Arikara[13] on the Missouri; and the Pawnee[14] and Osages[15] on, or south of, the Platte. This fact does not, however, invalidate the truth of the major proposition; for even these tribes had no other resource than the buffalo if their crops failed.[16] And either because of the uncertainty of agriculture, or because of a natural preference for buffalo meat when obtainable[17]—which may perhaps confirm the foregoing suggestion of agriculture having possibly been adopted perforce—the only accounts we possess of some of them from early (winter) sojourners describe them as 'buffalo' Indians solely.[18]

[7]See below, Appendix U, "Indian Vegetable Diet."

[8]Wissler, American Indian, 3, 12-14, 31-5, 64, etc.

[9]Ibid., 218-20.

[10]Perhaps in some cases the pressure of more powerful neighbours. The Mandans had the dreaded Sioux on one side and on another those 'Pananas and Pananis,' because of whom, they told La Vérendrye in 1738, 'the men would not undertake to go far . . .' (Report of Canadian Archives, 1889, 19, 21; Burpee (ed.), Journals of La Vérendrye, 335). Thought to be very probably the Arikara, who were themselves in part agriculturists.

[11]See on these, Burpee, ibid., 325; Thompson, Narrative, 231; Coues (ed.), Henry-Thompson Journals, I, 302, 323 seq., and on the neighbouring 'Souliers,' ibid., 348; Harmon's Journal, 101, 106; Catlin, Letters on the North American Indians, I, 89, 121, 127, etc.; Dale (ed.), Ashley-Smith Explorations, 57, 93, 110.

[12]Catlin, Letters on the North American Indians, I, 199; Maximilian, Early Western Travels, XXIII, 274, 289, 368.

[13]Maximilian, ibid., XXII, 335; cf. Bradbury, 1811, ibid., V, 175.

[14]On the Pawnees, see authorities cited, chap. XX, note 63.

[15]For the Osages, see Coues (ed.), Expeditions of Pike, II, 533; Long, Early Western Travels, XVI, 247.

[16]Maximilian on the Arikara having to desert their villages for this reason, 1832 (Early Western Travels, XXII, 335); cf. De Smet, ibid., XXIX, 196.

[17]Note this in a white man, John McDougall, 1864. In extenso above, chap. XIV, note 192.

[18]See the accounts of the Mandans, 1794-1806, by John McDonnell, F. A. Larocque, and Charles Mackenzie, in Masson, Les Bourgeois de la Compagnie du Nord-Ouest, I, 267-81, 299-313, 314-93.

I have alluded to the multiplicity of buffalo products used by the Indians. These were the amazement of the early Spanish explorers, as well they might be.[19] Out of a number of such descriptions of their uses in detail,[20] I quote that of Hornaday, as being probably the best:

If any animal was ever designed by the hand of nature for the express purpose of supplying, at one stroke, nearly all the wants of an entire race, surely the buffalo was intended for the Indian.

And right well was this gift of the gods utilized by the children of nature to whom it came. Up to the time when the United States Government began to support our Western Indians by the payment of annuities and furnishing quarterly supplies of food, clothing, blankets, cloth, tents, etc., the buffalo had been the main dependence of more than 50,000 Indians who inhabited the buffalo range and its environs. Of the many different uses to which the buffalo and his various parts were put by the red men, the following were the principal ones:

The body of the buffalo yielded fresh meat, of which thousands of tons were consumed; dried meat, prepared in summer for winter use; pemmican (also prepared in summer), of meat, fat and berries;[21] tallow, made up into large balls or sacks, and kept in store; marrow, preserved in bladders; and tongues, dried and smoked, and eaten as a delicacy.

[19]Perhaps the earliest ever printed in English (Cabeza de Vaca) ". . . of those which are not great, they make Garments to cover them, and of the greater they make shooes and Targets . . ." (i.e. shields: *Purchas his Pilgrimes*, XVII, 478). Coronado *et al*: ". . . in them consisteth the greater part of the sustenance of the people, for of the skinne they cloathe, and make Shooes, and Cords; they eate the flesh, and make tooles of the bones . . ." (*ibid.*, XIV, 482). "They are meat, drinke, shooes, houses, fire, vessels, and their Masters whole substance . . ." (*ibid.*, XVIII, 64). *In re* tools, buffalo shoulder-blades as hoes, see Thompson, *Narrative*, 231; Coues (ed.), *Henry-Thompson Journals*, I, 343; Bradbury, *Early Western Travels*, V, 175; Long, *ibid.*, XV, 77; Maximilian, *ibid.*, XXIII, 276; Catlin, *Letters on the North American Indians*, I, 121. In 1876 (buffalo then gone or going fast) a Cree chief at Fort Pitt, on the North Saskatchewan, said to Governor Morris: "I have no hoes; I make them out of the roots of trees . . ." (Morris, *Treaties with the Indians of Manitoba*, 289).

[20]Marquette (*circa* 1670), *Jesuit Relations*, LIX, 111-13; Henry, *Travels, 1760-1776*, 312; Coues (ed.), *The Expeditions of Pike*, I, 344; Butler, *Wild North Land*, 61; Allen, *American Bisons*, 191-201; Fletcher, "Buffalo," *Handbook of American Indians*, I, 169, etc.

[21]This was a superior kind, 'berry pemmican,' frequently made by the fur traders for the officers' use, and very highly prized. See on this, Allen, *American Bisons*, 193. The 'pemmican' furnished by the British Admiralty for Arctic expeditions was modelled on this, containing sugar, currants, raisins, etc. Sir George Simpson to Dr. Richardson, April 1847: "He informed me that the stock of provisions at the various posts in the Hudson's Bay Territories was unusually low, owing to the failure of the bison hunts on the Saskatchewan . . ."; requiring pemmican to be sent from England, as above (Richardson, *Arctic Expedition 1847-1850*, 32). See also on this, and on the common variety, Milton and Cheadle, *North-West Passage*, 53. On the digestive effects and later consequences of the

The skin of the buffalo yielded a robe, dressed with the hair on, for clothing and bedding; a hide, dressed without the hair, which made a tepee cover, when a number were sewn together; boats, when sewn together in a green state over a wooden framework. Shields, made from the thickest portion,[22] as rawhide; ropes, made up as rawhide; clothing of many kinds;[23] bags [that is, 'parfleches'] for use in travelling; coffins, or winding sheets for the dead, etc.

Other portions utilized were sinews, which furnished fiber for ropes, thread, bow-strings, snow-shoe webs, etc.; hair, which was sometimes made into belts and ornaments; "buffalo-chips" [that is, *bois de vache*], which formed a valuable and highly-prized fuel;[24] bones, from which many articles

latter, they observe that there are "few half-breeds who do not suffer habitually from dyspepsia." This has been suggested as an underlying cause of Indian ferocity.

Mackenzie, 1789, notes something similar concerning pemmican, but says that "a little time reconciles it to the palate . . ." (*Voyages, 1789-1793*, cxvi). Hearne, 1772, calls buffalo meat 'light and easy of digestion' (*Journey*, ed. Tyrrell, 262); but pemmican was notoriously richer and stronger, which was its recommendation. Chittenden describes it as "very palatable as well as nutritious food"; but this may have been a superior 'Army pemmican,' as above. (*American Fur Trade*, II, 811). The two best descriptions of its manufacture known to me are by Thompson, *circa* 1800 (*Narrative*, ed. Tyrrell, 434), and in Kidd, "Blackfoot Ethnography," 108. See also Coues (ed.), *Henry-Thompson Journals*, II, 593: and an important historical and dietetic study by Vilhjalmur Stefansson, "Pemmican," *The Military Surgeon* (U.S.A.), vol. 95, August, 1944, 89-98, very kindly drawn to my attention by the author. See Appendix M.

[22]The evidence appears uncertain. Bulls' hides, one would think; but the "Traslado de las Nuevas" or "Anonymous Document," and the "Relacion del Suceso" say 'shields made of cows' hides' (*Journey of Coronado*, 152, 194, 211). *Cows* frequently their generic term, but Father Allouez, Mississippi Valley, 1677, says the same without that proviso (*Jesuit Relations*, LX, 161), and Edwin James, 1820, states that the skins 'of cows only' were used. When specifying cows or bulls, he always signifies the sex (*Early Western Travels*, XV, 245). Thompson, however, notes that the Mandan shields, *circa* 1800, were of bull's hide (*Narrative*, 228, 411). James Mooney cites a practice of covering the bull's hide with a more flexible and workable cover of cowskin, which may explain the confusion (*Handbook of American Indians*, I, 88; II, 546).

[23]"It has been noted that certain peculiar styles of garments in the bison area were due to the natural form of the skins . . ." (Wissler, *American Indian*, 64). Kidd and others have noted that while buffalo skin was used in winter, antelope was preferred for summer ("Blackfoot Ethnography," 73-92).

[24]It is not difficult to conceive how its value probably became known. After a prairie fire, the night wind, blowing over the plain, fans them into a bright smoulder, which can be seen for some time at quite a distance. Rev. James Gilmour, 1870, found dried animal-dung used as fuel in Mongolia (*Among the Mongols*, 31), and cf. Gibbon (*Decline and Fall of the Roman Empire*, IV, 318) on camel-dung in Arabia. My late friend, Mr. D. E. Cameron, then Librarian of Alberta University, informed me that it is still so used in Egypt. Gilmour says it is 'quick but smoky' in (Mongol) tents (*Among the Mongols*, 178, 201). 'Quick' also and 'clear outside' (Hornaday, "Extermination of the American Bison,"

of use and ornament were made; horns, which were made into spoons;[25] drinking vessels, etc.[26]

Even this comprehensive survey does not exhaust the list. A modern investigator mentions several additional uses by the Blackfoot which were very probably familiar to other tribes. The tribe in question used the paunch as a container in cookery and carried fire about with them in buffalo horns. For more ornamental purposes, a yellow paint was prepared from buffalo galls, and the 'back-fat' was much favoured for hair grease.[27]

There was another practice also, which has been found over a huge expanse of the plains buffalo range; although the Blackfoot, in this instance, deny that this was followed by them.[28] It is nevertheless quite manifestly of Indian origin. Pedro de Castañeda records that the Indians of the Southwest drank the water, or 'juices' from the stomach

---

451). 'Burns like peat, producing no unpleasant effects . . .' (Parkman, *Oregon Trail*, 81, 100). Much less acrid than peat smoke, in my opinion, and a matter of draught. Cf. Palliser's description, *Palliser Journals*, 43; and Cowie's, *Company of Adventurers*, 208.

Its use was related with wonderment, as hearsay, by Fathers Dablon and Allouez, Mississippi Valley, *circa* 1670 (*Jesuit Relations*, LV, 207); and equally so by eye-witnesses, 1541 (*Journey of Coronado*, 194, 217). Matthew Cocking, October 6, 1772: "We made use of Buffalo dung for fuel and it answered very well . . ." (evidently his first time): "Journal," ed. Burpee, 108, 112. Similarly John McDonnell, "Account of Red River, 1793-1797" (in Masson, *Les Bourgeois de la Compagnie du Nord-Ouest*, I, 272); *Harmon's Journal*, 84; Irving, *Astoria*, 209; Marcy, *Prairie Traveller*, 155 (who also mentions its use in Tartary); Allen, *American Bisons*, 200; Hornaday, "Extermination of the American Bison," 451. Sir Richard Burton cites it as a Western *cliché*, 1855, that 'a steak cooked over them requires no pepper' (*City of the Saints*, 48).

Henday, 1754, describes the Indians as *smoking* 'dryed horse-dung' ("Journal," 339), but his editor, Burpee, doubts this (*ibid.*, 337), which is not mentioned by anybody else I have encountered.

'Buffalo chips' were gathered up for fuel by the Nebraska settlers in the eighties, so they have often told me.

[25]On spoons, see *Handbook of American Indians*, I, 83-6. According to Mr. Kidd's native informants, they were of buffalo horn boiled until soft, then cut open and dried to the required shape ("Blackfoot Ethnography," 116). Cf. below, Appendix N.

[26]Hornaday, "Extermination of the American Bison," 437-8; cf. *ibid.*, 449, 477.

[27]Kidd, "Blackfoot Ethnography," 87, 90, 113, 123. Paint brushes were also made by certain Plains tribes from 'a flat piece of spongy bone from the knee joint of a buffalo' (*Handbook of American Indians*, II, 186); cf. W. R. Wedel, *Smithsonian Miscellaneous Collections*, vol. 100, 1940, 337. Arrow-points were at one time made by the Hidatsa entirely from buffalo sinew (Hough, *Handbook of American Indians*, II, 575).

[28]Kidd, "Blackfoot Ethnography," 108, 170.

of a slain buffalo, when out on the thirsty plains.[29] This habit evidently became familiar to plainsmen. Dr. Gregg relates that William Becknell's party, the first to use the dreaded 'Cimarron cut-off' on the Santa Fé Trail (1821), saved their lives by this expedient when almost perishing from thirst.[30] Townsend mentions it, along the Oregon Trail, in 1833.[31] And it was on the northern plains, despite the Blackfoot disclaimer, where Harmon observed or learned of it.[32]

It may be considered certain that Hornaday's figure of 'more than 50,000' Indians is well within the mark, even for the somewhat late date when the United States Government began to (partially) feed and clothe them; for he himself gives a table, drawn from the census statistics of 1886, of 54,758 Indians of twenty-one tribes in the very heart of the former (U.S.) prairie buffalo habitat. And this enumeration, says Hornaday, ". . . leaves entirely out of consideration many thousands of Indians living in the Indian Territory and other portions of the Southwest who drew an annual supply of meat and robes from the chase of the buffalo, notwithstanding the fact that their chief dependence was on agriculture."[33]

It also leaves out of consideration various tribes in the United States, some apparently quite extinct, perhaps surviving as a mere remnant, or possibly incorporated in other tribes included in the table already mentioned; such as the Pottawatomies, Miamis, Illinois, Ponca or Puncahs,[34] Osages,[35] Konzas (? Kansas)[36] and Wico (or Wacoes) of Texas;[37] together with others still maintaining a tribal identity, as the Chippewas (Ojibwa) of northern Minnesota.[38] All these tribes, and many more, drew upon the buffalo resources in the recognized prairie habitat within known historical times; and no doubt bore a

[29]Castañeda, *Journey of Coronado*, 112.
[30]Gregg, *Early Western Travels*, XIX, 179.
[31]Townsend, *ibid.*, XXI, 169-72.
[32]*Harmon's Journal*, 279.
[33]Hornaday, "Extermination of the American Bison," 526.
[34]Catlin, *Letters on the North American Indians*, II, 42. The Ponca are a Siouan tribe, closely related to the Omahas, living at one time on a branch of the Red River, toward Lake Winnipeg. 'A dangerous tribe,' Missouri River, 1811 (Iriving, *Astoria*, 370). See *Handbook of American Indians*, II, 158.
[35]For the Osages, see *Lewis and Clark Journals*, I, 43; Coues (ed.), *Expeditions of Pike*, II, 533, 589; *Handbook of American Indians*, II, 158.
[36]Catlin, *Letters on the North American Indians*, II, 23; *Handbook of American Indians*, I, 389.
[37]Catlin, *Letters on the North American Indians*, II, 75; *Handbook of American Indians*, II, 887.
[38]See Coues (ed.), *Expeditions of Pike*, I, 346; *Handbook of American Indians*, I, 277.

part in the acquisition and transmission of general characteristics developed in them through the influence of the buffalo environment.

The large number of Canadian Indians depending on the buffalo must also be included. A careful historian, quoting from the census figures of 1885, gives the total of the Indians of Assiniboia, Saskatchewan, and Alberta as 20,270; and there were also "many thousands in Athabasca and the Great North West."[39] Some of these Athabaskan[40] Indians may possibly have contributed in the transmission of characteristics they have themselves since lost. For D. W. Harmon tells us (1820) that the Beaver Indians—whose name, in this particular instance, could indicate a geographical habitat quite as much as a totemistic or tribal identity—were 'formerly clothed with the skins of buffalo,' as well as moose and red deer.[41] By the time these many remaining or extinct[42] peoples have been accounted for in their former possible strength (even *circa* 1800), Catlin's estimates of 250,000,[43] or 300,000,[44] whether literally demonstrable or not, may not seem so utterly preposterous as might at first sight appear to be the case.[45]

2.

A great deal has been said at various times about the 'independence' of these buffalo Indians; almost every traveller of a philosophic turn of mind has indulged in some reflection concerning this. I quote one or two. The elder Alexander Henry remarks of the Assiniboines: ". . . the Asinipoilles are less dependent on our merchandise. . . . The wild ox alone supplies them with everything which they are accustomed to want. The amazing number of these animals prevent all fear of want, a fear which is incessantly present to the Indians of the north. . . ."[46]

Duncan McGillivray writes (1795): ". . . they have invented so many methods for the destruction of animals that they stand in no need of ammunition to provide a sufficiency for these purposes. It is then our luxuries that attract them to the Fort. . . ."[47]

Harmon comments similarly on the independence of the Plains tribes, attributing it to the ease with which they could obtain food;[48]

[39]Black, *History of Saskatchewan*, 285.
[40]Athabaskan, not 'Athapaskan'; locality, not linguistic stock, here referred to.
[41]*Harmon's Journal*, 149.
[42]On extinct buffalo tribes, see below, Appendix G.
[43]Catlin, *Letters on the North American Indians*, I, 122.
[44]*Ibid.*, 262, 263.
[45]See Appendix G, "Indian Populations Subsisting on Buffalo."
[46]Henry, *Travels, 1760-1776*, 312.
[47]*McGillivray's Journal*, ed. Morton, 47.   [48]*Harmon's Journal*, 81-2.

and Pike, writing in 1805, in his general description of the Sioux nation at that time, observes: "The Yanctongs and Titongs are the most independent Indians in the world; they follow the buffalo as chance directs, clothing themselves with the skins, and making their lodges, bridles, and saddles of the same material, the flesh of the animal furnishing their food. Possessing innumerable herds of horses, they are here at this day, 500 miles off ten days hence, and find themselves equally at home in either place, moving with a rapidity scarcely to be imagined by the inhabitants of the civilized world. . . ."[49] He also says of the Assiniboine: "They reside on the plains and follow the buffalo; consequently they have very little occasion for the traders or European productions. . . ."[50]

One might concede the argument for independence, on the supposition that *the source of supply was literally inexhaustible.* Regarded from this aspect, philosophic reflections (after the event) on the essential helplessness of the 'buffalo' Indian when deprived of buffalo are rather trite and obvious.[51]

What the Indians themselves may have thought of their own 'economic status' is not easy to decide.[52] But observers were not lacking

[49]Coues (ed.), *Expeditions of Pike,* I, 344.

[50]*Ibid.,* 354.

[51]'The Indian conquered by the hide-hunter' (*Buffalo Jones' Forty Years,* 91): "The systematic slaughter of millions of buffalo, in the years between 1866 and 1873 (1883), for the sake of their hides . . . destroyed the economic independence of the Indian . . ." (Turner, *The Frontier in American History,* 144). Cf. also E. S. Osgood on the economic problem for the Government as the herds dwindled (*Day of the Cattleman,* 142-7); and for Canada, above, chap. XVII, note 55 *seq.*

See also below, Appendix H, "Buffalo, Indian, and Legislation," for evidence indicating that even the hides were merely a side issue.

[52]Hornaday ("Extermination of the American Bison," 480) has much to say concerning the 'confident predictions of their disappearance,' *circa* 1850 onward, not only by observing white men in the West, but also by "nearly all the Indians and half-breeds who formerly depended upon this animal. . . ."

Chittenden takes a similar view of the Indian attitude: "It is also easy to understand with what prophetic vision the Indian saw the downfall of his race linked with the extermination of the buffalo, and could measure his own decline by the rate at which these animals were disappearing before the advance of civilization . . ." (*American Fur Trade,* II, 816).

Actually, there is very little direct evidence for the 'prophetic' view. Frémont in 1842 found the Sioux 'démontés' over the failure of the buffalo (*Narrative,* 142; above *in extenso,* chap. XIII, note 137); but this seems rather to have been connected with the white influx into their country, for many other similar disappearances have been noted, without such consequences. Crowfoot, the Blackfoot chief, to Denny, can scarcely be termed 'prophecy'—in 1876! (Denny, *The Law Marches West,* 99.) The only really philosophical early Indian forecast I have found is from an Assiniboine chief to Father De Smet, *circa* 1850 (*Life of De Smet,* III, 935). See below in detail, note 236.

among white travellers or residents who, at a time when the buffalo still roamed in vast numbers, could penetrate beneath the apparent independence of the Plains tribes and realize the actual precariousness of their condition. In the 1830's, Maximilian wrote:

The [Mandan, etc.] Indians residing in permanent villages have the advantage of roving hunting tribes, in that they not only hunt, but derive their chief subsistence from their plantations, which afford them a degree of security against distress. It is true these Indians sometimes suffer hunger when the buffalo herds keep at a great distance, and their crops fail; but the distress can never be so great among the Missouri Indians, as in the tribes that live further northward. . . .[53]

Catlin, at the very same time, formed similar opinions, and foresaw the ultimate disappearance of the buffalo;[54] as likewise did Parkman in 1846.[55] Marcy, in 1852, asked himself with reference to those Indians 'who follow the buffalo, and subsist almost exclusively upon the uncertain products of the chase . . . what will be the fate of these people when these animals shall have become extinct . . .?'[56] George McDougall warned the Saskatchewan Indians in 1863 of the impending extinction of the herds;[57] and in the same year, Milton and Cheadle were under no delusions concerning the 'independence' of the Plains Crees.[58] John McDougall emphasizes the true relationship more than once. He says of a Blackfoot party in whose camp he and his father were virtually prisoners (January, 1865):

These men were thoroughly buffalo Indians. Without buffalo they would be helpless, and yet the whole nation did not own one. To look at them and to hear them, one would feel as if they were the most independent of all men; yet the fact was they were the most dependent among men. Moccasins, mittens, leggings, shirts and robes—all buffalo. With the sinews of the buffalo they stitched and sewed these. Their lariats, bridle, lines, stirrup-straps, and saddles were manufactured out of buffalo hide. Their women made scrapers out of the leg-bone for fleshing hides. The men fashioned knife-handles out of the bones, and the children made toboggans out of the same. The horns served for spoons and powder-flasks. In short, they lived and had their physical being in the buffalo. . . .[59]

The Stoneys [Assiniboine] and Wood Crees could generally live anywhere, but the true plainsman would starve if the buffalo upon which he depended were not forthcoming. . . .[60]

[53]Maximilian, Early Western Travels, XXIII, 274.
[54]Catlin, Letters on the North American Indians, I, 247, 249, 256, 263.
[55]Parkman, Oregon Trail, 234.
[56]Marcy, Exploration of Red River, 93, 103, 105.
[57]McDougall, Forest, Lake, and Prairie, 195; also McDougall MS., 10.
[58]North-West Passage, 83-4.
[59]McDougall, Saddle, Sled, and Snowshoe, 261.
[60]McDougall, Western Trails, 195.

It would seem that in some instances at least, the woodlands Indians themselves endorsed McDougall's classification of the two types: "The Mountain and Wood Stoneys roamed from the northern tributaries of the Missouri to the Athabasca, and generally kept inside of the foothills. These Indians were more independent than the plains tribes, as they were, almost without exception, expert wood hunters. Moose, elk, caribou, small deer, big-horn, goat, all kinds of bear and lynx, as well as buffalo, made up their larder, and yet, like that of all hunters, this was often empty. . . ."[61] He writes again (Morley, upper Bow Valley, 1874); "We had . . . Blackfeet, Bloods, Piegans, and Sarcees from the plains, altogether depending on the buffalo; Wood Crees and Wood Stoneys, who because they could live independent of the plains, and were more individual in character, generally despised the plains tribes. . . ."[62]

The profound significance of this virtually complete neglect and abandonment by the Plains tribes of everything not derived from or connected with buffalo, an abandonment so far-reaching that fishing[63] and trapping[64] became lost arts, can scarcely be realized until we recollect that these 'buffalo tribes' were hardly ever in any sense of the term aboriginal in their historic territories in the prairie buffalo habitat. Tribe after tribe was of woodland (and distant) origin. In some cases— the Canadian Sarcees being a notable example, and the Apache another—they were even aliens from the racial stock near or among whom (as with the Sarcees and the Blackfoot) they settled; apparently, it would seem, in order to share in the easy subsistence so bountifully available.[65] In the face of such impressive testimony to the moulding

[61]*Ibid.*, 10.

[62]*Ibid.*, 199. Compare Milton and Cheadle on this: Keenamontiayoo (drunk) *loquitur*: "If I were an Indian of the Plains now, I should stab you to the heart if you dared to say no. . . ." Cheadle: "Yes . . . that's just the point of it; you are *not* a Plains Indian, and therefore won't do anything of the kind. The Indians of the Woods know better." Cheadle goes on to say regarding his answer, "This touched the right string . . ." (*North-West Passage*, 138).

[63]Absence of fishing in the 'bison area': Wissler, *American Indian*, 220.

[64]La Vérendrye, 1738: ". . . we were going among people who did not know how to kill the beaver, and covered themselves only with ox-skin . . ." (*Report of Canadian Archives*, 1889, 7; *Journals of La Vérendrye*, ed. Burpee, 301). Cf. also Katharine Coman, *Economic Beginnings of the Far West*, II, 77.

[65]The Sarcee, as is well known, although members of the Blackfoot Confederacy, are of the Beaver Indian stock (Athabaskan = paskan, while the Blackfoot (Siksika) are Algonkian. Rundle included the Sarcee among the 'Slaves,' the common Cree term for the Confederacy (*Journal, passim*). The best earlier accounts of them are in Coues (ed.), *Henry-Thompson Journals*, II, 531, 617, 656; *Palliser Journals*, 77, 87, 204. See also Maclean (who lived among them),

and modifying influences of the buffalo environment as this, it cannot be doubted that further investigation will almost certainly yield much more.

3.

The foregoing indicates clearly that the argument for the influencing and modification of type through environment is not confined for its basis to mere conjecture, even though it be rational and scientific conjecture of the highest order. Let us consider the Indian of the buffalo plains as a nomad. This aspect of Indian life and character has given rise to two distinct conceptions or schools of thought; although it might perhaps be suggested that the later of these is but an extended application of the earlier view. In the final analysis of Indian character into its primary and basic elements, its essential constituents have been regarded by erudite investigators as being so entirely anti-nomadic that a high authority in this field of inquiry almost refuses to bestow the term 'nomad' on any Indian. And this in spite of the profound changes wrought within and about him by a life which ordinary observers would probably agree was nothing if not nomadic, whatever its origin may have been. This denial of the applicability of the term to the Indian may seem like an ultra-fastidious refinement in scientific definition. For, after all, the learned critic was not required to acknowledge that his whale was a fish, but merely that it had developed into a marine animal. His view serves at least to emphasize the striking nature of the change. The late H. W. Henshaw, the scholar to whom I refer, says: "The term 'nomad' is not, in fact, applicable to any Indian tribe"; arguing that even Plains Indians had a certain generally-accepted territorial limit.[66] I do not know what exactly would be Henshaw's own definition of a nomad; but in so far as tribal boundaries in the plains buffalo habitat are concerned, much Indian history seems to show that these were very commonly determined by 'the good old rule, the simple plan, that they may take who have the power and they may keep who can.'

The later opinion to which I have referred accepts the Plains Indian as a nomad, but does not—broadly speaking—consider this character-

Canadian Savage Folk, 9-19; Dorsey and Goddard, "Sarsi," Handbook of American Indians, II, 467; and best of all Jenness, The Sarcee Indians of Alberta, tracing their migration southward to their present habitat, in a masterly study of this people. A recent commentator notes their persistant Athapaskan individualism after centuries of isolation among distant aliens. John J. Honigmann, "Parallels in the development of shamanism among northern and southern Athapaskans," American Anthropologist, LI, 1949, 512-14.

[66]Henshaw, "Popular Fallacies," Handbook of American Indians, II, 282.

istic to be traceable to the influence of the buffalo; preferring to ascribe its development to the essentially modern acquisition of the horse and the adoption of the equestrian life. The evidence adduced in support of this hypothesis is more archaeological than either historical or (in the strict sense) anthropological. While I do not suggest that my own historical objections dispose of the argument, they do at least present factors which must certainly be considered hand-in-hand with the archaeological data.

It is apparently—and in my view soundly—accepted that the consumption for food of the most numerous and important roaming (if not 'migratory') creature in the Plains area, the buffalo, should constitute a significant or leading test of the nomadic tendency in its human denizens. The opinion has been advanced that prior to the advent of the horse in the Plains area, the mass-slaughtering of the buffalo was not practised by the Indians of the region. A strong point is made of the fact that the bone-deposits in the ancient kitchen-middens in various localities of the area, particularly the Pawnee villages in the lower Platte territory, do not appear to indicate the buffalo as an early preponderating or material source of food-supply.[67] It may be well at this point to summarize briefly my own objections to the conclusions drawn from this circumstance, since such a summary may best enable the reader to judge in what measure they find support from the evidence which follows in detail in the present chapter. My principal objections are:

Social or economic history: In the absence of any stronger beast of burden than the dog, the ratio of buffalo bones in prehistoric village bone-deposits is of little value as evidence for buffalo consumption. The buffalo was too heavy an animal to transport whole; and in view of the Indians' familiarity with the well-known methods of drying meat for later use—which were noted by early observers and which

[67]Strong, "The Plains Culture in the Light of Archaeology," *American Anthropologist,* New Series, XXXV, 1933, 271-87. Strong's general conclusions may be compared with Wedel, "Culture Sequences in the Central Great Plains," *Smithsonian Miscellaneous Collections,* vol. 100, 291-352. I am indebted to Dr. D. Jenness, of Ottawa, for drawing my attention to these important papers. Kroeber (*Cultural Areas,* 88) considers that the ante-equine Plains Indians merely 'nibbled' at the buffalo, but he also notes cases where neither horse nor buffalo seems to have been the governing influence (*ibid.,* 76-88). Curiously enough, an even more recent scholar considers that so far from the horse inaugurating impounding mass-slaughter, this became of less importance among the Plains tribes after the horse made its appearance among them. John C. Ewers, "The last bison drives of the Blackfoot Indians," *Journal of the Washington Academy of Sciences,* XXXIX, November, 1949, 355-60. I have not seen this: noted in *Canadian Historical Review,* XXXI, 1950, 99.

must have been of long standing, since these usages persisted long after possession of the horse had obviated their strict necessity—it is most improbable that large masses of bones would ever be carried to the villages. Also, they were acquainted from the earliest historical ante-equine times with such hunting practices as the 'surround'; quite obviously an expedient for taking buffalo, etc., *wherever they might find them*.[68] This indicates a roving, nomad life, and, *ipso facto*, mass slaughter.

Historical chronology: The Indians, both on the buffalo plains and also in territories where the historic buffalo had not yet penetrated, were classed by the earliest European observers as nomads prior to the horse era.[69]

The time-element: Apart even from other evidence, the time available since the Indians' mastery of the horse seems utterly inadequate for such fundamental change in a conservative-minded race; particularly in the northern Plains Indians, whose use of horses dates only, *circa* 1700-40,[70] and who were quite as nomadic as other 'buffalo' tribes.[71] I do not consider their rapid, facile adoption of such innovations as the horse, firearms, or the repeating rifle, are relevant instances to the contrary; since in the final analysis these possessions only enabled the Indians to do *the same things* more easily.

There is some trace of Henshaw's hesitancy in other scholars. Two learned authorities describe the Cree as having been "attracted to the plains by the buffalo, the Cree, like the Chippewa, being essentially a forest people. Many bands of Cree were virtually nomads, their movements being governed largely by the food supply. . . ."[72] A later high authority thus defines their earlier home: "On the north they were bounded by the coast-line from the Eastmain river nearly to Churchill; on the east by lakes Mistassini and Nichikun. Their western limits are uncertain, but in the early sixteenth century they appear to have wandered over part of the country west of Lake Winnipeg, perhaps between the Red River and the Saskatchewan. . . ."[73]

[68]For the 'surround' in detail, see below, note 170 *seq.*

[69]See Roe, "From Dogs to Horses among the Western Indian Tribes," *Transactions of the Royal Society of Canada*, 1939, Sec. II, 209-75, for details on this.

[70]For dates at large, *ibid.*, 232 *seq.*

[71]Below, in detail, notes 74, 111 *seq.*

[72]James Mooney and Cyrus Thomas, *Handbook of American Indians*, I, 359; cf. *ibid.*, 813; II, 206, 414, 579; also C. Thomas, *History of North America*, II, 350.

[73]Jenness, *Indians of Canada*, 283-7. It may have been some recollection of the ancestral forest standards of life that led the Wood Crees to regard their Plains kindred as degenerates, fallen from grace, as above, note 62.

The statement defining their historical (Plains) condition as 'virtually nomads' is abundantly substantiated by the testimony of John McDougall and others, cited above.[74] This indicates a vital factor which is sometimes overlooked by the more purely archaeological inquirer. The environmental character of any hunter-people is definitely moulded and stamped, not by the possession of this or that facility—a limitation which human ingenuity has everywhere overcome; but by the character of the game animals upon which they subsist. The 'buffalo Indians' did not wander about the country *because* they were nomads; they were made nomads by having perforce to wander after the buffalo—to 'follow the cows around' it was termed in 1541—in order to subsist upon the buffalo resources. Any reader of the present essay will instantly realize that the whooping, yelling, 'buffalo Indian' of the Plains would have starved to death if he employed that technique on the 'Mountain Bison' of the easterly slopes of the Rockies, the Northern Wood buffalo,[75] or the moose,[76] all of them species which fled at the crackling of a twig!

This is set forth quite definitely by certain contributors to the *Handbook of American Indians*. O. T. Mason, a scholar who is a pronounced supporter of the regular migration and its trails (with which this present passage scarcely agrees) writes thus: "Dependence on the buffalo and the herbivorous animals associated with it compelled a meat diet, skin clothing and dwellings, a roving life, and industrial arts depending on the flesh, bones, hair, sinew, hide, and horns of these animals. . . ."[77]

Another contributor, A. F. Chamberlain, writes: "The appearance and disappearance of fur-bearing animals, their retreat from one part of the country to another, influenced the movements of various tribes. This is particularly true of the movements of the buffalo. . . . The occasional and finally complete disappearance of the buffalo from these regions has weighed heavily upon the tribes. . . ."[78]

When O. T. Mason speaks of a 'roving life,' he may of course signify a mere periodical change of scene from one familiar haunt to another at recognized intervals in accordance with the 'regular migration'; which would presumably find the tribe always resident in any par-

[74]See chap. XX, notes 206-24, 319-28, etc.

[75]Above, chap. III, on these two varieties, note 56 *seq.*

[76]The best description of moose-hunting tactic known to me is in Butler, *Wild North Land*, 206-10.

[77]Mason, "Environment," *Handbook of American Indians*, I, 428; see also Wissler, *American Anthropologist*, XVI, 1914, 447-505; Hewett, *Ancient Life in the American Southwest*, 23, 205, 251.

[78]Chamberlain, "Fur Trade," *Handbook of American Indians*, I, 478.

ticular locality at the same season in each year, like the Miamis in the Central States region,[79] and the Pawnee on the Platte.[80] There were, however, nomads in all parts of the North American continent in the more general acceptation of the term, as an abundance of evidence clearly indicates.

A scholarly Canadian historian, Norman Fergus Black, long ante-dating the archaeological conclusion of Strong, mentioned above, ascribes much of the change to the horse; which "made nomads of many tribes which there is abundance of evidence to show were formerly almost sedentary in character. . . ."[81] A somewhat later Canadian scholar, Dr. Jenness, who is one of the foremost living anthropologists on this continent (already cited in a passage[82] which in my

[79]Father Hennepin says (1679) the Miamis "hunt them toward the latter end of Autumn." In winter, he adds: "It is then their Custom to leave their Villages, and with their whole Families to go hunting wild Bulls, Beavers, &c. . . ." (New Discovery, I, 145, 146, 153). It may also be noted that the Miamis were within practicable reach of a warmer zone, in which Peoria Lake (supposedly) 'never froze' (see on this, Shaler, Nature and Man in America, 241 seq.); and this was known as Pimiteoui = 'a place where there is abundance of fat beasts' (Hennepin, New Discovery, I, 154, 155). In spite of their addiction to permanent villages when practicable, (see Parkman's description of the 'great Illinois town,' La Salle, 169, 221, 239), Hennepin states they were often nomads from force of circumstances (New Discovery, II, 490); despite being partly agriculturists, like most of the Algonkian tribes. See on this, Mooney and Thomas, Handbook of American Indians, "Agriculture," "Algonquian Family," "Maize," I, 24-7, 38-43, 790. G. E. E. Lindquist, Red Man in the United States, 278, 282, describes the Navajos as 'nomads, not from choice but from necessity.' Cf. above, note 16, on the Arikara.

[80]Henry, 1806, describes the Pawnee as 'a sedentary people like the Mandans, and [who] cultivate the ground in the same manner' (Coues (ed.), Henry-Thompson Journals, I, 338, 348, 354). Parkman, 1846, mentions 'the great trail of the Pawnees from their permanent villages on the lower Platte' to "their war and hunting grounds to the southward, but throughout the summer the greater part of the inhabitants are wandering over the plains . . ." (Oregon Trail, 74). See above, chap. XX, notes 63-4. The incident there recorded by Edwin James (1819) shows that even the presence of large buffalo-bone deposits in village-sites may require to be interpreted very cautiously. It was in their summertime role as 'nomads' that this herd was found at their villages. See also C. Hallenbeck, Journey of Cabeza de Vaca, 137-40, on nomads assembling for the pecan harvest, Texas—New Mexico, circa 1530.

The "Narrative of Jaramillo," 1541, mentions meeting near Quivira "some Indians who were going hunting, killing the cows to take the meat to their village, which was about three or four days still farther from us . . ." (Journey of Coronado, 234). These may have been Pawnee; but there was a 'Pawnee Piqua' (?) village on the upper Red River, Texas, 1820, whoever they may have been. Long, Early Western Travels, XVI, 95). Wichita, below, p. 791.

[81]Black, History of Saskatchewan, 94. See some instructive general remarks on the horse and nomads, in Gibbon, Decline and Fall, chap. XXVI, also in Milman, History of the Jews (Everyman ed.), I, 55.

[82]Above, note 73.

view strongly rebuts his present contention), writes in essential agreement: "The ease with which they could now run down the buffalo on horseback led many woodland tribes to move out on to the prairies. . . ."[83]

One of the material arguments in favour of the theory that the 'buffalo' Indians led earlier a sedentary life is the profusion of languages spoken in relatively small areas;[84] but against this inferential evidence (as applied retrospectively to prehistoric times) may be set direct testimony of several kinds. Among these are the use of the dog (and of foot travel) long before the appearance of the historic horse on the plains;[85] the confirmed addiction to the nomadic life in regions where the horse (as an Indian domestic animal) never penetrated; the migration of later 'horse' Indians from the forest territories (1) prior to the horse era;[86] and (2) after that epoch, but for other and quite distinct causes—as we learn from contemporary residents in the territory, sometimes the very men to whom we owe our historical knowledge of these events.[87]

As I have remarked, I have no key to Henshaw's definition of a nomad, but other observers, residents, travellers, and scientists, link the term itself with the hunter's life among the Indian tribes in various

[83]Jenness, *Indians of Canada*, 129; who also apparently considers the horse may have inaugurated wars *de novo* among the Plains horse tribes (*ibid.*, 256, 308, 316). I have discussed this in my paper, "From Dogs to Horses among the Western Indian Tribes," *Transactions of the Royal Society of Canada*, 1939, Sec. II, 262 *seq.*, and cf. remarks below, note 88.

[84]See below on this, Appendix V.

[85]See on this, Roe, "From Dogs to Horses among the Western Indian Tribes," *Transactions of the Royal Society of Canada*, 1939, Sec. II, 209-17; cf. also Fletcher, McGuire, Mason, *Handbook of American Indians*, II, 798-804. Wissler asks unanswerably, "Why should the Plains people have had the dog travois if they did not go on long journeys by land?" (*American Anthropologist*, XVI, 1914, 14.)

[86]For example, the Cree; as Jenness, etc., notes 72-3 above. Blackfoot, whom the Cree 'drove before them' from the northeast (Mooney, *Handbook of American Indians*, II, 570; see also Kidd, "Blackfoot Ethnography," who suggests the existence of a Plains culture, *circa* 1492, 10-16). According to McClintock, an adopted 'son' of the tribe, the tribal tradition is that "ages ago their people lived far to the north of their present country, where the dark fertile soil so discoloured their moccasins that they were called *Siksikaua* or Black Moccasins . . ." (*Old North Trail*, 2). Also the Sarcee (Jenness, *Sarcee Indians of Alberta*, 1-4); whose Athapaskan kindred, the Apache, long preceded them southward.

[87]On the Chippewa (Ojibwa) driving the Sioux out on to the prairies, see Mooney and Thomas, *Handbook of American Indians*, I, 277; Mooney and Swanton, *ibid.*, II, 575 *seq.* According to Peter Grant, the Sioux were 'emigrating' from the Chippewa country, 1790-1800 (Masson, *Les Bourgeois de la Compagnie du Nord-Ouest*, II, 346).

portions of the North American continent. A scholar who is far from being out of date, writes as follows:

When . . . the buffalo came to the semi-civilized inhabitants of the Mississippi system of villages, he brought a great plenty of animal food to the people, who had long been in a measure destitute of such resources, for they had no other domesticated animals save the dog. Not yet firmly fixed in the agricultural art, these tribes appear, after the coming of the buffalo, to have lapsed into the pure savagery which hunting entails. . . . With the rehabilitation of the Hunter's habit, and with the nomadic conditions which this habit necessarily brings about, came more frequent contests between tribes, and the gradual decadence of the slight civilization which the people had acquired. . . .

In the district south of the Tennessee the Indians long maintained agricultural habits in a measure not common with their northern kindred. Indeed when the settlements of the Creeks and the allied tribes about the Gulf were destroyed by the advancing tide of European life, the sedentary conditions of the population had not been destroyed by the invasion of the buffalo.

In general, north of the Great Lakes and the St. Lawrence, the climate is such as to make the development of people beyond the stage of savagery quite impossible, for the reason that agriculture, at least such as a primitive people could invent, is not possible in that country. We therefore find in the considerable Indian and Eskimo population of the high north of our continent much less trace of advance than in the southern section. We may say, indeed, that the possibilities of culture are in a descending scale from the subtropical districts of Mexico to the northern fields of the continent; the measure of advance depending on the ratio between the proportion of food-supply derived or derivable from hunting and from tillage. . . .[88]

This generalized view finds support (in respect of opinion) from such students as Dr. Richardson,[89] Thomas Simpson,[90] John McDougall[91] and General Chittenden,[92] to name only a few; and the broad conclusions of these men are abundantly substantiated by their own observations and those of others among the Indians in practically all portions of the northern continent. Champlain certainly describes the Indians as being 'sedentary' at 'Ochelaga' in Cartier's time (1534);[93] but the term was scarcely ever again applied to them for two centuries, until 1734. Father Nau, or Aulneau, observed: "Our Iroquois, like all other savage tribes, with the exception of the Sioux, are sedentary. . . ."[94]

[88]Shaler, *Nature and Man in America*, 184, 185, 187.
[89]Richardson, *Fauna Boreali-Americana*, I, 231.
[90]Simpson, *Narrative of Discoveries*, 13.
[91]McDougall, *Forest, Lake, and Prairie*, 213; *Saddle, Sled, and Snowshoe*, 52; *Red River Rebellion*, 17, 69; *Pathfinding*, 24, 89, 109, 259; *Western Trails*, 99, 123.
[92]Chittenden, *American Fur Trade*, II, 758.
[93]Hakluyt, *Voyages*, VI, 89; *Champlain's Voyages*, ed. E. G. Bourne, I, 13.
[94]Nau, or Aulneau, *Jesuit Relations*, LXVIII, 275.

The contrary classification finds abundant mention. Marc Lescarbot remarks (1612): ". . . game is not always to be found in abundance in a place where people are obliged to live on it, and where there is a permanent settlement. This is what makes nomads of the Savages, and prevents them from remaining long in one place. . . ."[95]

The nomadic habits of many tribes were a hindrance to the missionary efforts of the Jesuits. Father Le Jeune says (1637-39) "it is the same thing in a Savage to wish to become sedentary and to believe in God. . . ."[96] Almost exactly the same thing is said by Father Morain, of the Indians of Acadia in 1677.[97] The term 'nomad' is applied to the Montagnais in 1612 and 1670;[98] and likewise to the Algonkins in 1634 (and later).[99] It was said of the forest tribes at large,[100] and of those about Sault Ste Marie, *circa* 1670;[101] and its cause indicated; "Hunger is their great evil and destroys them. . . ."[102] Fathers Dablon and Marquette, both in 1671, describe the eastern forest Cree (? Ojibwa) as nomads;[103] and Father Marest, 1712, applies the phrase both to the eastern Cree and the eastern Assiniboine.[104] John Long, the North West Company's fur trader (1768-82), says of the forest 'Chippeways'—"I believe all the nation, with very few exceptions, may be called rovers in the strictest sense of the word. . . ."[105]

It is a rather remarkable fact that the northern Indians, dwelling as they did in a closely similar woodland habitat, should have been much more generally stationary than their eastern kindred. Harmon writes thus: "Every tribe has its own particular tract of country, and this divided again, among the several families which compose the tribe. Rivers, lakes and mountains serve them as boundaries, and the limits of the territory which belongs to each family are as well known by the tribe as the lines which separate farms are by the farmers in the civilized world. The Indians who reside in the large plains make no such subdivision of their territory; for the wealth of their country consists in buffaloes and wolves, which exist in plenty everywhere

[95]*Ibid.*, II, 167.

[96]Le Jeune, *ibid.*, XIV, 215. Compare him also, *ibid.*, XII, 169; XIV, 127, 205; XVI, 233, 249.

[97]*Ibid.*, LX, 269; cf. McDougall similarly, *Forest, Lake, and Prairie*, 76 (*in extenso* above, chap. XIV, note 186).

[98]*Jesuit Relations*, I, 319; II, 73, 167; LII, 219.

[99]*Ibid.*, VI, 133, 151; VII, 107; XV, 153; XXIII, 205.

[100]*Ibid.*, LIII, 87, 89.

[101]*Ibid.*, LIV, 131, 133.

[102]*Ibid.*, LIII, 87.

[103]Dablon, *ibid.*, LIV, 133-5; Marquette, *ibid.*, 193.

[104]Marest, *ibid.*, LXVI, 109.

[105]Long, *Early Western Travels*, II, 99.

among them. But the case is otherwise with the inhabitants of the woody countries. . . ."[106]

Harmon clearly indicates his opinion of the prairie tribes by the absence of the definite tribal boundary; the very test laid down by Henshaw,[107] A critic of high standing defines the Dakotas (Sioux) as 'genuine nomads.'[108] Parkman writes (1846): "The western Dahcotah have no fixed habitation. Hunting and fighting, they wander incessantly through summer and winter. Some follow the herds of buffalo over the waste of prairie; others traverse the Black Hills . . . emerging at last upon the 'Parks,' those beautiful but most perilous hunting-grounds. The buffalo supplies them with the necessaries of life. . . ."[109]

Elsewhere he describes the 'Ogillallah' (Oglala) as "the wildest of the hordes that roam over the remote prairie. . . ."[110] A later student (an adopted 'son') says of the Blackfoot: "When changing camp, the small ends of the lodge poles were fastened to the horses' sides, the large ends dragging behind upon the ground [that is, à la 'travois']. The Blackfeet changed camp so frequently that their poles were soon worn too short for the lodges, requiring a new set of poles every year. . . ."[111]

These were procured from the foothills and creek valleys; and Frémont, who also notices this renewal of poles every year (by other tribes[112]), mentions place-names doubtless conferred upon favoured resorts for this purpose.[113]

McClintock's account of the Blackfoot agrees with Henday, who writes in 1754: "They follow the Buffalo from place to place, and that they should not be surprised by the Enemy, encamp on open plains. . . ."[114]

[106]*Harmon's Journal*, 330; so also, Warburton Pike, *Barren Ground*, 156; Seton, *Arctic Prairies*, 278; Black, *History of Saskatchewan*, 449.

[107]*Harmon's Journal*, 293. Dodge describes the Plains tribes as 'nomads within their own territory,' and homesick out of it (*Our Wild Indians*, 49-50, 238-42, 311-14); possibly, when exiled from it by the Government, as were the Cheyennes (Grinnell, *Fighting Cheyennes*, 379); but what about their long voluntary journeys in earlier times? Dodge is sometimes unreliable concerning Indians.

[108]Thwaites, *Jesuit Relations*, introd., I, 12.   [109]Parkman, *Oregon Trail*, 177.

[110]*Ibid.*, 233.

[111]McClintock, *Old North Trail*, 518; cf. 1, 52, 175, 233.

[112]Frémont, *Narrative*, 211.

[113]'Lodge Pole Creek,' South Platte (followed by the Union Pacific Railway, west of Julesburg, Nebraska); 'Lodge Pole Fork,' *ibid.*, 24, 310. I find another Lodge Pole Creek, tributary of Grand River, in Perkins County, South Dakota.

[114]"Henday's Journal," ed. Burpee, 339. Likewise the Piegans, 1811: "The buffalo regulates their movements over this vast extent of prairie throughout the year, as they must keep near these animals to obtain food . . ." (Coues (ed.), *Henry-Thompson Journals*, II, 723).

Palliser leaves us in no doubt of his opinion. He calls the Blackfoot 'the Bedouin of the prairies';[115] and speaks elsewhere of the 'migratory' and 'nomadic' habits of the Plains tribes generally.[116] I have no knowledge of the (northern) Cheyennes prior to the nomadic stage, which Father De Smet's language seemingly implies. He says: "The Cheyennes have embraced the nomadic life, and follow the buffalo in his migrations. . . ."[117] If the Cheyennes ever changed from a sedentary to a nomadic life it must have been long ago.[118] Among other nomad tribes of the northern-central plains territory and westward were 'some of the Pawnees,'[119] the Shoshones or Snakes,[120] and 'formerly' (that is, before 1833) the 'Minatarees' or Gros Ventres (Hidatsa),[121] all of them 'buffalo' Indians.

The nomadic way of life is the distinguishing characteristic of many of the Southern Plains tribes. It was noted by the very first Europeans to gaze upon them (in so far as we are aware). Cabeza de Vaca writes as follows:

The greatest part of all this Nation drinks raine water, gathered together in certain Trenches. For although they have Rivers there, nevertheless, because they have never any certaine and settled place of abode, they have no particular water knowne to them, or appointed place where to take it. Throughout the whole Countrie there are many great and goodly fences, and of excellent pasture for flockes and herds of cattle, and it would be a very fruitful Countrie if it were manured and inhabited by a people which had reason and knowledge. . . .[122]

Similar opinions are expressed in the "Narrative of Juan de Jaramillo" (1541),[123] and by La Salle's followers (1687).[124] Practically all

[115]*Palliser Journals*, 204.

[116]*Ibid.*, 199, 200; cf. McClintock: "There is always so much uncertainty in the movements of Indians . . ." (*Old North Trail*, 175).

[117]*Life of De Smet*, I, 211; also *Early Western Travels*, XXVII, 160.

[118]'Nomads,' 1811: Irving, *Astoria*, 205; so also, 1839: Farnham, *Early Western Travels*, XXVII, 163; but cf. Kroeber, *Cultural and Natural Areas*, 81.

[119]Irving, *Tour of the Prairies*, 416.

[120]Irving, *Captain Bonneville*, 80.

[121]Maximilian states (1833) that the Minatarees 'are no longer nomadic' (*Early Western Travels*, XXIII, 368).

[122]*Purchas his Pilgrimes*, XVII, 480. 'Fences' = defences of some character, natural or otherwise; but the version of a later scholar (Fanny Bandelier) is worth quoting: "Most of the people drink rain-water that collects here and there, for, as they have never a fixed abode, they know no springs nor established watering-places, although there are rivers. All over the land are vast and handsome pastures with good grass for cattle, and it strikes me the soil would be very fertile, were the country inhabited and improved by reasonable people . . ." (*Journey of Cabeza*, ed. Bandelier, 97).

[123]*Journey of Coronado*, 234, 236.

[124]Hennepin, La Salle, Douay, Joutel: *Journeys of La Salle*, I, 64, 195, 224, 237; II, 78.

the scribes in Coronado's expedition noted that the Indians 'travelled around with the cows';[125] and many later observers have since commented on the nomadic habits of the southwestern Plains Indians.[126] Even the occasional mention of 'villages' does not, it would seem, necessarily always indicate a settled abode.[127]

I have dwelt upon this characteristic in some detail, because it can be traced, beyond reasonable doubt, to the influence of the proximity of the buffalo. The localized presence in buffalo territory of the Indian moveable dwelling—the tipi or 'tepee'—together with its manner of construction and its characteristics, proves this. A moveable habitation has apparently been recognized in the Old World as the conclusive test of the nomad;[128] and it has been authoritatively adopted as such in the scientific classification of the New.[129] This is in my view a sounder criterion than any primitive mode of native transport such as the dog-*travois*; since such means could obviously be used by a strictly non-nomadic people to migrate periodically from one 'permanent' (or fixed) home-site to another.[130]

[125]Castañeda, *"Traslado de las Nuevas"* ("Anonymous Document"); *"Relacion del Suceso"*; 'Coronado to Charles V'; 'Narrative of Jaramillo' (*Journey of Coronado*, 64; 194, 195; 205, 209, 210, 220, 230).

[126]See on this Gregg, *Early Western Travels*, XIX, 244; XX, 83, 242; Farnham, ibid., XVIII, 150, 163; Marcy, *Exploration of Red River*, 26, 94, 95, 106; Fynn, *American Indian*, 29-30, 41, 242; Wissler, *American Indian*, 218-20; etc. Cf. Pike on the efforts of the Spanish Government in Texas, 1807, to induce buffalo tribes to become in part agriculturists (Coues (ed.), *Expeditions of Pike*, II, 785).

[127]Irving (presumably on Bonneville's authority) writes: ". . . a *village* of Indians, in trappers' language, does not always imply a fixed community, but often a wandering horde or band . . ." (*Captain Bonneville*, 80). Quite logically so; the pitching of their tipis made them a village instantaneously.

[128]See Gibbon on this, among the ancient Tartars or Huns (*Decline and Fall*, chap. XXVI) and compare Herodotus on the Scythians (Bk. IV, chap. 46). Gibbon also on the Arabs of Mohammed's day (*Decline and Fall*, chap. L). Milman preferred the horse as the test of the nomad (*History of the Jews*, I, 55). Cf. below, note 130, on this.

In the *Book of Genesis* we may observe in the disputes between Lot and Abraham, and in the digging of Jacob's Well in the Vale of Shechem (as also other well-diggings), the gradual passing of the nomad hunter-herdsman—the two coalesced or conflicted in Esau—and the development of the sedentary shepherd and agriculturist, consequent upon the necessity for the delimitation, with other ex-nomads, of 'marches' for pasture-ranges, or from the tempting call of some specially attractive situation. Our western nomad never reached, or resumed, that stage naturally. See *Genesis*, chap. XIII; XXI, 25 *seq.*; XXVI, 12-33; XXXVI, 7; etc. Cf. also Dean Milman's remarks, *History of the Jews*, I, 46.

[129]See Mooney, "Tipi," *Handbook of American Indians*, II, 758; Wissler, *American Indian*, 218-20; *Encyclopaedia Brittannica*, 14th ed., *s.v.* North American Indians.

[130]Entirely apart from chronological or other objections suggested above (notes 67-71), I believe this factor rules out the horse from consideration as the originating cause of a true nomadic society.

The dwellings of various Indian tribes exhibit for us the progression from the forest peoples, through the semi-nomadic to what I shall call (with no disrespect to Professor Henshaw's classification) the completely nomadic state. In the forest lands on the northeast of the 'bison area' the very typical dwelling appears to have been the bark lodge or hut:[131] although among some tribes brushwood lodges were constructed of brush either bent over in semi-circular form as it grew, or cut down and so bent and thrust into the earth to be then covered with grass or bark,[132] or with hides.[133] The last covering would speedily suggest itself to any adaptable people like the Indians, after seeing the buffalo. Along the entire southern fringe, from Georgia in the southeast to New Mexico in the southwest, the dwellings of the more sedentary folk ranged from the 'wretched huts' of grass or earth which Luys Hernandez de Biedma, the factor of De Soto's expedition in 1539, refused to dignify as 'houses';[134] to the grass house or adobe 'pueblo' of the Rio Grande region.[135] In the northwestern regional frontier, the Northern Shoshonean tribes used a dome-shaped brush shelter—somewhat like that of the Micmacs, mentioned above, I should judge—'before the tipi became general,'[136] whenever that may have been. It appears, however, to corroborate the opinions cited above, for the comparatively late penetration of the buffalo west of the Rockies.[137]

[131]Wissler, *American Indian*, 109-15, 122; cf. Parkman, *La Salle*, 260.

[132]I find a description of the St. Lawrence tribes, 1594: "Here we found the houses of the Savages, made of firre trees bound together in the top, and set round like a Dovehouse, and covered with the barkes of firre trees . . ." (Hakluyt, *Voyages*, VI, 99).

A friend from the Maritime Provinces informs me that this is or was a custom among the Micmacs.

[133]The tipi of bark or of skins was noted in the St. Lawrence Gulf region by Father Biard, 1616; also by Father Le Jeune, 1634 (*Jesuit Relations*, III, 77; VII, 37). Jenness classifies the 'Migratory Tribes of the Eastern Woodlands' (*Indians of Canada*, 12, 118-32); and see his chapter on "Dwellings" (*ibid.*, 84-99); also *Handbook of American Indians*, I, 505, 515-19.

[134]*Narratives of De Soto*, II, 37.

[135]Wissler, *American Indian*, 237, 241; cf. "Narrative of Jaramillo" on Indians in the 'flat-roofed houses' at Cibola or 'Cicuye' (*Journey of Coronado*, 230); also Hewett, *Ancient Life in the American Southwest*.

[136]Wissler, *American Indian*, 224. Hancock (Feather River, California, presumably *re* 'Digger Indians'): "Here we found some very friendly Indians occupying several huts formed by digging holes in the ground and using the earth thrown out to cover saplings arranged in a pointed roof . . ." (*Narrative*, 71). Some further interesting details on local styles of dwellings, Klamaths, Hoopahs, Apaches, Comanches, etc., in Bancroft, *Native Races*, I, 334, 485. He states that 'Diggers' were not a tribe, but any Indians who lived in 'dug-out' habitations (*ibid.*, 326). Henshaw gives 'diggers' as root-eaters, who *dug* for food (*Handbook of American Indians*, I, 390; II, 557, 861). Cf. J. H. Steward, *Smithsonian Miscellaneous Collections*, vol. 100, 1940, 455 *seq.*

[137]See above, chap. XI, notes 11-13.

The exclusive or merely partial use of these permanent habitations constitutes a rough yet not wholly unscientific test of the extent of the nomadic impulse in their inmates. The inhabitants of the 'maize area'— both on the east and on the southwest of the 'bison area'[138] who abutted on the latter region, lived when 'at home,' so to speak, in one or another of the various types of permanent abode; but used the tipi when on their hunts, and then only.[139] The inhabitants of the 'bison area,' we are told, used the tipi solely;[140] but this statement is open to some exceptions, as we shall see. A similar distinction existed in the more northern regions of the same area, where it cut squarely across the lines of tribal relationship. Parkman states that the 'Issanti' (that is, Santee Sioux)[141] "cultivated the soil; but the extreme western bands subsisted on the buffalo alone. . . ."[142] The bark lodge was peculiar to the Eastern Sioux, who also used the skin tipi; whereas this latter solely was used by the Western bands.[143] The exception at which I hinted in reference to the tipi alone being used in the bison area as a whole, is somewhat curious, and apparently tends to indicate that among some tribes at least, however convenient as a purely moveable habitation the tipi might be, it fell below Indian standards of comfort as a permanent home, where readiness of transportation need not be considered. There is at least a possibility that this circumstance might furnish a clue to the relative eras in which the tribes arrived in the central buffalo habitat.

Some of these partly sedentary tribes in the heart of the 'bison area' used the tipi only on their hunts. Catlin's drawings and descriptions show this to have been the case with the Mandans.[144] Parkman relates

[138]This is the accepted classification (Wissler, *American Indian*, 3, 12-14, 31 *seq*., etc.

[139]*Ibid.*, 111, 115, 220, 222.

[140]*Ibid.*, 220, 237, 241, 272, etc.; see also Mooney, "Tipi" (*Handbook of American Indians*, II, 758); *Encyclopaedia Britannica*, *s.v.* North American Indians.

[141]It is of course well known that the Siouan family was a large one. Thomas and Swanton give 69 tribes or subdivisions ("Siouan Family," *Handbook of American Indians*, II, 577-9). The 'Sioux' of common parlance comprised the Dakotas proper, also the Brulé (or Burnt Hip), Blackfoot Sioux or Sihasapa, Minneconjou, Oglala, Santee (subdivided into the Wahpeton = 'men among leaves'; and Sisseton = 'men of prairie marsh'), Winnebago, Yankton or Yanktonais. See also Dodge, *Plains of the Great West*, 445; Maclean, *Canadian Savage Folk*, 104; *Encyclopaedia Britannica*, *s.v.* North American Indians; Wissler, *American Indians*; etc., etc.

[142]Parkman, *La Salle*, 260; cf. Coues (ed.), *Expeditions of Pike* (1805), I, 341-5.

[143]Parkman, *La Salle*, 260; Coues (ed.), *Expeditions of Pike*, I, 341-5.

[144]Catlin, *Letters on the North American Indians*, *passim*.

a Dakota (Sioux) warrior's exploit at the 'permanent winter villages' of the Pawnees on the lower Platte: ". . . clambering up the outside of one of the lodges, which are in the form of a half-sphere . . ." etc.[145] Denny recounts a curious tale of another ultra-nomadic people, the previously mentioned 'Bedouin of the prairies.' He was told by a Blackfoot chief that "Long ago the Blackfeet used sod houses and not tents, and that the remains of some of their old encampments, further back than they had any record, could still be seen across the river. . . ." At this place (near Blackfoot crossing, Bow River, some sixty miles below Calgary) tobacco was being grown in 1875, as it apparently had been for generations.[146] Had this been a tradition of a certain type of habitation in their former (more northern) home,[147] it might have been less difficult to comprehend; but it may be remarked that Denny elsewhere cites quasi-geological evidence tending to indicate a considerable antiquity for the practice of historic Indian buffalo-usages in the same general river-territory.[148] Quite possibly an immigrant people might use a semi-permanent fixed habitation for a period after their arrival on the buffalo plains before adopting the tipi. Indian traditions are frequently rather dubious and inconsistent, however.

In addition to the Sioux on the northeastern borders of the Plains area, Clark Wissler specified also the Plains-Ojibwa (or Chippewa) and the Plains-Cree: ". . . who have many traits of the forest hunting tribes, as well as most of those found in the Plains. Possibly a few of the little-known bands of the Canadian Assiniboin should be included in this group, in distinction from the Assiniboin proper. . . ."[149]

The local (that is, topographical) nomenclature of the Crees in general has been noticed already.[150] The woodland origin of even 'Plains-Chippewa'—in so far as historic or existent linguistic eras are concerned—seems to be established by the fact that the name *Chippewa* signifies 'men of the woods.'[151] The Assiniboine ('Stoneys'), who

---

[145]*Oregon Trail*, 74; see Dale (ed.), *Ashley-Smith Explorations*, 122.

[146]Denny MS., 83. Rundle mentions a 'Tobacco Weed Plain' and Creek (now Weed Creek, southwest of Edmonton some 20 miles): *Journal*, October, 1844. Frémont speaks of 'tobacco root,' perhaps the same root (*Narrative*, 129, 159, 160). Denny's reference is strangely followed by saying: "Tradition or history among the Blackfeet there was none" (MS., 84). McClintock's only definite tradition is of the migration from the north (as above, note 86). Kidd remarks that Blackfoot traditions are often contradictory and unsatisfactory ("Blackfoot Ethnography," 10).

[147]Above, chap. XI, note 120.   [148]Below *in extenso*, Appendix Z.

[149]Wissler, *American Indian*, 222.   [150]Above, chap. IV, note 5.

[151]Mooney and Thomas, "Chippewa," *Handbook of American Indians*, I, 277. 'Bois Forts'; so Maclean, *Canadian Savage Folk*, 171. See also below, Appendix W, "Indian Nomenclature."

are thought to have broken away from the parent Sioux nation *circa* 1640 or thereabout,[152] persistently displayed a woodland derivation in their trail-habits, unchanged during more than two centuries.[153] This sturdy conservatism[154] exhibits in even bolder contrast the effect of the buffalo influence upon their minds in their adoption of the moveable tipi as a dwelling. They revealed apparently an equal readiness in this particular with other tribes more generally adaptable to the unfamiliar environment of the western plains buffalo habitat.[155]

If there still remain in the critical mind any doubts as to the conclusions justly to be drawn from the development and use of the tipi itself, and whether the name of nomad can fittingly be given to its inventors, even these should be dispelled by another accompanying feature of these prairie dwellings. I refer to the beautifully ingenious device of the 'ear-flap,' that wonderfully simple but efficient contrivance by which the draft can be so regulated to suit the ever-changing prairie winds, that from whatever quarter they may blow, they are still the servant and not the master of the fire within.[156] The evolution of this appliance is in my view direct and conclusive evidence of the working of a nomad's mind. For practically anyone planning a permanent home of his own choosing in an open country selects the best probable situation against prevailing winds, and against the occasional exceptions commonly does as best he can.[157] Whatever modern critics may think, it is interesting and significant to note that the men to whom we owe our earliest notice of the skin tipi, before the freshness of the experience had been dulled by familiarity, and before narration had

[152]Thwaites, ed. note, *Jesuit Relations*, LXVI, 341.

[153]Their adherence to the forest 'Indian file' on the plains. Coues (ed.), *Henry-Thompson Journals*, I, 244; McDougall, *Saddle, Sled, and Snowshoe*, 69.

[154]See below, Appendix Y. Cf. above, note 65.

[155]See below, Appendix X, "Indian Tipis."

[156]See on this McClintock, *Old North Trail*, 233, 518, etc. Even this has had its 'improved patterns': Seton on the Chipewyan 'ear-flaps' (*Arctic Prairies*, 149). A tipi was preferred by Frémont before a tent, as mosquitoes 'were never seen' in one (*Narrative*, 50). The Indian tipi was General Sibley's model for the U.S. Army 'Sibley tent'; so Mooney, "Tipi,'" *Handbook of American Indians*, II, 759. Wissler states that the tipi has been found in Siberia (*American Indians*, 112). If this means the Mongol tent as described by Rev. James Gilmour—no grumbler, by the way—the 'comfort' did not obtrude itself, to say the least (*Among the Mongols*, 74, 103, 220, etc).

[157]I visited a camp of Wood Stoneys, on Battle Lake (source of Battle River) Alberta, October, 1897. Instead of using the warmer and drier side of the valley they were under the hill on the moist shady side. Shelter from the prevailing northwest winds across the lake and closer proximity to a patch of dry timber were apparently the supreme desiderata. In 1928, I had the pleasure of meeting some who (unknown to me) were boys in that camp. This, they told me, was a 'permanent' site (*i.e.* for many months, summer and winter).

given place to refining, had no hesitation (with a well-known example before their minds) in classifying its occupants. Pedro de Castañeda likens them to the Arabs,[158] one of the super-nomad peoples of all history; and his opinion was manifestly shared by his comrades.[159] At the very same time, another fellow-countryman, hundreds of miles away, records a precisely similar opinion.[160]

I have dwelt upon the Indian as a nomad hunter in the western buffalo habitat, in considerable—perhaps excessive—detail, in order first of all to show clearly that this conception rests upon an abundance of sound evidence. In relation to any hypothesis of the horse as the originating factor in such a development, I really do not see with what logical authority characteristics which are recognized as essentially concomitant features of the nomad society in post-equine times, can be denied that classification when encountered—and evidently as deeply rooted practices of long standing—by the very earliest historic observers prior to the Indian acquisition of the horse.[161] There is another phase of the Indian-and-buffalo relationship which it is the purpose of this chapter to examine, the significance of which has scarcely been realized; certainly the protagonists of the 'regular migration' have failed to come to grips with it. Since I have contested that conception so strongly, I am both entitled and required to emphasize its bearing on that argument. If necessity be the mother of invention, it is probably also the primary 'parental' influence in general (that is, racial) mental characteristics. If the 'annual,' 'general,' 'regular,' 'seasonal' (etc.) migration has any meaning, as applied universally to a species which unquestionably thronged in millions in its chosen habitat, it is difficult to conceive the necessity out of which the nomadic instinct arose. If the self-same well-defined routes—'migration trails,' 'buffalo-highways,' or what you will—were being uniformly followed by the immense hosts in their 'annual migrations' between the regular summer and winter abiding-places, what probable or reasonable ground is there for supposing that the Indians, whose mastery of the animal lore of

[158]Castañeda, *Journey of Coronado,* 65, 75, 111.

[159]"Anonymous Document," *ibid.,* 195; "Relacion del Suceso," *ibid.,* 209; "Narrative of Jaramillo," *ibid.,* 230. Some of Coronado's and De Soto's men may quite conceivably have served in Charles V's great expedition to Tunis in 1535.

[160]The Gentleman of Elvas, concerning 'the country farther on' (*i.e.* past the Mississippi River) "where the Indians wandered like Arabs, having no settled place of residence, living on prickly pears, the roots of plants, and game . . ." (*Narratives of De Soto,* I, 180, 181).

[161]See above, notes 67-71. While Dr. Strong's argument deserves consideration, equally so with evidence from any source, its conclusions certainly cannot be accepted as final or decisive.

their local habitat is everywhere extolled by all observers, would not be themselves the first to discover this, and to profit from the knowledge to the full? Some who dissent from Henshaw's classification might argue that the nomad trait was an inheritance brought with them from a former habitat to the buffalo plains—as doubtless in good measure it was. But on the supposition of the regularity of the buffalo movements, it should have perished from atrophy in the plains country long ago.

I am not competent, nor is it the province of this essay, to pronounce how long the Plains Indians of historical knowledge have dwelt in that region in which Europeans found them. Some of them have probably known the buffalo during only a minor portion of its existence on this continent. In any event, their amazing conquest of the horse proves what veritable miracles of adaption could be wrought in a wonderfully short time.[162] The testimonies cited above indicate that their mastery of the potentialities of the buffalo was as complete in Coronado's day as it was in the nineteenth century;[163] and doubtless it was ancient then. Among other details, the Indians had realized the necessity for 'following the cows around.' When it is borne in mind that it was not until the latter part of the sixteenth century—and perhaps considerably later[164]—that the earliest of them had anything more adequate than the dog to relieve their own backs of the bearing of burdens; one is not merely tempted, he is entitled to ask why such a folk did not utilize their incomparable knowledge of an animal of such uniform habits as the buffalo of tradition, to literally 'camp on his trail,' as the westernism has it; and save the toil, inconvenience, privation, and suffering so frequently involved in their nomadic life. They had mastered practically everything else about the animal;[165] why not this?

Had they possessed the horse from some vastly remote era, it might perhaps be urged with some show of plausibility that the 'love of the chase' was possibly the reason for this wandering. I suspect that this

[162]See Roe, "From Dogs to Horses among the Western Indian Tribes," *Transactions of the Royal Society of Canada*, 1939, Sec. II, particularly 214, 264 *seq.*, on the early use of horses for riding, hunting buffalo, etc.

[163]Above, notes 1-32.

[164]See Roe, "From Dogs to Horses among the Western Indian Tribes," *Transactions of the Royal Society of Canada*, 1939, 232 *seq.*, for probable conjectural dates. I may add that my rejection of the 'accidental' hypothesis of Indian horses, from strayed or stolen animals from Coronado, etc., is confirmed by independent research. "Coronado's Muster Roll" (tr. Arthur S. Aiton, *American Historical Review*, XLIV, 1938, 556-70) lists 550 horses and only *two* mares! I am greatly indebted to Professor Aiton's kindness for a reprint of this important document, which in 1939 was unknown to me.

[165]See below, note 351.

passion has little influence upon the minds of these who have to follow the chase for existence.[166] Railroading and the sea are romance to everybody except railroaders and seamen; and I doubt whether 'the call of the road' would awaken much enthusiasm in those walking postmen of whom we used to hear, who had 'encircled the globe' several times in their daily rounds during forty or fifty years.[167] I believe the prophets of the chase, whether in the wilds or in the study, have generally a well-stocked commissariat conveniently close at hand. The Indian wanderings after the buffalo were born of necessity; and to couple that necessity with their perfect understanding of everything relating to an animal of such supposedly uniform habits is virtually a contradiction in terms.

4.

There are certain striking and outstanding traits in the Indian character which have been noted by almost every reflecting observer who has encountered the 'buffalo' Indians in earlier or more recent times. They are generic in the race; and belong to that category the origin of which I suggested, in the opening of this chapter, may be sought in the environment. The first of these is their propensity to what we term wastefulness. Waste (and particularly by others) is such a cardinal sin in the estimation of commercial societies, and the energies of their leaders are so entirely—and rightly—concentrated upon its consequences and their prevention, as to leave but little time or effort available for inquiry into its origins. This, however, is scarcely the attitude of the scientific philosopher; and apart from additions to our abstract knowledge, it may even yet some day be proved that in the problem of waste, our 'practical' remedial methods are a mere tinkering with symptoms, while causes are left untouched.

Indian 'wastefulness' displayed itself in the two main forms of slaughter and consumption—or perhaps more correctly, utilization for necessary purposes. In addition to carefully stalking the prey, commonly resorted to in the case of individual animals or small bands of only a few, there were three principal methods of slaughter *en masse*. The deadliest procedure of all, the 'still-hunt,' required high-power

[166]Hornaday, at least, denies this predilection in Indians; not very logically, on his own premises ("Extermination of the American Bison," 506). Below, note 233.

[167]As I once retorted to an eager harangue in the orthodox verbiage of rod and gun, I have myself ridden and tramped too many miles through drenching scrub before breakfast in search of stray stock, for 'the breezy call of incense-breathing morn' to move me overmuch toward the hunter's joys.

repeating firearms; and does not appear to have been practised to any material extent by Indians, even after they became possessed of more modern weapons. The three methods in question were 'buffalo running'; the 'surround' by a band of hunters on the open plain; and 'impounding,' which was a driving or decoying between narrowly converging line-fences or piles of brushwood or other barrier-marks conspicuously placed in the same formation, either into a pen or 'pound,' or 'park,' made of brush or timber; or similarly into a narrow strait or isthmus which opened on the edge of a precipitous cliff or 'cut-bank' ('jumping-pound') over which the animals were hurled to destruction below.

Buffalo-running has been described so often both in travel-literature and in fiction that it is needless to enter upon it here, any further than to say that only with experts had it any chance whatever of becoming wasteful; since the novice in his excitement usually spent his powder for nothing, as man after man has told us.[168] Indians, however, were commonly among the more expert; although proficiency varied even among Indian hunters, with buffalo as with moose, as we learn upon unexceptionable authority.[169] In the catalogue of Indian crimes, therefore, doubtless 'running' must occupy a place.

The 'surround' in the open was obviously an immediate human counterpart, on the bare prairies, of the impounding method—very probably an earlier rudimentary form of that procedure;[170] and clearly designed for taking game wherever they might chance to find it, an indication in itself of the nomadic life. It was utilized where there was neither time nor material for erecting fences or 'markers,' however rude or ill-constructed. The names of the prairie tribes mentioned by

[168]See above, chap. XIV, notes 193-6.

[169]McDougall's friend, 'Muddy Bull' (1864) once killed seven buffalo "within 50 square feet [? feet square] of ground, and that with an old pot-metal flint-lock gun, muzzle-loading and single-barrelled. I have seen him with the same gun . . . at full gallop over a rough country, knock three buffaloes down one after another, almost as fast as an ordinary hunter would with a Winchester. . . ." He could pick his game, too (*Saddle, Sled, and Snowshoe,* 119). 'Joseph' also (*ibid.,* 205). Another Indian, 1862: 16 buffaloes with 17 arrows (McDougall, *Forest, Lake, and Prairie,* 144); Jerry McNab, half-breed interpreter at Fort Qu'Appelle, 1867, as a buffalo runner with an Indian 'trade gun' (Cowie, *Company of Adventurers,* 216). Such men were beyond doubt particularly expert, or they would hardly have been singled out for 'honourable mention.' On Indian archery, cf. below, Appendix T, "Late Survival of Indian Archery."

[170]A learned scholar sums it up thus: "The climax of this first class [*i.e.* of hunting—taking game with the hand, poacher's lore, etc.] was the communal game drive, in which a whole band or tribe would surround a herd of animals and coax or force them into a gorge, corral, or natural *cul-de-sac* . . ." (Mason, *Handbook of American Indians,* I, 580).

Hornaday as having used the 'surround' indicate this. He speaks of
Minatarees, Cheyennes, Arapahoes, Sioux, Pawnees, Omahas, "and
probably many other tribes. . . ."[171] Such a ready expedient was manifestly of immense usefulness to hunter-folk. The hunters formed a
cordon around the herd, enclosing presumably as many as they felt
themselves competent to handle, or one of those small herds of which
the large aggregates were commonly held to be composed:[172] and I
should judge by running (or riding) round and round, with the usual
Indian accompaniment of yellings galore, would head them in towards
the centre as cowmen seek to do with a bunch of range cattle, so that
there was nowhere any glimpse of open freedom to aim for. In this
predicament the Indian arrows and lances would soon do their work;
the earlier victims near the outside perhaps assisting to form a ring
of slain which the remainder would be unwilling to pass. Catlin mentions a surround at the mouth of the Teton River, in Dakota, shortly
before his arrival there in 1832. An 'immense herd' appeared on the
opposite side of the river from the post (apparently Fort Pierre);
whereupon some 500 or more Sioux crossed on horseback and attacked
them, returning to the post at sunset with 1400 fresh buffalo tongues.
These they threw down in a heap, requiring (and receiving) for them
a few gallons of whisky, which were soon consumed. Catlin adds that
from all he could learn not a skin nor a pound of meat was saved, other
than the tongues.[173]

Catlin elsewhere relates the following episode: "The Minatarees,
as well as the Mandans, had suffered for some months past for want
of meat, and had indulged in the most alarming fears that the herds
of buffalo were emigrating so far off from them that there was great
danger of their actual starvation, when it was suddenly announced
through the village one morning at an early hour that a herd of buffaloes was in sight. . . ."[174]

On this occasion likewise (which brings out very clearly the uncertainty of the buffalo, and also the probable origin of the surround,
as a rough and ready expedient) the entire herd was slain. Hornaday
comments on the occurrence as follows:

[171]Hornaday, "Extermination of the American Bison," 482. Lewis and Clark
observed it among the Mandans, 1804 (*Journals,* I, 198). Grinnell notes another
(? Blackfoot) method of pitching the tipis around the herd, then frightening
them into 'milling' around inside until exhausted, when they could be slain
easily (Kidd, "Blackfoot Ethnography," 93).

[172]See above, chap. V, note 68; chap. X, note 145.

[173]Catlin, *Letters on the North American Indians,* I, 256.

[174]*Ibid.,* I, 199-200 .

[This extract] serves well to illustrate not only a very common and very deadly Indian method of wholesale slaughter—the "surround"—but also to show the senseless destructiveness of Indians even when in a state of semi-starvation, which was brought upon them by similar acts of improvidence and wastefulness. . . . It is to be noticed that *every animal* of this entire herd of several hundred was slain on the spot, and there is no room to doubt that at least half (possibly much more) of the meat thus taken was allowed to become a loss. People who are so utterly senseless as to wantonly destroy their own source of food, as the Indians have done, certainly deserve to starve.[175]

It will be pertinent to discuss the critic later. Thirty years before Catlin's time, the younger Henry says of the Mandans, also a sedentary tribe:

They went away yesterday, and found buffalo in great abundance near at hand. These people always hunt in large parties, as the continual danger from their numerous enemies obliges them to be very cautious in leaving the villages. Another reason is that they are anxious to prevent the buffalo from being driven away. For this purpose it is customary for them all in a body to surround one herd only, which sometimes consists of several hundreds. Not one of the whole herd do they allow to escape, large and small, fat and lean, all must fall, to prevent alarming other herds. . . .[176]

We have here at least a reason of sorts, which I shall later examine in detail.

Even in the more wooded regions, the surround (of buffalo) afoot—necessarily, in the absence of the horse—was practised in fairly early times, and by tribes widely separated one from another. Father Hennepin (1680), after telling us that the buffalo were "so swift that no Savage can overtake them,"[177] observes in another place: "Sometimes they send the swiftest among them . . . who would drive whole Droves of wild Bulls before them and force them to swim the River. Of these they sometimes kill'd forty or fifty, but took only the Tongues, and some other of the best Pieces. . . ."[178] As with the Mandans, so also with the Illinois or Miamis: "These Bulls being very convenient for the Subsistence of the Savages, they take care not to Scare them from their Country and they pursue only those whom they have wounded with their Arrows. . . ."[179]

[175]Hornaday, "Extermination of the American Bison," 481, 482. Destruction of 'at least half' is apparently a gratuitous application of Hornaday's calculations from *one* Red River hunt (as above, chap. XIV, notes 198-241) to Indians at large. The 'cause' of their previous condition of semi-starvation is pure assumption. They were sedentary and agriculturists in part at this very time (Maximilian, *Early Western Travels*, XXIII, 274, 368, 375, 377. Cf. also above, notes 10-18.

[176]Coues (ed.), *Henry-Thompson Journals*, I, 336.
[177]Hennepin, *New Discovery*, I, 150.
[178]*Ibid.*, 242.   [179]*Ibid.*, 149.

Not many years later, Henry Kelsey witnessed a surround, which in that region, along the Saskatchewan or Carrot River prairies, might have been by Crees, Saulteaux, or Assiniboines. He writes (August 23, 1691):

This instant [that is, 'to-day'] ye Indians going ahunting Kill'd great store of Buffillo. Now ye manner of their hunting these Beast on ye Barren ground is where they see a great parcel of them together they surround them with men wch done they gather themselves into a smaller Compass Keeping ye Beast still in ye middle & so shooting ym till they break out at some place or other and so gett away from ym. . . .[180]

Nicholas Cresswell (Kentucky, May 24, 28, 1775) writes: "Surrounded 30 Buffaloes as they were crossing the river. . . ."[181]

It seems certain at least that the Assiniboine used the surround at an early period in their plains life; for a competent Indianologist states that the long enmity between that tribe and the Cheyennes is said to have originated in a quarrel about a herd of buffalo each was trying to surround.[182] This fairly wide prevalence of the practice makes Dodge's statement read rather strangely: "So far as I am able to ascertain, either from writers or by questioning Indians, the 'surround' of Buffalo was peculiar to the Cheyennes and Arapahoes. . . ."[183]

When we consider that the surround has been noted in various localities as being practised on deer,[184] elk,[185] and antelope,[186] it appears reasonable to assume that previous to the possession of the horse or the introduction of superior weapons, nothing but an entire absence of buffalo would prevent its being utilized for that species also. It would seem, in fact, that the surround by horsemen only accomplished more rapidly and easily what the Indians had already succeeded in doing for many generations without the horse.

There is a certain amount of testimony, particularly among the older writers, regarding the use of fire in surrounding buffalo and other game. Hennepin speaks of 'encompassing the Wild Bulls with fire' as

[180]*Kelsey Papers*, 13; cf. note at conclusion of chap. XII.

[181]*Cresswell's Journal*, 78, 80.

[182]Grinnell, *Fighting Cheyennes*, 5.

[183]Dodge, *Our Wild Indians*, 576. Several of Dodge's generalizations are apparently based on these two tribes alone. Frémont describes a surround by these (*Narrative*, 29). See also Allen, *American Bisons*, 206; Dodge, *Our Wild Indians*, 288-91; Hornaday, "Extermination of the American Bison," 480-3.

[184]In the Cœur d'Alene country, 1861 (*Life of De Smet*, III, 1021).

[185]'Both Middle Plains and Mountain Indians' (Dodge, *Our Wild Indians*, 577, 578).

[186]'Eutaws' (Utes), Dodge, *ibid.*, 578; Irving, *Captain Bonneville*, 336; Shoshones, 1843: Frémont, *Narrative*, 120.

a custom among the Miami and Illinois tribes;[187] and an earlier explorer in 'Virginia' (1607) refers there to 'environing the Deere with fire.'[188] These phrases point to the utilization of a fire-cordon for facilitating the capture of a single herd precisely as with a human cordon, but other references indicate the use of fire in a wider and more commonly understood sense. Father Hennepin himself mentions the firing of the prairies as an annual practice among the Miamis and other tribes of the upper Mississippi territory, on a larger scale than the 'environing' of any one herd.[189] The reasons for this wide-spread custom are variously stated (probably there was no one reason): 'To induce the buffalo to visit the locality,'[190] or possibly to induce them to remain when they did appear, by the tempting green of the recently-burnt prairie[191] (for the first supposition smacks too strongly of the aforementioned shark-and-invalid occultism);[192] or even, to compel them to concentrate upon the area carefully left unburnt.[193] In other cases, the burnings were quite evidently intended as an 'unfriendly act,' designed to embarrass some enemy tribe;[194] and one fairly early witness suspected the Crees (apparently) of firing the prairies near Fort George on the North Saskatchewan, October, 1794, "to frighten away the animals in order to enhance the value of their own provisions [that is, for sale]. . . ."[195] Not very long afterwards, an observer in the Ohio Valley and Kentucky territory explained it thus:

This custom of burning the meadows was formerly practised by the natives, who came in this part of the country to hunt, in fact, they do it now in the other parts of North America, where there are savannas of an immense extent. Their aim in setting fire to it is to allure the stags, bisons, &c., into the parts which are burnt, where they can discern them at a greater distance. . . .[196]

Seeing that buffalo are almost precisely of the brown smoky tint of a burnt prairie after the first breeze has blown away the charred grasses, and that their forms would show up much more clearly against

[187]Hennepin, New Discovery, I, 147.
[188]The redoubtable Captain John Smith of 'Pocahontas' fame (Purchas his Pilgrimes, XVIII, 444).
[189]Hennepin, New Discovery, I, 145, 146, 154; cf. Father Vivier, 1750, Jesuit Relations, LXIX, 209.
[190]So the Minatari to Lewis and Clark, 1804 (Journals, I, 230, 238).
[191]So Macoun, Manitoba, 232. He says 'this made it good all summer'; but that is a mistake. It depends upon the season's rain.
[192]See above, chap. IV, note 64.
[193]Dodge, Our Wild Indians, 288.
[194]This is implied in Hennepin's remarks (New Discovery, I, 145, etc.).
[195]McGillivray's Journal, 33.
[196]Michaux, 1802, Early Western Travels, III, 221.

the light tawny colouring of old dry grass than against the new dark green, the reason given is by no means apparent. Hind cites the practice, almost on the scale of major strategy on the part of the Crees, north of the Moose Jaw country, 1858:

One object in burning the prairie at this time of the year was to turn the buffalo; they had crossed the (South) Saskatchewan in great numbers near the Elbow and were advancing towards us, and crossing the Qu' Appelle not far from the height of land; by burning the prairie east of their course they would be diverted to the south, and feed for a time on the Grand Coteau before they pursued their way to the Little Souris, in the country of the Sioux, south of the 49th. parallel. . . .[197]

The burning of the plains by the Indians was noted by La Salle's followers in the Lower Mississippi territory and westward toward Texas;[198] by Lewis and Clark,[199] and also by Father De Smet,[200] on the Upper Missouri; and by Palliser and others in Western Canada.[201] The native informants of a recent investigator deny that this was practised in former times by the Blackfoot, 'as it frightened the buffalo from the country'; but nevertheless, he believes it actually was done.[202] It was doubtless from these causes, together with accidental fires such as those which narrowly endangered Father Lacombe in 1857,[203] and Milton and Cheadle in 1863,[204] that the 'almost yearly fires'[205] destroyed great numbers of buffalo, as we have seen on an earlier page.[206]

In the case of the Mandans, described by Henry, and of the Minatarees and Sioux, mentioned by George Catlin,[207] the reader will have noted that every single animal is stated to have been slain. In the latter instances, Hornaday has almost elevated this to the status of law *de facto* as well as *de jure*. A similar universalism appears to be implied by Dodge: "A white hunter, considered very reliable, told me he had once seen nearly 300 buffalo killed in one [Indian] surround, that the

---

[197]Hind, *Report, 1858*, 52. Many tracks 'to the east' where the buffalo had crossed, at the South Saskatchewan River (*ibid.*, 57, 63). He remarks elsewhere, it is true, that 'nothing but fire could divert them from their course' (*ibid.*, 106); but why the need for *diverting* them south, when he insists on the same page (p. 106) that their uniform direction was south at this very season? See above, chap. XIV, notes 51-2.

[198]Joutel, *Journeys of La Salle*, II, 112, 113, 133; see also Allen (*American Bisons*, 202), citing Hennepin, Charlevoix, Du Pratz, and some large kills.

[199]*Lewis and Clark Journals*, I, 230, 238.

[200]*Life of De Smet*, IV, 1347.

[201]*Palliser Journals*, 57; Hind, *Report, 1858*, 42, 52, 67-70, 128.

[202]Kidd, "Blackfoot Ethnography," 94.

[203]*Palliser Journals*, 57; Hind, *Report, 1858*, 42; Allen, *American Bisons*, 170.

[204]Milton and Cheadle, *North-West Passage*, 220-2.

[205]So, *Harmon's Journal*, 90.

[206]See above, chap. VII, notes 27-33.   [207]Above, notes 173-6.

whole affair occupied less than ten minutes after the signal was given, and that not a single buffalo escaped. . . ."[208]

We have also seen, however, that the earliest recorded English-speaking witness of a buffalo surround, anywhere, treats the escape of a number, perhaps even a considerable proportion, as being a very ordinary feature of the performance.[209] It may be urged that in Kelsey's case, inferior weapons, or possibly even (for anything we know, in that locality) an acquaintance with the species itself too recent for those Indians to have acquired proficiency in the art,[210] may be the true explanation. But the very latest description of a surround (by the Pawnees in 1872) known to me, and from no mawkish sympathizer with Indians, records the following, concerning a herd of 'at least two thousand head.' The witness concludes: "After the Indians had departed, I counted up their day's work. I had supposed, of course, from their demonstration and hurrahs, I would find at least a hundred dead Buffaloes, but imagine my disgust when the total numbered only forty-one!"[211]

Buffalo Jones himself, it would seem, expected only 'at least' 100 out of this herd of 'at least' 2,000. It is possible that many cases of 'total annihilation' in ten (or more) minutes, if subjected to the same cold analysis, might be found to resemble the famous instance of the 'million cats in our yard.' We have seen already that certain hypothetical annual bills of mortality, by whose authors the Indian surround is held up as an awful example, will not endure translation into plain arithmetical fact.[212]

5.

Impounding was a different and much more serious affair. Instead of merely surrounding and slaying the herd or a portion thereof wherever they might chance to encounter it, the hunters drove or decoyed

[208]Dodge, *Plains of the Great West*, 355.

[209]Henry Kelsey, 1691 (above *in extenso*, note 180).

[210]Matthew Cocking remarks (October 20-26, 1772) that 'we' (his Indians) are not so expert at pounding as the Archithinue Natives (*i.e.* the Blackfoot): "Journal," ed. Burpee, 109-10. It is difficult to draw any satisfactory conclusions *re* its antiquity from language. The Cree had terms for these: 'PARC, ou les sauvages font entrer les buffles = *pittukahan, a'*; 'il va chercher les buffles pour les faire entrer dans le parc = *natjipahaw, ok'* (Lacombe, *Dictionnaire de la langue des Cris*, 210, 304, 569). In English we could say, 'long enough for a description to crystallize into a phrase'; but in the polysynthetic Indian tongues a description *is* a phrase, and the foregoing may long antedate their knowledge of the buffalo specifically.

[211]*Buffalo Jones' Forty Years*, 97-102.

[212]Compare above, *in extenso*, chap. XVIII, note 56 *et seq.*

it to some previously selected spot, presumably convenient to the encampment (whether permanent or for some extended period) and there slaughtered it. This involved a considerable amount of preparation before-hand; both in the labour of building the pound and laying out the 'markers,' and in the performance of certain propitiatory rites, which were usually deemed highly beneficial if not indispensable. The only real distinction between the two methods, the 'pound' proper and the drive over a cliff or 'jumping-pound,' was that in the latter case the actual enclosure or 'corral,' stout enough to restrain the buffalo after they were trapped, was needless. The leap over the cliff or 'cut-bank' both 'confined' and killed them, or so maimed them that escape was virtually impossible and slaughter easy.

Concerning the brush-built pound, Hornaday writes as follows:

. . . such wholesale catches were of common occurrence among the Plains Crees of the South Saskatchewan country, and the same general plan was pursued, with slight modifications, by the Indians of the Assiniboine, Blackfeet, and Gros Ventres, and other tribes of the Northwest. Like the keddah elephant-catching operations in India, this plan was feasible only in a partially wooded country, and where buffalo were so numerous that their presence could be counted on to a certainty. . . .

It is some satisfaction to know that when the first "run"[213] was made, the herd of two hundred buffaloes was no sooner driven into the pound than a wary old bull espied a weak spot in the fence, charged at it at full speed, and burst through to freedom and the prairie, followed by the entire herd.

Strange as it may seem to-day, this wholesale method of destroying buffalo was once practiced in Montana. . . .[214]

There can be little doubt that the buffalo or game pound is of immemorial antiquity, as the phrase would be applied to peoples having no written records. In the very nature of things, the use of such an expedient points to a time when men not only lacked really adequate transport facilities for conveying heavy masses such as buffalo meat, but possibly had not yet even developed weapons sufficiently powerful against monsters of such tenacious vitality at any but the very closest quarters. Clark Wissler observes: ". . . we find scattered everywhere in the great central reaches of the [plains or 'bison'] area, circles and

---

[213]The term *run* seems inaccurate here. It was apparently confined by old plainsmen to buffalo 'running'; as by Norbert Welsh (1845-1933), *The Last Buffalo Hunter*, 82-4, 100, etc. But when was the 'first run' made, and who was its chronicler? The reader may also by this time share my own curiosity as to where this region was, where the buffalo could be 'counted on to a certainty.'

[214]Hornaday, "Extermination of the American Bison," 478, 480; cf. Allen, *American Bisons*, 206. The italics are mine; why any stranger in Montana than elsewhere?

lines of boulders. . . . The small circles are assumed to mark sites; but long lines of stones have been noted whose use is problematical, though in Montana the historic Indians claim them as markers for buffalo pounds. . . ."[215]

Whatever be the prehistoric antiquity of pounds, they were a device in familiar use among the 'Archithinue Natives' (Blackfoot) when Matthew Cocking sojourned among them in the winter of 1772-73. I quote his account (December 4, 1772):

The Archithinue Natives drove into the pound 3 male & one female Buffalo, & brought several considerable droves very near: [sic] They set off in the Evening: and drive the Cattle all night. . . . They are all well mounted in light Sprightly Animals. . . . They likewise use pack-Horses, which give their Women a great advantage over the other Women who are either carrying or hauling on Sledges every day in the year. . . .[216]

It is a curious commentary on Hornaday's remarks about pounds in regions where buffalo 'could be counted on to a certainty,' that despite 'singing their Buffalo Pound songs' they could discover no buffalo for a long time; and later, when they appeared, the Indians (who were apparently Assiniboines, 'not so expert' as the Blackfoot) could get but few to enter their pound.[217] Cocking also mentions a 'permanent' Blackfoot pound in the same neighbourhood, the particular significance of which will appear later.

Whatever may have been the individual expertness or otherwise of those Indians in Cocking's company, 'parcs' or pounds are frequently mentioned as 'an ancient custom' among the 'Assiniboils'[218] or 'Osini-poilles,'[219] no doubt antedating their knowledge of the buffalo. These

[215]Wissler, American Indian, 272; also see his paper in American Anthropologist, XVI, 1914, 492. On this, see also Appendix Z.

[216]"Cocking's Journal," ed. Burpee, 111. Based presumably upon this, Agnes Laut fathers the following on Cocking: "The Blackfoot hunters thought nothing of riding for a hundred miles to round up the scattered herds to one of these pounds or corrals . . ." (Conquest of the Great Northwest, I, 377). Although Cocking records frequent scarcities, September to December, 1772, and 'starving,' January, 1773 (Journal, 105-12), she says: "Of food there was always plenty from the buffalo hunts . . ." (Conquest of the Great Northwest, I, 378). A good specimen of 'popular' buffalo history. One could overlook mere slovenliness, as 'a revolver,' 1787 (I, 405), or those '600,000 beaver' of Radisson and Groseilliers (I, 101), if it were not for her contemptuous dogmatisms. Racy and thoroughly readable, she is impossible as a source of exact knowledge. See above, chap. IX, note 27.

[217]"Cocking's Journal," 108-16.

[218]John McDonnell, "Account of Red River," 1793-97, in Masson, Les Bourgeois de la Campagnie du Nord-Ouest, I, 279, 280;Cf. McGillivray's Journal, 38, 42-4.

[219]Alexander Henry (the elder), Travels, 1760-1776, 293-6, 312.

in fact, seem almost to have attained a pre-eminent fame in this respect; although, as we shall see, other tribes also practised impounding.[220] We have also some curious evidence concerning the construction of pounds, at times, of the most unexpected materials.[221] Personal descriptions by eye-witnesses, however, either of pounds in actual use,[222] or of surviving relics of such within comparatively recent times, all indicate the use of brush or timber, as mentioned below.[223]

The 'jumping-pound' was apparently identical with the ordinary brush or timber-built pound, in respect of 'wings' or 'markers' to guide or decoy the herds; or perhaps, to put it more accurately, to discourage attempts to escape by presenting a counterfeit appearance of a continuous barrier on either side. These markers, which were sometimes covered with a buffalo hide, or might even consist of a hide bunched up like a small tent or the like, served also to conceal the auxiliaries hiding behind them; who rose up successively as the herd passed one barrier after another, and by closing in on the rear, assisted in keeping them in the strait and narrow way which led to destruction.[224] There are numerous historical references to jumping-pounds;[225] which apparently represented the form in which Indian buffalo-impounding at large was known far beyond the limits of the Western buffalo territory.[226] I have treated the subject of impounding at some length in order to bring out clearly the facts in the case; without which it would be futile to attempt to consider this practice as a result of a lengthy reaction to the buffalo environment.

It is impossible to deny that the first impression created is that of utter wastefulness; and one cannot feel greatly surprised that writer after writer has emphasized this.[227] A careful and critical examination of their arguments yields some curious results in certain cases, both in respect of polluted channels of information,[228] and of sweeping assertion unsupported by adequate evidence; this last being evidently deemed superfluous, when the accused parties were only Indians![229] In fairness, however, it must be pointed out that many or most of these writers were but passing travellers; perhaps in a majority of instances

[220]See Appendix AA, "Buffalo Pounds."
[221]*Ibid.*
[222]*Ibid.*
[223]*Ibid.*
[224]McDougall, *Saddle, Sled, and Snowshoe*, 276-9.
[225]See Appendix AA.
[226]*Ibid.*
[227]See Appendix BB, "Indian Wastefulness with Buffalo."
[228]*Ibid.*
[229]*Ibid.*

possessing neither the capacity, the inclination, nor the material for any philosophical co-ordination of the evidence at large. Much of the last, in fact, did not even exist, until the travellers themselves, among others, had furnished it. Hornaday, however, belongs to a very different category; and historical justice demands that he be judged differently. On Indian wastefulness at large, he writes as follows:

During the last forty years [that is, ante 1889] the final extermination of the buffalo has been confidently predicted by not only the observing white man of the West, but also nearly all the Indians and half-breeds who formerly depended upon this animal for most of the necessities, as well as luxuries, of life. They have seen the great herds driven westward farther and farther, until the plains were left tenantless, and hunger took the place of feasting on the choice tid-bits of the chase. And is it not singular that during this period the Indian tribes were not moved by a common impulse to kill sparingly, and by the exercise of a reasonable economy in the chase to make the buffalo last as long as possible.

But apparently no such thought ever entered their minds, so far as *they themselves* were concerned. They looked with jealous eyes upon the white hunter, and considered him as much of a robber as if they had a brand on every buffalo. It has been claimed by some authors that the Indians killed with more judgment and more care for the future than did the white man, but I fail to find any evidence that such was ever the fact. They all killed wastefully, wantonly, and always about five times as many head as were really necessary for food. It was always the same old story, whenever a gang of Indians needed meat a whole herd was slaughtered, the choicest portions of the finest animals were taken, and about 75 per cent. of the whole left to putrefy and fatten the wolves. And now, as we read of the appalling slaughter, one can scarcely repress the feeling of grim satisfaction that arises when we also read that many of the ex-slaughterers are almost starving for the millions of pounds of fat and juicy buffalo meat they wasted a few years ago. Verily, the buffalo is in a great measure avenged already. . . .[230]

It is absolutely certain that if the Indians had been uninfluenced by the white traders, or, in other words, had not been induced to take and prepare a large number of robes every year for the market, the species would have survived very much longer than it did. But the demand proved to be far greater than the supply. The Indians, of course, found it necesary to slaughter annually a great number of buffaloes for their own wants—for meat, robes, leather, teepees, etc. When it came to supplementing this necessary slaughter by an additional fifty thousand or more every year for marketable robes, it is no wonder that the improvident savages soon found, when too late, that the supply of buffaloes was not inexhaustible. *Naturally enough*,[231]

[230]Hornaday, "Extermination of the American Bison," 480-2. See above (chap. XVII, notes 90-1) for some of the details—recorded by himself—which doubtless fed the manifestly *un*repressed 'feeling of grim satisfaction'!

[231]The two words italicized (by myself) contain practically the only admission I can find in Hornaday's monograph that in any sense can be construed as palliation or excuse for the Indian.

they attributed their disappearance to the white man, who was therefore a robber, and a proper subject for the scalping-knife. Apparently it never occurred to the minds of the Sioux that they themselves were equally to blame; it was always *the paleface* who killed the buffaloes; and it was always *Sioux* buffaloes that they killed. The Sioux seemed to feel that they held a chattel mortgage on all the buffaloes north of the Platte, and it required more than one pitched battle to convince them otherwise. . . .[232]

Let it be remembered, therefore, that the American Indian is as much responsible for the extermination of our northern herd of bison as the American citizen. I have yet to learn of an instance wherein an Indian refrained from excessive slaughter of game through motives of economy, or care for the future, or prejudice against wastefulness. From all accounts, the quantity of game killed by an Indian has always been limited by two conditions only—lack of energy to kill more, or lack of more game to be killed. White men delight in the chase, and kill for the "sport" it yields, regardless of the effort involved. Indeed, to a genuine sportsman, nothing in hunting is "sport" which is not obtained at the cost of great labor. An Indian does not view the matter in that light, and when he has killed enough to supply his wants, he stops, because he sees no reason why he should exert himself any further. This has given rise to the statement, so often repeated, that the Indian only killed enough buffaloes to supply his wants. If an Indian ever attempted, or even showed any inclination, to husband the resources of nature in any way, and restrain wastefulness *on the part of Indians*, it would be gratifying to know of it.[233]

I do not contend that one has any particular right to demand sympathy *per se* from a scientist more than from others; unless it be that he supposedly possesses in greater degree that knowledge which should be the parent and well-spring of true sympathy. But I do insist that from such a class we are entitled to expect understanding, even if it be only of the coldly intellectual order. Apart from whatever may be gleaned from the two words italicized by myself, above, I find nothing to indicate that the critic had even the faintest glimmering of perception that Indian conduct might possibly be amenable to other mental standards than ours. In this relationship, I see two possible explanations only. Hornaday was either ignorant of this fundamental psychological principle; or, he was not ignorant of it, but disregarded such knowledge. Either alternative involves as its logical consequence a total unfitness to pronounce upon the question. The intellectually unconvincing and morally revolting language he permitted himself to use demonstrates this. In addition to his painful ineptitudes where a truly effective criticism must be based upon sympathy or insight; as mere examples of careful or candid citation of evidence which an 'ex-

[232]Hornaday, "Extermination of the American Bison," 490.
[233]*Ibid.*, 506. Italics Hornaday's.

haustive' historian should have seen—and much of which he actually saw and used and extols as authoritative—his more purely historical pronouncements leave much to be desired.

The writer's position should not be misunderstood here. This is in no sense an attempt to flog a dead horse by passing strictures upon a 'classic' which has become in course of time a mere landmark in the history of opinion. Hornaday's monograph is no such thing. By virtue of Seton's uncritical endorsement as late as 1929, Hornaday still stands as the virtually unimpaired and premier authority on the buffalo; wherein the historian carries the weight which most justly belongs—and in relation to this species, solely belongs—to the zoologist. In its relationship to the subject of our present chapter, the interaction of buffalo and Indian in the history of Western American civilization needs no labouring. The efforts of modern research in that department are in constant danger of being vitiated by the circumstance that the political or social historian, or even (in some phases) the anthropological or ethnological student, is compelled in matters affecting the buffalo to rely upon the 'authoritative' *dicta* of an obsolete monograph.[234] It is in the hope of remedying this condition that the present criticisms are advanced.

6.

It will scarcely be denied by any thoughtful reader, that even if he were not in possession of the mass of detailed evidence which has been presented under various heads in the foregoing chapters, the present data covering pounds, buffalo tongues, etc., would suffice to create a very strong impression in the mind of the truly immense numbers of the buffalo. The actual historical evidence extant leaves it impossible to doubt that these very practices themselves, if they did not actually thus arise—which is not inherently improbable—were confirmed and strengthened in their hold by a precisely similar feeling in the Indian mind, that the buffalo were so many as to be virtually inexhaustible. Who were those prescient Indians and half-breeds, 'nearly all of whom confidently predicted' the disappearance of the buffalo? And at a time when Catlin was still exhausting his vocabulary in the effort to describe the huge throngs; and when such men as De Smet, Parkman, Dodge, Lacombe, or McDougall, had barely (or not even) seen them! I have noted above,[235] forecasts of the impending

---

[234]The earliest dissent from Hornaday's conclusions known to me is not until 1933, in a specialized publication which many general historians might never see (*in extenso* above, chap. III, note 55).

[235]Above, notes 53-61.

disappearance of the buffalo from a number of thoughtful white observers, and a solitary relevant instance from a red one. Hornaday might have cited some specific examples of this, from one or two among the host of red prophets! It has hitherto been his own contention that the red men did *not* foresee the coming catastrophe.[236] In this at least he finds abundant historical support. A mass of testimony proves conclusively that the Indians at large did not judge of the probabilities of buffalo survival as a species in mass, pro or con, by the white man's criteria of vital statistics. More than one Indian tribe believed that the buffalo 'emerged each spring from the earth';[237] as Hornaday himself noted.[238] We have some highly interesting evidence concerning this, from both North and South. Apropos of this belief, Sir William Butler remarks:

Nor looking at the annual havoc, and seeing still in spite of all the dusky herds yet roaming over the treeless waste, can we marvel that the Red man should ascribe to agencies other than mortal the seemingly endless numbers of his favourite animal.

South-west from the Eagle Hills [that is, south of Battleford, Saskatchewan], far out in the prairie, there lies a lake whose waters never rest; day and night a ceaseless murmur breaks the silence of the spot.

"See," says the red man, "it is from under that lake that our buffalo comes. You say they are all gone; but look, they come again and again to

[236]"No wonder that the men of the West of those days, both white and red, thought it would be impossible to exterminate such a mighty multitude . . ." (Hornaday, "Extermination of the American Bison," 391; *circa* 1870).

"Like the Indian and many white men also, the buffalo seemed to feel that their number was so great that it could never be sensibly diminished . . ." (*ibid.*, 429).

"Although half a million buffaloes were killed [*i.e.* annually] by Indians, half-breeds, and whites, the natural increase was so very considerable as to make it seem that the evil day of extermination was yet far distant . . ." (*ibid.*, 466, *circa* 1870).

My friend, Rev. P. G. Sutton, was told by Mrs. Whitford, widow of the famous John Whitford, of Whitford, Alberta (see *Place-Names of Alberta*, 134; *Palliser Journals*, 48; McDougall, *Red River Rebellion*, 80), that the idea of such incredible hosts as the buffalo ever becoming extinct seemed utterly inconceivable. See below, note 249.

Similarly, Warburton Pike, 1889, *re* caribou: "If one remonstrates with the Indians at the waste, the ready answer comes: 'Our fathers did thus, and have taught us to do the same; they did not kill off the caribou, and after we are gone there will be plenty for our children' . . ." (*Barren Ground*, 51-2). See Appendix F, "Caribou."

For other instances of the same readiness to use both sides of the argument (the Indian 'stopped'—and also did *not* stop—'when he had enough') see above, notes 230, 233; also chap. III, note 167.

[237]Hughes, *Father Lacombe*, 243.
[238]Hornaday, "Extermination of the American Bison," 391.

us. We cannot kill them all—they are there under that lake. Do you hear the noise which never ceases? It is the buffalo fighting with each other far down under the ground, and striving to get out on the prairie—where else can they come from? . . ."[239]

Similarly, John McDougall writes, in this case of Jackfish Lake, in the north Saskatchewan country, 1873: "We rolled past in sight of the great springs where it is said, whole bands of buffalo have disappeared and again emerged in mysterious fashion. Such is tradition. . . ."[240]

Dodge also states the following, concerning the southern area:

Every Plains Indian firmly believed that the buffalo were produced in countless numbers in a country under the ground, that every spring the surplus swarmed like bees from a hive, out of great cave-like openings to this country, which were situated somewhere in the great 'Llano Estacado' or Staked Plain of Texas. One Indian has gravely and solemnly assured me that he has been at these caverns, and with his own eyes saw the buffalo coming out in countless throngs.[241] Others have told me that their fathers or uncles, or some other of the old men have been there. In 1879, Stone Calf assured me that he knew exactly where those caves were, though he had never seen them, that the Good God had provided this means for the constant supply of food for the Indian and that however recklessly the white men might slaughter, they could never exterminate them. When last

[239]Butler, *Wild North Land*, 62-3. This should have been Sounding Lake, Alberta, which lies in the direction indicated, but the legendary origin of that name is otherwise given (*Place-Names of Alberta*, 118).

[240]McDougall, *Western Trails*, 29. *Re* Canadian tribes, presumably, Jenness writes: ". . . the 'power' of the buffalo became a supernatural King-buffalo that lived in a mysterious buffalo-land, and yet was immanent in every single buffalo . . ." (*Indians of Canada*, 170). I have met with nothing else quite so definitely 'personifying' or crystallizing the buffalo *idea* in form; but I acknowledge freely that a sympathetic scholar like my friend Dr. Jenness is much more likely to penetrate to the inner realm of that conception than the more superficial traveller-witnesses who furnish most of my historical source-material. Cf. Jenness's whole chapter on "Religion and Mythology" (*ibid.*, 167-84); also his *Sarcee Indians*, 41-75. See too on those subjects, J. N. B. Hewitt, *Handbook of American Indians*, I, 964; Franz Boas, *ibid.*, II, 365. Kidd, on Blackfoot religion, "Blackfoot Ethnography," 174-92; likewise McClintock, *Old North Trail*, 167, 352. For Indian religious practices among Osages, Comanches, and at large, see Gregg, *Early Western Travels*, XX, 285, 340, 351. The latter include sun-worship; on which see also Castañeda, 'sun and water' in Hernando de Alvarado's "Report," and 'water worship,' in "Coronado to the Viceroy Mendoza" (*Journey of Coronado*, 93, 180, 243); cf. also A. J. Fynn, *American Indian*, 211-29. See also at large, De Smet, *Early Western Travels*, XXIX, 384, 394; Maclean, *Canadian Savage Folk*, 452; Chittenden, *American Fur Trade*, II, 815.

[241]Before we deride, compare Loyola, *circa* 1525. "It is difficult to relate without a pitying smile that, in the sacrifice of the mass, he saw transubstantiation take place, and that, as he stood praying on the steps of the church of St. Dominic, he saw the Trinity in Unity, and wept aloud with joy and wonder . . ." (Macaulay's *Essay on Von Ranke*; and see Von Ranke himself, *History of the Popes*, I, 144).

I saw him, the old man was beginning to waver in this belief, and feared the Bad God had shut up the openings, and that his people must starve. . . .[242]

Something similar is traceable in the language of Sitting Bull to the Joint Commissioners in the famous conference at Fort Walsh (southern Alberta), in October, 1877: 'God Almighty has always raised me buffalo to live on';[243] this, too, at a time when it had become plain enough even to some red men,[244] that the Almighty's purposes were in grave danger of frustration by human wickedness and greed. The Minatarees in 1833 asserted to Maximilian that "the bones of the buffalo in the prairie sometimes come to life again."[245] Likewise in Canada's so-called 'Rebellion' of 1885—principally an all-too-successful rebellion of the bureaucratic mind against the dictates of justice and common sense[246]—"the Indians believed the days of the whites were numbered and the buffalo would return. . . ."[247] This view is confirmed by independent testimony concerning that era;[248] and has been strenuously maintained by men perhaps yet living.[249]

If such beliefs could so tenaciously persist after what such men had themselves witnessed in the seventies and eighties, it is perfectly certain—entirely apart from the utter lack of any contrary evidence—that they were unlikely to have been superseded in the forties and fifties by any economic reasonings on supply and demand. It is possible that

[242]Dodge, *Our Wild Indians*, 286; cf. *ibid.*, 580. Dodge's attitude toward Indian beliefs is much more tolerant here than in his earlier work (*Plains of the Great West*, 1877; on which compare below, note 385). In addition to authorities cited in note 240, see also on Indian beliefs J. N. B. Hewitt, "Nanabozho," *Handbook of American Indians*, II, 19-23; Maclean, *Indians of Canada*, 108; *Encyclopaedia Britannica*, *s.v.* North American Indians; etc.

[243]Black, *History of Saskatchewan*, 186.

[244]Crowfoot, the Blackfoot chief, to Denny, 1876 (*The Law Marches West*, 99). On Crowfoot, see Maclean, *Canadian Savage Folk*, 371-81.

[245]*Early Western Travels*, XXIII, 376; cf. Edwin James, *ibid.*, XV, 63.

[246]See two early Westerners on this: General Sam Steele, *Forty Years in Canada*, 208-31; and some pungent remarks in Professor John Macoun's *Autobiography*, 134; see also Stanley, *Birth of Western Canada*, 243 *seq.*

[247]Hughes, *Father Lacombe*, 304.

[248]Dr. Edmond Melchior Eberts of Montreal informs me that this was the firm belief concerning buffalo among the older Assiniboines about Indian Head, Saskatchewan, *circa* 1883. Similar 'old-timer' opinion cited by Harwood Steele, *Winnipeg Evening Tribune*, August 21, 1937; see also 'Canada Cavalcade,' *Winnipeg Free Press*, September 11, 1937.

[249]Dr. E. A. Corbett (then of Alberta University) was told, 1933, by a grandson of an old Hudson's Bay Company man, that the disappearance of the Plains hosts was due neither to extermination by man ('an impossibility') nor to disease. 'Where had all the bones gone to?' The buffalo 'vanished into the earth whence they came'!

the complaints of the Siouan tribes in southern Minnesota, *circa* 1835,[250] and of the Sioux along the Platte to Frémont in 1842,[251] if we understood them aright, were actually querulous inquiries as to when these miracles might be expected to recur; much after the manner of Dodge's old friend, Stone Calf.

'Springing out of the earth' would be a not-inappropriate poetical description—our English Bible is full of such—of some of those wondrous reappearances after inscrutable absences which had baffled their wisest hunters, of which I have presented evidence in sober fact;[252] and perhaps even more emphatically, of some of those phenomena in the field, which occurred under the very eyes of the hunters, both red[253] and white.[254]

Precisely similar considerations apply to Hornaday's strictures upon the impounding customs of the Indians. When we contrast his futilities with McDougall's description, not only of the visible *modus operandi*, but of the hidden motivating forces behind it, we are more than ever impressed with the utter inadequacy of the ordinary traveller, let him be as observant as he may, whose ignorance of the speech, customs, or mentality of the strange folk leaves him without the key to under-

[250]Ponca and Sioux proper (Catlin, *Letters on the North American Indians,* I, 212; II, 131.

[251]Frémont, *Narrative,* 142 (above *in extenso,* chap. XIII, note 137).

[252]Above, chap. XX, at large.

[253]Maximilian, 1834: "The Mandans told us they had gone, some days before, to hunt buffaloes, and had driven a herd of them toward the mountains, where there is a good opportunity to use the bow and arrows; they had, therefore, pursued the animals rapidly, but, on reaching them, they found but a very few buffaloes, the others, as they affirmed, having sunk into the ground; they had, doubtless, taken refuge in the nearest ravines. They assigned, as the cause of this sudden disappearance of the buffaloes, that their party was headed by a man who, in the preceding year, had caused five Assiniboins, who had come to them as messengers of peace, to be killed, and that, on account of this unjust act, he was now always unsuccessful in hunting . . ." (*Early Western Travels,* XXIV, 70).

[254]Parkman, Arkansas River country, 1846: "When I began the chase, the prairie was almost tenantless; but a great multitude of buffalo had suddenly thronged upon it, and looking up, I saw within fifty rods a heavy dark column stretching to the right and left as far as I could see. . . . The column itself consisted almost entirely of cows and calves, but a great many old bulls were ranging about the prairie on its flank . . ." (*Oregon Trail,* 422); cf. *ibid.,* 93, for an equally spectacular disappearance, like Maximilian, above.

The explanation is no doubt, as Maximilian suggests, Western topography. Along the deep river-valleys, a galloping herd could vanish almost instantaneously into one of the deep tributary coulees or gullies; and appear with almost equal suddenness. Compare Seton's excellent sketch of a herd trooping slowly down one to water (*Life-Histories of Northern Animals,* I, 295; *Game Animals,* III, 684).

standing. The distant arm-chair critic—unless he be a Frazer or a Kroeber to begin with—is commonly infinitely worse. McDougall shows (in a passage entirely too long for quotation:[255] his writings are not particularly difficult of access) that Indian habits which white men are prone to condemn very readily along our own mental lines of reasoning, may require a totally different explanation. Along with certain forms of religious or semi-religious emotion[256]—commonly 'superstition' in the phraseology of the censor—there went on these occasions a species of half-occult influence over the animals; which, if it be capable of any rationalized explanation whatever, can apparently only be referred to the accumulated traditional experience derived from age-long study of and familiarity with buffalo. This influence resembles in this respect phenomena known to us all, wherein there is no perceptible trace of relationship along scientific channels of reasoning between supposed cause and alleged effect, and yet curious happenings almost make us think, despite ourselves, that 'there must be something in it.' It would scarcely be correct to say that all this is lost on Hornaday. There is no visible indication that it ever crossed his mind—even as a prelude to immediate rejection—that the clue to Indian habitual traits might possibly be discoverable in Indian psychology.[257] While McDougall's books are in my judgment of particular value, as demonstrating what long intimacy can reveal to one who was not in the 'technical' sense an anthropologist, they were of course subsequent to Hornaday's own essay. But there was abundance of testimony in his own time, which he could have utilized. Some of this he must have seen—and ignored. Such as I have been able to discover will now be laid before the reader.

The testimony concerning what may conveniently be termed 'occultism' in connection with the decoying or driving of herds, is not unanimous. Some consider it to be a mixture of occultism and skill.[258] Others ascribe it to skill alone, if one may judge from their omission of other possible influences.[259] Similar beliefs prevail among the aborigines in other portions of the Canadian Northland in reference to

[255]McDougall, *Saddle, Sled, and Snowshoe,* 271-82.
[256]See authorities cited above, note 240.
[257]The Neutrals (of Ontario) ". . . had the strange custom, unknown elsewhere in Canada, of killing every animal they encountered, whether or not they needed it for food, lest it should carry a warning to other animals of its kind, and keep them out of reach when food was needed . . ." (Jenness, *Indians of Canada,* 300); Hewitt, "Neutrals," *Handbook of American Indians,* II, 60-3.
[258]See below, Appendix AA.
[259]*Ibid.*

other species;[260] and indeed the application of occult powers to the chase is merely a fairly logical extension of the scope of such forces, whose workings in other spheres seem to be curiously well attested in various localities.[261] Precisely as with the surround,[262] the total destruction of herds in the pounds, which Hornaday and others wrathfully stigmatize as waste, is really a resultant phase of the supernatural process of reasoning. They were destroyed, lest if they escaped they might warn other herds of the dangers of the pound.[263] And even apart from such potent arguments in favour of total destruction, if once the existence of impounding be established, there are reasons which might prevent the sternest of economists from slaughtering no more at once than his necessities dictated. No man who has ever faced the task will question whether it be easier to handle an entire herd or a few separated individuals thereof! As Dr. Hector pointed out in his account of the afore-mentioned pound near Vermilion, all the buffalo in the pound *had* to be killed in order to make it practicable or safe to enter to secure the meat.[264] In the case of jumping-pounds, the animals killed themselves, or were so maimed as to make slaughter easy; but it would

[260]Warburton Pike, 1889, on the superstitions clinging around the hunting of the musk-ox among the Yellow-Knives: 'They are said to understand every word of the Yellow-Knife language'; and a hunt failed 'because somebody called across the river in French' (*Barren Ground*, 183).

E. T. Seton: "I had offended Chief Snuff by not calling and consulting with him; he now gave it out that I was here to take out live Musk-Ox, which meant that all the rest would follow to seek their lost relatives . . ." (*Arctic Prairies*, 144).

David Thompson, when in the caribou country, was thought from his astronomical observations to know 'where the deer are' (*Narrative*, 104).

[261]On Indian occultisms at large: A Montagnais soothsayer's prediction fulfilled, 1637, 1640, etc. (*Jesuit Relations*, Le Jeune, XII, 229; XIV, 63; XX, 263). An Indian foretelling his own death (Morice, *Northern Interior of British Columbia*, Appendix E, 352). The Arkansas tribes, 1723 (Diron D'Artaguiette, in Mereness (ed.), *Colonial Travels*, 58). The Nipigon country, 1785, and the 'Sauteux,' 1800 (Duncan Cameron, Peter Grant, in Masson, *Les Bourgeois de la Compagnie du Nord-Ouest*, II, 264, 323). Arikara, 1830-1840 (Maximilian, *Early Western Travels*, XXIII, 393; De Smet, *ibid.*, XXVII, 80). Parkman, 1846 (*Oregon Trail*, 279). Southesk, 1859 (*Travels*, 80). Denny (an eye-witness) (Denny MS., 42, 91-5). Authenticated instances of Indian clairvoyance, in Seton (*Arctic Prairies*, 57-9); also Maclean (*Indians of Canada*, 94-104); Washington Matthews, "Magic," *Handbook of American Indians*, I, 783; *Encyclopaedia Britannica*, *s.v.* North American Indians, etc.

[262]Above, note 170 *seq.*

[263]McDougall, *Saddle, Sled, and Snowshoe*, 282; Coues (ed.), *Henry-Thompson Journals*, I, 336 (*in extenso* above, note 176).

[264]*Palliser Journals*, 70-1; see also Macoun on this phase: *Manitoba*, etc., 344; Audubon and Bachman, *American Quadrupeds*, II, 49-50.

have been virtually impossible either to divide a small herd in the open, or to bring them intact to the verge of the pound and then endeavour to secure some, without all escaping.

It is a curious fact that very little attempt has been made to ascertain the origin of the peculiar methods adopted by the buffalo decoy. The only suggestion known to me occurs in a work which it is difficult to classify, but which its author insists is not fiction. In this, the 'bringer-in' is covered with a buffalo-robe and squats 'on all fours' in the generally accepted fashion. He imitates the frenzied tactics of a cow that has lost her calf, edging meanwhile toward the direction of the pound. His behaviour first attracts and then distracts the herd; which finally follows him, ultimately to the pound, after the manner described by McDougall and others. The suggestion is provocative, and seems inherently very probable.[265] The same author is of opinion that the actual stampedes which from time to time arose spontaneously among buffalo herds—and which bore a close generic resemblance to the impounding frenzy—may have originated in the contagious 'temporary insanity' of some cow who really had lost her calf, perhaps by drowning or by wolves. The evidence for maternal affection, although contradictory, does not preclude this;[266] and stampedes were often so apparently inexplicable that such may have been the case.[267]

7.

The question may be asked whether the reasons commonly given for the fairly general custom of total extirpation in impounding practices may not have masked some more rationalistic origin. Such origins tend to extend themselves beyond the bounds of the earlier purposes; which are superseded by the 'higher' sanctions perhaps at first designed merely to enforce and strengthen them. It is, of course, well known that quarrels over buffalo have been the cause of many tribal feuds and terrible battles amongst Indians. I have no positive evidence to offer; but it seems at least not impossible that among warlike folk, some of those 'wasteful' exploits, destroying to the last head herds of which they themselves could only consume a portion (or of which at

[265]James Willard Schultz, *Apauk, Caller of Buffalo*, 1916.
[266]Above, chap. VII, notes 123-36.
[267]Buffalo Jones says they would stampede on the slightest provocation; sometimes "by the scent from a single hunter even four miles away [though how this could be identified at that distance as the actual cause passes understanding!] . . . frequently without any assignable cause . . ." (*Buffalo Jones' Forty Years*, 230-46).

a given moment, they perhaps were in no need whatever)[268] may have had their origin in totally different incentives. Even in historical times, their partially true explanation may have lain in 'military reasons,' of which during two generations the contemporary world has not lacked examples. Historical students are familiar with those broad belts of 'scorched earth' devastation which the Scots so often strewed across the Lowlands when an English invasion was anticipated; and whose modern counterpart has been witnessed in the German invasion of Russia in our own day. The wide geographical range over which these buffalo-engendered rivalries and conflicts have been recorded is practically co-extensive with the prevalence of 'wastefulness.' Coronado's party in 1541 noted that the 'Querechos' and the 'Teyas,' both of them buffalo tribes, were enemies.[269] They (or other Southwestern tribes) also practised impounding; in all probability with a similar 'wastefulness' to that of the northern folk, although this is not specifically stated.[270]

In the Lower Mississippi territory, 1687, according to Father Zenobius Membre, "the people on one shore are generally enemies of those on the other. . . ."[271] Their wars are directly ascribed by Father Hennepin to the buffalo as the exciting cause; although it is fairly certain that the hunts were the cause, rather than the effect, of the war. Hennepin says: "The Wild Bulls are grown somewhat scarce since the Illinois have been at War with their Neighbours, for now all Parties are continually Hunting of them. . . ."[272]

La Salle himself is quoted as follows: "The Indians do not hunt in this region, which is debatable ground between five or six nations who are at war, and, being afraid of each other, do not venture into these parts except to surprise each other, and always with the greatest precaution and all possible secrecy. . . ."[273]

[268]M. S. Garretson speaks of mange as 'the most common disease' of the species; and says the Indians killed buffalo afflicted with it, down to the last animal (American Bison, 75). This is the only allusion I have found to such a practice. See Appendix J, "Buffalo and Disease."

[269]So, Castañeda, "Relacion del Suceso," "Coronado to Charles V" (Journey of Coronado, 111, 210, 215).

[270]The chronicle translated in Purchas his Pilgrimes (XVIII, 78) has the following: ". . . when they had found a great multitude of these oxen, and would compasse them about and force them into certain inclosures or toiles, their enterprize prevailed but a little; they are so wild and so swift . . . they declared the wildnesse and innumerable number of these Oxen. . . ."

[271]Journeys of La Salle, I, 141.

[272]Hennepin, New Discovery, II, 627.

[273]Parkman, La Salle, 194. This may perhaps only signify that no hunting was going on there then. Edwin James writes, however (Canadian River, 1820):

William Bartram, the naturalist, noticed among the partly agriculturist tribes of the Southeastern States territory, 1773, that in addition to hunting-ground disputes, wars were caused partly by the necessity for newer and richer areas for plantations.[274]

In the northern regions, Alexander Henry the elder states: "The cause of the perpetual war carried on between these two nations [Chippewa and Sioux] is this, that both claim, as their exclusive hunting-ground, the tract of country which lies between them. . . ."[275]

A modern scholar states that the long enmity between the Cheyennes and the Assiniboine is said to have originated in a quarrel about a herd of buffalo which both were trying to surround.[276] We have seen, above, the case of the sedentary Mandans in 1738, who were afraid to go far from their villages because of those 'Pananas and Pananis.'[277] Father Marquette records a precisely similar situation in the Illinois Country about 1670; where apparently buffalo were likewise the *casus belli*. "These people are very obliging and liberal with what they have; but they are wretchedly provided with food, for they dare not go and hunt wild cattle, on account of their Enemies. . . ."[278]

On the Upper Missouri plains, this factor in tribal warfare was well recognized. It has been recorded by Lewis and Clark's expedition,[279] the Astorians,[280] and Father De Smet;[281] in addition to historians and

---

"Notwithstanding the astonishing numbers of bison, deer, antelopes, and other animals, the country is less strewed with bones than almost any we have seen; affording an evidence that it is not a favourite hunting ground of any tribe of Indians. The animals also appear wholly unaccustomed to the sight of man . . ." (*Early Western Travels*, XVI, 140). As against this view, Coues says 'good buffalo country . . . bad Indian country . . .' (*Expeditions of Pike*, II, 435). Chittenden says of the Judith Basin, upper Missouri River, that it was always one of the most popular regions of the entire West for buffalo; and the scene of many wars over hunting-grounds (*American Fur Trade*, II, 854). Cf. the 'Bayou Salade' (*ibid.*, II, 750; *Early Western Travels*, XXVIII, 209, 266; *in extenso* above, chap. XI, note 39).

[274]Bartram, *Travels*, 314.

[275]Henry, *Travels, 1760-1776*, 197. The Sioux were driven by the Chippewa (Ojibwa) from the forest region of South Minnesota out on to the plains (*Handbook of American Indians*, I, 277; II, 577). Peter Grant, *circa* 1790, on Sioux 'emigrating' westward from the 'Sauteaux' (Ojibwa) country (Masson, *Les Bourgeois de la Compagnie du Nord-Ouest*, II, 346).

[276]Grinnell, *Fighting Cheyennes*, 5. Buffalo are also said to have been the cause of the separation of the Manitari (Hidatsa) from the Crows (Maximilian, *Early Western Travels*, XXIII, 367).

[277]Above, notes 10, 176.

[278]*Jesuit Relations*, LIX, 157.

[279]*Lewis and Clark Journals*, I, 218, 220.

[280]Irving, *Astoria*, 231-3.

[281]*Life of De Smet*, I, 360; II, 533; IV, 1375.

plainsmen since their day.[282] I have already alluded to the retaliatory expeditions of the Blackfoot that the Flatheads, on either side of the Rocky Mountains.[283] Concerning these, an early traveller writes: "The only cause assigned by the natives of whom I write, for their perpetual warfare, is their love of buffalo. . . ."[284] Another observer says of the Nez Perces and Snakes (or Shoshone) about the same time: "Their occupations are war and buffalo hunting. . . ."[285] D. W. Harmon notes among the general causes of Indian wars: ". . . sometimes the members of one tribe have hunted on the lands of another. . . ."[286]

Among the Canadian Crees and Blackfoot, buffalo were the cause of numerous outbreaks; and probably engendered much of the hatred which frequently expressed itself in bloody affrays where the buffalo were not the immediate bone of contention. Edmonton and its neighbourhood were the scene of fearful wars between them, *circa* 1807-8;[287] and one of the most famous of its old-timers says that "many a frightful massacre took place under the shadow of its walls. . . ."[288] Paul Kane mentions fighting between the two tribes—or bands of them—in the Carlton country in the summer of 1848:[289] and a number of residents and historians have recorded similar occurrences down to much later dates.[290]

They were, of course, frequently at peace; and in some instances the exigencies of buffalo-hunting assisted to bring this about. In the eighteen-forties Rundle evidently considered the fact of sufficient moment to be noted in his *Journal*.[291] The winter of 1861-62 was so hard, we are told ". . . that the Indians and some traders had been in a state of semi-starvation for months. The Crees and the Blackfeet

---

[282]Dodge, *Our Wild Indians*, 380; Chittenden, *American Fur Trade*, II, 854.
[283]See above, chap. XI, notes 9, 43-4.
[284]Ross Cox, *Columbia River*, I, 216-19; II, 133.
[285]Alexander Ross (of Red River), *Early Western Travels*, VII, 215.
[286]*Harmon's Journal*, 309.
[287]Burpee, *Search for the Western Sea*, 545; Davidson, *North West Company*, 99. 'Old' (Lower) Fort Augustus, 20 miles down the Saskatchewan, was burnt by the Blackfoot, 1807, and not rebuilt, the post moving to the present Edmonton. See *Place-Names of Alberta*, 46; Thompson, *Narrative*, 432; and particularly Morton, *History of the Canadian West*, 463, 484, 511, 611-30, etc.
[288]McDougall, *Saddle, Sled, and Snowshoe*, 12.
[289]Kane, *Wanderings of an Artist* (Radisson Society ed.), 303, 305.
[290]For Cree and Blackfoot, 1866-74, see McDougall, *Red River Rebellion*, 118; *Western Trails*, 172; Hughes, *Father Lacombe*, 175 *seq.*; Cowie, *Company of Adventurers*, 239, 304, 314; General Sam Steele, *Forty Years in Canada*, 56, 57, 71, 76-80, 116, 137, 276; C. M. MacInnes, *In the Shadow of the Rockies*, 96-9; etc. A large party of Blackfoot slain by Crees, 1874 (Denny MS., 134). See also John Hawkes, *Saskatchewan and her People*, I, 149-55.
[291]*Rundle's Journal*, February 26, 1841.

made peace because they needed all their energies for the hunt. Fort Edmonton, in spite of its traditional stores, knew the nip of want toward the end of the winter. . . ."[292]

The peace was either very local or of short duration; for Milton and Cheadle remark at Fort Pitt (April 20, 1863): "Peace had just been concluded between the Crees and the Blackfoot; large camps of both nations were within a day or two's journey of the Fort . . . all anxious to avail themselves of the rare occasion of a peace, generally only of very short duration. . . ."[293]

The peace in this instance was probably to enable the Blackfeet to trade at Fort Pitt or other northern posts.[294] In the winter of 1864-65, McDougall's friend, the Cree Chief Masképetoon,[295] again made peace with the Blackfoot, who were following the buffalo northward, under circumstances like those of 1861-62, except that there is no mention of scarcity.[296] Later in the year hostilities were evidently resumed; for Father Lacombe, a peaceful visitor in the Cree camp on the Battle River, was very nearly slain in a night attack by the Blackfoot, to the utter consternation of the assailants on learning the news.[297] Two years later, in 1867, a historic peace was made, which is commemorated in a well-known Alberta place-name, Peace Hills, near Wetaskiwin, on the Battle River. At this place, McDougall tells us ". . . a camp of Crees

[292]Hughes, *Father Lacombe*, 89-90. For the 'traditional stores,' see below, Appendix M.

[293]Milton and Cheadle, *North-West Passage*, 170.

[294]*Ibid.*, 171.

[295]A famous character; then an old man, for Maximilian met him on the Missouri as a chief in 1833 (*Early Western Travels*, XXIII, 13). His name signified in Cree 'Crooked Arm,' from a hunting injury; and he is the 'Bras Croche' of Simpson's *Journey Around the World*, I, 126 (1841). During the same era, Rundle (*Journal, passim*) and Paul Kane (*Wanderings of an Artist*, orig. ed., 1859, 392-4) met him. He had great influence among the older Blackfoot, having accepted Christianity and forgiven his father's (Blackfoot) murderer. See McDougall, *Saddle, Sled, and Snowshoe*, 193-206, 237 *seq.*

[296]*Ibid.*, 237-70. Note 'coming *northward*' at this season; and cf. chap. XX, notes 206 *seq.*

[297]Hughes, *Father Lacombe*, 114-22; cf. McDougall, *Saddle, Sled, and Snowshoe*, 129, 191. The Battle River was a famous frontier; and is thought by Dr. Elliott Coues to have its name, not from any one fight (as apparently *Place-Names of Alberta*, 16); but from the frequency of such (Coues (ed.), *Henry-Thompson Journals*, II, 499). 'Red River' also, possibly of the same origin from its bloody record (*ibid.*, I, 45). His earlier note, however (*Expeditions of Pike*, II, 704) on the various 'Reds' and *Colorados* of the Southwest, derives them more probably from sound, alliteration, red soils, red colour at sunset (camping-time, when such matters attract attention). On red earths, and Vermilion Rivers, etc., see further his *Henry-Thompson Journals*, II, 563, 565. See also below, Appendix CC, "Night Attacks in Indian Warfare."

and a party of Blackfeet, in running buffalo, ran into one another, and the mutual surprise and the need of the Blackfeet to move on into Edmonton for trade purposes caused them to make a temporary peace. . . ."[298]

McDougall has also recorded that it was owing to the Crees and Blackfoot 'having been forced into proximity by the movements of the buffalo' that his old friend Masképetoon was murdered by the latter in March, 1869,[299] an event that produced the most terrible consequences in the years immediately following, and indeed until the coming of the Mounted Police in 1874.

It cannot be disputed that in the mass of evidence which has been presented in the foregoing pages we may perceive two entirely distinct and opposing factors working in the 'buffalo Indian' mentality. There is first the belief in the inextinguishable plenty of the buffalo; a conception expressing itself in various forms of 'wastefulness.' Co-existent with this is a readiness to fight to the death in many instances—and perhaps even more remarkable, a willingness in the face of these inveterate enmities to make peace[300] rather than that the precious herd should be lost to them in their need. I cannot see what other possible conclusion can be drawn from the latter of these truths than that which has already been established so abundantly by various classes of evidence—the utterly irregular character of the buffalo movements. It is obvious that those 'broad territorial limits' which are supposedly fatal to the argument for the nomadic character of the 'buffalo' tribes, would render any theory of tribal war on economic grounds quite untenable; were it not that the buffalo wanderings were characterized by a complete irregularity, rendering such boundaries valueless and essentially meaningless.

8.

Although Hornaday almost triumphantly proclaims his failure to find any evidence for frugality or care for the future among Indians, it none the less exists; furnishing considerable support to the conclusions presented above. It is, of course, open to any critic who may

---

[298]McDougall, *Western Trails*, 91, 220; *Wetaskiwin* = 'having peace' (*ibid.*); also *Place-Names of Alberta*, 99, 133, where the date is given. 'Peace' River has a similar origin (*ibid.*, 100). The Northern (*i.e.* Canadian) Blackfoot were compelled to come north to trade, as they had themselves broken up the trading posts in their own territory along the South Saskatchewan (or Bow) River.

[299]McDougall, *Red River Rebellion*, 50 *seq.*

[300]See Parkman, on a similar scarcity, for the time being, preventing a projected inter-tribal war from breaking out in the Sioux country, in the summer of 1846 (*Oregon Trail*, 159, 201, 203).

so desire, to urge that much of this evidence is itself merely contrary opinion. While this is partly true, one insuperable objection remains. This testimony comes from the same class of first-hand witnesses from whom our only really authentic knowledge of the wild buffalo is derived; men whose knowledge of Indians also, whether in Hornaday's own time or long before, was unquestionably far superior to his; and many of whom he himself cites readily, when they happen to support his own contentions. I have noted above, Dodge's remarks on 'exceptionally improvident' tribes as logically implying a degree of providence in some others, if not as a practice of fairly wide extent.

In what is perhaps the very earliest relation we possess concerning buffalo in their central northern (United States or Canadian) habitat immediately west of the Great Lakes, although the precise locality and even the identity of the species mentioned in this passage are uncertain, Pierre Esprit Radisson, apparently describing the 'fourth journey' of Groseilliers and himself, observes in his *Journal*: "This place hath a great store of Cows. . . . The wild men [*sauvages*] kill not except for necessary use. . . ."[301] For our present purpose, the identity of the 'cows' is immaterial. The significant factor is that the Indians are stated to have been careful in their use of them.

Father Hennepin, not long afterwards, seems to imply the same: "These Bulls being very convenient for the Subsistence of the Savages, they take care not to Scare them from their Country; and they pursue only those whom they have wounded with their arrows. But these Creatures multiply in such a manner, that notwithstanding the great Numbers they kill every Year, they are as numerous as ever. . . ."[302]

Father Dablon, citing Marquette in support, stated also (perhaps because of this carefulness): "The wild cattle never flee. . . ."[303] A century and a half later, Edwin James, referring to the more southerly of the plains buffalo tribes (1820), says expressly: "Every eatable part of the animal is carried to the camp and preserved, excepting the feet and the head. . . ."[304] Thirty years later, R. B. Marcy says of the buffalo in the same territory: "Their only enemy then was the Indian, who supplied himself with food and clothing from the immense herds around his door; but would have looked upon it as sacrilege to destroy more than barely sufficient to supply the wants of his family. . . ."[305]

[301]See above, chap. XII, notes 44-8, for a discussion of the problems arising from this rather vague reference.

[302]Hennepin, *New Discovery*, I, 149.

[303]*Jesuit Relations*, LVIII, 99.

[304]Long, *Early Western Travels*, XIV, 301.

[305]Marcy, *Exploration of Red River*, 104.

Dodge testifies very similarly: "During the spring and summer months the buffalo were but little disturbed by the Indians. Enough were killed to enable all to gorge themselves at will, but this was done quietly by crawling or stalking. The greatest care was taken not to alarm and drive the herds away from the vicinity of the camp and villages. . . ."[306]

The note of contempt in the foregoing ('gorging themselves') makes its favourable testimony the more unequivocal. He remarks elsewhere: "Even when the buffalo were plentiful, they were carefully protected by the Middle Plains tribes . . ." (that is, Cheyennes and Arapahoes; and perhaps also Kiowas and Comanches).[307]

A somewhat later Canadian plainsman states that the Sioux were more provident than the Cree, Saulteaux, or even their own kindred, the Assiniboine.[308]

A modern student of the red men writes also: "In no other instance in history has a race of wild animals been wiped out in so short a period as the buffalo on our western plains. In a dozen or fifteen years, millions had been destroyed, not by the Indian, for he was always a conscientious economist of food supply, and he killed merely to provide for the wants of his camp. . . ."[309]

Hornaday himself has quoted the following contemporary account from a Middle-Western journalist. This was cited by him for the express purpose of enabling a later generation to form some idea of the situation as it appeared to observant critics at the time; and was given without any suggestion of dissent or disapproval: "To the credit of the Indians it can be said that they killed no more than they could save the meat from. . . ."[310] We shall later note that similar opinions (cited also by Hornaday) were expressed in Congress; and again quoted by him precisely because of his manifest endorsement of their sentiments.[311]

The above may, I repeat, be taken as mere *ex parte* utterances, coming in some instances from writers already committed to the Indian-apologetic side. It will therefore be entirely pertinent to give

---

[306]Dodge, *Our Wild Indians,* 287; so also Ross, *Fur Hunters,* II, 126 (1855).

[307]Dodge, *Our Wild Indians,* 576.

[308]Cowie, *Company of Adventurers,* 188 (*circa* 1867).

[309]Byrne, *The Red Men's Last Stand,* 205.

[310]*Sioux City Journal* (Iowa), no date, May, 1881; quoted by Hornaday, "Extermination of the American Bison," 503. Given in full above, chap. XVI, note 36. It is uncertain if it be meant here as a general habit at all times, or only *circa* 1880.

[311]Hornaday, "Extermination of the American Bison," 513-21. See below, Appendix H, "Buffalo, Indian, and Legislation."

certain individual examples of this attitude of mind in Indians and their kin; the constituent material out of which tribal custom must be built. Our very earliest English-born witness on the far Western plains, 1754, notes Indian moderation in killing beaver—"only ten . . . when I am certain they might have killed 200. . . ."[312] We may compare Parkman's guide and friend, Henry Chatillon, who was apparently a half-breed: "Henry knew all their peculiarities, he had studied them as a scholar studies his books. . . . Nothing excited his indignation so much as any wanton destruction committed among the cows, and in his view shooting a calf was a cardinal sin. . . ."[313] Father De Smet records a similar magnanimity in an Assiniboine in the Missouri River territory, 1851.[314] Milton and Cheadle (whose general views are those of Hornaday) mention another instance of a half-breed, in 1862.[315] There is also McDougall's friend, the Stoney (that is, Assiniboine) chief, Cheneka; a well-known character, whose name has been perpetuated in Western Canada, as it deserved to be; who "never killed more than five or six at a time. . . ."[316] Ernest Thompson Seton likewise refers to a Northern Indian, *circa* 1907;[317] in a region where exactly a century earlier W. F. Wentzel and George Keith were agreed concerning the care of the Beaver Indians in the economical use of food.[318] These people were formerly buffalo-hunters.[319] I can see no good reason for supposing these to exhaust the list; but judging from his general tone, I doubt whether even these few would have 'gratified' our censor overmuch.

Although Hornaday stigmatizes the Indians as "too lazy and shiftless to cure much meat,"[320] historical evidence, based upon the reports or boastings of men who were no lovers of Indians, tells a very

[312]"Henday's Journal," ed. Burpee, 340. There were then no fur-posts in the West, clamouring for beaver. Compare this with the white hunters, Radisson and Groseilliers, and Agnes Laut's famous '600,000' beaver!—no misprint, for it is repeated several times with calculations on its proceeds (*Conquest of the Great Northwest*, I, 101-7. According to Arthur Dobbs, 1744, 100 beaver-skins = one canoe-load; about correct, thinks Tyrrell (Hearne. *Journey*, 247). Captain John Smith in Virginia, 1607, waxed enthusiastic over '1100 bever skinnes'; and 'neere 20,000' in six years was prodigious (*Purchas his Pilgrimes*, XIX, 297-311).

[313]Parkman, *Oregon Trail*, 425.

[314]*Life of De Smet*, II, 658.

[315]*North-West Passage*, 18.

[316]McDougall, *Western Trails*, 237; see also Morris, *Treaties with the Indians of Manitoba*, 372. Cheneka or 'Chiniki,' on the Bow River (*Place-Names of Alberta*, 32, 33).

[317]Seton, *Arctic Prairies*, 134.

[318]Masson, *Les Bourgeois de la Compagnie du Nord-Ouest*, I, 89; II, 68-70.

[319]*Harmon's Journal*, 149; cf. below, Appendix A, "Buffalo Synonymy."

[320]Hornaday, "Extermination of the American Bison," 499.

different tale.[321] Furthermore, he himself says elsewhere: "The Indians formerly cured great quantities of buffalo meat . . . in summer . . . for use in winter. . . ."[322] "The 'great fall hunt' was a regular event with practically all the Indian tribes living within striking distance of the buffalo. In the course of this great numbers of buffalo were killed, great quantities of meat dried and made into pemmican, and all the skins were tanned in various ways to suit the many purposes they were called upon to serve. . . ."[323]

Many tribes also developed customary laws against individual hunting; from some of whom, it has been suggested, the organized Red River Hunt borrowed the idea.[324] Hornaday has himself mentioned the existence of such laws among the Omahas[325]—no particularly advanced tribe, for a careful observer describes them in 1833 as "the most indolent, dull, unintellectual, and cowardly of the Missouri Indians. . . ."[326] These hunting regulations were enforced by 'soldiers,' who are recorded in a number of tribes.[327] These facts must surely point, in part at least, to a fairly general recognition of a sense of

[321]For buffalo meat destroyed by U.S. troops, see the following: In a Sioux camp of 'not less than 400 lodges,' 400,000 or 500,000 lbs. September 1863 (Dodge, *Our Wild Indians*, 476). Sand Creek, before the massacre by Chivington, November 27, 1864 (Taylor, *Frontier Life*, 53; Grinnell, *Fighting Cheyennes*, 133). Powder River, 1865—General Connor's 'mission of annihilation' (*ibid.*, 195-206; Hebard and Brininstool, *Bozeman Trail*, I, 256). Summit Springs. Upper Republican River, 1867 (Grinnell, *Fighting Cheyennes*, 307). General George A. Custer, Black Kettle's band (?), 1868 (Taylor, *Frontier Life*, 160; Byrne, *Red Men's Last Stand*, 63). Cheyennes, 1876 (Grinnell, *Fighting Cheyennes*, 346, 353, 368). 'Two Moon's band' of Sioux and Cheyenne, 1877 (*ibid.*, 379, 380). The 'incredible quantities' at the Arapaho camp, Arkansas River, 1846, whether voluntarily wasted or abandoned perforce, at least prove the mass that had originally been stored up by them (Parkman, *Oregon Trail*, 395).

[322]Hornaday, "Extermination of the American Bison," 449; cf. Grinnell, *Fighting Cheyennes*, 346.

[323]Hornaday, "Extermination of the American Bison," 477; cf. Dodge on this, *Our Wild Indians*, 287.

[324]See above, chap. XIV, note 34.

[325]Hornaday, "Extermination of the American Bison," 477.

[326]Maximilian, *Early Western Travels*, XXII, 276.

[327]See on this, among the Cree and Assiniboine, 1776: Henry, *Travels, 1760-1776*, 282, 288, 309; Piegans, 1800: Thompson, *Narrative*, 358; Mandans and 'Minatarees,' 1833: Maximilian, *Early Western Travels*, XXIII, 293; Cheyennes, 1850-60: Dodge, *Plains of the Great West*, 266, 277, 353, also his *Our Wild Indians*, 476; Saulteaux, 1876: Morris, *Treaties with the Indians of Manitoba*, 82; Omahas: Hornaday, "Extermination of the American Bison," 477. Remarks on Plains tribes in general: Chittenden, *American Fur Trade*, II, 812.

On 'soldier' police societies, see also Fletcher, *Handbook of American Indians*, II, 614; Jenness, *Indians of Canada*, 128, 314; and for Blackfoot, Kidd, "Blackfoot Ethnography," 38, 142.

uncertainty in the supply; a condition which we have seen is abundantly substantiated by historical evidence.[328]

9.

There is another particularly well authenticated trait in the Indian character at large which, if no other evidence of any description remained, would virtually suffice of itself to establish to the satisfaction of discerning critics, the presence, in a necessary degree of frequency and force, of those seasons of privation which alone could have developed it so noticeably in the Indian nature. I allude to the almost universal Indian capacity for starving; which was sometimes found to an amazing extent. The Indian might be described as one of the champion fasters of the human race.

The fact that this characteristic was noted from the very earliest era of historical contact with American aboriginal life, and in the buffalo range[329] as well as in practically every other portion of the North American continent, effectually precludes any argument which would except the buffalo Indians from the sphere and action of its workings. Nor can it be explained on the ground that in the Plains tribes it was an inheritance from a former less-favoured environment. This is doubtless true enough. But it must be remembered that our earliest witnesses belonged to an age when the researches of anthropological science had not yet begun; and were in many instances men of a type to whom in any age its very existence as a branch of knowledge would be utterly unknown. Such men could by no conceivable possibility have suspected the presence in their Indian companions of a latent capacity for enduring starvation, as an inherited trait, had they not witnessed it in actual operation.

The younger Henry somewhat cynically remarks concerning the Piegans, *circa* 1810: "They are seldom entirely out of food, for they kept a stock of dried provisions on hand for emergencies, as buffalo sometimes disappear, and it may be several days before they can get a fresh supply. When they are reduced to dried provisions, they call it starving. . . ."[330]

In whatever degree this may apply as a general truth, it in no way invalidates the argument concerning starvation. The development of

---

[328]Above, chap. XX, "Irregular Migration," see also below, Appendix DD.
[329]Cabeza de Vaca, *circa* 1530: "They are very well able to endure hunger, thirst, and cold, as they who are more acquainted therewith then any other . . ." (*Purchas his Pilgrimes,* XVII, 493).
[330]Coues (ed.), *Henry-Thompson Journals,* II, 725.

the practice of drying meat, and its exercise at that early era in such a locality as the Piegan tribal territory, are proofs in themselves of the irregularity of the buffalo supply. They are, in fact, as conclusive as literal starvation itself; and they furnish also an interesting sidelight on Indian 'improvidence.'

We are not, however, confined to inference, even of the most logical order. The prevalence of cannibalism among 'most,'[331] or 'all Indians formerly,'[332] points clearly to certain conclusions. It is of course well known that cannibalism as a rite was practised on prisoners of war by certain of the Eastern tribes, notably by the Iroquois confederacy.[333] Reasoning *a priori*, it might have been expected that in regions where the immense hosts of the buffalo did not penetrate, while cannibalism might exist as a rite, like anywhere else; there only would it be found as a last desperate resource in times of famine.[334] Whereas in the typical buffalo plains habitat, whether practised as a rite or not, it would never be seen as a mere expedient in distress, since in that land of plenty it would clearly be needless. Curiously enough, the actual evidence by no means supports such reasoning. In the West, occasional references to cannibalism appear only to indicate a final resort in the madness of hunger.[335] Among the Eastern tribes, it is recorded both as a rite,[336] and as an occasional necessity;[337] and among the Northwestern forest peoples, in the latter usage only.[338]

These relations concerning not only scarcity *per se*, but scarcity so severe and prolonged as to exhibit both the stoical capacity for endurance and also the descent to cannibalism when endurance failed, are the more remarkable, since they come to us from the self-same observers to whom we owe much of our knowledge of the Indian propensity towards what we term gluttony, in some cases.

Among the Eastern tribes, these 'gluttonous' feasts were sometimes of a semi-religious character, where everything must be consumed (*festins à tout manger*[339]), although even among the Eastern and

---

[331]Parkman, *Pioneers of France in the New World*, 367.

[332]Thomas Forsyth's description, *circa* 1800 (in Blair, *Indian Tribes*, II, 225).

[333]Father Le Jeune, 1637-40 (*Jesuit Relations*, XII, 255; XVI, 81; XVII, 75, 99; XIX, 81; etc.); also A. Hrdlička, "Cannibalism," *Handbook of American Indians*, I, 200; *Encyclopaedia Britannica*, *s.v.* North American Indians.

[334]See Appendix EE, "Indian Cannibalism."

[335]*Ibid.*   [336]*Ibid.*   [337]*Ibid.*   [338]*Ibid.*

[339]See Laut's account of Radisson's stratagem on the Iroquois, 1657, when he overpowered them either by repletion or by drugs (*Pathfinders of the West*, 60-3). See also Jouvency, 1610 (*Jesuit Relations*, I, 287). C. Lalemant, 1626 (*ibid.*, IV, 199). Le Jeune, 1634 (*ibid.*, VI, 209): "I have not seen any of these

Mississippi nations the early evidence is not uniform.[340] Among the Plains and Northern Indians, although feasting as a religious feature has been noted (in the former[341]), it is more frequently mentioned as a mere diversion in their lives; and no reference has been found to banquets *à tout manger* as a religious observance.[342] So far from this attitude, which implies an essentially sacred sanction for customs otherwise 'socially' inexcusable, in some instances 'gluttony' was defended upon strictly philosophical grounds;[343] to which it is not easy to furnish any more logical answer than that of our own differing customs.[344]

In so far as 'non-religious gluttony' is concerned—I use the phrase for convenience; without necessarily conceding its accuracy thereby— although its indulgence on any given occasion is obviously an indication of a momentary plenty, its origin seems clearly traceable to the precisely opposite condition. It is, I believe, not often found among agriculturists and herdsmen, whose food-supply, under normal conditions, is sufficiently abundant and uniformly available.[345] Drunken-

---

great fasters, but I have seen great diners. . . ." Compare Le Jeune also, 1634-40 (*ibid.*, VI, 249, 283; VIII, 127: Hurons; X, 179; XIV, 63; XX, 263). Marest, 1712 (Kaskaskias: *ibid.*, LXVI, 221).

[340]Chauchetière, 1687: ". . . what the savages eat during half the year is not sufficient to keep a man alive . . ." (*ibid.*, LXIII, 219). Father Râle noted, *circa* 1710, that the Illinois were not addicted to gluttonous feasts, where all must be eaten (*ibid.*, LXVII, 165). On reservations and under ordinary circumstances, they have been said to be moderate eaters (Blair, ed. note, *Indian Tribes*, II, 237).

[341]See Gregg, *Early Western Travels*, XX, 287, 334.

[342]See *Harmon's Journal*, 284; Hughes, *Father Lacombe*, 142-53; McDougall, *Western Trails*, 99, 120, 123, etc. In addition, most of the authorities cited above (note 329) *re* starving have something to say about gluttonous feasting.

[343]Warburton Pike's guide, the notorious 'King Beaulieu,' 1889, "criticized severely the habit of eating three regular meals a day, which he described as eating by the clock instead of by the stomach, a much more greedy habit than that of gorging when meat is plentiful, and starving at other times. On several occasions during our travels together I had reason to expostulate with him on the carelessness he displayed with provisions, but without making the least impression. 'What is this improvidence?' he would say, 'I do not like that word. When we have meat, why should we not eat *plein ventre* to make up for the time when we are sure to starve again?'" (Pike, *Barren Ground*, 84). Similarly, Matonabbee, Hearne's guide, 1770-72 (*Journey*, 113, 119, 152). See also Father Râle, 1710 (*Jesuit Relations*, LXVII, 141). The famous Jim Bridger never ate until he was hungry (Hebard and Brininstool, *Bozeman Trail*, II, 244).

[344]One might enlarge on the regular working periods of agricultural or industrial life, requiring regular eating or resting times. The anthropologists tell us, however, that the hunter preceded the herdsman or tiller of the soil; so that even here the Indian, with invincible logic, could plead 'right of prior user.'

[345]The Illinois themselves, as a case in point, were partly agriculturists. See above in this chapter, notes 7, 79, 340.

ness, we are told, is seldom seen in the wine countries; and few of us but have been familiarized with the argument—whatever be its worth in our midst[346]—that the surest way to lessen the consumption of alcoholic liquors is to make them readily available at all times.

It is a well-established trait in the Northerner from the Barren Lands who has been brought so near to death by starvation that his mind is temporarily affected, to steal and secrete supplies of provisions in some private cache of his own; in readiness for the famine which he cannot for some time be convinced—in a well-stocked post, or ocean steamship, or city hotel—is no longer to be dreaded. Milton and Cheadle have described very graphically how on reaching Kamloops in 1863, after narrowly escaping death from starvation in the dense and pathless forests along the Thompson River, 'the ordinary bountiful meals of the Fort were quite inadequate for their satisfaction' and they multiplied the orthodox 'three squares a day' into six by secretly dining with their henchman 'The Assiniboine' and his family, from early morn to dewy eve, between their appearances at the official board.[347] This experience, which was later repeated by another traveller at the very same place,[348] and could no doubt be widely paralleled from similar situations,[349] very appositely demonstrates my argument above, that while the indulgence is palpable proof of an immediate abundance, it originates from the exact contrary.

With the Miltons and Cheadles, *et al.*, such occurrences are purely temporary; but they serve to show how quickly necessity and want could override the normal instincts of cultured gentlemen, at least in something which inflicted no wrong upon others. Gluttony is an attribute of hunter peoples; and a hunter-society is not composed of cultured gentlemen. The hunter is in the human family what the carnivora are in the animal kingdom, and the rule for both is the same—stuff when you can and starve when you must. This has been recognized by philosophic observers in the wilds and in the study.[350]

[346]Whatever this be worth psychologically, it is historically dubious. The Anglo-Saxon tribes, *temp.* Tacitus (*Germania*, 22, 23), and their descendants long after, were hard drinkers, if not drunkards, *who brewed their own liquor!*

[347]Milton and Cheadle, *North-West Passage*, 318-19.

[348]Rev. George M. Grant at Kamloops, September (1872 (*Ocean to Ocean*, 328).

[349]I have noted a few instances. See Long's expedition 1820 (*Early Western Travels*, XIV, 134, 190). Frémont, at Sutter's Fort, California, 1843 (*Narrative*, 265). Some interesting examples in Dodge (*Our Wild Indians*, 271-81). H. Somers Somerset, Fort McLeod, B.C., in 1893 (*The Land of the Muskeg*, 217-19); Seton (*Arctic Prairies*, 143).

[350]See Umfreville, 1790: "The uncertainty of a savage life is such that perhaps he may be one day exulting in the midst of plenty, and the next day pining under the distress of penury and want . . ." (*The Present State of Hudson's*

In so far as the present essay is concerned, such citations of opinion are really superfluous, for the fluctuations in food supply have been demonstrated beyond dispute, as matters of historical fact.

It is needless to labour the argument that such privations cannot possibly be explained upon any supposition of an imperfect knowledge of the habits of the game animals from which the hunting tribes drew their subsistence. This also has been undeniably established by evidence, in addition to the appreciative comments of observers upon the Indians' .wonderful mastery of everything pertaining to the animal life of their habitat.[351] From this mastery, it has been shown that the buffalo were in no sense an exception. Among the 'buffalo' tribes, the true explanation of the riotous feastings in plenty, and the extraordinary capacity for stoical endurance in scarcity, lies in my opinion unquestionably in the relatively frequent and quite inscrutable absences and the general irregularity in the movements of the buffalo.

It seems to me scientifically inevitable that this must have persisted for a long time; nothing less than generations of such experience could have developed not merely the purely physical capacity for physical endurance, but also the instinct for that mental passivity which can wait uncomplainingly for better times. And we are expected to believe that this race, whose utter lack of the qualities of self-restraint has been emphasized *ad infinitum*, schooled themselves to this in face of the 'regular' migration, 'following along its well-known routes each year,' and so forth, in the well-worn shibboleths of the traditionary school; following, that is to say, a supposedly uniform cycle of events, of which (if they occurred at all) none could conceivably be more competent judges than the Indians themselves. They learned how to starve—or retained the power, obviously by practice—in a land where their mastery of the 'herd-psychology' of the buffalo was so complete that they could not only slay a herd at once, but herd after herd[352]

---

bay, 93). Alexander Ross: 'a hunter's life was one of feast and famine . . .' (*Red River Settlement*, 253). Marcy, *Exploration of Red River*, 93. McDougall, *Pathfinding*, 13-16; *Western Trails*, 10, 195 (*in extenso* above, notes 59-62). Pike, *Barren Ground*, vii, 50, 84, 131, etc. MacInnes: 'temporary scarcity always a feature of Indian life' (*In the Shadow of the Rockies*, 142).

[351]Hind: "It may truly be said that they exist on the buffalo, and their knowledge of the habits of this animal is consequently essential to their preservation . . ." (*Narrative*, II, 104). Warburton Pike (*re* Northern Indians): ". . . possessed of a thorough knowledge of the movements of various animals at different seasons . . ." (*Barren Ground*). McDougall, *Red River Rebellion*, 32. Butler, *Wild North Land*, 206. Jenness, *Indians of Canada*, 53; and a splendid description of caribou hunting, by Angus Buchanan, *Wild Life in Canada*, 134, 173-91.

[352]See above, Section 5 of this chapter. Chittenden notes "an enclosure of this sort within ten miles of Fort Union, and around it were the bones of thousands of buffalo slain there . . ." (*American Fur Trade*, II, 857). Fort Union

in a spot of their own previous choosing. They developed these various phases of practice which have been summed up as 'wastefulness'—both the fastidiousness in picking and choosing tongues and choice bits, and in the callous abandonment of large quantities (which the whites learned from them[353]) in a territory where apparently even the observance of their most solemn religious ceremonials was dependent upon the comings and goings of the buffalo.[354] If these paradoxes have any meaning at all, they can only indicate a general condition which is the utter antithesis of everything that is suggested by the term 'uniformity.'

Neither historical nor psycho-anthropological evidence furnishes any support worth considering to the traditional theory of the regular buffalo migration.

10.

Hornaday's position—almost unique in historical study—as the un-challenged authority on a subject for over half-a-century, renders it impossible for a critic to terminate the present chapter without some final remarks concerning his treatment of the general relation of the Indian to the buffalo; since his *dicta* may be said to constitute not only the popular, but even the scientific knowledge of the world at large on that, as on almost every other department of buffalo history.[355] There could scarcely have been a more unhappy era than that of his own publication for the appearance of any work on such a subject. The 'time-spirit' in the United States, *circa* 1889, was neither favour-able to the Indian, nor even to impartial justice concerning him, whether in affairs or in literature. Those portions of Hornaday's essay dealing with the Indian are the most unsatisfactory of the entire work. The exaggerations, the contradictions, the unsupported assertions, and the slovenly argumentation, which are only too frequently evident in his pages, are brought to bear in an aggravated form against the Red man. The truth appears to be that Hornaday, with an uncritical

---

was at the mouth of the Yellowstone. This may have been the very one seen by Lewis and Clark (*Journals*, I, 308). See below, Appendix AA.

[353]Buffalo Jones speaks of the Indians feasting on the flesh, "in former years regarded by the white man as repulsive and worthless . . ." (*Buffalo Jones' Forty Years*, 254). I should be glad to learn when this was. For abandonment by whites, see Henry, 1810 (below, Appendix M).

[354]According to McDougall, the time and locality for the 'Thirst Dance' (or 'Sun Dance,' *i.e.* tortures and initiations) was "determined largely by the proximity of the buffalo and the conditions of tribal war . . ." (*Pathfinding*, 80).

[355]Only one man since Hornaday has written at any length (Seton, 1910, 1929), and he professedly takes Hornaday for his guide. See above on this, chap. III, note 55, also note 234 of this chapter.

facility surprising in a scientific mind—which should lead and direct rather than tamely follow popular opinion—and in face of weighty evidence which he himself adduces,[356] allowed himself to conform to what might fairly be termed the vulgar conception of the Indian, on this continent. This has prevailed more particularly in the United States since the last great struggle for possession of the Mississippi; and in its most acute form after the Civil War; previous to which era it is much less marked.[357] One cannot evade the conclusion that much of this was a subtle form of propaganda, furthered by those who coveted the Indian lands, and designed for the 'education' of the Eastern States; in which latter territory were the majorities whose suffrages might make or mar any policy of expansion in the West, and in whom it was consequently desirable to create an unfavourable impression of Indian character.[358]

Hornaday dismisses with contempt the suggestion that the Indians did at times slay with some judgment and prudence; and 'fails to find any evidence' of such a thing. He admits that 'some authors' (unspecified) have testified on the Indian's behalf. This category includes one of his own foremost authorities, Dodge; and he further prints citations from politicians and journalists—neither of them an excessively sentimental class—showing that the belief had at least some defenders. The politicians are manifestly cited because of his endorsement of their contentions, which are considered sufficiently authentic then to command his approval.[359] With this one significant exception, his answer is a mere denial in toto. When his flank is in danger of being turned by a production of fact, he saves his retreat by discovering a motive for all this. If a white hunter refrains from utter extermination, this is humanity, economy, 'love of sport'; when an Indian is asserted by otherwise-accepted authorities to have done likewise, it is laziness! Why Hornaday's Indians, who are all as like as two peas, should not have felt the urge of laziness before some of their killings in open country were finished to the last buffalo, is

[356]See Appendix H, "Buffalo, Indian, and Legislation."

[357]See Dr. Marcus Whitman's successful Journey to Oregon, 1835 and back alone, 1843 (Catlin, Letters on the North American Indians, II, 109, 114, 243; Bancroft, History of Oregon, I, 104-13; Hebard and Brininstool, Bozeman Trail, I, 41). Despite the 'Covered Wagon' type of literature, the contemporary chroniclers of 1849 ridiculed the idea of danger from Indians. Hulbert (Forty-Niners, 164, 183, 216, 296, etc.). As late as 1859, along the Oregon Trail, General W. F. Raynolds, U.S. Army, stated that "the Indians were perfectly peaceful . . ." (Hebard and Brininstool, Bozeman Trail, I, 47).

[358]See below, Appendix FF.

[359]See Appendix H, "Buffalo, Indian, and Legislation."

not clear. The only support offered for these postulates is that "they all did—" "It was always the same old story—" This is considered as 'historical evidence'![360]

The present chapter has discussed in some detail the allegations concerning wastefulness. It has been shown that much which a fair-minded but uninformed observer of Indian methods, not to say a malignant critic with malice prepense, might seize upon as waste, is frequently referable to a psychological interpretation. In relation to this, there is one more word to be said. If any critic remains of the opinion after consideration of the present chapter, that its contentions are not proven, and that the conduct of the Indians toward buffalo was actually waste pure and simple, in our connotation of the term and no other, one may still ask a very pertinent question. Why should the Indian school himself to the practice of a hitherto-needless economy, simply in order to leave the more for utterly conscienceless white men?[361] A plea of ignorance would not avail here; for Hornaday applied his remarks specifically to the territory of the northern herd, of whose destruction he is himself the authoritative historian. One wonders how many readers, if they encountered his paragraphs cited by myself above, and having no other knowledge of the buffalo extermination in the Western habitat, would have the least suspicion of the actual truth. An historian's sympathies and point of view are his own affair; but he should at least present the facts.[362]

The rancour against the Indian reveals itself in his remarks about 'Sioux buffaloes';[363] as if this were anything but a perfectly natural attitude, which is neither confined to the Sioux, nor to the Indian race. Father Le Jeune, in 1634, mentions certain of the Indians complaining of other tribes "coming to hunt upon our very grounds;

[360]One is reminded of Mr. John Barsad, who had never been kicked downstairs in his life. It was established in *his* case that he had certainly once been kicked (at the top of a staircase), but he fell downstairs purely 'of his own accord' (Dickens, *Tale of Two Cities*, Book Two, chap. III).

[361]I am glad to find this view expressed by a particularly competent modern authority on Indians, who holds that Indians were not wasteful; no conservation of game among them, but none was necessary; they were not improvident, food was stored away when available and practicable (Jenness, *Indians of Canada*, 49-50). So also, Angus Buchanan, *Wild Life in Canada*: Indians were *not* wasteful, and these were the 'pure' Indians of the North (64, 79, 119, 131, 153, 195, etc.). Likewise, Hewitt, so long as he is giving his own conclusions (*Conservation of Wild Life of Canada*, 12-13, 128 *seq.*); but he elsewhere quotes Hornaday's authoritarian diatribes, without a word of criticism (*ibid.*, 118, 298). See below, note 372.

[362]Above, notes 230-34; also see Appendix BB.

[363]Above, note 232.

taking away our game and our lives at the same time. . . ."[364] In 1845, a Crow war-party told Samuel Hancock a similar thing: "These Indians said Sioux had been killing their buffalo and other game on their [the Crows'] lands, and that they were now in search of them to obtain redress for these injuries. . . ."[365] Dodge alludes to this point of view as a more or less general characteristic;[366] and Hind mentions it among the Plain Cree in the Qu'Appelle country, 1858.[367] There are several allusions in the same general territory to what is *in esse* the same point of view;[368] which was evidently so instinctive in the Cree mind that it crystallized as a phrase in their language.[369] Father Morice speaks of the Sekanais of northern British Columbia and 'our sheep,' that is, the mountain sheep 'which they regarded as their own lawful property'—"and most rightly so," he declares emphatically.[370] History has recorded the indignant query of a Governor of the Hudson's Bay Company, *circa* 1857: "What!—take away the fertile lands where *our* buffaloes feed . . ."[371] and one may wonder how many English (or other) poachers through the ages have suffered various penalties for 'stealing *my* game.' If it were possible to revert to first principles on this question, a title direct from Almighty God might be thought at least equal to those deriving from a Charles Stuart or a Henry Tudor.[372]

[364]*Jesuit Relations*, VII, 171.
[365]*Narrative of Samuel Hancock*, 18.
[366]*Our Wild Indians*, 380; cf. also his account of a Sioux hunt accompanied by soldiers, 1880 (*ibid.*, 581).
[367]Hind, *Report, 1858*, 56.
[368]See above, chap. XIV, note 70.
[369]*Ki mustusuminow* = 'notre bœuf' (*i.e.* buffalo = *mustus*): Lacombe, *Dictionnaire de la langue des Cris*, 389.
[370]Morice, *Fifty Years in Western Canada*, 132; see also *Harmon's Journal*, 330.
[371]Sir Edward Watkin, *Canada and the States*, 120, 125; Beckles Willson, *Great Company*, 474; Stanley, *Birth of Western Canada*, 31. The italics, of course, are mine.
[372]In "The Sportsman's Code of Ethics," compiled by Dr. Hornaday, 1908 (cited by Hewitt, *Conservation of Wild Life of Canada*, 298), I find the following: "(Article 5): An Indian has no more right to kill wild game, or to subsist upon it all the year round, than any white man in the same locality. The Indian has no inherent or God-given ownership of the game of North America, any more than of its mineral resources; and he should be governed by the same laws as white men. . . . (Article 8): The highest purpose which the killing of wild game and game fishes can hereafter be made to serve is in the furnishing objects to overworked men for tramping and camping trips in the wilds; and the value of wild game as human food should no longer be regarded as an important factor in its pursuit."
If *no* race has any God-given rights in its aboriginal home, then I suppose the Indian must take his chance, on "the good old rule, the simple plan, that they

Hornaday himself came perilously near to the same unlawful assumptions he was so ready to chastise in Indians. In his account of the Smithsonian expeditions of May and September, 1886, in search of museum specimens, he describes an experience after a kill:

As early as possible the next morning we drove to the carcass with the wagon, to prepare both skin and skeleton and haul them in. When we reached it we found that during the night a gang of Indians had robbed us of our hard-earned spoil. They had stolen the skin and all the eatable meat, broken up the leg-bones to get at the marrow, and even cut out the tongue. And to injury the skulking thieves had added insult. Through laziness, they had left the head unskinned, but on one side of it they had smeared the hair with red war-paint, the other side they had daubed with yellow, and around the base of one horn they had tied a strip of red flannel as a signal of defiance. Of course they had left for parts unknown, and we never saw any signs of them afterward. The gang visited the LU-bar ranch a few days later, so we learned subsequently. It was then composed of eleven braves (!), who claimed to be Assiniboines, and were therefore believed to be Piegans, the most notorious horse and cattle thives in the Northwest.[373]

This failure of the Assiniboine-Piegans to co-operate in the interests of science[374] may have pointed his strictures on the Sioux; but far worse atrocities arising out of similar hatreds, perpetrated however by our own forefathers—by Britons against Romans,[375] Saxons against 'Danes,'[376] by both against Normans,[377] or by English and Scots against each other [378]—are generally coupled in history with something about 'brave defenders of their country.'

Hornaday himself has printed evidence of strong official opinion that the lessons to be drawn from pitched battles would be ineffectual, as the event proved.[379] These particulars are actually no part of buffalo history *per se*; but since he makes them such, a critic is entitled to discuss them, and there can be no doubt that they have contributed to emphasize a false aspect of Indian-and-buffalo (as other) relationships.

may take who have the power and they may keep who can." So also, if the earth is the white man's and the fulness thereof, the foregoing may be conceded. Pending the establishment of these premises, I emphatically deny these postulates *in toto*.

[373]Hornaday, "Extermination of the American Bison," 537; for the two expeditions, *ibid.*, 529-48.

[374]Cf. the initial hostility and later cordiality of Red Cloud, the Sioux chief, to Professor O. C. Marsh: Hebard and Brininstool, *Bozeman Trail*, II, 185.

[375]Boudicca ('Boadicea') A.D. 60: Tacitus, *Annals*, XIV, 30-9; etc.

[376]The 'Massacre of St. Brice,' 1002: *Anglo-Saxon Chronicle, sub ann.*, etc.

[377]The massacres at York and Durham, 1069: *ibid., sub ann.*, etc.

[378]For example, 1297, 1308-10, 1319, 1327. See John Hill Burton, *History of Scotland*, II, 195, 253, 261, 298, etc., who gives the Scottish side amply and dispassionately, supplementing the somewhat better known English historians.

[379]See Appendix H, "Buffalo, Indian, and Legislation."

The unhistorical blatancy of this attitude has long been exposed and abandoned by the best minds of the United States.[380] At such a time, and in view of the somewhat smug pharisaism occasionally heard in Canada,[381] one is ashamed to note that perhaps the most contemptuous of all remarks I have encountered concerning Indians is from a born Canadian. Agnes Laut observes: "One hears much twaddle of the red man's noble state before he was contaminated by the white man. . . ."[382] This may or may not be true, but it comes most ungracefully from a writer who in the same book 'twaddles' about "the noble Black Douglas,"[383] a typical Front-de-Bœuf of a baronial house which furnished many such, and the unbridled ferocity of which was for three centuries the curse of Scotland.[384] Whether in relation to buffalo or to any other phase of North American history, the true understanding of the Indian factor is impossible to such minds, and so also to their readers, until such unworthy prejudice, which degrades chiefly those possessed by it, has been swept away.[385]

[380]It is no longer possible to doubt that Custer's defeat was the outcome of a deliberate violation of his own (or General Terry's) strategic design, in order to be in the field before his co-operating colleagues and to reap all the glory. This was inspired by a foolhardy contempt for Indians, which the event by no means justified. See on this, Dodge, *Our Wild Indians*, 478, 491; Taylor, who knew the principals, *Frontier Life*, 147-73; Grinnell, *Fighting Cheyennes*, 332-45; Byrne, *Red Men's Last Stand*, 81-105, 131, 151-60. As several authors observe *re* Custer, so also with the "so-called Fetterman massacre," Fort Phil Kearney, December 21, 1866, 'Massacre' is absurd where an armed force offers battle to another armed force, and merely suffers what it sought to inflict (Grinnell, *Fighting Cheyennes*, 221-35, the quotation being his; Hebard and Brininstool, *Bozeman Trail*, I, 320; Brady, *Indian Fights and Fighters*, 259, 281, etc.). See also on Indian leaders, Rain in the Face (whose 'Revenge' is designated a 'lie'), Crazy Horse, Red Cloud: Byrne, *Red Men's Last Stand*, 132, 165, 229; Hebard and Brininstool, *Bozeman Trail*, II, 175-204; and cf. Maclean on Poundmaker, the Cree, 1885, in *Canadian Savage Folk*, 381. There is an extensive critical literature on Custer, whose glory has departed.

[381]*In extenso* above, chap. XIV, note 181.

[382]Laut, *Conquest of the Great Northwest*, I, 348.

[383]*Ibid.*, II, 322.

[384]It is not necessary to cite any very recondite authorities in support of this opinion; see Scott's notes, *Lay of the Last Minstrel*, xxvi, lxv; *Marmion*, lxix, lxxxvi, lxxxvii; Burton, *History of Scotland*, II, 253, 325, 415, 422, 428; III, 27, 89, 138, 150, etc.; Buckle, *History of Civilization*, III, 16-18, 45-69. It is of course well-known that the original of 'Front-de Bœuf' was a Scottish baron, Kennedy, Earl of Cassilis, *circa* 1570, the 'King of Carrick'; of that very region which had long been terrorized by the Douglases, of whom the Kennedys were then and formerly allies: See Scott's note v in *Ivanhoe*; and cf. also Froude, *History of England* (Everyman ed.), VII, 251; VIII, 257; Burton, *History of Scotland*, IV, 38.

[385]Miss Laut's expression is also used by Dodge: "always much twaddle about the Great Spirit, Great Father, etc. . . ." (*Plains of the Great West*, 265; compare him in 1886, above, note 242). One may doubt whether a U.S. army officer *circa*

1876 *could* enter into the Indian mind. Dodge's later work, 1883-86, is much less harsh; but even there, he generalizes too broadly from particular tribes. Such books as James Willard Schultz's *Apauk, Caller of Buffalo*, may perhaps idealize Indians' religious attitude too much; and possibly Walter McClintock's *Old North Trail* may depict the more mellowed philosophy of aged men toward a friend of their race; but they certainly present an aspect of the Indian character sharply divergent from Dodge's earlier conception or that of Agnes Laut—an aspect, moreover, which Indians were little likely to acquire from their contact with the whites, say 1840-80.

Compare Miss Laut's remarks on Dr. Edgar Lee Hewett. His important and fascinating work, *Ancient Life in the American Southwest*, 1930, seems, to a layman at least, to have revealed the soul of the Indian, with an insight manifested by few indeed. He speaks of 'savage cruelty being a much-exploited tradition' (*ibid.*, 25); and of Indians as 'a genuinely noble race' (*ibid.*, 22-32, 136, 313, 357, etc.).

Miss Laut justly acclaims Dr. Hewett as probably the first authority on the tribes of the Southwest, but adds: "You will not, in fact cannot, agree with all his gentle conclusions . . ." (*Pilgrims of the Santa Fé*, 88-95). One is entitled to ask by what canon of moral or intellectual right the transient, hasty, inaccurate Lauts pronounce that 'we' (*i.e.* themselves) 'will not or cannot' agree on a question requiring knowledge, insight, sympathy—the precise *desiderata* which they typically lack—with the patient, penetrating, scholarly, scientific Hewetts, unless it be the right of evidence; and can there be any hesitation as to which school are the true masters of the evidence?

In another book Miss Laut describes the late Dr. Grace Raymond Hebard as 'one of the highest authorities' on the Plains section of the Oregon Trail (*Overland Trail*, 19, 90, 92, 124, etc.). She adds, however, concerning the 'modern sentimentalists' who say that the Indian was "friendly to the white man till white ruffians changed that attitude to one of deadly hate and bloody feud, . . . Nay-nay! Much as we would like to believe such explanations, such is not the truth . . ." (*ibid.*, 207; but cf. her own remarks, 17, 50-1, etc.). The evidence for her alleged 'liking' is extremely feeble; and compare Dr. Hebard's own opinions (Hebard and Brininstool, *Bozeman Trail*, II, 175-204, etc.). The Hebards and the Hewetts unfortunately belong to the despised class of 'maps and study-chair' scholars (Laut, *Overland Trail*, 19-20, 32, 98-9); and their matured conclusions clash with the pronouncements of such authorities as the *Arizona Kicker*, Ballyhoo Bill, Colonel Carbine, or Senator Sorghum. Finally, what is a 'sentimentalist'? It is defined as "one who appeals to sentiment (*i.e.* 'a thought prompted by passion or feeling') rather than reason." Since those I have cited, and also myself, *are* prompted by reason (evidence), while Miss Laut, a true sentimentalist, is not—I therefore on their behalf and my own, repudiate the stigma. On her authenticity, cf. above in this chapter, notes 216, 312.

For an early philosophic review of the Indian question at large, see Alexander Simpson, *Life of Thomas Simpson*, 403-24; and for a modern one, Dr. Cyrus Thomas's two most instructive chapters, "The Indian Policy of the United States," and "The Indians as a Race and as a Factor in American History" (*History of North America*, II, 399, 432).

Chapter XXII

CONCLUDING SUMMARY

THE object of this essay has been not so much to suggest conclusions as to present facts. Inevitably at times, however, in adducing and commenting upon evidence concerning the habits of the buffalo or the Indian, or in discussing the various beliefs or assertions respecting them, the character, the degree of inherent credibility, the contemporaneous authority or some such feature of the evidence under consideration, has naturally given rise (in a study professedly critical) to occasional utterances of a 'judicial' character. These have been more commonly negative, tending to illustrate the apparent influence of the testimony under discussion upon the fortunes of some perhaps widely accepted but not soundly authenticated belief. Such pronouncements will in all probability contribute to assist the reader in forming certain general conclusions of his own. It will be readily perceived, however, that the mere labour involved in the collection and arrangement of the evidence contained in the present work, could scarcely be performed during the space of several years without the author reaching broad conclusions. Some of these are provisional and tentative, in certain respects at least. Others are more fixed and definite. While no student should close his mind to the possibility of further evidence necessitating a recasting of his views on any subject—perhaps very drastically—I must acknowledge that I cannot conceive what the nature of the new evidence could be that would require the abandonment of the latter class of conclusions, which I have been driven to form from my study of the evidence now existing.[1] These I shall now place before the reader in a briefly summarized form.

First and foremost, if our evidence can be considered to bear any meaning whatever, it has demonstrated beyond disproof the inapplicability to the buffalo species, even to the degree of absurdity, of any

[1] I mean by this: The Plains buffalo are now, as a free wild species, extinct. With a living species in its natural freedom, there is a possibility of new phenomena being discovered, as for example the existence of long unsuspected tree-climbing habits in African lions. Further evidence concerning buffalo conduct, however, could only take the form, it would seem, of an addition to some one of the various types or classes of historical evidence already considered.

theory of uniformity or regularity in their habits. In every department in which this 'regularity' could operate or has been declared to operate, the buffalo have been shown to be erratic and unreliable to the last degree; frequently in the recorded experience of the very persons who proclaim their knowledge of buffalo as the basis for their own firm belief in the uniformity of the habits of the species.[2]

Even on *a priori* grounds entirely distinct from evidence, I see nothing in this conclusion to occasion surprise; much less to justify an insistent or acrimonious demand for proof, while the supposition of undeviating regularity is virtually considered to require no further verification than is implied in its mere reiteration.[3] It cannot be—and in fact is not—supposed that a hard and fast line can be drawn between the higher *genera* of the mammalian order and man; on one side of which is invariably nothing more than the common herd instinct, and on the other invariably nothing less than the individualized, personal intelligence. It would be incredible that knowledge,[4] which has abandoned the once universally accredited conception that modification in the structural formation of the earth is the result of a succession of abrupt cataclysmic changes, should seek to cling to any form of catastrophic theory concerning the evolution of mental faculty. Considered as a manifestation of this gradual progression, the dawning of the capacity for individual impulse *must begin somewhere.* I think that most people who have bred dogs, horses, or cattle, will require some very strong evidence to convince them that it is not frequently present in those species, sometimes in a very marked degree;[5] and at the same time with a range of individual variation which is difficult to explain except upon some such essential principles as we should apply to ourselves, as Darwin noted long ago.[6] I can conceive of no sound reasons why this should not apply to the buffalo species; unless it could be shown that such individualistic manifestations of intelligence were confined to domesticated animals.[7] Apart from the circum-

[2]Compare Hind and the Red River half-breeds (above, chap. XIV, notes 50-2) with chaps. XIX-XX, on "Migrations."

[3]Above, chap. XIX, notes 1-38.

[4]The term *science* has come to bear a restricted meaning of its own; consequently I prefer to use the more comprehensive English equivalent.

[5]". . . anybody who has ever kept a dog or seen an elephant . . ." (Leslie Stephen, quoted by Darwin, *Descent of Man,* 81). See also below, Appendix GG.

[6]"The individuals of the same species graduate in intellect from absolute imbecility to high intelligence . . ." (Darwin, *Descent of Man,* 81).

[7]See numerous instances, *ibid.,* 28-44, 66, 131; Morgan, *Animal Life and Intelligence,* 331-414, who cites examples from many post-Darwinian investigators. Dogs, quite naturally, furnish several instances; see on these, Darwin, *Descent of Man,* 28, 80, etc.; Morgan, *Animal Life and Intelligence,* 396-407; and a

stance that such a fact would discredit an evolutionary theory of mental development almost entirely, by confining its operation to a negligibly minute fraction of many species, while others again must be left out altogether—such is not the case; for its presence has been authentically recorded in many wild species living in their natural freedom.[8] In relation to buffalo in particular, the most philosophic and generally reliable historian of the species at large explicitly credits them with a degree of individual variation in conduct which can scarcely be ascribed to anything else than some form of personal intelligence, define it how we may.[9]

From this propensity to occasional (and seemingly imponderable) individual or sub-group action, not characteristic of the species as a whole, it has been seen that even the sacrosanct 'regular migration' was not exempt. These movements did not, as historical facts, invariably take place. Neither were they invariably along the same routes, nor even in the same 'strategic' directions. Even Hulbert, the archprotagonist of the north-and-south conception, had to acknowledge that fact; it was the only expedient by which the Ohio Valley, the chief natural artery in his own chosen region, could be admitted to the full dignity of a buffalo highway.[10] Further, where one of the principal directions *was* north and south, the southward journey was not the one commonly taken for the winter. And this was in the Saskatchewan territory;[11] where *a priori*—if anywhere—each autumn should have witnessed a panic-stricken rush to the south!

Hornaday's suggestion of climate, and the desire for a relatively cooler summer, as the impelling force behind the northward exodus from Texas in spring, may be correct; since that region generally is the only one where something approximating to a regular northward spring movement—as distinct from mere assertions of such—has been recorded.[12] And even this would not explain the return journey southward, in a species so entirely competent to endure a cold winter.

---

remarkable case in Sir William Butler's *Autobiography*, 48; etc., etc. Cf. the cats and 'dinner-time' (below, Appendix GG).

[8]I find the following in Darwin's *Descent of Man*, beaver (p. 68); monkeys (pp. 71-2); fur-bearing animals in North America (p. 82); also Morgan, *Animal Life and Intelligence*, 366. Foxes (Darwin, *Descent of Man*, 83); baboons, Abyssinia (*ibid.*, 84, 104); 'half-wild' cattle, South Africa (*ibid.*, 107); crabs (*ibid.*, 278-9); snakes, a cobra, Ceylon (*ibid.*, 364-5); a beetle (Morgan, *Animal Life and Intelligence*, 368); wild elephants (*ibid.*, 370).

[9]"The American bison presents a considerable range of what may be termed individual variations . . ." (Allen, *American Bisons*, 48).

[10]Above, chap. IV, note 71; chap. X, note 28; etc.

[11]Above, chap. XX, note 206 *seq.*

[12]Above, chap. XIX, notes 8-29; chap. XX, notes 16-31.

The objections which historical evidence presents against almost any other suggested cause have driven me to the conclusion already indicated: that these wanderings were utterly erratic and unpredictable and might occur regardless of time, place, or season, with any number, in any direction, in any manner, under any conditions, and for any reason—which is to say, for no 'reason' at all. As I have pointed out, their elimination from the category of true migrations (that is, breeding movements) not only as a scientific theory but as an historical fact, removes what we may either term a powerful anterior cause or an important logical necessity for regularity; and I do not know that the doctrine of buffalo uniformity in behaviour is so vitally essential to our comprehension of the species that we are under any necessity to invent another to replace the one we have lost. If more conclusive evidence yet is desired by any critic, it is (in my opinion) furnished by the mass of detail which has been presented on the influence of the buffalo environment upon the Indian. It is utterly incredible to me that such physical and psychological reactions could result from a contact of centuries' duration with conditions of supposedly uniform reliability; of which none could conceivably be more competent judges than the Indians themselves.[13]

A critic might very naturally and pardonably suggest that the widespread persistence and acceptance of the two cardinal buffalo theories—if I may so term them—of the regular migration and the buffalo origin of our roads, must surely indicate the influence of an authentic tradition, even though not vocal in literary record; on the general principle that with so much smoke there must be some fire. That aphorism, while frequently an effective weapon in colloquial disputation, is commonly of little service as a guide in serious investigations. A general pronouncement *pro* or *con* on the value of traditionary evidence is worthless; each case must be separately tested by its own evidence; and it seems to have been almost generally true that among European (and English-speaking) immigrants to this continent, the mental shock of change among long and deeply rooted peoples altered the *prima facie* value of tradition, among many other things, even in witnesses otherwise broadly equal. I mean that an ancient tradition among English folk (for example) is more likely, by and large, to be true in its native English setting, than would an American tradition among their grandchildren, after a century or so in the New World. The new environment was so entirely strange and wonderful that nothing was too impossible for belief; they had no experience

---

[13]Compare chap. XXI, at large, particularly sec. 9.

which could even suggest a check; and mere repetition would suffice to establish almost any marvel.[14]

Bancroft cites a number of Western traditions which appear to resemble facts in one respect at least—they are 'chiels that winna ding.' He mentions the tradition, belief, claim, or whatever it be, of Workman and Spencer having travelled from Santa Fé to California in 1809-10, as the first American citizens to make the journey; the first actually being not until twenty years later, in the opinion both of Bancroft and some of his critics.[15] Bancroft again, after critical discussion, considers there is no foundation for the 'popular idea' that Santa Fé is the oldest town in the United States; the order in popular chronology being Santa Fé, 1555; Tucson, Arizona, 1560; St. Augustine, Florida, 1565.[16] He gives 1776 as the actual date for the foundation of Santa Fé.[17] W. P. Webb (without discussing Bancroft's date) is equally opposed to the date of 1555; considering Santa Fé to have been permanently occupied after 1599.[18] The earliest place of European origin in Colorado whose date is unquestioned is Nuestra Señora las Nieves,[19] northwestward from Santa Fé and just inside the Colorado state line; named by Dominguez and Escalanté in 1776.[20] Yet Bancroft notes a tradition—for which he could find no historical basis—of Spaniards in Wyoming before 1650.[21] Dr. Elliott Coues discusses the persistent tradition of Pike 'viewing the Pacific' (which he never saw anywhere) from 'Pike's Peak' or some neighbouring height; itself an utter impossibility for reasons of distance and altitude.[22]

[14]For example, of what influence on the popular mind would be any criticisms of French scientists on the *Pisikious* of Dablon and Allouez (*Jesuit Relations* LV, 195-7); *in extenso* above, chap. IX, note 86)? They had not seen these animals for themselves! English 'scientific criticism' did indeed procure the discrediting of the fearsome brutes of David Ingram, 1568-9 (above *in extenso*, chap. IX, notes 56-63). But it is quite evident that among Elizabethan seamen and doubtless among many others less learned than Hakluyt's coterie, Ingram's monsters were accepted to the full.

[15]Stated in Coyner's *Lost Trappers*, edition of 1847 or 1859; so Bancroft, *History of Nevada*, 350, 677; *History of Arizona*, 300. Cf. Coman, *Economic Beginnings of the Far West*, II, 87, 211-12.

[16]Bancroft, *North Mexican States and Texas*, I, 129; *History of Arizona and New Mexico*, 158, 374. Coues is for these traditional dates (*Expeditions of Pike*, II, 734).

[17]Bancroft, *History of Arizona*, 618.

[18]Webb, *Great Plains*, 115.

[19]An interesting name to Canadians = 'Our Lady of the Snows.'

[20]Bancroft, *History of Nevada*, 672; cf. Webb also, *Great Plains*, 85-139.

[21]Bancroft, *History of Nevada*, 672.

[22]Coues (ed.), *Expeditions of Pike*, II, 470, 480. These may be compared with false but seemingly imperishable traditions in Kentucky of George Rogers Clark, Simon Girty, and Isaac Shelby (Bruce, *Daniel Boone and the Wilderness Road*, 182, 201, 252).

These fantasies are not confined to famous personages. Dr. Gregg, writing of the prairie mustangs, mentions a certain white stallion of universal fame, *circa* 1830-40, 'found' everywhere, but never seen.[23] "That famous white mustang stallion," as General Chittenden terms it, was 'still doing business at the same old stand' in his time, half a century later;[24] and this or another ranged all the way from the Rio Grande to Manitoba.[25] Finally, there is our old friend, the 'hoop-snake.' If smoke indicates fire, this creature should be no rarity. Since first coming to Alberta, I have lived throughout my life in familiar intercourse with many who had dwelt for years in the regions from the Platte southward to the Rio Grande and beyond. There is no possible doubt about the hoop-snake; it is a 'well-known fact.' Many of these good folk had known individuals who were personally acquainted with other people (or their sisters or cousins or aunts) who had met fellows who were said to have seen it. I remember reading as a boy, over fifty years ago, of a standing offer from the Smithsonian Institution of Washington of five thousand dollars for a living specimen. One cannot pretend to know everything that takes place; but I have never heard of any claimant. Every one of the instances mentioned is from what was at some historic period, 'buffalo-land.' I know of no inherent reason why any other tradition of that region, or any belief current—if such were the case—among the like uncritical classes, should be thought entitled to demand an implicit acceptance.

Certain phases of buffalo history are inseparable from the history of the Plains Indians. I have noted above,[26] what I consider to have been the evil effects on our knowledge of the true history of the buffalo, which followed from Indian haters' contemptuous rejection of anything and everything which Catlin had to say, whether concerning Indians or not. It does not appear to have been realized to what degree of absurdity this reckless anti-Indian attitude is reduced, when some of its disconnected assertions are brought into conjunction one with another. While the Indian Agent, the land-grabbing propagandist, and the distant arm-chair philosopher were proclaiming by pen and platform the 'improvidence' of the Indian;[27] the soldier was exulting

[23]Gregg, *Early Western Travels*, XX, 260-2.
[24]Chittenden, *American Fur Trade*, II, 833.
[25]White Horse Plains, west of Winnipeg, is said to have derived the name from some mythical white horse, equally elusive with its Southern congener (Coues (ed.), *Henry-Thompson Journals*, I, 288).
[26]See my introductory chapter, note 14.
[27]*In extenso* above, chap. XXI, at large.

over the destruction of hundreds of thousands of pounds of buffalo meat stored up by this or that tribe in readiness for winter;[28] the very thing which yet another so-called 'authority' declares they were 'too lazy' to do.[29] On the testimony of a passing traveller whose own integrity is unimpugned, but who stayed at the place for three or four days only, we are informed that a northern band drove forty or fifty buffalo into their own private pound 'every day.'[30] Without expressly saying so, this conveys a subtle implication of 365 days in the year, and assists to 'prove' Indian wastefulness to the entire satisfaction of the critic. Yet only three years before, and at the same identical season of the year, the same visitor on his way northward found that very same place almost starving![31] The Indians were 'lazy';[32] yet we are asked to believe—and by scientists!—that the able-bodied male proportion of a population estimated, *circa* 1850, at less than 55,000,[33] slew every year not less than 3,500,000 buffalo.[34] This means that some 11,000 individuals killed each year an average of 318.18 buffalo per man; or roughly a buffalo seven days out of every eight.[35] These figures take no account of the annual slaughter—similarly deadly, no doubt—by the tribes, say, south of the Platte; nor of the annual destruction by various physical agencies, more fatal, in the opinion of one inquirer, than man himself prior to the terrific final extermination.[36] Yet we have seen that an annual mortality totalling 2,000,000, from all causes combined, and deducted from a numerical datum liberally in excess of that required by other estimates, would have annihilated the breeding stock of the species thirty years before extermination actually came to pass.[37]

While a scientist was expanding the figures of Indian buffalo destruction to the extent of 'all the traffic would bear,' a soldier was contemptuously reducing Catlin's estimates of 'buffalo-Indian' population by some 20 per cent; for no other apparent reason than that being

[28]Above, chap. XXI, note 321.

[29]Hornaday, "Extermination of the American Bison," 499. *In extenso* above, chap. XV, note 108; chap. XXI, note 320 *seq*.

[30]Thomas Simpson, Carlton, 1837, 1840. *In extenso* below, Appendix AA.

[31]Above, chap. XX, note 269.

[32]Compare Hornaday's own description of the manifold uses to which the buffalo products were put, chap. XXI, note 20 *seq*.

[33]Maclean, *Canadian Savage Folk*, 293. Above, chap. XVIII, note 62.

[34]Professor Spencer F. Baird ('Missouri [River] tribes alone'). Chap. XVIII, note 61.

[35]11,000 x 318.18 = 3,499,980; cf. above, chap. XVIII, notes 56-63.

[36]Dr. Elliott Coues, above, chap. VII, note 150.

[37]See discussion above, chap. XVIII, notes 67-79, and Table of Buffalo Decrease at end of chapter.

Catlin, he must be shown to be wrong.[38] Yet a soldier might have reflected that it was neither logical nor wise, if only in view of those invariable victories with their terrific slaughters of the red men, in which the Indians 'vastly out-numbered the troops,' to incur any risk of a public suspicion that these inexhaustible hosts approximated the lesser rather than the greater computations.[39] Likewise a philosophic reasoner should have realized that by reducing the numbers of the Indians in such wise, he merely contributed to remove their alleged enormities concerning buffalo from the region of the incredible to that of the impossible.

Perhaps impartiality was not to be expected in 1889. But despite the splendid endeavours of American scholars who have honoured themselves and their country alike by their efforts to secure a posthumous justice for the Indian of the nineteenth-century era of wars and hatreds, it is painful to note a similar difficulty some twenty years later,[40] and even more nearly the present time.[41] The varied relationships of buffalo and Indian make it impossible to doubt that the determination to discredit the Indian in defiance of evidence, by fair means or foul, must have contributed to seriously distort the world's conception of many aspects of buffalo history. I remain of the opinion already indicated,[42] that this attitude has not been without its influence upon our more or less standardized conceptions of the Red River Hunt. We simply do not know what local spleens may or may not have found expression in some of the animadversions on this;[43] but we do know from a careful examination of comparative data that more than one critic has eagerly seized upon anything discreditable to the half-breed, and has ignored other evidence. I have endeavoured to set these facts in their true light.

[38]See on this Appendix G, "Buffalo-Using Indian Populations."

[39]See on this feature, Bancroft, *History of Oregon*, II, 406-9 (*circa* 1856); Hebard and Brininstool, *Bozeman Trail*, I, 126, 129, 247-54; II, 180; together with authorities cited above, chap. XXI, note 385; also below, Appendix FF. Theodore Roosevelt, in his *Winning of the West*, alludes very frequently and sensibly to this passion for exaggeration in the earlier Indian fighters.

[40]Hornaday, 1908: above *in extenso*, chap. XXI, note 372.

[41]Laut, 1918-31: above *in extenso*, chap. XXI, note 385.

[42]See chap. XIV, "The Red River Hunt," at large; especially note 235.

[43]See Father Morice's remarks on the partiality and unfairness of Alexander Ross (whose *Red River Settlement*, 1856, is the basic authority for the Hunt) in totally ignoring Bishop Provencher (Morice, *History of the Catholic Church in Western Canada*, I, 131). In his accounts of missionary linguistic work, Ross likewise omits any mention of the Tukudh syllabary of Archdeacon Robert McDonald, a Red River half-breed.

I may remind the critical reader that in my own ignorance of biology, I have steadfastly refrained from intrusion into that sphere. Where I ventured to criticize biologists or zoologists, it has been for their pronouncements as historians. In dealing with an animal now extinct as a free wild species in its most characteristic native habitat, the first task is to ascertain and classify the historical evidence; and not until this has been done can biological investigation proceed with much profit.

I have no apology to offer for what at first sight may seem like a petty cavilling over points of ·detail; a mere tithing of mint, anise, and cummin. If words possess any meaning, it is in my view not merely legitimate, but the very *raison d'être* of scientific criticism, to require, for example, that something which is persistently termed 'regular' shall exhibit regularity under the critical microscope. So also, that which is 'obvious' should have left some evidence at least which could not possibly bear any other meaning than the one which is put forward. As I have hinted already,[44] I am considerably strengthened in this belief by finding that I have authoritative scientific support for the view that it is precisely this somewhat rigidly logical method of analysis that any thesis must be prepared to sustain, before its propositions can be regarded as established. In relation to critical studies such as the present essay, one frequently meets with statements about 'certain broad conclusions remaining unimpaired.' The conclusions which it has been my task to examine seem to me excessively broad for the foundations upon which they rest; altogether too much like an attempt to build a pyramid upon its apex. The possible becomes the probable, and the 'probable' becomes a certainty, far too frequently; and often for no weightier reason, apparently, than because *we* cannot see how otherwise a certain condition could exist.[45]

[44]See above, chap. IV, note 67.

[45]For example, most philosophers would agree in principle that peace ,and security are essential to the development of trade and commerce. These conditions were notoriously uncertain during the Middle Ages in Europe; yet commerce expanded steadily.

Even so competent a scholar as Kroeber seems to me to have not entirely escaped this influence (*Cultural and Natural Areas*, 77).

EUROPEAN BUFFALO SYNONYMY

EUROPEAN

American Ox: Arthur Dobbs, 1741 (Audubon and Bachman, *American Quadrupeds*, II, 33).

American Wild Ox: Warden, 1819 (Richardson, *Fauna Boreali-Americana*, I, 279).

Armenta: De Laet, 1633, and others (Allen, *American Bisons*, 51).

Beasts ("of the bignesse of a Cowe . . .") : Thomas Morton, 1637 (in Marcy, *Exploration of Red River*, 104; Allen, *American Bisons*, 107); Henry Kelsey, 1691 (*Kelsey Papers*, 6-13); Matthew Cocking, 1773 ("Journal," ed. Burpee, 113).[1]

Beeves (Eng. trans.): La Hontan, 1687 (in Allen, *American Bisons*, 107; Douay, Joutel, 1687 (*Journeys of La Salle*, I, 224; II, 78, 79, 100, etc.).

Beuf: "Journal of Jean Baptiste Truteau" (or Trudeau), 1748-1829, Missouri River, 1794-95 (*American Historical Review*, XX, 1914, 299-333).

Bison (Le): French-Canadian (so Seton, *Life-Histories of Northern Animals*, I, 247).

Bison d'Amérique: early French (so, Allen, *American Bisons*, 51).

Bisonte: Spanish (*ibid.*).

Bœuf (Le): Canadian *voyageurs* (so Richardson, *Fauna Boreali-Americana*, I, 279).

Bœuf du Canada: Charlevoix, 1720 (*ibid.*).

Bœuf sauvage[2]: Allouez, 1666 (*Jesuit Relations*, LI, 42, 43); Marquette, 1673 (*ibid.*, LIX, 111); Binneteau, 1699 (*ibid.*, LXV, 73, 105); Marest, 1712 (*ibid.*, LXVI, 293); Du Pratz, 1758 (Allen, *American Bisons*, 51).

BUFFALO: Mark Catesby (first to use as here spelled in *Natural History of Carolina*, London, 1754, I; so, Garretson, *American Bison*, 10, 233); but see "Buffaloe," below, on this.

'Buffalo Ox': See on this chap. III, notes 158-70.

Buffaloe: Henry Fleet, Potomac River, 1624 (Hornaday, "Extermination of the American Bison," 373).[3] Salmon, 1749 (see '*Urus*' below).

Buf, Buff, Buffe: David Ingram, 1568 (in Hakluyt, *Voyages*, VI, 296-354; Allen, *American Bisons*, 80); Winsor (ed.), *Narrative and Critical*

*See Supplementary Synonymy, Appendix MM, 925-29.

[1]On the significance of 'beast,' see note on Henry Kelsey, at conclusion of chap. XII.

[2]On the possible meaning at this period of *sauvage* as woodland or in the modern sense of 'wild' animal (*i.e.* ferocious, dangerous), see below, Appendix B, "Buffalo and Wild Cows."

[3]Compare above on all this, chap. IX, notes 37, 47.

History, III, 64, 170, 186; Fiske, *Discovery of America*, I, 249); Dablon and Allouez, 1671 (*Jesuit Relations*, LV, 195, 197).[4]

Buffelo: Lawson, 1700; Brickell, 1730 (Allen, *American Bisons*, 51).

Buffillo: Henry Kelsey, 1691 (*Kelsey Papers*, 3).

Buffle: early French (so, Richardson, *Fauna Boreali-Americana*, I, 279; Allen, *American Bisons*, 51).[5]

Bufle: Boucher, 1663 (Thwaites, ed. note, *Jesuit Relations*, IX, 310-11); Binneteau, 1699 (*ibid.*, LV, 73).

Bullocks (Eng. trans.): Joutel, 1687 (*Journeys of La Salle*, II, 40-4, etc.); Allen (*American Bisons*, 95).

Bulls (Eng. trans.): Coronado *et al.*, 1541 (*Journey of Coronado*, *passim*); Hennepin, 1679 (*New Discovery*, ed. Thwaites, I, 145, etc., etc.).

Cattle (Eng. trans.): De Soto *et al.*, 1540 (*Narratives of De Soto*, *passim*; *Purchas his Pilgrimes*, XVII, 521-50; XVIII, 1-51); Coronado *et al.*, 1541 (*Journey of Coronado*, 83, 139, 237). "Cattle, as big as Kine . . .": Samuel Argall, west of Potomac River, 1612 (*Purchas his Pilgrimes*, XIX, 92).[6]

Cibola: Spanish (as a 'loan-word,' Allen, *American Bisons*, 51, *re* Coronado *et al.*, 1541);[7] Douay, 1687 (*Journeys of La Salle*, I, 224).[8]

Cibolo: Southwestern U.S. *circa* 1831 (Gregg, *Early Western Travels*, XX, 262).[9]

Cows (Eng. trans., as generic term): Cabeza de Vaca, *circa* 1530 (*Journey of Cabeza*, *passim*); Coronado *et al.*, 1541 (*Journey of Coronado*, *passim*); De Soto *et al.*, 1541 (*Narratives of De Soto*, *passim*); Radisson and Groseilliers, 1661 (Bryce, *Remarkable History*, 5).

Crooke-Backed Oxen: Coronado, 1541 (in Hornaday, "Extermination of the American Bison," 374); Gomara, trans. Hakluyt (Allen, *American Bisons*, 134).

Hump-backed Oxen: Winship (ed., in *Journey of Coronado*, introd., ix).

Hunch-backed Kine: Purchas (*Purchas his Pilgrimes*, XVIII, 64).[10]

---

[4]Wherever they derived it, it appears as an English term in the earliest use I have found following Ingram: Newfoundland and the East Indies, both 1583. See chap. IX, note 48.

[5]See on this, Appendix B below.

[6]On Argall's animals, see chap. IX, notes 34-52.

[7]Cibola is found as a place-name only, in the *Journey of Coronado*, ed. Winship; "beasts or Kine of Cibola . . .": Henry Hawks, 1572, in Hakluyt, *Voyages*, VI, 284; cf. *Purchas his Pilgrimes*, XIV, 482.

[8]It is not certain whether Father Douay heard the word (for buffalo) in Europe, where it was known to Martine Basanier of Paris, 1582 (Hakluyt, *Voyages*, VI, 234), or from the Indians, whom La Salle's party found using other Spanish words such as *caballi* for horses, etc. (*Journeys of La Salle*, I, 48, 292).

[9]From *Cibolo* came *ciboléro* = buffalo-hunter (Gregg, *Early Western Travels*, XIX, 235, 239; XX, 119, 136). The term *cibolas* was applied by early Spanish writers to any buffalo-hunting Indians; so, *Handbook of American Indians*, I, 299. Cf. *Querecho* as a pueblo term for buffalo-hunting Apaches (*ibid.*, II, 338).

[10]See *vacas jorabadas*, below.

Islinois Cattle (Eng. trans.): Bacqueville de la Potherie, *circa* 1700 (Blair, *Indian Tribes,* I, 366); Bonnecamp, 1750 (*Jesuit Relations,* LXIX, 177).[11]

Kine of Cibola: Cabeza de Vaca, *circa* 1530 (Eng. trans., in *Purchas his Pilgrimes,* XVII, 506; XVIII, 64-7); Coronado, 1541 (*ibid.,* XIV, 482); Henry Hawks, 1572 (in Hakluyt, *Voyages,* VI, 283).

Mexican Bull (Eng. trans.): De Solis, 1684 (Seton, *Life-Histories of Northern Animals,* 251), or 1724 (Allen, *American Bisons,* Appendix, 231; Hornaday, "Extermination of the American Bison," 373).

Montana Buffalo: Bancroft (*History of Washington, Idaho, and Montana,* 595).[12]

Mountain Bison (for the 'mountain'—or possibly 'wood'—variety described by hunters): authorities cited chap. III, note 49 *seq.*

Mountain Buffalo: see Mountain Bison.

Oxen (Eng. trans.): Cabeza de Vaca, *circa* 1530 (in *Purchas his Pilgrimes,* XVII, 478); De Soto *et al.,* 1540 (*ibid.,* XVIII, 31); Coronado, *et al.,* 1541 (*ibid.,* 64, 78, etc.); Alexander Henry the Elder, 1775: ". . . Ox-skins, which the traders call buffalo-robes..." (*Travels, 1760-1776,* 256, 265).

Oxen of Cibola: Toletus, trans. Hakluyt or Purchas (*Purchas his Pilgrimes,* XVIII, 78).

Prairie Beeves: Gregg (*Early Western Travels,* XIX, 205).

Shag-Haired Oxen: that is, the animal seen by Argall, 1612 ("A Discourse on Virginia," [1625], in *Purchas his Pilgrimes,* XIX, 250).[13]

Taureau sauvage (apparently a generic term including both sexes): Hennepin, 1679 (*New Discovery,* ed. Thwaites, *passim*).

Taurus Mexicanus: Hernandez, at the time of Philip II of Spain, 1651, etc. (Richardson, *Fauna Boreali-Americana,* I, 279; Audubon and Bachman, *American Quadrupeds,* II, 33; Bancroft, *Native Races,* II, 165, 476; III, 728).

Urus (or *Zorax*): ". . . described by Caesar, which the English improperly call a Buffaloe . . ." (Thomas Salmon; *A New Geographical and Historical Grammar,* 1749, *s.v.* 'Carolina' = both the Carolinas and Georgia, 537). Also William Bartram, Georgia, 1773 = 'the buffalo [*urus*]' (Travels, 62).[14]

---

[11]'The Islenois' was used at a territorial name, not merely for the river. Henry has 'the traders of the Islenois' as late as 1806 (Coues (ed.), *Henry-Thompson Journals,* I, 384). 'Ilinois oxen' and 'Ilinois cows' used, manifestly for domestic cattle, in "Detroit Mission Accounts," 1733-56 (*Jesuit Relations,* LXIX, 268, 269, 291). It is unlikely in my opinion that these were domesticated buffalo. Father Marest observes in much the same region, 1712, "We have tried to tame the wild oxen, but we have never succeeded . . ." (*ibid.,* LXVI, 293). Cf. below, Appendix C.

[12]They were not specially characteristic of Montana; perhaps a rather ornate phrase for 'mountain buffalo.' *In extenso* above, chap. III, note 63.

[13]See above, chap. IX, notes 34-52; cf. 'shag-haired sheepe' (*Purchas his Pilgrimes,* XIV, 469).

[14]On this supposed identity, see Richardson, *Fauna Boreali-Americana,* I, 280).

Vacas jorobadas: Cortez, Bernal Diaz, Gomara, etc., 1519-60; = 'hump-backed cows.'[15]

Vacca Indica: Theodore De Bry, 1598 (in Baillie-Grohman, *Sport and Life*, 169).

Vacche (Ital.): Father Bressani, 1653 (*Jesuit Relations*, XXXVIII, 241).

Vaches sauvages: Dablon and Allouez, 1671 (*ibid.*, LV, 195, 197).

Visent (*Bos europaeus*): modern term.

Wild Bulls: Hennepin, 1679 (*New Discovery, passim*); Alexander Henry, Sr., 1775 (*Travels, 1760-1776*, 273).[16]

Wild Cattle (Eng. trans.): Le Moine, 1654 (*Jesuit Relations*, XLI, 129);[17] Dablon, 1673 (*ibid.*, LVIII, 99); Marquette, 1673 (*ibid.*, LIX, 111); Douay, 1687 (*Journeys of La Salle*, I, 224); Diron D'Artaguiette, 1723 (*Journal*, in Mereness (ed.), *Colonial Travels*, 53).

Wild Cows (a generic term): Cabeza de Vaca, *circa* 1530 (*Journey of Cabeza, passim*); Coronado *et al.*, 1541 (*Journey of Coronado, passim*); perhaps Jean de Quens, 1656 (*Jesuit Relations*, XLII, 37).

Wild Ox ('The Ox Nation' = Eastern Sioux): Hierosme Lalemant, 1663 (*ibid.*, XLVII, 149, 316); Allouez, 1666 (*ibid.*, LI, 42, 43); Binneteau, 1996 (*ibid.*, LXV, 105); Gravier, 1700 (*ibid.*, 135); Marest, 1712 (*ibid.*, LXVI, 293); Poisson, 'aux Akensas' (that is, Arkansas), 1726 (*ibid.*, LXVII, 285); A. Henry, Sr., Saskatchewan River, 1775 (*Travels 1760-1776*, 248, 276-80, 292, 297, 312).[18]

Wilde Ochsen und Kuhe: Peter Kalm, 1749 (Allen, *American Bisons*, 51).

Wisent al. Visent (*Bos europaeus*): modern term.

Wood Bison: this from hunters, who applied term *bison* to the woodland and mountain varieties only (Richardson, *Fauna Boreali-Americana*, introd., I, xxxvii; Allen, *American Bisons*, 39-41).

Wood Buffalo: see Wood Bison.

Zorax: see Urus.

INDIAN ANIMAL SYNONYMY

The following list of animal names has been taken principally from Maximilian's vocabularies of twenty-five Indian languages (*Early Western Travels*, XXIV, 210-300), which his editor, Thwaites, characterizes as unique since many of the languages are now no longer spoken. I have also used the lesser ones of Alexander Henry (Coues (ed.), *Henry-Thompson Journals*, II, 534-8) and George Catlin (*Letters on the North American Indians*, II, 262-6). These principal sources are marked MAX, HENRY, CATLIN, respectively. Other contributors are indicated individually.

Although lamentably imperfect, the following table furnishes some instructive data. It is not surprising that the large and powerful Algonkian

[15]This is the source of the various 'hump-backed' synonyms.

[16]Henry, 1775—"supping on wild beef . . ." (*Travels, 1760-1776*, 278).

[17]Hewitt (*Conservation of the Wild Life of Canada*, 28) thinks these were 'undoubtedly wapiti.' This may be so; perhaps also Father De Quens, 1656 (below, *s.v.* Wild Cows). See *in extenso*, Appendix B.

[18]The elder Henry never uses the word *buffalo* as his own term; cf. 'Oxen,' above.

stock should furnish what seems to have been the generic 'buffalo' root, *pisik, peecheek, petay,* etc.,[1] over a vast extent of territory, when we remember that the Algonkians were apparently in close contact with the species along the general northeastern front of its historic habitat prior to the Siouans, for example. We have seen that tribal friendships and hatreds cut across the lines of family relationships in several instances;[2] and these attitudes are in some cases recent enough in the traditions of the race to be later than the period of time probably necessary for the assimilation of a foreign term in the language of a non-literary people.[3]

When we bear in mind that the Cree, in respect of their territorial distribution, and the even wider spread of their language—the Indian *lingua franca* from the Great Lakes to the Rockies and for 500 or 600 miles northward from the international boundary—may be considered to have been probably the largest and most representative tribe of the Algonkian stock, the remarkable thing is that apparently they did not use the Algonkian root-term themselves. There is in the Ojibwa-Cree what seems to be almost a fundamental root or etymon signifying *animal* or *beast* (that is, the word *mus,* or 'moose').[4] This term, capable of extension by Indian polysynthesis into a variety of animal names for many species might, if we possessed the etymological key, throw much light on the beginnings of Cree-buffalo relationships. It is a curious fact that in the two related Indian tongues which together covered a vast portion of the moose habitat, the root-element itself, *mus,* indicated the moose,[5] as though this were

---

[1]It can scarcely be doubted that the term for 'jumping-pound' in Blackfoot Pound, Alberta = a place-name), 69. The Ojibwa and Illinois term pisikiou is also given in Watkins' *Cree Dictionary* (1865; rev. ed. 1938) is the Swampy Cree for buffalo; their lands abutting on the Ojibwa (Saulteaux) territory. See below, 'Cree.'

[2]E.g. the inveterate hatreds of Cree and Blackfoot (both Algonkian) or

[3]The immemorial enmity between Cheyennes and Assiniboines is said to 1640. See above, chap. VI, on an alleged Blackfoot adoption of a Cree term for their first horse.

[4]Father Lacombe, writing as a French and classical scholar, has the Cree

[5]Moose as *moose, mooswa* (Cree) and *moose* (Ojibwa); so, Seton, *Life*-1607-22 (cf. description of one, *Purchas his Pilgrimes,* XIX, 281). Lacombe gives *ayâbew moswa* = bull moose, *notjimosowew* = 'chasse à l'orignal,' *nosémoswa, onitjaniwimoswa,* both = 'Femelle d'orignal,' *mosokiwan* = 'nez d'orignal' (*i.e.* 'the mouffle'), *apistimosus* = 'petit orignal' (Lacombe, *Dictionnaire de la Langue des Cris,* 325, 58, 147, 511, 200, 298, etc.; cf. *Handbook of the American Indians,* I, 940). But he also gives what may be (in view of the derivation of Cree from Ojibwa) an earlier or purer form, *monswa* = 'orignal,' *ayâbemonswa* = 'l'orignal mâle,' *monswegin* = 'une peau d'orignal' (*Dictionnaire de la Langue des Cris,* 470, 483, 216). The *n* form is given by Maximilian as the Ojibwa moose-name, *mons* (*Early Western Travels,* XXIV, 279); also in the 'Monsoni' (*mongso-aeythinyuwok*) = 'moose people,' an Algonkian tribe related to the Cree-Ojibwa, perhaps a phratry of the latter, on Moose River, Northern Ontario; whence

'the animal' of the region, a sense perhaps reproduced in the French orignal.[6] Some similarly 'indigenous' etymology may underlie the Algonkian root, which is present in the names of the three largest species in the Cree territory, and in others also, but not, it would seem, in those of the very small ones.[7] Somewhat similar parallelisms are present in other Indian tongues, not merely in relation to the horse, where it was naturally to be expected,[8] but also in respect of other wild species,[9] indigenous to the linguistic territory affected. For this reason, it has been thought that it would be of interest and value to the student to present a number of these in a comparative tabular form. Slight differences will be noted, due either to dialectal variation, or perhaps to an imperfect apprehension by the inquirer; and also the constant recurrence of the deer-dog-horse analogy in Indian thought. It may perhaps furnish some inferential evidence for an age-long acquaintance with the domesticated dog, as against a much more recent contact in many regions with the buffalo, that only in three direct instances, Osage, Quapaw, and Winnebago (all Siouan) and possibly in the Mohican (Algonkian) has there been found to be any resemblance between dog and wolf names, in the material I have had opportunity to consult. See Table of Animal Names below.

---

probably Moosonee (*monsone* = moose); J. Mooney, C. Thomas, *Handbook of Canadian Indians*, 312, 315.

[6]Orignac, which is like an Oxe' (Tadoussac, 1603); . . . said to bee like Oxen, perhaps Buffes. . . .' 'Orignacs are Ellans,' *i.e.* moose. So, Lescarbot, in *Purchas his Pilgrimes*, XVIII, 191, 209, 230, 246, 264.

[7]Moose, buffalo, bear. The last *maskwa* = 'ours'; *noje-maskwa* = 'femelle d'ours;' *maskweyán* = 'une peau d'ours'; etc. (Lacombe, *Dictionnaire de la Langue des Cris*, 154, 208, 442, etc.). Also as *musquash*: Bear's Hill, Alberta, as *muskwa-chi-si* or *Musquachis* (*Place-Names of Alberta*, 16). *Musquash* = 'musk-rat'; so, Chamberlain, *Handbook of Canadian Indians*, 317; but Lacombe has *watjask, watchask* = 'rat musqué' (*Dictionnaire de la Langue des Cris*, 237, 641; *watchusk*: *Place-Names of Alberta*, 132). Musquash is found as a trade-term for muskrat skins, 1841, 1842 (in Oliver (ed.), *Canadian North-West*, "Minutes of Council," II, 814, 827, 835, 847); but other terms are 'Musk Rat,' 1839, 1841 (*ibid.*, 789, 813), and 'Spring rats,' 1841, 1843 (*ibid.*, 827, 863). 'Musquash': Umfreville, *The Present State of Hudson's Bay*, 82, 87. Henry includes the *mus* root in the Cree term for 'cabbrie' (antelope), *ahpisemoosecuse* (Coues (ed.), *Henry-Thompson Journals*, II, 535); and both Maximilian (*Early Western Travels*, XXIV, 278) and Henry (Coues (ed.), *Henry-Thompson Journals*, II, 535) in the Ojibwa for dog: *animúss* and *animouche* respectively.

[8]Apart from one sent to the Governor, Montmagny, in 1647, the first horses reached Quebec, July 16, 1665. The Indians called them 'the moose of France' (*Jesuit Relations*, XV, 235; L, 81, 215, 319). For 'dog'-synonyms for the horse, see below in this table.

[9]The Sioux *tah-tank-kah, tatanga*, is stated to signify 'large moose' (McLean, *Canadian Savage Folk*, 28). Compare also Thlinkit 'buffalo' (*hootz*) and Haida 'wolf' (*ho-ootz*) below. Both are British Columbia tribes.

INDIAN ANIMAL NAMES

Tribe	Buffalo	Horse	Dog (D) or Wolf (W)	Cervidae: Antelope (A), Deer (D), Elk (E), Moose (M)	Author
Algonkin	peecheek; nochena peecheek = cow				Richardson, Fauna Boreali-Americana, I, 279[28]
Arapaho			háqihana = W		Handbook of American Indians, I, 73, 532
Arikara	wa-tash	ha wah rooh te	hahtch = D steerich = W	annoo notche = A a noo nach = D wah = E	Catlin
	hoh-kúss = bull watahesch = cow sahóhtsch = a buffalo robe	chawàhruchtä chawakàdu = mule	chahtsch = D pachkàtsch = W	nochnunàhts = D ua = E uànukúss = stag uauàtaesch = doe wah-suchàrut = M	Maximilian
	okos = 'band of bulls' (gens)				Handbook of American Indians, I, 86; II, 116
Assiniboine		shu-gar-tung	shong = D		Umfreville, Present State of Hudson's Bay, 202
	peetai	ahcanyecabe, or shonga-tanga	shonga = D	tahtogan = A opah = D (red deer) tàh = M	Henry
	tatanga; tatanka taha = buffalo horns	schón-atanga	schónka = D schunk-tógitsche = W	tatogana = A choià = E	Maximilian

[28] I am unaware whether the (linguistic) family name, Algonquian, later the modern Algonkian, was coined in 1829; or whether the Algonkins proper knew the buffalo.

Tribe	Buffalo	Horse	Dog (D) or Wolf (W)	Cervidae: Antelope (A), Deer (D), Elk (E), Moose (M)	Author
(Canadian 'Stoney')	tatanga = *b. at large* cha-t. = *wood b.* sena-t. = *prairie b.* mno-ga t. = *bull* wea-t. = *b. cow*				I am indebted for the Stoney forms to my friend, Rev. P. G. Sutton of Vancouver, formerly missionary at Paul's Reserve, Wabamun Lake, Alberta. Compare the Assiniboine forms with the Sioux, below
Atsina	enáhkïi	wau-ce-hoth	hudth-er = D		Umfreville, *Present State of Hudson's Bay*, vocabulary, 202[29]
		it-shou-ma-shunga (*red dog*)	hotewi = D kïatïssa = W	lasikge = D (*common*) buhe-i = D (*black-tailed*)	Maximilian
Bannock	kutshundika = 'buffalo-eaters' (*gens*)		kliñ = D chiyune = W		Butler, *Great Lone Land*, 267. Clearly a foreign 'loan-word,' however. *Shunga, shonga* (= *dog*) is Siouan *Handbook of American Indians*, I, 130, 743[30]
Beaver (Tsattine)	hakáï h. tayidze = *b. bull* h. toché = *b. cow* haka = *calf* tytyue = *ox*	kliñchok kliñtaché = *mare* kliñyaché = *calf* kliñyazi = *foal* kliñtayadzé = *stallion* soosoohlyen = *ass*		yathóne, tápi = *cabbree* (*i.e.* A) madzih = *reindeer* hátá = E or M h. tayidze = *buck* h. che = *doe* tsiye = *young moose*	From a MS. Beaver-Cree-English vocabulary, compiled by Rev. A. C. Garrioch (Church Missionary Society), Athabaska Diocese, 1875 *seq.* I am indebted for this to the kindness of Mrs. (Rev.) Robert Holmes of that diocese, 1902 *seq.* For the Beaver (*tsattine* = beaver) see *Handbook of American Indians*, II, 822
Blackfoot (Siksika)		pin-ne-cho-me-tar	amé-tou = D		Umfreville, *Present State of Hudson's Bay*, vocabulary, 202

[29] The Atsina are the Fall, Rapid, or 'Gros Ventres of Alberta,' a branch of the Arapaho; the 'Big Bellies' after whom the Belly River, south Alberta, is named (*Place-Names of Alberta*, 18). See Umfreville, *Present State of Hudson's Bay*, 197; *McGillivray's Journal*, 27; Coues (ed.), *Henry-Thompson Journals*, II, 531, 718, 733; Maximilian, *Early Western Travels*, XXIV, 70, and cf. *ibid.*, VI, 371; *Handbook of American Indians*, I, 113; etc.

[30] The root-term *ika, eka, ïta* signifies 'eaters of' among several Shoshonean tribes. See Ross, *Fur Hunters*, I, 130. Cf. below, "Comanche."

Tribe	Buffalo	Horse	Dog (D) or Wolf (W)	Cervidae: Antelope (A), Deer (D), Elk (E), Moose (M)	Author
	ainew	poonokometai	imnetai = D	owwahcass = A poonno kno = D (red deer)	Henry
	stomick = bull	purnakomitä	emitá = D sikkapehs = W sehnipàh = coyote	cikittisso = M purnokàh stomick = E sikitisuh = M	Maximilian. He mentions Indian chiefs: Tatsika-Stomik, Otsequa - Stomik, Stomik-Sosak, *Early Western Travels*, XXIII, 142-63
	eneuh	ponokah meta	a meeteh = D ahpace = W	saw kee owa kasee = A ouacasee = D ponokah = E	Catlin
	eininee				Richardson, in Franklin, (First) *Journey to the Polar Sea* (orig. ed.), 109
Blood (Kainah)	enewh = b. en masse stomach = b. bull		tasha = W (clan)	ponokix = E (a gens) siksinokaks = 'black elks' band'	McDougall, *Saddle, Sled and Snowshoe*, 262 *Handbook of American Indians*, II, 279, 571
Caddo					
Cherokee			aní' wa' ya = W (clan)	aní' kawi' = D (clan)	*Ibid*, II, 695
Cheyenne	hottúe = bull issiwóhn = cow wohksá = calf	woindo hámm akéhm = mule	chotónn = D hoh-ni = W hotámitä' nio = 'dog men' (band)	mo-úi = E	*Handbook of American Indians*, I, 247 Maximilian

Tribe	Buffalo	Horse	Dog (D) or Wolf (W)	Cervidae: Antelope (A), Deer (D), Elk (E), Moose (M)	Author
Chippewyan	adgiddah yawseh				'Little Bison' (Musk-ox); Richardson, *Fauna Boreali-Americana*, I, 275
	ed-jer-ay				'Bison,' Seton, *Life-Histories of Northern Animals*, I, 247; *Game Animals*, III, 641. 'Wood bison,' *ibid.*, 706. Probably they knew no other
	et-cherre = *bull*				C. of Great Slave Lake (Lefroy, 1844), Richardson, *Arctic Expedition, 1847-1850*, 514
	ettirrè-yá-nè = *bull* ettirre-su-ta-ha = *cow*				C. of Athabaska, *ibid.*, 508; cf. *Edjieretrukenade* = 'buffalo people' (of the Chippewyan group); *Handbook of American Indians*, I, 414
Comanche	cook-chow				Marcy, *Exploration of Red River*, 275
	kotsoteka = 'buffalo-eaters' (*gens*)			kwahari (*pl.*) = A (*a gens or division*)	*Handbook of American Indians*, I, 328, 728. See note 30, above, on *eka, eta, ita* = 'eaters of.' Both Bannock and Comanche are Shoshonean.
Cree	moostouche	mistahtim	ahtim = D	ahpisemoosecuse = A wahwasskais = D mooswah = M	Henry. *Note mista(h)tim* = horse: that is to say 'big dog'
	mostúss japòh m. = *bull* onintchah-oniuack = *cow*	mesatimm	atimm = D	apestat-jehkus = A uauasskéhsu = E eyapeu-uauasskehsu = E (*stag*)	Maximillian

Tribe	Buffalo	Horse	Dog (D) or Wolf (W)	Cervidae: Antelope (A), Deer (D), Elk (E), Moose (M)	Author
Dog Rib (Thling-chadinne)	et-cherri = *bull* et-cherri-ettzae = *cow*				Fort Simpson, N.W.T. (Lefroy, 1844). Richardson, *Arctic Expedition, 1847-1850*, 514
Flathead (Salish)	zotúnn chooth-lim = *buffalo bull*	punko-emáhhi-mia = *race-horse* chiltz-altz-kar	nachketsä = D ahgk a cheen = D	zinechkóhch = D chtónskutsiss = E choo ool le = A tae yetz a = *red deer* snae chiltz un = *doe*	Maximilian Henry[31]
Hidatsa (Minatari or 'Gros Ventres of the Missouri')	witá kihrapi = *bull* úichtia = *cow* nahksidi = *calf*	eisóh-waschukka eisóh or éhsu-wassuka-náhnka = *young horse* achichtia = *mule*	maschúkka = D sähscha = W (*gray*) bóh-sa = *coyote* säh-tschüpischá = W (*black*) sahschattácki = W (*white*)	sih-tatacke = D *in general* sih-tatacke-kihrape = *stag or buck* sih-tatackte-michka = *doe* apatapá = M	Maximilian. Note the similarity in 'dog' and 'horse' (*maschukka, waschukka*)[32]
Illinois	pisikious (*pl. ?*)				Illinois and (upper) Mississippi tribes. Dablon and Allouez, 1671, *Jesuit Relations*, LV, 195, 197; Marquette, 1673, *ibid.*, LIX, 111. Pizhiki (buffalo), a Chippewa chief, 1759-1855, *Handbook of American Indians*, II, 266.
Iowa	arukhwa = *buffalo or cow buffalo* cheyinyc = *b. calf*		michirache = W	khotachi = E hó-ma-yiñ' e = *young elks (a sub-gens)*	*Ibid.*, I, 99, 557, 614, 680
Iroquois			toryone = W		*Ibid.*, II, 786
Kadohadacho	tanaha		tasha = W (*clan*)		*Ibid.*, I, 639; II, 695. See tarahah (Pawnee) below

[31] 'Flathead,' like 'Snake,' is a vague, indefinite term. Those now officially designated Flathead (Salish) never flattened the head (see *Handbook of American Indians*, I, 465; and a list of those so called, *ibid.*, II, 1054).

[32] See following note (33).

Tribe	Buffalo	Horse	Dog (D) or Wolf (W)	Cervidae: Antelope (A), Deer (D), Elk (E), Moose (M)	Author
	moostoosh	mistatim mistatimoosio = *colt* kiskisis = *mare* soosoowi mistatim = *ass*	mahihkun = W atim = D	mooswa = M wawaskesio = A (*cabbree*) utik, utikwai (*pl.*), or atik, atikdai = *reindeer*	Franklin (First) *Journey to the Polar Sea*, 89, 668; Richardson, *Fauna Boreali-Americana*, I, 279 MS. Beaver-Cree-English vocabulary (Garrioch)
	moostoosh moostoosis = *calf*				
	oonichanio = *cow*				
	mustus pikwatchimustus = *bœuf sauvage* (wood b.) maskutewimustus = *b. des prairies*	mistatim ayekkwewatim = *gelding*	atim = D mahigan = W	mons, monswa, mooswah = M ayâbe-monswa = *bull* *moose* (*l'original mâle*)	Lacombe, *Dictionnaire de la Langue des Cris*, 43, 58, 149, 183, 200, 216, 278, 325, 427, 470, 483, 511, etc.
	ayâbe-mustus = *bull* onitjaniw = *cow*				
	nosta-mus-tus = *cow* oya-peyu-mustus = *bull*				Cree of Carlton House, Richardson, *Arctic Expedition, 1847-1850*, 508
	matheh-moostos = 'ugly bison' (*musk-ox*)				Also Chippewyan (as a loan-word): Richardson, *Fauna Boreali-Americana*, I, 275
	ah-thuk-ard moostoosh = *wood buffalo*				Cree and Ojibwa: Seton, *Game Animals*, III, 706, 709
Crow	mas-kootay moostoosh = *prairie b.*			o-hot-du-sha = A	Cree and northern Indians: E. Mignault to Seton, *ibid.* *Handbook of American Indians*, I, 111

Tribe	Buffalo	Horse	Dog (D) or Wolf (W)	Cervidae: Antelope (A), Deer (D), Elk (E), Moose (M)	Author
Kansa	chedunga = b. bull ? arukhwa = cow		shomakoosa = prairie wolf or coyote (a gens)	ta = D upan = E (a gens)	Ibid., I, 655; II, 553, 664, 871
Kiowa	pá-dó-gâ-i, padó-gâ = white-faced b. bull		? qui = W	kogui (pl.) = E (a clan)	Ibid., I, 721; II, 601. Drannan (Thirty-One Years on the Plains, 42) mentions a Kiowa chief, 'Black Buffalo,' 1847; but gives no native name. Handbook of American Indians (1, 394) also notes a Kiowa chief, Pá-dó-gâ-i or Padó-gâ = 'White - faced buffalo bull'
Kutenai	jiámmo		chatsin = D kachi, kachkin = W	zupka = D keskásse = E	Maximilian
Mandan	berockà = bull pthhnda, pthhnde = cow nihka = calf	ùmpa-menissä ù.-menissinihk asch = young horse schümpsi-manisseh = mule	chahratä-psih = W (black) c.chótta = W (gray) schähäckä, or schähäcke = coyote	kockbe rocká = A (buck) berockà = E (stag) òmpa-mihk-asch = E (doe) páhchubptapta = M	Maximilian[33]
	ptemday	ompah meneda	mones = D waroota = D harratta = W	ko ka = A mah man a coo = D omepah = E	Catlin
Menominee			hana (änä' m) = D moqwaio = W	apaq' soss = D ama' skos = E mons = M	Handbook of American Indians, I, 530, 843, 942; II, 121

[33] Maximilian notes dialectal variations in the two Mandan villages. 'One-year-old b. cow' was *ninkii-patu* and *ninkii-pätune* in Mihtutta-hangkusch and Ruhptáre villages respectively. Similarly, 'young cow' was *ptin-* ... *chanaka, ptin-ikinikä* (Early Western Travels, XXIV, 260). Compare also above, "Mandan." He gives *wahock-schukkä* = 'animal' in that language.

Tribe	Buffalo	Horse	Dog (D) or Wolf (W)	Cervidae: Antelope (A), Deer (D), Elk (E), Moose (M)	Author
Miami			chonga = D mowhawa *or* mahwäwa = W	shewea = E	*Ibid.*, I, 854, 953; II, 460, 912
Missouri	arukhwa			hotachi = E tam = A pim = D	*Ibid.*, I, 572, 911[34]
Mohican or Mahican			ndeyao = D mechchaooh *or* nehjao = W tooksetuk = W (*clan*)		*Ibid.*, I, 788; II, 784. Compare the Delaware wolf-clan, *ptuk-sit* (*ibid.*, I, 386; II, 784)
'Musquake or Fox'	moskutáck-nallusuá = *prairie cattle* nallusuá = *domestic cattle*	nákoto-kaschá	honémua = D	maschauáwe = E	Maximilian. These are more commonly, and in modern works, Fox; constituting with their close allies the Sauk, the well-known 'Sacs and Foxes'
Nez Percé	moose moose	she came, koosy tallow noot = *gelding*	koosy koosy = D	lums lums = D mo luck = E	Ross, *Fur Hunters*, I, 317-23
'Ogebois'	pecheke	paipaijikosk unghee	animouche = D	muchcataiwanou-ouish = A homashkose = D (*red deer*) mouse *or* mouze = M	Henry
Ojibwa	pizhiki ('Buffalo,' a chief, 1759-1855)	päbäjiko-caji	animúss = D maihngann = W	apisti-tigosch = A uauáschkess = D	Maximilian[35]

[34] Lewis and Clark mention a Missouri or Oto chief (both Siouan), 'Neswaunja' (the 'Big Ox'), whose name might yield another root-form, if we had the key (*Journals*, I, 89).

[35] John Long, the 'Nor'-Wester,' Nipigon country, 1768-82, mentions an Ojibwa named Ogashy = 'the horse' (*Early Western Travels*, II, 142). If we could run this instance to earth (*Ogashy = pabajik o-cajI*), it might furnish some data concerning the chronology of the horse, so far northeast. See above, chap. V. Compare the Ojibwa wolf-name (*Handbook of American Indians*, I, 279, 953, 964) with the Cree above.

Tribe	Buffalo	Horse	Dog (D) or Wolf (W)	Cervidae: Antelope (A), Deer (D), Elk (E), Moose (M)	Author
('Chippewa')	ouasouarini *or* ahwahsissa = *Bullhead (clan)*		myeegun *or* ma-i-ngun = W		Maximilian *Handbook of American Indians*, II, 172[38]
Omaha	téh *or* tăh tăh-ská = *European ox*	schongä-tónga schantón-schinga = *a young horse*	schinúda = D schanton = W mikasi = W (*gens*)	tahg-tchä = D (*common term*) onpah = E	Maximilian. *Mikasi* = 'wolf' is from *Handbook of American Indians*, I, 860. *Mikasseh* = 'coyote' is given by Maximilian, *Early Western Travels*, XXIV, 269[37]
Osage	tschetoga = *bull* tschéh = *cow* tschéh-schinga = *calf*	kawa (*sing. and pl.*)	schong-gä = D	opán = E opán tánga *or* hächága = *stag* opán-minga = *doe* opán-schinga = '*calf*' nanpanta = D (*a gens*) upkhan = E (*sub-gens*)	*Handbook of American Indians*, II, 24, 872
Oto	tjà	schong-äh non-tua-chonjä = *mule*	schonk-okämäh = D schanton = W	tahg-tsche = D hóma = E	Maximilian
	arukhwa = *buffalo or 'cow buffalo'*		mé-je-rä-ja = W	hooma = E	*Handbook of American Indians*, I, 99, 614; II, 166

[38] Exception has been taken to this name being of buffalo derivation, the true origin being thought to be the 'bullhead' (trout?). The Ouasouarini, 'people of the Bullhead clan,' were a Chippewa tribe about Georgian Bay, Ontario, 1640; probably identical with the Ouassi, found near Nipigon River, 1706 (*Handbook of American Indians*, II, 172). It would be of interest to learn what other animal than *Bison americanus* could suggest such a parallel to an Indian tribe *circa* 1640 in that region. Most probably the name was age-old then.

[37] See above, note 27. This Omaha (Siouan) name *tah* is apparently the same as the Dakota-Sioux buffalo-root *tah* = moose. See above, "Blackfoot," for *ponokamita* = 'elk dog,' *i.e.* horse; also Potawatami and Shawnee 'horse,' = elk. Horse in the Creek or 'Muscogulge' tongue (southeastern United States) = 'big deer': Bartram, *Travels*, 185.

Tribe	Buffalo	Horse	Dog (D) or Wolf (W)	Cervidae: Antelope (A), Deer (D, Elk (E), Moose (M)	Author
Pahni or Pawnee	taraháh	aruhsch kit-kehah-keh = *mule*			Maximilian
			tskiri = W; *whence* Skidi = '*Wolf Pawnee*'		*Handbook of American Indians*, II, 589. Compare *tanaha*, above ("Kadohadacho"). Both tribes are Caddoan.
Piegan			é-mi-taks (*pl.*) = '*dogs*' (*a clan*)		*Handbook of American Indians*, II, 422
Ponca	washaba, washabe = '*dark buffalo*'			nikapashna = E (*gens*)	*Ibid.*, II, 279, 919
Potawatomi			moah = W	míshiäwä = E	*Ibid.*, I, 872, 915; II, 291. Cf. Shawnee *meshawa*, Chippewa *mishewe*, Miami *shewea*, all = elk' (*ibid.*, I, 530, 843, 942; II, 121, 234, 536, 912)
Pueblos Acoma*	moshaich (*clan*)			kurts = A	*Ibid.*, I, 736, 948
Cochiti*			shrutsuna = *coyote* (*clan*)	kuts, kurts = A	*Ibid.*, 318, 736
Hopi			kwewu = W ishauu = *coyote*	chubia = A sowiinwa = D chaizra = E	*Ibid.*, 562, 747
Isleta			tuim = W		*Ibid.*, 624, 680

Tribe	Buffalo	Horse	Dog (D) or Wolf (W)	Cervidae: Antelope (A), Deer (D, Elk (E), Moose (M)	Author
Jemez			yang, yangtsaa = coyote (clan)		Ibid., I, 630; II, 788
Keresan					Ibid., I, 675. Keresans are a family, strictly speaking. Those marked with an asterisk are Keresan
Laguna*			kakhan = W, tsushki = coyote	kurtsi = A	Ibid., I, 752; II, 747
Pecos			ya = coyote	alu = A, pa = D, alawahku = E	
San Felipe*				kurts, kuuts = A, dya' ni = D	Ibid., I, 407, 736
San Ildefonso	koo			ton, tong = A, pang = D	Ibid., II, 440, 777
Santa Clara				pa = D	Ibid., 457
Sia*	moshaich, or mushach		shutsun = coyote	kuts, kurts = A, dyani = D	Ibid., I, 736, 948; II, 563
Taos			kahl = W, towha = coyote	turatu = E	Ibid., II, 670, 797, 840
Tewa	koo				Ibid., I, 725; II, 738

Tribe	Buffalo	Horse	Dog (D) or Wolf (W)	Cervidae: Antelope (A), Deer (D, Elk (E), Moose (M)	Author
Tigua			tuïm = W	tam = A	Ibid., II, 680
Zuni			sus'-ki-kwe = coyote (clan)	sho'-hoi-ta-kwe = D (clan)	Ibid., 553, 1018
Quapaw	te, tukhe = 'reddish yellow buffalo' (gens)		shangke = dog or wolf	nanpanta = D (gens) anpan = E (gens)	Ibid., I, 59; II, 24, 335, 336, 526. Cf. the Osage names, above
Sarcee		che-che-nun-to-er	tley = D		Umfreville, Present State of Hudson's Bay, vocabulary, 202
		chistli			Chistli = 'seven dogs': so, Butler, Great Lone Land, 267
	kanleklisata = buffalo en masse; kanamaka = cow				McLean, Canadian Savage Folk, 14
Sauk	nannosó	naketóhsh-kescháh		mäschauäh = E	Maximilian
Shawnee		pe-sa-wä' (from meshäwä = elk)	m'-wa-wä' = W	psake-the' = D (gens) also pishekethé (gens)	Handbook of American Indians, II, 234, 310, 536
Sioux	pe tay	shonka wakon	shonka = D	tah to ka no = A teh cha = D opon = E	Catlin
('Yanktonan')	tatánka = bull ptäh = cow ptah sidja = calf ('ptah' generally used)	schónka-uakán	schónka = D schuk-toketscha-tanka = W mihtschak-sih = coyote	tatóhkana = A upán = E achahka = stag upán (Teton Dakota) = E hächáhka = stag	Maximilian

Tribe	Buffalo	Horse	Dog (D) or Wolf (W)	Cervidae: Antelope (A), Deer (D, Elk (E), Moose (M)	Author
(Yankton, Oglala)	tah-tank-kah = *bull* ptay = *cow* tah-tank-ka-Coh-wah'-pee = *buffalo at large*				Seton, *Life-Histories of Northern Animals*, 1, 247
Snake	pishish	warack	sherry = D		Ross, *Fur Hunters*, II, 154
		shekum			Townsend, *Early Western Travels*, XXI, 252
Tahltan			cheona = W		Handbook of American Indians, 670 (a British Columbia tribe)
Tonkawa	awash (*gens*)		hatchukuni = W (*a clan*)		*Ibid*, I, 536; II, 782
Tuscarorà	hohats	tyanoots ruhuh	zir = D tskwarinuh = W	ojiruk = A awgway = D joowaroowa = E	Catlin
Winnebago	cheikikarachada		shungikkara-chada = W	chaikikarachada = D huwanikikarachada = E	Handbook of American Indians, II, 560, 961[38]
Yuchi			tä' la = W	weyon = D (*clan*)	*Ibid*, II, 677, 937, 1005 (S.E. United States)

[38] These are all gentile appellations. Note the almost identical *cheiki* (buffalo) and *chaiki* (deer). The meaning seems to be 'those who call themselves after the ...' (see *Handbook of American Indians*, II, 560, 961). Note also the dog-name (*shungi ...*) applied to the wolf gens. This, the Osage, and the Quapaw, and name (*shungi ...*) applied to the wolf gens. This, the Osage, the Quapaw, and possibly the Mohican (above), are the only instances I have found of what has been said to be a common usage, of one word for both dog and wolf; as by Father Hennepin, in 1680 (*Handbook of American Indians*, II, 460).

WHITE BUFFALO NAMES (Catlin)

Arikara	toh-n-hah-tah-ka[39]	Osage	tsecka[42]
Blackfoot	eneuh quisix sinnuum[40]	Sioux	
Mandan	woka da[41]	Tuscarora	ta his ka[43]
			owary-akuh

[39]Maximilian records an Arikara chief, *Tanahah-Takka* ('the White Cow') almost identical with Catlin's form: *Early Western Travels*, XXIII, 230.
[40]A Blackfoot or Sarcee chief, 'White Buffalo,' 1834 (*ibid.*, 87-8; Catlin, *Letters on the North American Indians*, I, 34); possibly the same mentioned by Paul Kane, 1847 (*Wanderings of an Artist*, orig. ed. 425, 430).

[41]For the Mandans and white buffalo. see below, Appendix D.
[42]La Flasche, *Osage Dict.*
[43]An Assiniboine chief, *Pteh-Skah* ('the White Cow'); Maximilian, *Early Western Travels*, XXIII, 203.

ALPHABETICAL INDEX OF INDIAN TRIBAL BUFFALO FORMS

Adgiddah yawseh	Chippewyan
Ah-thuk-ard moostoosh	Cree
Ahwahsissa	Ojibwa
Ainew Blackfoot (Confederacy)[1]	
Arukhwa	Iowa, Kansa,
	Missouri, Oto
Ayâbe mustus	Cree
Aў/ani	Navajo
Ayekkwe mustus	Cree
Berockà	Mandan
Cha-tatanga (Can.) Assiniboine	
Chedunga	Kansa
Cheikikarachada	Winnebago
Cheyinye	Iowa
Choth-lim	Salish
Cook chow	Comanche
Ed-jer-ay	Chippewyan
Eininee Blackfoot (Confederacy)	
Enáhkia	Atsina
Eneuh Blackfoot (Confederacy)	
Eneuh-quisix-sinnuum	
Blackfoot (Confederacy)	
Enewh Blackfoot (Confederacy)	
Et-cherre	Chippewyan
Et-cherri	Dog Rib
Et-cherri-ettzae	Dog Rib
Ettirrè-ya-nè	Chippewyan
Ettirre-su-ta-ha	Chippewyan
Goo-cho Ap-woo-ro-kae (N. Cal.)	
Goo-choo At-wum-we (N. Cal.)	
Goo-choo Ham-mah-we (N. Cal.)	
Goot-tsoo	Northern Paiute
Haka	Beaver (Tsattine)
Hakái	Beaver (Tsattine)
Hakái tayidze	Beaver (Tsattine)
Hakái toché	Beaver (Tsattine)
Hohats	Tuscarora
Hoh-kúss	Arikara
Hoots	Thlinkit
Hootz	Thlinkit
Hottué	Cheyenne

Ikòsi stoma	Kalispel
Issiwóhn	Cheyenne
Japóh mostúss	Cree
Jiammó	Kutenai
Kanamaka	Sarcee
Kanleklisata	Sarcee
Kawa	Ponca
Kíhrapi	Manitari-Hidatsa
Kocdl-hiw	Kiowa
Kō-chō	Comanche
Koo	Pueblos of
	San Ildefonso and Tewa
Kotsoteka	Comanche
Mashkodé pijiki	Ojibwa
Mas-kootay-moostoosh	Cree
Maskutewimustus	Cree
Matheh-moostoos	Cree
Mno-ga tatanga	Assiniboine
Moose moose	Nez Percé
Moostoosh	Cree
Moostoosis	Cree
Moostouche	Cree
Moshaich	Pueblos of Acoma
	and Sia
Moskutáck nallusuá	Fox
Mostó os	Cree
Mostúss	Cree
Mushach	Pueblos
Muskota	Plain Cree
Mustus	Cree
Nahksidi	Minatari, Manitari
	(Hidatsa)
Nannosó	Sauk
Nihka	Mandan
Ninkii-páhtune	Mandan
Ninkii patú	Mandan
Nocheena pecheek	Algonkian
Nosta-mustus	Cree
Nsá yinki	Biloxi
Nsá-yankí	Biloxi
O-kom	Comanche

Okos	Arikara	Tan	Haida (B.C.)
Onintchah oniuack	Cree	Tanaha	Kadohadacho
Onitjaniw	Cree	Taraháh	Pawnee
Oonichanio	Cree	Tatanga	Assiniboine[2]
Owary akuh	Tuscarora	Tatanka	Sioux
Oya-peya-mustus	Cree	Te	Quapaw
Pá-dó-gâ-i	Kiowa	Téh	Omaha
Padó-gâ	Kiowa	Tjà	Oto
Pecheke	Ojibwa	Toh n hah tah ka	Arikara
Peecheek: Algonkian (root form)		Tschéh	Osage
Peetai	Assiniboine	Tschéh-schinga	Osage
Pe tay	Sioux	Tschetoga	Osage
Pijiki	Ojibwa	Tse	Osage
Pikwatchimustus	Cree	Tsecka	Osage
Pishish	Snake	Tukhe	Quapaw
Pisokew	Swampy Cree	Tutanga	Assiniboine
Pisikious Illinois (*et al c.* 1670)		Uichtia	Minatari, Hidatsa
Pizhiki	Ojibwa, Sioux	Wa-dsu-ta-ton-ga	Osage
Ptah	Sioux	Was[3]	Natchez
Ptah-sidja	Sioux	Wash	Natchez
Ptemday	Mandan	Washaba	Ponca
Ptihnda	Mandan	Washabe	Ponca
Ptihnde	Mandan	Watahesch	Arikara
Ptin-chamaha	Mandan	Watash	Arikara
Ptin-ihinika	Mandan	Wea-tatanga	Assiniboine
Puskwá-we-mostó-os	Cree	Witá	Minatari, Hidatsa[4]
Sena-tatanga (Can.) Assiniboine		Wohksá	Cheyenne
Sha	Osage	Woka da	Mandan
Sha-ton-ga	Osage	Wun-nes-tow	
Skocdl-hiw	Kiowa		Blackfoot (Confederacy)
Stomach Blackfoot (Confederacy)		Yannash	Choctaw
Stomick Blackfoot (Confederacy)		Yinisa	Natchez
Ta-his-ka	Sioux	Yuko	Klamath
Tàh	Omaha	Zotúnn	Flathead

[1]The Blackfoot Confederacy comprised the Blackfoot proper (Siksika), the Blood (Kainah), the Piegan, the Sarcee or Sarsi, and intermittently, the Atsina or "Gros Ventres," after whom the Belly River in Alberta was named. The first four spoke the Siksika, but the Sarcee (who are Athapaskans) also had their own language, which the other three could never learn.

[2]The Assiniboine are Sioux who broke away about 1640 in the Great Lakes region. Note the persistent resemblance in their speech.

[3]The terms *was, wash* are used in the Natchez and other tongues for buffalo, horse, and dog.

[4]The Hidatsa were also termed the Gros Ventres, but "of the Missouri" to distinguish them from the Atsina.

BUFFALO AND 'WILD COWS'

It is by no means to be taken for granted that every reference to 'wild cows' (*vaches sauvages*) in the early French historical material necessarily indicates buffalo.

Father Le Jeune, writing in 1636, mentions among other animals of New France, "a kind of cow that appears to have some affinity with ours."[1] The learned editor of the series, the late Dr. R. G. Thwaites, thinks the reference is either to the elk or the moose. He remarks that the terms *vache sauvage, boeuf sauvage, buffe,* and *buffle,* were applied by early French writers to buffalo, moose, and elk. We have noted in the present essay that the name might almost logically be given to any species from which 'buff leather' could be obtained.[2] Dr. Thwaites quotes Boucher, 1663: "As for the animals called Bufles, they are only found in the country of the Outaouais, some four or five hundred leagues from Quebec, toward the West and North. . . ."[3]

While *buffe* or *bufle* most assuredly *might* be moose or elk, the foregoing quotation seems to me inconclusive as regards any identification with the deer species; '400 or 500 leagues' West and North from Quebec might or might not land one on the north-eastern fringe of the historic buffalo habitat, say somewhere west of Lake Winnipeg, or of Red River. It is doubtful if anything reliable was known about that region by Europeans in 1663; and this would tend to render it not less, but more probable that, if there were, the *bufles* of Boucher would be *Bison americanus* and not deer. Conversely, if his locality were some of the great forest regions of northern Ontario, neither then nor now could anyone maintain that moose or elk were 'only found' in some such distant territory, *circa* 1663. Furthermore, near 'the country of the Outaouais' (west of Green Bay, Wisconsin, etc.) is almost the very region where the historic buffalo first became known to the French, beyond any reasonable doubt, about 1660 or 1661.[4] The first direct reference to them under that name is in 1663; and in a region apparently somewhere near the southern end of Lake Michigan.[5]

There are possibly (but unlikely) allusions some years earlier. Father Simon Le Moine, south of Lake Ontario, and near its eastern end, September 2, 1654, observes: ". . . proceeding across vast prairies, we see in different places large herds of wild cattle; their horns resemble, in many respects, the antlers of a stag. . . ."[6]

[1]Le Jeune, 1636 (*Jesuit Relations*, IX, 165).
[2]See above, chap. IX, notes 48-50.
[3]Thwaites, ed. note, *Jesuit Relations*, IX, 310. (Outaouais = Ottawa.)
[4]Above, chap. IX, notes 81-95.
[5]Hierosme Lalemant, *Jesuit Relations*, XLVII, 147, 149, 316.
[6]Le Moine, *ibid.*, XLI, 129. 'Undoubtedly wapiti' (elk); so, C. Gordon Hewitt, *Conservation of Wild Life of Canada*, 28.

Describing the same trip, Father Jean De Quens writes two years later: "Soon after our departure, our travelers killed 18 Wild Cows (*vaches sauvages*) within less than an hour, on prairies prepared by nature alone for those ownerless herds. . . ."[7] The 'resemblance to the antlers of a stag' seems to settle the question *in re* buffalo, on this occasion. Elsewhere, however, criticism seems to have gone too far. Allen notes that John Gilmary Shea disputed the interpretation of Marquette's description of the "abundance of Wild Goats and Wild Bulls" on the Wisconsin River,[8] or the Upper Mississippi,[9] 1673, as 'buffalo.' *Vaches* might signify either deer or buffalo in this particular connection, and a clumsy translator, using the term as Hennepin (whose work he was translating) often does, as a generic expression, might even render it 'bulls.'[10] But there can be no doubt whatever that Marquette's description—if this be the passage in dispute—is of buffalo, and not of any deer.[11]

At the same time, the quite common use of *vache sauvage* for moose or elk is beyond dispute. That it is so used is not merely implied, as in the passage from Le Moine; it is explicitly stated. Hierosme Lalemant observes, 1646: "There is found here a species of deer, different from the common ones of France. Our French call them 'wild cows' [*vaches sauvages*] but they are really deer. . . ."[12] Again: "Deer, which our French call cows. . . ."[13]

Dr. Thwaites applies this interpretation to Du Peron's "Relation" of 1638-39, concerning the Indians: "They will go two or three hundred leagues into the woods to find game, such as bears, deer, or cows. . . ."[14]

The Indians, as we have seen in other analogous cases, reversed the process. An Indian who was taken to Paris, described coaches as 'rolling cabins drawn by moose.'[15]

The first horses in French Canada (apart from one sent to the Governor, Montmagny, in 1647) arrived July 16, 1665. The Indians called them 'the moose of France.'[16] After all, both white men and red merely gave a known name to the unknown thing, which men have done since language existed.

[7]De Quens, 1656 (*Jesuit Relations*, XLII, 37); cf. Chaumonot, 1656 (*ibid.*, XLII, 63).

[8]So, Thwaites, ed. note, in Hennepin, *New Discovery*, II, 643.

[9]So, Allen, *American Bisons*, 104; also, on Shea (*ibid.*).

[10]Hennepin, *New Discovery*, I, 222, *et passim*.

[11]Marquette, in *Jesuit Relations*, LIX, 111-13; *in extenso* above, chap. IX, note 87. Cf. also Dablon and Allouez (*ibid.*, notes 85-6); and Thwaites's notes on Marquette (*Jesuit Relations*, L, 322; LXXI, 400). The linguistic test, the term *pisikious*, is decisive; cf. Pizhiki = 'buffalo'; a Chippewa chief, 1759-1855 (*Handbook of American Indians*, II, 266).

[12]Lalemant, *Jesuit Relations*, XXIX, 220, 221.

[13]Paul Le Jeune, Lake St. Louis, 1657; *ibid.*, XLIII, 139.

[14]Du Peron, *ibid.*, XV, 183, 249; 'cows' also: *ibid.*, XVI, 83, 153; XXI, 197; XXVI, 311; etc.

[15]Le Jeune, 1639: *ibid.*, XV, 235.

[16]Le Mercier, *ibid.*, L, 81, 319.

It is interesting to note, however, that almost alone among terms applicable to the *cervidae*—and perhaps as an aftermath of the confusion of terms—'bull' and 'cow' moose have persisted, and are the accepted nomenclature today.[17]

[17]Compare Alexander Henry: 'buck moose' (Coues (ed.), *Henry-Thompson Journals,* II, 617, 634); 'doe moose' (*ibid.,* 609). McDougall has 'cow moose' (*Pathfinding,* 263); 'buck moose' (*ibid.,* 14, 158, 262); 'cow elk' (*ibid.,* 161); 'buck elk' (*ibid.,* 163). David Thompson also has *buck* and *doe* moose (*Narrative,* ed. Tyrrell, 448, 453).

APPENDIX C

EARLY BUFFALO DOMESTICATION

Such evidence as I have been able to collect regarding the question of buffalo domestication (which includes hybridization, or cross-breeding between the buffalo and domestic cattle), appears to indicate that its possibilities attracted the attention of European colonists at a relatively early date. Whether the Indians ever attempted it seems doubtful. Prescott cites a passage from Gomara, concerning a tribe or nation, dwelling about latitude 40° N.—the supposed limit, that is to say, of Coronado's northward excursion to 'Quivira'[1]—'whose chief wealth was in droves of these cattle'; oxen with a hump on the shoulders (*vacas jorobadas*).[2] De Soto's "Letter to the Magistrates of Santiago de Cuba," also, speaks of 'a town called Ocale' containing (among other things) "herds of tame deer that are tended. What this means, I do not understand, unless it be the cattle of which we brought the knowledge with us. . . ."[3]

I take the 'cattle' to be buffalo, and their knowledge to have been derived from Cabeza de Vaca, whom some of them, probably De Soto himself, had met in Spain.[4] There is nothing in either passage which necessarily implies domestication. 'Tending' might only signify that guarding at certain seasons, lest they be frightened from the tribal habitat, which has been noted above, in more than one region,[5] providing these 'tame deer' actually were buffalo. So also, 'their chief wealth' being in buffalo, could quite logically be said—it has been said[6]—of the nomad Plains tribes as we know them, whose only access to the herds was by hunting them as wild animals. The only conceivable addition to such 'wealth' would be from the milk, which would certainly involve domestication. Edwin James, of Long's expedition of 1820, tells us concerning the tribes of this very region: "Although the bison cow produces a rich milk, the Indians make no use of it. . . ."[7] It is not probable that any milking habits had been discarded in the three centuries from Coronado to Long, and the equally unmilkable range cows of a Western rancher could quite logically be designated 'his chief wealth.' There is a reference to 'tamed buffaloes' and also to cross-

[1]See above, chap. IX, notes 24-7.
[2]Prescott, *Conquest of Mexico*, II, 400.
[3]*Narratives of De Soto*, II, 162.
[4]*Ibid.*, I, 5-8, 180.
[5]See above, chap. XXI, sec. 8.
[6]"They are meat, drinke, shooes, houses, fire, vessels, and their Masters whole substance . . ." (*Purchas his Pilgrimes*, XVIII, 65, about Coronado, 1541—perhaps the first English translation of the very passage in question).
[7]Long, *Early Western Travels*, XIV, 305. 'Infinitely richer than that of the Jersey'; so, Buffalo Jones, in his *Forty Years of Adventure*, 49, 244.

breeding with domestic cattle in Chihuahua, Sonora, or Sinaloa[8]—the last of which provinces of Mexico would take the buffalo possibly to the Pacific seaboard: Gulf of California, 26° N., 108° 25′ W.[9] But the absence of any date for this statement leaves us wholly ignorant whether this movement was of Indian or Spanish origin.

The first authenticated attempts, actual or prospective, known to me, are both of French origin, and both *circa* 1700. In that year, by royal command (at d'Iberville's instigation) an effort 'was to be made' to propagate buffalo for the 'buffalo wool' in the young settlement at New Orleans.[10] In 1701, the Huguenots who had settled near Manikintown on the James River, some few miles above Richmond, Virginia, began domesticating buffalo.[11] Says Dr. Hornaday: "It is . . . a matter of historical record that in 1786, or thereabouts, buffaloes were domesticated and bred in captivity in Virginia, and Albert Gallatin states that in some of the northwestern counties the mixed breed was quite common. . . ."[12]

About 1815, Robert Wickliffe, of Lexington, Kentucky, entered upon a series of systematic experiments in domesticating and cross-breeding between the buffalo and domestic cattle. These continued for some thirty years, with a considerable measure of success, so he informed Audubon.[13] He could not have been the only one. William Bullock writes in 1827 of a certain Thomas D. Carneal, sometime member of the Kentucky State Legislature: "A few weeks before, Mr. Carneal had parted with a pair of American buffaloes. . . . which he had kept for some time, for the purpose of improving his breed of draft cattle. . . ."[14] What fortune Carneal may have had is not stated, and I know nothing further concerning him.

Colonel Dodge states that some cattalo (not then known by that name, which was coined later) were to be found in the 'Republican country,' as early as 1874.[15]

What is perhaps the most widely famed effort at buffalo cross-breeding —that of 'Buffalo Jones,' whence he obtained his cognomen—had its origin

[8]Bancroft, *North Mexican States and Texas*, II, 750. He cites as his authority, 'Amlegin, 142-4'; but most unfortunately, although Bancroft's bibliographies are voluminous, I can find nothing of Amlegin, unless he is lurking elsewhere under some other name.

I find 'Buffalo Tamer' (Fr. *Bride-les-Bœufs*) as the name of a chief of the Tunica or 'Toanikas,' Lower Mississippi, 1732: D. I. Bushnell, Jr., "Drawings by A. DeBatz in Louisiana, 1732-1735," in *Smithsonian Miscellaneous Collections*, vol. 80, 1927-28, no. 5. Probably a figurative name for one deemed invincible; and by implication indicating the (usual) untamability of buffalo.

[9]De Laet, 1633; in Prescott, *Conquest of Mexico*, II, 401.

[10]Winsor (ed.), *Narrative and Critical History*, V, 21.

[11]Prescott, *Conquest of Mexico*, II, 400; Hind, *Report, 1858*, 107; Allen, *American Bisons*, 215-21; Hornaday, "Extermination of the American Bison," 379, 451-64; Hewitt, *Conservation of the Wild Life of Canada*, 138.

[12]Hornaday, "Extermination of the American Bison," 451.

[13]See his own account, Audubon and Bachman, *American Quadrupeds*, II, 51.

[14]Bullock, *Early Western Travels*, XIX, 140.

[15]Dodge, *Plains of the Great West*, 149. For his description of the Republican country, see above, chap. XIX, note 72; chap. XX, notes 52-6.

in Canada. Seton's account gives the most detail, although its opening words read strangely, from one who quite manifestly had Dr. Hornaday's essay at his elbow as he wrote: "So far as I can learn, the earliest systematic effort to domesticate the buffalo took place in Manitoba. In 1877 some Indians returning to Winnipeg from the west brought with them 5 Buffalo calves (1 bull and 4 heifers). These became the property of James McKay, and were allowed to run about the outskirts of the town until 1882, when the herd, now numbering 23, came into the possession of S. L. Bedson. . . ."[16] This herd was sold to Buffalo Jones in 1888, perhaps for the purpose of infusing some new blood into his own existing herd, from a more northerly strain. It was not in any case his first buffalo herd, for he made four successful trips—three prior to his purchase—between 1886-89, to the Llano Estacado in quest of buffalo calves.[17]

The last breeder of cattalo as a stock-raising proposition of whom I have any knowledge—for occasional cross-breedings in zoological collections[18] are scarcely relevant, any more than such collections would themselves be admissible as 'domestication'—was the late Mossom Boyd, of Big Island Stock Farm, Bobcaygeon, Ontario, 1894-1914, the origin of whose herd is not stated. This herd was sold to the Dominion Government at his death in 1914, and moved to Scott, Saskatchewan, in 1915. It was afterward transferred to the Wainwright Buffalo Park,[19] in the later reports of which I have found no reference whatever to it, and it appears to be extinct, or likely to become so.[20]

The conflicting character of much of the evidence and the evanescent nature of many of these efforts, despite the sporadic enthusiasms of a few individuals,[21] render a suspicion almost inevitable that hybridization has

[16]Seton, *Life-Histories of Northern Animals*, I, 298. Commonly given as coming into Bedson's hands, 1877 (as Hornaday, "Extermination of the American Bison," 451; loc. cit. Hewitt, *Conservation of the Wild Life of Canada*, 138-40). Hewitt's historical sketch ignores Wickliffe, one of the most important of all. Dixon Craig (*Edmonton Journal*, January 17, 1929) gives some further particulars concerning the Bedson-Jones herd, with yet more variant details; and see also Seton, *Game Animals*, 1929, III, 672.

[17]Seton, *Life-Histories of Northern Animals*, I, 298; Hewitt, *Conservation of the Wild Life of Canada*, 138-40; *Buffalo Jones' Forty Years*, 246-65. The four trips were: April, 1886 (*ibid.*, 50); May, 1887 (p. 111); Spring, 1888 (p. 181); May, 1889 (p. 201).

[18]Hornaday gives a list of such in the U.S., Canada, and elsewhere, *circa* 1889 ("Extermination of the American Bison," 451-64). It has been much increased since then. See above, chap. XVIII, notes 68-72; and cf. Hewitt, *Conservation of the Wild Life of Canada*, 133-42 (1920). A very full list, itemized for America, in Seton, *Game Animals*, III, 670-3, showing for 1926 some 20,000 buffalo alive, and increasing about 20 per cent per annum. Finally, a very informative list, giving figures, in Garretson, *American Bison*, 1938, 215-30.

[19]Since moving them to Wainwright, Hewitt writes (1919): ". . . up to the present time, however, there have been practically no cattalo calves born . . ." (*Conservation of the Wild Life of Canada*, 142).

[20]*Ibid.*, 140-2.

[21]Compare Red River, *circa* 1821: "It will probably be found that the buffalo when tamed are sufficiently good milkers as well as the best workers. . . ." (letter to Andrew Colvile, Lord Selkirk's executor, in Oliver (ed.), *Canadian*

either been a total failure—that is, when viewed broadly over a period of years, and as a thing of abiding and permanent value for commercial utilization—or at best, precarious enough to make standard domestic types clearly preferable.

Hornaday writes as follows: "Almost from time immemorial it has been known that the American bison takes kindly to captivity, herds contentedly with domestic cattle, and crosses with them with the utmost readiness. . . ."[22]

Early French opinion seems to have been divided on the subject. Joliet (whose views may have influenced both d'Iberville and the Huguenots), observed in 1673: "[If the settler had no oxen from France] he could use those of this country, or even the animals possessed by the Western Savages, on which they ride as we do on horses. . . ."[23] Father Marest, however, (who, probably then, at least, would know nothing of the Huguenots' efforts) says in 1712: "We have tried to tame the wild oxen, but we have never succeeded. . . ."[24]

One must suppose that Nuttall, as a naturalist, would be fairly cognizant of the general achievements in this department in the United States, not then so large or so populous as now. He wrote in 1819: "The bison, entirely distinct from the buffalo of Europe, can scarcely be domesticated. . . ."[25]

Wickliffe's experiments were only in their early stages and probably of little significance in 1819. But the situation was scarcely the same in Maximilian's time—his work appeared in 1843[26]—and his remarks indicate a sharp divergence of opinion, if not on domestication proper, at least on cross-breeding. He observes:

I have been frequently told, in America, of hybrids of the buffalo (bison) and the tame race, but never saw any; and several naturalists, especially Mr. Thomas Say,[27] have always affirmed that no instance ever occurred of hybrids, capable of propagating their kind, of that animal and the tame species. He declares that every case into which he examined turned out to be unproved. Mr. Gallatin has, indeed, lately spoken on the subject, and pronounced against Mr. Say's opinion. He calls the bison a mere variety of the common ox, but this may be easily refuted. The bison is quite a different species from the ox, as is clear, not only from its outward form, high withers, short tail, the formation of the head, and the peculiarity of its long hair, but likewise from the osteology, the number of ribs and vertebrae being different in the two animals. . . .[28]

North-West, I, 212. For the failure of these hopes, see Morton, History of the Canadian West, 554, 568.

[22]Hornaday, "Extermination of the American Bison," 451.

[23]Joliet, Jesuit Relations, LVIII, 107. On horses (I know not what else they could be) among the 'Western Savages,' see my paper "From Dogs to Horses among the Western Indian Tribes," Transactions of the Royal Society of Canada, 1939, sec. II, 209-75; giving some dates.

[24]Marest, Jesuit Relations, LXVI, 293.

[25]Nuttall, Early Western Travels, XIII, 210.

[26]See my bibliography below, for title in full.

[27]This can be no one but Thomas Say, secretary of Captain Bell's detachment of Long's expedition, 1819-20 (see Early Western Travels, XVI, 192-291). If so, he was an experienced observer of the wild species.

[28]Maximilian, ibid., XXIV, 129.

After our experience of some phases of scientific opinion in relation to wood buffalo,[29] the dictum of no one man, scientist though he be, can be considered final. Here, however, dogmatism is roughly equal on either side, and such evidence as I have found is very contradictory. Wickliffe's experiences indicated some measure of uncertainty in the respective relations of the sexes in the two hybrid forms. He could not feel sure that the half-buffalo bull would reproduce; but the half-buffalo heifer did so undoubtedly.[30]

Our next witness (in chronological order) is Colonel Dodge, whose remarks must surely have reference to his cattalo in the 'Republican country' aforementioned. These were evidently being reared under domestic conditions, as otherwise the apparently systematized physical phenomena recorded by Dodge could scarcely have been observed. He states that the buffalo and domestic cattle would only cross successfully when the buffalo cow was the mother of the 'mule':[31] "The domestic cow will receive the attentions of the buffalo bull, but invariably dies, being unable to bring forth the calf. . . ."[32] This theory is contested by later definitions of cattalo. Buffalo Jones restricts the term to the offspring of male buffalo and domestic cow;[33] while an even later classification—that of Mossom Boyd, apparently—is, "the offspring of parents both of mixed blood"; though whether the parentage on both sides must, or may be, according to Jones's cross, or the reverse, or promiscuously either way, is not stated.[34]

Although I attach no value other than as expressions of individual opinion[35] to the generalizations of Jones (or of his chronicler, Inman) on any phase of buffalo *history*, yet the conclusions of a foremost breeder of the hybrid stock, based upon his own experience, can scarcely be disregarded. On the other hand, Dodge had (in 1874) twenty-five years experience of buffalo; and his work was in print before Jones had even commenced his experiments in cross-breeding. His assertion therefore

[29]See above at large, chap. III, "Variants of the Buffalo Species."

[30]Correspondence to Audubon, *American Quadrupeds*, II, 51.

[31]*Mule*—scarcely the right word, in view of Wickliffe's experiences; these however were perhaps unknown to Dodge. The term, if correct, would close any controversy concerning continuance of fertility.

[32]Dodge, *Plains of the Great West*, 149-50.

[33]*Buffalo Jones' Forty Years*, 243-5.

[34]Hewitt, *Conservation of the Wild Life of Canada*, 141. Compare the following: "A large dairy farm was maintained. Among the cattle was a buffalo heifer, seven years of age, procured for the purpose of crossing the breed, but every domestic bull had always appeared to be afraid of her . . ." (Sir George Simpson, Edmonton, July 27, 1841, *Journey Around the World*, I, 105). Experiments at Wainwright note "a natural antipathy of bison . . . bulls to domestic cows, unless they are brought up in association with each other . . ." (article on "Experimental Crossing of Buffalo with Domestic Cattle," *Good Roads*, 29-32). This clipping was among other material kindly lent me by my friend, Professor William Rowan, Alberta University, and the date was unhappily not preserved. The author speaks of Mossom Boyd's as the first scientific attempt, and mentions others by name.

[35]See their table of buffalo vital statistics above (chap. XVIII, note 2); and their dicta on white buffalo as 'cattalo' (Appendix D).

carries the initial weight of an original statement and is certainly not
intended to controvert Jones, nor, apparently, anyone else; for the general
history of buffalo hybridization is not even mentioned. Assuming a broadly
equal credibility in the statements of the two men, Dodge's opinion is
therefore (in my view) *a priori* the more probable of the two, if choice
is unavoidable. It is not impossible, however, that the domestic cows in the
Republican country may have been special breeds particularly favoured
by the settlers, perhaps even a relatively small milking type with which
such physical consequences would be virtually inevitable; whereas those
of Jones were larger beef breeds, selected for the purpose of raising a large
semi-native beef animal.

The evidence appears to indicate that in certain particulars the hybrids
leaned more to the buffalo than to the domestic ancestor. This is to be
expected, since our many domestic breeds—like the 'laying' breeds of poultry
—are themselves artificially created machines designed usually for some one
special object, only to be achieved by countless modifications; while the
buffalo retained their native prepotency unimpaired. Wickliffe wrote of
his hybrids: ". . . they still observe the habit of having select places within
their feeding grounds to wallow in. . . ."[36] This is the only reference I have
found, to wallowing habits. Jones remarks with reference to milking, "the
nearer they approach the full-blood buffalo the less quantity is produced."[37]
This also is entirely logical, since long-protracted milking capacity in a wild
animal—particularly an annual breeder—is essentially unnatural, as remarked
above. A great deal has been said about cattalo 'facing the blizzards' like
buffalo, in contradistinction to domestic cattle.[38] On general principles,
such behaviour is what one might expect, but the evidence for buffalo
themselves doing this as a uniform practice, is so contradictory, as we
have seen,[39] that little can be wisely based upon it.

The fundamental purpose of cross-breeding buffalo and cattle is not very
clear. Buffalo Jones describes this to be the production of an animal,
or rather a race of cattle "so clannish as never to separate and go astray . . .
that can water every third day and keep fat, ranging from twenty to thirty
miles from water. . . ."[40] It was manifestly to the buffalo that Jones and
his co-workers were looking to implant these qualities—above all, the 'clan-
nishness'—in the hybrid. Why not then simply domesticate the pure buffalo
race which already had them, and abandon cross-breeding altogether? Unless
it were that the buffalo had become so few, *circa* 1888, as to make this
process impracticably slow, there seems to be no satisfactory answer to
this question.

Much has been said about the tractability of the species, and the
consequent ease with which domestication and cross-breeding might be
prosecuted. Like everything else about buffalo, this is disputed. As I
have had occasion to note in another connection, Umfreville (1785)

[36]Wickliffe to Audubon (*American Quadrupeds*, II, 53).
[37]*Buffalo Jones' Forty Years*, 244.
[38]*Ibid.*, 245; Seton, *Life-Histories of Northern Animals*, I, 299.
[39]See above, chap. VIII, particularly notes 47-74.
[40]Hornaday, "Extermination of the American Bison," 457; see above on this,
chap. V, notes 56-64.

was of the opinion they might easily be 'tamed to the plough,' by being captured young;[41] and Audubon and Catlin mention a simple method by which they might readily be caught. Gregg also considered the calves tame.[42] Southesk thought them easily domesticable if caught young; but apparently based his opinion upon one solitary instance, observed during a single season (or part of a season) only.[43] Dr. Gordon Hewitt considered the buffalo in Wainwright Buffalo Park 'docile' *to those on horseback*.[44] As most people are aware, this was the only safe method of approach to the Western 'range cattle' in the old days. Anyone who has had experience—as I have—of their attitude toward those afoot may well doubt if such behaviour offered much encouragement to the hopes of domesticating (in the immediate future at least) a wild species. Dr. Hewitt's work contains photographs of buffalo eating hay in the barnyard at Elk Island Park, Lamont, Alberta, which are instanced as evidence of a ready adaptability to domestication.[45] This cannot be conceded. During the winter of 1932-33 the newspapers mentioned countless instances of deer and moose invading the farmers' barnyards and straw-stacks because of the prolonged and intense severity of the weather. This is no proof of readiness for domestication, any more than is the similar conduct in the woods in 'fly-time.' And in so far as buffalo specifically are concerned, in 1840 Thomas Simpson recorded the very same thing at Carlton (January 13): "The buffaloes were so numerous about this place that I found Mr. Small [the factor] removing his haystacks to the fort, to save them from being entirely devoured. . . ."[46]

The evidence (of opinion) for the intractability of the buffalo is by no means negligible.[47] Furthermore, it is supported by evidence of fact, furnished by those who, like Marest, had put the matter to the test; in striking contrast, to the general competence of the school of optimistic assumption. Buffalo Jones states that the calves were 'vicious, when caught and tied';[48] and Thompson Seton ascribes what he calls—and apparently with justice—'the failure of the cross-bred,' to its intractability.[49] The 'docile' animals at Wainwright are the descendants of the Pablo herd in Montana, of 621 animals, which required two years to round up for shipment to

[41]Umfreville, *Present State of Hudson's Bay*, 159.

[42]Gregg, *Early Western Travels*, XX, 268; above, chap. VII, notes 137-41.

[43]Southesk, *Travels*, 82.

[44]Hewitt, *Conservation of the Wild Life of Canada*, 138.

[45]*Ibid.*, 136.

[46]Thomas Simpson, *Narrative of Discoveries*, 402. Isaac Cowie mentions the haystacks at Fort Ellice (1868) needing watchmen—to keep away those buffalo 'which nothing could turn'! (*Company of Adventurers*, 182). So also in Pennsylvania, winter 1799-1800: Shoemaker, *Pennsylvania Bison Hunt*, 31. He laments that such a docile animal' was not domesticated (*ibid.*, 47-9); but seems entirely ignorant of the history of buffalo domestication, which might have modified his optimism.

[47]J. O. Pattie, 1825, *Early Western Travels*, XVIII, 64; J. K. Townsend, 1833, *ibid.*, XXI, 206.   [48]*Buffalo Jones' Forty Years*, 65.

[49]Seton, "Buffalo Summary," *Arctic Prairies*, 318.

Alberta, despite all the advantages of mounted approach;[50] and after they had been for some eighteen years in the Buffalo Park at Wainwright it became necessary to forbid pedestrians to enter the Park.[51] A similar unreliability has been recorded concerning buffalo elsewhere, after years of captivity.[52]

Whether we concede 'failure' or not, intractability seems in large measure undeniable; and if we dispute the latter, failure from some cause seems none the less to have been the result. For otherwise, where are the herds of cattalo, which by this time should have attained material proportions and an influential standing in the Western stock-breeding world? Apparently every one of those herds cited by the optimistic faithful as 'the substance of things hoped for' has either vanished silently from our ken, or is in parlous case, on the evidence of the true believers themselves.[53]

I am not competent to discuss the biological laws of generation and sterility; but even historical evidence tends to indicate the possible working of subtle genetic principles—or deviations from supposed principles—whether we understand them or not. In reference to another species of the genus *Bos* (*B. primigenius*; the ancient wild white cattle of Britain), Dr. Whitaker, writing in 1812, stated of the herd at Gisburne-in-Craven, in the West Riding of Yorkshire: "They breed with tame cattle. . . ." However, Harting, writing in 1880, informs us that this, and a subsequent attempt, proved failures.[54] We have here—together with its sequel—one of those enthusiastic forecasts so typical of the early stages of any enterprise; of which, in relation to the American buffalo, we have seen instances already—without the sequel.

The late Dr. Gordon Hewitt speaks of the 'eminently natural' conditions

[50]Denny MS., 47. The best account I have seen of the rounding-up of the Pablo herd for shipment from Montana to Alberta is in Seton, *Game Animals*, III, 658, 671—not specially suggestive of tractability. There is a fairly good one in Shepstone, *Wild Beasts of To-day*, 126-33. Westerners, however, will smile at "*dank* buffalo-grass" (p. 132); but Shepstone's language is all too frequently slovenly. See below, Appendix J, note 55.

[51]During several months in the summer of 1924, I spent every Sunday in Wainwright, and when it was fine usually in the Park. Even small children went about freely on foot, picnicking, and bathing in the lakes. It is a curious illustration of buffalo vagaries, that with thousands roaming at will and fresh tracks everywhere, I never once throughout that summer saw a herd or even a single buffalo.

[52]Some interesting particulars on the—occasionally fatal—unreliability of 'tame' buffalo, in Garretson, *American Bison*, 47-51. See an account of the breaking-out of the Silver Heights herd, Winnipeg (*Manitoba Free Press*, Winnipeg, August 2, 9, 1894). An Ontario friend, who knew Mossom Boyd (and his herd) well, informed me that similar breakings-out were incessant, and exceedingly troublesome. She was unaware whether these were occasioned by the pure buffalo or the hybrids.

[53]For example, Hewitt and Seton (above, notes 19-20, 49).

[54]Whitaker's *History of Craven*, quoted by Harting, *Extinct British Animals*, 236-9.

in Wainwright Buffalo Park.[55] I suggest that apart from climatic and topographical conditions, they are eminently unnatural. The supposed migratory instinct, so dear to the traditionalist, must surely receive a severe shock when the orthodox 'northward trek' in summer or southward in winter is suddenly terminated by a wire fence like the Deacon's—'horse high, bull strong, and pig tight.' Who can say what effect the semi-artificial environment created by man may have upon cross-domestication; or what hidden forces may operate to induce sterility, perhaps after two, and perhaps not before ten generations? Apart from the short interim of one year at Scott, the Mossom Boyd cattalo, after breeding with apparent success for twenty years, must have been in the most natural (buffalo) environment the herd had ever known since the very earliest buffalo ancestors were confined. Yet the transference to Wainwright seems to have put an end to calving.[56] N. S. Shaler, who could scarcely have been ignorant of the facts up to then, wrote in 1884 that buffalo 'were apparently not domesticable. . . ."[57] In 1891 he repeated this deliberately: "It was at first supposed possible for these new States to acquire a laboring class by enslaving the Indians; but all these efforts at subjugating the American savage have been as unsuccessful as the similar efforts to domesticate the buffalo. Both of these American creatures have a fair measure of physical vigor, but they are alike untamable."[58] Later history seems to support him.

[55]See his description, *Conservation of the Wild Life of Canada*, 134-6; cf. above, chap. VIII, notes 136-8.

[56]Hewitt, *ibid.*, 142 (above, notes 19-20). I since find Seton writing (1929): ". . . the continued infertility of the hybrids has not yet been proven, and is, indeed, much questioned by geneticists . . ." (*Game Animals*, III, 673).

[57]Shaler, in Winsor (ed.), *Narrative and Critical History*, IV, xv.

[58]Shaler, *Nature and Man in America*, 203. Some interesting particulars on this in Garretson, *American Bison*, 196-230. Dobie speaks of the Mexican *ciboléros* using young buffalo along with oxen in bull-trains (Dobie, *The Flavor of Texas*, 225). I have found no other mention of this.

ALBINISM IN BUFFALO

The occurrence of occasional albinism in many species of animals and birds which normally are otherwise coloured is of course a well-recognized phenomenon, entirely apart from any question of its frequency. Its presence in the former hosts of the buffalo (*Bison americanus*) has at various times aroused the interests of students. Certain rather dogmatic pronouncements have been put forth on the subject, both in earlier times when a reasonable sufficiency of data could scarcely have been expected; and down to our own day by writers who quite evidently had not even taken the trouble to consider adequately the evidence which is actually available. My purpose here is to present historical evidence concerning the presence and significance of white specimens in the wild native buffalo herds.

The *relative* rarity of such albinos will scarcely be regarded as requiring much discussion; it may almost be taken for granted. But we have seen that the numbers of the buffalo, in their palmy days, were so almost incredibly vast, that a very low percentage might quite easily yield a by no means negligible aggregate. As the commonly accepted premier authority on the species, Hornaday writes:

Cases of albinism in the buffalo were of extremely rare occurrence. I have met many old buffalo hunters, who had killed thousands and seen scores of thousands of buffaloes, yet never had seen a white one. *From all accounts* it appears that not over ten or eleven white buffaloes, or white buffalo skins, were ever seen by white men. Pied individuals were occasionally obtained, *but even they were* rare. Albino buffaloes were always so highly prized that not a single one, so far as I can learn, ever had the good fortune to attain adult size, their appearance being so striking, in contrast with the other members of the herd, as to draw upon them an unusual number of enemies, and cause their speedy destruction.

At the New Orleans Exposition, in 1884-'85, the Territory of Dakota exhibited, amongst other Western quadrupeds, the mounted skin of a two-year-old buffalo which might fairly be called an albino. Although not really white, it was of a uniform dirty cream-color,[1] and showed not a trace of the bison's normal color on any part of its body.

Lieut. Col. S. C. Kellogg, U.S. Army, has on deposit in the National Museum a tanned skin which is said to have come from a buffalo. It is from an animal about one year old, and the hair upon it, which is short, very curly or wavy, and rather coarse, is pure white. In length and texture the hair does not in any one respect resemble the hair of a yearling buffalo save in one particular,—along the median line of the neck and hump there is a rather long, thin mane of hair, which has the peculiar woolly appearance of genuine buffalo hair on those parts. On the shoulder portions of the skin the hair is as short as on the hind quarters.

[1]This, I have read, is the actual colour of the famous 'white elephant' of Siam (or must one say, *re* a past era, Thailand?).

I am inclined to believe this rather remarkable specimen came from a wild half-breed calf, the result of a cross between a white domestic cow and a buffalo bull. At one time it was by no means uncommon for small bunches of domestic cattle to enter herds of buffalo and remain there permanently.[2]

While the suggested explanation would present itself not unnaturally to one reasoning *de novo,* and may very probably have been the correct one in that instance and quite possibly so in others, certain other considerations force themselves forward irresistibly and require us to pause. Some of these at least should have been noticed by Hornaday, since in part they are derived from his own foremost authorities. Including one from almost the very earliest plainsman authority whom he cites, Dodge, we have noted some very definite pronouncements on this obscure question of sexual relationships between buffalo and domestic breeds.[3]

The testimony at large concerning the general contact of cattle with buffalo is widely inconsistent; entirely too much so to support any generalized explanation of such a phenomenon as white buffalo. We have noted Denny's account of the white Texas long-horn, at first thought to be itself a white buffalo, which had 'taken up' with a herd, or perhaps with a succession of herds.[4] Elsewhere Denny apparently contradicts himself. He states that domestic cattle 'never joined the buffalo; always appearing afraid of them.'[5] He also writes in another place: "While the buffalo roamed the plains it was useless to let range cattle run, as buffalo bulls would kill any animal they came across, and cows would be carried away in the great migratory herds; therefore what cattle were brought in the first five or six years the Police were in the country [that is, *post* 1874] were generally kept close along the river-bottoms and had to be herded. . . ."[6]

This view perhaps finds some confirmation from a fairly recent press report of a 'wild buffalo' in the Wood Mountain country, (49° N., 107° W.), thought to be—as it was later proved to be—a fugitive from some Montana 'park' herd, which stampeded the cattle and horses in the locality.[7] But we must also allow for a degree of unfamiliarity with the sight of buffalo on the part of the domestic animals; much greater in 1935 than it would be *circa* 1875.

Several writers besides Denny record cases of cattle which either 'joined' the buffalo, or at least could not escape from them even if they wished to do so; and which were evidently not killed by them until long afterward, if at all. Frémont in 1842 mentions a red ox which returned homeward a long distance through buffalo country.[8] And the aforementioned oxen on snowed-

---

[2]Hornaday, "Extermination of the American Bison," 414-15; italics mine; see note 27 below.

[3]Above, Appendix C, "Buffalo Domestication," notes 22-34.

[4]Above, chap. IV, note 37.

[5]Denny MS., 41.

[6]*Ibid.,* 260; also Denny, *The Law Marches West,* 90; similarly L. V. Kelly, *The Rangemen,* 110. Kelly is, however, a late and inaccurate writer, of no particular authority and without corroboration.

[7]*Edmonton Journal,* June 28, 1935.

[8]Frémont, *Narrative,* 17.

up trains which were 'turned loose to die' in the Platte Valley, 1858-59, 1864-65,[9] evidently survived the wild buffalo as well as the winter.

It is stated also that in 1878 or thereabouts, a freighting outfit of the well-known southern Alberta trading firm of Healy and Hamilton lost most of its oxen in one night through their 'wandering off' with a herd of buffalo.[10] This last might be supposed to be an ever present danger; yet we know that the annual Santa Fé caravans and the emigrant trains to the Pacific territories travelled successfully through the buffalo country.[11] The contradictory behaviour of the buffalo in their contacts with horses implies a variability which becomes quite credible even toward their domestic cousins.[12]

The general history of the hybridization of domesticated buffalo would seem to cast doubt upon the supposition that these alleged antipathies were an insuperable obstacle. The apparent failure of attempts at hybridization seems rather to arise from subtle and unknown genetic forces which tend to induce sterility after a few generations. Dodge's observations referred to certain hybrids in the 'Republican country'[13] circa 1874. If, in order to save Hornaday's argument, we prefer to assume that Dodge's dictum concerning the buffalo cow was erroneous,[14] we must further assume (1) that white domestic cows and the buffalo bull had a peculiar mutual affinity; or (2) that the former must have been so favoured by the early settlers and immigrants that their mere numbers of strays would be sufficient to supply the suggested probable quota of 'white buffalo.' For neither of these hypotheses have I found one fragment of evidence. Failing these provisos, the aggregate of female domestic strays must necessarily have been very large. Such strays would require to survive the perils of Indians, wolves, and other ferocious beasts, thirst in a strange environment (a common cause for straying), and probably unfamiliar poisonous vegeta-

[9]Above, chap. VIII, notes 51, 52.

[10]MacInnes, In the Shadow of the Rockies, 178.

[11]M. S. Garretson gives a print from a painting, "Indians Stampeding Buffalo Through an Emigrant Train in the Platte Valley" (American Bison, 76). In a fairly considerable amount of literature on the buffalo I have not found one single hint of such an occurrence, and in my judgment it may fittingly keep company with another piece of anti-Indian propaganda also preserved by Garretson ('2,000,000 for whisky,' ibid., 77; below, Appendix J, note 51).

Actually we have seen above that the common wail from the emigrants was 'No buffalo,' which they had been led to expect in unfailing swarms, while they themselves in turn were accused of having 'frightened the buffalo back from the [Oregon] trail.' Further, these are those buffalo which 'always fled in terror from the hated scent of the white man,' and the same which 'nobody could turn' from their own chosen path! The Mormons in 1847 noted the buffalo 'stampeding their yoke-cattle'; but nothing about Indians (Bancroft, History of Utah, 425). On all this, see above, chap. VI, at large; chap. XX, notes 89-102; etc.

[12]See above, chap. IV, notes 41-2.

[13]On this region, see above, chap. XIX, notes 72-6.

[14]I have suggested above (Appendix C, note 31 seq.) what might be a conceivable explanation of Dodge's assertion, but I have no evidence of its actuality in fact.

tion.[15] Yet the average albino proportion in this polychrome host—which furthermore had also to compete with the unquestionably higher reproductive prepotency of the buffalo; a pure race as against an infinity of nondescript ancestries—must be numerically sufficient to furnish the requisite contingent of 'white buffalo.' Here again, I have found no evidence of any such large numbers of stray cows, apart from any question of the possibilities of their survival. And whatever conclusions we may adopt concerning this particular phase of the question, chronological objections alone are fatal to any hypothesis of semi-domestic origin as a general explanation. It cannot account for the presence of white buffalo long prior to any domestic cattle in the buffalo country. Here the Canadian testimony is of the very first order. It is the earliest of all that we possess from experienced residents in the western territories, in contradistinction to visiting travellers; and among the latter even, many of them are earlier than the later misleading conventions which so often supplant or distort the actual evidence of fact.[16]

The earliest evidence known to me for the presence of domestic cows—not 'cattle'; which might only signify oxen—in the northern Plains territory, is that concerning Fort Edmonton, 1841, which has been noted, and which is decidedly unfavourable to any supposition such as Hornaday's.[17] There were oxen in use also at about the same time,[18] but not in the southern Alberta buffalo country until a much later date.[19] The easy believer in the Great Trek from Texas to the North Saskatchewan might readily explain such early phenomena—though scarcely prior to 1540—by referring sexual contacts to

[15]Something of the last-named may be indicated in the mysterious deaths among Coronado's horses, en route from Tiguex to Cibola and thence to Culiacan (Castañeda, *Journey of Coronado*, 128).

[16]See two outstanding examples above, chap. XVI, note 7.

[17]Above, Appendix C, note 34. There is also a fragmentary reference in Rev. James Evans's journal to being able to take frozen milk with him on some of his missionary journeys (December 14, 1840, in *Wesleyan Missionary Notices*, London, 1843, 229). This apparently implies cows being kept at Norway House, which of course was out of the buffalo habitat. The Hudson's Bay Company experimental farm at Red River in the thirties is well known, but our evidence concerning white buffalo from this precise region is far older. See below, notes 34, 35.

[18]*Rundle's Journal* (Edmonton, November 25, 1843; December 2, 5, 1845).

[19]The first ox-cart brigade, Fort Garry to Edmonton, 1862, organized by Father Lacombe (Hughes, *Father Lacombe*, 87; Oliver (ed.), *Canadian North-West*, II, 1002). Vaughan, *Life of W. C. Van Horne*, 93, prefers 1857, but Miss Hughes wrote from Lacombe's papers. First American traders across the boundary from Fort Benton, 1866; first 'bull-train' thence to Edmonton, 1870 (Dorothy Diller, "Early Economic Development of Alberta Previous to 1905," chaps. II, 12; IV, 2, 3). Dr. John McDougall (Alberta, 1862-1917) says the first cattle for stock-raising purposes were driven in by Shaw, 1875 (McDougall MS., 1875 *seq.*, 25). Denny says those of Shaw and Lee, 1875, were domestic cattle, sold for beef, and gives the date of the first range cattle as 1877 (Denny MS., 259, 303; cf. also Kelly, *The Rangemen*, 113). Denny's printed version varies somewhat, noting other 'first men' and 1876 for range cattle (Denny, *The Law Marches West*, 88, 100). Miss Diller has the respective dates 1875, 1878 ("Early Economic Development of Alberta Previous to 1905," chaps. IV, 8; V, 2).

the previous autumn in the South; but it has been abundantly shown that this grand movement has no historical basis. Apart from that having connection with the strictly practical utilization of the horse,[20] our buffalo-and-Indian evidence at large renders it improbable that the Indian buffalo rituals or practices were so recent as to be post-European.[21] Curiously enough, the very earliest direct reference to white buffalo is also the northernmost of all instances I have found.

The same chronologico-geographical reasoning applies also to Buffalo Jones's so-called 'solution of the problem' of white buffalo, as being cattalo.[22] Historical comparison was seldom any weighty feature in his conclusions; it can scarcely be disputed that if he were correct in this instance, there must have been a large number of *non*-white hybrids roaming the plains, which would surely have attracted the attention of somebody. The historical evidence shows that both the earlier true plainsmen and scientifically minded travellers were keenly observant of analogous variations and anomalies.[23] I have found no evidence at all suggestive of such 'natural' (undomesticated) cattalo.

It seems probable that Hornaday's views on white buffalo were derived from contemporary plainsmen whom he met, rather than from such earlier ones as Dodge or his antecessors, whom he ignores on this topic. Such men of the 'plainsman' type were unphilosophic as a class, and commonly very contemptuous of any suggestions not consonant with their own individual experience. The 'buffalo-hunters' to whom both Hornaday and a modern uncritical generalizer refer us[24] were more strictly 'buffalo-*butchers*' (as they were then actually termed) of the final days of extermination. Their observation of the species at a time, moreover, when Hornaday himself emphasizes a great change in buffalo characteristics, due to their incessant persecution,[25] was largely confined to those more or less narrow phenomena which, as it were, impinged upon the butcher's calling; and their 'always' and 'never' concerning buffalo may be dismissed as being usually worthless.

Hornaday's conclusions were certainly not derived from his own principal literary authorities on buffalo. Taken in chronological order, these write as follows: "The buffalo of the plains are not always of the dark and rich bright brown which forms their characteristic colour. They are sometimes seen from white to almost black, and a grey buffalo is not at all uncommon. . . ."[26] "White individuals are still more rare [that is, than pied

[20]See Roe, "From Dogs to Horses among the Western Indian Tribes," *Transactions of the Royal Society of Canada*, 1939, Sec. II, 209-75.

[21]See above, chap. XXI, at large.

[22]"Of late years Colonel Jones has figured out the solution of the problem of white buffalo . . ." (*i.e.* as cattalo). Inman (ed.), *Buffalo Jones' Forty Years*, 81. Jones never suggests explanations, he 'solves problems'; but Inman's *imprimatur* means little. On Inman himself, see chap. XVIII, notes 2-13, 80-100.

[23]See above, chap. III, on "Variants of the Buffalo Species."

[24]Garretson, *American Bison, passim*. An old buffalo-hunter 'doubted if there were any that were pure white' (*ibid.*, 31); apparently because *he* had never seen one.

[25]Above, chap. VI, notes 106-14, particularly.

[26]Hind, *Report, 1858*, 105; also in his *Narrative*, II, 104, from which Hornaday quotes it ("Extermination of the American Bison," 407).

ones] but are not unknown. A former agent of the American Fur Company, who had unusually favourable opportunities of judging, informed me that they probably occur in the proportion of not more than one in millions, he having seen but five in an experience of twenty years, although he had met *hundreds of pied ones.* Black ones are rather more frequent, but can only be regarded as very rare. . . ."[27] Five seen by one individual in twenty years indicates rarity, but is hardly suggestive of a total aggregate of 'not more than ten or eleven' throughout all the history of the buffalo; and Hornaday himself adds later: "A 'buckskin robe' is from what is always called a 'white buffalo,' and is in reality a dirty cream color instead of white. A robe of this character sold in Miles City in 1882 for $200, and was the only one of that character taken on the northern range during that entire winter. A very few pure white robes have been taken, so I have been told, chiefly by Indians, but I have never seen one."[28]

Taking them in chronological order, I cite below such historical references to white specimens as I have been able to discover.

La Vérendrye, on his visit to the Mandan villages (Bismarck, North Dakota) in 1738, was told that "cattle were abundant on the [more southerly] prairies, far larger and fatter than we had seen on their prairies; their coat white and of several colours. . . ."[29] Or, to quote another version: "a vast quantity of buffalo, large and heavy, some white, others of different colours. . . ."[30]

The early trader, Antony Henday, sojourning among the Blackfoot, probably in the lower Battle River country or thereabout in October, 1754, found a white buffalo skin used as a seat or seat-covering for the Blackfoot chief.[31] A century later "two fine albino examples of the prairie buffalo" are recorded from the same general territory, on the plains of the upper Saskatchewan River. These were in the possession of Chief Factors John Rowand and James G. Stewart of the Hudson's Bay Company.[32]

John McDonnell, the North West Company's man, records in his Journal (Assiniboine River and Fort Qu'Appelle country) November 23-24, 1793: "The men were in chace [sic] of a white Buffalo all day but could not get within shot of him. . . . The men commenced a fresh chase of the white buffalo, but with as little success as the preceding day. . . ."[33]

Alexander Henry the younger writes, December 1, 1800 (at his Red River post): "The Crees inform me they have seen a calf as white as snow in a herd of buffalo. White buffalo are very scarce. They are of inestimable

[27]Allen, *American Bisons,* 39; cf. Hornaday, above, note 2 (italics mine).
[28]Hornaday, "Extermination of the American Bison," 444. 'The only one taken that winter' almost conveys a sense of an unusual scarcity in the returns, rather than an article so rare that *one* was a lifetime experience.
[29]*Report of Canadian Archives,* ed. Brymner, 21, 27.
[30]*Journals of La Vérendrye,* ed. Burpee, 355. Burpee (*ibid.*) thinks this might possibly refer to Spanish domestic cattle. 'Larger' is a vague and purely relative term, but as a mere coincidence it has been noted that 'Washita' (River, south of the Arkansas) perhaps signifies 'country of large buffaloes' (above, chap. III, note 148).
[31]"Henday's Journal," ed. Burpee, 337.
[32]Mair and McFarlane, *Through the Mackenzie Basin,* 178.
[33]In Masson, *Les Bourgeois de la Compagnie du Nord-Ouest,* I, 285.

value among the nations of the Missouri, but of none to the Crees and Assiniboines, except to trade with other nations. . . ."[34] Henry writes again, April 24, 1804: "I bought a beautiful white buffalo skin from Le Cedre . . . the hair was long, soft, and perfectly white, resembling a sheep's fleece. The Saulteurs [that is, Saulteaux or 'Sauteaux' = Ojibwa] set no value on the skins. . . ."[35]

We have a considerable amount of evidence concerning the high estimation of white buffalo skins among the Mandans and their neighbouring allies, the 'Gros Ventres' (Minatari, Hidatsa); which latter tribe acquired their veneration for these articles from the Mandan, so Maximilian was informed.[36] Charles Mackenzie, another 'Nor-Wester,' mentions the 'Shawyens' coming to the Mandan villages in 1805, with a white buffalo skin for one or other of the two tribes.[37] These were the Cheyennes, and this notice is of particular interest, as an instance of acute sub-tribal or sectional individualism, since it tends to indicate that the Northern Cheyennes (or possibly the entire tribe before their separation, which had not occurred in 1805)[38] placed no value on the skin other than for trade; while the Southern Cheyennes valued it very highly indeed.[39]

Alexander Henry also mentions the Minatari chief, Le Borgne, 'sacrificing a white buffalo hide to the waters, an article of the highest estimation.'[40] Speaking elsewhere of the great regard of the 'Big Bellies' for their best

[34]Coues (ed.), *Henry-Thompson Journals*, I, 159.

[35]*Ibid.*, I, 242. Seton says that 'white' means *pied*. Yet he extols the immense value of this very work for precisely such exact information on buffalo, as we have noted above in our introductory chapter (notes 20-1). Compare further his own statement below, note 39.

Without subscribing literally to the 'hundreds of pied ones' seen by Allen's informant (above, note 27), it doubtless signifies a considerable number; and that witness carefully differentiates between the two. Allen is Hornaday's mentor (frequently without acknowledgment), and Hornaday is Seton's!

[36]Maximilian, *Early Western Travels*, XXIII, 371.

[37]Masson, *Les Bourgeois de la Compagnie du Nord-Ouest*, I, 382; cf. also Burpee, *Search for the Western Sea*, 378; *Journals of La Vérendrye*, ed. Burpee, 355, 366.

[38]See *Handbook of American Indians*, I, 253.

[39]Seton: "A magnificent and historical robe of pure white was the special medicine and personal adornment of the great Cheyenne Chief Roman-nose. He wore it in his last fight when he charged fearlessly at the head of his band to fall in the leaden hail of Forsyth's troops entrenched on Beecher Island . . ." (Republican River, September 19, 1868; Seton, *Life-Histories of Northern Animals*, I, 250). On the same page he says 'white' means *pied*, as above, note 35. Something like the foregoing in Walsh and Salsbury, *Making of Buffalo Bill*, 121; who are highly (and wisely) critical of such rhetoric concerning W. F. Cody (above, chap. XV, note 31). Grinnell, a much better authority on the Cheyennes, states that Roman Nose was never 'technically' a chief. He adds: "Roman Nose never wore a white buffalo robe. To the Cheyennes the white buffalo was a sacred object, which might not be handled or used by anyone. The flesh might not be eaten nor the hide tanned by a woman of the tribe. The flesh was left on the prairie, and the skin presented as a votive offering to the powers above . . ." (*Fighting Cheyennes*, 240, 271, 281).

[40]Coues (ed.), *Henry-Thompson Journals*, I, 395.

horses, the 'buffalo runners,' he says: "The only article that will induce them to part with a horse of this kind is a white buffalo hide. They have a superstition that many superior virtues are contained in a skin of this kind, and imagine it to be the most essential article an Indian can possess. Every individual who wishes to appear of any consequence must have at least one hide, and the more he has, the greater his importance. . . ."[41]

Maximilian confirms this pronouncement some thirty years later: "The skin of a white buffalo cow is. . . . an eminent medicine in the opinion of the Mandans and 'Manitaries.' He who has never possessed one of them is not respected. . . . These animals are very rare. . . ."[42] Maximilian furnishes some curious details showing various forms in which their regard manifested itself among the two tribes mentioned. For a young white buffalo cow as many as ten or even fifteen horses would be given, and one horse even to the man who skinned one for the successful hunter, whose own achievement surpassed the slaying of an enemy. Another informant specified 'ten horses, a gun, a kettle, and other matters,' given by himself for one. A white bull, or an old cowskin, was less valued, but a horse would be given even for a 'silk robe.'[43] Among the Mandan (perhaps in both tribes), white buffalo held an important place in secret society rituals. Both La Vérendrye[44] and Maximilian[45] mention the 'women's band of the white buffalo cow,' whose leader was wrapped in a white buffalo robe.[46]

This veneration was not confined to these tribes alone. It was shared by the Arikara,[47] Blackfoot,[48] Cheyenne (the Southern group at least),[49]

[41]Ibid., 353. At Fort Vermilion (North Saskatchewan River), 1810, he obtained a buffalo runner for twenty pints of rum (ibid., II, 619).

[42]Maximilian, Early Western Travels, XXIII, 289, 321, 371; XXIV, 48.

[43]Ibid., XXIII, 321-3, 371. On silk (or 'beaver') robes, see chap. III, note 187.

[44]Journals of La Vérendrye, ed. Burpee, 342.

[45]Maximilian, Early Western Travels, XXIII, 266, 297.

[46]Ibid., XXIV, 48, 62, 67.

[47]Ibid., XXIII, 350, 390; Coues (ed.), Henry-Thompson Journals, I, 354. Maximilian mentions them giving five horses for one. This implies an exceptionally high estimation, since the Arikara, who had plenty, were a stingy lot with their horses; 'sometimes one buried in the grave of an eminent man,' and three offered in exchange for three Arikara prisoners (Maximilian, Early Western Travels, XXIII, 387, 394; XXIV, 104).

[48]So, James Willard Schultz, Apauk, Caller of Buffalo, 90-7. The author insists that this work is not fiction, so perhaps it may be classed as freely paraphrased folk-lore. But the evidence is conflicting. Henday, 1754 (above, note 31) found one used as a seat or 'cushion'—scarcely indicative of veneration, for the Blackfoot have neither 'kings' nor 'thrones' (Kidd, "Blackfoot Ethnography," 134, 192); and Catlin refers to them bringing one to the Mandans in trade (Letters on the North American Indians, I, 133). Kidd, however ("Blackfoot Ethnography," 188) cites R. N. Wilson, "The Sacrificial Rite of the Blackfeet," in Transactions of the Royal Society of Canada, 1910, Sec. II, 3-21, on their veneration for the white buffalo robe. Maximilian also mentions Ohistahna, chief of all the Blackfeet' (Early Western Travels, XXIII, 158). One would like to know if Blackfoot in all these cases are the Siksika proper, or the Confederacy. As with the 'cushion,' and a cap of white buffalo skin worn by a Manitari chief (ibid., XXIV, 72), it is also difficult to distinguish between personal, non-reverential use, social dignity, or ritualistic adornment.   [49]Grinnell, Fighting Cheyennes, 281-2.

Omaha,[50] and Piegans.[51] Henry relates an instance, Rocky Mountain House, October 8, 1810: "These Piegans had a fresh hide of a bull they had killed at the foot of the Rocky Mountains. . . . The hair on the back was dirty white, the long hair under the throat and forelegs iron gray, and the sides and the belly were yellow. I wished to purchase it, but the owner would not part with it on any consideration. . . ."[52] Since Henry tells us that the herds above the Rocky Mountain House were the larger and wilder 'wood buffalo,'[53] the foregoing entry reveals the occurrence of albinism in that species. There is of course no reason why it should not occur. Another albino wood bison was shot in the winter of 1871-72 some thirty-five miles northwest of Fort McMurray.[54]

While I have found no direct notice of any actual specimen amongst them, myth and ritual clearly indicate a similar veneration in the Sarcee. Dr. Jenness notes in their Sun Dance myth, a white buffalo skin valued above all else, and therefore required by the 'Maker'; and in the 'Medicine Pipe Bundle,' a *white* blanket, 'in place of the former buffalo robe.'[55]

Maximilian states that they were 'feared' and not used—whatever that may precisely mean—by the Crows.[56] They were apparently neither feared nor used by the Northern Cheyennes, the Cree and their kindred Saulteaux or Ojibwa, and the Assiniboine, except as a source of gain.[57] The indifference of the last named may have been a Sioux characteristic, manifested in their kinsmen, for Maximilian observes (1833): "The Yanktonans showed us a beautiful skin of a young white female buffalo, which they intended as a present for the Mandans, by whom such skins are highly valued. They had already sent them a white buffalo calf. . . ."[58]

On the other hand, however, we find white buffalo worship among other branches of the Sioux. We have a description of the 'White Buffalo Festival of the Uncpapas' from a learned investigator;[59] and in a certain 'Sioux Calendar,' 1799-1870, the following occurs under the year 1811: "The 'Black Stone' band of Sioux made medicine with a white buffalo cow. . . ."[60] It may be noted also that the Mandan and the Omaha, if not the Sioux, are Siouan; but again, the Illinois, who at some era practised a 'white buffalo sacrifice,'[61] and the Cree, Ojibwa, and (Northern) Cheyenne, who did not,

---

[50]An Omaha gens, *dtesanhadtadhishan* = 'pertaining to the sacred skin of an albino buffalo cow' (*Handbook of American Indians*, I, 405).

[51]Schultz, *Apauk, Caller of Buffalo*, 90-7; Coues (ed.), *Henry-Thompson Journals*, II, 646.

[52]*Ibid.*   [53]*Ibid.*, II, 639-41, 660, 682, 739.

[54]Mair and MacFarlane, *Through the Mackenzie Basin*, 178.

[55]Jenness, *Sarcee Indians of Alberta*, 47, 81.

[56]Maximilian, *Early Western Travels*, XXII, 354.

[57]Above, notes 34-7.

[58]Maximilian, *Early Western Travels*, XXII, 343.

[59]Alice C. Fletcher, *Peabody Museum, 16th Report*, 1882, 260-75. I have not seen this.

[60]Cited by Dodge, *Our Wild Indians*, 400-4. On the general credibility of this, see remarks on "Indian Calendars" (Cyrus Thomas, *Handbook of American Indians*, I, 189). Some of its later entries, e.g. the appearance of Texas cattle on the Upper Missouri, *circa* 1867, seem to be borne out by other evidence (below, Appendix E, note 17).

[61]*Handbook of American Indians*, II, 403.

are all Algonkian. These diversities may be of very remote origin, for the white buffalo ceremonies are apparently an extension of an earlier 'White Dog Sacrifice.'[62] Their quite characteristic individualism detracts very seriously from the value of assertions concerning 'the Indians' believing that white buffalo were 'the especial property of the Sun'; and must very heavily discount similarly sweeping generalizations from such sources.[63]

These peculiar specimens were not always wholly white, as Hind remarked;[64] and as we might infer from Henry's account of the Piegans, cited above.[65] He says elsewhere: "I observed one . . . in the Mandane village, whose head was on one side of a lead colour, inclining to black, and upon the other perfectly white; upon the body were many large spots of the same hue, on a white ground. . . ."[66] Dr. Edwin James, the secretary and historian of Stephen H. Long's southern expedition of 1819-20, mentions a 'grayish-white bison' seen by a trader in the Pawnee village, and two other specimens having 'white stars'; all these being in the Platte region, or somewhat farther south.[67] In the southern territory also, Catlin records one along the Canadian River in 1834;[68] and Francis Parkman saw one on the Arkansas River in 1846.[69] Both of these were described as 'white.'

The actual frequency must have been largely a matter of opinion, doubt-less based upon the personal experiences of the particular witness of the moment. The person cited by Allen, who had seen five or so in twenty years, thought white ones 'not more than one in millions.'[70] George Catlin, who apparently saw but one living specimen in some eight years, suggested 'perhaps not one in 100,000.'[71] Henry records two (in the same local territory) in less than three-and-one-half years.[72] Parkman encountered a white

[62]*Ibid.*, 403, 939-44.

[63]Garretson, *American Bison*, 31. Much more logically, two learned scholars observe that it is impossible to make statements concerning 'Sioux' customs that would be true of all (C. Thomas, J. R. Swanton, "Siouan Family," *Handbook of American Indians*, II, 578). Garretson also says (*American Bison*, 31) that even a war-party from a hostile tribe would treat such sacred shrines with reverence. I consider this doubtful, say in the sack of a village, particularly by a non-buffalo-worshipping tribe.

[64]Above, note 26.

[65]Above, note 52.

[66]Coues (ed.), *Henry-Thompson Journals*, I, 354. Maximilian also states that buffalo skins with white spots were highly prized by the Mandans (*Early Western Travels*, XXIII, 323). Compare the photo in Garretson (*American Bison*, 13) of the "Head of a Pied Buffalo Cow."

[67]*Early Western Travels*, XV, 244. Compare the Pawnee folk-tale of the 'Buffalo-Wife' with its 'yellow calf' (Grinnell, *Indians of To-Day*, 73-89). This possibly indicates a worship of animals of an uncommon colour, but the young calves were of yellowish-tawny hue (see chap. V, note 28). See also the buffalo folk-lore in *The Indians' Book* (with music, ed. Natalie Curtis, 1907). Dr. Gregg (below, note 76), by implication at least, seems to restrict white buffalo worship to the *northern* tribes.

[68]Catlin, *Letters on the North American Indians*, II, 55.

[69]Parkman, *Oregon Trail* (1892 ed.), 415.

[70]Above, note 27.

[71]Catlin, *Letters on the North American Indians*, I, 133.

[72]December 1, 1800 to April 24, 1804 (above, notes 34-5).

one after some three or four months only, although of course he might have passed years without seeing another. And the 'Yanktonans' aforementioned would seem to have found their two specimens not very far removed in point of time.[73]

Henry M. Brackenridge, in discussing albinos, remarks: "A single deer or buffalo, I am well assured, has been met with of this colour. . . ."[74] Expressed thus by a visitor of a season (1811), and in the absence of any personal rhodomontade from his informant about what *he* had seen, this may be taken to indicate a general plainsmens' belief (that is, as apart from scientists') in their rarity. This would be strengthened by the prices which certain Indians were willing to pay for them. Dr. Josiah Gregg, one of the two earliest really philosophical students of the buffalo of any very lengthy personal experience—Catlin being the other—writing of them after nine or ten seasons' observation (1831-40), may be said to sum up the other side of the question. In the course of his very valuable remarks on the buffalo, he writes: "The phenomenon of a white buffalo has frequently been remarked upon the Prairies; but as the white skin is said to have been used in the mystic ceremonies of many of the northern tribes of Indians this probably created such a demand for them, that they have become nearly extinct. Their unusual colour has commonly been considered a *lusus naturae,* yet it is probable that they stand in about the same relation to the black or brown buffalo[75] that black sheep do to white ones. . . ."[76]

If it be correct—as Gregg's language seems to imply—that the white buffalo worship was not prevalent among the southern Plains tribes, this might possibly account for their being (or being thought to be) rather less rare than in the north. Even so, however, as a valuable article of trade among tribes who sometimes had to import their very bowstaves or tipi poles,[77] they might probably be in almost equal demand with the northern regions.

In Gregg's day, I think it may fairly be assumed that the occasional white specimens in the general neighbourhood of the Santa Fé Trail were

[73]Above, note 58.

[74]Brackenridge, *Early Western Travels,* VI, 56. *In re* deer, a big-game-hunting friend, the late T. G. Case, Esq., of Edmonton, informed me that he once saw near Mackay, Alberta (90 miles west of Edmonton), an adult bull moose whose body colour was gray, turning towards black below the knees. Professor William Rowan, Zoological Department, University of Alberta, tells me he knows of no similar instance. Denny mentions a white beaver—the only one he ever saw—brought into Fort Macleod by an Indian, 1875 (Denny, *The Law Marches West,* 60); and a white gopher was reported near Bawlf, central Alberta (*Edmonton Journal,* November 15, 1940). An albino caribou pelt reported from Yellowknife, North West Territories (*Victoria Daily Colonist,* April 26, 1946).

[75]'Black or brown' signified here the usual prairie type, and has nothing to do with any supposed 'black variety' (above, chap. III, notes 9-49). 'The plains black with buffalo' is a commonplace in the travel-literature. I note a Brulé chief, 1804—*Tahtónka-tsapa* = 'black buffalo bull' (*Handbook of American Indians,* I, 432). Cf. Allen, above, note 27; 'Black Buffalo,' a Kiowa chief, 1847 (Drannan, *Thirty-One Years on the Plains,* 42).

[76]Gregg, *Early Western Travels,* XX, 262.

[77]See below, Appendix X.

actually 'sports' of the true *Bison americanus*. The very late dates noted by M. S. Garretson for 'the only one recorded in Kansas' (1873), and the only one recorded south of the Arkansas River' (Texas, 1876)[78] render it at least possible that in these instances Buffalo Jones's 'solution of the problem' of white buffalo as being cattalo might conceivably apply, other conditions, such as have been discussed above, being favourable; perhaps the more so that the latter speaks of four being once seen together.[79]

But the identical testimony of two entirely independent early witnesses concerning the low social estimation of those aspirants to dignity in the Mandan villages who did not possess at least one—doubtless a tribal criterion of long standing—points clearly to a relative degree of frequency quite incompatible with Hornaday's 'ten or eleven' in all buffalo history. The present discussion cites twice that number, principally from sources not known to or not mentioned by him. And after his own rather definitive utterances on colour, he adds: "I have been informed that the late General Marcy possessed a white buffalo skin. If it is still in existence and is really *white*, it is to be hoped that so great a rarity may find a permanent abiding place in some museum where the remains of *Bison americanus* are properly appreciated."[80] One can sympathize with Hornaday's feeling on the question. At the same time, any scientific doubt which is implied in his remarks concerning whiteness in certain cases at least—in so far as anything is *white* except snow—may in my view be fairly set at rest by our foregoing evidence. It is scarcely credible that a specimen described by an experienced and shrewd fur-trader in a business transaction as being 'perfectly white'—a man, moreover, who elsewhere carefully defines 'dirty white' among several colours[81]—could have been artifically whitened, even had the Indians possessed the requisite practical facilities for doing this. The only recorded whitening medium in use by Western Indians was 'white earth' or clay; such as was used for whitening the buffalo skins of their tipis,[82] or their buckskin dress.[83] Nor could artificially whitened buffalo-skins have been passed off on keen bargainers of other tribes in exchange for their dearly prized horses; or in religious or social rivalry, upon envious competitors for the more exclusive honours conferred by such coveted possessions. It is impossible to doubt that the fraud would have been detected immediately.

It is hopeless to attempt to form any sound conclusions on the numbers of white buffalo from Indian nomenclature. Indian names were bestowed, and at widely varying times of life, for quite casual and incidental, some-

[78]Garretson, *American Bison*, 29-30. Cf. above, notes 68, 69.

[79]*Buffalo Jones' Forty Years*, 80-2.

[80]Hornaday, "Extermination of the American Bison," 415.

[81]Above, note 52.

[82]Lewis and Clark mention a village of "one hundred Teton [Sioux] cabins, made of white buffalo hide dressed" with clay (*Journals*, I, 137).

[83]An assembly at the Mandan villages, 1833, "the Indians wrapped in their white [ned] buffalo robes . . ." (Maximilian, *Early Western Travels*, XXII, 341. For the Blackfoot, Coues (ed.), *Henry-Thompson Journals*, II, 526; Kidd, "Blackfoot Ethnography," 84, 88; a Yanktonai chief, *Handbook of American Indians*, II, 990.

times—to us—utterly irrelevant and even fantastic, reasons.[84] 'White Buffalo' names might be given in some tribes, because of a dream or one's 'medicine'; or in other non-worshipping tribes, perhaps to the captor of a specimen, or even to some warrior slaying a chief or other foeman so called. The name seems to have been a not uncommon one, in the northern tribes at least. Lewis and Clark mention a Mandan chief in 1804, 'White Buffalo Robe Unfolded.'[85] Henry speaks of an Assiniboine (that is, a non-worshipper) at Fort Vermilion on the North Saskatchewan, 1809, named *Le Bœuf Blanc*; and a Piegan at Rocky Mountain House, 1810, named 'White Buffalo Robe.'[86] References to 'White Buffalo,' apparently a Blackfoot or Sarcee, are made in 1834 by both Catlin[87] and Maximilian;[88] and he is possibly the same individual of that name mentioned by Paul Kane in the Saskatchewan territory in 1847-48.[89] G. B. Grinnell prints a photograph of a Cheyenne (apparently of the late nineteenth century and presumably a chief) also named 'White Buffalo.'[90] Maximilian, again, mentions two chiefs on the Missouri River in 1833, named 'White Cow'; the one an Assiniboine (*Pteh-Skah*), and the other an Arikara (*Tanahah-Tahka*).[91] It is not clear in the case of *Ohistahna*, the 'chief of the womens' band of the white buffalo cow' aforementioned, whether this was the translation, or its bearer's position and dignity.[92] Denny (an eye-witness) records an unidentified Indian chief among those signing the treaty of September, 1877, at Blackfoot Crossing on the Bow River, named *Onistah-pokah* (White Calf), who from the name might possibly be a Blackfoot.[93] The name has also appeared in fiction,[94] and has furthermore been applied in cases which in some instances may not have been,[95] and in others were definitely not buffalo at all.[96] What would appear to have been true white buffalo (*B. americanus*) seem to have been known in the eastern territories, where of course they were just as likely to appear as anywhere else; from the fact that a name for them has been recorded in Tuscarora, as we have seen.[97]

[84]See Kidd, "Blackfoot Ethnography," 34, and authorities there cited. The famous Sitting Bull was 'Four Horns' until he 'made medicine' in 1857 (*Handbook of American Indians*, II, 583). The one name seems to us as irrelevant as the other.

[85]*Lewis and Clark Journals*, I, 175.

[86]Coues (ed.), *Henry-Thompson Journals*, II, 579, 597, 659, 719.

[87]Catlin, *Letters on the North American Indians*, I, 34. He also mentions *Wak-a-dah-ha-hee* = 'Hair of the white buffalo' (*ibid.*, 154-8).

[88]Maximilian, *Early Western Travels*, XXIII, 87.

[89]Kane, *Wanderings of an Artist* (orig. ed.), 425, 430.

[90]Grinnell, *Indians of To-Day*, 84.

[91]Maximilian, *Early Western Travels*, XXIII, 203, 230.

[92]*Ibid.*, 158; above, note 48.

[93]Denny, *The Law Marches West*, 115.

[94]*White Buffalo*, by Rev. Dr. John McDougall (Alberta, 1862-1917). I have not been able to see this, or to ascertain its *motif*. I have read McDougall's reminiscent material, frequently cited here, printed and unprinted, terminating with 1876 (McDougall MS. uncompleted). There is no mention of white buffalo in any of it.

[95]See below, Appendix N.

[96]*Ibid.* [97]Above, Appendix A, "Buffalo Synonymy."

I find two or three place-names of this order: White Buffalo Lake, North Dakota, White Buffalo Butte, Missouri River (1865);[98] also Grey Bull River (tributary of Big Horn River) 44° N., 109° W., Wyoming.[99] Doubtless these commemorate some occurrence relating to white specimens, but I have found nothing more concerning them.

While there can be no 'law of averages' in this field, it is of interest to note a specimen in our own day. A press notice records the following:

"A white bison bull, an animal rarer than the sacred white elephant of Siam, is an inmate of the National Bison Range near Moiese, Montana, and was presented to the park by the United States Biological Survey. White bison were great rarities even in the days of the vast herds on the western plains, a couple of generations ago. The Indians considered them sacred. One plains tribe, the Atsina, used to kill large numbers of bison by driving them over cliffs. But if they found one white animal in the mass they slaughtered wholesale, only the direst necessity could drive them to take the meat or hides of any part of the whole herd."[100]

[98]Taylor, *Frontier Life,* 41, 175.
[99]Cram's *International Atlas of the World.*
[100](Quoted from *Science,* no date given, in *Edmonton Journal,* November 26, 1938).

One would like to know the original writer's authority (1) for the generalization on 'Indians' (cf. above, note 63), or (2) for the specification of the Atsina in particular. I have found nothing to support this.

BUFFALO RITUALISM IN INDIAN LIFE

Allusion has been made above to the adaptation of the buffalo resources to Indian ritualistic purposes.[1] These may roughly be classified as follows: rites or practices for 'making the buffalo come,' and the 'totemistic' designation by some buffalo term of a gens or phratry in an Indian tribe. In the latter cases, membership in this body was accompanied by, or bound up with, the observance of certain practices or inhibitions, which, in so far as an outsider can judge, were probably nothing more than distinctive; and howsoever solemnly inculcated as being vital to the particular organization, served essentially the same purposes of identification and little else, as are served in our own polities by the regimental details in military uniforms, or similar minutiae in our fraternal societies.

Although few and fragmentary, the following notices may serve to indicate the prevalence of various religious practices for the first-named purpose, of 'making the buffalo come.' It is difficult in my opinion to reconcile the development and influence of such ceremonials with any conception of regularity in the comings and goings of the Indians' food supply. It is worthy of notice also, that these practices have been observed in those localities and among the tribes which are most typically associated with buffalo, as will be seen below.

Our information refers principally to the Missouri River and Saskatchewan tribes. Matthew Cocking, apparently somewhere in the Eagle Hills country, south of Battleford in October, 1772, mentions the Indians 'singing their Buffalo Pound songs' to attract the herds.[2] It is not certain whether these were Assiniboines or 'Archithinue' (Blackfoot), although more probably the former; but the southern Blackfoot of Montana also had a 'Buffalo Song.'[3] David Thompson, writing of the Piegans, *circa* 1800, says: "Others turn Dreamers, and tell . . . where the Bisons and Deer are most plenty. . . ."[4]

The Mandan and their associates were addicted to these rites. Patrick Gass noticed in 1804: "After they were done eating they presented a bowlful to a buffalo head, saying *eat that.*' Their superstitious credulity is so great that they believe by using the head well the living buffalo will come and that they will get a supply of meat. . . ."[5]

Maximilian, describing their religious practices thirty years later, mentions another feature: "Another very remarkable festival is that for attracting the herds of buffaloes, which is usually celebrated in the autumn

[1] Above, chap. XXI, note 4.
[2] "Cocking's Journal," ed. Burpee, 108-11.
[3] McClintock, *Old North Trail*, 81-3.
[4] Thompson, *Narrative*, ed. Tyrrell, 366; cf. Southesk, *Travels*, 80-3.
[5] Gass, *Journal of the Lewis and Clark Expedition*, ed. Hosmer, 66.

or winter. . . ."[6] One part of this was the prayer, or "address to the lord of life, in which he [the speaker] besought him to send buffaloes that they might not starve. . . ."[7] and Charles Mackenzie (1804) translates one of the Mandan invocations as follows: "Hooee! great bull of the meadow [that is, prairie] be thou there with thy white cow. . . ."[8] This bull-deity[9] is probably to be identified with the belief of which Dr. Jenness writes: ". . . the 'power' of the buffalo became a supernatural King-buffalo that lived in a mysterious buffalo-land and yet was immanent in every single buffalo. . . ."[10] The further association with the 'white cow' may also indicate the origin of the sanctity with which white buffalo were regarded by many tribes; and white cows *par excellence*, among the Mandan most particularly.[11] Our very earliest notice of this people (1738) records a society, 'the women's band of the white buffalo cow';[12] and Jenness mentions in reference to some such organization in some tribes, a ceremonial cutting of buffalo tongues after a hunt, 'by women who had dedicated themselves to this form of thanksgiving.'[13]

The Minatari (Hidatsa) also practised a ". . . buffalo medicine . . . with a view to prevent the buffalo from removing to too great a distance from them. . . ."[14] The Arikara[15] and other Missouri tribes[16] did the same.

In what seems to be a fairly acceptable 'Sioux Calendar' 1799-1870, cited by Dodge, it is recorded *sub anno* 1810-11—"The 'Black Stone' band of Sioux made medicine with a white buffalo cow. . . ."[17] In the same year, 1811, H. M. Brackenridge, on the Missouri, notes observing the remains of a Sioux 'medicine lodge,' where the rites 'for making the buffalo plenty' had been performed.[18] Maximilian mentions a pile of buffalo skulls near Fort Pierre (Pierre, South Dakota): "We are told that this was a medicine or charm, contrived by the Sioux Indians in order to entice the herds of

[6]Maximilian, *Early Western Travels*, XXIII, 334.

[7]*Ibid.*, XXIV, 57.

[8]Mackenzie, in Masson, *Les Bourgeois de la Compagnie du Nord-Ouest*, I, 379; cf. II, 103.

[9]No doubt the analogies of Aaron's Golden Calf, the bull Apis, the cow Io, the bull-faced deities of Mesopotamia, the Bull of Phalaris, etc., played a part in the supposed Jewish or Egyptian origin of the Indians, once so dear to many hearts.

[10]Jenness, *Indians of Canada*, 170.

[11]See above, Appendix D. "Albinism in Buffalo."

[12]*Journals of La Vérendrye*, ed. Burpee, 342; also a century later (Maximilian, *Early Western Travels*, XXIII, 266, 297).

[13]Jenness, *Indians of Canada*, 322.

[14]Maximilian, *Early Western Travels*, XXIII, 375, 377.

[15]*Ibid.*, 392.

[16]De Smet, *ibid.*, XXIX, 284, 394.

[17]Dodge, *Our Wild Indians*, 401. Some measure of reliability is suggested by a fairly close agreement with such events as the appearance of Texas cattle on the northern plains. See on this, Bancroft, *North Mexican States and Texas*, II, 559-63; *History of Nevada*, 544; Hebard and Brininstool, *Bozeman Trail*, I, 229; E. S. Osgood, *Day of the Cattleman*, 21, 31, 42-6; Webb, *Great Plains*, 216, 260. On "Indian Calendars," including this, cf. Cyrus Thomas, *Handbook of American Indians*, I, 189.

[18]*Early Western Travels*, VI, 109.

buffaloes. . . ."[19] There was a similar 'Assiniboine medicine' near Fort Union.[20]

It is significant that rites of this character were also practised by tribes in the southern buffalo territory below the Platte; that is to say, in the one region where something approximating a regular 'migratory' movement finds a measure of historical support.[21] Dr. Gregg noted observances 'to induce buffalo to visit the neighbourhood' among the Comanches and Pawnee.[22] Apparently among the latter, on the Platte, June, 1820, Edwin James mentions that the expedition's hunter, 'Mr. J. Dougherty,' ". . . saw in an Indian hut a bison head, very well prepared, which had a white star on the front; the owner valued it highly, calling it his great medicine; he could not be tempted to part with it, 'for,' said he, 'the herds come every season into the vicinity to seek their white-faced companion. . . .' "[23]

As may perhaps have been the case in the foregoing instance, these functions were sometimes of a semi-private or personal character, rather than public ceremonials at stated seasons. Parkman speaks of an old Sioux, 'consulting an oracle' to discover where the absent buffalo were;[24] and Catlin rather cynically indicates what may have been a potent factor in the consideration which the 'dreamers' acquired. He says the rites and incantations were continued *until the buffalo did come*; whereby the medicine men acquired merit, and in this way 'never failed.'[25]

'Buffalo-calling' ceremonies have been found among many tribes.[26] As with other tribal rites, these are not invariably as aboriginally ancient as their devotees commonly imagined.[27] A not uncommon feature in Indian folk-myths[28] is the assumption of the presence of the buffalo as an established denizen of a region previous to the tribe's own arrival there. In cases of relatively recent tribal migrations this could easily be true, as with the Crees and Assiniboine, for example; but the same circumstance demonstrates the recentness of their *buffalo* ceremonials, strictly speaking.[29] Other

[19]Maximilian, *ibid.*, XXII, 318.

[20]*Ibid.*, 383.

[21]Above, chap. XIX, note 69 *seq.*

[22]Gregg, *Early Western Travels*, XX, 351.

[23]Long, *ibid.*, XV, 244. For a curious commentary on the efficacy of these expedients, see above, chap. XX, note 64.

[24]Parkman, *Oregon Trail*, 257, 279. Lewis and Clark mention a Sioux chief named 'Buffalo Medicine,' *Tartongawaka* (*Journals*, I, 130, 150).

[25]Catlin, *Letters on the North American Indians*, I, 127.

[26]See R. H. Lowie, "Ceremonialism in North America," *American Anthropologist*, XVI, 1914, 602-31. The Winnebago, at the farthest northern limit of the central habitat, had a 'Buffalo calling' dance in the spring (*Handbook of American Indians*, II, 960; cf. *ibid.*, I, 382.

[27]See Lowie, "Ceremonialism in North America"; also Clark Wissler, *American Anthropologist*, XVI, 1914, 12.

[28]On Mandan and other legends on the buffalo preceding 'the making of the first man,' see Maximilian, *Early Western Travels*, XXIII, 252-395. Cf. also the Teenikashika, a 'buffalo gens' of the Quapaw, *i.e.* 'those who became human beings by means of the buffalo' (*Handbook of American Indians*, II, 717).

[29]Among the Illinois and Creeks, their 'white buffalo' sacrifice was an extension from an earlier white dog ritual (Swanton, *Handbook of American*

tribal stocks came from regions where the buffalo only penetrated very shortly before their extinction in those localities, and in negligible numbers; sometimes not at all. The very numerous and widespread Siouan family are a case in point. Their earliest ancestral home is considered by the most competent investigators to have been in the Carolinas, whence they spread westward to the Mississippi valley; dividing there into 'up-river' and 'down-river' folk, respectively.[30] The late arrival of the historic buffalo in the southeastern States has been shown above.[31]

Observances similar to the foregoing have been recorded with other game animals; and presumably for the purpose of attracting the particular species in question. Maximilian noted "a pyramid of elks' horns, to which every Indian made a point of contributing one, to insure success in hunting. . . ."[32] Such 'pyramids' have been remarked elsewhere;[33] and have even been commemorated in Western place-names[34]—not undeservedly, as they were a quite characteristic feature among the aboriginal inhabitants.

It has been said that these 'offerings to the Sun' were never disturbed even by hostile war-parties.[35] Having regard to the minute tribal distinctions so widely prevalent—of which, in relation to religion, the distinctive attitudes toward 'white buffalo' worship furnish an outstanding example[36]—and also to the many inveterate and implacable tribal hatreds, I require conclusive evidence before accepting this assertion.

Indians, II, 403). Similarly dog-standards of value are found antedating the horse-'tariffs' in other tribes. See Roe, "From Dogs to Horses among the Western Indian Tribes," *Transactions of the Royal Society of Canada*, 1939, Sec. II, 262-71.

[30]See on this Thomas and Swanton, "Siouan Family," *Handbook of American Indians*, II, 577; also *passim*, on Siouan tribes.

[31]See above, chap. IX, notes 38-60; chap. X, notes 103-120.

[32]Maximilian, *Early Western Travels*, XXIII, 34; so also, De Smet, *ibid.*, XXIX, 366.

[33]See an illustration of one, Hewitt, *Conservation of the Wild Life of Canada*, 27. Similar piles of stones, to which each Indian contributed one more, are recorded by Father Le Jeune, 1657 (*Jesuit Relations*, XLIV, 25); Hearne, 1771 (*Journey*, 162); Nuttall, 1819 (*Early Western Travels*, XIII, 207, 210); not to say in South America (C. R. Enock, *The Mystery of the Pacific*, 1912, 325); South Africa (Leo Frobenius, *Childhood of Man*, trans. A. H. Keane, 1909, 154); and England (S. O. Addy, *Sheffield Glossary*, English Dialect Society, 1888, xxi). Thought to be landmarks (Washington Irving, Osage country, 1832, *Tour of the Prairies*, 402; Hector, Bow River, 1859, *Palliser Journals*, 143) 'and nothing more' (Dodge, *Our Wild Indians*, 577); but Dr. G. M. Dawson, Old Man River, Alberta, noted such where they could not serve as landmarks (*Place-Names of Alberta*, 96).

[34]Antler (Red Deer River, west of Penhold, Alberta) translation of Cree name = 'pile of elk-horns' (*Place-Names of Alberta*, 12). Another 'Antler,' Southeastern Saskatchewan. Compare 'Pile o' Bones,' Regina (above, chap. XIII, note 111).

[35]Garretson, *American Bison*, 31.

[36]See above, Appendix D, "Albinism in Buffalo"; cf. *Handbook of American Indians* (*s.v.* Religion), II, 365 *seq.*; also authorities cited above, chap. XXI, notes 240, 385, etc.

APPENDIX F

CARIBOU

The movements of the caribou at different seasons are such as may correctly be designated 'migrations' in the rigidly 'technical' sense of recent scientific classification; that is to say—whatever may have been their origin, which we can probably never know—they are now apparently for the purpose of giving birth to the young in some selected summer habitat.[1] It seems to follow logically that a truly migratory movement of this character should *a priori* exhibit uniform regularity, if it is to be expected anywhere; and evidence to the contrary in such a species would tend strongly to establish an antecedent probability for irregularities in non-'migratory' wandering herds, such as buffalo. Evidence of this character confirms me in the belief that the interpretation I have placed upon the buffalo movements is correct.

At the time when I was engaged upon the preliminary research work for the present essay, the English-speaking world at large, and Canada and England in particular, were startled and shocked by the tragic fate of J. N. Hornby and his young companions in the North-West Territory between Great Slave Lake and Chesterfield Inlet on Hudson's Bay. A very few words will suffice to indicate the bearings of this event upon the theory of uniform caribou migration routes.

'Jack Hornby,' as he was universally known among Northmen, was the son of a man whose name was a household word among cricketers the world over;[2] and an experienced Northman of long standing in the Barren Lands.[3] In June, 1926, the party of three, Hornby, his nephew, E. V. Christian, and H. Adlard—the two latter being much younger and new to the Northland—set forth across Great Slave Lake on their way eastward towards Chesterfield Inlet on Hudson's Bay. As many months elapsed without any word from them, anxiety began to be felt; but the general consensus of opinion among competent judges was that 'Hornby would come out all right.'[4] Nevertheless, they were never again seen alive; and not until long after was their fate known, when a rescue party of the Royal North-West Mounted Police discovered their remains in a log shack at, or near the junction of Thelon and Hanbury Rivers, (about 63° N., 103° W.) in October, 1928.[5] From a diary which was found in the cabin, it was learned

[1]See 'migration' defined above, chap. IV, note 53.

[2]A. N. Hornby, sometime Lancashire county cricket captain, a contemporary of Grace in his palmy days.

[3]George M. Douglas, the author of *Lands Forlorn*, dealing with the Coppermine River country, lived several months with Hornby, winter 1911-12. The latter had then been 'several years on Great Bear Lake' (*ibid.*, 50, 139, etc.).

[4]October, 1928. See an opinion by a former comrade on Hornby's capacity and experience (*Edmonton Journal*, May 4, 1931).

[5]*Ibid.*, November 3, 1928; *ibid.*, January 24, 1929.

that the three died in succession between April 16, and June 3, 1927.[6] Their deaths were due to starvation, owing to their failure to connect with the migrating herds of caribou, as Hornby had expected to do.[7]

An event of this character, apart from its pathetic interest to the world at large, could scarcely fail to deeply impress a student then struggling through a mass of very imperfectly supported assertion concerning the 'regular' (etc., etc.) buffalo migration. This led to my collecting, as occasion offered, a little incidental evidence concerning caribou migrations, which is here set forth.

The earlier 'scientific' opinion seems to have been in favour of an undeviating regularity. Richardson writes as follows (1861): "They always follow the same routes and cross the rivers at the same place . . ." and, citing Baron Wrangel, "The migrations of the reindeer are as constant in Siberia as in America. . . ."[8] These routes were known to the Eskimos.[9]

I am led to suspect that here, too—as with the buffalo—this supposed ultra-regularity is based upon the assertions of uncritical local generalizers; perhaps supported by the chance experience of the particular years of Richardson's own visits. For the literature of the Northland at large by no means uniformly endorses his conclusions. Samuel Hearne remarked concerning the annual migrations of the caribou between the forest and the coast across the Cathawhachaga River (1770-71):[10]

The number of deer which crossed Cathawhachaga during our stay there, was by no means equal to our expectations. . . .[11]

The scarcity or abundance of these animals in different places at the same season is caused, in a great measure, by the winds which prevail for some time before; for the deer are supposed by the natives to walk always in the direction from which the wind blows, except when they migrate from East to West, or from West to East, in search of the opposite sex, for the purpose of propagating their species. . . .[12]

David Thompson speaks of 'vast herds' passing here and there quite by chance, and not being seen in places apparently on their direct line of march.[13] On the other hand, John McLean, the old Hudson's Bay man, makes the migrations very uniform, 'seldom deviating,' etc.[14]

[6]Printed in extenso, ibid., December 28, 1929. The notice of its discovery appeared in several English newspapers, October 3, 1929.

[7]Edmonton Journal, December 28, 1929. As a result, in part, of data gathered by Hornby and Captain J. C. Critchell-Bullock, the Thelon Game Sanctuary of 15,000 square miles is now closed to hunters (ibid., January 17, 1930; May 4, 1931).

[8]Richardson, Polar Regions, 275-6; cf. his Fauna Boreali-Americana, I, 233-51.

[9]Richardson, Polar Regions, 274.

[10]Hearne, Journey, ed. Tyrrell, note 87.

[11]Ibid., 88.

[12]Ibid., 214. Compare Hearne on 'deer-pounds' made on regularly frequented paths; but the deer did not keep on them! (ibid., 120, 126, 193). Also the well-known incident of his guide, Matonabbee, and the 'women being able to live on the lickings of fingers' (p. 102). Matonabbee knew where they were going!

[13]Thompson, Narrative, ed. Tyrrell, 100-1.

[14]McLean, Twenty-Five Years' Service (orig. ed.), II, 111-12.

Professor John Macoun, whose personal contact with Northmen dated (for this purpose) 1872-80, and who may be termed the earliest of the moderns, is in implied agreement with the 'irregular' view: ". . . herds that aggregate many thousands. In spring and fall, as they pass and repass, to their feeding grounds, they are met by the hunters and slaughtered in thousands. Should the fall hunt be a failure, as it sometimes is . . ."[15]

The Northland travel literature of the last forty years or so contains a number of works by particularly competent observers, who, as sportsmen, scientists, or explorers often dependent upon their weapons for subsistence, had a direct or even vital interest in the habits of caribou. It will be seen that among a considerable amount of detail, they present a strikingly unanimous body of testimony concerning irregularity in the species. Some of these I shall quote in chronological order. Warburton Pike writes thus (1889):

> The caribou are extremely uncertain in their movements, seldom taking the same course in two consecutive years and thus affording ground for the universal cry in the North that the caribou are being killed off. I think there is really much truth in the statement that they keep a more easterly route than formerly, as they seldom come in large quantities to the Mackenzie River, where they used to be particularly numerous in winter. . . .[16] One point that seems to bear out the theory of a more easterly movement is that within the last three years the caribou have appeared in their thousands at York Factory on the west side of Hudson's Bay, where they have not been seen for over thirty years; but I cannot believe, judging from the vast herds that I myself saw, that there is any danger of the caribou being exterminated. . . .[17]

J. W. Tyrrell describes them as follows (1893):

> Concerning the habits of the reindeer, they are both gregarious and migratory. During the summer season their resort is the open plain and the sea-cost, where, to some extent, they escape from their tormentors, the mosquitos and black-flies, and find abundance of food in the tender grasses, the ground birch, or the willow buds. In the autumn they turn their steps toward the woodlands or more sheltered districts, where they spend the long severe winters, subsisting on tree-buds, moss, or lichens. . . .[18]

Ernest Thompson Seton characterizes the caribou thus:

> The Caribou is a travelsome beast, always in a hurry, going against the wind. When the wind is west, all travel west; when it veers, they veer. Now the wind was northerly, and all were going north. . . .[19]

The main body winters in the sheltered southern third of the range, to avoid the storms, and moves north in the late spring to avoid the plagues of deer-flies and mosquitoes. The former are found chiefly in the woods, the latter are bad everywhere; by travelling against the wind a certain measure of relief is secured, northerly winds prevail, so the Caribou are kept travelling northward. When

[15]Macoun, *Manitoba*, 339.
[16]Owing to the lichens and other pasturage having been destroyed by fire, thinks Pike.
[17]Pike, *Barren Ground*, 50.
[18]Tyrrell, *Across the Sub-Arctics of Canada*, 88-9.
[19]Seton, *Arctic Prairies*, 209.

there is no wind, the instinctive habit of migration doubtless directs the general movement. . . .[20]

Dr. Gordon Hewitt's general conclusions are:

The great herds in the fall of the year perform a more or less regular movement in the nature of migrations, and within certain limits their course of travel and times of arrival at given points are well known. . . .[21]

While their migratory movements are very regular in point of time, the routes they take are not always the same, and they travel generally in a northerly or southerly direction. Their course cannot be predicted with any degree of certainty. They seldom follow the same course in two consecutive years. The Indians, such as the Yellow-knives and Dog-ribs, who are dependent upon the caribou to so great an extent for food, with all their experience of the caribou are sometimes unable to find them where they might be expected, with the result that distress and starvation follow. . . .[22]

The foregoing generalizations find abundant confirmation in the incidental travel jottings of the day; and—as with buffalo—it is notable that even the most diametrically opposite points of view can be buttressed by evidence. The mere belief of their routes being 'well known' to the Eskimo and Indians[23] could scarcely have obtained credence in a land where this was *uniformly* untrue; and some measure of physical (that is, topographical) justification is found in Thompson Seton's description of some of the caribou trails, which must have involved a certain amount of repeated use, whether uniformly annual or not. He writes ('Pike's Portage,' 1907): "The country here is cut up on every side with Caribou trails; deep worn like the buffalo trails on the plains, with occasional horns and bones; these, however, are not as plentiful as were the relics of the Buffalo. This, it proved, was because the Caribou go far north at horn-dropping time, and they have practically no bones that the Wolves cannot crush with their teeth. . . ."[24] J. W. Tyrrell remarks also (1893): "At certain seasons of the year, when travelling north or south, the deer cross streams, rivers, or lakes in great numbers, and these crossings are commonly effected year after year in the same place. The hunter, knowing their habits lies in wait at the crossings. . . ."[25]

It can scarcely be questioned that none would know their habits better than the aboriginal hunters. Warburton Pike speaks of the Northern Indians being "possessed of a thorough knowledge of the movements of various animals at different seasons. . . ."[26] Yet despite this they 'often starved';[27] precisely as we have seen in the case of the buffalo.[28] Thompson Seton,

[20]*Ibid.*, 257.

[21]Hewitt, *Conservation of the Wild Life of Canada*, 61.

[22]*Ibid.*, 63-4.

[23]According to David Thompson, *circa* 1790, the Indians said 'the Manito drove them on to the place where they were to go.' 'Where is that?' 'We don't know.' 'Instinct' was ridiculed (*Narrative*, ed. Tyrrell, 102).

[24]Seton, *Arctic Prairies*, 202; cf. Richardson, *Fauna Boreali-Americana*, I, 246.

[25]Tyrrell, *Across the Sub-Arctics of Canada*, 148. On their swimming powers, see *ibid.*, 84-5; Richardson, *Fauna Boreali-Americana*, I, 246. Seton, *Life-Histories of Northern Animals*, I, 201; etc.

[26]Pike, *Barren Ground*, preface, vii.

[27]*Ibid.*, 50-1, 84, 131-3, etc.

[28]See above, chap. XXI, sec. 9, etc.

speaking of Indian knowledge, observes: "Two weeks hence, they say, these hills will be alive with Caribou; alas! for them it proved a wholly erroneous forecast. . . ."[29] David Thompson, a century earlier, recorded the fact of his being thought, by reason of his astronomical observations, to know 'where the deer are.'[30] What can this mean, except that at times they themselves did not?

The utterly impredicable uncertainty to which these records clearly point is stated in so many words as an actual experience. G. M. Douglas, writing of the winter his party spent in the Coppermine River country (1911-12), says:

We had come through the best caribou country and seen only one. . . .[31]

. . . hoping to see some caribou on the plains. . . . there were no signs whatever. . . .[32]

Caribou were really very scarce; only a few small bands left their tracks in our vicinity through all the winter months. Perhaps the. . . . party hunting around here the previous winter may have frightened them away, or it may have been merely the chance of their movements, always very uncertain and capricious. . . .[33]

. . . week after week might pass without a sign of any caribou; but that did not prevent the hunter from having the most enthusiastic expectations the first day or so [that is, of his week, in regular rotation, as 'hunter' for the party]. . . .[34]

Thompson Seton wrote in 1907: "Other travellers have gone, relying on the abundant Caribou, yet saw none, so starved. I relied on no Caribou, I took plenty of groceries, and because I was independent, the Caribou walked into camp nearly every day, and we lived largely on their meat. . . ."[35] The fate of the Hornby party twenty years later is only too bitter a commentary upon the soundness of Seton's conclusions.[36]

There seems some reason to suppose that in part these variations in the numbers of caribou may have been due to what one can only term a systematic change of route—abandoning the regular use of one for the regular use of another. A Northman's journal records that caribou were seen at Reindeer Lake (57° N., 102° 30′ W.), their 'farthest point south' in that central region, each season from 1874 until 1884; and none from 1884 until the autumn of 1889.[37] Count Illa Tolstoi (a grandson of his famous namesake) is reported as stating that after a study of the northern caribou, he concludes that they are 'changing their habits.'[38] Something similar may be indicated in a later Press dispatch:

[29]Seton, *Arctic Prairies*, 189.

[30]*Narrative*, ed. Tyrrell, 104-5; cf. Sheldon, *Wilderness of Denali*, 230 (Alaska).

[31]Douglas, *Lands Forlorn*, 121.

[32]*Ibid.*, 147.

[33]*Ibid.*, 157.

[34]*Ibid.*, 164.

[35]*Arctic Prairies*, 221.

[36]See a friend and former comrade of Hornby on this (J. C. Critchell-Bullock, *Edmonton Journal*, May 4, 1931).

[37]Cited by Angus Buchanan, *Wild Life in Canada*, 108. On the Reindeer Lake region (Lac du Brochet) see Hewitt, *Conservation of the Wild Life of Canada*, 60. See also below, note 47.

[38]*Edmonton Journal*, March 16, 1929.

Observations made by explorers and investigators of the department of the interior, Canada, over a considerable period, indicate that a decided improvement has taken place in the condition of the caribou herds of Canada's northland. To the west in Yukon Territory and eastward almost to Hudson Bay the caribou are reported in large numbers, in many cases having re-appeared on their old migrational routes. . . .[39]

The extraordinary feature in fluctuations of this character is that they cannot be ascribed purely to the difficulty of locating small herds in a large territory. For it is evident that the numbers of the caribou were—probably still are—almost incredibly vast. We have two or three striking descriptions of the caribou en route. Warburton Pike witnessed the herd movement in 1889, when it occupied six days (October 20-25) in passing the camping-ground of his expedition:

This passage of the caribou is the most remarkable thing that I have ever seen in the course of many expeditions among the big game of America. The buffalo were for the most part killed out before my time, but notwithstanding all the tall stories that are told of their numbers, I cannot believe that the herds on the prairie ever surpassed in size *la foule* of the caribou. . . .[40]

J. W. Tyrrell (Carey Lake, July 29, 1893) writes:

. . . one of our party called attention to something moving on the distant shore to our right. It turned out to be not one but a band of deer. . . . Drawing nearer we found there was not only one band, but that there were many great bands, literally covering the country over wide areas. The valleys and hillsides for miles appeared to be moving masses of reindeer. To estimate their numbers would be impossible. They could only be reckoned in acres or square miles. . . .[41]

Buffalo Jones remarks concerning a caribou herd which he saw in 1897: "It appeared as if the whole face of the earth were alive and moving. . . ."[42]

There have been several estimates of the size of the herd or herds. David Thompson saw one which he computed 'by space'—a mathematician's estimate, moreover—to contain 3,564,000 head.[43]

H. T. Munn, in 1892, in three weeks saw 'not less than 2,000,000 head; the advance guard going south.'[44] Buffalo Jones's herd in 1897, was estimated to include "over 25,000,000 [sic]. Yet it is possible there are several such armies, in which case they must indeed outnumber the Buffalo in their palmiest epoch. . . ."[45]

[39]*Ibid.*, December 24, 1930.
[40]Pike, *Barren Ground*, 89-91.
[41]Tyrrell, *Across the Sub-Arctics of Canada*, 85-9. Tyrrell's photograph of this is found in several books. See Seton, *Arctic Prairies*, 222; Hearne, *Journey*, ed. Tyrrell, 234; Hewitt, *Conservation of the Wild Life of Canada*, 66.
[42]*Buffalo Jones' Forty Years*, 338.
[43]Thompson, *Narrative*, ed. Tyrrell, 102. Thompson severely criticized R. M. Ballantyne (*Hudson's Bay*, London, 1848) for the latter's 'myriads of wild animals' in the Territory (*Narrative*, 109, 298, ed. note). Compare the above! On the Piegan method of computation 'by the space of ground they stood upon'; cf. *ibid.*, 366.
[44]Seton, *Arctic Prairies*, 258.
[45]*Ibid.*, 258-9.

Thompson Seton draws an interesting comparison:

A year afterward [that is, after 1907], as I travelled in the fair State of Illinois, famous for its cattle, I was struck by the idea that one sees far more Caribou in the north than cattle in Illinois. This State has about 56,000 square miles of land, and 3,000,000 cattle; the Arctic Plains have over 1,000,000 square miles of prairie, which, allowing for the fact that I saw the best of the range, would set the Caribou numbers at over 30,000,000. There is a good deal of evidence that this is not far from the truth. . . .[46]

He adds in another place: "They number over 30,000,000, and may be double of that. . . ."[47]

Shortly after Seton, another explorer commented thus: "Warburton Pike says that he cannot believe that the buffalo herds on the prairies ever surpassed in numbers *la foule* of the caribou, and this statement is borne out by other travellers in the Barren Ground. Ernest Thompson Seton, who made a trip thither in 1907, estimated the total number of caribou in the region at thirty million, but his figures are probably too large. . . ."[48]

Haworth offers no reasons for his opinion. Seton (whose critical attitude towards a living species is much more satisfactory than are his more purely historical pronouncements concerning buffalo) brings forward some evidence for his faith:

And what a region it is for pasture. At this place, it reminds one of Texas. Open, grassy plains, sparser reaches of sand, long slopes of mesquite, mesas dotted with cedars and stretches of chapparal [sic] and soapweed. Only, those vegetations here are willow, dwarf birch, tiny spruce, and ledum, and the country as a whole is far too green and rich. The emerald verdure of the shore, in not a few places, carried me back to the west coast of Ireland. . . .[49]

Thompson Seton concludes as a whole: "This herd is said to rival in numbers the Buffalo herds of story, to reach farther than the eye can see, and to be days in passing a given point; but it is utterly erratic. . . ."[50]

What really seems to be nothing more than a typical instance of this erratic propensity is well illustrated in a fairly recent report from an official investigator, cited in the Press. In the self-same article which relates a great scarcity and consequent privation in the Coppermine River region and about Coronation Gulf in the season of 1928[51]—considered as

[46]*Ibid.*, 220.

[47]*Ibid.*, 261. Cf. also the following: "Winnipeg—Paul Reykdal, veteran northern fisherman and hunter, said that in his opinion there should be no alarm over the meat rationing question in Canada because of the 'millions of caribou up north.' Mr. Reykdal told of reports he had received from two fishermen from Reindeer Lake that steady columns of Caribou from 100 yards to half a mile wide migrated across the Lake in February. A rough estimate of the number seen in ten days, Mr. Reykdal said, was about 2,500,000 animals" (*Edmonton Journal*, April 20, 1943).

[48]Haworth, *Trailmakers of the Northwest*, 193.

[49]Seton, *Arctic Prairies*, 222.

[50]*Ibid.*, 255-6; cf. Hearne, *Journey*, 236.

[51]The region of G. M. Douglas's scarcity, 1911; above, notes 31-4.

evidence of the 'disappearing caribou'—it is stated that they were 'unusually plentiful' along Back's River and in the territory farther eastward.[52] A later report scouts the idea, and 'describes the vanishing caribou as a myth.' That the animals have become scarce in certain districts is ascribed to their wariness: "They have found them dangerous and now void those places. . . . The natives depend on the punctuality and regularity of the caribou migration and are often near starvation when the caribou fail to arrive . . . ."[53]

It is entirely consonant with our experience at large concerning generalizations on game, that even the wariness is not present at all times. Tyrrell writes: "At certain seasons of the year, when travelling north or south . . . occasionally vast herds of deer numbering many thousands, are met with, and at such times their numbers appear to give them confidence. The hunter then has no trouble in approaching them. . . ."[54] The opinions expressed concerning native consumption being really negligible imply vast numbers; and the suggested estimates put forward make the opinions on consumption at least credible.[55] It may be recalled that with the buffalo there is no indication that under aboriginal conditions the Indians ever could have exterminated the species.

One final problem remains, to which it is difficult to suggest an answer. As the movement of the caribou is a true migration (that is, a movement for breeding purposes), Dr. Hewitt's statement—that their migrations are 'very regular in point of time,' if not in place would seem to be almost necessarily true;[56] although even here, important authorities record absolutely fundamental variations.[57] But after making every allowance for an immense and little-known land, and for the possibility of tribal enemies refusing to transmit intelligence of observed changes of route, it still remains difficult to understand how such hosts could move along different routes at what must inevitably be the same approximate speeds (or for the same rough mileage totals) in order for breeding-season 'time-tables' to work out correctly. For we must

[52]W. H. B. Hoare, quoted in *Edmonton Journal*, April 20, 1929.

[53]Guy H. Blanchet, *ibid.*, June 14, 1930; cf. also *ibid.*, December 24, 1930 (*in extenso* above, note 39). 'Erratic' (Young, *Canoe and Dog-Train*, 107); 'no danger of extinction from Indians' (Pike, *Barren Ground*, 50); as also Seton, *Arctic Prairies*, 260-2; Hearne, *Journey*, ed. Tyrrell, himself an experienced Northman, 213-14.

[54]J. W. Tyrrell (brother of the above), *Across the Sub-Arctics of Canada*, 148, 187.

[55]Angus Buchanan (who considers Indians thrifty in slaughtering: Reindeer Lake region) allows about 40 per male Indian hunter per winter; that is, twice Seton's estimate (*Wild Life in Canada*, 131-8; cf. *ibid.*, 104-51, 195-203).

[56]Above, notes 20-5.

[57]*Re* the caribou-mating season: Tyrrell, 'young born before the winter quarters are vacated'; Pike, 'in June, after the northward migration has taken place.' See remarks in Hewitt, *Conservation of the Wild Life of Canada*, 61-2.

Pike speaks of meeting the bulls on their way to the cows, 1889, *Barren Ground*, 48-9, 54. Seton observes, 1907: "This year the Caribou cows went north as usual, but the bulls did not . . ." (*Arctic Prairies*, 189). This, or even the selecting of another route, seems astounding in males presumably following by scent.

bear in mind that while choice was possible to the caribou in respect of *destination* in this or that season, they had no choice in the period of time available to them between the commencement of their migration and their return to their winter feeding-grounds with their young of that summer.

When experienced native observers failed to co-ordinate the inevitable 'factors of regularity' in this annual process in a truly *migratory* species, the impredicability of analogous movements of such a character in a technically non-migratory animal is even greater. This seems unquestionable.

APPENDIX G

ESTIMATES OF INDIAN POPULATIONS SUBSISTING WHOLLY[1] OR PARTLY ON BUFFALO

1

IT IS not the object of this discussion to attempt to reach definite conclusions concerning Indian populations. First, the material at our disposal is often vague; and secondly, the task has already been essayed, and in some degree achieved, by Indianologists of the first rank, with whom I could not hope to compete.[2] At the same time, their point of view is somewhat different from my own, insomuch that one important essay embraces the entire North American continent north of Mexico. This includes large territories which have never been occupied by the historic buffalo, and leaves out the precise region which almost the latest generalizing authority on the species selects as the 'type locality'.[3] The demarcation is moreover a purely political and relatively recent one, having no significance whatever for some of the most typically 'buffalo' tribes of the Southwestern plains area.

It is, in my opinion, futile to attempt to treat our material as it is found in the early travel literature, as a census return in the rough. With one or two exceptions, the estimates of aggregate numbers are purely arbitrary; we commonly do not even know whose the original computation may have been, nor what was his competence to make one.[4] Further, the ratios of the (estimated) numbers of men, or warriors, or lodges, 'huts,' or 'cabins,' to the 'total numbers of souls' are themselves utterly empirical and variable. Among nations, living in a state of frequent inter-tribal war—waged as it was by Indians—the slaughter in one battle could reduce

[1] In using the phrase 'wholly,' I refer of course to the nomadic 'buffalo' tribes, without implying a meat diet solely, not to say a buffalo diet solely. Neither of these has been found. See chap. XXI, note 5.

[2] James Mooney, "The Aboriginal Population of America North of Mexico." The section on "Population" in A. L. Kroeber's important work, *Cultural and Natural Areas of Native North America*, 131-81, is admittedly a tentative critical commentary upon Mooney (p. 134) rather than a postulating of fresh data *de novo*.

[3] Seton, *Game Animals*, III, 641, 643.

[4] In some instances general estimates were remarkably close. Lewis and Clark, who do not appear to have actually visited the Osage villages, give the 'Great Osages' as 'about 500 warriors,' 1804 (*Journals*, I, 43). Pike writes, 1806: "I last evening took the census of the Grand [Osage] village, and found it to be, men 502; boys 341; women and girls 852; total 1695, lodges 214 [*i.e.* about 7.9 per lodge]" (Coues (ed.), *Expeditions of Pike*, II, 582). We are not told whether any number of men were absent; but the very high ratio, virtually 30 per cent, renders it improbable.

the ratio of warriors to souls in a community enormously.[5] A raid in a village involving a massacre of women and children in the warriors' absence would produce the reverse effect;[6] and a similar raid in which the tribe was absent or where the women and children might largely escape, but where a considerable number of dwellings were destroyed,[7] would raise the ratio of 'souls per lodge' in a huge disproportion until more were built. No one could predict in an Indian society when such events might occur; and if mentioned at all to a traveller coming shortly after, it would not be with the precise figures of a modern statistician.

In addition to the divergencies due to such 'catastrophic' causes, there are also to be considered the more normal everyday variations in the size of the dwelling or of the family as between tribe and tribe, or between individual households in the same community. These differed widely. One of the earliest descriptions I have found, apparently of the great village of the Illinois, *circa* 1670, speaks of a village of '500 or 600 fires, with more than 1500 men alone.'[8] Father Claude Allouez speaks of 350 'cabins' in the village of Kaskaskias, 1677;[9] and Father Dablon estimates the Mascouten village, 1679, at some '20,000 souls.'[10] If it were safe to pool these estimates, and to rank a 'fire' as being equivalent to a 'cabin,' the Illinois proportion of from 2.5 to 3 men per cabin would give the Kaskaskias a population roughly of some 965 men, and on the very commonly adopted ratio of one man to five individuals, a total of over 4,800 souls. Such an estimate is at least not incredible, when we consider Father Dablon's for a neighbouring tribe. As we shall see, however, these figures by no means find support from our modern investigators; although the early missionaries may have classified under one name confederacies which later scholars subdivide.

The one-in-five ratio per family is accepted by some inquirers too much as a matter of course. Even among tribes in the same general habitat, others have questioned this ratio, and such detailed evidence as I have been able to discover seems to support them in their doubts. General Henry Atkinson, *circa* 1825, estimated the Grand Pawnee at 5,500 souls and 1,100 warriors; and the Pawnee Loups at 3,500 souls and 700 warriors, respectively.[11] Long estimated the latter (P. Loups) in 1820

[5]September, 1804, 75 men of the 'Mahas' slain in one fight by the Sioux (*Lewis and Clark Journals*, I, 135); 250 of the Missouris 'destroyed by the Sauks at one contest' at their own village on the Missouri, 'a few years' *ante* 1804, perhaps 1774 (*ibid.*, 49-51).

[6]E.g. the Chivington massacre, 1864, '400 or 500, mostly women and children' (Taylor, *Frontier Life*, 57). 'Baker small-pox massacre,' Marias River, 1870, 18 warriors in 176 or 190 souls (Grinnell, *Indians of Today*, 19; *Fighting Cheyennes*, 105; Butler, *Great Lone Land*, 269).

[7]Lewis and Clark, September 26, 1804: "While on shore we saw 25 squaws, and about the same number of children, who had been taken prisoners two weeks ago [by the Sioux] in a battle with their [the prisoners'] countrymen, the Mahas. In this engagement the Sioux destroyed 40 lodges, killed 75 men . . . and took these prisoners . . ." (*Journals*, I, 135).

[8]Father Marquette, *Jesuit Relations*, LIX, 189; cf. *ibid.*, 123, 161.

[9]Allouez, *ibid.*, LX, 159.   [10]Dablon, *ibid*,. LXI, 149.

[11]Dale (ed.), *Ashley-Smith Explorations*, 120-2.

at 500 'families or approximately 2,000 souls in 100 'dirt lodges,' or one man in four persons.[12] Pike in 1806 found the figures to be as follows for the two bands mentioned: Grand Pawnees, 1,000 warriors, 1,120 women, 1,000 children; a total of 3,120 persons in 90 lodges, constituting one village; an average of 34.5 persons per lodge, and 32 per cent of the total population being men. The Pawnee Loups comprised 485 warriors, 500 women, and 500 children, a total of 1,485 persons in 40 lodges in one village; yielding averages respectively of 37.1 persons per lodge, and 30.6 men per hundred souls.[13] The general accuracy of these (Pike's) figures would seem to be established by their close agreement with those for the Republican Pawnees, recorded by Pike's own census: one village of 508 men, 550 women, and 560 children, a total of 1618 persons in 44 lodges;[14] an average, respectively, of 36.8 persons per lodge, and of 32 per cent men to the population. Yet their near neighbours, the Osage, were found by the same painstaking observer with an average of only 7.9 per lodge; their average ratio of men—naturally much less variable— being about 30 per cent.[15]

Very similar ratios, actual or estimated, are found in other Southern plains tribes. Pike's census of the Little Osage village showed 250 men, 241 women, 174 female children, 159 males; a total of 824 persons in 102 lodges, almost 8 per lodge, and 30 per cent of them men. So also in the Arkansas River village of the Wasbasha (Osage).[16] Pike gives an estimate as furnished to him by the Grand Osage chiefs, of 500 men, 700 women, and 300 male children in 200 lodges.[17] To this total of 1,500 we must surely add about 250 or 300 female children. This would yield something between 8.5 and 9 per lodge; with men comprising from 29 to 33 per cent of the population. Similarly, the Kans(a), another tribe of the Dhegiha group[18] of the Siouan family, are stated 'on information' to have contained 465 men, 500 women, and 600 children, a total of 1,565 souls in one village of 204 lodges;[19] an average of 7.66 per lodge, with men almost 30 per cent of the total. As a check against any tendency to interpret such

[12]Long, *Early Western Travels*, XVII, 153.

[13]Coues (ed.), *Expeditions of Pike*, II, 589.

[14]*Ibid.* The Pawnee are classified as (1) P. proper, Grand P., or Tcawi; (2) P. Republicans or Republican P., from the Republican River; (3) P. Loups, P. Mahas, P. Wolves, or Skidi ('Skedee or Wolf Pawnees'; Taylor, *Frontier Life*, 153); (4) Tapage or Pitahauerat. See Coues (ed.), *Expeditions of Pike*, II, 412, 532; *Handbook of American Indians*, I, 707; II, 213, 263.

The P. Mahas are not to be confused with the Mahars or Mahas of Lewis and Clark (*Journals, passim*). The latter are the Omahas, who are Siouan, not Caddoan like the Pawnee (*Handbook of American Indians*, II, 121).

[15]Above, note 4.

[16]'Osage' apparently French; Wasbasha = native name (*Lewis and Clark Journals*, I, 43; Coues (ed.), *Expeditions of Pike*, II, 589; *Handbook of American Indians*, II, 158).

[17]Coues (ed.), *Expeditions of Pike*, II, 589. Lewis and Clark, from Pike or hearsay, give Grand O. = 500 warriors; Little O. = nearly 250 (*Journals*, I, 43).

[18]For 'Dhegiha,' see *Handbook of American Indians*, I, 389; II, 579; etc.

[19]Coues (ed.), *Expeditions of Pike*, II, 589.

lodge-ratios as being assignable to Indian tribal or family idiosyncrasies[20] in a similar environment, the Comanche, or 'Tetau' as Pike calls them, are given as comprising 2,700 warriors, 3000 women and 2,500 children, in 1020 'lodges of roving bands'; a total of 8,200,[21] or almost exactly the same ratio of 8 per lodge as the Little Osage, with 32.9 per cent of the total population men. Jacob Fowler mentions a gathering of '20,000' Arapahoes, Snakes, Kiowa, and Comanche in 400 lodges, on the Arkansas River, 1821.[22] This can scarcely be admitted into any discussion of ratios, since the total aggregate of souls must have been pure guesswork; and the variation of 50 persons per lodge from apparent local plains ratios points to a condition of 'doubling up' and overcrowding, possibly for this particular expedition, which robs this instance of any statistical value or significance.

Lewis and Clark speak of the Sioux lodges as 'containing from 10 to 15 persons'; in this instance apparently Yanktonai or Yanktons.[23] Somewhat similarly, the 'Teton Okandandas' (Oglala[24]) had 100 lodges of 'white buffalo hide dressed' in a village consisting of 'about 150'[25] or 'about 200' men.[26] Pike gives the Sioux (meaning perhaps the more easterly bands) as comprising in 1804, 3,835 men, 6,433 women, 11,800 children, in 1,270 lodges;[27] a total of 21,068, with an average of 16.6 per lodge, and men 18.2 per cent of the population. Long reckoned them in 1823 at 28,100 of whom 7,055 were warriors, in 2,330 tents.[28] This gives an average of 12.6 per tent, and what seems like a highly conventional ratio of slightly more than 25 per cent men. Our suspicion of Long's figures is not diminished by his further estimates (or guesses) of their kindred, the Assiniboine, also *circa* 1823; that is, 28,000 souls, 7,000 warriors, 3,000 tents;[29] the same precise ratio of men per total population, and an average of 9.33 per tent. The Assiniboine were estimated by Pike in 1805 at 1,500 warriors, no suggested totals or proportions being mentioned.[30] The younger Henry gives a very precise enumeration of the 'tents' of each band throughout their enormous habitat, but is provokingly lacking in details. He merely suggests that the total, 880 tents, contained in all about 2,000 men capable of bearing arms, supporting this conclusion by the fact that in a grand war force assembled on the Missouri in 1809, they had

[20]Such as the wide variation in adjacent Pawnee and Osage (above, notes 14-15).

[21]Coues (ed.), *Expeditions of Pike*, II, 589.

[22]Coman, *Economic Beginnings of the Far West*, II, 77. I regret having had no opportunity to see Fowler's *Journal*, ed. Coues, 1898, at first hand.

[23]*Lewis and Clark Journals*, I, 100.

[24]So, *Handbook of American Indians*, II, 110.

[25]*Lewis and Clark Journals*, I, 104-6.

[26]*Ibid.*, 135.

[27]Coues (ed.), *Expeditions of Pike*, I, 346; misquoted as 21,575, by Maximilian (*Early Western Travels*, XXII, 304).

[28]Long, cited by Maximilian, *ibid.*, 304.

[29]*Ibid.*

[30]Coues (ed.), *Expeditions of Pike*, I, 354.

1,100 guns by actual count.[31] This yields an average of 2.28 *warriors* per tent, but offers no light on the problem of aggregates.

Their southern neighbours along the Missouri furnish little reliable information. The evidence concerning the Mandans, 1804-06, is highly contradictory. Lewis and Clark state that 'forty years ago' (that is, *circa* 1764) the Mandans lived in nine villages, since reduced by enemies and disease to three, and later to two, in which last number they found them.[32] Each village contained 'about forty or fifty lodges,' and about 350 men[33] or '1,000 souls.'[34] Henry's most interesting and detailed description (1806) seems clearly to indicate that although the Mandan huts were 'spacious,' only one family, consisting of its lord and master with several wives and children, occupied a hut. Such may possibly have been chiefs, but he makes no mention of anything like four men occupying one hut.[35] The household economy of the Minatari (Hidatsa, or 'Gros Ventres of the Missouri') appears to have been very similar, according to Henry. He describes the 'little village' and the 'great village' of the 'Big Bellies' as containing 60 and 130 huts respectively; the latter having at one time been of 900 huts, but reduced by smallpox and other causes.[36] Lewis and Clark state that the smaller contained 'about 150 men,'[37] and the larger '450 warriors';[38] and give the total for the tribe as '3,000 souls.'[39] This yields an average per hut of 15.8 persons. It was asserted that in 1796 the 'Manitaries' had 1,000 warriors in action.[40]

Similarly among the 'Ricara' (Arikara), Lewis and Clark's account of their three villages indicates a lack of uniformity even among themselves. The explorers mention that the first was of 80 lodges, and the two others of 60 lodges each,[41] containing between 150 and 200 men in 80 and 60 lodges respectively and 300 men in 60 lodges. Hence the first averaged about 2.3 men per lodge, the second about 3 per lodge, and the third 5 per lodge.[42] Lewis and Clark give the 'Ricara' total as 3,000 souls;[43] and are made responsible by a modern scholar for an estimate of 'about 3,600.'[44] Here again, an early *habitué* of their territory has 700 warriors

[31]Coues (ed.), *Henry-Thompson Journals*, II, 522.

[32]*Lewis and Clark Journals*, I, 186; see Coues's notes, *Henry-Thompson Journals*, I, 321-9. For their names and some dialectal variations, as given by Maximilian, see above, Appendix A, note 69.

[33]*Lewis and Clark Journals*, I, 186.

[34]Lewis and Clark's map.

[35]Coues (ed.), *Henry-Thompson Journals*, I, 337-40.

[36]*Ibid.*, 334, 344-8.

[37]*Journals*, I, 187.

[38]*Ibid.*

[39]Lewis and Clark's map. 'Estimated by L. and C. 1804 = 2500'; so, Maclean, *Canadian Savage Folk*, 290; Chittenden, *American Fur Trade*, II, 858.

[40]Maximilian, *ex inf.* Charbonneau, *Early Western Travels*, XXIII, 230.

[41]*Journals*, I, 149, 150, 152.

[42]*Ibid.*, 156.

[43]Lewis and Clark's map.

[44]Chittenden, *American Fur Trade*, II, 862.

in action in 1796.[45] On their mean basis (as between Lewis and Clark and General Chittenden) of 650 men, the explorers' total would indicate a ratio of 21.7 men per hundred of the total population, and 3.25 men to a lodge. The critic's total aggregate would yield 18 per cent men.

A similar discrepancy, within the same tribe is recorded by Henry amongst the 'Slaves,' 1809, the term signifying at that time the Blackfoot Confederacy without the Sarcee. One hundred tents of Bloods (Kainah) and 350 tents of 'Picaneux' or Piegans contained respectively 200 and 700 warriors, each group averaging two warriors per tent. But while one band of Blackfoot proper (Siksika) has the same ratio, 160 warriors in 80 tents, another band of 120 tents contained 360 warriors.[46] The total of 1420 warriors is translated by an eminent Indian scholar (now deceased, at one period resident among the Blackfoot) as signifying a population of '7100' souls![47] Their later associates, the Sarcees ('all in one camp,' and apparently counted), in 1809 comprised 90 tents containing only 150 men capable of bearing arms.[48] David Thompson gives the same number of tents, *circa* 1800, and about 650 souls,[49] which agrees very well with 150 warriors.[50] This constitutes an average of 7.22 persons per tent, and 25.33 men per hundred. These figures agree fairly well with Mackenzie. His estimates *circa* 1789 for Siksika and Piegans respectively are (1) 8 per *tipi* and 800 men in a population of *circa* 2500; and (2) less for the Piegans, whom he estimates at 1200-1500 (say 1,350) men in a total aggregate which Thompson, almost contemporary in this, placed at *circa* 8000 men, and a later commentator at 8500—that is, 17 per cent men or even less.[51] Thompson's own ratios of 3 men to 5 women, and one child for each adult, work out at about 18 per cent men in the population. Some of these early estimates can have been little more than guesswork, on an arbitrary ratio of 3 warriors per tent, whatever the tents might contain *in toto*. The Atsina in 1809 had 'about 80 tents with 240 warriors';[52] and at the same time, a detachment of the Plain Cree near Fort Vermilion (North Saskatchewan River) consisted of about 300 tents, "which may furnish 900 men capable of bearing arms."[53]

The transmontane and Pacific Coast tribes reveal even wider discrepancies in the ratios per lodge or 'house.' Lewis and Clark mention one band of Shoshones in the Salmon River country, Idaho, having about 300

[45]Charbonneau to Maximilian, *Early Western Travels*, XXIII, 230.

[46]Coues (ed.), *Henry-Thompson Journals*, II, 530. Mackenzie's figures thought more reliable than Henry's, as the latter missed some bands (Kidd, "Blackfoot Ethnography," 26). This however would affect ratios but slightly.

[47]Maclean, *Canadian Savage Folk*, 294.

[48]Coues (ed.), *Henry-Thompson Journals*, II, 532.

[49]*Narrative*, ed. Tyrrell, 327.

[50]See Jenness, *Sarcee Indians of Alberta*, 1-10.

[51]The commentator in question is E. Curtis, *The North American Indian*, (20 vols., 1907-30), VI, 5; cited by Kidd, "Blackfoot Ethnography," 25-6.

[52]Coues (ed.), *Henry-Thompson Journals*, II, 531; 1811 = 'over 100 tents' (*ibid.*, 733).

[53]*Ibid.*, 516.

souls;[54] or (elsewhere) 'about 100 warriors and three times that number of women and children,'[55] in 60 lodges, averaging either 5 per lodge and 33 per cent men, or say, 6.66 persons per lodge and 25 per cent men. They specify also seven bands of the Chopunnish (Nez Percé), who were comprised as follows:

Numbers (souls)	Houses	Averages per house
2000	33	60.6
1600	33	48.5
800	33	24.25
250	33	7.66
400	33	12.0
2300	40	57.5
7850	238	33.0[56]

It is apparent that a variation ranging from 7.66 to 60.6 would not justify any sweeping generalization on Indian averages. The Wappatoo Indians, consisting of 13 tribes or bands,[57] exhibit an even wider variability:

Tribes	Houses	Numbers	Average
Cathlacommatups (Cathlacomatup)[58]	3	170	56.66
Cathlacumups (Cathlacumup)[59]	6	450	75.0
Cathlamah (? Cathlamet)[60]	10(?)	300	30.0
Cathlanaquiahs (Cathlanahquiah)[61]	6	400	66.66
Clackstar (? Tlatskanai)[62]	28	1200	42.85
Clahinnata (Claninnata)[63]	5	200	40.0
Clannaqueh (Clahnaquah)[64]	4	130	32.5
Clannarminnamuns (Kathlaminimim)[65]	12	280	23.33
Multnomah (? Multnomah)[66]	6	800	133.33
Nechacokee (Nechacoke)[67]	1	100	100.00
Nemalquinner (Nemalquinner)[68]	4	200	50.00
Quathlahpotle (Cathlapotle)[69]	14	900	64.28
Shoto (Shoto)[70]	8	460	57.50
Totals and General Average	107	5,590	52.33

Here again this general average of 52.33 per house would be quite misleading in a range from 23.33 to 133.33.

[54]*Lewis and Clark Journals*, Appendix, III, 326.
[55]*Ibid.*, II, 115
[56]*Ibid.*, III, 326.
[57]Wappatoo = 'potato' in the Chinook jargon (in the wild potato region): *Lewis and Clark Journals*, ed. pref., III, v-vi; also *Handbook of American Indians*, II, 913. The names on the left are from Lewis and Clark, Appendix, III, 327-8. On the right, the identifications in the *Handbook of American Indians*.

[58]*Ibid.*, I, 216; II, 1037.
[59]*Ibid.*, I, 216.
[60]*Ibid.*
[61]*Ibid.*, 217; II, 1037.
[62]*Ibid.*, 763, 1045.
[63]*Ibid.*, I, 305; II, 1045.
[64]*Ibid.*, I, 302; II, 1045.
[65]*Ibid.*, I, 664; II, 1045.
[66]*Ibid.*, I, 956; II, 1095.
[67]*Ibid.*, 49, 1101.
[68]*Ibid.*, 54.
[69]*Ibid.*, I, 217; II, 1037.
[70]*Ibid.*, 558.

An equally intense but less surprising individualism in this respect may be noticed in separate and non-related tribes in the same general territory. Lewis and Clark recorded the following figures for tribes along their portion of the Columbia River and its principal tributaries, giving totals of houses and souls respectively,[71] as tabulated below:

Tribes	Houses	Numbers	Average
Cathlamahs (Cathlamet: Chinookan)[72]	9	300	33.33
Chilluckittequaws (Chilu-ktkwa: Chinookan)[73]	32	1,400	43.75
Eskeloot (Skilloots: Chinookan)[74]	21	1,000	47.60
Shahala (Shahala: Chinookan)[75]	62	2,800	45.20
Skilloots (Skilloots: Chinookan)[76]	50	2,500	50.00
Smockshop (Smackshop: Chinookan)[77]	24	800	33.30
Wahkiacums (Wahkiakum: Chinookan)[78]	11	200	18.20
Wheelpo (? Willopah: Chinookan)[79]	130	2,500	19.23
Chimnahpum (Shahaptian)[80]	42	1,860	44.28
Eneeshur (Tapanash: Shahaptian)[81]	41	1,200	29.25
Sokulk (Sokulk: Shahaptian)[82]	120	2,400	20.00
Tushshepah (Tushepaw: Salish or Shahaptian)[83]	35	430	12.28
Hohilpo (Tushepaw division? Shahaptian)[84]	25	300	12.00
Micksucksealton (Tushepaw division? Shahaptian)[85]	25	300	12.00
Ootlashoots (Tushepaw division? Shahaptian)[86]	33	400	12.12
Wahowpum (Wahowpun: Shahaptian)[87]	33	700	21.20
Wollawollah (Walla Walla: Shahaptian)[88]	46	1,600	34.80
Coospellar (?)[89]	30	1,600	53.33
Cutsahnim (?)	60	1,200	20.00
Hihighenimmo (?)	45	1,300	28.88
Killamucks (?)	50	1,000	20.00
Lahanna (? Lahanna)[90]	120	2,000	16.66
Lartielo (? Spokane)	30	600	20.00
Skeetsomish (?)	12	2,000	166.60
Totals and General Average	1,086	30,390	27.98

[71]*Lewis and Clark Journals*, II, 310-13; III, 326-30.
[72]*Handbook of American Indians*, I, 216, 274; II, 1037.
[73]*Ibid.*, I, 268, 274; II, 1042.
[74]*Ibid.*, 591; 'partly buffalo people': *Lewis and Clark Journals*, III, 64.
[75]*Handbook of American Indians*, I, 274; II, 1137.   [76]Above, note 74.
[77]Merely as 'Chinookans' (*Handbook of American Indians*, I, 274; II, 1137); but as the 'Smockshop band of Chilluckittequaws' (*ibid.*, II, 602), as by Lewis and Clark.   [78]*Handbook of American Indians*, I, 274; II, 890, 1168.
[79]*Ibid.*, I, 274; II, 955, 1172.   [80]*Ibid.*, I, 271, II, 520, 1042.
[81]*Ibid.*, I, 422; II, 691, 1053.   [82]*Ibid.*, 520, 614.
[83]*Ibid.*, 520, 853, 913. Perhaps Kutenai, or Nez Percé, or both.
[84]*Ibid.*, I, 556; II, 1061.   [85]*Ibid.*, I, 858.
[86]*Ibid.*, II, 137.   [87]*Ibid.*, I, 274; II, 520, 890.
[88]*Ibid.*, 520, 900.
[89]Those marked (?) have not been identified; perhaps Kalispel (Pend d'Oreille).   [90]*Handbook of American Indians*, I, 753.

The presence of a similar variability in Coast tribes clearly indicates that this individualism was quite as independent of topographical environment as it was of tribal affinities. The same explorers mention several tribes about the mouth of the Columbia River,[91] as given below:

Tribes	Houses	Numbers	Average
Chinnooks (Chinook: Chinookan)[92]	28	400	14.28
Clatsops (Clatsop: Chinookan)[93]	14	200	14.28
Killaxthokle ('Killaxthokle's town': Chinookan)[94]	8	100	12.50
Calasthocle (Quileute: Salishan)[95]	10	200	20.00
Potoashees (Potoashees: Salishan)[96]	10	200	20.00
Quiniilts (Quiniaelt: Salishan)[97]	60	1,000	16.16
Chilts (? Quileute: Salishan)[98]	38	700	18.50
Chillates (? Chehalis: Salishan)	8	150	18.75
Quieetso (Quieetso: Salishan)[99]	18	250	14.00
Clamoitomi (? Klumaitumsh)	12	260	21.66
Pailsk (?)	10	200	20.00
Totals and General Average	216	3,660	16.95

These yield the following comparative results:

Tribe	Souls	Houses	Minimum Average	Maximum Average	General Average
Nez Percés	7,850	238	7.66	60.60	33.00
Wappatoo	5,940	107	20.00	133.33	51.30
Columbia River Tribes	30,390	1,086	12.00	166.66	27.98
Coast Tribes	3,660	216	12.50	21.66	16.95
Totals and General Average	47,840	1,647			29.05

The wide discrepancies (in closely similar environments) indicated in the foregoing may be compared with some estimated ratios of population by Pike, 1805, of certain Prairie tribes dwelling in virtually the same 'cultural area.' I omit his figures for the Sioux proper,[100] as they manifestly extended far beyond the area of the eastern Sioux into the Plains cultural regions, which did not include the other tribes specified:

Tribe	Men	Women	Children	Total	Average of Men
Fox	400	500	550	1450	27.6
Iowa	300	400	700	1400	21.4
Menomenee	300	350	700	1350	22.2
Saut	700	750	1400	2850	24.6
Winnebago	450	500	1000	1950	23.1
	2150	2500	4350	9000	23.9
Chippewa	2049	3184	5944	11,177	18.33[101]

[91]*Journals*, II, 310-13; III, 326-30.
[92]*Handbook of American Indians*, I, 272, 274.
[93]*Ibid.*, 274, 305.　　　　[94]*Ibid.*, 274, 688; II, 1174.
[95]*Ibid.*, I, 688; II, 340, 416, 1035.　　[96]*Ibid.*, 293, 416.
[97]*Ibid.*, 342, 416.　　[98]See *ibid.*, 340, 416.
[99]*Ibid.*, 332, 418.　　[100]Given above, note 27.
[101]Coues (ed.), *Expeditions of Pike*, I, 346 (averages mine).

The only reference to lodges among the foregoing figures concerns the Menominee: 'large enough for sixty to shelter in and for twenty to reside in'; being of rush or rush-covered. He speaks elsewhere of forty-one in one lodge, including seventeen capable of bearing arms; and of a Council House, 'two large lodges, capable of containing 300 men.'[102]

Comparing the loose round-figure estimate for the five tribes with the very precise fractional numbers for the Chippewa (Ojibwa), it can scarcely be doubted that the latter represent something like an actual census. Pike's own variations in the estimated proportions of women to men, and of children to both, indicate in my view not only the erratic nature of Indian tribal individualisms, in this as in so many other respects, but also a *perceptible* manifestation of this, sufficiently striking to ordinary observation in a round estimate. Taking a proportion of 20 per cent men to total population as the hypothetical datum, it may be noted that the five tribes, with their separate estimates of adults and children, present an increase of virtually one-fifth above that commonly accepted ratio. The more authentic enumeration of the Chippewa (over a much larger aggregate; nearly 25 per cent greater than the five combined) reveals a ratio of men materially lower, when spread over a large body of people; and 23 per cent lower than the resultant general average of the five tribes from Pike's round numbers.

These broad conclusions are in no way invalidated by the possibility in the case of both exploring parties, that their figures may have been incorrect. In the case of Lewis and Clark, the figures on their map and in their tabular enumerations are frequently at variance. I have preferred the latter, because they include many records of dwellings, estimated or actual. The wide variations in the ratios of these to numbers of souls are conclusive proof (1) of a local, tribal, or individual diversity, fatal in itself to any hopes of reliable computations based upon averages; which would merely be using one assumption to prove another; and (2) of an honest attempt on the explorers' part to furnish the most trustworthy information obtainable. These men did their best, where careless sweeping generalization—too often found in writers professedly much more 'critical'—would have been much easier; and whatever the defects of their data, we have in most cases little or no testimony more sound. I do not believe in the existence of such a thing as an 'Indian average'; but it cannot be without value to note various estimates of Indian tribes in the buffalo habitat at large, at various eras down to the extermination of the wild species, together with such information as may serve to check or to corroborate these statements.

2

Concerning the ante-European Indian population at large, opinion differs. Two recent historians write thus:

Three hundred years after the arrival of the white man and the founding of Jamestown [that is, 1607] there were probably as many Indians in the area now embraced by the United States as there were when Captain John Smith landed on the shores of Virginia; and the latest census reported an increase within the decade. It is not exactly correct, therefore, to speak of the 'extermination' of the red man. Indeed it is doubtful whether the arms and whisky of his

[102]*Ibid.*, 341-5; cf. *ibid.*, 189, 197.

white competitor were more destructive than his own diseases, such as smallpox, his tribal wars, his clannish jealousies. . . .[103]

An earlier divergent view was well maintained by the late James Mooney, who must be considered a leading authority on the subject. He emphasized several considerations which are often overlooked. Citations from census returns very commonly begin at too late a period, when treaty relations had been established, and something like a faithful observance was being carried out, that is, when there was less likelihood of war or popular outbreaks with bloodshed arbitrarily disturbing Indian aggregates or ratios. Again, the Indian of the discovery period was a full-blood; while the modern 'Indian' is very often a 'mongrel,' with only one-sixteenth, one thirty-second, or even one sixty-fourth Indian blood in his veins.[104] Inter-tribal wars, in Mooney's opinion, "in most cases have not greatly diminished the numbers of Indians"; although he cites some very destructive ones in the area at large, east of the Mississippi. Concerning this region, a foremost American anthropologist differs from Mooney somewhat. He points out that the tribes there—perhaps others also—waged war, not for some definite acquisition such as territorial or economic aims, which when attained brought peace of more or less lasting duration; but in accordance with a state of mind, whose only real *raison d'être* was a desire for victory, in itself essentially insatiable.[105] Mooney summarizes thus:

The chief causes of decrease, in order of importance, may be classed as small-pox and other epidemics; tuberculosis; sexual diseases; whisky and attendant dissipation; removals, starvation, and subjection to unaccustomed conditions; low vitality due to mental depression under misfortune; wars. In the category of destroyers, all but wars and tuberculosis may be considered to have come from the white man, and the increasing destructiveness of tuberculosis itself is due largely to conditions consequent upon his advent. . . .[106]

It may be pointed out also, in relation to wars waged by powerful confederacies such as the Iroquois, that while in some instances the independent political existence of an enemy was utterly destroyed, at the same time the remnant of the vanquished was merged in the victors. Thus at one stroke a tribe could 'disappear'; while another could receive an augmentation of its numbers which (if taken to apply to Indians at large) might give rise to an entirely false conception of Indian ratios of increase.[107]

[103]Chas. A. and Mary R. Beard, *The Rise of American Civilization*, II, 147.

[104]See A. F. Chamberlain, "Mixed-bloods," "Negro and Indian," *Handbook of American Indians*, I, 913; II, 51.

[105]Kroeber, *Cultural and Natural Areas*, 148.

[106]Mooney, "Population," *Handbook of American Indians*, II, 286. See also his important essay, "The Aboriginal Population of America North of Mexico." A. L. Kroeber in the section on "Population" (*Cultural and Natural Areas*, 131-81), cites a number of papers on population, but still considers Mooney to be the soundest basis at present available.

[107]See on this the following important articles by J. N. B. Hewitt, and references therein cited: "Adoption" (*Handbook of American Indians*, I, 15); "Caughnawaga" (*ibid.*, I, 220); "Cayuga" (I, 223); "Clans and Gens" (I, 303); "Huron" (I, 584); "Iroquoians, Iroquois" (I, 615); "Mohawk" (I, 921); "Neutrals"

Smallpox and other epidemics have undoubtedly wrought havoc among the Indian peoples at different times; and the 'buffalo' tribes have probably borne a full share. Whether these epidemics have always been of the disastrous proportions reported by local testimony at or near the eras of such visitations is problematical, and has given rise to much discussion. As A. L. Kroeber points out with reference to population estimates in general, it is almost a fixed assumption with ethnologists that the great majority of figures given by contemporaries are too large; and that our 'direct data' (that is, statements from such witnesses) are almost always of low reliability.[108] His emphasis on the essential importance of balanced, discriminating judgment by competent ethnologists will be endorsed by any careful student. But in relation to our immediate topic of catastrophic destruction among the Indians arising from epidemic diseases, a word must be added. The type of witness to whom we have referred, the early missionary, trader, or traveller, was at least on the ground, and in many cases had known the tribe, or was in touch with others who had, both before and after the scourge. It is wholly unphilosophic and unjustified to assume that *in every case* such men were temperamentally incapable of fairly accurate observation. To put the case in concrete form, whatever opinion a critic may entertain concerning the early Jesuit's enthusiasm for the conversion of the heathen, if he imagines that this fervour blinded such men to the things about them, that critic should read the *Jesuit Relations* for himself. If he has already done so and still persists in his assumption of the inherent unreliability of such early witnesses as a class, he should abandon criticism for some more suitable occupation. While the views of the trained modern ethnologist must always command respect, the present writer is not in the least disposed to reject the early local witnesses merely in order to set in their place the (reduced) assertions *ex cathedra* of Indian fighters whose ignorance and hatred of Indians are only too evident; or of some 'scientist' whose own Indian-and-buffalo pronouncements fling millions about as if they were peanuts.

Mooney notes outbreaks of smallpox in the northern Atlantic States region in 1637-38, 1640, 1658, 1663, 1664, 1717, 1755, and 'later.' In the southern Atlantic States area, 'before 1696,' 1696, 1738, 1759, 1776. In the Gulf States, 1698, and 'several before 1776.' In the Central States, 'several times,' between 1700-1815, including one in 1782.[109] In the Ohio Valley region, roughly the centre of this last great territory, Nicholas Cresswell records 'terrible havoc' in 1775;[110] and farther north, among the Chippewa (Ojibwa) west of the Great Lakes, there was an outbreak in 1770.[111] East and north of the Great Lakes, in Eastern Canada, there were smallpox

(II, 60); "Oneida" (II, 123); "Onondaga" (II, 129); "Ottawa" (II, 167); "Seneca" (II, 502); "Totem" (II, 787); "Tribe" (II, 814); "Tuscarora" (II, 842). Also J. Mooney, "Tutelo" (*ibid.*, II, 855); C. Thomas, J. R. Swanton, "Siouan Family" (*ibid.*, II, 577).

[108]Kroeber, *Cultural and Natural Areas*, 180.
[109]Mooney, "Aboriginal Population," 3-11.
[110]*Cresswell's Journal*, 122.
[111]Coues (ed.), *Expeditions of Pike*, I, 170.

epidemics in 1639, 1670, 1702-03, 1799.[112] In the central Rocky Mountain territory, Mooney also mentions a devastating outbreak of smallpox and fever in 1853.[113] On the Pacific slope, he instances occurrences of the former in the Lower Columbia region, destroying 'one third to one half the population,' in 1782-83, 1846, 1852.[114] In British Columbia proper, there were epidemics in 1781-82, 1852-53, 1862.[115] Lewis and Clark record that a disease, apparently smallpox in their opinion, destroyed 'four chiefs and several hundreds' of the Clatsops, a Chinookan people.[116]

In the Plains area, the ravages of smallpox were deadly. La Vérendrye alludes to an outbreak in the Missouri territory about the Mandan villages in 1738-39.[117] Mooney refers to another in 1778, which swept the Plains area, and 'nearly destroyed several small tribes.'[118] The great epidemic of 1781-82 was of an appalling character. It raged 'over the whole of the Upper Missouri region, the Saskatchewan northward to Great Slave Lake, the Columbia territory to the Pacific, and eastward to Lake Superior, paralyzing the fur trade for two years.'[119] On the Saskatchewan, it was thought by the fur traders to have carried off 'half the Indians.'[120] John McDonnell, of the North West Company, believed there were 'not a third of the Crees remaining.'[121] David Thompson, recording what appeared to be an unusually acute shortage of buffalo and other game (which actually seems to have been nothing more than one of those inscrutable absences for a time, of which buffalo history furnishes so many examples[122]), says that the Indian explanation was that 'they were taken away by the Great Spirit, as they were not needed, owing to so many Indians dying of smallpox.'[123] It is curiously illustrative of buffalo vagaries that during the similar scourge of 1837-38 along the Missouri, 'buffalo were more plenty than had been known for years';[124] perhaps for the more mundane reason that there were fewer to kill them. The Cree and Chippewyans in the Ile à la Crosse and Lake Athabaska country were 'decimated' by the disease, '1779';[125] and the Cree were said in 1786 to be reduced (? by the outbreak of 1781) to 'less than half of their former numbers.'[126] The Blackfoot also suffered

[112]Mooney, "Aboriginal Population." 24.

[113]Ibid., 20.

[114]Ibid., 13-14.

[115]Ibid., 27; cf. Mooney, Handbook of American Indians, II, 286; Hancock, Narrative (Oregon, 1853), 181; and for some details, Bella Coola, B.C., in 1862, Lieut. H. S. Palmer, R.E., in Fleming, Explorations and Surveys for a Canadian Pacific Railway, 1874, 223.

[116]Circa 1800 (Lewis and Clark Journals, II, 310).

[117]Journals of La Vérendrye, ed. Burpee, 256, 320.

[118]Mooney, "Aboriginal Population," 12-13.

[119]Ibid.

[120]Umfreville, Present State of Hudson's Bay, 92, 203.

[121]McDonnell, "Account of Red River, 1793-7," in Masson, Les Bourgeois de la Compagnie du Nord-Ouest, I, 277.

[122]See above, chap. XX, "Irregular Migrations."

[123]Thompson, Narrative, ed. Tyrrell, 325.

[124]Chittenden, American Fur Trade, II, 626.

[125]Handbook of American Indians, I, 275, s.v. Chipewyan.

[126]Ibid., 359, s.v. Cree.

greatly in 1781;[127] and from the tone of Henry's references, which do not indicate a really recent date, it would seem to be this epidemic to which he alludes regarding the Atsina of southern Alberta—formerly 'very numerous,' but reduced by smallpox and war to about 240 warriors.[128] The same era seems also to be meant in regard to the Swampy Ground Assiniboines, in the 'strong wood' country west of Fort Augustus (Edmonton), 1809. They too had been 'very numerous'; but smallpox and murders had reduced them to about 30 tents.[129] As a result of smallpox, Pasquayah, Paskoyac, Pasquia River (The Pas), formerly a noted *rendezvous* of the Indians on the lower Saskatchewan, was in 1808 almost deserted.[130] Farther south, on the Missouri, it seems to have been the ravages of 1781 which reduced the 'Big Bellies' (Gros Ventres = Hidatsa) from '900 huts formerly' to 130 in 1806.[131] Lewis and Clark speak of the neighbouring Mandans being in nine villages 'forty years ago' (that is, *circa* 1764), and reduced through smallpox and other causes, to two villages in 1804.[132] They also allude to its effects upon the Mahas (Omaha) and Puncaras (Ponca) in 1780-81.[133]

Mooney mentions another visitation in 1801-02, when smallpox swept the whole Plains area from the Gulf of Mexico to Dakota, with especial destruction in Texas and among the Omaha.[134] Lewis and Clark refer to the Omaha ('Mahas') having lost 400 by the disease evidently about 1800;[135] and their kinsfolk, the Iowa, in 1803 lost 100 men besides women and children, that is, 33 per cent of their force of 1803-4.[136] It is difficult to decide whether Henry is referring to this or to the earlier period of 1781. He says of the Cree: "Small-pox some years ago made great havoc among these people, destroying entire camps; but they are again increasing very fast."[137] Similarly the Piegans—"reduced by small-pox about twenty years ago to only 150 tents; but now [1810] increasing fast."[138] L. J. Burpee speaks of smallpox outbreaks among the Western tribes in 1804— perhaps referring to mention of the disease by Lewis and Clark in that year, as given above—and in 1832;[139] on these outbreaks I have found no further precise information.

[127]*Ibid.*, II, 570, *s.v.* Siksika.

[128]Coues (ed.), *Henry-Thompson Journals*, II, 531, 733. Compare the Tonkawa in Texas: 1778 = 300 warriors; 1779 = 150 warriors (small-pox); so H. E. Bolton, *Handbook of American Indians*, II, 782. Even as estimates, such differences indicate a conspicuous *visible* change.

[129]Coues (ed.), *Henry-Thompson Journals*, II, 523; cf. *Handbook of American Indians*, II, 660.

[130]Coues (ed.), *Henry-Thompson Journals*, II, 470.   [131]*Ibid.*, I, 334, 345-8.

[132]*Lewis and Clark Journals*, I, 186.   [133]*Ibid.*, 112.

[134]Mooney, "Aboriginal Population," 12-13; cf. Coues (ed.), *Expeditions of Pike*, II, 714.

[135]*Journals*, I, 86; cf. *Handbook of American Indians*, II, 120 (est. 2800 in 1780; 300 in 1802).

[136]*Ibid.*, I, 613.

[137]Coues (ed.), *Henry-Thompson Journals*, II, 516.   [138]*Ibid.*, 722.

[139]Burpee, *Journals of La Vérendrye*, ed. notes, 256-8. Catlin says the Pawnee in his time were only half the number before the smallpox of 1832, when 10,000 perished (*Letters on the North American Indians*, II, 24).

In 1837-38, another disastrous epidemic of smallpox raged over the northern Plains area from the Missouri to Red River and the Saskatchewan.[140] Bancroft puts the mortality at 10,000 among the Blackfoot, Crows, Minatari (Hidatsa), and Mandan.[141] Thomas Simpson, writing at the time, says the Indians were 'dying by hundreds';[142] and the Mandan, according to Mooney, were 'practically exterminated.'[143] This conclusion finds support both from men on the ground at the time,[144] and from independent scholars of high repute.[145] Major Joshua Pilcher, Superintendent of Indian Affairs at St. Louis, and Mr. McKenzie of the American Fur Company, believed that among the Minatari, Blackfoot, Cheyennes, Crows, and Cree, 25,000 people perished.[146] Careful inquirers at or near the time cite from contemporary observers a reduction in the Southern Assiniboine of the Missouri of from 1000 to 1200 lodges to 'less than 400'; and of the people from some 8000 to 10,000 down to 4000.[147] Of the Plains tribes within the devastated area, competent students believe, 'at least half' to have perished.[148] Mooney's conclusion is that the northern Plains tribes were reduced by 'nearly one half.'[149]

General H. M. Chittenden rejects as 'impossible' such estimates of the total mortality at this time as 150,000, or even 60,000; preferring about 15,000.[150] When we consider the paucity of preventive or remedial facilities and the extreme difficulty of applying such if they had them,[151] an enormously high mortality seems inevitable; and even if one were to discount the absolute totals somewhat, it seems impossible in my view to suppose that the widely prevalent estimated ratios ('one-third,' 'one-half,' etc.), coming as they do from men of all types then on the ground, are *in all cases* mere exaggerations of a *visible* decrease of not more than 20 per cent and perhaps as little as 5 per cent of such estimated aggregates. This is scepticism riding rough-shod.

[140]Mooney, "Aboriginal Population," 12-13; also Mooney, *Handbook of American Indians*, II, 286.

[141]Bancroft, *History of Washington, Idaho, and Montana*, 692.

[142]Simpson, *Narrative of Discoveries*, 227.

[143]Mooney, "Aboriginal Population," 12-13.

[144]See Catlin's Appendix A, "Extinction of the Mandans" (*Letters on the North American Indians*, II, 257-9).

[145]Mandan = 1,600 souls, 1837; reduced by smallpox about then to 125-50 (Dorsey, Thomas, *Handbook of American Indians*, I, 798).

[146]Catlin, *Letters on the North American Indians*, II, 258. Pilcher, a well-known figure, was characterized by Rev. Samuel Parker, the Oregon missionary, *circa* 1835, as 'intelligent and candid' (Bancroft, *History of Oregon*, I, 128); cf. also Dale (ed.), *Ashley-Smith Explorations*, 70-87; Coman, *Economic Beginnings of the Far West*, II, 116, 373.

[147]Mooney, Thomas, "Assiniboin," *Handbook of American Indians*, I, 102. They cite S. G. Drake and Professor F. V. Hayden; for the dates of these see the Bibliography, *ibid.*, II, 1190, 1196.

[148]Mooney, Thomas, "Cree," *ibid.*, I, 359.

[149]Mooney, *ibid.*, II, 286.

[150]Chittenden, *American Fur Trade*, II, 619-27.

[151]See on this, for example, John McDougall, *Red River Rebellion*, 115-48. My friend, Mrs. (Rev.) Robert Holmes, Diocese of Athabaska, 1902 *seq.*,

Mooney mentions an outbreak among the Blackfoot in 1845,[152] and there were possibly others.[153] The only other direct allusion to that time or thereabout that I have found is to an Arikara band known as the Wanderers —perhaps in contradistinction to the more sedentary Arikara in general— who are stated to have been exterminated by smallpox, 1842.[154] Smallpox also, in the winter of 1852-53 carried off nearly one-quarter of the Kansa at Council Grove, Kansas.[155] Mooney furthermore notes another visitation among the Blackfoot in 1857-58;[156] on which I can find nothing further. A frontiersman-author says that the Mandan, Minatari, and Arikara (all sedentaries) were reduced by nine-tenths, 1800-70, by war, smallpox, and cholera.[157]

The last great epidemic seems to have been that of 1870-71. This is stated to have been very destructive among the Assiniboine, Cree and the Blackfoot Confederacy.[158] The Sarcee are said to have been before that 'several thousands'; afterward 300 or 400.[159] The earlier figures are impossible; but there can be no doubt that the mortality was very great.[160] The losses among the Cree on the Saskatchewan are placed by Butler, in his official Report to Governor Archibald at Red River, at 1200.[161] The Rev. Dr. John McDougall, who lost two sisters in the outbreak, describes some of the appalling details at first hand.[162] The rigid enforcement of quarantine by the authorities at Red River, while doubtless needful to prevent the contagion from spreading further, must inevitably have tended to increase the mortality, as a result of the difficulty of conveying supplies and assistance to the stricken area.[163] Altogether, one-third of the 'Plains Indians' (? of Canada) are said to have been swept away.[164]

Although smallpox may be considered to have been the principal epi-

---

described to me very graphically her hand-to-hand struggle with one of the Indian women from an infected camp, who could not understand why she was being (for the first time) refused admittance into the 'praying man's' home, at the time, of course, under quarantine.

[152]Mooney, "Siksika," *Handbook of American Indians*, II, 571.

[153]*Journals of La Vérendrye*, ed. Burpee, note, 256-8.

[154]Taylor, *Frontier Life*, 204.

[155]*Handbook of American Indians*, I, 654.

[156]*Ibid.*, II, 571. In 1856-57, Burton says the Assiniboines lost 1500 from smallpox (*City of the Saints*, 100) ? 1836-37.

[157]Taylor, *Frontier Life*, 59-71, 76-84, 121-31, 176-83.

[158]Mooney, "Aboriginal Population," 12-13, 25.

[159]MacInnes, *In the Shadow of the Rockies*, 76.

[160]According to Mr. (Rev. John ?) McLean: "An eye-witness told me that at the Marias River, in Montana, there stood fully 100 lodges, and not one containing less than ten bodies. His estimate of dead Sarcees was 1500 . . ." (Horatio Hale, 1885). Another estimate by a Sarcee was 'nearly 200 families' (Jenness, *Sarcee Indians of Alberta*, 7, 8). Jenness considers these accounts 'in no way exaggerated.'

[161]Butler, *Great Lone Land*, 202, 227, 250, 366-73.

[162]McDougall, *Red River Rebellion*, 115-48.

[163]Rev. E. R. Young (whose Norway House Indians conveyed food etc. up the Saskatchewan to the afflicted area): *Canoe and Dog-Train*, 191-8.

[164]MacInnes, *In the Shadow of the Rockies*, 76.

demic disease, others ravaged the tribes at various times.[165] Mooney refers
to an epidemic of unknown character, which raged through eastern Texas
and adjacent Louisiana in 1691; and which was officially reported as having
slain 3000 of the southern Caddo alone.[166] Henry mentions an epidemic of
'a sort of whooping cough,' which was prevalent about 1806 from Red
River to the Missouri and the Saskatchewan 'even to Fort des Prairies' (that
is, Lower Fort Augustus, below modern Edmonton), and of which many
people died.[167] It was estimated that 70,000 died from a fever epidemic in
California about 1830 or 1833.[168] In 1823, 1829-30, malarial fever—the later
visitation said to be due to breaking up ground around the trading posts;
a reason strongly suggestive of Indian disapproval—broke out among the
Oregon and Columbian tribes, almost exterminating the Chinookan stocks.[169]
In the same region, an outbreak of measles in 1847 is believed to have
played a part in arousing the hostile feeling resulting in the Whitman
massacre.[170] Measles are also mentioned among the Blackfoot, 1864.[171] We
have noted a fever epidemic in the central Shoshonean region, 1853;[172]
and fever, with smallpox, is described as 'almost periodical' in New Mexico
and Arizona for nearly a century.[173] In 1856 an epidemic of scarlet fever
decimated the Sarcee.[174] Cholera raged in the Central Plains area in 1849,
killing off about one-fourth of the Pawnee;[175] and (it was estimated) two-
thirds of the Cheyennes—some 200 lodges, equalling 2000 souls.[176] It is
mentioned as one of the prime causes in the virtual extermination of the
Mandans.[177] Its prevalence along the Oregon Trail and in the adjacent

[165]See A. Hrdlička, "Health and Disease," *Handbook of American Indians*,
I, 540.

[166]Mooney, "Aboriginal Population," 12.

[167]Coues (ed.), *Henry-Thompson Journals*, I, 343.

[168]Mooney, "Aboriginal Population," 19; also *Handbook of American Indians*,
II, 286.

[169]*Ibid.* Catlin observes in a note: "The Reverend Mr. [Samuel] Parker, in
his *Tour across the Rocky Mountains* says, that amongst the Indians below the
Falls of the Columbia at least seven-eighths, if not nine-tenths as Dr. McLaughlin
believes, have been swept away by disease between the years 1829, and the time
that he visited that place in 1836. 'So many and so sudden were the deaths
which occurred, that the shores were strewed with the unburied dead, whole and
large villages were depopulated, and some entire tribes have disappeared.' This
mortality, he says, 'extended not only from the Cascades to the Pacific, but from
very far north to the coast of California' . . ." (Catlin, *Letters on the North
American Indians*, II, 255).

[170]Bancroft, *History of Oregon*, I, 648. In the epidemic of 1637, the heroic
Brébeuf was in danger from the Hurons, for the same reason; and Jogues' death
from the Mohawks, 1646, is partly traceable to this. The Huron village of Ouenrio,
also in 1637, desired missionaries in the hope of averting the pestilence (*Handbook of American Indians*, I, 899, 923; II, 173).

[171]Mooney, *Handbook of American Indians*, II, 571.

[172]Mooney, "Aboriginal Population," 20.

[173]*Ibid.*, 21.

[174]Jenness, *Sarcee Indians of Alberta*, 6.

[175]Mooney, "Aboriginal Population," 12-13; Fletcher, *Handbook of American
Indians*, II, 216.

[176]*Ibid.*, I, 253.   [177]Above, note 157.

territory at that era can occasion no surprise. While it would be impracticable in these cases at large to attempt to determine the rate of decline in numbers without first possessing an exact census of the previous totals, I am of opinion, Indian aboriginal life being what it was, that the larger suggested ratios are inherently more probable than the smaller ones. In many cases, the marvel is that any escaped.

Other scholars dissent from Mooney's view concerning wars as well as from his opinion on the influence of various diseases. One prominent archaeologist thinks that *circa* 1492 they were slowly increasing, but that the 'frequent wars had a marked effect in limiting the increase.'[178] Since the European influx, it is difficult to see how the influence of war as an agent of destruction, and the virtual 'extermination of the Indian' over the eastern portion of the North American continent, can be seriously questioned. Mooney sums up as follows: "Among the wars most destructive to the Indians may be noted those in Virginia and in southern New England, the raids upon the Florida missions by the Carolina settlers and their savage allies, the wars of the Natchez and the Foxes with the French, the Creek war, and the war waged by the Iroquois for a period of thirty years upon all the surrounding tribes. . . ."[179] More sinister than war itself, he observes

[178]A. Hrdlička, "Health and Disease," *Handbook of American Indians,* I, 540.
[179]Mooney, *ibid.,* II, 287.
EXTINCT TRIBES: (Missouri River territory), Ahnahaways, *Soulier Noir* or 'Black Shoe' (wrongly 'Saulteur' by Henry, 1806; but cf. Coues, ed notes, *Henry-Thompson Journals,* I, 323-63, etc.), called by the Mandan, Wattasoons, Mahahas = 'Shoe Indians.' about 50 men, 1804: *Lewis and Clark Journals,* I, 168, 172, 187, 228, 231; III, 249. Their ancient village-site at Heart River and Missouri confluence, *circa* 1865; Taylor, *Frontier Life,* 128, 174, 250. 'Staitans' = 'Kites or Flyers,' apparently a division of the Cheyenne (Mooney, *Handbook of American Indians,* I, 251; II, 632). About 100 men, 1804; *Lewis and Clark Journals,* I, 73, 104; exterminated shortly after, Lodge Pole Creek country, South Platte (Taylor, *Frontier Life,* 24-7). 'Wetapahato' (with some 'Kiawa' = ? Kiowa) = 200 men, 1800 souls, 1804. 'Castahana' (perhaps Arapaho), 300 men, 1500 souls (*Lewis and Clark Journals,* I, 74, and map); '5000 souls in 500 lodges' (*Handbook of American Indians,* I, 212). 'Cataka' (probably the 'Cattacka' of La Salle = Kiowa-Apache; *Handbook of American Indians,* I, 702) = 75 men, 300 souls, 1804 (*Lewis and Clark Journals,* I, 74). 'Dotame or Dotami' (perhaps Kiowa; *Handbook of American Indians,* I, 399) 30 warriors, 120 souls, 1804 (*Lewis and Clark Journals,* I, 74, and map). These in the Upper Tongue River region "supposed to be remnants of the great Padouca nation, now lost even by name," 1804 (*ibid.,* but Padouca = Comanche; *Handbook of American Indians,* I, 328).
The inroads of the Sauk on the Missouri and Osage *ante* 1804 (*Lewis and Clark Journals,* I, 49, 51, etc.; cf. Parkman, *La Salle,* 285). 'Oseegah' or 'Waziah,' 1862; apparently Assiniboine or some tribe now extinct (*Handbook of American Indians,* s.v. Tschantoga, II, 823).
Compare "Extinct Tribes," in Mooney, "Aboriginal Population": 11 tribes in Florida and Gulf States, est. *circa* 1650 = 28,000 (p. 8); 9 tribes, Yazoo River and (modern) Louisiana, 1650 = 8,400 (p. 9); 2 tribes, Central States, 1650 = 5,500 (p. 11); 5 tribes, southern Plains region, 1690 = 19,000 (p. 13); 6 tribes, New Mexico and Arizona, 1680 = 14,600 (p. 22); one tribe, Missouri, as above, 1780 = 1,000 (pp. 22-3); 89 tribes or designations in 'Oregon,'

again: "In California the enormous decrease from about a quarter of a million to less than 20,000 is due chiefly to the cruelties and wholesale massacres perpetrated by the miners and early settlers."[180] The latest discussion of the population question at large (that is, Kroeber's) is particularly valuable for its masterly summaries (in relation to different cultural types and areas) of the various biological, ecological, or 'economic' influences, which might conduce toward an increasing population, or tend to keep it stationary.[181]

3

Perhaps partly as a natural reaction from 'extremists who have imagined an aboriginal population of millions';[182] perhaps also—with a logic of sorts—arising from those defenders of the régime of blood and iron who would rebut the charge of extermination with the plea that there were never very many Indians to exterminate, and possibly also from the fur traders, who might have found this a very convenient *dernier ressort* when pestered by uncomprehending boards of absentee directors concerning the year's 'unsatisfactory returns'; for whatever reason, disbelief in any but the most meagre numbers of Indians seems quite commonly to have been regarded as the very beginning of wisdom. I suspect that the last mentioned, or some kindred influence in the economy of the fur trade, may have been a potent cause, since out of a number of sceptical frontiersman-critics, the only one who offers any reason whatever for his conclusions, manifestly derived it from the fur-trading posts. Palliser, in discussing the estimated figures furnished by the Hudson's Bay Company in 1856, of some 64,000 souls for Rupert's Land (whatever area that term may denote), considers their number to be 'very much over-estimated, as the same Indians are counted over and over again at different posts'; his own estimate for the 'nomadic' population being 28,510.[183] Professor Hind, at the very same time, believed another estimate of 42,870 Rupert's Land Indians to be 'one-fourth too high'; and an estimated total east of the Rockies (in Canada) of 60,000, consisting of 35,000 'Thickwood Indians' and 25,000 Plains tribes, to be 'considerably over-rated.'[184] Similarly, with respect to the

---

1780 = 42,250; 1907 = 3,450 (pp. 16-18). De Smet, 1841: 'many of the Plains tribes only the miserable remnants of their former numbers' (*Early Western Travels*, XXVII, 159).

[180]Mooney, *Handbook of American Indians*, II, 286. On the extermination of the Karankawa, Texas, 1858-59, see Bancroft, *North Mexican States and Texas*, II, 408, 524; Thwaites, ed. note, *Early Western Travels*, XXVIII, 149. An attempted massacre of the Wichita-Caddo, also 1858, and of the Tonkawa (successful), 1862, both in Texas (Lindquist, *Red Man in the United States*, 181-5). For military massacres, see above, note 6; also chap. XXI, note 321. See also Wissler, *American Indian*, 237, 241, etc.; Kroeber, *Cultural and Natural Areas*, *passim*.

[181]*Ibid.*, at large.

[182]Mooney, *Handbook of American Indians*, II, 286.

[183]*Palliser Journals*, 199, 200.

[184]Hind, *Report, 1858*, 114-15.

United States tribes, Colonel Dodge, criticizing Catlin's estimate of 60,000 Blackfoot, *circa* 1835 (obtained from a well-known Indian Department official of high reputation, Major Joshua Pilcher[185]), reduces it to 'probably not more than a fourth of that number'; and remarks likewise concerning fifty years later, that the grand total of 253,000 in the last official report (1886) 'is probably at least one fifth too great.'[186] The only argument advanced in support of this condition is that "the number of Indians has always been and is now, very greatly overrated";[187] and in so far as I can discover the evidence for this pronouncement lies in the fact of the estimate of 1835 coming from Catlin—his informant is not mentioned—who is invariably wrong.[188] Possibly Catlin's (or Pilcher's) estimate may require a considerable reduction; but in 1835 the Indian population had yet to run the gauntlet of four epidemics of smallpox; 1837, 1845, 1857, 1870 (of which the first and the last are conservatively estimated to have reduced them by one-half and one-third respectively);[189] and an outbreak of measles, 1864. Yet General Chittenden—no believer in extravagant figures, who himself cuts down the estimate of smallpox mortality on the worst of these occasions to two-fifths or even one-tenth of the figure popularly accepted— notes 14,000 souls in the Blackfoot Confederacy, about 1900.[190]

The plain truth appears to be that although in many respects our contemporary observers are the best authorities we can hope to command, some of them are in matters beyond mere superficial observation of no real authority at all. Dodge's thirty-five years 'among the Indians' (if one can call it that) did not save him from most egregious error concerning Indian linguists.[191] I have pointed out also the damning effect of the scanty-population argument upon the huge aggregates of buffalo supposedly destroyed by Indians,[192] and also upon the repeated victories with terrific slaughter over Indians who 'vastly outnumbered the troops.'[193] Still less can Palliser or Hind be considered authorities on matters Indian outside the scope of their personal observation. As I suggest, it might for various reasons be either a common cliché or even an article of faith among the fur traders that Indians, as Palliser intimates, were commonly duplicated or multiplied. I have met with nothing which supports that idea. Indians seem to have been commonly classified as 'Somebody's band' of (approximately) so many men or souls,[194] whose numbers were as well known as

[185]On Pilcher, see above, note 146.   [186]Dodge, *Our Wild Indians*, 48-9.
[187]*Ibid.*, 48, 317.
[188]*Ibid.*, 43, 54, 63, 305; cf. above, chap. 1, note 14.
[189]Above, notes 140-60, 171.
[190]Chittenden, *American Fur Trade*, II, 851; cf. Coues (ed.), *Henry-Thompson Journals*, II, 524.
[191]Dodge on the 'practically universal ignorance' among Plains Indians of any language but their own (*Our Wild Indians*, 42-51, 382-94). Elsewhere: "I have never yet seen an Indian who had mounted the ladder of human progress sufficiently far to have observed that there is one star which never perceptibly changes its place . . ." (*ibid.*, 551). Both generalizations are disproved by abundant evidence, from 1610 onward.
[192]Above, chap. XVIII, notes 56-79.
[193]See Appendix FF.
[194]Coues (ed.), *Henry-Thompson Journals*, II, 530; cf. also 522-3.

ranchmen know the estimated total of So-and-so's cattle or horses. I have
found no recorded instance of a trader failing to recognize a chief; or even
attempting to individually acquaint himself with his followers. The chief
answered for them.[195] These visits to fur posts were not social calls. They
were made to obtain advances on the winter's hunt, and to trade its proceeds
in the spring. We are required to believe that the traders, who in the
cant phrase were 'nobody's fools' to begin with, and whose transactions at
this very time were watched and checked with a lynx-eyed scrutiny such
as a (supposedly) modern 'efficiency expert' might envy,[196] even ran the
risk of dissipating their stock-in-trade among strangers of whom they knew
nothing, except that they might never see them again and would be unable
to recognize them if they did.[197] We may recollect that (where we discussed
the danger of having implicit belief in everything heard at fur-posts) it was
remarked that at the same places Butler never found the least hint of
any recognition of the agricultural potentialities of the country.[198] Taken
as a whole, even the fur traders themselves, despite their long residence
in the country, can scarcely be considered very high authorities on any
question requiring sympathetic insight. For sympathy scarcely existed. It
is hardly ours to distribute blame or praise; but the fact, in the great
majority of cases, cannot be denied.[199] The good Indian was the one who
brought in plenty of furs; the 'lazy' or 'indolent scoundrel' was the one
who did not.[200] In so far as the Red race was concerned, it is quite clear
that in the Shorter Catechism of the fur trade, the chief end of man was
to serve the trader and enrich him forever. It is of interest, however, to
note that one of the few authorities at our command who possessed the
knowledge which is quickened by sympathy, held a totally opposite opinion
from the foregoing ones concerning population. Father Morice considered
that Indian populations were 'commonly underestimated.'[201]

[195]*Ibid.*, 539-53, particularly p. 546. Their usual trading-places were known
(*ibid.*, 508, 655, 737, etc.).

[196]If anyone doubts this, let him read the Minutes of the Northern Council,
Hudson's Bay Company, 1830-43 (Oliver (ed.), *Canadian North-West*, I, 643-88;
II, 689-871). Chief Factors 'directed to charge to private account' any unusual
expenditure which Sir George Simpson—months afterward, hundreds of miles
distant, and not faced with the situation—pronounced 'unnecessary.' Cf. Henry,
North West Company, 1810 (Coues (ed.), *Henry-Thompson Journals*, II, 559).

[197]Compare Henry (*ibid.*, 575).

[198]Butler, *Great Lone Land*, Report, 381; *Autobiography*, 138.

[199]See Coues, ed. pref., *Henry-Thompson Journals*, xviii; cf. also *ibid.*, I, 46,
343-8, 401; II, 452, 526, 617, 656-9, 700-37, etc. Cf. George Simpson, 1821:
"Philanthropy is not the exclusive object of our visits to these Northern Regions ..."
(*Simpson's Athabaska Journal*, 356). A reviewer caustically observes: "There is
nothing in the Journal to indicate that it was even a secondary object . . ."
(W. J. Ghent, *Canadian Historical Review*, XX, 1939, 320).

[200]Coues (ed.), *Henry-Thompson Journals*, I, 241 (pro); contra: *ibid.*, II,
531, 532, 724, 737, etc.; Duncan McGillivray, 1795, on the Gros Ventre (Atsina):
"a worthless indolent tribe, entirely addicted to sloth and laziness . . ." (*Journal*,
27).

[201]Morice, *Northern Interior of British Columbia*, 195.

Hind's term, 'Thickwood Indians,' is so hopelessly vague as to require some elucidation, before his estimate of their numbers can have any even approximate value. Indians designated themselves by native names indicative of various topographical distinctions;[202] and on precisely the same essential principles as our 'St. John's Wood' or 'Covent [that is, Convent] Garden' in the heart of modern London,[203] they often retained these distinctive names after the topographical or local significance had ceased to have any meaning. Thus the younger Henry, in his valuable enumeration of the numbers, habitat, and 'tents' of the various bands of Assiniboine,[204] mentions 24 tents of 'Red River Assiniboines,' whose home region was west of Qu'Appelle Lakes. Literally speaking, they were no longer *Red River* Assiniboines. There were also 40 tents of 'Strong Wood Assiniboines' who dwelt 'on Battle River and between that and the South Branch [of the Saskatchewan].' He specifies the location of their camp as 'one long day's ride S. [from his Fort Vermilion[205]]'; that is to say, probably somewhere on Battle River between 'The Narrows,' 40 miles south of Vermilion, and the Big Bridge near Wainwright, Alberta—the precise type of country where 'strong wood' is conspicuous by its absence, and where hardly any wood whatever is to be seen, even along the river-bottoms. 'Strong wood' and 'thickwood' are very indefinite terms, and may mean almost anything.[206]

[202]The Cree have their own names for Plains, Wood, and Swampy Cree: *Paskwawininiwug* (prairie), *Sakawithiniwuk* or*Sakawiyiniwok* (wood), *Maskegon* (marshes, swamps = 'muskeg'); see *Handbook of American Indians*, I, 361, 813; II, 206, 414, 579. One division at least of the Strongwood Assiniboines (Hind, *Report, 1858*, 115), or Thickwood A. (*Palliser Journals*, 18), or Thickwood Stoneys (Sullivan, *ibid.*, 88) was self-named evidently: *Tschantoga* = people of the woods (*Handbook of American Indians*, II, 823). 'Mashquegie Assiniboines' (Henry, in Coues (ed.), *Henry-Thompson Journals*, II, 509, 571) must certainly have been so named by the Cree.

[203]Covent Garden (the 'Seven Acres') was the orchard and kitchen garden of the Abbey of St. Peter's, Westminster, now 'Westminster Abbey.' St. John's Wood belonged, at the time of the Dissolution, to the great monastic house of St. John's, Clerkenwell.

[204]Coues (ed.), *Henry-Thompson Journals*, II, 522; see also II, 508, 597, and his admirable notes on the region, II, 497-509.

[205]*Ibid.*, 508, 523.

[206]Henry speaks of the 'strong woods' as one might of the 'forest land,' the 'wood country,' the 'woods,' the timber' (as himself, *ibid.*, 552, 570, 580, 582, 593), meaning a large territory north of the Saskatchewan River (*ibid.*, 540-53, 567-9, 587-93, 637, 639, 652, etc.). He also has 'a space of strong wood,' and 'covered with strong wood' (pp. 546, 562), as if indicating *large* timber (*bois fort*) aparently; as this is geographically meaningless. He further mentions a party fearing pursuit from Cree, who 'kept along the strong woods' in that very locality noticed in the text, where there are now none (pp. 576, 591). This must mean any tiny bluff which could afford shelter in such a territory. He also uses 'the thick woods' (*not* 'thickwood') precisely as we do today (*ibid.*, 565, 569, 633-51, etc.).

Palliser and Hector refer to the Thickwood Hills, northwest of Carlton, evidently as a place-name (*Palliser Journals*, 63, 64, 81). This might possibly localize the 'Thickwood Crees' (*ibid.*, 18, 65, 80, 115, 117, 201); but could scarcely do so for 'T. Assiniboines' (p. 18) or 'T. Stoneys' (pp. 88, 202, 204). The party at large also have 'thickwood hills (common noun, pp. 64, 81), 't.

Henry also mentions the 'Swampy Ground Assiniboines, who inhabit the strong wood W. of Fort Augustus [Edmonton].'[207] This name may probably have been brought with them, or even been bestowed by some other people, as 'Mashquegie or Mashquegon' Assiniboines[208] (Ojibwa = Cree) might indicate. Later, when he is living in their territory, he calls them Strong Wood Assiniboines[209] and Canoe Assiniboines.[210] with reference to questions of population, these are not merely matters of academic minutiae. When Henry tells us, *circa* 1810, that the 'Strong Wood Assiniboines' (that is, the foregoing, and those 'between the Battle River and the South Branch') comprised two bands of 70 tents all told;[211] and when two later traders, perhaps more authoritative—for they had then lived in the country much longer than Henry did—tell us *circa* 1842, that there were some 3020 Strongwood Assiniboines,[212] after a most disastrous visitation of smallpox, it is quite evident that the two computations were based upon very different data. The Assiniboine occupied a vast territory,[213] and it is doubtful whether any one man (or estimate) could be sure of including all. So too with Hind's 'Thickwood Indians,' *circa* 1856. The only 'authorities' at that era would in the final analysis be Hudson's Bay Company officers. A very closely detailed estimate of that year, printed by Dr. Bryce,[214] is based upon the administrative divisions of the Company's districts, and clearly ignores not

---

animals' (pp. 12, 92), 't. hunters' (p. 99), 't. plants' (M. Bourgeau, botanist, p. 250), 't. reindeer' (p. 201); 'thick-wood buffalo' (p. 148), 'thick-wood wolf' (timber wolf, pp. 63, 126). Comparing their uses, it is difficult to decide just what it meant to them; whether a recognized tribal, geographical, botanical, or zoological classification, or merely the type of country where certain phenomena were encountered. It is interesting to note its use as a place-name in England; Thickwood, Wiltshire, in various spellings from Domesday Book (1086) to 1339 (*Place-Names of Wiltshire*, English Place-Name Society, 1939, 94).

[207]Coues (ed.), *Henry Thompson Journals*, II, 523.

[208]*Ibid.*, 509, 571.

[209]*Ibid.*, 615. *Gens du Bois*, p. 549; *Gens du Bois Fort*, p. 575, 597.

[210]*Ibid.*, 652. I cannot identify 'Grand River A.' (p. 624). 'Cree-Assiniboines' are half-bloods of those tribes (p. 597).

[211]*Ibid.*, 523.

[212]John Rowand, J. E. Harriott, in Hind, *Report, 1858*, 115. Rowand (1787-1854), North West Company, 1804; Chief Factor, Saskatchewan District, Hudson's Bay Company, 1826; Harriott (1797-1877), Hudson's Bay Company, 1809; Chief Trader, 1829; Chief Factor, 1846 (Wallace, "Biographical Dictionary," in *Documents Relating to the North West Company*, 455, 496).

[213]"Their lands may be said to commence at the Hair Hills [*i.e.* Pembina Mountain] near Red River, thence running W. along the Assiniboine, from that to the junction of the North and South branches of the Saskatchewan, and up the former branch to Fort Vermillion; then due S. to Battle River, then S.E. to the Missourie, down that river to the Mandane villages, and finally N.E. to the Hair Hills again. All this space of open country may be called the lands of the Assiniboines . . ." (Henry, 1809, in Coues (ed.), *Henry-Thompson Journals*, II, 516). In J. H. Taylor's time, 1864, the head-waters of the Mouse (Souris) River were 'the country of the South Assiniboines . . .' (*Frontier Life*, 39).

[214]*Remarkable History of the Hudson's Bay Company*, Appendix C, 489.

only geographical or topographical, but tribal boundaries.[215] The Blackfoot, for example, occupied as their 'permanent' home, territory as far south as the Missouri.[216] It is perfectly certain, after the abandonment of Piegan Post, Bow Fort, and Chesterfield House, that there must have been numbers of the southern members of the Blackfoot Confederacy who were never seen at Rocky Mountain House, Edmonton, or Fort Pitt, and would not be on their books; probably those who are now classed as United States bands of those tribes. It was in the endeavour to persuade the Confederacy in general to cease trading at the Missouri River posts that Piegan Post was established in 1832 by the Hudson's Bay Company, and various inducements offered.[217] These factors, taken as a whole, demonstrate the virtual impossibility of reaching reliable definite conclusions concerning numbers. Notwithstanding, various tribal or chronological estimates made by observers on the spot, or those of critical scholars commenting on such, cannot be without interest and value in a study of the present character. These, as our title indicates, include none who do not appear to have utilized the buffalo, in part at least. For convenience, I have arranged them in periods of approximately a century, representing natural divisions. I have also subdivided them regionally in general accordance with Mooney's classification. The final estimate, if printed in italics, is in each case that of A. L. Kroeber (1939);[218] representing either an independent conclusion, or a tentative acceptance of Mooney's figures, pending further demonstration.

---

[215]The Saskatchewan District comprised Edmonton (7500 Indians), Carlton (6000), Fort Pitt (7000), Rocky Mountain House (6000), Lac la Biche (500), Fort Assiniboine (150), Lesser Slave Lake (400), Jasper's House (200), Fort à la Corne (300) = 28,050 (*Report from the Select Committee on the Hudson's Bay Company, 1857*, 365).

[216]Henry, 1809: "The tract of land which they call their own at present begins on a line due S. from Fort Vermilion to the South Branch of the Saskatchewan and up that stream (Bow R.) to the foot of the Rocky Mountains; then goes N. along the mountains until it strikes the N. Branch of the Saskatchewan, and down that stream to the Vermillion river . . ." (Coues (ed.), *Henry-Thompson Journals*, II, 524). The Sarcee then dwelt "commonly S. of the Beaver Hills . . ." (*i.e.* about Wetaskiwin and Camrose, Alberta), so Henry, *ibid.*, 532; cf. Jenness, *Sarcee Indians of Alberta*, chap. I. Simpson met them on the Red Deer River in 1841, an unthinkable spot 50 years later (*Journey Around the World*, I, 110). Yet Lewis and Clark encountered Blackfoot on the Missouri, and Maximilian mentions meeting Ohistahna, 'principal chief of the Blackfeet,' at Fort McKenzie, Upper Missouri, 1833, as if this were their headquarters region (*Early Western Travels*, XXIII, 158).

[217]Opened by Harriott, 1832. See Oliver (ed.), *Canadian North-West*, I, 662, 678, 679; II, 693, 695, 730. There is, however, some confusion as to whether this place is identical with Bow Fort, at the junction of the Kananaskis with the Bow River, or a separate post on the International Boundary. See on all this, J. E. A. Macleod, "Piegan Post and the Blackfoot Trade," *Canadian Historical Review*, XXIV, 1943, 273-9.

[218]Kroeber, *Cultural and Natural Areas*, 134-46. Kroeber's general conclusion is that Mooney's figures require some reduction, but it is not easy in our present knowledge to specify just where. Mooney was apparently in the process of reducing them at his death (Kroeber, *ibid.*; also preface to Mooney's essay, by John R. Swanton).

4. ESTIMATED NUMBERS PREVIOUS TO 1700

SOUTH ATLANTIC STATES

1600: Maryland and Delaware combined = 4700. Virginia = 15,100. North Carolina = 17,300. South Carolina = 15,100. (*MO.*, p. 6)[219] The two latter States include the Tuscarora and Catawba; each estimated *c.* 1600 at *c.* 5000 souls. Catawba 1682 = *c.* 4600 (*MO.*, pp. 4-6; *HAN.*, I, 215). Total, *c.* 1600 = 52,200 souls.

GULF STATES

1650: Cherokee = 22,000. Yuchi = 1500. Creek Confederacy, including the Seminole, a later off-shoot from the Creeks = 18,000. Yamasee = 2000 (E. 1907;[220] *HAN.*, II, 986). Mobile and Tohome = 2000 (E. 1907; the latter est. 350 warriors, 1702; *HAN.*, II, 771). Total in Georgia, Alabama, Tennessee = 45,500 (*MO.*, pp. 8-9). 1650: Chickasaw = 8000. Choctaw = 15,000. Natchez = 4500. Lower Yazoo River tribes—Tunica, Yazoo, Koroa, Ofogoula = 2000 (the last three E. 1907). Upper Yazoo River tribes—Chakchiuma, Ibitoupa, Taposa, Tiou[221] = 1200 (E. 1907). Biloxi, Pascagoula, Moctobi = 1000 (E. 1907). Total in Mississippi = 31,700 (*MO.*, pp. 8-9).

1650: Acolapissa (including Tangipahoa) = 1500. Atakapa = 1500. Chitimacha = 3000. Houma = 1000. *Les Gens de la Fourche*: Bayogoula, Chawasha, Mugulasha = 1500. Quinipissa, Washa = 1400. Opelousa or Okelusa, Taensa = 800 (E. 1907). Total in Louisiana, excluding Caddo tribes = 10,700 (*MO.*, p. 9).[222]

Grand Total for the Gulf States, *c.* 1650 = 87,900.[223]

[219]For key to these symbols, see bibliography.

[220]E. signifies extinct.

[221]Mooney includes the Tiou with the Chakchiuma; Swanton with the Natchez (ed. note in Mooney, "Aboriginal Population," 9-10).

[22]Cf. Kroeber, *Cultural and Natural Areas*, 138.

[223]This, as stated, signifies Indians in States where the historic buffalo has been found. Mooney notes 24,000 in Florida *circa* 1650, now extinct, whom I do not include. He also includes the Quapaw or Arkansa in (modern) Arkansas, whom I give below with the Southern Plains tribes.

Swanton also questions Mooney's figures for the following ("Aboriginal Population," 9).

Tribe	Swanton	Mooney
Creek Confederacy	7,000	18,000
Mobile and Tohome	1,225	2,000
Chickasaw	3,000-3,500	8,000
Choctaw	15,000	15,000
Natchez	3,500	4,500
Chakchiuma, Ibitoupa, and Taposa	750	1,200
Tunica, Yazoo, Koroa, and Ofogoula	2,450	2,000
Biloxi, Pascagoula, and Moctobi	875	1,000
Houma	1,225	1,000
Chitimacha	2,625	3,000
Acolapissa	1,050	1,500
Atakapa	2,000	1,500

NORTH ATLANTIC STATES, INCLUDING EASTERN CANADA, NORTH OF
THE GREAT LAKES

c. 1600: New York State = 17,500; including 5000 'Iroquois' and 3000
Mahican. Pennsylvania and New Jersey = 13,000; including 8000 Delawares. (*MO.*, pp. 3-4).[224]

CONESTOGA, 1647: 1300 men capable of bearing arms in one village alone;
hence *c.* 4500 souls. (*HAN.*, II, 132; but cf. *HAN.*, I, 335).[225]

ERIE: '3000 to 4000 combatants' defending Riqué, 1654, exclusive of women
and children; all their warriors not likely to be there; hence 14,500 souls
'probably a conservative estimate at this time' (Hewitt, *HAN.*, I, 431,
588).

HURON: 1615 = 30,000 (Champlain; later 20,000); *c.* 1620 = 30,000
(Sagard); 1626 = 35,000 (Brébeuf); 1648 = *c.* 20,000 (Hewitt, all
HAN., I, 587); 1653 = 'more than 1000 Christian Hurons [prisoners]
among the Onondaga alone' (*HAN.*, I, 588); 1649 onward–'never more
than 500 Hurons [*i.e.* a free settlement] in one body' (*HAN.*, I, 590).

IROQUOIS: *c.* 1595 (after almost incessant war by the League of the Iroquois
since *c.* 1570) = 8000 warriors or perhaps *c.* 36,000 souls (Hewitt, *HAN.*,
I, 587, 616, 618); 1600–5000 in New York State (*MO.*, p. 3); 1648 =
2000 warriors against the Hurons (Mooney, *HAN.*, I, 900); 1654 = 1800
warriors against the Erie at Riqué; 1657 = about 24 villages; 1659 = 700
warriors at the Long Sault (all, Hewitt, *HAN.*, I, 431, 618, 589); *c.*
1660 = 25,000 people (Maclean, *Canadian Savage Folk*, 160); 1677 =
1685 = 16,000 souls; 1689 = 2250 warriors, 12,850 souls; 1698–'more
than half' (in U.S.) lost by war and by desertions to Canada = 1230
warriors (all Hewitt, *HAN.*, I, 619).

IROQUOIS CONFEDERACY

CAYUGA: 1660 = 1660 = 1500 (Mooney and Hewitt, *HAN.*, I, 223);
1663 = '800 Cayuga and Seneca warriors' (*HAN.*, II, 505); 1670 =
3 villages (*HAN.*, I, 223).

MOHAWK: 1643 = 3 villages, probably 700 or 800 warriors (Hewitt,
HAN., II, 505); 1650 = est. 5000 souls; 1660 = 'about 500 warriors,
2500 total numbers'; 1677 = '1500 souls' (all, Hewitt, *HAN.*, I, 922).

ONEIDA: 1660 = 500 souls; 1677 = 1000 (Hewitt, *HAN.*, II, 125).

ONONDAGA: 1660 = 1500 souls; 1677 = 1750 (Hewitt, *HAN.*, II, 132).

Bayogoula, Mugulasha, and Quinipissa	875	1,500
Washa, Chawasha, and Okelousa		
(not Opelousa, as Mooney above)	700	1,400
Opelousa	455	....
Taensa and Avoyel	1,155	800
TOTALS	44,385	62,400

[224]Mooney's figures for the Iroquois are considered 'disproportionately low'
(Kroeber, *Cultural and Natural Areas*, 133). On buffalo utilization by the
Iroquoians, see Wissler, *American Anthropologist*, XVI, 1914, 461. The Seneca
had a 'Buffalo Indian' society (Hewitt, *Handbook of American Indians*, II, 502).

[225]Both J. N. B. Hewitt. The respective accounts of the Conestoga scarcely
seem to agree.

SENECA: 1648 = '300 warriors in one expedition'; Senecas, "the larger part of the Iroquois warriors who in 1648-9 assailed . . . the Huron tribes. . . ." 1660 = 5000 souls; 1663 = 800 Seneca (and Cayuga) warriors; 1677 = 5000 souls; 1686 = 200 warriors sent against the Miami; 1687 = '600 or 800 warriors' in their home-region; 1677= 4 villages (all, Hewitt, *HAN*., II, 502-8).

MAHICAN: *c*. 1600 = 3000 in New York State (*MO*., p. 3).

'NEUTRALS': 1616 = 4000 warriors (Champlain); 1626 = 28 villages; Brébeuf and Chaumonot, 1640-41 = 40 villages, 4000 warriors, 12,000 souls: they visited 18 villages, stayed in 10, est. *c*. '500 fires' and 3000 population;[226] 1643 = 2000 warriors sent against the *Nation du feu*;[227] 1653 = Neutrals and 'Tobacco Nation'[228] more than 2000 warriors (all, Hewitt, *HAN*., II, 60).

OTTAWA: 1615 = 300 men met at one time (Champlain's *les cheueux releuez*); 1670 = 'a generic name for more than 30 different tribes' (so, Allouez); 1670 = 30 villages, 3000 warriors (Mooney, Hewitt, *HAN*., II, 167-71, 472).

CENTRAL STATES TERRITORY

ERIE: 1650 = 4000 (? souls) E. 1907 (*MO*., p. 11).[229]

FOX: 1650 = 3000 (*MO*., p. 11); *c*. 1665 = a settlement of 600 lodges near Green Bay, Wisconsin (*HAN*., II, 474).

ILLINOIS CONFEDERACY: 1650 = 8000 (*MO*., p. 11). [230] 1660 = 60 villages, with 20,000 men and 70,000 souls (*HAN*., I, 597).[231] 1670 = 'a village of 500 or 600 fires, with more than 1500 men alone' (Marquette, *JR*., LIX, 189; cf. *ibid*., 123, 161).

ILLINOIS: 1673 = one village of 74 cabins, of one tribe only (so, Marquette); 1680 = est. 400 houses, 1800 warriors, 6500 souls (Hennepin); 1690 = 350 cabins; 1692 = 300 cabins, of four fires each, two families per fire, est. *c*. 9000 souls (Râle), 'perhaps excessive' (Mooney, Thomas, *HAN*., I, 598).

[226]See remarks on 'fires' (above, notes 8-10). Here we have apparently a fire per family; but Daillon, 1626, noted also 'long houses' like those of the Hurons, 25-30 fathoms long, and 6-8 wide. These contained 'about 12 fires and 24 firesides . . .' (*Handbook of American Indians*, II, 61).

[227]The Mascoutens, an Illinois people (*ibid*., I, 811).

[228]The Tionontati, later part of the Wyandot-Huron (*ibid*., 585; II, 755).

[229]I have classified these regionally, as in Mooney. Cf. above on Erie numbers. Unless these were wholly isolated bands, the discrepancy in numbers seems so great that one may ask whether Mooney really meant warriors here instead of souls (cf. Hewitt, *ibid*., I, 430).

[230]It is difficult to determine in a given instance whether we are dealing with the Illinois proper, or one of the Confederacy, or all of them, as apparently Mooney, above. In 1643, the *Nation du Feu* (a name later applied to the Mascoutens) was said to be 'alone more populous than all the Neutral nation [then of some 12,000 souls], all the Hurons, and all the Iroquois' (*Handbook of American Indians*, II, 62, 473). The *Nation du Feu* here included 'all the so-called Illinois tribes' (*ibid*., 62). Compare Parkman on 'the great Illinois town' (*La Salle*, 221-41).

[231]'An extravagant estimate' (*Handbook of American Indians*, II, 62, 473).

KASKASKIAS: 1677 = '350 cabins in their village' (Allouez, *JR.*, LX, 159).[232]

KICKAPOO: 1650 = 2000 (*MO.*, p. 11).

MASCOUTEN (*i.e. Nation du Feu*): 1642 = est. 900 warriors (Hewitt, *HAN.*, II, 473); 1650 = 1500 warriors (?) (E. 1907; *MO.*, p. 11); 1679 = their village est. at 'some 20,000 souls' (Dablon, *JR.*, LXI, 149).[233]

MENOMINEE: 1650 = 3000 (*MO.*, p. 11).

MIAMI (? including WEA and PIANKASHAW): 1650 = 4500. (*MO.*, p. 11) 'probably never exceeded 1500' (Mooney, C. Thomas, *HAN.*, I, 854).

OJIBWA (CHIPPEWA, etc.): 1650 = 35,000 (*MO.*, p. 11); 'in early times scattered over a region extending 1000 miles from E. to W.' (Mooney, Thomas, *HAN.*, I, 280).

POTAWATOMI: 1650 = 4000 (*MO.*, p. 11); 300 warriors at once met by Allouez; 'probably never over 3000 souls' (Mooney, Hewitt, *HAN.*, II, 290, 291).

SAUK: 1650 = 3000 (*MO.*, p. 11);[234] 1671: 1000 warriors, Sauk, Fox, Potawatomi, and Huron, against the Sioux (*HAN.*, II, 474).

SHAWNEE: 1650 = 3000 (*MO.*, p. 11).

WENROHRONON: (perhaps of the Erie Confederacy of tribes, south of Lake Erie): weakened by smallpox, 1639, when 600 sought refuge with the Hurons; *ante* 1639 = probably 1200-1500, perhaps 2000 people (Hewitt, *HAN.*, II, 932-4).

WINNEBAGO: 1650 = 3000 (*MO.*, p. 11).

SOUTHERN PLAINS AREA

AKOKISA: 1690 = 500 (E. 1907; *MO.*, p. 13).

ARANAMA: 1690 = 200 (E. 1907; *MO.*, p. 13).

ARIZPE (Rio Sonora, Mexico): 1678 = 416 (Hodge, *HAN.*, I, 87).

ARKANSA (Quapaw or Arkansa): 1650 = 2500 (*MO.*, p. 9).

BIDAI: 1690 = 500 (E. 1907; *MO.*, p. 13).

CADDO (including HASINAI, etc.): 1690 = 8500 (*MO.*, p. 13).

'COAHUILTECAN tribes': 1690 = 15,000 (E. 1907: *MO.*, p. 13).[235]

COMANCHE: 1690 = 7000 (*MO.*, p. 13).

KARANKAWA: 1690 = 2800 (E. 1907: *MO.*, p. 13).

KICHAI: 1690 = 500 (*MO.*, p. 13).

LIPAN: 1690 = 500 (*MO.*, p. 13).

MESCALERO: 1690 = 700 (*MO.*, p. 13).

NATCHEZ: 1682 = probably *c.* 6000, 1000-1200 warriors. (Henshaw, Swanton, *HAN.*, II, 35).

---

[232]The preceding Illinois 'village of 74 cabins' perhaps Kaskaskias.

[233]See above, note 230, also Swanton, ed. note, in Mooney ("Aboriginal Population," 11). Here again, Dablon is possibly referring, under cover of the tribal *Nation du Feu*, to the Illinois confederates so termed. We need a more definite chronology here.

[234]Cf. Swanton, ed. note, in Mooney ("Aboriginal Population," 11).

[235]These, which occupied both sides of the lower Rio Grande (*Handbook of American Indians*, I, 314), would presumably be some aggregation or confederacy roaming over Coahuila and Texas at large.

NATCHITOCH: 1682 = 'a powerful nation' (Douay: Alice C. Fletcher, Swanton, *HAN.*, II, 37).

QUAPAW: (? 1541) = 5000 or 6000 (C. Thomas, *HAN.*, II, 335).[236]

TONKAWA: 1690 = 1600 (*MO.*, p. 13).

TUNICA: 1699 = est. 260 cabins. Gravier, 1700 = '50 or 60 small cabins, in 7 hamlets' (*HAN.*, II, 838).

WICHITA: 1690 = 3200 (*MO.*, p. 13).

NEW MEXICO AND ARIZONA[237]

'YUMAN' stocks:

ALCHEDOMA: 1680 = 3000 souls (E. 1907; *MO.*, p. 22).

CAJUENCHE (Cawina): 1680 = 3000 (E. 1907; *MO.*, p. 22).

HAVASUPAI (Suppai, Cohonino): 1680 = 300 (*MO.*, p. 22).

MARICOPA: 1680 = 2000 (*MO.*, p. 22).

MOJAVE: 1680 = 3000 (*MO.*, p. 22).

QUIGYUMA (Jalliquimay): 1680 = 2000 (E. 1907: *MO.*, p. 22).

WALAPAI (or 'Hualapais'): 1680 = 700 (*MO.*, p. 22).

YAVAPAI (Mojave Apache): 1680 = 600 (*MO.*, p. 22).

'PIMAN' stocks:

PAPAGO: 1680 = 6000 (*MO.*, p. 22).

PIMA: 1680 = 4000 (*MO.*, p. 22).

SOBAIPURI: 1680 = 400 (*MO.*, p. 22).

'ATHAPASCANS':

APACHE proper: 1680 = 5000 (*MO.*, p. 22).[238]

NAVAJO: 1680 = 8000 (*MO.*, p. 22).

PUEBLANS:

ACOMA 'province' (mod. Acoma, Laguna): 1680 = 1500 (*MO.*, p. 22); 1583? = 6000 (*HAN.*, I, 11). [239]

HOPI 'province' (excluding Hano, but including Awátobi): 1680 = 2800 (*MO.*, p. 22); Awátobi, 1680 = 800 (*HAN.*, I, 119).

JEMEZ 'province' (mod. Jemez): 1680 = 2500 (*MO.*, p. 22); 1694 = 84 warriors slain, 361 prisoners (*HAN.*, I, 630).

KERES 'province' (mod. Cochiti, San Felipe, Santa Ana, Santo Domingo, Sia): 1680 = 2500 (*MO.*, p. 22). Cochiti (formerly on the *Potrero de las Vacas*[240]): 1680 = 300 at the San Buenaventura mission; 1692

[236]See Arkansa, above.

[237]Some of these Southwestern tribes may never have been, and others may have ceased long ago to be, 'buffalo Indians' in any really material sense; but it is difficult to disentangle them. Many not on the buffalo range itself might obtain buffalo products in trade. See above on this, chap. XI, note 117.

[238]On the Apache (eastern bands) or buffalo users, the Vaqueros or 'Querechos' (1541, 1894: Coues (ed.), *Expeditions of Pike*, II, 748), a Pueblo term for all the buffalo-hunting Apache; comprising the Faraones, Jicarilla, Lipans, Llaneros, Mescaleros (see *Handbook of American Indians*, II, 337, 338). On the classification of the Apache, see Kroeber's admirable summary, *Cultural and Natural Areas*, 34-8.

[239]These had a 'buffalo clan' (*Handbook of American Indians*, I, 11).

[240]*I.e.* 'Little Cow [buffalo] Meadow' (*ibid.*, I, 317, 370; II, 189). Sia had also a 'buffalo clan' (*ibid.*, 563).

= 200 women captives (*HAN.*, I, 318). Keres, 1630 = 4000 (*HAN.*, I, 675).

PECOS 'province': 1541 = 2000-2500 (*HAN.*, II, 221); 1680 = 2000 (E. 1907: *MO.*, p. 22).[241]

PIROS 'province' (mod. Senecú, Mexico): est. 6000 in 1630. "The entire Piros division of the Tanoan family probably numbered about 9000 early in the seventeenth century" (Hodge, *HAN.*, II, 262); 1680 = 9000 (*MO.*, p. 22).

TANO 'province': 1583 = 40,000 (Espejo = 'grossly exaggerated': Hodge, *HAN.*, II, 686); 1630 = 4000 (Benavides: *ibid.*); 1680 = 4000 (E. 1907: *MO.*, p. 22).

TAOS 'province' (mod. Taos, Picuris): 1540 = 15,000 ('greatly exaggerated'); 1680 = c. 2000 (*HAN.*, II, 689); 1680 = 1500 (*MO.*, p. 22); Picuris: 1680 = est. 3000 (*HAN.*, II, 245).

TEWA 'province' (mod. Nambe, San Ildefonso, San Juan, Santa Clara, Tesuque, Hano of the Hopi group): Tewa, 1628 = 6000 in 8 pueblos (*HAN.*, II, 737); 1680 = 2500 (*MO.*, p. 22).

TIGUA, TIQUA 'province' (mod. Isleta, New Mexico; Sandia and Isleta, Texas): 1680 = 3000 (*MO.*, p. 22). 1680 = c. 2000; 1681 = 519 captives taken (*HAN.*, I, 623); Tigua province, 1629 = 8 pueblos, 6000 people; 1681 = Puaray = 200, Sandia = 3000, Alameda = 300, Isleta = 2000, 500 captives (Hodge, *HAN.*, II, 748); Tigua, 1630 = est. 6000; 1680 = 3700 (*ibid.*).

ZUNI 'province' (mod. Zuni): 1583 = 20,000 (Espejo = 'greatly exaggerated': Hodge, *HAN.*, II, 1017); 1680 = c. 2500 (*HAN.*, II, 1018); 1680 = 2500 (*MO.*, p. 22).[242]

5. ESTIMATED NUMBERS, 1700 TO 1811

I have selected 1811 as the end of the period for what are broadly, eighteenth-century estimates, instead of 1800, for the purpose of including our witnesses so often cited, Lewis and Clark, Zebulon M. Pike, and the younger Henry. Several of their recitals represent the first, or very early visits by white men; and since no known epidemics (on any large scale) intervened between 1800 and 1811, their accounts represent substantially the eighteenth century at large, or virtually aboriginal conditions. The Lewis and Clark figures for Central Mountain tribes will be given in the period 1811-1911, for reasons stated below. I again follow Mooney's regional classification in general.

ATLANTIC[243] AND CENTRAL STATES

CHEROKEE: 1708 = '60 villages, at least 500 men'; 1715 = 4000 warriors, 11,210 souls; 1720 = 3800 warriors, 10,000-11,500 souls; 1729 = 6000 warriors, 20,000 pop.; 1730 = c. 20,000 pop.; 1739 = 1000 warriors; 1758, 7500 pop. (Mooney, *HAN.*, I, 247).

[241]A 'buffalo clan' in Pecos also (*ibid.*, 221).

[242]Zuni = 'Cibola' of Coronado, *et al.*, 1541. Zuni as the 'buffalo province,' at the time of Philip II of Spain: Bancroft, *Native Races*, IV, 673; *History of Arizona*, 42, 44, 85, 195, 229.

[243]It is impossible to suggest, even approximately, the degree of subsistence on the buffalo in this territory *circa* 1700-1800. We have noted that the Tuscarora

CHICKASAW: 18th cent. = 2000-6000 variously est.; 1744 = ?900 warriors, 3000-4000 people (Gatschet, C. Thomas, *HAN.*, I, 261).

CHOCTAW: 1700 *seq.* = 15,000-20,000 people (Swanton, Thomas, *HAN.*, I, 289).

CATAWBA: 1728 = 400 warriors, *c.* 1400 persons; 1743 = less than 400 warriors; 1761 = 300 warriors, *c.* 1000 pop.; 1775-84 = 400-490-250 souls (Mooney, *HAN.*, I, 215).

CREEK: *c.* 1775 = *c.* 20,000 in 40 to 60 towns; 1789 = *c.* 6000 warriors, 24,000 pop.; 1775 = est. 11,000 in 55 towns; 1785 = 5400 men, *c.* 19,000 pop. (*HAN.*, I, 364).

HURONS: 1736 = 1300; 1748 = 850, also 500; 1765 = 1250; 1794-95 = 1500 (Hewitt, *HAN.*, I, 590).

'IROQUOIS': 18th century = 10,000-12,000 souls (the 'Six Nations' and their colonies[244]); 1774 = est. 10,000-12,500 (Hewitt, *HAN.*, I, 619).

IROQUOIS CONFEDERACY:

CAYUGA: 1778 = 1100 (Mooney, Hewitt, *HAN.*, I, 223).

MOHAWK: *c.* 1700 = *c.* 1500; 1736 = 400; 1741 = 500; 1765 = 800; 1778 = 500; 1783 = 1500 (Hewitt, *HAN.*, I, 924).

ONEIDA: 1721 = 1000; 1770 = 410; 1776 = 628; 1795 = 660 ('decreasing for a long time': Hewitt, *HAN.*, II, 125).

ONONDAGA: 1721 = 1250; 1736 = 1000; 1765 = 1300; 1778 = 1150 ('not including those on the St. Lawrence':[245] Hewitt, *HAN.*, II, 133).

SENECA: 1721 = 3500; 1736 = 1750; 1765 = 5000; 1778 = 3250; 1783 = 3000, also 2000; 1796 = 1780 (Hewitt, *HAN.*, II, 507).

TUSCARORA (Confederacy after 1722): 1708 = 15 towns, 1200 warriors, *c.* 4800 pop.; so, Lawson, *c.* 1708 = 1200-1400 warriors, *c.* 5600 souls; so, Barnwell, 1736 = 250 warriors, *c.* 1000 total pop.; so Chauvignerie; but only ·those living near Oneida, N.Y. 1765 = 1000; 1778 = 2000; 1783 = 1000; 1796 = 400 in U.S. (Hewitt, *HAN.*, II, 851).

TUTELO, SAPONI, and others of the 'Tutelo Confederacy' (Siouan, Virginia —North Carolina): 1701 = 750 souls; 1763 = *c.* 1000 (Thomas, Swanton, Mooney, *HAN.*, II, 579, 856).

YUCHI: 1792 = 500 warriors, 1000-1500 pop. (Speck, *HAN.*, II, 1004) 'Indians under the French Govt.' 1736 = est. 82,000 souls[246] (Maclean, *Canadian Savage Folk*, p. 290).

BETWEEN THE GREAT LAKES AND THE MISSOURI
(NOT INCLUDING THE SIOUX)

Fox: 1728 = 200 warriors; 'most estimates *ante* 1750' = *c.* 1500-2000 souls; 1804 = 300 warriors, 1200 souls (Mooney, Thomas, *HAN.*, I, 474); 1804 = 1800 souls (*LE*, map); 1805 = 400 men, 500 women, 550 children (Pike, *CS*1., I, 346).

---

had a native name for buffalo, apparently not borrowed from any of the commoner root-forms (see Appendix A). The Tutelo had 'plenty of buffaloes' in their country, *circa* 1700 (Mooney, citing Lawson, *Handbook of American Indians*, II, 856).

[244]Originally 'Five Nations.' Six after the admission of the Tuscarora, 1722 (see *Handbook of American Indians*, II, 847).

[245]These last are probably the 'Saint Regis' Iroquois (*ibid.*, 412).

[246]This is hopelessly vague: ? So claimed by the government, acknowledged by its 'vassals,' or somebody's opinion.

ILLINOIS: 1750 = est. 1500-2000 souls (Mooney, Thomas, *HAN.*, I, 598).
KASKASKIA: 1764 = 600 persons; 1778 = 60 warriors, 210 total pop.
(Mooney, Thomas, *HAN.*, I, 598, 662).
KICKAPOO: 1759 = est. 3000 (Mooney, Jones, *HAN.*, I, 685).
MASCOUTEN: 1718 = 200 men (M. and Kickapoo); 1736 = 60 warriors
(Mooney, Thomas, *HAN.*, I, 811).
MENOMINEE: 1805 = 300 men, 350 women, 700 children (Pike, *CS1.*, I,
346).
MIAMI: 1764 = est. 1750; 1765 = est. 1250; 'probably never exceeded
1500' (Mooney, Thomas, *HAN.*, I, 854).
OJIBWA (CHIPPEWA): 1764 = 25,000 souls; 1783, 1794 = *c.* 15,000
(Mooney, Thomas, *HAN.*, I, 280); 1797 = 665 souls at Pembina Post,
Red River, 420 at Rainy River House (so Thompson, *Narrative*, p.249);
1804 = 500 on Red River, 48° N. (*LE.*, map); 1805 = 2049 men,
3184 women, 5944 children, total 11,177 (Pike, *CS1.*, I, 346).
PEORIA: 1736 = est. 250 souls (Chauvignerie: Mooney, Thomas, *HAN.*,
II, 228).
PIANKASHAW: P. Wea, Pepicokoa, together, 1736 = *c.* 1750 souls
(Chauvignerie); P. alone, 1759 = 1500; 1764 = est. 1250; 1780 = 950;
1795 = 800 (Mooney, *HAN.*, II, 240).
POTAWATAMI: 1765 = est. 1500; 1766 = 1750; 1778 = 2250, 1783 =
2,000; 1795 = 1200 (Mooney, Hewitt, *HAN.*, II, 290).
SAUK (1804 = Mississippi, below Rock River): 1736 = *c.* 750 persons;
1759 =1000; 1766 = 2000; 1783 = 2250; 1810 = 2850 (all, Hewitt,
HAN., II, 479); 1804 = 3000 (*LE*, map); 1805 = 700 men, 750
women, 1400 children (Pike, *CS1*, I, 346).
SHAWNEE: 1732 = 1750; 1736 = 1000; 1759 = 1765; 1778, 1783, 1794,
1812 = 1500; 1794 = 1000 (Mooney, *HAN.*, II, 536).
WINNEBAGO: 1805 = 450 men, 500 women, 1000 children (Pike, *CS1.*,
I, 346); 1806 = 1750 (Pike: Dorsey, Radin, *HAN.*, II, 961).

'BUFFALO INDIANS,' EAST OF THE ROCKY MOUNTAINS

'ALGONKIANS' (? Saulteaux—Ojibwa): 1804 = 600 souls, Fort Garry (*LE*,
map).
AMAHAMI (or 'AHNAHAWAYS'):[247] 1804 = *c.* 50 men, 250 souls (*LE*, I,
168, 172, 187, 188, 228, 231; III, 249-52; *TA.*, pp. 128, 174, 250).
APACHE (Maricopa and Pima: 1742 = 6000; 1775 = 3000 (Hodge, *HAN.*,
I, 806).
ARAPAHO: 1780 = 3000 (*MO.*, p. 13); see KANINAVIESCH, below.
ARIKARA: 1780 = 3000 (*MO.*, p. 13); 1804 = 3 villages, 80, 60, 60
lodges respectively; *c.* 175, 175, 350 men = *c.* 3600 souls (*CH.*, II,
862); 1804 = 3000 souls (*LE*, map); 1796 = 700 warriors; 1804 =
600 warriors (Maximilian, *EWT.*, XXIII, 230).
ARIZPE: 1730 = 316; 1777 = 359 (Hodge, *HAN.*, I, 87).
ARKOKISA: 1756 = 50 families; 1760-70 = 80 men (Fletcher, *HAN.*, I,
87).

---

[247]An extinct tribe, long merged with the Hidatsa: see Coues (ed.), *Henry-Thompson Journals*, I, 323; *Handbook of American Indians*, I, 47, 548; *Canadian Historical Review*, XV, 43.

Assiniboine: 1780 = 10,000 (*MO.*, p. 13); 1799-1800 = 3200 (*TH.*, 326); 1804 = 'between the Assiniboine and the Missouri rivers' 4 bands of 200, 250, 450, 500 (men) respectively; one, 200 men, 'roving on the Saskatchewan. . . .' (*LE.*, I, 205), *i.e. c.* 1600 men, 8000 souls; 1804 = west of Brandon, Manitoba, '1000 souls'; west of Assiniboine River lat. 50° N., '1200 souls'; Cypress Hills, lat. 49° N., '2000 souls' (all, *LE.*, map); Nov. 14, 1804: '70 lodges of one band of Southern A. at the Mandan villages' (*LE.*, I, 182); 1805 = 'A. computed at 1500 warriors,' *i.e. c.* 7500 souls (*CS1.*, I, 354); 1808 = 12 bands, 880 tents, 'perhaps *c.* 2000 men capable of bearing arms' (*CS2.*, II, 522) 'Probably 10,000 souls' (Maclean, *Canadian Savage Folk*, pp. 21-3).

Atsina: 1780 = 3000 (*MO.*, p. 13); 1798 = *c.* 500-1000 souls (*TH.*, p. 304); 1808 = 'about 80 tents, 240 warriors' (*CS2.*, II, 531); 1811 = 'over 100 tents; formerly very numerous, but smallpox carried off most of them' (? 1781: *CS2.*, II, 531, 733).

Beaver: 1770 = est. 1250 (*MO.*, p. 26).

Blackfoot (proper = Siksika): 1780 = 3000 (*MO.*, p. 13); 1754-55 = '200 tents of Archithinue Natives' ("Henday's Journal," p. 337); '*c.* 9000 in ancient times' (Jenness, *Indians of Canada*, p. 324); *c.* 1790 = 2250-2500 warriors, ?9000 souls (Alexander Mackenzie: Mooney, *HAN.*, II, 571); far greater *ante* 1781, but the total given is perhaps for the Confederacy; 1789 = 800 Siksika men (Mackenzie, *Voyages 1789 and 1793*, p. xci); 1804 = '3000 souls' (*LE.*, map); 1808 = 2 bands, 120, 80 tents; 360, 160 warriors, respectively; *c.* 2600 souls (Henry: *CS2.*, II, 530; cf. Maclean, *Canadian Savage Folk*, p. 294).

Blood (Kainah): *c.* 1789 = 50 tipis (Mackenzie, *Voyages 1789 and1793*, xci); about 250 men, 1000 individuals (*ibid.*; accepted by Kidd, "Blackfoot Ethnography," p. 25); 1808 = 100 tents, 200 warriors, *c.* 1000 souls (Henry: *CS2.*, II, 530); 200 tents, 400 warriors in two bands (*ibid.*).

Caddo: 1699 = 8 gentile divisions; 1716 = 11 (Fletcher, *HAN.*, I, 181); *c.* 1800 = 100-200; reduced by smallpox, 1801 to *c.* 25 (souls ?) in 1825. (*CS1.*, II, 711-14).

Carrizo (Coahuiltecan, a distinct tribe, 1742: *HAN.*, I, 209).[248]

Castahana: (Upper South Platte, 1804)[249] = '300 men' (*LE.*, I, 74); '1500 souls' (*LE.*, map); '5000 souls in 500 lodges' (*HAN.*, I, 212).

Cataka (Upper Tongue River, 1804): '75 men' (*LE.*, I, 74); '300 souls' (*LE.*, map).[250]

[248]Carrizo, Karankawa, Tonkawa = 'almost true buffalo Indians'; so Wissler, *American Anthropologist*, XVI, 1914, 462.

[249]These and others supposed, 1804, to be 'remnants of the great Padouca nation, whose very name was lost' (*Lewis and Clark Journals*, I, 74); but returning, 1806, they are 'a small band of Snake Indians' (*ibid.*, III, 232). The 'Padouca' are identified as Comanche (*Handbook of American Indians*, I, 328); which might pass the 'Snake' relationship—both Shoshonean. But the Castahana are considered probably Arapaho (*ibid.*, 212), and the Arapaho are Algonkian. See below, note 256.

[250]Identified by Mooney with the 'Gattacka' of La Salle, as Kiowa-Apache (*ibid.*, 702).

CHEYENNE: 1780 = 3500 souls (*MO.*, p. 13); 1804, 'Sharha or Chayenne'[251] = 'now reduced,' but still 300 men (*LE.*, I, 344); '3000 souls' (Upper Big Cheyenne River: *LE.*, map).

CHIPPEWYAN: 1670 = 2250 souls (*MO.*, p. 26) 'decimated by small-pox, 1779'; est. 1812 = 7500 (*HAN.*, I, 276).

COMANCHE (TETAU of Pike): 1806 = 2700 warriors, 3000 women, 2500 children; 8200 souls 'in 1020 lodges of roving bands' (*CS1.*, II, 589).

CREE: 1670 (including Maskegon = 'Swampy Cree')[252] = 15,000 souls (*MO.*, p. 26); 1776 (Cree proper, without Maskegon) 'before small-pox had greatly reduced them' = 15,000 (Mooney, Thomas, *HAN.*, I, 361); 1786, 'less than half their former number' (Umfreville: *ibid.*, 360); 1797 'not a third now remaining' (McDonnell, in Masson, *Les Bourgeois de la Compagnie du Nord-Ouest*, I, 277); 1809 = not including those north of Beaver River, Alberta, 'about 300 tents, *c.* 900 warriors, or 4500 souls, of Plain Crees' (Henry: *CS2.*, II, 516).

CROW: 1780 = 4000 souls (*MO.*, p. 13); 1804 = 350 lodges, 3500 souls (*HAN.*, I, 368).

DOTAME or DOTAMI: 1804 = 'supposed to be a remnant of the great Padouca nation,' no number given (*LE.*, I, 74); 120 souls, Upper Tongue River, Wyoming (*LE.*, map); 'possibly Kiowa' (so *HAN.*, I, 399).

HIDATSA ('true' Minatari, Gros Ventres of the Missouri): 1780 = 2500 souls (*MO.*, p. 13); 1797 = *c.* 1600 souls (*TH.*, p. 236);[253] 1804 = *c.* 550 warriors, ? 1950 souls (Mooney, *HAN.*, I, 548); 1804 = 3000 souls (*LE.*, map);[254] 1806 = formerly 900 huts; reduced by small-pox, etc., to 130 huts; apparently one family per hut, polygamous in many or most cases (*CS2.*, I, 334).

IOWA: 1760 = 1100 souls (*HAN.*, I, 613); 1780 = 1200 souls (*MO.*, p. 13); 1804 = 300 men (*LE.*, I, 48); 1804 = 200 warriors, 800 souls (100 men, also women and children, lost by smallpox, 1803; so J. O. Dorsey, Thomas, *HAN.*, I, 613); 1805 = 300 men, 400 women, 700 children, total of 1400 (*CS1.*, I, 346).[255]

KANINAVIESCH or KA-NE-NA-VISH (as *LE.*, map): supposedly a 'Ricara band' of emigrants from the Pawnee = 400 men (*LE.*, I, 73, 142, 155); '1800 souls,' west of the Forks of the Platte (*LE.*, map).[256]

KANS, KANSA, KANSAS: 1702 = est. 1500 families (Iberville: *HAN.*, I, 654); 1780 = 3000 souls (*MO.*, p. 13) 1804 = 2 villages, Kansas River

[251]Known as 'Chaa,' 1680; so, *Handbook of American Indians*, I, 251.

[252]See on these, Mooney, Thomas, *ibid.*, 361, 813.

[253]Counted in conjunction with the Atsina (Gros Ventre of modern Alberta) as 2200-2500, 1797 (Thompson, *Narrative*, 236). Atsina then 500-1000, or *circa* 750 (*ibid.*, 304); cf. 1330 souls, 1797 (*ibid.*, 228).

[254]Lewis and Clark cited as '2500 souls' by Maclean, *Canadian Savage Folk*, 290; Chittenden, *American Fur Trade*, II, 858.

[255]These are the Ayauway, Ayauwa, Ayoway, Ayaway, of Lewis and Clark (*Journals*, I, 48, 90; II, 81; III, 293), the Aouays of De Smet (*Early Western Travels*, XXVII, 166). 'A branch of the Otoes,' so Lewis and Clark (*Journals*, I, 75), at that time apparently correct (see *Handbook of American Indians*, I, 612).

[256]The Arikara and Pawnee are Caddoan, but the Kaninaviesch are identified as Arapaho, who are Algonkian (Coues (ed.), *Henry-Thompson Journals*, I, 384; *Handbook of American Indians*, I, 74; Wissler, *American Indian*, 403, 405).

= *c.* 300 men, 1500 souls; 'the old village (site) must once have been a large town.' (*LE.*, I, 55-9); 1804 = '1200 souls' (*LE.*, map); 1806 = 465 men, 500 women, 600 children, 1565 in one village of 1204 lodges (Pike, 'on information': *CS1.*, II, 589).

KARANKAWA: E. 1858. Seven probable and 32 possible villages enumerated (Fletcher, Swanton, *HAN.*, I, 658).[257]

KEE HEETSA (CROWS):[258] Big Horn River, 1804 = 4000 souls (*LE.*, map).

'KEYES or KEYCHIAS' (KICHAI): 1772 = 30 houses, 80 warriors; 1778 = 100 warriors (Fletcher, *HAN.*, I, 683); 1805 = 60 men, *c.* 300 souls (Sibley: *CS1.*, II, 708).

'KIAWA' (apparently KIOWA): 'Wetapahato and Kiawa' associated, Upper South Platte, 1804 = 200 men (*LE.*, I, 74); '1800 souls' (*LE.*, map).

KIOWA: 1780 = 2000 souls (*MO.*, p. 13); 1807 = '1000 men strong' (Pike: *CS1.*, II, 744).

KIOWA APACHE: 1780 = 300 souls; 1804 = 300 in 25 tipis (Mooney, *HAN.*, I, 702).[259]

LIPAN: 1805 = 3 bands, totalling 750 men alone (Hodge, *HAN.*, I, 768).

MANDAN: 1780 = 3600 souls (*MO.*, p. 13); 1797 = 5 villages, 220 warriors, 1520 souls (Thompson, *TH.*, p. 228); 1804 = 40 years ago (*i.e.* *c.* 1764) were in 9 villages; now in 2 only, each about 40 or 50 lodges, 'about 350 men,' or *c.* 1550 souls (*LE.*, I, 186); '1000 souls' (*LE.*, map); *c.* 1804 = 1250 souls (Dorsey, Thomas, *HAN.*, I, 798).[260]

MESCALERO (*HAN.*, I, 846): no numbers available.

MISSOURI: 1702 = 200 families (Dorsey, Thomas, *HAN.*, I, 911); 1780 = 1000 souls (*MO.*, p. 13); 1805 = 300 souls (Lewis and Clark: *ibid*); 1805 = 'about 30 families of this once great and powerful nation. . . .' (*LE.*, I, 49).[261]

NATCHEZ: 1731 = 450 captured; 1735 = 'third and most numerous division,' 180 warriors, or *c.* 700 total; 1799 = 'gun-men' est. 50 (Henshaw, Swanton, *HAN.*, II, 36).

NATCHITOCH: 1730 = 200 cabins (Fletcher, Swanton, *HAN.*, II, 37); *c.*

[257]See above, note 248.

[258]So, *Handbook of American Indians*, "Synonymy," II, 1071.

[259]". . . thought to be a distinct tribe, not closely related to the Apaches of the mountains . . ." (Grinnell, *Indians of To-day*, 103, 119). See also *Handbook of American Indians*, I, 701; cf. Kroeber, *Cultural and Natural Areas*, 37, 47, 48, 79-86, 187.

[260]Mandans = '6000 in the earliest known times' (? 1738): Chittenden, *American Fur Trade*, II, 860. On the computation above of *circa* 775 souls per village, nine of about equal size = *circa* 7000 population, *circa* 1764. But were they equal, 1804—or ever? Henry, 1806, speaks of 'the great village of the Mandanes . . .' (Coues (ed.), *Henry-Thompson Journals*, I, 329). Cf. above, notes 36-43.

[261]On the inroads of the Sauk on the Missouri and Little Osage, 'a few years' *ante* 1804, see *Lewis and Clark Journals*, I, 49, 51. The 30 families lived with the Oto, 'whose language resembled theirs' (*ibid.*, 72, 75, 89). Virtually identical (*Handbook of American Indians*, I, 612; above, note 255).

1750 = c. 300 souls (*CS1.*, II, 714); 1805 = 50 (Sibley: *HAN.*, II, 37); E. soon after 1805.[262]

NAVAJO: 1806 = 'supposed to be 2000 warriors strong'; or about 9000-10,000 souls (Pike: *CS1.*, II, 746).[263]

OMAHA: 1780 = 2800 souls (*MO.*, p. 13); 1802 = c. 300 souls (small-pox); 1804 = 150 warriors, 600 total (both, *HAN.*, II, 120); 1804 = 'about 200 Mahas' (? men or souls); 'once about 300 cabins'; 75 men slain by Sioux in one fight, Sept. 1804 (*LE.*, I, 86, 112, 135); 'the Mahar village = 1500 souls' (*LE.*, map).

OSAGE (Wasbasha): 1780 = 6200 souls (*MO.*, p. 13); 1701 = probably 1200-1500 families; 1719 = one band, 100 cabins, 200 warriors (Du Tisne: Swanton, *HAN.*, II, 157).

GRAND OSAGE: 1804 = c. 500 warriors (*LE.*, I, 43-4); Pike 1806: "I last evening took the census of the Grand village, and found it to be: men 502; boys 341; women and girls 852; total 1695; lodges 214. . . ." (*CS1.*, II, 582, 589); 1805 = 400 (Sibley: *HAN.*, II, 158).

LITTLE OSAGE: 1804 = 'nearly 250 warriors': (*LE.*, I, 43); 1805 = 250 (? warriors–Sibley: *HAN.*, II, 158); 1806, census by Pike = 250 men, 241 women, 159 male children, 174 female, 824 souls in 102 lodges (*CS1.*, II, 589).

ARKANSAS RIVER WASBASHA: 1804 = 600 warriors (*LE.*, I, 43); 1805 = 600 (Sibley: *HAN.*, II, 158); 1806 *ex inf.* Grand Osage chiefs to Pike = 500 men, 700 women, 300 male children (? 300 female children also) = 1800 souls in one village of 200 lodges (*CS1.*, II, 589).

OTO: 1780 = 900 (*MO.*, p. 13); 1805 = 200 men (this including the 30 families of Missourie then living with them: *LE.*, I, 49, 72); 1805 = 500 (Lewis and Clark: *HAN.*, II, 160).

PAWNEE: 1702 = est. 2000 families (Iberville: Fletcher, *HAN.*, II, 216); 1780 = 10,000 souls (*MO.*, p. 13).[264]

GRAND P.: 1804 = c. 500 men (*LE.*, I, 72); 1806 = 1000 warriors, 1120 women, 1100 children, 3120 souls in one village of 90 lodges (Pike: *CS1.*, II, 589).

P. MAHAS, P. LOUPS, WOLF P., SKIDI: 1804 = 280 warriors (*LE.*, I, 72); 1806 = 485 warriors, 500 women, 500 children = 1485 in one village of 40 lodges (Pike: *CS1.*, II, 589): 1805 = '1500 souls' (Pawnee Loup River: *LE.*, map; *HAN.*, II, 216, 589).

P. REPUBLICANS: 1804 = 'nearly 250 men' (*LE.*, I, 72); 1806 = 508 men, 550 women, 500 children = 1558 in one village of 44 lodges (Pike: *CS1.*, II, 589).

[262]An elderly French gentleman (to Sibley, 1805) 'remembered the time when the Natchitoches were 600 men strong . . .' (Coues (ed.), *Expeditions of Pike*, II, 708, 714).

[263]Very probably buffalo-users in part, by trade. See above, note 237.

[264]See *Handbook of American Indians* (I, 532) on 'Harahey,' apparently a Pawnee community, 1541. Cf. *taraháh* = buffalo (Pawnee: above, Appendix A). Was Harahey by chance another 'buffalo province'? as above, note 242.

TAPAGE P. or PITAHAUERAT (*HAN.*, II, 214, 216, 263): no numbers available.

'P. OF THE ARKANSAS' ('P. Piqua' or 'P. Picts'): 1804 = 400 men (*LE.*, I, 72).[265]

PIEGANS: 1790 = 'reduced by small-pox to only 150 tents; but now [*c.* 1810] increasing fast' (Henry: *CS2.*, II, 722); much more numerous *ante* 1781; est. 1789 = 1200-1500 men, 8000-8500 souls (Mackenzie, *Voyages 1789 and 1793* p. cxi; E. Curtis, *North American Indian,* VI, 5; Kidd, "Blackfoot Ethnography," pp 25-6); 1810 = Piegans 'the most numerous' of the Confederacy: having 350 tents, 700 warriors, *c.* 3500 souls (*CS2.*, II, 530).

PONCA: 1780 = 800 souls (*MO.*, p. 13); 1804 = 'about 50 men; once *c.* 400 men; decline owing to small-pox and Sioux' (*LE.*, I, 112); 1804 = '200 souls' (Rivière qui Court, trib. Missouri River; *LE.*, map: as also Dorsey, Thomas, *HAN.*, II, 278).

QUAPAW (Akansa, Arkansas): 1750 = 400 warriors; est. 1400-1600 souls (Thomas, *HAN.*, II, 335).

SARSI, SARCEE: 1670 = est. 700 souls (*MO.*, p. 26); 1790 = 'one of the leading tribes trading with H. B. Co.' = 35 tents, 120 warriors (Mackenzie, *Voyages 1789 and 1793,* p. lxx); "always a small tribe, apparently. . . ." Jenness, *Sarcee Indians,* p. 6); *c.* 1800 = '650 souls,' or *c.* 500-1000 (Thompson, *TH.*, pp. 304, 327); 1809 = 90 tents, *c.* 150 warriors (Henry *CS2.*, II, 532); 'about 700 souls' (Maclean, *Canadian Savage Folk,* pp. 9-19).

'SIOUX': 1780 = 25,000 (*MO.*, p. 13); 'late 18th century, south of the Missouri' = *c.* 18,000 (*CH.*, II, 863); 1796 = 1300-1400 'Sioux' (or again 1000-1200) attacking the Mandan villages (Maximilian, *EWT.*, XXIII, 230; XXIV, 21).

MDEWAKANTON: 1804 = 300 men, 'nearly 300 men' (*LE.*, I, 104, 204); '1800 souls' (*LE.*, map); 300 warriors, 1200 souls (Dorsey, Thomas, *HAN.*, I, 827).

SISSETON: 1804 = 200 men, *c.* 200 warriors (*LE.*, I, 104, 204); 200 men, 800 people (Lewis and Clark: so Thomas, Swanton, *HAN.*, II, 581); 900 souls (Upper Red River, below Wahpekute: *LE.*, map).

TETON (*a*) Sichangu or Brulé: 1804 = *c.* 300 men, 200 warriors (*LE.*, I, 104, 204); '1500 souls' (Great Bend of the Missouri: *LE.*, map);

   (*b*) HUNKPAPA (Teton Saone of 1804?[266]): 1804 = 120 *tipis,* 300 men, *c.* 900 souls (*HAN.*, I, 579);

   (*c*) MINICONJOU: 1804= *c.* 250 men (*LE.*, I, 104, 204); 250 men = 850 souls, 'probably many more' (so Dorsey, Thomas, *HAN.*, I, 868); '1000 souls' (Missouri River, 45° N.: *LE.*, map).

   (*d*) OGLALA: 1804 = 150 men (*LE.*, I, 104, 204); '200 men, in 100 cabins' (*ibid.*, p. 135) 600 souls (Big Cheyenne River: *LE.*, map);

---

[265]Apparently not Pawnee at all. See 'Waco,' below, p. 791.

[266]So *Handbook of American Indians,* I, 579. The Yanktons and 'Titons' est. 600 tents, *circa* 1790 (Coues (ed.), *Henry-Thompson Journals,* I, 358). Tetons, 1804 = *circa* 1000 men, 4000 souls; probably much less than the true number (Thomas, *Handbook of American Indians,* II, 737).

(e) SIHASAPA (Blackfoot Sioux), or OOHENONPA (Two Kettle Sioux[267]):
1804 = c. 300 men (*LE.*, I, 104, 204); '1500 souls' (Missouri River,
above 46° N.; *LE.*, map).[268]

WAHPEKUTE: 1804 = 150 men (*LE.*, I, p. 104; *HAN.*, II, 890); 'not
more than 100 men' (*ibid.*, I, 204); '600 souls' (*LE.*, map).[269]

WAHPETON: 1804 = '200 men,' 'nearly 200 men' (*LE.*, I, 104, 204);
'1000 souls' (St. Peter's River: *LE.*, map).

YANKTON: 1804 (Y. of the Plains) = c. 500 men = c. 2200 souls (*LE.*,
I, 104, 204); 1807 = 700 (? men: so Lewis, *HAN.*, II, 989); '1000
souls' (Jacques, or James River: *LE.*, map).

YANKTONAI (? 'Yankton of the South'): 1804 = 200 warriors (*LE.*,
I, 104); 1806 = 500 men, c. 1750 total (Lewis: so Thomas, *HAN.*,
II, 990); 1805 = Yanktonai and Yankton together = 4300 (Pike:
ibid.).

STAITANS ('Kites' or 'Flyers'): 1804 = '100 men, 500 souls' (Upper Tongue
River: *LE.*, map) or Lodge Pole Creek;[270] E. shortly after.

TONKAWA ('Tancards' of Pike[271]): 1778 = est. 300 warriors; 1779 = 150
warriors (following small-pox); 1782 = '600 Tonkawa present'—men
or souls?; 1805 = 200 men (Sibley: *CS1.*, II, 705; Bolton, *HAN.*, II,
782); 1805 = '600 men strong' (*CS1.*, II, 785); 1809 = 200 families
(*HAN.*, II, 782).

TUNICA: 1700 = 7 hamlets, '50 or 60 small cabins'; 1802 = 120 men, c.
450 total pop. (*HAN.*, II, 838).

UTE (see *HAN.*, II, 874).

WETAPAHATO (and KIAWA = Kiowa): 1804 = 200 men (*LE.*, I, 74);
'1800 souls' (Upper South Platte River: *LE.*, map).

6. ESTIMATED NUMBERS 1811 TO 1911

EAST OF THE MISSISSIPPI RIVER

East of the Mississippi, the buffalo were virtually extinct in 1811; and
tribal numbers given for what may formerly have been buffalo territory
can have no significance in relation to buffalo *consumption* at this time.
They may serve, however, to assist as a possible check upon earlier and

[267]Apparently; but neither were mentioned by Lewis and Clark (so, *ibid.*,
136, 568).

[268]Lewis and Clark's total for the Sioux = 9900 souls; Pike, 1805 = 3835
men, 6433 women, 11,800 children, total 21,068 (Coues (ed.), *Expeditions of
Pike*, I, 346).

[269]These and the Mdewakanton constitute the Santee (*Handbook of American
Indians*, II, 579).

[270]Apparently a division of Cheyenne (so Mooney, *Handbook of American
Indians*, I, 251). 'Lodge Pole Creek' is from Taylor, *Frontier Life*, 24-7. The
likeliest in Taylor's own range is the one in Perkins County, South Dakota; but
the Cheyenne identification may admit the other—a tributary of the South Platte,
used by the Union Pacific main line.

[271]'A *colluvies gentium* or fusion of tribes': Major J. W. Powell, cited by
Coues (ed.), *Expeditions of Pike*, II, 705; cf. Wissler, *American Indian*, 237; also
above, note 248.

more speculative estimates; but we should bear in mind the warnings concerning admixtures of other blood in many so-called 'Indians.'[272]

CATAWBA (Virginia, Carolina[273]): 1882 = 450; 1826 = 110; 1881 = 120 (*HAN.*, I, 215); 1907 = 90 (*MO.*, p. 6).

CHEROKEE: 'Several years' *ante* 1835 = 6000-7000; 1835 = 22,000, 6000 in Georgia (*CAT.*, II, 119, 120); 1838 = *c.* 22,500; 1885 = *c.* 19,000; 1902 (including mixed bloods) = 28,016 (*HAN.*, I, 247); 1907 (Gulf States) = 25,000 (*MO.*, p. 8).

CHICKASAW: 1822 = 3265; 1865 = 4500; 1904 = 4826 (*HAN.*, I, 261); 1907 (Mississippi) = 5000 (*MO.*, pp. 8-9).

CHOCTAW: 1822 = 25,000; 1700 onward = variously from 15,000-20,000; 1904 = 17,805 (*HAN.*, I, 261, 289); 1907 = 18,000 (*MO.*, p. 8).

CREEK CONFEDERACY: *c.* 1835 = 20,000 (Creeks or Mus-ko-gees: *CAT.*, II, 122); *c.* 1840 = about 15,000-20,000; 1904 = 9905 'Creeks by blood,' Oklahoma (*HAN.*, I, 364); 1907 = 11,000 (*MO.*, p. 8).

DELAWARES: 19th century estimates = 2400-3000; 1836 = 800, 'once 10,000-15,000' (*CAT.*, II, 102); 1906 (Pennsylvania, New York, New Jersey) = *c.* 1900 (*HAN.*, I, 386).

FOX: 1907 = a band of 345 in Iowa (*HAN.*, I, 474; *MO.*, p. 11); 1911 = 541 in Oklahoma (*GN.*, p. 285).

HURON: 1812 = 1000; 1885 (Oklahoma) = 251; 1905 = 378 (Hewitt, *HAN.*, I, 590); Canada, 1911 = 487 (*Handbook of Canadian Indians*, p. 212).

ILLINOIS CONFEDERACY:

PEORIA: 1835 = *c.* 200 (*CAT.*, II, 101); 1896 (Oklahoma) = 192 (*HAN.*, II, 228).

PIANKASHAW: 1825 = 234 (*HAN.*, II, 240); 1835 = *c.* 170 (*CAT.*, II, 101).

WEA: 1835 = *c.* 200 (in Kansas: *CAT.*, II, 99).

In 1854 the four consolidated tribes (as above with Kaskaskia) = 259; 1885 = 149; 1909 = *c.* 200 (*HAN.*, I, 598; II, 228, 240, 925); see also, MIAMI.

'IROQUOIS': 1896 = '8000 in Canada' (Maclean, *Canadian Savage Folk*, p. 160); 1904 (U.S.) = 5290; 1911 (Canada) = 10, 738; total, 16,028 (Hewitt, *HAN.*, I, 619; *Handbook of Canadian Indians*, p. 228).

IROQUOIS CONFEDERACY:

CAYUGA: 1906 (U.S.) = 175; 1910 (Canada) = 1063 (*HAN.*, I, 223; *Handbook of Canadian Indians*, p. 83; *GN.*, p. 246).

MOHAWK: 1851 = *c.* 1200; 1884 = 965 (Canada); 1910 = 1473 (Canada: *HAN.*, I, 924; *Handbook of Canadian Indians*, p. 310; *GN.*, p. 246).

ONEIDA: *c.* 1835 = 500-600 (*CAT.*, II, 103); 1906-10 = 2430 (U.S.), 1140 (Canada); so *HAN.*, II, 125; *Handbook of Canadian Indians*, p. 364; *GN.*, p. 246.

ONONDAGA: 1851 (Canada) = *c.* 900; 1906-10 = 553 (U.S.), 367 (Canada); *HAN.*, II, 133; *Handbook of Canadian Indians*, p. 368; *GN.*, p. 246.

[272]See above, note 104.
[273]These localities refer to the active historical period.

SENECA: 1825 (U.S.) = 2325; 1835 = 1200; 1850 = 2712; 1909-10
=2749, 2735; (Canada): 1850 = 210; 1911 = 219 (*CAT.*, II, 104;
HAN., II, 507; *Handbook of Canadian Indians*, p. 419; *GN.*, p. 246).

ST. REGIS: 1909 = 1501 (Canada); 1349 (U.S.); 1910 = 1368 (? U.S.
alone; *HAN.*, II, 413; *GN.*, p. 246).

TUSCARORA: *c.* 1835 = 500 (*CAT.*, II, 103); 1885 (U.S.) = 414; 1910
= 368; Canada, 1885 = 414; 1910 = 416; 1911 = 421 (*HAN.*,
II, 852; *Handbook of Canadian Indians*, p. 496; *GN.*, p. 246).

KICKAPOO: 1817 = 2000; 1825 = 2200; 1835 = 600-800; 1875 = *c.* 800;
1885 (U.S. and Mexico) = 700; 1905 (same) = 832; 1907 (same) =
830; 1910 (Kansas) = 209 (*CAT.*, II, 97; *HAN.*, I, 685; *GN.*, p. 215;
MO., p. 11).

MENOMINEE: 19th cent. commonly est. 1600-1900; 1835 = *c.* 3000 (*CAT.*,
II, 147); 1907 = 1375 (*MO.*, p. 11); 1909 = 1600 (*HAN.*, I, 843);
1910 = 1509 (*GN.*, p. 213).

MIAMI: 1825 = 1400 (327 WEA: *HAN.*, I, 854); 1907 = 530 (*MO.*,
p. 11); 1910 = 527 (*GN.*, pp. 293, 342).

MOHEGAN: 1804-09 = 84-69; 1825 = 300; 1832 = 350; 1835 = 400
(*HAN.*, I, 786, 926; *CAT.*, II, 103).

NATCHEZ (Mississippi): 1907 = ? 25 (*MO.*, pp. 8-9).

OJIBWA, or CHIPPEWA: 1835 = '3000 at one treaty' (*CAT.*, II, 161);
1840 = est. 15,000 souls (Thwaites, *EWT.*, XXIII, 191); 1843 = *c.*
30,000 (Mooney, Thomas, *HAN.*, I, 280); 1844 = 2298 'Chippewas,
Pottawatomies, and Ottawas of the North' (Report, Commissioner for
Indian Affairs, cited by Gregg, *EWT.*, XX, 341); 1851 = *c.* 28,000
(*HAN.*, I, 280), 'probably exclusive of more remote bands'; 1884 = *c.*
16,000 in U.S. (*HAN.*, I, 280); 1905 = 15,000 in Canada, 17,000 in
U.S. (*ibid.*); 1907 (U.S. and Canada) = 36,000 (*MO.*, p. 11); 1910,
13 bands or reservations in U.S. = *c.* 18,800 (*GN.*, pp. 158, 181,
222-5, 243, 267, 275, 333, 341); in Canada, 1884 = 9000 (Ontario),
17,129 (Manitoba and N.W.T.); Chippewa = Cree (*HAN.*, I, 280);
1912 (Canada) = 21,000 (*Handbook of Canadian Indians*, p. 98).

OTTAWA: 1906 = *c.* 4700 (U.S.); ?750 (Canada); 1910 = 208 (Oklahoma: Mooney, Hewitt, *HAN.*, I, 280; II, 171; *GN.*, p. 293).

POTAWATOMI: 1812 = 2500; 1820 = 3400; *c.* 1835 = 2700 (*CAT.*, II,
99); 1843 = 1800; 1844 = *c.* 750 (Gregg, *EWT.*, XX, 341; as above,
s.v. OJIBWA); 1908 (U.S. and Canada) = 2522, 220 = total, 2742
(*HAN.*, II, 291); 1910 (Kansas and Oklahoma) = 2379 (*GN.*, pp. 267,
296).

SAUK: 1825 = *c.* 4800; 1834 = 2500 (Sauk alone); 1835 (Sauk and Fox)
= 5000-6000 (*CAT.*, II, 211); 1820 (both) = 3000; 1825 = 6400;
1834 = 5300; 1837 = 5000; 1844 = 2762 (Gregg, *EWT.*, XX, 341);
1885 = 930; 1909 = 975 (*HAN.*, II, 479); 1907 = 608 'Sauk' (*MO.*,
p. 11); 1910 (Sauk Reserve, Iowa) = 365 (*GN.*, p. 282).

SEMINOLE: *c.* 1835 = 3000-4000 (*CAT.*, II, 218); 1907 = 2200 (*MO.*,
p. 8); 1910 = *c.* 500 (*GN.*, p. 292).[274]

SHAWNEE: 1812 = 1500, 1600; 1817 = 2000; 1835 = *c.* 1200 (*CAT.*,

[274]This wide discrepancy is probably to be ascribed to inclusion or exclusion
of mixed bloods; on which see *Handbook of American Indians*, II, 501.

II, 116); 1907 = -1500 (*MO.*, p. 11); 1909 = 1400 (*HAN.*, II, 536); 1910 = 558 (also another band, not enumerated: *GN.*, p. 293).

TUNICA: 1907 = ?50 (*MO.*, pp. 8-9; *GN.*, p. 137).

WINNEBAGO: 1820 = 5800; 1835 = 4000 (*CAT.*, II, 146); 1837, 1843 = 4500; 1844 = 2183 (Gregg, *EWT.*, XX, 341); 1867 = 2450; 1876 = 2323; 1886 = 2152; 1907 = 2333 (*MO.*, p. 11); 1910 = 2323, 2333 (*HAN.*, II, 961; *GN.*, pp. 135, 249, 345).

YUCHI (Gulf States): 1907 = 700 (*MO.*, pp. 8-9); 1909 = less than 500; (Oklahoma: *HAN.*, II, 1005); 1910 = 'several hundred' (*GN.*, p. 138).

MISSISSIPPI RIVER TO THE ROCKY MOUNTAINS

APACHE:[275] *c.* 1850 = 4000 (exclusive of Gila River or *Gileños*, non-buffalo bands:[276] *BA4*, p. 462); 1880 = '3000 in Arizona' (*ibid.*, p. 727); 1894 = *c.* 6000 (*CS1.*, II, 748); 1907 = 4500 (*MO.*, p. 22); 1910 = 400 (? 4000: *GN.*, p. 162).

'APACHES':

CHEMEHUEVI: 1853 = 1500; 1866 = 750; 1903 = 'over 300' (*HAN.*, I, 242); 1907 = 144 (*MO.*, p. 22); 1910= 199 (*GN.*, pp. 140, 172).

HUALAPAI or WALAPAI: 1867 = *c.* 1500; 1894 = *c.* 750 (*CS1.*, II, 736); 1889 = 728; 1897 = 631; 1907 = 525 (*MO.*, p. 22); 1910 = 498 (*HAN.*, II, 899; *GN.*, p. 207).

JICARILLA: 1850 = '*c.* 17,000' (*BA4.*, pp. 462, 658, 665, 736, 781); 1894 = 800 (*CS1.*, II, 748); 1905 = 795 (*HAN.*, I, 632) or 750 (Thwaites, ed. note, *EWT.*, XX, 70); 1907 = 776 (*MO.*, p. 18).

LIPAN: 1805 = 3 bands, 750 men (*HAN.*, I, 768); 1907 = 25 (*MO.*, p. 13).

MARICOPA: 1894 (exclusive of Cocopas) = *c.* 300 (*CS1.*, II, 736); 1905 = 350 (*HAN.*, I, 806); 1907 = 383 (*MO.*, p. 22); 1910 = 94 (*GN.*, pp. 119, 140, 286).

MESCALERO: 1894 = c. 5000 (*CS1.*, II, 748); 1907 = 466 (*MO.*, p. 13); 1910 = 453 (*GN.*, p. 230).

MOJAVE: 1834 = 4000, 'probably an overestimate' (*HAN.*, I, 921); 1894 = *c.* 1850 (*CS1.*, II, 736); 1905 = 1589 (*HAN.*, I, 921); 1907 = 1309 (*MO.*, p. 22); 1910 = 1390 (*GN.*, pp. 140, 162, 171, 172).

WHITE MOUNTAIN APACHE: 1894 = *c.* 1900 (*CS1.*, II, 748); 1910 = 2269 (*HAN.*, II, 945: *GN.*, p. 189).

YAVAPAI (also Mojave): 1903 = 500-600; 1906 = 520 (*HAN.*, II, 994); 1907 = 655 (*MO.*, p. 22); 1910 = 7 (*GN.*, p. 162).

YAVASUPAI or HAVASUPAI: 1869 = 300 (*HAN.*, I, 538); 1894 = *c.* 200 (*CS1.*, II, 736); 1902 = 233; 1905 = 174 (*HAN.*, I, 538); 1907 = 172 (*MO.*, p. 22); 1910 = 177 (*GN.*, pp. 140, 206).

[275]It is almost impossible to decide what early writers mean by 'Apache' without particularization, e.g. Dr. Gregg quotes from the Report of the Commissioner for Indian Affairs, 1844: '100 Apaches' (*Early Western Travels*, XX, 341). Whether this is a misprint for 1000 or 10,000, or has some special application, nobody can say. Those above are mentioned as Apaches, *sans phrase*.

[276]The best classification is that of Kroeber, *Cultural and Natural Areas*, 34-8. See also *Handbook of American Indians*, I, 63; Coues (ed), *Expeditions of Pike*, II, 735, 746; Wissler, *American Indian*; etc.

'YUMA APACHE' or YUMA: 1853 = 3000 (*HAN.*, II, 1010); 1894, Yuma proper, Cuchans = *c.* 1300 (*CS1.*, II, 736); 1910 = 677 (*GN.*, pp. 162, 340).

ARAPAHO: 1843 = 2000 (Report, Comm. Ind. Affairs, cited by Gregg, *EWT.*, XX, 342); 1876 = 2294 Northern A. and Cheyennes, *c.* 1100 Arapaho (*BA8.*, p. 777); 1894 = 2638; 1904 = 2283 (Mooney, *HAN.*, I, 73); 1904 also = *c.* 1700 (Thwaites, *EWT.*, XV, 157); 1907 = 1774 (*MO.*, p. 13); 1910 = 892, 861 (*GN.*, pp. 165, 300).[277]

ARIKARA: 1832 = *c.* 4000 souls, 500-600 warriors; or 3000 to 4000 souls, 500 warriors (both, Maximilian, *EWT.*, XXII, 336; XXIII, 387); 1841 = *c.* 1000 (De Smet, *ibid.*, XXVII, 166); 1843 = 1200 (Report, Comm. Ind. Affairs, cited by Gregg, *ibid.*, XX, 341); 1871 = 1650; 1888 = 500; 1904 = 380 (*HAN.*, I, 84); 1907 = 389 (*MO.*, p. 13); 1910 = 411 (*GN.*, p. 193).[278]

ARKANSA, KWAPA, QUAPAW (see QUAPAW, below).

ASSINIBOINE: '28,000 in the best days of the fur trade' (? 1830: *CH.*, II, 857); 1835=7000 warriors in 3000 tents; or 'eight divisions' = 28,000 (Maximilian, *EWT.*, XXII, 304, 387); '20,000 [1833] not too high,' based upon Long's 25,000, with 6,000 warriors, in 1825 (*ibid.*); 1829 = 8000 (Porter); 1835 = 6000 (*CAT.*, I, 53); 1836 = 10,000 (Drake); 1836 = 6000 (Gallatin);[279] South Assiniboines 'up to 1838' = 1000-1200 lodges (Hayden; all *HAN.*, I, 104); 1839 = 8000 (Farnham, *EWT.*, XXVIII, 156); 1839 (South Assiniboine of the Missouri) = 400 lodges (*HAN.*, I, 103); 1841 (Saskatchewan District H. B. Co.[280]) est. Simpson = 580 tents, 4060 souls (Simpson, *Journey Around the World*, I, 102); 1842, Lefroy, 'A. in N.W. Canada' = 3600; Shaw, = 4000 (both *MCSF.*, p. 23); 1842 (Rowand, Harriott[281]), Plains A. = 240; Strongwood A. = 640 (*MCSF.*, p. 23); 1842 (the same two authorities) Strongwood A. = 3020 (*HI.*, p. 115); 1843 (U.S. Indian Report) =7000 (*HAN.*, I, 104); *c.* 1850 'A. from the Missouri into Rupert's Land': ? Schoolcraft) = 8900 (*HI.*, p. 117); 1850 (Upper Missouri and tributaries, *i.e.* U.S. Assiniboine only ?) = *c.* 4800 (*MCSF.*, p. 23); 1856 (Southern A., Hayden) = 250 lodges; 1862 (Northern A., Hayden) = 250-300 lodges (both, *HAN.*, I, 103); 1866 = 1200 (*BA2.*, p. 692); 1890 (N.W. Canada, *Dominion Blue Book*) = 1342 (*MCSF.*, p. 23); 1890 (U.S. and Canada) = 3008; 1904 (U.S.) = 1234 (both, *HAN.*, I, 104); *c.* 1896 (U.S. = 1673; Canada =1337)

---

[277]Such wide variations indicate that our authorities are reasoning from different data. Below, note 281.

[278]De Smet (*Early Western Travels*, XXVII, 166), gives 3000 Mandans, 'Big Bellies,' and Arikara, as though one community. For convenience, although it is probably not strictly correct to do so, I have given them one-third each. Taylor notes an Arikara band, the 'wanderers' of 1804, exterminated by smallpox, 1842 (*Frontier Life*, 204).

[279]Drake's figure, before the smallpox, when 4000 perished; Gallatin's apparently after (so, *Handbook of American Indians*, I, 104). On Catlin's low estimate of 6000 (1835) see remarks below, conclusion of this Appendix.

[280]For the definition of this area, 1856, see above, note 215.

[281]On these as authorities, see above, note 212. Here again for 1842, these wide variations are either for different groupings, or are due to a misprint or other error.

=3010 (*CS2.*, II, 522); 1907 (? U.S. and Canada) = 2080 (*MO.*, p. 13); 1910 (U.S.) = 1350 (*GN.*, pp. 190, 201); 1911 (Canada) = (*Handbook of Canadian Indians*, p. 46); 1915 = *c.* 1400 (*TH.*, pp. 178, 326).

ATAKAPA: (mod. Louisiana): 1907 = ?25 (*MO.*, p. 9).[282]

ATSINA: 1833 = 260 tents, 200 tents, 400-500 warriors, (both, Maximilian, *EWT.*, XXIII, 71, 76); 1904, 'steadily decreasing' = 535 (Mooney, *HAN.*, I, 113); 1907 = 553 (*MO.*, p. 13); 1910 = 501 (*GN.*, p. 190).

BLACKFOOT, and B. CONFEDERACY: 1820 = 350 tents (Franklin, (First) *Journey to the Polar Sea*, p. 169); 1833 = 'thought to be more than 18,000 or 20,000,' 5000-6000 warriors (Maximilian, *EWT.*, XXIII, 94-6); 1835 = 'not far from 40,000 under the general designation of B.' (*CAT.*, I, 52[283]); 1842 (est. Harriott) = 13,000 (*HI.*, p. 115); *c.* 1850 ('*temp.* Schoolcraft,' in Nebraska?) = 9530[284] (*HI.*, p. 117); 1858 (est. Hayden) = 2400 warriors, 6720 souls;[285] 1858 (U.S. official estimate) = 7300 souls (both *HAN.*, II, 571); *c.* 1858 = 10,000 (*BA2.*, p. 691); 1859 = 10,000-12,000 present near Fort Benton, Montana (De Smet, *Life.*, II, 792; III, 952); 1874 = 8000 (Denny MS., p. 212); 1890 *seq.* = 2000 Siksika (Denny: MacInnes, *In the Shadow of the Rockies*, p. 127); 1896, B. Confederacy, U.S. = 1800; Canada = *c.* 5000 (*CS2.*, II, 524); 1900, B. Confederacy, U.S. = 14,000 souls (*CH.*, II, 851); 1907 = 4560 (*MO.*, p. 13); 1909, B. Confederacy, U.S. = 2195; Canada = 795 Siksika (both, *HAN.*, II, 571); 1910 (U.S. Blackfoot, Piegans) = 2269 (*GN.*, p. 156); 1911 (Canada) = 767 Siksika (*Handbook of Canadian Indians.* p. 427; *TH.*, p. 327).

BLOOD (Kainah): 1820 = 300 tents (? = 2400 souls[286]); *c.* 1840 = 400 tents (Douglas: Jenness, *Indians of Canada*, p. 324); 1850 (Upper Missouri) = 1612 souls (*HI.*, p. 117); 1858 (Report, U.S. Comm. Ind. Affairs) = 300 tipis, 2400 persons (*HAN.*, I, 643); 1890-1905 = 3000 (Denny: MacInnes, *In the Shadow of the Rockies*, p. 127); 1909-11, Canada = 1174, 1122 (*Handbook of Canadian Indians*, pp. 233, 427; *HAN.*, I, 643; II, 571).

CADDO or 'CADDOANS' (Texas): 1825 = 'about 25' (*CS1.*, II, 711-14); 1844 = 500 'Caddoes and Inyes' (Iniies = Hainai:[287] Report, Comm. Ind. Affairs, cited by Gregg, *EWT.*, XX, 341); 1855 = 794 Caddoes, Anadahkos, Tahwaccorroes, Wacos, and Tonkahwas on 'the first Indian Reservation in Texas' (*BA5*, II, 407); 1859 'Wichita'–Caddo (attempted

---

[282]On these, as culturally Texan, see Kroeber, *Cultural and Natural Areas*, 63, 70.

[283]Maclean cites Catlin (*circa* 1835) = '23,400 Crees and Blackfeet, in the N.W. alone'—meaning Canada alone? (*Canadian Savage Folk*, 293).

[284]In Nebraska surely 'Blackfoot Sioux' (Sihasapa) is more probable. De Smet, 1841: 1500 of these (*Early Western Travels*, XXVII, 166; cf. Coues (ed.), *Henry-Thompson Journals*, II, 522).

[285]Unless the men had contrived to escape smallpox, etc., by deserting the camps, the ratio of men to souls seems incredibly high.

[286]The (Siksika) ratio of 8 per tipi is endorsed by Kidd ("Blackfoot Ethnography," 25).

[287]So, *Handbook of American Indians*, II, 1065.

massacre: Lindquist, *Red Man*, p. 184); 1907 = 555 'Caddo, including Hasinai, etc.' (*MO.*, p. 13); 1910 = 1021 Wichita–Caddo (*GN.*, pp. 104, 216).

CHEYENNE: *c.* 1835 = *c.* 3000 (*CAT.*, II, 2); 1835 = est. 3250 souls (Dr. Morse: Maximilian, *EWT.*, XXII, 333); 1841 = 2000 souls (De Smet, *ibid.*, XXVIII, 160); 1844 = 2000 (Report, Comm. Ind. Affairs, cited by Gregg, *ibid.*, XX, 342); 1849 = est. 3000 souls; 1850 = 1000 (small-pox: Culbertson, cited in *HAN.*, I, 253); 1864, 'one division,' with some Arapahoes, Chivington massacre = 130 lodges (*TA.*, p. 53); 1876 = 2294 Northern C. and Arapaho (? 1200 Northern C., *BA8.*, p. 777); 1904 = 1903 Southern C.; 1409 Northern C. = 3312 (*HAN.*, I, 253); 1907 = 3351 (*MO.*, p. 13); 1910 = 3235 (*GN.*, pp. 165, 308).

CHIPPEWYAN: 1812 = 7500 (Drake: *HAN.*, I, 276); 1873 = 600 (*ibid.*); 1904 = 1200, 1800 (*ibid.*); 1907 = 1520 (*MO.*, p. 26); 1910 = 1885 (N.W.T., Canada; *Handbook of Canadian Indians*, p. 95).

CHITIMACHA (mod. Louisiana): 1881 = *c.* 50 (*HAN.*, I, 286); 1907 = ?60 (*MO.*, p. 9); 1910 = 'less than 50' (*GN.*, pp. 104, 108).

COMANCHE: 1832 = est. 30,000-40,000, 6000-7000 warriors (*CAT.*, II, 68); 1839 = 'supposed to be 20,000 strong' (Farnham, *EWT.*, XXVIII, 149); 1844 = 'about 10,000 souls' (Report, Comm. Ind. Affairs, cited by Gregg, *ibid.*, XX, 342); 1849 = 12,000 (*BA4.*, p. 462); 1850 = 'probably about 10,000' (Thwaites, ed. note, *EWT.*, XVI, 233); 1868 = *c.* 2500 (warriors or souls? *CS1.*, II, 412); 1886 (U.S. Census) = 2756 'Kiowas and C.' (*HO.*, p. 526); 1907 = 1430 (*MO.*, p. 13); 1904 = 1400 (Mooney, *HAN.*, I, 327);[288] 1910 = 1476 (*GN.*, p. 216).

CREE (including MASKEGON = 'Swampy Cree'): 1833 = 1800-2400 men, *i.e. c.* 10,000 souls, 600-800 tents (Maximilian, *EWT.*, XXIII, 14); 1835 = 3000 (men or souls? *CAT.*, I, 53); 1841 (Saskatchewan District, H.B. Co., est. Governor Simpson) = 500 tents, 3500 souls (Simpson, *Journey Around the World*, I, 102); 1842 = 2000 Plain Cree, 4000 Strongwood C., about Edmonton (Rowand: *HI.*, p. 115); 1842 = 'over 12,000' (Lefroy: *MCSF.*, pp. 68-85);[289] *c.* 1850, Cree of the Upper Missouri = 800 (*HI.*, p. 117); 1896 = 'over 10,000' (*MCSF.*, p. 69); 'most estimates for the 19th cent. give from 12,500 to 13,000' (Mooney, Thomas, *HAN.*, I, 361);[290] 1907 = 14,200 (*MO.*, p. 26); 1911 = *c.* 18,000 (Canada: *Handbook of Canadian Indians*, p. 119).

MASKEGON: 1889 = 1254 'living with Chippewa on reserves in Manitoba' (*HAN.*, I, 813); 1911 = 2641 on Manitoba reserves, a large proportion M. (*Handbook of Canadian Indians*, p. 276).

CROW: 'not over 10,000 at their best' (no date: *CH.*, II, 855); *c.* 1827 = 1000 warriors; est. Donald McKenzie, 1830 = 300 lodges, 3000 souls; *c.* 1833 = 400 tents, 1200 warriors (all, Maximilian, *EWT.*, XXII, 351;

[288]Thought to be 'never a very large tribe' (Mooney, *Handbook of American Indians*, I, 327). The official and local estimates scarcely support this.

[289]Given by Maclean (*Canadian Savage Folk*, 69) as '1852'; but as Lefroy was in the North West Territories 1843-44 that must surely be the date.

[290]Given as '2500 to 3000' in *Handbook of American Indians*, I, 361. Thought in *Handbook of Canadian Indians* (p. 119) to be a misprint, which it evidently is. I have given the latter's figures as those intended by Mooney and Thomas.

XXIV, 222); 1829, 1834 = 4500 souls (*HAN.*, I, 368); 1835 = *c.* 7000 (*CAT.*, I, 43); 1862 = 460 lodges, 'formerly about 800 lodges or families' (Hayden, *HAN.*, I, 368); 1866 = 2000 (*BA2.*, p. 692); 1871 = 4100 (*HAN.*, I, 369); 1886 (U.S. Census) = 3226 (*HO.*, p. 526); 1890 = 2287; 1904 = 1826 (both, *HAN.*, I, 368); 1907 = 1787 (*MO.*, p. 13); 1899 = 1962; 1910 = 1740 (both, *GN.*, p. 175).

DAKOTA (see SIOUX).

HIDATSA (Minatari, 'Gros Ventres of the Missouri'): 1835 = 1500 (est. Catlin: *MCSF.*, p. 290); *c.* 1850 ('*temp*, Schoolcraft, between the Missouri and the Saskatchewan'; apparently including the Atsina)[291] = 2500 (*HI.*, p. 117); 1841 = *c.* 1000 (De Smet, *EWT.*, XXVII, 166); 1886 = 856 (*HO.*, p. 526); 1888 = 502 (*MCSF.*, p. 290); 1905 = 471 (*HAN.*, I, 548); 1907 = 468 (*MO.*, p. 13); 1910 = 466 (*GN.*, p. 193).

IOWA: 1829 = 1000; 1832-36 = 1400, 992 (both, Catlin, *HAN.*, I, 613; *CAT.*, II, 22). 1843 = 470 (Report, Comm. Ind. Affairs, cited by Gregg, *EWT.*, XX, 341); 1884 = 143; 1905 = 225 (*HAN.*, I, 614); 1907 = 339 (*MO.*, p. 13); 1910 (Oklahoma) = 80 (*GN.*, p. 285).

KANSA(s): 1820 = *c.* 1500 souls (Long, *EWT.*, XVII, 154); 1822 = 1850; 1829 = 1200; 1830 = 1500 (Gallatin: Maximilian, *ibid.*, XXIV, 229); 1843 (Report, Comm. Ind. Affairs, cited by Gregg, *ibid.*, XX, 341) = 1700; or 1588 (*HAN.*, I, 654); 1840 = 1560 (*CAT.*, II, 23); 1850-1905 = 1700 to 209 (*HAN.*, I, 654); 1907 = 196 (*MO.*, p. 13); 1910 = 231, 70 full-bloods (*GN.*, p. 212).

KARANKAWA (Texas): 1817 = 3000 (Farnham, *EWT.*, XXVIII, 149); 1840 = '10 or 12 families,' also 100 (*HAN.*, I, 657); exterminated by settlers, 1858-59 (so, *BA5.*, II, 408, 524; cf. Thwaites, ed. note, *EWT.*, XXVIII, 149; *HAN.*, I, 657).

KICHAI (Keyes, Kichias, etc.): 1843 = 'Keechyes' one of the five tribes totalling 1000 (Report, Comm. Ind. Affairs, cited by Gregg, *EWT.*, XX, 342); 1852 = 'Keechies' about 100 warriors, *c.* 450 souls (*MAI.*, p. 93); 1906 = 'about 50' (*HAN.*, I, 683); 1907 = 30 (*MO.*, p. 13); 1910 = 'less than 100'; or, one of five Caddoan tribes totalling 1021 (*GN.*, pp. 106, 216).

KIOWA: 1843 = 2000 souls (Report, Comm. Ind. Affairs, cited by Gregg, *EWT.*, XX, 342); 1886, K. and Comanche = 2756 (*HO.*, p. 526); 1904 = 1100 (Thwaites, *EWT.*, XV, 157); 1905 = 1165 (*HAN.*, I, 700); 1907 = 1220 (*MO.*, p. 13); 1910 = 1366 (*GN.*, pp. 114, 152, 216).

KIOWA APACHE: *c.* 1820 = 3000 (Long, *EWT.*, XV, 211);[292] 1891 = 325; 1905 = 155 (*HAN.*, I, 702); 1907 = 156 (*MO.*, p. 13).

MANDAN: *c.* 1833 = '600 warriors in the field at any time,' *i.e.* M. and Hidatsa (Maximilian, *EWT.*, XXIV, 262); 1837 = 1600; reduced by

[291]The common early use of 'Gros Ventre' for both tribes leads to frequent confusion, not always easy to untangle.

[292]'Kaskias' or 'Bad Hearts,' here identified as Comanche; but actually Kiowa Apache (so *Handbook of American Indians*, I, 701; II, 1070). The Kiowa proper are said by Drannan to be (*circa* 1847?) 'the most numerous tribe' in the United States: *Thirty-One Years on the Plains*, 45. A preposterous and worthless assertion; see Note, conclusion of chap. XV.

smallpox to 145, 125, or 31 (*HAN.*, I, 798); 1841, three tribes, M., Hidatsa, Arikara = 3000 (De Smet, *EWT.*, XXVII, 166); 1850 = 150; 1852 = 385 (*HAN.*, I, 798); 1870 = the above three tribes ('a mere remnant, reduced nine-tenths by war and disease, 1800-70') = 500 (*TA.*, pp. 59-71, 76, 82, 121-31, 176-83); Mandan, 1871 = 450; 1877 = 420; 1885 = 410; 1886 = 283 ·(*HO.*, p. 526); 1905 = 249 (*HAN.*, I, 798); 1907 = 263 (*MO.*, p. 13); 1910 = 255 (*GN.*, p. 193).

MUSKOGEE: *c.* 1835 = '20,000 Creeks or Mus-ko-gees' (*CAT.*, II, 122); 1843 = 931 Oto and M. (Report, U.S. Comm. Ind. Affairs, cited by Gregg, *EWT.*, XX, 341); 1885 = 40 M. (*HAN.*, I, 911); 1905 = 385 M. and Oto (*ibid.*); 1907 = extinct (*MO.*, p. 13); 1910 = 411 Oto and M. (*GN.*, p. 255).

MUSKOGEE: *c.* 1835 = '20,000 Creeks or Mus-ko-gees' (*CAT.*, II, 122); 1860 = 'some 500 Alabamas, Coashattas, and Muscogees,' in Texas (*BA5.*, II, 442); 1910 = 'practically extinct' (*GN.*, p. 117).

MUSKHOGEAN Family: est. 50,000 *c.* 1492; 1890, pure bloods = 26,490; 1905 (with mixed bloods) = 55,213 (*HAN.*, I, 962).

NAVAJO:[293] 1849 = 10,800 (*BA4.*, p. 462); *c.* 1860 = 40,000 (Laut, *Pilgrims of the Santa Fé*, p. 77); 1867 = 7300 counted at once; 1869 = 'less than 9000' counted at once (*HAN.*, II, 41); 1880 = 16,000 (*BA4.*, p. 727); 1890 = 17,204 (*ibid.*; *CS1.*, II, 746); 1900 = 'over 20,000'; 1906 = est. 28,500 (*HAN.*, II, 42); 1907 = ?25,000 (*MO.*, p. 22); 1910 = 25,433 (*GN.*, pp. 103, 239).

OMAHA: 1820 = est. 1500 (Long, *EWT.*, XVII, 151); 1829 = 1900; 1843 = 1600 (*HAN.*, II, 120); 1843 = 1301 (Report, Comm. Ind. Affairs, cited by Gregg, *EWT.*, XX, 341); *c.* 1833 = 300-400 warriors, 1500 souls (Maximilian, *ibid.*, XXII, 277; *CAT.*, II, 24); 1851 = 1349; 1857 = 1200; 1880 = 1200; 1906 = 1228 (all *HAN.*, II, 120); 1886 (U.S. Census) = 1160 (*HO.*, p. 526); 1907 = 1246 (*MO.*, p. 13); 1910 = 1276 (*GN.*, p. 249).

OSAGE: 1820 = 4000 (Long, *EWT.*, XVII, 155); 1834 = *c.* 5200 (*CAT.*, II, 40); 1821, Grand O. = 4200; Little O. = 1000; 1843 = 4102 (*HAN.*, II, 158; Report, Comm. Ind. Affairs, cited by Gregg, *EWT.*, XX, 341); 1851 = 3758 (incomplete); 1877 = 3001; 1884 = 1547; 1886 = 1582; 1906 = 1994 (all *HAN.*, II, 158); 1907 = 1246 (*MO.*, p. 13); 1910 = 2104 (851 full-bloods: *GN.*, p. 253).

OTO: 1820 = 1400 (Long, *EWT.*, XVII, 150); 1833 = 1200 (Catlin: so *HAN.*, II, 166); 1833 = 600 (*CAT.*, II, 24); 1843 = 931 Oto and Missouri (Report, Comm. Ind. Affairs, cited by Gregg, *EWT.*, XX, 341); both tribes, 1849 = 900; 1862 = 708; 1867 = 511; 1877 = 457; 1886 = 334; 1906 = 390 (all *HAN.*, II, 166); 1907 = 390 'Oto' (*MO.*, p. 13); 1910 = 411 O. and Missouri (*GN.*, p. 255).

PAWNEE:

GRAND P.: 1820 = 500 souls (Long, *EWT.*, XVII, 152); 1825 = 1100 warriors, 5500 souls (General Atkinson: *DAS.*, p. 120).[294]

---

[293]Possibly at some time buffalo-users at least in part, by trade.

[294]Long's figure given by Dale as 3500 souls (*Ashley-Smith Explorations*, 100).

P. Loups: 1820 = 2000 souls (Long, *EWT.*, XVII, 152); 1825 = 700 warriors, 3500 souls (Atkinson: *DAS.*, p. 120); 1835 = *c.* 3500 (Dale, ed. note, *ibid.*, p. 122).

P. Republicans: 1820 = *c.* 1000 (Long, *EWT.*, XVII, 153).

'Pawnees': 1835 = *c.* 10,000-12,000, half the number prior to smallpox of 1832 (*CAT.*, II, 24); 1835 = est. 10,000 or 12,500 souls (*HAN.*, II, 216); 1839 = est. 2500 warriors (Farnham, *EWT.*, XXVIII, 148); 1844 = 12,500 souls (Report, Comm. Ind. Affairs, cited by Gregg, *ibid.*, XX, 341); 1849 = 4500 left out of 6000 (cholera); 1856 = 4686; 1861 = 3416 (all, *HAN.*, II, 216); 1870 = 'the main tribe,' *c.* 3000 (*GN.*, p. 106); 1879 = 1440 (*HAN.*, II, 216); 1886 (U.S. Census) = 998 (*HO.*, p. 526); 1904 = *c.* 650 (Thwaites, *EWT.*, XV, 215); 1906 = 649 (*HAN.*, II, 216); 1907 = 644 (*MO.*, p. 13); 1910 = *c.* 700, 635 (*GN.*, pp. 106, 258).

Piegan: 1820 = 400 tents (Franklin, (First) *Journey to the Polar Sea*, p. 169); *c.* 1840 = 500 tents (Douglas: Jenness, *Indians of Canada*, p. 324); 1841 = 350 tents, 2450 souls (Saskatchewan District, H. B. Co.: Simpson, *Journey Around the World*, I, 102); 1858 = 400 tents (*HI.*, p. 115); 1858 = est. 3700 in U.S.; 1861 = 2520 (Hayden: both, *HAN.*, II, 246); 1886 (U.S. Census), P., Bloods, Blackfeet = 2206 (*HO.*, p. 526); 1890 *seq.* (?Canada) = 1000 Piegans (Denny: MacInnes, *In the Shadow of the Rockies*, p. 127); 1906 = U.S., 2072; Canada, 493 (*HAN.*, II, 246); 1910 = in U.S. 2269 Blackfeet and P. (*GN.*, p. 156); 1911 (Canada) = 448 (*Handbook of Canadian Indians*, p. 386).

'Piman':

Papago: 1890 = 5163 (*CSI.*, II, 735); 1900 = 859 (Mexico: *HAN.*, II, 200); 1906 = 4981 (*ibid.*); 1907 = 4037 (*MO.*, p. 22); 1910 = '4000,' 1150, 74 (*GN.*, pp. 256, 260, 286).

Pimas: 1890 = 4464 (*CSI.*, II, 735); 1906 = 3936 (*HAN.*, II, 253); 1907 = 5800 (*MO.*, p. 22); 1910 = 3179, 826 (*GN.*, pp. 260, 286).

Ponca: 1829 = 600; 1842 = 800 (*HAN.*, II, 278); 1843 = 777 (Report, Comm. Ind. Affairs, cited by Gregg, *EWT.*, XX, 341); 1871 = 747; 1880 = 825; 1906 = 833 (all, *HAN.*, II, 278); 1907 = 845 (*MO.*, p. 13); 1910 = 583 (*GN.*, p. 265).

Pueblans:

Acoma: 1902 = 566 (*HAN.*, I, 10); 1907 = 2190, A. and Laguna (*MO.*, p. 22); 1910 = Acoma 818, Laguna 1551 = 2369 (*GN.*, p. 269).

Jemez: 1890 = 428; 1904 = 498 (*HAN.*, I, 630); 1907 = 521 (*MO.*, p. 22).

Keres: 1907 = 1971 (*MO.*, p. 22); in this are included Cochiti (*c.* 1906 = 300: *HAN.*, I, 318); San Felipe (1890 = 544; 1910 = 514: *HAN.*, II, 433; *GN.*, p. 269); Santa Ana (1890 = 253; 1905 = 226; 1910 = 211: *HAN.*, II, 454; *GN.*, p. 269); Santo Domingo (1910 = 819: *HAN.*, II, 462); and Sia (1890 = 106; 1910 = 119: *HAN.*, II, 562).

Moki, Moqui (Hopi, etc.):[295] 1680 = 2500; 1904 = 2338 (*HAN.*, I,

---

[295]Besides the *Handbook of American Indians* (I, 560-7, etc.) see also Coues's excellent notes, *Expeditions of Pike*, II, 741-5.

562); 1907, not including Hano (*i.e.* 1900 = 160: *ibid.*) = 1970 (*MO.*, p. 22); 1910 = 1804 (*GN.*, pp. 124, 128, 236).

PIROS (Senecú, Mexico): 1907 = *c.* 60 (*HAN.*, II, 262; *MO.*, p. 22).

TAOS (Taos, Picuris): 1907 = 590 (*MO.*, p. 22); 1910 = 515 (*HAN.*, II, 689).

TEWA: including Hano, 1900 = 160 (*HAN.*, I, 562); Nambe, 1890 = 79; 1904 = *est.* 100 (*ibid.*, II, 15); San Ildefonso, 1910 = 110 (*ibid.*, 440); San Juan, 1782 = 500 deaths from pestilence; 1910 = 404 (*ibid.*, 443, 457); Santa Clara, 1910 = 277 (*ibid.*, 457); Tesuque, 1906 = 80 (*ibid.*, 735). 1907-10 = 1200 (*HAN.*, II, 738); or 1215 (*MO.*, p. 22).

TIGUA: Isleta (New Mexico) 1909 = 1110 (*HAN.*, I, 623); 1910 = 998 (*GN.*, p. 269); Isleta (Texas) 1909 = 'very few' (*HAN.*, I, 624); total, 1907 = 1108 (*MO.*, p. 22).

ZUNI: 1880 = 1650 (*HAN.*, II, 1018); 1907 = 1682 (*MO.*, p. 22); 1910 = 1640 (*HAN.*, II, 1018; *GN.*, p. 269).

PUEBLAN TOTALS: 1907 = 11,297 (*MO.*, p. 22); 1910 = 9167 (*GN.*, p. 269).

QUAPAW: 1828 = 150 families in Texas; 1829 = 500; 1843 = 476 (*HAN.*, II, 335); 1852 = 'only about 25' (*MAI.*, p. 93); 1885 = 174; 1890 = 198 (*HAN.*, II, 335); 1895 = *c.* 250 (*CSI.*, II, 559); 1907 = 290 (*MO.*, p. 9); 1909 = 305, including mixed bloods (*HAN.*, II, 335); 1910 = 307 (*GN.*, p. 293).[296]

SARSI, SARCEE: *c.* 1830, Tsattine (*i.e.* Beavers) and Sarsi = '150 hunters,' *c.* 650 souls (*HAN.*, II, 467); 1820 = 100 tents of Sarsi (Franklin, (First) *Journey to the Polar Sea*, p. 170); *c.* 1840 = 100 tents (Douglas: Jenness, *Indians of Canada*, p. 24); 1871 = est. 1500 died of smallpox; 1885 = 'less than 500' (Jenness, *Sarcee Indians*, p. 7); 1889 = 336 (*MCSF.*, pp. 13-14); 1901 = 205 (Thwaites, *EWT.*, XXIII, 90); 1907 = 200 (*MO.*, p. 26); 1909 = 197 (*HAN.*, II, 499); 1911 = 205 in Canada (*Handbook of Canadian Indians*, p. 409; *TH.*, p. 304).

SIOUX:

BLACKFOOT SIOUX (SIHASAPA; perhaps 'Etasapa,' below):[297] 1841 = 1500 (De Smet, *EWT.*, XXVII, 166); 1851 = 450 lodges, thought to be an exaggeration; 1856 = 165 lodges; 1862 = 220 lodges (*HAN.*, II, 568); 1869 = *c.* 1000 individuals (*TA.*, p. 87);[298] 1878 = 814 souls (*HAN.*, II, 568); 1910 = *c.* 700 (*GN.*, p. 167).[299]

BRULÉ SIOUX: 1841 = 2500 (De Smet, *EWT.*, XXVII, 166); 1856 = est. 150 lodges (*HAN.*, I, 167); 1876 = *c.* 7000 (*BA8.*, p. 777); 1890 =4271 (*HAN.*, I, 167); 1900 = 472; 1910 = 469 (? of a total of 5096, Rosebud Agency, South Dakota: *GN.*, pp. 228, 276).

---

[296]Akansa or Arkansa: Father Poisson, 1726–'Aux Akensas' (*Jesuit Relations*, LXVII, 285). Their habitat was the lower Arkansas River (Coues (ed.), *Expeditions of Pike*, II, 559; *Handbook of American Indians*, II, 333).

[297]Minneconjous, Sans Arcs, Etasapas, nearly 3000 in 1869 (Taylor, *Frontier Life*, 87). The conjecture is Coues's (*Henry-Thompson Journals*, II, 523).

[298]As in the previous note.

[299]Blackfoot Sioux, Minneconjous, Sans Arc, Two Kettle (on Cheyenne River Reserve), 1910 = 2590 (Grinnell, *Indians of Today*, 167). I have compared De Smet's proportions broadly (*Early Western Travels*, XXVII, 166).

MDEWAKANTON: 1822 = 1500 souls (Long: HAN., I, 827); 1841 = 500 (De Smet, EWT., XXVII, 166); 1890 = 1161; 1905 = 929 (HAN., I, 827); 1910 = 350 (200 full bloods: GN., p. 229).

MINICONJOU: 1841 = est. 2000 souls (De Smet, EWT., XXVII, 166); 1850 = 270 lodges, i.e. 2150 total; 1856 = 200 lodges, 1600 souls; 1863 = 1280 = Indian Report (all, HAN., I, 868); 1869 = c. 1300 (TA., p. 89); 1910 = c. 900 (GN., p. 167).

OGLALA: 1825 = est. 300 warriors, 1500 souls (HAN., II, 109); 1841 = 1500 (De Smet, EWT., XXVII, 166); 1876 = 9087 (BA8., p. 777); 1906 = 6727 (HAN., II, 110); 1910 = ?3454 (GN., p. 306).

SANS ARC: 1841 = 1000 'Lack-bows' (De Smet, EWT., XXVII, 166); 1869 = c. 700 (TA., p. 87); 1910 = c. 550 (GN., p. 167); cf. HAN., II, 453.

SANTEES: 1841 = 300 'Jantons' (Yanktons) and Santees (De Smet, EWT., XXVII, 166); 1910 = 1155 (GN., p. 290).[300]

SAONE: 1841 = 2000 (De Smet, EWT., XXVII, 166).[301]

SISSETON: 1824 = 2500; 1853 = 2500; 1886 = 1496 S. and Wahpeton; 1906 = 985; 1909 = 980; 1909 = 1936, the same two and 'Pabaksa' (HAN., II, 181, 581, 892); 1910 = 1994 S. and Wahpeton (GN., p. 303).

TWO KETTLE (Oohenonpa): 1841 = 800 (De Smet, EWT., XXVII, 166); 1843 = 800; 1850 = 60 lodges; 1856 (Indian Report) = 100 lodges; 1887 = 652 souls (HAN., II, 136).

(H)UNKPAPA: 1841 = 2000 (De Smet, EWT., XXVII, 166); 1850 = est. 320 tipis; 1855 = 365 tipis, 2920 souls; 1891 = 571 souls (HAN., I, 579, 580).

(H)UNKPATINA: 1866 = est. 2100; 1905 = 1009; 1909 = 1019 (HAN., I, 580; II, 991); 1910 = 997, or 1102 (GN., pp. 189, 201).

WAHPEKUTE: 1824 = 100 lodges, 200 warriors, 800 souls (Long: HAN., II, 891); 1834 = c. 150 warriors; 1856 = 2379 W. and Mdewakanton (ibid.).

WAHPETON: 1835 = c. 1500 souls (HAN., II, 892); 1841 = 2000 (De Smet, EWT., XXVII, 166); '19th century estimates vary from 900-1500'; 1909 = 1936 Sisseton and W. (HAN., II, 892); 1910 = 1994 Sisseton and W. (GN., p. 303).

YANKTON: 1842 = 2500 (Indian Report);[302] 1862 = 3000; 1867 = 2530; 1886 =1776; 1909 = c. 2000 (HAN., II, 989); 1910 = 1753 (GN., p. 338).

[300]It is almost impossible to be sure just what any early writer means by Santee. It comprised the Mdewakanton, Wahpekute, Wahpeton, Sisseton (Handbook of American Indians, II, 460, 581).

[301]A somewhat vague term, comprising variously the Teton divisions, Sans Arcs, Sihasapa, Oohenonpa (Two Kettles), Hunkpapa (ibid., 464). The Tetons considered circa 1833 = 50 per cent of all the Dakota (Maximilian, Early Western Travels, XXII, 305).

[302]'Yanktonans' = 20 per cent of all the Dakota (ibid.). De Smet's '300 Jantons and Santees,' 1841 (ibid., XXVII, 166) can refer only to some isolated body.

YANKTONAI: 1823 = 5200 (Long: *HAN.*, II, 990); 1841 = 4500 (De Smet, *EWT.*, XXVII, 166); 1842 = 6000 (Indian Report); 1856 = 6400; 1867 = 4500 (*HAN.*, II, 990, 991); 1850 = 4000 'Ihankton-wanna' (Schoolcraft: *HI.*, p. 117); 1875 = 2266; 1885 = 6618; 1886 = 5109; 1909 = 1019 Lower Y. or Hunkpatina; 1909 = 3500 Upper Y., Yanktonai, and others; Montana, 1909 = 1082 (*HAN.*, II, 991).

'SIOUX' in general: 1805 (Lewis and Clark) = 9900 souls; or (Pike) = 21,068 (*CS1.*, I, 346); 1825 = 7055 warriors, 28,100 souls, in 2330 tents (Long: Maximilian, *EWT.*, XXII, 304);[303] 1833-43 = 'still reckoned at 20,000, or by some, 15,000 warriors,' which 'seems rather too high' (*ibid.*); 1846, south of the Missouri River = 5000-6000 warriors, 60,000 to 80,000 souls (De Smet, *Life*, II, 792; cf. *ibid.*, III, 956);[304] 1852 = 'c. 25,000 Sioux' (Rev. Dr. S. R. Riggs: *PN2.*, p. 261); 1860 = '13,000 warriors strong' (*BA2.*, p. 693); 1869, con-federated bands, exclusive of Assiniboine = c. 40,000 (*TA.*, p. 62); 1876 = est. 2500-3000 Indian warriors on the Little Bighorn, 'more than 2000' surrendered later (*HAN.*, II, 109); 1876 = 'about 35,000 souls' (*BA8.*, p. 777); 1886 (U.S. Census) = 30,561 (*HO.*, p. 526); 1907 = 28,060 (*MO.*, p. 13); 1910 = 18,958 (specified: *GN.*, pp. 167, 179, 201, 229, 276, 290, 303, 306, 338).

TAWAKONI: 1844, 'Towockanoes,' one of five tribes totalling 1000 (Report, Comm. Ind. Affairs, cited by Gregg, *EWT.*, XX, 342); 1855, 'Tahwac-corroes' one of five tribes, partly the same, in Texas = 794 (*BA5.*, II, 407); 1910, one of (? the same) five tribes in Oklahoma = 1021; 1910 = 'less than 100' (*GN.*, pp. 106, 216).

TONKAWA: 1828 = est. 80 families; 1847 = 150 men; 1862 = c. 300, 137 massacred; 1884 = 92 (*HAN.*, II, 782); 1870 = 500 T. and Lipan (*BA5.*, II, 525; cf. *BA9.*, I, 593); 1907-8 = 45 8 (*MO.*, p. 13; *HAN.*, II, 782); 1910 = 'less than 50,' or 53 (*GN.*, pp. 137, 265).

TAWEHASH or 'TOWYASHES' (*HAN.*, II, 705).

WACO, WICHITA (*i.e.* 'Pawnee Picts': *HAN.*, II, 949, 1118):

WICHITA-CADDO: 1805 = c. 2600 souls, including 60 Kichai; 1809 = 2800; 1824 = c. 2800 (*HAN.*, II, 948); 1834, 'the main Waco village' = 33 grass houses, c. 100 men, or 400-500 souls (*ibid.*, 888); 1835, 'Pawnee Picts' (Wichita) = 3000 warriors, 8000-10,000 souls, or, by some, 12,000 souls; Wichita, Waco, Kiowa, Comanche = 30,000 to 40,000 (*CAT.*, II, 73, 83); 1843 = 1000 'Waco, Wichita, Towock-anoes, Towyashes, and Keechyes' (Report, Comm. Ind. Affairs, cited by Gregg, *EWT.*, XX, 342); 1852 = c. 80 Wacoes; Wichita = c. 100 warriors, 'not more than 500 souls' (*MA1.*, p. 93); 1855 = 794 Anadahkos, Caddoes, Wacoes, Tahwaccorroes, and Tonkahwas in

[303]Maximilian uses Pike's total as his datum, but gives it as 21,575. He also cites Long's totals for Assiniboines = 6000 warriors, 25,000 souls; therefore 20,000, *circa* 1833, 'not too high.' But elsewhere he gives 28,000; a grand total with the Sioux of 14,055 warriors, 56,100 souls, in 5330 tents (*ibid.*, XXII, 304).

[304]De Smet's ratio of warriors to souls is too low, and his aggregate (Sioux alone?) too high; 1850, 54,550 Indians est. for the Upper Missouri and tributaries (Maclean, *Canadian Savage Folk*, 293).

Texas (reserve: *BA5.*, II, 407); 1859 = 204 Tawakoni, 171 Waco (*HAN.*, II, 949); 1860, the same two, 572, plus 123 Kichai = 695 (*ibid.*); 1907 = 310, plus 30 Kichai (*ibid; MO.*, p. 13); 1910, Wichita, Caddo, Tawakoni, Kichai, Hueco (*i.e.* Waco) = 1021 (*GN.*, pp. 106, 216).

7. BUFFALO-USING INDIAN TRIBES IN THE CENTRAL MOUNTAIN TERRITORY (FROM THE EARLIEST TIMES)

If it is borne in mind that the references are to peoples using buffalo products, and not necessarily to the actual presence of the species itself within the limits suggested, this area may roughly be defined as follows: In the northern transmontane territory, the boundary may be considered as following (rather more closely than along the lower Columbia River) the actual limits of the buffalo habitat itself, in so far as we have been able to ascertain them, that is, from about 50° or 57° N. in the headwaters region of the Peace River and the northern tributaries of the upper Fraser, and working downward along the Columbia Valley. Along the lower Columbia, the line may be extended practically to the Willamette Valley, judging from the localities assigned by Lewis and Clark on their map to the buffalo-hunting 'Shoshonees or Snakes.'[305] We have seen that the actual presence of the species has been noted as far west as the Boisé Valley (Boisé, Idaho, 116° W.); and vestiges have been recorded much farther west, up to 119° W., or possibly even to beyond 123° W.[306] It seems probable, however, that the penetration of buffalo in these regions would only be in the nature of wedge-like 'thrusts,' and farther south, the western limits of use or presence would lie much nearer to the main Rocky Mountain range. Our present southern limit of use—certainly in any material degree—may be considered as the State of Utah or possibly northern Nevada.[307] The tribes in the regions beyond that have already been included in our figures for the Plains area. The actual situation of the tribes indicated by Lewis and Clark is of more importance for our present purpose than their identification under more scientific or better-known names; I have, however, added such wherever obtainable. It may be noted in the case of the Wappatoo Indians (above, p. 748) that the close agreement between the Lewis and Clark and the scientific nomenclatures is an important item in the general evidence for the explorers' broad reliability.

BANNOCK (Shoshonean):[308] *c.* 1829 = 1200 lodges, 8000 people (*HAN.*, I, 130); 1845 = 1000 (*MO.*, p. 18); 1869 = est. 500, but only 50 lodges, probably *c.* 350 souls (*HAN.*, I, 130); 1885 = 422 at Fort Hall (*ibid.*); 1886 'Bannock and Shoshone' (U.S. Census) = 2000 (*HO.*,

---

[305]*Lewis and Clark Journals* (map, III, 329). Their description, "Shoshonees, a small tribe of the Nation called Snakes . . ." (*ibid.*, II, 115) shows that this was not meant for 'Shoshoneans,' a purely scientific term unknown in their day, which is applied to a group whose members occupied wide areas of the unquestioned buffalo territory. See *Handbook of American Indians*, II, 555; Kroeber, *Cultural and Natural Areas*, 43-4, 52-3, 189-93, etc.

[306]See above, chap. XI, notes 103-6.   [307]See chap. XI, notes 117-27.

[308]*Kutshundika* = 'Buffalo Eaters'; a Bannock division (*Handbook of American Indians*, I, 130, 743).

p. 526); 1901 = 513 (*HAN.*, I, 130); 1907 = 530 (*MO.*, p. 18); 1910, B. and Shoshoni = 1273 (*GN.*, p. 194).

CALLAHPOEWAH (Calapooya: *HAN.*, II, 1035): Multnomah, *i.e.* Willamette River, 1805 = 2000 souls (*LE.*, III, 329); 3000 souls (*LE.*, map).

CAULDRONS (Colville: *HAN.*, II, 1038): 1841 = 600 (De Smet, *EWT.*, XXVII, 166).

CATHLACUMUP (Chinookan): mouth of Willamette R., 1805 = 450 (*HAN.*, I, 216); still existing, 1850 (*ibid.*).

CATHLAKAHECKIT (Chinookan): Columbia R. Cascades, 1812 = est. 900 (*HAN.*, I, 216).

CATHLAMET (Chinookan): near Columbia River mouth, 1805 = 300; 1849 = 58 (*HAN.*, I, 216).

CATHLANAHQUIAH (Chinookan): Multnomah County, Oregon, 1805 = 400 souls (*LE.*, III, 327; *HAN.*, I, 217).

CATHLAPOTLE (Chinookan): Clarke County, Wash., 1806 = 900 (*HAN.*, I, 217).

CATHLATHLALAS (Chinookan): below Cascade, Columbia River, 1812 = 500 (*HAN.*, I, 217).

CAYUSE (Waiilatpuan: *HAN.*, II, 893): Washington-Oregon, 1841 = 2000 (De Smet, *EWT.*, XXVII, 166); 1805 = 250 (*HAN.*, II, 66).

CHARCOWAH (Chinookan): Willamette River above the Falls, 1806 = 200 souls (*LE.*, III, 329; *HAN.*, I, 235).

CHILLUCKITTEQUAW (Chinookan): Columbia River below the Dalles, 1806 = 1400 souls (*LE.*, III, 329); 2400 (*LE.*, map; *HAN.*, I, 268).

CHIMNAPUM (Shahaptian): Columbia River near Snake confluence; 1806 = 1860 souls (*LE.*, III, 326; *HAN.*, I, 271); 2000 (*LE.*, map).

CLACK-A-MUS (Clackama: *HAN.*, II, 1045; Chinookan): Clackamas County, Oregon, 1806 = 1800 (*LE.*, III, 329; *LE.*, map also); 1851 = 88 (*HAN.*, I, 302).

CLAHCLELLAH (Chinookan): near the Cascades, Columbia River, 1806 = one village of seven houses (*HAN.*, I, 302).

CLAHNAQUAH (Chinookan): near Willamette River mouth, 1806 = 130 souls (*HAN.*, I, 302).

CLANINNATA (Chinookan): Multnomah County, Oregon, 1806 = 200 (*HAN.*, I, 305).

CŒUR D'ALENE (Skitswish: *HAN.*, II, 594, 1046): SKEETSOMISH or SKET-SO-MISH, 1806 = 2000 souls (*LE.*, III, 330); 2600 (*LE.*, map); 1841 = 700 'Pointed Hearts' (De Smet, *EWT.*, XXVII, 166); 1845 = 1000; 1907 = 506 (both, *MO.*, p. 16); 1903 = 533 (*HAN.*, II, 594); 1910 = 537 (*GN.*, p. 169).

'COLUMBIA' Indians (Colville Reservation): 1910 = 521 (*GN.*, p. 173; see also *HAN.*, I, 326, on these).

COLVILLE (Salish: *HAN.*, I, 326): 1806 = 2500 (*ibid.*); 1904 = 321 (*ibid.*); 1910 = 294 'Flat Bows and Colville'; also on Colville Reserve, 418, 'South half of Colville' (*GN.*, p. 173).

CUSHOOK (Chinookan): above the Falls of the Willamette, 1806 = 650 (*LE.*, III, 329).

ENEESHUR (Shahaptian): Columbia River near Deschutes confluence, 1806 = 1200 (*LE.*, III, 327; also *LE.*, map).

ESKELOOT, E-CHE-POOT (Tlakluit: *HAN.*, II, 762, 1053; a Chinookan tribe):
Deschutes River opposite the 'Eneeshur,' 1806 = 1000 souls (*LE.*, III,
327; also *LE.*, map); *c.* 1909 = 150 (*HAN.*, II, 762).

FLAT BOWS (Lower Kutenai; also Kitunahan family: *HAN.*, I, 740; II,
1054; also 'Lake Indians,' and 'Skalzis': *ibid.*, I, 742; II, 1081, 1142):
1841 = 500 'Savages of the Lake' (De Smet, *EWT.*, XXVII, 166);
1910 = 294 'Lake and Colville Indians' (*GN.*, p. 173); 1911 = 154
Flatbow (*Handbook of Canadian Indians*, p. 257).

FLATHEAD (Salish[309]): 1835 = 800 souls (Rev. Samuel Parker; in Maximilian, *EWT.*, XXIV, 227); 1845 = 600 (*MO.*, p. 16); 1853 = 325
(*HAN.*, II, 416); 1907 = 623 (*MO.*, p. 16); 1909 = 598 (*HAN.*, II,
416); 1910 = Flathead, one of five tribes, Salishan = 4, Kitunahan = 1,
totalling 2265 (*GN.*, p. 185).
1909 (U.S. and Canada): Coast Salish = 8474, interior S. = 10,378,
total = 18,852 (*TH.*, p. 328).

GOSIUTE: see UTE, below.

HANNAKALALS: Columbia River above the Willamette and near the Shahala,
below, 1806 = 600 souls (*LE.*, III, 312; *LE.*, map).

HE-HIGH-E-NIMI-MO (Sanpoil: *HAN.*, II, 451, 1060; Salishan): Clark's
Fort of the Columbia, 1806 = 1300 souls (*LE.*, III, 330); 1500 (*LE.*,
map); 1905, 1909 = 324, 178 (*HAN.*, II, 451).

HOHILPO (Salish: *HAN.*, I, 556; II, 1061; 'a tribe of the Tushepah'):
Clark's River, above the Micksucksealton, 1805 = 300 souls (*LE.*, III,
330; *HAN.*, I, 556); 600 souls (*LE.*, map).[310]

KALISPEL, PEND D'OREILLE ('Coospellars' of Lewis and Clark, Salish):
1805 = 1600 souls (*LE.*, III, 329); 1845 = 1200 (*MO.*, p. 16); 1851,
Upper and Lower K. = 520, 480, totalling 1000 (*HAN.*, I, 646); 1905,
combined = 935 (*ibid.*). 1910 = 2265 in Montana, 95 in Washington
(*GN.*, pp. 173, 185).

KLAMATH (possibly in part):[311] 1905 = 755 (*HAN.*, I, 712); 223, including Modoc (*ibid.*, 919); 1910 = 1126 Klamath, Modoc, and Yahuskin
band of Shoshoni (1877, 1891, 1909 = 166, 135, 103 respectively: *ibid.*,
II, 983), on Klamath Reserve, Oregon (*GN.*, pp. 204, 219).

KUTENAI: 1811 = 'not more than 50 families' (Henry: *CS2.*, II, 707);
1798 = *c.* 750 (*TH.*, p. 304); 1835 = probably not over 1000 (Rev.
Samuel Parker: Maximilian, *EWT.*, XXIV, 233); 1841 = '4000 Kootenays
and Carriers,' *i.e.* Takulli, below (De Smet, *ibid.*, XXVII, 166); 1843 =
800 (Rowand: *MCSF.*, p. 140); 1845, 1859 = 'over 1000 K. and Flat-

---

[309]For numerous tribes to whom the term has been applied, see *ibid.*,
II, 1054. The large Salishan family, 1909-10 = 18,630 (*ibid.*, 417) or 20,000
(Grinnell, *Indians of Today*, 124). See also Bancroft, *Native Races*, I, 252-91;
Coues (ed.), *Henry-Thompson Journals*, II, 708. Lewis and Clark (*Journals*,
III, 321) speak of the Kooskooskee or 'Flathead's River,' now the Clearwater
(*ibid.*, prefaces, II, vii; III, vi). In practically the exact situation given 47° 30' N.,
114° W.), they have the 'Tushepahs,' 800 souls; on whom see below, TUSHEPAH.

[310]Clark's River as Cokalahiskit = 'river of the road to buffalo' (*Lewis and
Clark Journals*, III, 164), or Isquet-co-qualla = 'the road to the buffaloes' (Gass,
Journal of the Lewis and Clark Expedition, 254).

[311]See references, notes 306, 307, above.

bows, *i.e.* Lower K. (De Smet, *MCSF.*, p. 140); 1890 (U.S.) = 400-500 (*HAN.*, I, 742); 1896 (425, U.S.; 539, Canada) = 964 (*CS2.*, II, 550); 1904 (Canada) = 553 (*HAN.*, I, 742); 1905 (U.S.) = 554 (*ibid.*); 1910 = K. one of five tribes totalling 2265 (*GN.*, p. 185); 1911 = 517 in Canada: 'a decrease of 150 in 13 years' (*HAN.*, I, 742) or '185 in 20 years' (*Handbook of Canadian Indians,* p. 257); but Maclean gives 655 only in 1891 (*MCSF.*, p. 140).

LOWER KUTENAI (including Shushwap intermarried with K. families): 1904 = 172 in British Columbia, 79 in Idaho (*HAN.*, I, 776); see also FLATBOW, above.

LAHANNA: (?) 'both sides of Columbia River above the entrance of Clark's River,' 1805 = 200 souls (*LE.*, III, 329).[312]

LARTIELO (*LE.*, III, 330): see below, SPOKANE.

LEMHI (Shoshone): Fort Hall Reserve, Idaho, 1910 = 449 (*GN.*, p. 194; *HAN.*, II, 557; Kroeber, *Cultural and Natural Areas*, pp. 51, 57).

MICK-SUCK-SEAL-TON (? Kutenai: *HAN.*, II, 853): Clark's River, above the Hohilpo, *c.* 48° 30′ N., 116° W., 1805 = 300 souls (*LE.*, III, 330; *LE.*, map).

MONO-PAVIOTSO (Shoshonean): 1903 = *c.* 5400 (*HAN.*, I, 932).

MOY . . ., or '. . . MOY':[313] headwaters, Gallatin Fork of the Missouri River, 1805 = 600 souls (*LE.*, map).

NEZ PERCÉ (Shahaptian; the 'Chopunnish' of Lewis and Clark): 1805 = 7850 (*LE.*, III, 326);[314] 1805 = *c.* 6000 (*HAN.*, II, 66); '8000 souls' on Kooskooskee (Clearwater) River, *c.* 46° 30′ N., 117° 30′ W., *i.e.* Clark's measurements, 1805 (*LE.*, map); 1841 = 2500 'Pierced Noses' (De Smet, *EWT.*, XXVII, 166); 1845 = 4000 (*MO.*, p. 16); 1849, Chopunnish = *c.* 3000 (Wilkes: *HAN.*, II, 66); 1853 = over 1700 (Gibbs: *ibid.*); 1885 = 1437 (*ibid.*); 1886 (U.S. Census) = 1460 (*HO.*, p. 526); 1906 = over 1600 (*HAN.*, II, 66); 1907 = 1563 (*MO.*, p. 16); 1910 = 1530 (*GN.*, pp. 173, 195).

OKANAGAN, OKINAGAN (Salishan): 1841 = 1100 (De Smet, *EWT.*, XXVII, 166); 1855 = 'six bands'; 1906 = 527, U.S.; 824, Canada (both *HAN.*, II, 114); 1910 = 538 (? U.S: *GN.*, p. 173); 1911 = 795, Canada (*Handbook of Canadian Indians,* p. 360).

OOTLASHOOT (Shahaptian): headwaters of Clark's River, *c.* 45° 30′ N., 112° 30′ W., 'a band of the Tushepahs,' 1805 = about 80 men (*LE.*, II, 141); 400 souls (*ibid.*, III, 326); 430 souls (*LE.*, map).

PAIUTE, PAH-UTE (Shoshoncan): 1845 (including Paviotso and 'Snake' Oregon)[315] = 7500 (*MO.*, p. 18); 1900 = 3700 non-agency Paiutes in Nevada; 1906 = 1436 agency Paiutes in Nevada, 350 Arizona; 500 (non-agency), Utah (all, *HAN.*, II, 187); 1907 = 5605 (*MO.*, p. 18); 1910 = 3 bands of Paiutes,' 83 Kaibab P., over 100 San Juan P. (*GN.*, pp. 155, 211, 289, 328, 331; *HAN.*, I, 641).

[312]'Lahanna' not identifiable (*Handbook of American Indians*, I, 753).
[313]Not identifiable.
[314]1600 deducted from this total for the Pelloatpallah (*q.v.*) and 250 for the Yeletpo (Wailetpu = Cayuse, above): Henshaw, Farrand, *Handbook of American Indians*, II, 66.

PALOOS, PELLOATPALLAH of Lewis and Clark (Shahaptian: *HAN*., II, 195):
on the Columbia, just above Lewis River confluence, 1805 = 1600 souls
(*LE*., III, 326); 3000 souls (*LE*., map); 1841 = 500 'Palooses' (De
Smet, *EWT*., XXVII, 166); 1854 = 500 (*HAN*., II, 195).[316]

PISHQUITPAH (Shahaptian): Columbia River, below the Walla Walla, *c*.
46° N., 119° 30' W., 1805 = 2600 souls (*LE*., III, 326; *LE*., map);
'1600,' not 2600, suggested (*HAN*., II, 262).

POHAH, 'a band of Snake Indians' (*i.e.* Bannock: *HAN*., II, 1122): headwaters of South Fork of Lewis's River, *c*. 43° 40' N., 113° W., 1805 =
1000 souls (*LE*., map).

SAN POIL (Salish: *HAN*., II, 451, 1060; same as Hihighenimmo, above):
1905 = 324; 1909 = 178 (*HAN*., II, 451); 1910 = 189, Colville
Reserve, Washington (*GN*., p. 173); they had been estimated by Thompson, July 1, 1811 = 60 families, *c*. 420 souls (*TH*., p. 476).

SCIATOGAS (Shahaptians, dwelling west of the Nez Percés, *c*. 1814; buffalo
Indians, having 'great numbers of horses':[317] Irving, *Astoria*, p. 82):
cf. *HAN*., II, 413, 520; *CS2*., II, 818, 853.

SEKANI, SEKANAIS (Athapaskan; Headwaters of Peace and other rivers):
1820 = est. 1000; 1888 = 151, Mackenzie River region; 1887 = 500,
half in British Columbia (Morice: *HAN*., II, 499); 1893, S. group =
1300: S. proper = 500, Tsattine (Beaver) = 700, Sarsi = 100 (Morice,
ibid.); see, however, SARSI, above; also Morice, *History of Northern
British Columbia*, p. 38.

SHAHALA (Chinookan; north side of Columbia River, 122° W.; including
Clahclellah, Neerchokioon, Wahclellah, Yehuh, on whom see *HAN*., I,
302; II, 51, 519, 996, etc.): 1805 = 2800 souls (*LE*., III, 327); 1000
souls (*LE*., map).

SHAHAPTINS: 1811 = a village of 66 families (*TH*., p. 485); an unitemized
total of 2679 'Shahaptians' on Yakima Superintendency, Southern Washington, 1910 (*GN*., p. 336).

SHALLALAHS (Silela: *HAN*., II, 572; south of Columbia River, beyond the
Willamette, or on lower Umpqua River, West Oregon: *ibid*.)[318] 1806

---

[315]Lewis and Clark mention three bands of 'Shoshonees or Snakes' (as on
map), totalling 10,600, dwelling on the Multnomah (Willamette) River and
tributaries, some 'high up on the said river' and not well known to the Columbia
Indians (*Journals*, III, 329). Perhaps some of the same.

[316]In 1805—Pelloat-Pallah, "a band of Chopunnish [Nez Percé] on the
Kooskooskee [Clearwater] above the forks, and on the small streams which fall
into that river, west of the Rocky Mountains and Chopunnish river [apparently
west side of Bitter Root Mountains *circa* 47° N., 116° 30' W.] and sometimes
pass over to the Missouri" (*Journals*, Appendix III, 326 = 1600 souls. Not on
their map, which gives the tribe as above, *circa* 46° 20' N., 120° W., Clark's
measurements).

[317]Thought by Coues (probably by reason of the horses) to be very probably
the Cayuse (*Henry-Thompson Journals*, II, 818, 853) but cf. *Handbook of
American Indians*, I, 224; II, 413, 520. 'Sciatoga, Saituka' = 'camas eaters.'

[318]I should feel very diffident about including as 'partly buffalo-using Indians'
any tribe so far down the Columbia were it not that the explorers mention the
Skilloots as being such (*Lewis and Clark Journals*, III, 64). The village shown
on their map is well below the Willamette, toward the coast; but they were first

= 1200 souls (*LE.*, II, 312; III, 328; not on *LE.* map).

SHANWAPPOM (Salish, a division of the Pisquows: *HAN.*, II, 263, 527): Yakima Valley, *c.* 46° 30′ N., 121° W., 1806 = 400 souls (*LE.*, III, 329; also *LE.*, map).

SHOSHONI (SHOSHONEES or SNAKE INDIANS, 1805[319]): 1805 = 4000 souls along tributaries of South Fork of Lewis's River (*ibid.*); 2000 along upper John Day River, *c.* 45° N., 118-119° W. (*ibid.*); 1000 along upper tributaries of North Fork of Lewis's River, *c.* 44° N., 112° 30′ W. (*ibid.*); 'MOY (?) band of Snakes,' headwaters, Madison-Gallatin Forks of the Missouri = 600 souls (*ibid.*); 'POHAH band of Snakes,' headwaters, main South Fork of Lewis's River, *c.* 43° 30′ N., 113° W. = 1000 souls (*ibid.*); 'YEPPE band of Snakes,' Yellowstone headwaters, *c.* 43° 20′ N., 110° W. = 1000 souls (*ibid.*); SHOSHONES and SNAKES on *LE.* map = 19,600 souls.

Five bands of 'Shoshonees' = 13,900 souls (*LE.*, III, 326, 329); 1845 = 4500 Shoshoni and 'Sheep-eater'[320] (*MO.*, p. 18); 1907, the same = 2265 (*ibid.*); 1909 = 1766 S. and Bannock, Idaho, *c.* 1000 in Nevada, 816 in Wyoming, total, less 500 Bannock = *c.* 3100 (all *HAN.*, II, 557); 1910 = 1092; 1126 Klamath, Modoc, and 'Yahooskin band of Shoshoneans' in Oregon (*GN.*, pp. 219, 252, 300).

SKADDAL (a division of the Pisquows; Yakima Valley, 46° N., 121° W.): 1805 = 200 souls (*LE.*, III, 329; *HAN.*, II, 585); 400 souls (*LE.*, map); 1846 = 400 (*HAN.*, II, 585).

SKILLOOT (Chinookan): Columbia River below the Willamette, *c.* 46° N., 123° 30′ W., 1806 = 2500 souls (*LE.*, III, 328; also *LE.*, map); almost exterminated by fever, 1823; 1850 = 200; shortly afterwards disappeared (*HAN.*, II, 591).

SMACKSHOP (Chinookan; 'a band of Chilluckittequaws,' Columbia River, near the Dalles): 1806 = 800 souls (*LE.*, III, 327; also *LE.*, map; *HAN.*, II, 602).

SOKULK (Shahaptian; Columbia River, above Snake River confluence): 1806 = 2400 souls (*LE.*, III, 326); 3000 (*LE.*, map); *c.* 1909 = 150-200 (*HAN.*, II, 614).

SPOKANE (Salish, the 'Lartielo' of 1806: *HAN.*, II, 625, 1081, 1145): south tributary of Clark's River, *c.* 48° 30′ N., 117° W., 1805 = 600 souls (*LE.*, III, 330; *HAN.*, II, 625); 900 (*LE.*, map); 1853 = 450; 1908 = 539 in Washington, 95, Idaho; 1909 = 509 in Washington, 104, Idaho (*HAN.*, II, 625).

SQUANNAROO (Yakima: *HAN.*, II, 629): Yakima Valley, 46° N., 121° W., 1805 = 120 souls (*LE.*, III, 329; *HAN.*, II, 629); 240 souls (*LE.*, map).

---

found at a village east of the Eneeshur, below the Dalles (*ibid.*, 60-4). Below, note 323.

[319]Shoshones = a descriptive term, signifying 'inlanders,' according to Alexander Ross (see Coues (ed.), *Henry-Thompson Journals*, II, 794). 'Origin not known'; no mention of Ross (Henshaw, *Handbook of American Indians*, II, 556).

[320]Tukuarika; cf. the Shoshonean *Yamparika* = yampa-eaters; *Shirrydika* = dog-eaters; *Warrarika* = fish-eaters; *Kutshundika* = buffalo-eaters (see Ross, *Fur Hunters*, I, 249; Coues (ed.), *Henry-Thompson Journals*, II, 818; *Handbook of American Indians*, I, 130, 743, etc.).

TAKULLI, or CARRIERS (Athapaskan: Peace River headwaters and Stuart Lake region, British Columbia): 1820 = one band of 100; 1835 = est. 5000; 1839 = 897 men, 688 women, 578 sons, 462 daughters, total 2625 (*HAN.*, II, 676); 1841 = '4000 Kootenays and Carriers' (De Smet, *EWT.*, XXVII, 166); 1889 = 1600 (Morice); 1902 = 1551; 1909 = 1614 (all, *HAN.*, II, 676).

TSATTINE, or BEAVER[321] (Athapaskan: Peace River headwaters and east): 1889 = 800; 1906 = 700 (both, Morice, *HAN.*; II, 822); evidently much reduced: cf. *ibid.*

TUSHEPAW (probably Kutenai: *HAN.*, II, 853): on Clark's River, *c.* 48° N., 114° W. = 'a numerous people of 450 tents' (*LE.*, II, 141); 1806 = 430 souls (*ibid.*, III, 330: 'Tushepaw proper,' so *HAN.*, II, 853); 1806 = 800 souls (*LE.*, map).

UTE (Shoshonean): 'a band of several thousands, thought to be Ute, Bear River (Utah or Wyoming), 1825 (*DAS.*, p. 144); 1839 = 'at least' 10,000 (Gregg, *EWT.*, XX, 83); 1841 = *c.* 4000 souls (De Smet, *ibid.*, XXVII, 166); combined total 'probably never exceeded 10,000' (*HAN.*, II, 875); 1845 = 4500 (*MO.*, p. 18); *c.* 1849 = 4000 or 5000 (*BA4.*, p. 462); 1870 = *c.* 4000; 1885 = 3391 (both, *HAN.*, II, 875); 1886 (U.S. Census) = 978 (*HO.*, p. 526); 1907, including Gosiute and Pahvant = 2068 (*MO.*, p. 18); 1909 = 2014 in Colorado and Utah (*HAN.*, II, 875); 1910 = 2388, '815 Southern Utes' (*GN.*, pp. 167, 305, 315).

GOSIUTE: 1861 = '200 men'; 1873 = 460; 1885 = 256 (*HAN.*, I, 497).

PAHVANT: 1885 = 134 (*HAN.*, II, 185).

WAHKIAKUM (Chinookan): north bank, Columbia River, near the mouth, 1805 = 200 (*HAN.*, II, 890).

WAHOWPUM (Shahaptian): Columbia River, above the Dalles, 1805 = 700 souls (*LE.*, III, 327); 1000 souls (*LE.*, map).

WALLA-WALLA (Shahaptian): on lower Walla Walla River, Washington, 1805 = 1600 souls (*LE.*, III, 326; *HAN.*, II, 900); 2500 souls (*LE.*, map); 1841 = 500 (De Smet, *EWT.*, XXVII, 166); 1910 = 461 (*HAN.*, II, 900; *GN.*, p. 317).[322]

'WAPPATOO' Indians (Wappatoo or Sauvies Island, mouth of Willamette River): 1805 = 13 tribes, 5 being Multnomah (Willamette) River tribes, totalling 5490 souls (*LE.*, III, 327); not on *LE.* map.[323]

WASCO (Chinookan): Columbia River, near the Dalles, 1822 = est. 900 (*HAN.*, II, 917); 1910 = Wasco, Tenino, and 'Confederated Warm Springs,' last two Shahaptian, totalling 780 on Warm Springs Reserve, Oregon; *c.* 200 Wasco (*HAN.*, II, 917; *GN.*, p. 330).

[321]*Tsaotine; tsa* = beaver (Garrioch, Beaver MS. Vocabulary).

[322]Lewis and Clark included the Umatilla with the Walla Walla; incorrectly, so *Handbook of American Indians*, II, 866. 151 Umatilla in 1910 (Grinnell, *Indians of To-Day*, 317).

[323]The names given in *Handbook of American Indians*, II, 913, with identifications. Here also the proximity of the buffalo-hunting Shoshoni, and of buffalo-using tribes (Skilloots, etc.) farther down the Columbia, probably justifies their inclusion as buffalo-users in some degree; or even by distinct bands perhaps moving for the purpose. Lewis and Clark note 50 houses of Skilloots on the Lower Columbia (as above, *Journals*, III, 328), and also a 'Skilloot village' of 23 houses above the Dalles (*ibid.*, 323) not on their map. Above, note 318.

WASHO (Nevada): 1845 = 1000 (*MO.*, p. 18); 1859 = *c.* 900 (*HAN.*, II, 920); 1907 = *c.* 300 (*ibid.*; *MO.*, p. 18).

WENATCHI (Salish, probably a band of the Pisquows: *HAN.*, II, 932): 1850 = said to be 50 (*ibid.*); 1910 = 66, Colville Reserve, Washington (*GN.*, p. 173); said in 1811 to be *c.* 120 families, 800 souls (*TH.*, p. 482).

WHEELPO or WHE-ET-PO (Colville; Salish: so, *HAN.*, I, 327; II, 1172): on Clark's River at its northernmost point, 117 ° W., 1805 = 2500 souls (*LE.*, III, 329); 3500 souls (*LE.*, map).

WILLEWAH (Nez Percés: *HAN.*, II, 953): Willewah, apparently Grand Ronde River, tributary of Lewis River, *c.* 46° N., 117° 30' W., 1805 = 500 souls (*LE.*, III, 326; *HAN.*, II, 953); 1000 souls (*LE.*, map).[324]

YEPPE ('a band of Snakes'): Yellowstone headwaters, *c.* 43° 20' N., 110° W., 1805 = 1000 souls (*LE.*, map); Yeppe = Yampa (*HAN.*, II, 1176).

8. ESTIMATED AGGREGATES, IN CHRONOLOGICAL ORDER

1736: Indians 'under the French Govt.' est. 82,000 souls (*MCSF.*, p. 290).[325]

1805: Prairie and Plains tribes of the Mississippi, and from the Kansas River to the Assiniboine River (Manitoba) = 56,300 (*LE.*, map);[326] 80,000 'West of the Rocky Mountains' (*ibid.*, III, 326-30);[327] Sauks and Foxes, 'Chipeways,' Menominees, Winnebagoes, Iowa, 'Sues' (? Sioux) = 45,152 on the Mississippi from its source, including Red Lake and Lower Red River, to St. Louis (Pike: *CS1.*, I, 346).

1806: 20,007 (Osage, Kansa, Pawnee, Comanche) in 'that part of Louisiana visited by Z. M. Pike in the years 1806 and 1807' (*CS1.*, II, 590).

1811: 13,615 souls (seven per family) 'in the valley of the Columbia' (Thompson, *Narrative*, p. 529).

1820: est. 526,592 Indians (*MCSF.*, p. 290).[328]

1825 (*circa*): est. 140,000 souls in 'the Oregon Territory' (Thomas Hart Benton: *BA6.*, II, 426).[329]

1830: 20,000-30,000 Indians in California (*MCSF.*, p. 291).

1833: est. 70,000 died of fever in California (*MO.*, p. 19).

1835: est. 330,000 Indians in U.S. and Mexico (*MCSF.*, p. 293); 1835 (*circa*): est. 60,000 Blackfoot (Pilcher: Catlin, so Dodge, *Our Wild Indians*, p. 48);[330] 'more than 250,000' (*i.e.* buffalo Indians: *CAT.*, I,

---

[324]Given in *Lewis and Clark Journals* (map) as 'Wil-le-wah river and tribe, 1000 souls'; in their abstract as 'Willewah band of Chopunnish' (Nez Percé: *ibid.*, III, 326).

[325]See remarks above, note 246.

[326]Entirely too low. The Sioux alone total over 16,000, on Lewis and Clark's map; cf. SIOUX (above, sec. 5).

[327]Their map for that territory gives 73,940, exclusive of 20,370 (III, 327-9) not shown on the map; a total of at least 94,310.

[328]Doubted by Maclean; for what reason is not mentioned.

[329]I am unaware just what constituted the Oregon Territory in 1825. Lieut. Wilkes's Report to the Secretary of the Navy, 1842, defines Oregon as the region west of the Rockies (Thwaites (ed.), *Early Western Travels*, XXIX, 94).

[330]In the same passage the statement is criticized by Dodge; 'probably not more than a fourth of that number.' I have been unable to identify the passage

122); 300,000 (buffalo Indians: *CAT.*, I, 263).

1839: 'about 135,000 Indians inhabiting the Great Prairie Wilderness' (Farnham, *EWT.*, XXVIII, 117).

1840-41: '80,000 Indians in Texas' (Maillard, an English author; 'very unreliable,' so Bancroft: *BA5.*, II, 141, 214, 346).

1842: 17,000 in the Valley of the Saskatchewan (Governor Simpson, cited in *MCSF.*, p. 293).[331]

1844: 'nearly 40,000' Blackfoot, Cree, and kindred tribes in Manitoba and N. W. Territories (citing Lefroy: *MCSF.*, p. 293); 'not more than 23,400 Indians on the British plains' (computation by Lefroy: *BL.*, p. 72).

1846: 'about 110,000;' the total number in the Oregon territory (De Smet, *EWT.*, XXIX, 143).

1850: est. 54,550 Indians, Upper Missouri and tributaries (*MCSF.*, p. 293).

1856: 64,000 (pop. of Rupert's Land, H.B. Co.); almost entirely Indians ('very much over-estimated': *PL.*, p. 199).

1856: 25,500 Indians in (part of) the Saskatchewan District, H.B. Co. = Edmonton, 7500; Rocky Mountain House, 6000; Fort Pitt, 7000; Carlton, 5000 (*Canadian Indians Blue Book*, cited in *HI.*, p. 115).[332]

1856: 150,000 in 34 H.B. Co. Districts (*BR.*, pp. 489-90). The Indian population in the 14 buffalo-using districts was distributed broadly as follows:

ATHABASKA (Fort Chipewyan, Dunvegan, Vermilion, Fond du Lac) = 1550.

COLUMBIA (in part, probably F. Vancouver) = *in toto*, 2200.

COLVILLE (Washington: Fort Colville, Pend d'Oreille River, Okanagan, Flat Heads, Kootenay) = 2500.

CUMBERLAND (Cumberland House, Moose Lake, The Pas) = 750.

ENGLISH RIVER (Ile à la Crosse, Rapid River, Green Lake, Deer's Lake, Portage la Loche) = 1370.

LAC LA PLUIE (Rainy Lake; in part: Fort Frances, Fort Alexander, Rat Portage, White Dog, Lac du Bonnet, Lac du Boisblanc) = 2850.

MACKENZIE RIVER (in part; probably, Fort Simpson, Fort au Liard, Fort Rae, Fort Resolution) = *in toto*, 10,430.

NEW CALEDONIA (in part, probably Stuart Lake, McLeod's Lake, perhaps Fort George) = *in toto*, 12,000.

NORWAY HOUSE (Norway House, Beren's River, Nelson River) = 1080.

RED RIVER (Fort Garry, Lower Fort Garry, White Horse Plain, Pembina, Manitoba House, Reed Lake) = 8250 (including half-breeds and white residents).[333]

SASKATCHEWAN (Edmonton, Carlton, Fort Pitt, Rocky Mountain House, Lac la Biche, Lesser Slave Lake, Jasper's House, Fort Assiniboine, Fort à la Corne) = 26,550.[334]

---

in Catlin. For the latter's two estimates immediately following (made, be it noted, before the terrific smallpox epidemic of 1837) see remarks below.

[331]Simpson's own (*Journey Around the World*, I, 102) is 16,730 in the Saskatchewan District, Hudson's Bay Company; which is a very different thing.

[332]See note 334.

[333]See above, chap. XIV, for Red River population, 1831-46.

[334]Given by Bryce (*Remarkable History*, Appendix C, 489) as 28,050; but the last five posts total only 1550, in addition to 25,500 as given above, note 332. These are all from the *Report from Select Committee on Hudson's Bay Company, 1857*, 365.

SNAKE COUNTRY (Walla Walla, Fort Hall, Fort Boisé) = 700.[335]

SWAN RIVER (Fort Ellice, Fort Pelly, Qu'Appelle Lakes, Shoal River, Touchwood Hills, Egg Lake) = 2200.

YORK (York Factory, Churchill, Severn, Trout Lake, Oxford House) = 1500.[336]

Total = 73,880.

1856: 42,870 Indians in Rupert's Land ("one-fourth too high": *HI.*, p. 114).

1857: 43,000 Indians in Rupert's Land (*MCSF.*, p. 294).

1858: 35,000 'Thickwood Indians' east of the (Canadian) Rockies (*HI.*, pp. 114-15); '25,000 Canadian Plains tribes' ("considerably over-rated": *HI.*, pp. 114-15);[337] 28,510 'nomadic Indians' in Rupert's Land (*i.e.* principally buffalo-users: *PL.*, p. 200); 1483 Reservation Indians in Texas (*BA5.*, II, 408).

1865 (*circa* ?): 'more than 50,000 when the U.S. Govt. began to support the (Plains) Indians' (*HO.*, p. 437); '25,000 warriors on the war-path' (? *circa* 115,000 souls: Hebard and Brininstool, *Bozeman Trail*, I, 147).

1875: 300,000 Indians in 17 Western States, as follows: Arizona = 28,179, Colorado = 9265, Dakota = 36,031, Idaho = 10,291, Indian Territory = 75,200, Kansas = 400, Michigan = 9412, Minnesota = 9490, Montana = 25,896, Nebraska = 4406, Nevada = 3318, New Mexico = 25,918, Oregon = 6915, Utah = 4864, Washington = 11,784, Wisconsin = 15,139, Wyoming = 15,814 (Ado Hunnius, *Table of Indians living in the United States of America in 1875;* cited in *DOl.*, pp. 441-8).[338]

316,000 Indians in U.S.: 'civilized' = 100,000, 'semi-civilized' = 135,000, 'barbarous' = 81,000 (Hunnius: *ibid.*, p. 448).

1876: '19,000 or more' of all tribes, in Wyoming (*BA8.*, p. 777); 2938 Indians in the 'Athabaska district' (*MCSF.*, p. 295); 20,998 Indians, Manitoba and N.W.T. (*MCSF.*, p. 295).

1881: 246,417 in U.S. Official Census (*MCSF.*, p. 291).

1884: 2038 in 'Peace River district' (*MCSF.*, p. 295).

1885: 20,170 in N. W. Territories and Canada, as follows: Assiniboia = 4492, Saskatchewan = 6260, Alberta = 9418 (Canadian Census: *BL.*, p. 285).

1886: 253,000 in U.S. per Official Report ("probably at least one-fifth too great": *DOl.*, p. 49); 54,758 'buffalo Indians' of 21 tribes (*HO.*, p. 526).[339]

[335]This could only mean 'on the H.B. Co. books.' As a population estimate, it would be farcical. Doubtless true elsewhere also, *re* estimates.

[336]For movement of buffalo products in that direction, see above, chap. XII, note 73; chap. XVII, notes 36-7.

[337]Presumably the 25,500 instanced above, notes 332, 334.

[338]See remarks below regarding this date. *Ante* 1840, many more (modern) States might be added. I regret I know nothing more about Hunnius.

[339]Dr. Hornaday adds: "This leaves entirely out of consideration many thousands of Indians living in the Indian Territory and other portions of the Southwest who drew an annual supply of meat and robes from the chase of the buffalo, notwithstanding the fact that their chief dependence was on agriculture . . ." ("Extermination of the American Bison," 526). Add to these the Central States and Canadian areas; and compare *circa* 1700-1800. Even among the buffalo tribes, Hornaday gives only Apache = 332; Arapaho = 1217; Arikara = 517; Assiniboine = 1688; Bannock-Shoshone = 2001; Blackfoot, Blood, Piegan = 2026;

1891: 244,704 Indians in U.S., including some mixed bloods (*MCSF.*, p. 291); *c.* 8000 in the 'Athabaska district' (*MCSF.*, p. 295); 25,195 Indians, Manitoba and N.W.T. (*MCSF.*, p. 295).

1895: 256,000 Indians (? North America or U.S.: *MCSF.*, p. 290).

1907: 3450 in western Oregon (*c.* 1780 = 89 tribes, 42,250 pop.: *MO.*, pp. 16-18); 4203, East Washington (*c.* 1780 = 36 tribes, 17,950 souls: *MO.*, pp. 15-16); 3943, West Washington (*c.* 1780 = 42 tribes, 22,750 souls: *MO.*, pp. 15-16).

1910: *c.* 90,000 Algonkians (40,000, U.S.; 50,000, Canada: *HAN.*, I, 43).

Mooney's final summaries are of interest:

	Early Figures	Late Figures (*i.e.* 1907)
North Atlantic States	55,600	21,900
South Atlantic States	52,200	2,170
Gulf States	114,400	62,700
Central States	75,300	46,126
Northern Plains	100,800	50,477
Southern Plains	41,000	2,861
The Columbia Region	88,800	18,797
Central Mountain Region	19,300	11,544
New Mexico and Arizona	72,000	53,832
'California'	260,000	15,431
Eastern Canada	54,200	27,000
Central Canada	50,950	28,770
British Columbia	85,800	25,588
Greenland	10,000	11,000
Alaska	72,600	28,310
	1,152,950	406,506
United States proper	840,000	266,000
British America	221,000	101,000
Alaska	73,000	28,000
Greenland	10,000	11,000
	1,153,000	406,000

(*MO.*, p. 33).[340]

To these may be added for my present purpose, a considerable number in northern Mexico, up to say *circa* 1810.[341]

Cheyenne = 3477; Crow = 3226; Gros Ventre = 856; Kiowa-Comanche = 2756; Mandan = 283; Nez Percé = 1460; Omaha = 1160; Pawnee = 998; Sioux = 30,561; Ute = 978; Winnebago = 1222 (not a specially buffalo tribe).

[340] I subjoin Mooney's later note: "nearly 1,150,000 [*circa* 1492] . . . which is believed to be within 10 per cent of the actual number. Of this total, 846,000 were within the limits of the United States proper, 220,000 in British America, 72,000 in Alaska, and 10,000 in Greenland. The original total is now reduced to about 403,000, a decrease of about 65 per cent. The report of the Dept. of Indian Affairs for 1911 states that the total native population of Canada is 108,261—including 4600 Eskimos" (Mooney, *Handbook of American Indians*, II, 286; *Handbook of Canadian Indians*, 390).

[341] See Kroeber, *Cultural and Natural Areas*, 131-81, etc.

Kroeber would reduce Mooney's (early) general aggregate total to about 900,000. This reduction, coming from an ethnologist of the very first rank, is not lightly to be questioned; particularly since Kroeber readily acknowledges his predecessor's high competence as a cautious critic.[342] In their relation to the question of 'buffalo' Indian population at large, the figures of Ado Hunnius and particularly their date, 1875, are of great importance. They may be compared with those of Catlin, *circa* 1835-40. At the later date the tribes, as we have seen, had been scourged by a number of devastating epidemics. Also, the period falls within the era of decimating wars and of massacres both of an organized military character and of a more sporadic 'popular' nature which involved considerable numbers of non-combattants. Further, relations in the West were then scarcely such as to suggest any fictitious bolstering up of nominally 'Indian' populations through intermarriage; and removals of other tribal remnants into the Western States territory could hardly offset the decrease in the numbers of the original residents from various causes. The possible inaccuracy of Hunnius is irrelevant for the moment; the point is that Dodge, of all critics perhaps, was not unwilling to print such an estimate for such a period without adverse comment. Catlin may not have been so far astray after all.

Catlin's estimates (as in the crowning instance of the 60,000 Blackfoot, after Pilcher) were quite often furnished to him by others; his own offence being merely that of endorsing them. It will be noted that his contemporary figures for the Central States and Middle West tribes do not differ materially from those accepted for neighbouring eras by the scholarly contributors to the *Handbook of American Indians*. Nor was he always in excess. We may compare his 6000 Assiniboine, 3000 Cree, 7000 Ojibwa; with the 10,000 Assiniboine of Drake, or the 28,000 of Maximilian and Chittenden; the usual 12,000 Cree; the conjectural maximum 10,000 Crow of Chittenden; or the estimated 15,000 or 30,000 Ojibwa of Thwaites or Mooney. The study in the present Appendix was not entered upon for the purpose of vindicating Catlin. But his testimony has been very frequently cited in the course of our inquiry as coming from the most reliable witness known to me of all those who studied the buffalo species in detail in its natural (prairie) habitat. It can scarcely be denied that to convict Catlin of reckless extravagance in one particular would be to seriously lessen the weight and authority of his evidence in other departments. Instead of his figures discrediting his general trustworthiness, however, the case is reversed; the latter entitles his figures to respectful consideration, whether finally acceptable *in toto* or not.[343]

I have stopped at 1911, as any variations in the population of Indian tribes since that time, besides being partly artificial owing to admixtures of races, would be meaningless in relation to buffalo.

[342]*Ibid.*, 132-4.
[343]See above, chap. I, note 14.

APPENDIX H

BUFFALO, INDIAN, AND LEGISLATION

A serious historical study of the buffalo would not even approximate completeness without some reference to the official attitude toward their extermination. Hornaday has made the plea for game preservation so conspicuously his own (to an extent where even I myself cannot follow him[1]), and my own critical remarks concerning his positions on various aspects of buffalo history have been at times so severe, that common justice demands a similar publicity and emphasis for his utterances on our present subject. This is the more true, since he was contemporary with the final manifestations of the abuses he denounced; and since also (in so far as I have been able to discover) no better summary has ever been presented to the public. I shall first quote the section of his essay dealing with "Congressional Legislation for the Protection of the Bison":[2]

The slaughter of the buffalo down to the very point of extermination has been so very generally condemned, and the general Government has been so unsparingly blamed for allowing such a massacre to take place on the public domain, it is important that the public should know all the facts in the case. To the credit of Congress it must be said that several very determined efforts were made between the years 1871 and 1876 looking toward the protection of the buffalo. The failure of all those well-meant efforts was due to our republican form of Government. Had this Government been a monarchy, the buffalo would have been protected; but unfortunately in this case (perhaps the only one on record wherein a king could have accomplished more than the representatives of a people) the necessary act of Congress was so hedged in and beset by obstacles that it never became an accomplished fact.[3] Even when both houses of Congress succeeding in passing a suitable act (June 23, 1874), it went to the President[4] in the last days of the session only to be pigeon-holed, and die a natural death. . . .
    [Mr. R. C. McCormick, of Arizona, speaking on April 5, 1872] mentioned a then recent number of *Harper's Weekly*, in which were illustrations of the slaughter of buffalo, and also read a partly historical extract in regard to the same. He related how, when he was once snow-bound on the Kansas Pacific Railroad,[5] the buffalo furnished food for himself and fellow-passengers. Then he read the bill introduced by him March 13, 1871, and also copies of letters furnished him by Henry Bergh, president of the America Society for the Prevention

[1]Above, chap. XXI, note 372.
[2]Hornaday, "Extermination of the American Bison," 513-21.
[3]One cannot doubt his sincere belief in this, *circa* 1888; but he would have some ado to establish his thesis. The extermination of men and things by Spaniards in the Indies or by Turks in Palestine were scarcely the achievements of republicans; and Dickens's own particular 'Circumlocution Office' was — if I mistake not — situated not far from London, though it has relatives everywhere.
[4]Grant.
[5]Known as the 'Buffalo Route,' *circa* 1873 (Seton, *Game Animals*, III, 423).

of Cruelty to Animals, which were sent to the latter by General W. B. Hazen, Lieut. Col. A. G. Brackett, and E. W. Wynkoop. He also read a statement by General Hazen to the effect that he knew of a man who killed ninety-nine buffaloes with his own hand in one day. . . .

[Another bill was introduced by Mr. Fort, of Illinois, to protect the buffalo on January 5, 1874.] Mr. Cox [opposing: March 10, 1874, with reference to females in the bill] said he had been told by old hunters that it was impossible to tell the sex of a running buffalo. . . . Mr. Fort. . . . had been told that the sexes could be distinguished while they were running.[6]

Said Mr. Fort [March 10, 1874], "So far as I am advised, gentlemen upon this floor representing all the Territories are favorable to the passage of this bill."

Mr. Cox wanted the clause exempting the Indians from the operations of the bill stricken out, and stated that the Secretary of the Interior had already said to the House that the civilization of the Indian was impossible while the buffalo remained on the plains.

The Clerk then read for Mr. McCormick the following extract from the *New Mexican*, a paper published in Santa Fé:

"The buffalo slaughter, which has been going on the past few years on the plains, and which increases every year, is wantonly wicked, and should be stopped by the most stringent enactments, and most vigilant enforcements of the law. Killing these noble animals for their hides simply, or to gratify the pleasure of some Russian duke or English lord, is a species of vandalism which cannot too quickly be checked. United States surveying parties report that there are two thousand hunters on the plains killing these animals for their hides. One party of sixteen hunters report having killed twenty-eight thousand buffaloes during the past summer [1873]. It seems to us there is quite as much reason why the Government should protect the buffaloes as the Indians."

Mr. McCormick . . . read the following extract from a letter he had received from General Hazen:

"I know a man who killed with his own hand ninety-nine buffaloes in one day, without taking a pound of the meat. The buffalo for food has an intrinsic value about equal to an average Texas beef, or say $20. There are probably not less than a million of these animals on the western plains. If the Government owned a herd of a million oxen they would at least take steps to prevent this wanton slaughter. The railroads have made the buffalo so accessible as to present a case not dissimilar." . . .

Mr. Potter desired to know whether more buffaloes were slaughtered by the Indians than by white men.

Mr. Fort thought the white men were doing the greatest amount of killing.

Mr. Eldridge thought there would be just as much propriety in killing the fish in our rivers as in destroying the buffalo in order to compel the Indians to become civilized.

Mr. Conger said: "As a matter of fact, every man knows the range of the buffalo has grown more and more confined year after year; that they have been driven westward by advancing civilization." But he opposed the bill![7] . . .

Mr. Parker, of Missouri, intimated that the policy of the Secretary of the Interior was a sound one, and that the buffaloes ought to be exterminated, to prevent difficulties in civilizing the Indians. . . .

[6]"I know of no greater affront that could be offered to the intelligence of a genuine buffalo-hunter than to accuse him of not knowing enough to tell the sex of a buffalo 'on the run' by its form alone" (footnote by Hornaday, "Extermination of the American Bison," 515).

[7]Comment by Hornaday, *ibid.*, 517.

The bill was reported to the Senate, ordered to a third reading, read the third time, and passed. It went to President Grant for signature, and expired in his hands at the adjournment of that session of Congress. . . .

On February 2, 1874 [? 1875], Mr. R. C. McCormick, of Arizona, introduced in the House a bill (H. R. 1728) restricting the killing of the bison, or buffalo, on the public lands; which was referred to the Committee on the Public Lands, and never heard of more.

On January 31, 1876, Mr. Fort introduced a bill (H. R. 1719) to prevent the useless slaughter of buffaloes within the territories of the United States, which was referred to the Committee on the Territories.

The Committee on the Territories, reported back the bill without amendment on February 23, 1876. Its provisions were in every respect identical with those of the bill introduced by Mr. Fort in 1874, and which passed both houses.

In support of it Mr. Fort said: "The intention and object of this bill is to preserve them (the buffaloes) for the use of the Indians, whose homes are upon the public domain, and to the frontiersmen, who may properly use them for food. . . . They have been and are now being slaughtered in large numbers. . . . Thousands of these noble brutes are annually slaughtered out of mere wantonness. . . . This bill, just as it is now presented, passed the last Congress. It was not vetoed, but fell, as I understand, merely for want of time to consider it after having passed both houses. . . .

Mr. Crounse . . . thought Indians were to blame for the wanton destruction.

Mr. Fort. . . . stated that he was informed that the Indians did not destroy the buffaloes wantonly. . . .

The Clerk read . . . a letter from A. G. Brackett, lieutenant-colonel, Second United States Cavalry, stationed at Omaha Barracks, in which was a very urgent request to have Congress interfere to prevent the wholesale slaughter then going on.

Mr. Reagan thought the bill proper and right. He knew from personal experience how the wanton slaughtering was going on, and also that the Indians were *not*[8] the ones who did it. . . .

Mr. Throckmorton . . . had several objections. He also thought a cow buffalo could not be distinguished at a distance.

Mr. Hancock, of Texas, thought . . . the sooner the buffalo was exterminated the better.

Mr. Fort replied by asking him why all the game—deer, antelope, etc.—was not slaughtered also. Then he went on to state that to exterminate the buffalo would be to starve innocent children of the red man, and to make the latter more wild and savage than he was already. . . .

On February 25, 1876, the bill was reported to the Senate, and referred to the Committee on Territories, from whence it never returned.

Dr. Hornaday comments as follows:

This was the last move made in Congress in behalf of the buffalo. The philanthropic friends of the frontiersman, the Indian, and of the buffalo himself, despaired of accomplishing the worthy object for which they had so earnestly and persistently labored, and finally gave up the fight. At the very time the effort in behalf of buffalo protection was abandoned, the northern herd still flourished, and might have been preserved from extirpation.

At various times the legislatures of a few of the Western States and Territories enacted laws vaguely and feebly intended to provide some sort of protection to the fast disappearing animals. One of the first was the game law of Colorado,

---

[8]Italics Hornaday's.

passed in 1872, which declared that the killers of game should not leave any flesh to spoil. The western game laws of those days amounted to about as much as they do now; practically nothing at all. I have never been able to learn of a single instance, save in the Yellowstone Park, wherein a western hunter was prevented by so simple and innocuous a thing as a game law from killing game. Laws were enacted, but they were left to enforce themselves. The idea of the frontiersman (the average, at least) has always been to kill as much game as possible before some other fellow gets a chance at it, *and before it is all killed off!*[9] So he goes at the game, and as a general thing kills all he can while it lasts, and with it feeds himself and family, his dogs, and even his hogs, to repletion. I knew one Montana man, north of Miles City, who killed for his own use twenty-six black-tail deer in one season, and had so much more venison than he could consume or give away that a great pile of carcasses lay in his yard until spring and spoiled.

During the existence of the buffalo, it was declared by many an impossibility to stop or prevent the slaughter. Such an accusation of weakness and imbecility on the part of the General Government, is an insult to our strength and resources. The protection of game is now, and always has been, simply a question of money. A proper code of game laws and a reasonable number of salaried game-wardens, sworn to enforce them and punish all offences against them, would have afforded the buffalo as much protection as would have been necessary to his continual existence. To be sure, many buffaloes would have been killed on the sly in spite of laws to the contrary, but it was wholesale slaughter that wrought the extermination, and that could easily have been prevented. A tax of 50 cents each on buffalo robes would have maintained a sufficient number of game-wardens to have reasonably regulated the killing, and maintained for an indefinite period a bountiful source of supply of food, and also raiment for both the white man of the plains and the Indian. By judicious management the buffalo could have been made to yield an annual revenue equal to that we now receive from the fur-seals— $100,000 per year.

During the two great periods of slaughter—1870-'75, and 1880-'84—the principal killing-grounds were as well known as the stock-yards of Chicago. Had proper laws been enacted, and had either the general or territorial governments entered with determination upon the task of restricting the killing of buffaloes to proper limits, their enforcement would have been in the main, as simple and easy as the collection of taxes. Of course the solitary hunter in some remote locality would have bowled over his half-dozen buffaloes in secure defiance of the law, but such desultory killing could not have made much impression on the great mass for many years. The business-like, wholesale slaughter, wherein one hunter would openly kill five thousand buffaloes and market perhaps two thousand hides, could easily have been stopped forever. Buffalo hides could not have been dealt in clandestinely, for many reasons, and had there been no sales for ill-gotten spoils, the still-hunter would have gathered no spoils to sell. It was an undertaking of considerable magnitude, and involving a cash outlay of several hundred dollars to make up an 'outfit' of wagons, horses, arms and ammunition, food, etc., for a trip to 'the range' after buffaloes. It was the wholesale hunters, both in the North and the South, who exterminated the species, and to say that all such undertakings could not have been effectually prevented by law is to accuse our law-makers and law-officers of imbecility to a degree hitherto unknown. There is nowhere in this country, nor in any of the waters adjacent to it, a living species of any kind which the United States Government can not fully and perpetually protect from destruction by human agencies if it chooses to do so. The destruction

[9]Italics Hornaday's.

of the buffalo was a loss of wealth perhaps twenty times greater than the sum it would have cost to conserve it, and this stupendous waste of valuable food and other products was committed by one class of the American people and permitted by another with a prodigality and wastefulness which even in the lowest savages would be inexcusable.[10]

I have quoted Hornaday's utterance *in extenso,* since without doing so, certain other items of historical evidence could scarcely be set in their proper light. It will be noted that he makes no mention of the buffalo as a possible obstacle to the agricultural development of the Plains area; but since the defenders of the slaughter appear to have been similarly silent, that phase may be passed over. One cannot but be struck by the practical wisdom with which Hornaday provided a workable remedy, instead of being content merely to denounce the abuse. This suggests certain considerations. It cannot be supposed that some such methods as those he suggested would not be obvious to the executive officers of the country; or to other public men who had ever carried on with any measure of success—even if it were only that of successful routine administration— an essentially similar task. Give such men the will and they would quickly find a way. They may, I think, be acquitted of the charge of 'imbecility'; although at the same time, the stigma would be thoroughly well deserved by the executives of any great country, with an accumulated fund of political and administrative experience upon which to draw—in addition to abundant material resources—if their implied plea of the impossibility of prevention were put forward in good faith as their only answer to the problem.

Actually, however, there appears to have been some measure of method in the madness of the executives of the United States government. The confident tone of the appeals to the dictum of the Secretary of the Interior concerning 'the impossibility of civilizing the Indian while the buffalo remained,' indicate with sufficient clearness (in my opinion) that he had what might be termed a constructive policy—of sorts; whatever we might think of it from the political, economic, or humanitarian standpoint. Evidence appears to indicate that influences were at work behind the scenes which Hornaday very probably did not suspect; or I cannot but think that so courageously outspoken a critic of an official policy would have mentioned them. One is glad to be able to record the names of any military men of western experience on the humanitarian side. It is idle at the same time to ignore the fact that we look in vain for defenders of the buffalo among the outstanding military chiefs in Indian warfare. It is equally idle to suppose that if these men—many of them Civil War heroes and the idols of the nation—had been opposed to the extermination policy, its opponents in Congress would not have ranked these great names in the forefront of their argument, and that Hornaday would not have emphasized the fact. The President of the day was an old comrade-in-arms of many of these men, with no Western military experience of his own;[11] and a man who—

[10]Compare a later opinion: "Its extermination was one of the most shameful examples of man's greed and a nation's lethargy that is furnished in the history of any country . . ." (Stone and Cram, *American Animals,* 1913, 67).

[11]Compare Grant's attitude toward Custer, one of his most energetic officers,

with all respect to a gallant soldier and one who bore without abuse the grand old name of gentleman—gave very little indication of that political insight which can see above and beyond the war cry of the hour.[12]

The two supreme military chieftains of that era were Sherman and Sheridan. Competent Western and historical critics have deposed these great figures from their position as authorities on matters Indian to which Civil War hysteria had elevated them, and in which a hasty and uncritical journalism would retain them.[13] To Sheridan is ascribed the glory of the well-known formula that 'the only good Indian is a dead Indian'; and the facility with which this creed could be propagated scarcely admits of doubt. A modern scholar writes of the anti-Indian attitude: "This conception was based upon the intermittent warfare that began in 1862. It was kept vivid by the propaganda of bordermen and army officers. Through every means of civilized communication, press, mail, telegraph, and public exhibition, they strengthened the public belief in Indian brutality and treachery. Their gospel was Sheridan's, 'The only good Indian is a dead Indian.' . . . The Indian had no medium of publicity through which to reply. . . ."[14]

Sherman, who is, by the way, the author of the classic definition of war, is placed upon record as follows: " 'We must act with vindictive earnestness against the Sioux,' General Sherman wrote to Grant, 'even to their extermination, men, women, and children. . . .' "[15] We have already considered the ethics of such a position.[16] It is sufficient to say here that to suppose a soldier of Sherman's experience to be ignorant of the value of starvation in forwarding the accomplishment of that *desideratum* would indeed be to accuse him of military 'imbecility, to a degree hitherto unknown.' One thing is self-evident from Hornaday's recital: some influence, compared with which the passage of a bill through both Houses of Congress was as nothing, was able to nullify a measure which we cannot doubt would have passed into law with alacrity at the earliest moment that constitutional requirements permitted, had legislative and executive opinion been in accord on the subject.

Whatever of quasi-secrecy this vindictive spirit might have maintained in Washington, in the Western territory at large its protagonists were much less reticent. As far back as 1867, Sir William (then Lieutenant) Butler found Colonel Dodge in command at North Platte, Nebraska. Butler writes:

---

and with an Indian campaign in prospect; spring, 1876 (Taylor, *Frontier Life*, 161).

[12]I do not forget the essential political wisdom in Grant's chivalrousness to Lee at Appomattox; but I doubt whether chivalry toward an Indian was very often thought of.

[13]Sherman and Sheridan as authorities, in Laut, *Pilgrims of the Santa Fé*, 249, 275; 'ignorant of Indians' (Grinnell, *Fighting Cheyennes*, 288). Cf. Walsh, below.

[14]Walsh and Salsbury, *Making of Buffalo Bill*, 43-4. Cf. above, on the mutually-destructive theses—repeated 'defeats of overwhelming forces of Indians with terrific slaughter' (chap. XXI, sec. 10), and of tribes which were almost invariably 'vastly over-rated' in point of numbers. See Appendix G, "Indian Populations."

[15]Walsh and Salsbury, *Making of Buffalo Bill*, 101.

[16]Above, chap. XXI, sec. 10.

"We told him of the week's hunting we had had on the Platte prairies. More than thirty buffalo bulls had been shot by us, and I could not but feel some qualms of conscience at the thought of the destruction of so much animal life, but Colonel Dodge held different views. 'Kill every buffalo you can,' he said; 'every buffalo dead is an Indian gone.' "[17] Following upon this, it is difficult to avoid the conclusion that when Colonel Dodge writes, ten years later, that "Congress talked of interfering, but only talked. . . ,"[18] we are listening, not to regret of the scientist or the humanitarian, but merely to the exultation of the soldier.

It is quite safe to assume that an officer of no higher than regimental rank would not have been so outspoken to an alien visitor, had there been any doubt of the opinions of his chiefs. At a somewhat later time (when the Sioux under Sitting Bull had moved over into Canada after the defeat of Custer in June, 1876, and whence they refused to return for a considerable time),[19] similar opinions were looked upon as being no secret. A careful historian of Western Canada, who drew upon a large mass of (then) living reminiscence and tradition, states that the extermination of the buffalo was believed by North West Mounted Police officers and well-informed traders to have been planned by the United[1] States military authorities as the only means of bringing the Sioux to submission.[20] This is corroborated by others, somewhat more precisely,[21] and whether filtering through from such 'inspired' sources, or as an original consensus of opinion held by the Westerners at large and adopted from them by the army men—it is quite commonly found among all classes.[22]

[17]Butler, *Autobiography*, 97; see also his *Great Lone Land*, 63, 241, 318-20. Ten years later (for public consumption), Colonel Dodge was indicating conscientious scruples *re* buffalo slaughter (*Plains of the Great West*, 120-1; quoted *in extenso* above, chap. XIII, note 143). One may contrast the earlier attitude of the U.S. authorities toward the slaughterings of Sir George Gore and party, Fort Berthold, winter 1855-56 (Bancroft, *History of Washington, Idaho, and Montana*, 609; Hebard and Brininstool, *Bozeman Trail*, II, 228; Garretson, *American Bison*, 101-2). The last-named thinks that this official view was expressed more to avert Indian resentment than to protect the buffalo; but—as will be seen below in this Appendix—'Indian resentment' imposed no restraints later on.

[18]Dodge, *Plains of the Great West*, 132.

[19]See above, chap. XVII, notes 60-63.

[20]Black, *History of Saskatchewan*, 200.

[21]MacRae, *History of Alberta*, I, 377; 'on the authority of a highly-placed Mounted Police officer.' This was Colonel Herchmer; so, Diller, "Early Economic Development of Alberta," IV, 4.

[22]"Some American frontiersmen believed that the more buffalo they killed the sooner would the hated Indians disappear, and so zest was added to the holocaust . . ." (MacInnes, *In the Shadow of the Rockies*, 143). He adds elsewhere: "Many of them [Indians] knew that certain Americans had openly avowed the policy of exterminating the Indians, and facts were not wanting to confirm their belief that these individuals represented the will of the American people generally . . ." (*ibid.*, 62).

'Commonly understood, *circa* 1879, that the U.S. Govt. desired the extermination of the buffalo' (Osgood, *The Day of the Cattleman*, 79; cf. also Turner, *Frontier in American History*, 144).

One of our very latest historians of the species, Thompson Seton, cites and seemingly endorses the more recent opinion that the buffalo were the real bone of contention (from the Indian standpoint) in the virtually final war with the Sioux, 1866-76. For practical purposes, this war may be said to have broken out as a result of the disastrous defeat of Fetterman at Fort Phil Kearney, December 21, 1866; and to have culminated in the extermination of Custer's force on the Little Big-Horn, June 25, 1876. The exciting cause has been very generally accepted as having been the discovery of gold in the Black Hills, with the resultant advance of the whites over the Bozeman Trail, in defiance of the treaties made with the Sioux, under Red Cloud and other leaders. This view has been held to be incorrect. Thompson Seton cites the following:

"They [the Indians] say that from the year 1864 onward till after the Sitting Bull—Custer battle they—the Western Sioux Indians—kept the Buffalo herded back into Montana or the extreme western part of the present North Dakota. This statement, strange as it may seem, is confirmed by numerous white frontiersmen.

"The old Indians say, and other evidence shows, that these Sioux Indians extended their herd line as far north only as the Killdeer Mountains. . . .[23] and to the point on the Missouri River just north of these mountains. Meanwhile, the Buffalo, now quite safe from ruthless depredation by white men, increased greatly in numbers; and in the summer of 1875, many of these Buffalo crossed the Missouri from the south side to the north side—from the present McKenzie County to the present Williams County and Mountrail County—and thus escaping the Indian herd line, they roamed up and down the Missouri, often swimming the river forth and back, and going as far down the river as Painted Woods, 60 miles up river from Bismarck, North Dakota.

"All white frontiersmen know well that from 1864 onward till after the Sitting Bull—Custer battle, no Buffalo were to be found on the vast plains west of the Missouri River and east of the Indian herd line, except a very few that occasionally slipped through the herd line and were not followed by Indians and killed for food. But from 1875 on, large numbers of Buffalo were sometimes found in the north country which was beyond this Indian herd line, and some of them wandered as far east as the Turtle Mountains country. . . .

"After the Sitting Bull—Custer battle, which was the end of this careful attention given to the Buffalo by the Western Sioux Indians, the Buffalo that had thus increased in numbers came freely eastward, and seemed, at times, almost to fill the plains country, west of the Missouri River in North Dakota. In old times, Indians never ruthlessly slaughtered Buffalo, or other animals. They used what was necessary and preserved the rest. The Buffalo were the Indians' cattle.

"The Western Sioux Indians regarded Buffalo stealing about as a Dakota Cattle-rancher regards Cattle-stealing—as a crime deserving death. This Buffalo stealing by white men in the Dakotas was many times more the cause of trouble with the Sioux than all the gold in the Black Hills. I know this from hearing old Indians freely talk among themselves. That the trouble was caused chiefly by the Black Hills gold is an erroneous notion of the matter originated by white men. This notion has become fixed in written history, but it is incorrect."[24]

One hesitates to criticize statements from an authority in touch with the Indians themselves; and it is scarcely to be doubted that the wanton

[23]Killdeer, Dunn County, North Dakota; *circa* 47° 30′ N., 103° W.
[24]Father A. McG. Beede, "In the Days of the Buffalo," *Forest and Stream*, June, 1921, 248; cited by Seton, *Game Animals*, III, 668. I have not seen Father Beede's article myself.

slaughter of the buffalo may have played on the Indian mind in the era
of wars and hostilities. But considered as general conclusions and almost
sole causes, the foregoing conflict with other pronouncements which cannot
be disregarded. I am dubious, *a priori*, about generalizations by Indians;
the Indian is not a generalizer. Corroboration from 'all white frontiersmen'
is practically of no more value; the same class corroborated the legend of
the hoop snake, almost to a man. Furthermore, they do not all corroborate
this view of the buffalo history.

It seems probable that in many instances, the absences of the buffalo
described above were of that inscrutable character, of which we have seen
so many examples.[25] General W. F. Raynolds (U.S. Army) is quoted as
saying: "As late as 1866, they occupied much of the country between Fort
Union and Fort Pierre. . . ."[26] Father De Smet records them as having
'disappeared' from the Missouri River, from Yankton Agency to 'above
Fort Randall,' 1867.[27] J. H. Taylor, our frequently cited plainsman-author,
writes of 1868: "As the timbered points from Fort Randall to Fort Benton
at that time contained large numbers of deer and elk, and the prairies for
the greater part of the same distance ranged numerous herds of antelope,
besides occasional droves of buffaloes, the task of plentifully supplying the
boats [that is, steamboats] with fresh wild meats, was not a difficult
one. . . ."[28]

He writes in another place: "Around these elevated plains of the Dog
Den country the buffalo continued in large numbers until about the year
1868, when they disappeared, and only now and then after that year that
a herd could be seen there [sic]. In 1874, a band of sixty buffalo were
discovered near Prophet's Mountain, a butte ten miles south of the Dog
Den, and a few miles west of that place, by a hunting party of Sissetons.
The buffalo were surrounded and slain by the red hunters. The destruction
of this band ended the buffalo among the lakes and buttes of the Coteau du
Prairie, with a very few straggling exceptions."[29] The great southern bend,
or 'bight' of the Souris (that is, Mouse) River touches its lowest point,
Mouse River, North Dakota (some little distance east of Minot, on the
Great Northern main line), at about 48° N., 101° W. The Dog Den is a
well-known landmark of the early days, the *Maison du Chien* or 'Dog's
House' of the younger Henry, 1806;[30] apparently some ten or fifteen miles
south of the bight of the Souris, a high hill, a flank or outlier of the Missouri
Coteau.

The foregoing passages seem to indicate the continuous presence (that is,
broken only by such intervals as are recorded practically everywhere
throughout their history) of buffalo, down to 1868, or perhaps in some
measure down to 1874, at points beyond the Indian herd-line, and far
below the Painted Woods. This place was situated, as Father Beede
observes, some sixty miles up-river from Bismarck, North Dakota, near the

[25]See above, chap. XX, "Irregular Migrations."
[26]Allen, *American Bisons*, 161.
[27]*Life of De Smet*, III, 872.
[28]Taylor, *Frontier Life*, 240-1.
[29]*Ibid.*, 262.
[30]See Henry, and Coues's notes, *Henry-Thompson Journals*, I, 316, 406.

later town of Washburn.[31] Father Beede seems also to have overlooked the influence of the annual Red River hunts in sweeping the buffalo progressively westward at this time, across a huge front extending roughly from the line of the lower South Saskatchewan (north of the Elbow; about 107° W.), to the Missouri. The hunters, as we have seen, followed a general route not far north of latitude 49°, and spread considerably to the south, if occasion seemed to warrant it.[32] It has been noted also that in 1874 the buffalo were not found on the Canadian hunters' route east of Cypress Hills (*circa* 108° 30′ W. to 110° W.), or on the international boundary itself until about 107° 20′ W.[33] The secretary of the U.S. contingent of the International Boundary Commission of that year was our invaluable authority, Dr. Elliott Coues. I have so far found nothing from him or from anyone else concerning buffalo as far east as Turtle Mountain, later than 1875; nor any allusion of any character to the herding by Indians on so grand a scale. When the Boundary Commission encountered the buffalo later on, several other tribes besides the Sioux were attacking the immense herd as common property.[34]

A hot resentment at the loss (or prospective loss) of the buffalo for the moment, and the guarding or policing of local herds to preclude this, are well attested.[35] But such a movement as this would seem to have been, a gathering up of their resources lest the coming of the white folk should leave them destitute forever, implies an Indian reaction toward buffalo which finds no support whatever from Indian psychology, as we have seen in abundant detail.[36] At much later periods, 1877, 1885, when, as we know now, the herds were almost, and at the second date actually exterminated, Indians (including Sitting Bull himself) regarded the preservation or the return of the buffalo as a matter totally independent of what we should designate economic laws.[37] Curiously enough, almost as this was being written, the following item appeared in the press (from Wood Mountain, Saskatchewan, December 6, 1933):

Buffalo have returned to Saskatchewan plains.

Unknown in these parts since at least a quarter century,[38] the bison came back to the Elm Spring country and were reported seen Saturday and on several occasions since then.

At least six buffalo are in the small herd seen. Old Indians are all agog. They tell each other that prophecies of their old medicine men will come true.

Buffalo roaming in their wild state in southern Saskatchewan lend color to the belief of the Indians, that once again they will possess the happy hunting grounds of their forefathers. In the 50's and 60's buffalo by thousands roamed these prairies.

Police are a little skeptical.

[31] Taylor, *Frontier Life*, 124. It often appears in his reminiscences.
[32] See above, chaps. XIV, XVII, at large.
[33] Above, chap. XIV, notes 174-80.
[34] Chap. XIV, notes 178-80.
[35] Above, chap. XIV, notes 34-38; chap. XXI, sec. 8.
[36] Above, chap. XXI, sec. 6.
[37] See chap. XXI, notes 237-49.
[38] See above, chap. XVII, notes 77-82, 99-102, etc.

They think the buffalo came from the Montana range country across the border and belong to a private rancher.[39]

This apparently proved to be the case.[40] It is precisely this belief in the supernatural replenishing of the stock of buffalo which, in the case of Indians, removes into a totally different category what would unquestionably be 'waste' in the case of white hunters. I have endeavoured to set this matter in its true light, in some detail;[41] but to say that Indians never slew more than could be utilized, either at the time or by curing, is simply incorrect as a statement of fact; whatever extenuating circumstances or temperamental explanations may be validly adduced in defence.

For more than one reason, in addition to the foregoing, the hostility toward the miners seems much more authentic than Father Beede's informants would make it to be. Bad blood between miners and Indians is well attested, long before any destruction of the buffalo on a scale that could reasonably be termed 'extermination.'[42] While it is true that historical misconceptions concerning the West have only too frequently obscured actual truths, a critical student cannot consent to degrade careful and scholarly historians to the category of 'writers' in order to set the nameless authority of 'white frontiersmen' in their place; the more so, when such historians utilize (and much more critically) a considerable amount of frontiersman material themselves.[43] If one section of white opinion can fabricate 'an erroneous version' of certain events, another section—drawn from the same class, moreover—may do likewise. I do not for one moment question Father Beede's good faith; but the statement of the informants looks very much like a desperate attempt to evade responsibility for an era that few right-minded people mention today without shame, by pleading at the bar of History that 'Codlin's the friend, not Short.'

As usual, chronology is the stumbling-block. The semi-legitimate extermination (that is, by professional fur hunters, and traders, who furnished something at least to the Indians in return for their share in the traffic) had been increasing since *circa* 1830.[44] The hide-hunter pure and simple, of the final era, did not make his appearance in the Southern buffalo territory until the advent of the railway made marketing possible, about 1867.[45] This type of indiscriminate butcher does not appear to have cursed the North with his presence until the Southern extermination was virtually complete. In fact, there was actually an interval of four or five years (1875-80) between the termination of the one and the commencement of

---

[39]*Edmonton Journal*, December 6, 1933.

[40]*Ibid.*, December 16, 1933.

[41]Above, chap. XXI, sec. 6.

[42]See on this Marcy, *Exploration of Red River*, 19, 69; Bancroft, *History of Oregon*, II, 311; *History of Utah*, 467-71; *History of Washington, Idaho, and Montana*, 695-8; *History of Nevada*, 718-24; Butler's Report (*Great Lone Land*, 363); *Place-Names of Alberta*, 39; etc., etc. Some personal details in Taylor, *Frontier Life*, 12-22, 156-8.

[43]For example, Hebard and Brininstool, *Bozeman Trail;* see particularly, I, 201-63; II, 113-48.

[44]See above on this, chap. XVIII, notes 28-50.

[45]Above, chap. XV, notes 53-59.

the other, in the opinion of their leading historian, Hornaday.[46] It is hard to evade the conclusion that it was not the buffalo stealing in the Dakotas which caused the trouble with the Sioux, but the trouble with the Sioux which caused the buffalo stealing in the Dakotas.

The movement into Montana, which marked the opening of the Bozeman Trail, was in some measure a march of settlers; but it seems to have been the miners who gave it the character of a resistless rush, not to be stemmed by any such feeble obstacle as an Indian treaty which forbade entrance into the territory. The influx was principally, it would seem, of miners and those who drew their living from the miners. Either as miners *per se*, or as buffalo slaughterers who attacked the herds on their way, as they journeyed to the gold-fields, miners and their associates are practically the only ones who could furnish cause for (localized) Indian hatreds at that time. Even the military advance, marked by the establishment of such posts as Forts Phil Kearney and C. F. Smith, was not until 1866.[47] Miners (that is, of course, gold seekers) in a Western gold rush have not been remarkable for pausing on their way for any purpose; and we have seen that long before this time, it was almost proverbial along the great homeseekers' route of the West, the Oregon Trail, that the buffalo were chiefly conspicuous by their absence, they had been 'frightened from the road,' even although they might be found some few miles back, by a more leisurely class of travellers.[48] Buffalo extermination, at a later date, doubtless constituted a contributory cause in the bitterness of the red race toward the invaders; as the sole explanation, or the 'real truth,' it is, with the accompanying exoneration of the miners, unconvincing.

The reader has doubtless noted, from yet another angle of the endless contradictions concerning buffalo, that these Sioux herds which were seemingly swept from a huge area and confined for ten years in a territory not of their own choosing, are the same headstrong species 'which nothing could turn from their course,' etc.[49]

I feel, at the same time, that the strictures of Hornaday and of Messrs. Stone and Cram, on 'a nation's lethargy,' and 'a disgrace to the American *people*,' are unduly severe. In many cases, as the former himself has observed, things could be and were done before they were even known to the nation at large.[50] Even in those cases where the facts were supposedly laid before them—or their representatives—and their sanction formally requested, at that time more often than not the sources of information whence

[46]Hornaday, "Extermination of the American Bison," 505-6 (*in extenso* above, chap. XVI, notes 8-10).

[47]Hebard and Brininstool, *Bozeman Trail*, I, 263, 346; II, 39-109.

[48]See above, chap. VI, notes 109-11; chap. XV, notes 37-41; chap. XX, notes 89-99; etc.

[49]See above, chap. VI, at large. Hornaday's account reads quite differently, whoever is right (chap. XVI, notes 8-10). Possibly his informants, themselves largely buffalo butchers, might over-emphasize Indian slaughter; cf. on this, chap. XV, note 89. We have seen also the suspicious character of an assertion concerning drought in the Concho country, Texas, 1875 (chap. V, note 69).

[50]Hornaday, "Extermination of the American Bison," 511 (above, chap. XVI, note 40).

alone the ordinary man could obtain the 'authenticated' evidence by which he must approve or condemn, were poisoned. We have seen reason to suppose that even a well-informed critic like Dr. Hornaday himself was unaware of the extent of this cancer.[51] In passing our judgment, these factors must not be overlooked.

[51]Above, note 10, and my own comments following. For a specimen of anti-Indian propaganda, 1872, see a cartoon reproduced in Garretson, *American Bison*, 77: Indians slaying 2,000,000 per annum 'for Robes to get Whisky.'

BUFFALO PLACE-NAMES

While 'buffalo' place-names have been bestowed upon a large number of physical features or 'political' divisions (towns, etc.) on the map of North America, I have found one word only of Indian origin which has taken its place along with Spanish, French, and English derivatives in the historical terminology of buffalo at large. That word is Cibolo, Cibola.[1] This was thought by earlier scholars to be from *sibú lodá* = 'buffalo,' in the dialect of the Pueblo of Isleta, New Mexico;[2] but a later learned authority gives *Cibola* = *Shí-vo-la*, from *Shíwona*, or *Shí-winakwin* = 'the land that produces flesh'; or, 'buffalo-land.'[3]

We are not here concerned with the 'Seven Golden Cities of Cibola,' in which relationship no map of the Indies in Shakespeare's time was complete without this famous name. But it must have become virtually synonymous with *buffalo* or *cattle* in Spanish ears; for it has been noted as a Spanish (loan-word) place-name in a territory in Peru which was famed for its hides.[4] Consequently it seems rather curious that while 'Kine of Cibola' was perhaps the first English term for the buffalo,[5] I have found only two Hispano-Indian place-names embodying this word. These are the Rio Cibolo, or tributary of the Rio San Antonio, which with its co-partner, the Rio Guadalupe, debouches into Matagorda Bay, Texas; and the Arroyo del Cibolo, about 25 miles northeast of the San Antonio River, some distance farther up.[6] The Spaniards may in many cases have had a definite repugnance toward bestowing names drawn from the nomenclature of an enslaved race; there are indications that some of the forms in current use may have borne a contemptuous connotation. While it seems logical enough to term buffalo hunters *Ciboléros*,[7] the use of *cibolos* for Mexicans at large, apparently prior to the American (U.S.) era in Santa Fé, carries an unmistakeable suggestion of the *plebs,* the 'common herd,' as mere 'cattle.'[8]

[1]*Cibolo* = masc.; *Cibola* = fem.; so Bancroft, *History of Arizona and New Mexico*, 44.

[2]Bancroft, *ibid.; Journey of Coronado,* ed. Winship, 91.

[3]Hodge, *Handbook of American Indians,* II, 1016.

[4]Bancroft, *History of Arizona and New Mexico,* 44.

[5]See Appendix A, "Buffalo Synonymy."

[6]Bancroft, *History of North Mexican States and Texas,* II, 203, 228, with map, 249; Coues (ed.), *Expeditions of Pike,* II, 697, 703. See below, note 10. 'Arroyo del Cibolo' is noted by a learned Texas scholar, Bolton, *Handbook of American Indians,* II, 422.

[7]Gregg, *Early Western Travels,* XIX, 235, 239-40; XX, 119.

[8]In the revolutionary outbreak at Santa Fé and Taos, 1847, "the cibolos took advantage of the slaughter . . ." (an old MS. cited by Bancroft, *History of Arizona and New Mexico,* 434). I find an Indian tribe termed Zibolos (? a nickname), Bancroft, *Native Races,* I, 611, 672, "N.E. Mexican Tribes." See following note.

The name, in several variant or extended forms, apparently occurs in numerous instances.[9] The other fundamental Spanish buffalo-name, *vaca*, *vacas*, is also well represented.[10]

[9]CIBOLA; also Cebola, Sibola, Zibola (Coues (ed.), *Expeditions of Pike*, II, 742). Cevola, Civola (*Purchas his Pilgrimes*, XVIII, 62, 63, etc., etc.). Ceuola (Michael Lok, 1592; in Bancroft, *History of North Mexican States and Texas*, I, 151). Cebolia (?) River, Saguache County, Colorado (Bancroft, *History of Nevada, Colorado, and Wyoming*, 636).
Cebolleta, pueblo near Albuquerque, New Mexico (Bancroft, *History of Arizona and New Mexico*, 67, 247, 285, 422, 656; Coues (ed.), *Expeditions of Pike*, II, 619, 630). Given also as *La Joya de Cibolletta* (*ibid.*, 619, 628, 632, 739); and again Sibilleta or Sevilleta, and hence 'possibly Spanish in origin' (Bancroft, *History of Arizona and New Mexico*, 296, 312); but cf. Coues (ed.), *Expeditions of Pike*, II, 619, 630. Coues also mentions the pueblo of *Cebolletita*, in the region of ancient Cibola (Zuni) (*ibid.*, 630). See on all this, Hodge, *Handbook of American Indians*, II, 1016.
[10]VACAS. Rio de las Vacas, Alvarado, 1540 = the Canadian River; so Hallenbeck, *Journey of Cabeza de Vaca*, 143. Martin Lopez de Ibarra, 1564—"reached some great plains adjoining those of the Vacas—the buffalo plains— . . ." (Bancroft, *History of the North Mexican States and Texas*, I, 109). Vargas, 1583, mentions the *Valles de las Vacas*, along the *Rio de las Vacas*, and Espejo, also 1583, describes the region along the same river (Rio Pecos): "*esta provincia confina las vacas que llaman de Civola . . .*" (Bancroft, who considers the river to be the Gallinas, the eastern and larger branch of the Pecos: *History of Arizona and New Mexico*, 59, 72, 85, 90, 796; also his *History of the North Mexican States and Texas*, I, 127). On Espejo's journey, see also *Purchas his Pilgrimes*, XVIII, 65-7; Thomas, *History of North America*, II, 44-6; and particularly Hallenbeck, *Journey of Cabeza de Vaca*, 89, 140-4, 200, 209, *et passim*, with reference to the journal of Perez de Luxan, and the tribe '*de las Vacas.*'
There was the *Potrero de las Vacas* (*potrero* = 'little mesa,' table-land, 'cow-pasture') 25 miles northwest of Santa Fé (Coues (ed.), *Expeditions of Pike*, II, 745; *Handbook of American Indians*, I, 317, 370; II, 184, 189). There were also in Sinaloa the missions of *Vaca* (with *Baca* to the northward; B = V in Spanish) and *Toro* (Bancroft, *History of North Mexican States and Texas*, I, 660, 687; II, 629, 657, with maps). These may not necessarily have been from buffalo; since there were 'wild cattle' in great numbers in northern Sinaloa, though not buffalo, *circa* 1600; as well as in the Peninsula of Baja California, across the Gulf, *circa* 1775 (*ibid.*, I, 210, 712, 716, 737-51). At a later period, not clearly specified, however, 'tamed buffaloes' are mentioned in Sinaloa, Sonora, or Chihuahua, and cross-breeding with cattle (*ibid.*, II, 750). Whether wild herds were in those parts at that time is not indicated (cf. *ibid.*, I, 407-91). See above, Appendix C, note 58.
I note also *Mesa La Vaca* in Arizona (36° 30' N., 111° W.). This name, together with Skull Valley Station above, furnishes, I believe, the only (inferential) evidence we possess for the possible presence of *Bison americanus* in Arizona formerly. There is a *La Vaca* River in Texas, also sometimes *La Baca* (as in Bancroft, *History of North Mexican States and Texas*, II, 69); a Spanish phonetic usage which is present also in *De Baca* County, New Mexico (*Cram's International Atlas*). This *La Vaca* is the Rio San Antonio, or River Guadalupe, whichever name it bears at the mouth. It is also the *Rivière Aux Bœufs* of La Salle, 1686 (Joutel, *Journeys of La Salle*, II, 69, 78); ". . . stream and (Matagorda) bay are still known as Lavaca, from the Spanish equivalent . . ." (Coman, *Economic Beginnings of the Far West*, I, 384).

With reference to buffalo place-names in general, as given below, while it is not always possible to distinguish them, it may be taken for granted that they fall into three principal categories. Apart from 'political' names in some instances, those in the extreme outlying regions of the habitat may reasonably be accepted as evidence of the buffalo having penetrated at least to that point. Some of those within the more central portions probably refer to famous resorts where buffalo 'could always be found'—in popular supposition at least. And I have no doubt that some others in the plains territories commemorate occasions when buffalo *were* found, perhaps after a period of privation; or some striking specimen seen (as probably 'White Buffalo Lake,' below).

1. CREEKS

Bœuf Creek, Missouri (*Cram's International Atlas*, 1924).

Big Buffalo Creek, tributary of Osage River, Kansas (Coues (ed.), *Expeditions of Pike*, II, 377).

Big Bull Creek, Kansas; perhaps the same (*ibid.*, 519).

Buffalo Creek, Alberta, tributary of Pembina River, 1859 (Southesk, *Travels*, 170).[11]

———— Battle River, Alberta (White (ed.), *Altitudes in Canada*, 471).

———— Colorado, Jefferson County; Arkansas-South Platte headwaters (Bancroft, *History of Nevada, Colorado and Wyoming*, 621; Coues (ed.), *Expeditions of Pike*, II, 468).

———— Georgia, *circa* 1770 (Allen, *American Bisons*, 225).

———— Great Slave Lake, near Slave River (Richardson, *Arctic Expedition, 1847-1850*, 97).

———— Kansas, tributary of Republican River (Coues (ed.), *Expeditions of Pike*, II, 404-20).

———— 205 miles west of Leavenworth, Kansas Pacific Railway, 1867 (Grinnell, *Fighting Cheyennes*, 247).

———— Minnesota, Upper Red River, near Georgetown (John McDougall, *Forest, Lake, and Prairie*, 67).

———— Mississippi; near Natchez (Cuming, *Early Western Travels*, IV, 327).

———— Missouri River above St. Charles (Maximilian, *ibid.*, XXII, 240).

———— Montana (*Cram's International Atlas*).

———— Nevada, Washo County, *circa* 40° 45' N., 119° 50' W. (*ibid.*).[12]

———— New Mexico, tributary of Pecos River, De Baca County (*ibid.*). See below, note 10.

———— New York, city of Buffalo (Allen, *American Bisons*, 107).

In cases of simple *Vaca* or *Toro*, there is always the possibility of a direct transplanting from Spain. I have not found *Vaca* there, though the personal name was common enough, as Cabeza de Vaca, Vaca de Castro, Peru, *circa* 1540, etc.; but I note *Toro*, in Leon, in the civil wars, 1476 (Prescott, *History of the Reign of Ferdinand and Isabella*, 1872 ed., I, 248-63).

[11]Probably the present Lobstick River, draining Chip (late 'Lobstick') Lake into the Pembina, 60 miles west of Edmonton.

[12]See above on this, chap. II, notes 27, 42.

———— Erie County (*Handbook of American Indians*, I, 409).

———— North Carolina (Hornaday, "Extermination of the American Bison," 379).

———— Pennsylvania, Upper Conemaugh River (Michaux, *Early Western Travels*, III, 340; Allen, *American Bisons*, 108).

———— Pennsylvania or Virginia, 1753 ("Diary of the Moravians," Mereness (ed.), *Colonial Travels*, 340, 342; Michaux, 1795, *Early Western Travels*, III, 33).[13]

———— West Virginia (Thwaites (ed.), *Early Western Travels*, I, 129, note).[14]

———— Wisconsin, 1805 (Coues (ed.), *Expeditions of Pike*, I, 103, 290).

———— Wyoming, tributary Powder River, Park County (*Cram's International Atlas*).

Buffalo Ford, North Carolina (Hornaday, "Extermination of the American Bison," 379).

———— Virginia (Garretson, *American Bison*, 20).

Buffalo Fork, West Virginia (six instances; *ibid.*, 20).

———— Wyoming, tributary Snake River (Bancroft, *History of Nevada, Colorado, and Wyoming*, 666; *Cram's International Atlas*).

Buffalo Hide Creek, Wyoming; Little Powder River (*ibid.*).

Buffalo Horn Creek, Des Moines River, 1804 (map, *Lewis and Clark Journals*).

Bull Creek, Wyoming; Niobrara County (*Cram's International Atlas*).

Bull Lake Creek, Wyoming; tributary Wind River, Frémont County (*ibid.*).

Bullock Creek, South Carolina (*ibid.*; Allen, *American Bisons*, 95).

Bullpound Creek, Alberta; tributary Red Deer River, south of Hanna, Canadian National Railway (*Place-Names of Alberta*, 26).

Bullshead Creek, Alberta; tributary of South Saskatchewan River, west of Dunmore Junction, Canadian Pacific Railway (*ibid.*, 26).

Cow Creek, Kansas, 1806; tributary Smoky Hill River (Coues (ed.), *Expeditions of Pike*, II, 545).

———— Kansas; Santa Fé Trail, 16 miles east of the Arkansas River (*ibid.*, II, 424-6, 519; Gregg, *Early Western Travels*, XX, 92-3; Chittenden, *American Fur Trade*, II, 537).

———— Oregon; tributary Snake River, Malheur County, 43° N., 107° 20' W. (*Cram's International Atlas*).

———— Oregon; tributary fork of Umpqua River, rising *circa* 42° 40' N., 123° 15' W. (Bancroft, map, *History of Oregon*, II, 380).[15]

———— Wyoming; Carbon County (*Cram's International Atlas*).

Jumpingpound Creek, Alberta; tributary Bow River, west of Calgary (*Place-Names of Alberta*, 69, and map).

'Little Buffloe Creek,' Georgia, 1772 ("Journal of David Taitt," Mereness (ed.), *Colonial Travels*, 562; Wm. Bartram, *Travels*, 55).

Little Buffalo Creek, Kansas, 1806; tributary Big Buffalo Creek, above (Coues (ed.), *Expeditions of Pike*, II, 377).

[13]Seven 'Buffalo Creeks' in Virginia; so, Garretson, *American Bison*, 20.
[14]Sixteen 'Buffalo Creeks' in West Virginia; *ibid.*
[15]If authentic, the most westerly buffalo reference in the United States; see remarks above, chap. XI, notes 102-6. The position given marks only the source. The buffalo may have been encountered considerably farther west.

Little Bull Creek, Kansas, 1806; tributary Big Bull Creek, above (*ibid.*, II, 424-6, 519).

Pile o' Bones Creek, 1883 (now Regina, Saskatchewan); Wascana Creek, Regina, is from *Wascana* = 'pile of bones' in Sioux; so Armstrong, *Place-Names in Canada*, 236.

2. HILLS

Bison Peak, Park County, Colorado (Garretson, *American Bison*, 155).

Bone Pile Butte, Wainwright Buffalo Park, Alberta (*Ottawa Journal*, September 27, 1928).

Buffalo Bull Knob, West Virginia (Garretson, *American Bison*, 20).

Buffalo Buttes, Taos County, New Mexico (Coues (ed.), *Expeditions of Pike*, II, 597; *Cram's International Atlas*).

Buffalo Head Hills, Alberta; south of Peace River, 57° 30' N., 116° W. (White, *Altitudes in Canada*, 518; *Place-Names of Alberta*, 26, and map).

Buffalo Hill, Alberta; Bow River, near Gleichen (*ibid.*).

———— Virginia (Garretson, *American Bison*, 20).

Buffalo Hills, Alberta; on a tributary of South Saskatchewan River, 50° 35' N., 113° 13' W. (White, *Altitudes in Canada*, 517).

———— West Virginia (Garretson, *American Bison*, 20).

Buffalo Hump, Idaho County, Idaho (Bancroft, *History of Washington, Idaho, and Montana*, 396, 506; *Cram's International Atlas*).

Buffalo Mountain, Alberta, 1837; on Buffalo Lake, Portage La Loche—Ile à la Crosse (Simpson, *Narrative of Discoveries*, 56, 57).

———— West Virginia (two: Garretson, *American Bison*, 20).

Buffalo Mountains, Alberta; south of Peace River, *i.e.* 'Buffalo Head Hills' above (Butler, *Wild North Land*, 167, 172).

———— Pennsylvania, *circa* 1800 (Shoemaker, *Pennsylvania Bison Hunt*, 12).

Buffalo Peak (or 'Mountain'), 'Parks' region, Colorado (Bancroft, *History of Nevada, Colorado, and Wyoming*, 336).

Buffalo Point, Lake Claire, North-West Territories, Canada (Soper, "History of the Northern Bison," 360).

———— Lake of the Woods, *circa* 1800 (Coues (ed.), *Henry-Thompson Journals*, I, 23, 69; 1873, Morris, *Treaties with the Indians of Manitoba*, 320).

Buffalo Pound Hill (Lake), Qu'Appelle Valley region, Saskatchewan, 1853 (Hind, *Report, 1858*, 53).

Buffalo Ridge, Virginia (two: Garretson, *American Bison*, 20).

———— West Virginia (two: *ibid.*, 20).

Buffalo View, Alberta; near southern boundary, Wainwright Buffalo Park (*Place-Names of Alberta*, 26).

Bull's Head, Alberta; a hill 'shaped like a bull's head,' south of Medicine Hat (*ibid.*, 26).

———— southern Manitoba, *circa* 1800 (see Calf Mountain).

Calf Mountain, South Manitoba; formerly Bull's Head = *Tête de Bœuf* (Coues (ed.), *Henry-Thompson Journals*, I, 68).

Death Bull Mountain, Oregon; Linn County, 44° N., 122° 20′ W. (*Cram's International Atlas*).

Hair Hills, Southern Manitoba; *i.e.* Pembina Mountain (Coues (ed.), *Henry-Thompson Journals*, I, 81, 103).

Hairy Hill, Alberta, north of Vegreville (*Place-Names of Alberta*, 61).[16]

Horn Mountains (possibly) near Mackenzie River, Great Slave Lake, *circa* 63° N.

Jumping Buffalo, Alberta; Bow River, below Gleichen, east of Calgary (*Place-Names of Alberta*, 69).[17]

Jumpingpound, Alberta, on 'Jumpingpound Creek,' above (*ibid.*).

Roche à Bosche, Alberta; Athabaska River, below Jasper; possibly 'hump rock' (*bosse*; so *ibid.*, 22).[18]

Roche de Bœuf, Ohio; Maumee River, *ante* 1830 (*Handbook of American Indians*, II, 170, 393).

———— Upper Mississippi River, 1805 (Coues (ed.), *Expeditions of Pike*, I, 228).

White Buffalo Butte, Missouri River, 1865 (Taylor, *Frontier Life*, 175).

3. ISLANDS

Buffalo Island; Missouri River, above St. Louis, formely *Ile au Bœuf*, sometimes 'Shelton's Island,' 1895 (Coues (ed.), *Expeditions of Pike*, II, 365).

———— south of the Platte confluence, 1805; perhaps the same (Brackenridge, *Early Western Travels*, VI, 68).

Buffalo's Head, island in Lake Winnipeg, 1775 (Henry, *Travels, 1760-1776*, 252); 1877 (Young, *Canoe and Dog-Train*, 159).

Bull's Head, 1808 (the same; Coues (ed.), *Henry-Thompson Journals*, II, 454).

Cow Island, Missouri River, near Leavenworth, Kansas (Ile au Vache, 1820: Long, *Early Western Travels*, XIV, 175).

———— Missouri River, near the Musselshell River (Bancroft, *History of Washington, Idaho, and Montana*, 512).

Isle aux Bœufs, lower Missouri River, 1811; perhaps identical with Pike's, above (Brackenridge, *Early Western Travels*, VI, 38).

4. LAKES

Buffalo Bay Lake, Alberta, apparently Lesser Slave Lake region (*Edmonton Journal*, April 22, 1938).

Buffalo Chip Lake, Alberta, 1859; now Chip Lake, 70 miles west of Edmonton (Hector, *Palliser Journals*, 130).

Buffalo Dung Lake, 1810; *i.e.* Chip Lake, above (Coues (ed.), *Henry-Thompson Journals*, II, 585, 652).

[16]These 'hair' names are very probably derived from some exceptionally matted growth of scrub, which caught the hair from the buffalo at shedding-time. See above, chap. XIV, note 107.

[17]Given as a translation from Blackfoot; but in the very locality of Denny's jumping herd, 1876 (above, chap. IV, notes 36-7).

[18]Cf. 'Buffalo Hump,' above. Very probably from a similar resemblance.

———— now Yellowhead Lake, summit of that pass, Canadian National Railway, 1865 (Milton and Cheadle, *North-West Passage*, 245). So also George Simpson, 1824 (in Merk (ed.), *Fur Trade and Empire*, 37).

Buffalo Hump Lake (*Pekaukaune Sahkiegun*) above head of Pembina River, southern Manitoba (Coues (ed.), *Henry-Thompson Journals*, I, 81).

Buffalo Lake, Alberta, south of Battle River (*Place-Names of Alberta*, 26). In 1894 = 'Buffalo Hide Lake'; whence 'Tail Creek,' outlet into Red Deer River, see 'Bull Lake,' below.

———— Ile à la Crosse, Alberta (Mackenzie's *Lac du Bœuf*, *Voyages 1789 and 1793*, lxxx; maps in *Harmon's Journal*, *Place-Names of Alberta*, etc., etc.).

———— Wood Buffalo Park, North West Territories, Canada (Soper, "History of the Northern Bison," 360).

———— northern Minnesota (Coues (ed.), *Henry Thompson Journals*, I, 147).

———— Wisconsin, near Portage, Wisconsin (Coues (ed.), *Expeditions of Pike*, I, 301).

————, or 'Musk-Ox Lake,' 1770; 69° 30′ N., 120° W. (Hearne, *Journey*, ed. Tyrrell, 164, 204).

Bison Lake, Wood Buffalo Park, North West Territories, Canada (Soper, "History of the Northern Bison," 360).

Bull Dung Lake, Alberta; *i.e.* Chip Lake, above (Hector, 1859, *Palliser Journals*, 182).

Bull Lake, 1810; now Buck Lake, Alberta (Coues (ed.), *Henry-Thompson Journals*, II, 741).

————, now Buffalo Lake, Alberta; as above, south of Battle River (1860: *Palliser Journals*, map).

Chip Lake; the foregoing (*Place-Names of Alberta*, 33).

Cow-Dung Lake; now Yellowhead Lake, in that Pass (Hector, 1859, *Palliser Journals*, 129; Grant, 1872, *Ocean to Ocean*, 278).

Cow Creek Lake, Oregon; 43° N., 117° 20′ W. (*Cram's International Atlas*).

Cowhead Lake, southern Oregon (Bancroft, *History of Oregon*, II, 504).[19]

Dirt Lake, Alberta; *i.e.* Chip Lake, above (1859; map in Southesk, *Travels*).

Dried Meat Lake, Battle River, Alberta (*Place-Names of Alberta*, 44).

Mustus Lake (*i.e.* Buffalo Lake),[20] Alberta; 58° 6′ N., 116° 25′ W. (*Place-Names of Alberta*, map).

Pimiteoui = Peoria Lake, Illinois; 'a place where there is abundance of fat beasts,' *circa* 1680 (Hennepin, *New Discovery*, I, 154; Father Le Clercq, *Journeys of La Salle*, I, 100).

White Buffalo Lake, North Dakota (Taylor, *Frontier Life*, 41).

5. POLITICAL DIVISIONS

Bison: Oklahoma, South Dakota (*Cram's International Atlas*).

Buffalo: Alberta (2), Arkansas, Colorado, Georgia, Illinois, Iowa, Kansas,

[19]See remarks above, chap. XI, notes 105-6.
[20]Cree *mustus* = buffalo. See Appendix A, "Buffalo Synonymy."

Kentucky, Minnesota, Montana, Nebraska, New York, North Dakota, Oklahoma, South Carolina, South Dakota (2), Texas, West Virginia, Wisconsin, Wyoming (*ibid.*).
Buffalo Center, Iowa (*ibid.*). ·
Buffalo City, North Carolina (*ibid.*).
——— Wisconsin (Coues (ed.), *Expeditions of Pike*, I, 23, 24, 57).
Buffalo County: Nebraska, South Dakota, Wisconsin (*Cram's International Atlas*).
Buffalo Forge, Virginia (Garretson, *American Bison*, 20).
Buffalo House, on Buffalo Lake, Ile à la Crosse, 1872 (Macoun, *Autobiography*, 121).
Buffalo Mills, Virginia (Garretson, *American Bison*, 20).
Buffalo Park, Kansas (*Cram's International Atlas*).
Buffalo Station, Virginia (*ibid.*; Garretson, *American Bison*, 20).
Buffaloville, Illinois (*Cram's International Atlas*).
Bullshead (village), Alberta, south of Medicine Hat (*Place-Names of Alberta*, 26).
Grey Bull, Wyoming (*Cram's International Atlas*).

6. RIVERS

Buffalo Ford, Manitoba; Red River, above Fort Garry, 1793 (John McDonnell, in Masson, *Les Bourgeois de la Compagnie du Nord-Ouest*, I, 269).
——— North Carolina (Hornaday, "Extermination of the American Bison," 379).
——— Virginia, *circa* 1775 (Allen, *American Bisons*, 86; Garretson, *American Bison*, 20).
Buffalo Lake River, North West Territories, Canada, 11 miles from Hay River, southern end of Great Slave Lake (Richardson, *Arctic Expedition 1847-1850*, 99).
——— North West Territories, Canada; flowing north, paralleling Slave River, into Great Slave Lake (*Everyman Historical Atlas of America*, 52).[21]
Buffalo Landing, Wood Buffalo Park, North West Territories, Canada (Soper, "History of the Northern Bison," 360).
Buffalo Rapid, upper North Saskatchewan River, 1810 (Coues (ed.), *Henry-Thompson Journals*, II, 683).
Buffalo River, Alberta, now apparently Lobstick River, tributary of Pembina River, draining Chip Lake, above (*Palliser Journals*, 182).
——— northern Minnesota (Coues (ed.), *Henry-Thompson Journals*, I, 147).

[21] The existence of two—apparently quite distinct—'Buffalo Lake Rivers,' both flowing into Great Slave Lake, leads one to suspect that the latter may at some time have been known locally as 'Buffalo Lake,' perhaps in some Indian tongue. I have found no reference, however, to any such usage. The present Peter Pond Lake, 56° N., 109° W., was formerly 'Buffalo Lake' (Tyrrell, ed. note, *Hearne and Turnor Journals*, 367).

———— New York State (Allen, *American Bisons,* 88).

———— North West Territories, Canada (2); one flowing northeast into Great Slave Lake, southeast of the Mackenzie River outflow (Hewitt, *Conservation of the Wild Life of Canada,* map, 132; apparently also, Franklin, *Second Journey to the Polar Sea,* 11).

———— Tennessee; tributary of Tennessee River (Allen, *American Bisons,* 102).

———— Virginia (Garretson, *American Bison,* 20).

'Buffillo' River; Kelsey, July 10, 1689 (*Kelsey Papers,* 28).

'Buffalo (river) Branch,' Virginia (Garretson, *American Bison,* 20).

Buffalo Shoal, Upper Missouri River, 1806 (*Lewis and Clark Journals,* III, 235, 240). Probably a 'rapid.'

Cowdung River, *i.e.* Miette River, Jasper, Alberta (Simpson, 1824, in Merk (ed.), *Fur Trade and Empire,* 32).

Grey Bull River, Wyoming; tributary Bighorn River (*Cram's International Atlas*).

Horn River, tributary Mackenzie River, below Great Slave Lake (*ibid.*).

Little Buffalo River, North West Territories, Canada; paralleling Slave River into Great Slave Lake (Hewitt, *Conservation of the Wild Life of Canada,* map, 132).[22]

Ox-Portage Rapids (?), upper Mississippi River region, 1805 (Coues (ed.), *Expeditions of Pike,* I, 142).

Park (*i.e.* 'pound') River; tributary of Red River, above Fort Garry (Coues (ed.), *Henry-Thompson Journals,* I, 89-95, etc.).

Rio de las Vacas ('Cow River'); the Pecos or Canadian River.[23]

Rivière des Bœufs; sometimes applied to Buffalo *Creek,* above; city of Buffalo, New York.

Rivière aux Bœufs, northern Minnesota (Coues (ed.), *Henry-Thompson Journals,* I, 147).

———— tributary of Missouri River, 1806; now Buffalo River; 'Bœuf' or 'Buffalo' Island at the confluence, as above (Coues (ed.), *Expeditions of Pike,* II, 365).

———— Texas, 1686; see above, note 10.

———— (*i.e.* Wisconsin River, 1680) = 'so named from the abundance of buffalo' (Hennepin, *New Discovery,* I, 222).

Slaughter River; next tributary of Missouri River, above Judith River, Montana (Maximilian, *Early Western Travels,* XXIII, 71).

Tongue River, Manitoba, 1800; tributary of Red River, or Pembina River (Coues (ed.), *Henry-Thompson Journals,* I, 230, etc.).

———— Montana; tributary of Yellowstone River, 1806; confluence at Miles City, Montana (*Lewis and Clark Journals,* III, 234).

'Two Medicine River,' Montana, or 'Two Piskun River,' from a double *piskun* or 'jumping-pound'; *i.e.* at a river-confluence, a precipitous 'cut-bank' facing both streams (McClintock, *Old North Trail,* 438, 520).

---

[22]Quite evidently the same as the Buffalo Lake River of the *Everyman Historical Atlas of America* (cited above); and very probably the same as Back's 'Little Buffalo River' of 1820 (in Franklin (First) *Journey to the Polar Sea,* 284).

[23]See above, note 10; also chap. IX, note 24.

Wood Buffalo River, Wood Buffalo Park, North West Territories, Canada (Soper, "History of the Northern Bison," 360).

7. Springs,[24] Wallows, 'Licks'

Buffalo Springs, Colorado; 'Parks' region, headwaters of South Platte River (Bancroft, *History of Nevada, Colorado, and Wyoming*, map, 409).

—————— 'south of Fairplay,' Colorado (Allen, *American Bisons*, 40).

—————— North Dakota (*Cram's International Atlas*).

—————— Texas (*ibid.*).

—————— Virginia (2) (Allen, *American Bisons*, 86; Garretson, *American Bison*, 20).

'Buffalo Springs Ranch,' 19 miles west of Julesburg, Nebraska, South Platte River (Grinnell, *Fighting Cheyennes*, 191).

Buffalo Pond (?) (Atlantic States area).[25]

Buffalo Tank, Colorado; Jefferson County (Bancroft, *History of Nevada, Colorado, and Wyoming*, 621).[26]

Skullspring, Oregon; Malheur County, 117° 45' W., 43° 30' N. (*Cram's International Atlas*).

'Buffalo Wallow' ('The'; *i.e.* a place-name), Texas; near Amarillo, and 'Adobe Walls,' battle, June 24, 1874 (*Handbook of American Indians*, II, 204, etc.).

—————— ('The'), Minburn, Alberta, Canadian National Railway (locally so called).

Buffalo Lick, Kentucky, 1780 ("Col. Wm. Fleming's Journal," in Mereness (ed.), *Colonial Travels*, 652).

—————— Virginia, near Roanoke, 1753 ("Diary of the Moravians," *ibid.*, 344).

—————— West Virginia (6) (Garretson, *American Bison*, 20).

Big Bone Lick, Kentucky, 1763 *seq.* (*Simon Kenton*, 63; Croghan, *Early Western Travels*, I, 135; Captain Harry Gordon, in Mereness (ed.), *Colonial Travels*, 466-70.

'Great Buffalo Lick,' Georgia, 1772-1773 ("Journal of David Taitt," *ibid.*, 562; Bartram, *Travels*, 55).

'Grinin's Lick,' Kentucky, 1775 (*Cresswell's Journal*, 86).

Bayou Bœuf, near Biloxi, Mississippi, 1795 (*Handbook of American Indians*, II, 205).

Bayou Salade, 'North Park,' Colorado, 1839 (Farnham, *Early Western Travels*, XXVIII, 209, 266).

Beef Slough, Wisconsin; Chippewa River, 1805 (Coues (ed.), *Expeditions of Pike*, I, 58-60).

Buffalo Bayou, Harrisburg, Texas (Bancroft, *History of the North Mexican States and Texas*, II, 228, 252, 362, 455, 568-70).

[24]Always favourite resorts; it was about such places in the Central Alberta territory (1894 *seq.*), that the very latest collections of bones, or complete skeletons, were found. On large quantities at a spring near High River, South Alberta, 1858, see *Palliser Journals*, 91.

[25]Reference lost. West Virginia, *circa* 1780.

[26]The meaning of *tank* is obscure. It might be a spring or small lake, or even a deep narrow valley in the hills; doubtless famous for buffalo.

Buffalo Swamp, Pennsylvania, 18th century (Allen, *American Bisons*, 108).
────── South Carolina, 18th century (*ibid.*, 95).[27]

8. VALLEYS, COULEES, ETC.

Buffalo Bottom, Little Kanawha River, West Virginia, 1765 (Croghan, *Early Western Travels*, I, 132).
Buffalo Coulee, Alberta; Battle River, 10 miles north of Wainwright (White, *Altitudes in Canada*, 273; *Place-Names of Alberta*, 26).
Buffalo Flats, Colorado, Summit Country (Bancroft, *History of Nevada, Colorado, and Wyoming*, 637).
Buffalo Gap, Illinois (Hulbert, *Historic Highways*, VIII, 23-7).
────── Pennsylvania, Union County circa 1800 (Shoemaker, *Pennsylvania Bison Hunt*, 22).
────── South Dakota, Custer County (*Cram's International Atlas*).
────── Texas (*ibid.*).
────── Virginia (4) (Garretson, *American Bison*, 20).
Buffalo Path, Pennsylvania, circa 1800 (Shoemaker, *Pennsylvania Bison Hunt*, 12, 22, 46).
Buffalo Run, Pennsylvania, circa 1800 (*ibid.*).
────── Virginia (Garretson, *American Bison*, 20).[28]
────── West Virginia (7) (*ibid*).
Buffalo Tent (*Loge des Bœufs*); a famous haunt, Pembina River, South Manitoba, 1800 (Coues (ed.), *Henry-Thompson Journals*, I, 68).
Buffalo Valley, Pennsylvania, 18th century (Allen, *American Bisons*, 87).
'The Bull Pen,' North Park, Colorado; same as 'Bayou Salade,' above (Farnham, *Early Western Travels*, XXVIII, 209, 266).
Bullhorn Coulee, Alberta; Belly River, south of Pincher Creek (*Place-Names of Alberta*, 26).
Bull's Gap, Tennessee (*Cram's International Atlas*).
Skull Valley, Utah or Nevada, 1855 (Burton, *City of the Saints*, 330, 454, 511).
Skull Valley Station, Arizona, west of Prescott (*Cram's International Atlas*).

9. MISCELLANEOUS

Buffalo Cart Plain, Saskatchewan; north of Touchwood Hills; circa 51° 30′ N., 104° 30′ W. (Hind, *Narrative*, I, 410).
────── Cross Roads, Pennsylvania, 1801 (Shoemaker, *Pennsylvania Bison Hunt*, 40; Garretson, *American Bison*, 89).[29]
────── Plain, Smoky River, North West Territories; circa 1815 (*Letters of Colin Robertson*, ed. Rich, 109).
────── Plains, west side of Mississippi River, above the Falls of St. Anthony, 1805 (so Pike and Schoolcraft in Allen, *American Bisons*, 104).[30]

[27]Allen remarks (*American Bisons*, 95), that the South Carolina 'buffalo-names' are "all old; not on recent maps" (of circa 1876).
[28]Compare 'Bull Run,' Virginia (battle, 1861).
[29]See above on this name, chap. X, note 157.
[30]'Plains' scarcely a place-name proper; where 'Buffalo-land' began.

———— Meadows, Washo County, Nevada (*Cram's International Atlas*).[31]

———— Robe Plain, 1825; same region, southeast from Carlton, as Buffalo Cart Plain, above; perhaps identical (Simpson's Journal; in Merk (ed.), *Fur Trade and Empire*, 155).

———— 'Stamps' (Ohio Valley region, *circa* 1800).[32]

Fort de la Rivière aux Bœufs (Ohio Pennsylvania, *circa* 1750); 'Fort' but no 'river' mentioned (Thwaites (ed.), *Early Western Travels*, I, 102, ed. note).

La Prairie de la Graisse,[33] Alberta, 1840; south of Red Deer River along the Little Red Deer, "so called from often being well stocked with buffalo . . ." (Simpson, *Journey Around the World*, I, 112).

Mesa La Vaca, Arizona (36° 30' N., 111° W.: *Cram's International Atlas*).

Prairie de la Vache, Alberta; Upper Athabaska River, above Jasper, 1817 (Cox, *Columbia River*, II, 175, orig. ed.).

Prairie des Vaches = the same, 1859, 1872 (Hector, *Palliser Journals*, 128; Fleming, *Explorations and Surveys for a Canadian Pacific Railway, 1874*, 168, 170).

Prairie de la Tête de Bœuf, S. Manitoba, near Manitou, 1800 (Coues (ed.), *Henry-Thompson Journals*, I, 166, 198, 419).

Blind Bull Lake, Wood Buffalo Park, N.W.T. (Soper, "History of the Northern Bison," 404).[34]

[31]On this place, see above, note 15.

[32]A name given to places such as the Blue Licks, in Kentucky; where the buffalo had stamped the earth down around the trees, etc. See above, chap. X, note 46.

[33]*Prairie de la Graisse* = 'Grease Prairie.'

[34]This lake was so named from an unfortunate blind bull which was drowned in it in 1923; a tragical commentary on the supposed ease (above, p. 158) with which such animals could find their way about.

BUFFALO AND DISEASE[1]

Attention has recently been drawn to the possibility that epidemic disease played a part in the disappearance of the historic species of the plains buffalo, as the following newspaper extract indicates (from Cloverdale, British Columbia, January 16, 1932):

It now develops that the vast herds of buffalo which once roamed western plains were not entirely wiped out by avaricious hunters. The real villain in the piece has just been discovered.

Dr. E. A. Bruce, Dominion pathologist, Agassiz experimental farm [B.C.], revealed to British Columbia dairymen in the course of an address, that the noble bison may have been killed off almost to the point of extinction by a dread disease which is today taking fierce toll of herds and flocks throughout the continent.

Hemorrhagic septicaemia is the name given to a germ which flourishes in unclean barn-yards, filthy hog wallows and neglected hen houses, ramshackle sheep corrals and insanitary rabbit hutches.[2]

It is somewhat curious (from the standpoint of an Edmonton student) that almost the only reference to disease among the wild species that I have found is in this very region: in the upper North Saskatchewan foothill country. I have pointed out, in my discussion of that portion of the habitat,[3] the general improbabilities (1) of disease in such a region "*following* the fires, in the light of actual experiences in the territory; (2) of '*all* the animals' being affected thereby; and (3) of the historical accuracy of the supposedly really vast quantities of game before, and of the virtual disappearance of the game animals after, the alleged epidemic, *circa* 1847. In my paper referred to,[4] I also emphasized, and may briefly notice here, the fact that while epidemic disease on a scale sufficiently large to constitute any appreciable force in the extermination of the buffalo must surely have left some visible indications of its ravages in large masses of dead carcasses, in situations where mass destruction by fire, water, or snow (as in coulees, for example) was obviously inapplicable, I have not found the least hint of allusion to such conditions; neither in the form of direct witness of such actual (or even supposed) effects, or of any second-hand testimony to such, that might set in motion a train of question-

[1]The general substance of the first part of this Appendix has been printed in the *Canadian Historical Review*, XV, 1934, 1-23.

[2]*Edmonton Journal*, January 16, 1932; and doubtless elsewhere. On hemorrhagic septicaemia among domesticated herds, see Garretson, *American Bison*, 75-8.

[3]See above, chap. XII, notes 167-8; cf. chap. XVII, notes 85-6.

[4]*Canadian Historical Review*, XV, 1934, 1-10, particularly.

ing or reminiscence likely to elicit unlooked-for information; or even any tradition to that effect without specific examples, save this one uncorroborated instance. Nor does it seem reasonable—as an explanation of this silence—that such results would manifest themselves for the first time only among the very latest generations of the buffalo, when the supposed causes must have prevailed for ages. The testimony concerning disease among the wild *ungulata* of the buffalo territory in general (which as a class might reasonably be supposed to exhibit something of a similarly uniform susceptibility to epidemic complaints indicated for domestic species by Dr. Bruce), appears to be fully as variable as that noted above in reference to domestic animals in the supposed epidemic of 1847.[5] Speaking as a layman, it seems to me more probable that the danger and the 'impartiality 'of hemorrhagic septicaemia may be ascribed to the confinement of animals in filthy pens— confinement itself being a wholly unnatural existence.[6] From such local

[5]Seton, re diseases among wild species: 'epidemics' with antelopes (*Game Animals*, III, 451); white goat = 'no disease' (*ibid.*, 483); bighorn = 'scab or mange' (p. 568); buffalo = 'no epidemics' (p. 676); confirming his earlier verdict, 'apparently unknown amongst them' (*Life-Histories of Northern Animals*, I, 267); moose = 'disease among them' (*Game Animals*, III, 158, 185). No tuberculosis in many wild buffalo examined by Charles Aubrey (*ibid.*, 676).

Alexander Henry mentions the following (Red River, October 4, 1800): "I found to-day, in the kidney of a bull, a small solid substance of the size and shape of a bean, and as hard as a pebble [renal calculus]. On breaking it open, it showed shining particles of the nature of a stone. I had often abstracted the same substance from the kidneys of bulls, generally like a bean, but some perfectly round . . ." (Coues (ed.), *Henry-Thompson Journals*, I, 110).

Garretson writes thus: "Mange was the most common disease of the buffalo, and when infested animals were found by the Indians, [they] were killed to the last individual . . ." (*American Bison*, 75). While there are references to scabby mangy bulls in hard winters (above, chap. V, note 34, etc.), I have found no other allusion to such a practice, either as an opinion or as an observed fact. I find a reference to the *Oi-vimána* (= 'scabby people'), a division of the Cheyenne. "The name originated about 1840, when a band . . . became infected from having used a mangy buffalo hide for a saddle-blanket . . ." (*Handbook of American Indians*, I, 255; II, 112). This occurrence hardly indicates any pronounced abhorrence then; but might conceivably have originated a practice in that tribe of slaying mangy animals.

[6]Dr. Gordon Hewitt speaks of the 'eminently natural conditions' in Wainwright Buffalo Park (*Conservation of the Wild Life of Canada*, 134-6). I share the view of Henry Fairfield Osborn (*Age of Mammals*, 502) and R. K. Scharff (*Distribution and Origin of Life in America*, 66) that such conditions are essentially unnatural. See quotation in Osborn (p. 503) regarding a herd of Urus, Aurochs, 'Wisents,' *Bison bonasus*, in the forest of Bieloviejsha or Bialowitza, Grodno, Lithuania, Russia (1895, 1910; since exterminated, it is said, by the Soviet Government). Their life and environment, as a forest species (Osborn, *Age of Mammals*, 408, 414, etc.) in a forest preserve, were, I should suppose, at least as natural as those at Wainwright; yet conditions *circa* 1895 were thought to be responsible for diminished fertility, malnutrition resulting in an excess of male calves, and consequently inbreeding; cf. remarks above, chap. XVIII, note 75.

Professor William Rowan, again, informs me in conversation that in his opinion (and that of others) many evils commonly attributed to inbreeding *per se*

or potential plague-spots the wild buffalo—like any other species roaming in freedom—could readily escape.[7]

Ernest Thompson Seton records a rather remarkable statement from one who might be supposed to know:

As I sat up in his log museum, in the mountains during the blizzard of Oct. 30, 1899, Edwin Carter, the naturalist of Breckinridge, Colorado, made a curious observation. He was familiar with the buffalo in the '60's, and said:

"In my opinion, the Buffalo was a dying race. In their palmiest days, calves were comparatively scarce in the herds, showing that sterilization, the first process of natural extinction, had set in. In the Lost Park herds, calves were rarely seen."[8]

However, I can find no one who agrees with him in this belief. Experience in our Buffalo Parks is a sufficient refutation.[9]

It seems certain that a scarcity of calves could not have continued long as a chronic condition, from the 'sixties onward. Governor Laird, in August, 1877, noted 'very few of that season's calves' to be seen; but the herds were 'mostly small.'[10] This, moreover, was on the very eve of extinction, so that it is impossible to draw any conclusions from the latter case. It seems at least possible that Edwin Carter (after so many years' lapse of time) may have generalized from his observations of some one particular herd, which perhaps had recently lost a large proportion of calves in a flooded river, or even by fire. The wide variability in buffalo, which our historical evidence has placed beyond question, was seldom realized by the local observer. It scarcely could be; and in most cases he would have treated with contempt the suggestion that *his* experiences needed qualification, or comparison with those of others. Be the explanation what it may, all the evidence indicates that Seton's view is the correct one.

The general question of buffalo and disease, however, took on a new aspect, by the release of a large quantity of buffalo from the Wainwright Park in the Northern Wood Buffalo Park. The proposal to do this aroused what Thompson Seton terms 'a storm of protest' from scientific circles,[11] of such proportions and with so many variations in the available evidence pro and con, that some notice of it cannot be omitted from a general survey of disease as a possible factor in the extermination of the buffalo.

---

are more probably the result of unnatural conditions in domestication. Certainly natural inbreeding *must* have prevailed among buffalo, on the 'clan' theory (see above, chap. V, note 68).

[7]McDougall, south of Carlton, September, 1862: ". . . around us multiplying evidence of the recent presence of thousands of buffalo, the country in some places smelling like a barn-yard" (*Forest, Lake, and Prairie,* 202). We have seen testimony above (chap. V, notes 81-9) to the buffalo indifference in polluting their drinking-places, etc.; but there is no hint of infectious consequences.

[8]On the 'parks' region, see Bancroft, *History of Nevada, Colorado, and Wyoming,* 322-37, 495, 629; cf. also Farnham on the 'Bayou Salade' (chap. XI, note 39).

[9]Seton, *Game Animals,* III, 684. See table above (chap. XVIII, note 70) giving percentages of increase at Wainwright Buffalo Park, 1909-27.

[10]Between Battleford and Blackfoot Crossing, Bow River (east of Calgary). See Morris, *Treaties with the Indians of Manitoba,* 252.

[11]Seton, *Game Animals,* III, 661, 712.

As I have hinted above, the controversy was noticed by Seton, whose account may be said to constitute the principal popular source of information. A critical examination of his synopsis of the case reveals some strange misconception on his part, which can scarcely fail to result in a wrong impression reaching the public, or even scientists not previously conversant —to some extent at least—with the details of the controversy. In order to do no injustice either to Seton or to the policy he defends, I quote his account, as given in his latest standard work on buffalo, verbatim.

After giving some figures on annual slaughterings of surplus animals at Wainwright, 1922-23,[12] he continues as follows:

It occurred to the officials . . . that although they could not accommodate the annual increase by adding to the [Wainwright] Park in the adjoining territory, they had at their disposal a 10,000 square mile tract of the Wood Buffalo Park recently created [1922]. To this, they proposed to send the annual surplus, and turn them loose.

As soon as their plan was known, a storm of protest from many scientists broke about the Dominion officials. These onlookers maintained that the Wood Buffalo was a rare, interesting and valuable species, and the introduction of Plains Buffalo in such numbers would virtually and unnecessarily wipe out the Wood Buffalo form.

To this, the Northwest Territory Branch of the Department [that is, of the Interior, Ottawa] made reply: In the Wood Buffalo Park are two quite distinct herds, in widely separate parts of the country. That in the North is the pure Wood Buffalo—if there is such a thing. That in the south is half-way between the Wood and the Plains Buffalo. It is to the latter that the surplus of Wainwright is to be added. Furthermore, if the protesting scientists agree in disapproving this plan, let them propose another that is more satisfactory and yet practical.

To this challenge, no reply has been made; so that in 1924, the Northwest Territories and Yukon Branch of the Department demonstrated the wisdom and practicability of the scheme by safely shifting per rail and scow, 1,634 Buffalo from Wainwright to the Peace River end of the Buffalo Park, where with the trifling loss of 8, they joined the herds of their Kinsmen. . . .

Since the above was written, I learn from Director O. S. Finnie, that in the late fall and early winter of 1925, some 400 head of Buffalo wandered southward out of the Park boundaries and wintered in the Baril and Clair Lakes districts, a low-lying country with abundance of hay. They continued sleek and fat all winter, and in the spring returned northward across the Peace River, and are once more in the original Park.

As it is possible that this migration may take place yearly, the Government is adding this new region to the Park. It will increase the area from 10,500 to 17,000 square miles. In this, the Buffalo will be protected and, no doubt, thrive and multiply. . . .[13]

Again in order to preclude misrepresentation, I quote Seton's further observations, verbatim also:

In Sept., 1914, Dr. Francis Harper, of the Canadian Geological Survey, assisted by the Buffalo Guardian, Peter McCallum, spent a week in the Wood Buffalo country; and estimated them at 500.

[12]*Ibid.*, 661 (cf. above *in extenso*, chap. XVIII, note 70).
[13]Seton, *Game Animals*, III, 661-2.

The following appears in his Report:[14] "According to McCallum, the Wood Buffaloes are divided into two main groups. It was the southern herd whose territory we had entered, while the range of the other lies northwest of Fort Smith near Little Buffalo River. Part of the northern herd was reported to have been seen within 20 miles of Great Slave Lake during the winter of 1912-13.[15] The two ranges are separated, McCallum said, by a strip of jack-pine country 20 or 30 miles wide, in which he has seen hardly a trail. He estimated there were about 500 animals in the two herds, the northern one being slightly the larger. . . ."[16]

Follows again, Thompson Seton *in propria persona*:

Before leaving the subject, it is well to remind scientists that in this Park there are two separate herds of the Buffalo—the northern herd, which is the typical group of true *athabascae*; and the Peace River herd, which, *according to some*[17] is between the Wood and Plains Buffalo. It is to this southern herd that the surplus from Wainwright is being added at the rate of 1,500 per annum. . . .[18]

It is only fair to add that many scientists strongly disapprove the importation of the Wainwright Buffalo to the Wood Buffalo Park. Among those who have entered vigorous protests are Dr. Francis Harper, Prof. Wm. Rowan, H. E. Anthony, and many others. They forecast that it will mean the absorption and total loss of that superb sub-species, the Wood Buffalo.[19]

If Seton's designation of his fellow-zoologists by the contemptuous term 'onlookers' was not intended to prejudice the ordinarily critical but not necessarily specialist reader, by suggesting interference in some subject the critics did not understand, it certainly tends to produce that effect. So also does his 'reply' of the Department concerned to the storm of scientific protest; clearly implying a triumphant retort, to which the discomfited critics could furnish no rejoinder, in the form of a practicable alternative scheme. No doubt the practicability of any scheme which does not actually break down in the very process of operation is automatically demonstrated by carrying it into effect; but how the 'wisdom' of a scheme contrived in 1923 and executed in 1924[20] can be demonstrated against a criticism whose very foundation and essence lies in the slow and gradual action of the biological laws of heredity, passes my understanding, albeit I am no biologist nor zoologist. Seton himself appears to be the only one of the latter class to whom the demonstration has been satisfactory. One is

[14]Given by Raup (*Range Conditions in Wood Buffalo Park*, bibliography, 45): "The Athabasca-Great Slave Lake Expedition, 1914" (*Summary of Report of the Canadian Geological Survey*, 1914, 161-2). I have not seen this.

[15]Note the northward migration for the *winter* season.

[16]Seton, *Game Animals*, III, 712.

[17]Italics mine.

[18]Seton, *Game Animals*, III, 712; cf. Soper, "History of the Northern Bison," 376, 383.

[19]Seton, *Game Animals*, III, 712-14. Cf. below, notes 43, 54, 60.

[20]So Seton, above; but apparently a misprint for 1925, the year of the literature of the protests, as we shall see, and of government pamphlets, Canada, Department of the Interior, *Bringing Back the Buffalo*; also of my own observation of the 'buffalo trains' from Wainwright, Canadian National Railway. I was stationed in Wainwright myself during the summer of 1924.

accustomed to such pronouncements from official departments. Nobody ever heard of any new departure which was not 'an unqualified success.'[21] But from a man of science! Let us review the actual facts.

The 'two herds' to which Thompson Seton has referred are described by him (as a feature in the argument of the Department of the Interior)[22] as "two quite distinct herds"; the one to the north "pure Wood Buffalo—if there is such a thing"; and the southern one "half-way between the Wood and the Plains Buffalo." Later, he endorses these particulars in person, without the dubious query for the first herd, which he now terms "the typical group of the true *athabascae*"; and classifies the second (southern) one as being between the Wood and Plains buffalo "according to some." Who these persons are neither he nor the Department tells us.[23]

So far as the general publication of these statements is concerned, they will be found in a paper by Maxwell Graham,[24] of the Department in question, published in December, 1924, in which it was emphasized that the respective herds in the two ranges did not mingle (in 1916; so reported by Dr. Charles Camsell, in the *Report of the Canadian Geological Survey* for that year);[25] and that according to McCallum in 1914, the two ranges were separated by a strip of jack-pine country 20 or 30 miles wide, in which he had seen hardly any trails.[26] This information appears to trace back ultimately to an account given to Inspector Jarvis of the North West Mounted Police, in 1897.[27] It was confirmed, or at least repeated, to the same officer in 1907.[28]

These reports therefore obviously refer to two native wild herds; one 'pure,' the other 'half-way,' presumably so bred or interbred 'from time immemorial,' to use Graham's own expression for the herds in the Northern region (1922).[29]

I have remarked that neither the Department nor Seton cites any authority for the existence of this crossbred race or herd.[30] They have the best of reasons for their silence. It has been shown above that never at any time, as a result of either geographical or of zoological exploration

[21]So, *Bringing Back the Buffalo.* "The entire movement has more than justified itself . . ." (D. H. Christie, Department of the Interior, Ottawa, in *Edmonton Journal,* July 28, 1928; cf. *ibid.* March 9, 1926.

[22]Seton, *Game Animals,* III, 661.

[23]*Ibid.,* 712.

[24]Maxwell Graham, "Finding Range for Canada's Buffalo," *Canadian Field Naturalist,* XXXVIII, 1924, 187; cf. Canadian Zoologist, "Passing of the Wood Bison."

[25]See Raup, *Range Conditions in Wood Buffalo Park,* 27-32, 44; also Canadian Zoologist, "Passing of the Wood Bison"; Kitto, "Survival of American Bison in Canada," 436.

[26]Above, note 16; cf. Raup, *Range Conditions in Wood Buffalo Park,* 31, 45. Graham emphasizes in his 1922 trip, trails 'being re-opened' (*Canada's Wild Buffalo,* 9-10).

[27]Raup, *Range Conditions in Wood Buffalo Park,* 29, 46. I have not seen the *Report* for 1897.

[28]Jarvis, in Royal North West Mounted Police *Annual Report,* 1907, 122-9.

[29]Graham, *Canada's Wild Buffalo,* 8.

[30]See above on all this, chap. XII, notes 100, 240-42.

or arising from contact with the northern buffalo by hunters, has there been recorded in any source I have been able to discover, any vestige of allusion to such an intermediate breed. Dr. Francis Harper, who explored part of the buffalo range in 1914, in company with their official guardian (whose views on trails were put forward in support of the long-continued isolation theory), has not a single word to say about crossbreds. It will be observed that in 1914 Harper's notes are confessedly based upon McCallum's authority;[31] when next he appears in the buffalo arena it is as a strong critic of the Department's policy. These crossbreds must have been recognizable, or how were they recognized as such? Moreover, the baseless assertion that a crossbred race (or herd) existed, emanated from the self-same officials who in 1922 laboured to establish a virtual identity in appearance between the two *pure* races;[32] and who in 1924, at the very time when this preposterous dictum was being advanced, informed the world that the theory of "the so-called wood-bison being a sub-species has recently been considered doubtful,"[33] or tacitly classified him as *Bison americanus*, without any further distinction.[34] In so far as evidence serves to guide us, even if the two propositions were not mutually destructive, neither is true. The Plains and the Wood buffalo are distinct;[35] and the 'two herds' were two in a geographical sense only, and not zoologically. We have seen above that E. Mignault, Seton's original source of information, whose experience dates from a time (1865-75) when any supposed modifications of habit arising from the persecutions of the 'final days' do not enter into the case, stated that 'only one Prairie buffalo' had ever been seen in Peace River valley.[36] It has furthermore been reported locally, I understand, that the herd of the newly-arrived immigrants which in official phraseology 'wandered

[31]Above, note 16.

[32]Graham, *Canada's Wild Buffalo*, 8.

[33]Graham, "Finding Range for Canada's Buffalo," 189; cf. Canadian Zoologist, "Passing of the Wood Bison."

[34]Kitto (Department of the Interior), "Survival of American Bison in Canada."

[35]Concerning Maxwell Graham, and the 'doubts of the wood bison being a sub-species,' I quote the trenchant essay of 'Canadian Zoologist' ("Passing of the Wood Bison"): "The inference to be drawn from this remark in light of the supplementary text is that the two forms are considered to be identical and obliteration of the wood bison would then matter but little. Now as a matter of fact, were Mr. Graham conversant with Canadian zoology, he would find that his statement is literally correct, but so far from any doubts arising because the animals are so alike, they arise on account of their very marked differences. There is truly some doubt about their being sub-species; but the question is not, Are they identical? but, Are they not actually full species?—an entirely different matter. . . ."

Professor H. M. Raup (who may have known the writer) characterizes his paper as 'authentic' (*Range Conditions in Wood Buffalo Park*, 51). Edmond Seymour, President of the American Bison Society, 1932, maintains that the two are not distinct (*ibid.*, 52). The latter is supported by the Society's secretary, M. S. Garretson (*American Bison*, 5-7) who claims that 'the best authorities' (unspecified) endorse that conclusion. H. J. Shepstone, an uncritical popular writer, is also for 'only one species' (*Wild Beasts of To-Day*, 127).

[36]See above, chap. III, notes 90-9.

southward' across Peace River in the early winter of 1925 (and to accommodate which the Park area was enlarged about 62 per cent), actually fled in panic on their first encounter with the Wood species.[37] If this be correct, it is further evidence of an antipathy which is unquestionably indicated by former evidence of geographic limits, by similar limitations in the hitherto discovered skeletal remains of both 'races' in the North and by historical references at large from experienced judges, as we have already seen.[38]

The statement that the protesting scientists had no constructive and practicable policy to offer is entirely incorrect. It is inherently improbable that North American and British zoologists of recognized standing in the scientific world would stultify themselves by mere denunciation of a scheme to which they could suggest no feasible alternative.[39] As a matter of actual fact at least one definite proposal was made. I quote once again from the vigorous essay of 'Canadian Zoologist':

> As has already been emphasized, the wood bison are rapidly increasing in numbers. There is no doubt that if the present adequate protection is continued the park in comparatively few years will not only be fully stocked with pure wood bison but will be overflowing and populating adjacent territory. This is in fact the only area in the north in which the release of the Wainwright animals would be entirely superfluous.
>
> It is popularly believed that the chief object in making the transportation is to guarantee the far north a certain meat supply for the future. If this actually is the primary object, the Wainwright animals should surely be turned down on some spot other than the one that already has its supply of bison. Even though the contract has been let and full arrangements made, and money has been expended on the necessary preparations, all this need not matter, for the general programme can be retained but the beasts released elsewhere. The Birch Hills country, on the Athabaska River, the Peace River country to the south and west of the Caribou Mountains, even the eastern bank of the Slave River, all at one time supported buffalo. The experiment of releasing semi-domesticated animals could be attempted on any one of these areas without endangering the welfare of the wood bison. And thus buffalo could be reinstated on the big game list of Alberta and high priced hunting licences be made to pay for the necessary warden service. . . .[40]

When the opponents of a policy are also the final judges of its feasibility, it will seldom be found 'practical.' In this case, the man of science even provides an expedient for recouping the financial outlay which his proposals would involve. The same essay (which is doubtless fairly typical of the

[37]*Ex inf.* Professor William Rowan to the author.
[38]See above in detail, chap. III, notes 85 *seq.*
[39]Seton himself mentions Dr. Francis Harper, H. E. Anthony, Professor William Rowan, 'and many others' (above, note 19). Professor Raup cites Harper, A. B. Howell, and W. E. Saunders, protesting in *Canadian Field Naturalist*, XXXIX, 1925, 45, 118; and Canadian Zoologist, "Passing of the Wood Bison"; Raup, *Range Conditions in Wood Buffalo Park*, 46, 50, 51. Professor Rowan mentions Dr. Ritchie in *Nature* (London) 'and others': "Canada's Buffalo," (*Country Life*, LXVI, 1929, 358-60).
[40]"Passing of the Wood Bison"; cf. Raup, *Range Conditions in Wood Buffalo Park*, 18-19, etc.

general character of the protests) includes data concerning such factors of extermination as winter food supply and extreme weather conditions; which there seems reason to believe have affected the native herds in the region in former times,[41] and which one cannot suppose a large increase in numbers could render more favourable.

The following paragraph, forming part of a press despatch at the time, indicates the nature of the official response: "The Department of the Interior at Ottawa, while admitting that they have received protests from zoologists and mammalogical societies of the United States and Canada, against the sending of 2,000 plains bison yearly for the next five years, into the Wood Bison preserve at Fort Smith, are going ahead with their plans, claiming that their own experts are better qualified to judge the policy, because of experience and practice, than are zoologists at a distance. . . ."[42] The same newspaper item includes a statement from the then Minister of the Interior, the Hon. Charles Stewart (if he be correctly reported) that "it is not the intention to mix breeds in any way."[43]

The defenders of the Departmental policy did not seem to realize that their arguments involved them in a dilemma. A great deal has been said about the 'two herds' in their respective ranges; these 'in widely separate parts of the country' according to Thompson Seton's version of the Department's 'challenge';[44] or separated by 'a strip of jack-pine country 20 or 30 miles wide' in Dr. Francis Harper's Report of 1914, cited by Seton.[45]

Whatever the intended meaning, the implication seems clearly to be that the Wood buffalo would not cross this belt, because it was a jack-pine country or for some other reason. Maxwell Graham noted the fact that in 1916 Dr. Charles Camsell found that the northern of the two Wood bison herds did not migrate beyond their own (northern) range. From this Graham assumed that they would remain isolated and uncontaminated for ever.[46] In Thompson Seton's hardy but illogical defence of the departmental action this inference was supported by implication, in Peter Mc-Callum having seen 'hardly a trail' in this particular strip.[47] Now jack-pine country can hardly be considered a barrier to the Wood bison; since F. V. Seibert and Soper print photographs of buffalo, in what is quite apparently, and in the latter instance is definitely stated to be, coniferous country.[48] Further, the country at large is not unbrokenly jack-pine; other trees and vegetation are intermingled, and Seibert and Soper both show that grass grows very abundantly not only in the openings but throughout

[41]See *ibid.*, 19-33; cf. Kitto, "Survival of American Bison in Canada." The latter is less discriminating and more enthusiastic.

[42]*Edmonton Journal*, May 5, 1925; and doubtless elsewhere.

[43]*Ibid.*, May 5, 1925. They are already mixed, virtually beyond the possibility of defining any scientific distinction. See below, notes 54, 60.

[44]Above, note 13.

[45](In inverted commas; above, notes 14-16).

[46]Graham, "Finding Range for Canada's Buffalo."

[47]Above, note 16.

[48]"Appendix" to Graham, *Canada's Wild Buffalo*, 16. Similar photographs in coniferous areas in Soper, "History of the Northern Bison," 355, 359, 361, 364, 372, 386, 387.

the bush as well.[49] In addition to this, trails *do* cross this supposed barrier, and both Maxwell Graham and his collaborator, Seibert, noted their abundance;[50] the former, at least, emphasizing also the 'new trails that are being broken out.'[51] This, however, was in 1922; when the Department was not committed to any necessity for proving the contrary supposition.

The two herds, therefore, will either intermingle, or they will not. If they do, the assumption that intermingling will not occur, of course, falls automatically to the ground. If they never did, and will not, mix with their 'full' or 'half-kindred' native to the region, still less would they be likely to mix with the alien importations from Wainwright. This would remove another possible objection to the proposal to release buffalo in another district of the great Northland.

With reference to the official disclaimer of any 'intention to mix breeds in any way,' this can only signify that its reputed author does not recognize the existence of the most minute varietal distinction; and even this cannot very well be reconciled with the statement published by his own Department in the following year (1926) that the imported animals were 'mingling with the Wood buffalo.'[52] Whether the Wood buffalo in the case be the 'pure' *Bison bison Athabascae* Rhoads of the 'northern' herd (virtually identical, they themselves tell us, in any case, with the Prairie type), or this illusory 'hybrid' half-and-half product, of the 'southern' herd, matters little; it is difficult to see how 'mixing of breeds,' whatever intentions may have been, could be avoided. Perhaps they would instruct the well-disciplined creatures to go and play together, as little cousins should; but not misbehave! It may—it unhappily often does—lie within the province of politicians to govern scientific policy; but without personal competence or expert instruction they would be wise to refrain from public pronouncements on such topics.

If such ineptitudes are the result of trusting to 'their own experts,' one cannot wonder at the indignant outburst of our 'Canadian Zoologist':

It may possibly be prudent, but it is nevertheless greatly to be regretted, that when a government department finds occasion to make reference to its experts it refrains from divulging their names. . . . But we are vouchsafed neither the names of the experts nor given their reasons. We know that numerous government geologists have visited the wood bison park from time to time. But even if a thousand geologists had investigated conditions there, their collective opinions on the race *athabascae* would not be of equal value to the conclusions derived from a single skull by a single trained zoologist, even if he had made his investigation in Honolulu or at the south pole. We can hardly believe that it is geological opinion to which the Minister of the Interior alludes.

[49]Seibert, "Appendix" to Graham, *Canada's Wild Buffalo*, 16; Soper, "History of the Northern Bison," 359, 364, 372, 390, etc. See also Inspector Jarvis, Royal North West Mounted Police, *Annual Report*, 1907, 122-9; Canadian Zoologist, "Passing of the Wood Bison"; Raup, *Range Conditions in Wood Buffalo Park*, 19-33.   [50]*Canada's Wild Buffalo*, 9-10, 17.

[51]*Ibid.*, 10; the 'network of buffalo trails' Siebert, *ibid.*, "Appendix," 17; also Kitto, "Survival of American Bison in Canada," 437, but the last apparently meaning Park rangers' trails since made.

[52]Canada, Department of the Interior, Ottawa, *Bringing Back the Buffalo*, 1926.

Nor can it surely be the opinion of local trappers and rangers. They may be familiar with local conditions, with breeding, feeding and other problems, but what do they know of comparative osteology or taxonomy?[53]

It is not necessary that a reader of the foregoing should himself be a zoologist to appreciate the relative soundness of the two respective positions; a reasonably logical mind, and the least acquaintance with the history or methods of any specialized branch of knowledge, will suffice to establish the crushing and unanswerable force of the scientific argument. At the present time, the 'mongrelization' of the animals in Wood Buffalo Park— despite the continued use of the conventional term, Wood buffalo—is treated as commonplace, however regrettable as a scientific fact. It is recorded as merely incidental to other general inquiries, and is scarcely a *conclusion* even. It is more like a starting point.[54]

Finally, there is one more phase of the question; and it is wholly independent of any opinions concerning species, varieties, or hybridization, being strictly one of disease. I quote the same critic once again:

It is a perfectly well known and authenticated fact that tuberculosis is rampant in the Wainwright herd. Somewhere over 10% of the animals killed in 1923 were condemned as unfit for human consumption on this account. It is true that the Government intends to ship only healthy young animals north, but they come from tainted stock. Every breeder knows the significance of that statement. I have been quite unable either by conversation with men from the north or by hunting through published literature, to find the slightest evidence of even a suspicion of tuberculosis in the northern herds.[55]

" The foregoing was written in 1925. The following, dated 1932, indicates that while the Department remained possibly unmoved, the protesting scientists were neither silenced nor convinced. In a review by an outstanding zoologist, the following passage occurs:

[*Wild Beasts To-Day*: Harold J. Shepstone, 1932]: The book abounds in inaccuracies. . . . There is one other fault, which in truth is really harmful, and this is the amount of space and praise devoted to the transfer of bison from southern Canada into the northern wood bison reserve. This, one of the most tragic examples of bureaucratic stupidity in all history, was done against the protests of both Canadian and American naturalists who would rather have seen the surplus southern bison killed. They were known to be infected with bovine tuberculosis and they are certain to interbreed [with] as well as infect the wood bison, which is a far finer animal and one of greater zoological interest because in some respects it seems more like the European wisent [that is, aurochs, *urus*, etc.] than the common American bison. The book would have done well to have shown up this transfer in its true light as a real tragedy and not as a triumph of

[53]Canadian Zoologist, "Passing of the Wood Bison."

[54]See Raup, 1933 (*Range Conditions in Wood Buffalo Park*, 18-19); Soper, 1941 ("History of the Northern Bison," 375-6); Skinner and Kaisen, 1947 ("Fossil Bison of Alaska," 166). See also below, note 60.

[55]Canadian Zoologist, "Passing of the Wood Bison." We have seen that this view is equally sound with reference to Plains buffalo (above, note 5). See my paper also, *Canadian Historical Review*, XV, 1934, 1-10; and cf. Raup's remarks, *Range Conditions in Wood Buffalo Park*, particularly 18-19.

conservation. The public as a matter of fact has never had the true story, and Shepstone might easily have given it as he could have gotten it from any intelligent mammalogist on this continent. . . .[56]

Considering the standing of the foregoing critic, his views cannot be dismissed as a mere bug-bear of a few hole-and-corner recalcitrants; although this was attempted, not only in Canada[57] but in England also.[58] I quote from an English journal: "These fears have proved groundless. Mr. Raup,[59] an American naturalist who recently studied the bison in the Wood Buffalo Park, reported that the newcomers were doing well and that there was no evidence that crossing produced any degeneration; he only recommended that some specimens of the pure woodland race, the *Bos americanus athabascae*, should be obtained for museums *before the mixed breed had become predominant*. . . ."[60] The whole question is logically surrendered in that statement; and six or seven years are insufficient for any pronouncement on 'degeneration,' other than is inherent in any form of cross-breeding. One would prefer Professor Raup's own report before any journalistic abstract, perhaps from 'inspired' sources.

After all this, the two following press notices are of interest:

There are no definite plans to close Wainwright Buffalo Park in Alberta, it was stated officially [Ottawa]. . . .

It was admitted that the Wainwright herd is considerably affected by bovine tuberculosis, and that the grazing is none too good. . . . it may be closed a few years hence.[61]

[Calgary, January 29, 1940]: Arising from a discussion at the annual meeting of the Alberta Fish and Game Association . . . a reason for the slaughter of the 12,000 buffalo at Wainwright park was claimed.

[56]Review by Professor Thomas Barbour, Harvard University, in *Science*, LXXVI, November 25, 1932, 490. Professor Barbour represents the Museum of Comparative Zoology on the 'Advisory Committee' of the American Commission for International Wild Life Protection.

His general strictures on Shepstone's book are fully deserved. It is a readable but slovenly performance, which can never have been revised. It contains ludicrous errors in grammar (pp. 14, 54), and in proper names (pp. 100, 193). European Bison, "erroneously termed aurochs *by sportsmen*, aurochs being the extinct European wild ox" (p. 7, italics mine). In our modern age, what is a 'wild *ox*'?

[57]Professor Barbour's criticisms 'entirely without foundation'; so, departmental officials, Ottawa (*Edmonton Journal*, December 2, 1932). Yet six months previously a Press notice stated that J. Dewey Soper, a well-known naturalist, was then in the Wood Buffalo Park, studying the habits *and diseases* of the buffalo (*ibid.*, June 6, 1932).

[58]As we have seen above (note 39), British naturalists had participated in the scientific protests.

[59]Professor H. M. Raup of Harvard University, author of *Range Conditions in Wood Buffalo Park, with notes on the Northern Wood Bison* (1933); frequently quoted above.

[60]London *Times*, November 18, 1937 (italics mine).

[61]*Edmonton Journal*, June 2, 1939 (closed that year). See on this Soper, "History of the Northern Bison," 396.

Dr. William Rowan, professor of zoology at the University of Alberta, said the animals were riddled with tuberculosis and that their hides were infested with numerous parasites.[62]

After such long-immovable official obscurantism, one cannot but wonder whether the (wholly unsupported) thesis of disease as the 'real exterminator' of the prairie hosts[63] may not have had some connection with a desperate attempt to show that any imported disease among the Wood bison is really no new thing—they 'have always had it'!

[62]*Edmonton Journal*, January 29, 1940. This assertion passed uncontradicted.

[63]A correspondent, Dr. Edmond Melchior Eberts, of Montreal, informs me of a 'prevalent theory' that they had been exterminated by disease, apparently existing around Indian Head, Saskatchewan, *circa* 1883. This is the only allusion I have found to such a belief at that date. I have encountered it occasionally in recent years. See above, chap. XVII, note 85.

APPENDIX K

BUFFALO AS A POSSIBLE INFLUENCE IN THE
DEVELOPMENT OF PRAIRIE LANDS

It has been suggested on more than one occasion that the buffalo may be in part responsible for the formation or extension of the prairie lands of the North American continent by their action in rubbing down and destroying the trees. Ernest Thompson Seton stated, for example, that there is "little doubt that the Buffalo have helped to extend the prairies, and to reduce the woodland country by rubbing down the trees. . . ."[1]

A question of this character can be discussed only in the light of such evidence as we can discover: largely historical evidence. This would seem to group itself more or less naturally under three principal heads: evidence for the general prevalence of the "rubbing" practice; evidence for the existence at some time of woodlands in the "buffalo" prairie regions; evidence governing the condition of woodlands in regions where the buffalo had only penetrated in small and virtually negligible numbers, or perhaps not at all.

There can be little room for doubt of the buffalo's fondness for rubbing, in regions where trees were available for the purpose; and it is quite certain that, where groves of trees were to be found, they were sought for shade, if not for rubbing. One of our earliest observers writes with regard to the Mississippi and Illinois river country (1679): "For the convenience of these Creatures, there are Forests at certain distances where they retire to rest and shelter themselves against the violence of the sun. . . ."[2] A frontiersman author of first-hand experience mentions the "Painted Woods," a well-known spot on the Missouri above the "Mandan villages" (now Bismarck, North Dakota), as a favourite buffalo retreat in the heat of the summer.[3] Neither of these witnesses alludes to them rubbing down trees. Other witnesses do so, however; and their observations pertain to the same general types of country. An old pioneer writes thus of the Cumberland river region in Tennessee: "The open space around and near the sulphur or salt springs, instead of being an old field, as had been supposed by Mr. Mausker [Mansker], at his visit here in 1769, was thus freed from trees and underbrush by the innumerable herds of buffalo and deer and elk that came to these waters. . . ."[4] John Filson describes the Blue Licks,

---

[1] Seton, *Game Animals*, III, 676.

[2] Hennepin, *New Discovery*, I, 148; cf. Joutel, *Journeys of La Salle*, II, 100.

[3] Taylor, *Frontier Life*, 125.

[4] John Donelson, *Journal of a Voyage from Fort Patrick Henry on the Holston River to the French Salt Springs on the Cumberland River in December, 1780*; cited by Garretson, *American Bison*, pp. 22-3. But who is our guarantor for Donelson's superior accuracy? 'Mausker' was most probably the truer interpreter.

Kentucky, 1784 (in part) as follows: ". . . the vast space of land around these springs desolated as if by a ravaging enemy, and hills reduced to plains; for the land near these springs is chiefly hilly. . . ."[5] Fortescue Cuming's "old-timer" host, Captain Waller, with reference to the same approximate period said that "about the salt licks and springs they frequented, they pressed down and destroyed the soil to a depth of three or four feet, as was conspicuous yet in the neighbourhood of the Blue Lick, where all the old trees have their roots bare of soil to that depth . . ."[6] (1789-1809).

In these cases, it appears to have been more a matter of "packing down" the soil by the convergence of numbers at a favoured haunt than of actual assaults upon the trees themselves. In fact, if Waller's remarks are to be considered as anything more than vague reminiscent generalizing and can be taken precisely, one would suppose that the "old trees" (which were "conspicuous yet") would have fallen and rotted long before twenty years had elapsed. We have a considerable amount of testimony from a number of witnesses in the period 1765-1809, as to the "great roads" worn into the Blue Licks; but the evidence has not chanced to allude to the destruction

---

See Roosevelt (who gives his name more authentically as Mansker, 'Old Mansco'), *Winning of the West*, I, 129, 143, 172; II, 26. Allen (*American Bisons*, 114) cites no authority, as if the rectification were his own.

Garretson, who is seldom critical, follows Colonel H. W. Shoemaker, who is even less critical, in glossing Clearfield, Pennsylvania, as 'a space cleared by buffalo' (Shoemaker, *Pennsylvania Bison Hunt*, 30-3; Garretson, *American Bison*, 22-3). Shoemaker places Clear Creek, Pennsylvania, in the same category. Now 'Clearfield' is virtually pleonastic (or tautological) to begin with, for *field* is itself an open space clear of timber, a 'clearing'—natural or artificial—in the woods. The countless *field* place-names of England are found thickest in the historically heaviest-wooded regions, such as the Weald of Kent and Sussex (*weald* = 'wood'), the Middlesex, Hertfordshire, and Essex Weald, Sherwood, Arden, Dean, etc. Clearfield, Buckinghamshire, and Clearwood, Wiltshire, are English place-names dating back at least to 1305 and 1348 respectively; and probably much farther (English Place-Name Society, *Buckinghamshire Place-Names*, 119; *Wiltshire Place-Names*, 156). What authority have we, then, for confining the place-name *field* to fields 'cleared *by buffalo*'? There were plenty of old Indian fields in the Atlantic States, even extending into regions where buffalo hardly penetrated. See Bartram, *Travels*, 173, 314-15; 'Chickasaw Old Fields,' Mississippi or Alabama: *Handbook of American Indians*, I, 262; Adair, *History of American Indians*, 435, *seq*.

'Clear Creek' is even more preposterous. How would buffalo 'clear' a *creek*? 'Clear Creek' is the etymological significance of most of the numerous Skirbecks, Sherburns, and Sherbrookes of Anglian and Saxon England. See Allen Mawer, *Chief Elements in English Place-Names*, 52; E. Ekwall, *English River Names*, 361, 367. Cf. the many Clearwaters and Eau Claires of North America. Garretson (*American Bison*, 20) draws attention to the numerous 'Buffalo' place-names of the Virginias as proof of a former abundance there. Why not then a similar wealth of 'Clearfields'? I have found this one only in the 'buffalo' forest-territory. In all probability it is an importation from England. On such folk-etymology, see a specimen, chap. X above, note 116.

[5]Allen, *American Bisons*, 113; Hornaday, "Extermination of the American Bison," 387. For a critic's opinion of Filson, see above, chap. X, note 59.

[6]Cuming, *Early Western Travels*, IV, 175-8; Allen, *American Bisons*, 113.

(or injury) wrought among the trees.[7] Hornaday cites an instance on the authority of Thomas Ashe (1806), in which an old man, Ashe's informant, had his cabin in the Pennsylvania woods "rubbed down in a few hours"; apparently in two successive years, "when he first went there," which appears to signify about 1770-75.[8] Colonel Shoemaker mentions an even more tragic affair, nearer to the end of the century. Almost the last herd in that region (Pennsylvania also) stumbled in its blind heedless fashion into a settler's cabin which stood in the way with its door open; and trampled the mother and children to death in the ruins of their home.[9] But there is nothing, even in a terrible occurrence like that, which necessitates *absolutely* large numbers. The very prominence given by these writers (and presumably by their informants) to such episodes raises an almost inevitable presumption that they were quite exceptional. I have noted above Shoemaker's etymology of Clearfield.[10] My feeble faith in Shoemaker's etymological flights is nowise strengthened by his evidence for the numbers which did these mighty works.[11] Nobody seems ever to have seen this process in any really unmistakable stage of deforestation. Whatever its origin, Mansker's field was "old" in 1769; and more than a decade older when Donelson so boldly pronounced the true interpretation. In the remainder of the quotation from Ashe, indeed, there is no hint of the buffalo killing the trees by rubbing.[12]

In the very same year in which Ashe was in Pennsylvania (1806), the younger Alexander Henry describes a lake, south of Turtle Mountain, in North Dakota: ". . . at the south end, adjoining the foot of the hill, is a delightful little wood, which runs about three acres up the hill, and for the same distance[13] along the lake. This is a great resort for buffalo and

[7]See above, chap. X, notes 45-62; chap. XIII, notes 11-78.

[8]Hornaday, "Extermination of the American Bison," 420; for contemporary and later critical estimates of Ashe, see above, chap. III, notes 25-6.

[9]Shoemaker, *Pennsylvania Bison Hunt*, 30-3.

[10]Above, note 4.

[11]The 'last buffalo'—or one of the usual multiplicity of 'last buffaloes'—was killed in Buffalo Valley, Pennsylvania, January 19, 1801, at a place called 'Buffalo Cross Roads' (Seton, *Game Animals*, III, 658). This type of local name has furnished the Hulbert school with material for much disquisition on 'great buffalo routes, with here and there a great cross road' (Hulbert, *Historic Highways*, I, 131, etc., etc.). But Seton's authority, Colonel Shoemaker, says this last buffalo was killed by Colonel John Kelly "at a cross-roads, *afterwards called* from this occurrence, 'Buffalo Cross-roads'" (Shoemaker, *Pennsylvania Bison Hunt*, 40; italics mine). One wonders whether Shoemaker's own 'Buffalo Path' (*ibid.*, 22, 46-7) had any more relevant origin; it is on the strength of such names as these that his Pennsylvanian 'vanished millions' are largely built (*ibid.*, 10, 38). On similar principles, an escaped elephant from a circus, re-captured on a later-christened 'Elephant Corner,' could 'prove' a former abundance anywhere you please.

For a detailed analysis of the purely relative significance of 'vast herds,' etc., east of the Mississippi, see above, chap. XIII, notes 1-78.

[12]Allen, *American Bisons*, 109-10; Hornaday, "Extermination of the American Bison," 387, 420.

[13]Note 'distance' of *acres;* a most interesting example of the persistence in 'American-English' of the old Middle-English (and later) use of *acre* and *rood*

other animals, to shade themselves from the heat of the sun, and may serve as a shelter from storms in winter. The state of the ground in this little wood shows that there are always animals in it; for the grass does not grow, and the bark of the trees to the height of an animal is worn smooth by their continuous rubbing. . . ."[14] Here again, we are faced by the fact that an observant resident, well acquainted with the animals of his region, makes no other allusion which throws light on the subject of our discussion. These few meagre notices constitute all that I have been able to discover in the form of positive evidence for a rubbing against the trees, sufficient to give any likelihood of bringing about deforestation.[15]

We have an abundance of references to the general character of the continent from the Atlantic seaboard to the Mississippi. Again and again our authors mention "the woods," which varied from "fine groves,"[16] in what is now so often termed "parkland," to what were no doubt considerable forests: outliers of the mighty woodland which in 1680 and later, spread almost unbrokenly across the eastern portion of the continent.[17] This huge tract was by no means uniformly impenetrable. It has been well said that the significance of that phrase depends very largely upon what the intruder's purpose may be. For military operations—previous to such as those which

---

—the latter still common in Cumberland—as a term of long measure. The early English acre must be so long (one furlong = 220 yards), and it must be so wide (four roods = 66 feet; *i.e.* same as four *rods*). Our 'superficial measure,' which achieves an equivalent of 160 square rods in any conceivable shape, was not understood for centuries. Cf. the following: "A request by the North West Company for a grant of land one acre in width [*i.e.* 66 feet] from Lake Superior to 'Long Lake' for the purpose of constructing a wagon road . . ." (adversely reported on by the council at Quebec, June 30, 1788): Davidson, *The North West Company*, 23, 119.

[14]Coues (ed.), *Henry-Thompson Journals*, I, 409; cf. *ibid.*, 64, 99, 119.

[15]For some of the humorous aspects of rubbing, and other details, see above, chap. XV, note 107.

[16]Amongst others, see Joliet, 1673 (*Jesuit Relations*, LVIII, 107); Father Marquette, 1673 (*ibid.*, LIX, 103, 107, 161); Hennepin, 1680 (*New Discovery*, II, 641-3); also *Journeys of La Salle*, II, 100, etc., etc.

[17]'Florida' (which comprised the whole Atlantic seaboard from Mexico northward and inland indefinitely; as above, chap. IX, notes 29-32) was 'a land of woods and bogs,' 1540 (*Purchas his Pilgrimes*, XVII, 526, 531). So also was 'Virginia' (the same expanse; chap. IX above, note 39) in 1625 (*Purchas his Pilgrimes*, XIX, 242). Compare New France, 1606: "the thicknesse of the wood and greatnesse of Forrests doe hinder the sun from warming of the ground . . ." (*ibid.*, XVIII, 275). New France also (De Monts, 1607): "These Countries are not the Plaines of Champaigne, nor of Vatan, nor the ingrateful wood of Limosin. All is there covered with woods that seem to threaten the clouds . . ." (*ibid.*, 291). See also Lescarbot, *History of New France*, II, 131, 281, 321, 342, 346; III, 9, 194). Father Biard, 1616: ". . . the whole country being but an interminable forest . . ." (*Jesuit Relations*, III, 41). Cadwallader Colden, *circa* 1730: "the vast forest which everywhere covers the country, and which in many places is impenetrable . . ." (*History of the Five Nations*, II, 262; cf. *ibid.*, I, 18, 180, 243). Compare Michaux, *père et fils* (Early Western Travels, III, at large); and authorities cited by John Fiske, *Discovery of America*, I, 250; an admirable ecological summary by A. L. Kroeber, *Cultural and Natural Areas*, 60-7.

in 1917 annihilated Delville Wood, at least—a very little obstructive resistance would render almost any wood impenetrable.[18] Opinions, however, differ somewhat. N. S. Shaler writes as follows:

> From Maine to Alabama the woods were unbroken and impassable. This great Appalachian forest was in primitive days an exceedingly dense tangle. At a few points the aborigines had worn narrow footways through it; but these trails were not adapted to pack-animals, the original means of transportation brought by the Europeans, but for the use of men who journeyed on foot, and could thus climb steeps inaccessible to a burdened beast. . . . The undergrowth of this forest country is far more dense than that which is commonly found in European lands. The shrubby plants and the species of smilax or green briar and other creeping vines make the most of our Appalachian forests very nearly impassable, even at the present day. Only once during the Civil War—in the retreat of George H. Morgan's army in 1862, from Cumberland Gap to the Ohio—did any considerable body of troops make an extended march through our trackless forests, and this redoubtable enterprise was accomplished in a portion of the Alleghany district where the woods are far more open than they are in the more eastern part of the country. Although this march extended for only two hundred miles and was partly over roads, it wore out the well-trained army which had part in it. . . .[19]

A. B. Hulbert, in contradistinction to Shaler, is all for the view that there was a "vast network of trails" in the forest territory.[20] But this, as he himself shows, would do little toward opening the forests:

> The bed of an Indian trail was very narrow, since made by only one traveler passing at a time. The trees and bushes encroached closely upon the path, and it was generally impossible to see ahead more than a rod or two. There were, probably, no such vistas as those along our woodland roads. Surprises were easily achieved.
> The narrowness of these early thoroughfares with heavy forests on either side combined to render such passage-ways frequently impassable. Zeisberger, who came westward as a missionary for the Moravian brethren [that is, about 1760], relates that much of the journey was accomplished on hands and knees—such was the impenetrable growth that choked the slender trails which were the only roads over the Alleghanies. It is evident that a single windstorm, in such aged forests as those which covered the country a century ago, could easily fill a narrow roadway with fallen branches, so that it would be well-nigh as impassable as the jungle itself. . . .[21]

[18]This has been well worked out, in relation to English mediaeval military history, by H. W. Mackinder, *Britain and British Seas* (2nd ed.), 230 *seq.* Compare also Dr. Gregg's description of the 'impenetrable forest' of the Cross Timbers, 1831, with others (above, chap. XX, note 422).

[19]Shaler, *Nature and Man in America*, 195-6.

[20]Hulbert, *Historic Highways*, I, 23; II, 14-15, 80-1; VIII, 73-4; etc. So also, Winsor (ed.), *Narrative and Critical History*, III, 186; Fiske, *Discovery of America*, I, 250; O. T. Mason, "Travel," *Handbook of American Indians*, II, 802; and for an extension of the same unsupported assumption into the Plains region, see Thwaites, ed. note, *Early Western Travels*, XVI, 230, *re* the Santa Fé Trail; with which compare Pike, 1806 (Coues (ed.), *Expeditions of Pike*, II, 400-546), and discussion above, chap. IX, note 24.

[21]Hulbert, *Historic Highways*, II, 19. Unfortunately Hulbert never tires of telling us that the historic Indian "followed the routes of that first great traveler,

This is borne out by historical evidence concerning more pretentious highways. Hulbert remarks elsewhere: "In the primeval forests it did not take long for a road to become impassable, if unused. Braddock's Road over the Alleghanies, cut in 1755, was impassable in 1758. . . . The Old Portage Road, cut in 1749, was cut out again in 1752 . . ." (by Marin's expedition).[22] The general evidence for eastern Canada proper indicates that conditions such as those suggested above prevailed in that region also.[23] But again, further evidence suggests that both in Canada[24] and in the eastern parts of the United States "open woods" were to be found. Two regional geographers write thus: "The coast plain forests, particularly the

---

the bison . . ." (*ibid.*, VIII, 17, etc., etc.). These old routes, *circa* 1900, were still so plain that their course could be traced (*ibid.*, I, 20, 66, etc.; so also Shoemaker: "very plain after 115 years," with a photo (*Pennsylvania Bison Hunt,* 12, 22, 46-7). Yet about 1760, when Shoemaker's 'vanished millions' (*ibid.,* 10, 38; for his dates see my chap. XIII, notes 1-78) were still going strong, and when 'everybody knew that the buffalo-Indian trails were the best,' and when Zeisberger himself was on "the great buffalo migration-route" on this very journey (Hulbert, *Historic Highways,* I, 18-134, *passim*; II, 15-20, 64; VIII, 16, 34; X, 53; XI, 26, 157, 164; XII, 25-9; etc.), he had to resort to crawling on his hands and knees! As we have seen, there is no evidence that the historic buffalo of Hulbert's postulates had penetrated into the area east of the Mississippi and south of Tennessee as late as 1542 (above, chap. IX, note 18 *seq.*); the Indian was there first. In his fervour, Hulbert (or some enthusiastic contributor) pushes his Indian trails in all directions "from the Gulf of Mexico to the country of the Eskimo . . ." (Hulbert, *Historic Highways,* II, 80), even into the canoe area. Lescarbot, Champlain, *The Jesuit Relations,* Hudson's Bay Company men, engineers, missionaries, travellers, east of Lake Winnipeg, tell another tale; well summarized by Jenness, *Indians of Canada,* 100. Finally, in his later delightful 'composite chronicle' of contemporary sources (Hulbert, *Forty-Niners*), neither he himself, nor any single one of his pilgrims, so much as mentions the buffalo-Indian-highway-railroad supposition. Hulbert's later volumes of his great series *are* historic and of high value. The first two (of pre-history) are a mass of contradictions.

[22]Hulbert, *Historic Highways,* VII, 156.

[23]Father Biard, 1616: "the whole country being but one interminable forest . . ." (*Jesuit Relations,* III, 41). Charles Lalemant, 1626: "nothing but forests . . ." (*ibid.,* IV, 195). Le Jeune, 1633-36: "a forest more than 800 leagues in extent at Kebec . . ." (*ibid.,* V, 73, 183); "800 to 1000 leagues . . ."; "vast forests . . .", "infinite forests . . ." (*ibid.,* VII, 107; VIII, 177; IX, 37). Vimont, Lalemant, 1644-46: "their great forests . . ." (*ibid.,* XXVII, 205, 207; XXIX, 65, 221). Paul Ragueneau, 1650: "vast forests . . ." (*ibid.,* XXXV, 265, 273, 275). Father Bressani's interpretation of *Canada* is unacceptable as etymology, but unexceptionable as physico-historical testimony, 1653: *hà nada* = 'nothing but woods' (*ibid.,* XXXVIII, 227).

[24]*Prairie* (*i.e.* meadow) was pressed into service by the French and by later usage for anything from a 'beaver-*meadow*,' sometimes of a few acres only, to the great plains. In the smaller sense, probably, Father Du Peron, 1638, speaks of the Huron country as being "tolerably level, with many prairies" (*Jesuit Relations,* XV, 153). Doubtless also the 'Prairie de la Madeleine,' Montreal, was little more than an open glade in the woods. See Nicolas Perrot and Bacqueville de la Potherie in Blair, *Indian Tribes,* I, 201; II, 81; also Colden, *History of the Five Nations,* I, 181; II, 44.

pine belts, were entirely open and free from undergrowth. It is incorrect to think of them as being in any sense impenetrable, though forests deserving such an epithet were found by the early pioneers who attempted to penetrate the upper Piedmont and Appalachian ridges. . . ."25 This is corroborated by another high authority: "The Piedmont [of Virginia and the Carolinas] was by no means the unbroken forest that might have been imagined, for in addition to natural meadows, the Indians had burned over large tracts. . . ."26

The "open woods" on the western fringe of the great territory we have been discussing are well attested. The same competent scholar gives this description:

> Ohio, Indiana, southern Michigan and central Wisconsin were almost covered with a growth of noble deciduous trees. In southern Illinois, along the broad bottom lands of the Mississippi and the Illinois, similar forests prevailed. To the north, in Michigan, Wisconsin, and Minnesota, appeared the sombre white pine wilderness, interlaced with hard woods, which swept in ample zone along the Great Lakes, till the deciduous forests triumphed again, and, in their turn, faded into the treeless expanse of the prairies. In the remaining portion were openings in the midst of the forested area, and the grassy ocean of prairie that rolled to west and northwest, until it passed beyond the line of sufficient rainfall for agriculture without irrigation, into the semi-arid stretches of the Great Plains. . . .27

This graphic outline sketch finds historical support in many early references. Fathers Membre and Douay, in La Salle's last fatal expedition of 1686, speak of "lofty woods and groves, through which you might ride on horseback."28 In the Illinois country, Father Claude Allouez, in 1672, emphasized the freedom from underbrush in many of the woods;29 as likewise did Colonel George Croghan in 1765,30 and Edmund Flagg in 1836.31 The common conception of the vast forests finds unconscious confirmation in the references to the "wide," "great," or "vast prairies" which confronted the early travellers in the country of the Illinois, when the enormous expanse of woodland at last began to break away through "oak openings"32 and "parklands" into stretches of treeless meadow.33 Such expressions, which are relative and do not necessarily imply areas of really great extent,34

25Jones and Bryan, *North America* (regional geography), 72; on the western yellow pine forests, cf. *ibid.*, 163.

26Turner, *Frontier in American History*, 89. See also Allen, *American Bisons*, 86; D. Huger Bagot, "The South Carolina up-country at the end of the eighteenth century," *American Historical Review*, XXVIII, 1922, 682-98.

27Turner, *Frontier in American History*, 130; cf. on 'oak openings,' *ibid.*, 137, 341, 346.

28*Journeys of La Salle*, I, 152, 263.

29*Jesuit Relations*, LVI, 123.

30Croghan's *Journal*, in *Early Western Travels*, I, 140; Hulbert, *Historic Highways*, I, 149, 151.

31Flagg, *Early Western Travels*, XXVI, 211.

32Turner, *Frontier in American History*, 130, 137, 341, 346.

33Marquette, Dablon, Allouez, 1670: 'great prairies in the country of the Illinois . . .' (*Jesuit Relations*, LIV, 185, 229, 231). Dablon, Allouez, 1671: 'beautiful prairies . . .' (*ibid.*, LV, 193-5). Allouez, 1672, 1677: 'vast prairies . . .' 'great prairies which extend farther than the eye can reach . . .' (*ibid.*, LV, 99; LVI, 123; LX, 157). Marest, 1712: 'prairies stretching farther than the eye can

sprang instinctively to the lips of men who had traversed a thousand miles of forest or wood-girt waterways. Charles Dickens, a century after Bonnecamp or Croghan, viewing them after the long journey from the Atlantic seaboard, calls them "immense prairies."[35] Audubon saw them in the very same year, 1842; but before his work was published he had seen the "Great Prairie" of the Missouri; and he designates them "the small and beautiful prairies of Indiana and Illinois."[36]

The general results of the foregoing review would seem at first sight to point to the "groves," "open woods," "oak openings," parklands, or whatever name one may give them, being more pronounced on the western borders of this huge territory than on the Atlantic slope; that is, more numerous on the side towards which the buffalo approach was made.

But we have also seen that such open glades, and "open woods" were likewise found (a) in regions where the buffalo have been recorded in such small numbers that their influence would be negligible; (b) in other regions where the buffalo had apparently never been known when the first Europeans (De Soto, 1539-42) passed through, at which time they were occupied by natives dependent in part on agriculture; and (c) in localities where buffalo of either historic or fossil species have never been recorded at all. Certain of these open spaces, moreover, are in vast expanses of the coniferous woods; and these woods wherever they occur have generally been held to mark roughly the frontiers of the buffalo habitat.

It is clear, therefore, that phenomena such as might be attributed to the buffalo in regions where they occurred were to be found in other areas where the buffalo were unknown; precisely as "open woods" may be found in older lands where herds of large and heavy animals have long been unknown, and where the forest denizens have been considered by expert opinion to have been at least as beneficial to woodland growth through the action of some species, as they were destructive through that of others.[37] A great portion of the historical source-material bearing

reach' (ibid., LXVI, 269, 271). Diron D'Artaguiette, 1723: 'a vast prairie on the Kaskaskia River'; also 'beautiful wide prairies . . .' (Journal, in Mereness (ed.), Colonial Travels, 67, 68, 70). Bonnecamp, 1750: 'vast prairies' among the Miamis; 'vast plains,' Detroit (Jesuit Relations, LXIX, 69, 187-91). Croghan, 1765: 'large savanahs . . .' (Journal, in Early Western Travels, I, 140).

[34]Estwick Evans, 1818, mentions 'Pilkawa Prairie,' Indiana, seven miles long by three broad (ibid., VIII, 283). Cf. also 'The Big Prairie,' Wabash River, and 'The Long Prairie,' Illinois, circa 1818 (Hulme, ibid., X, 258, 260; Faux, ibid., XI, 246).

[35]"From St. Louis we cross to Chicago, traversing immense prairies . . ." (Letters of Charles Dickens, 62).

[36]Audubon and Bachman, American Quadrupeds, II, 36; cf. Edmund Flagg, 1836 (perhaps after a similar experience): ". . . the lesser prairies" (of Illinois; Early Western Travels, XXVI, 340).

[37]Woods 'through which you might ride on horseback' were a characteristic of England. See the photo of the 'Haywood Oak' at Blisworth in Sherwood (Cox, Royal Forests of England, 220). Such trees cannot stand close; cf. also Roe, "The Winding Road," Antiquity (England), XIII, June, 1939, 191-206. John Nisbet, a practical forestry expert and also a learned authority on mediaeval forest history, thinks that natural regeneration of the mediaeval woods was fostered by the

on our topic is in the form of reports from missionary-ecclesiastics to their official superiors, who required guidance for future policy as well as reports of the year's expenditures in "blood and treasure" (sometimes no mere figure of speech!). When we reflect on this and also on the insatiable curiosity usually shown by educated stay-at-homes for everything about a strange land, it seems incredible that their voluminous writings would not contain more notice of the destruction of trees by buffalo if it occurred on any extensive scale.

In my view it is more probable that the prime cause of the destruction of trees was the immemorial custom of Indians in many regions, of frequently firing the country for various reasons—their primitive agricultural or economic necessities, or the demands of military strategy. It may be noted that one of our earliest witnesses records this practice among the Miamis and other tribes in the very territory under consideration, the Mississippi valley country.[38] The practice of using fire-cordons for "environing the Deere" was noted in "Virginia" (then practically conterminous with "Florida"[39]) in 1607;[40] in a locality where the buffalo had then probably never penetrated.[41] Anyone who has lived in Alberta during the last twenty or thirty years particularly, has had exceptionally good opportunities of witnessing the rapidity with which fire can convert woodland into "prairie." In a long-grass country, the charred butts and stumps standing out above a growth which is the more rank and lush since the sun obtained free admission, are often the only visible feature which can distinguish a *brulé* of five years' standing from some adjacent tract which was never known to have been wooded. I am glad to find myself in general agreement on this question with an eminent scientist already quoted; whose work has by no means been wholly superseded by the scientific progress of half a century. Shaler writes:

Thus the deforested condition of our prairies, which gives a very peculiar physiographic condition to the central basin of the continent, is probably to be accounted for by the interference of man. It is an effect, though unintended, of the savage's action in relation to an important wild beast. If the advent of European folk in the Mississippi valley had been delayed for another five centuries, the prairie country would doubtless have been made very much more extensive. Thus in western Kentucky a territory of about five thousand square miles in area had recently been brought to the state of open land by the burning of the forests.

---

trampling-in of acorns, beech-nuts, etc., by swine and cattle; but that rabbits and deer (which latter were fed branches in winter—'deer browse'—and also ate such for themselves) destroyed much. See on this, G. J. Turner, *Select Pleas of the Forest;* Cox, *Royal Forests of England, passim*; Nisbet, *Our Forests and Woodlands,* 117, 159, 298, 312; cf. also R. G. Albion, *Forests and Sea Power,* 119. Below, note 51.

[38]Hennepin, 1680, *New Discovery*, I, 145, 146, 154; cf. Father Vivier, 1750, *Jesuit Relations*, LXIX, 209; also F. J. Turner, *Frontier in American History,* 89.

[39]See above, chap. IX, note 39.

[40]By the doughty Captain John Smith, of 'Pocahontas' fame (*Purchas his Pilgrimes*, XVIII, 444). So also among the Central Mississippi tribes (Hennepin, *New Discovery*, I ,147).

[41]See above on this, chap. IX, notes 18-63.

All around the margin of this area there were only old trees scarred by the successive fires, there being no young of the species to take the place as they fell. It is probable that with another five hundred years of such conditions the prairie region would have extended up to the base of our Alleghanies, and in time all the great Appalachian woods, at least as far as the plain-land was concerned, would probably have vanished in the same process. . . .[42]

The hypothesis of fire origin was accepted by many scientific and essentially scientifically minded observers,[43] as well as by the less-educated,[44] concerning United States territories; and also—by similarly diverse minds—with reference to more than one region in Canada.[45] And it may be pointed out that in northern woodlands, where heavier shade and colder, damper soils, makes fires of the sporadic unsystematized Indian character less prone to run than might be suspected among the *conifera*; and where at the same time—partly owing to this very circumstance of the damp "moss" in which the *larvae* are deposited—mosquitoes are even more intolerable than on the plains, the suggestion of buffalo destroying the trees seems never to have been advanced.

The apparent rapidity with which large areas in the buffalo country were deforested can in my view be readily explained by the hypothesis of fire. It is much more difficult to find grounds for considering the buffalo as even a secondary cause of any material importance. Dr. Hector, "two short days" westward from Fort Ellice (at the junction of the Assiniboine and Qu'Appelle rivers; almost on the Manitoba-Saskatchewan boundary, near Lazare, on the Canadian National main line between Winnipeg and Saskatoon), in September, 1857, wrote as follows: ". . . we crossed several detached plains of considerable size, covered with clumps of very fine poplars, some of them measuring two feet in diameter, and reaching a great altitude. This is the only place on the plains where we have seen wood of any size. . . ."[46] Professor Henry Youle Hind, in the following year, makes mention of something even more remarkable: "An old Indian . . . born in this part of the country, told us he remembered the time when the whole of the prairie through which we had passed since leaving Fort Ellice [that is, to Indian Head, Saskatchewan, a distance westward of

[42]Shaler, *Nature and Man in America*, 186-7.

[43]Father Vivier, 1750 (*Jesuit Relations*, LXIX, 209); F. A. Michaux, 1802 (*Early Western Travels*, III, 221); Brackenridge, 1811 (*ibid.*, VI, 157); Dr. Edwin James, with S. H. Long, 1820 (*ibid.*, XX, 256); Wyeth, 1833 (*ibid.*, XXI, 49); · Flagg, 1836 (*ibid.*, XXVI, 162, 212, 234, 302, 342-7).

[44]This was the opinion of the Illinois settlers, *circa* 1818 (Faux, *ibid.*, X, 280).

[45]See on Canada, G. M. Dawson, *re* southern Manitoba and Peace River, in Macoun, *Manitoba*, 43, 125; Thompson, *Narrative*, ed. Tyrrell, 441; Henry, 1811, in Coues (ed.), *Henry-Thompson Journals*, II, 741, 743; D. W. Harmon, *circa* 1819, *Harmon's Journal*, 90; *Palliser Journals*, 1857-60, 7, 13, 57, 59 (Palliser); *ibid.*, 83 (Hector); *ibid.*, 86, 89 (Sullivan); *ibid.*, 245 (M. Bourgeau). McDougall, *circa* 1865, *Pathfinding*, 53. It is cited as an Indian tradition by MacRae, *History of Alberta*, I, 92. For areas with remains of ancient fire-scarred trunks, *circa* 1800, 1880, see Thompson, *Narrative*, 248; Macoun, *Manitoba*, 91, 111.

On the common Indian practice of firing the country, see chap. XXI, notes 187-206.

[46]Hector, in *Palliser Journals*, 50.

practically one hundred miles] was one continuous forest, broken only by two or three intervals of barren ground. . . ."[47]

It is pertinent to note that buffalo could not have been responsible for the changes. The large size of the timber growth noted by Hector, and the fact that no such alleged or even traditional results are asserted concerning much smaller growths in an aboriginally occupied territory, the Northern Wood Buffalo Park, may be considered virtually conclusive evidence[48] for the Fort Ellice region. As for the statement itself, it comes within the category of direct evidence, quite fundamentally different from "tradition," whatever our views upon Indian traditions may be.[49] Apart from any question of its truth, it would at least be admissible upon oath—from a white witness at all events—in a court of law. And if, without other reasons, it is to be rejected because of its Indian origin, this logically entails the exclusion of any and every statement from Indian sources, regardless of its character. Hind apparently saw no reason for disbelieving it; nor do I. Dr. E. H. Moss, of the University of Alberta, who has conducted some authoritative investigations into the botanical and ecological history of the province, considers the buffalo were "doubtless an important factor" as a check upon woodland growth.[50] This is inherently quite probable; and is consonant with phases of woodland history.[51] But that buffalo were enemies to regeneration, and that they were the authors of the "original" deforestation—in any material degree—are two very different arguments.

[47]Hind, Report, 1858, 48; cf. ibid., 7, 17, 30.

[48]See the excellent photographs, clearly indicating the nature of the woodland growth, together with the author's sketches of 'rubbed' or broken-down trees (3 in. in diameter) in Soper, "History of the Northern Bison" (i.e. the Wood buffalo); 355, 359, 361, 372, 386, 387, 395.

[49]After a careful examination of several, I confess that my faith in the average traditions of plainsmen, red or white, is very weak. See chaps. III, notes 9-39; VIII, notes 9-28; XII, notes 167-8; XVII, notes 85-6; XXII, notes 14-25; also Appendix J, "Buffalo and Disease."

[50]Francis J. Lewis, Eleanor S. Dowding, and E. H. Moss, "The Vegetation of Alberta" (Journal of Ecology, England, 1926, 1928, 1929, 1930; part IV, by Moss, 405).

[51]Dr. R. G. Albion notes a project for planting oak in Suffolk, England, 1791: "Oak would pay, but the Crop to be Timber only, and no Cattle ever admitted . . ." (Forests and Sea Power, 119). J. D. Soper, after careful examination, considers damage in Wood Buffalo Park to be slight (as above, note 48); offset, or more than offset, by natural regeneration from manuring, etc. (Soper, "History of the Northern Bison," 388). Compare my remarks above (chap. XVIII, notes 23-7), which were written some months before seeing Soper's most valuable essay.

FOSSIL BISON IN BRITISH COLUMBIA (pp. 20, 309)

Max H. Ruhmann, in his article "The Bison in the Okanagan Valley" (*First Annual Report of the Okanagan Historical and Natural History Society*, September, 1926, p. 6) writes:

In June 1919, Mr. Harry Mills, while prospecting on Mission Creek, 12 miles from Kelowna, discovered some large bones in deposits of the Pleistocene period on bedrock twelve feet below the surface of the soil. The bones, seven in number, consisted of two Cannon bones (united metapodials), two Tibia (hind leg) one Hemerus [*sic*] and two Ulna (fore leg). Besides these bones a considerable quantity of broken fragments were found. According to an affidavit signed by Mr. Harry Mills, the bones were covered by five strata consisting of: 1 blue clay; 2 coarse gravel; 3 yellow clay; 4 fine gravel; 5 a sandy loam. Each stratum averaged over two feet in depth with a total depth of twelve feet above the bones. These bones were placed at the disposal of the Okanagan Historical and Natural History Society in the Fall of 1925 so that they might be identified. Dr. M. Y. Williams, Palaeontologist of the B.C. University, determined their period as Pleistocene. The bones were identified as the limb bones of a species of Bison by Dr. D. W. Mathews, Curator-in-Chief of the American Museum of Natural History, New York City. These findings were brought to the attention of Dr. Rudolph Anderson, Mammologist of the Canadian Biological Survey, who states that this interesting find will possibly extend the known range of the bison.

This is certainly the case, and in a most significant degree. There appears to be no record of bison of any species, fossil or otherwise, crossing the Rocky Mountains into British Columbia at any point south of approximately 56° N., with this one exception. Kelowna lies approximately 49° 30' N., over 450 miles to the south. Pending the possible discovery of further bison vestiges in the intervening territory, the locality would seem to suggest a specific approximation to the fossil species of the Columbia drainage basin (in Oregon). See Skinner and Kaisen, *Fossil Bison of Alaska*, 165-80.

APPENDIX M

PEMMICAN AND BUFFALO MEAT AT THE FUR POSTS (p. 289)

The profusion at the fur posts may convey some idea of the buffalo plenty. Duncan McGillivray's '500 thighs and shoulders' in store at Fort George, 1795 (*Journal*, ed. Morton, 41-54); Henry, Fort Vermilion, 1810: '550 thighs and 380 shoulders' in the ice-house, and '400 limbs' left behind, on leaving (Coues (ed.), *Henry-Thompson Journals*, II, 582, 601). De Smet: '500 buffalo' stored at Edmonton, 1846 (*Early Western Travels*, XXIX, 234-51, also *Life of De Smet*, II, 533). Edmonton, 1848, '700 or 800': Kane, *Wanderings of an Artist*, (orig. ed.), 367.

Harmon records 70 persons eating at least 450 pounds per day, February 7, 1805 (*Journal*, 103). At 'Panbian' (Pembina) River Post, South Manitoba, North West Company, September 1, 1807 to June 1, 1808, 17 men, 10 women and 14 children (together with 45 dogs) consumed 147 buffalo, weighing in all 63,000 pounds, plus 410 pounds of grease, and 140 pounds of 'beat meat' (that is, as prepared for pemmican before adding hot fat), besides other meat and vegetables. The voyageur's daily allowance was eight pounds of fresh meat, or a pound and a half of pemmican (Coues (ed.); *Henry-Thompson Journals*, I, 444; cf. Thompson, *Narrative*, ed. Tyrrell, 435). At Henry's Fort Terre Blanche, near Pakan, Alberta, 1810, 90 pounds of pemmican per day were consumed (*Henry-Thompson Journals*, II, 604). Franklin at 'La Montee,' 1820, notes 70 men, 60 women, and children, consuming 700 pounds of buffalo meat daily, 8 pounds per day being one man's allowance (First) *Journey to the Polar Sea*, 117. At Edmonton, 1857, 'two buffalo' were served out every day (Hector, *Palliser Journals*, 72, 78).

Cowie gives a detailed description, Fort Qu'Appelle, 1867-68: ". . . the daily allowance for each child was one-quarter, and for a woman one-half that for a man, which was twelve pounds fresh buffalo meat, or six pounds dried buffalo meat, or three pounds pemmican, or six rabbits, or six prairie chickens, or three large whitefish, or three large or six small ducks, . . . with a weekly allowance of tallow or fat [besides potatoes, milk, sometimes berries]. . . . Daily to feed the establishment required in the form of fresh meat, the tongues, bosses, ribs and fore and hind quarters of three animals, for the head, neck, shanks, and inside were not considered worth freighting from the plains to the fort. The product of three buffalo in the concentrated form of pemmican was equivalent to the daily issue of fresh meat. . . ." There were at Fort Qu'Appelle that winter 53 men, women, and children, drawing rations from the Hudson's Bay Company; also 30 train dogs, equal to 20 man's rations (Cowie, *Company of Adventurers*, 214-16). See also R. O. Merriman, "The Bison and the Fur Trade," *Queen's Quarterly*, July-September, 1926, 78-96; Innis, *Fur Trade in Canada*, 240. For recent investigations into the nutritive value of 'pemmican' (of modern manufacture), see Vilhjalmur Stefansson, "Pemmican," *The Military Surgeon*, vol. 95, August, 1944, No. 2, 89-98.

I am favoured with the following further information from my friend Henry Stelfox, of Rocky Mountain House (Alberta), to whom I have referred above. It forms part of the data on pemmican furnished by him (at my own request) to Stefansson, and I am kindly permitted to use it.

As with ordinary pemmican, the preparation of an improved quality containing fruits or other vegetable ingredients was acquired from the Indians. Their ratios of such in the season's manufacture were not large. Stelfox considers that probably not more than some five per cent among the prairie tribes and from seven to ten per cent in the Foothill country would be of this superior class. The fact that such 'berry pemmican' was regarded as a delicacy for 'higher-ups' in the tribe and their friends may have been partly the cause and partly the effect of this.

These additions or condiments were apparently obtained from whatever the local resources might furnish. In the Foothill regions saskatoons (*Amelanchier Canadensis var.*) were the chief or sole item. In other areas such natural commodities (of which Macoun, *Manitoba*, 177-95, gives a lengthy list) as dried herbs or wild vegetables, nuts, wild rice, etc., were utilized. Considering how wide was the liking for this dainty fare, both for its own excellence and no doubt as a sort of social 'hall-mark,' it seems probable (as Stelfox considers) that the low ratios suggested were largely due to seasonal conditions. Most of the pemmican had to be made before the vegetable auxiliaries were available (see above, p. 473, on this).

The keeping qualities of pemmican seem to have been virtually unlimited. They were at any rate practically so from the standpoint of the traders who at least expected some day to need their own reserve stocks. Chittenden (*American Fur Trade*, II, 811) and General Sam Steele (*Forty Years in Canada*, 69-70, 89-90, 95-6) cite some informative data on this. Steele notes (p. 95) having seen the hide bags of pemmican (*taureaux*) from which the outer hair had been worn away by 'decades' of repeated handling in trans-shipment, leaving the hide quite smooth and shiny; yet the meat was quite unaffected, and as good as ever.

Stelfox mentions an instance of a 'cache' of pemmican near the Red Deer River, being uncovered by a farmer while ploughing, about 1933; apparently somewhere in the Red Deer district itself. I recall a similar discovery being made in the Wainwright country, but have lost the newspaper reference. In the latter case at least, the fact was emphasized that there were no visible indications of decay or putrefaction. The bags turned up 'as hard as stone.' It is regrettable that—in so far as I am aware—no attempt was made to cook or analyse the contents and ascertain their suitability as food. They must necessarily have been fifty years old, and were probably far more.

APPENDIX N

MUSK-OX (AND OTHER SPECIES) AS 'BUFFALO' (p. 302)

Henry Kelsey on his first journey, July 9 to 10, 1689, mentions ". . . Buffillo . . . seen neear yt River wch they call Buffillo River. . . ." These animals are considered to be Musk-oxen (*Kelsey Papers*, xix, 27-28, 29).

Compare Hearne's 'Buffalo or Musk-Ox' Lake; about 69° 30′ N., on his map (*Journey*, 164, 204). Hearne seems to have used the two names rather loosely and indifferently as, for example, ". . . bowls and spoons made of buffalo or musk-ox horn . . ." (*ibid.*, 190).

The following suggests the musk-ox also: "There is no wood to the Northward of Slave Lake, there is only a little low Brush which is filled with a species of Buffaloes which have no Tails, but have long Hair on the Back of their Thighs & Legs that resemble a Tail. They are smaller than the common Buffaloes . . ." (Letter of Isaac Ogden, Quebec, November 7, 1789, in *Report of Canadian Archives*, 1889, 30).

Sir Alexander Mackenzie, 1789, mentions the 'buffalo of the Coppermine River,' from whose horns, presumably, a white horn spoon in the Indians' possession was made (*Voyages 1789 and 1793*, 198). He says of the region near the Mackenzie Delta, that the country at this point "did not abound in moose-deer and buffaloes . . ." (*ibid.*, 83; cf. 38, 72, 82; July 6 to 27, 1789). Whether this means there were some, or none whatever, it is difficult to say. They could scarcely be bison, however; Richardson states that 'the Bison was unknown to the Esquimaux of the Polar Sea' (*Fauna Boreali-Americana*, I, 279). He also says: "The districts inhabited by the musk-ox are the proper lands of the Esquimaus; and neither the Northern Indians nor the Crees have an original name for it, both terming it *bison* with an additional epithet . . ." (*ibid.*, 276). The names are, in Cree, *matteh-moostoos* = 'ugly bison'; and among the Chippewyan and 'Copper' Indians, *adgiddah-yawseh* = 'little bison' (so, *ibid.*, 275). Seton classes the musk-ox as 'Musk Buffalo, Arctic Buffalo, or Polar Cattle.' He says: "It is nearer to the American Buffalo in anatomy than to any other existing animal; and may be described as a form of Buffalo specialized for life on the Polar Plains. . . ." He gives its French names as *Bison musqué, le bœuf musqué*, and its Chippewyan and 'Slavey' names as *Et-jer-ré* or *Ota-Et-jir-er*, the same in Chippewyan as *Bison americanus* (Seton, *Game Animals*, III, 596-637). I find 'musk-buffaloe' in George Keith's "Letters" (Masson, *Les Bourgeois de la Compagnie du Nord-Ouest*, II, 103, 1807-17).

The 'white buffaloes' of Mackenzie, 1789 (*Voyages*, 198: Willson, *Great Company*, 335; etc.) are thought by Allen to be musk-oxen (*American Bisons*, 39). This might find some basis in Richardson, above, on Chippewyan and Cree names for that animal. Richardson himself believed Mackenzie's white buffaloes to be mountain sheep (*Fauna Boreali-*

Americana, I, 272); and Lewis and Clark found mountain sheep termed 'white buffalo' in the Rocky Mountain territory in 1806 (*Journals*, III, 162). Such usages are perfectly natural and logical. Cresswell, *in re* mastodon remains, Big Bone Lick, Kentucky, 1775, writes: "All the traditionary accounts by the Indians is that they were White Buffaloes that killed themselves by drinking salt water . . ." (*Journal*, 86).

BUFFALO IN THE ROCKY MOUNTAIN PASSES (p. 306)

I have consulted Richardson's *Fauna Boreali-Americana* concerning buffalo. This is the only work of his cited by Allen; and it is quoted by Hornaday, who here is clearly following Allen and not the original, as will be seen below. I have also consulted Richardson's contributions in Franklin, (First) *Journey to the Polar Sea, 1819-22* (London, 1825), and *Second Journey to the Polar Sea, 1825-27* (London, 1828). Richardson's observations on this matter have been given above (at the commencement of chap. XII). He speaks of buffalo finding out "a passage across the mountains near the source of the Saskatchewan. . . ." There is nothing about the Kananaskis or Kicking Horse passes, the latter of which is the Canadian Pacific Railway route; and for good reason. In Richardson's day, and for years after, there was no used—perhaps no known—pass between the Athabaska Pass, about 52° 30′ N. (that is, 'Boat Encampment') and the Kootenay Pass, 49° N., 114° W. White Man Pass (50° 45′ N., 115° 29′ W., directly south from Banff, Alberta) is stated to have derived the name from being 'probably' the one used by Father De Smet in the autumn of 1845, en route to Rocky Mountain House and Edmonton, where he wintered (*Place-Names of Alberta*, 134). I can find nothing further on this. Palliser's parties 'discovered' (or examined) the Howse Pass of Thompson (1800: see Burpee, *Search for the Western Sea*, 537), the Kananaskis, and the Kicking-Horse passes, 1859-60. (See on this *Palliser Journals*, 1863, *passim*; Bryce, *Remarkable History*, 339; Bancroft, *Northwest Coast*, chapter XX, "Passes and Routes," I, 616-65; Burpee, *Search for the Western Sea*, introd., xli-xlv). Hornaday frequently errs concerning Canada; and he may have confounded 'the source of the Saskatchewan' with the Canadian Pacific Railway through the Rockies. For although the identity of the Bow and the South Saskatchewan River was known early to some (see John McDonald of Garth, *circa* 1800, in Masson, *Les Bourgeois de la Compagnie du Nord-Ouest*, II, 20), I suspect that to Hornaday—probably to Richardson also—the 'Saskatchewan' was (as generally) the North Saskatchewan. Many people in Alberta today are still unaware of the identity of the other two, the South Saskatchewan and the Bow.

As for "the numbers which crossed the mountains at that point [being] sufficiently noticeable to constitute a feature of the fauna" on the western side—I can find no such statement in the *Fauna Boreali-Americana*, the logical place for such. Richardson's own words are as given above (chapter XII): ". . . their numbers to the westward are *said to be* annually increasing. . . ." The three crucial words in italics are Richardson's own; the italics, of course, being mine. They are omitted by Allen (*American Bisons*, 166-8), and the omission is repeated by Hornaday "Extermination of the American Bison," 384) with a photographic fidelity too often lacking elsewhere. I may add that I can find nothing whatever on this particular question in Richardson's other works in volume form, *The Arctic Searching Expedition of 1847-1850* and, *The Polar Regions*. It seems improbable that a writer not mentioning these would be quoting from unidentified, lesser-known papers in scientific periodicals.

See also, for similar omissions by Hornaday of important qualifying clauses in quotations at second hand, above, pp. 35, 61, 283-4, 306; *cf.* below, p. 880.

APPENDIX P

PREFERENCE OF INDIANS AND WHITE MEN
FOR BUFFALO COWS (p. 375)

Allusions to the preference for cows, both among Indians and those who came after them, are numerous and virtually unanimous. This unanimous 'preference' for the skins of cows, however, may be regarded as really more or less forced upon them. The bull-hides were practically unworkable; and more cow-hides (slain for food) were naturally available. On the preference for cow-beef, see "Relacion del Suceso," 1540, in *Journey of Coronado*, 208. Hennepin, 1680, *New Discovery*, ed. Thwaites, I, 146. Pike, 1806, in Coues (ed.), *Expeditions of Pike*, II, 516. Henry, 1808, in Coues (ed.), *Henry-Thompson Journals*, II, 490. Thompson, 1810, *Narrative*, ed. Tyrrell, 408, 431. Astorians eastbound, 1813, Irving, *Astoria*, 360-8, 377. Richardson, 1820, *Fauna Boreali-Americana*, I, 282. Long's expedition, 1820: a bull, 'too ill-savoured to eat'; another (likewise, but eaten): *Early Western Travels*, XVI, 30, 103. In 1833: Irving, *Captain Bonneville*, 123. In 1842: Frémont, *Narrative*, 23. In 1848: 'not desirable in winter, when the female can be procured . . .' (Kane, *Wanderings of an Artist*, Radisson Society ed., 267). In 1857: "killed a young bull, of which we were able to eat a little . . ." (*Palliser Journals*, 53). Hind, 1858: 'very poor' (*Report*, 46; also *ibid.*, 106, citing Major Long, 1825). Hughes, *Father Lacombe*, 148-50. Denny MS., 42, 88. McDougall, *Saddle, Sled, and Snowshoe*, 106; *Western Trails*, 92, 121, 171. Hornaday, "Extermination of the American Bison," 492.

These are occasional exceptional views. Allen says: "the tongue, even of an old bull, is always regarded as a delicate morsel . . ." (*American Bisons*, 193). Father Râle, *circa* 1720: "When they have killed an ox [that is, buffalo] that seems too lean, they are satisfied to take its tongue (*Jesuit Relations*, LXVII, 169). Hearne, 1771: "The tongue is very delicate; and what is most extraordinary, when the beasts are in the poorest state, which happens regularly at certain seasons, their tongues are very fat and fine; some say, fatter than when they are in the best order; the truth of which I will not confirm . . ." (*Journey*, ed. Tyrrell, 258). 'Bulls eaten only in the months of May and June' (Long, *Early Western Travels*, XIV, 301). 'Bulls of all ages, if fat, make good beef . . .' (Gregg, *ibid.*, XX, 264). Henry, Red River, 1806: "more palatable in rutting-time than the cows"; but contra, North Saskatchewan River, 1808 (Coues, (ed.), *Henry-Thompson Journals*, I, 310; II, 490). 'Rank in rutting-time' (Audubon and Bachman, *American Quadrupeds*, II, 41). Ross: "In the early part of the season the bulls are fat and the cows lean. In autumn . . . the bulls are lean and the cows fat . . ." (*Red River Settlement*, 262). McDougall, 1865: a bull killed, 'not eatable'; another, shortly afterward (probably a young one), 'prime beef' (*Pathfinding*, 189, 255).

Concerning the use of cows' hides alone, this was noticed—even for shields—in the letter from the Viceroy, Antonio de Mendoza, to Charles V (*Journey of Coronado*, 152); and also by Father Claude Allouez along the Mississippi Valley, 1677 (*Jesuit Relations*, LX, 161). Thompson, however, found shields of bulls' hides among the Mandans, *circa* 1800 (*Narrative*, 228, 411); and according to Wissler, and Kidd's native informants, Blackfoot shields were made from the breast of a buffalo bull (Kidd, "Blackfoot Ethnography," 129). An eminent American scholar states that shields were ordinarily of thick buffalo hide *covered* with soft dressed buffalo (or other) skin. Mooney, *Handbook of American Indians*, II, 546. Parkman, 1846: ". . . no scruple about killing bulls. . . . Against the bulls we waged unrelenting war. . . . their numbers greatly exceed those of the cows . . . it is the hides of the latter alone which are used for the purposes of commerce and for making the lodges of the Indians; and the destruction among them is therefore greatly disproportionate" (*Oregon Trail*, 91, 419). This was probably what made the cows faster runners (so, Marcy, *Exploration of Red River*, 24; cf. Audubon and Bachman, *American Quadrupeds*, II, 39, 41).

Hornaday comments as follows: "With a recklessness of the future that was not to be expected of savages, though perhaps perfectly natural for civilized white men, who place the possession of a dollar above everything else, the Indians with one accord singled out the cows for slaughter, because their robes and their flesh better suited the fastidious taste of the noble redskin . . ." ("Extermination of the American Bison," 492; cf. 506).

BUFFALO HIDE, MEAT, AND BONE TRAFFIC (p. 438)

It is extremely difficult to reach any reliable conclusions concerning this. One can do little more than give such data as he has been able to collect, and leave readers to form their own ideas on the question. The table cited above (chap. XV, note 101) is taken from Dodge (*Plains of the Great West*, 142). It is cited also by Hornaday ("Extermination of the American Bison," 499), to whom these calculations are credited by Garretson (*American Bison*, 110); who only mentioned Dodge once throughout his book, for a contemptuous denial (p. 39). From some source not indicated, Allen secured some detached figures on the Kansas Pacific Railway for 1871. 'Dry hides' shipped, 341,150 pounds at 25 pounds per hide = 13,646 buffaloes. (At Dodge's ratio for 1871, this would perhaps equal 68,230 animals killed). Meat, 1,161,419 pounds at 200 pounds per 'saddle' = 5,807 buffaloes: "far below the actual number," so Allen (*American Bisons*, 177). In General Meigs' "MS. Notes on Buffalo" (which I have not seen) there were 'reputed to be 180,000 hides over the Santa Fé road in a single season' (Allen, *American Bisons*, 178). Garretson states that in 1871 one firm in St. Louis bought 250,000 skins (*American Bison*, 110). These, however, would not necessarily be all from the southern range. As early as 1833, Maximilian notes 15,000 hides in two shipments only, bound for St. Louis (*Early Western Travels*, XXII, 327; XXIII, 11).

The following is of interest, although for reasons given at the conclusion of chapter XV, I hesitated to insert it in my text: "Steel was laid into Dodge in September of '72, and that fall the buffalo trade began. Over by the railhead station . . . was Wright and Rath's store yard for buffalo hides. I've seen forty or fifty thousand hides piled up there at one time awaiting shipment. Wright and Rath didn't do all the business, but they'd ship 400,000 hides and 2,000,000 pounds of buffalo meat in a season. The Santa Fé hauled more than 3,000,000 hides out of this camp in four winters. Hides meant $2. to $3. each to the traders, not to mention five or ten million pounds of buffalo meat at five cents a pound and, later, 'about $2,000,000 in buffalo bones, which were legal tender in Dodge at $6. a ton. . . .'" (Quoted from "Straight-Shooting Dodge," reminiscences of an old-timer coterie, told to, or compiled by Stuart N. Lake, *Saturday Evening Post*, March 8, 1930).

Inman (*The Old Santa Fé Trail*, 203) says the average price was $8. per ton. In Kansas alone, 1868-81, $2,500,000 was paid out for buffalo bones, representing (100 buffalo = one ton of bones) the skeletons of over 31,000,000 buffalo. In neither account can one find any definite authority for such round sums. These two contemporary authorities differ in the price by 33 per cent.

But even these are out-done by 'Bob Davis': 2,000,000 *hides* a year between 1865-75 ("Canada Cavalcade," *Winnipeg Free Press,* September 11, 1937).

Garretson accepts such figures as they stand, although some of his aggregates vary; as well they might, for no two informants agree or come near agreement. He has 200,000 hides for Wright and Rath in 1872; "and others shipped as many more . . ." (*American Bison,* 114).

McCreight's information varies again. He prints a photograph of the 40,000 hides in Wright and Rath's yard; and says: ". . . it is claimed that nearly four million animals were killed and their hides shipped out over the Santa Fé railroad, while the carcasses were left to rot on the plains— all in two years. . . ." (*Buffalo Bone Days,* 10).

This claim ignores Dodge's—or any—estimate of the proportion of ruined hides; it also ignores meat shipped; and compresses the 4,000,000 hides into *two* years! As against the $6. per ton for bones, given above, McCreight prints accounts from the Nebraska and Kansas Historical Societies respectively (one of the two, contemporary), which give the price as 'averaging $8. per ton': and '$7. to $9. per ton.' Further, 'five cents a pound for meat, which was a drug in the market, coming from a witness sixty years after; the more nearly contemporary newspaper cited above (note 69) says 'from 1 to 2 cents per pound.' (Cf. also Garretson, *American Bisons,* 114).

In my opinion, many of these colossal figures are their own refutation. 'Any man worth his salt' killed his 100 a day. In the Dodge City area 'over 75,000 were killed in 1872' by some 2600 hunters; that is, about 30 per man *per season*. In the Medicine Lodge district, '216,000 slaughtered in two months'; this only required 36 hunters at 100 per day. That ratio would give an aggregate for the four-month season, from the mean of the '8000 or 10,000' hunters on the range, of some 96,000,000! (See Garretson, *American Bison,* 108-29, and other authorities cited in this appendix and in chapter XV.) Extreme estimates—'claims' only to begin with—are treated too much as ordinary occurrences (as McCreight, *Buffalo Bone Days,* 9-10). It seems to be forgotten that such loose extravagances would be the common phraseology of the time. But their mere use of course testifies to vast numbers.

BUFFALO HIDE NUMBERS (p. 444)

It is difficult to reduce the vague dimensional assertions concerning masses of buffalo hides into even approximately trustworthy numbers. Professor Thompson's calculation of a pile equal to 120 cords furnishes a starting point, however (see above, chap. XV, note 131). A cord being eight feet long, four feet wide, and four feet high, or 128 cubic feet, 120 cords (15,360 cubic feet) would be equal to a pile 80 feet long, 24 feet wide, and 8 feet high. I have no direct data as to what this would represent in numbers. McCreight (*Buffalo Bone Days*, 10) and Garretson (*American Bison*, 124) give a photograph of '40,000 hides' in Wright and Rath's yard, at Dodge City, 1874.

The distance to the end of the corral from the commencement of the stack seems to be not more than 100 feet; it is of irregular shape, like an ill-built and uncompleted haystack, some twelve feet wide, and about ten feet high in a dome or hay-stack form at its highest point, which occupies in a finished condition about one-third of the length. A triangle would be one half a square of those dimensions. This, being a blunt convex form, may be allowed three-quarters for say forty feet in length; and half the square for sixty feet. This yields a space, say 40 x 12 x 8, together with 60 x 12 x 6 = a combined total of 7160 or 7200 cubic feet (56¼ cords). Let this be assumed at 60 cords for 40,000 buffalo hides. Garretson writes as follows: "In Cheyenne, Wyoming, in 1872 there was a shed at the Union Pacific tracks that measured 175 feet long, 60 feet wide, and 30 feet high, that was literally so packed with buffalo hides that the walls bulged . . ." (*American Bison*, 110). These dimensions constitute a space of 315,000 cubic feet = 2461 cords; 41 times the computed cubical space of the 40,000 hides at Dodge City: that is, 1,640,000 hides.

According to Hornaday (who, however, is incorrect here), Cheyenne was a frontier, east of which the buffalo were extinct in 1867 (Hornaday, "Extermination of the American Bison," 492; but cf. chap. XV, note 40; also above, chaps. VII, VIII). We are not told who measured the building, nor who authenticated the 'bulging' walls. Lest my own conjectural dimensions, which necessitate a total of 80,000 hides in the pile measured at Dodge City in 1878, should seem too narrow to conform to such an aggregate at that late date, we may even halve the estimate in the Union Pacific shed at Cheyenne. I still consider 820,000 in one place at one time to be incredible. There is no contemporary mention of any such total; nor do those recorded by Garretson (*American Bison*, 110-12, etc.) or anyone else, bear any relation to such figures. I suggest that this may keep company with Daniel Ott's piles 100 feet high! (See above, chap. XV, note 11).

Dodge, a cautious contemporary observer, believed that the Union Pacific handled a much smaller quantity than either of the other two principal 'buffalo' systems. (See above, chap. XV, note 99).

At the famous battle of Adobé Walls, June 24-7, 1874, where 28 men are said to have withstood 700 Indians for three days, the defenders were entrenched 'behind stacks of buffalo hides' (Grinnell, *Fighting Cheyennes,* 308-15); or 'in three of the largest buildings' (Garretson, *American Bison,* 120-2). Frank Dobie quotes 'Billy Dixon,' one of the defenders, as saying there were 'thousands upon thousands of buffalo . . .' (*The Flavor of Texas,* 237). In November, 1876, 'there were thousands of them where Amarillo, Texas, now stands . . .'; so, Raine and Barnes, *Cattle, Cowboys, and Rangers,* 172. The same authors give a very spirited account of the Southern slaughter in general (*ibid.,* 113-27).

GAME IN WESTERN CANADA OTHER THAN BUFFALO (p. 483)

This is another example of Hornaday's propensity for basing most significant pronouncements upon very insufficient evidence. In this instance the evidence consists of an isolated expression of opinion from *one* witness, at a very late date. In 1881, the Canadian buffalo were virtually exterminated, and the scarcity of other game noted by Professor Kenaston was, most probably, directly attributable to that cause. The chronology is hopelessly confused. Probably nobody but the author of the passage would recognize any connection between the respective eras of a 'paternal government' (that is, in Washington) and when aboriginal hunting customs or preferences were in process of formation.

Concerning game in western Canada *circa* 1862 Milton and Cheadle write: "With the exception of wolves and buffalo, wild animals of any kind are rarely seen in the Hudson's Bay Territories unless they are carefully tracked up. They are so constantly hunted by the Indians, and whenever they encounter man are so invariably pursued, that they are ever on their guard, and escape unseen on the slightest alarm. It is only when the snow betrays their numerous footprints, that a novice can bring himself to believe there really is any four-footed game in the country . . ." (*North-West Passage*, 85).

Even Milton and Cheadle are relatively late. According to Agnes Laut, Henday, in 1754, found 'red deer in myriads' on the plains about 100 miles south of The Pas (*Conquest of the Great Northwest*, I, 341); although I cannot identify the allusion in "Henday's Journal" (ed. Burpee). The elder Alexander Henry notes tracks of 'large herds of deer' south of Fort des Prairies (Forks of the Saskatchewan River?) in February, 1776 (*Travels, 1760-1776*, 277). *Harmon's Journal* (141, 153, 156, 226, 285) records their frequent abundance in the Northland *circa* 1808-17. Mackenzie observed the same thing, 1789, 1793 (*Voyages*, 23, 148); and see Hector's remarks of their disappearance in Mackenzie's region only 'some twenty years' before 1858 (*Palliser Journals*, 126). David Thompson described the Bow River *circa* 1800, as "the great resort of the Bison and the Red Deer" which possibly gave the tributary so-called—one of several of such place-names—its name (*Narrative*, ed. Tyrrell, 188). The younger Henry says that moose and red deer 'were very numerous at all seasons' between La Salle and Assiniboine Rivers (Coues (ed.), *Henry-Thompson Journals*, I, 56, 61, 62); on eastern tributaries of Red River (I, 70, 130, 131, 138, 139, 141, 143, 145, 286); Pembina River (I, 84); Park River (I, 88-95, 108, 120, 129); Shayenne or Schian River (I, 151); Tongue River (I, 155, 229); Salt River (I, 254); Souris River, July, 1806 (I, 305); and near latitude 49° toward the Missouri. His two last are *cabri*, that is, jumping deer or antelope (I, 310); and also toward the Mandan country (I, 374, 410).

In the north Saskatchewan country, between Smoky Lake and Sturgeon River, October, 1809 (*ibid.*, II, 564); October, 1810, near Gull Lake, south of Battle River, he notes a recent Sarcee camp of 25 tents: "They must have made a good hunt here in beaver, bear, moose, red deer, and buffalo, as a great quantity of bones lay about their camp . . ." (*ibid.*, II, 637, 638). Rundle describes the region between Carlton and Fort Pitt as "a fine country for Red Deer . . ." (*Journal*, June 17, 1841); and Kane noted in that precise locality, September, 1846, "an immense number of cabrees, or prairie antelopes" (*Wanderings of an Artist*, Radisson Society ed., 85). John Schott, to Seton *re* antelope on the White Horse Plains, Manitoba, 1855 (Seton, *Arctic Prairies*, 7). Great quantities of moose and deer, *ante* 1847, on the Upper North Saskatchewan River, 57 moose shot in a single season by one man *circa* 1857 (Hector, in *Palliser Journals*, 102-11). Wapiti, Pigeon Lake country, September, 1858: "the Indians told us these deer have already commenced to go in large bands, which is a sign of an early winter" (*ibid.*, 295-8). Hector also, between Little Red Deer and Bow Rivers, December, 1858: "band after band of deer, just as if we were passing through a deer park. This is the only time I have ever seen game in such plenty in the country, excepting of course buffalo herds" (*ibid.*, 121). Deer similarly, upper Bow River, 1859 (*ibid.*, 146). Hind, Bend of the Souris, 1858: "Deer are very numerous . . . it appears to be a favourite watering-place"; "cabri . . . used to abound on the Qu'Appelle . . ." (*Report, 1858*, 42, 48). McDougall, 1868: "large and small flocks of antelopes" (*Pathfinding*, 249); at which time, or a little earlier, Seton thinks they exceeded the buffalo (*Life-Histories of Northern Animals*, I, 214-22). Reverend E. R. Young, 1873: "Buffalo and deer, once so abundant . . ." (west of Lake Winnipeg: *Canoe and Dog-Train*, 239). Denny, Alberta, 1874: "Game of all kinds abounded in the river-bottoms and foothills; elk, deer, antelope; often seen in bands of many hundreds; not much hunted by the Blackfeet, as they had abundance of buffalo . . ." (Denny MS., 28, 50). Macoun on the former abundance of elk and cabri (*Manitoba*, 337, 338). A later scholar on the same in Canada (Hewitt, *Conservation of the Wild Life of Canada*, 72-4). On wapiti, *ibid.*, 26-37, also (United States and Canada) Seton, *Game Animals*, III, 9-12. On 'cabri,' *ibid.*, 417-26.

These things cannot be ignored in estimating Hornaday as an authority on matters concerning Canadian zoological history.

LATE SURVIVAL OF INDIAN ARCHERY (p. 503)

Apparently, most Indians, tribally and individually, were expert bow-men, learning archery as children. See on this, among the Illinois and Abenaki, *circa* 1720, Father Râle, *Jesuit Relations,* LXVII, 139, 169; and among the Sarcees, in the nineteenth century, Jenness, *Sarcee Indians of Alberta,* 19. Lescarbot remarks it among the Atlantic forest tribes (*History of New France,* III, 266); and Father Morice among the Carriers of British Columbia (*Northern Interior of British Columbia,* 47). Henday, 1754, comments on expert Blackfoot archery ("Journal," ed. Burpee, 354); and the skill of the Sioux, 1763, is noticed by Cyrus Thomas (*History of North America,* II, 328). Charles Mackenzie, at the Mandan villages, 1804, observes: "The Indians in this quarter seldom use guns for buffaloes and wolves; for these they make use of arrows . . ." Masson, *Les Bourgeois de la Compagnie du Nord-Ouest,* I, 331).

Pike, 1807, extolled Apache archery (Coues (ed.), *Expeditions of Pike,* II, 749). Irving's informant said of the Pawnees: "The Pawnee could shoot with unerring aim 300 yards, and send his arrow clean through and through a buffalo; nay, he had known a Pawnee shaft pass through one buffalo and wound another . . ." (Irving, *Tour of the Prairies,* 432). So also, *re* Pawnees and Nez Percés, Townsend, 1833 (*Early Western Travels,* XXI, 165, 218); likewise Farnham, Santa Fé Trail, 1839 (*ibid.,* XXVIII, 86); Gregg, 1831-40 (*ibid.,* XX, 265, 323); and Bonneville on the Bannacks, 1833 (Irving. *Captain Bonneville,* 207).

Of the Comanches, to whom Castañeda very probably refers in 1541 (*Journey of Coronado,* 75), R. B. Marcy remarks, 1852: "The bow was the favourite arm and constant appendage of the prairie Indian . . ." (*Exploration of Red River,* 98; cf. also his *Prairie Traveller,* 221). Colonel Dodge, writing in 1875, says the shot-gun was less effective against buffalo than the bow in the hands of an Indian (*Plains of the Great West,* 114); and cf. Maximilian, Missouri River, 1833 (*Early Western Travels,* XXIII, 119). We may remember of course that many of their early fire-arms were 'trade guns,' like that described by McDougall: "an old pot-metal flintlock gun, muzzle-loading and single-barrelled . . ." (*Saddle, Sled, and Snowshoe,* 119). Even with this, its owner, an expert hunter, worked wonders; but all Indians (says McDougall) were not experts. There is an excellent account of Blackfoot training in archery, arrow-making, etc., in Kidd, "Blackfoot Ethnography," 37, 124-9; another, equally good, in Garretson, *American Bison,* 177-80, 242. Indian hunting arrows (among some tribes) had the heads vertically parallel with the feathering, to pass between the (vertical) ribs of the great game quadrupeds; while war arrows had the heads trans-verse to the feathering, to penetrate between the (horizontal) ribs of human foes, without glancing off (Dodge—who in this later work belittles Indian archery and marksmanship—*Our Wild Indians,* 415-20); see also Garretson, *American Bison,* 179; Burton, *City of the Saints* (1860), 52, 119-20, 143.

A more recent and very comprehensive historian cites some interesting data on the Indian adoption of fire-arms and disuse of the bow, from early times in French Canada and thence westward (Innis, *Fur Trade in Canada,* 14, 16-18, 31, 99, 127, 139, 274, 290, etc.). 'Iron arrowheads' were being imported in 1626 (*Jesuit Relations,* IV, 207); but Innis's last mention of these is 'two grosse' to Hudson Bay, in 1671 (*Fur Trade in Canada,* 127). Despite this, it was thought in 1822 that by withholding ammunition for a year the Indians of the Hudson Bay Territory would 'recover' the use of the bow (*ibid.,* 290). This opinion, however, was expressed by Nicholas Garry, the Hudson's Bay Company magnate; a visitor in Rupert's Land, with no knowledge of Indians. Probably they had never lost it.

In the United States territories, it is believed that many 'Indian raids' were principally to obtain hoop-iron, etc. for arrowheads; and steel arrowheads were an important article of trade down to much later times (Garretson, *American Bison,* 179, 180). This implies a very late date for the bow, which is historically substantiated. Dr. Hector recorded some fine archery by a Stoney (Assiniboine) in 1858 (*Palliser Journals,* 120). McDougall notes a Cree (1862) killing 16 buffalo with 17 arrows (*Forest, Lake, and Prairie,* 144). Cowie mentions very skilful Indian archery at Fort Qu' Appelle, 1867 (*Company of Adventurers,* 218, 241). Garretson gives a most interesting account of Sioux archery as late as 1872, at the hunt arranged under Buffalo Bill (Cody) for the Grand Duke Alexis of Russia. The noble guest wondered why the Indians 'carried those absurd toys,' but changed his mind when the Sioux chief sent a shaft practically (or entirely) through a buffalo! (Garretson, *American Bison,* 130-4; Inman, *The Old Santa Fé Trail,* 209, who says 'through'). The significant factor in all this is that such things could not be done at a moment's notice as 'exhibition stunts' by men not in constant practice. Garretson here emphasizes the Indian preference for the bow against big game; but elsewhere (*ibid.,* 80) echoes the conventional shibboleths about the vast increase in buffalo slaughter after fire-arms appeared among the tribes.

Seton gives some revealing data on the modern use of archery by big-game sportsmen, and its astonishing deadliness, probably with expert bowmen (*Game Animals,* II, 58); but it proved a fiasco at a buffalo hunt at Rawlins, Wyoming, on February 13, 1947; rifles were finally required (*Victoria Daily Colonist,* February 13-14, 1947).

These alleged Indian exploits have been termed "an oft-repeated Plains *cliché.*" There was one of these that assuredly did not belong to any such category, for it was recorded by the very first Europeans to penetrate into the enormous territory east of the lower Mississippi. "One shot," says Frank Dobie, "was so mighty that De Soto had it notarized; the arrow went clean through the largest and fattest horse in camp and stuck in the ground beyond..." (Dobie, *The Mustangs,* 1952, 31).

INDIAN VEGETABLE DIET (p. 603)

Even such meagre details as I have been able incidentally to note in our early authorities reveal numerous uses of vegetable food among various tribes.

Coronado's several chroniclers say of the Indians 'in the country where the cows are,' that they 'neither sow nor plant corn' (*Journey of Coronado*, 194, 205, 209, 214, 230). They must also have crossed the adjacent 'S.W. maize area,' however (so classified by Wissler, "Material Cultures of the North American Indians," *American Anthropologist*, XVI, 1914, 447-505; *American Indian*, 12-14); for Coronado himself mentions the Indian 'worship of water, because it makes the corn grow' (*Journey of Coronado*, 180). Father Claude Allouez, 1677, mentions '14 kinds of roots' and '42 different kinds of fruits' eaten by the Illinois, who were also in part agriculturists (*Jesuit Relations*, LX, 161), as were likewise the Eastern Sioux (see Parkman, *La Salle*, 260). A. F. Chamberlain enumerates 70 plants to which the prefix 'Indian' has been added, from their use by Indians or for other reasons (*Handbook of American Indians*, I, 605). Some valuable details are also given in Jenness, *Indians of Canada*, 40-66, 288 *seq.*

On the plains the well-known 'pomme blanche' or prairie turnip (*psoralea esculenta*) was used at least from the Platte to the Saskatchewan. Mentioned by Bradbury, 1811 (*Early Western Travels*, V, 154); Long, 1820 (*ibid.*, XV, 217); Catlin (*Letters on the North American Indians*, I, 56, 122); Frémont, 1843, 'prairie potatoes' (*Narrative*, 95). Northward, Rundle found it on the menu at a Blackfoot camp (*Journal*, April 17, 1841); and Hind calls it 'Indian turnip, an important article of diet in the Qu'Appelle Country' (*Report*, 1858, 48). Dr. C. N. Bell notes French experiments with it as a substitute for potatoes, which proved unsatisfactory (*Journal of Henry Kelsey*, 20). Chittenden describes this—as 'Indian turnip' —and also Camas root (*camassia esculenta*, *American Fur Trade*, II, 806). The latter found at 'Kamas Prairie,' Utah, and 'much used for food . . .' (1833); so Townsend, *Early Western Travels*, XXI, 250; Dale (ed.), *Ashley-Smith Explorations*, 153. Frémont notes 'kooyah,' (*valeriana edulis*) and 'yampah' (*anethum graveolens*) among the 'Snakes' or Shoshones 1842 (*Narrative*, 116, 150). See also A. J. Fynn, *American Indian*, 209.

Some interesting details on Blackfoot vegetable foods, in W. McClintock, *Old North Trail*, 529; and more fully, K. E. Kidd, "Blackfoot Ethnography," 101-13.

APPENDIX V

MULTIPLICITY OF INDIAN LANGUAGES (p. 617)

The profusion of Indian languages spoken in relatively small areas was used many years ago as an argument in favour of a formerly sedentary life among North American Indians at large (Black, *History of Saskatchewan*, 94). Compare a later scholar: "It may be suggested that in addition to inherent instability, Shoshonean languages did not diverge more rapidly because a seminomadic life kept local groups in constant contact with one another. A similar situation seems to prevail in areas like the Arctic, Canada, and Patagonia. By contrast, peoples who travelled only within a restricted orbit, like the relatively sedentary peoples of the Pacific coast, have enormous linguistic diversity . . ." (Steward, "Native Cultures of the Intermontane (Great Basin) Area," *Smithsonian Miscellaneous Collections*, vol. 100, 1940, 476).

This is an obscure subject, here as everywhere. The linguistic *stocks* have been very generally accepted as relatively few. But the foregoing argument would in my view be fatal to any attempt to claim a *recent* (post-equine) nomadic origin for the two great northern families of the Ojibwa-Cree and Dakota-Sioux-Assiniboine, whose respective languages were considered by the earliest European observers to be sufficient for intercourse with the aboriginal peoples over the (northern) continent; as by Father Marest (*Jesuit Relations*, 1706, LXVI, 107). Whether the enmities which tend to produce variant languages were or were not as pronounced in the non-buffalo as in the buffalo area is not very material; for in any case they were largely fixed before the appearance of the horse. The question is, perhaps, which were languages and which dialects. *Circa* 1890, estimates of their number varied, according to the criterion adopted, from 400 to 1264 (Fiske, *Discovery of America*, I, 38, 48). See among others, Franz Boas, "Languages," *Handbook of American Indians*, I, 757; Chamberlain, "Linguistic Families," *ibid.*, I, 766; *Encyclopaedia Britannica, s.v.* North American Indians; and some interesting facts on Indian languages, even if his theories have required revision, in Bancroft, *Native Races of the Pacific States*, III, 574-722. An admirable review, summarized to date, will be found in Jenness, *Indians of Canada*, 19-27. Dr. Franz Boas considers attempts to reduce Indian tongues to a *few* linguistic stocks 'not very satisfactory' (*American Aborigines*, ed. Jenness, 367).

John McDougall says of Edmonton, 1862: "Thirteen different peoples, speaking eight distinct languages, made this post their periodic centre . . ." (*Saddle, Sled, and Snowshoe*, 12). Elsewhere he states that six languages were spoken at Morley, upper Bow River, in 1874 (*Western Trails*, 199).

APPENDIX W

INDIAN NOMENCLATURES (p. 625)

Indian tribal names fall into two principal categories: the 'nickname,' either local (usually topographical) or habitual, bestowed by others; and the self-laudatory type, on the Greek-and-Barbarian principle, bestowed upon themselves, itself almost a nickname again (see *Handbook of American Indians*, II, 16-18).

Of the first, like the Chippewa, there are the numerous branches of the Cree, already mentioned (note 150 above). The Potawatomies *circa* 1670 = 'people of the small prairies,' or 'fire people' (*Handbook of American Indians*, II, 289; Blair, *Indian Tribes*, I, 302, 329). The Slaves called themselves, or were known as *Etshtawut-dinni* = 'thickwood men,' or Franklin's 'Brushwood Indians,' 1824, 1856 (*Handbook of Canadian Indians*, 152). *Tschantoga* = 'people of the woods' (*Handbook of American Indians*, II, 823). 'Stick Indians' used by British Columbia tribes to designate other inferior tribes (*ibid.*, II, 636).

Some of the 'habitual' nicknames are uncomplimentary. *Mohawk* is said to signify 'cannibal' (Fiske, *Discovery of America*, I, 51; *Handbook of American Indians*, I, 921). Chippewyans, *ouant chipouanes* = 'dwellers in holes' (*Jesuit Relations*, LXVIII, 251, 332). Atsina (a branch of Arapaho) = 'beggars or spongers' (*Handbook of American Indians*, I, 113). Sarsi or Sarcee = *sa arsi*, 'not good' in Siksika = Blackfoot (*ibid.*, II, 467). The famous Sioux is from *Nadowe-is-iw*, French *Nadessioux* = in Chippewa, 'snake, or adder'; that is, 'enemy' (*ibid.*, II, 577; Maclean, *Canadian Savage Folk*, 103-20).

The classic instance of an habitual or custom-nickname is that of the Assiniboine (Stone or Stoneys), commonly derived from their use of hot stones in cooking (*Handbook of American Indians*, I, 102, 468; Maclean, *Canadian Savage Folk*, 354). But why should this become a distinctive designation for these folk in particular? For the same practice was noted by Cabeza de Vaca *circa* 1530 (*Purchas his Pilgrimes*, XVII, 507); by Jouvency, 1610, and Bressani, 1653, in New France (*Jesuit Relations*, I, 285; XXXVIII, 256); the Northern Indians *circa* 1770 (Hearne, *Journey*, 305); the Slaves and Dog-Ribs, Mackenzie River, 1789 (Mackenzie, *Voyages 1789 and 1793*, 35); the Chinooks, Fort Vancouver, 1846 (Kane, *Wanderings of an Artist*, 127). General Sam Steele has the name from hot stones used in sweat-lodges (*Forty Years in Canada*, 132); but this brings us no nearer a solution, for if anything this practice was even more common (see Jenness, *Indians of Canada*, 89).

Among the self-bestowed names, we find the Illinois (Illiniwek = 'people who are men'; Hennepin, *New Discovery*, I, 153; II, 506; Marquette, *ibid.*, II, 651; *Jesuit Relations*, LIX, 125; Blair, *Indian Tribes*, I, 295). Cf. the Tinneh (Butler, *Wild North Land*, 127), more properly Déné = men (so Morice, *Northern Interior of British Columbia*, 4; as also Thompson, *Narrative*, 78, 128, 166). The Crees designated themselves Naheyowuk = 'the exact people' (so Maclean, *Indians of Canada*, 1892, 254). Similarly, the Blackfoot spoke of themselves as *Sâke-tupiks* ='the people of the plains'; while the Confederacy at large were *Netsepoye* = 'the people that speak the same language' (*ibid.*, 130, 254). 'The people!' Cf. *Job*, XII, 2.

There is a good note on this principle of nomenclature in Indians, ed. note, *Jesuit Relations*, LIX, 309. See also the *Handbook of American Indians*, for names given by themselves and others to Abenaki (I, 2), Athabaska (I, 108), Bloods (I, 643), Chippewyan (I, 275), Minatarees (I, 508), Kutenai (I, 740), Piegan (II, 246), Potawatamies (II, 289), Sarsi (II, 467) etc.; also for most Indian topics, *Encyclopaedia Britannica*, *s.v.* North American Indians; and a host of similar examples from all ages, lands, and races, in Isaac Taylor's chapter, "Names of Nations," *Words and Places*, 55-79.

INDIAN TIPIS OR 'TEEPEES' (p. 626)

To speak of anything that followed 'when the tipi became general' opens a wide field of inquiry.

It is difficult to say precisely when the tipi did become general. With its concomitant paraphernalia of lodge-poles, etc., it was evidently a long-standing feature in 1541. The "Narrative of Jaramillo" says: "We found Indians among these first cows, who were, on this account, called Querechos by those in the flat-roof houses. They do not live in houses, but have some sets of poles which they carry with them to make some huts at the places where they stop, which serve them for houses. They tie these poles together at the top and stick the bottoms into the ground, covering them with some cowskins which they carry around, and which, as I have said, serve them for houses. From what was learned of these Indians all their human needs are supplied by these cows, for they are fed and clothed and shod from these . . ." (*Journey of Coronado*, 230). This admirable description, which could instantly be recognized by anyone who had ever seen a tipi or a picture of one, is borne out less fully but quite unmistakably by others of the party ("Traslado de las Nuevas"), and by Coronado to Charles V (*ibid.*, 194, 220).

McClintock describes its construction (among the Blackfoot) as follows: "It required eight buffalo skins to make a small lodge, and from twenty to thirty to make a very large one. The average size was about sixteen feet in diameter at the base, while large ones measured twenty-five feet. From fourteen to twenty-six poles were used for the supporting framework, and two others as 'ear-poles' for facilitating the escape of smoke. The best poles are made of the slim and straight mountain pines, which the women cut and peel and season slowly, to keep them straight. Their length varies from fifteen to thirty feet, according to the size of the tipi. A good set of poles having been secured, it is carried everywhere in their wanderings" (*Old North Trail*, 233). See his remarks above (chap. XXI, note 111) on poles needing renewal each year because of the incessant wanderings.

The size of the tipis is disputed, like most other details. Colonel Dodge —who often generalizes too widely on Indians from his own evidently restricted experience—says that "even the very largest lodge is scarcely ever more than 18 feet in diameter . . ." (*Our Wild Indians*, 214); '12 to 18 feet in diameter, 12 to 15 feet high' (*ibid.*, 232); or, in his earlier work, '12 to 20 feet diameter, about 15 feet high' (*Plains of the Great West*, 311). Henry, 1808, says 'about 17 poles generally, 10 to 15 skins, 20 feet diameter' (Coues (ed.), *Henry-Thompson Journals*, II, 513). Catlin gives '25 or 30 poles, about 25 feet high' (*Letters on the North American Indians*, I, 43). The Astorians mention a tipi 'forming a circle capable of admitting fifty persons' (Irving, *Astoria*, 203). This may seem excessively large; but

McDougall mentions a feast at which he was present, for the 'dedication of a new lodge' (Cree, 1864): "The twenty or more buffalo-skins had been dressed soft and white as possible and then cut into shape by some pattern carried in the brain of one of the older women. . . . There may have been forty or more guests. We sat in a ring around the tent . . ." (*Saddle, Sled, and Snowshoe,* 92). According to McClintock and Grinnell, an even number of cowskins was always used by the Blackfoot. I can find nothing specific on this point elsewhere, though it is disputed by inference (see Kidd, "Blackfoot Ethnography," 118). Butler mentions having "a leather tent of eight skins, small of its kind . . ." (*Wild North Land,* 59); while Grant, also in 1872, gives '5 to 6 skins, small; 14, medium; 20 to 25, large' (*Ocean to Ocean,* 173). Palliser mentions 12 to 20 skins as 'a common size'; 40 or 50 'not uncommon'; and 13 poles for the smallest (*Palliser Journals,* 204). 'Often 40 or more skins' (Blackfoot probably; Denny MS., 78). Welsh, who describes the erecting process, calls Poundmaker's tipi (Cree, 1863) 'very large,' of 16 skins and 24 poles (*The Last Buffalo Hunter,* 29-30). Ten skins was apparently the number among the Nez Percés, 1833 (Townsend, *Early Western Travels,* XXI, 225). Mooney specifies '15 to 18 dressed skins for the cover, renewed every one or two years'; for which I can find no confirmation other than *poles,* as above ("Tipi," *Handbook of American Indians,* II, 758). He also states (*ibid.*) that northern tipis were fewer in number (to a band) and larger in size than southern ones, horses being fewer. The reason given seems to me paradoxical; and Palliser states the precise contrary, that the Blackfoot lodges were much larger than those of the Cree. Blackfoot chiefs' tents were 20 to 22 feet diameter; some council tents nearly 30 feet across (*Palliser Journals,* 138; similarly, Steele, *Forty Years in Canada,* 104). Kidd says that exceptionally large Blackfoot tipis had as many as forty skins ("Blackfoot Ethnography," 118). For a painted tipi for Blackfoot newlyweds, the recognized price was four dogs (that is, less than one horse: *ibid.,* 55). Jenness gives the Sarcee tipi as of '12 to 16 hides . . . on 14 to 24 poles . . .' (*Sarcee Indians of Alberta,* 13).

Lodge-poles in the South were sometimes obtainable only by trade. James says, 1820: "The poles necessary for the construction of these movable dwellings are not to be found in any part of the country of the Kaskaias, but are purchased from the Indians of the Missouri; or others inhabiting countries more plentifully supplied with timber. We were informed . . . that five of these poles are, among the Bad Hearts (that is, Kaskaias = Kiowa Apache) equal in value to a horse . . ." (Long, *Early Western Travels,* XVI, 110). These lodge-poles were '20 to 30 feet long; and 6 or 8 to a lodge' (*ibid.,* 109). These Kaskaias were Comanches (*ibid.,* XV, 211; but see Appendix G, note 292); and their country, where no poles were to be had, was about 'the source of the Platte, Arkansa, and Rio del Norte' (*ibid.,* XVI, 117). Marcy mentions "the Comanches, with their portable lodges, which they trail with them, having no wood suitable for lodge-poles in their country" (*Exploration of Red River,* 25). I cannot think Marcy was ignorant that the 'trailing' was common to all wandering tribes living in tipis. The length and fewness of the imported 'Comanche' lodge-poles indicate a thrifty desire to make the most of them. Marcy elsewhere has '8 or 10' poles' (*Prairie Traveller,* 141). But such numbers, even if approximate, clearly exhibit a contrast with those used by tribes having their own plentiful supply near at hand. Burton terms the tipi the 'Comanche lodge,' as though it were a Comanche device. See some interesting details, *City of the Saints,* 85-7.

Re traffic in wood, Maximilian says of the Blackfoot (of all people! who ranged along *Bow* River: = *Munuchaban* = 'the place one gets bows from': *Place-Names of Alberta,* 23, 83; McDougall, *Western Trails,* 17): "Their country does not produce any wood suitable for bows; and they endeavour to obtain, by barter, the bow wood or yellow wood, from the River Arkansas" (*Early Western Travels,* XXIII, 119). This is the familiar 'Osage orange,' *Maclura Aurantiaca* (*ibid.*), or *Toxylon pomiferum* (Chamberlain, *Handbook of American Indians,* II, 159).

SIOUX AND ASSINIBOINE KINSHIP (p. 626)

The linguistic affinity or identity of the Assiniboines with the Sioux was noted long ago. Father Marquette, 1671, writes: "The Assinipouars, who have almost the same language as the Nadouessi [oux] . . ." (*Jesuit Relations*, LIV, 193). Also Marest, 1706: ". . . the language of the Assiniboëls . . . is the same as that of the Scioux . . ." (*ibid.*, LXVI, 107). Similarly, Alexander Mackenzie (the ('Nadowasis') in *Voyages, 1789 and 1793*, lxvii.

John McDougall was able to converse with the Sioux in Stoney, 1872 (*Red River Rebellion*, 269); and the Stoneys have little difficulty in reading Sioux in the Syllabic. See specimen words, Appendix A, "Buffalo Synonymy" (*ex inf.* Rev. P. G. Sutton, late of Paul's Reserve, Wabamun Lake, Alberta). See also Catlin, on the physiognomical resemblance to the Sioux (*Letters on the North American Indians*, I, 53, etc.). Palliser, not a negligible judge, thought otherwise (*Journals*, 202). Comparing Sioux portraits with former Stoney friends of my own, I am decidedly for Catlin.

Their westward migration appears to indicate (in the Canadian Stoneys at least) a preference for a woodland habitat, judging from their chosen haunts and various designations. The *Handbook of Canadian Indians* notes a number of such: 'Assiniboine of the South,' 1741 (p. 48); 'A. of the Meadows' (prairies), 'A. of the Woods' (both Dobbs, 1744; p. 45); 'A. of the North,' *ante* 1800 (p. 355); 'Eagle Hills A.' (dwelling there, 1808; p. 137); 'Saskatchewan A.' (p. 410); 'Strongwood A.,' 1808, 1860 (pp. 485, 486); 'Swampy Ground A.,' 'they inhabit the strong wood west of Fort Augustus' (that is, Edmonton), 1808; so Henry (*ibid.*, 442); 'A. des Plaines' (De Smet, 1848: *ibid.*, 45-8); 'Thickwood A.' or Mountain Stoneys (p. 48); also 'Wood A.' and 'Wood Stoneys' (Maclean, *Canadian Savage Folk*, 486); 'Mountain and Wood Stoneys' (McDougall, *Saddle, Sled, and Snowshoe*, 77).

It would not be difficult to imagine them, if left to their own unaided resources, turning once more since the buffalo are gone either to the ancestral bark lodge or, in localities where sufficiently large timber was not procurable, perhaps to the aforementioned dome-shaped brush shelter used by the Northern Shoshoneans 'before the tipi became general' (Wissler, *American Indian*, 224).

APPENDIX Z

INDIAN STONE RINGS AND POUND SITES (p. 638)

Dr. John Maclean writes: "There are several rows of stones several miles in length on the northern side of Belly River [southern Alberta], near the Blood Indian Reserve, and within three miles of the Slide Out, which can be seen when the prairie is burned. The Indians are unable to give any account of their history. A line of boulders may still be seen, stretching from St. Mary's River northward for more than one hundred miles. In some places they are quite close together, and at intervals are separated by several miles. Some of them have been worn smooth by the action of the weather, and by the buffalo using them as rubbing-posts. Indeed, you may see them lying in hollow spots on the prairie, the soil having been loosened by the tramping of the buffalo and then blown away by the wind.

"Upon the summit of a limestone hill on Moose Mountain, Assiniboia [written in 1896; now Saskatchewan] there is a group of cairns. The central cairn is composed of loose stones, and measures about thirty feet in diameter and four feet high. This is surrounded by a heart-shaped figure of stones, having its apex toward the east, and from this radiate six rows of stones, each terminating in a small cairn. Four of these radiating lines nearly correspond with the points of the compass, and each of the lines of different lengths terminates in a smaller cairn. The Indians know nothing of the origin of these lines and cairns, but state that they were made by the spirit of the winds . . ." (*Canadian Savage Folk*, 579).

According to Bonneville (Platte River, below the Forks, June 1852): "At one place they observed a field decorated with buffalo skulls, arranged in circles, curves, and other mathematical figures, as if for some mystic rite or ceremony. These were almost innumerable . . ." (Irving, *Captain Bonneville*, 39).

Denny thinks pounds are of an immemorial age. He mentions a layer of old buffalo bones found on the Elbow River, ten miles above Calgary, in 1875. These were covered with many feet of soil, and flint arrowheads were found among them (Denny MS., 42). Something similar was observed at the Forks of the Assiniboine and Little Souris Rivers, Manitoba, 1858 (Hind, *Report, 1858*, 42).

Denny would likewise put the rings of stones back to an age ere the Indians had any steel cutting tools, hatchets, etc., to cut and sharpen stakes for tipis. They naturally left the stones behind on changing camp, and they settled into the ground (Denny MS., 86). This may not necessitate a really remote antiquity. Mackenzie, on that river, 1789, observes: "Near us were two Indian encampments of the last year. By the manner in which these people cut their wood, it appears that they have no iron tools . . ." (*Voyages, 1789-1793*, 27). He might at least have told us how they did cut it! See on this, *Handbook of Canadian Indians*, 43, 53; on the labour

878

involved by stone axes, Jenness, *Indians of Canada*, 30; also his *Sarcee Indians of Alberta*, 14; and on Piegan methods of tearing down dead branches by lines thrown over them, Coues (ed.), *Henry-Thompson Journals*, II, 724; and cf. also Kidd, "Blackfoot Ethnography," 121.

Tipi sites, rings of stones, etc., were noted by Parkman, Laramie Creek, 1846 (*Oregon Trail*, 220); Coues, Missouri Coteau, 1873, correspondence to Allen (*American Bisons*, 158). In 1896 I myself noted an old encampment site on the right bank of the Bow River, about eight miles below Calgary. The rings of stones were in straight rows, forming 'streets,' and were sunk into the ground too firmly to be dislodged without a crowbar. This was on the western (that is, wooded) side of the river, which there is flowing south. Cf. Hind, Qu'Appelle Valley, 1858: "When this camp ground was occupied by the Crees, timber no doubt grew in the valley below, or on the prairie and ravines in detached groves, for their permanent camping-grounds are always placed near a supply of fuel. . . . It may have been a camping-place for centuries" (*Report, 1858*, 53). Compare above, chap. XXI, note 157.

See Jenness, *Sarcee Indians of Alberta*, 13, on Blackfoot parallel camp-lines; also Kidd, "Blackfoot Ethnography," 61, 118, 119. Jenness considers that 'camp rings' are often burial rings (*Indians of Canada*, 320). Cf. *Handbook of American Indians*, I, 163, on boulder lines.

APPENDIX AA

BUFFALO POUNDS (pp. 639, 647)

As 1 have observed above (chap. XXI), impounding practices were followed by many tribes and with considerable diversity in details. See in this connection, *Harmon's Journal*, 285; Franklin, (First) *Journey to the Polar Sea*, 112; Maximilian, 1833, *Early Western Travels*, XXII, 390; Audubon, 1842, *American Quadrupeds*, II, 49-50. Even men as far away as Gregg (1843) had heard of the Assiniboines (*Early Western Travels*, XX, 268).

Thomas Simpson relates that at Carlton (January, 1840), the Assiniboines of three camps had each their separate buffalo pound, into which they drove forty to fifty animals daily (*Narrative of Discoveries*, 402, 404). This is cited by Allen (*American Bisons*, 206); who says merely '1840,' and no month. Allen's statement is faithfully so copied by Hornaday ("Extermination of the American Bison," 460); blissfully unaware of the season of the year, when according to his own migration doctrine there were no buffalo within 300 or 400 miles from Carlton southward!

For incidental references to parks or pounds among other tribes besides those already mentioned, such as the Sioux, Pawnees, Piegans, etc. see Dodge, *Our Wild Indians*, 291, 577; Coues (ed.), *Henry-Thompson Journals*, II, 725; Allen, *American Bisons*, 206. The last observes (p. 206) that along the upper Yellowstone they were used (he was informed) "in entrapping the elk and deer as well as the buffalo; and according to Charlevoix, the Indians of Canada formerly hunted the moose, the caribou, and the deer, in a somewhat similar manner. . . ." Impounding the moose seems incredible! Jenness notes drives for Caribou among the Copper Eskimo ("Copper Eskimo," *Report of the Canadian Arctic Expedition, 1913-1918*, XII, 1923, 148-51). Maximilian mentions 'parks' to catch antelope, but not buffalo (just like a buffalo pound) among the Mandans and Minatarees (*Early Western Travels*, XXIII, 347); and Lewis and Clark noted pounds for 'goats' among the Mandans also (*Journals*, I, 180). 'Goats' are commonly antelope (that is, 'cabrie' = *capri*). Bonneville saw pounds for antelope among the 'Digger' Indians (Irving, *Captain Bonneville*, 219-20); and Pike records the use of pounds with 'wings' (the converging approaches) in Mexico *circa* 1807, to capture wild horses (Coues (ed.), *Expeditions of Pike*, II, 783).

Thomas Simpson, following on the three Assiniboine pounds at Carlton, January 1840, adds: "I afterwards learned that in other places these pounds were actually formed of piled-up carcasses" (*Narrative of Discoveries*, 402, 404). At that season, '40 or 50 per day' would soon result in piled-up carcasses, frozen stiff! Paul Kane says of the Crees, near Fort Pitt, January 1848: "These Indians had a buffalo pound within a short distance of their encampment, which was literally crammed with the dead frozen carcasses they had slaughtered in it . . ." (*Wanderings of an Artist*, 277). Why Simpson did not see something like that himself, if he actually witnessed the daily drives, is not clear. Kane himself remarks elsewhere: "I heard of a pound, too far out of my road to visit, formed entirely of the bones of dead buffaloes that had been killed in a former pound on the same spot, piled up in a circle similarly to the logs . . . described . . ." (*ibid.*, 81).

Attention has been drawn to the account given by Thomas Ashe (1806) of buffalo in Pennsylvania shunning forever a spot where a great buffalo slaughter had occurred (see above, chap. X, note 145); and also to that of Colonel Dodge, on buffalo deserting the Laramie Plains after great numbers had perished there in the deep snow, 1844-45 (above, chap. VIII, note 9). I should certainly not reject the testimony of Simpson and Kane merely because of its disagreement with that of Ashe or Dodge; my own researches and my general thesis concerning such discrepant evidence preclude that. But I am highly suspicious of loose hearsay concerning Indians. What about the effect of the sight—perhaps of scent also, on milder days—on the herds following? Finally, I have found nothing confirmatory of the accounts of Simpson or Kane in any form whatever, from eye-witnesses or anyone else.

Concerning pounds in actual use, see Duncan McGillivray's description of the Assiniboine pound on the 'Paint' (Vermilion) River, and the Cree pound in the Beaver Hills, 1795 (*Journal*, 38, 42, 49). Henry, on the North Saskatchewan tribes (1808) in Coues (ed.), *Henry-Thompson Journals*, II, 516-20; also 'Slaves' (that is, Blackfoot Confederacy), south of Fort Vermilion, and on the upper Red Deer River, 1809-11 (*ibid.*, II, 530, 576, 670, 723, 725). Hector on a Cree pound south of Fort Vermilion, Christmas, 1857 (*Palliser Journals*, 70). Hind, on Crees in the Qu'Appelle Valley, July 1858, *Report, 1858*, 55, 113. Norbert Welsh (same region, 1865), *The Last Buffalo Hunter*, 43-5. John Macoun, *Manitoba*, 344-6. And above all (known to me), John McDougall (1862 *seq.*), *Saddle, Sled, and Snowshoe*, 271-82.

Allen writes regarding impounding: "This method, if not still practised in the Yellowstone country [1876], was in use there at no distant date, since while with the Yellowstone Expedition of 1873 I several times met with the remains of these pounds and their converging fences in the region above the mouth of the Big Horn River . . ." (*American Bisons*, 207).

And Dr. C. N. Bell observes: "I saw such a structure south of the Battle River, in Saskatchewan, in October, 1872, and the quantities of bones left in the neighbourhood were amazing . . ." This was about the region of the Blackfoot permanent pound of Cocking, exactly a century earlier, October, 1772, and may even possibly have been the very spot.

Dr. Bell adds: "I saw another buffalo trap in the form of a high steep cut bank over which the buffalo were driven to pile up at the bottom dead and dying. The piles of skulls and bones at the foot of the cut bank must have represented tens of thousands of animals . . ." (Bell, *Journey of Henry Kelsey*, 24). Another was observed, south of Carlton, 1857 (*Palliser Journals*, 57), also somewhere near Cocking's pound of 1772.

Another account comes from Dr. John Maclean: "Here and there along the Old Man's River and other places in Alberta may be seen layers of buffalo bones, marking the spot where the Indians drove the herds over the precipices and they perished in thousands . . ." (*Canadian Savage Folk*, 51). On an ancient buffalo pound at Macleod, on the Oldman River, see *Canadian Historical Review*, V, 1924, 193.

They persisted to a very late date. "The ordinance of 1877 forbade the use of buffalo pounds, the wanton destruction of buffalo at any season, the killing of animals under two years of age, or the slaughter of female buffalo during a stated close season—briefer for Indians than for others. This bill was framed in the best interests of the Indians and half-breeds, but their very destitution made the protection of the waning herds a hardship, and it was found necessary to repeal the measure in the following year . . ." (Black, *History of Saskatchewan*, 196, 247). See also Denny MS., 273; Morris, *Treaties with the Indians of Manitoba*, 175-272, *passim*; *Canadian North-West*, ed. E. H. Oliver, II, 1046, 1051.

I am inclined to think that most 'permanent' pounds were jumping-pounds, where the remains of previous holocausts would not confront the entrapped herd until it was too late to retreat. The Crees had one at Horse Hills, just below Edmonton, January, 1810 (Coues (ed.), *Henry-Thompson Journals*, II, 581). The Piegans made one on Red Deer River, January, 1811, for Henry's post at Rocky Mountain House; and 'Kootenay Parc,' above there, seems to have got its name from the Kootenai having a (jumping) 'parc' or pound there (*ibid.*, II, 670, 691, 723-5).

Some of the instances cited in this appendix may have been jumping-pounds. Dodge notes the practice among the Sioux and Pawnees (*Our Wild Indians*, 291, 577); and Edwin James mentions it on the South Platte headwaters, 1820 (*Early Western Travels*, XV, 282). McClintock gives the Blackfoot name as *piskun* (or *piskan*), and states that Two Medicine River, Montana, got its name from a 'double piskun' or 'two piskuns'— evidently a jutting-out point or headland, possibly a creek confluence— where buffalo could be driven either way (*Old North Trail*, 438, 520). See the word also in Jumping-pound, Bow River, Alberta (*ninapiskan*, *Place-Names of Alberta*, 69). The word seems to embody the great Algonkian root-form for buffalo, *pisik, peecheek*, etc. See Appendix A, "Buffalo Synonymy." Colloquial local forms such as Jumpingpond, Dog Pond, etc. (Alberta) should always be *pound*.

Their wide notoriety is revealed by the following which comes from William Faux (then in North Carolina, 1818): "Buffaloes . . . are thus decoyed and taken; but not alive. A man dresses himself in one of their skins, and walks on all fours to the brink of a stupendous precipice, so concealed as to be unobserved by the hurrying animals. The decoy steps aside, and down rush and tumble the herd, and break their necks or legs in falling. The skins and tongues are then taken, and the carcasses left . . ." (*Early Western Travels*, XI, 86).

On the general subject of occultism in impounding, see Audubon and Bachman, *American Quadrupeds*, II, 49-50 (Gros Ventres, Assiniboines, Blackfoot); Allen, *American Bisons*, 204 (Minatari, Cree, etc.); Parkman, on the old Sioux 'consulting an oracle' where to find buffalo (*Oregon Trail*, 257, 279). Cocking, 1772, mentions Indians 'singing their Buffalo Pound songs,' but no buffalo! (*Journal*, 108). According to Catlin, *re* 'making the buffalo come,' the incantations continue *until they do come,* whereby the medicine men acquire merit, and in this way 'never fail' (*Letters on the North American Indians,* I, 127). David Thompson, *re* Piegans, *circa* 1800, says: "Others turn Dreamers, and tell . . . where the Bisons and Deer are most plenty" (*Narrative,* 366); also on this, Southesk, *Travels,* 80-3.

McDougall describes old Chief Samson, a Cree (then young, 1869), and his occult skill in the handling of herds (*Red River Rebellion,* 94); and Southesk mentions a half-breed similarly, 1859 (*Travels,* 104). 'Partly occultism, partly skill, dexterity, knowledge of buffalo'; so Franklin, (First) *Journey to the Polar Sea,* 112; Kane, *Wanderings of an Artist,* 80; De Smet, *Life,* III, 1025-32; Macoun, *Manitoba,* 344; McDougall, *Saddle, Sled, and Snowshoe,* 271-82; Chittenden, *American Fur Trade,* II, 812. Doubtless the origin of such a name as 'Poundmaker,' the Cree chief; 1885.

There were various incidental beliefs connected with impounding. According to John McDonnell (Red River, 1793-97), "the chief of the park thinks that if he were to eat any of the meat thus killed, it would be out of his power to make buffaloes enter his park ever after; so he must have meat killed in the open field for his own use . . ." (Masson, *Les Bourgeois de la Compagnie du Nord-Ouest,* I, 280). I have not found this elsewhere; and McDougall implies quite the contrary for the 'bringer-in,' whoever the 'chief' may be (*Saddle, Sled, and Snowshoe,* 280). These are of course merely tribal variations; cf. Jenness: "The master of a buffalo pound apportioned the meat equally among all the tents except his own, which nevertheless received the largest share through the gifts offered by each household in payment of his services . . ." (*Indians of Canada,* 65). So also, *re* Assiniboines, Coues (ed.), *Henry-Thompson Journals,* II, 520; cf. Blackfoot usage, in Kidd, "Blackfoot Ethnography," 97-101.

Dr. Hector (near Vermilion, Alberta, December 26, 1857): "When first captured and driven into the pound, which difficult matter is effected by stratagem, the buffalo run round and round violently, and the Indians affirm always with the sun. . . . There are many superstitions connected with the whole business, and the Indians always consider their success in procuring buffalo in this manner to depend on the pleasure of the Manito . . ." (*Palliser Journals,* 71). According to McDougall, "running always as the medicine man had walked, and that was with the sun . . ." (*Saddle, Sled, and Snowshoe,* 281). So also Henry, "never against the sun . . ." Coues (ed.), *Henry-Thompson Journals,* II, 519; Assiniboines). Practically every witness mentions the central tree or post, around which the decoy turned, in a built pound. Similar beliefs among the Netsilingmiut Eskimo (*Canadian Historical Review,* XVI, 1935, 90). Kidd's Blackfoot informant (born *circa* 1900) considered the 'sun-turning' absurd ("Blackfoot Ethnography," 98).

Henry (also near Vermilion, Christmas, 1809) notes the difficulty of getting them into the pound with the wind blowing contrary. This is evidently not occultism but scent (Coues (ed.), *Henry-Thompson Journals,* II, 576); and on manoeuvering for scent, cf. McDougall, *Saddle, Sled, and Snowshoe,* 281.

Paul Kane writes: ". . . the man now rides up alongside of the herd, which, from some unaccountable propensity, invariably endeavours to cross in front of his horse. I have had them follow me for miles in order to do so. The hunter thus possesses an unfailing means, wherever the pound may be situated, of conducting them to it by the dexterous management of his horse . . .". To this L. J. Burpee subjoins an editorial note: "This curious propensity has been noted also among some of the deer family in Mongolia" (*Wanderings of an Artist*, Radisson Society ed., 327). One cannot dispute an explicit statement like this; but I have found no hint of such a thing elsewhere, throughout the buffalo literature. Moreover, Kane's is a *drive*, and not a decoying after the 'bringer-in,' who is always on foot, so far as I have found (although Jenness, *Sarcee Indians*, 16, implies the possibility of horses in this). Finally, with this ready expedient at hand, why did 'horse' Indians ever fail when impounding buffalo, as Cocking, Rundle, and others tell us sometimes occurred (see below).

McDougall says that if a herd succeeded in breaking away before reaching the entrance to the pound, "the driver will be humiliated, the new pound made unlucky, and the whole camp sadly disappointed . . ." (*Saddle, Sled, and Snowshoe*, 279). It was also considered, by the Crees, unlucky to burn up an old pound, as he once did when in straits for firewood (*ibid.*, 19, 28). Among the Blackfoot, ". . . the buffalo pound seems to have been the property of the group who constructed it . . . so long as it was utilized. As in the case of territory, title lapsed with disuse . . ." (Kidd, "Blackfoot Ethnography," 147).

Cocking, 1772, remarks on his 'Assinipoet' companions not being "so expert at pounding as the Archithinue Natives" (that is, Blackfoot). Later, even the 'Natives' were unsuccessful, March to April, 1773. "They bring droves to the pound, but only few enter into it . . ." ("Journal," 109, 116).

Similarly, Rundle: "Went in the morning to visit Buffalo Pond [pound; near Beaver Lake, southeast from Edmonton], situated a short distance from the camp. The pond was strewn with half-devoured carcasses of the animals, the spoils of previous captures; these fragments afforded a fine feast for the wolves, which came during the night season and gorged themselves at pleasure. I had hoped to see the capture of buffalo by the method of decoying them, but was doomed to disappointment. Two or three herds were driven near the entrance whilst I remained there but they escaped by rushing off in a contrary direction to that of the mouth of the pond . . ." (*Journal*, January 16, 1841).

The elder Henry mentions a pound which he witnessed (North Saskatchewan country, 1776), in which 72 were slain; apparently in this instance through skill in decoying (*Travels 1760 and 1776*, 293). His nephew's description (same region, 1808) emphasizes skill rather than occultism (Coues (ed.), *Henry-Thompson Journals*, II, 517-20). Hind's account of the big pound along the Qu'Appelle Valley, 1858, ignores occultism, 'skilled hunters,' etc. (*Report, 1858*, 55, 113). Compare above, chap. XXI, note 269.

Hearne describes the Chippewyans impounding deer, in pounds made on regularly frequented paths. One was so made, March, 1771; 'but the deer did not keep on it' (*Journey*, 120, 126, 193, 309).

INDIAN WASTEFULNESS WITH BUFFALO (p. 639)

I have already examined the historical evidence for wastefulness in the Red River half-breeds, and noted the fatal effects of arithmetical analysis on the conventional claptrap (above, chap. XIV); and also on the huge aggregates of buffalo which, it is asserted, were slaughtered by the Indians (chap. XVIII).

Many of the writers already cited concerning buffalo pounds include some moralizings on Indian wastefulness. *Circa* 1820, the proportion killed by the white men, out of 200,000 per annum, has been genially computed at five per cent! (Coman, *Economic Beginnings of the Far West*, II, 30, 34). Gregg says (1843): ". . . for every one killed by the whites, more than a hundred, perhaps a thousand, fall by the hands of the savages . . ." (*Early Western Travels*, XIX, 244). Kane has the Indians 'impounding for pleasure; not one in twenty used' (*Wanderings of an Artist*, 80-2); see also Southesk, 1859 (*Travels*, 264). Colonel Dodge speaks of the Dakotas (Sioux) as "an exceptionally improvident people"; the Pawnees also wasteful; and states that "the Crows, and some other far northern tribes, are said to be as improvident as the Sioux . . ." (*Our Wild Indians*, 576, 577). See Parkman also, on the vast quantity of buffalo meat left behind at the Arapaho camp on the Arkansas River, 1846 (*Oregon Trail*, 395). We are not informed *why*; but 1846 was a troublous year, with Doniphan's and other marchings. They might have been forced to abandon it. Its very presence indicates some provision for future needs. So also, a people 'exceptionally improvident' logically implies some degree of providence as a general rule.

Edwin James, 1820: "Our guide informed us that the Indians, a few years ago, destroyed every individual of a large herd of bisons, by driving them over the brink of one of these precipices . . ." (*Early Western Travels*, XV, 282). Western guides were frequently very ready with anti-Indian information; but James and Stephen H. Long, after personal observation, desired measures to restrain the wastefulness of *white* hunters (*ibid.*, XV, 256). H. M. Brackenridge was also 'informed' (1811): "such is the wanton destruction of the buffalo, that, I am informed, the Indians will kill them merely for the purpose of procuring their skins for these canoes . . ." (that is, 'bull-boats': *ibid.*, VI, 108). This thoroughly practical use, common to so many 'buffalo' tribes, although, curiously, unused by the Blackfoot (Kidd, "Blackfoot Ethnography," 129), was 'waste' by Indians! Brackenridge travelled with the Astorians, perhaps the informants in question. John Bradbury, on the same journey, noted *their* wastefulness, killing buffalo when not in need of food (*Early Western Travels*, V, 148); precisely as did Catlin (an eye-witness) with the U.S. troops on the Canadian River, 1834 (*Letters on the North American Indians*, II, 46, 76). Maximilian also records wastefulness (in taking tongues only) by the American Fur Company's men, 1833 (*Early Western Travels*, XXII, 382). Inman, no mawkish sympathizer with Indians, cites an early plainsman, 1861, who stated that the Indians ate everything 'even to the intestines'; and that their grievance in Kansas was not what the white men *ate* but what they wasted (*Old Santa Fé Trail*, 154). Similarly in Garretson (*American Bison*, 119) *re* wastefulness. The unfortunate Indian might well have exclaimed, like Ophelia:

> "Do not, as some ungracious pastors do,
> Show me the steep and thorny way to heaven,
> Whilst, like a puff'd and reckless libertine,
> Himself the primrose path of dalliance treads
> And recks not his own rede . . ." (*Hamlet*, I, 3).

L. V. Kelly asserts as follows: "Thousands of buffalo, even as late as 1875 and a year or two later, were annually slaughtered by the red men for the sake of the unborn calves, which were considered a great dainty . . ." (*The Rangemen*, 106). He cites no authority for the statement, and his unreliability in other details has already been noticed (see above, chap. XVI, note 32).

It is true they were considered a delicacy. See Hearne, 1772, *Journey*, ed. Tyrrell, 257, 307, 308. Paul Kane partook of this at Fort Edmonton, Christmas Day, 1847 (*Wanderings of an Artist*, 263); but says nothing of such a practice, albeit a severe critic of Indian wastefulness (*ibid.*, 80-2). John McDougall gleefully relates how his father unsuspectingly ate of this dish in a Cree lodge, and pronounced it good (*Saddle, Sled, and Snowshoe*, 109); but nowhere else mentions it to my knowledge. In the fall and winter hunts thousands of cows must necessarily have been so slain; but I have found no evidence that it was for the sake of their unborn calves, nor indeed any allusion whatsoever, other than the above. Blackfoot cookery is described by Kidd ("Blackfoot Ethnography," 105). Jenness merely notes that Sarcee boys and girls might "on no account" eat of this meat (*Sarcee Indians of Alberta*, 19); cf. Hough, "Food," *Handbook of American Indians*, I, 466.

The predilection for the tongues is of course well authenticated. Hennepin noted it in 1679 (*New Discovery*, I, 242). Father Râle, *circa* 1720, and Diron D'Artaguiette, 1723, both in the Illinois River territory (*Jesuit Relations*, LXVII, 169; Mereness (ed.), *Colonial Travels*, 83-5). Father Poisson, 'Aux Akensas,' 1726, mentions "a Canadian bringing down to new orleans [*sic*] 480 tongues of cattle that he and his partner had killed the previous winter . . ." (*Jesuit Relations*, LXVII, 285). This is the earliest allusion I have found to buffalo tongues in trade.

Henday found the practice of taking 'tongues and titbits' in the north, September, 1754 ("Journal," 333, 336). At the Mandan villages, Christmas, 1804, Charles Mackenzie says: "Large parties who went daily in pursuit of the buffaloe often killed whole herds, but returned only with the tongues . . ." (Masson, *Les Bourgeois de la Compagnie du Nord-Ouest*, I, 331). This was not so far above the region of the surround and the '1400 tongues' related by Catlin and scourged by Hornaday (above, chap. XXI, notes 174-5); and about where Maximilian, a year later, 1833, similarly scourges the wastefulness of the American Fur Company's own men (*Early Western Travels,* XXII, 382). The same thing, 'nothing but tongues and choice bits,' was said of the Kentucky settlers long before, by Michaux, 1800, and Faux, 1820 (*ibid.,* III, 234; XII, 19); but Colonel Fleming's contemporary Journal, 1779-80, casts doubt on this (Mereness (ed.), *Colonial Travels,* 629). Even among the Athabaskan tribes, Hearne found the practice of taking buffalo for their tongues—when they had the chance! (*Journey,* 258). James, 1820, and Gregg, 1843, agree that in the south 'thousands every year were slain for the tongues alone'; the former ascribing this principally to the whites, the latter blaming the Indians (*Early Western Travels,* XV, 257; XX, 264). The white folk soon learned to like buffalo tongues. In 1847 or 1848—perhaps both—25,000 salted tongues were sent to St. Louis (Chittenden, *American Fur Trade,* II, 817; *Life of De Smet,* II, 635); see also above, chap. XV, note 86, on men in Kansas *circa* 1872, bringing in barrels of salted tongues and nothing else. It seems very probable that such a name as 'Tongue River' (Miles City, Montana; also Red River tributary, near Latitude 49°: Coues (ed.), *Henry-Thompson Journals,* I, 230) may commemorate some episode such as the 1400 tongues.

Tongues played a part in Plains Indian rituals connected with the buffalo. 'Tongues only, used in the medicine lodge'; so Frémont, *Narrative,* 23; Denny MS., 42, 88; Hawkes, *Saskatchewan and her People,* I, 126. Jenness mentions a 'ceremonial' cutting of buffalo tongues 'by women who had dedicated themselves to this form of thanksgiving' (*Indians of Canada,* 322). Cf. Kidd's native informants on Blackfoot usages ("Blackfoot Ethnography," 100). Among the Assiniboines, the chief claimed the tongues (*ibid.*). In the earlier fur-trading economy, the tongue 'generally belonged to the hunter' (Henry, in Coues (ed.), *Henry-Thompson Journals,* I, 446).

NIGHT ATTACKS BY INDIANS (p. 653)

The *night* attack mentioned above (chap. XXI, note 297) is also of some interest. Colonel Dodge says that night attacks by Indians were very uncommon; the Indians having an aversion to them, believing that one slain in darkness would dwell in darkness throughout eternity (*Plains of the Great West*, 286; *Our Wild Indians*, 181). Dr. John Maclean is partly corroborative, though for more mundane reasons: "Just before sunrise, or after sunset, an attack is made, as travellers are tired at night and drowsy in the morning, consequently not able successfully to resist the enemy. . . . Very rarely do the Indians make an attack during the day or night, or make war in the winter . . ." (*Indians of Canada*, 1892, 51-2).

Father Jacques Buteux, however, records night attacks by the Iroquois, 1651 (*Jesuit Relations*, XXXVII, 69); and Maclean himself notes (*Indians of Canada*, 51-2) that the Moravian Mission at Gnadenhutten was attacked at night, "just as they had finished supper." That might easily be after dark, in spring or autumn. Hulbert relates an account of a night attack on Boone's camp on the Kentucky River, March, 1775, apparently by Shawanese, 'the most bloodthirsty and cruel on the continent' (*Historic Highways*, III, 58; VI, 84, 85, 96). He also cites "Henderson's Diary," April 11, 1775: "We keep Sentry this Night for fear of the indians [*sic*] . . .", showing what experienced Indian fighters thought about it (*ibid.*, VI, 113).

On the plains, Dr. Gregg says of the Comanches: "Different from the 'prowling' tribes, they seldom attack at night or in timbered or rough regions, for they would then be unable to manoeuvre their coursers to advantage . . ." (*Early Western Travels*, XX, 347). Yet he himself says that night attacks were the 'most common' on the Santa Fé Trail (*ibid.*, XIX, 200, 201); as also Coman, *Economic Beginnings of the Far West*, II, 84; while Laut denies it (both *re* Santa Fé)—"Desert Rovers seldom fought at night" (*Pilgrims of the Santa Fé*, 103).

Among the northern plains tribes, Edward Umfreville says that night attacks were favoured (*Present State of Hudson's Bay*, 187). A night attack and battle between Hidatsa and 'Fall' (Atsina) Indians, told to Lewis and Clark (*Journals*, I, 188). A night attack in a rainstorm by the Arikara, 1824 (Pattie, *Early Western Travels*, XVIII, 52); and another night attack by the Blackfoot in the Cypress Hills country, June, 1868 (Cowie, *Company of Adventurers*, 330-2).

When generalization concerning Indians is so utterly unreliable in an abstract characteristic, it is *a fortiori* more so in assertions involving discredit to the Indian.

APPENDIX DD

INDIAN FASTING (p. 659)

Fasting, as practised by the Indians, was noted by Lescarbot, *circa* 1610 (*History of New France*, III, 28). Also the Jesuit fathers: Jouvency, 1610 (*Jesuit Relations*, I, 285); Le Jeune, 1635-38, who says the Hurons "could easily pass a week without eating," giving two examples, one of them 'a woman of 80' (*ibid.*, VII, 127; XIV, 273; XVI, 213). Vimont, 1644, says: "We have seen some who have wandered in the woods for ten, fifteen, or twenty days without other food than a piece of bark or of skin . . ." (*ibid.*, XXV, 107). Compare Rundle on the starving Assiniboines, Edmonton district, 1841—a family 'with nothing to eat but old skins for eighteen days' (*Journal*, December 13, 1841). Vimont is corroborated by Father Bressani, 1653: 'They endure hunger for ten or fifteen days . . .' (*Jesuit Relations*, XXXVIII, 259). Cf. Le Mercier, 1668, Crepieul, 1686 (*ibid.*, LI, 259; LXIII, 253). In the territory west of the Great Lakes, it was noticed by Hennepin, 1679 (*New Discovery*, II, 469, 488); not unnaturally, for at the very time he was taken prisoner by the Sioux, his captors were starving (*ibid.*, I, 228; Parkman, *La Salle*, 263). It is also related by Nicolas Perrot and Bacqueville de la Potherie, *circa* 1670-1700, in their descriptions (Emma H. Blair, *Indian Tribes*, I, 58, 250, 369). Christian Frederick Post, the missionary, mentions 'learning the Indian custom of girding their bellies tight,' when no food was to be had, 1758 (*Early Western Travels*, I, 282). It was apparently north of the Great Lakes where the elder Henry observed it in 1764 (*Travels 1760-1776*, 149).

In the more typical plains habitat, Cocking remarked that "the natives suffered hunger with surprising patience"—this in a Saskatchewan winter! ("Journal," ed. Burpee, 113). Umfreville, in the same region, *circa* 1785, also alludes to it (*Present State of Hudson's Bay*, 38, 93). Likewise Franklin, 1819 (First) *Journey to the Polar Sea*, 69, 110); Rundle (*Journal*, December, 1841–April, 1842; October 18, 1845; May 19, 1847); Milton and Cheadle (*North-West Passage*, 143); Macoun: Blackfoot, 1879 (*Autobiography*, 149); McDougall (*Western Trails*, 99, 120, 123); Hughes (*Father Lacombe*, 142-53); Black (*History of Saskatchewan*, 82).

On the Missouri plains, it is mentioned by Catlin and Maximilian among the Mandans, Minatari, and Assiniboines (*Letters on the North American Indians*, I, 127, 199; *Early Western Travels*, XXII, 390; XXIII, 274, 346).

For the North, see Hearne, *Journey*, 102, 113; *Harmon's Journal*, 289 (Carriers); Butler, *Wild North Land*, 129 (Beavers). Re 'patience,' Warburton Pike (1889) relates a quarrel between two wives. "If the men are alone [that is, when starving] they are quiet; but when there are women, there is no peace . . ." (*Barren Ground*, 172). Even this apparently varied among tribes.

INDIAN CANNIBALISM (p. 660)

Indulgence in cannibalism as a rite and also to allay hunger *by the same individuals* is an obscure subject, which has not (I believe) been very deeply investigated. David and his men eating the shewbread (I Samuel, XXI, 1-6) might furnish a loose analogy. The act must have required tremendous courage. See an allusion, J. Mooney and C. Thomas, "Chippewa," *Handbook of American Indians*, I, 277. Edwin James remarks (1820) that among the Missouri River Indians, cannibalism was 'almost unknown,' save from hunger: 'Ioway and Sioux' instances known (*Early Western Travels*, XIV, 304). It had been known among the Bloods, 1810 (Coues (ed.), *Henry-Thompson Journals*, II, 736); but apparently from hunger alone.

Dr. Gregg writes thus (1840): "It seems there were anciently occasional cannibal tribes in those [prairie] regions, but not a vestige of cannibalism, as I believe, now remains; except such an inhuman appetite may be ascribed to some of the more savage warriors, who, as I have heard, in the delirium of exultant victory, have been known to devour the hearts of their bravest victims, at once to satiate their blood-thirsty propensities, and to appropriate to themselves, as they fancy, the valor of the slain enemy. . . . A diminutive tribe on the Texas border, called Tonkewas, made food of human flesh within the present [nineteenth] century, and, it may be of late years, though I have not heard it mentioned . . ." (*Early Western Travels*, XX, 332). On the Tonkawas (extinct) see *Handbook of American Indians*, II, 778-83.

An aversion to cannibalism in the Southwestern tribes is perhaps revealed by Cabeza de Vaca's account of the Indians being 'greatly offended' by the Spaniards' lapse into this; but it may have been in the degradation of such godlike beings (*Purchas his Pilgrimes*, XVII, 463, 487, 502). See also Hallenbeck, *Journey of Cabeza de Vaca*, 53, 62.

Cannibalism in the ritual or sacrificial sense is, among Indians, very closely bound up with the torture of prisoners. Gregg adds that the prairie tribes seldom did this; and says "the practice of burning their captives alive, said to have prevailed many years ago among some prairie tribes, seems now to have grown quite out of use . . ." (*Early Western Travels*, XX, 320). Maximilian says: "The Mandans, Manitaries, and Crows never torture their prisoners like the Pawnees and the eastern nations" (*ibid.*, XXIII, 351). Colonel Dodge also says the Plains Indians 'never burned at the stake' (*Our Wild Indians*, 524); although he cites an Apache instance (*ibid.*, 189). Kidd's native informants (with some dissentients) mention burning alive as a former occasional punishment for incorrigibles (Kidd, "Blackfoot Ethnography," 146). On torturing of prisoners, cf. *ibid.*, 174; and for torturing of Blackfoot prisoners by Flatheads, which would doubtless provoke reprisals, see above, chap. XI, note 44. See also *Encyclopaedia Britannica, s.v.* North American Indians.

With reference to cannibalism as a rite, among Eastern tribes, see Fathers Le Jeune, 1637-40 (*Jesuit Relations*, XII, 255; XVI, 81; XVII, 75, 99; XIX, 81), Du Peron, 1638 (*ibid.*, XV, 173), Chaumonot, 1640 (*ibid.*, XVIII, 33, 45), H. Lalemant, 1642 (*ibid.*, XXII, 129, 253), Vimont, 1642-45 (*ibid.*, 129, 253; XXVI, 33; XXVII, 239, 299).

Among the same Eastern tribes it is also recorded as an occasional (hated) necessity. On this phase, see Le Jeune, 1635, 1657 (*ibid.*, VIII, 29-31; XLIV, 81, 173). Vimont, 1640 (*ibid.*, XVIII, 227). H. Lalemant, 1647 (*ibid.*, XXXI, 85). Ragueneau, 1649-50 (*ibid.*, XXXIV, 217; XXXV, 189). Bressani, 1653 (*ibid.*, XXXIX, 59, 81, 221). Le Mercier, 1665-68 (*ibid.*, L, 57; LII,123, 171). Anonymous writer, 1670—perhaps Dablon or Allouez (*ibid.*, LIII, 139). Lamberville, 1681 (*ibid.*, LXII, 59, 71). Marest, 1712 (*ibid.*, LXVI, 275). Anonymous writer, 1757 (*ibid.*, LXX, 125); also Thwaites, ed. note, *ibid.*, LXIX, 299.

The elder Henry mentions a cannibal at Sault Ste Marie, 1767, an object of horror to the other Indians, who finally slew him (*Travels 1760-1776*, 207-10). Duncan Cameron, Nipigon country, *circa* 1790, says there were 'many cannibals' among Indians (Masson, *Les Bourgeois de la Compagnie du Nord-Ouest*, II, 249). Hearne states that among the Northern tribes, cannibals, even from necessity, were detested (*Journey*, 85). Alexander Mackenzie says that among the Chippewyans and other Northern Indians, it never occurred, except from necessity (*Voyages 1789 and 1793*, cxxii). Rev. Egerton Young mentions that one of his native assistants (Norway House, 1870), a Wood Cree, 'had been a cannibal in his day'; which almost seems to imply a habit, rather than a single desperate extremity (*Canoe and Dog Train*, 163); and David Thompson says that 'forest Indians only' were cannibals (*Narrative*, 259). Cannibalism among the starving northern Crees in 1886 has already been noticed (Hornaday, "Extermination of the American Bison," 526-7; *in extenso* above, chap. XVII, note 90).

There are three recorded instances of Northern cannibalism, but all by Iroquois. The famous case of the one shot by Richardson in Franklin's expedition: (First) *Journey to the Polar Sea*, 451-9; another one mentioned by Paul Kane (*Wanderings of an Artist*, orig. ed., 329); and in 1875 Brother Alexis Reynard was slain and partly eaten by an Iroquois halfbreed in the lower Athabaska country (Morice, *Catholic Church in Western Canada*, II, 103). Jenness notes a 'Cannibal Society' in the Tsimshians of British Columbia (*Indians of Canada*, 338). Cf. *ibid.*, 285, 305; also A. Hrdlička, "Cannibalism," *Handbook of American Indians*, I, 200; Mooney and Thomas, "Chippewa," *ibid.*, I, 277; Hewitt, "Mohawk," *ibid.*, I, 921.

ANTI-INDIAN PROPAGANDA (p. 665)

Bancroft long ago noted the existence of anti-Indian propaganda (re 1826: *North Mexican States and Texas*, II, 104; 1855: *History of Oregon*, II, 404); see also Thwaites's remarks on the 'education' of Eastern public opinion (ed. note, *Early Western Travels*, XIV, 21). A modern student writes: "Later legends picture life in the West as one long reign of terror, with Indians constantly hovering about and swooping down in sudden assault. This conception was based upon the intermittent warfare that began in 1862. It was kept vivid by the propaganda of border-men and army officers. Through every means of civilized communication, press, mail, telegraph, and public exhibition, they strengthened the public belief in Indian brutality and treachery. Their gospel was Sheridan's: 'The only good Indian is a dead Indian.' The Indian had no medium of publicity through which to reply. As Frederic L. Paxson says: "The scalped and mutilated pioneer with his haystacks burning and his stock run off, is a vivid picture in the period, but is less characteristic than the long-suffering Indian, accepting the inevitable and moving to let the white man in. . . . After the Civil War it was easy to gain credence for any invention about Indian attacks, and to date it as far back as the purposes of the narrator might dictate . . ." (Walsh and Salsbury, *Making of Buffalo Bill*, 43). I cannot identify Paxson's utterance, but he is a well-known scholar of high standing.

Walsh and Salsbury add: "President Grant's Commission, looking back in 1869, said: 'The history of the border white man's connection with the Indians is a sickening record of murder, outrage, robbery, and wrongs committed by the former, as the rule; and occasional savage outbreaks and unspeakably barbarous deeds of retaliation by the latter, as the exception. . .'" (*ibid.*, 71). Yet following upon this, General Sherman wrote to Grant: "We must act with vindictive earnestness against the Sioux . . . even to their extermination, men, women, and children . . ." (*ibid.*, 101). It was Civil War idolatry that placed Sherman and Sheridan in such authority. 'They were ignorant of Indians'; so, Grinnell, *Fighting Cheyennes*, 288.

Grinnell's work contains one account after another of reprisals upon Indians (even 'friendlies,' as Ash Hollow, 1855, *ibid.*, 102) for what other tribes or individuals had done; of 'official accounts' of victories invariably won against heavy odds by U.S. troops (as Crook on the Rosebud, 1876, *ibid.*, 316-32; see also Byrne, *Red Men's Last Stand*, 38-57, 155, 180, 202; and cf. Appendix G, "Indian Populations"); of general ignorance, callousness, and brutality—as in the Sumner campaign of 1875; the Chivington massacre, 1864; the Powder River expedition, 1865; and the Baker small-pox butchery, Marias River, 1870 (*Fighting Cheyennes*, 93-411).

Grinnell also cites the following: "The official reports all agree that the woman surrendered at Laramie was Mrs. Eubanks, captured on the Little Blue, August 11, 1864 (*ibid.*, 148; originally by Cheyennes, so, J. H. Taylor, *Frontier Life*, 44). Grinnell adds: "The two Sioux . . . had bought the woman and her child at their own expense from the Indians who had captured them, and had brought them to the fort and given them up to prove their friendliness. The drunken officer in command of the post ordered the two Indians hanged in chains, and this was done . . ." (*Fighting Cheyennes*, 181). The account of this in Hebard and Brininstool (*Bozeman Trail*, I, 148) differs materially. They cite several versions, and should at least have mentioned Grinnell's, since he is one of their accepted authorities in various other details.

The foregoing are not merely post-dated slobberings from arm-chair sentimentalists. Walsh writes: "Some few of the professional Indian fighters were honest enough to admit, as one of the best of them, Kit Carson, said under oath, that 'as a general thing, the difficulties arose from aggressions on the part of the whites. . . .'" Similarly, Cody himself in his later days on tour: "In interviews, he would say that in disputes with the Indians, the white man was to blame nine times out of ten . . ." (Walsh and Salsbury, *The Making of Buffalo Bill*, 71, 254). Cf. Dodge, *Our Wild Indians*, 639-53) who was no admirer of Indians (above, chap. XIII, note 143). I might also cite a plainsman, J. H. Taylor, *Sketches of Frontier and Indian Life*, 1889, often ludicrous in style but splendid in spirit, sometimes an eye-witness.

INTELLLIGENCE VERSUS HERD-INSTINCT IN BUFFALO AND OTHER ANIMALS (p. 672)

A particularly competent Alberta zoologist, and a world-authority on bird-migration, writes as follows: "It is useless, for instance, to bestow on a bird human powers of thought, if the structure of its brain obviously precludes any such possibility. Whether we wish to credit it with powers of long-sustained flight or with such a simple thing as the appreciation of color, we are not justified in doing so merely on the strength of a personal opinion . . ." (William Rowan, *The Riddle of Migration*, 5).

I am not ignorant of the danger, to a layman in these regions, of making a fetish of Darwin, and citing him as being unchangeably final on any question. Yet one cannot suppose that so competent a student and so cautious a reasoner would be ignorant or unmindful of the structural or morphological limitations indicated by my friend, Professor Rowan. The authenticated facts and incidents of animal intelligence noted by Darwin in his two chapters on the "Comparison of the Mental Powers in Man and the Lower Animals" (*Descent of Man*, 66-131) still stand, however; and are supplemented by G. J. Romanes, Lloyd Morgan, and others (see Morgan, *Animal Life and Intelligence*, 331-414, etc.).

The question is of course that of the correct interpretation of the true motive forces behind these phenomena noted above (chap. XXII, note 5). I cannot pretend to be abreast of contemporary opinion on this subject; but the average layman finds it difficult to understand how the workings of a fundamentally similar reasoning power, differing in degree rather than in kind, can be denied in such cases. In some instances, the dissenting critic appears to base his denial of a supposed process, on our inability to explain not *how* merely, but *why* it occurs. Can we always explain this in man?

Lloyd Morgan, in a searching examination of the problem in its many phases, differentiates upon philosophical and logical grounds between *intelligence* and *reason*; the latter human only, and broadly defined as the capacity to form abstract concepts from one or more experiences. While one could accept this hypothetically as being difficult, perhaps impossible, to the animal, in some of his arguments and instances in proof, the shades of distinction are so finely drawn as to be dangerously near the imperceptible to the lay vision. In a locomotive shop of my acquaintance, the roundhouse cats converge daily from various directions at the dining room door *before the noon whistle blows*. Is not this an abstract concept—of time—formed from particular experiences of something else?

Morgan also, in the very act of stressing 'the danger of anthropomorphism,' is compelled to use it, in speaking of the 'look of conscious dignity' on the face of a lioness (*Animal Life and Intelligence*, 339). Our limitations of speech render this inevitable; but we do not thereby necessarily assert a *feeling* of conscious dignity in the lioness, though it may be present.

Fortunately for my present purpose, however, it is the visible manifestation of these individualisms by buffalo, and not their philosophical classification, which concerns us here.

APPENDIX HH

BUFFALO TWINS (p. 115)

I have consulted the Annual Reports from the various buffalo parks (Wood Buffalo Park, North-West Territories; Wainwright Buffalo Park, and Elk Island, Alberta), from their inception until the closing of Wainwright Park (1909-40); but have found no mention of twin calves in any of them. The statistics given are somewhat meagre and uninformative; often not even the respective numbers of the sexes in adults being indicated, while almost the only reference to calves is the surmise that the sexes are about equal in numbers. This might leave room for the possibility of twin calves having been passed over without recorded mention.

I am informed, however, by Dr. Winnifred Hughes, of the Department of Zoology, University of Alberta (who has, I believe, enjoyed the advantage of personal intercourse with the Wainwright Park staff), that no twin buffalo calves have ever been known among any of the Park herds.

Since the publication of the first edition of this work, the *Victoria Daily Colonist* (May 7, 1964) reported the following from Sault Ste. Marie, Ont.: "A bison has given birth to twins at Bellevue Park Zoo here in what zoo authorities describe as a 'rare occurrence.' The calves, each weighing 60 and 70 pounds [*sic*] were born Tuesday night [i.e. May 5, 1964]."

"BUFFALO" AND "BISON" (pp. 3-4)

Most people speak of the "buffalo," as I have done throughout this book. Scientists, however, refer more commonly to the "bison." As a result, one frequently hears people saying—"If those animals the Indians lived on were buffalo, what were the *bison?*" I shall try to make this clear. We have seen above that there was an animal in the Colorado "Parks" country (in the South Platte headwaters region) which the old mountaineers called the "mountain bison," this being the only use known to me of the term *bison* for buffalo of any species by anyone but scientists. We are dealing here with the ordinary Plains buffalo.

Both names belong to the selfsame creature, the North American animal. The reason why scientists do not use the name *buffalo* for these is because that name had already been given to another species more than 2000 years before the North American animal became known. Our familiar term "Indians" is a precise parallel to this, and illustrates the case exactly. Logically speaking, the name of Indians should belong to the native inhabitants of India, just as we speak of Europeans, Africans, Americans, or Australians. But we simply do not use it for India because the name had already been appropriated (even though incorrectly) for the aboriginal inhabitants of the North and South American continents.

Although both the North American buffalo and the immemorial buffalo or buffaloes of the Old World belong to the family of the *Bovidae* (oxen), they are quite unalike in many important respects. They differ widely in appearance, and as men came to know our North American creature better it was found to differ even more widely from the earlier buffalo in temperament. For the Old World buffalo, which—in so far as we know—apparently originated in India and spread thence into western Asia, southern Europe, and northern Africa, could be domesticated and broken to the plough, like the well-known "water buffalo" which is familiar in Hawaii, the Philippines, and the Far East at large. Its use on the plough in India and Italy was known to English travellers at least as early as 1588. The earliest printed account of the American animals in English and perhaps in any language was not published until 1589. There is one notable exception to the generally docile nature of the Old World buffalo species. This is the African (or South African) wild creature, *Bubalus caffer*, which is utterly untamable, and is perhaps the most ferocious animal upon the face of the earth.

From about 1700 onward various attempts were made in several localities to domesticate and tame the North American monarch, but before very long it became apparent that, like the South African species, *Bison americanus* was fundamentally untamable. For though they have more than once been (as was thought) successfully broken to harness, they have almost always sooner or later turned on their trainers, and some of these latter have been killed by them. The large herd formerly in the Wainwright Buffalo Park (Alberta) were for many years apparently docile and accustomed to man. Even children from the town could wander unattended and swim in the lake, as I myself have frequently done. After eighteen or twenty years in the park, the herd suddenly turned cross and dangerous, and the gates had to be closed against visitors afoot. The basic ferocity of our native species revealed itself in the ultimate failure of the numerous efforts to domesticate it in any real sense (i.e., for any working purpose, on which, see above: Appendix C, Early Buffalo Domestication, 706-14).

The term *Bison* is actually the more correct term by virtue of long descent. There flourished in ancient Europe, long before Caesar's time and long after, an animal which bore a closer resemblance to the Northern Wood Buffalo of Canada than the Wood Buffalo bear to our Plains type. This statement would no longer be true in the exact scientific sense. Since the transfer of the Plains herd from the (former) Wainwright Buffalo Park to the Wood Buffalo Reserve at Fort Smith (North West Territories), the two species have intermingled—or "mongrelized"—and the Wood Buffalo as a pure species can no longer be said to exist.

The European animal is classed as *Bos europaeus*. A small herd of these, in addition to the North American species *Bison americanus*, may be seen in the Duke of Bedford's zoological park at Woburn Abbey, Bedfordshire (England). The local name in the European habitat was originally *wisent* or *wissent*. By certain well-known phonetic laws, V and W are interchangeable in certain languages. This is conspicuously the case in Russian and German. We are hearing every day over the radio about "Vàgner's" music, which indicates the name spelt as "Wagner." That of the great German scientist Virchow is pronounced "Weerkov"; in which instance the change is exactly reversed at the two ends of the same name. It so happened that Russian and German were the precise languages of the *wissent* habitat; hence *visent* was the term used as often as not.

In other languages, and in Spanish perhaps above all, V and B are similarly interchangeable. As we may see any day if we take the trouble, a box of Havana cigars is always labelled *Habana*. Mobile, Alabama, is held by many scholars to be the place where De Soto fought his great battle of *Maubila* or *Mauvila* with the Indians. Vaca-Baca, Ovando-Obando, Saavedra-Saabedra, Quivira-Quibira, Cibola-Civola, Balparaiso, Baldivia, etc. litter the pages of Hakluyt and Purchas. The usage even spread into English. We find *Malavar* and *Martavan* in *Hakluyt's Voyages* (III.240,311;IV. 248, Everyman's Library ed.); and I have myself heard old road-builders talk of "putting a *culbert* under a road" for drainage.

The use of *wissent* apparently lapsed in its native region, though it was revived later by scientists. The animal came to be known as the *zuhr*, *urus*, or *aurochs*, under some of which terms it is mentioned by Caesar about 50 B.C. For the year 28 A.D. we have an account of what is obviously the same creature from the Roman historian Tacitus (*Annals*, IV, 72). Tacitus writes as follows:

A moderate tribute, such as suited the poverty of the [Frisian] people, consisting of raw hides for the use of the legions, had formerly been imposed by Drusus. To specify the exact size and quality of the hide was an idea that never entered the head of any man, till Olennius, the first centurion of a legion, being appointed governor over the Frisians, collected a quantity of the hides of forest bulls, and made them the standard both of weight and dimension. To any other nation this would have been a grievous burden, but was altogether impracticable in Germany, where the cattle, running wild in large tracts of forest, are of prodigious size, while the breed for domestic uses is remarkably small. . . .

These animals are also mentioned by Pliny about 70 A.D. Gibbon notes them in the German forests nearly five centuries later. A note runs thus:

> Without losing myself in a labyrinth of species and names—aurochs, urus, bisons, bubalus, bonasus, buffalo, etc. (Buffon, *Histoire Naturelle*, supplement, III, VI, also XI), it is certain that in the sixth century, a large wild species of horned cattle was hunted in the great forests of the Vosges in Lorraine and the Ardennes (Gregory of Tours, tome II, lib. X, cap. X, 369. Theodebert, King of the Franks, was overthrown and slain by a wild bull while hunting in the Belgic or German forests (*circa* 538 A.D.). [Gibbon, *Decline and Fall*, etc., III, Ch. XLI, 534.]

Another reference is over a thousand years later: at Königsberg in East Prussia (bordering on Lithuania) on one of the young Frederic's royal journeys with his terrible father, July 1731, one of the spectacles arranged for the King of Prussia was a combat between two wild bisons and two bears [Carlyle, *Frederic the Great*, 10 vols. (London, 1873), III, 19]. A Polish friend tells me there is a considerable Polish literature on the subject.

While the name *wissent*, *visent* apparently ceased to be current in the German forests, it was passed on through the Latin countries by a regular series of phonetic transmutations as *wisent*, *visent*, *bisent* into central and southern Europe. On the way, so to speak, it must have impinged upon the territory of a kindred species mentioned long before by Herodotus (*History*, VII, 124-6). He notices the presence of "wild bulls" in the borderlands of Macedonia and northern Greece, just across the Adriatic from Italy. These have been classed as *bonasus*, and "slightly different" from the *aurochs* or *urus* (*Herodotus*, Everyman's Library ed., II, 165, note). It seems highly probable, virtually certain, that these would be the "Caucasian bison," which are defined in practically identical terms.

These phonetic modifications culminated ultimately in the Spanish *bisonte* and the French *bison*. At just what date this final form became current I am unaware, but it was applied quite logically by French zoologists or classical scholars such as Martine Basanier of Paris in 1582 to a North American animal which evidently was almost or completely identical with the creature described by Caesar and Pliny.

The history of the term *buffalo* seems less enlightening. The various species which are classed by zoologists as "true" buffalo are termed, as a family, *Bubalus*. This is the Latin form of the Greek *Boubalos*, the root of which is *bous*, ox. Yet strangely enough, the name *boubalos* was originally applied to a species of deer or antelope, and only later was it given to wild *bovidae*. History repeated itself in this. More than 2000 years later the early French in Canada did much the same thing. They applied the name "wild cows (*vaches sauvages*) both to deer and to buffalo (see above, Appendix B, 703).

Long before our North American buffalo or even their country were known to Europeans, both names were applied by English writers to wild animals, possibly in Bohemia (the modern Czechoslovakia) to the *wissent* itself. John of Trevisa wrote in 1398 (printed 1495) of "*bubali* and *bisontes*"; and in 1601, Philemon Holland, the famous "translator-general" of Pliny's *Natural History*, mentions "those neat or buffles called *uri* or *bisontes* . . . ," in each case using the plural form. In the Book of Deuteronomy (xiv, 5), among the cloven-hoofed chewers of the cud which the children of Israel were permitted to eat, we find "the ox . . . and the pygarg, and the wild ox." In a marginal note the "pygarg" is glossed as being in Hebrew "*dishon* or bison." What this animal may have been is difficult to conjecture. It could scarcely in itself be a wild ox, since that creature (or what the translators took to be such) is mentioned specifically. The European bison of the Caucasus, while not impossible—and certainly the nearest—seems rather far-fetched geographically.

We have noted the transition from V to B. There is an analogous slurring in the softer Southern English between V-B and F. *Vauxhall* in London was an estate of the notorious *Fawkes* de Breauté in 1220; and the aristocratic English family, the Vanes are one and the same with the Fanes. By this phonetic process *Bubalus* became *Boeuf* (beef, beeves; cf. thief, thieves), *buff* (a common term in Shakespeare's time for any animal, even including the manati or "sea cow," that would yield "buff leather" suitable for making the soldier's famous "buff coats" (see above, 216), and finally *buffalo*, variously spelt. The *Oxford Dictionary* states that *bison* "was hardly English before the seventeenth century"; and *buffalo* seems to have been at first rather an educated person's expression. The very first English description of the North American animal, by Henry Hawks, 1572, and printed by Richard Hakluyt, 1589, called them "the Kine of Cibola"; Cibola, by general agreement of competent scholars, being Zuni, New Mexico, where they first became known to Coronado's party in 1540. Coronado's men were not classical scholars, any more than was Henry Hawks. Their name for the buffalo was *vacas jorobadas*—"hump-backed cows."

The earliest use of *buffalo* is said to be by Mark Catesby, 1754, but Dr. Thomas Walker, 1750, seems possible. A book in the present writer's possession, by Thomas Salmon, 1749, has *buffaloe*.

APPENDIX JJ

WESTERN PENETRATION OF THE HISTORIC BUFFALO
IN THE UPPER BOW RIVER VALLEY* (p. 316)

When visiting the well-known Luxton Museum at Banff in 1955, the curator, J. G. ("Red") Cathcart, showed me an interesting portion of a buffalo skull, together with a steel spear-head or lance-head which was originally found embedded in the skull.

On the tang of the weapon is stamped the mark of the makers: "I. & H. Sorby." The museum inscription reads: "Part of buffalo head and steel spear found on Seventeen-Mile Flat, west of Banff, by Ulysses Le Casse, who was a game warden in Banff National Park for many years." This is the farthest westward point at which buffalo vestiges have been found in the Bow River valley.

The site and character of this discovery present several most interesting and quite distinct problems. First, the circumstance of a *steel* spear-head obviates at the outset any discussion about whether the animal was of the historic or of some fossil species, such as has occasionally arisen where the weapon in similar finds was of flint. The (relatively) modern weapon and the broad chronology of European penetration into the region make it quite clear that we are dealing with one of the historic races of buffalo—which of them may be another matter.

The probable geographical penetration route by which this animal reached the area depends very particularly upon the species to which the skull belongs, whether Plains or Wood buffalo. While the shape and length of the horn-cores suggest the latter, this can only be decided definitely by a competent zoologist. As I have shown elsewhere, the existing historical evidence for the westward penetration of the Upper Bow Valley is rather scanty, and takes the buffalo no farther west than a point which has been thought to be near Banff, where the Rev. Robert Terrill Rundle, the pioneer missionary, noted them as "numerous," April 14, 1841.[1]

There were white men on the Upper Bow before Rundle; James Edward Harriott opened "Old Bow Fort" (or Peigan Post) for the Hudson's Bay Company in 1832.[2] This post was situated at the junction of the Kananaskis River with the Bow, but the hostility of the Blackfoot compelled its abandonment in a very short time; it was not again reopened until 1873-4, when the

*Reprinted from paper by F. G. Roe in the *Alberta Historical Review*, v (Winter, 1957), 21-24.

[1]*Rundle's Journal*, Fort Edmonton, 1840-48. Ed. by Rev. J. P. Berry and F. G. Roe.
[2]See E. H. Oliver citing "Minutes of the Northern Dept." in *The Canadian North-West*, I, 662, 678-79; II, 693, 695, 730; cf. J. E. A. Macleod, "Peigan Post and the Blackfoot Trade," *Canadian Historical Review* (Sept., 1943), 273-79.

Company "took another chance" under the protection of the McDougalls—
this time more successfully.[3] While buffalo beyond doubt were plentiful
enough for subsistence purposes—since the latter family was living "principally upon buffalo" at the neighbouring mission station at Morley as late
as 1876[4]—yet buffalo in the foothills territory farther west were clearly not a
reliable staple source to the local tribes, without going to the plains for that
purpose. John McDougall himself says of these:

> The Mountain and Wood Stoneys roamed from the northern tributaries of
> the Missouri to the Athabasca, and generally kept inside the foothills. These
> Indians were more independent than the plains tribes, as they were, almost with-
> out exception, expert wood hunters. Moose, elk, caribou, small deer, big-horn,
> goat, all kinds of bear and lynx, as well as buffalo, made up their larder, and yet,
> like that of all hunters, this was often empty. . . .[5]

Whether by reason of the relative propinquity of the familiar route by
Boat Encampment to the Columbia River, or for some other cause, white
contacts with the Bow River headwaters route seem to have been rare in
the pre-railway era; and these few seem to have been more across it than
along it. This appears to have been more commonly the case in Rundle's
southern journeys (1840-8). Governor Simpson, on the famous journey
around the world in 1841, struck southwesterly from Edmonton on no route
that was then in common use by those crossing the Rockies; for Rundle
(then himself returning from Rocky Mountain House) met Simpson at the
"Sarcee Hills" on the upper Battle River, July 29, 1841.[6] Father De Smet,
the eminent Jesuit missionary, reached Rocky Mountain House *en route* to
Edmonton in October, 1845, by a route via "White Man Pass," directly
south of Banff (50° 45′ N., 115° 29′ W.).

In none of these instances is there any reference to buffalo having been
seen in any of the foothill localities westward of the Banff position. In the
case of Father De Smet, the scarcity of buffalo was so noticeable that he
reached the conclusion that "these animals had now disappeared" from
the "Hudson territory." Rundle states that the Assiniboines (Stoneys) were
then starving at Rocky Mountain House (October 18, 1845); and had been
starving for "two or three autumns." Father De Smet had evidently no desire
to chance that territory again, for on his return journey (March, 1846) he
followed the Athabasca route by way of Fort Assiniboine and Jasper House.[7]

Practically the first party that is definitely known to have crossed the
summit by the Bow River (Kicking Horse) Pass is the Palliser Expedition
of 1857-60. No mention was made of buffalo there, neither does McDougall
for the years 1873-76, when his memoirs terminate. His references practically all indicate the lower stretches of the Bow Valley near Calgary, and
throw no light on any possible penetration of the Bow headwaters region
by the Plains herds at any time.

[3]John McDougall, *Western Trails &c.*, 10.
[4]McDougall ms, Provincial Library, Edmonton, 33.
[5]McDougall, *Western Trails &c.*, 10.
[6]*Rundle's Journal*, 1841; Simpson, *Journey Around the World*, 1, 110.
[7]De Smet, *Early Western Travels*, XXIX, 250.

Although the identity of the South Saskatchewan and the Bow Rivers was known to some of the early voyagers (such as John McDonald of Garth, who established Chesterfield House near the Red Deer Forks in 1792), historical and place-name evidence suggest very strongly that the Bow Valley from perhaps the Belly River forks west was very much of a *terra incognita* until a late era.

The two names for the same stream, which have persisted to the present day, tell clearly enough a tale of their own. For the early fur-traders working their way up the Saskatchewan to christen the two streams—of broadly equal volume, which converged at the Saskatchewan Forks—the North and South Saskatchewan was natural and logical. Whether either the North or the South branch bore the name Saskatchewan aboriginally (to the exclusion of the other), I have been unable to learn definitely. If such were the case, however, the North branch running as it does through the Cree territory would be the more logical, since the river bears a Cree name. But there is nothing in the word *Kisiskatjiwan* ("great swift-flowing river," or "swift current") which contains or indicates *north*.[8] It is therefore quite probable that the South branch originally also bore an independent name of its own. Names possess a tenacious vitality of their own, and are not easily suppressed, but it does occur; and in this instance the traders would be the only ones giving a very wide publicity to the name in the form of written record. At a certain—or uncertain—point the name Saskatchewan "disappears," and that of the Bow becomes the accepted usage. I had myself been some years in the West before I learned of the identity, from maps. The average man in the street is not much of a map-reader; judging from my own experience in putting the question to others, I have no doubt whatever that even now in Saskatoon and Calgary respectively, any number of citizens would be very much surprised to hear their river called the "Bow" or the "South Saskatchewan," as the case might be.

In the case of the Bow, this river had an aboriginal name, and we know what it was: "Bow" is a translation of the Cree *Munuhchaban* ("the place one takes bows from"; or elliptically, "Bow River").[9] This name in the south had evidently attained a dominating position in men's thoughts, comparable to the great Saskatchewan in the north. It seems a fairly logical inference that if the traders at Chesterfield House had pushed westward along their "South Saskatchewan" to its headwaters and made it a main line of communication, that name would have submerged the aboriginal designation; and that the survival of the latter may be taken as a fair index of the general European ignorance of the Bow headwaters territory, such as would sufficiently explain our ignorance of Plains buffalo penetration of the region by that route.

When we come to the consideration of our animal as being more probably a Wood buffalo, we find ourselves on more satisfactory ground. The geographical location of the find is very nearly 51° 25′ N., 115° 55′ W.—some twenty miles east of the Canadian Pacific station at Lake Louise. Wood buffalo vestiges have been found at points along the Banff-Jasper

[8]Rev. Albert Lacombe, *Dictionnaire de la langue des Cris*, 201, 418.
[9]McDougall, *Western Trails &c.*, 17.

Highway. In 1859 Dr. Hector of the Palliser Expedition was told by his guide that two years previously (1857) he had killed a Wood buffalo cow —one of a band of seven animals—on Pipestone Creek, given by Hector as being 51° 38. 5 N. This is presumably Pipestone River, which would appear to flow from Lake Louise (see *Place-Names of Alberta*, 103, and Provincial Department of Lands and Mines map, 1941).

On the same exploring trip Hector observed a fresh buffalo track along the Sifleur River.[10] This river rises about 51° 25′ N., 116° 10′ W., directly north of Lake Louise, and flows northward into the North Saskatchewan. Hector does not specify the exact whereabouts on the river he saw this, but the source would only be some twenty miles from Seventeen Mile Flat.

This renders the identification as Wood buffalo extremely probable. If this be both the farthest west up the Bow River (as it is) and the farthest south, working along the main mountain range from the Upper Athabasca Valley at Jasper, it constitutes in itself a significant find from the angle of the buffalo archaeologist.

The identification of the spear-head proved at first unfruitful. The surname of Sorby is probably of Yorkshire origin (very possibly from the several village names of Sowerby); and is almost a household word in Sheffield, the present writer's native place. Inquiries made to W. G. Ibberson, the (then) Master Cutler of Sheffield, and to Miss Alice Johnson, archivist for the Hudson's Bay Company, produced no tangible results.

However, acting on a suggestion from Dr. Douglas Leechman of the Glenbow Foundation, a letter was sent to the Director of the Sheffield City Museum, H. Raymond Singleton. His reply stated in part:

In about the year 1790 John Sorby set up a workshop in The Wicker, Sheffield, where he made edge tools, sheep shears, etc. John Sorby had three sons, Edwin, John and Henry, who all became toolmakers. In the 1814 and 1822 directories of Sheffield the firm is recorded as John Sorby & Sons, of Spital Hill, Sheffield. In 1827 Henry Sorby joined the family business and the trade mark "I. & H. Sorby" was adopted: the letter I being commonly used instead of J in trade marks of this and earlier times. Before 1827 the trade mark "I.S." was used.

In 1837 Henry Sorby set up on his own account as a merchant, probably concerned with the export trade, but the mark "I. & H. Sorby" continued to be used by John Sorby & Sons on their edge tools, shears, saws, spades, shovels, etc. I have been able to find no evidence here that they made spearheads, but in view of the general character of their products this would not seem improbable. There was certainly a steady export trade in operation at this time, supplying knives and spears to trading posts in all parts of the Empire.

In about 1845 John Sorby & Sons went into partnership with Messrs. Lockwood Brothers, who eventually took over the firm and registered the "I. & H. Sorby" mark in their own name in 1877. The firm of Lockwood Brothers still flourishes in Sheffield, but the edge tool section of their business was sold to Messrs. Turner Naylor & Company in 1934. This firm, which also flourishes today, is a subsidiary of another edge tool concern, William Marples & Sons Ltd., of Hibernia Works, Sheffield, who are therefore the present holders of the trade mark.

The date of your spear-head could therefore be anywhere between 1827 and

[10]Hector, in *Palliser Journals*, 148-49.

perhaps the end of the century, or whenever this particular trade came to an end.

You may be interested to know that about two years ago I received a similar enquiry regarding an identical spear-head with the same trade mark, from Mr. Colin Clarke of the Saskatoon Archaelogical Society, 135 7th Street Saskatoon. The Secretary of the Society has since sent me details of others, and would I am sure be interested to hear of your acquisition.

While any definitely final decision is unattainable, the Director's letter furnishes a broad potential solution as to the date of the spear-head.

In view of the chronological data furnished from Sheffield and the geographical situation of the find, we may, perhaps, tentatively assume that the weapon was supplied from Piegan Post (H.B.Co.). This establishment was situated at or near the confluence of the Kananaskis River with the Bow, some thirty or forty miles from the site of the discovery. Its date would necessarily be (relatively) early, since Piegan Post was abandoned shortly after 1832.

APPENDIX KK

THE HISTORIC BUFFALO (*BISON AMERICANUS*) IN THE
AMERICAN SOUTHWEST WITHIN THE HISTORICAL
PERIOD[1] (p. 274)

The question of the presence or "penetration" of the historic buffalo into the territories "west of the Rocky Mountains" in the southwestern United States, or across the Rio Grande into Mexico, is one upon which there has been considerable disagreement. In the opinion of some critics the matter cannot be considered definitely settled even yet. Certainly no such claim will be made for the present discussion. At the same time there are various items of evidence which may very relevantly be adduced, more or less in the nature of an interim report; such as must—to say the least—be included in any attempt to pronounce a final verdict.

Much of the history of the buffalo in New Mexico can scarcely be said to belong to the territory "west of the Rockies" in the sense in which dwellers at a distance, anyhow, commonly use that phrase. Several contemporary Southwestern scholars, moreover, are inclined to question or to deny that the species occupied western New Mexico beyond the Rio Grande—perhaps not even beyond the Pecos—or onward westerly toward the Gila River watershed. The problems of the identification of this or that river or route have also to be faced, and these have occasioned much controversy. In the judgment of many scholars, both earlier and contemporary, it was on the Pecos that Antonio de Espejo encountered the buffalo in 1583. As old Purchas's version of 1625 expresses it, Espejo returned " . . . by another way, downe a river, called De la Vaccas, or of Kine, an hundred and twenty leagues, still meeting with store of those cattell."[2] Another more recently published journal of the same expedition, by Diego Pérez de Luxán, is considered by some modern critics to discredit the account given by Espejo very materially, but in my own opinion by no means to the degree their strictures might suggest.[3] None the less, in the lack of more precise particularization, the extended course of the Pecos (if that river be accepted) necessarily leaves Espejo's recital somewhat inconclusive as between New Mexico and Texas.

---

[1]This appendix, which was read before the Royal Society of Canada (Section Two) in June, 1962, presents supplementary evidence to Chapter XI of the original edition of *The North American Buffalo* (1951). It consists of material not then known to the author, or appearing since the above work was published.

[2]*Purchas his Pilgrimes*, XVIII, 65-7.

[3]*The Expedition into New Mexico made by Antonio de Espejo in 1582-1583, as revealed in the Journal of Diego Pérez de Luxán, a Member of the Party*, ed. George P. Hammond and Agapito Rey (1929). For criticisms of Espejo, see particularly Hallenbeck, *Journey and Route of Cabeza de Vaca*, 89, 140-4, 200, 209.

Espejo was not the first explorer after Coronado, and some of the others are considered to be rather more specific in their reports. The expedition of Martin López de Ibarra records seeing buffalo in 1564[4]; so also Barrundo and Escalanté[5] (or Barrando[6] and Escalona)[7] in 1581. Later explorers include Vicenté de Zaldívar in 1598,[8] Juan de Oñaté in 1604,[9] Fernando de Bosque in 1675 (who gives the earliest noted description of the buffalo's curious "oblique" vision mentioned by several buffalo students[10] and Diego de Vargas in 1694.[11]

While there appear to have been no inherent reasons for the buffalo not extending their range from a generally similar and adjacent region into Arizona, the evidence for this having actually occurred is meagre and largely inferential.

J. A. Allen (1876) cited Dr. Elliott Coues in support of the supposition of their presence in that State at some period; but Coues' evidence proved to be exceedingly vague and unsatisfactory.[12]

A later scholar notes a possible knowledge of the buffalo in 1540 among the tribes of the lower Colorado River, below the Grand Canyon. This is a distance from the Rio Grande of about eight degrees of longitude (107-15° W.); equivalent at that latitude (c. 35° N.) to some 450 miles. It was said that an Indian of some tribe had been to Cibola.[13] Whether this would be sufficient to postulate a "knowledge of the buffalo" at that remote distance remains problematical, without personal contact in some reasonable degree.

The local tribes are stated to have informed Juan de Oñaté in 1604 that there were buffalo on the Gila headwaters.[14] A very learned Southwestern critic demurs to this, pointing out that Oñaté was not in or near the Gila headwaters country in 1604.[15] There is nothing in the statement that requires him to have been. And apart from any questions of historical authenticity, it was not at all unknown for the early explorers to be assured by Indians or others of the presence of buffalo *somewhere else* than in their own country; probably a highly convenient method of "steering" a ruinously large hunting party away from their own territory.[16] It is a familiar fact

[4]Bancroft, *North American States and Texas*, I, 109.

[5]Bancroft, *History of Arizona and New Mexico*, 75, 77, 89.

[6]Bolton, *Spanish Exploration in the Southwest*, 142.

[7]Bancroft, *History of Arizona*, bibliography, xxix.

[8]*Ibid.*, 138; *New Mexico in 1602*, ed. Hammond and Rey, 27, 50-8.

[9]Bancroft, *History of Arizona*, 346-8.

[10]Bolton, *Spanish Exploration in the Southwest*, 298. For others, see above, 124, notes 21-2.

[11]Bancroft, *History of Arizona*, 210.

[12]Allen, *American Bisons*, 125-8. Cited *in extenso* above, 275. The earliest printed account in English, that of Henry Hawks, 1572 (*in extenso* above, 211, note 26) calls them "the kine of Cibola." From this came *cibolo* = buffalo, and *ciboléro* = buffalo-hunter.

[13]Bolton, *Coronado*, 162.

[14]*Ibid.*, 275.

[15]Dr. Erik K. Reed (Santa Fé, New Mexico), correspondence to the author, October 13, 1961.

[16]See the present work, 189, 246, 302, 339.

that in 1539 Fray Marcos de Niza found "ox-hides" among the Indians on the tributaries of the Gila. These had been obtained from the "Kingdom of Cibola,"[17] which of itself would rather imply that there were few or none in that particular region along the Gila waters at that time. This does not necessarily entail, however, that if there were none along the Gila in 1539, there could not have been any in 1604.

It appears to be very much of a fixed opinion with some scholars (if I have interpreted them correctly) that the buffalo had been shrinking both in numbers and in territory, "for a long time," which in the light of their context seems to imply—even before the European invasion—while the species were still exposed to none but the aboriginal influences. I cannot understand upon what this view is based.[18] I have found no evidence that the Plains tribes would ever have been able to exterminate the Plains hosts prior to the intensive hunting of the post-European trans-Mississippian era. Two basic circumstances may be mentioned: I have never yet heard of a single discovery of fossil remains of the historic species (*Bison americanus*) in any region where they have never been known as living creatures; in the southeastern United States east of the Mississippi and south of the Ohio Valley, where in the years 1539-42 De Soto's expedition found neither the living animals, buffalo products, nor even any tradition of a former presence,[19] by 1730—if not earlier—the buffalo had journeyed virtually to the Georgia coast, a distance of nearly 600 miles as the crow flies.[20] This presents a direct analogy to the Gila River possibility, 1539-1604. In addition to such major movements, there is also the utterly unpredictable caprice or whatever it was, of the herds; whereby in the very heyday of the vast hosts, even the regions of (alleged) "unfailing plenty" might experience a buffalo famine, as Indians and whites knew only too well![21]

With respect to one important Arizona people, however, that is to say the Navajo, the evidence is somewhat more specific. Bancroft states that Vildosola's expedition in 1758 found the Apache in Arizona obtaining buffalo skins from a people (supposed to be Moqui) seven days northward from the Gila River, "where there were many cattle and cultivated lands."[22] The Hopi-Moqui Reservation is or was down to 1924 situated some

[17]Stanley A. Fishler, *El Palacio* (Santa Fé, N.M.), LXII, Feb., 1955, 47; cf. Erik K. Reed, *Journal of Mammalogy* (New York), XXXIII, Aug., 1952, 391.

[18]A. S. Romer (1932): "The living species (*B. bison*) is known to have ranged much more widely in the past than in historic times. . . . " in Jenness, ed., *American Aborigines*, 53. No evidence is adduced for this assertion. The only shrinkage brought forward prior to historic times (to my knowledge) is that given below in this appendix, note 88.

[19]Even H. E. Bolton, who (contrary to virtually everyone else, and citing no authority for the conclusion) thinks that De Soto's party saw the buffalo, puts the occurrence west of the Mississippi, at Coligua, near Little Rock, Arkansas (Bolton, *Coronado*, 275-81).

[20]For buffalo in Georgia, see above, 242-4.

[21]See above *in extenso*, Chs. XIX-XX, 521-600.

[22]Bancroft, *North Mexican States and Texas*, I, 558. Fossil species have been found in Arizona. On *B. arizonica* see Skinner and Kaisen, *Fossil Bison of Alaska*, 150, 204, 207, 210; see also E. K. Reed, *Texas Journal of Science*, 1955, 130-5.

180 miles north of the upper Gila River. In this precise territory, on the boundary between the Moqui and Navajo reservations, and on a line directly north from Winslow, Arizona, there is *Mesa la Vaca*, that is, "Cow Plain."

A Southwestern scholar informs me that the Hopi had cattle in the eighteenth century, and is disinclined to attach any weight to the place-name I have instanced.[23] But it is to be noted that the *vaca* place-names as a class are identified by Southwestern scholars in general as referring to buffalo, the common generic term for cattle (wild cattle, range cattle, or domestic cattle more strictly) being *ganado*. Reasoning *à priori*, it seems unlikely that the Spaniards would apply the term *vaca* to cattle they had themselves taken with them to such a locality. It seems equally improbable that *early* parties—the more likely to bestow the name—would convey cattle with them; similarly, if Vildosola's party were not the first, but had merely traversed a territory in which (European) cattle were familiarly known, it is remarkable that they did not mention the fact *en route*. And unless the *Mesa la Vaca* really indicates buffalo, why bother amid the general silence, to mention the denizens of this spot at all, whoever may have named the place.

The use of the term *vacas*, "the cows," as a generic (not sexual) designation for buffalo as a species—precisely as Father Hennepin a century and a half later uses "bulls"—does not seem to have been entirely arbitrary and unreasoning on the Spaniards' part. Although the first encounter of the Coronado expedition (to whom we owe the earliest authentic description of the animal at first hand) was actually with the bulls *en masse* at a season when the sexes very commonly separated, so that "it was more than forty leagues from where we began to see the bulls to the place where we began to see the cows . . . ,"[24] yet they appear to have taken the sexes on the Indians' own valuation. While young bulls not yet come to maturity could be eaten readily enough—and older ones *were* eaten when the commissiariat was *in extremis*—yet it was the cows alone that furnished any needs of housing, harness, clothing, bedding, etc., that were derived from the skins.[25] *Vacas jorobadas*, "hump-backed cows," is the standard name with Cortés, Bernal Díaz, Gomara, etc. The cumulative weight of the foregoing particulars may in my judgment be considered as contributory evidence for the presence of the historic buffalo in northern Arizona.

[23]Dr. E. K. Reed, correspondence to the author, October 13, 1961. A century after Vildosola, a place-name, *Ojo la Vaca* ("Buffalo Spring") was recorded on the El Paso—Fort Yuma wagon road, west of the Rio Grande and in Arizona (*Report on Pacific Wagon Roads: Report to Second Session of 35th Congress*, Exhibition Document, No. 108, 1859), 78. A Southwestern geographer, Prof. Donald D. Brand, notes the use of the term *estancias de vacas* in Querétaro and Durango. But these, by the name, were doubtless breeding centres (i.e. *vacas* in the sexual sense) and in any case date 1533, before Coronado had ever seen buffalo (Brand, "The Early History of the Range Cattle Industry in Northern Mexico," *Agricultural History*, Washington, D.C. XXXV, 1961, 132-9).

[24]Quoted above *in extenso*, 348-9.

[25]See above, 375, 394, 548, 601-7. Under 11 subheadings, Ewers tabluates 87 uses of buffalo products other than food, by Blackfoot and other tribes (*The Horse in Blackfoot Indian Culture*, 150-1, 223-4).

Such conclusions are immensely reinforced by the evidence of a modern scholar, writing in 1955. Stanley A. Fishler, in an important paper on the *locale* and cultural technique of Navajo buffalo-hunting, presents a mass of data from tribal tradition and other sources, such as in my opinion tend to establish the former presence of the animals in the Navajo territory in Arizona well into the nineteenth century.[26] Dr. Erik K. Reed, himself a Southwestern scholar and critic on buffalo history, was opposed to this conclusion, pointing out that the Navajo were known to have gone buffalo hunting both to the San Luis Valley and eastward to the plains in the seventeenth and eighteenth centuries. Following upon this, "their knowledge and traditions furnish no proof of the recent former presence of bison in the Navajo Reservation. . . ."[27] This of course is perfectly true, but neither is it—particularly in view of our earlier remarks on buffalo fluctuations—any proof that there were *not*; and it may be noted that *Mesa la Vaca*, to which Dr. Reed attaches no weight, is itself situated in the Navajo Reservation.

These factors in combination impose a heavy burden of proof upon critics who reject them, since what has been perhaps loosely termed "tradition" consists in part of direct reminiscence only two generations back, and such as in our own societies—and in relation to Western history most specifically—frequently constitutes an important feature in "historical source-material" so called, and from not much more literate informants. Randolph B. Marcy wrote concerning the Comanche (*c.* 1850):

The knowledge they possess of their early history is very vague and limited, and does not extend farther back than a few generations. They say that their forefathers lived precisely as they do and followed the buffalo: that they came from a country toward the setting sun, where they expect to return after death. . . .[28]

It must be left to anthropological scholars, more competent than myself, to pronounce whether such traditions would justify any extension of the buffalo habitat beyond their authenticated range. I should hesitate to venture upon the hazardous task of either vindicating or refuting Indian buffalo traditions at large. Some Indian traditions appear to have been established by scientific investigation, while in other cases tradition has failed to preserve any memory of what must have been really striking events.[29] In any case I do not consider we have any justification for

[26]Fishler, *El Palacio* (Santa Fé, N.M.), LXII, Feb., 1955, 43-57.

[27]Dr. E. K. Reed, correspondence to the author, October 13, 1961.

[28]Marcy, *Exploration of the Red River of Louisiana in 1852*, 107; cf. also Bancroft, *Native Races of the Pacific States*, 111, 528.

[29]See above, Ch. XI; also Roe, *The Indian and the Horse* (1955), 101-3, 117, 207-18, 236. See Fiske's remarks on the tradition of Cabeza's companion, the negro Estévanico, the "Black Mexican," preserved after 350 years (since Coronado) in the Southwest (*Discovery of America*, II, 507; also Bishop, *Odyssey of Cabeza de Vaca*, 161). Coronado's visit of 1540-1 was found to be quite forgotten at Cibola, according to Juan de Oñate, 1596. Cabrillo, 1542, and Drake, 1579, were not remembered in California: so Fathers Crespi and Serra, 1769 (Bancroft, *Native Races*, III, 27).

adopting either point of view *en bloc*; each tradition must be examined on its own merits.

Many buffalo tribes have traditions of the buffalo being already in the country when the tribe reached it. Nothing can be more certain in the history of the North American continent than the fact that the Indian preceded the buffalo. For the Indians penetrated to many areas long before the buffalo, and to other areas where the historic buffalo at least, never penetrated at all. But we have to remember that the buffalo tribes as history knows them have migrated over vast distances to their historic habitats. For example, the Algonkian linguistic family stock had their homeland in Labrador and the lower St. Lawrence region, whence some of them were driven by the Iroquois perhaps as late as *circa* 1300. The Ojibwa, Cree, and Blackfoot in western Canada, the Cheyenne and Arapaho in the Western States, and the Kootenay and Kalispel in British Columbia are all Algonkians. The buffalo were certainly here when these tribes reached their historic Plains areas; it is quite conceivable that the shattering impact of such a tremendous phenomenon, revolutionizing their lives as it did, could really take form in their minds as a "first arrival" and obliterate all remembrance of a former existence. Thus their traditions could be both "true" and "untrue." The Mandan—and probably other tribes also—had both their mystics and their rationalists. They told David Thompson *circa* 1790 about earlier generations, when "the Bison and the Horse were not known to them. . . ."[30] Forty years later the Mandan legends told to Maximilian had the buffalo" preceding the making of the first man. . . ."[31]

In the present (Comanche) instance, one would like to know more about the season of the year for those "setting suns." "Coming from the west" could quite legitimately be said in the region of the upper or central Red River (of Texas), where Marcy found them. Unfortunately, the consensus of critical opinion seems to derive the Comanche (who are Shoshoneans) from some northern or northwestern homeland nearer to the northern Shoshonean territory, where the evidence indicates a relatively recent arrival of the buffalo species.[32] Curiously enough, too, for the horsemen *par excellence* of the southern territory, their acquaintance with the horse only dates from about 1700.[33]

Concerning Utah, Dr. Hornaday remarks: "It is well known that buffaloes, though in very small numbers, once inhabited northeastern Utah, and that a few were killed by the Mormon settlers prior to 1840 in the vicinity of Great Salt Lake. . . ." I am unaware who "the Mormon settlers prior to 1840" may have been,[34] but Ashley and Smith's party found that very region "well supplied with buffaloe" in May, 1825.[35] Perhaps even more curious, in view of the evidence for a relatively recent invasion of

[30]Thompson, *Narrative of Explorations* (ed. Tyrrell), 230-1.

[31]Maximilian, *Early Western Travels*, XXIII, 252-395.

[32]See above, 257-64.

[33]See Roe, *Indian and the Horse*, 213-16, and sources there cited.

[34]Hornaday, "Extermination of the American Bison," 383. The earliest Mormons reached Utah in 1847 (so Bancroft, *History of Utah* (1889).

[35]H. C. Dale, *Ashley-Smith Explorations*, 155.

the transmontane area at large, and a less forward advance westward in its more southerly portions is the circumstance that the buffalo occupation of the Salt Lake Valley was thought by an eminent American paleontologist to date back to a very remote period "since their skulls occur wholly buried in the marshes about the lake, where the deposition appears to have been quite slow. . . ."[36] Joel A. Allen (1876) summed up the evidence for their final disappearance from the region as follows:

The buffalo seems, however, to have lingered longer on the headwaters of the Colorado than in either the Great Salt Lake Valley, or the valley of Bear River, or on the headwaters of the two main forks of the Columbia. Frémont found them on St. Vrain's Fork of Green River and on the Vermilion in 1844, and [Captain Howard] Stansbury in 1849 found them on the northern tributaries of the Yampah [i.e. Bear River] and the upper tributaries of Green River,[37] but the scarcity of water seemed to have forced the greater part of them southward. . . . They have, however, long since disappeared from the headwaters of Green River, and, indeed, from all the country drained by the tributaries of the Colorado. Although their bleached skulls are still found throughout the valleys, I was informed by old hunters whom I saw there in the autumn of 1871, that no buffaloes had been seen in this region for more than twenty years. . . .[38]

What may be termed the local or popular history of their final disappearance is less clear. There were no buffalo among the 1229 wild animals of various species slain by the Mormon "hunting companies for the extermination of wild beasts" in the winter of 1848-9.[39] In a discussion of various routes in the vicinity of Salt Lake City, neither buffalo nor buffalo placenames occur, nor are they mentioned by John W. Gunnison in 1852.[40] A well known (later) "Danite," one Bill Hickman, afterwards "claimed" to have killed the last buffalo in Salt Lake Valley in 1838,[41] but I can find no evidence that he was there at that early date. Putting aside the Munchausenlike details, one must presume there must have been some factual basis for the prodigious buffalo mortality described by old Bridger. If we accept his date the animals had vanished in 1830, years before Hickman.[42]

A solitary bull appeared in 1875 near Fort Bridger (Uinta County, Wyoming, in the extreme southwest corner of the State, about 40° 25′ N., 110° 20′ W.), where it was said to have been the first one seen for thirty years.[43] The "last one" in the adjoining northeastern portion of Utah is declared to have been shot in 1844 on Henry's Fork of the Green River, which it joins about 109° 35′ W. on the Utah-Wyoming state line, some thirty miles

[36]Prof. Henry W. Henshaw, cited by Allen, *American Bisons*, 119-20.

[37]About 110° W. (n.e. Utah—s.w. Wyoming). Green River lower down is the Colorado of the Grand Canyon.

[38]Allen, *American Bisons*, 120-1.

[39]Bancroft, *History of Utah*, 287.

[40]*Ibid.*, 258, 323.

[41]"The notorious Bill Hickman" (*ibid.*, 564, 663; Bancroft, *History of Nevada, Colorado, and Wyoming*, 205).

[42]See the tale *in extenso* above (from Bancroft), 181.

[43]Allen, *American Bisons*, 125.

southeast of Fort Bridger.[44] Since Fort Bridger itself dates only from 1843, this report compares curiously with the unsupported assertion of a characteristically hasty writer, that the "frequency of buffalo" was one reason for Bridger's choice of the location.[45] With respect to such claims as these, Hornaday remarks sarcastically concerning the final extirpation in the United States, that in 1883 "the last buffalo had already been killed about a score of times."[46] The history of "the last wolf" in England inclines one to agree with him.[47]

In the state of Nevada (which was once included within "California"[48]) nothing whatever of any definite character has apparently been recorded concerning the historic buffalo at any time during their active existence, although fossil species have been found there.[49] Later evidence, however, appears to indicate that the historic animal may have occupied portions of Nevada even as late as the early part of the nineteenth century. Two writers of our own time (1913) give their "original range" as being "to Nevada."[50] It is difficult to decide just what this means. It may be intended to include that state, or perhaps merely to signify the western confines of Utah, but there seems at present to be no extant evidence of buffalo being found very nearly on either side of the Nevada state line, except perhaps in a small section northwest of Great Salt Lake. In the westernmost part of Nevada, however, in Washoe County, about 40° 15′ N., and just short of the California state line, I find a place-name, Buffalo Meadows, on Buffalo Creek.[51] At one time I thought this name very possibly commemorated the discovery of the fossil vestiges hitherto associated with Nevada, the actual site of which is unknown to me.[52] But there seem to be good grounds for connecting these names with the historic species. These are considered by contemporary Californian scholars to have penetrated into the (modern) State of California almost in this precise region. If their conclusions be correct, this establishes the first known connection of the historic buffalo with modern California.

The former presence of *Bison americanus* in California was first made

[44]Prof. O. C. Marsh to Allen (*ibid.*, 125). Waldo R. Wedel, re bison remains in Promontory Cave, Utah ("which is full of them"), considers that "bison occurred in some number in the area until about 1832" (*Smithsonian Miscellaneous Collections*, C, 1940, 472). I can find nothing further regarding this dating.

[45]Agnes C. Laut, *The Overland Trail*, 121.

[46]Hornaday, "Extermination of the American Bison," 521, 525.

[47]See above *in extenso*, 279-80.

[48]See Bancroft, *History of Nevada, Colorado, and Wyoming*, 66.

[49]*Ibid.*, 247-8. See also above, 20, note 42; Skinner and Kaisen, *Fossil Bison of Alaska*, 185-6.

[50]Stone and Cram, *American Animals* (1913), 66. There is also a reference by Sir Richard Burton, the Orientalist, which one could wish were more precise. He speaks (1855) of buffalo being in "Utah Valley" (?) fourteen to fifteen years ago . . . and later still on the Humboldt River. . . ." (*City of the Saints*, 50). The Humboldt River apparently rises in Nevada north of Elko, *c.* 41° 10′ N, 116° W. Burton also mentions a certain "Skull Valley," which may possibly be west of the Utah–Nevada state line, the allusion being vague (*ibid.*, 330, 454, 511).

[51]Cram's *International Atlas* (1924), *s.v.* "Nevada."

[52]See above, 18, 20, notes 27, 42.

known by C. Hart Merriam in 1926. Merriam obtained his information from ancient members of the local Indian tribes, some of whose parents had actually hunted the animals nearly a century before. Merriam also obtained the native names for them in the Achomawi, Atsugewi, Klamath, and Paiute languages.[53] In 1951, Francis A. Riddell was able, as a result of a careful field investigation in the area, not merely to substantiate Merriam's data, but to supplement them materially. The region in question is in the vicinity of Eagle Lake, Horse Lake, Madeleine Plains, and Honey Lake, all of which are in Lassen County, northeastern California. In addition to the linguistic evidence and the reminiscent matter with respect to buffalo hunting *per se*, several informants described an old buffalo wallow on the western shore of Honey Lake.[54] S. A. Barrett and E. W. Gifford, two independent investigators prior to Riddell, furnish an intresting connecting link with the aforementioned "Buffalo Meadows" in Washoe County, Nevada. They found that the Miwok, a local tribe, formerly obtained buffalo skins in trade from the Washo.[55] From the general consideration of the various data, Riddell dates the extinction of the buffalo in California about 1830.[56] This is the only section of California in which the historic buffalo have ever been identified, despite various statements to the contrary.[57]

It is possibly a feature in the general argument against acceptance of the historic species anywhere west of the Rio Grande, that a leading Southwestern archaeologist already mentioned in these pages, Erik K. Reed, some few years ago refused to accept their presence in Mexico at any time since the era of European contacts.[58] This is to run counter to earlier accepted opinion, and also (in my judgment) to some very weighty evidence, while at the same time the arguments by which the critic supported his contention were seriously defective.

Too much emphasis has been laid upon the fact—quite correct in itself—that for a long time prior to the Mexican War of 1847, "Mexico" included territories which are now part of the United States. As we have already noted, our earliest really authentic description of the buffalo at first hand

[53]C. Hart Merriam, *Journal of Mammalogy*, VII (1926), 211-14. Merriam also noted several buffalo place-names in the locality: B. Creek and B. Spring, 20 miles N. of Pyramid lake; B. Meadows, on B. Creek, 20 miles above its mouth; "B. Salt Works," apparently on B. Creek; B. Cañon, 119° 55′ W., in Nevada, east of the California state line).

[54]Francis A. Riddell, "The Recent Occurrence of Bison in Northeastern California," *American Antiquity*, XVIII, 1952, 168-9.

[55]Barrett, S. A. and E. W. Gifford, "Miwok Material Culture"; cited by Riddell, *American Antiquity*, XVIII.

[56]Riddell, *American Antiquity*, VIII, 1952, 169.

[57]See note above, 280-2.

[58]E. K. Reed, *Journal of Mammalogy*, XXXIII, 1952, 391. Dr. Reed was not alone in this view. Vernon Bailey wrote in 1931: "No good evidence is found that [the historic] buffalo . . . inhabited the Rio Grande Valley or the country west of it." Bailey, *Mammals of New Mexico* (*North American Fauna*, 53, U.S. Biological Survey, Washington, 1931), 12. So authoritative a statement may have influenced others. I owe this reference to Dr. Reed; see below, note 82.

comes from the scribes of Coronado's party (1540-1).[59] It is quite true that it was not until they had penetrated northward into the present United States, very probably east of the Pecos River in New Mexico, that they actually saw the animals. From this there seems to have sprung a tacit assumption that since the expedition had been traversing "Mexico" before reaching the Pecos, and had seen no buffalo—ergo, there were then no buffalo in Mexico. This hypothesis overlooks a vital consideration.

Arthur S. Aiton published many years ago his translation of "The Muster-Roll of Coronado," which gives the *personnel* of the force and also records the number of its horses and their owners. These were recorded at a review of the troop before the Viceroy, Antonio de Mendoza "the good" (*El Bueno*), Sunday, February 22, 1540. This review was held at Compostela, on the western seaboard of Mexico, at the extreme south of the State of Nayarit (formerly Tepic), about 21° N., 105° W.[60] It is quite evident, even to a distant critic, from the fact that their route going and returning lay through Culiacán, that for a long distance at least they kept to the coast *littoral*; and there seems to have been an old highway through the area, now probably followed in the main by the Southern Pacific Railway route from Tucson and Nogales to Guadalajara. The general direction of their approach to the "buffalo plains" by way of "Cibola" (Zuni, New Mexico, 32° 20′ N., 107° 30′ W.) reveals the broad features of the route clearly enough. For the whole of their journey "northward" (i.e., northwestward) they had been widely flanking the portions of Mexico in which buffalo were later stated to have been encountered.

Apart from the "field notes" of the Coronado expedition, or the brief description by such men as Henry Hawks,[61] and doubtless based upon common gossip in Mexico, the first really scientific account of buffalo is apparently in the great work on natural history, *Rerum Medicarum Novae Hispaniae Thesaurus Francisci Hernandez*, written by Dr. Hernández for Philip II of Spain (1527-98). The name given by Hernández to *Bison americanus* is *Taurus mexicanus*, "the Mexican Bull."[62] This is a case in point where the relevance of the term *Mexico* has been questioned. Dr. Reed wrote thus: "Hernández very probably, I imagine, placed the bison in 'New Spain,' which included Mexico but also included the western and southern United States."

It is of course possible that in writing *mexicanus* Hernández meant (or perhaps even *said*) "New Spain." I do not know whether Linnaeus, who classified the "type-locality" of the species (*Bison bison*) as Mexico,[63] took

[59]See above, note 24. Dr. Reed draws my attention to the fact that the *first* published description of the animals was that of Gonzales Fernández de Oviedo, in his *Historia General y Natural de las Indias* (1535). I have had no opportunity to see this. See below, note 62.

[60]Arthur S. Aiton, "The Muster-Roll of Coronado," *American Historical Review*, XLIV, 1938, 556-70. I am indebted to Prof. Aiton's kindness for a copy of this important document.

[61]Hawks, in Hakluyt, *Voyages*, &c (Everyman's Library ed.), VI, 283. Given *in extenso* above, 211.

[62]For Hernández, *see* Bancroft, *Native Races*, II, 165, 476; III, 728.

[63]So E. Thompson Seton, *Lives of Game Animals*, III, 641, 643.

this from Hernández, though it seems probable. However, the term *type-locality* is not necessarily applied—as some people appear to suppose—to the region where any species was first encountered, and which in this instance of buffalo was somewhere in the southwestern United States; but rather to the region from which it was derived for scientific appraisal and classification. And the whole case for interpreting "Mexico" as signifying really the United States somewhere northeast of the Rio Grande is pure hypothesis, and demands authentic confirmation.

A Mexican manuscript work on the mammals of Mexico (now lost) is much more specific on behalf of the opposing contention. Dr. Berlandier's work has been accepted by Joel A. Allen (1876),[64] the most judicious of all the earlier generalizers on buffalo, and Allen's judgment has been endorsed by Hornaday,[65] Thompson Seton, and a learned lady scholar of high standing in her time, Alice C. Fletcher.[66] Berlandier writes thus (in part) :

> In 1602 the Franciscan monks who discovered Nueva León encountered in the neighborhood of Monterey numerous herds of these quadrupeds. Also in Nueva Biscaya (States of Chihuahua and Durango) and sometimes in the extreme south of that country [i.e. of Durango ?]. In the eighteenth century they concentrated more towards the north, at the beginning of the nineteenth receding more into the interior . . . in the south, although they may have reached as low as 25°, they scarcely passed beyond the 27th. or 28th. degree (north latitude), at least in the inhabited and known parts of the country. . . .[67]

I am unaware of the precise date of Dr. Berlandier's treatise, but it was manifestly written between 1828 and 1847, since he mentions the earlier date, and also refers to "the States of Coahuila and Texas" exactly as he refers above to "the States of Chihuahua and Durango," quite obviously as though the former were two Spanish provinces under the same rule. This of course ceased to be the case after the Mexican War of 1847. The definite mention of Nueva León, Chihuahua, and Durango, which were never at any period included in the United States, precludes any argument concerning ambiguous interpretations of "Mexico."

Berlandier was actually cited by Dr. Reed, who in this instance made no reference to the "Mexico" ambiguity. Yet he was strangely unwilling to accept Berlandier's testimony. His comment was that Berlandier "seems to stand almost alone and unsupported. . . ." Reed goes on to say:

> Until I find a positive contemporary reference, I shall be very dubious as to early-historic (1500-1700) bison beyond the Rio Grande. . . . The closest to such documentation is the statement by Obregón that in the 1565 expedition to "Paquimé" with [Martin Lopez de] Ibarra they saw hides, bones, and manure of "the cattle"; but the local people, *querechos*, told them the cattle were four days' march away and that they themselves were enemies of those *querechos* who "lived among the cattle; also that the cattle came up into the slopes and sheltered places to get away from the cold in the open country." This all sounds rather

---

[64]Allen, *American Bisons*, 72-3, 129-30.
[65]Hornaday, "Extermination of the American Bison," 382-3.
[66]For Alice Fletcher's summary and that of Hornaday, see above, 204-5. See also Skinner and Kaisen, *Fossil Bison of Alaska*, 149, 154.
[67]Quoted *in extenso* above, 522.

peculiar and slightly confused, and I am not sure that the traces they saw were really of bison. "Paquimé" is thought to have been the Casas Grandes vicinity in Chihuahua [*circa* 30° 30′ N., 107° 45′ W.].[68]

A dissenting critic who doubts whether the traces these men saw "were really of bison" should at least suggest what else they might be. I am unaware whether or not there had been other expeditions into Nueva España between Coronado and Ibarra, but I have met with no allusion to such among some very competent students. Certainly, in the mid-sixteenth century in Mexico, there would be nothing like the present consensus of general knowledge, such as enables the commonly uninformed man in the street to recognize at a glance whether a certain animal encountered is a buffalo or not. But we can scarcely doubt that Coronado's "cows" would be well known by repute, at a time when some of his force were probably still living,[69] and the very paucity of exploration in the intervening years would of itself preclude or minimize any likelihood of the Coronado descriptions having to struggle for survival against contradictory rival species. Obregón's competence to recognize buffalo can scarcely be legitimately questioned.

What Obregón records, however, were merely "traces." A non-zoological observer could certainly be deceived by bones,[70] and perhaps even more easily by dung. But it is utterly inconceivable that there could have been any doubt about the hides, even had there been any domesticated or semi-domesticated bovine breeds in the territory to create confusion. This last contingency seems, however, clearly implied in the suggestion of Dr. Reed's doubts. On this question some very recent evidence may relevantly be cited.

In a richly informative paper by a Southwestern geographer who apparently possesses a wide mastery of the literature and doubtless a complementary knowledge of the *terrain*, Professor Donald D. Brand discusses this important question of the advance of cattle ranching into northern Mexico from the time of the Conquest onwards. He cites a considerable mass of evidence showing that in point of chronology, there were large herds both of range cattle and of "wild" cattle ranging in many parts of Mexico, and certain regions had been reached as early as 1563-4; yet these were far removed from any neighbourhood of Casas Grandes, and Brand shows that northern Chihuahua as a whole cannot be dated earlier than *circa* 1663. There are notices of "vast droves of wild cattle" at the very time of Francisco de Ibarra in 1564, the progeny of animals abandoned in the 1530s and 1540s, but the region is southern Sinaloa, far away from northern

---

[68]E. K. Reed, *Journal of Mammalogy*, 1952, 392. Note "the cattle" *coming* up; not even "going up" (somewhere else).

[69]I am unaware of the exact date of Pedro de Castañeda's account of the Coronado expedition, but he speaks of writing "at a time when many of the men who saw [the buffalo] are still living. . . ." Such language suggests a material lapse of time (*Journey of Coronado*, 139).

[70]Maximilian of Wied (1834) defines the osteology in part in *Early Western Travels*, XXIV, 129. See Chap. III, also Appendix J, of this work.

Chihuahua. If that last-named locality was really "Paquimé," there is thus a definite lack of evidence for (European) cattle in any category, in that region *circa* 1564.[71]

Then, too, there are the *querechos,* from whom "the cattle" were at four days' distance, in the enemy territory of other *querechos.* This term has itself been recorded as a pueblo name for buffalo hunters.[72] This interpretation is disputed; it is affirmed that "the name Querechos has no connection with buffalos or hunting; it simply means wild or mountainous tribes."[73] I do not wish to be captious, but this seems to be begging the question, which is one of association rather than etymology. We could equally argue that the Cree *mistatim* ("horse") had nothing to do with the horse, because the name means "big dog."[74] Why could not these "mountainous" tribes be buffalo hunters when opportunity offered, precisely as the "Mountain Cree" and "Mountain Stoney" (·Assiniboine) were in Alberta? And while the Apache territory as a whole was broadly mountainous, the buffalo term was only applied to five divisions of the Apache, Faraones, Jicarilla, Lipan, Llanero, and Mescalero; and Coronado noted the "Querechos" as "buffalo Indians" in 1540. We may note also that in the very citation we are considering, the "cattle" *came up into the slopes. . . ."* These mountain men could still hunt buffalo in their own "etymological" environment.

This last proviso seems to dispose of any possible contention that the animals were always four days distant. The absence of buffalo at a given moment even from commonly-favoured haunts (for quite lengthy periods and in unknown directions) is a commonplace of buffalo history,[75] and there are not lacking instances where the direction *was* broadly known, yet the dread of powerful enemies kept the starving people from seeking the herds.[76] Dr. Reed's contention seems clearly to be that the buffalo were (at least) four days distant as a fixed condition, which in that region, about the Casas Grandes, could easily put them across the Rio Grande and disprove the Mexican occupation. If that were the case, in an area where dog-traction was virtually negligible,[77] the conveyance of buffalo products would be something of a severe strain upon the people. Meat and some amount of skins for the various uses that buffalo tribes made of them would be almost imperative. There might even be a minor traffic in bones, for mechanical, ceremonial, or social uses.[78] But under such conditions it becomes unthinkable to conceive of packing *dung* such distances! Moreover, it was on this expedition, apparently, that Spaniards were *met* for the first time by

[71]D. D. Brand, "Early History of the Range Cattle Industry in Northern Mexico," *Agricultural History,* 1961, 132-9. Were there *two* Ibarras? Bancroft has "Martin Lopez de Ibarra," *History of the North Mexican States and Texas,* I, 109. Compare below, note 79.

[72]*Handbook of American Indians,* II, 338.

[73]Dr. E. K. Reed, correspondence to the author, October 13, 1961.

[74]Rev. Albert Lacombe, O.M.I., *Dictionnaire et Grammaire de la Langue des Cris* (Montreal, 1874), 37, 60, 317, 329, 558.

[75]See above, Chaps. XIII, XIV, XX.

[76]See above, Ch. XXI.

[77]See Roe, *Indian and the Horse,* Ch. I, "From Dogs to Horses."

[78]See above, note 25, on Indian buffalo uses in addition to food.

mounted Indians who had acquired the horse on their own unauthorized initiative, totally independent of active or passive Spanish approval.[79] It is incredible to me that Obregón or some other member of the Spanish force would not have specified European cattle, had such been seen. It would have been an equal marvel.

With respect to another section of Mexico, two centuries or more later, Dr. Reed seemed similarly disposed to explain away what appears in itself to be a perfectly simple and straightforward statement. I quote his paragraph *verbatim*:

Another relevant contemporary source is an eighteenth-century account of Sonora by the Jesuit friar Pfefferkorn, which describes bison in the region to the northeast—"*In den Wildnissen, welche gegen Nordosten in die Gebirge der Apaches beruhen*"—a rather general term which could in fact refer to eastern New Mexico and West Texas; he evidently based this on information from others. . . .[80]

Dr. Reed did not indicate just what made it evident that Pfefferkorn based his statement on second-hand information, but if the missionary actually did, does it necessarily follow that this proves his informant to be unreliable? Why could not that northeastern wilderness in the mountains of the Apaches be taken to mean what it says—some mountainous portion of the Apache tribal territory, and hence most probably on the western side of the Rio Grande. It is difficult to see any reason for Dr. Reed's purely gratuitous suggestion that this specified *terrain* lies within the plains areas of eastern New Mexico and western Texas beyond a seemingly fixed determination to rule out Mexico by any argument that might offer. While the Apache country on either side of the Rio Grande-Gila watershed is not Mexico, once the formidable—and to some critics apparently fetish-like—obstacle of the Rio Grande has been passed, there seems no reason and certainly none is offered, why the buffalo could not have continued to wander southward through a broadly homotypical *terrain*. Any alleged lack of evidence is irrelevant while the evidence we have reviewed continued to be treated in such a manner, in clear conformity with an apparently settled determination to dismiss it.

Actually, there is further (inferential) evidence for buffalo in Mexico which Dr. Reed did not mention. In reference to the same broad era as that of Pfefferkorn, Bancroft cites an allusion to "tamed buffaloes," and also to cross-breeding with domestic cattle, in Chihuahua, Sonora, and Sinaloa.[81] This latter notice calls for more definite comment. It is admittedly conceivable that a mention of one species only (?*vacas*: *sans phrase*) could

[79]In 1567 (?), Francisco de Ibarra encountered mounted Indians in Sonora Valley (R. M. Denhardt, *The Horse of the Americas*, 87-92); cf. Roe, *Indian and the Horse*, 73; cf. above, note 71.

[80]Theodore E. Treutlein, translator and editor, *Pfefferkorn's Description of the Province of Sonora* (Ignaz Pfefferkorn, *Beschreibung der Landschaft Sonora*, Koln, 1794, 234), University of New Mexico, Albuquerque, N.M., 1949, 102. Cited by E. K. Reed, *Journal of Mammalogy*, 1952, 392.

[81]See above, 707, 818; citing Bancroft, *History of North Mexican States and Texas*, II, 750.

readily signify "cattle" almost as easily as *Bison americanus*. But I consider that the introduction of two differing species puts the case into another class of evidence. We know there was not at that time in frontier Mexico our modern wealth of *varying* European breeds upon which to draw for such purposes. The only other imaginable "cross-breeding" that could occur would be the intermixing of the ranging "wild cattle" of Mexico with their more strictly domesticated kindred in the village herds, and this, through the various accidents of flood and field—escape, negligence, etc.—would be too commonplace to attract notice.

Even this does not exhaust the historical evidence. Howsoever vague or unreliable the testimony of illiterate Hispano-Indian or Indian informants might be by reason of confusion or indifference, we have no ground for imputing such defects to Zebulon Montgomery Pike. Pike was perfectly aware of the visible distinctions between buffalo and European breeds. He was sent into the Spanish territories partly at least (whatever his ostensible mission may have been) to spy out the land, and certainly its faunal wealth and resources would not be ignored in the fulfilment of his purpose. Pike's competence and accuracy in other phases of his task have been acknowledged by authoritative critics; and Pike includes buffalo among the *fauna* of Coahuila in or about the year 1807.[82] It is inherently unlikely that he would either accept or reject such information on the assurance of one informant only; and if the intention had been to deceive the inquisitive *Americano*, it appears *à priori* much more probable that they would deny the presence of buffalo rather than affirm it falsely to an intruder whom they clearly held in suspicion.

A contemporary Southwestern scholar shows, however (on Spanish authority), that at this very time there really were buffalo in Coahuila, and quite apparently in sufficient quanties as to create a social/economic problem of some concern to the governing authorities of the country. J. Frank Dobie, whom I quote *verbatim*, records the following:

About 1934, Don Alberto Guajardo of Piedras Negras, Coahuila, showed me a document proving the existence of bison in Coahuila early in the last century. I have a translation of this document from which I quote. I think the original is in the archives of the University of Texas. The document is a letter from the Alcalde or some other official at Monclova, Coahuila, dated January 24, 1806, and transmits to the proper authority at Santa Rosa an order from the governor as follows:

"Buffalo hunting expeditions in the settlements of this province are the cause of the neglect of families. The expeditions cause settlers to lose interest in stock raising. They disrupt friendship with the Indian tribes. Hereafter, settlers are not to go out in organized parties for the sole purpose of hunting buffaloes.

"You are to circulate this order among the citizens of your community."[83]

Dobie adds: "There is a well-known arroyo in northern Coahuila called *Arroyo de los Cibolos*, which means Buffalo Creek."[84]

---

[82]*Expeditions of Pike*, ed. Coues, II, 738, 777. I am surprised at such an authority as Vernon Bailey (above, note 58) neglecting Pike, the first literate American in the territory, and so easily accessible!

[83]Dobie, *Journal of Mammalogy*, XXXIV (1953), 150.

[84]Correspondence to the present writer.

Dr. Reed attaches little or no weight to this testimony. But is not this the very thing to which Pike is alluding in 1807? He mentions attempts by the Spanish Government to convert buffalo-hunting tribes—in part at least— towards agriculture.[85] Pike instances these as having to do with Texas, but we have noted above that "Texas and Coahuila" were described very much as sister provinces, as naturally allied as "Kansas and Nebraska" or "Saskatchewan and Alberta."[86] And Pike is justly regarded by Dr. Reed as a reliable authority, within the scope of his own observation.

In a later paper, Dr. Reed modifies his position considerably, but to the present writer he still appears to pronounce too definitively from disputable data. He notes a statement by Father Francisco Garces (1776) concerning the hunting of "cibolas" by the Havasupai (Apache) of northern Arizona in the eighteenth century, on the Little Colorado River. Dr. Reed comments on this as follows:

This sounds like genuine local occurrence rather than long trips into Utah. Perhaps this could conceivably refer to wild (feral) cattle, but the term "cibola" is used. Statements by Walapai [or Hualapai] informants are quoted or summarized . . . as: "Only a few buffalo ever straggled into the Walapai country. . . . Buffalo were too large to hunt successfully, but in the old days the Walapai would now and then see a few. . . . Their occurrence in California also tends to support the idea of bison ranging . . . possibly even to northwestern Arizona fairly late. . . .[87]

The Havasupai Reservation is—or was in 1924—situated in an area bounded on the north and northeastward by the Grand Canyon of the Colorado itself and by the tributary Little Colorado River; the confluence being only some sixty miles or thereabouts southwest from the aforementioned *Mesa la Vaca*. The interesting feature in the Little Colorado testimony is that on the general argument for a further *westerly* penetration of the species in these latitudes than has been hitherto the accepted view; it is quite possible that the herds had to traverse the *Mesa la Vaca* locality to reach the Little Colorado.

Dr. Reed sums up thus:

Bison disappeared from central and western Mexico, no doubt long before historic times. Evidently they disappeared in much of Arizona before the Christian era. To about 1200 or 1250 A.D. there were still buffalo west of the Rio Grande in western New Mexico, abundant in the high enclosed basin of the plains of San Augustin and perhaps occasional in valleys further west; undoubtedly also in Coahuila and Chihuahua; very likely they were still present in the San Luis valley of southern Colorado, and possibly to be found on the western slope of Colorado and in central and southern Utah and perhaps also in northwestern Arizona.

The drought period of 1276-1299 A.D. may have seriously affected the bison (as Dr. Remington Kellogg suggests, letter of August 8, 1950) and other large

[85] *Expeditions of Pike*, ed. Coues, II, 785.

[86] See above, note 67.

[87] E. K. Reed, "Bison Beyond the Pecos," *Texas Journal of Science*, VII, 1955, 130-5; citing the *Diary and Itinerary of Francisco Garces*, ed. Coues, 1900, II, 403. 406. I have not seen this. The Little Colorado enters the main Colorado River about 50 or 60 miles Southwest from *Mesa la Vaca* (above, note 23).

animals, as it apparently did the human occupants of certain parts of the Southwest. The bison were all gone or were certainly very rare by historic times, west of the Pecos River; the last remnants must have disappeared at various times between 1300 and 1500 A.D. in various districts. Further south, however, west of the lower Rio Grande in Coahuila and northern Tamaulipas, bison survived to the nineteenth century.[88]

In querying the use of such a term as "a few" in the Walapai country for example, I do not suggest that the region ever saw the enormous hosts of the Plains, though there may have been no inherent reason why it should not have done so. But one would like to know just what constituted a *few* in the various informants' minds, where no estimates of numbers were mentioned. We may note that while leading generalizers on the buffalo are—I think soundly—agreed that the numbers east of the Mississippi were "mere stragglers,"[89] only one-twelfth of the aggregate host;[90] yet the herds were considered prodigious by those who encountered them in that territory, at a time when the Spanish or other descriptions of the truly huge masses were unknown.[91] So likewise, the drought period of 1276-99 might quite conceivably "seriously affect the bison," but is this expression to be accepted automatically as being something synonymous with extinction? And after all, this is only something which "may have" occurred.

Criticism is disarmed by the admirable candour with which Dr. Reed acknowledges earlier misconceptions. Other evidence may of course appear later which might necessitate a drastic revision of the present conclusions. But the net results—as based upon Dr. Reed's final summing-up, even had no other evidence been presented—can only be the critical rehabilitation of such early and *local* witnesses as Garces, Pfefferkorn, Berlandier, and Pike, whose accounts may be taken broadly to mean what they say. And of these, Dr. Berlandier, the one zoological student among them, describes the buffalo as being "numerous" near Monterey in 1602.[92]

---

[88]E. K. Reed, *Texas Journal of Science*, VII, 132-4.
[89]Hornaday, "Extermination of the American Bison," 388.
[90]Ernest Thompson Seton, *Life-Histories of Northern Animals*, I, 259, 262; *Game Animals*, III, 654-7.
[91]See above, Ch. XIII.
[92]Quoted above, Ch. XIX (see also above, note 67).

FOSSIL VESTIGES OF EXTINCT "SUPERBISON" FOUND IN SASKATCHEWAN (p. 19)

The discovery is announced (almost certainly the first of its kind any-where in the Canadian prairie territory) of the fossilized horns and a por-tion of the skull of a giant bison in the Province of Saskatchewan, of which the particulars are given in the original description below. While this deposit is neither the farthest west nor the farthest south in Canada (see above, Appendix L), it is none the less a discovery of immense importance. We are not informed whether or not the name of "superbison" is of their own choice; although I have never previously encountered it as being a recognized term for any of the (commonly) much larger fossil species. The huge size of the horns, and the broad frontal dimensions, in comparison with the historic prairie animal (*Bison americanus*), which are revealed by the happy inspiration of the photograph, perhaps tend to identify this specimen with *Bison crassicornis* ("the heavy-horned") or *Bison latifrons* ("broad-fronted"); two well-known classes among the fairly numerous fossil species. Since neither of these have ever been found in Canada, the exact identification of the Saskatchewan discovery will be of interest to palaeon-tologists. Below are the details of the discovery and some figures.

The account as printed, is from Bruce A. McCorquodale of the Provin-cial Museum and Archives of Alberta, Edmonton, Alberta:

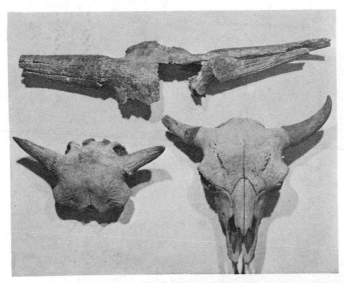

Cine-Graphic Division, Province of Saskatchewan

Fragment of the skull of an extinct "superbison" (above) and the skull of a large modern bison (below). Note great difference in size.

One of the most outstanding fossil discoveries ever made in Saskatchewan is a portion of the skull of a giant bison known as "superbison." Mr. B. DeVries in co-operation with the Bliss brothers, excavators, recovered this specimen from a gravel pit near Fort Qu'Appelle during gravel removal in August 1956. The genus "Superbison" is the largest known bison, being much larger than its modern relatives. (See photo.) Although a few others have been found in the Yukon, Alaska and the southern U.S.A. this is believed to be the most southerly and easterly record in Canada.

A complete study of this specimen remains to be made but preliminary judgment indicates that it is probably of interglacial age and at least one hundred thousand years old. This belief is supported by studies of the geological formation and the other fossil animals with which it was associated. It is worthy of note that this type of bison probably became extinct before man came to North America; no artifacts have ever been found in association with its bones.

The span of the tips of the horn cores if complete would be approximately five feet; with the horn shells present the span of the horns of this great bison would have been at least six feet. Imagination can scarcely conceive a bison with horns of such a dimension. The presence of this animal together with a musk-ox-like bovid, numerous large native horses and many elephants (mammoths), as indicated by the fossil evidence, presents a picture of a strange fauna, indeed, for the southern region of Saskatchewan.

Reprinted from *The Blue Jay*, XV, I (March, 1957), 42.

SUPPLEMENTARY BUFFALO SYNONYMY (p. 681)

Tribe	Buffalo	Horse	Dog (D) or Wolf (W)	Cervidae: Antelope (A), Deer (D), Elk (E), Moose (M)	Author
CALIFORNIANS					
Ap-woo-ro-kae	Goo'-choo				C. Hart Merriam, *Journal of Mammalogy* (U.S. 1926), 212
At-wum-we	Goo'-cho				
Ham-mah-we	Goo'-choo				
Klamath	Yuho'				
Northern Paiute	Goo-choo *or* Goot'tsoo				
Biloxi	yĭnisa, yn-nisahe'	tohoxk; ta indoke' + ita indoke toho 'xk, nixuxw naske' = *mule* (i.e. "long-eared horse")	D = tcuñki (*or* atcû-ñki) $W = ayih^n$	D = ta	Dorsey and Swanton, *Biloxi and Ofo Dictionary*, 1912. Wak, *cow* from Sp. *vaca*: so, Dorsey and Swanton, *op. cit.*
	nsa' intoki' = *B bull*				
	nsa' yanki' = *B cow*				
	nsa' yiñki = *B calf*				
Choctaw	Cow (domestic) wak, wax, waka	isuba	D = ipaf, ofi, ofi puta; *male* = ofi nakni; W = nashoba, *male* = nashoba nakni; *fem.* = washoba tek; Wolf-dog = nashoba iklanna	isi	Byington, *Choctaw Dictionary*, 1915
	B = yannash				
	B = calf *or* young = yannash				
	ushi. Cow (domestic) = wak, wak tok				
Clickitats	Kó-chō	Shecum			Rev. Samuel Parker (183) in Hulbert, *Marcus Whitman*, I, 125
Comanche	O-kom = *Buffalo bull*	Tā-ha-yēr-quoīp ("Horse's back," a chief, *circa* 1867)	W ēs-ā	Par-ri-ä	Richardson, *Comanche Barrier*, 19, 81, 279, 307, 363

Tribe	Buffalo	Horse	Dog (D) or Wolf (W)	Cervidae: Antelope (A), Deer (D), Elk (E), Moose (M)	Author
Cree	Mosto 'os; or puskwa' nemosto 'os	mistutim = *male*; napas' tim (fem.) nosā 'stim	D = utim, *male* napa 'stim; *fem.* nosa 'stim, koskanukos kunis	A kwa skwuti–a chikosis D utik. *Buck* = eyapa wutik, eyapa e. *Doe* = noosatik. E = wawa skasiw. M = mooswa	Rev. E. A. Watkins, *Cree Dictionary*, 1865; rev. 1938
Plain Cree	muskota' wemosto 'os		W = muhe' kun Coyote' = mastucha		
Swampy Cree	pisikew		Fox = muka' sew		
"Flathead" (Kalispel)	Ikoai stoma	Sachilzask-àgae. Esmilmilko epils = *stallion* smomshin = *mare* = soips, ka' gae = *American horse*	D = nkokos. W = ltamkae Coyote' = snkazos	A *male* = kaelschin; *fem.* = sta'an. D *male* = sgotech' chin. *fem.* = szooligu. E *male* = shetse; *fem.* = snechelze M = sgasalks	*Dictionary of the Kalispel or Flathead Language* (Societatis Jesu, 1879)
Haida			D = qa W = ghi 'ate	D = g'at E = tsi'cku	Grasserie, *Cinq Langues de la British Columbia*. Tolmie and Dawson, *Five Comparative Vocabularies* (1884)
Haida (Kaigani Sept.)	tan	kaiu-tin	D = ha W = ho-ootz	D = kauit E = wut-tsish	
Haida (Masset dialect)			D tsei-hiw, tsei-gu n, SH'-dl-ei. *male* tsei hiw, kiw. *fem.* tseihiw-me		
Kiowa	B = sk oc dl-hiw, B (as "*cattle*") = oc ga-piw, k oc dl. B *bull* = t oc p̀-p 'wdl	tsei	Coyote hou, kou'm; kue, sywn, m t'ou tsou-hi'	A = th-p, t oc p, t̂ oc n D = kwe-qu oc n	Harrington, *Kiowa Dictionary*, 1928

Tribe	Buffalo	Horse	Dog (D) or Wolf (W)	Cervidae: Antelope (A), Deer (D), Elk (E), Moose (M)	Author
Kwagiutl			D = wāts, watsa, uatsē, wats; W = tewha, koosheils, atllulum, atlunem; Fox = hatse iŭh	D = kulhum, kulhamin, sikwuno, khe'was; E = tlols	Grasserie, *Cinq Langues*, 1902
Natchez	was, wash (= "cow") Stem-word	was, wash	D = was, wash		Swanton, *American Anthropologist*, IX (1907), 521
Navajo	aў' ani	li	D = lichā-i, lechai, li'-chāi. W = mâ-itso; *Coyote'* = mâli, ma'ists' ŏ'si	A = jădi; D = bi'; E = dzĕ	*Vocabulary of the Navaho Language* (1912)
Nootka			D = ainítl; W = kh'ā'natla	D = A' tuc; E = tlō 'nem	Grasserie, *Cinq Langues*
Ofo		atchŭ' ñgasi; atcu' ñgasi; atcu' ngas; nashu 'sita (*mule*)	D = atchŭ 'ñki	D = i ya	Dorsey and Swanton, *Biloxi and Ofo Dictionary*, 1912
Ojibwa, Otchipwe, Chippewa, Sauteux, Saulteaux	Mashkode', pijiki; piji-kiwegin = B *robe*; cf. Cree mustusweyan *Cow* (*domestic*) pijiki, ikwe-pi-jiki	bebejigoganji (*i.e.* "*one-hoofed animal*")	D = animosh enim, animokadji; W = maingan, mainganika (*plural*)	D = wâwas-keshi; E = moose; M = mons	Baraga, *Grammar and Dictionary of the Otchipwe Tongue* (1879)
Osage	sha-ton-ga = *bull*; sha = *cow*	Kou-o-la = *horse*; Kou-o-la mingã = *mare*; Kou-o-la shinga = *colt*	D = shon-ga; W = sho-na ca-sa	D *male* = taw-ton-gă; *fem.* = taw min-ga; E *male* = o-pa-tongã; *fem.* = o-pa mingã	Bradbury, *Early Western Travels*, V, 216 (1811)

Tribe	Buffalo	Horse	Dog (D) or Wolf (W)	Cervidae: Antelope (A), Deer (D), Elk (E), Moose (M)	Author
Osage	wa-dsu-ta-ton-ga = B *bull.* tse = B *cow.* tsecka = *white* B	Ka-wa (corruption of Sp. *caballo*) So, La Flesche, *Osage Dictionary*, 82, 279	D = sho^n ge W = sho^n ge *Coyote* = sho'-mi-ka-çi	D = ta; wa'-dsu-ta zhi^n ga	F. LaFlesche, *Osage Dictionary* (1932) G. E. Hyde, *North Dakota History*, XVIII (1951), 201
Ponca	kawa (*plural*), *circa* 1730				
Thlinkit	hootz		D kyetl W ghoute, kowtsh D = kyetl W = ghoute, kowtsh D = hä-as W = hä-as	D khooká'n, kuakan E wut-sish tsish^n D = kua-kan E = wut-sish tsish D = wunn E = wit-zi, wid-si	Grasserie, *Cinq Langues* Tolmie and Dawson, *Five Comparative Vocabularies* *Ibid.*

BIBLIOGRAPHY

This is not intended as an exhaustive catalogue of sources for the history of the buffalo. It is confined to those works I have consulted, the last edition indicated being the one I have used.

Adair, James. *History of the American Indian* (orig. ed., London, 1775), ed. Samuel Cole Williams. Johnson City, Tenn., 1930.

Aiton, Arthur S. "The Later Career of Coronado." *American Historical Review*, XXX (1924), 298-304.

—— "The Muster Roll of Coronado." *Ibid.*, XLIV (1938), 556-70.

Albion, Robert G. *Forests and Sea Power*. Cambridge, Mass., 1926.

Allen, Joel A. *The American Bisons, Living and Extinct*. (*Memoirs of the Museum of Comparative Zoology*, IV, No. 10).Cambridge, Mass., 1876.[1]

—— "The Northern Range of the Bison." *American Naturalist*, XI (1877), 624.

American Anthropologist. In progress, 1895 *et seq.*

American Explorers (orig. ed., J. B. McMaster, 1904), 21 vols. New York, 1922.

American Historical Review. In progress, 1895 *et seq.*

American Naturalist. 1877.

Antiquity. England, in progress, 1927 *et seq.*

Armstrong, G. H. *The Origin and Meaning of Place-Names in Canada*. Toronto, 1930.

Ashe, Thomas. *Travels in America, Performed in the Year 1806*. London, 1808.

Audubon, John James, and Bachman, Rev. John. *The Quadrupeds of North America*, 2 vols. New York, 1846, 1854.

Baillie-Grohman, W. A. *Sport and Life*. London, 1900. Hunting reminiscence.

Ballantyne, R. M. *Hudson Bay: Everyday Life in the Wilds of North America . . . in the Territories of the Honourable Hudson's Bay Company* (orig. ed., 1848). London, 1879.

Bancroft, Hubert Howe. *Works*, 38 vols. San Francisco, Calif., 1883-90.

Native Races of the Pacific States. I-V, 1883.

History of the North Mexican States and Texas, 1531-1889. XV, 1884; XVI, 1889.

History of Arizona and New Mexico, 1530-1888. XVII, 1889.

History of California, 1542-1890. XVIII-XXIV, 1890.

---

[1]Identical matter also quoted by Hulbert (*Historic Highways*, I, 123-3) as from J. A. Allen, *Ninth Annual Report of the Department of the Interior* (Washington), 467. Likewise by E. T. Seton (*Game Animals*, III, 656, 664, 703, 708), as from J. A. Allen, "History of the American Bison," in *U.S. Geological and Geographical Survey, 1875*, Part III, "Zoology," 1877. I have not seen these.

BA8.   *History of Nevada, Colorado, and Wyoming.* XXV, 1890.

BA7.   *History of Utah.* XXVI, 1889.

BA1.   *History of Oregon, 1834-1888.* XXIX, 1885; XXX, 1888.

BA2.   *History of Washington, Idaho, and Montana, 1845-1889.* XXI, 1890.

BA6.   *History of the Northwest Coast,* 2 vols. 1886.

           History of Pastoral California, 1769-1849. XXIV, 1888.

Bartram, William. *The Travels of William Bartram, 1773-78* (orig. ed., 1791), ed. Mark Van Doren. New York, 1928.

Beard, Charles A. and Mary R. *The Rise of American Civilization,* 2 vols. New York, 1927, 1930.

Bell, Dr. Charles N. *The Journal of Henry Kelsey, 1691-1692.* Winnipeg: Historical and Scientific Society of Manitoba, 1928.

Bishop, Morris. *The Odyssey of Cabeza de Vaca.* New York, 1933.

BL.   Black, Norman Fergus. *A History of Saskatchewan and the Old North West,* 2nd edition. Regina, Sask., 1913.

Blair, Emma Helen. *Indian Tribes of the Great Lakes and Mississippi Valley Regions,* 2 vols. Cleveland, 1911. Comprises the descriptions of Nicolas Perrot, Bacqueville de la Potherie (English translations), Thomas Forsyth, and Morrell Marston, 1670-1815.

Blakiston, Capt. Thomas. "Report on the Exploration of the Kootanie and Boundary Passes of the Rocky Mountains in 1858." *Occasional Papers of the Royal Artillery Institution* (Woolwich, 1860), 118-20, 237-54.

Blue, John. *Alberta Past and Present,* 3 vols. Chicago, 1924.

Bolton, Herbert E. "Odoesmades." *Handbook of American Indians* (*q.v.*), II, 106.

Borrodaile, L. A. *The Animal and its Environment.* London, 1923.

Brackenridge, Henry M. *Journal of a Voyage up the Missouri, 1811* (2nd edition, 1816), ed. R. G. Thwaites (*q.v.*). (*Early Western Travels,* VI). Cleveland, 1904. The author journeyed partly with the westbound Astorians.

Bradbury, John. *Travels in the Interior of North America* (orig. ed., 1817). (*Early Western Travels,* ed. R. G. Thwaites (*q.v.*)., V). Cleveland, 1904. Westward with the Astorians under Wilson P. Hunt.

Brady, Cyrus T. *Indian Fights and Fighters.* New York, 1909.

Bringing Back the Buffalo. Ottawa: Department of the Interior, 1926. *Re* Wood Buffalo Park, North West Territories.

British-American Magazine, ed. H. Y. Hind (*q.v.*). Toronto, 1863 *et seq.*

Brittain, Alfred. *Discovery and Exploration.* (*History of North America* (*q.v.*), I). New York, 1903.

Brooks, C. E. P. *Climate through the Ages.* London, 1926.

Bruce, H. Addington. *Daniel Boone and the Wilderness Road* (orig. ed., 1910). New York, 1922.

BR.   Bryce, George. *The Remarkable History of the Hudson's Bay Company* (orig. ed., 1900). Toronto, 1904.

Buchanan, Angus. *Wild Life in Canada.* London, 1920.

Buckle, H. T. *History of Civilization* (orig. ed., 1861), 3 vols. (World's Classics). London, 1903-11.

Bullock, William. *Sketch of a Journey through the Western States of North America, 1827* (orig. ed., 1827) (*Early Western Travels,* ed. R. G. Thwaites, (*q.v.*), XIX). Cleveland, 1905.

Burke, Ulick R. *A History of Spain from the Earliest Times to the Death of Ferdinand the Catholic* (orig. ed., 1894), ed. Martin A. S. Hume, 2 vols. London, 1900.

Burpee, Lawrence J. "Grand Portage." *Proceedings of the Minnesota Historical Society* (1931), 359-77. Address to the State Historical Convention.

—— "Highways of the Fur Trade." *Proceedings and Transactions of the Royal Society of Canada*, 2nd Ser., VIII (1904), Sec. II, 183-92.

—— (ed.). "The Journal of Antony Hendry" (Henday, 1754-55). *Ibid.*, 3rd Ser., I (1907), Sec. II, 307-54.

—— (ed.). *The Journal of F. A. Larocque* (1805). (Publications of the Canadian Archives, No. 3.) Ottawa, 1910.

—— (ed.). "The Journal of Matthew Cocking" (1772-73). *Proceedings and Transactions of the Royal Society of Canada*, 3rd Ser., II (1908), Sec. II, 89-121.

—— *The Search for the Western Sea*. New York, 1908.

Burton, John Hill. *History of Scotland*, 2nd edition, 9 vols. Edinburgh, 1874.

Burton, Sir Richard F. *The City of the Saints*. New York, 1860.

U1.   Butler, Sir W. F. *The Great Lone Land* (orig. ed., 1872), 17th edition. London, 1910.

U2.   —— *The Wild North Land* (orig. ed., 1874), 7th edition. London, 1878.

—— *An Autobiography*, edited by his daughter. London, n.d.

Buttrick, Tilly, Jr. *Voyages, Travels, and Discoveries, 1812-1819* (orig. ed., 1851). (*Early Western Travels*, ed. R. G. Thwaites (*q.v.*), VIII.) Cleveland, 1904.

Y.   Byrne, P. E. *The Red Men's Last Stand*. London, 1927. Some important critical revisions of 'Custer' fables, etc.

Cabeza de Vaca. *The Journey of Alvar Nuñez Cabeza de Vaca and his Companions from Florida to the Pacific, 1528-1536*, ed. Fanny Bandelier. (*American Explorers* (*q.v.*).) New York, 1922. His own narrative translated and edited by Fanny Bandelier with an introduction by A. F. Bandelier. *See also* Bishop, Morris, *and* Hallenbeck, Cleve.

Canada, Commission of Conservation. *Annual Reports*. Ottawa.

——, Department of the Interior, Parks Branch. *Reports*. Ottawa, annually.

——, Department of Public Archives. *Reports*. Ottawa, annually.

Canadian Field Naturalist. In progress.

Canadian Forum. In progress.

Canadian Geological Survey. *Memoirs*. Ottawa, annually.

Canadian Historical Association. *Annual Reports*. Ottawa.

Canadian Historical Review. In progress, 1920 *et seq.* Indispensable for Canadian history, particularly its very full bibliographies.

Canadian Pacific Railway. *See* Fleming, Sandford, *et al.*, Gibbon, J. M., *and* Innis, H. A.

AT.   Catlin, George. *Letters and Notes on the North American Indians*, 8th edition, 2 vols. London, 1851.

Champlain, Samuel de. *Voyages and Explorations of Samuel de Champlain, 1604-1616, narrated by himself*, ed. Edward G. Bourne, 2 vols. (*Trailmakers of Canada*.) Toronto, 1911. Translated by Annie Nettleton Bourne.

———— *Voyages and Explorations of Samuel de Champlain, 1604-1616*, ed. H. P. Biggar, 6 vols. Toronto: Champlain Society, 1922-36.

CH.   Chittenden, H. M. *The History of the American Fur Trade of the Far West*, 3 vols. New York, 1902. *See also* De Smet.

Christy, Miller. "The Last of the Buffaloes." *The Field* (London, November 10, 1888), 698.

Cocking, Matthew. *See* Burpee, L. J.

CN.   Colden, Cadwallader. *The History of the Five Indian Nations of Canada* (orig. ed., 1730), 2 vols. (*American Explorers* (*q.v.*).) New York, 1922.

Coman, Katharine. *Economic Beginnings of the Far West*, 2 vols. New York, 1912.

JC.   Coronado. *The Journey of Coronado, 1540-1542*, ed. George P. Winship. (*American Explorers* (*q.v.*).) New York, 1922. Comprises the accounts of Coronado and his followers, as translated by G. P. Winship: the Chronicle of Castaneda, Coronado to the Viceroy Mendoza, Coronado to Charles V, Narrative of Jaramillo, the "Relacion del Suceso," the "Anonymous Document" ("Traslado de Las Nuevas"), and the Report of Hernando de Alvarado.

CS1.   Coues, Elliott (ed.). *The Expeditions of Zebulon Montgomery Pike* (1805-6-7), 3 vols. New York, 1895.

    ———— (ed.). *The Journal of Jacob Fowler.* New York, 1898.

CS2.   ———— (ed.). *New Light on the Early History of the Greater Northwest*: *The Henry-Thompson Journals* (1799-1814), 3 vols. New York, 1897.

Country Life. London, in progress.

Cowie, Isaac. *The Company of Adventurers.* Toronto, 1913. Comprises Hudson's Bay Company reminiscence, 1867-74.

Cox, J. Charles. *The Royal Forests of England.* London, 1905.

CX.   Cox, Ross. *The Columbia River*, 2nd edition, 2 vols. London, 1832.

Cresswell, Nicholas. *The Journal of Nicholas Cresswell, 1774-1777* (orig. ed., 1924), ed. A. G. Bradley. New York. 1928.

Croghan, Col. George. *Journals* (1750-65). (*Early Western Travels*, ed. R. G. Thwaites (*q.v.*), I.) Cleveland, 1904.

Cuming, Fortescue. *Tour to the Western Country, 1807-1809* (orig. ed., 1810). (*Early Western Travels*, ed. R. G. Thwaites (*q.v.*), IV.) Cleveland, 1904.

DAS.   Dale, H. C. (ed.). *The Ashley-Smith Explorations, and the Discovery of a Central Route to the Pacific, 1822-1829.* Cleveland, 1918. Includes the original journals.

Darwin, Charles. *The Descent of Man* (orig. ed., London, 1871). New York, 1898.

    ———— *Journal of Researches during the Voyage of the 'Beagle.'* (Everyman's Library.) London, 1906.

    ———— *The Origin of Species* (orig. ed., London, 1859). New York, 1897-98.

Davidson, G. C. *The North West Company* (University of California Publications in History.) Berkeley, Calif., 1918.

Davis, Thomas M. "Building the Burlington through Nebraska." *Nebraska History*, XXX (1949), 317-47.

Davis, W. H. H. *The Spanish Conquest of New Mexico.* New York, 1867.

Denhardt, Robert M. *The Horse of the Americas.* Norman, Okla., 1947.

Denny, Sir Cecil E. *The Law Marches West, 1874-1905,* ed. W. B. Cameron. Toronto, 1938.

—— Manuscript reminiscence in Provincial Legislative Library, Edmonton, Alta. Cited as Denny MS.[2]

De Smet, Rev. Father Pierre Jean. *Letters and Sketches with a Narrative of a Year's Residence among the Indian Tribes of the Rocky Mountains* (orig. ed., 1843). (*Early Western Travels,* ed. R. G. Thwaites (*q.v.*), XXVII.) Cleveland, 1906.

—— *Life, Letters, and Labours of Father P. J. DeSmet, 1801-1873,* eds. H. M. Chittenden and A. T. Richardson, 4 vols. New York, 1905.

—— *Oregon Missions and Travels over the Rocky Mountains, 1845-1846* (orig. ed., 1847). (*Early Western Travels,* ed. R. G. Thwaites (*q.v.*), XXIX.) Cleveland, 1906.

De Soto, Hernando. *Narratives of the Career of Hernando de Soto, in the Conquest of Florida, 1539-1542,* ed. E. G. Bourne, 2 vols. (*American Explorers* (*q.v.*).) New York, 1922. Comprises the narrative of the Gentleman of Elvas, the "Relacion" of Luys Hernandez de Biedma, and Oviedo's account from the *Historia General,* based upon the Diary of Rodrigo Ranjel, De Soto's secretary.

Dickens, Charles. *Letters* (orig. ed., 1882), edited by his daughter. London, 1909.

Diller, Dorothy. "Early Economic Development of Alberta previous to 1905." Unpublished Master's thesis, University of Alberta, 1923. Manuscript in Provincial Legislative Library, Edmonton, Alta.

Ditmars, Raymond L. *The Reptile Book.* New York, 1908.

Dobie, J. Frank. *The Flavor of Texas.* Dallas, Texas, 1936.

—— *Mustangs and Cow Horses.* Austin, Texas, 1940.

Dodge, Col. Richard Irving. *Our Wild Indians.* Hartford, Conn., 1883, 1886.

—— *The Plains of the Great West,* New York, 1877.

Donkin, John G. *Trooper and Redskin in the Far Northwest.* London, 1889. *Re* the Royal North West Mounted Police, 1884-88.

Douglas, George M. *Lands Forlorn.* New York, 1914. *Re* expedition to Hearne's Coppermine River, 1911-12.

Dowling, D. B. *The Southern Plains of Alberta.* (*Memoirs of the Canadian Geological Survey,* No. 93.) Ottawa, 1917.

Drannan, William F. *Thirty-One Years on the Plains and in the Mountains* (1847-78). Chicago, 1900.

Dunham, S. A. *A History of Spain and Portugal,* 5 vols. London, 1832.

Early Western Travels. See Thwaites, R. G.

Edmonton Bulletin. Edmonton, Alta., daily.

Edmonton Journal. Edmonton, Alta., daily.

[2]There are two manuscripts by Denny in the Provincial Legislative Library, Edmonton, containing much identical matter, but not wholly so. Instead of printing either *in toto,* they should in my judgment have been collated. The unprinted one contains a chapter on the buffalo. In this, while the author's generalizations are of little value, owing to insufficient comparative study, there is first-hand reminiscence of actual experiences, some of it absolutely unique in the buffalo literature. This is most deplorably omitted from the printed work.

Eiseley, Loren C. "Did the Folsom Bison Survive in Canada?" *Scientific Monthly* (New York), LVI (May, 1943), 468-72.
—— "Post-Glacial Climate Amelioration and the Extinction of Bison Taylori." *Science* (New York), XCV (June 26, 1942), 646.
Ekwall, Eilert. *English River-Names.* Oxford, 1928.
Encyclopaedia Britannica, 11th and 14th editions.
English Historical Review. In progress, 1886 *et seq.*
English Place-Name Society, annual publications 1924, *et seq.* Cited by counties, e.g. *Place-Names of Buckinghamshire,* 1925; *Place-Names of Worcestershire,* 1927, etc.
Ermatinger, Edward. "York Factory Express Journal: Being a Record of Journeys made between Fort Vancouver and Hudson Bay in the Years, 1827-28." *Transactions of the Royal Society of Canada,* 3rd Ser., VI (1912), Sec. II, 67-132.
Evans, Estwick. *A Pedestrious Tour Through the Western States and Territories, 1818* (orig. ed., 1819). (*Early Western Travels,* ed. R. G. Thwaites (*q.v.*), VIII.) Cleveland, 1904.
Everyman Historical Atlas of the World, 3 vols. London, 1906 *et. seq.*
Ewers, John C. "The Last Bison Drives of the Blackfoot Indians." *Journal of the Washington Academy of Sciences,* XXXIX (November, 1949), 355-60.
Farnham, Thomas J. *Travels in the Great Western Prairies, 1839* (orig. ed., 1843). (*Early Western Travels,* ed. R. G. Thwaites (*q.v.*), XXVIII-XXIX.) Cleveland, 1906.
Faux, William. *Memorable Days in America, 1818-1820* (orig. ed., 1823). (*Early Western Travels,* ed. R. G. Thwaites (*q.v.*), XII.) Cleveland, 1905.
Field, The. London, in progress.
Fiske, John. *The Beginnings of New England.* New York, 1894.
—— *The Discovery of America,* 2 vols. New York, 1892.
Flagg, Edmund. *The Far West, 1836-1837* (orig. ed., 1838). (*Early Western Travels,* ed. R. G. Thwaites (*q.v.*), XXVI-XXVII.) Cleveland, 1906.
Fleming, Sandford, *et al. Report of Progress on the Explorations and Surveys for a Canadian Pacific Railway, up to January 1, 1874.* Ottawa, 1874.
Fletcher, Alice C. "Buffalo." *Handbook of American Indians (q.v.),* I, 169-70.
—— "Trading Posts." *Ibid.,* II, 798.
Flint, James. *Letters from America, 1818-1820* (orig. ed., 1822). (*Early Western Travels,* ed. R. G. Thwaites (*q.v.*), IX.) Cleveland, 1904.
Flower, Richard. *Letters from Lexington and the Illinois, 1819* (orig. ed., 1822). (*Early Western Travels,* ed. R. G. Thwaites (*q.v.*), X.) Cleveland, 1904.
Ford, Richard. *Gatherings from Spain* (orig. ed., 1846). (Everyman's Library.) London, 1907.
Forest and Stream. New York, in progress.
Fortier, Alice, and Ficklen, John R. *Central America and Mexico* (*History of North America* (*q.v.*), IX.) New York, 1907.
Franchère, Gabriel. *A Voyage to the Northwest Coast of America, 1811-1814*

(orig. ed., 1854). (*Early Western Travels*, ed. R. G. Thwaites (*q.v.*), VI.) Cleveland, 1904.

N.   Franklin, Sir John. *Narrative of a Journey to the Shores of the Polar Sea, in the Years 1819, 1820, 1821, and 1822.* London, 1825.
———— *Narrative of a Second Expedition to the Shores of the Polar Sea, in the Years 1825, 1826, and 1827.* London, 1828.

Fraser, Simon. "First Journal of Simon Fraser," ed. A. G. Doughty. *Report of the Canadian Archives, 1929* (Ottawa), 109-59.
———— "Letters from the Rocky Mountains." *Ibid.*

R.   Frémont, John C. *Narrative of the Exploring Expedition to the Rocky Mountains in the Year 1842; and to Oregon and North California in the Years 1843-44.* London, 1846.

Froude, James Anthony. *History of England* (1520-88), 10 vols. (Everyman's Library.) London, 1906 et seq.

Fynn, A. J. *The American Indian as a Product of Environment.* Boston, 1908.

Galbraith, J. S. "The Hudson's Bay Company under Fire, 1847-1862." *Canadian Historical Review*, XXX (1949), 322-35.

Ganong, W. F. (ed.). *A New Relation of Gaspesia*, by Father Christian Le Clercq. Toronto: Champlain Society, 1910.

Garretson, Martin S. *The American Bison.* New York, 1938.

Garrioch, Rev. Alfred. Beaver-Cree-English Vocabulary (manuscript). Mr. Garrioch was a missionary (Anglican) in the Diocese of Athabaska, *circa* 1875.

.   Gass, Patrick. *Journal of the Lewis and Clark Expedition* (orig. ed., 1811), ed. J. K. Hosmer. Chicago, 1904.

Gates, C. M. (ed.). *Five Fur Traders of the Northwest.* University of Minnesota, 1933. Comprises the narrative of Peter Pond, and the diaries of John McDonnell, Archibald N. McLeod, Hugh Faries, and Thomas Connor.

Geographical Journal. London, in progress.

Geographical Magazine. London, in progress.

Gibbon, Edward. *The Decline and Fall of the Roman Empire* (orig. ed., 1776-88), ed. H. H. Milman, 5 vols. New York, n.d.

Gibbon, John Murray. *Steel of Empire. Toronto*, 1935. A history of the Canadian Pacific Railway.

Gilmour, Rev. James. *Among the Mongols.* London, 1885.

Goodwin, George G. "Buffalo Hunt—1935." *Natural History* (New York, September, 1935), 156-63.

Graham, Maxwell. *Canada's Wild Buffalo.* Ottawa: Department of the Interior, 1923. Includes an appendix by F. V. Seibert.

Graham, R. B. Cunninghame. *The Conquest of the River Plate.* London, 1924. A history of Cabeza de Vaca.
———— *The Horses of the Conquest.* London, 1930.

Grant, Rev. George M. *Ocean to Ocean* (orig. ed., 1873), ed. W. L. Grant. Toronto: Radisson Society, 1925. An account of Sandford Fleming's expedition across Canada, 1872.

Greenbie, Sydney. *Frontiers and the Fur Trade.* New York, 1929.

Gregg, Josiah. *The Commerce of the Prairies, 1831-39* (orig. ed., 1845).

(*Early Western Travels*, ed. R. G. Thwaites (*q.v.*), XIX-XX.) Cleveland, 1905.

Grinnell, George B. *The Fighting Cheyennes*. New York, 1915.

——— "Horses." *Handbook of American Indians* (*q.v.*), I, 569-71.

GN. ——— *Indians of To-Day* (orig. ed., 1900). New York, 1911.

Hakluyt, Richard. *The Principall Navigations, Voyages [Traffiques], and Discoveries of the English Nation* (orig. ed., 1589), 8 vols. (Everyman's Library.) London, 1907.

Hallenbeck, Cleve. *The Journey and Route of Alvar Nuñez Cabeza de Vaca*. New York, 1940.

Hamilton, Peter J. *The Colonization of the South* (*History of North America* (*q.v.*), III.) New York, 1907.

Hamilton, W. J. *American Mammals*. New York, 1939.

Hancock, Samuel. *The Narrative of Samuel Hancock, 1845-1860*, ed. A. D. Howden Smith. New York, 1927.

HAN. *Handbook of American Indians North of Mexico*, ed. F. W. Hodge, 2 vols. Washington, 1910.

Handbook of Canadian Indians. Ottawa: National Geographic Board, 1913. Includes many reprints from *Handbook of American Indians*.

Handbook of South American Indians, ed. Julian H. Steward. Washington: Bureau of American Ethnology, 1945 *et seq.*

Hargrave, Letitia. *Letters of Letitia Hargrave*, ed. Margaret Arnott McLeod. Toronto: Champlain Society, 1947. Hudson's Bay Company reminiscence.

HAR. Harmon, Daniel Williams. *A Journal of Voyages and Travels in the Interior of North America* (orig. ed., 1820). (*American Explorers* (*q.v.*).) New York, 1922.

Harrison, William. *A Description of England, 1577* (originally prefixed to Holinshed's *Chronicle*, 1587), ed. F. J. Furnivall, 3 vols. London: New Shakspeare Society, 1877.

Hart, Albert Bushnell. "Imagination in History." *American Historical Review*, XV (January, 1910), 230.

Harting, J. E. *Extinct British Animals*. London, 1880.

Hawkes, John. *Saskatchewan and her People*, 3 vols. Chicago, 1924.

HAW. Haworth, Paul L. *Trailmakers of the Northwest*. Toronto, 1921.

Hearne, Samuel. *A Journey from Prince of Wales's Fort in 1770, 1771, and 1772*, ed. J. B. Tyrrell. Toronto: Champlain Society, 1911.

——— and Turnor, Philip. *Journals* (1789 *et seq.*), ed. J. B. Tyrrell. Toronto: Champlain Society, 1934.

Hebard, Grace Raymond, and Brininstool, E. A. *The Bozeman Trail*, 2 vols. Cleveland, 1922. A scholarly work, embodying much research.

Helps, Sir Arthur. *The Spanish Conquests in America* (orig. ed., 1855-61), 4 vols. London, 1900-4.

Henday. *See* Burpee, L. J.

HE. Hennepin. *See* Thwaites, R. G.

Henry, Alexander ('the elder'). *Travels and Adventures in Canada and the Indian Territories between the years 1760 and 1776*. New York, 1809.

Henry, Alexander ('the younger': nephew of the above). *See* Coues, E.

Hewett, Edgar Lee. *Ancient Life in the American Southwest*. Indianapolis, 1930.

Hewitt, C. Gordon. *The Conservation of the Wild Life of Canada.* New York, 1921.

Hind, Henry Youle (ed.). *The British-American Magazine.* Toronto, 1863 *et seq.* An early attempt at a Canadian *Quarterly Review,* which apparently did not long survive.

———— *Narrative of the Dawson and Hind Expedition,* 2 vols. London, 1860. The same material as in the following work, with a few additional episodes and in more attractive literary form.

———— *Report on the Assiniboine and Saskatchewan Exploring Expedition of 1858.* Published by authority of the Legislative Assembly, Toronto, 1859. Invaluable for the territory east of the South Saskatchewan River.[3]

History of North America, The, eds. Lee, G. C. and Thorpe, F. N., 20 vols. New York, 1903-7.

Honigmann, John J. "Parallels in the Development of Shamanism among Northern and Southern Athapaskans." *American Anthropologist,* LI (1949), 512-14.

Horan, J. W. *On the Side of the Law.* Edmonton, 1944. A biography of J. D. Nicholson, formerly of the Royal North West Mounted Police.

Hornaday, William T. "The Extermination of the American Bison, with a Sketch of its Discovery and Life History." *Smithsonian Report, 1887* (Washington, 1889), Part II, 367-548.

Hubbard, A. J. and G. *Neolithic Dew-Ponds and Cattle Ways.* London, 1905.

Hudson's Bay Company. *Report from the Select Committee on the Hudson's Bay Company, 1857.* London, 1857.

———— *The Beaver.* 1920 *et seq.* Hudson's Bay Company quarterly.

Hughes, Katherine. *Father Lacombe, the Black-Coat Voyageur.* Toronto, 1911.

Hulbert, Archer Butler. *Forty-Niners.* Boston, 1931. Contemporary letters, narratives, reminiscences, etc., of the Overland Trail journey of 1849, skilfully and delightfully woven into semi-continuous form.

———— *The Historic Highways of America,* 16 vols. Cleveland, 1902-5. Severe criticism of the author's prehistoric speculations must not obscure the high value of his more purely historical research.

Indians' Book, The, ed. Natalie Curtis. New York, 1907. Indian folk-songs translated, with the original music.

Ingram, David. "The Land Travels of David Ingram and others in the years 1568-69," edited from the original manuscript (Sloane MSS., British Museum, No. 1447, ff. 1-18) by Plowden J. C. Weston. *Documents connected with the History of South Carolina* (London, 1856), 14.

Inman, Henry. *The Old Santa Fé Trail.* New York, 1898. *See also* Jones, 'Buffalo.'

Innis, Harold. *The Fur Trade in Canada.* New Haven, 1930. A masterly survey.

[3]There are either one or two reprints of Hind's *Report,* printed 1859 or 1860, identical in subject matter, and almost but not exactly the same sized pages, which produced a slight difference in page-numbering. This gives rise to some confusion as the book progresses, and requires careful checking.

———— *A History of the Canadian Pacific Railway.* Toronto, 1923.

———— *Peter Pond, Fur Trader and Adventurer.* Toronto, 1930.

———— "Rupert's Land in 1825." *Canadian Historical Review*, VII (1926) 302-3.

International Atlas of the World. New York: Cram Publishing Co., 1924.

IR3. Irving, Washington. *Adventures of Captain Bonneville* (orig. ed., 1836). (*Complete Works*, XI, 1-358.) New York, n.d.

IR2. ———— *Astoria* (orig. ed., 1834). (*Ibid.*, VIII, 1-464.) New York, n.d.

———— *Complete Works*, 12 vols. New York, n.d.

IR1 ———— *A Tour of the Prairies* (orig. ed., 1832). (*Ibid.*, VII, 369-527.) New York, n.d.

James, Edwin. *An Account of an Expedition from Pittsburg to the Rocky Mountains, Performed in the Years 1819, 1820; Under the Command of Major Stephen Long, 1823.* (*Early Western Travels*, ed. R. G. Thwaites (*q.v.*), XIV-XVII.) Cleveland, 1905.

Jenness, Diamond (ed.). *The American Aborigines, Their Origin and Antiquity.* Toronto, 1933. Essays by expert scholars.

———— *The Copper Eskimo.* (*Report of the Canadian Arctic Expedition, 1913-1918*, XII.) Ottawa, 1923.

———— *The Indians of Canada.* (National Museum of Canada, Bulletin 15.) Ottawa, 1932.

———— *The Sarcee Indians of Alberta.* (National Museum of Canada, Bulletin 90; Anthropological Series, No. 23.) Ottawa, 1938.

JR. *Jesuit Relations.* See Thwaites, R. G.

JO. Jones, C. J. *Buffalo Jones' Forty Years of Adventure*, ed. Col. Henry Inman. London, 1899.

Jones, L. R., and Bryan, P. W. *North America* (orig. ed., 1924). London, 1928. Regional geography.

Journal of Ecology. England, in progress.

KA. Kane, Paul. *Wanderings of an Artist among the Indians of North America* (1846-48). Toronto, 1859.

———— *Wanderings of an Artist among the Indians of North America*, ed. L. J. Burpee. Toronto: Radisson Society, 1925.

Kelly, L. V. *The Rangemen.* Toronto, 1913.

Kelsey, Henry. *The Kelsey Papers*, eds. A. G. Doughty and Chester Martin. Ottawa, 1929. *See also* Bell, C. N.

Kendall, George Wilkins. *Narrative of the Texas Santa Fé Expedition* (orig. ed., 1844), ed. Milo M. Quaife. New York, 1929.

Kenton, Edna. *Simon Kenton, His Life and Period* (1755-1836). New York, 1930.

Kidd, Kenneth E. "Blackfoot Ethnography." Unpublished Master's thesis, University of Toronto, 1937. Pp. 223, with a rich bibliography. A most valuable monograph, embodying much research.

Kitto, F. H. "The Survival of the American Bison in Canada." *Geographical Journal* (London), LXIII (1924), 431-7.

Kroeber, A. L. *Cultural and Natural Areas in Native North America.* Berkeley, Calif., 1939.

Lacombe, Rev. Father Albert, O.M.I. *Dictionnaire et Grammaire de la Langue des Cris.* Montreal, 1874.

LaSalle. *The Journeys of Robert René Cavelier, Sieur de la Salle*, ed. I. J. Cox, 2 vols. (*American Explorers* (*q.v.*).) New York, 1922. Includes the accounts of Henri de Tonty; Fathers Zenobius Membre, Anastasius Douay, Christian Le Clercq, and Louis Hennepin; La Salle's brother, Jean Cavelier, and his trusted subordinate, Henri Joutel. Also various memorials, etc.

Laut, Agnes C. *The Conquest of the Great Northwest* (orig. ed., 1908), 6th edition, 2 vols. New York, 1918.

———— *The Overland Trail.* New York, 1929.

———— *Pathfinders of the West.* New York, 1904. Re Radisson and Groseilliers.

———— *Pilgrims of the Santa Fé.* New York, 1931.

———— *The Romance of the Rails*, 2 vols. New York, 1929. These works exhibit the characteristic merits and defects of the author's profession. She has the quick eye for a story, and the sure dramatic touch, with a style always readable, often rich and racy. But there is also the newspaperman's haste and resultant inaccuracy, and a disdain of revision in subsequent editions. Her works may be history among journalists; they are merely journalism among historians.

La Vérendrye. *Journals and Letters of Pierre Gualtier De Varennes, Sieur de la Vérendrye, and his Sons*, ed. L. J. Burpee. Toronto: Champlain Society, 1927.

———— "La Vérendrye's Journey of 1738," ed. D. Brymner. *Report of Canadian Archives, 1889* (Ottawa), 1-27.

Legardeur de Saint Pierre (Jacques Repentigny). "Journal," ed. D. Brymner. *Report of the Canadian Archives, 1886* (Ottawa).

Lescarbot, Marc. *A History of New France* (3rd ed., 1618), ed. H. P. Biggar, 3 vols. Toronto: Champlain Society, 1907-14.

Lewis, Merewether, and Clark, William. *Journals of the Expedition of 1804-1806* (orig. ed., Nicholas Biddle, 1814), 3 vols. (*American Explorers* (*q.v.*).) New York, 1922.

Lewis, Francis J., Dowding, Eleanor S., and Moss, E. H. "The Vegetation of Alberta." Part I (Lewis, Dowding), *Journal of Ecology* (London), XIV (1926), No. 2; Part II (Lewis, Dowding, Moss), *ibid.*, XVI (February, 1928), No. 1, 19-70; Part III (Dowding), *ibid.*, XVII (February, 1929), No. 1, 82-105; Part IV (Moss), *ibid.*, XX (August, 1932), No. 2, 380-405.

Lindquist, G. E. E. *The Red Man in the United States.* New York, 1923.

Lloyd Morgan, C. *Animal Life and Intelligence.* London, 1891.

Long, John. *Voyages and Travels, 1768-1782* (orig. ed., 1791). (*Early Western Travels*, ed. R. G. Thwaites (*q.v.*), II.) Cleveland, 1904.

Long, M. H. *A History of the Canadian People*, I. Toronto, 1942.

———— *Knights-Errant of the Wilderness.* Toronto, 1920.

Long, Stephen H. *See* James, Edwin.

Loudon, W. J. *A Canadian Geologist.* Toronto, 1930. A biography of J. B. Tyrrell.

Lowie, Robert H. "Ceremonialism in North America." *American Anthropologist*, XVI (1914), 602-31.

Lucas, F. A. "The Fossil Bisons of North America." *Proceedings of the*

U.S. National Museum (Washington), XXI (1899), No. 1172, 755-71. With 20 plates.

Lydekker, R. *Wild Life of the World,* 3 vols. London, 1915.

MacInnes, C. M. *In the Shadow of the Rockies.* London, 1930. A history of southern Alberta.

MacKay, Douglas. *The Honourable Company.* Indianapolis, 1936. Hudson's Bay Company history.

Mackenzie, Sir Alexander. *Voyages from Montreal, on the River St. Lawrence, through the Continent of North America to the Frozen and Pacific Oceans, in the Years 1789 and 1793* (orig. ed., London, 1801), including the *General History of the Fur Trade,* prefixed. Philadelphia, 1802.

Mackenzie, Rev. John. *Day-Dawn in Dark Places.* London, 1882. An account of missionary labours in South Africa, 1858 *seq.*

Mackinder, H. W. *Britain and the British Seas* (orig. ed., 1902). London, 1915.

MCSF. Maclean, Rev. John. *Canadian Savage Folk.* Toronto, 1896.

ME. ———— *The Indians of Canada,* 3rd ed. London, 1892.

———— *McDougall of Alberta.* Toronto, 1927. A biography of Rev. Dr. John McDougall.

Macleod, J. E. A. "Piegan Post and the Blackfoot Trade." *Canadian Historical Review,* XXIV (1943), 273-9.

Macoun, John. *Autobiography.* Memorial volume published by the Ottawa Field Naturalists' Club, Ottawa, 1922.

MN. ———— *Manitoba and the Great North West.* Guelph, Ont., 1882.

MacRae, A. O. *History of Alberta,* 2 vols. Calgary, 1912.

Mair, Charles, and McFarlane, Roderick. *Through the Mackenzie Basin.* Toronto, 1908.

MA1. Marcy, Gen. Randolph B. *Exploration of the Red River of Louisiana, in the Year 1852.* Washington, 1854.

MA2. ———— *The Prairie Traveller.* New York, 1859. A guide-book.

Masson, L. R. *Les Bourgeois de la Compagnie du Nord-Ouest,* 2 vols. Quebec, 1889, 1890.

Mawer, Sir Allen. *The Chief Elements Used in English Place-Names.* Cambridge: English Place-Name Society, 1924. Sir Allen was Director of the English Place-Name Society survey, 1924-42.

Maximilian, Prince of Wied. *Travels in the Interior of North America, 1833-1834* (orig. ed., 1843). (*Early Western Travels,* ed. R. G. Thwaites (*q.v.*), XXII-XXV.) Cleveland, 1906.

Maxwell, Marius. *Stalking Big Game With a Camera.* London, 1924. Experiences in Africa.

MC. McClintock, Walter. *The Old North Trail.* London, 1910. On the life, legends, and religion of the Blackfoot Indians.

McCreight, M. I. *Buffalo Bone Days.* Published by the author, Dubois, Pa., 1939. Contains valuable data from an old buyer on the buffalo bone traffic.

MD3. McDougall, Rev. Dr. John. *In the Days of the Red River Rebellion* (1865-68; orig. ed., 1903). Toronto, 1911.

———— *Forest, Lake, and Prairie* (orig. ed., 1895). Toronto, 1910. Re frontier life in Western Canada, 1842-62.

———— MS. (1875-76), unfinished at his death, 1917; now in the Provincial Legislative Library, Edmonton, Alta. Cited as McDougall MS.

{D2.	———— *Pathfinding on Plain and Prairie* (1865-68). Toronto, 1898.

{D1.	———— *Saddle, Sled, and Snowshoe* (orig. ed., 1896). Toronto. *Re* pioneering on the Saskatchewan in the 'sixties (1862-65).

{D4	———— *On Western Trails in the Early Seventies* (1873-75). Toronto, 1911. McDougall's writings are not professedly 'scientific'; their unpretentious accuracy makes them so. As unconscious revelations of a long experience they are of unrivalled authority for daily life in their region.

McGee, W. J., and Thomas, Cyrus. *Prehistoric North America.* (*History of North America* (*q.v.*), XIX.) New York, 1905.

'G.	McGillivray, Duncan. *The Journal of Duncan McGillivray,* ed. A. S. Morton. Toronto, 1929. An account of experiences with the North West Company, Fort George, North Saskatchewan River, 1794-95.

McLean, John. *Notes of a Twenty-Five Years' Service in the Hudson Bay Territory,* 2 vols. London, 1849.

———— *Notes of a Twenty-Five Years' Service in the Hudson Bay Territory,* ed. W. S. Wallace. Toronto: Champlain Society, 1932.

Mereness, Newton D. (ed.). *Travels in the American Colonies, 1690-1783.* New York, 1916.

Merk, F. (ed.). *Fur-Trade and Empire. See* Simpson, George.

Merriman, R. O. "The Bison and the Fur Trade." *Queen's Quarterly* (Kingston, Ont., July-Sept., 1926), 78-96.

Michaux, André. *Travels into Kentucky, 1796* (orig. ed., 1804). (*Early Western Travels,* ed. R. G. Thwaites (*q.v.*), III.) Cleveland, 1904.

Michaux, F. A. (son of the above). *Travels into Ohio, Kentucky, and Tennessee, 1802* (orig. ed., 1804). (*Early Western Travels,* ed. R. G. Thwaites (*q.v.*), III.) Cleveland, 1904.

Milman, Rev. H. H. *History of the Jews,* (orig. ed., 1830), 2 vols. (Everyman's Library.) London, 1906 *et seq.*

J.	Milton, Viscount, and Cheadle, W. B. *The North-West Passage by Land,* (orig. ed., 1863), 9th edition. London, 1901.

Minutes of Council, Northern Department of Rupert's Land, 1821, ed. R. Harvey Fleming. (Hudson's Bay Company Series.) Toronto: Champlain Society, 1940.

Mississippi Valley Historical Review. In progress.

.	Mooney, James. *The Aboriginal Population of America North of Mexico,* ed. J. R. Swanton. (Smithsonian Miscellaneous Collections, vol. 80, No. 7.) Washington, 1928.

Morice, Rev. Father A. G., O.M.I. *Fifty Years in Western Canada.* Toronto, 1930.

———— *History of the Catholic Church in Western Canada,* 2 vols. Toronto, 1910.

———— *History of the Northern Interior of British Columbia.* Toronto, 1906.

Morris, Governor Alexander. *Treaties with the Indians of Manitoba and the North-West Territories.* Toronto, 1880.

Morris, Capt. Thomas. *Journal, 1764* (orig. ed., 1791). (*Early Western Travels,* ed. R. G. Thwaites (*q.v.*), I.) Cleveland, 1904.

Morton, Arthur S. *A History of the Canadian West to 1870-71.* New York, 1939. An encyclopaedic masterpiece.

Morton, W. L. "Agriculture in the Red River Colony." *Canadian Historical Review,* XXX (1949), 305-21.

Moseley, Edwin L. *Our Wild Animals.* New York, 1928.

Nebraska History. In progress, 1920 *seq.*

New English ('Oxford') *Dictionary,* ed. Murray, Bradley, Craigie, etc. Oxford, 1888-1928.

Nisbet, John. *Our Forests and Woodlands,* 2nd ed. London, 1909.

Notes and Queries. London, in progress, 1849 *et seq.*

Nuttall, Thomas. *A Journal of Travels into the Arkansa Territory, 1819* (orig. ed., 1821). (*Early Western Travels,* ed. R. G. Thwaites (*q.v.*), XIII.) Cleveland, 1905.

Oliver, Edmund H. "The Beginnings of Agriculture in Saskatchewan." *Transactions of the Royal Society of Canada,* 3rd Ser., XXIX (1935), Sec. II, 1-32.

——— (ed.). *The Canadian North-West,* 2 vols. (Publications of the Canadian Archives, No. 9.) Ottawa, 1914, 1915. A most important collection of original documents.

Osborn, Henry Fairfield. *The Age of Mammals. New York,* 1910.

Osgood, E. S. *The Day of the Cattleman.* Minneapolis, 1929.

PL. Palliser, John, *et al. Journals, Detailed Reports, and Observations, relative to Palliser's Exploration of British North America, 1857, 1858, 1859, 1860.* (Parliamentary Blue Book.) London, 1863. A mine of inestimable information.

Palmer, Joel. *Journal of Travels over the Rocky Mountains, 1845-1846* orig. ed., 1847). (*Early Western Travels,* ed. R. G. Thwaites (*q.v.*), XXX.) Cleveland, 1906.

Parkman, Francis. *A Half-Century of Conflict* (orig. ed., 1892), 2 vols. Boston, 1910.

PN2. ——— *La Salle and the Discovery of the Great West* (orig. ed., 1878). Boston, 1910.

PN1. ——— *The Oregon Trail* (orig. ed., 1847). Boston, 1892.

——— *Pioneers of France in the New World* (orig. ed., 1865). Boston, 1910.

Pattie, James O. *Personal Narrative, 1824-1830* (orig. ed., 1831). (*Early Western Travels,* ed. R. G. Thwaites (*q.v.*), XVIII.) Cleveland, 1905.

Pike, Warburton. *The Barren Ground of Northern Canada* (orig. ed., 1891). London, 1917.

Pike, Zebulon M. *See* Coues, E.

Place-Names of Alberta. Ottawa: Geographic Board of Canada, 1928.

Post, Christian Frederick. *Journals, 1758-1759* (orig. ed., 1759). (*Early Western Travels,* ed. R. G. Thwaites (*q.v.*), I.) Cleveland, 1904.

Prescott, William H. *History of the Conquest of Mexico* (orig. ed., 1843), 2 vols. (Everyman's Library.) London, 1906 *et seq.*

——— *History of the Conquest of Peru* (orig. ed., 1847). New York, n.d.

——— *History of the Reign of Ferdinand and Isabella* (orig. ed., 1837), 3 vols. Philadelphia, 1872.

Preston, W. T. R. *Life of Lord Strathcona.* Toronto, 1916.

Purchas, Rev. Samuel. *Hakluytus Posthumus, or Purchas his Pilgrimes: Contayning a History of the World in Sea Voyages and Lande Travells by Englishmen and Others* (orig. ed., 1625), 20 vols. Glasgow, 1905-7.

Queen's Quarterly. Kingston, Ont., in progress, 1893 *et seq.*

Railway Magazine. London, in progress, 1897 *et seq.*

Raine, Wm. Macleod, and Barnes, W. C. *Cattle, Cowboys, and Rangers.* New York, n.d.

Raup, Hugh M. *Phytogeographic Studies in the Peace and Upper Liard River Regions, Canada.* Arnold Arboretun, Harvard University, 1934.

—— *Range Conditions in the Wood Buffalo Park of Western Canada, with Notes on the History of the Wood Bison.* (Special Publication of the American Committee for International Wild Life Protection.) New York, 1933.

Regina Star. Regina, Sask., daily.

Richardson, Sir John. *Arctic Searching Expedition through Rupert's Land and the Arctic Sea in Search of Sir John Franklin, 1847-1850.* London, 1852.

—— *Fauna Boreali-Americana,* 4 vols. London, 1829-37.

—— *The Polar Regions.* London, 1861.

Robertson, Colin. *Robertson's Letters, 1817-1822,* ed. E. E. Rich. (Hudson's Bay Company Series.) Toronto: Champlain Society, 1939.

Roe, Frank Gilbert. "From Dogs to Horses among the Western Indian Tribes." *Transactions of the Royal Society of Canada* 3rd Ser., XXXIII (1939), Sec. II, 209-75.

—— "The Hudson's Bay Company and the Indians." *The Beaver,* September, 1936.

—— "The 'Wild Animal Path' Origin of Ancient Roads." *Antiquity* (England), III (Sept., 1929), 299-311.

—— "The Winding Road." *Ibid.* (June, 1939), 191-206.

Rogers, Joseph M. *Thomas Hart Benton.* Philadelphia, 1905.

Roosevelt, Theodore. *African Game Trails.* New York, 1910.

—— *Hunting Trips of a Ranchman* (orig. ed., 1885). New York, 1927.

—— *Winning of the West,* 4 vols. New York, 1889, 1910.

Ross, Alexander. *Adventures of the First Settlers on the Oregon or Columbia River, 1810-1813* (orig. ed., 1849). (*Early Western Travels,* ed. R. G. Thwaites (*q.v.*), VII.) Cleveland, 1904.

—— *Fur Hunters of the Far West,* 2 vols. London, 1855.

—— *The Red River Settlement.* London, 1856.

Rowan, William. "Canada's Buffalo." *Country Life* (London), LXVI (1929), 358-60.

—— *The Riddle of Migration.* Baltimore, 1931.

Royal Canadian Mounted Police. *Annual Reports.* Ottawa.

Royal Society of Canada. *Transactions* and *Proceedings.* Annually.

Rundle, Rev. Robert Terrill. "Journal" (1840-48). MS. edited by Rev. J. P. Berry and F. G. Roe. McDougall Memorial Museum, Edmonton, Alta. *Re* Fort Edmonton and Saskatchewan River territory. Cited as "Rundle's Journal."

Salmon, Thomas. *A New Geographical and Historical Grammar.* London, 1749.

Saturday Evening Post. Philadelphia, Pa., in progress.

Scharff, Robert F. *Distribution and Origin of Life in America.* London, 1911.

Schultz, James Willard. *Apauk, Caller of Buffalo.* New York, 1916.

Science. Washington, D.C., in progress.

Seibert, F. V. *Natural Resources.* Ottawa: Department of the Interior, 1922.

────── "Some Notes on Canada's So-called Wood Buffalo." *Canadian Field Naturalist,* XXXIX (1925), 204-6.

────── "A Reconnaissance in the Home of the Wood Buffalo." Appendix to Maxwell Graham, *Canada's Wild Buffalo. See* Graham, M.

Seton, Ernest Thompson. *The Arctic Prairies.* New York, 1911.

────── *Life-Histories of Northern Animals,* 2 vols. New York, 1910.

────── *Lives of Game Animals,* 4 vols. New York, 1929.

Setzler, Frank M. "Archaeological Perspectives in the Northern Mississippi Valley." (Reprint from *Smithsonian Miscellaneous Collections,* vol. 100.) Swanton Anniversary Volume (Washington, 1940), 253-90.

Shaler, N. S. *Nature and Man in America* (orig. ed., 1891). New York, 1900.

Sheldon, Charles. *The Wilderness of Denali.* New York, 1930. *Re* Alaska.

Shepstone, Harold J. *Wild Beasts To-Day.* London, 1932.

Shetrone, H. C. *The Mound Builders.* New York, 1931.

Shoemaker, Henry W. *A Pennsylvania Bison Hunt.* Middleburg, Pa., 1915. Pamphlet, pp. 60.

Shufeldt, Dr. R. W. "The American Buffalo." *Forest and Stream* (New York), June 14, 1888.

Simpson, Alexander. *Life of Thomas Simpson.* London, 1845.

Simpson, Sir George. *Fur-Trade and Empire,* ed. F. Merk. (Harvard Historical Studies.) Cambridge, Mass., 1931. Simpson's Journals for 1824-25.

────── *Narrative of a Journey Around the World in the Years 1841 and 1842,* 2 vols. London, 1847.

────── *Simpson's Athabaska Journal, 1820-21,* ed. E. E. Rich. (Hudson's Bay Company Series, No. 1.) Toronto: Champlain Society, 1938.

Simpson, Thomas. *Narrative of Discoveries on the North Coast of America.* London, 1843. Dease and Simpson, Hudson's Bay Company Expedition, 1836-40.

Skinner, Alanson. "The Culture of the Plains Cree." *American Anthropologist,* XVI (1914), 68-87, 314-18.

Skinner, Morris F., and Kaisen, Ove C. "The Fossil Bison of Alaska and Preliminary Revision of the Genus." *Bulletin of the American Museum of Natural History* (New York), volume 89 (1947), Article 3, 123-256. With plates, maps, and statistical tables.

Somerset, H. Somers. *The Land of the Muskeg.* London, 1895.

Soper, J. Dewey. "History, Range, and Home Life of the Northern Bison." *Ecological Monographs,* XI (October, 1941), 347-412. The most comprehensive study of the northern Wood buffalo in print.

SO.   Southesk, Earl of. *Saskatchewan and the Rocky Mountains.* Edinburgh and Toronto, 1875. Travel, etc., 1859-60. Cited as Southesk, *Travels.*

Stanley, George F. G. *The Birth of Western Canada.* London, 1936.

Steele, Gen. Sam. B. *Forty Years in Canada.* London, 1915. Reminiscences of the Northwest, 1874 *seq.*

Stefansson, Vilhjalmur. "Pemmican." *The Military Surgeon* (U.S.A.), vol. 95 (August, 1944), 89-98. A study of nutritive values in relation to modern 'pemmican.'

Steward, Julian H. "Native Cultures of the Intermontane (Great Basin) Area." (Reprint from *Smithsonian Miscellaneous Collections*, vol. 100.) Swanton Anniversary Volume (Washington, 1940), 445-502. *See also Handbook of South American Indians*, above.

Stone, Witmer, and Cram, W. E. *American Animals* (orig. ed., 1902). New York, 1913. Popular guide to the mammals of North America, north of Mexico.

Strong, W. D. "Plains Culture in the Light of Archaeology." *American Anthropologist*, XXXV (1933), 271-87.

Swanton, John R., and Dixon, Roland B. "Primitive American History." *American Anthropologist*, XVI (1914), 376-412.

Taylor, Isaac. *Names and their Histories*. London, 1896.

Taylor, Joseph Henry. *Sketches of Frontier and Indian Life* (orig. ed., 1889). Washburn, N. Dak., 1895. Sometimes actually ludicrous from a purely literary standpoint, but a valuable human document from an experienced and outspoken observer.

Thevet, André. *Les Singularitez de la France antarctique*. Paris, 1558.
———— Thevet MS. (1586).

Thomas, Cyrus. *The Indians of North America in Historic Times*. (*History of North America* (*q.v.*), II.) New York, 1903.

Thompson, David. *Narrative of Explorations in Western America, 1784-1812*, ed. J. B. Tyrrell. Toronto: Champlain Society, 1916. Of supreme interest and value as an early guide.

Thwaites, Reuben Gold (ed.). *Early Western Travels, 1748-1846*, 32 vols. Cleveland, 1904-1907.
———— (ed.). *The Jesuit Relations and Allied Documents, 1610-1791*, 73 vols. Cleveland, 1896-1901.
———— (ed.). *A New Discovery of a Vast Country in America* (1679-81), by Louis Hennepin (orig. ed., 1683), 2 vols. Chicago, 1903. English translations in facsimile reprint of second London issue of 1698. Dr. Thwaites's masterly works are beyond criticism.[4]

Townsend, John K. *Narrative of a Journey across the Rocky Mountains, 1833-1834* (orig. ed., 1839). (*Early Western Travels*, ed. R. G. Thwaites (*q.v.*), XXI.) Cleveland, 1905.

Turner, F. J. *The Frontier in American History*. New York, 1920.

Turner, Geo. J. *Select Pleas of the Forest*. (Selden Society Publications, 1899.) London, 1901.

Tuttle, Charles R. *Our North Land*. Toronto, 1885.

Tweedie, Mrs. Alec. *Mexico as I Saw It* (orig. ed., 1897). London, 1911.

Tyrrell, James W. *Across the Sub-Arctics of Canada*. Toronto, 1897.

Umfreville, Edward. *The Present State of Hudson's Bay*. London, 1790.

Vancouver Daily Province. In progress.

Vanderhoof, V. L. "A Skull of Bison latifrons from the Pleistocene of

---

[4] *The Early Western Travels* have been given in this bibliography under authors' names also, as they were almost all originally published independently in book form. *The Jesuit Relations* were not. Except when citing editorial notes, it has not been thought necessary to add "ed. Thwaites" to each reference in the footnotes. His editions are perfectly well known.

Northern California." *University of California Publications in Geological Science* (1942), 1-23.

Vaughan, W. *The Life of Sir W. C. Van Horne.* New York, 1920.

Victoria Daily Colonist. British Columbia, in progress.

Wallace, J. N. *The Wintering Partners on Peace River up to the Union of 1821.* Ottawa, 1929.

Wallace, W. Stewart (ed.). *Documents Relating to the North West Company.* Toronto: Champlain Society, 1934. A most valuable "Biographical Dictionary of the Nor-Westers," Appendix A, 425-505.

Walsh, Richard J., and Salsbury, N. S. *The Making of Buffalo Bill.* Indianapolis, 1928. *Re* W. F. Cody.

Watkin, Sir Edward. *Canada and the States.* London, 1887. Recollections, 1851-86.

Webb, Walter Prescott. *The Great Plains.* New York, 1931.

———— *The Texas Rangers.* New York, 1936.

Wedel, Waldo R. "Culture sequences in the Central Great Plains." (Reprint from *Smithsonian Miscellaneous Collections,* vol. 100.) Swanton Memorial Volume (Washington, 1940), 291-352.

Welsh, Norbert (1843-1933). *The Last Buffalo-Hunter,* ed. Mary Weekes. New York, 1939.

Wesley, John. *Journals* (1737 *seq.*), 4 vols. (Everyman's Library.) London, 1906 *seq.*

White, James (ed.). *Altitudes in Canada.* Ottawa: National Geographic Board, 1939.

Williamson, J. A. *Sir John Hawkins.* London, 1927.

Willson, Beckles. *The Great Company.* Toronto, 1899.

Winsor, Justin (ed.). *Narrative and Critical History of America,* 8 vols. Boston and New York, 1884-89.

Wissler, Clark. *The American Indian* (orig. ed., 1916). New York, 1922.

———— "The Influence of the Horse in the Development of Plains Culture." *American Anthropologist,* XVI (1914), 1-25.

———— "Material Culture of the North American Indians." *Ibid.,* 447-505.

Woods, John. *Two Years' Residence in the Settlement on the English Prairie* (orig. ed., 1822). (*Early Western Travels,* ed. R. G. Thwaites (*q.v.*), X.) Cleveland, 1904. *Re* the Illinois Country, United States, 1820-21.

Wyeth, John B. *Oregon, 1832* (orig. ed., 1833). (*Early Western Travels,* ed. R. G. Thwaites (*q.v.*), XXI.) Cleveland, 1905.

Young, Rev. Egerton Ryerson. *By Canoe and Dog-Train.* London, 1892. *Re* missionary work among the Cree and Saulteaux, 1868 *seq.* Like McDougall, reminiscent rather than 'scientific'; but of unimpeachable authenticity.

Zoologist, A Canadian. "The Passing of the Wood Bison." *Canadian Forum,* V (1925), 301-5. A trenchant criticism of the policy of the Department of the Interior *re* the mongrelization of the aboriginal race in Wood Buffalo Park, North West Territories, by an anonymous but manifestly competent observer.

SUPPLEMENTARY BIBLIOGRAPHY (p. 929)

Agricultural History, quarterly (Washington, D.C.). In progress.
All.erta Historical Review (Calgary, Alberta). In progress, 1952 *et seq.*
Bailey, Vernon. *Mammals of New Mexico*, 12. *North American Fauna*, 53; U.S. Biological Survey, Washington, D.C. 1931.
Baraga (Bishop) Frederic. *A Grammar and Dictionary of the Otchipwe Language*. Montreal, 1879.
Bolton, Herbert Eugene. *Spanish Exploration in the Southwest, 1542-1706.* New York, 1916.
———— *Coronado, Knight of Pueblos and Plains.* New York and Albuquerque, N.M., 1949.
Brand, Donald D. "The Early History of the Range Cattle Industry in Northern Mexico." *Agricultural History*, Washington, D.C., XXXV (1961), 132-9.
Byington, Cyrus. *A Dictionary of the Choctaw Language*, ed. John R. Swanton and Henry S. Halbert, Bureau of American Ethnology, Bulletin 46. Washington, D.C., 1915.
Chittenden, Hiram M. *History of the American Fur. Trade*. New ed. by Stallo Vinton, 2 vols. New York, 1935.
Dale, Harrison C. "Did the Returning Astorians Use the South Pass?" *Oregon Historical Quarterly*, XVII (1916), 47-51.
Denhardt, Robert Moorman. *The Horse of the Americas.* Norman, Okla., 1947.
Diaz del Castillo, Bernal. *The Conquest of the New World*. Trans. and ed., A. P. Maudslay. Hakluyt Society, 5 vols., London, 1908-16.
Dictionary of the Cree Language, based upon the foundations laid by Rev. E. A. Watkins, 1865; ed. Rev. Archdeacon R. Faries, Toronto, 1938.
Dictionary of the Kalispel or Flathead Language. Compiled by the Missionaries of the Society of Jesus, St. Ignatius Mission, Montana, 1879.
Dobie, J. Frank. "Bison in Mexico." *Journal of Mammalogy*, XXXIV (1953), 150.
Dorsey, James O. and John R. Swanton. *A Dictionary of the Biloxi and Ofo Languages*, Bureau of American Ethnology, Bulletin 47, Washington, D.C., 1912. Biloxi: 169-318; Ofo: 319-40.
Edmonds, Walter D. *The Musket and the Cross*. New York, 1967.
Ewers, John C. "Were the Blackfoot Rich in Horses?" *American Anthropologist*, XLV (1943), 602-10.
———— "The Last Bison Drives of the Blackfoot Indians." *Journal of the Washington Academy of Sciences*, XXXIX (1949), 355-60.
———— *The Horse in Blackfoot Indian Culture*. Bureau of American Ethnology, Bulletin 159. Washington, D.C., 1955.
Fishler, Stanley A. "Navaho Buffalo Hunting." *El Palacio* (Santa Fé, N.M.), LXII (1955), 43-57.

947

Grasserie, Raoul de la. *Cinq Langues de la Colombie Britannique.* Paris, 1902.

Hammond, George P. and Agapito Rey. *The Expedition into New Mexico made by Antonio de Espejo, 1582-1593; as revealed in the Journal of Diego Pérez de Luxán, a Member of the Party.* Quivira Society, I. Los Angeles, Calif. 1929.

────── *New Mexico in 1602. Relacions* by Juan de Oñaté, Vicente de Zaldívar, and Juan de Montoya. Quivira Society, VIII, Los Angeles, Calif., 1938.

Harrington, John P. *Vocabulary of the Kiowa Language.* Bureau of American Ethnology, Bulletin 84. Washington, D.C., 1928.

Havighurst, Walter. *The Land of Promise, the North-West Territory* (i.e. the Great Lakes and Ohio Valley region). New York, 1946.

Hulbert, Archer B. and Dorothy P. Hulbert. *Marcus Whitman, Crusader.* 3 vols. Denver, Colorado, 1936-9.

La Flesche, Francis. *A Dictionary of the Osage Language.* Bureau of American Ethnology, Bulletin 109. Washington, D.C., 1932.

Larpenteur, Charles. *Forty Years a Fur Trader on the Upper Missouri; The Personal Narrative of Charles Larpenteur* (ed. Coues), 2 vols., 1898.

Merriam, C. Hart. "The Buffalo in Northeastern California." *Journal of Mammalogy,* VII (1926), 211-14.

Oregon Historical Quarterly. In progress, 1900 *et seq.*

Radin, Paul. *The Indians of South America.* New York, 1942.

Reed, Erik K. "The Myth of Montezuma's Bison and the Type-Locality of the Species." *Journal of Mammalogy,* XXXIII (1952), 390-2.

────── "Bison beyond the Pecos." *Texas Journal of Science* (June, 1955), 130-5.

Riddell, Francis. "The Recent Occurrence of Bison in Northeastern California." *American Antiquity,* XVIII (1952), 168-9.

Roe, Frank Gilbert. *The Indian and the Horse.* Norman, Okla., 1955.

────── "Early Agriculture in Western Canada in Relation to Climatic Stability." *Agricultural History,* Washington, D.C. (July, 1952), 104-23.

────── "The Alberta Wet Cycle of 1899-1903." *Ibid.* (July, 1954), 112-20.

────── "Early Opinion on the 'Fertile Belt' of Western Canada." *Canadian Historical Review,* XXVII (1946), 131-46.

────── "Western Penetration of the Historic Buffalo in the Upper Bow River Valley, Alberta." *Alberta Historical Review,* V (1957), 21-4.

────── "Some Historical Evidence on the Earlier Physiography of the North American Prairies." *Transactions of the Royal Society of Canada* (1961), Section Two, 9-35.

Rollins, Philip Ashton, ed. *The Discovery of the Oregon Trail* (Robert Stuart's Narrative of 1812-13). New York and London, 1935.

Tolmie, W. Fraser and George M. Dawson. *Five Comparative Vocabularies of Indian Tribes of British Columbia.* Montreal, 1884.

Vocabulary of the Navaho Language. By the Franciscan Fathers, 2 vols., St. Michaels, Ariz., 1912.

Young, Frederic George. "The Oregon Trail," *Oregon Historical Quarterly,* I (1900), 339-70.

INDEX

The dates following names of persons cited are intended to indicate the era to which the citations broadly refer, apart from general authorities such as Allen, Hornaday, Seton, etc.

Italics indicate the more important references, containing subject-matter in the witness's own words, or the like.

ABERT, Col. J. J. (U.S. Army, 1842), 548

Aboriginal contacts with buffalo, 312–13

'Abundance,' relative meaning of, 334–46

Acosta, Father (1588), *206*

'Acre of buffaloes, an,' 359, 507–11

'Acres,' distance of (1788, 1806), 844–5

Adair, James (1775), 244, 245, 843

Addy, S. O., 732

Adirondacks, b. in, 220–1

Adlard, H., 733

Adobe Walls, battle of (1874), 865

Advance of b. west of the Rockies, *305–9*

Agriculture (Indian), 603, 632

Aiton, Prof. Arthur S., 212, 348, 628

Alabama, b. in, *see* REGIONS

Alaska, b. in, *see* REGIONS

Albanel, Father Charles (1672), 292

Alberta, b. in, *see* REGIONS

Albinism in b., 715–28; *see also* White buffalo

Albinos (non-buffalo), 725

Albion, Prof. R. G., 28, 850, 852

Alexis, Grand Duke, of Russia (1872), 434–5, 869

'Alleghanian buffalo,' 27, 54

Alleghanies, 204, 205, 242, 244, 256, 503, 846, 847

Allen, Joel A., 3, 5, 7, 9, 12–3, 17, 19, 22, 28, *30*, 31, 33, 36, *39–40*, *47*, 59, *60*, 62, 66–7, 76–7, 93, 95, 96, *103*, 106, 109, 113, 114, 120, *121–2*, *124*, *126*, *128*, *149–50*, 162, 172, 173, *175*, 177, *181*, 182, *187*, 194, 195, *196*, 200, 204, 205, *206*, 207–8, 215–6, *217*, 218, 220, *222–3*, 225–6, *228*, 229, *230*, 231–4, *235*, *236*, 237, 238, 240–2, *243*, *244*, 245, 247–8, *249*, 250–1, *253*, 254, *256*, 257, 260, *262*, 263–4, 269–70, 272,

273, *275*, 278, *279*, *284*, 286–7, *294–6*, 298, 301, *307–8*, 318, 325, 333, *335*, 338, *340*, 341, 342, 343, 348, 351, *356–7*, 369, 371, *373*, 377, 393–4, 396, *397*, 400, 402, 410, *412*, 418, *419–20*, 421, 424, 437, 441, *451–2*, 453, *454*, 469, 472–3, 493, 499–502, *503*, *506*, 515, *521–2*, 524, 527, 529–30, *533–4*, 552, 554, 556-7, *566–7*, 585, 596–9, 604, 606, 633, 635, 637, *673*, 681–4, 704, 707, 720–1, 812, 843–4, 856, 858, *860*, 862, *880–2*

Allouez, Father Claude (1665–?), 96, 219, *224*, 605, 675, 681–2, 684, 692, 743, 818, *848*, 861, 870, 891

Alvarado, Hernando de (1541), 209–10, 350, 644, 818

Amarillo, Texas, 865

America (eastern) 'all forest' (1534 *seq.*), 845

American Fur Company (1830 *seq.*), 498, 501, 565, 886

Anderson, Dr. R. M., 61, 853

Andrews, Harry (Kansas, 1874), 420, 442

'Annual hunts' frequently failures, 370, 381, 383–4, 386–7, · 388, 389, 391–3, 395, 410, 543–95

'Annual itineraries' of b., 185, 378–86, 387–94, 543–95, 635

Antelope, 492, 866–7, 880

Anthony, Dr. H. E., 833, 836

Anticosti (island of), b. there (?), *219*

Anti-Indian manifestations: allegations, 501–6; in Canadians, 399, 669–70; generalization, 637, 639–42, 664–70, 805–6, 816, 888; propaganda, 665, 892

Appalachians (forests), 846, 848

Appomattox (1865), 809

Arabs, Indians likened to, 621, 622, 627

INDIANS: agriculture, 603, 632, 843, 850; archery, 186, 503, 630, 868–9; b. hunting regulations and 'soldiers,' 116, 374, 375, 658; b. mythology, 643–8; b. rituals, 729–32; camping habits and sites, 626, 638, 878–9; cannibalism, 660, 890–1; castrating b., 63–4; clothing (northern), 500; dogs, 407, 731–2; endurance of privation, starving, 659–64, 889; epidemic diseases, 752–60, 789, 797, 799; extravagance, 482–5, 885–7; fasting, 659, 889; firearms, replacing bows, 139, 154, 493, 503; 'gluttony,' 660–4; half-breed b. hunters disliked, 371, 382, 391, 410; horses, 614, 617, 627–8, 682, 709, 722, 731–2; influence of b. environment on, 88, 601–70; languages, 625, 871; manners (Mandans), 170–1; marksmanship, 630; mastery of game lore, 197, 663–4; methods of b. hunting, 629–49, 663–4; mixed-bloods among (late), 752; moderation, 654–9; names, 625, 872; nomads (pre-equine), 612–29; not harassing b. in summer, 116–18, 154, 374–5, 658; numbers (adult ratios) and population, 502, 607–8, 742–803; pounding practices, 639, 647, 880–4; pre-Columbian b. hunting methods, 503, 630–9, 646–9, 871, 880–4; prudence with b., 116–18, 374–5, 654–9; psychology (b. and game), 632, 642–9, 663–4, 880–4; ratios of b. and hides utilized, 439–41; religious practices, 644–8, 660–1, 721–4; repeating rifles and b., 186, 450, 503, 630, 868–9; resentment against b. hunters (1841–78), *424, 428, 433, 804–16*; slaughter-totals, 449–51, 493, 499–503; 'soldiers' and b. hunting, 116–18, 374–5, 658;

Nevada: b. in, *see* REGIONS; once in 'California,' 277, 280

New Jersey, *see* REGIONS

New Mexican (Santa Fé, N.M., 1874), 805

New Mexico, b. in, *see* REGIONS

New Orleans, La., 559, 886

New York, *see* REGIONS

Newfoundland ('Baccalaos,' 1550 *seq.*), *see* REGIONS

Newton, Dr. Robert, 83

Nicholson, J. D. (N.W.M.P., 1885), 468, 487

Night attacks (Indian), 888

'Nipigon country' (1770–1790), 294, 891

Nisbet, John, 28, 849, 850

Nixon, Tom (Kansas, 1870), 421, 423

Nomads: b. Indians, 399–400, 612–29; early, pre-equine, 622; and pecan harvest (Texas), 616

North America, climates of, 70–3, 75, 80–6

North Park, Colorado, 554

North Platte, Nebraska, 357, 809

North West (Fur) Company, 762, 845

North West Mounted Police, 468–9, 477–8, 573, 810, 834, 838

North West Territories (Canada), *see* REGIONS, Athabaska and N.W.T.

'Northern' and 'Southern' herds (U.S. 1870), 361–5

Northern extermination (U.S.), 449–50, 453–7

Northern Wood b., 39–57, 286, 294, 299–305, 316–29, 429, 469, 615

Norway House, a b. supply depot (H. B. Co.), 299, 718, 757, 800

'Nuestra Senora las Nieves' ('Our Lady of the Snows,' Colorado, 1776), 675

Nueva Biscaya (Chihuahua, Durango, Mexico), 204, 522

Nueva Leon (Mexico), 210, 351, 522

Numbers of buffalo: in Canada, 137–8, 363–4, 383, 396–7, 472–4; E. of Mississippi River, 256, 336–44; seen dead on small areas, 418–20; mathematical estimates, 353–5, 357–9, 363; in N.W.T., Canada, 301–5; general surveys, 334–6, 340, 364–5, 383, 454, 472–4, 490, 506–11, *568* (U.S.); W. of Mississippi, 345–66; wild (1865–89), 490, 506–11; *see also* Hides

Nuttall, Thomas (1819), 12, 70, *104*, 120, *165*, 240, 521, 709, 732

OAKES, North Dakota (1888), 463

Occultism (Indian) in b. pounding, 639, 647–9, 882–4

'Ochelaga' (Hochelega, 1534), 618

Ogallala, Nebraska (town: 1885), 442

Ogden, Isaac (1789), 856

Ogden, Peter Skene (1826), *273*

Ogilby, John (Maryland, 1670), 248

Ogilvie, William (N.W.T., 1890), 187

Oglethorpe, Gen. James E. (1733), *243*

Ohio, b. in, *see* REGIONS

Ohio Valley, 91, 146, 230–2

Ohistahna (Blackfoot, 1833), 722, 727, 765

Ojo del Cuerbo (Salt lakes, Rio Grande), 598

Okanagan (B.C.), fossil b. remains, 20, 309, 853

Oklahoma, b. in, *see* REGIONS

'Old Cline's Trail,' 313–14

'Old Portage Road' (Alleghanies, 1749–52), 847

Olds, Alberta, 583

Oliver, Rev. E. H., 72, 297, 310, 314, *368–9*, *371–2*, 375, *410*, *476*, 686, 708, 718, 762, 765, 882

Oliver, Hon. Frank, 40, 86, 90, 486

Omaha, Nebraska, 427–8, 806

Oman, Mitchell (1780), 162

Oñate, Juan de (1604), 274, 277

'One herd only,' 386 (Western Canada, 1860), 424 (U.S.),

'One vast charnel house' (Kansas, 1873), 418–19

Onistah-pokah (Blackfoot chief, 1876), 727

Ontario, b. in, *see* REGIONS

'Open woods,' 847–50

Oregon: b. in, *see* REGIONS; definition of (1842), 266, 270, 799

Oregon–California Trail, 76, 83, 120, 124, 183–4, 270–1, 356, 424–5, 464, 532, 554–8, 607, *665*, *670*, 717, 759

'Osage orange,' 876

'Osage Trace,' 559

Osborn, Henry Fairfield, 3, 15, *18–23*, 61, 202, 335, 505, 830

Osgood, E. S., 609, 730, 810

Ott, Daniel, 419, 445, 864

'Overcrowding of the b. range,' 492–8

Overton, Dr. Richard C., 464

'Regular migration' of b., 70–5, 84, 90–1, 163–7, 185, 193–5, 377–8, 521–42, 627
Reighard, George W. (1870), 358, *360*, *511–12*, *516*, 529, 533–4
Reindeer Lake (N. Saskatchewan), 737, 739
Relacion del Suceso (1541), 211, 348–50, 860
Religious ceremonials (Indian): *re* b., 660–1; conditional on b., 664
Reminiscent material, critical examination, 419, 425–6, 444–6, 479–82, 488
Repeating rifles and Indians, 450, 493, 503, 868–9
Reproduction in b., 505–6
'Republican country,' 95, 540–2, 550–1, 707, 710, 717
Reykdal, Paul, 739
Reynard, Brother Alexis (1875), 891
Rhoads, Samuel N., 14, 19, 24, 33, 44, 53–4, 66–7, 252
Richardson (Dr.) Sir John (1819–50), 7, 16, 19, 23, *35*, 39, *57*, 92, 115, *131*, 145, 156, 165, 168, *200–1*, *204–6*, *246*, *260*, 263, 280, 283–4, 289, 300, *304*, 306, *308*, 321, 323, 399, 521, 523, 604, 618, 681–4, 687–700, 734, 736, 856, 858–60, 891
Rifle-fire to divert stampeding b., 136, 357; contra, 137
Riggs, Rev. Dr. Stephen R., 791
Ritchie, Dr., 836
Rituals (Indian) *re* buffalo, 721–4 (white b.), 729–32
River crossings and b., 154–5, 160–79
RIVERS (R. = river; C. = creek):
    Alabama R., 241; Alatamaha R., 244; Alleghany R., 31; Arkansas R., 60, 77, 81, 91, 95, 101, 104, 110, 113, 134, 136, 165–6, 259,